Contemporary
Literary Criticism

Guide to Gale Literary Criticism Series

When you need to review criticism of literary works, these are the Gale series to use:

If the author's death date is:

You should turn to:

After Dec. 31, 1959
(or author is still living)

CONTEMPORARY LITERARY CRITICISM

for example: Jorge Luis Borges, Anthony Burgess,
William Faulkner, Mary Gordon,
Ernest Hemingway, Iris Murdoch

1900 through 1959

TWENTIETH-CENTURY LITERARY CRITICISM

for example: Willa Cather, F. Scott Fitzgerald,
Henry James, Mark Twain, Virginia Woolf

1800 through 1899

NINETEENTH-CENTURY LITERATURE CRITICISM

for example: Fedor Dostoevski, Nathaniel Hawthorne,
George Sand, William Wordsworth

1400 through 1799

LITERATURE CRITICISM FROM 1400 TO 1800
(excluding Shakespeare)

for example: Anne Bradstreet, Daniel Defoe,
Alexander Pope, François Rabelais,
Jonathan Swift, Phillis Wheatley

SHAKESPEAREAN CRITICISM

Shakespeare's plays and poetry

Antiquity through 1399

CLASSICAL AND MEDIEVAL LITERATURE CRITICISM

for example: Dante, Homer, Plato, Sophocles, Vergil,
the Beowulf Poet

Gale also publishes related criticism series:

CHILDREN'S LITERATURE REVIEW

This series covers authors of all eras who have written for the
preschool through high school audience.

SHORT STORY CRITICISM

This series covers the major short fiction writers of all
nationalities and periods of literary history.

POETRY CRITICISM

This series covers poets of all nationalities, movements, and
periods of literary history.

DRAMA CRITICISM

This series covers dramatists of all nationalities and periods of
literary history.

BLACK LITERATURE CRITICISM

This three-volume series presents criticism of works by major
black writers of the past two hundred years.

ISSN 0091-3421

Volume 71

Contemporary Literary Criticism

Excerpts from Criticism of the
Works of Today's Novelists, Poets,
Playwrights, Short Story Writers, Scriptwriters,
and Other Creative Writers

Thomas Votteler
EDITOR

Laurie DiMauro
Sean R. Pollock
Bridget Travers
Robyn Young
ASSOCIATE EDITORS

Gale Research Inc. DETROIT • LONDON

STAFF

Thomas Votteler, *Editor*

Marie Lazzari, Roger Matuz, Sean R. Pollock, Bridget Travers, Robyn Young, *Associate Editors*

Jennifer Brostrom, Ian A. Goodhall, Christopher Giroux, Elizabeth P. Henry, Kyung-Sun Lim,
Dale R. Miller, Brigham Narins, Alexander C. Sweda, Janet M. Witalec, *Assistant Editors*

Jeanne A. Gough, *Production & Permissions Manager*
Linda M. Pugliese, *Production Supervisor*
Paul Lewon, Maureen A. Puhl, Camille P. Robinson, Jennifer VanSickle, *Editorial Associates*
Donna Craft, Rosita D'Souza, Brandy C. Johnson, Sheila Walencewicz, *Editorial Assistants*

Victoria B. Cariappa, *Research Manager*
Maureen Richards, *Research Supervisor*
Mary Beth McElmeel, Tamara C. Nott, *Editorial Associate*
Andrea B. Ghorai, Daniel Jankowski, Julie Karmazin, Robert S. Lazich, Julie Synkonis, *Editorial Assistants*

Sandra C. Davis, *Permissions Supervisor (Text)*
Maria L. Franklin, Josephine M. Keene, Denise M. Singleton, Kimberly F. Smilay, *Permissions Associates*
Brandy C. Johnson, Michele Lonoconus, Shelly Rakoczy, Shalice Shah, *Permissions Assistants*

Margaret A. Chamberlain, *Permissions Supervisor (Pictures)*
Pamela A. Hayes, *Permissions Associate*
Amy Lynn Emrich, Karla Kulkis, Nancy Rattenbury, Keith Reed, *Permissions Assistants*

Mary Beth Trimper, *Production Director*
Shanna Heilveil, *Production Assistant*

Art Chartow, *Technical Design Services Manager*
Cynthia Baldwin, *Art Director*
Nick Jakubiak, C. J. Jonik, *Keyliners*

10 9 8 7 6 5 4 3 2 1

Contents

Preface   vii

Acknowledgments   ix

Preface

Named "one of the twenty-five most distinguished reference titles published during the past twenty-five years" by *Reference Quarterly,* the *Contemporary Literary Criticism (CLC)* series provides readers with critical commentary and general information on more than 2,000 authors now living or who died after December 31, 1959. Previous to the publication of the first volume of *CLC* in 1973, there was no ongoing digest monitoring scholarly and popular sources of critical opinion and explication of modern literature. *CLC,* therefore, has fulfilled an essential need, particularly since the complexity and variety of contemporary literature makes the function of criticism especially important to today's reader.

Scope of the Series

CLC presents significant passages from published criticism of works by creative writers. Since many of the authors covered by *CLC* inspire continual critical commentary, writers are often represented in more than one volume. There is, of course, no duplication of reprinted criticism.

Authors are selected for inclusion for a variety of reasons, among them the publication or dramatic production of a critically acclaimed new work, the reception of a major literary award, revival of interest in past writings, or the adaptation of a literary work to film or television.

Attention is also given to several other groups of writers—authors of considerable public interest—about whose work criticism is often difficult to locate. These include mystery and science fiction writers, literary and social critics, foreign writers, and authors who represent particular ethnic groups within the United States.

Format of the Book

Each *CLC* volume contains about 500 individual excerpts—with approximately seventeen excerpts per author—taken from hundreds of book review periodicals, general magazines, scholarly journals, monographs, and books. Entries include critical evaluations spanning from the beginning of an author's career to the most current commentary. Interviews, feature articles, and other published writings that offer insight into the author's works are also presented. Students, teachers, librarians, and researchers will find that the generous excerpts and supplementary material in *CLC* provide them with vital information needed to write a term paper, analyze a poem, or lead a book discussion group. In addition, complete bibliographical citations note the original source and all of the information necessary for a term paper footnote or bibliography.

Features

A *CLC* author entry consists of the following elements:

• The **author heading** cites the form under which the author has most commonly published, followed by birth date, and death date when applicable. Uncertainty as to a birth or death date is indicated by a question mark.

• A **portrait** of the author is included when available.

• A brief **biographical and critical introduction** to the author and his or her work precedes the excerpted criticism. The first line of the introduction provides the author's full name, pseudonyms (if applicable), nationality, and a listing of genres in which the author has written. Since *CLC* is not intended to be a definitive biographical source, cross-references have been included to direct readers to these useful sources published by Gale Research: *Short Story Criticism* and *Children's Literature Review, Contemporary Authors, Something about the Author, Dictionary of Literary Biography,* and *Contemporary Authors Autobiography Series* and *Something about the Author Autobiography Series.* Previous volumes of *CLC* in which the author has been featured are also listed in the introduction.

• A list of **principal works,** usually divided into genre categories, notes the most important works by the author.

• The **excerpted criticism** represents various kinds of critical writing, ranging in form from the brief review to the scholarly exegesis. Essays are selected by the editors to reflect the spectrum of opinion about a specific work or about an author's literary career in general. The excerpts are presented chronologically, adding a useful perspective to the entry. All titles by the author featured in the entry are printed in boldface type, which enables the reader to easily identify the works being discussed. Publication information (such as publisher names and book prices) and parenthetical numerical references (such as footnotes or page and line references to specific editions of a work) have been deleted at the editor's discretion to provide smoother reading of the text.

• A complete **bibliographical citation** designed to help the user find the original essay or book follows each excerpt.

• A concise **further reading** section appears at the end of entries on authors for whom a significant amount of criticism exists in addition to the pieces reprinted in *CLC*. In some cases, this annotated bibliography includes references to material for which the editors could not obtain reprint rights.

Other Features

• An **Acknowledgments** section lists the copyright holders who have granted permission to reprint material in this volume of *CLC*. It does not, however, list every book or periodical reprinted or consulted during the preparation of the volume.

• A **Cumulative Author Index** lists all the authors who have appeared in the various literary criticism series published by Gale Research, with cross-references to Gale's biographical and autobiographical series. A full listing of the series referenced there appears on the first page of the indexes of this volume. Readers will welcome this cumulated author index as a useful tool for locating an author within the various series. The index, which lists birth and death dates when available, will be particularly valuable for those authors who are identified with a certain period but whose death date causes them to be placed in another, or for those authors whose careers span two periods. For example, Ernest Hemingway is found in *CLC*, yet a writer often associated with him, F. Scott Fitzgerald, is found in *Twentieth-Century Literary Criticism*.

• A **Cumulative Nationality Index** alphabetically lists all authors featured in *CLC* by nationality, followed by numbers corresponding to the volumes in which they appear.

• A **Title Index** alphabetically lists all titles reviewed in the current volume of *CLC*. Listings are followed by the author's name and the corresponding page numbers where the titles are discussed. English translations of foreign titles and variations of titles are cross-referenced to the title under which a work was originally published. Titles of novels, novellas, dramas, films, record albums, and poetry, short story, and essay collections are printed in italics, while all individual poems, short stories, essays, and songs are printed in roman type within quotation marks; when published separately (e.g., T.S. Eliot's poem *The Waste Land*), the titles of long poems are printed in italics.

• In response to numerous suggestions from librarians, Gale has also produced a **special paperbound edition** of the *CLC* title index. This annual cumulation, which alphabetically lists all titles reviewed in the series, is available to all customers and will be published with the first volume of *CLC* issued in each calendar year. Additional copies of the index are available upon request. Librarians and patrons will welcome this separate index: it saves shelf space, is easy to use, and is disposable upon receipt of the following year's cumulation.

A Note to the Reader

When writing papers, students who quote directly from any volume in the Literary Criticism Series may use the following general forms to footnote reprinted criticism. The first example pertains to material drawn from periodicals, the second to material reprinted from books:

[1]Anne Tyler, "Manic Monologue," *The New Republic* 200 (April 17, 1989), 44-6; excerpted and reprinted in *Contemporary Literary Criticism,* Vol. 58, ed. Roger Matuz (Detroit: Gale Research Inc., 1990), p. 325.

[2]Patrick Reilly, *The Literature of Guilt: From 'Gulliver' to Golding* (University of Iowa Press, 1988); excerpted and reprinted in *Contemporary Literary Criticism,* Vol. 58, ed. Roger Matuz (Detroit: Gale Research Inc., 1990), pp. 206-12.

Suggestions Are Welcome

The editors welcome the comments and suggestions of readers to expand the coverage and enhance the usefulness of the series.

Acknowledgments

The editors wish to thank the copyright holders of the excerpted criticism included in this volume, the permissions managers of many book and magazine publishing companies for assisting us in securing reprint rights, and Anthony Bogucki for assistance with copyright research. We are also grateful to the staffs of the Detroit Public Library, the Library of Congress, the University of Detroit Library, Wayne State University Purdy/Kresge Library Complex, and the University of Michigan Libraries for making their resources available to us. Following is a list of the copyright holders who have granted us permission to reprint material in this volume of CLC. Every effort has been made to trace copyright, but if omissions have been made, please let us know.

COPYRIGHTED EXCERPTS IN *CLC*, VOLUME 71, WERE REPRINTED FROM THE FOLLOWING PERIODICALS:

The Advocate, January 29, 1991 for "Ellis in Blunderland" by Merle Rubin. Reprinted by permission of the author.—*American Book Review,* v. 11, January-February, 1990. © 1990 by *The American Book Review.* Reprinted by permission of the publisher.—*The American Book Review,* v. 5, September-October, 1983. © 1983 by *The American Book Review.* Reprinted by permission of the publisher.—*Analog Science Fiction/Science Fact,* v. CXI, November 11, 1991 for "Tehanu" by Tom Easton. © 1991 by Davis Publications, Inc. Reprinted by permission of the author.—*Book World—The Washington Post,* August 15, 1971. © 1971 Postrib Corp. Reprinted by courtesy of the *Chicago Tribune* and *The Washington Post.*/ August 23, 1987; February 2, 1990; March 3, 1991; July 14, 1991; September 8, 1991. © 1987, 1990, 1991, *The Washington Post.* All reprinted with permission of the publisher.— *Callaloo,* v. 9, Fall, 1986. Copyright © 1986 by Charles H. Rowell. All rights reserved. Reprinted by permission of the publisher.—*The Canadian Fiction Magazine,* n. 65, 1989. Copyright © 1989 by *The Canadian Fiction Magazine.*—*The Canadian Forum,* v. LXVIII, April, 1989 for "In the Aftermath of Empire: Identities in the Commonwealth of Literature" by Keith Garebian. Reprinted by permission of the author.—*Canadian Literature,* n. 119, Winter, 1988 for "Images of India" by Amin Malak. Reprinted by permission of the author.—*Chicago Tribune— Books,* April 9, 1989 for "Back in Top Form: Tough, Honest Elmore Leonard" by Andrew Vachss; September 15, 1991 for "China's Human Side" by John Maxwell Hamilton. © Copyrighted 1989, 1991, Chicago Tribune Company. All rights reserved. Both reprinted by permission of the respective authors./ April 9, 1989. © copyrighted 1989, Chicago Tribune Company. All rights reserved. Used with permission.—*The Christian Century,* v. 106, July 5-12, 1989. Copyright 1989 Christian Century Foundation. Reprinted by permission from *The Christian Century.*— *The Christian Science Monitor,* September 27, 1962; October 4, 1991. © 1962, 1991 The Christian Science Publishing Society. All rights reserved. Both reprinted by permission from *The Christian Science Monitor.*/ July 5, 1951; November 10, 1955. Copyright 1951, renewed 1979; copyright 1955, renewed 1983 by The Christian Science Publishing Society. All rights reserved. Both reprinted by permission from *The Christian Science Monitor.*— *Commentary,* v. 92, July 1991 for "PC & the Ellis Affair" by Carol Iannone. Copyright © 1991 by the American Jewish Committee. All rights reserved. Reprinted by permission of the publisher and the author.—*Commonweal,* v. CIV, December 9, 1977. Copyright © 1977 Commonweal Publishing Co., Inc. Reprinted by permission of Commonweal Foundation.—*The Commonweal,* v. XLII, April 20, 1945; v. LIV, July 1951. Copyright 1945, renewed 1973; copyright 1951, renewed 1979 by Commonweal Publishing Co., Inc. Reprinted by permission of Commonweal Foundation.—*Educational Theatre Journal,* v. XV, May, 1973. © 1973 University College Theatre Association of the American Theatre Association. Reprinted by permission of the publisher.—*Éire-Ireland,* v. XX , Summer, 1985 for a review of "A Writer's Ireland: Landscape in Literature" by Steve Connelly.; v. XXIII, Spring, 1988 for " 'Only the Truth': The Short Stories of William Trevor" by Michael Ponsford. Copyright © 1985, 1988 Irish American Cultural Institute, 2115 Summit Avenue., No. 5026, St. Paul, MN 55105. Both reprinted by permission of the publisher and the respective authors.—*Esquire,* v. 100, December, 1983 for "The Flight of Rachel Carson" by Geoffrey Norman. Copyright © 1983, Esquire Associates. Reprinted by permission of the author.—*Feminist Studies,* v. 6, Summer, 1980. Copyright © 1980 by Feminist Studies, Inc. Reprinted by permission of the publisher, c/o Women's Studies Program, University of Maryland, College Park, MD 20742.—*Film Comment,* v. 27, May-June, 1991 for a review of "American Psycho" by Richard Corliss. Copyright © 1991 by the author. Reprinted by permission of the author.—*The Hudson Review,* v. XLIII, Winter, 1991; v. XXXVI, Summer, 1983; v. XLIV, Summer, 1991. Copyright © 1983, 1991 by The Hudson Review, Inc. All reprinted by permission of the publisher.— *Journal of the Short Story in English,* n. 9, Autumn, 1987. © Universite d'Angers, 1987. Both reprinted by permission of the publisher.—*Library Journal,* v. 116, January 1991 for " 'American Psycho' Is Not the Problem" by John N. Berry III. Copyright © 1991 by Reed Publishing, USA, Division of Reed Holdings, Inc. Reprinted from *Library Journal,* published by R. R. Bowker, Co., Division of Reed Publishing, USA, by permission of the publisher and author.—*The Listener,* v. 117, April 9, 1987 for "Which Are the Bad Guys?" by Clancy Sigal. © British Broad-

Chingiz Aitmatov

1928-

(Also transliterated as Aytmatov) Russian short fiction writer, novelist, filmmaker, playwright, translator, essayist, journalist, and editor.

The following entry provides an overview of Aitmatov's career through 1990.

INTRODUCTION

A prominent figure in Soviet literature and the first Kirghiz author to earn international recognition, Aitmatov is best known for works in which he combines Soviet literary traditions with elements of the folklore and oral history of his native Kirghizia, a region in Central Asia. While Western commentators often emphasize Aitmatov's criticism of the Stalin era, Soviet critics note that his frequent use of positive heroes exemplifies the practices of socialist realism, which aims to present a favorable view of Soviet life and the struggle to establish a truly socialist society. Aitmatov's works are generally considered a valuable commentary on the social problems of the Soviet Union, and Evgeni Sidorov praised Aitmatov as "one of the first Soviet writers to deal with the tragic conflicts of Soviet times."

Born in Sheker in the Kirghiz Republic, Aitmatov was raised by his mother after his father, a political activist, disappeared during the Stalinist purges of 1937. Aitmatov's aunt and grandmother taught him the oral history and legends of the Kirghiz people, who had no written language of their own until the late 1920s, and he became fluent in Russian at an early age. One of the few literate persons in his village, Aitmatov served in a variety of clerical positions from the ages of fourteen to eighteen. After World War II, he attended a veterinary school in Kazakhstan. Aitmatov's first story was published in Russian in 1952, and he continued to write while working as a livestock specialist from 1953 to 1956. During the next two years he studied literature at the Gorky Institute in Moscow; he later worked as a correspondent for the newspaper *Pravda*. As a member of the Communist party, Aitmatov has served as a deputy to the Supreme Soviet and held editorial positions on several prominent Soviet and Kirghiz literary journals.

Aitmatov wrote most of his early works in Kirghiz and later translated many of them into Russian. He was awarded the Lenin Prize in 1963 for his collection *Povesti gor i stepei (Tales of the Mountains and Steppes),* which reprints several of his best known early stories, including *Dzhamilia (Dzhamilia)* and *Pervyi uchitel' (The First Teacher.)* Often considered Aitmatov's first major work, *Dzhamilia* focuses on a young Kirghiz peasant woman who, while awaiting her husband's return from war, real-

izes that she never loved him and leaves her village with another man. *The First Teacher* relates the struggles of Duishen, a veteran of the Russian Revolution, to establish a school in a rural village. Often opposed by the villagers, he nevertheless succeeds in making a positive difference in the lives of his pupils, one of whom becomes a prominent scholar. While Kirghiz commentators have frequently attacked Aitmatov for portraying women in unconventional and non-subservient roles and for having many of his characters engage in conflicts with state authorities, Soviet critics have praised his protagonists for their attempts to fulfill socialist ideals under adverse conditions.

Beginning with the publication of *Proschai, Gul'sary! (Farewell, Gul'sary!)* in 1966, Aitmatov began writing primarily in Russian and later translated some of his works into Kirghiz. Awarded the State Prize for Literature in 1968, *Farewell Gul'sary!* concerns the intertwined fates of Tanabai, an elderly Kirghiz peasant, and Gul'sary, a racehorse once owned by Tanabai. Although Tanabai played an important role in organizing collective farms, he was subjected to a series of demotions during the Stalin era and ultimately lost his membership in the Communist party. Tanabai reminisces about these events while watching over the dying Gul'sary, who was confiscated by party officials, castrated, and used as a work horse. While some critics consider *Farewell, Gul'sary!* a provocative indictment of Josef Stalin's policies, others note that Tanabai's continuing commitment to socialist objectives throughout his ordeals places him within the tradition of positive Soviet heroes.

Set in the Lake Issuk-Kul region of Kirghizia, *Belyj parokhod (Posle skazki) (The White Ship)* focuses on a young boy who sees a deer that he identifies with the Horned-Deer Mother, which, according to legend, saved the boy's ancestors from extinction by guiding them to the area, but disappeared when hunters began killing deer for their antlers. After a relative who does not value the old legends forces his grandfather to shoot the deer, the boy becomes distraught and drowns while attempting to swim to a white steamship on which he believes he will find his long-lost father. Aitmatov later revised the ending slightly in response to Soviet critics who found the death of the young protagonist overly pessimistic; nevertheless, *The White Ship* has often been praised for exploring the consequences which arise when a group neglects its cultural heritage.

Aitmatov's novel *I dol'she veka dlitsia den' (The Day Lasts More Than a Hundred Years)* comprises three major subplots and blends elements of Kirghiz folklore, Soviet history, and science fiction. The first subplot relates the unsuccessful efforts of a railway worker to honor a co-worker's request that he be buried in an ancient cemetery associated with *mankurts*—prisoners of foreign invaders who, according to legend, were turned into mindless slaves after being brutally tortured. The second focuses on a former Russian soldier who is being persecuted for writing his memoirs of World War II. In the third subplot, astronauts on a joint Soviet-American space mission discover an advanced utopian civilization on another planet but are prevented from returning to Earth by their own governments, both of which fear the cultural changes that might result from this contact. Critics have recognized this work as a highly complex treatment of intellectual freedom and cultural identity open to numerous thematic interpretations. Joseph P. Mozur observed: "Taken in its entirety, [*The Day Lasts More Than a Hundred Years*] enunciates a powerful plea for freedom of conscience. It condemns the psychology of obsequious careerism and mutual mistrust that characterized the Stalin years and, as the author implies, finds expression in Soviet society today."

Aitmatov's 1986 novel, *Plakha (The Place of the Skull)*, continues his interest in the moral and social problems of Soviet Union, especially drug trafficking, bureaucratic corruption, and the destruction of nature. The two major narrative lines of the novel focus on Avdiy Kallistratov, an ethnic Russian who has been discharged from a seminary, and Boston Urkunchiev, a Kirghiz herdsman. Avdiy's attempt to infiltrate the Central Asian drug trade ultimately leads to his being severely beaten by workers who are slaughtering wild antelope in the region. Simultaneously, Boston's efforts to save a pack of wolves bring him into conflict with party officials. While the social emphasis of *The Place of the Skull* has been praised, Western

reviewers found its narrative structure disjointed. Soviet commentators also objected to Aitmatov's pessimistic social outlook, his use of religious symbolism, and his favorable portrayal of a spiritually motivated character.

Aitmatov collaborated with Kaltai Mukhamedzhanov on *Voskhozhdenie na Fudzhiamu (The Ascent of Mount Fuji)*, an anti-Stalinist drama that examines the issues of conscience and personal responsibility among a group of friends, one of whom has secretly denounced another member of the group for treason. An important figure in Kirghiz cinema, Aitmatov has also produced film adaptations of many of his works.

PRINCIPAL WORKS

SHORT FICTION

Dzhamilia   1958
   [*Dzhamilia* published in *Tales of the Mountains and Steppes,* 1969]
Litsom k litsu   1958
Rasskazy   1958
Topolek moi v krasnoi kosynke   1961
   [*Pretty Poplar in a Red Kerchief* published in *Tales of the Mountains and Steppes,* 1969; also published as *To Have and to Lose* in *Piebald Dog Running along the Shore, and Other Stories,* 1989]
Verbliuzhii glaz   1961
   [*The Camel's Eye* published in journal *Soviet Literature,* 1962]
Pervyi uchitel'   1962
   [*The First Teacher* published in *Tales of the Mountains and Steppes,* 1969; also published as *Duishen* in *Piebald Dog Running along the Shore, and Other Stories,* 1989]
Povesti gor i stepei   1962
   [*Tales of the Mountains and Steppes,* 1969]
Materinskoe pole   1963
   [*Mother Earth* published in *Mother Earth, and Other Stories,* 1990]
Proschai, Gul'sary!   1966
   [*Farewell, Gul'sary!,* 1970]
Povesti   1967
Belyj parokhod (Posle skazki)   1970; also published as *Posle skazki (Belyj parokhod)* [revised edition], 1971
   [*The White Ship,* 1972; also published as *The White Steamship,* 1972]
Povesti i rasskazy   1970
Rannie zhuravli   1975
   [*The Early Cranes* published in the journal *Soviet Literature,* 1976; also published as *The Cranes Fly Early* in *Piebald Dog Running along the Shore, and Other Stories,* 1989]
Pegil pes, begushchij kraem moria   1977
   [*Piebald Dog Running along the Shore* published in *Piebald Dog Running along the Shore, and Other Stories,* 1989]

NOVELS

I dol'she veka dlitsia den'   1980; also published as *Buran-
    nyi polustanok,* 1981
    [*The Day Lasts More Than a Hundred Years,* 1983]
Plakha   1986
    [*The Place of the Skull,* 1989]

OTHER

V soavtostve s zemleiu i vodoiu   (essays and lectures)
    1978
Voskhozhdenie na Fudzhiamu   [with Kaltai Mukhamed-
    zhanov]   (play)   1973
    [*The Ascent of Mount Fuji,* 1975]
Sobraniye sochineniy v 3-kh tomakh.   3 vols.   (collected
    fiction and journalism)   1982-84

CRITICISM

Ronald Hingley

From time to time, apparently on some form of rota, writers from the 'Fraternal Republics' of Central Asia, Cauca-
sia etc are represented in organs of the central Soviet Russian press by works of *belles lettres* lavishly bespattered
with the local colour of their area. The system resembles
that whereby manufacturers of household commodities
are said to allocate the award of competition prizes on a
regional basis: so many to West Country housewives, so
many to garage mechanics in the East Riding, and so on.

Not all specimens of this exotic genre are necessarily de-
spicable from a literary point of view, as *Farewell
Gul'sary!* shows. It is the work of a Kirgiz author writing
in Russian and concerns the joint tribulations of an elderly
Kirgiz, Tanabai, co-starring with his aged, dying horse:
the great pacer and ex-stallion Gul'sary, once famed down
Frunze way and a frequent symbol in the games of Kirgiz
boys frolicking beneath the *karagach* (a species of elm).

There is a distant whiff of Hemingway's *The Old Man and
the Sea*—not to mention Tolstoy's famous horse-story
Kholstomer or even Paul Gallico's *Snow Goose*—about
this plain tale from the yurts. Typically of Soviet works
of fiction (was ever anything less forward-looking?) the
whole affair is a flashback from the first paragraph: 'The
old man was riding on an old cart. And Gul'sary, the
pacer who drew it was an old, a very old horse.' Things
were not always so, however, for the now-gelded Gul'sary
was once a great seducer of Kirgiz mares, as was his master of Kirzig widows. In youth Tanabai had committed a
grave sin by denouncing his step-brother to the authorities
as a kulak counter-revolutionary, and many of his troubles
seem to him a just retribution for this ancient act of
treachery. They include the official withdrawal of his
party card, as the penalty for a tantrum provoked by his
failure to maintain the norm in lamb-raising, in impossible
conditions, during his period as a shepherd—after previous, more glorious spells as soldier, blacksmith and herdsman.

The mystique of the 'party card' as a sort of Holy Grail,
and the general message that 'All is well down on the Collective Farm', stamp [*Farewell Gul'sary!*] as one of the
less daring publications to appear (truncated) in the otherwise adventurous journal *Novy mir* in recent years. Yet it
has its sterling, not to say sturdy, virtues as a piece of unpretentious narrative meritorious within its admittedly
narrow conventions. Moreover, what is humdrum and everyday in Kirgizia may seem the height of exoticism in
Potters' Bar. The translator's otherwise unaccountable
policy of bestrewing his text with such transliterated arca-
na as *partorg, zavkhoz* and *lapsha* may, one hopes, kindle
poetic inspiration among connoisseurs of the quaint far
from Frunze, where these things are as unromantic as are
town clerks and fish and chips elsewhere. With 'zootech-
nics' for what should presumably have been 'veterinary
practice' we enter lush pastures indeed. (pp. 105-06)

> *Ronald Hingley, "Down Frunze Way," in* The
> Spectator, *Vol. 225, No. 7414, August 1, 1970,
> pp. 105-06.*

The Times Literary Supplement

As in much contemporary Soviet literature, the urge in
Chingiz Aitmatov is to grapple with a sleazy Stalinist past
in order to come to terms with the present. In this respect,
Georg Lukács has even nominated him as someone who
can stand alongside Solzhenitsyn; Aitmatov could be a deliberate counterweight, if one sees Solzhenitsyn—a disaf-
fected Russian, writer of the traditional "loose, baggy
monster" Russian novel, feted in the West, but spurned
by officialdom at home; winner of the Nobel Prize—
balanced by a loyal non-Russian, Soviet writer of small-
scale regional novellas, having had little impact in the English-speaking world, yet groomed as an exemplary author
by the Soviet regime, winner of the Lenin Prize for literature in 1963 at the age of thirty-five.

It is in the "Library of Lenin Prize Winners" series that
Aitmatov's four early tales—*Dzhamilya, My Red Ker-
chiefed Young Poplar, Camel's Eye,* and *The First Teacher*—appear in their latest honoured guise [in *Povesti gor
i stepei*]. They are all translated from their original Kirghiz and set among the common people of Kirghizia, the
Central Asian republic bordering on Sinkiang; only in the
last tale does the point of view move away to the Moscow
intelligentsia when a woman academic, born in a backward Kirghiz settlement, tells the story of her rescue from
there by a semi-literate young revolutionary "teacher" in
the early 1920s.

As an outsider, conscious of her uprooting from her people, Altynai Sulaimanova throws the ordinariness of the
characters in the stories into a sharper focus. Similarly,
her recollection of the heroic Leninist period of the revolution sharpens the awareness of the grubbiness of the moral
climate of the postwar period in which the other three
tales are set.

It is a past shared and suffered in common with Kirghizia,
yet reappearing in strange and distant foreign ways, which
disturbs and enthralls the metropolitan Russian reader.
For Aitmatov is a pugnaciously regional writer not only

singing the beauty of his land but stressing—sometimes, it would seem, unnecessarily in tales written for Kirkghiz readers—the customs and social idiosyncrasies of his people. This emphasis of nationality on the periphery (it echoes Solzhenitsyn's emphasis on Russianness) is a corrective to Stalinist denationalizing and finds an understanding in the Russian heartland. So does the pain and bewilderment of the swift change from a backward Muslim nomadic peasantry to the citizenry of an industrialized state: the noble horse-riding *dzhigit* is now the long-distance lorry-driver grinding over the mountains with supplies for China. Heroic politics have proved illusory: the idealist "first teacher" is now an inglorious country postman treated with patronizing condescension by local worthies.

An added rawness is given to them by the deliberate naivety of the storytelling. Only in *Camel's Eye* is there an echo of belles-lettres with the Chekhovian description of an impersonal steppe. Elsewhere, the echoes are of the folk tale with its evil and innocent characters, its mysterious outsiders, its quests for the impossible, the set-piece proving of strength; of the novelette where hearts throb and storms rage; of the popular cinema, for Aitmatov's montage is cinematographic in its sharp angles and direct cuts. Unappetizing as this may sound as a mixture, Aitmatov makes it work. Under his apparent naivety lies the arch sophistication of primitive painters—two of them, significantly, act as the main narrators of the first and last tale.

In a ruggedly simple prose, understatement, such as the expatriate academic's plaintive "When did we lose the ability really to respect a simple man as he was respected by Lenin?", becomes a natural weapon to deal with the enormities of Stalinism. Respect for ordinary men, the triumph of warm personal relationships in an uncaring society—Aitmatov has simple but effective remedies for social wounds. The understatement strikes home at the Soviet reader with his experience, yet it is Aitmatov's understatement, filtered of necessity through two translations, which, oddly enough, would probably fail to make contact with English readers.

> *"Lost Simplicities," in* The Times Literary Supplement, *No. 3658, April 7, 1972, p. 384.*

The Times Literary Supplement

Those who know Aitmatov's previous regional novels will need no acclimatizing for *The White Steamship.* The setting in the grandeur of the Kirghizian landscape is unchanged. So is the spiritual landscape among men living at subsistence level on the fringes of Soviet society: the good, innocent and pure in heart stand meekly under boorish, tin-pot Stalinist bullies. Familiar too is the literary topography—the juxtaposition of folk-tale and documentary, lyrical pathos and colloquial roughness, the use of simple yet extraordinarily evocative symbols.

Central to the novel (its alternative Russian title is *After the Tale*) is the telling by Momun, the kindly grandfather to his grandson, of the folk-legend of the Horned Deer-Mother who suckled the child founders of the Kirghiz nation. The legendary deer, although hunted to extinction by the Kirghiz, makes a brief reappearance in the forest na-

ture reserve where Momun works, only to be shot on the orders of Orozkul, the brutal overseer, and butchered in a savage scene. Aitmatov's symbolism is transparent: the folk-tale is about "conservation", both natural and cultural.

Alongside Momun's national legend there is his seven-year-old grandson's private fairy-tale of becoming a fish and swimming away to the great lake and its white steamship. Against the old man's conservative dream, to which Aitmatov is critically sympathetic, is set the unformulated, innocent aspiration of youth. Both dreams are shattered by the reality of petty Stalinist brutality and lawlessness: the butchering of the deer shot on the reserve.

With all this we are in familiar Aitmatov country. It is the resolution of the novel which unexpectedly takes us into uncharted territory. From Aitmatov's previous work, one might have expected Momun and his grandson to be rescued from their tragedy by a caring Communist Party. This time there is no salvation: the boy and innocence are swept away in the river rapids as the Stalinist brutes carouse over their venison.

This bitter, pessimistic ending has led, of course, to anguished public debate in the Soviet Union, well documented in the translators' afterword; although mention should have been made of Aitmatov's subsequent revised ending which does make a slight concession to his critics while yielding no significant point of principle. The afterword places Aitmatov, admired by both the intelligentsia and party machine, for English readers. But eliciting a response in readers unaccustomed, perhaps, to his intelligent, probing naivety depends far more on conveying Aitmatov's acute control of tone which directs his disparate material. This the present version fails to do. There are mistranslations—one makes the river Yenisey rise in Kirghizia!—and the tenses are muffed in the crucial ending. "Hey you gas-bags, what are you chirping about here?" is hardly the English to put on the lips of a bard singing a competitive elegy in an heroic rage. And Momun, who should remain simply "an old man", appears as an old "fogey", "duffer", "codger" and "geezer"—antique slang which lies uneasily with "odd-ball", "goofy" and "whacky".

Yet, with its symbols, motifs and moral force *The White Steamship* miraculously survives—as many Russian novels have had to in the past—the betrayals of translation.

> *"Dreams and Reality," in* The Times Literary Supplement, *No. 3677, August 18, 1972, p. 961.*

Chingiz Aitmatov [Interview with N. N. Shneidman]

[The following interview was conducted on April 7, 1976 at the offices of the House of the Writers' Creative Activity of the Union of Soviet Writers.]

[Shneidman]: *What is the main trend in the development of your creative activity?*

[Aitmatov]: I view the development of my creative activity as a transition from romanticism to realism. One of my early works *Litsom k litsu* was realistic, but later, and in particular in *Dzhamilia,* there are strong traits of romanticism. This is not to say that I am against romanticism in general. Not in the least, but I am against the so-called *Izhe*-romanticism in which certain aspects and traits of man's nature and activity are overemphasized at the expense of problems of real life.

Could you elaborate on the specific traits of the so-called Izhe-romanticism?

I believe that the main objective of art is to render a picture of life which is as close to reality as possible. *Izhe*-romanticism presents often an idealized picture of life in which reality could be deformed. It is possible to say that certain works of socialist realism of the Stalin period have been written in this spirit.

You write in two languages: in your native Kirghiz as well as in the Russian. In what language do you prefer to write and why?

It makes little difference to me in what language I write. Everyone is aiming at perfection which is difficult to achieve. Good literature is difficult to write in any language.

Could you comment on your style and your methods of work?

When I write I correct a lot in the process of creating. I do not write, let us say, thirty pages and later start correcting and editing. I usually correct and introduce many changes while I write. I consider it a waste of time going over the same text a number of times, but it may happen that I spend as much, if not more, time and waste even more paper in search for a proper image or for the right description of a certain scene. I aim in my writing at a compactness of style, at a concentration of ideas and words, at an intensity of narration. I am against unnatural descriptiveness *(protiv napusknoi opisatel'nosti)*. I try to find an artistic image for everything I describe. In the process of writing changes are inevitable, but usually I try to keep to the initial conception intended for a given work. In my early stories I often wrote in the first person, making use of outside narrators. Presently I am writing mostly in the third person. I consider writing in the first person an easy way out. One should write in the first person only when dealing with one's personal and intimate problems, and in particular when one writes about himself.

How would you explain the fact that evil is often victorious in your works and that the positive heroes go down to defeat?

I regard tragedy as the highest form of artistic expression and a tragic ending of a given work may often be the only honorable way out for the positive hero from the existing situation. This does not mean, however, that the tragic ending of a given work is necessarily its main concern. Thus, for example, the story *Rannie zhuravli* ends on a tragic note; the main hero goes down to defeat, but the main theme of the story is the birth of a poet in man. I endeavor to show in this work how a young teenager grows and develops into a true poet. The moving force, leading him onto this path is love. In *Rannie zhuravli* it is the love

for life in general, as well as the growing love of the main hero for his young girl-friend.

What is in your opinion the role of the positive hero in contemporary Soviet literature?

The image of the positive hero in literature should change continuously. There could be no standardization or stabilization of the image of the positive hero. As soon as the positive hero becomes a static unchangeable character, he dies. Such an unimaginative approach to the depiction of the positive hero undermined to a degree the development of the literature of socialist realism of the Stalin period. In my works the positive hero may be a representative of any segment of Soviet society and I find no particular place in my art for the new hero of the period of the so-called scientific and technological revolution *(NTR)* in our country. My main objective in creating a positive hero is to create the image of a true man, a man who could be called a real human being.

What is, in your opinion, the main concern of contemporary Soviet literature in general, and of your creative activity in particular?

The social significance of literature should not be underestimated but personally I do not aim at solving in a certain work of art one particular problem only. My writings encompass and deal with a number of ethical, social, ideological, and other problems which are interwoven in my works, and which are difficult to separate from each other.

Soviet literature, in which contemporary reality is depicted, is in general concerned with the fate of man in contemporary society. Society is in a state of constant change. It appears that capitalism will not exist forever; socialism will be replaced by communism, and later, perhaps, there might be even further changes. All these changes become even more complicated due to the existing disparities between the nature of man and the very essence of society of which man is a part.

In the process of history man tries continuously to perfect himself, but by overcoming certain shortcomings, in the process of correcting previous errors man is bound to make new mistakes. Man endeavors always to become a true human being, but his efforts are influenced by his environment: by social, economic, and ideological problems with which he is faced and which are not always easy to solve.

How do you view the interaction of Soviet theory of literature and contemporary literary practice?

In the past Soviet theory of literature devised guidelines for the development of contemporary literature and literary practice followed closely these theoretical premises. It appears that the situation has changed by now. Soviet theory of literature is presently late in summarizing and generalizing the experience of literary practice and the literary output of contemporary writers is ahead of the theoretical premises for contemporary literature. Theorists of literature, in turn, endeavor to adapt the new theoretical premises to the needs of literary practice. The interaction of theory and practice of Soviet literature in contemporary conditions is often complicated because certain representatives of the past in our literature endeavor to hold back its development.

In what way is the freedom of artistic expression related to theoretical requirements?

Soviet writers have presently an opportunity to write as they wish, regardless of what the theorists of literature say. The task of innovating, however, of moving the development of Soviet literature ahead, of prompting its progress, is entrusted to those writers who have reached a high level of artistic mastery and have proven beyond doubt their dedication to our cause. It would be difficult to imagine what would happen if anyone, regardless of his ability and literary mastery, would write and publish whatever comes to his mind. Many such experimental works would certainly be harmful to society.

How do you view Western criticism of your work?

In general terms I consider it fair. It is usually good criticism which is, however, in many ways different from our Soviet literary criticism. I read it very attentively. It brings to my mind many new aspects of my work not pointed out by Soviet critics. It alerts me to those features of my art which have been overlooked by my compatriots. Sometimes Western critics express opinions similar to those expressed by Soviet critics but they do it more openly and candidly. Personally I am very interested to learn how people living in different countries and in different social systems react to my art.

What are, in your opinion, the objectives of literature in the shrinking world of the twentieth century?

It seems to me that literature plays in the Soviet Union a more important role than it does in the West. We seldom hear that a work of art, a novel or a play, would excite the people in the West as much as it often does in the Soviet Union; that people would discuss and argue about it in the West the way we do it here. This is probably due to the fact that literature is in the Soviet Union a vehicle of ideology and it stimulates the development of the ideological and political consciousness of our people.

The mission of literature is to express the essence of the human spirit, of man's spiritual quest. Russian nineteenth century literature, for example, is a peculiar phenomenon of unparalleled height and of unsurpassed power of the peoples' spirit. Regardless of circumstances and conditions there are always possibilities for the creation and development of true art.

Since literature is to play an important role in the rapprochement between different nations and different social systems, and since it could assist in a better understanding between people residing on different continents the problem of translating literature from one language into another one becomes very important. It is imperative that a work of art would reach the reader in a perfect translation; that a translation would render the content and spirit of a work as it is intended by its author. We, in the Soviet Union, make a concentrated effort to acquaint our readers with the best literature appearing in the West. We have a special school for translators, and I am sure that our readers benefit from being exposed to the works of Western

writers in translations of high quality. It appears that in the West, on the other hand, the selection of Soviet works for translation is sometimes haphazard and it is often performed by people who are not adequately qualified for such duties. It is in the interest of Western readers and Soviet writers alike that the people in the West be exposed to the best Soviet works of art in the best possible translations. (pp. 265-68)

Chingiz Aitmatov and N. N. Shneidman, in an interview in Russian Literature Triquarterly, *No. 16, 1979, pp. 265-68.*

Joseph P. Mozur

"The mission of literature is to express the essence of the human spirit, of man's spiritual quest," remarked Chingiz Aitmatov in an interview several years ago [published in *Russian Literature Triquarterly,* 1979]. Aitmatov's deep concern for man's spirituality in Soviet society brings his art into close association with that of Valentin Rasputin and the late Yuri Trifonov, whose works transcend the problems of the Siberian village and the *byt* (manners and milieu) of the Soviet metropolis respectively, to confront the reader with profound ethical questions concerning one's relationship to one's fellow man. Most of Aitmatov's work is set in Soviet Middle Asia, in his native Kirghizia, yet his treatment of eternal questions and his innovative spirit have combined to make him one of the most popular writers in the Soviet Union today. Aitmatov's works have been published in the leading Soviet literary journals, and their subsequent appearances in book form enjoy large editions. . . . Not a very prolific writer, Aitmatov is very serious about his art, and, motivated by a Tolstoyan sense of duty to man and society, he does not shy away from controversial issues. Thus the appearance of each new work by the author has been a literary event, often provoking intense discussion in the Soviet press concerning his fresh approach to socialist realism.

The combination of Aitmatov's Kirghiz heritage and his assimilation of the wealth of classical Russian literature make his art truly unique. The folklore and rich epic tradition of his people have made him keenly sensitive to esthetic problems in literature. His prose is highly lyrical, and at times its style is clearly reminiscent of the Kirghiz national epos *Manas.* Yet the symbols and recurring motifs in Aitmatov's prose do not have merely ornamental function, as is the case in many inferior literary works from Soviet Middle Asia, but serve to give each work its peculiar structure and to dramatize dilemmas and conflicts common to all of mankind.

Thanks to his parents, both of whom had studied in Russian schools, Aitmatov was introduced at an early age to Russian language, literature and culture. He grew up to be bilingual—in a short autobiographical sketch he writes humorously about his first experience at interpreting at age five—and today he writes and translates freely in both Kirghiz and Russian. Although he tends to avoid direct answers to questions concerning the language in which his later works are written (his early works of the 1950s and 60s—*Dzhamilia, The First Teacher, Mother Earth*—were written in Kirghiz), it is a fact that beginning in 1966 with *Proščaj Gul'sary! (Farewell, Gulsary!)* his works have appeared first in Russian.

Although Aitmatov's early work was written in Kirghiz, the folklore of his native country played only a modest role in its esthetic conception. Beginning with *Belyj paroxod (The White Steamer;* 1970), however, a much more conscious effort to present human situations and conflicts on both a realistic and a mythical level is evident, with the latter structuring and interpreting the action on the realistic plane. The appearance of *Belyj paroxod* in *Novyj Mir* during the last month of Tvardovsky's editorship of the journal can be considered a turning point in Aitmatov's career in another way as well. In the novella an unnamed boy drowns when he "flees" the real world of brute force created by his sadistic uncle, an embodiment of cynical tyranny, and attempts to reach his own dreamworld of love and beauty embodied in the symbol of the white steamship. Aitmatov's portrayal of the triumph of evil over good was so powerful that an intense controversy concerning the possibility of the tragic under socialist conditions arose in *Literaturnaja Gazeta.* The author successfully defended his work against accusations of pessimism and lack of justice to socialist reality, and his victory has proved to be not insignificant for the course of Soviet letters. One must note, however, that Aitmatov later weakened his position somewhat by altering the conclusion of *Belyj paroxod* in its first edition in book form (*Čingiz Ajtmatov: Povesti i rasskazy;* 1970) to introduce a ray of light in the novella's dark world. The role of a minor character, Kulubek, is stressed by the narrator as having offered a possible unrealized alternative for the doomed boy.

Aitmatov has continued to write in the spirit of *Belyj paroxod.* His last three works—*Rannie žuravli (Early Cranes:* 1975), *Pegij pës, beguščij kraem morja (A Spotted Dog by the Seashore;* 1977) and *I dol'še veka dlitsja den' (And the Day Lasts Longer Than a Century;* 1980)— all combine myth and legend with everyday reality to accentuate man's precarious situation in the world. Likewise his belief that man is essentially a tragic creature is maintained in his latest work.

Rannie žuravli is set in a small Kirghiz village during World War II. The novella is based on Aitmatov's boyhood experiences in his native *ail,* Sheker, and reflects the hardship his village suffered during the war when women and children were called upon to do the labor of men in the fields. The author portrays the struggle of five Kirghiz youths in an isolated *ail* to do the work of their fathers, who are away at the front. The boys are requested by the kolkhoz chairman to drop out of school in the winter to prepare the kolkhoz's neglected plows, the few half-starved horses and themselves to do the spring plowing and sowing on the vast Aksai steppe situated in the foothills of the Manas mountain range. The theme of the work itself can hardly be considered very original for postwar Soviet literature, yet Aitmatov modifies it significantly. The mountain, for example, is a constant reminder of the Kirghiz epic poem *Manas,* in whose images of bravery and grandeur the author casts the boys and their "mission."

Even the rhythm of the narration is in a number of passages clearly reminiscent of epic solemnity.

As winter turns to spring the boys become men, and the main character, Sultanmurat, manages to whip his companions into a disciplined *kollektiv.* Uniting the boys is their intense yearning for their fathers and their desire to live up to their idealized conceptions of them. But Aitmatov was not intent on applauding the boys' patriotism or crowning their efforts with well-deserved success. In the final pages of the novella the reader is jolted from his position of serene observer when tragedy suddenly befalls the boys almost immediately after they have finally begun their "mission" in the Aksai steppe. After four days' labor the boys find themselves entirely alone and exhausted, yet encouraged by the hope that the harvest will be bountiful. Their dreams are dashed, however, when horse thieves attack and rob them of their plowhorses, an act which also threatens to deprive the village of sorely needed grain. Sultanmurat pursues the armed men on the one remaining horse (his father's). But the horse is shot from under him, and the story ends with Sultanmurat left alone at the mercy of a wolf that has scented the blood of the dying horse.

The abrupt change of fate in *Rannie žuravli* is typical of Aitmatov's later prose. His works are characterized by long expositions and a deliberate narrative pace, both of which are dramatically brought to an end by a sudden crisis. The novella, however, is an uneven work. The epic background does not adequately compensate for the lack of depth of the characters, nor is it as successfully integrated into the structure of the novella as was the case of myth and legend in *Belyj paroxod.*

These inadequacies are fully overcome in Aitmatov's next novella, *Pegij pës, beguščij kraem morja,* the first of Aitmatov's major works to be set outside his native Kirghizia. *Pegij pës* can best be described as a lyrical and philosophical story of life and death in mythic form. The novella relates the sea journey and fate of three Nivkh fishermenhunters and the boy they take along to initiate in the hunt and in life at sea. As in all of Aitmatov's later works, the action takes place in a highly isolated area—this time on the sparsely inhabited coast of the Sea of Okhotsk among the Nivkh people in far northeastern Siberia. As in his earlier works, Aitmatov chooses a very dramatic situation to test man's humanity under extreme conditions. The three hunters and their boy initiate, Kirisk, paddle out into the open sea beyond sight of land in order to reach three rocky islands where the hunt is to take place. The men's losing sight of land is marked by the disappearance from view of their orientation point on land, a rocky knoll with spots of trees and snow, which from the distance has the appearance of a piebald dog. The moment is an important one for Kirisk, for he now enters the world of men, who in order to provide for their wives and children must venture out to sea.

Accompanying the boy are his father, his uncle and the elder, Organ, the most experienced fisherman-hunter in the hamlet, whose primitive, animistic understanding of the world is shared by all in the boat. Organ's thoughts and daydreaming during the course of the journey transport the reader into a mythical world. One dream that never leaves the elder is his dream of the great Fish-Woman, the mythological mother of the Nivkh tribe, with whom he yearns to unite. This longing finds expression in a number of erotic images. In his dreams Organ follows her into the sea, swimming along with her until they reach a haven on land where, "overcome by passion, they were to be one at last to experience in one lightning-like instant all the pleasure and bitterness of the beginning and end of life." Yet when they finally reach the haven, their unification cannot be consummated, for the Fish-Woman cannot leave her element and must return to the sea, where Organ can never reach her. The dream is important for the structure of Aitmatov's novella, for it emphasizes the eternal opposition of the sea and the land as expressed in the opening and closing paragraphs: "Along the shoreline of the Sea of Okhotsk, along the whole front between the land and the sea, the fierce battle of the two elements raged—the land impeded the movement of the sea, the sea tirelessly besieged the land." Also, the dream is in a sense a death wish, and as such it foreshadows the catastrophe that will befall the four men in the kayak.

After reaching the first island, where Kirisk's incautious actions spoil the hunt, the men set off for the second island. Immediately upon losing sight of land again they become engulfed by dense fog and must wrestle with a terrifying storm. They survive the storm yet lose their way in the fog. The fog settles down motionless over the sea, and the little drinking water the men have brought with them is soon to run out. Realizing their plight might last for days, Organ steps into the icy water to his death in order to save drinking water for the others in the boat. As time goes on and the fog continues to hang low over the sea, the boy's uncle and then father imitate the elder's act of self-sacrifice, leaving Kirisk the last remaining drops of water. Yet for Kirisk the men never die; they live on in his animistic world—Organ as the wind, his uncle as the waves, his father as the guiding star that the boy, alone and exhausted, sees when the fog finally lifts. Kirisk is saved on the seventh day as the winds drive the fragile kayak within sight of the "spotted dog" again.

Aitmatov's novella deliberately gives no clear indication of the time when the story takes place. This vagueness of time, of course, gives the story its mythological context. The self-sacrifice of the men is not military or revolutionary heroism, which has often been the theme of socialist-realist works. The sacrifice, although not easy, is still a natural act determined by a harmonious pagan view of the world that, odd as it may seem, has Christian undertones as well. The image of Christ walking on water, for example, is evoked prior to Organ's stepping into the sea.

A Spotted Dog can be compared to Hemingway's *The Old Man and the Sea.* In both works individual men stand for mankind, and the external action can take on mythological interpretation. If the creed of Hemingway's Santiago in essence calls upon men to preserve their dignity in defeat, then for Aitmatov's Nivkh fishermen the call is to "remain true to one's humanity"; and in the final analysis the three men's choice is not a choice at all, for it is their only way to live as men in their understanding of the

world. Another interesting parallel can be drawn between *Pegij pës* and Stephen Crane's "The Open Boat." Yet in Crane's story blind fate determines which of the five shipwrecked men makes it alive to the shore, whereas in Aitmatov's novella the men themselves actively create their fate.

The publication of *Pegij pës* with its heavy reliance on myth and symbolism quickly brought forth voices of strong criticism. In a brief survey of mythological and allegorical currents in recent Soviet literature, for example, L. Anninsky criticized the use of myth and legend by writers because in his view it distracts them from their chief goal— the realistic portrayal of reality (*Literaturnaja Gazeta,* 1 March 1978). Another critic asserted that to resort to myth in literature is far easier than to write "honest straightforward prose" (*Literaturnaja Gazeta,* 12 April 1978). Aitmatov countered by reaffirming his staunch loyalty to socialist realism, yet pointing out that his detractors have an oversimplified, naïve understanding of realism (*Literaturnaja Gazeta,* 29 March 1978). In an interview with Larissa Lebedeva he expressed the view that literature should break with obsolete one-dimensionality by using legend and myth, thus making the reader's experience of reality a deeper one (*Družba Narodov,* 1977).

Indeed, in his most recent work, *I dol'še veka dlitsja den',* Aitmatov continues to move away from one-dimensionality by creating a remarkable "symphonic" novel based on the counterpoint of several motifs and temporal planes. The central motif that determines the novel's structure and meaning is Aitmatov's peculiar interpretation of the Kirghiz legend of the Zhuanzhuany, a cruel nomadic tribe that tortured its prisoners by pulling taut leather skullcaps over their heads, thus depriving those that survived of their memory. The survivors, called "mankurt" by the tribe, thereafter became submissive slaves, obediently fulfilling their masters' most whimsical desires. According to the legend as presented in the novel, one such *mankurt* even kills his own mother, Naiman-Ana, at the behest of his captors, when she desperately seeks to revive her son's memory by repeating his name to him and by constantly asking him to tell her his father's name—Donenbai. According to the legend, as Naiman-Ana fell, pierced by her son's arrow, her scarf turned into a white bird that even today flies over the steppe crying, "Donenbai, whose son are you? Donenbai, Donenbai." The place where she was buried became known to the inhabitants of the Sarozek steppes of Kazakhstan—where the novel is set—as Ana-Beiit (Mother's Repose). Through the centuries Ana-Beiit became the sacred burial ground of the nomadic peoples populating the vast steppes.

The burial ground and the legend associated with it tie together three temporal planes: the legendary past, the recent past and the present, and the near yet hypothetical future. The main character, Edigei Zhangildin, a railwayman at an isolated hamlet in the steppe, represents Aitmatov's conception of the positive hero—a simple man devoted to his labor. Edigei is a *malen'kij čelovek* (little man), similar to the many variations of the type known to us from classical Russian literature. Like them he strives to live with dignity and conscience in a world in which forces are active that he can neither control nor fully comprehend. In the early 1950s Edigei tries to preserve his personality and humanity in the face of Stalinist henchmen, who even in the isolated Sarozeks manage to destroy an innocent family dear to him. Likewise in the present era he is confronted with another type of *mankurt* when he decides to honor a deceased friend's last wish to be buried at legendary Ana-Beiit. The funeral is to take place according to Moslem ritual, but Edigei soon discovers that his deceased friend's son, who arrives from the city, cares little for his father's heritage or Edigei's world view, which encompasses both life and death. The son, Sabitzhan, reveals himself to be a petty party careerist whose unlimited faith in technological progress envisions a world of human robots subserviently following orders from above.

After quarreling with Edigei, however, Sabitzhan grudgingly agrees to join the funeral procession, which is to go deep into the steppe. Yet the procession never reaches the burial ground. Unknown to Edigei, Ana-Beiit has been incorporated into the off-limits zone of the top-secret Sary-Ozek space center. The officers at the gate show little concern for Edigei's plight, and a Kazakh lieutenant, refusing to speak to him in his native Kazakh, tells him brusquely in Russian that Ana-Beiit will soon be liquidated to make room for a new housing project for the personnel of the space center. Edigei has no choice but to leave, and with deep sorrow and anger he solemnly buries his friend in a ravine within sight of the barbed-wire fence that has separated him from Ana-Beiit.

Paralleling the drama at the funeral procession is an unprecedented crisis, one which Edigei knows nothing about, that unfolds on the third narrative plane. For the first time Aitmatov introduces the fantastic into his prose. An American and a Soviet astronaut, as part of a joint USA-USSR mission, have discovered intelligent life on another planet. Choosing not to inform their superiors on Earth, they visit the planet on their own initiative before deciding to break the news to mankind, which, given its political and ideological differences, they doubt will be inclined to embrace a more advanced civilization. When Mission Control is finally contacted by the insubordinate astronauts, it learns that the "new world" is a virtual utopia, free of disease, civil strife and war. Yet the discovery threatens to throw the world into a dangerous crisis. When the U.S.-Soviet crisis commission is requested to allow representatives from the other planet to visit Earth, it rejects the offer; and to ensure the Earth's inviolability, the commission initiates "Project Hoop," which is to blot the discovery of a better way of life from the Earth's memory by cutting off all contact with the two astronauts, by casting a cloak of secrecy over all aspects of the mission and by setting up an impenetrable ring of explosive orbiters around the Earth to ward off any attempted interference from outer space.

Yet before Project Hoop is put into action, the narrative returns to Edigei, who now stands alone at the barbed-wire fence of the space center. He has vowed to himself not to give up the fight for Ana-Beiit. Deserted by all who had accompanied him in the procession, Edigei decides to

go back to the gate, only to turn and flee in terror in the closing apocalyptic scene of the novel, as the Soviet Union commences its part of the project and rocket after rocket thunders from the nearby launch site. Amidst the fire and roar of the rockets the cry of the white bird Donenbai is heard, symbolically warning man to remember his heritage.

Thus in the closing lines of *I dol'še veka dlitsja den'*, a work considered to be Aitmatov's first full-length novel, the author brings all the mythic currents and temporal planes together. The "cosmic myth" created by Aitmatov contains a number of contradictions, but it essentially parallels the myth of Naiman-Ana. The Earth dons a *mankurt*'s cap when it tries to cut itself off from all external influence. The cries of the stranded astronauts are clearly reminiscent of the call of the bird Donenbai.

Taken in its entirety, the novel enunciates a powerful plea for freedom of conscience. It condemns the psychology of obsequious careerism and mutual mistrust that characterized the Stalin years and, as the author implies, finds expression in Soviet society today. Similar to Czesław Miłosz, who in his Nobel Prize address warns Western man of the consequences of a "refusal to remember," Aitmatov urges his readers to resist becoming a *mankurt*, without memory, personality or conscience, and as such a pliable tool in the hands of those who have little respect for human dignity. This is the meaning of Edigei's simple life, the courageous act of the astronauts and the legend of Naiman-Ana.

I dol'še veka dlitsja den' is a complicated novel and, as such, not without deficiencies. Aitmatov has received justifiable criticism for his occasional inappropriate use of archaisms and neologisms in the narration. Furthermore, a number of important characters are sketchily portrayed—in particular, Edigei's wife and the Russian geologist Elizarov. Several sections in the exposition might seem to Western readers unduly sentimental and drawn-out.

Soviet criticism speaks with one voice in lauding Aitmatov's success at creating a believable positive character. Edigei's simple life takes on epic proportions, reaching deep into the heritage of his ancestors and at the same time calling upon modern man to remember whence he has come before rushing blindly into the future. The cosmic myth, however, has become the object of diverging opinions. Some reviewers do not question the justification of the Earth's decision to sequester itself from any contact with the "new world," considering its inhabitants no more than "highly humanistic Zhuan-zhuany" (*Oktjabr'*, 1981) or looking upon the planet as a dangerous Trojan horse (*Oktjabr'*, 1981). Others admonish Aitmatov for not being more specific as to which of the two partners on the U.S.—Soviet space commission bears responsibility for the Earth's unwillingness to embrace a more advanced form of life (for example, *Voprosy Literatury*, 1981, and *Pravda*, 16 February 1981). Significantly, the novel leaves such questions open, for in Aitmatov's prose all men bear responsibility for life on this planet. Moreover, a number of other burning questions are left unanswered as well. Thus, *I dol'še veka dlitsja den'* will certainly continue to be mentioned in literary discussion in the USSR for some time yet.

Aitmatov's official status in the Soviet Union—in addition to editorial responsibilities at *Novyj Mir* and *Literaturnaja Gazeta,* he represents Kirghizia in the Supreme Soviet and is chairman of the Kirghiz Union of Cinematographers— no doubt enables him to write with more artistic freedom than other Soviet writers. He has consistently criticized primitive didacticism and cliché-ridden style in Soviet letters and has become very vocal in recent years in advocating a more imaginative approach to socialist realism, one in which myth, legends and the fantastic are all to be granted a place (see, for example, his interview in *Družba Narodov,* 1977). If in the past Soviet literature has been straitjacketed by theorists trying to direct the way its development is to go, today there are signs that literary practice in the Soviet Union is beginning to relegate literary theory to an ever-increasing interpretive role. In an interview with N. N. Shneidman Aitmatov sums up this complicated evolution:

> The literary output of contemporary writers is ahead of the theoretical premises for contemporary literature. Theorists of literature, in turn, endeavor to adapt the new theoretical premises to the needs of literary practice. The interaction of theory and practice of Soviet literature in contemporary conditions is often complicated because certain representatives of the past in our literature endeavor to hold back its development.

Chingiz Aitmatov's role in this evolution should not be underestimated. And there is good reason to believe that his art will continue to challenge Soviet literary conservatives in the future. (pp. 435-39)

> *Joseph P. Mozur, "Chingiz Aitmatov: Transforming the Esthetics of Socialist Realism," in* World Literature Today, *Vol. 56, No. 3, Summer, 1982, pp. 435-39.*

Nina Kolesnikoff

Any reader familiar with the novellas of Chingiz Aitmatov is aware of the important role children play in his writing. Children are not only the protagonists of many of his novellas, but often become the narrators: they not only tell the story but evaluate everything and everyone in it.

Perhaps the clearest example of the child narrator appears in *Dzhamilia,* which is told in the first person by the fifteen-year-old Seit; he witnesses the story of the growing fascination between his sister-in-law Dzhamilia, whose husband is at war, and Daniiar, a demobilized soldier. Seit reports only what he can see and hear, or what he can guess, and is unable to penetrate the innermost feelings of the lovers. The advantage of this method is an unusual freshness and poetic beauty in the depiction of the love story, reflecting Seit's lack of prejudice and his innocent perception of the world.

Moreover, the choice of Seit as a narrator allows Aitmatov to introduce the other theme of the novella—that of the importance of art. Under the influence of Daniiar, Seit responds to the beauty of nature and experiences a strong desire to paint it. He leaves his native village to go to a city to study art. In the frame which opens and closes the novella, Seit is already a recognized painter, reminiscing about the events that made him an artist.

The frame establishes a dual temporal perspective, that in which Seit talks about his painting, and that in which he enacts his childhood experience. The past perspective predominates in the novella, and most of the story is filtered through the consciousness of the young Seit. But at the same time the narrative constantly reflects the point of view of the mature Seit, who comments on the events. Thus *Dzhamilia* offers a dual point of view which is perfectly reasonable, and which allows Aitmatov to transcend the limits of the innocence of his hero and to present values very close to his own.

By comparison with the clear first-person narration in *Dzhamilia,* the narration in Aitmatov's latest novellas about young protagonists is not as easy to define. Written in the third person, they seem at first to employ an omniscient narrator who presents the story, comments on the events, and sketches the characters. But a closer look at the narrative reveals that the predominant point of view in these novellas is not that of the omniscient author, but that of the young hero. While retaining the third-person narration, the narrator identifies himself with his young protagonists and reproduces their perception of the world around them.

The most consistent use of the child narrator occurs in *Rannie zhuravli* (*The Early Cranes*) written almost entirely from the point of view of a fourteen-year-old youth experiencing the hardships of war in a distant Kirghiz village. Like his predecessor Seit, Sultanmurat is forced to leave school in order to help the kolkhoz with farming. Together with his four friends, he forms "a landing force," responsible for the plowing and sowing of the spring crops in the Aksai steppe.

From the beginning of the novella the narrative transmits the point of view of Sultanmurat as he reflects on the harsh life in the village, the self-sacrificing work of women and children, and on his own responsibility as head of his family. As a contrast to these pictures of the difficult life on the homefront appear Sultanmurat's recollections of the happy days before the war; he remembers his father, their trip to the city, and their stay overnight in the steppe.

The two temporal planes of the present and the past are artfully interwoven in the novella, but there is also a third dimension—that of the future. Basically a daydreamer, Sultanmurat often escapes into fantasies, imagining the return of his father from the front and a happy life after the war. At the end of the novella, however, his dreams are crushed when he pursues horse thieves, loses his horse, and faces an uneven fight with a hungry wolf.

The child narrator also predominates in *Belyi parokhod* (*The White Steamship*), which renders the point of view of a seven-year-old boy deserted by his parents and living with his relatives in a mountain forest preserve. Through the eyes of the child the reader sees the cordon itself, its inhabitants, and events that lead to his tragic death. In the course of the novella the reader learns the innermost feelings of the boy, who feels rejected by everyone except his grandfather Momun. To escape this cruel reality he creates a tale in which he becomes a fish and swims to the white ship on which his father is working. He has another favorite tale told to him by his grandfather. That tale depicts the fate of the legendary Horned Deer Mother, who once had helped the Kirghiz people but had had to escape with its offspring when people began hunting for its horns. In the boy's childish perception there are no strict boundaries between the real world of the cordon and the world of fairy tales, and when a deer and family appear in the preserve, he mistakes her for the legendary Deer Mother. The killing of the deer is a blow to the boy's dream, and he decides to turn into a fish and swim away. As in *Rannie zhuravli,* the beautiful world of the child is crushed by the brute forces of real life.

By comparison with these two previously discussed novellas, the role of the child narrator diminishes in Aitmatov's latest work, *Pegii pes, begushchii kraem moria (The Skewbald Dog Running along the Seashore),* in which the voice of the young protagonist is combined with the voices of other characters, as well as with the voice of the omniscient narrator. But even here the child narrator outshines the others. The initial pages register the excitement of eleven-year-old Kirisk, going for his first sea hunt. The boy recalls his preparation for the hunt and imagines the celebration that will follow his happy return home. It is through the eyes of Kirisk that the reader sees the sea, calm and serene at first, but later raging and powerful. Through the boy's eyes the reader watches the desperate struggle of the three men in a tiny boat against the sea. Miraculously the men survive the storm, but are unable to find their way home in the thick fog that follows it. Faced with a shortage of food and drink, the men throw themselves one by one into the sea, hoping to prolong the life of the boy even for several days. The final pages of the novella transmit the despair of Kirisk, alone in the boat, delirious and raving for fresh water. But the novella ends on an optimistic note—after several days of ordeal the boy spots the familiar silhouette of his native bay with its snowy mound resembling a skewbald dog running along the seashore.

Despite the differences in the narrative technique, itself, and the degree to which the narrative is filtered through the consciousness of a young hero, all the above novellas testify to Aitmatov's predilection for the child narrator. Why is the writer so attached to this method of narration?

One of the most obvious advantages of the child narrator is an unusual vividness of description. A child sees the world in a unique way, not influenced by any habits or misconceptions. Using the arguments of Victor Shklovskii we can say that a child sees the old and the habitual as if it were new and unusual. A writer reproducing the child's vision defamiliarizes ordinary things and makes the reader see them instead of merely recognizing them. This is exactly what happens in the following passage in *Belyi parokhod:*

> The lad ran quickly, hopping over bushes and around the boulders he wasn't able to jump. He

didn't dally anywhere, even for a second—not near the high grass, nor near the rocks, although he knew that they were far from ordinary. They could feel insulted and even trip people. "The motor-market's arrived. I'll come back later," he tossed off while rushing past "lying camel," as he called a ginger, hunch-backed piece of granite sunk into the earth up to its chest.

> Ordinarily, the lad wouldn't pass without patting his "camel" on its hump. He patted him in the manner of an animal's master, like grandfather his short-tailed gelding—just a casual, off-handed tap as if to say, "You wait around, I'm off to take care of something nearby." He had a boulder called "saddle"—half white and half black, a skewbald rock with a saddle-like hollow on which you could mount, as on a horse. There was also a "wolf" rock which looked very much like a real wolf—tawnyish and flecked with gray, with powerful withers and weighty brows. He would steal up to him on all fours and take aim. But his favorite rock was the "tank," an indestructible boulder on the very bank of the river, which was hollowed away by the current. Any second now the "tank" would charge from the bank and plunge on, and the river would seethe, boiling with whitecaps.

The familiarization is motivated here by the age and character of the protagonist. The only child in the cordon, not spoiled by any toys, he had learned how to play and communicate with natural objects: rocks, plants and grasses. His closest "friends" are his binoculars, through which he can see the white ship in the distant Issik'kul Lake, and his briefcase to which he can confide all his injuries and worries.

Like all Aitmatov's other children, the boy is very close to nature. He knows a lot about the trees and animals in the forest, and through the teaching of his grandfather, respects all living things. Such an attitude towards nature is of great importance to Aitmatov, who stressed that by writing *Belyi parokhod* he wanted to make people aware of the need to establish a harmonious relationship with nature, "to preserve the wealth and beauty of the world around us." The boy in the novella expresses perfectly this idea, without any additional authorial comments or generalizations.

In a similar way, the child narrator allows Aitmatov to convey in his novellas the idea of the necessity to preserve the link between tradition and the new way of life. In all these novellas the young protagonists have a close relationship with their real or surrogate grandfathers, who pass on to them the old traditions. Grandfather Momun in *Belyi parokhod,* the old man Organ in *Pegii pes,* the team leader Chekish—all these old and wise men tell the youngsters about life in the past and by their own example teach them how to live.

Throughout all these novellas the colorful details of the local customs are transmitted not in authorial descriptions, but through the eyes of the young protagonists. Thus the local color does not burden the narrative, but adds to its vividness. As in descriptions of nature, Aitmatov often defamiliarizes local customs by filtering them through the consciousness of his young heroes, who do not understand the true meaning of what they witness:

> We walk home and hear: somebody starts singing a song. A young shepherd probably, or maybe an old one. Grandfather stops me. "Listen. You can't always hear those songs." We stand still and listen. Grandfather sighs. The song makes him nod his head.
>
> Grandfather says that long ago one khan had another khan prisoner. And this khan said to the captive khan: "If you want to you can live as my slave. Otherwise I'll fulfil your most cherished wish and then kill you." The other one thought before answering: "I do not wish to live as a slave. I'd rather you kill me, but before this, summon the first shepherd you meet from my homeland." "Why do you want him?" "Before my death, I want to hear him sing." Grandfather says that these people give their lives for their native songs. Who are these people? I'd like to see them. I guess they live in big cities?

It is important to note that local color as used by Aitmatov is devoid of the usual exotic flavor: it reproduces realistically the setting, customs, and way of thinking of the Kirghiz people. Moreover, this local color is not mere decoration, but an essential element of the structure, strengthening the characterization and revealing truths about human nature.

The child narrator is used by Aitmatov not only as a means to describe the settings vividly, but also as a vehicle for his ideas. In an interview given to *Literaturnaia gazeta* the writer stressed that as his creative goals had become more complex, he was looking for heroes that could express his ideas naturally, by their own essence. He had found such heroes in children:

> At the very essence of man's inner self lies the full value of childhood. The unity between adults and children, the selfless love of a mother, father, sister, and a grandmother, creates the impression of a loving, good world. Hence, the child's capacity to experience someone else's grief, his belief in truth . . . But the integral child's nature is confronted in life with lies, egoism and compromises. And a young person is not capable of sophistry. Here an artist can find the dramatic material and the sharp conflicts. By looking at the events with the eyes of youth, he can reveal the drama of life in a new, ingenious way.

The dramatic conflict between the child's innocent vision and the cruelty of the real world is the underlying principle of Aitmatov's recent novellas. In all of them he portrays extremely dramatic situations which reveal the true character of the protagonists. Depicted at the moment of their first serious trial, Aitmatov's young heroes prove themselves not only idealistic, but strong enough to defend their principles.

Faced with the killing of the deer, the boy in *Belyi parokhod* decides to swim away from the cruel people. He prefers to die rather than to live in the immoral and hypocriti-

cal world of adults. The boy dies, but the moral victory is his.

A similar effect is achieved by the tragic ending of *Rannie zhuravli,* portraying Sultanmurat in the pursuit of the horse thieves. The boy loses his horse and has to face an uneven fight with a wolf. Although he is likely to lose this fight, his death symbolizes his willingness to die to defend his principles.

The confrontation depicted in *Pegii pes,* unlike that in the other two novellas, is not between the idealistic world of the young and the immoral world of the adults, but between men and nature. The sea represents here the cruel force that crushes the boy's dream of a successful hunt which would initiate him into the world of adults. The adults, on the other hand, exemplify the highest moral standards possible—they sacrifice their own lives in order to save the boy. At the time of the events Kirisk does not comprehend the full meaning of their action, but eventually he will grasp the value of their self-sacrifice.

The change of the dramatic collision in *Pegii pes* forced Aitmatov to change the narrative method. In order to reveal the full meaning of the sacrifice of the adults, he could not rely exclusively on the perception of his young hero. Therefore, Aitmatov introduced into the novella the points of view of the other characters as well, primarily of Organ, an old man who is summing up his life while preparing for death, and of Emraiin, Kirisk's father, who, before dying, contemplates his responsibility towards his son.

Moreover, Aitmatov combined the concealed narrator with an omniscient one who describes the setting, introduces characters, and comments on the uneven struggle between the four men and the sea. In addition, the narrator renders the myths and legends which help to endow the concrete events described in the novella with cosmic dimensions. Because of the presence of the omniscient narrator *Pegii pes* reads like a philosophical tale about the meaning of life and the responsibilities of people towards each other.

In the other two novellas the author is more consistent in the use of the child narrator, but even here he occasionally introduces other points of view. In *Belyi parokhod* he renders the thoughts of Momun, the boy's grandfather and protector, and of Orozkul, the forest warden and the virtual ruler of the three families in the cordon. The character of Orozkul is univocal—he is the symbol of the hypocrisy and immorality of the adults, which shatter the boy's dreams of beauty and goodness. The character of Momun is more complex—he represents the good forces in life, but because of his inability to defend his principles he becomes an unwilling instrument in the death of his grandson. The convincing psychological portrayals of Momun and Orozkul throw into relief the opposing forces in the conflict and prepare the reader for the tragic ending of the novella.

The superficial treatment of minor characters, on the other hand, weakens the artistic impact of *Rannie zhuravli,* where the figures of the horse thieves are depicted one-sidedly, without a trace of psychological substance. They are brought into the novella suddenly, without any prehistory, simply to illustrate the evil forces that destroy the beautiful dreams of youngsters.

In addition to using the points of view of several characters, Aitmatov also introduces the voice of a narrator, very close to himself, who occasionally comments on the events and reveals their importance. In **Rannie zhuravli** the narrator draws a parallel between his young protagonists and the brave warriors of Manas, legendary heroes of the Kirghiz epos, thus emphasizing the heroic aspect of the boys' hard labor. In **Belyi parokhod** the narrator takes over the story after the death of the boy. In a peculiar epilogue, the narrator reiterates the moral message of the novella:

> I can only say one thing now: you rejected what your child's heart could not reconcile itself to. And that's my consolation. You lived like a bolt of lightning which once—and only once— flashed and expired. But lightning strikes from the sky. And the sky is eternal. This too is my consolation. And that a child's conscience in a person is like an embryo in a particle of grain: the grain won't grow without the embryo. That whatever awaits us on earth, truth will endure forever, as long as people are born and die.

The narrator concludes by repeating the words of the boy, addressed to the white steamship, thus suggesting that he had fulfilled the dreams of his hero by reaching the ship and telling it about the boy's short life, about his indestructible belief in the Deer Mother, and the principles of beauty and justice.

Nowhere do the voice of the narrator or the voices of other characters outweigh the voices of the protagonists. In all the novellas discussed, the child narrator remains the chief storyteller, describing the main events and forwarding the action. Moreover, the child narrator performs an important ideological function—through the child's innocent vision the writer penetrates the essence of life's complexities and contradictions. In order to make these contradictions more apparent, Aitmatov supplements the voice of the child narrator with the voices of other characters.

The role of the authorial narrator, on the other hand, is to strengthen the ideological message by transplanting the ordinary events depicted in the novellas into the philosophical framework. All three novellas force the reader to think about such eternal questions as the meaning of life and the responsibilities of men towards nature and towards each other. And the position of Aitmatov is very clear—he believes that good will triumph over evil, and that truth will endure forever. (pp. 101-09)

> *Nina Kolesnikoff, "The Child Narrator in the Novellas of Chingiz Aitmatov," in* Russian Literature and Criticism: Selected Papers from the Second World Congress for Soviet and East European Studies, *edited by Evelyn Bristol, Berkeley Slavic Specialties, 1982, pp. 101-10.*

Aitmatov on *The Day Lasts More Than a Century:*

I feel that I am not simply a representative of a particular national literature but am bound to say something more.

This "something more" I attempted to express in my new work, the novel ***The Day Lasts More Than a Century.*** Now that the book is written, I feel the need to reflect on what served as my guiding star.

A writer cannot precisely formulate what his creation is about. It always seems to him that there are no words to express his intentions fully. But nevertheless, I will try. The inner thought of my novel is not new, but it is still pertinent today: the essence and major creation of the Universe is man. One can write of the social, international, or scientific conditions of contemporary society, but only Man on Earth should concern and inspire the writer. Without this, art is dead.

> *Chingiz Aitmatov, in his "Everything Concerns Everyone" (1980), published in* On Craftsmanship, *Raduga Publishers, 1987.*

Constantin V. Ponomareff

Poetic vision in conflict, as understood in this paper, is taken to occur whenever a conscious and *non-* or *anti-aesthetic* manipulation of fictional material interferes with the natural thematic flow of an author's poetic imagination, which may, as it does on occasion in Aitmatov's work, cause psychological lapses in the credibility of literary characters. To a sensitive reader these manipulations of theme and character can be recognized as a lessening of the tragic tension of the poetic whole.

Before proceeding further it will be useful to establish the essential nature and direction of Aitmatov's creative energy, that which holds his work together, the better to indicate later any conscious shifts away from his natural poetic vision. His major work, written between 1957 and 1970, offers the best examples.

As I have tried to show in my previous work on Aitmatov [in *The Silenced Vision: An Essay in Modern European Fiction*], the essential poetic structure of Aitmatov's fiction is built by the presence and positive function of female figures and their children in human or animal guise. In his first significant novella **Litsom k litsu (Face to Face,** 1957), a vicious father figure stands in direct contrast to the mother and child configuration. His love story **Dzhamilia** (1958), which brought him an international reputation, revolves about the morally and emotionally exceptional character of Dzhamilia, who left an unloving husband for a man who understood and appreciated her. In his more tragic love story **Topolek moi v krasnoi kosynke (My Little Poplar in the Red Kerchief,** 1962), Asel took her child and left a young husband who lacked moral stamina for an older, but more selfless man. In **Materinskoe pole (Mother Field,** 1963) the whole action revolves about the lot of women who lose their husbands and their sons to war. Finally, in his major novels **Proshchai,**

Gul'sary! (Farewell Gul'sary, 1966) and *Belyi parokhod (The White Ship,* 1970), he metaphorized the female figure into animal forms, a device which gives his work a further mythical and symbolic dimension.

In each of these works woman as virgin, mistress, or mother is the creative focal point around which Aitmatov's fictionalized world turns. The men who are worthy figures are only those who remain in a positive relationship to the female figure at the center. Those who lose her love lose their humanity and become negative counter figures, a development which is not without significance for Aitmatov's creative process with its female orientation. The confrontation of a negative male with the feminine element is a formula valid in varying degrees for all of these major writings by Aitmatov. We see this most easily in his novellas *Face to Face, Dzhamilia* and *My Little Poplar in the Red Kerchief.* In *Mother Field* the men are away at war and thus do not have an immediate role to play. Curiously, an earlier tale, *Pervyi uchitel' (The First Teacher,* 1957), which had a man at the center, was not a deviation from Aitmatov's creative orientation, because Diuishen the village teacher actually functioned as a surrogate "mother" figure to all the schoolchildren. Though the female motif was muted in *Farewell, Gul'sary!* it explodes in full force in *The White Ship* where the central core of the novel is energized by a legend about the Horned Deer-Mother and her children.

It is perhaps not an accident that what I call Aitmatov's tampering with his poetic and lyrical art coincided with his official rise in the Soviet literary establishment, an ascent marked by his receiving the Lenin Prize in 1963 and the State Prize in 1966. It is also surprising how very few of the Soviet critics writing on Aitmatov in the last two decades have dealt with the problem of the conscious manipulation of literary material in his writing.

Though one can find earlier instances of Aitmatov's conscious attempts to manipulate the psychology of his characters, as for example in *My Little Poplar in the Red Kerchief* the lack of credibility of the psychological motivation of the truck driver Il'ias, it was not until his *Farewell, Gul'sary!* and especially his *The White Ship* that the conscious interference with character and theme became more apparent. In this respect it is primarily women among Soviet critics who have been most perceptive of this aspect of Aitmatov's writing. Thus, V. Stanislavleva writing about Aitmatov's novel, *Farewell, Gul'sary!* was first to point to the crucial break in the psychology of Tanabai, the herdsman, at the point where he is expelled from the Party. Why, she asked, did Tanabai not protest his expulsion from the Party (which would have been more in keeping with his character), but instead became suddenly inert? Stanislavleva's answer is that the reason for such a sudden psychological inertia in Tanabai lay in the fact that the literary character and the author had parted ways:

> And it was here [at the point of the expulsion and after] that the author violated the logic of the development of Tanabai's character, entrusting his favorite hero with too much of what he himself thought as author. Here, the dialectical

way of portraying Tanabai's character gave way to the conclusions the author had set for himself, for whom his own subjective evaluations and ideas about events become more important than the true delineation of character *(pravda kharakterov)* and of circumstances. The artistic exploration of life was interrupted. And that is why everything subsequent to this in the novel turns out to be not shown but told by Ch. Aitmatov and, therefore, is not artistically convincing.

This conscious reshaping of a character in greater consonance with what we might call Socialist Realist decorum and to the detriment of the artistic whole, suggests Aitmatov's capacity for the ideological manipulation of literary material. In this connection his *The White Ship* is a very interesting case in point showing how a gifted Soviet writer tried to correct the natural impact on his readers of what remains to date his greatest novel.

The original impact and ending of the novel as it appeared in the first issue of *Novyi mir* for 1970, when it was entitled *Belyi parokhod (Posle skazki) (The White Ship [After the Fairy Tale]),* was tragic and hopeless both for the boy, who committed suicide after the brutal slaying of the Horned Deer-Mother, and symbolically, for man in general. For a writer who had claimed (in 1967 [in his essay in *Voprosy literatury*], in connection with *Farewell Gul'sary!*) that it is the function of modern Soviet literature to solve "the problem of creating the image of our contemporary . . . ," the ending and impact of *The White Ship* could only mean public embarrassment as a Socialist Realist writer. His attempt to exculpate himself in his **"Neobkhodimye utochneniia" ("Necessary Clarifications"),** which he published shortly afterward in the July issue of *Literaturnaia gazeta,* subtly though it was argued, could not do away with the tragic human import of the novel.

Aitmatov, for whom according to L. Lebedeva the development of the novel had in some sense come as a surprise (no doubt a mark of its artistic authenticity), was clearly worried about the impact of this novel on the Soviet reader. He therefore came to a decision, hallowed by Soviet literary practice, to revise certain key sections leading up to and including the end of the novel. Taisa Napolova, who based her findings on the revised 1971 Kirghizstan edition of the novel—where Aitmatov even deemphasized the original title by inverting it to read *Posle skazki (Belyi Parokhod)*—showed the actual changes made by Aitmatov. In effect the changes were meant to weaken the Horned Deer-Mother theme by giving more resonance to Kulubek, who was a substitute father figure to the boy. As a result, Aitmatov undermined the tragic inevitability and artistic power of the original version of the novel. It may also be interesting in this context to remind ourselves that a 1975 collection of important articles on Aitmatov's work included only those written between 1962 and 1967, thus leaving out any mention of *The White Ship* altogether. Aitmatov's utter artistic failure (in our opinion) in *Early Cranes* (1975) due to his trend toward the father figure and his forcing masculine motifs into the female mold of his poetic imagination, only further destroyed the poetic unity of his work and made him regress to his groping beginnings of before 1957.

Indeed, if one looks back at Aitmatov's early writing before 1957, one becomes aware of the fact that it was during that time that his awakening creativity became defined by a tension between male and female figures. And that by the time he had written his first mature work in 1957, the female orientation of his poetic vision had finally overcome the initial male-centered tendency of his earliest stories.

Aitmatov's pre-1957 and artistically immature writing thus gives us a preview of those thematic and structural ingredients which were both to shape and, on occasion, to disrupt his future creative development. Aitmatov's early stories already utilized father and/or mother figures (and their children) in thematic and structural terms. In "Sypaichi" (1954), for example, Aitmatov centered his fiction around a father and son relationship. After a conflict between the proud and old-fashioned father and his more modern-minded son over the best method for preventing river floods, the son triumphs and the two finally become reconciled to one another. The son's victory reaffirmed the inherent idealization of the male in this story. In *Belyi dozhd' (White Rain,* 1954), however, the action had already shifted to one between mother and daughter. But the mother's position remained "inferior" to man's, both in the sense that her only daughter, Saadat, left her to marry, but even more so because it was left to the mother's brother, Tokoi-Ake, to justify Saadat's action and to heal the break between mother and daughter.

With *Soperniki, (The Rivals,* 1955) Aitmatov was definitely moving in the direction of his later, mature work. Though much of the action had to do with the competitive conflict between two men—the jealous Karatai and the much more responsible Sabyrbek on how effectively to irrigate their respective Collective State Farms—a new emphasis was placed on the tender and loving relationship of the mother (Karatai's wife) with her small son, as well as on the now somber and hostile father figure Karatai. For example, at one point Karatai "coldly glanced at his wife and son" while the mother, a forerunner of Seide in *Face to Face,* "stood stunned, pressing the child to her breast." Portrayed as repulsive and beast-like, the father's hostility to the mother is unmistakable: "With a face distorted by rage he turned to this wife and stared at her with a ferocious look filled with hate." The climax of the story came when Karatai's wife, Kanymgul, moved by love and compassion, physically struggled with her husband and managed to overpower him. In this story it was she, a woman and not a man, who played the crucial role in bringing Karatai and Sabyrbek together again. Finally, in *Na reke Baidamtal, (On the River Baidamtal,* 1955) Aitmatov found his major theme: Woman. For here it is the young girl Asiia's moral strength that has an exemplary and formative influence on the selfishly irresponsible and, at first, cowardly, Nurbek. Nurbek ultimately was able to overcome his weakness, but this was only due to Asiia, to Woman, who is envisaged as a marvelous source of moral strength, love, knowledge and happiness.

It remains for us to discuss Aitmatov's latest novella *Pegii pes, begushchii kraem moria (The Skewbald Dog Running at the Edge of the Sea,* 1977). It provides us with an interesting confirmation of our view that not only is Aitmatov's poetic vision feminine in orientation, but that in order for him to avoid conflict within his creative process, he cannot *neglect* or abandon Woman who is at the very nerve center of his creative world.

This holds true in spite of the fact that *Skewbald Dog Running at the Edge of the Sea* seems at first sight to run counter to our view because Aitmatov here succeeds for the first time in his fiction in giving us a moving and *sustained* portrayal of a father and his son during a tragic sea hunting expedition where all, save the son, Kirisk, perish. But in our view, Aitmatov was able to draw this sustained relationship precisely because he did not try to abandon his Mother oriented universe (as he had attempted to do in the revised *The White Ship* and in *Early Cranes*). Though the immediate focus is on the father and son, there is essentially no shift away from his natural poetic perspective and therefore no possibility for poetic conflict. That Aitmatov had found a way back to the true poetic sources of his vision is suggested in several ways. For one, the frequent hostility in Aitmatov's fiction of the father to the mother is totally absent in this novella. Instead, a deep and loving bond unites Kirisk's parents whether they are together or apart. Even more significant is the fact—reminiscent of the Horned Deer-Mother—that the whole conception of the novella is bound up with the image of Fish-Woman who is the progenitor of Kirisk's tribe. As such she pervades the story from beginning to end. She is present symbolically and culturally in the waking thoughts of the protagonists and especially, figuratively, in the dreams of Kirisk's grandfather who is also in the boat. Her haunting and commanding presence therefore unifies the whole and creates a female world in which the characters live and die. More significant, still, is that the novella, metaphorically and creatively speaking, is actually about the *death* of the Father and the miraculous return of the Son to his Mother. Consequently, Aitmatov has, at least temporarily, healed the conflict within his creative vision which for a time threatened the future development of his art. (pp. 158-64)

> *Constantin V. Ponomareff, "A Poetic Vision in Conflict: Chingiz Aitmatov's Fiction," in* Russian Literature and Criticism: Selected Papers from the Second World Congress for Soviet and East European Studies, *edited by Evelyn Bristol, Berkeley Slavic Specialties, 1982, pp. 158-66.*

Stewart Paton

Aitmatov came to national and international prominence with the publication in 1966 of the *povest': Proshchay, Gul'sary! (Farewell, Gul'sary!).* Before that he had aroused considerable attention throughout the Soviet Union, as well as in his native Kirgiziya, with a number of *povesti,* written for the most part originally in Kirgiz and then translated into Russian, often by the author himself. Between these early stories and *Gul'sary* lies a gap of four to five years but the themes of *Gul'sary* and the technique used to express them are clearly announced in the earlier work. (p. 496)

The relevance of [Aitmatov's] early experiences to the issues he explores is clearly visible in his work. He was brought up without a father, mainly by loving and devoted female relatives. It was through his grandmother and his aunt, who were both illiterate, that he became acquainted with the oral literature of his native people, and the harsh circumstances of his adolescence and youth inculcated in him a sense of duty to his people which is clearly his dominant moral trait. For all the true 'heroes' of his early stories, and indeed to some extent of his later ones too, are outstanding examples of virtuous devotion to duty. Aitmatov obviously identifies totally with their moral canon and many of the stories have a first person narrator who, we feel, is very like what the young Aitmatov must have been. All are set in Kirgiziya and depict the struggles of working people against the hardships caused mainly by the war and its aftermath. Nevertheless, although the physical hardships are there and are graphically described, it is the emotional deprivation of women without husbands and of children, particularly sons, without fathers that is stressed. The moral courage required to persist in the midst of such physical and emotional difficulties is the supreme virtue.

However, what sustains this courage and this persistence is the consciousness of belonging to one, usually very small, community, all of whose members are suffering equally. Loyalty to this group on a human level is the mark of the good man—for with it goes a sense of the need to defend the oppressed, to defend those who cannot defend themselves: women in the first place (especially in a society which had traditionally treated them as inferior) and of course children, whose right to self-development and education must be maintained. Such community solidarity can only be based on a common creed of mutual respect. This creed extends to paying due respect to the dead, for in this act people consciously acknowledge their debt to their forefathers and their awareness of the importance of the past. Finally, for such a community living close to nature, the treatment of animals—truly innocent victims who are unable to protest—is used as a touchstone to distinguish the good man from the bad. Indeed nature itself must be treated as a sacred trust, for a man who defiles nature is unlikely to possess any of the other virtues.

From these early stories [*The First Teacher, Face to Face, Dzhamilya, My Little Poplar in the Red Kerchief, The Eye of the Camel* and *Mother's Field,* plus the two short stories "Rendez-Vous with my Son" and "The Little Soldier"] it is apparent that Aitmatov is above all a moralist who has no doubt that good men exist and need to be praised. A clear view of what is good leads also to a clear view of its absence. Evil exists in these stories in an equally clear-cut way. Principally it is seen in the rejection of the values listed above and the figure of the deserter, in the story *Litsom k litsu (Face to Face)* (1958), is the embodiment of betrayal of the group.

One distinction that Aitmatov makes between his evil characters points to a problem that particularly concerns him. Whereas the deserter's evil actions can be explained

as consequences of weakness and fear (they are actions which, had there not been a war and its pressures, he would not have committed) what worries Aitmatov more is the existence of pure, unmotivated evil. The real focus of interest in the story *Verblyuzhiy glaz (The Eye of the Camel)* (1961) is Abakir. Aitmatov makes it clear, reporting through his adolescent boy narrator, that Abakir is young, good at his work, has a loving wife, and yet he hates everyone and everything, including himself. 'Why is this so?' asks Aitmatov: 'Why did Abakir turn out to be so harmful, so much in a rage (*zlyushchim*)?' Such evil, as his wife eventually realizes, cannot be mollified or conciliated by love and affection.

This very clear-cut view of good and evil, of heroes and villains, may be unfashionable in the West but is less out of place in the prevailing literary climate in the Soviet Union. However, in Aitmatov's case, the origins of this view of the world have less to do with the canons of socialist realism than with the literary tradition he has inherited: the tradition of the oral epic. Like many other oral traditions, that of Kirgiziya sang the praises of heroic virtue triumphing over adversity and villainy. It is this mode of writing which is so clearly dominant in Aitmatov's work and which represents on his part a conscious attempt to shape a written literature on the basis of his people's rich oral epic tradition.

In his early stories Aitmatov achieved considerable success in the difficult task of making his 'positive heroes' interesting and sympathetic. He does this mainly by presenting them to us as victims—of the war, for the most part, and by rarely showing us virtue triumphant. Aitmatov uses his gift for lyrical and emotional writing, often in an elevated style appropriate to moments of great grief, to reinforce the pathos of the hero's or heroine's situation.

Whatever successes Aitmatov achieved with his early stories, the style and method chosen entailed certain risks, imposing restrictions on the author's range. Concentration on a main character who is both a type and a hero makes it very difficult to present at the same time a credible individual. What is more, his literary conventions are to some extent at odds with the realistic, contemporary settings of his stories and this is most apparent when he does attempt a quasi-conventional, didactic, Soviet type of *proizvodstvennaya povest'*, such as *Topolyok moy v krasnoy kosynke (My Little Poplar in the Red Kerchief)* (1962).

One particular aspect of his literary technique and one of his most striking features as a writer makes it difficult for Aitmatov to deal with a typical, modern, workaday subject: the use at emotional moments (often in the narrator's recollections of past events) of an incantatory verbal technique, with repeated phrases or leitmotivs, a conscious adaptation to contemporary themes of the narrative style of the folk songs and fairy tales of his oral tradition. This tends to formalize what is being depicted and set it at some remove.

Moreover, the division by Aitmatov of his characters (even of his minor figures) into heroes and villains tends to eliminate any shades of grey. We are faced with extremes of human behaviour. One reads that Aitmatov sings the praises of the 'ordinary working man', and it is true that every one of his heroes comes from this stratum of society, but in his stories one is made constantly aware of how exceptional each of these heroes is—imbued with the highest sense of morality, people of the greatest sensitivity, but in particular capable of heroism, of those deeds which can inspire us as an ideal to emulate, but which are beyond the reach of mere ordinary mortals.

Characters on this heroic scale can only be shown at their best in extreme situations—and these are the circumstances in which Aitmatov places them: circumstances which test to breaking point, where it is a question of death, betrayal or disaster, or of an attempt to conquer insuperable difficulties. Aitmatov is quite clear what kind of people he prefers to write about:

> It seems to me that there has always existed and that there still exists, an art dealing with powerful characters (*sil'nykh kharakterov*). In all probability there exists, to the same degree, an art dealing with every-day characters (*obydennykh kharakterov*), depicted in their usual surroundings. Both have an equal right to exist.

The overwhelming characteristic of his early writing is its emotionalism. The power of his writing conveys his often total identification with, or hatred of, the characters he portrays. When this method is applied with skill and restraint, as in his later work, the effect is like an emotional bombshell. But the danger, sometimes not avoided, is over-use of the method, leading to exaggerated calls on our sympathy, which are ultimately counter-productive. To evoke our sympathy for an innocent victim, the tendency, in his early work, is to idealize the victim's virtue while increasing the number and severity of the blows inflicted by a malign fate. To read these stories is like running an emotional marathon: exhaustion sets in from the excess of emotion and of the language used to evoke it.

However, the emotion expressed in Aitmatov's first major work *Farewell, Gul'sary!* cannot be considered excessive and seems to be fully justified by the scale of the subject. In this work one can see clearly, in the narrative and literary style used, the continuing influence of his native oral/epic tradition: more particularly one sees his continuing attachment to the heroic in life and literature and his sharp division of characters into good and evil—but there are significant changes of emphasis. The hero-narrator, Tanabay, is no idealized figure. He is honest, upright, direct, of somewhat fiery and impatient temperament but above all an idealist, and this is the primary cause of his difficulties. As a young man he believed all the promises and responded to all the demands made by the party in the thirties—even to the extent of denouncing his step-brother as a kulak. The book charts his increasing disillusionment with the party during the post-war Stalinist period. He is eventually expelled for a physical attack on one of its representatives, an attack so fully justified that the reader can only applaud it as just retribution.

From the vantage point of old age Tanabay looks back over his life and his close links with his favourite horse, a stallion pacer, Gul'sary, now dying. The party's treatment of the horse parallels its treatment of him. The party took Gul'sary from him—when he had trained it and ridden it to victory, making it a champion—and castrated it, breaking its spirit. As in Aitmatov's earlier stories we are invited to identify with the hero, as the embodiment of approved qualities, and to hate what is evil. And we see clearly the face of evil—but the crucial shift of emphasis is that it is seen here in the shape of Stalinist party officials. The narrative technique underlines the point—the gelding of the stallion is the emotional high point of the story and Aitmatov takes the trouble to make clear that it is an act of personal revenge and savagery by the new chairman, Aldanov, against the hated horse, the symbol of resistance to his will:

> And now his new master hopped up to the pacer who was stretched out on the ground, squatted down beside his head, bringing with him again yesterday's smell of raw spirit, and grinned, with an open expression of hate and triumph, as if he had before him not a horse but a man who was his worst enemy.

The hero then, like the horse, is a hero-victim, whereas the portraits of all those in power, of whom there are a number in the story, make it clear that they are of the same stamp as the detestable Aldanov.

In this work we have also, for the first time, a fine portrait of a character drawn in various shades, a devoted party worker who is the soul of goodness, full of sympathy and human concern for the people he works with, Tanabay's lifelong friend, Choro. In spite of these human qualities, when he comes up against people in power in the party, of whose actions he disapproves, he fails to oppose them, accepting their decisions like blows of fate while attempting to mollify the effects. His feelings towards the party and its officials eventually come to be the same as Tanabay's, but he lacks the passion and directness which turn Tanabay into a rebel.

If the good men are unable to act against those who are evil and who are not worthy of the power they wield, where does Aitmatov see hope for the future? In *Farewell, Gul'sary!* these hopes are centred on the new generation of men coming forward to take the positions of power in the party, such men as Choro's son, Samansur, who, it is hinted, will be his father's worthy replacement. One of these younger men, Kerimbekov, plays a larger part in the story. He speaks valiantly in Tanabay's defence at the meeting which eventually votes to expel Tanabay from the party. After the expulsion he moves the motion to censure the party official Tanabay had attacked. At the end of the meeting he expresses the hope that Tanabay will one day be able to return to the party—a hope no one shares. Kerimbekov himself becomes party secretary in the changed atmosphere after Stalin's death and he then visits Tanabay, seven years after his expulsion, to invite him to rejoin the party. By the end of the story Tanabay has not taken up the invitation.

Given the emotional weight behind the crises experienced by Tanabay and Choro, one must conclude that the story is an attack on the Stalinist distortions of party ideals, repudiated as evil by the heroes with whom the readers identify. The optimism enshrined in the figures of Samansur and Kerimbekov strikes the reader as the expression of a pious hope rather than a real expectation. One is tempted to think that Tanabay's hesitation about returning to the party is a hint that for him (as for Aitmatov?) the party has not yet changed enough.

After a further interval of four years 1970 saw the publication of *Belyy parokhod* (*The White Steamship*), later published separately in a slightly different version with the title *Posle skazki* (*After the Fairy Tale*). This remarkable work is a contemporary fairy tale in which the elements have been cunningly woven together but whose message is clear: the story is about the destruction of the innocent by evil and is therefore tragic. Because of this it aroused much controversy and discussion when it appeared. Aitmatov himself took part in the discussion in *Literaturnaya gazeta* and his final article in defence of tragedy is mentioned below.

The hero of this story is a truly helpless innocent victim, a boy of seven, deserted by his parents, living in a remote community of foresters, and attached only to his grandfather, whom he loves and reveres. The grandfather, Momun, is kindness personified: indeed he is so willing to be of service to others that he is treated with scant respect. Aitmatov puts it as follows:

> His zeal was not appreciated by anyone—just as no one would appreciate gold, if it was given away for nothing.

The boy loves and believes his grandfather's tales— particularly the one about the 'Horned Mother Deer' who once saved the remote ancestors of his people and who first brought them to their country round Lake Issyk-Kul.

The small community lives in terror of the chief forester, Orozkul, who is married to the boy's aunt, his grandfather's daughter, Bekey. In Orozkul we have the most striking portrait of an evil man that Aitmatov has yet given us. He is a man with a gnawing grievance that nothing can remedy: his wife is barren and he takes this out on her, beating her violently when he is drunk—a frequent occurrence. He abuses and humiliates the grandfather, and Momun responds by attempting to conciliate him and thus alleviate the fate of his daughter.

Orozkul is compounded of all the vices. He is self-centred, corrupt, violent, a drunkard, a boaster, an exploiter and tormentor of those beneath him. He takes pleasure in exercising his power, enjoys the privileges of his position to the full, despoiling the forest for his own gain, but in particular losing no opportunity to humiliate his wife and her father.

Clearly neither the grandfather nor the boy can stand up to this kind of person. Like Abakir's wife in the early story *The Eye of the Camel,* the grandfather simply cannot understand: 'Why do people become like that? You do him good, and he does you evil in return.' As for the boy the only remedy he can see is to pray to the Horned Mother Deer—to beg her to bring a child to Aunt Bekey: then everything would change. The gloomy conclusion is that there is no one in this community who can deal with Orozkul. The story is tragic because it shows, apparently, evil

triumphant over good. The *dénouement* is impressive. Three deer appear, a mother, a stag and their offspring. The boy is in ecstasy for he believes, according to legend, that the Horned Mother Deer has returned to them, as a sign of her favour. But Orozkul forces grandfather into the position where he has to shoot and kill the deer. The boy, horrified by this and by what he construes as betrayal by his grandfather, dies when he dives into the stream which he believes will take him to Lake Issyk-Kul, to meet his father on the White Steamer.

In the middle of this finely written concluding scene there is an episode which hints at a possible way of seeking help against Orozkul. In his delirium the boy has a dream that a young lorry driver, Kulubek, who had once come to transport hay from the valley, who was clearly such an influential and powerful leader of his group, and who had befriended the boy, comes again at his summons, takes vengeance on Orozkul by humiliating him, and drives him away. This imaginary rescue by an almost unknown young hero, Kulubek, has striking parallels with the situation in *Farewell, Gul'sary!:* like Kerimbekov (an equally vague figure) Kulubek is representative of the new generation which will be strong enough to overcome Orozkul. But, as in *Farewell, Gul'sary!,* it seems that this is only a gesture towards some kind of optimistic solution, very insubstantial when compared with the graphic portrayal in both stories of evil in action. Aitmatov however clearly attaches great importance to this expression of hope, as is evident from the way he concludes his story.

Aitmatov's reply to some of his critics [In an article in *Literaturnaya gazeta,* 29 July 1970] is a staunch defence of the story as he wrote it. The victory, he asserts, is not finally to Orozkul. The reader is called upon to fight to create those circumstances in which Kulubek can achieve the victory of good over evil, a victory of which the boy can only dream. And the boy's death *is* a triumph, a triumph of the principle of non-acceptance of evil in its most unacceptable form. The boy is therefore truly heroic in his refusal to compromise. The real defeat is that of the grandfather—his total failure to realize that conciliation and appeasement is not the way to deal with evil of this kind. Like Choro in *Farewell, Gul'sary!* he realizes this bitter truth too late: that, in compromising with such evil, one not only betrays all the values one holds dear but even loses what one is trying to preserve.

If *The White Steamship* represents a remarkable artistic success, Aitmatov's recent major work is his most ambitious undertaking to date. *I dol'she veka dlitsya den'* (*And One Day Lasts Longer Than An Age*), is the first one he has called a novel and this is an indication of its greater range and complexity. It not only develops and deepens many of the themes which have preoccupied him hitherto but expands into new areas with boldness and skill. While using the same narrative technique as in *Farewell, Gul'sary!,*—that of an elderly hero-narrator who looks back over the trials of a long life—Aitmatov gives us in the figure of this hero, Yedigey, a man who embodies all the qualities he admires. Like some of the earlier heroes, he is the underdog, fighting against abuses in the system and subject to fits of passion and of impotent rage. Yedigey combines the honesty and abrasive temperament of Tanabay (in *Farewell, Gul'sary!*) with the kindness of Choro in the same story and the goodness of the grandfather in *The White Steamship.* Unlike the latter, however, he is a man who evokes respect in the small community of workers where he is the dominant figure. But this respect is earned, not forced from the people, for he holds no official party or administrative position.

The important difference in emphasis between Yedigey and Tanabay is well illustrated by the parallel stories of the animals to which they are both linked: Tanabay to the pacer Gul'sary and Yedigey to his camel, Karanar. Whereas Gul'sary is, at the whim of a party official, taken away from Tanabay and gelded, Yedigey himself is responsible for deciding the fate of Karanar, a present from his old work-mate, Kazangap. As Karanar grows older he becomes more difficult to manage and Yedigey is faced with the decision whether to geld or not. Kazangap says to him:

> It is your affair. If you want a quiet life, then geld him. If you want the glory—don't touch him. But then, take all the responsibility on yourself if anything happens. If you have enough strength and patience—hang on, he will be a rebel for three years or so and after that will obey you.

> [*I dol'she veka dlitsya den'*]

So Yedigey does not touch him, he makes his own decision and accepts personal responsibility for the consequences. He decides that a whole animal with all its passions and the trouble they cause is better than a neutered version.

The narrative framework of the novel is also, so to speak, a consequence of a decision by Yedigey. He resolves to give a fitting burial to Kazangap, who dies as the novel begins. The two have worked together for many years at an isolated small railway halt, in the middle of the steppes. Yedigey is determined to transport the body in procession with friends and relatives to the ancient cemetery of the people of the region, half a day's journey into the desert. For the procession he insists on decking out in all its finery his camel, Karanar, and, during the preparations and the procession itself, the novel takes us, using the recollections of the hero, into the past of Yedigey and Kazangap, and into the remoter historical past of the area, re-telling some of the legends of the peoples of the region.

The story of the procession to the cemetery is interwoven with the difficulties of the joint U.S.S.R./U.S.A. mission in space—from this we learn that the novel is set in the (perhaps idealized?) future. A 'cosmodrome' to launch the Soviet rockets for the joint project has been built in the steppes and, although Yedigey does not at first know it, prevents access to the cemetery. When the procession is eventually turned back at the boundary fence they are forced to bury Kazangap (although with appropriate religious ceremony) in the open steppe.

This insistence on paying our dues to the dead members of the community, already mentioned in reference to earlier works by Aitmatov, here assumes even greater importance. It is linked with the notion of the importance of memory, and, by implication, of history. On a personal level to remember is to be involved in the fate of others. Yedigey refuses to forget the forty-four years he worked with Kazangap, the many occasions when Kazangap helped him, hence his insistence on a ceremonial funeral. The horror of the man without memory is graphically portrayed in the legend of the *mankurt* (robot): the tale is that of a savage tribe in the steppes who tortured their prisoners by compressing their skulls with a band of animal skin until they lost all memory and—if they survived the torture—became totally obedient slaves who remembered nothing of their former lives. Whereas Aitmatov's heroes are the men of the older generation, like Yedigey and Kazangap, who do remember each other, feel mutual respect and involvement, and have a sense of duty and obligation, the younger generation is shown as the exact opposite, lacking in consideration above all, because of indifference and apathy. Indeed Yedigey is so disgusted at the sort of man that Kazangap's son, Sabitzhan, has become (he shows a total lack of interest in giving his father an appropriate funeral, for example) that Yedigey refers to him as a real *mankurt,* a real automaton. ('God help us all', says Yedigey, 'if such people get into positions of power.') [The critic adds in a footnote: "This is almost word for word the remark that the grandfather makes about Orozkul in *The White Steamship.*"] For the son, duty to one's fellow man does not exist. But for Yedigey and those like him behaviour towards one's fellow men—particularly when they are in trouble—is the touchstone. This seems to be the issue he is underscoring in the emotional high point of the novel, the story of the teacher Abutalip, which Yedigey recalls with undiminished bitterness as the funeral procession moves over the steppe.

The story of Abutalip, his wife, and two young sons, is a violent shout of horror at the excesses of Stalinism. Aitmatov uses his considerable emotional and literary power to maximum effect in this tale of injustice, perpetrated by Soviet society against former prisoners of war and using informers and unfeeling automata (*mankurts?*) to carry out 'orders from above'. The principal agent is a security policeman, referred to as the *krechetoglazyy,* (the 'vulture-eyed one'), although we do learn that his name is Tansykbayev. This key section of the novel reaches a dramatic culmination, and one that produces a truly remarkable effect, on 5 March 1953, the day of Stalin's death.

When at last the funeral procession reaches the boundary fence of the cosmodrome and is halted, the soldier on guard insists that permission to go further can only be given by his superior, Lt. Tansykbayev. Yedigey rejects this omen as mere coincidence. But when this Tansykbayev refuses access he bursts out: 'Listen, who is your father?', then goes on: 'Can it be that you fathers are not dead or that you yourself will never die?' For Tansykbayev the matter is routine—he is merely carrying out orders which he has no right to question, whereas Yedigey insists that he (and every citizen) *does* have such a right and demands that Tansykbayev transmit to his superiors—those who hold the power—that he, Yedigey, will make representations to those who have made the incredible decision to destroy the ancient cemetery of his people in order to replace it with housing.

Aitmatov is clearly concerned that people like the new Tansykbayev and members of the younger generation such as Kazangap's son Sabitzhan are narrow-minded, servile careerists. He is worried that they continue to surface in Soviet society and wield power, for they are precisely the kind of people who carry out orders like the *mankurt*—any orders, even Stalin's. Perhaps, in fact, they are even worse, perhaps they are evil, taking an active pleasure in frustrating or crushing man's nobler aspirations. Aitmatov seems, indeed, to be posing a question of a religious nature: is evil always with us?

This is in fact one of the main points raised by Aitmatov when he is describing the older Tansykbayev's disgrace and Abutalip's posthumous rehabilitation. Yedigey receives the news in a letter from his highly placed party friend in Alma-Ata, Yelizarov. (This letter is a crucial event in Yedigey's life, Aitmatov tells us, a kind of watershed, and his life divides into two periods, before and after the letter.) It had been established that Abutalip had in fact been denounced by the railway inspector. Yelizarov goes on:

> Why did he do it? What caused him to commit such an evil act? I have thought a great deal about this, bearing in mind what I myself knew of similar cases and what you told me, Yedigey. Picturing the whole thing to myself I tried to grasp the motives for his action. But I find it difficult to give an answer. I cannot explain the cause of such hatred on his part for such a total stranger as Abutalip Kuttybayev was. Perhaps it is some kind of illness or epidemic which seizes hold of people at certain periods of history. Or perhaps man, because of his nature, has buried within him a destructive spirit—envy, which little by little eats away his soul and brings him to such acts of cruelty. But what kind of envy could be caused by the figure of Abutalip? For me, this remains a mystery. As for the means used—they are as old as the hills. At one time it was enough to denounce someone as a heretic and in Bukhara he was stoned in the market place while in Europe he was burned at the stake. You and I spoke about this, Yedigey, during your visit. After establishing the facts in Abutalip's case I am more than ever convinced that it will take a long time for people to rid themselves of this vice—hatred of personal qualities in another man. How long it will take is difficult to guess. In spite of all this I rejoice in the fact that justice can never be extinguished on this earth. And in this case again it has triumphed. Even if it was at a high price, it triumphed in the end. As it always will—as long as the world lasts. I am pleased, Yedigey, that you strove unselfishly for justice and were successful in obtaining it . . .

Apart from this letter Yedigey also remembers the profession of faith in the future expressed by Yelizarov shortly before Yedigey left Alma-Ata:

> No matter how painfully and bitterly we have to pay for past mistakes and failures we have not ceased to make progress as pioneers along an unknown road—that is the meaning of history. And he [Yelizarov] also said that now this progress would continue with renewed strength. A

> guarantee of this was society's ability to correct its own faults and to purify itself. 'If we are able to say this to ourselves this means that we do have the strength for the future', said Yelizarov.

A somewhat different view of the future is also given in this novel in what for Aitmatov is a venture into new territory 'the fantastic'. As was mentioned, the novel is set in the not too distant future, when a joint U.S.S.R./U.S.A. space authority maintains a space research station to investigate alternative mineral sources on a planet 'X'. The two astronauts manning the station, one American and the other a Soviet citizen, have decided to accept an invitation extended to them to visit this distant planet. The reasons why the astronauts decided on such a breach of discipline are difficult to formulate—but are hinted at in the following quotation:

> We have been forced to act in this way since we have no difficulty in imagining what attitudes, disputes and passions would erupt as soon as those forces went into action which see a political victory in an extra goal at ice-hockey (since it demonstrates the superiority of their own system). Alas, we know only too well the reality which exists on earth today. Who can guarantee that this opportunity of contact with another civilization will not become the reason for the mutual slaughter of the inhabitants of the earth?

The astronauts' first message from the unknown planet soon arrives. This distant place is a rational Utopia, the inhabitants having advanced beyond Earth's petty squabbles and representing a higher stage of evolution. (They have for example no states and no arms—and therefore no wars.) A sign of their superiority is the range of their forward planning and concern for the future of their planet—for it is drying up from the core and they can either attempt to reverse the process by scientific means or find another home. They request a visit to Earth, but will not come unless they are invited. The joint decision, by the two power blocks, when it comes, is brutal and final: to break off all contact with the astronauts and the other planet and to erect a shield of satellite rocket-robots, like a ring round the Earth, which will hermetically seal off and protect it from any contact, the whole matter then being buried in total secrecy and all records of the two astronauts and their contact being destroyed. The world community on Earth, even at that time in the future (says Aitmatov), will be incapable of making any other decision—no agreement could possibly be hoped for between the two power blocks on a joint programme to deal with the approach from the other planet, given the precarious nature of the existing agreement on joint research.

If one attempts in conclusion to offer a tentative interpretation of the main themes of this complex novel it would appear that Aitmatov sees the good life (and the future progress of mankind) depending on men like Yedigey, Kazangap and Yelizarov. They are involved with their fellow men and imbued with a sense of solidarity—they will actively intervene on behalf of others and are deeply concerned that justice should be done. That such men come to the fore and wield influence is of primary importance.

And yet, the most powerful image in the novel—the horror of the *mankurt,* the man deprived of his memory and his history and reduced to the status of a robot—expresses Aitmatov's fear that people like Tansykbayev and Kazangap's unworthy son Sabitzhan still exist and will continue to flourish. Could it even be that Aitmatov is expressing a fear in this novel that this figure is, alas, more typical of contemporary (Soviet) man? (Certainly there is no indication in this novel of the hope for the future which in the earlier works is embodied in young Soviet heroes such as Kerimbekov in *Farewell, Gul'sary!* or Kulubek in *The White Steamship.*)

The clear parallel in images between the savage crushing band of skin round the forehead, which deprives the captive of all memory of the past, and the tight ring of satellite robots which destroys the possibility of a 'memory of the future', so to speak, is another expression of Aitmatov's fear: that the human race is afraid of contact with the unfamiliar and that those who 'play safe' are in charge of our destinies, not realizing that to 'play safe' means not security but stagnation. As Aitmatov comments bitterly at the end of his story, they took this decision to cut us off from the future, to establish a *cordon sanitaire,* 'so that nothing should change in our affairs here on Earth, so that everything should stay as it is.'

This novel is an ambitious work, but Aitmatov's belief in the benefits to society which accrue from the honest efforts of honest men comes over as politically naive. However, it is conveyed with considerable force because of his hatred of the evil he knows, a hatred expressed with such violence in his images and in the portraits of men he detests. Aitmatov takes the view that the world is in a perilous situation because of what he regards as the trivial differences (in comparison with the dangers we face) between the two power blocks. Perhaps it is indeed naive of Aitmatov to insist that it is more important to realize the danger than to establish which of the two sides is more to blame for the situation. Perhaps it is naive to contrast the unreasonableness of mankind with the rational behaviour the situation demands: but it is remarkable that such a powerful expression of this point of view has appeared in the U.S.S.R. (pp. 497-510)

> *Stewart Paton, "Chinghiz Aitmatov's First Novel: A New Departure?" in* The Slavonic and East European Review, *Vol. 62, No. 4, October, 1984, pp. 496-510.*

Evgeni Sidorov

Aitmatov's prose expands outwards and skywards, only when it portrays human crises, dramas, treachery and unnatural deaths does it become cramped and suffocated. Once these outbursts of evil perpetrated by man are over, everything again grows tranquil in the world, nature is at peace with man and man is at peace with nature.

The author sees life as a moment of eternity which contains, in condensed form, the history of the human race. That became especially evident, even demonstratively so, when the novels *A Day Lasts Longer than an Age* and *The Executioner's Block* came out, and in some cases was even detrimental to the purely artistic aspects of his latest works. Aitmatov regards an individual life as reality and metaphor simultaneously. Unless we are aware of that, we will not understand his prose.

His heroes' isolation in some out-of-the-way spot like a forest cordon *(The White Steamer),* a boat in the boundless sea *(A Skewbald Dog Running Along the Edge of the Sea)* or a godforsaken railway passing track *(A Day Lasts Longer than an Age),* is not coincidental in the plots of Aitmatov's works. The author does not deal with solitude in the existentialist sense; on the contrary, he stresses a steadfast sense of life and human solidarity that wins no matter what. It wins in spite of the deliberately emphasised outward isolation which the author uses only to bring out in greater relief and to accentuate more fully the centre of his own artistic universe, from which warm waves of kindness, hope and conscience emanate into the world.

Chinghiz Aitmatov has turned to the genre of the novel relatively recently. Actually, *Farewell, Gulsary!* and *The White Steamer* could already be counted as novels if we are to judge by the author's intentions, the wide range of events, and the artistic concept of man and time revealed in them. Yet the author was in no hurry to define his extensive, socio-philosophical parables as novels. He seemed to be only preparing to launch himself into a new and more complex realm of creativity.

The launching took place when he published the novel *A Day Lasts Longer than an Age,* a complex book which combines day-to-day life and legend, reality and fantasy, a day and a century. As previously in his *Tales of the Mountains and the Steppes,* the author finds support in legends and myths and verifies contemporaneity by comparing it with the ethical experience of past generations. But unexpectedly for many people, he introduced an element of fantasy into his prose for the first time, a kind of "outer-space" story which, in his words, was created for the sole purpose of "intensifying in a paradoxical, hyperbolised form, a situation fraught with potential danger for people on earth".

He wants us to imagine simultaneously some tiny spot on earth and the boundless, starry firmament and understand how closely the two are linked in the eternal cosmos of life. Such an understanding is characteristic of the author of the novel, and it is conveyed to the reader, who begins to see the universal and philosophical content through the individual concrete images of the book. The grand scope of the author's conception called for a new artistic expressive device, and Aitmatov took the risk of introducing dry informative journalism into his colourful style. Our ideologically complex epoch has introduced into the novel the inescapable struggle between war and peace, the conflict between two differing socio-political systems, in which every representative of thinking and suffering human race is involved, whether he likes it or not.

One of these is Edyghei Zhangeldin, the main character, who was born in 1917, the year of the Socialist Revolution, and who works as a simple railwayman. His whole life is inseparably tied up with the life of the country and the tragic history of the building of socialism. He is placed at the centre of the novel and, later, at the centre of the whole universe created by Aitmatov's imagination.

The author gives a detailed portrayal of Edyghei's character, which may be called heroic by rights, though he does not appear to perform any heroic acts. Actually, his whole life, humble and conscientious, is a moral feat. Aitmatov expresses his notions of human dignity through the image of this modest working man. Edyghei is a genuine hero, without a hint at idealisation, since the author has no intention whatsoever of embellishing reality.

A deep-rooted faith is the motivating force behind the best characters in Aitmatov's works. Hardships and suffering only serve to temper their spirit. Such were Duishen in *The First Teacher,* Tolgonai in *Mother's Field,* Tanabai in *Farewell, Gyulsary!* and Edyghei, a hardworking man and philosopher, a human from the planet Earth.

The narrative of the novel is conducted on two different planes; one deals with earthly life and the other, with a Soviet-American space odyssey. The slow trains that Edyghei comes out to meet seem to encircle the earth from east to west and from west to east. From a cosmodrome in the steppes nearby spaceships are launched to the American-Soviet "Parity" orbital station. The cosmodrome has expanded its premises and Edyghei is unable to bury his old friend, Kazangap, in the old family cemetery. Edyghei addresses a prayer to God and men as he stands by the open grave of his friend, dug in a wild, god-forsaken place.

Conscience and memory, sad and enlightened thoughts about the meaning of human life are Edyghei's God. What can one say to oneself and to others at the solemn hour of death? One can only fathom the depths of human essence by raising one's thoughts so high that every man suddenly appears to be a God, equal in intellect and feelings to all living things.

Aitmatov's legend about the "mankurt", a man who has been robbed of his memory, leaves a lasting impression. The motif of the people's memory, which is so persistent in modern Soviet multi-ethnic prose, has in Aitmatov's writings a strong intonation of warning, wrath and compassion. "With hatred and pity in his heart" Edyghei thinks of Sabitzhan, the son of Kazangap, who has lost all spiritual contact with the land of his fathers. The old Ana-Beiit cemetery, made "off limits" by the expanding cosmodrome, reminds the reader of Matyora, the island in Valentin Rasputin's book, *Farewell to Matyora,* forever submerged under the water. The life stories of Abutalip and millions like him who were unjustly persecuted in Stalin's times, are impossible to forget, because time does not forgive the silence and oblivion that hides their names, demanding that the terrible wounds of the past be brought to door of the living today.

Earth and space coexist easily in Aitmatov's Nature and its rotating cycles of births and deaths. Exceptionally striking is the fierce and irrepressible camel, Karanar, a creature that is quite perfect in his wild, unruly strength; he is as free as the elements and submits only to man's goodwill. The other denizens of the steppes are described with equal mastery: the hungry and sensitive fox, and the hawk who makes the round of his territory twice a day. They seem to have been living in the steppe ever since the beginning of Creation, lending everything around them an intransient meaning, not always comprehensible to men with their limited, vain and too practical consciousness.

The cosmic myth about the planet "Forest Bosom", that was discovered by Soviet and American spacemen, belongs in the same category as the folk legends. The camel, the fox, the hawk and man find themselves involved in the mystery of never-ending life which, possibly, exists outside Earth as well, and is good, just and free to a far greater extent than life on Earth, for the simple reason that it was born of poetry and an ideal human dream.

Planet Earth is another matter. In his preface to the novel, Aitmatov wrote: "The most tragic contradiction of the late 20th century has to be the infinity of human genius and the impossibility of its realisation due to political, ideological and racial barriers . . . "

The great discovery of the American and Soviet spacemen comes too early. In the face of the sudden threat of military conflict, both sides reach a compromise, whereby they reject all contacts with the new civilisation and decide not to allow the spacemen from the "Parity" station to return to Earth.

The reader's logic accepts the decision, but his heart does not. He is infinitely sorry for the fellows who bravely send signals to Earth, which has rejected them.

"The rockets sped on in space, creating a constantly active cordon round the globe so that nothing should change on it, so that everything should remain as it was . . ."

But can everything around really remain unchanged? Can the tragedy enacted in space pass unnoticed by humankind, without teaching it anything, without opening new horizons for struggle and aspiration? It does not engender pessimism and apocalyptic moods, it engenders quite different, constructive emotions. As long as people like Edyghei and Kazangap, the geologist Elizarov and the teacher Kuttybayev are born on this earth, life, no matter how tragic it may be, will gain increasing force and steadily stretch upward, towards the sky, towards the cosmos of human unity.

The idea of future communist fraternity shines like a star for Aitmatov's favourite heroes, just like a bright star over the steppes where they have spent the centuries and days of their lives full of selfless work and dramatic tribulations. Extra-terrestrial civilisations also send their inconspicuous light, yet we must build our earthly destiny ourselves, through trials and tribulations without the participation of the miracle-working extra-terrestrial reason. That is one of the chief messages of the metaphorical novel, a novel that may serve as a warning.

Earlier this year I have had occasion to write about *The Executioner's Block,* the novel's consistent theme of the unbreakable link between man and nature. The connecting link is demonstrated in the story of the wolves, a couple of superb, powerful animals doomed to die at the hands of man. But man brings doom and destruction upon himself if his life is not inspired by a higher ideal, if he crosses the border between good and evil.

I would like to repeat that a clean conscience and goodness do not automatically guarantee man happiness on this earth. On the contrary, destiny had prepared the "executioner's block", a fate in keeping with the laws of ancient tragedy, for both Avdiy, the young man who intended to become a priest, and the herdsman Boston. Good is doomed in its battle against evil and people who have violated moral laws, because it cannot resort to the means that contradict its high ideals and aims. If it takes up the weapon of vengeance, it perishes like Boston, who accidentally becomes the murderer of his own son.

Avdiy, the central character in the novel, aroused heated argument. The novel would have been impossible without him. He is incorporeal like any beautiful idea placed in a world that rejects everything ideal. He seems to soar between heaven and earth, rejected by the Church and deprived of earthly bearings. He seems to be a stranger on this earth, an envoy from the planet "Forest Bosom" from the author's preceding novel.

The hero's incorporeal quality was necessary for Aitmatov to lay bare social contradictions with special sharpness. Avdiy's presence magnifies the madness that seizes men who have forgotten all about goodness and conscience.

Boston is a character who personifies earthly good; he is a traditional Aitmatov hero. Yet, despite the high artistry of the third part of the novel, I cannot rid myself of the feeling that the author has "forced" the material. My mind comprehends the tragedy of Boston, but amid the string of deaths, the bullet that kills his son, an innocent child, seems too great a sacrifice to necessity, which is only a step away from rationalism. The mechanism of the drama has been contrived to such an extent that sometimes the feeling of unpremeditation and freedom of life seems to disappear, yet we know that life is far more elevated and unpredictable than we can ever imagine it to be.

Aitmatov's question: "Why does evil almost always triumph over good?" should be answered by social practice only, and not by verbal explanation. There are no ready answers to eternal questions, and history is, in fact, a collective attempt to find a way to establishing harmony between the individual and society, between nature and man.

I make bold to quote again my own words, "Aitmatov's new novel reflects the crisis of the humanistic consciousness of the present day, which will not be reconciled with the existing state of things but at the same time sees no other outlet but the recourse to the mainstays of the people's age-old moral values." However, we see that even they are being lost by the people and no longer serve as mainstays. (Victor Astafyev's *A Sad Detective Story,* Valentin Rasputin's *The Fire* and a number of other books deal with the same subject.)

Aitmatov's new novel is an attempt at finding a way out of the crisis. It is not free of purely artistic shortcomings (critics have written about that already), but it provokes serious reflection.

Chinghiz Aitmatov has been one of the first Soviet writers to deal with the tragic conflicts of Soviet times. In the most general philosophical form we may imagine the tragic conflict as the *irreconcilable* contradiction between the future which is not ready to take over yet, and the past which has already outlived itself. Therefore, the tragic is the most profound and all-embracing expression of life's truth, understood as *development and the process of existence.*

Aitmatov's works, starting with *The White Steamer,* are high tragedy and as such they enter into dialogue with world literature in a universal quest for the meaning of life and the meaning of history. (pp. 128-32)

> *Evgeni Sidorov, "On Chinghiz Aitmatov and His Characters," in* Soviet Literature, *No. 488, 1988, pp. 127-32.*

Herbert Mitgang

In the shifting world of Soviet fiction, *The Place of the Skull* by Chingiz Aitmatov falls somewhere between the traditional and the daring, the cautious past and the glasnost present. Half of the novel is about humans—incidents in the lives of a former seminarian and peasants brushing up against bureaucracy in the Kirghiz Soviet Socialist Republic, the author's home region in Central Asia. The other half is about wolves—thinking, anthropomorphic animals whose lives reach beyond (in Jack London's phrase) the law of the club and fang. On the people level, the novel stumbles; strangely, the story of a wolf family with near-human characteristics is filled with poignancy and is the better half of the book.

A number of themes are constructed but not mortised together very well by the author: the hold of old-fashioned religion even in a Communist country; the intrusion of the helicopter into the rugged but beautiful landscape; drug smuggling and greedy small-time operators; cruelty against wildlife and lack of concern for the environment; the wall of misunderstanding between project officials in control and ordinary workers and peasants.

Since the dialogue, translated from the Russian, sometimes takes the form of proletarian sound bites, Mr. Aitmatov invites the reader to assess his novel within the context of the new openness. (The day may come when glasnost is not relevant, but that day is still to come.) The fact that much of the story is presented as a parable says something about the author's masked style. Unfortunately, parable can be a cloak concealing boldness and directness; it acts as a wink of disguise for the reader. In this respect, parable resembles Russian science fiction, which for a long time has been used by Soviet writers to expose authoritarianism—in other galaxies, of course.

Mr. Aitmatov's method worked well in his play *The Ascent of Mount Fuji,* set on a sacred mountaintop in Kirghizia, when it was presented at the Arena Stage in Washington in 1975. The play dealt directly with the moral dilemmas of the Soviet past, noting that some people who lived through the Stalinist era did not face up to their personal responsibilities. Like Fyodor Abramov writing about the Archangel region, Valentin Rasputin about Siberia, or Mikhail Sholokhov on Cossack life in the Don area, Mr. Aitmatov's strength is as a regional author. Several passages in his novel that stick close to his Central Asian landscape and mountainscape are haunting.

But a fundamental fault with the human side of *The Place of the Skull* is its evasiveness. It is only a quasi-glasnost novel. By contrast, Anatoly Rybakov's current novel, *Children of the Arbat,* has a grander narrative sweep and Stalin himself appears as a character with a speaking role. Mr. Aitmatov attempts to come in through the side door of fiction; Mr. Rybakov hardly bothers knocking before coming in the front entrance. It isn't possible to foretell which sort of Soviet novel will be more durable as art a decade or so from now but in the present political climate, a reader hopes for a new boldness, even in fiction.

The Jerusalem section of the novel that gives the book its title sticks out as if it were uprooted from another story and replanted. The more-or-less central character, a former seminarian who has tried to reform a group of hashish smugglers and is half killed by them for his effort, lies in a state of delirium. His mind wanders to "The Place of the Skull"—Golgotha on the day of the Crucifixion. The dialogue between Jesus of Nazareth and Pontius Pilate is almost embarrassing to read. The Nazarene is chatty and cheerful; the Roman sounds like a parody of a biblical epic starring Charlton Heston, or whoever plays him at Soviet studios.

The first half of *The Place of the Skull* is called "Man," the second half "Wolf." Suddenly the novel's angle of narration shifts in the second half and develops new strength. "Wolf" brings to mind *Call of the Wild* and *White Fang,* which also dealt with survival and domestication in a wolf pack. Although Mr. Aitmatov's wilderness story can stand on its own, it is interesting to recall that London has been one of the most widely read authors in the Soviet Union for many years.

In the story, a dimwitted individual on the steppes has stolen four wolf cubs from their parents. The adult wolves go mad searching for their cubs and, in their sorrow, begin to turn on humans as prey. The she-wolf exists in a state of unrelieved anguish, no different from a human parent. In the background are coldblooded hunters—authority figures. The climax of "Wolf" is so suspenseful that it should not be revealed. Remarkably, the author gets inside the minds of the wolves; the reader is willing to accept their human behavior. For this, and this alone, *The Place of the Skull* is a novelistic achievement.

> *Herbert Mitgang, "Humans and Wolves in Soviet Novel," in* The New York Times, *May 6, 1989, p. 15.*

Tom Clark

This unusual and highly uneven novel [*The Place of the Skull*], powerfully evocative of place, is set in remote regions of Central Asia that will seem as exotic to most Western readers as distant planets: the Issyk-Kul Ridge of Kirghizia, a wild upland country of treacherous, forbidding glaciers and ravines, and the vast steppes of Moyun-Kum in neighboring Kazakhstan, in summer a bountiful,

sun-baked expanse of wild grasses, reigned over by noble birds of prey and grazed by fleet *saigak,* or antelope, and in winter a desolate, "boundless white ocean, frozen in waves."

It is a deep love of these lands, along with a strong faith in the redemptive power of unorthodox Christian religious beliefs, that forms the basis of values used by 61-year-old Soviet novelist Chingiz Aitmatov—himself a Kirghiz native son—as a platform for this extended moral tract in the form of a novel. Hailed in the West as a progressive literary breakthrough made possible by the new freedoms of expression brought on by *glasnost* (and excerpted by *Time* for its putative controversial content), *The Place of the Skull* is in fact, and in method, far more traditional than modern, laden with sermonizing and severely limited by old social realist narrative modes. The strength of the book lies not in its political critique, but in its moments of poetic vision, contained in passages of lyric response to the natural world.

The book is divided into two complementary parts, titled "Man" and "Wolf." At the outset of "Man," Aitmatov follows the fortunes of a she-wolf and her mate, driven by man's intrusions out of savannah hunting grounds whose beauties are limned in an uplifting prose disclosing the novelist's evident familiarity with and affection for the pristine wilderness of the Moyun-Kum.

> In that evening hour a whole flock of white-tailed kites was circling high above the earth. They flew smoothly and aimlessly, simply for the joy of it, in the faint haze of the cool, cloudless heights. Round and round they circled, as though to symbolize the eternal stability of the land and of the sky, silently observing the life down below them on the earth. Thanks to their exceptional, omnipotent vision (their hearing is vastly inferior), these aristocratic birds of prey live their whole lives in the heavens above the savannah, descending to the sinful earth only to eat and sleep.

The vantage soon descends, however, to that sinful Earth. Breaking into the peaceful natural paradise is a raiding party of armed mercenary roughnecks in jeeps and helicopters, dispatched by local officials to top off the regional Five-Year-Plan meat quota by slaughtering the *saigak.* Caught in the ensuing stampede, the wolves' cubs are crushed, the parents wounded and forced to flee.

The only one of Aitmatov's human intruders to approach the wild lands with an interest not arising from sheer rapacity, a deacon's son and former seminarian named Avdiy Kallistratov, becomes the focus of the action through the remainder of the book's first part. A self-appointed, well-meaning ethical crusader bent on the moral reformation of a band of teen-age drug smugglers, Avdiy joins their expedition into the steppes to gather *anasha,* the wild cannabis plant that grows there in profusion. When his companions discover his motive is not the profits of the weed but his own obscure idealism, they beat him up and fling him from a speeding train in the middle of nowhere. At this point the persecuted Avdiy is seized by a vision of Christ conversing with Pontius Pilate. The scene carries obvious echoes of the Christ-Pilate confrontation in Bulgakov's *The Master and Margarita* and seems to confirm a link with Dostoevsky as well (though Aitmatov's Christ-like Avdiy, it must be said, is drawn with little of the subtlety of his famous Russian forerunner's saintly Alyosha).

Rescued and recovered, Avdiy is briefly consoled by a comely scientific researcher who shares his hatred of *anasha* (in fact she's employed in a government campaign to eradicate the "evil weed"). But their romance ends when a misunderstanding bred of a missed rendezvous leads to his rash enlistment in the *saigak* hunt, which proves as disastrous for him as for the defenseless antelope.

In "Wolf," the setting shifts to the Issyk-Kul mountains, where the migrating she-wolf and her mate are found dwelling in uneasy proximity to local shepherds. Here Aitmatov introduces a second main character, the "model worker" Boston Urkunchiev. Urkunchiev, another goody-good with an earnest conscientiousness to match Avdiy's religious fervor, clashes with the inflexible head of the state collective farm. The latter figure refuses his request for private grazing lands and colludes with Noigutov, the teetotalling Urkunchiev's envious, vodka-swilling rival, to bring about his downfall. There is one last fatal encounter between man and wolf, after which the reader is left to ponder the "eternal riddle of why evil almost always triumphs over good."

Human evil and virtue are indeed Aitmatov's chosen protagonists, but his human characters come off seeming hardly more real than cartoon stick-figures, and his true heroes, righteous intentions aside, are the animals.

Certainly the principal message put forward in Aitmatov's preachings—a stern injunction against contemporary people's wasteful, foolhardy and thoughtless defilement of the Earth, and of each other—is a commendable one. The problem with **The Place of the Skull** is that the message is given entirely too much sway over the novelistic medium, unfortunately (and ironically) turning the latter into its own kind of oppressed beast of burden.

> *Tom Clark, "A Canticle for Kirghizia," in* Los Angeles Times Book Review, *June 18, 1989, p. 4.*

Anthony Olcott

Chingiz Aitmatov has long been a powerful figure in Soviet literature, but few critics in the west or the Soviet Union have treated him as a serious writer. Many of the reasons why Aitmatov's reputation is not commensurate with his achievement are clear enough; the few westerners who have bothered with Aitmatov tend to agree that he offers "a somewhat new mix from the old patterns of Soviet literature with an admixture of Central Asian lore, but the game he is playing is as old as socialist realism itself." Critics in the Soviet Union, however much they may praise him, still generally relegate Aitmatov to the ranks of the national writers and leave him outside of Russian literature. Indeed Aitmatov began as a Kirghiz writer, and his early works were standard, if accomplished, examples of what Rasul Gamzatov scorns as "dagger and bracelet lit-

erature," or local color exotica. For at least two decades, however, Aitmatov has written in Russian, has addressed issues of importance to the Soviet Union as a whole, and has increasingly claimed the role of great novelist, which in Russia means, of course, that he should be moralist, philosopher, and politician, as well as artist. *Plakha* [translated into English as *The Place of the Skull*] is Aitmatov's most ambitious attempt to describe both cause and cure for the Soviet malaise, but the confusion, as well as hostility, that the book has provoked illustrates clearly the fundamentally different cultural assumptions that, for all he and his readers may share the Soviet experience, still separate Aitmatov from the greatest part of his audience—native Russians.

Soviet critics have greeted *Plakha* with a diversity of opinion unusual even in the era of glasnost. After the first installment appeared in *Novyi mir,* Aitmatov was accused of "flirting with God" and of "incompetence" in his chosen subject matter. Following the next two installments, some critics rhapsodized: One gushed, "we are on the eve of the end of the second millennium, and Aitmatov's book comes like an accounting of the second millennium before the first, an accounting for all of our era," while another, more measured, called the novel "a difficult success." Far more common was the opinion that for all the strengths of certain portions, the book as a whole is a jumbled pastiche without coherent structure.

Indeed the novel is difficult even to paraphrase. *Plakha* contains two wholly separate, nonintersecting plots, with distinct locales, characters, and even narrative styles. The shorter, occupying the last third of the novel, tells of Boston Urkunchiev, a leading shepherd on a Kirghiz sovkhoz, and, like other Aitmatov heroes, "a real laborer . . . one of those on whom, as the saying goes, the earth must rest." The longer, and more sensational, plot is the story of Avdii Kallistratov, a unique Aitmatov hero in that he is a Russian, and surely a unique Soviet hero in that he is a Christian. Expelled from seminary for heresy, Avdii becomes a freelance undercover journalist, investigating the illegal trade in *anasha,* a Central Asian variety of wild hemp. Since Boston and Avdii never meet, indeed are never even in the same republic, only one element can be said to unite the book, the story of a wolf pair, Akbara and Tashchainar. The novel opens with the destruction of the wolves' first litter in the Moiunkum steppe, where Avdii is an unwilling participant in a mass slaughter of wild antelope. The novel ends as the female, her third litter destroyed and her mate dead at Boston's hand, steals Boston's only son. With no other choice before him, Boston shoots, wounding the wolf, but killing his own child. [The critic adds in a footnote: The close similarity of this ending to the ending of the 1985 Kirghiz film *Descendants of the Snow Leopard,* which was based on the *Mannas* legend, suggests that this theme—man countering nature only to kill his own offspring—is recurrent in Kirghiz thought.]

There is plainly some justice in the observation that "if the author really had no whole, internal, organic seed of an idea which might in fact have united these parts expressively, in a way the reader could understand, then probably he ought not to have written a novel, but a cycle of stories." Even Aitmatov admits tacitly that the book was produced in great haste. *Novyi mir* offered the novel in its June, August, and September issues, skipping July because, as Aitmatov explained, "things weren't completely ready yet"; moreover, the text of the novel in *Novyi mir* differs somewhat from the excerpts published in *Sovetskaia Kirgizia,* suggesting that Aitmatov shoved *Plakha* through an unexpected "window of opportunity" for publication.

For all the novel's apparent chaos, other critics have sensed it to be a whole, pointing out that Aitmatov's previous novel also had two noncontiguous plots and, more substantively, that what *Plakha* lacks in unity of setting and character it more than amply supplies in "unity of authorial position, of authorial thought." There has been very little agreement, however, on the organizing principles of *Plakha,* beyond the obvious one that the novel is a jeremiad, exposing and condemning ecological despoliation, drug and alcohol abuse, moral degeneration, and a myriad of other evils—a general crisis of society and man. In itself, this is unremarkable, for doomsaying has become a fashion in recent Soviet literature; in the words of one critic, "our most popular prose is that which answers not the question 'how' (quality, level, or achievement) but rather the question 'what' or 'about what' (the theme, social daring, or, as we say, biting commentary)." *Plakha* is distinguished by Aitmatov's attempts to portray these evils of the day as symptomatic of a larger evil—the Soviet Union has abandoned religion.

As early as the novella *Belyi parakhod* (1970) Aitmatov began portraying religion as a force that organizes and gives meaning to human life; his novel before *Plakha, I dol'she veka dlitsia den',* demonstrates clearly that the hero's virtues as a worker and citizen were rooted precisely in his knowledge of and respect for traditional religious practice, just as the villains' vices stem from their ignorance of it. Neither book, however, was perceived as a challenge to the official atheism of the USSR. The religions Aitmatov was illustrating, a mixture of Islam and pre-Islamic primitive religion, were of little interest or importance to most Soviet readers.

Not so with *Plakha,* where Aitmatov has chosen not only to have a Russian Orthodox adherent as his hero, but also openly to model him on Christ. Avdii, who is in his early thirties, is even called "the new Christ." He has "a high pale forehead . . . wore his hair to his shoulders, and had a thick chestnut beard which, though it didn't much become him, did give his face a sympathetic expression"; he travels with twelve other marijuana gatherers; he is a carpenter, a trade taught him by his father; and most pointed of all, Avdii is quite literally crucified, arms and feet bound to a tree "like a big bird with outstretched wings, straining to rise into the heights, but now killed and tossed into the bushes."

The simple novelty of such a hero in a Soviet novel has eclipsed most discussion of what Aitmatov may have meant by his choice. No Soviet critic has yet felt secure enough in glasnost to praise *Plakha* for offering Christianity as the antidote to the ills of the USSR (though Evgenii Evtushenko came close), but several hostile to the novel

have accused Aitmatov of pro-Christian propaganda. At least one critic has been offended that Aitmatov seems ignorant of Russian Orthodoxy, and a number have seized upon such statements as "God is the higher essence of man's own existence" as meaning that Aitmatov is advocating those functional elements of the Christian tradition that will improve society; in the words of one western critic:

> Avdy wants to resurrect the *idea* of God in modern society in order to improve the quality of living. His message is less about the immanent [*sic*] presence of a transcendent Deity than about a definition of the nature of god-consciousness, and of the ways this can assist man to live in a post-industrial era.

At the same time Aitmatov confounds any attempt to relegate Avdii's view of God to the hoary revolutionary conceit of Man-Become-God: He capitalizes the word *God* throughout the novel, illustrates the value of prayer, and insists that Avdii is in search of a God that is transcendent, larger than man, and powerful enough to give meaning to the modern world.

Aitmatov's choice of Christ as a model, both directly and in Avdii's paler reflection, has led most Soviet critics (and such western ones as have taken up this novel) to see Aitmatov's message in *Plakha* to be approximately that:

> repentance is an idea which grows in proportion to the experience of life, the magnitude of the conscience, a magnitude acquired, nurtured, and cultivated, by human reason. No one other than man has the capacity to repent. Repentance is the eternal and inescapable preoccupation of the human spirit about itself.

Avdii himself might be called an embodiment of repentance, for he is capable of such intense sympathy that "when he learned the story of Christ in the seminary he so suffered His torment that he sobbed when he read how Judas had betrayed Him." Not satisfied with the ability of the church to make people, especially youth, realize the significance of Christ's death, Avdii begins a search for "a new contemporary form of God," which he attempts to take to the people whom he considers suffer most from the absence of God, the wild marijuana gatherers. His goal in doing so is twofold, to write about narcomania and its effects so that "the many would cry out, as if it were a matter of their own blood, a fire in their own home, a danger to their own children" and to convince the drug runners themselves to "repent right here, right here in the steppe, under the wide blue sky, and promise yourself to give this up forever . . . and seek reconciliation with yourself and with that which we call God."

Unfortunately, *Plakha* presents significant hindrances to this reading of Aitmatov's message, which repeatedly portrays repentance as an activity that has no practical consequence. The repentance of good characters like Avdii is of no avail against evil characters like Grishan, head of the marijuana gatherers, or the Ober, head of the gang that is machine-gunning antelope. Nor does Avdii's repentance prompt anything other than contempt for Avdii in those whom he would change, the weak and wandering youth who follow Grishan and the Ober. This contempt may in part be due to Avdii's general bloodlessness; several critics have found Avdii to be a schematic, unconvincing figure. Some of the character's lack of focus is factual; as I. Kryvelev pointed out, in the USSR an expelled seminarian could not become a freelance, undercover journalist. It also seems unlikely that Avdii, the son of a priest, would read of Judas's treachery for the first time only upon entering seminary. Perhaps more damaging is the symbolic weight Avdii must bear, as what one critic terms "a typical hero-ideologue." Even the name declares Aitmatov's intentions for his character; *Abdi* is a Hebrew name meaning of God, while *Kallistratov* is Greek for good soldier. His patronymic, for good measure, is Innokentievich. In the words of critic E. Sidorov, "Avdii is fleshless, just as every beautiful idea that comes into a world that rejects idealism is without flesh. It is as though he sails between heaven and earth, torn away by the church and deprived of earthly soil, of daily life."

The futility of repentance shows equally clearly in *Plakha*'s other story, that of Boston Urkunchiev, who is as real and fully realized as Avdii is ethereal. Boston is one of a line of positive Aitmatov characters, all of whom share the same virtues. He is a fanatically hard worker, with an unusually well-developed sense of responsibility, as well as the integrity to insist on doing his job the correct way even when to do so is politically inexpedient. *Plakha* differs from earlier works in that, far from bringing the hero satisfaction and repose, these qualities are shown to be the cause of Boston's death. Boston, whom one critic has called "a practical attempt to realize the values which Avdii preaches," is in his afflictions almost a Kirghiz Job, a man cursed to have his best efforts bear evil fruit. He and an equally conscientious companion go high into the mountains to seek new pasture for the hungry sheep; the companion disappears into a crevice, and the others blame Boston. Boston's wife soon dies of cancer; on her deathbed she urges him to marry the friend's widow. This marriage causes another character to sneer "who are you after that, you and that bitch of yours, Guliumkan? Ernazar is up on the divide, frozen in ice, without a grave, like a dog, while you, you snake, you're hugging that shameless wife of his, damn rentable bitch, and you're living on top of the world!" Boston's best efforts to improve the economic efficiency of his sheep band get him accused of being a kulak, while his attempt to return the stolen wolf cubs to the she-wolf results in the wolves identifying Boston's home as the place where their cubs disappeared. Because their howling makes life impossible for Boston and his family, he is forced to fight them, with the final consequence that he accidentally kills his own son, then murders Bazarbai, the drunken, boastful conniver who, in Boston's opinion, first set in motion the events that led to the tragedy. Despite every evidence of "magnitude of conscience," Boston is, in Aitmatov's depiction, as incapable of changing the actions of those around him as he is of controlling the circumstances of his own life. Conscious of the mistakes that have caused evil, scrupulous in his own behavior, and demanding of the behavior of others, Boston seems nevertheless an illustration of the incompleteness, if not the complete inutility, of repentance.

The most telling failure of repentance, however, comes in the scenes in which Aitmatov depicts Christ before Pilate. The close similarity of this scene to the one in Mikhail Bulgakov's *Master i Margarita* may well be the aspect of *Plakha* that has irritated Russian readers the most. Christ, an accused criminal facing a slow and painful death, shows no sign of repentance for his "crime," even though his apology for wrongdoing would gain him Pilate's pardon and save his life: "Let everything be as it is meant to be" Christ says, rejecting clemency. Anyone raised in the western tradition will, of course, understand that what Jesus means here is his crucifixion, in turn suggesting that Jesus is rejecting repentance out of divine duty. He must die in order to become the Redeemer. *Plakha,* though, offers good reason to believe that this assumption is false— Aitmatov after all was not raised in western tradition. Soviet criticism has not explored the nature of Aitmatov's religious antecedents, nor has the writer spoken much about them, but his works show plainly that he is thoroughly familiar with traditional Kirghiz belief and practices. Earlier works show pre-Islamic elements of those beliefs, but *I dol'she veka dlitsia den',* the novel preceding *Plakha,* shows that Aitmatov's knowledge of Islam is thorough.

Plakha makes no direct mention of Islam, however, which is especially odd since the novel refers to virtually every other religious or cultural tradition that can be found in the USSR. In addition to Avdii and his Orthodoxy, Aitmatov also introduces the Kirghiz pre-Islamic pantheon, makes passing reference to Buddhism, and even introduces a "wolf-goddess" to whom the grieving she-wolf prays. Two other references are not exactly religious, but nevertheless recall the ethnic and cultural diversity of the USSR: These are to Georgians, in a short story included within the text of the novel, and to the Germans, of which nationality Avdii's girlfriend is a member. Even the Jews appear in some measure, in Aitmatov's portrayal of Jerusalem. The only major religious tradition to which Aitmatov does not refer (save for a single greeting of "Salam") is Islam.

This omission is even more striking because *Plakha* has one detail that is inarguably, and significantly, Islamic: For all its similarities to Bulgakov's novel, Aitmatov's scene with Christ has the major difference that Christ is not crucified. It may be, of course, that Aitmatov simply considered the crucifixion unnecessary to depict, but it seems more likely that this omission is deliberate, since the Koran makes very plain that Jesus was *not* crucified:

> and for their unbelief, and their uttering against
> Mary a mighty calumny, and for their saying,
> "We slew the Messiah, Jesus son of Mary, the
> Messenger of God"—yet they did not slay him,
> neither crucified him, only a likeness that was
> shown to them . . . they slew him not of a certainty—no indeed; God raised him up to Him.

This difference from the Christian version of Christ's life is more profound than simple narrative disagreement: Islam not only rejects crucifixion but sees it as an insult, impossible to imagine for the prophet whom only Muhammed outranks. As one Muslim theologian states, "I know of nobody who has been so impudent towards God as [the Christians]. No, by God! There is no disgrace more shocking than that of a people who believe that God the Knower was buried. They affront God by actually making that statement."

In fact, a great deal about *Plakha* suggests that Aitmatov's critique of the modern world, and hence his prescriptions for remedying its failings, depend upon an Islamic understanding, not only of the Christ story, but of the world. For example, what makes the Christian doctrine "impudent" is that Islam draws a much closer connection between physical well-being and spiritual correctness than does Christianity:

> The assurance that Islam holds out to the faithful comprehends not only the eventual destiny of mankind in another world to come but has meaning in this world, as well. The way of the Muslim is the best way of life, necessarily so, because it reflects an ageless divinely ordained pattern. It follows, therefore, that it must also be a successful mode of life for those who follow it truly. As people who cooperate, as it were, with the creative forces of the universe, Muslims may reasonably expect to enjoy well-being here and now in addition to bliss in the hereafter. [Charles J. Adams, "Islamic Faith," in *Introduction to Islamic Civilization,* ed., R. M. Savory.]

In Islam pain, disease, and early death are marks of failure, of improper comprehension of God's will; they could not have been suffered by the prophet who preceded Muhammed. Conversely, the sign of God's favor lies precisely in success. It is probably in this context that we are to understand Aitmatov's portrayal of Jesus recalling a time from childhood in Egypt, when he and his mother were mysteriously lent a boat, to take a ride on the Nile. Drifting helplessly, the two are set upon by an enormous crocodile and then miraculously find themselves safe on the shore. Mary's reaction is telling: "Jesus! Jesus! My beloved son! Your Father recognized you! He saved you! It's Him who saved you! He loves you, you are His beloved son, Jesus! You will become wise, Jesus, you will become a Teacher! And you will open people's eyes, Jesus!" For all its similarity to Christian rhetoric, Mary's words contain the additional Islamic notion of Jesus being marked out, set apart by God, and so spared the struggles of other men, who in Islamic tradition must suffer the eternal competition between a personal angel and personal devil, or *shaytan.*

Aitmatov's insistence on calling Jesus a teacher more often than he does a savior is also consonant with Islamic theology. The Islamic Jesus is an object lesson, whom believers are obligated to contemplate, just as they are Adam, Abraham, and Moses, as illustrations of the ever-present human potential for ignorance and ungodliness. After all, the reason Allah had to make Muhammed his Prophet was that humanity had distorted and ignored these earlier prophets. Aitmatov probably seems to imitate Bulgakov in his presentation of Christ because each author's message requires that Christ be understood as a living, flesh and blood man. Where Bulgakov seems to be illustrating the power of the written word, in the distance between Eshua Ga-Nostri and the Jesus of the Gospels, Aitmatov is attempting to present Jesus in a manner that

both retains his mythic aura and makes him comprehensible as a man of today. Critics who have lambasted the Christ scenes of *Plakha* for clumsy, jargonized prose, overlook that Aitmatov presents the scene as Avdii's hallucination. A character like Avdii, who is of good heart but little education, a man who is both a religious and a journalistic crusader, would naturally imagine the figure he most holds in awe, Jesus Christ, as a very modern, slightly pompous moralizer, much in the mold of the scolds of perestroika.

Aitmatov's translation of a figure whom everyone can recognize but no one knows into a more familiar and topical Jesus offers an understanding of history fundamentally different from that of an orthodox materialist. *Plakha* argues that history is not a series of events dictated by economic forces and is decidedly not a progression, as Aitmatov's Jesus chides Pilate:

> Since the founders of Man were driven from Eden what an abyss of evil has yawned open, what wars, cruelties, murders, persecutions, injustices, and insults people have suffered! . . . What is the prime significance of history but the movement of reasoning beings to the blessed heights of love and sympathy? But how many terrible trials have there been in human history, and there is no end visible to the evil acts which rise up like waves in the ocean.

Grishan, the leader of the marijuana band, is even more pointed in his rejection of history:

> So much has been held out to Man since the day of creation; what miracles haven't been promised to the insulted and injured? Now it's the Kingdom of God coming, now democracy, now equality, now brotherhood, and now even happiness in a collective—if you want, go live in communes and if you're industrious, on top of it all they'll promise everybody heaven. And what do you really get? Nothing but words!

What Aitmatov wants to offer in place of history-as-progress is history as a series of lessons, a book that people are obligated to study. It is this that Jesus calls "Real history . . . the history of the flowering of humanity" that "has not yet begun on earth."

Here too Aitmatov would seem to be a reasonably orthodox Muslim, since for a Muslim "the essence of God's message for humanity today . . . is the same as it has been for all time." One commentator has called this "Koranic time":

> History in the Qur'an becomes unified time. . . . The walls that separate the past, the present, and the future collapse and the three times commingle in a common destiny. Even the earth and the heaven, temporal time and divine time, the story of Creation and the Day of Judgement . . . always meet in the present moment in the Qur'an.

Aitmatov would seem to be saying essentially the same thing in his observations that "the same unchanging problem confronts every man—to be a man today, tomorrow, and always." In fact, in a recent interview Aitmatov has suggested that the purpose of art is precisely to introduce humanity into this atemporal world:

> But art can also aspire to another and, I think, higher level, when it acquires universal significance . . . and then it refers not only to details of the everyday, not only to what is happening in daily reality, but also refers to myth, to legend, to the big philosophical concerns, the big historical conceptions, relating what is imagined not only to the realia of some small region and defined environ, but also trying to spread this over the whole of human reality.

Plakha demonstrates that moral contemplation of the past, which Aitmatov calls historical synchronism, is the only reliable compass for human behavior:

> [This] is to some degree possible for every person who is not wholly without imagination. The person, though, for whom the events of the past are as close as the reality of the moment, the person who suffers the past as though it were part of his blood, that person is a martyr, a tragic figure, since in knowing in advance how this or that history ends and the consequences it brings, seeing all this in advance the person can only suffer, unable to influence the course of events, and so he makes himself a sacrifice to a triumph of justice which will never occur. But this passion to confirm the truth of the past is holy, for it is precisely thus that ideas are born, that the spiritual struggle of new generations with the preceeding ones, and the ones that preceded them, on which the world stands, and the experience of life constantly grows larger, develops . . . good and evil are transmitted from generation to generation in the infinity of memory, the infinity of time and space in the human world.

Such an understanding of history is an implicit challenge to Soviet authority, perhaps to any temporal power, in that it requires the companion conviction that absolute definitions of good and evil exist independent of time, territory, and politics. Most governments, and certainly the Soviet one, reject such arguments, as did one of Aitmatov's more acute, and more hostile, critics: "Marxism-Leninism . . . does not admit any posing of a general question other than in a concretely political and social way. The concrete-historical approach is the only justified one, while the rest are relegated to those of which V. I. Lenin said 'We don't believe in absolutes!' " The point of Aitmatov's "history of the flowering of humanity" is precisely that it is based upon absolutes of good and evil.

Aitmatov's understanding of these absolutes is more Islamic than Christian, as can best be seen in the story of the two wolves, Akbara and Tashchainar. Critics have long remarked Aitmatov's sympathetic renderings of animals, but generally understand them as an "opposition of man to nature [that] is at least two hundred years old . . . 'the fate of the pursued' [which] our generation of readers learned about way back in Seton-Thompson." The choice of wolves in *Plakha* makes particularly clear that this interpretation is incorrect. Aitmatov's understanding of nature is neither Seton-Thompson's—humanity is bad and nature good—nor the earlier Christian one—nature is the dominion of humans, given for their use. In the former scheme, the wolf would be good, in the latter, evil. Aitmatov, for all the sympathy with which he portrays the wolves, makes very clear that they are neither good nor bad; they simply *are*. The wolves' every action, from the drive to reproduce to the fury of the hunt, is presented as the expression of a natural condition. Paralleling wolf and human in some detail (even to the point of giving Boston a name which means, we are told, "grey coat"), showing both with their offspring, at the hunt, and enjoying the intoxication of *anasha*, Aitmatov in each instance shows that wolves, unlike men, observe a natural limit in all things: killing only when hungry, attacking only when threatened, and menacing people only after three of their litters have been destroyed by humans. This presentation too is consonant with an Islamic understanding of the world; to call any animal bad or good, is impossible to a Muslim:

> Allah is both the creator of the universe and its ruler. The laws instituted by him govern the motion of the stars and the planets, the sun and the moon, the natural processes of animal and vegetable worlds. In this essentially harmonious and beneficial world, all created things, except human beings, submit to their Creator. James Dickie, an English Muslim convert, has expressed this aspect of the Quranic vision succinctly . . . by stating that 'all animals and insects are already Muslims.' Humans alone have a propensity to violate God's laws because, unlike the animals, they have consciousness and therefore freedom of choice. [Malise Ruthven, *Islam in the World*.]

Aitmatov makes the same point symbolically by giving both the she-wolf and Jesus the same unusual piercing blue eyes.

Critics with western assumptions find *Plakha* confusing because Avdii and Boston each possess some consciousness of God. Each attempts to exercise his freedom of choice in the way that God would presumably prefer, and yet both come to grievous ends for reasons that they cannot control and of which they may not even be aware. Much of the apparent formlessness of *Plakha* stems from Aitmatov's effort to demonstrate that, as Avdii says, "any evil act, any human crime in any part of the world touches all of us, even if we are far away and have no suspicion of it, and don't want to know about it." To readers raised in an intellectual tradition that understands guilt, responsibility, and repentance to be individual, the inability of a good character like Boston or Avdii to overcome evil will seem paradoxical. To someone from a Muslim tradition, however, the failure of these characters is wholly comprehensible, because Islam has at its center not the individual, but the community, the *umma*.

In religious dogma the *umma* is elastic, encompassing family, neighbors, fellow citizens, and all other Muslims into a common unit of faith, life, and understanding that ought, theoretically, to make impossible any human conflict more serious than an argument. The piety of the *umma*, not that of any one individual, determines the beneficence of God; a pious individual may suffer because he or she lives in an impious community. It is, of course, folly to argue that Aitmatov is attempting to picture a religious *umma* in *Plakha,* but it seems very likely that one of the chief purposes of the novel is to demonstrate graphically that the state of our deeply troubled world results from the sins of a collective human community. In his previous novel, *I dol'she veka dlitsia den',* Aitmatov held the Soviets and Americans equally responsible for earth's cowardice; set in the USSR, *Plakha* criticizes the failures of modernity in east and west alike. Avdii ruminates:

> How crowded man is on this planet, how he fears that he will find no place for himself, that he won't get enough to eat, that he won't find a life with others like himself. And isn't this the reason that prejudice, fear, and hatred reduce the planet to the size of a stadium in which all the spectators are hostages, for both teams, in order to win, have brought nuclear bombs with them, while their fans, indifferent to all, scream "Score! Score! Score!"

In fact, one of the major points of Aitmatov's novel is that humanity's danger to itself is so great that ideology is irrelevant, a point made vivid by Jesus' nightmare:

> It was as though I was flying over the earth and neither night nor day did I see a single living person. Everything was dead, everything was covered entirely over with the black ash of burnt-out fires, the land lay wholly in ruin, without forests, field, or ships on the sea, and only a strange, endless barely audible ringing carried from afar, . . . and I was horrified by this terrible riddle— could this be the reward for my love for people, for making myself a sacrifice? Could it really be that the savage world of men had killed itself in its own savagery, as the scorpion kills itself with its own poison?

On its surface, Jesus' nightmare is of course the sort of antinuclear propaganda that has become almost obligatory in Soviet prose and seems, no matter how heartfelt the fear or actual the threat, to be bathetic. Nuclear devastation, however, is only one of the ways in which this horrible future might come about. *Plakha* clearly suggests that there are others. Narcomania, having devastated the east, is now well begun in the west. Ecological despoliation and frivolous uses of resources play havoc with the land. Ideology interferes not only in time-tested ways of living but actually works against man's ability to provide himself with food and shelter.

The fear that man has lost any sense of collective responsibility animates *Plakha.* Aitmatov repeatedly presents images of individuals who, in pursuit of private ends, ignore the larger whole: "The youth of today don't want to work in filth and live in the sticks," frets Boston Urkunchiev, "and the pay there [in the sovkhozes] wasn't much, a young fellow or a girl could get a lot more for an eight-hour day in a factory or a building site." In another place he laments that "it's as though people don't understand how much of the unhappiness and poverty of their lives flows and has always flowed from laziness." The bad shepherd, Bazarbai, steals the wolf cubs solely to buy himself

vodka, just as the Partorg in the sovkhoz attempts to get Boston disciplined because he feels personally offended, masking his animus in political rhetoric. Avdii is ejected from the seminary because dogma takes precedence over the realities of today; he then discovers that his hard-won knowledge about the dangers of the narcotics trade cannot be published for reasons of prestige. "How long are we going to pretend that even our catastrophes are the best?" Avdii wails in despair.

How humanity might avoid this disastrous future is more difficult to extract from *Plakha* than are the many ways of reaching that future. Aitmatov provides hints about a possible way to avoid disaster through an "extraordinary prayer," composed by a woman who becomes a nun after her husband's ship is sunk during the war. The strange thing about her plea to God is that she requests no salvation for her husband, no repose for his soul—only that the ship be allowed not to sink: "Let the waves beat against the bow and . . . the ocean foam wash the ship with whistling rain," she entreats, let it not even reach paradise, but please let it keep sailing into eternity. Strikingly, Akbara addresses a very similar prayer to the "wolf-goddess," asking only that she be allowed to grieve indefinitely for her lost cubs, not that they be returned to her.

Plakha contains a third prayer—the one uttered by Avdii on his "cross." Although closely modeled on Christ and identified as a Christian, Avdii moans his last prayer not to God, but to the she-wolf. Moreover, when she arrives at his "cross" Avdii dies, content. Aitmatov makes Avdii commit such apostasy to underscore the change that Avdii had undergone after his first encounter with evil, when the marijuana gatherers fling him from a moving freight train. Avdii emerges from this brush with death a disillusioned man. Part of this change is no doubt due to his realization of the strength of evil, but a large part too seems to come from his realization that, in his words, "no one needs anybody." Shunned by proper Soviet citizenry and denied by his fellow *anasha* gatherers, now jailed, and his article rejected on inconsequential political grounds, Avdii suffers a crisis of faith in his "God-contemporary," for which he compensates by falling deeply, irrationally in love with Inga Fedorovna, a botanist also working on *anasha.* Pouring out his thoughts in letters to her, Avdii persuades Inga that he should move to her town in Kazakhstan. When he arrives, however, she has had to leave on some legal business, precipitating suicidal depression:

> Avdii's depression became extreme. He felt as though he was in a dark and gloomy forest. Alone, completely alone. An autumnal wind was rattling the upper branches of the trees, soon snow would come, to cover the forest, and him, Avdii, to bury everything in snow, to efface everything . . . Avdii wanted to die . . . without a second thought he would have gone out and lain beneath the first train to pass by.

This suicidal frame of mind seriously weakens the parallel between a Christian Christ and Avdii; Avdii's death is not a triumph but a defeat, which Aitmatov further emphasizes by trivializing its causes. Though he is taunted to "renounce that God of yours," the real cause of his crucifixion is that Avdii refuses to drink alcohol with the meat-harvesting crew, suggesting clearly that Avdii dies not to redeem humanity, but because humanity has excluded him.

For purposes of understanding *Plakha,* the more important aspect of Avdii's death is that it clearly parallels that of Boston. The comparison lies not so much in the manner of death, though each is in its way a suicide, but in the cause. Avdii finds himself excluded and denied by his fellow men: Boston makes himself an outlaw: "Boston suddenly understood that from that moment [when he shot Bazarbai] he had crossed some line and so had separated himself from everybody else." Both men are separated from the human community.

One of the ironies arising from the cultural assumptions that separate Aitmatov from his readers is that the novel's final scene, in which Boston wades into Lake Issyk-Kul' to drown himself, has different implications in western and Islamic traditions, making Aitmatov's fears about such separation appear obscure. To most western readers, the tragedy of Boston's death will probably be in his destruction as an individual; Aitmatov's description seems to imply that the tragedy lies in Boston having *become* an individual:

> "So it's the end of the world," Boston said aloud, a horrible truth opening before him. Until now the whole world had been within him, and now he, this world, had come to an end. He had been the sky and the earth and the mountains . . . and all that he had lived and seen in his time, all of this had been his universe, had lived in him and for him, and now, even though all this would be as it had always been, but without him. It would be another world, while his world, unrepeatable, unreplaceable, was lost, not to be reborn in anyone or anything. It was a great catastrophe, it was the end of his world.

Read from a perspective that values the individual only within the greater context of the community, Boston's realization does not involve a western conception of solipsistic individualism but the tragic awareness that individuality has reduced the world to insignificance. If each individual is separate, if the world also dies when each one dies, then human life has no meaning. If, however, each individual lives within a community and for a community, in harmony with the eternal design, then it is death that becomes insignificant. Aitmatov touches upon this idea at the death of Boston's wife and his own death, by picturing the waves on Issyk-Kul', that "boil up, disappear, and once again emerge from within themselves." Avdii's dying appeal to the she-wolf thus clarifies the significance of the other two prayers, that the only way for an individual's death not to become "the end of the world" is for him or her to become part of the greater harmony of humanity and nature.

Most of *Plakha* is a demonstration of what happens when people do not live in harmony with nature. One incident in the novel, however, suggests the possibilities for human achievement foreseen by Aitmatov if people were no longer to put themselves outside the natural order. The scene comes early in the novel, when Avdii chances on a concert of an a cappella church chorus in Moscow's Pushkin Museum:

> These ten [singers], joined together by God, sang to submerge us within ourselves, in the circling depths of unconsciousness, to resurrect within ourselves the past, the spirit and trials of vanished generations, so that we might then rise up, to soar above ourselves and above the world, to find the beauty and meaning of our own predestination—once having appeared in life, to adore its miraculous structure.

Aitmatov, however, is not sanguine that this harmony is something humanity can easily achieve. As he listens Avdii recalls a Georgian short story he had read, "The Six and the Seventh": Recognizing defeat, a tattered band of anti-Soviet guerrillas spend a final night together before separating to leave now-Soviet Georgia forever. In a final celebration of their nationality, they sing traditional songs, using the same vocal harmonies as does church music. Among the seven is a Soviet undercover agent assigned to kill the others. He does kill them, but only by leaving the circle of singers. The real force of the story for Aitmatov lies in the effect upon the agent, who then also kills himself: "And so once more the vicious circle of killings, and once more blood spilled for spilled blood."

In the context of this short story, the three prayers of *Plakha* become intelligible. In Jesus' words, "all people, taken together, are the image of God on earth"; the prayers in *Plakha* are in effect addressed to humanity, requesting the only thing that in Aitmatov's understanding this "God-contemporary" can truly grant: continuity into the future of the natural order that existed in the past. It no doubt is an overstatement to claim that Aitmatov sees the age-old structure of the world to be literally ordained by God (or Allah), but *Plakha* leaves little doubt that the author understands life on earth to be a kind of harmonious cycle that man can join but not change; his every interference only causes destruction. The only possible prayer that may then be offered is to have the chance to continue that harmony. This interpretation explains Aitmatov's odd addition to the Christ story, when Avdii attempts to "save the Teacher! I will take him to Russia, to a forgotten little island in a river of ours, the Oka." Avdii fails, of course, since "he had still to be born in the far-off twentieth century." As noted, Aitmatov is ambiguous as to whether or not that failure leads to crucifixion, but wholly unambiguous that the story of that death should be a lesson in the consequences of stepping outside the natural order. Jesus tells Pilate:

> In eternal repentance let there come generations who will each time shudder anew at the price which I will pay today to redeem human sinfulness, in the illumination and stimulation within them of their divine origins. That is why I am born in this world, to serve as an unfading example to people.

Jesus would appear to be the impetus for *Plakha*'s unexplained title, which has variously been rendered in English as "scaffold" or "chopping block," but which ought more accurately to be "place of execution." Execution by definition is a violation of the natural order, one person taking on the ending of another's life; man is set against man. Aitmatov's novel argues that if people would set themselves against others, as individuals concerned only for their own selves, then every death becomes a kind of execution, and every person an executioner, in violation of the "miraculous structure" of life. On the other hand, and perhaps paradoxically, it is only within that collective harmony that people can achieve the true value of the individual, as Aitmatov makes clear by having Avdii find his double among the singers:

> I suddenly discovered that one of them . . . resembled me very much. . . . Grey-eyed, narrow-shouldered . . . with long light-colored hair, with the same thin, veiny hands he probably was overcoming his shyness with singing, just as I must overcome my reserve when I turn the conversation to the theological themes that are close to me.

Only when we "flow as one into the chorus," Aitmatov argues, will individuals find their "aroused, powerful and triumphant voices [ascending] to the heavens and the earth beneath [their] feet firm and unshakeable. And then we will sing as long as there are songs to sing, sing into eternity."

Properly understood, Aitmatov's novel presents an interesting problem for Soviet ideologists. In one sense profoundly collective in mentality. *Plakha* is at the same time profoundly hostile to ideology: All of the troubles on earth, Jesus tells Pilate, come from the "incompatibility of people with people, the incompatibility of imperial borders, the incompatibility of ideas, the incompatibility of prides and ambitions, the incompatibility of absolute power-mad Caesars." Moreover, as a recent interview makes even clearer, the collectivism of the present-day USSR and the "miraculous structure of life," even if related by intention, are most often widely separated in fact:

> In the past man could get by with a natural economy, relying primarily upon himself, on his own labor, his own property, on his own land. Now everything is completely different, the government must take care of everything. On the one hand such an approach is a phenomenon of the principles of socialism, but on the other hand I am disillusioned that we have not been able to organize properly many spheres of our existence.

Plakha challenges readers to orient themselves upon the eternal, upon those constants that join person to person, not only through the expanse of our world today, but also through the temporal expanse of the past and the future. Aitmatov argues that to concentrate upon temporary differences that set each person apart from the other is to set out, each of us alone, to individual places of execution, where each will die a death as meaningless as that of Avdii or of Boston. The only salvation, Aitmatov makes clear, lies in that harmony of each person with all people and eternal nature, the "God-Contemporary" that all the characters of *Plakha* seek in one way or another.

In *Plakha* Chingiz Aitmatov fulfills the duty of a Soviet novelist, to diagnose the gravest ills of the USSR and then to offer the prescription he thinks will best cure them. In doing so he not only continues the traditions of the great Russian novelists, using his art to alarm, educate, and inspire his countrymen, but even offers a solution that would seem to have deep roots in both Soviet and Russian culture. Wholly a product of the Soviet Union, having both suffered the evils of Soviet history and enjoyed its benefits, Aitmatov meant *Plakha* to be for all his fellow citizens. The novel's reception, however, suggests strongly that the underlying cultural assumptions of an Aitmatov and his Russian reader, for all they may share as Soviets, are still so different as to make Aitmatov's passionate appeal seem merely incoherent to the Russian. In other words, *Plakha* suggests very clearly that in the Soviet Union of today, even so ecumenical a construct as "the God-Contemporary" will still be of a defined denomination, which in this case seems to be Islam. (pp. 213-26)

> Anthony Olcott, "What Faith the God-Contemporary? Chingiz Aitmatov's 'Plakha'," in Slavic Review, Vol. 49, No. 2, Summer, 1990, pp. 213-26.

Joseph Mozur

Chingiz Aitmatov, one of the most important non-Russian cultural figures in the Soviet Union today, has been an unfailing spokesman in support of the linguistic and cultural rights of the country's numerous non-Russian nationalities. The collection *Piebald Dog Running along the Shore* reflects the author's pride in his non-Russian cultural heritage as well as his indebtedness to the Russian and Soviet literary traditions.

The title story, first published in 1977, is an enchanting tale of a rite de passage set among the Nivkh hunter-fishermen, who inhabit the harsh coastline of the Sea of Okhotsk in northeastern Siberia. Accompanying the boy Kirisk on his first hunt at sea are his father, his uncle, and the village elder. While crossing the sea to their island hunting grounds, the men and the boy are overtaken by a dense fog and for days seek in vain to find their way back home. When their drinking water begins to run out, the men sacrifice themselves one by one by stepping into the icy sea and leaving Kirisk the last remaining drops of water. In the boy's animistic world, however, the men live on as the wind, the waves, and the star that guides the fragile boat to the snow-spotted hills of the coastline. Kirisk is saved on the seventh day of his lonely trial when the winds drive the boat to his seaside hamlet, nestled at the foot of a hill, which from afar resembles a piebald dog. Through the integration of folkloric and mythical elements into a "realistic" plot Aitmatov seeks to efface the time and space of his narration, thereby elevating his tale to the stature of a parable on man's plight in the twentieth century. If so read, *Piebald Dog* becomes an urgent appeal for human solidarity in the nuclear age.

A boy is also the hero of the second major novella in the collection, *The Cranes Fly Early* (1975). The most autobiographical of Aitmatov's works, the story is set in a small

Kirghiz village during World War II. A group of young boys—whose portrayal is based on Aitmatov's boyhood friends—are called upon to do the plowing for their fathers, who are fighting at the front. The boy heroes see their enthusiastic and selfless efforts come to naught, however, when their plow horses are stolen by black marketeers. The frustration of their hope to accomplish a man's task and to be worthy of their fathers' sacrifice at the front is depicted as a supreme tragedy. The realistic plot—no doubt chosen to coincide with the thirtieth anniversary of the Soviet victory in World War II—is couched in an epic style, with reminiscences from the Kirghiz epos *Manas* woven into the narrative. In the attempt to give his story universal significance Aitmatov also prefigures various aspects of the plot with allusions to the Christian Book of Job and the Buddhist *Theragatha*. Unfortunately the epic associations are too diverse to give the work its needed unity, and the martial imagery from *Manas* clashes with the Buddhist world view evoked by the act of plowing, to which the epigraph from the *Theragatha* refers. *The Cranes Fly Early* is perhaps the mature Aitmatov's weakest novella, yet its autobiographical nature makes it an important work in the author's fictional oeuvre.

Of the other three stories included in the volume—*To Have and to Lose* (1961; translated earlier as *Pretty Poplar in a Red Kerchief*), *Duishen* (1962), and *Mother Earth* (1963)—the last is the most accomplished. In lyric prose a widow confesses to the Earth her unrelenting grief over losing her husband and three sons in the war. The story is a condemnation of all wars, and when it first appeared Aitmatov was criticized for "compromising" the proper Soviet ideological position. In *Duishen* Aitmatov transforms the positive hero of socialist realism into the more human "little man" of the nineteenth-century Russian literary tradition. The hero, a half-educated Komsomol member, goes to a Kirghiz *ail* in the early 1920s to teach the children to read and write. He makes up for his lack of education with enthusiasm for the ideals of the revolution. During the debate over "youth prose" in the early 1960s Aitmatov saw his hero as a counter to the more popular antiheroes of Yevtushenko, Aksyonov, and Voznesensky.

Piebald Dog brings together for the English-language reader good translations of a number of important works Aitmatov wrote before publishing his two major novels, *The Day Lasts More Than a Hundred Years* and *The Place of the Skull*. The stories show the development of his fiction over the course of twenty years. It is thus highly unfortunate that the publisher fails to indicate the year in which a particular story first appeared. Aitmatov's fiction is embedded in the politics and cultural policies of his time, and therefore some chronological reference is imperative for Western readers. (pp. 485-86)

> *Joseph Mozur, in a review of "Piebald Dog Running along the Shore and Other Stories," in* World Literature Today, *Vol. 64, No. 3, Summer, 1990, pp. 485-86.*

FURTHER READING

Bibliography

Shneidman, N. N. "Bibliography of Works by and about Chingiz Aitmatov." *Russian Literature Triquarterly,* No. 16 (Fall 1979): 340-41.
　　Lists primary and secondary sources from 1952 to 1976.

Criticism

Aitmatov, Chingiz. "The Age of Repentance." *Encounter* LXXII, No. 4 (April 1989): 71-73.
　　Translated text of a talk Aitmatov gave on Soviet television concerning the controversy over religious elements in *Plakha*.

Asanaliyev, Keneshbek. "Prose Has Two Wings." *Soviet Literature* 2, No. 443 (1985): 166-69.
　　Briefly discusses the importance of *The Day Lasts More than a Hundred Years* and some of Aitmatov's other works in the development of Kirghiz literature.

Clark, Katerina. "The Mutability of the Canon: Socialist Realism and Chingiz Aitmatov's *I dol'she veka dlitsia den'*." *Slavic Review* 43, No. 4 (Winter 1984): 573-87.
　　Argues that *The Day Lasts More than a Hundred Years* "provides a case study of the ways authors can play with the formal conventions of the socialist realist tradition to produce meanings that are highly suggestive but open to radically different interpretations, so that it is not hard for critics to make their accounts of the novel respectable."

————. "*The Executioner's Block:* A Novel of the Thaw." *Times Literary Supplement,* No. 4395 (26 June 1987): 696.
　　Analyzes *Plakha* as a representative text of Mikhail Gorbachev's *perestroika* movement.

Dadazhanova, Munavvarkhon. "Both Are Primary: An 'Author's Translation' Is a Creative Re-creation." *Soviet Studies in Literature* XX, No. 4 (Fall 1984): 67-79.
　　Discusses the phenomenon of bilingualism in Soviet literature, focusing primarily on Aitmatov's works that have appeared in both Kirghiz and Russian.

Fuller, Edmund. "A Morality Theme In Cautious Hands." *Wall Street Journal* CLXXXVI, No. 32 (14 August 1975): 8.
　　Review of Nicholas Bethell's 1975 translation of *Voskhozhdenie na Fudzhiamu* (*The Ascent of Mount Fuji*).

Gardner, Anthony. "Religious Instincts, Sacred Landscapes: Two Russian Novels." *Encounter* LXXIII, No. 3 (September-October 1989): 42-5.
　　Studies religious themes in Leonid Borodin's *The Third Truth* and Aitmatov's *The Place of the Skull*.

Garnes, Stephen. "Steppe Brothers." *Manchester Guardian Weekly* 140, No. 10 (5 March 1989): 29.
　　Favorable review of *The Place of the Skull*.

Jagusztin, László. "In the Widening World of Parables." *Acta Litteraria Academiae Scientarum Hungaricae* 25, Nos. 3-4 (1983): 353-58.
　　Examines the use of parables in Aitmatov's works.

Novikov, V. *Chingiz Aitmatov*. Moscow: Raduga Publishers, 1987, 182 p.

Critical study of Aitmatov's works. Includes a selection of essays by and interviews with Aitmatov.

Ponomareff, Constantin. "Chingiz Aitmatov, 1928- : Reincarnations of the Virgin and Child." In his *The Silenced Vision: An Essay in Modern European Fiction,* pp. 26-38. Frankfurt am Main: Peter Lang, 1979.

Discusses the Virgin-and-Child motif in Aitmatov's works.

Porter, Robert. "Chingiz Aitmatov—The Provincial Internationalist." In his *Four Contemporary Russian Writers,* pp. 52-86. Oxford: Berg Publishers, 1989.

Overview of Aitmatov's works.

Scammell, Michael. "Wolf and Man under Socialism." *New York Times Book Review* (30 April 1989): 22-3.

Unfavorable review of *The Place of the Skull.*

Seton-Watson, Mary. "Protest and Prayers." *Times Literary Supplement* No. 4205 (4 November 1983): 215.

Favorable review of *The Day Lasts more than a Hundred Years.*

Shneidman, N. N. "Soviet Literature at the Crossroads: The Controversial Prose of Chingiz Aitmatov." *Russian Literature Triquarterly* 16 (1979): 244-63.

Discusses Aitmatov's works in relation to the changing requirements of socialist realism.

———. "Chingiz Aitmatov: Myth and Reality." In his *Soviet Literature in the 1970s: Artistic Diversity and Ideological Conformity,* pp. 32-46. Toronto: University of Toronto Press, 1979.

Examines Aitmatov's works and critical reputation through the 1970s. Shneidman comments: "[Aitmatov's] position in Soviet literature is special because he represents a new and growing breed of Soviet writers who embody the fusion of ideological conformity and linguistic and cultural diversity in the Soviet Union."

———. "Innovation and Experiment." In his *Soviet Literature in the 1980s: Decade of Transition,* pp. 191-208. Toronto: University of Toronto Press, 1989.

Discusses developments in Soviet literature during the 1980s, focusing primarily on *The Day Lasts More than a Hundred Years* and *The Place of the Skull.*

"For the Want of a Horse." *Times Literary Supplement,* No. 3613 (28 May 1971): 610.

Review of *Povesti i rasskazy,* focusing primarily on *Farewell, Gul'sary!*

Traub, Rainer. "The 'Indispensable' Aitmatov." *World Press Review* 35, No. 2 (February 1988): 60.

Brief overview of Aitmatov's career.

Interviews

Fruntelată, Nicolae Dan. "The Field in Which Your People's Culture Grows." *Romanian Review* 42, No. 2 (1988): 79-82.

Interview with Aitmatov conducted by Fruntelată and Feodosy Vidrashku, editor-in-chief of the journal *Novyi mir.* Discussion revolves around the reception of Aitmatov's works in Romania, the influence of Kirghiz folklore, and the novel *The Day Lasts more than a Hundred Years.*

Jaggi, Maya. "Voice from the Republics: An Interview." *Third World Quarterly* 12, No. 1 (January 1990): 194-200.

Examines Aitmatov's childhood and early works, the Kirghiz tradition of oral storytelling, and *The Place of the Skull.*

Khokhlov, Nikolai. "Chinghiz Aitmatov: A Feeling for the Times." *Soviet Literature* 4, No. 421 (1983): 159-65.

Report of a conversation with Aitmatov exploring his views on America, his life, and his works.

Korkin, Vladimir. "Time to Speak Out." *Soviet Literature* 5, No. 434 (1984): 139-50.

Discusses Aitmatov's opinions on major philosophical and social issues in world literature.

Salganik, Miriam. "India Has Become Near." *Soviet Literature* 453, No. 12 (1985): 135-40.

Explores Aitmatov's views on India and the aims of literature.

Additional coverage of Aitmatov's life and career is contained in the following sources published by Gale Research: *Contemporary Authors,* Vol. 103; *Major 20th-Century Writers;* and *Something about the Author,* Vol. 56.

Simone de Beauvoir

1908-1986

(Full name Simone Lucie Ernestine Marie Bertrand de Beauvoir) French philosopher, novelist, autobiographer, nonfiction writer, short story writer, editor, and dramatist.

The following entry covers major works in Beauvoir's career. For further information on her life and work, see *CLC,* Vols. 1, 2, 4, 8, 14, 31, 44, and 50.

INTRODUCTION

Beauvoir is a highly acclaimed twentieth century writer who is recognized as an important contributor to the French intellectual movement known as existentialism, which sought to explain human existence and the individual's situation in a purposeless, absurd universe. In her influential study *Le deuxième sexe (The Second Sex)*, she utilized existentialist concepts concerning personal freedom and the relationship of the self to others to examine the status of women throughout history. Beauvoir posited that traditionally a woman must assume the role of the "other," or the inessential being, in relation to a man, the essential being, and analyzed this inferior position of women from biological, psychological, and social perspectives. In addition to her philosophical studies, Beauvoir wrote distinguished fictional and autobiographical works in which she explored aspects of contemporary Western society, particularly those relating to women. Her writings, which have been praised for their intellectual integrity, represent a milestone in feminist theory and politics.

Born in Paris to middle-class parents, Beauvoir was raised a Roman Catholic. In early adolescence, however, she perceived certain hypocrisies and fallacies of bourgeois morality and rebelled against her class, privately disavowing her belief in God. Following her undergraduate studies at the Institut Catholique and the Institut Sainte-Marie, Beauvoir attended the Sorbonne in 1928, where she specialized in literature and philosophy, and later audited classes at the prestigious Ecole Normale Supérieure. In 1929 she met fellow student Jean-Paul Sartre, and together they prepared for the *agrégation* examination in philosophy. Finding that they were intellectual equals, each of whom desired a lasting relationship free of conventional restraints, she and Sartre agreed to a shared life outside the institution of marriage and also mutually consented to "contingent relationships."

After graduating from the Sorbonne, Beauvoir taught in Marseilles, Rouen, and Paris. She and Sartre settled in Paris in the late 1930s and became prominent figures amid the intellectual society of the Left Bank, associating with such writers and thinkers as Albert Camus, André Malraux, Raymond Queneau, and Michel Leiris. During World War II, Beauvoir and Sartre organized a resistance

group to oppose the Nazi occupation in France. She relegated most of her time during the war years to writing and published her first novel, *L'invitée (She Came to Stay)*, in 1943 and the philosophical essay *Pyrrhus et Cinéas* the following year. In 1944 Beauvoir resigned from teaching and, together with Sartre, founded the leftist journal *Les temps modernes.* At this time she began writing *Le sang des autres (The Blood of Others)* and *Tous les hommes sont mortels (All Men Are Mortal)*, philosophical novels on the subjects of ethics and mortality published in the immediate postwar period. Writing theoretical essays concomitantly with her fiction, Beauvoir contributed significantly to the development of an existentialist philosophy. In *Pour une morale de l'ambiguité (The Ethics of Ambiguity)*, which appeared in 1947, she defined existentialism in terms of ambiguity, examining the uncertainty of living in the present while being aware of one's mortality. In *L'existentialism et la sagesse des nations,* an essay collection that was published the next year, Beauvoir defended existentialism against critics who denounced it as frivolous, emphasizing the importance of merging an authentic philosophy with one's personal life. She applied these theories to her next work, *The Second Sex,* which achieved widespread notoriety immediately following publication in 1949 for what was then considered a candid portrayal of women and sexuality.

During the 1950s Beauvoir engaged in numerous social causes and attempted to live out the committed existence that she espoused in her writings by protesting the French-Algerian War, documenting French military atrocities in *Les temps modernes,* and signing a public manifesto against the war. Beauvoir maintained her involvement in social issues during the 1960s and, in particular, supported the radical student uprisings of 1968. Although she joined the Mouvement de la Libération des Femmes (MLF) in 1970 to participate in demonstrations supporting legalized abortion, Beauvoir did not declare herself a feminist until 1972, after which time she began writing a column on sexism in *Les temps modernes* and became president of the French League for Women's Rights. Beauvoir continued to promote various social movements, especially those concerning women, until her death in 1986.

Critical discussion of Beauvoir's works of fiction focuses primarily on *Les Mandarins* (*The Mandarins*), for which she received the Prix Goncourt in 1954 and which continues to elicit praise from critics. Considered a *roman à clef* by most commentators—though Beauvoir denied the designation—*The Mandarins* depicts the lives of a group of left-wing French intellectuals between 1944 and 1947 and reflects the intellectual malaise felt by many when the initial euphoria following the Liberation of Paris had subsided. The two male protagonists, writers committed to supporting Communism, face a conflict of individualism and political choice when they learn of the existence of labor camps in the Soviet Union and must decide whether or not to reveal this fact in their work. The novel also examines questions of individualism and moral choice as they apply to love and sexual relationships. Narrated mainly from the point of view of the female protagonist, Anne Dubreuilh, *The Mandarins* conveys the unhappiness Anne feels upon realizing that in relationships based solely on sexual passion, a woman's emotional well-being is far more precarious than a man's. Beauvoir's later fictional works, published in the late 1960s, reflect an increasingly negative view of society and of relationships between men and women. For example, in her last novel, *Les belles images,* she delineated a bourgeois, technocratic milieu, presenting, according to critic Mary Evans, "a portrait of an affluent, decadent, and essentially valueless society." In the three stories that are included in her short fiction collection, *La femme rompue* (*The Woman Destroyed*), Beauvoir characterized women whose dependencies on men have crippled their abilities to create positive identities and construct autonomous lives.

Beauvoir's major theoretical study, *The Second Sex,* appeared in 1949 and is often said to represent the first full-length sociophilosophical examination of the status of women in society. In this work she incorporated existentialist concepts concerning personal freedom, or individual guidance by choice alone; responsibility, or accepting the consequences of one's choices; bad faith, or denying one's freedom by shifting responsibility to an outside source; and the role of the other, or the relation of an inessential being to an essential being. Perhaps the most repeated postulate from *The Second Sex* is Beauvoir's statement, "One is not born, but rather becomes, a woman." Several commentators have interpreted this to mean that Beauvoir believes women are socialized to assume a secondary status to men. Thus, she asserted, in order to attain equality with men, women must reject the conventional female roles of wife and mother, whereby a woman is economically dependent on a husband and bound to the repetitive tasks of nurturing. Positing that men have achieved the favorable status of transcendence while women have assumed that of immanence, Beauvoir proposed assimilation into the male universe as a means of achieving gender equality. Further, she called the existence of essentially feminine and maternal traits a myth and presented the female body in extremely negative terms, highlighting ways in which a woman's freedom is inhibited by her sexuality and fertility. *La vieillesse* (*The Coming of Age*), an examination of the elderly in contemporary Western culture, appeared in 1970. Considered a companion piece to *The Second Sex,* though not as popular or critically esteemed as her earlier study, this work incorporates similar themes and methods of analysis into Beauvoir's investigation of the devalued status of the aged.

From the time of its publication, when it provoked the ire of both conservative and liberal critics, *The Second Sex* has dominated discussion of Beauvoir's theoretical position. Despite the initially negative reaction of critics to the work, it has attained widespread recognition and has proved vastly influential. Today *The Second Sex* is generally regarded as fundamental to the development of the women's movement of the 1960s as well as to the discipline of feminist studies. With the rise in the 1970s of new French feminists extolling feminine physical and psychological differences, *The Second Sex* was dismissed as out-of-date, and many feminists decried Beauvoir as a Sartrean revisionist, condemning her adoption of a masculine identity. More recently critics have begun to reassess her importance as a pioneering thinker who established the groundwork for the study and liberation of women in modern Western society. Representing this position, Ellen Willis wrote: "Nearly four decades after it was first published in France, despite all the commentary the feminist movement has produced in the meantime, dated and parochial as it is in many respects, *The Second Sex* remains the most cogent and thorough book of feminist theory yet written."

PRINCIPAL WORKS

NONFICTION

Pyrrhus et Cinéas   1944
Pour une morale de l'ambiguité   1947
  [*The Ethics of Ambiguity,* 1948]

L'Amérique au jour le jour   1948
   [*America Day by Day,* 1952]
Le deuxième sexe. 2 vols.   1949
   [*The Second Sex,* 1953]
La longue marche: Essai sur la Chine   1957
   [*The Long March,* 1958]
La vieillesse   1970
   [*The Coming of Age,* 1972; also published as *Old Age,*
   1972]

AUTOBIOGRAPHIES

Mémoires d'une jeune fille rangée   1958
   [*Memoirs of a Dutiful Daughter,* 1959]
La force de l'âge   1960
   [*The Prime of Life,* 1962]
La force des choses   1963
   [*Force of Circumstance,* 1965]
Tout compte fait   1972
   [*All Said and Done,* 1974]

ESSAYS

L'existentialisme et la sagesse des nations   1948
Privilèges   1955

NOVELS

L'invitée   1943
   [*She Came to Stay,* 1949]
Le sang des autres   1945
   [*The Blood of Others,* 1948]
Tous les hommes sont mortels   1946
   [*All Men Are Mortal,* 1955]
Les mandarins   1954
   [*The Mandarins,* 1956]
Les belles images   1966
   [*Les Belles Images,* 1968]

SHORT FICTION

La femme rompue   1968
   [*The Woman Destroyed,* 1969]
*Quand prime le spirituel   1979
   [*When Things of the Spirit Come First: Five Early Tales,*
   1982]

OTHER

Les bouches inutiles   (play)   1945
   [*Who Shall Die?,* 1983]
Une morte très douce   (reminiscences)   1964
   [*A Very Easy Death,* 1966]
*La céremonie des adieux: Suivi de entretiens avec Jean-
   Paul Sartre*   (reminiscences)   1981
   [*Adieux: A Farewell to Sartre,* 1984]

*The stories of this collection were written between 1935 and 1937.

CRITICISM

Simone de Beauvoir with Alice Schwarzer

[*Schwarzer is a German feminist and journalist. In the
following 1972 interview, Beauvoir declares herself a
feminist.*]

[*Schwarzer]: Your analysis of the situation of women is still
the most radical we have, in that no author has gone further
than you have since your book* **The Second Sex** *came out
in 1949, and you have been the main inspiration for the new
women's movements. But it is only now, twenty-three years
later, that you have involved yourself actively in women's
actual, collective struggle. You joined the International
Women's March last November. Why?*

[Beauvoir]: Because I realised that the situation of women
in France has not really changed in the last twenty years.
There have been a few minor things in the legal sphere,
such as marriage and divorce law. And the availability of
contraception has increased—but it still does not go far
enough, given that only seven per cent of all French
women take the Pill. Women haven't made any significant
progress in the world of work either. There may be a few
more women working now than there were, but not very
many. But in any case, women are still confined to the low-
grade jobs. They are more often secretaries rather than
managing directors, nurses rather than doctors. The more
interesting careers are virtually barred to them, and even
within individual professions their promotion prospects
are very limited. This set me thinking. I thought it was
necessary for women who really wanted their situation to
change to take matters into their own hands. Also, the
women's groups which existed in France before the MLF
[Mouvement de la Libération des Femmes] was founded
in 1970 were generally reformist and legalistic. I had no
desire to associate myself with them. The new feminism
is radical, by contrast. As in 1968, its watchword is:
change your life today. Don't gamble on the future, act
now, without delay.

When the women in the French women's movement got
in touch with me, I wanted to join them in their struggle.
They asked me if I would work with them on an abortion
manifesto, making public the fact that I, and others, had
had an abortion. I thought this was a valid way of drawing
attention to a problem which is one of the greatest scandals in France today: the ban on abortion. [Schwarzer
adds in a note: "A new law was passed in 1975 which permitted abortion in the first ten weeks of pregnancy."]

So it was quite natural for me to take to the streets and
to join the MLF militants in the march [in November
1971] and to adopt their slogans as my own. Free abortion
on demand, free contraception, free motherhood!

*You refer to the situation in France, yet you have visited sev-
eral socialist countries. Has the situation of women undergone any fundamental changes there?*

It's somewhat different. Almost all Russian women work,
and those who do not (the wives of highly placed functionaries and other important men) are held in contempt by
the others. Soviet women are very proud of the fact that

they work. They have considerable political and social responsibilities and a real sense of these responsibilities. All the same, if you take into account the number of women in the Central Committee or the People's Assemblies who have any real power, the figure is very low compared with men. The same is true in the professions. The most unappealing and least prestigious jobs are done by women. Almost all doctors in the Soviet Union are women because medical treatment is free, the state does not pay well and the job is extraordinarily hard and tiring.

Women are consigned to medicine and education, but the really important jobs, like those in science and engineering, are much less accessible to them. On the one hand, they are not the professional equals of men. On the other, there is the same scandalous situation in Russia as there is everywhere else, which the women's movements are currently fighting—housework and looking after children are exclusively female preserves in the USSR too.

This comes over very strikingly in Solzhenitsyn's *Cancer Ward*. There is a woman in the hospital who is very senior, a very important member of the medical profession; after doing her rounds and after an exhausting day at the hospital, she rushes off home to cook dinner for her husband and children, and to do the washing-up. In other words, she takes on household chores on top of all her heavy professional responsibilities, just as in other countries. Indeed, perhaps even more so than in France where a woman in a similar position would have some domestic help.

The condition of women is, in one sense, better than in the capitalist countries, but it is also more difficult. One concludes that there is no real equality between men and women in the Soviet Union either.

Why is that?

First and foremost, because the socialist countries are not really socialist. In other words, they have not achieved the kind of socialism that transforms mankind, which was Marx's dream; what they have done is to change the means of production. But as time goes on, we realise that simply altering the means of production is not sufficient to transform society, to transform people. So despite the different economic system, traditional roles are still allotted to men and women. This is linked with the fact that men in our societies have internalised what I term a superiority complex, an image of their own superiority. They are not prepared to surrender it. They need the inferiority of women to enhance their own status. They need to see women as inferior. And women are so accustomed to think of themselves as inferior that only very rarely do they fight for equality.

The term 'feminism' is much misunderstood. What is your definition of it?

At the end of **The Second Sex** I said that I was not a feminist because I believed that the problems of women would resolve themselves automatically in the context of socialist development. By feminist, I meant fighting on specifically feminine issues independently of the class struggle. I still hold the same view today. In my definition, feminists are

women—or even men too—who are fighting to change women's condition, in association with the class struggle, but independently of it as well, without making the changes they strive for totally dependent on changing society as a whole. I would say that, in that sense, I am a feminist today, because I realised that we must fight for the situation of women, here and now, before our dreams of socialism come true. Apart from that, I realised that even in socialist countries, equality between men and women has not been achieved. Therefore it is absolutely essential for women to take their destiny into their own hands. That is why I have now joined the Women's Liberation Movement.

There is another reason—and I believe that it is one of the reasons why so many women have come together to found the movement—namely, that a profound inequality exists between men and women even in left-wing and revolutionary groups and organisations in France. Women always do the most lowly, most tedious jobs, all the behind-the-scenes things, and the men are always the spokesmen; they write the articles, do all the interesting things and assume the main responsibility. So, even within these groups, whose theoretical aim is to liberate everybody, including women, even there women are still inferior. It goes still further. Many—not all—men on the left are aggressively hostile to women's liberation. They openly despise us. The first time a feminist meeting took place at Vincennes, a number of male leftists broke into the room shouting, 'Power is at the end of the phallus.' I think they are beginning to revise that position, but only because women are taking militant action independently of them.

What is your general position regarding the new feminists, these militant young women who are more radical than ever before?

There is a wide range of tendencies within the women's movements, at least in America, where they have made the most progress. It ranges from Betty Friedan who is fairly conservative to SCUM [the Society for Cutting Up Men] which favours the emasculation of men. And there are any number of positions between the two. In France it seems there are also various tendencies within the movement, and my choice would be one which endeavoured to link women's liberation with the class struggle. I believe that although the women's struggle is unique, it is certainly linked to the struggle women have to conduct along with men. As a result, I reject the total repudiation of men.

In that case, what do you think—at the present stage of the conflict—of the exclusion of men from women's meetings, as is the case in most women's movements?

It is, as you have just said, a question of the stage reached. At the moment it's a good thing, for several reasons. First, if men were admitted to these groups, they would not be able to stifle their male reflex to give all the orders and to take charge. On the other hand, many women have a certain feeling—even if they won't admit it—of inferiority, a degree of shyness, and often they know it. Many of them wouldn't dare to speak freely in front of men. It's particularly important for women not to feel judged by the men who share their lives, precisely because they must liberate themselves from them as well . . .

. . . and analyse their own specific oppression?

Exactly. At the moment, neither the male mentality, nor the female one, allows a truly honest discussion in a mixed group.

Is the exclusion of men at this stage simply a practical question for you, because women would be more inhibited or whatever? Or is it also a political question? Given that men represent the system, and, furthermore, that men as individuals oppress women, are they not therefore seen as Enemy Number One in the initial stages?

Yes, of course, but it is fairly complicated, because what Marx says about capitalists applies here. They are victims too. Of course, it is too abstract to say, as I did for a time, that one must only fight the system. Of course one must fight men as well. After all, one is an accomplice, one still profits by the system, even if one hasn't created it oneself. The man of today didn't set up this patriarchal society but he profits from it, even if he is one of those who are critical of it. And he has made it very much a part of his own unconscious thinking.

One must fight the system, but at the same time one must approach men, if not with hostility exactly, then at least with suspicion, and with caution, and not let them trespass on our activities, our own potentialities. Women must attack both the system and men. Even if a man is a feminist, one should still keep one's distance and be wary of paternalism. Women don't want to be granted equality; they want to win it, which is not the same thing at all.

Have you ever felt this suspicion, this hatred of men?

No. I have always got on very well with the men in my life. Indeed, many of the women I know in the MLF don't hate men either, but they do take a cautious attitude, and are determined not to let men devour them.

Do you think that it's a good thing, politically, for some women to go further than that?

Perhaps. Perhaps it's not a bad thing that some women are really totally, totally radical and repudiate men completely. These women might be able to win over those who out of a lack of personal motivation might otherwise be ready to compromise. That's entirely possible.

In most women's movements there is a homosexual element—by no means the majority, incidentally, as is so often said, but a minority—which is a source of important ideas nonetheless. Do you believe that female homosexuality— the most radical way of excluding men—can be a political weapon in the current phase?

I haven't thought about that. I think it's a very good thing that some women are very radical. Lesbians could play a useful part. But when they put too much emphasis on their homosexuality, they risk alienating the heterosexuals from the movement. I find their mystique of the clitoris fatuous and irritating, as well as the sexual dogmas they try to impose.

These homosexual women have taken it upon themselves to refrain from all sexual relations with men because under current conditions they must necessarily be oppressive . . .

Is it true that all sexual relations between a man and a woman are necessarily oppressive? Instead of refusing such relations, could one not work at them so that they are not oppressive? I'm shocked when people tell me that intercourse is always rape. I don't believe it. When one says that intercourse is rape, basically one is adopting male myths. That would mean that the male sex organ really is a sword, a weapon. It's a question of inventing new, non-oppressive sexual relations.

You said in a comment on **The Second Sex** *that the problem of femininity had never affected you personally, that you found yourself 'in a position of great impartiality'. Do you mean to say that individually a woman can escape her female condition? Professionally, as well as in her relationships with her fellow human beings?*

Escape one's female condition completely? No! I have the body of a woman—but clearly I have been very lucky. I have escaped many of the things that enslave a woman, such as motherhood and the duties of a housewife. And professionally as well—in my day there were fewer women who studied than nowadays. And, as the holder of a higher degree in philosophy, I was in a privileged position among women. In short, I made men recognise me: they were prepared to acknowledge in a friendly way a woman who had done as well as they had, because it was so exceptional. Now that many women undertake serious study, men are fearful for their jobs. Admitting, as I have done, that a woman doesn't necessarily have to be a wife and mother to have a fulfilled and happy life, means that there will be a certain number of women who will be able to have fulfilled lives without suffering the enslavement of women. Of course they have to be born into a privileged family or possess certain intellectual abilities.

You once said, 'the greatest success of my life is my relationship with Sartre' . . .

Yes.

. . . yet all your life you have always had a great need for your own independence and a fear of being dominated. Given that it is very difficult to establish relationships between men and women that are based on equality, do you believe that you personally have succeeded?

Yes. Or rather, the problem never arose, because there is nothing of the oppressor about Sartre. If I'd loved someone other than Sartre, I would never have let myself be oppressed. There are some women who escape male domination, mostly by means of their professional autonomy. Some have a balanced relationship with a man. Others have inconsequential affairs.

You have described women as an inferior class . . .

I didn't say class. But in *The Second Sex* I did say that women were an 'inferior caste', a caste being a group one is born into and cannot move out of. In principle, though, one can transfer from one class to another. If you are a woman, you can never become a man. Thus women are genuinely a caste. And the way women are treated in economic, social and political terms makes them into an inferior caste.

Some women's movements define women as a class outside the existing classes. They base this on the fact that housework, which has no exchange value, is done exclusively by women for nothing. As they see it, patriarchal oppression is therefore the main contradiction, not a subsidiary one. Do you agree with this analysis?

I find the analysis lacking on this point. I'd like someone to do some serious work on it. In *Women's Estate,* for example, Juliet Mitchell showed how to ask the question, but she doesn't claim to resolve it in that book. I remember it was one of the first questions I put when I first came into contact with the militant feminists in the MLF: what, in your view, is the exact connection between patriarchal oppression and capitalist oppression? At the moment, I still don't know the answer. It's a problem which I'd very much like to work on in the next few years. I'm extremely interested in it. But the analyses which regard patriarchal oppression as the equivalent of capitalist oppression are not correct in my view. Of course, housework doesn't produce any surplus value. It's a different condition to that of the worker who is robbed of the surplus value of his work. I'd like to know exactly what the relationship is between the two. Women's entire future strategy depends upon it.

It's very right to emphasise unpaid housework. But there are many women who earn their own living, and who cannot be considered as exploited in the same way as housewives are.

But even when a woman does work outside the house, she is paid less than a man for the same job.

Yes, wages are not the same. That's true. But to return to my point. The exploitation of women doing housework is not the same thing as worker exploitation. This is a point that neither Kate Millett nor Germaine Greer nor Shulamith Firestone pays enough attention to.

They bring nothing new to the analysis . . .

No. Not in the case of Millett or Greer. But Firestone, who is less well-known, does include something new in her book *The Dialectic of Sex.* She links women's liberation with children's liberation. That is correct, because women will not be liberated until they have been liberated from their children, and by the same token, until children have also been liberated from their parents.

You've also been very active in the class struggle, since May 1968. For instance, you've assumed responsibility for a radical left magazine. You've taken to the streets. In brief, what is the connection between the class struggle and the war between the sexes, in your opinion?

What I have been able to establish is that the class struggle in the strict sense does not emancipate women. That has made me change my mind since *The Second Sex* was published. It doesn't matter whether you're dealing with Communists, Trotskyists, or Maoists, women are always subordinate to men. As a result, I'm convinced of the need for women to be truly feminist, to take their problems into their own hands. A serious analysis is needed to try to establish the relationship between worker exploitation and the exploitation of women, and to what extent the overthrow of capitalism would create better conditions for the emancipation of women. I don't know. It still remains to be done. I'm certain of one thing though, which is that the overthrow of capitalism would create more favourable conditions for the emancipation of women at a stroke. But there would still be a long way to go to achieve it.

Overthrowing capitalism does not mean overturning the patriarchal tradition so long as the family is left intact. I believe that one must not only overthrow capitalism and transform the means of production, but that one must also change the structure of the family. And that has not been done, not even in China. Of course, the feudal family has been abolished, and by the same token a change in the position of women has been achieved. But in the sense that they accept the nuclear family, which is, in fact, the successor to the feudal family, I really don't believe that women in China are liberated. I think that the family must be abolished. I'm in complete agreement with the attempts made by women, and indeed sometimes by men too, to replace the family either with communes or with other forms which have yet to be invented.

So could one say that the class struggle doesn't necessarily change women's condition, but conversely that radical feminism—calling society and the relations between men and women into question—will destroy the classes?

No, not necessarily. If you start by destroying the family and related structures, then there's a possibility that capitalism will start to teeter at the same time. But I don't want to go too far along those lines either, without having thought about it properly. I don't know to what extent the destruction of patriarchal society by women would affect all aspects of capitalism and democracy.

If feminism makes radical demands and if it manages to implement them, then it really will be a threat to the system. But that will not be enough to reorganise the means of production or the conditions of work or the relationships of men—by which I mean human beings—to one another. There hasn't been enough analysis of this point; and that is because the women who have been active in feminism have mostly been middle-class women who conducted their struggle within the political system.

I'm thinking of the suffragettes, who sought the right to vote. They were not thinking of themselves in economic terms. And, in economic terms, we have tended to settle for Marxist formulas and to assume that socialism, when it came, would mean equality between men and women at a stroke. When I wrote *The Second Sex,* I was very surprised at the bad reception it got from the left. I remember one discussion I had with the Trotskyists who said that the women's problem was not a true problem, and that it simply didn't exist. When the revolution came, women would automatically find their place.

It was the same with the Communists, with whom I was in very bad political odour at the time, and who exposed me to a great deal of ridicule. They wrote articles saying that the working-class women in Billancourt really couldn't give a damn about the women's problem. Once the revolution had taken place, women would be equal with men. But they were not interested in what would happen to women in the time it took for the revolution to come.

I also hoped that things would be a great deal better in the socialist countries than in the capitalist ones. Well, that hope was pretty smartly dashed—apart from the few shades of difference that I referred to earlier.

After **The Second Sex** *was published, you were often accused of not having developed any tactics for the liberation of women and of having come to a halt in your analysis.*

That's right. I admit it was a shortcoming in my book. I finish with vague confidence in the future, the revolution and socialism.

And today?

I have changed my views now. As I've been telling you, I really am a feminist.

What concrete possibilities do you see for the liberation of women on an individual and on a collective level?

On an individual level, women must work outside the home. And, if possible, they should refuse to get married. I could have married Sartre but I think we were wise not to have done so, because when you are married, people treat you as married and eventually you think of yourself as married. As a married woman, you simply do not have the same relationship with society as an unmarried woman. I believe that marriage is dangerous for a woman.

Having said that, there can be reasons for it—if you want to have children, for example. Having children is still very difficult if the parents are not married because the children encounter all sorts of difficulties in life.

What really counts, if one wants to be truly independent, is work, a job. That is my advice to all women who ask me. It is a necessary precondition. If you are married and want a divorce, it means you can leave, and support your children, and have a life of your own. Of course, work is not a miracle cure. Work today does have a liberating side, but it is also alienating. As a result, many women have to choose between two sorts of alienation: the alienation of the housewife and that of the working woman. Work is not a panacea, but all the same, it is the first condition for independence.

And what about the women who are already married and have children?

I think there are some women who really don't stand much of a chance. If they are thirty-five, with four children to cope with, married and lacking any professional qualifications—then I don't know what they can do to liberate themselves. You can only talk about the real prospect of liberation for future generations.

Can women who are struggling for their liberation do so as individuals, or must they act collectively?

They must act collectively. I myself have not done so up to now because there was no organised movement with which I was in agreement. But all the same, writing *The Second Sex* was an act which went beyond my own liberation. I wrote that book out of concern for the feminine condition as a whole, not just to reach a better understanding of the situation of women, but also to contribute to the struggle and to help other women to understand themselves.

In the last twenty years I have received an enormous number of letters from women telling me that my book has been a great help to them in understanding their situation, in their struggle and in making decisions for themselves. I've always taken the trouble to reply to these women. I've met some of them. I've always tried to help women in difficulties.

What is your general opinion of the way the existing women's movements have developed?

I think they'll make progress. But I'm not sure. In France, like everywhere else, most women are very conservative: they want to be 'feminine'. All the same, I think that the modern conditions of housework are liberating women a little and giving them a little more time to reflect: they must be led into revolt. In professional terms, there is no doubt that women will never get work in a capitalist country while men are unemployed. That's why I think women will never achieve equality unless there is a complete overthrow of the system.

I think the women's movement could have the same effect as the student movements, which were also limited to begin with, but later set off a wave of strikes throughout the country; it could cause an explosion. If women get a foothold in the world of work, they could really shake up the system. At the moment, though, the weakness of the French movement, and of the American movement too, I believe, is that there are so few working-class women in it.

Isn't it a case of the stage reached in the struggle?

Of course. Everything is connected. When women go on strike, as they did in Troyes and Nantes, they become aware of their power and their autonomy, and they are much less ready to submit at home.

So you think there is a need to develop this sense of solidarity?

Absolutely. Liberation on an individual level is not enough. There must be a collective struggle, at the level of the class struggle too. Women fighting for women's liberation cannot be truly feminist without being part of the left, because even though socialism is not sufficient to guarantee the equality of the sexes, it is still necessary.

Indeed, for the first time in history feminist movements are also revolutionary movements. They don't believe there can be any changes in the lot of women without changes to society as a whole.

True. There was a slogan I saw in Italy which I found very apt: 'No revolution without women's liberation, no liberation of women without revolution.'

In **The Second Sex** *you quoted Rimbaud's vision of a fu-*

ture world in which women would be liberated. Do you have a vision of this new world?

Rimbaud was imagining that women would contribute something entirely different to the world after their liberation. I don't believe that. I don't think that, having achieved equality, women will develop any specifically feminine values. I've discussed this with some Italian feminists. They say we must reject masculine values and models, we should invent some that are entirely different. I don't agree. The fact is that culture, civilisation and universal values have all been created by men, because men represented universality. But just as the proletariat rejects the notion that the bourgeoisie is the universal class, though without rejecting the entire bourgeois heritage, so women should make use of some of the tools men have created, from a position of equality with men. I think that a degree of suspicion and vigilance is necessary here too.

In creating universal values—by which I mean mathematics, for example—men have often left their specifically masculine, male, virile stamp on them. They have combined the two in a very subtle and devious way. So it's a question of separating one from the other and of getting rid of this confusion. It is possible, and that is one of the tasks women face. When it comes down to it, what do we mean by rejecting the male model? If a woman learns karate, it is a masculine thing. We ought not to reject the world of men, because, after all, it is our world too.

I believe that liberated women will be just as creative as men. But I do not think women will create new values. If you believe the opposite, then what you are believing in is a feminine nature—which I have always opposed. We must totally reject all concepts of that kind.

Of course, women's liberation will lead to new kinds of relationships between human beings and men and women will certainly be changed. Women, and men too, must become total human beings. The differences between them are no more important than the differences between men and women on an individual level.

Do you believe in the need for violent tactics in bringing about the liberation of women?

In the present situation, yes—up to a point. Because men resort to violence against women—in their use of language, in gesture. They rape them, insult them, even the way they look at them can be aggressive. Women should use violence to defend themselves. Some women are learning karate or other forms of self-defence. I'm entirely in favour of that. They'll feel much more at ease in themselves and in the world if they don't feel helpless in the face of male aggression.

You often talk about American women. Has your main contact with feminism been through them?

Yes; primarily through their books. There are many of them, apart from those we've already mentioned, Kate Millett and Germaine Greer—although they are not American—and Shulamith Firestone. I've read their books. So far French women have not published anything. It has to be said that the American women's movement is more advanced. I've also had a lot of letters from Ameri-

can women and invitations to visit America. But my reply to them is that I'm working with French women, and that I must work at home first. (pp. 29-47)

The struggle of the women's liberation movements is often linked with the struggle for free abortion. Do you personally want to go beyond this stage?

Of course. I think the women's movements, including me, will have to work together on many things. We are not only fighting for free abortion but also for widespread availability of contraceptives, which will mean that abortion will only play a marginal role. On the other hand, contraception and abortion are only a point of departure for the liberation of women. Later on, we will be organising other meetings at which we will expose the exploitation of female labour, be it as a housewife, a white-collar worker, or a working-class woman. (pp. 47-8)

> *Alice Schwarzer, in her* After the Second Sex: Conversations with Simone de Beauvoir, *translated by Marianne Howarth, Pantheon Books, 1984, 120 p.*

Michèle Le Doeuff

I have been rereading the Introduction to *The Second Sex.* Incisive, forceful, and wonderfully clear, such a text scarcely calls for the pretensions of an exegesis. "To be read, and reread" would seem to be the only possible commentary. Instead, I would like to explicate certain impressions prompted by reading it, and simply give voice to these impressions, the signs no doubt of a mute reworking of the text by a reading which progressively rewrites it. I have sought to elucidate my own, contradictory responses to de Beauvoir's discourse, and from this I have embarked on a series of considerations that are more complicated than I might have liked.

For a feminist reader, that is to say, for an *interested* reading by one principally concerned with finding elements of reflection that might underpin a possible practice, this book has today the appearance of a curious mixture. And thus I feel tempted to try and separate out the elements in the book that I evaluate now as "positive." Very empirically, it seems to me that one finds in this work a host of observations, descriptions, and analyses which I, for my part, can only endorse. When Simone de Beauvoir describes the repetitive nature of housework, when she analyzes the censorious treatment of aggressiveness in little girls, when she sets out notions on female frigidity, when she examines the prevailing conception of women's wages as "salaire d'appoint" supplementing the husband's earnings, she provides essential elements of a *detailed* and *precise* consciousness of women's oppression. And this attention to detail is certainly what gives the book its greatest utility because oppression always also exists where it is least expected and where there is the danger that it will not even be noticed.

And yet, along with these highly valuable analyses of the feminine condition, one also finds in *The Second Sex* a whole conceptual apparatus that is now a trifle obsolete. What is one to make of this, for instance:

Every individual preoccupied with justifying his existence experiences this existence as an indefinite need for self-transcendence. Now what marks the specificity of woman's situation is that, while being, like every human being, an autonomous freedom, she discovers and chooses herself in a world where men force her to assume herself as the Other: they claim to fix her as an object and to vow her to immanence, since her transcendence is itself to be perpetually transcended by an other, essential and sovereign consciousness.

Indeed . . . ! Is it really necessary to have recourse to such concepts as these in order to reveal the nature of women's oppression? Supposing one were unwilling to concede any sense to these categories? Isn't it taking a strategic risk to tie the study of oppression to considerations of this order?

The senescence of a philosophy fashionable in 1949 and out of favor today, and the confused perception of the dangers involved in utilizing such a perspective, are two reasons for the temptation to read this feminist *summa* in a selective manner, skipping the passages excessively marked by this philosophy. But it is more instructive if one confronts the malaise directly and tries to articulate these two sides of de Beauvoir's work to determine in what respect, if any, is the choice of this or that philosophical reference point a decisive factor in feminist studies? Over the last few years, we have been witnessing a certain philosophist inflation in the domain of theoretical productions. Thus, Luce Irigaray's books insist that because it is philosophical discourse that lays down the law for all other discourses, the discourse of philosophy must first of all be overthrown and disrupted. At a stroke, the main enemy comes to be idealist logic and the metaphysical *Logos*. Simone de Beauvoir's book leaves me with the opposite impression because within a problematic as metaphysical as any, she is still able to reach conclusions that at the very least have reactivated women's movements in Europe and America over the last thirty years.

My intention is to show how the ethic of authenticity functions as a pertinent theoretical lever, an operative viewpoint for exposing the character of women's oppression. Consequently, one cannot, as I confess I am in the habit of doing, dissociate the philosophical substratum of de Beauvoir's work from that more empirical dimension, which I see as more relevant today than the conceptual grid via which this feminist investigation is executed. But even if they cannot be divorced, there is still no preestablished harmony between this philosophical position and the results to which it leads in *The Second Sex.* As I shall show, Jean-Paul Sartre's *Being and Nothingness,* where the same problematic of authenticity leads to entirely opposite consequences, offers proof of this. In a word, de Beauvoir's text cannot be totalized except dialectically.

Let us first give a summary characterization of the conceptual grid employed by de Beauvoir. It is a dualist one, the notions function in pairs: immanence/transcendence, in-itself/for-itself, authentic/inauthentic, responsibility/bad faith, subject-project/object. It is an ethical ontology: the individual *is* subject, and when he affirms himself as such

he assumes his freedom and transcendence and is in a state of authenticity. But the individual may also feel the "temptation to flee his freedom and constitute himself as a thing," thus evading "the anguish of existence authentically assumed." Thereupon the for-itself is degraded into an in-itself and freedom into facticity, and in short, there is bad faith. Lastly, this is a problematic of consciousness: "The subject only posits itself by opposing itself. It claims to affirm itself as essential and to constitute the other as the inessential."

On this basis, the fundamental thesis of the book becomes that every woman is from the start constituted as inessential; dominated, she has been obliged to submit herself to this alien point of view of her. Hence, the description of an oppression that derives from a relation of force and yet is also capable of producing the same effect as moral error: "Each time that transcendence collapses back into immanence, there is the degradation of existence into an 'in-itself'. . . . This collapse is a moral fault if it is consented to by the subject. If it is inflicted on the subject . . . it is an oppression." The analogy between moral fault and oppression seems to have the effect of dramatizing oppression: what is grasped here as oppression is what would under other circumstances be moral error. The theoretical problem with oppression is that oppression is hard to grasp, and is generally unnoticed, so we must emphasize the power of this analogy between oppression and moral fault. The analogy provided de Beauvoir with a first set of reference marks to help her find her way through the mists of dominant ideology—she can see oppression where the dominant discourse says there is protection, or seduction, or, worse, duty. The reference to ethics remains, in any case, central.

The ethic in question is not hard to identify because de Beauvoir's point of view is that of existentialist morality. Without laying any but the lightest stress on it, one may recall that *The Second Sex* is also a labor of love and that de Beauvoir brings as one of her morganatic wedding presents a singular confirmation of the validity of the Sartrian philosophy—your thought makes it possible to think the feminine condition, your philosophy sets me on the path of my emancipation, your truth will make me free.

No doubt, at the relational level, this gesture is a matter of course; one has here a stereotype of philosophical liaisons. But it is less of a matter of course from a theoretical point of view. To confirm this, it is enough to single out two aspects of Sartrianism as of 1943: no oppression can be thematized as such in the existentialist system, women's oppression no more than any other; and at the same time, the terrifying relation of men with women's bodies, expressed in this system grounds an ontological-carnal hierarchy of "the masculine" and "the feminine." Hence de Beauvoir's utilization of this viewpoint emerges as a tour de force deserving of recognition.

The ethic of authenticity denies the efficacy of social or historical determinations in favor of a classical form of voluntarism: "Constraint can have no possible hold on a freedom." Bad faith consists in the refusal to recognize oneself as a free subject and the pretense of being determined by external circumstances. Such a position carries a certain number of piquant consequences.

1. "It is senseless to dream of complaining, since nothing alien to us has decided for us what we feel, what we live, what we are. . . . Isn't it myself who decides the coefficient of the adversity of things?" "Everything that happens to us may be considered as good fortune," that is, as a means of realizing that being which is in question in our being.

2. Revolutionaries are materialistic, "serious," and of bad faith because they evaluate the situation of humanity on the basis of a world to which they attribute more reality than to themselves. The principal figure of this bad faith is Marx, to whom Sartre opposes a Kierkegaard who has properly grasped how play posits freedom and brings escape from *natura naturata*.

3. Every feeling of inferiority derives from a free choice. "It is up to us to choose ourselves as great or noble or as base and humiliated." Certainly it is not through free volition that one chooses to be or not to be a Michelangelo. But to choose inferiority is to choose an order of work, a domain of activity in which I will be the lowest. The inferiority Sartre is thinking of is that of the mediocre artist who has chosen to manifest himself in art *because* in it he is inferior, whereas in some other domain he would without difficulty have been able to "equal the norm": if I choose to be a modest artisan because in that domain my talents permit me to "equal the norm," this is not by a masochist choice of inferiority, but as a simple example of the choice of finitude. Inferiority is not thought of in terms of the social hierarchy of tasks, but in terms of the psychological perversion of the model of successful socioprofessional career choice—a model presupposing congenital aptitudes.

4. Frigid women suffer from pathological bad faith. They take pleasure in denying their pleasure. The proof is that their husbands (!) interrogated by the psychoanalyst revealed that their wives have betrayed objective signs of pleasure. "And these are the signs which the woman, when questioned, insists on fiercely denying." It is they who have decided to be frigid, but they dissimulate the deliberate character of their attitude under the guise of facticity by declaring: "I am frigid," not "I have decided to mask my pleasure."

If the doctrine of authenticity leads to such a miscomprehension of every form of constraint, using it to describe the oppression of women must already seem paradoxical. But the most picturesque part is yet to come.

Sexual metaphors abound in the passage in which Sartre explains in what sense knowledge is appropriation. "To see is to deflower," and "Knowledge is at once a penetration and superficial caress." The description of the appropriative delight (*jouissance*) in knowledge tends toward images that are indeed far from innocent: "The knower is the hunter who takes a blank nudity by surprise and violates it with his gaze." The reference to the "sleek, blank, polished, womanly body" on which possession leaves no traces (how irritating, is it not?) manifests a set of fantasies, which in 1943 had no claim to be taken seriously as epistemology any longer because by that time critical philosophy had already demonstrated that in the course of every knowledge process, reason is transformed and must adapt itself to the particular form of rationality constructed by the conditions of a specific knowledge. This antiquated conception of "knowledge," in which a mind obstinately endeavors to appropriate the object, can have no further basis except in a system of fantasies. It forms, moreover, one wing of a diptych whose pendant is located at the very end of the book, which closes with some considerations on the slimy and holes. The slimy reveals the possibility of an "envenomed possession," "there is the possibility that the in-itself may absorb the for-itself . . . the slimy is the revenge of the in-itself." Here again the sexual metaphors abound: the revenge is a "sickly-sweet feminine" one. Like "the honey which slides off my spoon on to the honey contained in the jar," this viscosity is a "collapse" "comparable to the flattening out of the over-ripe breasts of a woman lying on her back"; "it sucks at me. . . . It is a soft, yielding action, a moist and feminine sucking. . . . In one sense it is like the supreme docility of the possessed, the fidelity of a dog who *gives himself* even when one does not want him any longer, and in another sense there is underneath this docility a surreptitious appropriation of the possessor by the possessed," and so forth. Next the nightmare slides into the figure of the hole, of which the female sex is only a particular case. The hole "is originally presented as a nothingness to be filled with my own flesh"; "to plug up a hole means originally to make a sacrifice of my body in order that the plenitude of being may exist." "A good part of our life is passed in plugging up holes, in realizing and symbolically establishing a plenitude." This "tendency to fill" is "one of the most fundamental tendencies of human reality."

> It is only from this standpoint that we can pass on to sexuality. The obscenity of the feminine is that of everything which gapes open. . . . In herself woman appeals to a flesh which is to transform her into a fullness of being by penetration and dissolution . . . the experience of the hole envelops the ontological presentiment of sexual experience in general; it is with his flesh that the child stops up the hole.

Let us note that here, as usual, it is only masculine adult sexual experience that is in continuity with the child's "ontological presentiment of sexual experience in general." The female child will no doubt have to trade in her ontological presentiment and abandon the "fundamental human tendency," which is to fill, in order to become instead that which is to be filled and identify herself with the hollowed, sucking in-itself. This phenomenology founds an ontological hierarchy, on the basis of which, for all eternity, woman can be posited as the in-itself and man as the for-itself. The masculine/feminine roles deduced from this phenomenology place woman outside the subject.

What place within the existentialist system are these pronouncements to be accorded? I believe that they are more than a simple projection of the personal anguishes of Monsieur Sartre and that, far from being an accidental accretion, they form an indispensible part of the metaphysic of authenticity. Sartre needs those sexual metaphors to give closure to his system.

It was indeed necessary that, by some means or other, the for-itself should "find itself compromised" in such a way that "man-in-the-world" can succeed in realizing only "a missing God." The conclusion of *Being and Nothingness* revolves around considerations on the perpetual failure of the integration of the in-itself by the for-itself "an ideal which one can term God." It is necessary for a counter-figure to undo the labor of integration, to regularly compromise the for-itself in such a fashion as to ensure the interminable character of the conquests proposed itself by the for-itself, and hence to guarantee that conservation of the very identity of the for-itself which is an absolute condition for the *reiteration* of the system.

Thus, sexist reveries appear in the text in a contradictory manner. They appear first in the theory of knowledge, which marks the weak point in Sartre's megalomaniacal ravings, as a means of reassurance where it was, for historical reasons, somewhat shaky. And the reveries occur in the conclusion to endow that megalomania with a necessary weakness, an encounter with death, with woman as the "sugared death of the for-itself," which permits everything to begin over again—because a metaphysical system can proceed only through the reiteration of its beginning. Sexism takes charge of the inadmissible, unthinkable contention that is nevertheless necessary for the system to work.

Then, if it, is not so much a matter of Monsieur Sartre as it is of existentialism as such, it was certainly not enough for this theory to pass from a man's to a woman's hands to change from the phallocratic discourse it had hitherto been into the theoretical tool of a feminist investigation. De Beauvoir operates a series of transformations on the existential problematic. The primary transformation seems to be transposing this *Weltanschauung* from the status of *system* (necessarily turning back on itself) to that of a *point of view* oriented to a theoretical intent by being trained on *a* determinate and partial field of experience. Thus the necessity for the counter-figure of the sugared death of the for-itself comes here to be eliminated.

Moreover, there is this little sentence in the Introduction: "Woman does not assert her demands as a subject because she lacks the concrete means." In Sartrianism it is above all a question of denying the effect of exteriority as an obstacle, constraint, adversity or alienating cause. De Beauvoir here poses a displaced problem: it is not enough not to be persecuted by exteriority, it is also necessary for exteriority to furnish the means for one's self-affirmation as a subject. If she insists so heavily in the course of *The Second Sex* on feminine narcissism, this is directly in line with this initial observation. Woman, is, first and foremost, deprived of exteriority; she cannot be "conquering," as the problematic of the for-itself demands. Being deprived, for example, of rights, what activity could she propose herself in the social world? Even her clothes "were primitively destined to vow her to impotence."

This situation itself still remains to be explained. The requirement, which assumes that the feminine condition is not a matter of course, could be posed by de Beauvoir in its fully radical form only thanks to the ethic of authenticity. The ethic enabled her to sufficiently *distance herself*

from the lot of women to be able to describe it as a shocking contingency, a strangeness, something nonnatural to be transformed as rapidly as possible.

The subject defined by its transcendence is neither a being nor a nature. The existentialist ethic has the effect of expelling from the sphere of the person every possible determination, projecting them on to the exterior plane of the situation that is to be transcended. In principle, there can be no valid existentialist anthropology or psychology. Or rather, existentialist morality demands a nonpsychology, an annihilation of every anthropological determinedness. For a break passes between the subject devoid of all density (a mere mathematical point, the site of a freedom and the origin of the vector of the "project," in the face of which all is alien) and everything else, which is thing, "in-itself," immanence, etc. This perspective enables de Beauvoir to escape essentialism: There is no such thing as an "eternal feminine," nor a "Dark soul," because there is no such thing as "human nature," freedom being the only character of human condition. It is no longer possible to justify a given state of things by reference to a psychological nature that would be fulfilled by a state of things. In other words, it is too easy for the dominant male ideology to say that women *are* such and such, with these given psychological tendencies, these given needs; and a woman is not happy until she is in a given situation corresponding to this nature, for example, married, mother, and housewife. The existentialist ethic that requires a nonpsychology, and prohibits, by the same token, posing the question of happiness, makes it possible to avoid this misleading ideology.

Thus whatever is observed is only result: "One is not born a woman, one becomes a woman." Everything is contingent in the face of freedom: there is no longer any question of justifying such and such a state of things by reference to any nature or necessity whatever. Rather, it is in a matter of setting before oneself every determination, referring it to an exterior situation ruled by the culturally arbitrary, and demonstrating its strangeness and its possibilities of variation: there is no destiny, everything can therefore lend itself to an objectivizing description—a description via which the subject (writer or reader) withdraws from implication in, and deprives of subjective sanction, that which is no more a sign or an institution. Undoubtedly, the liberating value of the book comes from this movement.

If the existentialist ethic demands a nonpsychology, at the same time it prohibits posing the question of happiness. The only value is "the freedom which must invent its ends unaided." Now the notion of happiness is one of the barriers to any investigation of domination and subjection. One can always declare a people whom one subjects to be happy. Moreover, the problematic of happiness inevitably reintroduces the idea of psychological tendencies (declared as being fulfilled by such and such a situation); it immediately reinstates the notion of a specified nature, a determinate "character," of assignable needs. De Beauvoir rightly mistrusts the easy recourse to declaring happy a situation which one imposes oneself. But the radical quality of her rejection is underpinned, I think, by the neo-

Kantianism of her ethic: it would be a lapse into the pathological determination of the will to pose the problem of choice on the terrain of pleasures and pains.

There rests the fundamental point. This world has always belonged to men. Even if women are—potentially at least—subjects, they do not contest the enserfing that men have imposed on them. What is the origin of such a situation? In the manner that de Beauvoir treats this problem, it seems as though the oppression of women is a scandal so unthinkable that she cannot manage to assign it to any origin or sufficient cause. Take the method used in Book I: she examines in succession three possible types of explanation—and rejects them all. Perhaps some readers will recall Rousseau's procedure in the *Social Contract.* Whence comes the social order that sets humans in chains? From nature? No. From the right of the stronger? The very phrase is a non-sense. By right of war? *Petitio principi!* Similarly, de Beauvoir eliminates, in turn, biology (insufficient to found a hierarchy of the sexes), psychoanalysis ("the phallus assumes the value it does because it symbolizes a sovereignty realized in other domains": *petitio principi,* then), historical materialism (manifest inadequacy); and, as each of these explanations proves inadequate, oppression comes to appear increasingly groundless and bizarre. In the end, the text leaves us in the lurch because the "key to the mystery" supplied in Book II is worth no more and no less than the explanations previously rejected. Moreover, de Beauvoir founds nothing on this foundation, she does not utilize it as the starting point for a deduction or a construction: Ultimately, in order to retrace the history of the feminine condition, she borrows much more from Engels than from this Hegelian "key."

One ends up then with the image of an oppression without a fundamental cause. Now this void has a very powerful, very dialectical effect. Because this oppression is founded on nothing, everything happens as though it has consequently been necessary to set in place a host of apparatuses and institutional props to create and sustain it. Lacking any basis on the side of the involuntary (nature, economy, the unconscious), the phallic order must secure itself against every circumstance with a forest of props—from the upbringing of little girls to the repressive legislation of "birth control," and from codes of dress to exclusion from politics. Certainly, I am interpreting here and describing above all an effect which the book has for me. But I would wager that de Beauvoir herself doesn't believe in her own "key," and this is what gives rise to her minute attentiveness to the polymorphous network of limitations imposed on women. Daily life is all the more narrowly policed because the subjection of women has at each moment to be reinvented.

This depiction of an oppression ultimately without a cause is, in part, a corollary of the existentialist maxim already cited: "Constraint can have no possible hold on a freedom"; it was surely not any original relation of forces at the outset that enabled men to impose on women to the extent of making them renounce an affirmation of themselves as subjects. A truism, indeed: founding itself on the negation of determinism, the existentialist perspective has no means for thinking a causality. But in strict orthodoxy,

it would then have been necessary to conclude that this oppression does not exist—unless in the bad faith of certain women, spiritual sisters of the revolutionaries with whom they share the mistake diagnosed by Sartre as "seriousness." Because de Beauvoir does not draw this conclusion, I see in this the proof of the primacy of involvement in the real over the philosophical reference point. Once applied to a field of conflicts, by one who is engaged in the struggle and who posits practical aims in relation to it, every philosophy undergoes remarkable modifications. In *The Second Sex,* one finds none of the Sartrian incapacity to thematize oppression, apart from the bankruptcy of the speculations on the origins of that oppression. And, ultimately, what do these speculations (which are in any case always liable to be merely mythical) matter to us here when the very impossibility of accounting for the origin of women's vassalage makes the aberrant character of this subjection all the more striking?

For against the background of the Hegelian-Sartrian problematic (every consciousness pursues the death of the Other, which opposes to it a reciprocal hostility), masculine/feminine relations appear as an incomprehensible exception. The philosophical reference point which de Beauvoir holds to be absolutely true is the least adequate to explain the phenomenon and, for this very reason, the most suitable for its denunciation.

Should one then draw the conclusion of indifferentism? Small matter whether you appeal to one philosophical position or another. Once our practical aspirations are clearly defined, these aspirations will suffice to remodel your initial perspective. Or should one accept the logic of "worse is better": the inaptitude of such and such a philosophy for the requirements of a theory of female oppression serving as a kind of springboard for illuminating that oppression? Either way would be to close the issue a little too rapidly.

Simone de Beauvoir made existentialism work "beyond its means" because she got more out of it than might have been expected. The choice of this reference was not without its drawbacks, and one must reflect on the type of miscomprehension which, in spite of everything, the limitations of this theoretical instrument brought about.

First of all one can see the *liberal* nature of de Beauvoir's critique: "Woman has never been given her chance in any domain." This question of chances, announced in the Introduction and reiterated through the book, is readily identified: It is a matter, in a quite strict sense, of the problematic of liberalism which demanded that the distribution of roles should not be preestablished by law (written or unwritten), because every artificial regulation of the destiny of individuals impedes the free play of competition; and we know that thanks to this free play of competition, individual tend to occupy the social place corresponding to their capacities. De Beauvoir pays a number of tributes to John Stuart Mill, and indeed the political tenor of her discourse is very close to that of *The Subjection of Women.* This is one stumbling block, politically this time, for me. Here is another: "on the whole, we have won out." Who is "we"? And when is this supposed to have happened, what is the historic mutation that has occurred? I do not seek to denounce this optimism as an illusion, but to delineate a gap in the analysis, a historical and sociological gap. This "we" is quickly replaced by "many among us"; but which ones? And are there really any? Some of us may indeed have the impression of "personally escaping," as they say, from such and such an aspect of alienation. But these partial liberations are scarcely effective—even at the level of the individuals who appear to benefit from them. The free disposal of one's salary, for instance, does not *ipso facto* cause the attitude of submission toward parents or husband to crumble, even if it affords the means for doing so. Correlatively, we are beginning today to recognize that—once again, only as an example—the fact that a high percentage of women stay "in the home" is not without its effects on those who do not. The class/sex of women is not as dispersed as it seems, and there is a globalization which needs to be examined: the common lot falls to each woman via a causality that passes through global society.

A classic schema then: existentialism, focused on the question of the individual, cannot arrive at posing all the problems, even on the individual level. In *The Second Sex,* ev-

erything happens as though, from the moment a minute gap is opened in the cage, it becomes the duty of the woman benefiting from it to make use of the escape to the maximum extent so as to posit herself as a subject condemned to be free. Every time de Beauvoir speaks of a woman who has had some means of affirming herself, of creating, and has not been fully capable of exploiting her opportunity, down at once comes the moral reprobation, and such themes as compliance, auto-compliance, narcissism, and the easy way out are invoked. The analogy drawn between oppression and moral error has a boomerang effect. It supports a miscomprehension of the same type as that of the teachers of yesteryear in the universal, free, nondenominational schools who equated failure in school with a moral infraction, but were unconscious of the sociocultural mechanisms that produced that failure.

In order to think through these problems one needs another problematic than that of the subject, and another perspective than that of ethics or ethical inquiry. It is permissible moreover to think that traces of this other philosophy begin to show in de Beauvoir's more localized interventions over the past few years. (pp. 277-88)

Michèle Le Doeuff, "Simone de Beauvoir and Existentialism," translated by Colin Gordon, in Feminist Studies, *Vol. 6, No. 2, Summer, 1980, pp. 277-89.*

Mary Evans

In *The Second Sex* de Beauvoir charts the excitement and nervous anticipation that adolescent girls entertain towards the possibility of entering social and sexual relations with men. The adolescent girl regards this possibility, according to de Beauvoir, with a mixture of excited anticipation and dread. On the one hand there lie the varied possibilities that men can offer to women and the wider social world that women, given male protection, can enter. On the other, negative, side is the cost of association with men—domestic tyranny and responsibility, pregnancy, the care of children, and a life of endless household drudgery.

The creatures who can both unlock the door of the world, and turn the key which shuts women out of it for ever, do not appear in *The Second Sex* as a particularly attractive group. Men possess what de Beauvoir describes as the 'original aspiration to dominate the Other', and, she argues, they have more than adequately demonstrated this proclivity in the past two thousand years of western history. Frequently careless and uncaring in their dealings with women, men emerge as insensitive and selfish creatures, content to brutalize women, and hypocritical in the moral systems which they erect to control women's behaviour. Men, as de Beauvoir points out, will frequently persuade or threaten women into adultery, abortion, moral compromise, and unprincipled action, yet are the same people who construct savage laws against divorce, or abortion, or women's economic independence. Relations between the sexes are therefore constructed around a dialectic of male dominance and female passivity, a form of relationship which encourages men in unthinking authoritarianism

---

Jean-Paul Sartre on Beauvoir:

It's very hard to tell what you owe someone. In a way, I owe [Beauvoir] everything. On the other hand, I would obviously have written even if she hadn't existed, since I wanted to write. But why is it that my complete confidence in her has always given me complete security, a security which I couldn't have had if I'd been alone, unless I were puffed with pride, as many writers are and which I am not, though I may be in other areas? When I show her a manuscript, as I always do, and when she criticizes it, I get angry at first and call her all kinds of names. Then, I accept her comments, always. Not as a matter of discipline, but because I see that they're always pertinent. They're not made from the outside, but with an absolute understanding of what I want to do and, at the same time, with an objectivity that I can't quite have.

She's in perfect agreement with what I say, even though she may think that it ought not to be said at that particular time. She trusts my judgment, since I want to write that particular thing. And since I want to write it, she's completely involved in it too. She's very severe, and so am I. After reading the first version of *The Respectful Prostitute,* she exclaimed: "Oh, it's disgusting! I now see all your tricks. It hasn't a leg to stand on."

I revised the play within twenty-four hours, and she finally said it was very good. Once she gives me, as it were, the "imprimatur," I have complete confidence in her. Other people's criticism has never made me change my mind about what I've written. To some extent, it can be said that I write for her, or, to put it more accurately, I write so that she can filter what I've set down. I then feel that it's fit for the public. You know, that's a very rare feeling. A man like Camus wrote in a state of doubt. That's natural, and it's even a virtue which I recognize he had.

Jean-Paul Sartre, "Sartre Talks of Beauvoir," in Vogue, *July, 1965.*

---

and dominance, and women in passivity and deviousness. Neither sex is free to express its true needs, each is constantly in danger of acting in bad faith towards the other. Yet the paradox of this analysis of existing relations between the sexes is that de Beauvoir seems to advocate the assumption by women of many male characteristics: . . .de Beauvoir wants women to escape from their subordinate and passive relationship to men by assuming precisely those habits and attitudes of rationality, independence, and emotional autonomy that have constituted the means by which men have been able to oppress women. Because men have generally been free of those ties to others which have traditionally been the lot of women, they have had both the time and the energy to develop intellectually, to explore the social world, and to organize the ideology of each and every society. If women are ever to imitate this activity, reasons de Beauvoir, they too must live independent lives and reject those relationships which constrain social action and mobility.

This prospect may seem to many to be less than appealing, particularly after almost two decades of western feminism have emphasized the values which women's traditional lives entail, values of nurturing, mutuality, care for others, and a morality which is less concerned with absolute, formal values than with the maximization of personal happiness and well-being. The activities of women in the household and particularly in child care are seen as positive; far from imprisoning women it is now suggested that these activities, and the values associated with them, are ones that men might well copy. The argument is not, therefore, that women should be more like men, but that men should be much more like women. The man who appears in *The Second Sex,* and indeed the traditional male of the west, is now seen as emotionally inexpressive, incapable of shared egalitarian relationships with others, and locked in futile competition and dreams of greatness and power. This 'macho' male, on feminist examination, looks quite unlike an enviable prototype of a human being. On the contrary, he appears as emotionally undeveloped, selfish, and, when given power, a real danger to the lives of others.

It is thus that a contemporary reading of *The Second Sex* might conclude that the very last thing that women should do to improve their lot in life is to become more like men. Becoming the equal partners of men in the kind of relationships which de Beauvoir outlines in the conclusion to *The Second Sex* involves the taking on of many characteristics of men, and almost certainly the abandonment of maternity which remains a trap and a prison for women. Work (in the sense of paid work outside the home) is the salvation of both sexes, sexuality remains heterosexuality and yet becomes an unproblematic meeting of two bodies of two different sexes. The disappearance of the economic dependence of women on men is followed by the disappearance of differing values, assumptions, and interests between the sexes. It is not, perhaps, unreasonable to ask quite what women have gained from this new, Utopian arrangement. Granted they have been freed from rearing children, but what they have been liberated into appears to be a world in which they may well be wage slaves rather than house slaves, and be forced into the kind of emotional narrowness that men have frequently been accused of illustrating, since their emotional relationships are limited exclusively to sexual relationships with other adults.

The elaboration and discussion of relations between the sexes is, of course, a central theme of *The Second Sex.* Yet it is in her novels and short stories that de Beauvoir most fully develops her views of male/female relationships: in fiction she is able to show the history, and something of the emotional complexities, of relationships between men and women in a way that is impossible in *The Second Sex,* where individual instances or relationships serve to illustrate a particular thesis. But it is clear that de Beauvoir's novels are very much by the author of *The Second Sex:* in both contexts a dichotomy is invoked between men and women, and in both the only transcendence possible between the sexes is through rational activity rather than emotional or sexual life. In the novels, just as much as in *The Second Sex,* women have to 'escape' from the limits of their biology; in fiction just as much as in fact there is no suggestion that men might be asked to integrate women's biology into their understanding and the arrangements of the social world in such a way that women are not trapped in a determining relationship with their anatomy.

If de Beauvoir's fiction is examined in its entirety, from the first full-length novel to *The Woman Destroyed,* a general pattern can be observed in which women stay much the same (in the sense that some of the female characters appear over and over again in different novels under different names) while the men become increasingly morally unattractive and unsympathetic. Pierre, of *She Came to Stay,* is a complex and morally sensitive man, while Maurice, of 'The Woman Destroyed', is little more than a stereotypically selfish, adulterous husband. And at the same time as the men become increasingly distant from moral concerns or emotional sensitivity, so the relationships between the sexes become more and more unhappy. The relationship between Françoise and Pierre in *She Came to Stay* (or Anne and Lewis in *The Mandarins*) are hardly romantic idylls, but they do contain an integrity and a concern for the other which is significantly absent in *The Woman Destroyed.* Since de Beauvoir's fiction spans a period in which women in western Europe achieved a measure of formal emancipation, and the sexual 'revolution' challenged accepted mores about sexuality, it is interesting that a perceptive and well-informed author sees these changes—and reflects these changes in her fiction—as losses rather than gains for women and portrays an overall worsening in male/female relationships.

Essentially, three stages exist in de Beauvoir's fiction: the first is that of the existentialist novels (*She Came to Stay, The Blood of Others,* and *All Men Are Mortal*), the second is that of the social novel (*The Mandarins*), and the third is that of what is perhaps best described as the stage of the novels of despair and moral anarchy: the collection of stories entitled *The Woman Destroyed* and the novel *Les Belles Images.* In these three stages of de Beauvoir's work we can detect quite different kinds of heterosexual relationships, and very varied pictures of men and women. In the first group of novels, de Beauvoir portrays heterosexual relationships as intensely passionate, sexually expressive, and above all collaborative: men and women are brought together by common interests and values. For example, in *She Came to Stay,* Françoise and Pierre, like Jean and Hélène of *The Blood of Others,* are united by common intellectual and political commitments, mutual agreement about how to live, and a shared moral code that operates between them and in their dealings with the rest of the world. De Beauvoir once wrote that she and Sartre had the 'same sign on their brows' and this description of the central relationship in her own life accurately summarizes the kind of relationship that exists between Françoise and Pierre, or Jean and Hélène. It is a pact against the world: an agreement between two people that they are united in the ways which they identify as absolutely central to their being.

But against these morally committed couples, de Beauvoir also poses the kind of couple which is to become, in *The Woman Destroyed,* a central theme. It is the couple in which the woman is totally emotionally dependent on the man, and is unable to achieve any kind of autonomous existence without reference to the relationship which she has with a particular man. The agonies for women of this kind of relationship are hinted at in all de Beauvoir's novels; thus Elizabeth, in *She Came to Stay,* describes her feelings after she has seen a momentary touch of the hand between her lover Claude and another woman:

> for a moment or so, she stood motionless at the back of the auditorium. Claude was helping Suzanne to slip off her mink cape; then he sat down beside her; she leaned towards him and laid her hand on his arm. A sharp stabbing pain suddenly shot through Elizabeth. She recalled that December evening when she had walked through the streets drunk with joy and triumph because Claude had said to her: 'You're the one I really love'. . . . He loved her, but that had changed nothing.

Elizbeth, like other female characters in de Beauvoir's later novels, suffers agonies of jealousy and misery because the loved one whom she still regards as central to her life is demonstrably no longer hers alone.

It is possible to find in the first stage of de Beauvoir's fiction all the problems in heterosexual relationships that she is to explore at greater length in her later work. But one further feature of all her novels, already apparent in her earliest work, deserves mention—de Beauvoir's assumptions about the nature and the extent of male and female sexuality. What emerges as a pattern in all the novels is that male sexual desire and expression are far less problematic than those of women. It is, moreover, men who show the greatest apparent inclination towards infidelity, or at least towards greater variety in their sexual partners than women. In *The Second Sex* de Beauvoir argued that male sexuality is far less beset with problems than that of women; thus in her novels she gives this statement of fact a fictional expression and repeatedly suggests a pttern of sexuality in which women invariably become deeply attached to the men with whom they have sexual relations, while the men are far more inclined to dismiss sexual encounters as unimportant, or at any rate place them at a far lower level of significance than do women. This pattern reflects the commonplace ideology of the west—that men have 'natural' sexual needs which have to be expressed (and have to be expressed with women) while women's sexual needs are far more generalized than those of men, and a great deal more emotionally charged. The 'ideology of male sexual needs' as Mary McIntosh has described it, is able to see fleeting male infidelities, female prostitution, or male sexual promiscuity as expressions not of major moral failing but simply as features of a world in which boys are expected to be boys.

Few of de Beauvoir's male characters are, in fact, sexually promiscuous in any extravagant sense. Nevertheless, while not extending their sexual favours widely, they do inflict considerable emotional damage on their female partners by the encounters which they embark on. Some of these encounters are deeply charged and tortuous affairs, others are presented quite straightforwardly as indulgences of the flesh rather than the spirit. A shift occurs here between the first, existentialist, novels and *The Mandarins:* in the existential novels sexual relations are always seen as emotionally significant, while in *The Mandarins* passing sexual encounters are seen as precisely that, implying no commitment between the parties and certainly not indicative of any strong affection. Thus in *She Came to Stay* Pierre deliberates for some considerable time about embarking on a sexual relationship with Xavière while in *The Mandarins* two of the central (and sympathetically portrayed) characters—Anne and Henri Perron—apparently attach far less significance to their sexual encounters. A different attitude to sexuality is therefore apparent between the two stages of the fiction (and a gap of some seven years separates *The Mandarins* from *All Men Are Mortal*), and sexual relationships lose some of the emotional and social significance which had been a characteristic of the earlier fiction.

In *The Mandarins* it is noticeable that there is, in general, more diversity in the range of heterosexual relationships than in *She Came to Stay, All Men Are Mortal,* or *The Blood of Others.* While the archetypal relationship between men and women in these novels is that of the committed, sexually expressive couple, in *The Mandarins* something of a dichotomy emerges between relationships in which men and women share the same commitments (to political values or moral concerns), and yet are not sexually active partners, and those couples in which sexual passion and attraction is a major, if not the single, factor in the relationship. Thus in *The Mandarins,* these two kinds of relationships between men and women are represented by the relationships between Anne Dubreuilh and her husband Robert, and that between Anne and her American lover, Lewis Brogan. Side by side with the history of Anne's romance with Lewis, de Beauvoir portrays the end of the romance between Henri Perron and his mistress of ten years, Paula. The moral of the history of the relationship between Paula and Henri is quite clearly that, for women, to live for love is to die for love. When Anne turns her back on Lewis and the United States, and decides to return home to Robert and their somewhat austere life together, it is a decision that the reader cannot but endorse, given the terrible sufferings of Paula, a woman who abandoned everything for love. At the beginning of

The Mandarins a brief conversation between Paula and Henri suggests the kind of stasis which their relationship has developed. The scene takes place just before a party, Paula appears dressed for the festivities in a violet dress:

> 'You're so positively dedicated to violet!' he said smiling.
>
> 'But you adore violet!' she said. He had been adoring violet for the past ten years; ten years was a long time. . . . It was all so useless, he told himself. In green or yellow he would never again see in her the woman who, that day ten years earlier, he had desired so much when he had nonchalantly held out her long violet gloves to her.

The emotional dependence of Paula on Henri traps them both into a deadly game: Henri cannot bring himself to tell Paula that he wishes to leave her, and contents himself with small, open infidelities (including, since this is a novel about intellectual life, a somewhat incestuous affair with the Dubreuilhs' daughter Nadine). Because Paula in a sense 'allows' Henri these affairs he becomes even more trapped; Paula gives him freedom, he cannot ask her for more, and so how is he to explain that what he wants is total disengagement? Eventually, their relationship ends, Paula becomes deeply involved in social life, and Henri is left with Nadine.

Against the unhappy relationships of Paula and Henri, de Beauvoir sets the relationship of Anne and Lewis Brogan. As de Beauvoir has acknowledged, the depiction of this affair is a fictionalized account of her own affair with the American novelist Nelson Algren—an account which Algren has condemned, both for its very existence and its content. Despite this controversial use of personal experience (and indeed the experiences of another party) in fiction, the affair is portrayed in essentially positive and romantic terms. But more surprising than the elements of either romance or commitment in the telling of the tale is the conventional nature of the sexuality and the sexual experience that occurs. Perhaps for some contemporary readers the most conventional aspect of the affair is that it is heterosexual; aside from that qualification it is also the case that the descriptions of the physical love of Anne and Lewis follow many of the conventions of romantic fiction. Thus de Beauvoir portrays the sexual encounters of Anne and Lewis in terms which suggest that female sexual drive is only brought to life by men. Rather like the heroines of the novels of Barbara Cartland or Denise Robins, Anne finds herself 'transformed' by male sexual desire. It is true that in the previous pages Anne had been preoccupied with wondering whether or not Lewis would initiate any sexual activity between them, but even if de Beauvoir does allow that Anne might have had more than a passing interest in whether or not Lewis wanted to sleep with her, the moves towards this state are all for Lewis to make. Anne can desire, she can gaze longingly, but, as much of chapter six makes clear, it is Lewis who is expected to make the crucial, resolving gestures towards his bedroom. And once there, the transformation of Anne from disembodied self to a physically delighted human being occurs. Like lovers in romantic fiction, Lewis and, particularly, Anne sink into a rosy haze of delight.

But in de Beauvoir's work, as in romantic fiction, sexuality has to be organized in an appropriate, conventional, manner. This is the second surprising element of de Beauvoir's portrayal of sexuality, and is illustrated by the symbolic claiming by Lewis of Anne in a permanent relationship, expressed both through the expected 'language of love' in which the parties exchange, at appropriate moments, words of affection and commitment, and through his giving her a ring. After their night together, certain doubts seem to arise in Anne's mind, but 'There was no need to be upset; he was caressing my hair, speaking gently, simple words, slipping an old copper ring on my finger'. And again, only three pages later, when Anne is beset with doubts about the relationship Lewis is there with reassurance and the ring: 'At the lakeside, Lewis had spoken to me as if I were never going to leave him, and he had slipped a ring on my finger'. So love is 'organized' in the expected way, and the exclusivity and commitment which western culture expects in sexual relations between men and woman are reaffirmed. Yet what is surprising about this particular case (apart, of course, from the fact that some of the passages are astonishingly romantic for the author of *The Second Sex*) is that both Anne and Lewis fall so rapidly into conventional patterns in their affair, notably into the pattern that says that it is only possible for a human being to have one significant relationship with another person. Lewis is as jealous of Anne's life in Paris with Robert as Anne is of Lewis's ex-wife: they both have intense feelings towards the intimate friends of the other, and their relationship with each other moves rapidly towards the moment when Anne has to choose Lewis or Robert. De Beauvoir does not assume that Anne must love any man that she sleeps with (the encounter with Scriassine in chapter one is acknowledged as a compartmentalized affair of 'carnal pleasure') but what is to be found in *The Mandarins* (and elsewhere) is the assumption that love, passion, and mutual physical pleasure are the sources of feelings, and needs, of exclusivity and commitment. Whether or not this is actually the case about human emotional life is unknowable; all that can be asserted is that western culture values monogamy and yet allows compartmentalized, adulterous sexuality—the kind of sexual relations advocated by Sartre and de Beauvoir are deeply threatening to bourgeois society since they involve choice, and possibly the frequent change of sexual partners. [De Beauvoir] and Sartre faced in their own lives all the problems of people wishing to live outside conventional morality. The problems of their 'open' relationship were solved by Sartre through conventional deceit, and by de Beauvoir largely through abstaining from threatening relationships. Both advocated openness, honesty, and freedom in personal relations, but found (and de Beauvoir illustrated the problems in her fiction) that this blueprint was woefully inadequate for the emotional realities of relations with others. Human beings are capable of amazing intellectual feats, great rational understanding, and concern for others—but add sexuality into any relationship, de Beauvoir seems to be suggesting, and all these excellent characteristics disappear.

In all, none of the sexually active relationships in *The Mandarins* can in any sense be described as happy or fulfilled, and the costs to all parties, in terms of emotional turmoil, empty days, sleepless nights, and enervating misery are considerable. It is true that Anne and Lewis Brogan have their moments of romance and intense sexual satisfaction, but all the time a question hangs over their affair of how their relationship is going to develop. Lewis is perhaps understandably moody at the thought that his love for Anne can only be temporary while Anne is appalled by the prospect of years of emotional and sexual sterility with Robert, and yet is unable to relinquish her loyalties and commitments to him, Paris, and the professional life which she has established there. The best that she can offer Lewis is a permanent, yet part-time arrangement. She would return to Paris and Robert for most of the year, while continuing to spend holidays and other free time with Lewis. The idea does not appeal to Lewis, and the affair ends. The end of the affair is also very nearly the end of Anne, since she is overwhelmed by grief and contemplates suicide. But finally she achieves a kind of *modus vivendi,* she makes a conscious decision to relinquish what she decides were the false dreams and hopes which her love was based upon; in particular the illusion that love can ever provide lasting happiness:

> Dead is the child who believed in paradise, dead the girl who thought immortal the books, the ideas, and the man she loved, dead the young woman who walked overwhelmed through a world promised to happiness, dead the woman in love who would wake up laughing in Lewis's arms.

The best thing to do with dreams, Anne concludes, is to bury them. The infinite promises which the world seems to offer are all illusory, particularly if they happen to be dreams of transcendence, of discovering another individual with whom one becomes one united human being. Indeed, the greater the hope of this transcendence, the more, the novel suggests, it is doomed to failure.

Yet if the final chapters of *The Mandarins* are bleak, what is offered to Anne is at least her interest in her work and the happy memories of the life which she and Robert have shared, and which they still have. Something, therefore, is still left to her, and she knows nothing except love and consideration from the men with whom she is involved. Robert and Lewis are both, in their different ways, deeply fond of her, and concerned for her welfare. Whatever the difficulties of heterosexuality, compassion, concern, and mutual companionship still exist as possibilities between men and women. But in her final novel and short stories, de Beauvoir abandons the fictional portrayal of any such possibilities, and portrays instead heterosexual relationships that are based on mutual exploitation and manipulation. Furthermore, in the three short stories that make up the collection *The Woman Destroyed,* the theme of women destroyed by love for men (the Elizabeth and Paula theme of the earlier novels) is brought to its fullest and most vivid representation in the short story **'La Femme rompue'**.

Although in these final works there is a major shift towards pessimism and negative expectations about heterosexuality there is a further and equally significant development in that the milieu which de Beauvoir writes about is no longer that of the liberal, intellectual world. Instead, she places the characters in managerial or technocratic jobs, gives them quite different preoccupations from her earlier characters, and divorces them completely from the values of the previous novels. Thus in *Les Belles Images* the heroine is a woman called Laurence, who works in advertising. Her husband Jean-Charles is an architect, and quite unlike any of the previous men in de Beauvoir's fiction in that he has no ideas other than a determined commitment to industrial capitalism, which has provided him with a comfortable and secure life. He is predominantly interested in making money, acquiring the material possessions appropriate to a well-paid fashionable male, and making sure that his family life conforms to the stereotypical picture of conventional society. He does not demand from Laurence that she shares any ideal with him: what he wants is an attractive wife who does not damage his car too often.

The title of the novel is, like that of all de Beauvoir's novels, most apt. The characters are devoted to images of themselves, their motivation derives from maintaining those socially constructed fictions about how people 'like them' should behave, act, and even appear in certain circumstances. Thus Laurence arranges her pose of appropriate wifely gratitude when Jean-Charles has given her an expensive present:

> She bowed her head a little so that he could fasten the necklace again: a perfect picture of the couple who still adore one another after ten years of marriage. He was buying conjugal peace, the delights of the home, understanding, love; and pride in himself. She gazed at herself in the mirror. 'Darling you were right to insist: I'm wild with happiness'.

Others, as much as Laurence, are conscious of the correct demeanour to adopt in particular situations and moods: one puts on the role of concerned wife, adoring mistress, anxious mother, and so on, as is demanded. All such behaviour is light years away from that of the tortured lovers of *She Came to Stay* or the deeply committed political activists of *The Mandarins.* Liberal humanism has disappeared under a barrage of affluence and consumerism, and has been replaced by what has been described as 'the consciousness of the Club Mediterranée', or thought which is attractive, not too demanding, and just different enough to be titillating [Lucien Goldmann, *Power and Humanism*].

The attack on the consumer society and on the repressive tolerance of advanced industrial capitalism in *Les Belles Images* is, for some critics, not quite sharp enough. Whether or not they are right, the novel is convincing as a portrait of an affluent, decadent, and essentially valueless society—a society which is not necessarily immoral in any conventional sense (indeed most of the characters would be horrified by any truly unorthodox behaviour) but is quite ruthlessly without values if a concern for public, general issues is regarded as a fundamental and essential ingredient of morality. Nobody in *Les Belles Images,* with the exception of Laurence (whom her husband regards as slightly sentimental in her views), ever has any twinges of interest or conscience in matters which do not affect their own interests. But when their own interests are attacked, they can fight with quite ferocious determination, as is illustrated by the case of Laurence's mother, Dominique. For some years, Dominique has been living with the rich and powerful Gilbert. Suddenly, Gilbert decides to abandon Dominique for a much younger woman, and in a mood of vindictive anger and spite Dominique writes to the woman, giving full details of Gilbert's past, and attempting, as far as she is able, to cast an extremely long shadow over what is left of his future. Dominique is, of course, one in the long line of de Beauvoir's heroines who become unbalanced, violent, or at least temporarily insane when abandoned by their male lover, but Dominique's reaction is both more furious (and in a way more spiteful, since it is directed against a third party) and more superficial, since she eventually recovers her composure and without any apparent sense of emotional loss continues with her life.

Emotional life for the characters in *Les Belles Images* is, as the case of Dominique demonstrates, both intense and yet largely fleeting: there is a great deal of desire, both innate and also constructed, for close personal relationships ('a woman without a man is a half-failure', says Dominique at one point) and yet many of the relationships that result from these needs are largely about the acquisition of the state of being involved with another person. A man or a woman thus becomes valued at least in part because it is socially appropriate to be married, or have a lover, or simply have 'a relationship'. Any individual characteristics that the person might have, or the shared values and views that a couple might possess, are largely subservient to the possession of a sexual partner. Inevitably, since a market-place in sexual relationships operates (and has operated for some time, and is not an invention of monopoly capitalism), it is important that the man or woman is attractive, and has the right sort of job for a particular social milieu; but more fundamental questions, the kind of questions asked in *The Mandarins* or *She Came to Stay* about moral choices or an individual's capacity for good or evil, are no longer asked.

The bleakness of personal relationships in advanced industrial capitalism has been a subject that has preoccupied many writers besides de Beauvoir. The loss of the sense of individual commitment to others, the contradictory demands within the family of the man, the woman and the children, and the increasing penetration of all areas of social and personal life by economic and material values have all contributed to a situation in which individual, long-term relationships seem increasingly redundant. Given that many of the social constraints (other than material ones) on remarriage and divorce have disappeared or lessened, it is now perfectly possible for individuals to exchange one partner for another, to say of a human being, as one might of an object, that she or he is 'past its best' or can no longer satisfy a certain set of desires. But as de Beauvoir rightly perceives, this situation is not the equal preserve of the sexes: she had always identified the problem of women abandoned by men; now, in *Les Belles Images* and more significantly in *The Woman Destroyed*, she identifies the culture in which people become objects, but the objects least able to manipulate their fate are women. The consumer society is, therefore, a general background, but its effects are far from equally distributed between the sexes.

In *The Woman Destroyed*, and especially in the short story which bears the same name, de Beauvoir continues her theme of the woman who has given all for a man, and is deserted by him. Monique, the heroine of 'The Woman Destroyed', is now in her forties, and is told by her husband, Maurice, that he is having an affair with another woman. At first, Monique decides to tolerate the relationship, remain the understanding and loving wife, and hope that Maurice will come back to her. As the story continues, it becomes increasingly obvious that Maurice is going to do no such thing: his lover, Noëllie, satisfies all his current desires for a chic, cosmopolitan woman of the world, just as Monique once wholly satisfied his need for a loving and supporting wife who was prepared to provide the emotional stability and reassurance wanted by a man in the early stages of a demanding professional career.

Maurice does not emerge from 'The Woman Destroyed' as a sympathetic or likeable character; on the contrary he is, like Jean-Charles in *Les Belles Images*, obsessed by professional success and the establishment and gratification of his own self-image. But de Beauvoir's argument is not that all men are necessarily corrupt, or bad, or the enemy of women, although they can certainly act like that. Her point remains that although women are often the victims of male behaviour, they themselves construct the conditions of their own victimization. Monique, just as much as Paula in *The Mandarins*, deludes herself into supposing that she can live simply through the love of a man, and that in sacrificing her time, her energy, and even on occasion her own values, she has a right to expect total commitment in return. So de Beauvoir is not suggesting an analysis in which men are wrong, and women are right, but a much more complicated pattern in which men and women construct their own mutual self-destruction. Women therefore abandon all for the man they love, men accept this abandonment and self-abasement, since a particular culture accepts that that is a fitting pattern for male/female relations. The price for both sexes is, however, high. Women are never able to develop any capacity for independent or autonomous thought or action, since everything must be done with reference to the beloved. Men are trapped by guilt and social pressures into maintaining relationships that are no longer in any way rewarding.

Many contemporary feminists might argue that the situation of male independence and female dependence is one in which men are always the privileged sex, and women always the losers. De Beauvoir does not attempt to maintain this absolute dichotomy, however, and she suggests in all her novels that both sexes suffer from the excessive commitments demanded of women in love. Her existentialist values do not in fact disappear, and she maintains throughout her work a belief in individual freedom and an individual capacity for the choice of freedom. But what does change during her career as a writer, between *She Came to Stay* and *The Woman Destroyed*, is her presentation of the extent to which men and women, and particularly women, can choose their fate. Between the active, morally assertive Françoise of *She Came to Stay* and the passive suffering of Monique of '*The Woman Destroyed*' there is a vast distance in the range of human action; perhaps there is also a major difference in de Beauvoir's view of the relative freedoms of men and women.

Again, it is important to emphasize that de Beauvoir is not saying what some radical feminists might say—that men are free, and women unfree. In all her novels she shows that men and women are both constrained by social pressures. If Maurice in '*The Woman Destroyed*' is free in the formal sense of being able to leave his wife to live with a mistress, he is far from genuinely free in that he has to maintain all the appropriate poses of the professional man, the lover to his mistress, and the man with a 'great love' for another woman to the world at large. With his mistress, as de Beauvoir suggests, he is even less free than with his wife, since he has to be able to match all her expectations of professional distinction, sexual competence, and social sophistication. Compared to the agonies of heartache endured by Monique at her husband's departure this price might not seem particularly high to some readers, but de Beauvoir is showing us that there are costs, albeit different ones, for both sexes in sexual relations as they are now constituted.

Yet as we have seen, a shift has occurred, between *She Came to Stay* and *The Woman Destroyed,* in social values about human relationships, and it is possible that the loss of liberal, humanist values in the world after the Second World War has intensified patriarchy. In many ways, of course, evidence would suggest an increasing emancipation of women—better contraception, more widely available abortion, increased access to education and paid work, all these changes could be construed as improvements in the lot of women. But at the same time as these changes have taken place (and their impact has been far from universal or complete even in north-west Europe) other changes in the social construction of sexuality have arguably brought about a deterioration in the status and situation of women, in that the demands on them have increased. De Beauvoir suggests in *The Woman Destroyed* and *Les Belles Images* that the old image of the 'home-making' woman no longer accords with the myths and fantasies of a technocratic society. It is now demanded that women should be—to produce an exaggerated stereotype—brilliant brain surgeons, superb cooks, wonderful wives and mothers, and active socialites. Sexually attractive (and constantly available), intellectually able, and socially popular, the woman of the dream world of technocratic patriarchy inevitably fails to exist, except in the smallest number of cases. But like all myths, the potency of this dream lies not in its fulfilment, but in the measure it represents for reality. Thus the woman who fails to meet all, or some, of the expected attributes of the super-woman is seen as a failure, and a failure in a society which values success very highly. As Monique in '*The Woman Destroyed*' quite rightly perceives, the attraction of Noëlle is not her intrinsic moral qualities, but the way in which she meets Maurice's fantasies of the bright, active, professionally successful woman. That Noëlle is bright and active about issues that are not of any intrinsic value in a general political or social sense is of no concern to Maurice; what he admires is the reassurance of success and socially recognized competence. As Monique realizes, the activities to which she has devoted herself, the care of their children and the establishment and running of a home, are now dismissed as unimportant and time wasting. The care of children and housework have no material value, and are thus easily dismissed by a society in which all social relations and all work are increasingly assessed in terms of the market-place. Just as it was once a matter of status for a man to have a wife whom he could support economically, so it now becomes a matter of equal importance for a man to have a wife who 'achieves' and can demonstrate skills that have a market value. This change is, however, complex as far as its repercussions for women are concerned: on the one hand it encourages them to seek economic independence from their husbands or male others, while on the other it adds to the responsibilities (including child care and the maintenance of the household) which women are deemed to bear.

De Beauvoir would no doubt see that within this change there exists the possibility for the emancipation of women from an exclusive identification with the household. Nevertheless she also acknowledges that entry into paid labour does not, in itself, guarantee any great extension in women's freedom. The question then remains of what else has to change before women can leave that state of emotional dependence on men that was so widely condemned in *The Second Sex* and illustrated in the fiction. One answer that might be introduced—that women should abandon sexual relationships with men and choose either chastity or what contemporary feminism describes as 'political lesbianism'—is categorically rejected by de Beauvoir, who writes:

> All feminists agree that love and sexuality must be redefined. But some of them deny that men have any part to play in a woman's life, particularly in her sexual life, whereas others wish to keep a place for them in their lives and in their beds. I side with them. I utterly revolt at the idea of shutting women up in a feminine ghetto.

So heterosexuality is to continue, even if 'love and sexuality' must be redefined.

In de Beauvoir's fiction we do not find, and can hardly expect to find, a programme for this redefinition of heterosexuality. Suggestions about alterations in male/female relationships are given, albeit briefly, in the conclusion to *The Second Sex,* but these remain essentially superficial and are largely related to changes in ideology. The material world, as much in *The Second Sex* as in the fiction, is largely a background (albeit sometimes an inconvenient one) against which individuals attempt to work out their metaphysical differences. So most of the campaigns of contemporary feminism for equal participation in work and child care by men and women, for equal pay for the sexes, and for the ending of discriminatory legislation against women find little place in de Beauvoir's work. That is not to say that she would condemn any of the changes—on the contrary, she has consistently advocated the majority of them—but that she undervalues the part that these issues play in the determination of a woman's (or a man's) life. But most striking of all is the absence in de Beauvoir's fiction of any discussion of women as mothers or men as fathers. It is true that Anne in *The Mandarins* has a daughter, and Monique in 'The Woman Destroyed' has two daughters, but these relationships between fictional mothers and daughters is, at best, distant. What is missing from the account of male/female relations, and the lives of both sexes, is a portrayal of the desire to bear children, and the costs and rewards of being a parent. None of the men in the novels has anything to do with children; Robert and Perron in *The Mandarins* have fleeting encounters with their offspring, but family life in any significant sense is not part of their experience.

Such a portrayal of men's relationships with their children can hardly be described as entirely unrealistic. Numerous feminists have pointed out that many men have little to do with their children and that the burden of child care falls almost exclusively on women. So what is interesting about de Beauvoir's account of maternity and paternity is that it is markedly matter of fact: children are sometimes simply in existence but apparently constitute little of emotional significance. Monique is attached to her children, yet they offer little compensation for the loss of Maurice; Anne is often irritated and appalled by Nadine's behaviour but generally adopts towards her an attitude of complete objectivity. The central female characters of the novels never express their attitudes towards their own mothers: strong, assertive, and (in the case of Françoise and Anne) independent women arrive in the world and in the novels with little or no explanation of why they should have those characteristics and why they are so markedly different from the miserably dependent Monique or Paula. Why, we might ask, do the daughters of Monique turn out to be so different—the one traditional and the other aggressively independent and assertive? Equally, there is little explanation for the constant, often spiteful, delinquency of Nadine. Certainly, a previous lover had been killed during the war, but this scarcely explains the petty vindictiveness of her behaviour towards other women—particularly Paula and Anne.

But this feature of *The Mandarins,* that is the behaviour of Nadine towards Anne and Paula, illustrates particularly clearly an important and striking feature of de Beauvoir's fiction: that women do not, on the whole, behave particularly well towards each other. When a man is involved with two women, or a woman is involved in competition for a particular man, women act markedly badly. Quite how badly varies from murdering the other woman in *She Came to Stay,* to coquetry and competitive sexuality in the case of Nadine in *The Mandarins* or Noëlle in **'The Woman Destroyed'**. This feature of de Beauvoir's fiction departs from a general feature of much fiction written by women, in which women, and especially sisters, are bound together by ties of loyalty and concern. For example, Austen and Eliot do not always show women who are well disposed towards each other (competition for men reaches heights of intensity and moral compromise in Austen's *Mansfield Park* and *Sense and Sensibility*) but they do show women who are capable of genuine and even, on occasions, unselfish concern for other women. It is interesting that de Beauvoir quotes a male author—Tolstoy—to illustrate a point about women's lack of common identity, and uses, from the fiction of women authors, only examples which suggest female independence (Maggie Tulliver of *The Mill on the Floss* or Jo of *Little Women*) or female enslavement (the women portrayed by Colette). There is no mention of the altruism of Dorothea in *Middlemarch,* with her real generosity of spirit towards the clinging and vapid Rosamond, or the quiet moral strength of Anne in *Persuasion,* who is capable of acknowledging the freedom of the man whom she still loves to choose another woman. These women do not act as 'the other' but very much as individuals who have confronted and accepted the possibilities of women's capacity for moral choice and action. Even if they are constrained within circumstances that none of de Beauvoir's heroines knows, they nevertheless show an alternative to the assumptions that de Beauvoir has made about women, in that they do not blindly follow accepted standards and conventions, and are, most importantly, prepared to make the kind of moral decision that promises neither security nor comfort nor male approbation.

To read literature as de Beauvoir does in *The Second Sex* is largely to ignore the assertiveness of which women have been shown to be capable. This does not answer the question of whether or not literature is in any sense a mirror of reality, but it does suggest that there exists an alternative perception to the dominant ideology of male power and female powerlessness. Increasingly, women's 'resistance' has been discovered by historians and literary critics, and this recent discovery of the female past has alerted many people against assuming that what is taken as the 'great' literary tradition or the conventional version of history is necessarily a comprehensive or even accurate view. In the case of de Beauvoir's novels we have to ask, therefore, if they do not reflect, in a fictional form, some of the generalizations about male power and female powerlessness that are outlined in *The Second Sex.* Given that this is the theme that informs de Beauvoir's novels, we must ask next how adequate de Beauvoir's novels are in their portrayal of individual personal relationships between the sexes. In terms of what could be described as 'feminist realism' and its judgements about literature, de Beauvoir's fiction would be highly rated, since she shows in fictional terms precisely those aspects of female emotional dependence on men which feminists have for so long attacked. Equally, de Beauvoir portrays the different standards of sexual morality that exist for men and women, and provides more than one instance of men's laack of interest in certain fundamental aspects of women's existence. For example, the unfaithful Maurice in 'The Woman Destroyed' takes no interest, or part in, the home which he has been so content to enjoy.

But while de Beauvoir's fiction passes this test of portraying what is assumed to be a reality of male power and female subservience, it is also necessary to ask if she adequately portrays some of the complexities of motivation and compromise which are a feature of many people's lives. Literature would be very dull if it were about the humdrum daily life which never involved choice or change, but de Beauvoir does suggest a world in which emotional life is always active and always a matter of idealized choice. Wives and husbands do not stay together because of material necessity, let alone for 'the sake of the children', and all the characters act with a complete lack of interest in the material circumstances of their individual choices. Money, as almost all the great European novelists have appreciated, is an important, if not a determining, feature of human existence, and few characters of this tradition are shown without some reference to the means by which they acquire their livelihood and maintain themselves. Further, as was so well portrayed by Eliot, Austen, the Brontës, Flaubert, and Mann, money made the person: men and women were not born with grace, or ease, or perfect composure, these attributes were provided by a culture which was in its turn created by wealth. Emma Bovary was not attracted to the facile Roland for any reason other than those aspects of his person which had, in a very real sense, been bought. Whatever the virtues of the homely Charles Bovary, they counted for nothing in his wife's eyes against his rough manners and untutored behaviour. Emma, like many other heroines, could find what she thought was 'love' and 'beauty' in the sight of expensive clothes and the acquisitions of wealth.

This aspect of women's behaviour, their interest in what men can provide for them in material terms and what men themselves appear as in terms of the material world, is a feature of male/female relations that is largely absent from de Beauvoir's world. Only in '**The Woman Destroyed**', in the portrayal of Maurice and Noëlle, do we find it suggested that human beings do not make abstract, individualized judgements about each other, but that social values and aspirations are an extremely important part of sexual relations. In the other novels, judgements about others, the affection of one for another, are about the characteristics of the individual and those characteristics alone. The problem, of course, is that no individual exists in such a highly individualized sense, and it is not, therefore, either cynical or materially over-deterministic to point out that what individuals can love or value in each other has often little to do with the other person but a great deal to do with the projection of individual needs or aspirations on to another. The way in which women would project on to men their own needs, and the possibilities for the realization of what they wished to become, was expressed very clearly by a number of nineteenth-century female novelists. George Eliot in particular brilliantly portrayed the way in which women would locate in men what they themselves wanted. Seldom in fiction has the bending of one will to another been more accurately portrayed than in the depiction in *Middlemarch* of the courtship between Lydgate and Rosamond Vincy. Lydgate has no wish to marry Rosamond, Rosamond has absolutely no interest in Lydgate's ideas or aspirations. And yet:

> she looked at Lydgate and the tears fell over her cheeks. There could have been no more complete answer than that silence, and Lydgate, forgetting everything else, completely mastered by the onrush of tenderness and the feeling that this sweet young creature depended on him for her joy, actually put his arms around her, folding her gently and protectingly; he was used to being gentle with the weak and the suffering.

From that moment on, Lydgate is the hopeless captive of Rosamond's whims. He can no more refuse to concede her wishes than he can fly, and although he may occasionally vent his dissatisfactions in ill humour he cannot in any substantial sense act as a free man.

Yet many feminists would point out, here, that a measure of Rosamond's lack of freedom, and dependence on men, is that she has to make men do what she wants for her, since she is incapable of achieving her own aims through her own efforts. Petit-bourgeois women in nineteenth-century Europe could not establish a household or a secure place in society without a husband—men had a social as well as an economic function as far as women were concerned. That they have not lost this function is an endless complaint of contemporary feminism. A woman without a man may be like a fish without a bicycle in terms of political slogans, but in terms of social reality a woman without a husband is generally poor, and her children are certainly regarded as illegitimate. Attachment to men, and confirmation by men, is therefore as much now as in the nineteenth century a feature of women's existence. Given that this is the case and was the case when de Beauvoir wrote her fiction, what remains interesting about her novels is the way in which she constructs the attraction that men have for women. Material provision is not given prominence, neither is sexuality. She shows in *She Came to Stay, The Blood of Others,* and *The Mandarins* how men and women might be bound together by rational and political ties, but still the issue remains of what the sexes want from each other that they cannot gain from members of their own sex. In the relationships that seem to be offered as the most developed and fulfilled (Françoise and Pierre of *She Came to Stay,* and Anne and Robert Dubreuilh of *The Mandarins*) sexuality is absent, and what exists between the two parties is a long-standing friendship that might equally well exist between two men or two women, and might be less likely to entail the kind of jealousies, drama, and high passions that beset these two couples. It is, perhaps, a reflection on the undeveloped state of the intellectual and political lives of most women that exceptional women (the Françoise or Anne of intellectual/Bohemian life) can only gain from men the kind of companionship that they seek? But if this is the case, we must also ask if the power that men have over women in the novels of de Beauvoir is no longer a power of economic dominance or superior social standing, but the possession of intellectual and mental power. The symbolic phallic power of Robert of *The Mandarins* and Pierre of *She Came to Stay* is not, therefore, the same as it might be for women with more conventional domestic and reproductive ambitions, but it is nevertheless power—an ability to offer the kind of coherent understanding of the world which women themselves are never portrayed as capable of. That is not to say that they are not competent, hard working, talented, and capable—in the cases of Hélène of *The Blood of Others* or Françoise of *She Came to Stay*—of brave and determined action, but that they do not possess the same capacities for coherence and the systematization of the social world as the men with whom they are associated.

The temptation, at this point, to shift from a discussion of de Beauvoir's fiction to a discussion of de Beauvoir's relationship with Sartre is very strong. So much of de Beauvoir's fiction is autobiographical that it is difficult not to see the positive relationships between men and women in her fiction as fictional portrayals of her own life with Sartre. *She Came to Stay* is openly admitted as autobiographical. *The Mandarins* contains endless examples of people and places whom de Beauvoir has described in either *The Prime of Life* or *Force of Circumstance.* It is impossible not to read de Beauvoir for Anne in *The Mandarins,* or Sartre for Robert in the novel. Nevertheless, the temptation to list the similarities between fact and fiction will be resisted, not the least because it is a commonplace of fiction that novelists tend to write about the people and the circumstances they they know best (and generally write badly when they try and write about cultures that are foreign to them—as in the case of de Beauvoir in her *All Men Are Mortal*). What is interesting about the relations between men and women in de Beauvoir's fiction is not, therefore, how far it follows the details of her own experience but how the organization, and fictional portrayal, of reality in her novels can be said to be patriarchal or feminist. The issue, then, is whether she shows male/female relations in ways that are genuinely illuminating and progressive, or merely suggestive of ways in which women might be more like men, and measure more nearly that independent woman who dominates the conclusion of *The Second Sex.*

The case for the patriarchal nature of de Beauvoir's novels is that they show women as more fulfilled, and only able to be free in any significant sense, when they follow closely male patterns of professional commitment. Further it has to be said that although de Beauvoir is very accurate in her portrayal of female weaknesses—their dependence and deviousness in particular—she is less than equally critical in her portrayal of men. She does not condemn Pierre for his infatuation with Xavière in *She Came to Stay,* nor is it suggested that this man who was held up as a model of moral strength and integrity must have been less than perfectly perceived and understood if he is now capable of a consuming passion for someone as transparently anxious to test her powers of sexual attraction as Xavière. Nor is Robert condemned for the emotional distance and detachment that almost drive Anne into Lewis's arms: if she perceives her life as emotionally sterile and less than happy, it does not seem implausible that she might question Robert's relationship to her rather than seeking another man, and eventually causing both him and herself a good deal of pain. But Robert's preoccupation is never questioned, and here is to be found an instance of an unthinking acceptance of patriarchal ideology: that it is perfectly legitimate, even admirable, for men to be so much concerned with their careers, or political ambitions, or whatever else, that they have no time for emotional life. Indeed, part of Anne's admiration for Robert is that he is committed and preoccupied—yet she does not connect this preoccupation with the lack of satisfaction of her own needs or her joy in meeting Lewis. Nor is any connection ever made in the novel between Nadine's delinquency and her petty and selfish seeking for attention, and the professional commitments of her parents. It is a commonplace of anti-feminism that women are always blamed for the failures and failings of their children, but

at no point does de Beauvoir ever examine this or suggest that Nadine's desire for male attention and confirmation might have some roots both in the distance between her and her father, and in the model offered to her by her mother of the 'successful' woman, a person indistinguishable, in certain crucial respects, from the successful professional male. Neither parent in the Dubreuilh household can have offered a great deal in terms of emotional engagement, identification, or warmth.

So apparently 'good' men in de Beauvoir's fiction are men who are emotionally distant from their children, or capable of infatuation that harms others, or too self-absorbed to question the commitment of others to them—as is the case of Henri in *The Mandarins.* What this illustrates is the long-standing dichotomy which the west has made between public men and private women—if men are to be assessed as 'good' then this is done largely in terms of their public lives. There has always been an excellent case for keeping the long arm of the state and public morality away from the private lives of citizens, yet feminism has raised, as much now as in its earlier days, the question of how morality, or moral standing, is to be assessed. Clearly, de Beauvoir might well regard Robert as a 'good' man, yet a contemporary feminist might say that no man, whatever his political and public virtues, could be regarded as 'good' while he was so neglectful of the emotional needs of his wife and daughter. Thus again we find that de Beauvoir reflects male standards and assumptions in her assessment of what constitutes virtue. Pierre and Robert emerge as morally acceptable even if the former has, through his infidelity, caused immense suffering, and the latter has been guilty, if not of sins of commission, then at least of sins of omission. Care for others (in a more than cerebral sense) and a personal commitment not to an abstract ideal of 'freedom' but to another person, whose feelings affect one's actions, are not always features of the 'good' men of de Beauvoir's world.

That the moral worlds and moral standards of men and women are not the same has now become a common observation of contemporary feminism. The importance of a man's behaviour in his private world has become widely accepted, and although none of the men in de Beauvoir's fiction ranks as an out-and-out villain, some of them do not meet the exacting, or different, standards that feminism has now introduced into our understanding of morality. It is arguable that the stress which feminism lays on private behaviour (often summed up in the slogan 'the personal is political') sometimes entails the danger that public questions may be overlooked: a stress on individual behaviour at the cost of the consideration of the actions of the collectivity. But this is not a charge that could be levelled against de Beauvoir: whatever the shortcomings, or determinants, of her view of morality—either in the real world or as portrayed in her novels—she has often acted with courage and determination in stating her political convictions. . . . In real life, therefore, she has been an example of the way in which women are as capable as men of moral and political conviction. That example is, perhaps, her most lasting contribution to feminism. . . .(pp. 76-98)

Mary Evans, in her Simone de Beauvoir: A Feminist Mandarin, *Tavistock, 1985, 142 p.*

Dorothy Kaufmann

For partisans and adversaries alike, Simone de Beauvoir's statement in *The Second Sex* that "One is not born, but rather becomes, a woman" has become the most familiar formulation of her position on sexual difference. It clearly defines her view of woman's Otherness as fabricated, imposed by culture rather than biology. If any doubts are possible about the pejorative implications of woman's difference for Simone de Beauvoir, they are immediately dispelled in the sentence that follows: "No biological, psychological or economic fate determines the figure that the human female presents in society; it is civilization as a whole that produces this creature, intermediate between male and eunuch, which is described as feminine." Both "the feminine" and "woman," as she uses the terms here, are cultural signs for the male-created product she calls the second sex.

Simone de Beauvoir's feminism, which views sexual difference as necessarily a source of oppression, has been most seriously called into question by the theoretical writings that emerged with the French women's movement in the 1970s. For writers otherwise as diverse as Hélène Cixous and Luce Irigaray, it is precisely woman's difference, repressed by the phallocentric discourse of the Western humanist tradition, that is the source of her potential liberation. Although, so far as I know, there is no explicit reference to Beauvoir in the work of either Cixous or Irigaray, their theories of feminine specificity mark a complete break with the philosophical and cultural assumptions of Simone de Beauvoir's feminism. Against the existentialist humanism that informs her work, the starting point for Cixous and Irigaray is the post-structuralist theoretical model that foregrounds language and deconstructs the notion of a coherent self. Lacan's psychoanalytic discourse defines the terms of their revolt even as their work seeks to subvert the Lacanian symbolic Father. Denouncing the rule of the phallus as privileged signifier, their writing attempts to celebrate and bring into being another signifier, that they call feminine difference.

In the work of both Irigaray and Cixous there is a constant slippage in the meaning of feminine difference, from an affirmation of biological woman to woman as a metaphor for the unconscious of culture, everything that has been left out of the masculine libidinal economy. In relation to that ambiguous "woman," sometimes body and sometimes archaic signifier, Simone de Beauvoir's feminism inhabits another language and an earlier, more confident relation between words and things. Her focus is on referential women as they exist in the social order. In contrast to contemporary French discourse, there is still for her the assumption of a world outside the text; she can talk about reality and lived experience without quotation marks.

Despite that gap, Luce Irigaray has chosen to ally herself, however ambivalently, with the struggle that calls itself feminist. Indirectly alluding to Simone de Beauvoir's model of feminism, Irigaray writes: "Women must, of course, continue to struggle for equality of salaries, social rights, against discrimination in employment, studies, etc. But that is not enough: women simply equal to men would be like them and therefore not women. Once more, the difference of the sexes would thus be annulled, unrecognized, covered up." For Irigaray, then, the ideology of equality is necessary but insufficient. Her relative acceptance of Simone de Beauvoir's positive role is indicated by the fact that she contributed an essay to *Les Temps Modernes,* the journal founded by Sartre and Beauvoir. Hélène Cixous, on the other hand, defines her position as against rather than beyond feminism, declaring categorically "I am not a feminist." As Cixous sees it, feminism is nothing more than a demand for power from the patriarchy and thus a cooptation of women by the system.

The most virulent attack against Simone de Beauvoir from an ideology of difference appears in *des femmes hebdo,* the journal of the group originally called "Psychanalyse et Politique," which was closely associated with Hélène Cixous between 1975 and 1982. In their report of the twenty-fifth anniversary colloquium on *The Second Sex* held in New York in 1979, they feature its author as no less than the Big Bad Wolf. The article headlines this exchange with a gullibly feminist Little Red Riding Hood: "O grandmother, what fine concepts you have!" "The better to retard you with, my child!" *Des femmes* mocks what it calls the "ambitious sons" of Simone de Beauvoir's phallic feminism, proclaims the nonexistence of feminist thought and asserts that the obvious source of women's oppression is not difference but the denial and scorn of difference.

A more suggestive context in which to consider Simone de Beauvoir's devalorization of feminine difference is provided by Julia Kristeva's 1981 essay on "Women's Time," in which she speaks of two generations of European feminist movements and looks to the possible forming of a third generation. Her use of the word "generation" implies not so much a chronology as a "signifying space," in which different generations can be parallel or interwoven. Existential feminists, in Kristeva's account, belong to the first generation beginnings, when women were aspiring to gain a place in social institutions on an equal footing with men. Part of the logic of that insertion into history, as Kristeva sees it, was the necessity of rejecting attitudes traditionally considered feminine or maternal when they proved incompatible with political struggles. Kristeva's second generation links younger women who came to feminism after 1968 to women whose aesthetic or psychoanalytic experience led to what she calls an "exacerbated distrust of the entire political dimension."

The attack against Simone de Beauvoir's devalorization of the feminine—characterized by "Psych et Po" and many others as misogyny—has tended to ignore the historical context in which *The Second Sex* was conceived. When she began to write her pioneering work in 1947, France was still emerging from the trauma of Occupation and the Vichy regime. It was only in 1944 that French women obtained the right to vote, legislated in part in reaction to the misogynist policies of Vichy and in recognition of women's active participation in the Resistance. However, male rejection of Vichy propaganda did not go so far as to consider women's right to control their bodies. In 1949, the publication date of *The Second Sex,* not only abortion but even the sale of contraceptives was still strictly illegal, going back to a law that was put in place in 1920 as part of France's natalist policies after the devastating losses of men in World War I. In spite of these policies, the birth-rate in France continued to remain low, almost equaled by the rate of illegal abortions. After the defeat of 1940, a favorite refrain of Vichy was that the French lost the war because they didn't have children, that the Germans were making cannons and babies while the French were just having a good time. After the war, pronatalist policies, in the form of subsidies to families, were continued by governments of both the right and the left. It was not until 1967 that the sale of contraceptives was made legal, but under such restricted conditions that in the early seventies, only seven percent of French women were using them. In 1974 the law forbidding abortions was repealed, due primarily to the militant activism of feminists—including Simone de Beauvoir who played a prominent role.

It has been noted, often with a sense of scandal, that Simone de Beauvoir begins her chapter "The Mother" in *The Second Sex* with a passionate polemic against the conditions under which women must undergo abortion in those countries where it is illegal. She points out that in France, at the time of her book, abortions were averaging about one million per year. That statistic achieves its full impact when we realize that in the United States, with a vastly larger population than France, the estimated number of abortions performed annually was about two-thirds of a million.

Simone de Beauvoir's consistent hostility to the biological as well as the cultural conditions of maternity is unmistakable. In *The Second Sex* she evokes the "quivering jelly which is elaborated in the womb (the womb, secret and sealed like the tomb)" and compares it to the "soft viscosity of carrion." The pregnant woman is described as "ensnared by nature," "a stockpile of colloids," "plant and animal." One aspect of her hostility to biological femininity, which I have discussed elsewhere, is her adoption of Sartrean existentialism and its rejection of the natural as antivalue. Another crucial factor in this hostility is her sensitivity to the personal trauma of an unwanted pregnancy when abortion is not a legal option. In 1971 Simone de Beauvoir signed and collected signatures for the Manifesto of 343 writers and celebrities who declared that they were among those million French women each year forced to have recourse to dangerous and illegal abortions. At the controversial Bobigny abortion trial in 1973, she chose to incriminate herself further. Asked if she herself had aborted, she replied "Yes, a long time ago. What I have been doing for a long time and frequently since then is to help women who come to ask me how to abort. I give or lend them money and I give them addresses. Sometimes I even lend them my home so that the intervention can take place in good conditions." [The critic adds in a footnote: "As Marie-Claire Pasquier has pointed out to me, Simone de Beauvoir's statements do not necessarily indicate that she has had an abortion. They are intended as political expressions of solidarity, comparable to the May '68 slogan 'We are all German Jews'."] When I asked her in 1982 about the gains of feminism during the seventies, her first response was to point to contraception and abortion, which she clearly sees as crucially important victories: "These are profound changes which completely alter women's lives." In answer to my question about the certainty of those gains should a right-wing government replace the Socialists, she compared the status of the right to abortion with the forty-hour work week (now thirty-nine hours) and the right to paid vacations, gains acquired in 1936 that have never been called into doubt since then, whatever the government in power.

Simone de Beauvoir's personal history illuminates her political priorities and her cultural assumptions. Growing up as a dutiful daughter in the early part of the century, her childhood relation to her parents was in keeping with the traditional expectations and family structure of the time. Her mother took care of her moral welfare and day-to-day needs, while her father was the authority figure who embodied the Law and worldly knowledge. Françoise de Beauvoir, as evoked by her daughter, was a pious woman who lived her married life in accordance with the accepted middle class codes of propriety and devotion. Completely dependent on her husband, she resigned herself to his numerous trivial affairs as part of the inevitable double standard of marriage. She accepted without question her prescribed duties as wife and mother, renouncing any self-expression outside those roles. Simone de Beauvoir describes her mother's growing resentment as she becomes aware of Simone's loss of religious faith and her beginning assertions of independence. She draws the portrait of her mother as a woman turned stranger to herself in the name of religious and moral principles of devotion. Françoise de Beauvoir becomes for her daughter a warning, the image of what she wants her own life not to be. The maternal, even as metaphor, will always look to Beauvoir like a trap, in which women lose their autonomy and their happiness.

In the recent film script about her life, Simone de Beauvoir is asked about her relationship with Sylvie Le Bon, a woman in her forties who has been her closest companion for the past several years. It is suggested that their friendship could be considered a kind of mother-daughter ersatz. Simone categorically denies such a bond: "Absolutely not," is her response. "We have a much better relationship than what generally exists between mothers and daughters. . . . I have always been for chosen relationships as against those that are imposed." Her response does not even consider any positive interpretation of the maternal metaphor, only the aspect of compulsion.

Simone de Beauvoir's fear of maternal engulfment is such that her early impulse of identification with her mother, the "petite maman chérie" of her early childhood, is buried in her adult life. She releases those feelings only in a few unguarded spaces of *A Very Easy Death,* the most moving of her autobiographical writings. As her mother is dying of cancer, she suddenly falls into a spell of uncontrollable sobbing and describes her "stupefaction" at feeling such overwhelming grief: "When my father died, I didn't shed a tear. I had said to my sister, 'It will be the same for mother.' Up to that night, I had understood all my sorrows. Even when they submerged me, I recognized myself in them. This time, my despair escaped from my control: someone other than myself was weeping inside me." It is her surprise more than her despair that is revealing. At the end of the book she makes one of her rare allusions to dreams: "In my sleep," she writes, "where my father appeared very seldom and in an insignificant way, [my mother] often played the essential role: she became confused with Sartre, and we were happy together." The dream then turns into a nightmare as she panics that she will again be taken over by her mother, as she was in childhood. The impulse toward maternal identification, with her mother and Sartre fused into one, is not explored further. Simone de Beauvoir's repression of the feminine, perhaps the deepest limitation of her writing, produces the kind of rationalist framing of her thought, the ordering of painful and ambiguous experience into neat and manageable categories, that theoreticians of difference now characterize as masculine.

The celebration of feminine difference in the name of women's liberation seemed to explode all at once in France in the mid-1970s. Cixous's "Rire de la Méduse" and *La Jeune née,* Leclerc's *Parole de femme,* Herrmann's *Les Voleuses de langue,* Kristeva's *Révolution du langage poétique,* and Irigaray's *Speculum de l'autre femme* and *Ce sexe qui n'en est pas un* were all published between 1974 and 1977. Whether the feminine is understood in these writings as the unconscious, or the maternal body, or as a metaphor for the silences in Western discourse, the impulse is to give birth to that feminine difference. It is not by chance that these celebrations found expression in the midseventies when in the political domain, women were achieving control over their bodies for the first time in history. To experience the feminine as liberation, a necessary condition is to have the possibility to live one's sexuality freely and, if heterosexual, to be able to separate sexual expression from reproduction. The maternal metaphor can only be privileged as liberating if the social world permits the actual experience of maternity as choice and desire.

It has not yet been demonstrated that the textual inscription of woman's imaginary can have a revolutionary effect on the real, as the theoreticians of difference proclaim. What is already clear, however, is that the real changes in women's situation in the past decade have altered women's imaginary. To the extent that any woman can be singled out as inspiring those changes in women's situation, Simone de Beauvoir should be there first. *The Second Sex* is where contemporary feminism begins. Its totalizing theory, however problematic, allowed for translation into a political praxis to which it gave philosophical support. Since the publication of *The Second Sex,* she has been actively involved in all the major political struggles against women's oppression, in France and elsewhere. It is ironic that she should now be dismissed by so many as not really a feminist, or even as a misogynist. Such accusations willfully confuse her distrust of the feminine with hostility to women, ignoring her efforts on behalf of women throughout her writing career, from the campaign to legalize family planning in France in the late fifties to her preface in 1982 for a book that protests the still widespread practice of genital mutilation in many Third World countries.

Simone de Beauvoir's identification with the world of women in struggles we usually call political emerged clearly and unexpectedly in my interview with her in June 1982. I asked her why, in our previous conversation, she seemed to disregard her commitment to feminism, insisting that she had never been very involved in politics. Feminism, she replied, is different:

> It's politics, but it's the kind of politics that touches me deeply. Perhaps, in spite of everything. I've shared the reticence of many women in regard to politics because politics is a man's world. I've never formulated it to myself in these terms but if I try to understand why I've had little interest in politician politics ("la politique politicienne"), it's perhaps because it's a world of men. Feminism is a world of women. It's the cause of women and that interests me passionately. I was loath to enter the politician world of men, whereas a feminist world of women's revolt—although I myself haven't had occasion in my adult life to rebel—that I understand with my heart, I'm completely in agreement and I can become wholeheartedly involved.

In the *Memoirs,* Simone de Beauvoir expresses on a personal level this sentiment of preference for women's values, noting that in many respects she set her women friends above her men friends, "for they seemed to me more sensitive, more generous, more endowed with imagination, tears, and love"—an indirect tribute to the "feminine" qualities her ideology does not allow her to acknowledge directly.

In the past decade, changing social conditions have produced new theories of discourse and new theories of the feminine that are not dreamed of in Simone de Beauvoir's philosophy. Her feminism does not take into account the role of language and of the unconscious as forces of oppression and of potential liberation for women. In that respect, as in so many others, she is a product of her generation. She reflects on the individual in society and does not offer the seductions of a feminine text. In antithesis, the work of the new feminine discourse, which has transformed our thinking about texts and the symbolic order, has had little to offer to the referential suffering of women in the social order. Nor has this discourse been able to reconcile the contradictions between the demand for equality and the demand for the recognition of feminine difference.

Simone de Beauvoir's view of feminine difference as a cultural fabrication is consistent from *The Second Sex* to her most recent interviews. It is not easy to find in her writing even the suggestion of any positive effects of that fabrication. One such suggestion does emerge in her "interview" with Sartre on women. Beauvoir asks him whether the status of woman's oppression has not developed in women certain qualities as well as certain faults that differ from those of men. When I asked her for her own response to the question, she enumerated those qualities which she thinks have developed out of woman's situation, what she calls "qualities of heart and of compassion": "Women are often more altruistic; they have more the sense of others; they tend to have a more ironic sense of the human condi-

Beauvoir at work in the Café de Flore, where she routinely wrote during her early career.

tion. These attitudes should be kept, outside a situation of oppression, and communicated to men as well." When I remarked that she rarely addresses these positive differences, she explained that her reticence was a question of "prudence": "If one insists too much on difference, even positive differences, one risks imprisoning woman once again in a feminine nature. And yet if we want to see clearly and look at things in their totality, without either fear or complacency, we have to admit that there are also feminine qualities." Insofar as feminine qualities are positive, they must become universalized as values rather than being used to perpetuate what she calls the "ghetto of difference."

In contrast to what Simone de Beauvoir sees as the regressive dangers of a claim to sexual difference, she presents the claim to equality as a demand having radical implications. The feminist struggle, in her view, is not an effort to become like men and take their place, but a way to change the world as it has been made by men. Women's access to all human potentialities would change the structure of the family, of work, of political and personal relations. "If women really did have complete equality with men," she asserts, "society would be completely overturned." For Simone de Beauvoir, the alternative to sexual difference is not sameness, as her enemies insist, but for women to be "singular and universal at the same time." It is a claim to liberate the plurality and unexplored possibilities of individual difference, independent of sexual definitions. From that perspective, *The Second Sex* has been an acknowledged source for such radical and radically heterogeneous utopian visions as Dorothy Dinnerstein's

The Mermaid and the Minotaur and Monique Wittig's "One is not born a Woman."

French male theory of the past two decades, asserting itself against the ideologies of humanism, the self and representation, has sought, quite successfully, to overthrow the authority of the Father who dominated intellectual France in the 1940s and 1950s: Jean-Paul Sartre and Sartrean existentialism. The daughters seem to be imitating the masculine model as they seek to overthrow the feminist Mother, in the name, paradoxically, of feminine difference. Up to now, there has been no translation of theories of difference into a politics of feminine praxis, with the dubious exception of "Psych et Po." Simone de Beauvoir's feminism, inseparable from the struggle for sexual equality, speaks to philosophic and cultural issues that are far from being resolved. As we move through linguistic and psychoanalytic explorations of Kristeva's "exploded, plural, fluid" feminine produced by the second generation to a third generation of daughters, we would do well to keep alive the connection with our first generation feminist Mother, even as we move beyond her limitations. (pp. 121-31)

Dorothy Kaufmann, "Simone de Beauvoir: Questions of Difference and Generation," in Yale French Studies, *No. 72, 1986, pp. 121-31.*

Michael Walzer

Simone de Beauvoir's intellectual achievement has been obscured by her relationship with Sartre—more accurately, by her own account of that relationship. Writing about the philosophical opinions and political commitments that they shared, she almost always describes herself walking a step or two behind Sartre, sometimes dragging her feet, sometimes hurrying to catch up. She is, for a socialist and a feminist, rather excessively concerned to prove his primacy, as if she is worried that unless the matter is settled, their partnership won't endure. Contemporary feminists, recognizing the anxiety, have been critical of de Beauvoir for expressing it so naively (and critical of Sartre, sometimes, who must have done something to require the expression). A few feminist writers have argued for the originality of her philosophical work, but these arguments always seem to stretch the point; she was at best a Sartrean revisionist, working within his categories even when she resisted his conclusions. And in politics, from the very beginning of their commitment, when he decided for the two of them that commitment was morally necessary, she was a follower: "A radical change had taken place in him," she wrote [in *The Prime of Life*] of Sartre on leave from the French army in 1940, "and in me too since I rallied to his point of view immediately."

As a social critic, however, de Beauvoir undoubtedly comes first. There is nothing in Sartre's wide-ranging work that equals *The Second Sex* or even de Beauvoir's later, and much inferior, *Old Age.* All his life, Sartre was a savage critic of bourgeois society, but what he had to say about the bourgeoisie could have been said by a hundred others, and probably was. De Beauvoir's criticism is more original and at the same time more attentive to her own and other people's actual experience. Her anger is less ideological than Sartre's and more firmly and interestingly focused. And for all his influence, the first of her critical books, *The Second Sex,* has touched more lives and started more arguments than anything he ever wrote.

De Beauvoir's importance has a lot to do with the groups for which she chose to speak: groups not yet mobilized, not represented by organized parties or movements, without militants of their own, without a political "line." When, by contrast, she writes about the French working class or about Algerian nationalists (or about Cubans or Vietnamese or Chinese communists), she seems content to follow Sartre and defer not exactly to the people she was writing about but to their militants and political leaders. She writes with conviction, even passion, but with little intellectual engagement, hence without subtlety. She sounds shrill, fitting herself too easily into a bad stereotype. Her books about women and the elderly, however, are quite different. They are entirely her own—in part because she is herself one of the people she is writing about (she was sixty-two in 1970 when *Old Age* appeared in France), even if she is distanced from the fate of the others; in part because she isn't led to acquiesce, guiltily, in their politics. They have no explicit politics; they are "inert." De Beauvoir was a feminist before there was a significant feminist movement in France, and she was one of the first to recognize elderly men and women as victims of a society fixated on youth, power, and efficiency. She doesn't make the unconditional commitment recommended by Sartre to either of these groups; she doesn't have to do that since she is already a member, and she can't do it since there are no organizations or militants to define the conditions for her. She is set free for creativity by another fact: gender and age are not Marxist categories. From some point in the 1940s or early 1950s, she and Sartre were in principle committed to Marxism as the only adequate framework for social criticism. In *Old Age,* she tries to adapt herself to Marxist doctrine, as Sartre does also in most of his major works after *Being and Nothingness.* But she finds herself compelled to write against the Marxist grain, liberated by her subjects, despite their subjection. Presumably, the oppression of women and the cruel neglect of the elderly will be brought to an end by the triumph of the proletariat: de Beauvoir sometimes repeats this dogma. If she really believed it, however, she would have written a book about the proletariat. Instead, she looked more freshly at the world around her and made a different choice.

Her choice of women as a subject derives, she tells us, from her choice of herself, that is, from her decision to write an autobiographical account of her childhood and youth. But I suspect that the choice also has a philosophical source in her uneasiness with Sartre's conception of freedom. She meant to describe herself in her autobiography as a free human being, but she sensed that her freedom had been won in a different way than Sartre's. It was won, so to speak, against all the odds, despite her female body and the situation of women in her society. She did not share her freedom with other women but with men, and while she relished the sharing, she also understood its problems. So her book is a critique of the unfreedom of women, an unfreedom undreamt of in Sartre's philosophy.

But the freedom she defends is the freedom she achieved side by side with him. She assumes that other women should be free, and should want to be free, in just this way. The force of her analysis, but also its difficulties, derive from this crucial assumption, which is at once a sign of generosity and of arrogance. These two qualities made her critique possible at the time she wrote it, in the absence of a feminist movement. They also guaranteed that once there was a movement, the terms of that critique would be called into question. It is said now that she wrote from a male perspective and at too great a distance from the experience of women. That may well be true, but what she wrote reflected her own experience as a woman. Had it not done that, her book would never have had the impact it did on other women; nor would it serve today as the necessary theoretical counterpoint for a different feminism.

Existentialist ethics is rooted in a peculiarly essentialist claim: that man is by nature free, radically, absolutely, universally free. His life is his project; he makes himself, and he is fully responsible for how he turns out. Any effort to blame anyone else, any reference to external determinations, is an act of bad faith. Planning our future lives, we justify our present selves—and leave ourselves, now and forever, without excuses. "There is no justification for present existence," writes de Beauvoir, faithful here to Sartrean doctrine, "other than its expansion into an indefinitely open future." But is woman's existence justified in the same way? Is the existentialist understanding of our essential humanity gender-neutral? With regard to these questions, *The Second Sex* constitutes, it seems to me, a sustained and brilliant equivocation. On the one hand, de Beauvoir believes that women, herself the prime example, are free exactly as men are, responsible for their own fate; and if most of them are in fact unfree, passive, subordinate, then they are responsible for *that,* complicitous in their own subordination. On the other hand, she believes that women, herself excluded, are doubly oppressed, by nature and by man, victims of their biological condition and their social situation. "I have escaped many of the things that enslave a woman," she told an interviewer in the 1970s, "such as motherhood and the duties of a housewife" [Alice Schwarzer, *After "The Second Sex": Conversations with Simone de Beauvoir*]. Her book, though, is an analysis of the enslavement, not the escape—a grim analysis that piles cause on cause until woman's fate seems overdetermined. But isn't the plea of overdetermination one more act of bad faith?

In her opening chapter, "Destiny: The Data of Biology," de Beauvoir comes very close to the claim that woman is not free, hence not complicitous, not capable of bad faith. She simply is what she is; she never consciously chooses what she will be. Understood as a physical body, a generic sexual being, woman represents the existentialist *en-soi,* being-in-itself, rather than the *pour-soi,* being-for-itself. These are dangerous terms; they suggest the problems of existentialist philosophy as a language of social criticism. For the existentialists seem constitutionally (I mean, because of their doctrine, not because of their bodies) incapable of recognizing the experience of oppression: the literal *pressing down* of a person who, despite the pressure, is still a being-for-herself. Applied socially, the idea of the *en-soi* serves only to replicate the conventional masculine view of gender difference. Or worse, it provides a metaphysical ratification of that view. But de Beauvoir is not concerned to deny the conventions; she wants to explain them and then to find some way to alter the conditions that give rise to them. The first of these conditions, however, is biological. A hard truth, according to de Beauvoir, but one that she will not avoid: the "enslavement" of women has biological foundations. She equivocates on the force of those foundations, not on their reality. Indeed, some of her most vivid prose is devoted to what can best be described as a denunciation of the female body.

Man's body always provides the exemplary contrast. He seems shaped for purposeful activity: "He is . . . larger than the female, stronger, swifter, more adventurous." He is "a being of transcendence and ambition." His body opens for him the opportunity "to take control of the instant and mold the future. It is male activity that in creating values has made of existence itself a value." Woman's body, on the other hand, is shaped for immanence, not transcendence, for repetition rather than invention and adventure. She is designed in the interest of the species, not the individual. She doesn't construct a project; she serves a purpose. "From puberty to menopause woman is the theater of a play that unfolds within her and in which she is not personally concerned." De Beauvoir's portrayal of human reproduction is extraordinary in its savagery—for reproduction on her accounting is cost-free to the male, deadly for the female. "First violated, the female is then alienated . . . tenanted by another, who battens upon her substance." While men contend against nature and one another, "seeking always to exercise . . . sovereignty in objective fashion," women merely reproduce the agents (and the victims) of this exercise: "Giving birth and suckling are not *activities,* they are natural functions; no project is involved, and that is why woman found in them no reason for a lofty affirmation of her existence—she submitted passively to her biologic fate . . . imprisoned in repetition and immanence."

Having said all this, there doesn't seem much point in saying anything more. The detailed ethnography of women's lives, which takes up most of the second half of the book, can be read as a mere extension and elaboration of the biological argument—a passage, as it were, from physical to social anthropology, where the first explains all but the surface variations of the second. De Beauvoir's description of housework, for example, directly parallels her description of childbirth and suckling: "Few tasks are more like the torture of Sisyphus than housework, with its endless repetition; the clean becomes soiled, the soiled is made clean, over and over, day after day. The housewife . . . makes nothing, simply perpetuates the present. She never senses [the] conquest of a positive Good." Of course, women are not biologically designed for housework in the same way as they are designed for childbirth. But pregnancy and lactation confine them to the house, which then becomes their social "domain" or, more realistically, their prison (and remains so however much they commit themselves to its interior decoration). The argument has a marked deterministic tone, but de Beauvoir is nevertheless set against determinism. Even in the chapter on biology,

she insists that woman "has the power to choose between the assertion of her transcendence and her alienation as an object." What transcendence requires is the rejection of woman's life in the service of the species; she must live for herself.

De Beauvoir believes that she can't criticize her society unless she repudiates her body. More exactly, she cannot criticize the social construction of gender unless she can find a way to escape the biological determinations that underlie it. It is men, mostly, who create and enforce gender roles, but this is not creation *ex nihilo;* it begins from the fact of woman's bodily immanence, from her reproductive biology. Listen again to de Beauvoir's voice describing female sexuality and the experience of pregnancy:

> Feminine sex desire is the soft throbbing of a mollusk. Whereas man is impetuous, woman is only impatient; her expectation can become ardent without ceasing to be passive; man dives upon his prey like the eagle and the hawk; woman lies in wait like the carnivorous plant, the bog, in which insects and children are swallowed up. She is absorption, suction, humus, pitch and glue, a passive influx, insinuating and viscous.
>
> . . . . .
>
> Ensnared by nature, the pregnant woman is plant and animal, a stockpile of colloids, an incubator, an egg; she scares children proud of their young, straight bodies and makes young people titter contemptuously because she is a human being, a conscious and free individual, who has become life's passive instrument.

Passages like this have a familiar ring to my ears; they ring with self-dislike. De Beauvoir joins the ranks of the assimilated Jew, Albert Memmi's "colonized" man, the American black before the age of "black is beautiful," whose standards of physical attraction and cultural excellence are borrowed and derivative. She doesn't mean to pass, obviously, else she would never have written a book calling attention to herself as a militant of the second sex. Nor, however, does she want to live like a woman or even to be thought of (by the men with whom she spends most of her time) as a woman. It is, she decides, her own rejection of conventional womanhood, of marriage and mothering, that points the way to female liberation. She chooses her lovers like a man, and she refuses to bear children. The result is a double achievement. She ceases to be a mollusk, a bog, a passive instrument, that is, she escapes biological determination; and then she ceases to be a "woman" as men conceive women—the natural, mysterious, frightening, and enticing Other—and becomes a human individual.

The second achievement is, so to speak, her official program, for herself, for other women, and for any future feminist movement: to replace the social construction of gender with the individual project. It is a quintessentially liberal program, though she would disdain the adjective. It is also a program that somehow misses the extent to which the individual project is itself a social construction. "To take control of the instant and mold the future" (the verbs are important, as much so as in "dives upon his prey") is not what human beings do by nature; it is what men do in the world de Beauvoir inhabits—or better, what men are supposed to do. It is also, according to de Beauvoir, what women want to do. "Woman also aspires to and recognizes the values that are concretely attained by the male. He it is who opens up the future to which she also reaches out." The repetitive "also" captures her meaning. She is not a critic of the world that men have made for themselves but only of the exclusion of women from that world. She demands woman's admission; that is her public message. But there is another message, not exactly concealed but also not quite brought to the fore: that women must qualify for admission. And while man qualifies with his body—"his sexual life is not in opposition to his existence as a person"—woman can only qualify by leaving her body behind.

This is an offensive and deeply dissatisfying message, and since it is offensive and dissatisfying, one has to honor de Beauvoir for delivering it. She does believe, of course, that women (or at least some women) can qualify—as she herself has done—and this must have been what made her book an inspiration to so many of its readers. Home and family, woman's domain and woman's prison, despite their biological foundations, are not escape-proof. And if escape is difficult ("I think there are some women who really don't stand much of a chance"—where "some women" seems to encompass most married women), then it is at least possible to avoid the original lockup. Don't marry and don't have children; or have children only on your own terms, by yourself. Though she is not a technological determinist, de Beauvoir places a great deal of faith in contraception and artificial insemination. The achievements of a universal science will rescue women from their sexual and gendered particularity. Better, some women will rescue themselves, using the achievements of a universal science, and then they will enter the realm of universality.

The concrete expression of woman's freedom is work outside the home. "Protected from the slavery of reproduction, she is in a position to assume the economic role that is offered her and that will assure her of complete independence." It is only outside, in the marketplace and the public forum, that she can avoid immanence and repetition; it is only outside that work becomes an activity and life a project. De Beauvoir doesn't seem to have looked very closely at what economic roles were actually being "offered" to women in the late 1940s. Her conception of work and life outside the home derives in large part from her own experience; it can hardly be emphasized too much that she was living the life she advocated.

She repeatedly describes that life in terms suggesting a metaphysical melodrama: it is the acting out of "the imperialism of the human consciousness, seeking always to exercise its sovereignty in objective fashion." "Each separate conscious being aspires to set himself up alone as sovereign subject." In fact, that is a bit more than the ordinary aspiration of working women. De Beauvoir herself, in her autobiographical volumes, manages to take pride in achievements that fall well short of sovereignty. Her intention is to evoke (once again with the vocabulary of existen-

tialism) a world of struggle: competitive rankings, harsh choices, continual risk, solitary victories. But this has been, and still is mostly, a man's world. One might think it unattractive, but it plainly has its attractions. The ambition of women, according to de Beauvoir, is to share the ambition, the risks, and the victories of men. That means, to earn money, write books, make scientific discoveries, rule nations, and win glory. The great majority of women have been excluded from these activities, and that is the chief injury that men have done to them. It seems entirely possible, however, that this injury can be overcome and nothing else be changed. When women are "completely independent," they will simply be what men are now. De Beauvoir sometimes suggests an alternative (socialist) vision, but her immediate goal is this imitative independence. "The future can only lead to a more and more profound assimilation [of women] into our once masculine society."

De Beauvoir is an assimilated woman, and then a critic of exclusion; she is most powerfully critical when she writes about the obstacles that women like herself encounter on the road that leads from (female) immanence to (male) transcendence. How, then, should we describe the standpoint from which she writes? She herself claims a kind of objectivity—because she has reached the end of the road. One might think, she says, that only an angel, "neither man nor woman," could be objective, but an angel would "be ignorant of all the basic facts involved in the problem." What is necessary is someone who knows "what it means to a human being to be feminine," who has "roots" in the feminine world, but who is at the same time "fortunate in the restoration of all the privileges pertaining to the estate of human being." De Beauvoir is that someone, though she acknowledges that there are other contemporary women who share her good fortune. Having "won the game," they can "afford the luxury of impartiality." It seems to me extraordinary that anyone writing in the 1940s (or before or since, for that matter, though the 1940s was a particularly hard decade) could possibly think that she had won the game and was in full possession of the privileges of humanity. De Beauvoir means to say simply that she is living like a man, sharing what she hardly recognizes as a badly depleted estate.

She writes about the second sex as if she were one of the first. There is nothing secretive or perverse about this identification; it is entirely open and innocent. She makes no special claim for herself; she simply assumes that all liberated women will be like existentialist men (much as she assumes that liberated Algerians will be like French leftists). There is, after all, only one universal life, and it is men—beings of "transcendence and ambition"—who have lived it. If these same men, encountered as individuals, commonly have to be opposed and resisted, their achievements can only be imitated. "The fact is that culture, civilization, and universal values have all been created by men, because men represent universality." Brave words from a feminist writer—especially brave in that the sentence I have just quoted comes from a conversation tape recorded in 1972, when many French feminists were in the process of repudiating just this argument, which they rightly identified with *The Second Sex:* they took it as an acquiescence in secondness. For de Beauvoir this acknowledgment of male universality is the only way to overcome secondness. What modern women want (or should want) is "not that they be exalted in their femininity" but rather "that in themselves, as in humanity in general, transcendence may prevail over immanence." Or, more concretely, the modern woman "accepts masculine values: she prides herself on thinking, taking action, working, creating, on the same terms as men; instead of seeking to disparage them, she declares herself their equal."

The central purpose of de Beauvoir's book is to make this declaration of equality. Nevertheless, her ethnographic account of inequality and immanence is a more powerful and moving achievement. When she is not belaboring the bad faith, she has a keen sense for the pain of women whose hopes and ambitions are first deferred, then repressed, then turned into sentimental fantasy. She writes about these women with a mixture of sympathy and repugnance that very few male students of women's lives could possibly match. The volatility of the mix suggests the intensity of her feelings, though personal reference is severely repressed throughout the account. We can tell from her memoirs how much of her own experience and the experience of her female friends is reflected at least in the early chapters of part 2 of *The Second Sex.* But there is no clue to the reflection in the text itself—except for the obvious fact that this universal ethnography is concerned almost entirely with Western, middle-class women. Her tone throughout is firmly impersonal: these, she reports, are the attitudes and customs of the natives. De Beauvoir deliberately distances herself from her material. Perhaps she has to do that since she is writing about experiences of immanence that she has escaped or that, having escaped early, she has missed entirely. From her new vantage point, the story she has to tell is a story of defeat and of complicity in defeat. "It is said that woman . . . wallows in immanence; but she has first been shut up in it." De Beauvoir describes the method of the shutting up, and then she describes, in great detail, the wallowing.

As with woman's body, so with her situation and her life, the standard of comparison is always that of the generalized male. "If we compare these situations . . . we see clearly that man's is far preferable; that is to say, he has many more opportunities to exercise his freedom in the world." Once again, de Beauvoir reveals the essentially liberal, individualist, and universal politics that her existentialism requires. Equal opportunity for men and women to compete in the world that men have made— that is her feminist platform. But it is only fair to describe it in her own terms. She wants women's lives to "expand," like men's lives, "into an indefinitely open future." Since she expects nothing new from this expansion, however, no new activities, understandings, or evaluations, the openness hardly seems indefinite. In fact, she is not proposing a reiteration of male experience, which might in principle produce genuine novelty, but only, again, an imitation. With regard to the present, the two formulations, equal opportunity and indefinite expansion, make for an identical rejection of woman's condition; and with regard to the future, they make for an identical acceptance of man's.

Since de Beauvoir is philosophically committed to the proposition that "inner liberty is complete in both [men and women]," and at the same time to the proposition that immanence is slavery, any acceptance of the female situation as a situation of value or even potential value would be an act of bad faith—an "abdication" of transcendence. Give women the same "opportunities to exercise their freedom" that men have had, and they will behave exactly as men have done throughout history (de Beauvoir's ethnography is pretty much ahistorical). "When woman is engaged in an enterprise worthy of a human being, she is quite able to show herself as active, efficient, taciturn— and as ascetic—as a man." How does one know what enterprises are worthy of a human being? Worthy enterprises are those in which men have been active, efficient, taciturn, and so on; de Beauvoir attempts no independent evaluation. It is more important to win equal opportunity than to worry about what this opportunity is for. So the indefinitely open future is programmatically empty, or better, it is wholly determined by the male past.

As soon as one recognizes alternatives to transcendence and universality as these have conventionally been understood, that is, understood by men, de Beauvoir's "objectivity" disappears. She writes from a particular perspective, from a time and a place-in-the-world. This is, as her critics commonly say, a male perspective. But one can't stop there: it is a rare man who could have written a book like *The Second Sex;* most men, reading it, are made acutely uncomfortable by its argument. For male comfort has historically required the belief that women are contented with their situation and that they are contented *with reason,* that the lives they lead are right—for them. De Beauvoir doesn't deny the contentment ("wallowing in immanence") of at least some women, but she denies the rightness, and the denial is hard for male readers to resist. Her portrait of female immanence hardly invites imitation: what man would want to live like that? And yet the argument toward which male readers are driven is, after all, not very difficult, at least in principle: let women (if they can) live like us! De Beauvoir holds out the possibility of a masculine feminism, male universality made truly universal.

She may well be right to suggest that this masculine feminism is better expressed by a woman like herself who has adopted male values and "won the game" than by a disabused and alienated man. "In order to change the face of the world," she says in *The Second Sex,* "it is first necessary to be firmly anchored in it." The case is the same with the criticism that precedes change: a woman who has found her anchorage will be a better critic than a man who has lost his—and this even if the woman is trying only to win the game while the man is trying to act justly. For she can more readily recognize "the values . . . concretely attained by the male," which he may feel bound to disparage and renounce. Many contemporary feminists would prefer the disparagement and renunciation of male values, but whatever the justice of their argument, it is an argument that can only be made after de Beauvoir. To disparage values from which one has been excluded is the classic form of *ressentiment:* it is, or it will commonly be experienced as, the politics of sour grapes. Better first to criticize and overcome the exclusion and then to judge the fruits of victory. When we consider the situation of oppressed human beings, our first demand (and theirs too) is simply that they be admitted to the rights shared among their oppressors. These will be called, as in *The Second Sex,* universal or human rights. In fact, they are always a particular set of rights, and admission to their enjoyment, even if everyone in the world were admitted, would not mark the end of political argument and contention. It will turn out that the male representation of universality is false, or at least that it is radically incomplete. But this male universality won't even be tested so long as women are excluded from its attainments. Hence the priority of de Beauvoir's "assimilationist" politics.

But de Beauvoir insists also upon the finality of her politics—for women, if not for humankind generally. Indeed, women could do worse than to imitate male achievements in mathematics, science, literature, and even philosophy (just as Algerians could do worse than to imitate the politics of French leftists). It would be a mistake, however, to insist that these imitative efforts, and only these, can count as liberation. "I do not think," de Beauvoir told an interviewer in the 1970s, "[that] women will create new values. If you believe the opposite, then what you are believing in is a feminine nature—which I have always opposed." But that can't be right. Surely the bourgeoisie, for example, created new values, significantly different from those of the aristocracy, even though there is no such thing as a bourgeois or an aristocratic nature; there are just different social experiences. De Beauvoir argues that women won't create new values because of her beliefs about their experience, not their nature (though she is more ambivalent than she admits here about natural, that is, bodily determinism): first, that the experience of immanence is entirely uncreative; second, that the experience of transcendence is or will be exactly the same for men and women. It follows, then, that there is no feminist politics beyond assimilation.

But both these beliefs are wrong. Social critics "firmly anchored" in the world of women seem more likely to see the mistake than critics already assimilated into the world of men. At least, the criticisms of de Beauvoir that I now want to rehearse come from women working within a feminist movement. These women obviously don't accept as their own the social domain of home and family to which gender makes them heir; if they did, they would never have been moved to create feminism as a political project. But they keep up connections there; they are committed to "the self-understanding of female subjects," even if these subjects, most of them, are wives and mothers who "don't stand much of a chance," as de Beauvoir said, in the struggle for transcendence. It is the conviction of de Beauvoir's critics that woman's life before transcendence is already in its own way transcendent, that women, as they are, are beings-for-themselves. But what does this mean? And why doesn't it constitute an acquiescence in subjection?

One can as easily ask the opposing question: isn't it subjection that has led women, following men, to devalue their own experience? When de Beauvoir writes in *The Second Sex* that, despite "all the respect thrown around it by soci-

ety, the function of gestation still inspires a spontaneous feeling of revulsion," is she expressing a liberated sensibility? Her critics, by contrast, are likely to begin with a more affirmative view of mothering. Sometimes the affirmation has the form of a Beauvoirist revisionism. According to *The Second Sex,* writes Mary O'Brien [in *The Politics of Reproduction*], contemporary contraceptive techniques make only for sexual freedom. Their real importance, however, is to open up "the choice of parenthood, the voluntary acceptance of a real as opposed to a philosophical risking of life." Contraception, O'Brien suggests, makes pregnancy into an existentialist adventure. But she goes on to ask, more sensibly, "if passivity is an accurate description of any form of reproductive consciousness at any time, in any society?" It isn't, and that means that immanence has no social reality. Human reproduction is always different from that of plants and animals because it is always susceptible "to the interpretations of a rational consciousness." A complete ethnography of women's lives would provide us with an account of these interpretations—an account that did not simply assume them to be ideological in character, concealing the grim truth of biological determinism and/or bad faith. Biology determines that only women will bear children, but what women make of the experience, given the many different things they have made of it, cannot be biologically determined.

The most interesting philosophical argument made by (some) contemporary feminists is the argument for pluralism in transcendence. De Beauvoir, as her assimilationist politics suggests, was always a monist. Women have never succeeded, she writes in *The Second Sex,* "in building up a solid counter-universe." Since there is no creative potential in immanence, they never will succeed. And since the universe that men have "built up" is already universal in principle, and women have only to enter it to make it universal in fact, there is no need for success. But what if this counter-universe already exists—not wholly different from the world of men, overlapping with it, but giving social embodiment, or even a variety of different embodiments, to whatever is different in women's experience? De Beauvoir doesn't see the counter-universe because she is writing from too far away, with too great a burden of dislike. She "portrays woman only as victim—maimed, mutilated, dependent," writes Iris Marion Young, "confined to a life of immanence and forced to be an object. She rarely describes the strength that women have had and the earthly value of their work: the ways [they] have formed networks and societies among themselves, the lasting beauty of the caring social values [they] often exhibit" ["Humanism, Gynocentrism, and Feminist Politics," *Hypatia: A Journal of Feminist Philosophy,* 1985].

I have called this critical view of de Beauvoir pluralistic because it suggests the existence of different, though equally "transcendent," moralities. But when contemporary feminists go on to claim that "masculine values exalt death, violence, competition, selfishness, a repression of . . . sexuality and affectivity," they don't seem very securely committed to pluralism. Then it is necessary to insist that while some men may have values of that sort, others don't. Nor do all women display or even recognize the "lasting beauty" of nurturance and cooperation, "the caring social values." A pluralism of two, the first ranked negatively, the second positively, is no different from an antipluralism of one. It is possible, however, to acknowledge differences without ranking them, and differences there seem to be: expressed not so much in two distinct sets of values as in a range of ethical sensibilities and orientations, with men and women distributed unevenly across the range. And then women's oppression "consists not in being prevented from participating in full humanity, but in the denial and devaluation of specifically feminine virtues and activities." On this view, the very idea of a universal humanity is itself oppressive insofar as it holds subordinate groups to standards they have had no hand in shaping. "Only an explicit affirmation of difference and social plurality . . . offers the hope of overcoming sexism."

De Beauvoir cannot provide an affirmation of that sort. But she was brought to make concessions to the idea of difference in the 1970s; they take a characteristic form that is worth looking at closely. Certain "male failings," she told Alice Schwarzer in 1976, are absent in women:

> For example, that grotesque masculine way of taking themselves seriously, their vanity, their self-importance. . . . And then the habit of putting down all the competition—generally women don't do that. And patience—which can be a virtue up to a certain point, though after that it becomes a weakness—is also a female characteristic. And a sense of irony. And a straightforward manner, since women have their feet on the ground because of the role they play in daily life. These "feminine" qualities are a product of our oppression, but they ought to be retained after our liberation. And men would have to learn to acquire them.

It is interesting that de Beauvoir's list omits the "caring values." A number of feminist writers, rather in her spirit, have criticized her for falling into the conventional female role of caring for Sartre, especially in his last years. Kate Soper makes the right response to this criticism: "It is a *human* convention—or should be—to minister to a dying lifelong lover or companion. Any feminism that would sacrifice such a practice to its ideological purity would seem to hold out little promise of bliss to either sex" ["The Qualities of Simone de Beauvoir," *New Left Review,* 1986]. But if the sacrifice is to be resisted, it is probably important to acknowledge, even to take pride in, the fact that this *human* convention has been sustained largely by women. For the rest, de Beauvoir's list is attractive enough. Her last sentence makes it clear, however, that she doesn't intend to affirm a pluralist position. It's as if she regards morality as a kind of United Fund to which liberated women will make a (somewhat marginal) contribution. And then men "would have to" accept the contribution—else the fund would cease to be united. This is still the assimilationist view, even if women are no longer seen as empty-handed petitioners. Given this view, de Beauvoir is right: after liberation, when men and women live identical lives, seize the same opportunities, expand into the same indefinite future, neither sex will be more patient, ironic, or straightforward than the other. All such qualities will be valued generally and distributed randomly.

But is it possible, after liberation, that men and women will live different lives? Is liberation compatible with difference, that is, with nonrandom distributions? There seems no necessary incompatibility so long as the distributions arise within more or less freely chosen or cooperatively shaped ways of life. Hence, again, the priority of de Beauvoir's argument for equal opportunity in politics, business, science, and literature—the career open to talents extended, finally, to women; the triumph at last of the French Revolution. Any defense of difference that obscures this priority is dangerous indeed: "a return to the enslavement of women," says de Beauvoir in a 1982 interview, "pure and simple!" She has no patience with "femininity," whether it is described in the old language of passive acquiescence or in the new language of active creation. And she despises any feminism that rejects the politics, business, science, and literature that men have made in the name of alternatives that have never yet been tested. This is to reject too much, since "this male world . . . is, quite simply, the world itself." Some women, she goes on, "won't do anything the man's way: whether it be organization, career, creative work or concrete action. I've always thought that one should simply borrow and make use of the systems men have at their disposal." Borrowing is sensible enough, so long as one doesn't just stop there, as de Beauvoir seems content to do. She still draws her conclusions from the ethnography of immanence she wrote in 1948, when she was already what she hoped all women would become, a transcendent being—which is to say, manlike—studying the benighted natives. The natives cannot do anything more than imitate the culture and technology of more advanced people.

Is de Beauvoir really manlike? Is her politics merely borrowed? It is hard to imagine a male social critic taking as the central subjects of his criticism women and the elderly. There is in de Beauvoir's work a quality of nonideological compassion (entirely missing, for example, in Sartre's) which must have something to do with her gender. I don't mean with her female essence; I don't want to defend the claims that de Beauvoir so tellingly mocks: that "woman has a particular closeness with the earth, that she feels the rhythm of the moon, the ebb and flow of the tides . . . that she has more soul, or is less destructive by nature, etc." Still, there is a story one can tell about the experience of women that explains de Beauvoir's intellectual choices better than the story she tells, focused on the imitation of men. Her imitation, indeed, provides her with critical standards. She attacks the male world from the inside, exploiting its "universal" values. But she is also a critic of women, from the outside. And here her criticism needs to be supplemented by critics differently positioned, who explicitly defend different values, who speak "in a different voice"—a voice that is just barely audible, though always repressed, in her own best work. (pp. 153-69)

Michael Walzer, "Simone de Beauvoir and the Assimilated Woman," in his The Company of Critics: Social Criticism and Political Commitment in the Twentieth Century, *Basic Books, Inc., Publishers, 1988, pp. 153-69.*

Beauvoir on feminism:

I think that when women really begin to consider liberating themselves seriously, they will take more of an interest in politics. And since liberation is a democratic concept, they will become more democratic and thus more radical. Men must be made to understand that, in the final analysis, feminist behavior is not gratuitous but serious. Feminists are not useless and silly hysterics. They have studied and thought, and they want to make changes that will benefit all of society. Throughout the world, women are still being sold, beaten, raped, and killed, so this is a struggle that must be in the minds of all women and be the basis of all feminist behaviour. We can no longer tolerate anti-feminist behaviour, from other women or from men.

Simone de Beauvoir, in 1984 Britannica Book of the Year, *Encyclopedia Britannica, 1984.*

Elizabeth Fallaize

The Mandarins, the novel for which Beauvoir was awarded the 1954 Goncourt Prize, was also Beauvoir's own personal favourite. The longest and perhaps the richest and most complex of her novels, it was the fruit of her experience and reflections in the postwar period on a number of fronts. Politically, her interest in the broad consequences of her discovery of the individual's historicity, the dominating subject of **All Men Are Mortal,** gave way, in the postwar period, to a concern with the role of the intellectual in politics, with the problem of co-operation with the French Communist Party and the problem of the interrelation between morality and political action. The late 1940s and early 1950s were rich with issues which act in the novel as a focus for this reflection—the dropping of the first nuclear bomb, the Cold War, the emergence in the West of details of the Soviet labour camps, the issue of the *épuration* (the 'purge' or meting out of justice to those who had collaborated with the Germans during the war).

But Beauvoir's thinking had also undergone a quite different kind of transformation and radicalisation in between the writing of **All Men Are Mortal** and **The Mandarins;** in between the two she had written—and discovered—**The Second Sex.** Sexual politics, hitherto virtually invisible to Beauvoir, opened up a new way of looking at the world. In **Force of Circumstance** Beauvoir describes how she began to

look at women with new eyes and found surprise after surprise lying in wait for me. It is both strange and stimulating to discover suddenly, at forty, an aspect of the world that has been staring you in the face all the time which somehow you have never noticed.

Gender role construction, the question of the ways in which men and women can construct relationships with each other, the problems of the mother-child relationship—all these issues which had already figured in Beauvoir's fiction reappear in **The Mandarins** in a more consciously organised way.

As in the **The Blood of Others** (1945), the problems which the characters encounter in the construction of different types of heterosexual couples are posed in parallel to the characters' problems of political commitment. Both political and sexual choice come to be governed by the notion of 'preference', the key value around which the text is organised, and the enunciation of which is entrusted to the novel's sage figure, Robert Dubreuilh. 'Commitment is nothing other than a choice, love is nothing other than a preference. If you wait until you meet absolute perfection before committing yourself, you'll never love anyone and never achieve anything', he claims. In the climate of black-and-white choices produced and thematised by the Cold War, Dubreuilh's conviction eventually prevails, if only precariously: politically, he and Henri decide to swallow their doubts and moral preoccupations in favour of action in tandem with the Communists, whilst on the interpersonal level first Henri and then Anne abandon romance and sexuality with politically or geographically remote partners, in favour of a 'preferred' companion.

The notion of 'preference' is underpinned by—and develops out of—the basic structure of repetition, already employed in **The Blood of Others** and **All Men Are Mortal.** In both their personal and political lives the characters have, or take on, commitments which are abandoned or thrown into question in the course of the novel, only to be eventually 'preferred' despite all their drawbacks and difficulties. This structure of meaning becomes insistent in **The Mandarins,** and is underlined both at the level of the characters' discourse, and in the author's exegesis of the novel in **Force of Circumstance:**

One of the principal themes that emerges from my story is that of *repetition* in the sense in which Kierkegaard uses that word; truly to possess something one must have lost it and found it again. At the end of the novel, Henri and Dubreuilh (. . .) return to the point they started from, but (. . .) instead of being content with a facile optimism, they take upon themselves all the difficulties, the failures, the scandal implied in any undertaking. Their old enthusiastic adherences are replaced by preferences.

The preferences of the wider political stage and those of the characters' interpersonal relations are bound together in the double narrative structure alternating between male and female focus, which is equally familiar from the two previous novels. However, in **The Mandarins** the female narrative attains parity with the male in terms of length, and has the concluding chapter of the narrative within its remit. Even more importantly, the female narrative focus becomes, for the first time in Beauvoir's novels, a narrative voice. In a reversal of the narrative situation of **The Blood of Others,** the female character (Anne) narrates her sections in the first person as a homodiegetic (internal) narrator, whilst the male character acting as narrative focus (Henri) is deprived of a voice and is subjected to the discreet authority of an external narrator. However, neither of the characters through whom the narrative is focused is entrusted with an authoritative interpretation of events which the reader is invited to accept. Anne therefore does not inherit the authority of Blomart in *The Blood of Others* and of Fosca in *All Men Are Mortal.*

Accompanying this change is the abandonment of the retrospective time structure. Instead of being recapitulated from a single fixed point in time, story and narrative time roughly coincide, moving forward together and giving a greater sense of the open nature of the characters' future. The historical period with which the characters engage is at the same time compressed to the four-year span of 1944-48. The novel's construction of the era is extremely detailed and depends heavily on autobiographical material, on Beauvoir's perceptions of the intellectual, political and literary dimensions of the four or five years preceding the writing of the novel (1944-49), as well as on emotional experience. The dilemmas of Henri and Robert are alimented by the twists and turns which marked Sartre and Beauvoir's relationship with the Communist Party after the War, by the bid to redefine the values of traditional humanism in which Sartre engaged, and by his attempt in 1948-49 to work within an independent left-wing grouping—the RDR, transmuted in the novel into the SRL. The pleasure which Beauvoir took in the running of *Les Temps Modernes,* the review which she and Sartre launched in 1945 as a forum for writers of the left, is clearly reflected in the characters' enthusiasm for *L'Espoir* and *Vigilance.* Beauvoir's visits to the States and her relationship with the American writer Nelson Algren (which began in the spring of 1947) are recounted with a minimum of fictionalisation in Anne Dubreuilh's relationship with Lewis Brogan.

But the text does not simply draw on events which took place before Beauvoir began writing in the autumn of 1949—it also reflects events and changes taking place during the four-year writing process. The news of the existence of the Soviet labour camps, for example, broke at the end of 1949. Beauvoir's relationship with Algren was still in full swing as she began writing (she had spent part of the summer travelling in Europe with him); the painful summer in the house on Lake Michigan which began with Algren's announcement that he no longer loved her and which Anne lives through with Lewis in Chapter 10 did not take place until the summer of 1950, when the writing had been going for almost a year. Beauvoir completed her first version of the novel in June 1951, but it was only in October of that year, after a return visit to Lake Michigan, that she found herself faced with the fact that her relationship with Algren was definitively over. Did Anne abandon Lewis in this version of the novel? The use of the writing process to work through immediate and painful personal experience is abundantly clear, as is its effect on the final shape of the work. (pp. 88-91)

It was not until the completion of the manuscript that Beauvoir chose its title. Deciding against *Les Suspects* ('The Suspects') and *Les Survivants* ('The Survivors'), she eventually selected [Claude] Lanzmann's suggestion, *Les Mandarins.* The choice of this routine metaphor, with its semi-ironic distancing effect, is a tactic which Beauvoir was to repeat in later work. Through its potentially pejorative implication (milder, however, than *Les Suspects* would have been), doubts are raised about the status of the

intellectual and about his or her actual influence on the centres of power. The reader is left uneasy, unclear about the author's relation to her text. Questioned about this in a 1954 interview with J. F. Rolland, Beauvoir said that though the title was intended to convey a mild and sympathetic irony, she was in total sympathy with her characters' political positions. The question itself, however, is evidence of the unease which this irony produces in the reader. Nevertheless, the title does point clearly to the whole problem of the conciliation of the role of the intellectual with that of political activist—one of the two principal spheres of choice in which the structure of preference is enacted.

The problematic of this conciliation is dealt with in both of the text's narratives, but largely in terms of the dilemmas of the two principal male characters, Robert Dubreuilh and Henri Perron; since both are writers, the question of the intellectual's role in politics often becomes that of the relationship between literature and politics (thus the problem of defining what is meant by an intellectual, a problematic area in Anglo-Saxon thinking at least, does not really arise). The question is raised in the opening scene of the novel, where Scriassine warns Anne that Henri and Robert will have to choose between sacrificing all their time and energy to political activities, or withdrawing into writing and risking cutting themselves off from the realities of their era. Though she does not write herself, Anne has an absolute belief in the power and value of literature. For her, it is impossible that Robert should give up writing. The two men, however, have acclimatised themselves to the rigours (and rewards) of political action in the Resistance struggle. Robert is ready to concede that, in the period of rapid social transformation which he hopes the world is about to traverse, literature may not be on the agenda. Henri has experienced a sense of solidarity in the War which he needs to feel he can go on earning. On his trip to Portugal in the third chapter he is abruptly faced with the opposition between this duty—this need— and literature: the novel celebrating the pleasures of peace and the beauties of the world which he had planned to write seems impossible in the face of the poverty and the hardships which he meets. How can he celebrate the pretty little lights on the Tagus river when he is fully aware of the misery and poverty which the lights conceal? For a period, both Henri and Robert stop writing, and Robert begins the process of rethinking their prewar values. He decides that it had been too optimistic to look for a conciliation between the revolution and the old humanist values; the concepts of literature, truth, freedom, individual morality and judgement would have to be 're-invented' to avoid jettisoning them entirely.

In the early chapters of the novel, discussion along these lines remains largely theoretical. However, it is brought into sharp focus by the issue which dominates the seventh chapter, of whether to publish documentation on the Soviet labour camps. For Anne, again, the issue is clear: 'As an intellectual, you've taken on certain commitments—to tell the truth, among others,' she tells Robert. Henri's reaction appears hardly less certain in its moral absolutism: 'In what measure had George told the truth?—that was the only question'. The consequences of this attitude do, however, disturb him; in the past he has felt able to affirm that his duty as a journalist is to tell the truth without regard for what uses might he made of it. Now, he faces the fact that he believes that the truth he has to tell may damage the hopes of a thousand million people living in subhuman conditions whose only hope for the future is the Soviet Union. Can 15,000 people in labour camps be sacrificed for the sake of a thousand million other people? Neither Henri or Anne can bring themselves to make this calculation. Their fundamental belief in individualism leads them to the position which Anne argues, that such calculations are false: 'One individual plus another individual doesn't make two; it will always make one plus one'. Despite his fear of the political consequences, Henri, like Anne, opts for individualism and the primacy of moral value: ' "It has to be brought out into the open," Henri concluded. "If not I'll be an accessory" '.

This decision leads the character into the second term of the structure of preference, as he rejects his initial commitment in the light of an absolute, and finds himself as a result in an impasse. Robert ends up at the same destination by a different route. When Anne tells him that it is his duty as an intellectual to tell the truth he invokes in the balance against the truth the fate of all the starving millions in the world, the fate of all those ravaged by disease and epidemics, all those enslaved by exploitative political regimes before declaring, ' . . . my duties as an intellectual, my respect for the truth—that's all twaddle! The only question is to know whether, in denouncing the camps, you're working for mankind or against it'. He is even more dismissive of moral considerations in discussion with Henri: ' "Those are moral considerations; they don't touch me," he said. "I'm interested in the results of my actions, not in what they make me appear to be" '.

Unlike Henri, therefore, Dubreuilh thus deliberately breaks the connection between the intellectual on the one hand and individual morality and truth on the other. But he still joins Henri in the wilderness because he cannot bring himself to *act* on his conviction. In the book which pushes his line of argument to its limits Robert writes, 'Today a French intellectual can do nothing', and he goes on to condemn the 'old humanism' in favour of a new one 'in which force figured large and the concepts of justice, freedom, truth, hardly at all'. This is the only set of moral values viable in today's situation, he claims—but at the same time he admits that he personally could never adopt them. The years of struggle for the triumph of values which he himself now judges to be inappropriate, constitute an impossible barrier for him to cross. He thus declares himself condemned to inaction and silence. Even the writing of literature is impossible for him; he had thought that literature could avoid doing harm, even when it did no good. But, he tells Anne, 'At the moment all literature that aspires to give man something besides bread is exploited to prove that he can very well do without bread'.

Both Anne and Henri are quick to grasp that Robert's disassociation between what he feels personally capable of and what ought to be done is suspect—and one could add that his description of the 'new humanism' remains very vague. Robert does not maintain for long the absolutism of this position, which is above all a cry of frustration. Henri's position of absolute morality fares no better. Even when making the choice over the labour camps he is aware that he is choosing not between right and wrong but between two evils: 'if evil were everywhere, innocence didn't exist. Whatever he did he'd be wrong,' he tells himself in an echo of Blomart in *The Blood of Others.* Two issues bring him up against the limits of moralism. In the Mercier affair, Henri is faced with the choice of inventing evidence to get an ex-Nazi collaborator acquitted, or allowing the fragile Josette to face investigation of her love affair with a German officer during the war.

> On the one side, there was Josette, on the other, qualms of conscience (. . .) At any rate, there was damned little to be gained from having a clear conscience. The thought wasn't new to him: you were just as well off being frankly in the wrong. Now he was being offered a fine opportunity to say to hell with morality; he wasn't going to let it go by.

But this cynicism is far from natural to Henri; he finds it sickening to have to throw doubt on the evidence of the two women sent to Dachau as a result of Mercier's treachery. He remains uneasy despite Dubreuilh's assertion that the incident is an illustration of the impossibility of individual morality. Dubreuilh's argument that 'personal morality just doesn't exist' because 'you can't lead a proper life in a society which isn't proper' is too generalised for Henri; the key question for him is to know what Dubreuilh—as an individual—would have done in his place.

The second event which strains Henri's faith in moral principles is the issue of what to do with Sézénac: 'Four years earlier everything would have been simple. When action means something, when you believe in certain objectives, then the word justice has a meaning: you execute traitors. But what do you do with a traitor from the past when you've lost all hope?' The issue is settled by the abrupt intervention of Vincent, who has no hesitation in killing Sézénac; 'you've got to know what side you're on (. . .) You've got to get your feet wet,' he argues succinctly. Without approving Vincent, both Henri and Robert are struck by the fact that their moral uncertainty stems from their lack of situation and commitment: 'If we were still active, there would be no problem. Only now we're on the outside, so our decision will necessarily be arbitrary'.

When the situation which Henri is lacking presents itself in the form of the Tanarive trials, his whole perspective changes; even the smell of the flowers in the garden 'didn't have the same savour as before'. He moves into the final term of the structure of preference when he takes the decision not to retire into exile in a sunny corner of Italy, but to work instead with Dubreuilh on a new left-wing journal. However, this return to commitment does not mean that Henri really abandons his individualism and his moralism. 'You don't prevent a war with words,' he admits—but for him words are not simply 'a way of changing history', they are 'also a certain way of living it'. How he feels about his own stance is thus valued just as highly as the effects of his action. In *L'Espoir* he had always aimed to educate his readers into making informed judgements—there is no indication that he will do anything other than this in his new venture. The idea of moral principles is not abandoned, even if he now sees morality as inseparable from a commitment and a situation rather than deriving from an absolute. Dubreuilh, in apparent contrast, emerges from his blind alley declaring that he is after all prepared to drop the old values and personally assume the 'new humanism': 'You can no more reject it than you can reject the world'. The world political situation has deteriorated in his view to a point where he has to prefer the Soviet Union over the United States without concerning himself with what the Soviet Union *ought* to be like: 'on the one hand there's reality, and on the other, nothing. And I know of no worse error than preferring nothing to something'. He thus appears to be essentially using his 'preference' theory to divest himself of moral considerations and choose the Soviet Union. However, Dubreuilh's jettisoning of the 'old' values is also more apparent than real. He overcomes a specific moral scruple—accepting the existence of the labour camps in the Soviet Union—but it takes him months to arrive at this position. It is clear that moral or intellectual scruples could interrupt his co-operation with the Communists at any moment—as indeed the Soviet invasion of Hungary did for Sartre only two years after the novel's publication, in 1956.

The humanistic aspect of Dubreuilh's projects for the future also emerges in the salvaging of literature, which both men ultimately agree on. For Henri, the problem of a 'pure' versus a 'political' literature, symbolised by the lights-on-the-river dilemma, is compounded by the problem of individualism. Dubreuilh settles the lights problem by cutting through the dichotomy:

> 'if you make a thing of beauty out of those lights
> and forget what lies behind them, you're a bas-
> tard. But that's just it: you've got to find a way
> to write about them which differs from the way
> right-wing aesthetes write; you've got to bring
> out at one and the same time the fact that they
> are pretty and that they shed light on misery.
> That's exactly the task that writers on the left
> should set themselves,' he said excitedly. 'Mak-
> ing us see things in a new perspective by setting
> them in their true place. But let's not impoverish
> the world. Personal experiences—what you call
> mirages—do exist.'

Literature and individual experience need not be abandoned, as long as the individual is not seen in isolation from a wider context. The novel which Henri had begun and then abandoned immediately after the war is now seen to be located within this problematic; he had tried to 'talk about himself without setting himself in either the past or the present. But the truth of one's life is outside oneself, in events, in other people, in things; to talk about oneself, one must talk about everything else'. His play, in contrast, is a play 'set in a definite place, at a definite time, a play that meant something'.

Thus the ethos of preference, the rejection of idealism in the name of a modest praxis, by no means prevents the redemption of the individual, the beautiful and the literary. Although the 'old humanism' of the intellectual is severely strained in the novel, many of its values survive, though not as absolutes. Morality becomes a function of a situation, and a specific role is defined for literature. Sartre had come round by the early 1950s to the view that morality 'is a collection of idealistic tricks', and Beauvoir writes of herself under Lanzmann's influence 'gradually [liquidating] my ethical idealism'. The attitudes of the characters of *The Mandarins* lag well behind this position. On the question of the role of literature, however, Henri's stance is very close to Beauvoir's; she frequently feels the need to justify the practice of taking her own experience as a starting point for writing, in terms which are virtually identical to those of Henri and Robert. Henri's novel is clearly the mirror image of Beauvoir's intentions for *The Mandarins* itself: 'a story of today in which the readers would find their own worries, their own problems' and for which he draws heavily, like Beauvoir, on autobiographical material. In an evident desire to ward off any attempt to treat her novel as a *roman à clef,* Beauvoir has Henri explain to Nadine that his book is nothing of the sort:

> I didn't write about us. You know very well that
> all the characters are made up . . . Of course,
> I tried to depict present-day people, men and
> women who are in somewhat the same situation
> as ours. But there are thousands of people like
> that; neither your father nor I is specifically por-
> trayed. On the contrary, in most respects my
> characters don't resemble us at all.

Whilst Beauvoir's situation may not have been so easily identifiable as identical to that of 'thousands' of people, the concept put forward here of a novel which would be a portrait of the times is central to *The Mandarins* itself, so that the very concept of the work and its construction echo the characters' conclusions. The issues of the postwar era, as Beauvoir saw them, are employed as a defining context for the characters and their struggles—Anne, depressed by the deaths in the War of those close to her; Henri and Robert, full of the optimism and idealism which the successful struggle of the Resistance has instilled in them; Nadine, Vincent and Sézénac, destabilised by the brutalities with which they had come into contact at a very young age. The heritage of the War thus continues to be a defining factor for the characters, but, as the novel develops, the situation which increasingly dominates and structures their lives is the climate of the Cold War, forcing the characters out of neutrality in areas of their lives extending well beyond the political.

The two power blocks centering on the United States and the Soviet Union, which constitute the binary political universe of *The Mandarins,* both figure powerfully in the novel, embodying at different moments political, cultural and emotional options. (pp. 92-9)

The choices to be made in the novel in world politics are played out with equal starkness in the personal choices of sexual relationships. The use of the United States as the location of a pole of choice in both political and sexual terms underlines the parallelism between the two sets of options. The account of the relationship between Lewis and Anne, and the choice which Anne has to make between what Lewis and Robert represent which dominates the second half of Anne's narrative, is often taken as a marginal episode of the novel. To take this view is to ignore both the central role which the exploration of types of male-female couples occupies in the text, and the way in which sexual choice in the novel is just as governed by the structure of preference as is political choice. Anne's eventual choice of Robert is echoed by Henri's choice of Nadine; in a sense both choose Dubreuilh, but in broader terms both follow the pattern of preference.

Of the two, the Anne-Robert couple is the dominant model, and is characterised from the point of view of Anne in her first section of narrative. For Anne, Robert represents security ('I had only to speak his name and I would feel safe and secure'), and total identification with herself ('I've lived with him as if from the inside, with no distance between us'). More than 20 years older than Anne, Robert is literally her teacher when she meets him, and he soon assumes a Pygmalion role in other areas of her life, assigning moral and political meaning to the world about her through their conversations and his writing. After revealing to her that she loves him, he goes on to teach her the pleasures of sexuality: 'It seemed a simple and joyous thing to me to become a woman in his arms; when the pleasure was frightening, his smile would reassure me'. But he also teaches her that desire wanes and that in giving up the sexual aspect of their relationship they have 'so to speak lost nothing'. For him, sexuality and love are naturally separable: 'Picking up a good-looking girl in a bar and spending an hour with her seemed perfectly natural to him'.

Anne takes up the career that Robert encourages because he 'believes that psychoanalysis can play a useful role in bourgeois society and that it might still be of use even in a classless society'; she also has the baby that Robert wants. But Anne has great difficulty in assuming caring roles; she is unable to love her daughter, resents her couple with Robert being turned into a trio by Nadine, and feels increasingly hostile towards her patients. To these difficulties are added her problems in coping with Robert's lack of need of her: despite her pupil status Anne does not in fact share all Robert's values, and is a romantic and an absolutist. The tale of the mermaid who sells her immortal soul for love and who becomes, after death, 'a bit of white foam without memory and without voice' recurs in Anne's imagination; on the one hand it represents Anne's fear of death as a void—a fear against which Robert partially secures her—but it also represents Anne's identification with a symbol of absolute love: 'I was the mermaid'. Anne often evokes what she thinks of as ideal couples—Nadine and Diego, Lambert and Rosa—and for her the thought that Robert might not have loved her had he met her in different circumstances or that he might have met someone else is a terrifying notion which she dispels from her mind with speed.

Anne's meeting with Lewis Brogan throws her couple with Robert into sharp relief. The most evident difference is the intensely sexual relationship which she sets up with him, reviving a part of her life which she has repressed for years. Other contrasts also emerge, however: Lewis needs security, permanence, fidelity. He likes having dinner with Anne at home, tries to create the illusion that they are married, slips a ring on her finger, is distressed by the infidelities which occur during the long months of Anne's absence. Anne compares her image of the two men: Lewis, waking in bed to a room 'destroyed' by her absence, Robert working in his study in which there is 'no place' for Anne. Robert and Anne's relationship maintains a constant even keel; Anne and Lewis hurt each other and suffer deeply. Language and rationality are of no help to them: 'We only get things in a muddle when we talk about them,' says Lewis as one of their conversations leads nowhere. The contrast with Robert, who uses language to make the world for Anne 'coherent, like a book' is striking and, in the end, decisive. When Anne finds that she will not be able to maintain both options, and that choice is inevitable, she consults Robert—effectively seeks his permission to choose Lewis. Robert makes no appeal on his own behalf, confirming Anne's feeling that he has no need of her, but argues, in an echo of Anne's own twice-repeated statement that 'love isn't everything', that the other aspects of her life which France represents are more important than love. However, it is not this argument which in the end holds Anne back; she *is* prepared to view love as an absolute and does eventually decide to go to Lewis if he summons her. It is in the absence of this summons that her confidence that Lewis has an absolute need of her deserts her, and she finds herself unable to abandon the security of Robert, the security and power of the *logos*. Discourse and reason, not the body and emotion, prevail.

Anne's choice is heavily supported by the development of the other couples in the novel. The pattern of commitment interrupted by an interlude with a third party and ending in reunion is echoed by the Henri-Nadine couple, but this time the pattern is viewed from the male partner's point of view. The Henri-Nadine couple echoes the Robert-Anne structure in the age gap between the two, in the strong Pygmalion element ('He had wanted to help her. He had told himself that if he could make her happy he would free her of that confused resentment which was poisoning her life'), and in the move from sexuality to verbality. In the first stage of their relationship, the sexual element is uppermost for Henri: 'Nadine would have been astonished had she known just how indifferent he was to her problems'; 'all he wanted was to get into bed with her'. In one of the last scenes of the novel between them, when they are already married, Henri effects his 'preference' for Nadine: 'Yes, the thing you prefer to all others, you love, and he was fonder of her than anything else in the world. He loved her, and he had to convince her of it'. He employs all his verbal skills to convince her, and then, with this achieved, 'he helped put her to bed, tucked her in, and went back to his room. Never had he talked so frankly with Nadine, and it seemed to him as if something had given way in her. He had to persevere'. Two points emerge from this: firstly, the entire relationship is now conceived in terms of Nadine's needs (as perceived by Henri) and of Henri's strength. Secondly, and most strikingly, the terms of preference again operate emphatically on the verbal level as a preferred alternative to the sexual. 'Talking frankly' appears to automatically preclude the sexual. Thus Nadine, who 'has to put her life into words', learns to depend on Henri's word, just as Anne does on Robert's.

The choice between the verbal and the sexual is in fact heavily loaded against the sexual. There are of course some lyrical scenes between Anne and Lewis, in which Anne describes a sense of transfiguration, of recovery of the body in its most elemental form, and in which desire, happiness and love mingle. 'Between us, desire had always been love,' says Anne—but this paradise contains a serpent. As Lewis begins to resent Anne's refusal to commit herself to him, their lovemaking is perceived by Anne as first bizarre and incongruous, and later brutally divorced from all tenderness as she feels treated 'as a pleasure machine'. Anne is surprised and distressed by this development, yet the presentation of sexual relations earlier in the novel clearly prepares this fall. In the scene between Anne and Scriassine, in Chapter 2, the grotesque aspect of sexual relations is doubled by an aggressivity which anticipates later scenes with Lewis. This scene is positively pleasant, however, in comparison with the one which takes place in the first chapter between Henri and Paule, and which is truncated in the published English translation. Henri's lack of desire for Paule shifts female sexuality into a grotesque and obscene mode: Paule is metamorphosed into 'a corpse or a madwoman' (omitted in the translation), 'a woman beside herself mouthing obscene words and clawing him painfully' (omitted in the translation). When Henri enters her, 'to get it over with as quickly as possible', he finds that 'inside her it was red just as her studio was red' (omitted in the translation). Dubreuilh calls Paule's red studio her 'brothel'; thus the red room—the place of the death of the child, of the abortion of the foetus and of Denise's madness in *The Blood of Others*—re-emerges here as a figure of female sexuality viewed as an obscene phenomenon.

In *The Blood of Others* the perception of the female body as obscene is specifically connected with woman's reproductive functions; in *The Mandarins,* it focuses on a fear of women being viewed by men as sexual predators, of women desiring and not being desired in return. Just as Elisabeth is used in *She Came to Stay* as the embodiment of everything that Françoise fears becoming (and as Denise functions to a lesser extent for Hélène in *The Blood of Others*), so Paule functions as a warning, as an image of what Anne might become. 'If ever I lost Lewis, when I lost Lewis, I would immediately and forever stop believing myself a woman,' Anne swears to herself, as she witnesses Paule and Claudie making seduction attempts on handsome young men. This negative image of woman is not confined, however, to Paule: Nadine also plays the role of woman as sexual aggressor, crudely manoeuvring Henri into bed with her and taking control of the sexual situation whenever possible. In *Force of Circumstance* Beauvoir states openly that she had intended to 'avenge myself on Nadine for certain traits that had offended me in Lise [i.e. Nathalie Sorokine] and some of my other younger women friends—a sexual coarseness that revealed rather nastily their underlying frigidity, an aggressiveness that was a poor compensation for their feeling of inferiority'. This view of sexual assertiveness as related to a basic frigidity is clearly at work in the presentation of Nadine. Despite her apparently liberated attitudes to sex, she is shown to regard it as 'a tedious occupation', and she is subjected to the male criticism that she should be content to allow her-

self to be 'gently lulled by pleasure instead of romping about in bed with determined shamelessness'. This kind of judgement, like Henri's horror of Paule, implicitly shores up Anne's sexual passivity, and her need to be the object of desire.

The function of other women characters as a negative pole to Anne operates not only in loading her choice against sexuality, but also as a pressure against the romantic absolute which, for Anne and Lewis, accompanies sexuality. Paule is the complete example of *The Second Sex*'s analysis of the *amoureuse* (the woman who makes a cult of love) who tries to attain her own being vicariously through that of the loved one. In the sections of narrative focused through Henri, the weight of the burden that Paule's refusal to make her own life places on the object of her attention is fully apparent. Her refusal to relate directly to the outside world entraps her in myths and rituals which at first entrance and later infuriate Henri; both he and Anne react strongly against Paule's mythmaking use of language, which converts Henri's ambitions into his 'mission' and her life with Henri into 'a kind of experience that's simply incommunicable'. Anne is not tempted to follow Paule down the road of mythifying discourse, or to imitate her refusal of the passage of time. But other aspects of Paule's behaviour are echoed as danger signals in Anne's relation to Lewis: Paule's narcissism and belief in the illusion of clothes occasionally tempt Anne, and Paule's bizarre interpretations of Henri's behaviour are echoed in Anne's misunderstandings of Lewis's increasingly desperate signals that he cannot cope with her double life.

The connections between Paule and Anne become most insistent in the eighth chapter, where Paule's descent into folly is interspersed with Anne's reflections on her own situation with Lewis. Faced with Paule's distress she searches for 'meaningless' words of comfort: 'You'll get well, you've got to get well. Love isn't everything'. Anne repeats these 'meaningless' words to Lewis later in the chapter: ' "If you love me the way I love you, why waste three-fourths of our life waiting?" Lewis said. I hesitated. "Because love isn't everything," I said'. But, before she even pronounces these words to Lewis, Anne knows that she does not believe them. Though Anne herself is frightened by Paule's delusions she knows that 'in her place I would never want to get well and bury my love with my own hands'. She values feeling and suffering more highly than the triumph of 'reason and routine', which she feels Paule's psychiatric treatment will bring about. She regards with hostility the bovine and resigned person which Paule becomes and revolts against sanity, against the sanitisation of feeling: 'I had less and less stomach for my work; often I felt like saying to my patients, "Don't bother trying to get better, you'll soon get better enough" '. As she herself sinks to the edge of suicide, the idea of explaining away her feelings as 'a depression' revolts her; she determines to 'make truth triumph', and her means will be Paule's little brown vial. She will do what Paule should have done and carry out the suicide which will represent the truth of her feeling.

Of course Anne does not in the end act on her belief in the truth of suffering, of folly, of death. She is wrested from this position by the sound of voices; the power of language again triumphs, bringing with it the sense of guilt which almost permanently accompanies Anne. However, in *Force of Circumstance* Beauvoir remarks that Anne's return from the edge of suicide 'seems more like a defeat than a triumph'. Anne is 'betraying something'— something which Anne sees expressed in the delusions of Paule, and perhaps in the more permanent folly of Maria who, like Paule, struggles to express her feelings through writing. Although Anne chooses to return to life, and acts within the structures of preference by renouncing the absolutes of death and sexuality, by preferring Robert to Lewis, life to death, she does so with little conviction. She does not share Robert's credo that love is nothing but a preference. When one remarks that Henri does not explain to Nadine that he is 'preferring' her—for the evident reason that Nadine would be unlikely to be satisfied with this—it becomes apparent that the novel's structure of preference is essentially a male structure, against which a female aspiration to absolutes occasionally breaks into revolt.

The playing out of the structure of preference on the level of the couple creates tensions in the text between certain types of femininity and, in particular, masculinity. In the wake of *The Second Sex,* the novel shows a much greater awareness than the earlier fiction of questions of gender role construction. Lambert and Nadine are both examined specifically in the text from this point of view. Nadine, the unloved daughter who, in her turn, becomes a punctiliously cold mother to her own daughter, bitterly resents any identification with the feminine. Her fury as an adolescent over the onset of menstruation is later translated into an attitude of contemptuousness towards the female body— an attitude which she parades with ostentation at the strip show which she presses Henri into taking her to. The beautiful Josette—equally unfortunate in her mother— has almost as many problems as Nadine in coming to terms with her body, experiencing her beauty as a humiliation and tortured by problems of what to wear. 'Girls are weighed down with restrictions, boys with demands—two equally harmful disciplines,' comments Anne. Despite this, the difficulties of becoming a woman are presented with more sympathy than those of becoming a man. Anne appreciates that Lambert is becoming adult in a period where 'being a man' means knowing how to kill, how to make others suffer and how to take suffering himself, but the character is nevertheless discredited through Anne's detailing of physical traits such as 'his grimaces, his comical voice, the sweat which streamed down his cheeks' and by his inability to cope with drinking alcohol. Lambert turns at first to the strongly masculine Henri as role model, but eventually replaces Henri by Volange, so that the character who has experienced difficulties 'becoming a man' is devalued and made to take a political wrong-turning.

If Robert and Henri play strong masculine roles, the non-Latin softly named Lewis with his attachment to security and fidelity is considerably more feminised. It is tempting to point to this feminisation as an unspoken element of the character's rejection, given the positive coding attributed in the text to the kind of stereotypical masculine role played by Henri. Combining commitment to political action with a strong moral concern, Henri is the undisputed hero of the novel, whose masculine credentials are firmly established from the beginning of the text by his image as Resistance leader. His automatic response to meeting women is to appraise them sexually: 'for him, there were desirable women and others who weren't. This one wasn't'. He frequently generalises about women in authoritative terms, and adopts a possessive attitude towards the women in his life, assuming that his role is to help and support them. The morning following the first night that he spends with Josette he feels 'wonderfully happy to have this woman for himself, and to be a man'. He asks himself, 'What can I do for her?' and concludes that what would be needed would be for him 'to be in love with her; all women are like that; they need loving with an exclusive love'. His plans for Nadine are very similar. However, when women step outside the boundaries he defines for them, his impulse is often towards violence; when he learns that Josette had loved a German officer, Henri 'felt like reviling her, beating her'. With Paule, he grabs her wrists in a fury, imagines shaking her and ripping her cigarette holder from her mouth, and feels 'like beating her' when she takes up his time in his office.

The relationship with Paule places Henri in a particularly unsympathetic light. Although he spends a great deal of energy on the moral problem of whether to publish details of the Soviet labour camps, he generally avoids considering the problem of his responsibilities towards Paule in moral terms. He misleads Paule, lies to her, even makes reluctant love with her, reasoning that 'it would take a lot less time to satisfy her than to have it out with her' (omitted in the English translation). He accepts that he ought to make the situation clear to Paule, but his honesty disappears when Paule senses danger and offers concessions. ' "I'm blackmailing her, that's just what it amounts to," Henri thought. "It's rather disgraceful," ' he indulgently concludes, before excusing himself with an ease and rapidity that he would never permit himself over an issue that did not concern his personal relations with a woman. Eventually, his relationship with Josette drives him into the open: 'it's impossible for a man to desire the same body indefinitely,' he explains, echoing Robert in this definition of male sexual needs as essentially promiscuous in nature and divorced from all emotional needs. Since Anne's narrative tends to reinforce the negative perception of Paule's attitudes (though not of her suffering) which Henri's narrative offers, the text suggests clearly that Henri is simply trapped in a situation for which he bears minimal responsibility.

With Josette, Henri goes through the period of sexual temptation that Anne also passes through, in this instance clearly damned through the moral and political guilt associated with it. His return to Nadine signals a return to probity, as well as a move away from the primacy of sexuality. Nadine is a much less strongly feminine character than either Paule or Josette: 'Nadine was not pretty. She looked too much like her father, and it was disturbing to see that truculent face on the body of a young girl'. The extent to which this relationship is caught up with Henri's attitude to Dubreuilh is clear from the beginning: 'What would

Dubreuilh's head on a pillow look like?' Henri wonders. The friendship between the two men is one of the strongest relationships of the novel, and echoes the pattern of commitment, withdrawal and recommitment of the other central relationships. It is quite unmatched by any relationship between women in the novel; neither Nadine nor Josette has any women friends, Anne and Paule's friendship seems to have come to an end and the mother-daughter relationship offers little but guilt and hostility. Anne's glacial attitude towards her daughter, combined with her interventions in Nadine's life behind her back, even to the extent of discussing Nadine's sexual needs with her daughter's current lover Lambert, bring the mother-daughter relationship to a nadir. It is little wonder that the indulgence which, in contrast, Anne is able to demonstrate towards the penitent Marie-Ange drives Nadine into a fury of jealousy.

Anne does castigate herself for her lack of feeling towards Nadine, Henri accepts an element of guilt towards Paule—but these traits are marked as marginal, almost natural errors. Maternal frigidity (or alternatively over-possessiveness) is an almost inevitable result for Beauvoir of the immense difficulties which she describes in *The Second Sex* as embroiling mother-child relations. The question of Henri's sexism is more difficult, but it seems quite likely that Beauvoir was simply endowing her character with traits she perceived in her male entourage, and which she did not identify at the time of writing as sexist. The fundamental thesis of *The Second Sex* that femininity is a social construct naturally implies that the same is true of masculinity, and Anne's remarks show that Beauvoir had taken this idea on board. However *The Second Sex,* whilst devoting a series of chapters to the socialisation of women, did not engage in an investigation of the construction of masculinity, and it is not really surprising to note Beauvoir's uncritical portrayal of sexist and stereotypical masculine traits in a positively coded male character.

The male-female counterpoint which emerges from this analysis is foregrounded in the novel's narrative organisation. The balance between male and female points of view, more nearly attained here than in any of Beauvoir's other novels, mimics the essentially verbal relationship between the sexes set up by the structure of preference. In *Force of Circumstance,* Beauvoir draws attention to the dual narrative structure of *The Mandarins* and describes the two narratives as '[establishing] between them a sort of counterpoint, each reinforcing, diversifying, destroying the other'. In order to unfix meaning Beauvoir needed Anne to 'provide me with the negative of the objects that were shown through Henri's eyes in their positive aspects'. In fact this 'counterpoint' does not effectively undermine the ethos of choice, responsibility and action which prevails in the novel. Anne herself does eventually enact the structure of preference—albeit with extreme reluctance, and when she reflects on the choices which Henri and Robert are faced with, her views often support those of Henri. Indeed, it is the coincidence of these two characters' views on matters such as Paule's mystifications, on Robert's godlike status, on the moral imperatives of the intellectual's function which largely establishes the text's system of values.

However, when Anne's narrative is examined in detail, it can be seen to consist of two rather different elements. The element which dominates in terms of numbers of pages is the one which consists of first-person narrative of events in the past (*récit*), in which Anne uses the past tense (frequently the past historic). However, this account, in which the disassociation between narrating and experiencing self is visible, is accompanied by a monologue in the present tense in which narrative time and story time coincide, and in which experiencing and narrating selves come together. It is this monologue which opens Anne's narrative as she lies in bed at night reflecting on death and on her anxieties about Robert, and which closes it in the final chapter of the novel where she comes to the brink of suicide: 'Who knows? Perhaps one day I'll be happy again. Who knows?' Anne's monologue, with its accent on suffering, folly and death, is the predecessor of the monologues of the women of Beauvoir's last two fictional works. The narratives of Anne and Henri, despite their similarities in some areas, thus remain differentiated by their gender marking. In *Force of Circumstance,* Beauvoir describes how she divided autobiographical traits between the two characters acting as narrative focus, one male, one female—and they are distributed strictly according to gender role. Henri has her optimism, her appetites, her taste for activity—and, of course, the pen. Anne has fear and shame, and the 'negative aspects of my experience'. In *The Mandarins* these 'negative aspects' are thus labelled female and more or less vanquished by the masculine structure of preference which, in political terms, means action not idealism, and within the couple means shared values and companionship, not sexuality and romanticism.

Henri is the only male character in Beauvoir's novels with a substantial role to play who acts as narrative focus for an external narrator (the other very minor example is Gerbert in *She Came to Stay*). Anne is the first female character to voice her own narrative through the 'I'. What these developments seem to signal is a shift of anxiety about the 'I'. Whereas Blomart and Fosca used the 'I' to examine the problem of the individual's relation to others and to history, these problems are thrown in *The Mandarins* into the more public arena of Henri's externally voiced narrative. The 'I' examines the 'negative aspects' of experience—it becomes the voice of suffering and of the temptation of folly and death which Anne shares with Paule, the fears of a 'secondary being', as Beauvoir calls her character.

In the last two works of fiction which follow *The Mandarins* this female narrative voice of suffering and folly is the only voice to be heard. Male characters neither voice the narrative nor act as its focus. The shift of the male voice from first-person narrative to third-person focus of the narrative is thus the prelude to its disappearance. However, it still has a role to play in *The Mandarins,* and is supported by the power of language on which the choices of the novel so heavily depend; writing itself also remains a male preserve. Women's writing in *The Mandarins* is an expression of suffering and madness (Paule's writing before her cure, and the mad woman Maria's), and if the suffering is removed, it becomes 'as empty, as flat as a story in *Confidences',* in other words becomes a writing fit only for other women's consumption. In Anne, a female character does achieve a narrative voice, a voice posited as reliable and which delivers judgements on many of the other characters. However, the emergence of the female voice brings with it in Beauvoir's fiction a growing focus on the illusory, the delusionary—held in check in *The Mandarins* by the structure of preference, but which reigns in the final period of her fiction writing. (pp. 105-15)

> *Elizabeth Fallaize, in her* The Novels of Simone de Beauvoir, *Routledge, 1988, 200 p.*

Kathleen Woodward

Like *The Second Sex,* Simone de Beauvoir's *The Coming of Age* is an original and prodigious contribution to critiques of the oppression of one social group by another in the twentieth-century industrial West. Importantly for our purposes, both books arose out of Beauvoir's desire to write from the base of her own experience, which led her, unerringly, to two of the most pressing social issues of our time: the subjection of women and the devaluation of the elderly. Yet while *The Second Sex* is still read today, *The Coming of Age,* which went out of print several years ago, has been virtually ignored by intellectuals and academics in the United States—even by those who are interested in the work of Beauvoir. This lacuna I have long found puzzling. More generally, among the categories of social division in a given culture and historical period (we may include race, gender, class, and age) only *age* has remained invisible, not subject to analysis. Yet for women it is especially important to think carefully about what it means to grow old in Western culture, because it is then that we are necessarily subject to—at the minimum—a double marginality. Aging—how we define ourselves as women as our social roles, our bodies, and our subjectivities change over time—is one of the great autobiographical themes, and one which has not received sufficient attention.

The encyclopedic *La Vieillesse* (the title under which the book was published in France in 1970) explores the roots of the dismaying treatment of the elderly in the West with a breadth of investigation that is stunning. Beauvoir's research extends to ethology, anthropology, biology, psychology, and psychoanalysis, as well as to the literary and artistic record. Significantly, in refusing to sentimentalize old age, she calls received opinion into question, concluding (among other things): that tribal cultures and the ancient civilizations of Greece and Rome did not sanctify old age per se, but rather granted status to the elderly on the basis of their power; that the elderly are without value in capitalist societies because they do not contribute significantly to the business of production; and that today's evaluation of the elderly is yet another symptom of the decay of Western civilization as a whole. An omnibus volume of research (much of which was conducted at the Bibliothèque Nationale in Paris), *The Coming of Age* is a manifesto for social action. Its tone is passionate, not balanced. But Beauvoir's salutary polemical purpose would not seem to fully account for her hostile and bitterly dark portrait of old age.

Thus *The Coming of Age,* notwithstanding the undeniable importance of its contribution to the study of aging and the politics of the elderly, must be read critically and, given the concerns of this book, in the context of her other writing as well. I read her representation of old age, in great part, as a symptom of personal concerns and obsessions, as a *figure* on which she has both projected her subjectivity and displaced her anxieties. For as we will see, her personal concern with aging manifested itself long before she began systematic research on the subject at the age of sixty. Beauvoir perceived herself as aging—as an old woman, in fact—long before anyone (except, of course, a child) could possibly have considered her old. This is all the more noteworthy because one of her major points in *The Coming of Age* is that we are made aware of our old age only by the gaze of the other, by seeing ourselves reflected in the eyes of others or by seeing ourselves in the mirror as though through the eyes of a stranger. She theorizes that the shock of recognition of our own old age comes to us from outside ourselves. But in her other work, she speaks of aging and old age as a depressive state of mind that periodically invades the imagination just as old age will ultimately take up residence in the body. (pp. 90-1)

Throughout Beauvoir's life as a writer, old age served her as a metaphor for disease, depression, and death. When she undertook the study of old age as a literal condition, it remained charged with the intensity with which she had earlier invested it. To be sure, there is a truth here: the category "old age" is rooted in the personal imagination as well as the physical world of the body and the social order. But in *The Coming of Age,* Beauvoir makes the mistake of unconsciously merging the metaphorical and the literal. (Unlike Susan Sontag, whose *Illness as Metaphor* shows how harmful it is to use such words as "cancer" to describe conditions other than the clinical disease, Beauvoir, I think, would have been incapable of writing a book on old age as metaphor.) While I do not deny the tragic view to which she subscribes, for me the real questions are what lies behind her obsession and how does it bias her view of old age? In the following pages I focus on three aspects of old age in *The Coming of Age*—physical deterioration, memory loss, and the loss of others—in the context of her work, especially her memoirs. My purpose is not to accuse Beauvoir of contradictions between what might be called the theory of *The Coming of Age* and her experience as presented to us in her more overtly autobiographical writing. Rather, it is to show that these disparities, or continuities, can help us understand how the theoretical and the autobiographical, in the extended sense of the term, are always and inevitably intertwined.

A recurring theme in *The Coming of Age* is the mutilation of the body by old age, a disfiguration that Beauvoir theorizes is repugnant both to others and to oneself because aging is an unambiguous sign of our mortality. Although she qualifies this assertion by cautioning that she is referring to the decrepitude of *advanced* age only, in fact the overwhelming weight of her book—pages upon pages of testimony of well-known cultural figures who voice their disgust at their aging bodies—suggests that Beauvoir is abnormally sensitive to the physical changes that accompany old age, even before it has advanced very far. This seems strange in a book whose mission is to rescue old age from contempt, and it is all the stranger because I do not think we can attribute her view to undue personal vanity; throughout her life Beauvoir did not seem to have even a conventional concern with her personal appearance (on the contrary, in her memoirs she presents herself as a woman unconcerned with her appearance, to the point of carelessness). Nor were her childhood and youth characterized by profound and negative experiences with the elderly. But if we turn to the first volume of her memoirs and to *The Second Sex,* we find a surprising source for her attitude toward the aging body.

The opening pages of *Memoirs of a Dutiful Daughter,* published in France in 1958, are among the most captivating in all of her memoirs. Her sensibility as a child (or so she tells us as an adult) was Keatsian—but with a gaiety untouched by melancholy. She was enchanted by sweets and dazzled by the sensuality of feminine fabrics, by laces, taffetas, silks. She was also subject to tantrums that would shake her entire body and to physical revulsions. Certain tastes and consistencies revolted her, and the details she provides are fascinating. She remembers, for example, that whenever her aunt served pumpkin pie she "would rush from the table in tears." Nor would she eat cheese. She further reports that "the insipidity of milk puddings, porridge, and mashes of bread and butter made me burst into tears, the oiliness of fat meat and the clammy mysteries of shellfish revolted me; my repugnance was so deeply rooted that in the end they gave up trying to force me to eat those disgusting things." The lack of firmness and solidity, that is, the indeterminate identity of a substance—is it solid or liquid?—was offensive to her. Such substances she found inane, innocuous, banal, lacking in originality or character, insipid. Her reference to the "clammy mysteries of shellfish" is telling. That something was hidden inside, the internal workings concealed, destroyed her composure, as did outer dampness and unusual coolness, which repelled her sense of touch.

Her extreme reactions lead us to ask what is involved in the attraction—or power—of what one finds horrible. Is it not possible that the feeling of horror is structured by a norm, which may very well be hidden to us? This would explain why we are simultaneously attracted to the horrible and repelled by it, and thus it would help us understand Beauvoir's obsession with the aging body as repellent. Her obsession conceals a norm: for her the ideal body—that is the "normal" body—is young and active. By contrast, the body of a person of advanced age, a decrepit body, is marked by imminent dissolution, by a lack of firmness, by frailty, by decay, and hence by a lack of identity.

But Beauvoir's obsession is not limited to her disgust with an aged body. Its roots are deeper, its territory wider than that. Throughout *Memoirs of a Dutiful Daughter* the word "repulsion" resounds, and most of her associations are to changes in the human body *in general.* As an adolescent the very word "development," which she associated with menstruation, repelled her, as did menstruation itself. She detested the thought that her breasts would swell (she would not even use the word "breasts," substituting the more clinical "chest"). She admits forthrightly (her

candor occasionally comes close to a sense of humor about herself and is one of her most engaging qualities) that as an adolescent sexuality frightened her and that as a young adult she found physical desire "repulsive," "a shameful disease." Indeed, in four volumes of memoirs noteworthy for their frankness, we find next to nothing about her sexual life with Sartre or [Nelson] Algren or with [Claude] Lanzmann, the only man with whom she ever shared living quarters. In short, it would seem that changes in the body in general arouse in her a deep-seated dislike of what is, for her, a sign of transformation as well as the thing itself. This view is confirmed in *The Second Sex.*

Although I agree with Beauvoir's major arguments about the oppression of women in Western culture, I find her attitude toward the reproductive nature or function of women quite odd, even bizarre. In *The Second Sex,* she writes at great length about menstruation as humiliating and painful, about pregnancy as an invasion by an alien being, and about childbirth as dangerous as well as painful. She asserts that this is the condition of women and concludes that, relative to the bodies of men, the bodies of women are characterized by weakness, instability, lack of control, and fragility. According to Beauvoir, woman's body is a burden, and only after menopause is a woman truly herself. Only then are a woman and her body one, as they were when she was a young child—when her body was firm and active and had not undergone any of the changes associated either with maturation or aging. Just as Beauvoir associates old age with death (she relates men's horror of decrepitude in women "logically" to their own fear of death), so too she links woman's capacity to give birth with death: "the function of gestation," she believes, "still inspires a spontaneous feeling of revulsion" in men. Nauseated as a child by the soft substances of cheese and pumpkin pie, Beauvoir was also repelled by any transformation in the female body toward softness and the unfirm (dangerously close in her mind to infirmity, to sickness).

The root of her disgust of the decrepit body is not so much a theoretical position as an aversion to bodily transformation, a loathing which may have had its origin in her early childhood. Just as some children are shy from birth and we cannot say why they are (that is, we cannot explain their temperament on the basis of their environment, their social context, or their place in history), Beauvoir seems to have been temperamentally repelled by changes in the body. This aversion then surfaces in her theoretical position—whether on women or on the elderly—in another guise. She generalizes without justification: "Men and women all feel the shame of their flesh; in its pure, inactive presence, its unjustified immanence, the flesh exists, under the gaze of the other, in its absurd contingence." Concealed within the language and theory of existentialism is her prudery (self-confessed in *The Prime of Life*) and distaste for the human body in any state which is not the *ideal* state. We may now wonder less at the source of an anecdote told in passing early in *Memoirs of a Dutiful Daughter.* There Beauvoir tells of the good times she and her younger sister had during summer vacations in the country, and she pauses just long enough to recall: "We despised mature *ceps* whose flesh was beginning to go soft and produce greenish whiskers. We only gathered young ones with nicely curved stalks and caps covered with a fine nigger-brown or bluish nap."

In *The Coming of Age* Beauvoir flatly rejects any fruitful role memory might play in the lives of the elderly. Given her existential posture, of course, she sees identity (it is her word) as created by actions: one is defined by what she calls one's projects or activities. Thus, she argues that women can achieve selfhood only through production, not reproduction, and that anything having to do with a woman's biological self has nothing to do with the authentic creation of her self. As she writes in *The Second Sex,* "giving birth and suckling are not *activities,* they are natural *functions;* no project is involved." I will not pause here to consider her position; I will only observe that in *The Second Sex* Beauvoir valorizes male labor as it has been traditionally defined in the West and is contemptuous of what we have traditionally called women's work. But what is important for our present purpose is her dismissal of a certain kind of psychological work which may be associated with a biological stage in life—for, like motherhood, old age is a distinct stage in the biological life of a person. Beauvoir does not ignore this point. Indeed, she makes much of the physical suffering which is likely to ac-

Beauvoir with demonstrators at the International Abortion March in Paris, 1971.

company old age. But just as she refuses to lend any cultural dignity or meaning to childbearing, so she denies that memory may play a critical role in one's psychological life when one approaches death.

Beauvoir thus necessarily sees old age as a tragedy, a view in great part prescribed by the dictates of her inflexible existentialism. In *The Second Sex,* she asserts bluntly that "there is no justification for present existence other than its expansion into an indefinitely open future," explaining that "every time transcendence falls back into immanence, stagnation, there is a degradation of existence into the '*en-soi.*' . . . It is an absolute evil." In *The Coming of Age,* she continues this line of reasoning. The tragedy is that the elderly can only escape stagnation by undertaking projects, but those very projects require "an indefinitely open future," and a future is precisely what the elderly will not have. Therefore they are doomed. The tragedy of old age has an ontological dimension that can never be avoided or escaped, because the very definition—or meaning—of old age is that one is at the end of one's life span and does not possess a future. Predictably, Beauvoir counsels the elderly to pursue projects and activities, but she is not sanguine about the outcome. Although she recounts with admiration the activities of many productive people in their old age (among them Georges Clemenceau, Victor Hugo, Lou Andreas-Salomé, and Francisco Goya), the accounts are gloomy. As we learn from her memoirs, so is her view of her own experience. Over and over she repeats that the body of her work is essentially formed. To write another book would be merely additive; it would not appreciably change that body of work—her measure of her identity— in any way. The past she refers to as a weight, a burden that grows heavier as one grows older, a prison.

In Beauvoir's view, memory by its very nature is the antithesis of the future-oriented project and thus is an ignoble means of escape from the present. She is contemptuous of the elderly who look back, and she offers stereotyped pictures of tedious old men and women who tell the same stories over and over. Although she has an intuitive grasp of the psychological impetus for the turn of the aged mind toward the past, she rejects *la vie intérieure.* Her interest is in social oppression, not psychic repression, in liberation, not happiness. Certainly her view of memory is linked to her existential philosophical posture, but, again, I think she devalues memory for more personal reasons as well, reasons that have to do with the *texture* of her own mind rather than the *logic* of a philosophy.

In *The Coming of Age* Beauvoir asks to what degree the elderly can recover the past. This is a strange question to pose, peculiar because it supposes a scientific, objective, qualitative criterion for measuring the success of memory. The way in which Beauvoir defines the problem—and the very fact that she defines it as a *problem*—is telling. Viewed as a process of information retrieval, it is a project bound by definition to fail. For Beauvoir, the appropriate or valuable form of memory is not *personal* memory, but rather *social* memory, described as "an intellectual operation that reconstructs and localizes past facts, basing itself upon physiological data, images and a certain knowledge, and making use of logical categories. This is the only one that allows us to some degree, to tell ourselves our own history." In order to tell a life story well, she continues, certain conditions must be met, the most important of which is that "this history must have been recorded," that is, it must have already been written.

Memory, to Beauvoir, is not a matter of considering one's relationship to the past—to work, mates, children, parents, community—in terms of affect. She converts the psychological task of memory, of recovering one's personal past, into the project of what we would call today social history, of taking oneself as a document of the times. Memory is defined as a form of archival research. It is clinical and pictorial in nature, and the results can never be perfectly pure, flawlessly eidetic. The further we stand from an event in our past, she argues, the less likely we are to perceive it with clarity. Beauvoir has no theory of perspective, no sense of needing time and space to see clearly, no belief in a wisdom achieved over time. Thus the elderly are doubly damned: they lack a future and they lack an unobstructed vision of the past.

Memory for Beauvoir is thus basically limited to the retrieval of the factual record and linked to the presentation of a public self, if often under the guise of a private self. I call this *archival memory*. Here I want to distinguish between two other forms of memory, both of which are, in my judgment, crucial to autobiographical practice: *reminiscence,* which I associate with remembrance and the private self; and *knowledge,* in the sense of *savoir,* which I associate with the achieved understanding of one's psychic past (and present) in the psychoanalytic mode. I want further to suggest that Beauvoir's belief that memory (in the sense of archival memory) dims over time is one of the reasons why she was able to write memoirs only (they are a combination of archival memory and reminiscence), and not autobiography (with, we will see, one important exception).

Here I go against the grain of some recent work in women's autobiography as well as against what we might call postmodern or post-structuralist definitions of autobiography, which have expanded to include virtually every form of writing. In her introduction to *Women's Autobiography: Essays in Criticism,* Estelle Jelinek, noting that male autobiography is more connected to a public world than is female autobiography (this, of course, is not the case for Beauvoir, who wrote her memoirs, she tells us, in order to show how she came to be a writer), makes the interesting observation that we have long erred in assuming that the autobiographical mode is necessarily an introspective and intimate one, characterized by a self-conscious and sustained effort to make sense of the narrative (I would add, the *narratives*) of one's life. Instead female "life stories"—the term she uses to cover the vast span of different forms—are more often discontinuous and fragmentary, written in a straightforward, objective manner, yet nonetheless emphasizing the personal rather than the public. I reserve Jelinek's characterization of the female life story for the *memoir*. For *autobiography* I still insist on the dimension of the interpretive, on a hermeneutics of the texts narrating a life; I agree with Karl Weintraub [in "Autobiography and Historical Consciousness,"

Critical Inquiry, 1975], that autobiography derives its "value from rendering significant portions of the past as *interpreted past*" where the past so interpreted gives knowledge (*savoir*) in the psychoanalytic sense. At the same time I want to insist—and this has been my implicit assumption and strategy all along—that the memoir as well as more explicitly theoretical works contains autobiographical materials or, as Marcus Billson and Sidonie Smith put it, that "the memorialist's vision of the outer world is as much a projection and refraction of the self as the autobiographer's" [*Women's Autobiography: Essays in Criticism,* edited by Estelle C. Jelinek]. In the psychoanalytic sense, then, I would add that in Beauvoir's writing, the theoretical works (*The Coming of Age, The Second Sex*), the four memoirs of her own life, and the memoir of Sartre present the *acting out,* while autobiography (as we find it in *A Very Easy Death*) presents, and represents, the *working through.* I believe that autobiography has a *plot,* in Peter Brooks's sense of the term, but just what kind of plot remains to be seen.

As Beauvoir reveals in the introduction to *Force of Circumstance (La Force des Choses),* she felt compelled to record events and feelings in the present because she was convinced that in her old age, "serene or sour, the influence of decrepitude would keep me from grasping my subject: that moment when, hard upon a still vibrant past, the decline sets in." Throughout her memoirs, what at first appears to be an interpretive impulse to autobiography turns into the wish to paint an accurate portrait of herself at an earlier age. At times Beauvoir believed that an earlier self had disappeared entirely. Whereas in *The Prime of Life,* for example, she refers to one of her earliest childhood memories (it had come back to her with particular force when she was in her thirties), in *Force of Circumstance,* which appeared only two years later, she can no longer grasp the child she once was. Poignantly she tells us: *"The little girl whose future has become my past no longer exists. There are times when I want to believe that I still carry her inside me. . . . She has disappeared without leaving even a tiny skeleton to remind me that she did once exist."*

We should not be surprised by such a statement. Beauvoir's memoirs suggest that her relationship to her past is not a particularly personal one. Indeed, one of the reasons her memoirs fail as autobiography is that she chronicles the past in a monotone—the names of the people and movies she saw in a given year, the details of her various trips abroad, a catalog of recent political events in France. Only rarely does she *evoke* her past. For the most part, she plods through it. Her pace is the result, in part, of her practice as a writer of memoirs. She kept voluminous diaries, and in preparing to write her memoirs (her method is not meditative but bibliographical) she spent days, she tells us, in the Bibliothèque Nationale reading old newspapers and journals, immersing herself in the public period of her memoir, refreshing her memory of the historical record. As she confesses, in a fascinating passage from *Force of Circumstance,* her secret dream was not to discover the pattern of her past but to possess the complete record of every detail of her life: *"I have always had the secret fantasy that my life was being recorded, down to the tiniest de-*

tail, on some tape recorder, and that the day would come when I should play back the whole of my past."

"So many memories are failures," Virginia Woolf once remarked, "because they leave out the person to whom things happened." Beauvoir's memoirs disappoint us because they are too connected with the outside world and do not seem motivated by a need to discover her own past. Although she does describe her feelings about her friends and her thoughts about old age—presumably intimate topics—the descriptions read as if she is not present in her own past. She admitted as much in a documentary movie: "I don't have," she said, "very warm, lively memories of what happened to me in the past." We may judge her memoirs by the standard Walter Benjamin set for the storyteller and find them lacking. Benjamin claimed that "not only a man's knowledge or wisdom, but above all his real life—and this is the stuff that stories are made of—first assume transmissible form at the moment of his death" ("The Storyteller" [in his *Illuminations*]). In her memoirs, Beauvoir's life never assumed this "transmissible form." And unfortunately, in ***The Coming of Age,*** she concludes that images of the past are impoverished and colorless for everyone, and that they only become more so as one grows older. (Here again we see the danger of projecting onto old age in general the attitudes, beliefs, and texture of mind that may be idiosyncratic to us as individuals.)

Beauvoir's memoirs reveal a person for whom coming to terms with a personal past is simple, not an important concern; they present us with a portrait of a well-adjusted and confident woman who—at least at the time that she wrote them—did not need to do the kind of psychic work that Robert Butler theorizes is especially important in old age [*Middle Age and Aging,* edited by Bernice L. Neugarten]; the author harbors almost no discernible nostalgia for the past and seems to have no pressing need to ingratiate herself with herself. What, then, compelled her to write her memoirs? They seem to function as a diary, as a collection of events that will help her recall the past, should she ever want to or need to. But my guess is that she wrote them for another reason as well. We should remember that Beauvoir's great ambition was to be a writer. Yet throughout her life as a writer she continually questioned what she should write about and what form her writing should take. The form of the memoir provided her with inexhaustible, ready-made material. It may well have satisfied her need to write *something, anything* to fill page after page as she sat in cafés, in her hotel room, in her studio. The memoir also allowed her, or so she thought, to avoid something she despised in an artist: repetition. Of course, it is ironic that the very person who inveighed against the return to the past which occupies many elderly people should herself have written four volumes of memoirs.

Of the many contradictions between Beauvoir's theoretical positions and her experience as represented in her writing, I will point to two only. The first is by far the most important because it involves ***A Very Easy Death,*** the only book of Beauvoir's which, to my mind, attains the status of a small masterpiece in the autobiographical mode. Of all Beauvoir's books, this narrative, occasioned

by her elderly mother's painful death from intestinal cancer, is the most accomplished in terms of style, structure, voice, and subtlety of observation. It is also the most reflective in its remembrances, with its chapters alternating between the anguished present in the hospital and the past of childhood, with Beauvoir the daughter coming to understand her mother and thus *to be present with her mother* in a way that we are given to understand had never happened before. The space of the book encompasses a moment of *savoir.* For the book is as much about Beauvoir as it is about her mother. In its pages Beauvoir discovers (or should we say, creates?) a meaning to her mother's death and a pattern to her life—to both of their lives. This book has the ring of deep affective truth, the truth which, as Elizabeth Bruss wrote in *Autobiographical Acts,* must always characterize the intent of the writer of autobiography.

In one magical passage Beauvoir, who all her life had resisted identification with her mother, embraces it. The woman who had *reasoned,* logically, that her mother, now in her seventies, was after all of an age to die was quite unprepared for the storm of emotions that overtook her as she kept watch over her dying mother in the hospital. The watching transformed her. "I had put Maman's mouth on my own face and in spite of myself, I copied its movements," she wrote. "Her whole person, her whole being was concentrated there, and compassion wrung my heart." It is an uncanny moment: the daughter taking on the suffering body of the mother, incorporating the mother in what we may conclude was an unconscious act of reparation in the Kleinian sense. For Beauvoir tells us that she was not consciously aware of her gesture—it was Sartre who, watching Beauvoir, recognized the body of the mother in the daughter. It is Beauvoir the writer who incorporates that moment in self-conscious reflection. Perhaps even more important, Beauvoir, who in a later conversation with Alice Schwarzer revealed that she had always understood herself to have played the role of a son to her mother, here assumes the role of the daughter. It is as if, for a moment, the daughter becomes the mother and the mother, the daughter. If the most excruciating test to which a woman can be put is the loss of her child, then Beauvoir suffers here as if from the death of the child she never had. It is only in ***A Very Easy Death*** that Beauvoir reinserts herself into the fabric of the family, her only family, since she did not desire to make one for herself. It is important that she dedicates the book to her only sibling, her sister.

A Very Easy Death is the only book in which Beauvoir permits the past to have an effect on the present, in which she allows a reciprocity between the past and the present in the psychoanalytic sense. When Beauvoir refers to her mother's death in her memoir, ***All Said and Done,*** she reduces it to a colorless, unambiguous event that serves to illustrate the threats of today's medical technology. In both ***The Coming of Age*** and ***All Said and Done,*** she does not recall that her need to write about her mother was a need to reestablish a bond between them—precisely in the mode of psychic work which she would deny to the elderly.

My second example of the contradictions between Beauvoir's theory and her writing practices is found in *All Said and Done.* In this book, published only two years after *The Coming of Age,* in which she rejected reminiscence, Beauvoir on the contrary admits to the pleasures of reminiscence, just as she mentions for the first time the gratification she derives from dreams precisely because "they have no dimension in the future." In her early sixties at the time of writing *All Said and Done,* she tells us her concern is "recovering my life—reviving forgotten memories, re-reading, re-seeing, rounding off incomplete pieces of knowledge, filling gaps, clarifying obscurities, gathering scattered elements together. Just as though there had to be a study on the moment when my experience was to be summed up, and as though it mattered that this summing-up should be done." She speaks warmly of the Left Bank of Paris as a place rich in memories and observes that she has always taken pleasure in talking over old times with her sister, Sartre, and her friends. Whereas before she vehemently denied any link between identity and reminiscence, now she embraces such a link, and her concern with reminiscence sounds very much like Butler's notion of the life review. Yet Beauvoir does not seem to be aware of a change in her thinking. In this matter, her thought lacks dialectical insight. After the first few chapters of *All Said and Done,* incipient autobiography breaks down into the half-life and soon thereafter the quarter-life of the march of events. What seems to have begun as a life review in Butler's sense devolves into a chronicle, a recitation of events, a diary.

I think Beauvoir's inability to see this contradiction, to take into account the lie her experience gave to her theory over time, is related to her sense of the human life span as ideally unchanging. She never considered, seriously or even indifferently, notions of psychological stages in human development such as those proposed by Erik Erikson. Yet throughout her life she was fascinated with the relationship of identity to time. Her intuitions were precocious. In *Memoirs of a Dutiful Daughter* she tells us that at age three or so, gazing at her mother's empty armchair, she understood that time would wrench her from the secure world of her mother's body, her presence, and she thought to herself: " 'I won't be able to sit on her knee any more if I go on growing up.' Suddenly the future existed; it would turn me into another being, someone who would still be, and yet no longer seem myself." This mystery of human identity, the shadowy relation we adults bear to our childhood, captivated her. One fairy tale in particular enchanted her—the story of Charlotte, whose body shrinks to miniature proportions and then swells to gigantic dimensions. As a little girl, Beauvoir imagined herself to be Charlotte and commented with palpable relief: "I came out of the adventure *safe and sound* after having been reduced to a foetus and then blown up to matronly dimensions" (emphasis mine). Almost obsessively she associates the miniature and the *gigantesque* with changes in the body, with a condition to be feared and avoided—with, in short, pregnancy and motherhood. Surely it is not insignificant that neither as an adolescent nor as an adult did she see motherhood as part of her future.

As a woman in late middle age, the author of *The Coming of Age* advised the elderly to remain involved in the activities of their middle years. She was committed to this philosophy, but I would again observe that she was projecting onto old age in general a quality unique to her—the way she had led her own adult life up to age sixty. Despite Beauvoir's transformation from a rather solitary university student into a public figure, her life is remarkable for its *lack* of change. As she is fond of noting, she lived her entire life in the same "village," a small section on the Left Bank of Paris. Until his death in 1980 Jean-Paul Sartre was her constant companion. Throughout her adult years she pursued the same occupation—writing—and had many friends to whom she remained attached for years. Her life was never punctuated by the birth and growth of children. It was, in other words, distinguished by remarkable continuity. Her own experience must have reinforced her philosophical conviction that the ideal life span is one that is not marred by intrusive change, whether biological change (puberty, motherhood, old age) or an abandonment of the goals defined for oneself in the early years of adulthood.

I have argued that Beauvoir's dark portrait of old age is due in part to her personal revulsion for changes in the human body and to her particular temperament, which does not value certain forms of memory. I also think that her grim view of old age may have sprung from the working out of one of her personal obsessions—that of death and the concomitant fear of loss which she believed advancing years would inevitably bring. In *The Coming of Age,* Beauvoir details the various forms melancholia may take in old age. But more important for our present purposes is her observation that the death wish is a strong urge present in all of us, not just in those who suffer from the chronic and increasingly painful condition of dispossession in old age.

I have already mentioned that a preoccupation with death saturates Beauvoir's work and life. This preoccupation has been amply discussed by Elaine Marks [in her *Simone de Beauvoir: Encounters with Death*] and others, and there is no need to trace that theme here. Instead I should like to suggest that at the root of her fears about old age—fears expressed through her obsessively catastrophic view in *The Coming of Age*—is not so much panic at the prospect of her own death but rather her dread of losing Sartre to death.

Here I turn to the psychoanalyst Gregory Rochlin's theory of the loss complex. Although Freud's speculations on the relationship between mourning and melancholia are seminal, he devoted only a few pages to the problem, and I have long wished for a more extended treatment of it. Rochlin's wise, book-length *Griefs and Discontents: The Forces of Change* fills this gap with a general theory that has a developmental basis: Rochlin concludes that our relationship to loss changes over the course of the life span. He argues that our lives are marked by an ongoing, continuous cycle of loss and restitution, which he calls the loss complex. Although the foundation of his theory is Freud's distinction between mourning and melancholia, Rochlin's contribution to an understanding of these two psychological states pivots on Freud's earlier insight that we never willingly give anything up. "Really we never can relinquish anything," Freud declared in an essay published almost a decade before his 1917 essay on mourning and melancholia; "we only exchange one thing for something else. When we appear to give something up, all we really do is to adopt a substitute" ("Relation of the Poet to Day-Dreaming"). The work of mourning is completed only when all libido has been withdrawn *and* attached to a new object, a substitute for the lost object—a loss which can never be tolerated and which is but one in a series of losses, of substitutions, in an infinite regression. The work of mourning, then, is to restore what has been lost, to bring us back to our previous condition.

Rochlin casts Freud's distinction between the psychological states of mourning and melancholy onto another plane, differentiating between the cycle of *loss and restitution,* which I would call the normal process of mourning, and the cycle of *loss and impoverishment,* which indeed may not be a cycle at all but instead a dead end, the cessation of restitution, the pathological state of melancholia understood clinically as depression. According to Rochlin, the stage of life known as old age is almost invariably marked by impoverishment. It is characterized by a series of severe losses for which we cannot reasonably expect to find substitutes.

Rochlin believes that throughout our lives we work, consciously and unconsciously, to shore up our defenses against future losses. His clinical research has led him to conclude that old age is a special phase of development whose psychological work is triggered by the combination of the loss of physical function (degenerative processes) and the loss of loved objects. "Paradoxically," he judges, "the intensified defenses of this period are more attached to the *fantasies* of loss than to the reality of losses" (emphasis mine). In its simplest form, the loss complex is an expression of the dread of abandonment. In old age as well as throughout the life span, the work of the loss complex is thus in great part *prospective,* a technique of mastering deprivation in anticipation of a final loss. It is anticipatory grief.

Beauvoir associates old age in general with melancholia, a terrible solitude and loss, and, specifically, with the death of Sartre, which for her would be catastrophic. Unlike Proust, who was obsessed with the recovery of the past, she was obsessed with the tragedy that she believed the future would inevitably bring. This concern hovered between fear and hysteria and sprang, I think, from the all-important role which a close mate played throughout her life. At the precocious age of three, Beauvoir reports in *Dutiful Daughter,* she "had forebodings of all the separations, the refusals, the desertions to come, and of the long succession of my various deaths." This intimation of loss was repeated over and over again, rehearsed in her fiction and her memoirs, played out in her critical writing. Throughout her life, the death of the self—her self—is linked indissolubly to the loss of others, to abandonment, to aging, to solitude, to death. Beauvoir explains in *Dutiful Daughter* that at an early age—when she was only about six—she understood that "a partner was absolutely essential to me if I was to bring my imaginary stories to life."

She was speaking of her relationship with her younger sister Poupette, the only member of her family to whom she was really close.

Beauvoir's feelings of panic at the thought of the loss of a loved one seem to have been reinforced by World War I. Although she had never experienced the loss of someone important to her, she fantasized what such a loss would mean: "I used to choke with dread whenever I thought of mortal death which separates forever those who love one another." Until Beauvoir met Zaza at school, Poupette was her only "partner," her only close friend. In her relationship to Zaza, we see Beauvoir playing out in fantasy the cycle of loss and impoverishment followed by the cycle of loss and the attempt at restitution. She imagines the absence of Zaza. In *Dutiful Daughter* she tells us how one day she walked into school and, staring with stupefaction at Zaza's empty seat, thought to herself, " 'What if she were never to sit there again, what if she were to die, then what would happen to me?' " This experience is for her a "blinding revelation," the realization that a future loss will have apocalyptic force for her. But this realization, generated by the imagination, will also blind her to a more balanced view of life processes. It is her blind spot. I am not suggesting that hers are idle imaginings or petty forebodings—indeed Zaza did die at a very early age—but rather that they were particularly intense and functioned blindly as well as presciently in the economy of her imagination. The very strength and force of this insight concealed as much as it revealed.

Although the two had drifted somewhat apart, Zaza's death devastated Beauvoir. It was through her relationship with Zaza that she had come to value the pleasures of a daily, intimate companionship and intellectual exchange with another person. Their friendship would be, for the rest of her life, the model of a meaningful relationship with another person—a relationship with an equal partner, not with a parent or a child. It is not surprising that Beauvoir concludes the first volume of her memoirs with the death of Zaza, whom she tried again and again to resurrect in the imagination, in the world of her writing; that resurrection would be, for her, a form of restitution for the loss.

As an adult Beauvoir was convinced that harm could come to her from Sartre only if he were to die before she did. His imperfect health frightened her. She dismissed the prospect of sharing old age with him as an impossible fantasy. It was, as she put it in *Force of Circumstance,* a "refuge" from reality, an absurd, "far-off, well-behaved dream." Her association of the terror of old age with the death of Sartre is seen even more clearly later in *Force of Circumstance,* when she recounts what the experience of Sartre's dreadful illness in 1954 meant to her. Seeing him in the hospital in Brazil, she suddenly realized that "he was carrying his own death within him," that death was no longer, for her, "a metaphysical scandal, it was a quality of our arteries." Later when he falls ill in Paris—exhausted, confusing his words, mumbling presciently and aphasically about his trouble with the "thickets of the heart"—his death is more than an intimate presence to her: now it possesses her. She writes: "This subjection, this possession, had a name . . . old age." As she had written earlier in *The Prime of Life,* "my greatest wish was to die with the one I loved." Beauvoir had an intuition amounting to conviction that Sartre would die before she did and that the loss would be intolerable. Her fiction enacts that dread of abandonment. One of the major themes of her short fiction is the loss of a mate due to dependency. Her fictional preoccupation with abandonment is so emphatic that we can read it as a symptom of her obsession with the loss of Sartre.

I am arguing that much of Beauvoir's writing took place under the sign of anxiety, not desire. In *Beyond the Pleasure Principle,* Freud distinguishes between fright, fear, and anxiety. Whereas both fear and fright are associated with the present (for fear there must be a definite object of which one is afraid, and fright is the state of encountering a danger unprepared), anxiety is associated with the future. Anxiety is a state of expecting a danger and preparing oneself for it, although the danger may be unknown to oneself, that is, not consciously known.

In a fundamental sense, of course, as Freud and Lacan have taught us, all narrative has to do with loss in the past. But it is wrong, I think, to read all narrative under the sign of desire—that ubiquitous word—for the originary lost object. André Green, in his essay "The Double and Its Absent," writes without hesitation that "the work of writing presupposes a wound and a loss, a work of mourning, of which the text is the transformation into a fictitious positivity." The emphasis is on past loss. But the wound itself may be "fictitious," or yet to come. In *Reading for the Plot,* Peter Brooks, like Green, reaches certain conclusions about narrative based on his reading of Freud, and in particular on his reading of *Beyond the Pleasure Principle.* In Brooks's view, narrative essentially has to do with the recovery of the past (with this I, of course, agree), but with *desire* as its motive force. He makes an excellent distinction, I think, between repetition as the assertion of mastery (the *fort-da*) and repetition as a "process of *binding* toward the creation of an energetic constant-state situation which will permit the emergence of mastery and the possibility of postponement." The thematic and figural repetition of old age throughout Beauvoir's writing works precisely, it seems to me, to permit both mastery and postponement. It is as though she creates the symbolic world in which she fears to live so as to acquaint herself with, and thus inure herself to, future loss. But her model is not desire; it is, rather, anxiety. We may speculate that the narrative of desire is a traditional male model, and the narrative of anxiety a female model. Freud has written that the most important event in a man's life is the death of his father, a death that frees a space for the enactment of desire. But, as I have already proposed, for a woman—a mother—is not that event the death of her child, a loss that is always projected in the future, a possible loss encircled with anxiety? And did not Sartre represent in Beauvoir's life father, husband, and child?

Restitution may be accomplished in actuality or in fantasy, consciously or unconsciously, by the process of symbolization or by the process of substitution. Beauvoir saw her book *The Coming of Age* as a means of alerting West-

ern society to the perils of old age. She believed that the book might result in efforts to alleviate the disgraceful treatment of the elderly by society as a whole. By writing that book—an act unconsciously informed by fear of her personal loss of Sartre—she also may have accomplished, in the world of words, a kind of restitution.

In *Force of Circumstance,* Beauvoir muses that her severe anxiety attacks "were a last revolt before resigning myself to age and the end that follows it." She opens the epilogue to this volume of her memoirs with a paean to her life with Sartre: "There has been one undoubted success in my life: my relationship with Sartre. In more than thirty years, we have only once gone to sleep at night disunited." She concludes the volume with an emotionally charged evaluation of what aging has meant to her. Her epilogue is indeed a sign or symptom of an anxiety attack.

She writes of aging as a mutilation, as the most "irreparable" thing that has happened to her since the end of World War II. She laments that the world has contracted for her. She chafes against the fact that her experience of human suffering and injustice in the world has led to a lessening of her horror at human misery. The result of having made choices in living her life is that she has been limited by those choices, and she is saddened by this. Her imagery is of calcification, hardening, imprisonment. Aging is "petrification," a "pox." And she detests the physical signs of it. "I loathe my appearance now: the eyebrows slipping down toward the eyes, the bags underneath, the excessive fullness of the cheeks, and that air of sadness around the mouth that wrinkles always bring." She speaks of her strengths having "dimmed," of the coming "deteriorations," of pleasures having "paled," of the loss of all desire, all sexuality. In this sense her very body is absent to her, dead—"it's strange not to be a body any more"—at the same time as it is ominously present as a prison. "I try not to think: in ten years, in a year. Memories grow thin, myths crack and peep, projects rot in the bud." These words, melancholic and near-hysterical at once—we read also of the "furious gallop to the tomb"—were written, we must not forget, when Beauvoir was only in her mid-fifties.

But by the time she wrote *All Said and Done,* the fourth volume of her memoirs, when she was sixty-three, a sea change had taken place. Her crises ceased. The woman who had always been contemptuous of a philosophic calm, who had always raged and hammered against old age and death, now speaks of her peace with death and of the heroic quality of Freud's resignation in his last years. With the publication of *All Said and Done,* the woman who had always defined herself as a writer virtually gave up writing— it now seemed pointless to her—and turned to active political work. Beauvoir tells us that it was in her early fifties that her aging had become apparent to her. Now, in her early sixties, she found she had reached an unanticipated plateau. She writes: "The first thing that strikes me when I look back at the ten years that have passed since I finished *Force of Circumstance* is that I do not feel that I have aged." She admits that her long-held fears about old age have in great part been proven wrong. Although she sees her life as a chronicle of losses, she realizes anew that it is also characterized by the continual creation of new friendships.

In *All Said and Done,* Beauvoir implicitly acknowledges two stages of old age. The first has come as a surprise to her: it is characterized by health and by changes in attitude which she had not foreseen. This is what gerontologists in the United States now refer to as the period of the "young old." The second stage is that period of tragic decline and ill health which she had believed characterized old age as a whole; this is more or less what gerontologists now call the period of the "old old," seventy-five and over. Having entered old age and discovered that it did not accord with her bleak and grim expectations, she defers her original view of old age as a period of decrepitude until later.

Later, as it turns out, will indeed come much later. In mourning for Sartre, Beauvoir turned again to writing, chronicling the last ten years of his life in *Adieux: A Farewell to Sartre.* She did survive his loss—so well that she could astonish me with her words of 1982 in which she passes, we might say, from the world of men (that is, Sartre) to the world of women, telling Alice Schwarzer that she believed that, whereas love affairs between men and women often do not last, by contrast great friendships between women often endure. She asserts in complete confidence, in the same conversation with Schwarzer, that "up to my death, I will never be alone" (translation mine).

But I want to insist again, in closing, that it was not only the reality of Beauvoir's experience of old age that led her to these conclusions. A lifetime of the projection of loss and anxiety in writing may well have constituted significant psychological work. Although that work took the form of melancholia (Julia Kristeva has theorized that all writing is melancholic), it may also have served the purpose of mourning in advance of actual loss—mourning that helped her overcome the actual loss of Sartre and that prepared her for other losses to come in her own old age. (pp. 93-111)

> Kathleen Woodward, "Simone de Beauvoir: Aging and Its Discontents," in The Private Self: Theory and Practice of Women's Autobiographical Writings, *edited by Shari Benstock, The University of North Carolina Press, 1988, pp. 90-113.*

Yolanda Astarita Patterson

It is in *The Second Sex* that Simone de Beauvoir first goes beyond a fictional transposition of her observations of the female condition to an analysis of the many elements which contribute to explaining it. The author began to work on this book when she realized that before she could be ready to write her own autobiography she needed to understand what difference the fact that she was born a woman had made in her life. Published in 1949, this monumental text explores the biological, psychological, social, and economic factors which have traditionally limited woman's access to independence and equality. The childbearing function is a recurrent theme in Beauvoir's analysis of the problems inherent in being born a woman and her comments about maternity provoked outrage in many of the early readers of her study.

Speaking of woman's destiny, the author presents female biology as a battle between the individual and the species, with the latter inevitably prevailing. Puberty is described as the moment when "the species reaffirms its rights" over the previously carefree young girl. In a comparison of the human and animal worlds, Beauvoir notes that, for females, only in the higher monkeys and in human beings is the reproductive process a recurrent monthly phenomenon rather than a seasonal one. The biological cycles are thus regarded as an unending series of crises for the individual woman, who progresses from the onset of menstruation through pregnancy, childbirth, and child care to the negation of her reproductive usefulness at the time of menopause.

In the two lengthy volumes of *The Second Sex,* Simone de Beauvoir follows the female child from birth through old age. She highlights the strong influence which the mother-child relationship has on the future development of the individual, pointing out that although the mother is the first love object for both boys and girls, boys quickly realize at an early age that they must break away from the maternal sphere of influence and are indeed encouraged by family and society to do so. Little girls, on the other hand, are expected to remain close to their mothers, to emulate them, eventually to help them with their daily chores. Traditionally, they play at being "Mommy," using their dolls as surrogate offspring. Children of both sexes are fascinated by their mother's ability to produce a new human being from her stomach, the author notes. "It's as beautiful as a sleight-of-hand trick. The mother appears endowed with the awesome power of fairies," she remarks somewhat ironically. In early childhood, according to Beauvoir's research, a little girl generally considers herself privileged to belong to the sex capable of performing this magical feat.

In a later chapter on lesbianism, Simone de Beauvoir acknowledges the importance certain psychoanalysts of the period attached to the mother's treatment of her daughter in the development of the latter's sexuality. Overly possessive or overtly hostile, the mother is cast as the culprit in turning her child toward homosexuality:

> There are two cases in which the adolescent girl has difficulty escaping from [her mother's] grasp: if she has been passionately protected by an anxious mother; or if she has been mistreated by a "bad mother" who has left her with a deep feeling of guilt. In the first case, their relationship was often bordering on homosexuality. . . . The girl will seek this same happiness in a new embrace. In the second case, she will feel a burning desire for a "good mother" who can protect her from the first one, who can take away the curse hanging over her head.

Words such as "grasp," "anxious," "mistreated," and "curse" suggest the negative feelings experienced by the author when she considers the extremes of mothering she has witnessed during her own childhood and adolescence.

Although Beauvoir does not completely concur with the

above explanation of lesbianism, the paragraphs which she devotes to it underline her awareness of the overwhelming influence of the maternal attitude on the development of the captive child. Heterosexual or homosexual, the maturing girl's search for a love object will often be an attempt to recreate the comfortable paradise of her childhood, according to *The Second Sex:*

> A woman does not wish to reincarnate one individual in another, but rather to revive a situation: the one she knew as a little girl protected by adults. She has been a complete part of the life of her family, has enjoyed in her home the peace of quasi passivity. Love will give her back her mother as well as her father. It will give her back her childhood.

Beauvoir is here drawing on her own experience as part of a loving and supportive family and as the daughter of an affectionate, committed mother. Her perceptive analysis challenges the Freudian theory that all women are seeking a father substitute in the men they love and marry. It suggests that beyond the obvious physical attraction which draws one human being to another lies the nostalgia of childhood, the desire to return to a phase of one's life clearly dominated by the figure of a mother who absorbs all cares and all responsibilities.

It is only in the very early years of childhood, however, that the female child accepts her mother unquestioningly. As she matures, she begins to wonder, as did the Beauvoir sisters, about her mother's limited role in society, to suspect that it is rather her father's activities which are validated by public opinion. The narrow confines of her home suddenly appear suffocating. The adjective *étouffant* is used repeatedly by Beauvoir to describe the family circle. Like the young Simone, the little girl is portrayed as detaching herself from her mother's dominion in order to fill her life with more meaningful tasks than the daily repetition of never-ending household chores. As her father grows in her esteem, her opinion of her mother's worth diminishes. With the approach of puberty, pregnancy and childbirth become frightening rather than miraculous phenomena: "Often it no longer seems marvelous but rather horrible to her that a parasitical entity is to grow inside her own body; the idea of this monstrous growth terrifies her. . . . Visions of swelling, of tearing, of hemorrhaging come to haunt her." This description of the reproductive process is a very personal one of Beauvoir's and can be found in numerous passages of her fictional works. The mother-child symbiosis which some women crave becomes in the author's eyes "parasitical," "monstrous," "horrible," and "terrifying." *The Second Sex* suggests that everything associated with her mother is devalued and distasteful in the young girl's mind as she becomes biologically capable of supplanting the woman who has most influenced her life.

With adolescence comes ambivalence about one's female identity. On the one hand there is the frightening prospect of pregnancy and childbirth described above, the haunting image of the parasitic embryo . . . in *When Things of the Spirit Come First* and *The Blood of Others.* On the other hand there is the familiarity of the role of wife and mother for which the girl has been psychologically prepared since the first years of her life. Convinced that she is "destined to keep the human race going and the home fires burning," she views marriage as a welcome escape from the decisions she must otherwise make about her future. Beauvoir here presents a point of view which will be reinforced by Betty Friedan in *The Feminine Mystique* more than a decade later. This comfortable choice of marriage and motherhood is seen by the author as an acceptance of passivity:

> The first twenty years of a woman's life are extraordinarily rich; the woman . . . discovers the world and her destiny. At age twenty, she is a housewife permanently attached to one man, with a child in her arms; her life is over forever. Real action and real work are done only by men.

For Beauvoir, a willingness to take on the expected traditional female roles is thus interpreted as a rejection of vitality, as a reluctance to commit oneself to meaningful participation in the real world. There are undoubtedly many contemporary women who would disagree with her bias in evaluating women's options, particularly those currently labeled "superwomen" by the media who have somehow managed to juggle families and careers successfully.

When Simone de Beauvoir was writing *The Second Sex,* many women had indeed tasted the freedom and independence afforded by a career, or at least by being active participants in a wartime marketplace which needed their contribution. Like Betty Friedan, Beauvoir was one of the first to emphasize the psychological satisfaction derived from pursuing a career and being paid for one's efforts. The author cites the childbearing function as the culprit in keeping women from continuing to participate in the work of their choice: "In most cases, the birth of a child obliges them to retreat to their matron's role. It is extremely difficult at the present time to juggle work and maternity." Persuaded by society that the path to true fulfillment requires the assumption of responsibilities as wife and mother, the working woman of the 1940s readily abandoned her career goals as extraneous to what she had been led to consider the more essential part of her existence. Although the atmosphere has changed considerably in the decades since the publication of *The Second Sex,* young women of the 1980s are still torn between their desire to forge ahead in their careers and the lure of participating in the creation of a new generation.

Many pages of *The Second Sex* are devoted to an analysis of the pressures brought to bear upon women by a society eager to keep them at home as wives and mothers. The unmarried woman has traditionally been treated as a useless appendage in many families, an attitude which leads young girls to assume that any husband is better than none. Until relatively recent advances in methods of contraception and abortion, a married woman was obliged to consume her youth and her energy in an endless series of pregnancies. According to Beauvoir: "The woman cannot actually be forced to bear children: all one can do is enclose her in situations where maternity is the only way out for her. The law and custom force her to marry, contraception and abortion are forbidden, as is divorce. . . ." In the conservative atmosphere of the 1940s, motherhood thus became an imprisonment rather than a choice freely and joyfully made. Highlighting the physical weakening of women through menstruation, pregnancy, childbirth, and child care, Beauvoir ascribes the development of male dominance to women's inability to assume an equal share of the work of the community. Motherhood traps the woman at home, where countless chores repeated at exhaustingly frequent intervals gradually erode away her youth, her vitality, and her interest in the realm of life that extends beyond her doorstep. The author paints a rather grim picture here, a demystification of the media presentation of serenely happy mothers beaming at their rosy-cheeked, gurgling babies.

The perceptive wife and mother soon finds herself caught in "a most ingenious paradox," as Gilbert and Sullivan would put it: the society which has led her to believe that she will find fulfillment, respect, and admiration in her current situation values violence, danger, and risk of one's life far more highly than the creation and preservation of life. In Beauvoir's estimation "it is not by creating life, but rather by risking one's life that man proves himself superior to animals; that is why humanity grants superiority not to the sex which gives birth but to the sex which kills." In Fosca's frustrated plans for his son Antoine in *All Men Are Mortal,* [we observe] the discrepancy between the lip service paid to creativity and peace and man's drive to prove his value through danger and violence. It is of interest to note that in a number of Jean-Paul Sartre's fictional works, the existential hero proves himself by killing someone else: Mathieu in *Troubled Sleep,* Oreste in *The Flies,* Hugo Barine in *Dirty Hands,* Goetz in *The Devil and the Good Lord.* Beauvoir's early female protagonists follow suit as Françoise Miquel turns on the gas and leaves Xavière to suffocate, as Hélène Bertrand chooses a much more masculine mode of action when she throws a grenade at the Nazi soldiers. In each case, the protagonists find fulfillment and a sense of identity in their acts of violence.

Having been raised by a devoutly Catholic mother, Beauvoir discusses the added pressure to bear many children felt by women raised in predominantly Catholic countries. Glorifying purity and abstinence, the church of the author's childhood has traditionally looked upon marriage as a concession to human weakness, justified primarily as a necessary evil for the perpetuation of the species. Women of Beauvoir's generation were therefore encouraged to marry young and to produce as many children as possible. The strong religious stand against planned parenthood reverberates in Saint Augustine's proclamation quoted in *The Second Sex:* "Any woman who takes any measures to prevent herself from giving birth to as many children as she can bear is guilty of that many homicides. . . ." The fact that such an authoritative statement comes from a man who has never had first-hand experience with the childbearing process does not escape Beauvoir's perceptive eye.

Having capitulated to religious and societal pressures, the young married woman depicted in *The Second Sex* finds herself faced with the physical discomforts of pregnancy. Beauvoir sees problems like morning sickness as an indica-

tion of "the revolt of the organism against the species which is taking possession of it." The modern gynecologist might well take issue with this assumption and rather attribute such symptoms to chemical imbalances.

Beauvoir discusses in considerable detail male ambivalence toward the whole reproductive process. The husband who has himself been programmed to sire a new generation often has little emotional support to offer his pregnant wife, according to her research. From childhood he has been alternately fascinated, frightened, and repulsed by female fertility: "Man is repulsed by finding in the woman he possesses the qualities which he has feared in his own mother." This analysis foreshadows the theme of Dorothy Dinnerstein's *The Mermaid and the Minotaur.* The mysteries attached to conception and childbearing have been surrounded by taboos and superstitions from primitive times on. In Simone de Beauvoir's opinion, "Underlying all the respect with which society endows it, the childbearing function inspires spontaneous repugnance." If both husband and wife have ambivalent feelings about the pregnancy, there is little mutual comfort which they can offer one another as she experiences a series of physical changes over which she appears to have no control. "Repugnance" is a very strong word in this context, indicating once again Simone de Beauvoir's personal bias. Her analysis of the sense of helplessness which may overcome a young couple expecting their first child is, however, extremely perceptive.

The author suggests that throughout the centuries men have attempted to divest women of any autonomy in the childbearing process. She has uncovered a revealing quotation from the Greek playwright Aeschylus in support of her argument: "It is not the mother who gives life to what people call her child. She only nourishes the germ poured into her breast. The father is the one who creates life. Woman, like a foreign receptacle, receives the germ and, if the gods so will, she becomes its guardian." Aeschylus would thus deprive women of any claim to an active contribution to society. Christianity, according to Beauvoir, is scarcely more generous. She sees in the cult of the Virgin Mary "the supreme male victory . . . the rehabilitation of woman through the accomplishment of her defeat." Mary's eagerness to kneel down before her son thus represents for the author the ultimate capitulation of female to male. The cult of the virgin contributes to the myth of the ideal Mother, created, in the author's opinion, to allow man to avoid recognizing the woman who gave him life as an essentially carnal being. Deified, purified, sterilized, woman becomes less threatening. In this passage one is aware of echoes of Françoise Miquel's reluctance to play divinity for Xavière and Pierre in *She Came to Stay.* The glorified image of motherhood becomes a haunting standard for the all-too-human women often unwittingly cast in that role, women who quickly realize that they will never be able to conform to all of the expectations with which religion and bourgeois society have encumbered maternity.

Psychological studies point out that the attitude of the mother toward her newborn daughter is fraught with ambivalence: "The daughter is both a double and an Other for the mother. The mother feels both a fierce attachment and hostility toward her." Treating the daughter as a double is effective as long as the child is willing to accept such a role. Gradually, however, each little girl begins to grow up and to pull away from her mother's sphere of influence. "The more the girl matures, the more cumbersome her mother's authority seems to her," Beauvoir notes. The adolescent girl will often focus her admiration and affection on an older girl woman or woman outside of the family circle, thereby arousing jealousy and resentment in a mother whose maternal role has been the only justification for her existence.

Simone de Beauvoir is painfully aware of the frustrations inherent in the mother-child relationship. For some new mothers, the newborn baby represents a love object to whom they utter "words that are almost those of a lover." For others, a child provides a long-awaited opportunity to dominate another human being and may be treated like a miniature slave or a performing circus animal. . . . Still another group revels in the role of martyr, dwelling on the sacrifices demanded by motherhood and creating a gnawing sense of guilt in its offspring: "the *mater dolorosa* creates from her suffering a weapon which she uses sadistically." No matter what its nature, however, any obsessive attachment to one's children is destined to meet with disappointment and futility. "Whether a mother is passionately affectionate or hostile, her child's independence destroys her hopes," the author warns.

It is the very lack of reciprocity in the mother-child relationship which accounts for both the problems and the "grandeur" of maternal love, according to Beauvoir. In a very revealing passage, she interprets the search for domestic bliss as an attempt to curb the passage of time, to insulate family members from the real world:

> The ideal of happiness has always taken concrete shape in the form of a house, be it a hut or a castle. The home is an incarnation of permanence and of separation. It is between its walls that the family establishes itself as an isolated cell and asserts its identity beyond the flow of generations. The past, preserved in the form of furniture and family portraits, prefigures a future without risk. . . .

It is the mother alone, however, who operates only within the four walls of her home. Her husband leaves for work each morning, her children soon go off to school. She is left striving frantically to find fulfillment in an encapsulated existence which she shares only with other nonworking mothers. In her solitude she bravely assumes the burden of creating "happiness" for the members of her family.

The Second Sex traces the gradual separation between mother and child which begins dramatically at the moment of childbirth: "The mother wants both to keep this treasure of flesh which is a precious part of herself in her womb and to free herself of something bothersome." The recurrent emphasis on the bothersome aspect of childbearing in Beauvoir's work is echoed in this passage, which labels the developing embryo a *gêneur*. The author's attitude toward pregnancy and childbirth may be partially explained by the fact that a pregnant woman does not seem to have any control over what is taking place in her body. She cannot, for example, choose to keep the child inside of her womb. An irreversible biological process expels it and sets it on the path to independence. Never again can the mother completely recapture the intimacy of the nine months during which the developing entity has been an integral part of her physical being. She must gradually resign herself to seeing her son move beyond her limited sphere of influence into a broader world of masculine values, to watching her daughter develop into a young woman whose sexuality threatens to supplant the energy and vitality of her parents' generation. In Beauvoirian terms, the mother of an adolescent has no alternative but to "accept her defeat."

The more her identity is tied up in her children, the more difficult it will be for the mother to allow them to have an individual existence of their own. It is the exceptional mother, according to Beauvoir, who has the "rare mixture of generosity and detachment which allows her to find enrichment in her children without becoming a tyrant for them or allowing them to tyrannize her." During her own adolescence, Beauvoir watched her classmate Zaza be tyrannized and manipulated by the mother she adored and at the same time resented her own mother's awkward attempts to dominate the lives of her two creative and independent daughters. Although she had undoubtedly observed children who tyrannized their mothers, it is of interest that she did not choose to use any of them as models for her fictional characters. In her fiction, mothers are consistently manipulative or martyred, but the martyrdom is of their own choosing and never blamed by the author on ungrateful children.

Just as Nancy Friday analyzes [in her *My Mother/My Self*] the threat a daughter's budding sexuality represents for her mother, Simone de Beauvoir observes many years earlier that for women who look to motherhood for the sole justification of their existence, the birth of a new generation can be extremely unsettling. The pregnancy of either her own daughter or a daughter-in-law can remind such a mother of her relative insignificance: "Life will go on without her; she is no longer THE Mother: just a link . . . she is no longer anything but an outdated, finished individual." Brought up to seek fulfillment in caring for and serving others, she suddenly finds herself with no one left who requires her attention. A continuance of the nurturing role with grandchildren or with protégés of a younger generation may help fill the void, although Beauvoir considers it "very unusual for the woman to find in her posterity—be it biological or handpicked—justification for her declining role in life. . . . She knows that she is useless." It is in this feeling of futility and uselessness that the author finds the explanation for the depression which sometimes accompanies menopause.

Beauvoir's own pessimism is apparent in the change of tone that has occurred between her play *Who Shall Die?* and *The Second Sex.* The French title of the play highlights the assumption that there are indeed no "useless mouths," that everyone in Vaucelles, women, children, and the aged, has an important part to play and a compelling reason to go on living. The author is much more severe in her application of the term "useless" (*inutile*) to the family-oriented women without careers whom she describes in *The Second Sex.*

How then is the woman of the mid-twentieth century to deal with motherhood? It is significant that Simone de Beauvoir devotes the first fourteen pages of her chapter entitled "The Mother" to a discussion of contraception and abortion. The author reiterates throughout the two volumes of *The Second Sex* her firm conviction that motherhood should be assumed only willingly and joyfully. She casts a perceptive spotlight on the hypocrisy of a bourgeois society which on the one hand waxes lyrical about the glories of maternity and on the other hand is quick to pressure a pregnant female whose condition might undermine the financial and social ambitions of her partner into doing away with the product of their sexual union:

> Since her childhood, the woman has been told again and again that she is made to have children and has heard hymns to the splendor of motherhood. . . . Everything is justified by the marvelous privilege of bringing children into the world which is hers alone. And now a man, in order to keep his freedom, . . . asks a woman to give up her feminine triumph.

This is very much the dilemma facing Sartre's Mathieu in *The Age of Reason* when his mistress Marcelle becomes pregnant and wants to have the child. Mathieu spends the entire duration of the narrative rushing here and there trying to raise money for an abortion and is finally greatly relieved when his homosexual and masochistic friend Daniel offers to marry Marcelle so that she can keep the child.

Although Simone de Beauvoir is totally in favor of legalizing abortion so that it may be equally available to women of all social classes, she is also very much aware of the trauma it represents for those brought up with traditional middle-class values. She describes the emotional aftermath of abortion in graphically naturalistic terms: "The only thing [the woman] remembers for certain is that foraged and bleeding womb, those bits of red life, that absent child." Between the exterior pressure to do away with the child and the inner sense of frustration at being unable to carry the pregnancy to full term and thereby complete the creative process it represents, the woman who has undergone an abortion is left with extremely ambivalent feelings about maternity.

Simone de Beauvoir chastizes Western mentality for denying women an active role in society while at the same time entrusting to them "the most delicate, the most serious undertaking one can imagine: the formation of a human being." She sees fulfillment through motherhood as a possibility only for the altruistic woman capable of respecting her child as an individual: "Nothing is more rare than the woman who genuinely respects the human being in her child, who recognizes his freedom even in his failures, who assumes with him the risks implicit in any commitment." Children bring joy rather than continual frustration only to "the woman capable of desiring the happiness of another person in a disinterested way," according to Beauvoir. The author implies that since such individuals are truly

exceptional, one should think seriously before having children simply because of social and family pressures.

Beauvoir sees great strides being made in modern woman's ability to control her reproductive functions. For those who willingly choose to have children, she advocates increased assumption of child care responsibilities by the society rather than by the individual family. "Because of a dearth of conveniently organized child care centers and nursery schools, all it takes is one child to paralyze a mother's activities completely," she proclaims. Beauvoir's use of the verb "paralyze" in this context underlines the depth of her feeling about women who never realize their full potential because of the social and familial roles they are trapped into playing.

In her concluding chapter, entitled "The Independent Woman," Simone de Beauvoir emphasizes the need to disentangle modern motherhood from the emotional and often pathological bonds inherent in the closed circle of the nuclear family. A child raised in a more communal atmosphere, one that would allow men and women to participate more equally in the activities needed to assure the smooth functioning of the society in which they live, "would sense that she is surrounded by an androgynous rather than a masculine world," the author asserts. This androgynous society is indeed the goal toward which Beauvoir directed all of the arguments presented in the two volumes of *The Second Sex,* the goal toward which she led innumerable groups of modern feminists after its publication in 1949. Her work, which inspired committed feminists of the next generation like Yvette Roudy, Elisabeth Badinter, Kate Millett, and Betty Friedan, was an eye-opener for women all over the world and did much to demystify the aura surrounding the idea of motherhood in the mid-twentieth century. (pp. 115-25)

> *Yolanda Astarita Patterson, in her* Simone de Beauvoir and the Demystification of Motherhood, *UMI Research Press, 1989, 445 p.*

FURTHER READING

Bibliography

Bennett, Joy, and Hochmann, Gabriella. *Simone de Beauvoir: An Annotated Bibliography.* New York: Garland Publishing, 1988, 474 p.
    Comprehensive annotated bibliography of secondary sources published between 1940 and 1986 in English, French, German, Italian, and Spanish.

Biography

Appignanesi, Lisa. *Simone de Beauvoir.* London: Penguin Books, 1988, 170 p.
    Biography tracing Beauvoir's life and development as a writer.

Ascher, Carol. *Simone de Beauvoir: A Life of Freedom.* Boston: Beacon Press, 1981, 254 p.

Biographical and critical study of Beauvoir's life and works, intended as "a mixture of the personal and the analytical."

Bair, Deirdre. *Simone de Beauvoir: A Biography.* New York: Summit Books, 1990, 718 p.
Authorized biography.

Cottrell, Robert D. *Simone de Beauvoir.* New York: Frederick Ungar, 1975, 168 p.
Overview of Beauvoir's life and works.

Francis, Claude and Gontier, Fernande. *Simone de Beauvoir: a Life . . . a Love Story.* Translated by Lisa Nesselson. New York: St. Martin's Press, 1987, 412 p.
Biography incorporating information gleaned from Beauvoir's unpublished letters and numerous interviews with Beauvoir.

Criticism

Bieber, Konrad. *Simone de Beauvoir.* Boston: Twayne Publishers, 1979, 198 p.
Monograph focusing on the originality of Beauvoir's writings.

Brée, Germaine. *Women Writers in France: Variations on a Theme.* New Brunswick, N.J.: Rutgers University Press, 1973, 90 p.
Historical overview of French women writers from the twelfth to twentieth centuries in which Beauvoir is designated an important intellectual and moralist.

Butler, Judith. "Variations on Sex and Gender: Beauvoir, Wittig and Foucault." In *Feminism as Critique: On the Politics of Gender,* edited by Seyla Benhabib and Drucilla Cornell, pp. 128-42. Minneapolis: University of Minnesota Press, 1987.
Discusses Beauvoir's theory of sex and gender as implied in her statement that "one is not born, but rather becomes, a woman" and compares it with the ideologies of Monique Wittig and Michel Foucault.

Dallery, Arleen B. "Sexual Embodiment: Beauvoir and French Feminism (*écriture féminine*)." *Women's Studies International Forum* 8, No. 3 (1985): 197-202.
Examines "the deployment of woman's sexuality in Beauvoir's *The Second Sex* and in the writings of Irigaray, Cixous and Kristeva, proponents of *écriture féminine.*" Posits that Beauvoir asserts a phallocentric basis as the norm for woman's sexuality, whereas the latter feminists identify "woman's sexuality as radically other and heterogenous."

DuPlessis, Rachel Blau, and Rapp, Rayna R., eds. "A Symposium: In Commemoration of the 30th Anniversary of the Publication of Simone de Beauvoir's *The Second Sex.*" *Feminist Studies* 6, No. 2 (Summer 1980): 245-313.
Includes essays by Mary Felstiner, Michèle Le Doeuff, Sandra Dijkstra, and Jo-Ann Fuchs, commemorating the thirtieth anniversary of *The Second Sex.*

Hatcher, Donald L. *Understanding "The Second Sex".* New York: Peter Lang, 1984, 281 p.
Introduction to the study of *The Second Sex.*

Heath, Jane. *Simone de Beauvoir.* New York: Harvester Wheatsheaf, 1989, 153 p.
Textual analysis of *She Came to Stay, The Mandarins, Les Belles Images,* and the autobiographies, focusing on

the paradox of Beauvoir's adoption of a masculine identity in her delineation of the feminine.

Keefe, Terry. *Simone de Beauvoir: A Study of Her Writings.* London: Harrap, 1983, 247 p.
Overview of Beauvoir's life and analysis of her writings.

Labovitz, Esther Kleinbord. "Simone de Beauvoir: *Memoirs of a Dutiful Daughter.*" In her *The Myth of the Heroine: The Female Bildungsroman in the Twentieth Century,* pp. 73-143. New York: Peter Lang, 1986.
Examines fictional elements in Beauvoir's autobiography *Memoirs of a Dutiful Daughter,* presenting the work as a bildungsroman.

Le Doeuff, Michèle. *Hipparchia's Choice: An Essay Concerning Women, Philosophy, etc.* Oxford: Basil Blackwell, 1991, 364 p.
Expands Le Doeuff's discussion of Beauvoir's ideas first put forward in her "Simone de Beauvoir and Existentialism," translated by Colin Gordon, in *Feminist Studies,* Summer, 1980 (see excerpt above).

Leighton, Jean. *Simone de Beauvoir on Woman.* Cranbury, N.J.: Associated University Presses, 1975, 230 p.
Analyzes Beauvoir's portrayal of woman in her novels, *The Second Sex,* and the first three volumes of her autobiography, attempting to illumine "such perplexing questions as her ambivalence toward women and also call into question perhaps some of her feminist doctrines, which may themselves be ever so slightly tarnished with an excessive adulation of 'masculine' values as established and revered for centuries in a male-dominated world."

Marks, Elaine. *Simone de Beauvoir: Encounters with Death.* New Brunswick, N.J.: Rutgers University Press, 1973, 183 p.
Studies Beauvoir's treatment of death and the absurd in her writings.

————, ed. *Critical Essays on Simone de Beauvoir.* Boston: G. K. Hall & Co., 1987, 263 p.
Comprehensive collection of articles and reviews on Beauvoir, offering varying perspectives on her works from critics in Canada, France, Great Britain, and the United States between 1943 and 1986.

McCallum, Pamela. "New Feminist Readings: Woman as *Ecriture* or Woman as Other?" *Canadian Journal of Political and Social Theory* IX, Nos. 1-2, (Winter-Spring 1985): 127-32.
Considers the direction of new feminist theory, contrasting Beauvoir's emphasis on woman as an autonomous being with new theories based on post-structuralist analyses.

Moi, Toril. *Feminist Theory and Simone de Beauvoir.* Oxford: Basil Blackwell, 1990, 120 p.
Includes an interview with Beauvoir as well as lectures that incorporate analyses of her works based on feminist, Marxist, psychoanalytic, and deconstructionist theories.

Okely, Judith. *Simone de Beauvoir: A Re-Reading.* London: Virago Press, 1986, 174 p.
Examines the changing perception of Beauvoir and her works, focusing on Okely's own reading of *The Second Sex* in the early 1960s and her reappraisal in the 1980s.

Pagès, Irène. "Simone de Beauvoir and the New French Feminisms." *Canadian Women Studies* 6, No. 1 (1984): 60-2.

Review of *New French Feminisms,* edited by Elaine Marks and Isabelle de Courtivron. Pagès contrasts the assimilationist feminist ideology as espoused by followers of Beauvoir with that of more radical theories expounded by such new French feminists as Hélène Cixous, Luce Irigaray, Monique Wittig, and Annie Leclerc.

Sankovitch, Tilde A. "Simone de Beauvoir: The Giant, the Scapegoat, the Quester." In her *French Women Writers and the Book: Myths of Access and Desire,* pp. 101-24. Syracuse, N.Y.: Syracuse University Press, 1988.

Studies *Memoirs of a Dutiful Daughter,* appraising Beauvoir's delineation of herself, events of the time, and underlying mythic elements.

Simons, Margaret A. "Sexism and the Philosophical Canon: On Reading Beauvoir's *The Second Sex.*" *Journal of the History of Ideas* 51, No. 3 (July-September 1990): 487-504.

Explores a prevailing bias against including discussion of Beauvoir's contribution to philosophy in critical studies of moral and social theory.

Whitmarsh, Anne. *Simone de Beauvoir and the Limits of Commitment.* Cambridge: Cambridge University Press, 1981, 212 p.

Considers Beauvoir "the doyenne of existentialism" and "focusses upon the ethical, social and above all political implications" of her Sartrean existentialist commitment both in her life and her work.

Winegarten, Renee. *Simone de Beauvoir: A Critical View.* Oxford: Berg Publishers, 1988, 142 p.

Assesses and challenges "the value of Simone de Beauvoir's activity and writings in the spheres of feminism, politics, and literature."

Yale French Studies, Special Issue: Simone de Beauvoir, No. 72 (1986).

Gathers essays by such critics as Yolanda A. Patterson, Isabelle de Courtivron, Deirdre Bair, and Elaine Marks as well as an interview with Beauvoir conducted by Hélène Vivienne Wenzel. Wenzel writes in the introduction: "[These] articles, as far-ranging and diverse as their various foci may be, when read as a collection, reflect decidedly feminist and contemporary revisions of the life, work, and influence of Simone de Beauvoir."

Additional coverage of Beauvoir's life and career is contained in the following sources published by Gale Research: *Contemporary Authors,* Vols. 9-12, rev. ed., Vol. 118 [obituary]; *Contemporary Authors New Revision Series,* Vol. 28; *Contemporary Literary Criticism,* Vols. 1, 2, 4, 8, 14, 31, 44, 50; *Dictionary of Literary Biography,* Vol. 72; *Dictionary of Literary Biography Yearbook,* 1986; and *Major 20th-Century Writers.*

Rachel Carson

1907-1964

(Full name Rachel Louise Carson) American nonfiction writer, novelist, and short story writer.

The following entry presents an overview of Carson's career.

INTRODUCTION

A seminal figure in the environmental movement, Carson is best known as the author of *Silent Spring*, a controversial study of pesticide misuse, and as a crusader in the fight for conservation and ecological awareness. A marine biologist and conservationist who emphasized the interconnectedness of all creation in her writings, Carson attempted to educate readers by instilling in them her own love of nature. Although primarily recognized for the scientific accuracy of her nonfiction, Carson also employed such literary devices as metaphor and allusion in her work, leading some critics to classify her as a participant in the naturalist school of literature.

Born in Springdale, Pennsylvania, Carson was a solitary child who spent much of her time outdoors. She often submitted pieces of fiction to the children's magazine *St. Nicholas*, in which she published her first story by age thirteen. Although Carson had intended to study English at the Pennsylvania College for Women, her interest in the natural sciences led her to change her major to biology despite her advisor's warning that writing afforded women greater opportunities. After graduating in 1929, Carson briefly worked at the Woods Hole Marine Biological Laboratory in Massachusetts and in 1932 earned an M.A. from Johns Hopkins University. She was subsequently hired by the United States Bureau of Fisheries, where she wrote and edited pamphlets, booklets, and radio scripts. To supplement her income, Carson began publishing articles as a free-lance writer, and the success of "Undersea," a short piece which appeared in the *Atlantic* in 1937, prompted her to write her first novel, *Under the Sea-Wind: A Naturalist's Picture of Ocean Life*. In 1949 she was appointed Editor-in-Chief of publications for the Fish and Wildlife Service, but relinquished her post in 1952 to devote herself to her own writing. Her most famous work, *Silent Spring*, was serialized in the *New Yorker* in 1962. Representatives of pesticide companies and other industry-related interest groups denounced *Silent Spring* and questioned Carson's credibility, but when the book was published in its entirety, Carson's findings were substantiated by other scientists, including the Science Advisory Committee appointed by President John F. Kennedy. Carson died in 1964, leaving behind several unfinished manuscripts. In 1980 President Jimmy Carter recognized Carson's contributions to the environmental movement by

posthumously awarding her the Presidential Medal of Freedom.

Carson's first book, *Under the Sea-Wind*, focuses on the dynamics of the marine world as experienced by a salmon, a migratory waterfowl, and an eel. Critics noted that Carson's use of anthropomorphism enabled her to create an emotional bond between her readers and protagonists. *The Sea around Us*, which won the National Book Award for nonfiction and became the basis for an Academy Award-winning documentary, examines the ocean's physical features, geologic development, mysteries, and inhabitants. The National Book Award judges called *The Sea around Us* "a work of scientific accuracy presented with poetic imagination and such clarity of style and originality of approach as to win and hold every reader's attention." Likening her descriptions of the sea to those of Joseph Conrad and Herman Melville, reviewers asserted that Carson's use of color, sound, and an objective tone convincingly evinced the sights, rhythms, and cycles of the underwater world. They also noted that the book's literary allusions, analogies, and occasional use of first-person plural point of view eased readers into what was for many unfamiliar material.

The Edge of the Sea focuses on the tidal zones and shallow waters of the United States' eastern seaboard. While some critics deemed the book of lesser literary value than its predecessor due to its narrowly defined subject, others cited Carson's use of imagery, repetition, alliteration, and rhythm as evidence of the work's merit. Carol B. Gartner, who has compared Carson to Henry David Thoreau, noted that the opening passage of the book can be read as a poem: "And so in that enchanted place / on the threshold of the sea / the realities that possessed my mind / were far from those of the land world / I had left an hour before." Like Carson's other books, *The Edge of the Sea* emphasizes the interdependence and sanctity of all forms of life; Charles J. Rojo observed: "To Miss Carson, the edge of the sea conveys a haunting sense of communicating some universal truth as yet beyond our grasp; a sense that through this region, in which Life began, we can approach the ultimate mystery of Life itself."

Silent Spring was the last of Carson's books to be published in her lifetime. An exposé of the dangers of pesticides, *Silent Spring* examines how humans, animals, plants, the soil, and the earth's food and water supplies have been affected by toxic chemicals during the twentieth century. Carson illustrated her thesis with numerous examples, attributing the worldwide rise in cancer rates to the use of pesticides and proposing ecologically safe methods of pest control. Despite its technical emphasis, *Silent Spring* makes use of literary technique; the book opens with a fable, takes its title from a poem by John Keats, and has been compared to such works of social consciousness as Harriet Beecher Stowe's *Uncle Tom's Cabin* and Sinclair Lewis's *The Jungle*. The book's greatest achievement, however, was in alerting international audiences to the dangers of pollution. Loren Eiseley called *Silent Spring* "a devastating, heavily documented, relentless attack upon human carelessness, greed, and irresponsibility—an irresponsibility that has let loose upon man and the countryside a flood of dangerous chemicals in a situation which, as Miss Carson states, is without parallel."

PRINCIPAL WORKS

NONFICTION

The Sea around Us 1951; also published as *The Sea around Us* [revised edition], 1961
The Edge of the Sea 1955
Silent Spring 1962
The Sense of Wonder 1965

OTHER

Under the Sea-Wind: A Naturalist's Picture of Ocean Life (novel) 1941

CRITICISM

William Beebe

The purpose of [*Under the Sea-Wind*] is to make the sea and its life a vivid reality, says Miss Carson, and she has succeeded. Her method is to write a series of short narratives around certain fish and birds, and in some cases to follow the life history of individual creatures from egg to death. Her more important actors are given special names, such as Blackfoot and Silverbar the sanderlings, Ookpik the snowy owl, and Anguilla the eel.

There are three "Books," each with three to seven chapters. The first Book is laid on the North Carolinian coast and the Arctic tundra, with black skimmers, shad, and sanderlings as the chief protagonists. The second division is almost wholly concerned with the life of Scomber, the mackerel, and the third deals in a similar way with the unique eel and its wonderful migration.

The author is at her best in her complete life histories. There, her attention is concentrated upon a single individual organism, about which environment, experiences and enemies, are made to revolve, and on which they focus. The account of the surface plankton, and the gauntlet drifting of the egg and larval mackerel is full of excitement. Indeed, the helpless young fish is threatened in turn by almost every predator of those waters known to science.

I have thoroughly enjoyed every word of the volume, but I found difficulty in trying to read it aloud. The plethora of facts occasionally smothers the smoothness of diction, and distracts the attention from the word picture itself. For example, in the first paragraph of the eel saga, in the description of a pond, we find the names of nine plants, from mountain ash to pickerel weed, and a second reading is almost necessary to refocus and visualize the general picture. This is not captious criticism, but an appeal for more simple words, fewer terms of physical and faunal geography, and a greater leisureliness in description in the author's second volume. Miss Carson's science cannot be questioned; I have been unable to detect a single error.

William Beebe, in a review of "Under the Sea Wind," in The Saturday Review of Literature, *Vol. XXIV, No. 56, December 27, 1941, p. 5.*

Jonathan Norton Leonard

When poets write about the sea their errors annoy scientists. When scientists write about the sea their bleak and technical jargon paralyzes poets. Yet neither scientists nor poets should object to *The Sea around Us.* It is written with precision more than sufficient for its purpose, and its style and imagination make it a joy to read. . . .

[Miss Carson] must have read many bristling books about tides and ocean currents and felt the thrill and mystery that lie deeply buried in them. She must have learned how to talk with oceanographers, those salty and crusty scientists who go down to the sea in ships to probe the sea's insides. While doing all this she must have read a fine variety of literature, for her chapters are headed by unusually apt quotations from authors as diverse as Homer, Matthew Arnold and The Venerable Bede.

The product of Miss Carson's learning is a book packed with information expressed in charming language. She tells how old the sea is and how all life came from it. The land in those old years was as bleak as the mountains of the moon, but the sea was as full of churning life as it is today. Then, little by little, plants learned to live on land. Animals followed to eat them. At last land animals developed that could sail on the sea in ships and measure the flowing tides and drop ingenious instruments into the deep ocean basins. Those prying animals are the oceanographers, Miss Carson's friends.

Miss Carson has other friends, and she obviously loves them all. She tells with a gardener's tenderness of the "blooming" of the northern seas, a magic moment in spring when the winter-chilled surface water sinks into the depths. Bottom water rises, bringing to the surface the salts that are needed by all living things. Then microscopic plants (diatoms) sprout by billions and trillions. Slightly larger animals multiply to devour them. Shrimps, squids, fish and whales struggle for the living broth and add their young to enrich it. Everybody eats everybody, and Miss Carson enjoys and describes it all.

"The symbols of hope are not lacking," she writes,

> even in the grayness and bleakness of the winter sea. . . . Already, from the gray shapes of cod that have moved, unseen by man, through the cold sea to their spawning places, the glassy globules of eggs are rising to the surface waters. Even in the harsh world of the winter sea those eggs will begin the swift divisions by which a granule of protoplasm becomes a living fishlet. Most of all, perhaps, there is assurance in the fine dust of life that remains in the surface waters, the invisible spores of the diatoms, needing only the touch of the warming sun and fertilizing chemicals to repeat the magic of spring.

Miss Carson loves mysteries too, and the sea has plenty of them. She tells of the black depths where no ray of light ever penetrates. All sorts of strange things live there, she says. Besides the giant squid that are hunted by sperm whales, the deeps are swarming with mysterious creatures that have, so far, evaded man's efforts to capture them. They are known only by clues picked up by the most modern instruments. What are these deep-living phantoms? How big are they? How shaped? Miss Carson seems glad that she does not know, and her reader is glad too.

The sea is alive with rhythm and cycles, some of them centuries long. This branch of science is formidable, but Miss Carson explains it in language that is soft and disarming. . . .

Each of Miss Carson's chapters is worth sampling and savoring, and her book adds up to enjoyment that should not be passed by. Every person who reads it will look on the sea with new pleasure. He will know that it is full of lights and sounds and movements, of sunken lands and mountains, of the debris of meteors, of plains strewn with ancient sharks' teeth and the ear-bones of whales.

Jonathan Norton Leonard, "—And His Wonders in the Deep," in The New York Times Book Review, *July 1, 1951, p. 1.*

Harry B. Ellis

In *The Sea around Us,* Rachel Carson has achieved that rare, all but unique, phenomenon—a literary work about the sea that is comparable with the best, yet offends neither the natural scientist nor the poet. Her book is a translation of the science of the sea into terms so imaginative and stirring as to evoke thoughts of those masters of the sea tale, Conrad and Melville.

The gigantic task Miss Carson set herself was to recount the geology and the fauna of the sea, that measureless liquid body which covers so much more than half the earth's surface. This task she approached, and accomplished, with the reverence of a natural scientist steeped in the lore of her subject, and with the kindling light of an artist whose imagination never ceased to be stirred by the wonder of the facts she uncovered.

One has the feeling of modesty in Miss Carson's book, partly in the way she calls upon other authors—including that newest titan of the sea, Thor Heyerdahl—to substantiate her views, or to present theirs. Yet her own art is fully equal to the almost fathomless challenge of her subject.

She has given us a textbook that is a work of art—simple, sparse of verbiage, as lucid as certain crystal waters she herself describes.

Now what is her book? It is an attempt to record the origin of the sea in geologic time; the evolution of the waters; the qualities of the sea's surface, its continental slopes, its Stygian deeps; a description of the life which teems and abounds all through the seas, and, finally the relation of mankind to "mother sea," from which all that the material senses know of life has sprung, and down to which, along the river valleys of the world, the forces of nature, slowly and slowly, are carrying the eroded earth.

From her book emerges a correct sense of the ageless, almost illimitable, liquid surface of the earth's crust, upon which the land seems at times a mere incursion, and the activities of mankind a tiny blurred fragment in the great skein of time.

"For," as the author herself says,

> the sea lies all about us. The commerce of all lands must cross it. The very winds that move over the lands have been cradled on its broad expanse and seek to return to it. The continents themselves dissolve and pass to the sea, in grain after grain of eroded land. So the rains that rose from it return again in rivers. . . . For all at last return to the sea—to Oceanus, the ocean river, like the ever-flowing stream of time, the beginning and the end.

Mankind has come far in probing the mysteries of the deep, as Miss Carson points out. There is, at the rocky tip of Lands End, England, an instrument which dissects the history of each wave that rolls across the glistening rocks—where each wave was formed, how strong the wind that formed it, how soon storm warnings must be posted along the coast of England.

We have learned that the bottom of the sea is no flat plain, but as complex with mountains, valleys, peaks, and cliffs as the land above the sea. There is many an area, now "drowned" beneath the waves, as striking topographically as the Grand Canyon of Arizona.

We know also, as Miss Carson so graphically writes, that "the conception of the sea as a silent place is wholly false." Measuring instruments, she records, have discovered "an extraordinary uproar produced by fishes, shrimps, porpoises, and probably other forms not yet identified." One hydrophone, lowered into deep water off Bermuda, "recorded strange mewing sounds, shrieks, and ghostly moans, the sources of which have not been traced." . . .

For its sense of adventure and of beauty, Miss Carson's book is a joy to read. Consider the titles of some of her chapters—"The Gray Beginnings," "The Pattern of the Surface," "The Sunless Sea," "The Long Snowfall," "The Birth of an Island," "The Shape of Ancient Seas." . . .

In the pages those headings describe are to be found concepts poetical, wonderful, and exciting, from the battle of whales and giant squid, "in the darkness of the deep water," to Miss Carson's descriptions of the "snowfall" of the sea, that "steady, unremitting, downward drift of materials from above, flake upon flake, layer upon layer . . . so little in a year, or in a human lifetime, but so enormous an amount in the life of earth and sea."

Miss Carson, a celebrated naturalist before writing this book, now takes her place also in the realm of letters with a work of which she may well be proud. As Herman Melville wrote: "There is, one knows not what sweet mystery about this sea. . . ."

> *Harry B. Ellis, "Science and Literature of the World's Vast Seas," in* The Christian Science Monitor, *July 5, 1951, p. 11.*

Francesca La Monte

The story of the sea with its islands and mountains and depths and of man's attempts to solve its mystery and exploit its treasures has been told before and often. But Rachel Carson has made of it one of the most beautiful books of our time. Her skill and the basic certainty of her knowledge has made it possible for her to write with simplicity, rhythm and sweeping force. In [*The Sea around Us*] she conveys not only her well substantiated information but the mixture of terror and attraction of the unlit ocean depths, the waves, the tides, the strange salt domes and the great undersea mountains and, on our land, the wonder of the ever present traces of the ancient seas.

Although thoroughly aware of the great progress made by man in his study of the oceans, Miss Carson is also impressed with man's helplessness in the face of this medium in which he cannot live, whose "every gesture . . . makes man aware that he cannot control or change the ocean, as

in his brief tenancy of the earth he has subdued and plundered the continents."

One of the most fascinating parts of this wholly fascinating book is the story of the oceanic islands, their births, their erratic appearances and disappearances, the tragedy of "the uniqueness, the irreplaceability of the species they have developed by the slow processes of the ages" whose total elimination has so often been due to man's instinct to explore, to acquire and to change.

Some of these human instincts, however, have led to our present day knowledge of the oceans; a knowledge comparatively rapidly developed since the first explorers set down their accounts. . . .

This is a stimulating and somewhat terrifying book in its emphasis on man's helplessness against this enormous mass of water whose continuing rise along the coasts of our own country might submerge most of the Atlantic seaboard with its cities and towns ("and there is more than enough water now frozen in the land ice to provide such a rise"). If such a rise should amount to a hundred feet

> the surf would break against the foothills of the Appalachians. The coastal plain of the Gulf of Mexico would lie under water; the lower part of the Mississippi Valley would be submerged. If, however, the rise should be as much as 600 feet large areas in the eastern half of the continent would disappear under the waters.

This story of the sea is developed from its shadowy beginnings through our present day knowledge. The book contains an immense number of facts and is an orderly, scientifically accurate work, but its charm lies in Miss Carson's apparently effortless ability to show the drama of her story, for, as she says,

> the sea lies all about us. The commerce of all lands must cross it. The very winds that move over the lands have been cradled on its broad expanse and seek ever to return to it. The continents themselves dissolve and pass to the sea, in grain after grain of eroded land. So the rains that rose from it return again in rivers. In its mysterious past it encompasses all the dim origins of life and receives in the end, after, it may be, many transmutations, the dead husks of that same life. For all at last return to the sea—to Oceanus, the ocean river, like the ever-flowing stream of time, the beginning and the end.

> *Francesca La Monte, "One of the Most Beautiful Books of Our Time: The Story of the Sea," in* New York Herald Tribune Book Review, *July 5, 1951, p. 3.*

Philip Burnham

[*The Sea around Us*] is a suave volume of blended fact and speculation, approached with a fashionably modern research romanticism, quite safely unrelated to the average reader's problems. And its immemorial sea parts provide a rather dreamy narcotic to minds and consciences overburdened with the earthy concerns of day to day.

Book habits are generally unphilosophical. But whatever serious dangers escape-literature may bring, one need not, in the particular instance, worry much about a brief escape to sea, particularly with a pilot who permits the passenger to apprehend without undue constraint the wonder and mystery of nature.

The main thing this book is, is a compilation of thoroughly interesting facts and theories about oceans. There are fourteen chapters, divided into three parts, covering from the time the moon began, up to the most recently issued Sailing Directions. It is a work of radical simplification, organization and popularization. For each reader, it will be somewhat uneven, according to his own experience and knowledge. If a person has read a fair amount about exploration and discovery and charting and mapping, for example, Chapter 14, "The Encircling Sea," may seem condensed to the point of superficiality. Chapter 13 goes into "Wealth from the Salt Seas" not as productively as some publications and publicity about Dow Chemical. Thousands of graduates of Army Weather Observer courses, or equal civilian schooling, will not find Chapter 12, "The Global Thermostat," unusually helpful in explaining climate and weather. And so on, back to the first chapter— "The Gray Beginnings"—which Geology "majors" and theologians might find something less than a university text or the Book of Genesis.

The nature of the job demands a somewhat common denominator production, but it is an example of the best. While the information given has uneven novelty and interest for a single reader, the remarkably good organization of the whole material, and the even, clear prose style throughout, provide consistent, sustained pleasure. It has been widely remarked with amazement that such good prose and clear and lively presentation are the work of the Editor-in-Chief of the United States Fish and Wildlife Service—Miss Carson's current and unlikely title. The Editor, however bureaucratic her post, is a genuinely literary craftsman who knows reading and writing.

The unusual momentum of Miss Carson's writing is proved by the way it carries over, without being caught or hurried, numberless color passages which in a less disciplined book would stop the music.

> But we know now that the conception of the sea as a silent place is wholly false. . . . There is an extraordinary uproar produced by fishes, shrimps, porpoises and probably other forms not yet identified. . . .

She proceeds to tell about croakers ruining submarine detection on Chesapeake Bay early in the war and about the deafening "shrimp-crackle" heard "around the world between latitudes 35° N and 35° S, and about "high-pitched resonant whistles and squeals, varied with the ticking and clucking sounds slightly reminiscent of a string orchestra tuning up, as well as mewing and occasional chirps," which white porpoises make in the St. Lawrence. And this kind of story does not throw the writer off pace, any more than her opening sounding of the depths of the Week of Creation in a hundred page geologists' counterpoint to the Bible.

Readers and writers should notice the greater challenge to her composition presented by the movement which had to be described in Part II: three chapters on "The Restless Sea." This tells how the sea acts, rather than what it is and what it contains. One of the special passages of the kind mentioned above that would block the progress of an ordinary book, shows how much more there is to the tide than the ready answer "twice daily movement of the waters in response to the moon's gravitational attraction." There are the sun, the moon and the other stars; and the tidal basins with water oscillating around their focusing nodes; and the "all-important" local topography.

In her modest acknowledgments, the author speaks of her "absorption in the mystery and meaning of the sea." That is an element it is hard to get directly from her clear book. [*The Sea around Us*] is a book about oceans, interesting and expert in its rendering of information about oceans. The mystery and meaning of the sea cannot be obtained by examination of the sea itself. However encompassing, "like the ever-flowing stream of time," the sea cannot bear its own explanation, and cast up its own meaning. Looking at it, contemplating it as Rachel Carson permits us to do, can raise in our minds and imaginations very fundamental questions whose study is no escape, but rather a closer approach to more profound reality, which relates the seas to other creation. (pp. 387-89)

> *Philip Burnham, in a review of "The Sea around Us," in* The Commonweal, *Vol. LIV, July 27, 1951, pp. 387-89.*

Never silent herself in the face of destructive trends, Rachel Carson fed a spring of awareness across America and beyond. A biologist with a gentle, clear voice, she welcomed her audiences to her love of the sea, while with an equally clear determined voice she warned Americans of the dangers human beings themselves pose for their own environment. Always concerned, always eloquent, she created a tide of environmental consciousness that has not ebbed.

—President Carter, on awarding Rachel Carson the Presidential Medal of Freedom, 1980.

Jonathan N. Leonard

The Edge of the Sea lacks the organ tones of Miss Carson's *The Sea around Us.* It deals not with the sea as a majestic whole but with the narrow strip of part-time sea bottom that rings the land between high and low tide marks. No habitat on earth is more fiercely contended; none supports more teeming and more varied life. The tidal strip has, also, a philosophical importance. It was the cruel training ground where sea creatures learned to live on the hostile land. Miss Carson points out forms that are making that great transition today and also a few that are returning from the dry land to the sea.

The Atlantic Coast of the United States, the author explains happily, has almost every kind of shore, from the hard rocks of Maine, pounded by icy surf, to the coral reefs and mangrove swamps of the tropical Florida keys. She seems to love the Maine coast best, and she takes her readers there when the tide is high and the waves are tossing spray among the shoreside junipers. No sea creatures are in sight except the waiting gulls. "But the gulls," says Miss Carson, "know what is there."

When the ebb begins (Miss Carson can *hear* the tide turn) she and the gulls follow the water line down the dripping rocks. The gulls are looking for clams and crabs big enough to be edible. There is nothing too small for Miss Carson to note and make interesting. She points out a dark line high on the rocks. It was drawn by blue-green algae, perhaps the oldest plants on earth, and it is likely that the rocky shores of one billion years ago had that same dark line.

Little by little the sea retreats, followed by Miss Carson. She pays loving respects to each species as it emerges: the crowding barnacles, the rock weeds, the mussels, starfish, snails and crabs. Each has a fascinating history and each its own way of life. Most of the animals are carnivorous, eating each other and smaller things with untiring gusto. This slaughter is not horrifying. Clams do not cry for mercy when fierce whelks bore holes in their shells. Even when there is visible struggle Miss Carson takes it philosophically. It is part of the feeding cycle, the steady mainspring of life.

"The shore," Miss Carson writes,

> is an ancient world, for as long as there has been an earth and sea there has been this place of the meeting of land and water. Yet it is a world that keeps alive the sense of continuing creation and of the relentless drive of life. Each time that I enter it, I gain some new awareness of its beauty and its deeper meanings, sensing that intricate fabric of life by which one creature is linked with another, and each with its surroundings.

On Carolina beaches and limey Florida reefs Miss Carson shows her readers the beauty and oddness of the living things peculiar to those places: eyeless worms that prowl through the mud glowing with phosphorescence, bright-colored clams that dance in the surf, sea urchins that point their venomous spines toward an approaching shadow. Each form is stranger than the last; there is no end of strangeness.

Miss Carson's book is beautifully written and technically correct. People who get bored by too much lolling on beaches should read it as a guide book. All around them, even beneath them, are fascinating worlds. A little wading, searching and poking will open their doors.

> *Jonathan N. Leonard, "Between the Mark of High Tide and Low," in* The New York Times Book Review, *October 30, 1955, p. 5.*

Harry B. Ellis

The enduring quality of the sea is a central theme of Miss Carson's writing; the sea which almost, but not quite, subjugates and dominates the land; the vast and unplumbed sea from which life as naturalists see it sprang; the sea, pressing always against the land, lapping higher, until, in some shadowy future, more and more land crumbles away again into the sea, and material life marches once more into the watery depths from which it came.

In the Edge of the Sea, Miss Carson's latest book, the enduring quality of the sea again is a theme, though in a different way. In this book Miss Carson has left the deep sea world, in which the sperm whale and giant squid, titans of the deep, battle in a midnight abyss, and has turned toward the shore, to that intertidal world which belongs at high tide to the sea and at low tide to the land. . . .

Though the author preserves in this book the essential mystery of the sea, *The Edge of the Sea* portrays a world more nearly understandable to the average reader than is the deep water world of *The Sea around Us.* The intertidal world has been glimpsed by every reader who has walked along a beach or sea coast. If that beach has been a sandy one in the temperate zones, the reader will remember strings of kelp and other weeds along the high tide line, will have marveled at the structure of minute shells, will have watched the primordial horseshoe crab tracing its way across the sands, will have seen a dozen forms strange and new to him. . . .

The Edge of the Sea is pitched, perhaps, in a lesser key than was *The Sea around Us,* if only because of the intertidal world is a more limited subject than was the whole sea itself. In her new book, however, Miss Carson's peri is as poetic as ever, and the knowledge she imparts is profound. *The Edge of the Sea* finds a worthy place beside Miss Carson's masterpiece of 1951.

> *Harry B. Ellis, "Between Pounding Surf and Dry Land," in* The Christian Science Monitor, *November 10, 1955, p. B8.*

Jacquetta Hawkes

The sea makes one of the greatest and most ancient symbols known to man. Everywhere and at all times it has been seen as expressing the feminine and unifying, the infinite and eternal.

Happily, scientific discovery has tended to enrich rather than detract from the sea's power to convey symbolic meaning. The task of a book such as *The Edge of the Sea* is at once to describe what is actual, the fascinating varieties of marine existence that nature has contrived to fit into every coign of vantage, and to invoke the poetic meaning lying behind, making fact glow with a greater significance, elusive but certainly radiant.

That Rachel Carson succeeded in achieving this illumination of facts in *The Sea around Us* is well known. Most readers nowadays having lost direct access to poetry love to reach it in this way, by means of the scientific facts whose significance and value are accepted in the modern world. Hence the enormous popularity of Miss Carson's first book. I think she has succeeded again, although with enough weakening and diminishment for even this success to appear a little sad. The truth is expressed in the title: Miss Carson having exhausted the heart of her subject, has been forced to move out to gather what was left round the periphery.

Although they have nothing to compare with the weird majesty of the oceans themselves, the seashores of the world still offer an abundance of subjects worthy of Rachel Carson's high descriptive powers. The rocky, the sandy and the coralline varieties of coast make the threefold division of her book; as all three occur in succession down the eastern seaboard of North America, the most detailed and personal descriptions are set there, yet always with a wider reference to comparable coasts throughout the world.

Moon and tides control the harmonies of time and space that give so satisfying a regularity to the life of the shore. The semi-diurnal rhythm of the tides along the beach causes a zoning of its life as regular and easily recognizable as the notes of a scale. Some of the most delightful passages in *The Edge of the Sea* describe the opening and closing of shells and tubes, the expansion and contraction of feelers and flagellæ, the stillness and quick activity of mobile creatures, that accompany the ebb and flow of the tides.

Beyond this rapid tidal rhythm, moreover, the moon conducts life with a slower beat. Thus there is a sea urchin of the Tortugas that spawns only at full moon, a hydroid that releases its medusae offspring always during the third lunar quarter, and the famed Palolo worm among whose many peculiar habits is that of spawning always at the same lunar phase of the same one month in every year. So hours, days and nights, weeks and months are marked as though by clock and calendar, a marking of time and season that has gone on with only the slowest of changes through vast geological ages.

At the heart of it all revolves that wheel to which we, too, are bound, the wheel of consuming and being consumed. Algae, sea weeds and the microscopic myriads of the plankton form the basis of the marine eating order, just as grass and other types of vegetation do on land.

Hosts of mild little creatures have devised means for gathering and trapping them, while many others feed on waste and carrion. Tyrannizing over this peaceful life are predators as fierce as the fanged and clawed carnivores of the land. The picture of the wide muscular foot of the welk enveloping its prey while the radula saws through the shell to reach the helpless inmate, is pitiless as any in nature.

Miss Carson succeeds admirably in conveying a sense of the richness and intricate interrelatedness of the life she describes. No jeweller could create a work so delicately interlocked and encrusted. The ingenuity of the different means devised for feeding, mating, breeding and preying is overwhelming—perhaps even repellent—yet the author contrives to unify it as an expression of the wholeness of life and its unwearying energy. She has been successful in this, and also in avoiding the chief dangers of this kind of writing—the lure of the purple patch and the false poetic. Perhaps she is not quite so innocent of dressing up the obvious in some of her generalizations, as, for example, when she says "as long as there has been an earth and sea there has been this place of the meeting of land and water." But such lapses are very few. What she could not hope to avoid in treating a subject without climaxes is a certain monotony. Reading her book through is like eating a meal composed of a succession of beautifully prepared hors d'oeuvres.

This sense of repetitiveness will not trouble those who dip into *The Edge of the Sea* savouring the finely exact accounts of sea lives strange as fairy tales; nor will it be felt by those who use the book (as it can well be used) to add to the interest of a seaside holiday. Yet it would be very wrong to recommend such intermittent attention. Those who are willing to risk some surfeit by reading through can be rewarded by gleams of the symbolic radiance of the sea, and by a vision of the whole of life in time, evolving towards its hidden, mysterious ends. (pp. 17-18)

Jacquetta Hawkes, "The World Under Water," in The New Republic, *Vol. 134, No. 4, January 23, 1956, pp. 17-18.*

Robert C. Cowen

Rachel Carson, noted author of *The Sea around Us,* has produced another thought-provoking book.

This time she has tackled a subject far more serious for humanity and more controversial than in her poetic portrait of the sea. Indeed, so controversial is her subject that her book [*Silent Spring*] has, in a sense, been widely reviewed before it was issued.

She is dealing with the fast-growing indiscriminate use of chemical insecticides and weed killers. She asks the question whether such use may not be dangerously affecting our environment, gravely damaging wildlife and creating a hazard to men. She answers this question with a disturbing "yes," which is documented by vivid case histories.

Because of this, and because much of the substance of her book was published in the *New Yorker* last June, a strong debate over her presentation is already gathering momentum and has been widely reported. For example, a full page was devoted to it in this newspaper last month.

It is in this sense that her book has been pre-reviewed.

Understandably, some of her most vocal critics have been from within the pesticide industry.

They charge that she has grossly distorted the picture, telling only the bad and discounting the great benefits the chemicals have brought to agriculture and public health. They point out that she amassed cases from widely scattered geographical areas and over a number of years in time, then put them together to paint an exaggeratedly black picture.

One might discount such criticism somewhat if it came only from those with a vested interest in the chemicals.

But reputable scientists, who recognize the dangers in misusing pesticides, make similar criticisms too.

These critics have a point.

Their assessment is based on the *New Yorker* articles, which drew mainly on Miss Carson's dramatic analysis of the dangers of pesticide misuse. She does deal with the beneficial aspects as well, in her book. But this is subordinate to her main theme, which the articles reflected.

On the other hand, the critics may have missed the most important point of all.

Miss Carson has undeniably sketched a one-sided picture. But her distortion is akin to that of the painter who exaggerates to focus attention on essentials. It is not the half-truth of the propagandist.

She has used shock tactics to try to alert an apathetic public opinion to an important and neglected issue. Her critics concede that she has her basic facts straight in doing this. They object to her dealing largely with the negative side of the question. But is the author really amiss?

There unquestionably is widespread misuse of pesticides. Wildlife has been seriously affected in many cases. Moreover, this misuse raises an as yet unevaluated question of hazards to humans themselves.

Miss Carson does not suggest that modern pest control be abandoned. She urges that dangers be assessed and misuses curbed. She is pressing for a thoroughgoing research program to enable men to learn to use pesticides safely and effectively and to reduce their use to a minimum by developing alternative means of keeping bugs in check.

Certainly she has underscored an urgent need. It is understandable that, in order to do this she has rung a loud alarm bell.

One hopes that her book will be read in this perspective. If the debate to which it is giving rise will take up the basic issue and stimulate broad research into all aspects of pest control, Miss Carson will have done a great service to her critics as well as to mankind.

> *Robert C. Cowen, "Yevtushenko in English-Housewifery—Miss Carson's 'Silent Spring',"* in The Christian Science Monitor, *September 27, 1962, p. 11.*

Robert B. Downs

Comparable in its impact on public consciousness, and demand for instant action, to Tom Paine's *Common Sense,* Harriet Beecher Stowe's *Uncle Tom's Cabin,* and Upton Sinclair's *The Jungle* was Rachel Carson's **Silent Spring** (1962), describing the disasterous effects on the balance of nature caused by the irresponsible use of insecticides and other pest controls.

Actually, the dark picture painted by Miss Carson, an eminent marine biologist, was part of a larger canvas—the overwhelming problem of pollution of the air, water, and land which was increasingly disturbing the conscience of the American people. Public-spirited citizens everywhere were realizing with alarm that man was ruining his environment by fouling the air he breathes, the water he drinks, the soil that produces his food, and the food itself. Automobiles were filling the cities with lethal fumes; smog was settling down in choking volume on virtually all large urban centers; human and industrial wastes were being dumped into lakes, rivers, and streams, killing fish and steadily reducing potable water resources; oil wastes dumped in the sea were killing millions of seabirds and ruining beaches, and further pollution of the ocean was resulting from the dumping of industrial atomic wastes. Beginning with World War II, the dangerous fallout from nuclear bomb explosions had posed an even more serious dilemma for the world at large.

This was the background against which Rachel Carson wrote. She begins her shocking story with a fable, in which she tells of a small American town, set in the heart of prosperous farmland, with its wild flowers, numerous songbirds, and well-stocked trout streams. "Then a strange blight crept over the area and everything began to change. Some evil spell had settled on the community: mysterious maladies swept the flocks of chickens; the cattle and sheep sickened and died. Everywhere was a shadow of death." Doctors discovered new kinds of sickness appearing among their patients. "There was a strange stillness. The birds, for example—where had they gone? . . . On the mornings that had once throbbed with the dawn chorus of robins, catbirds, doves, jays, wrens, and scores of other bird voices there was now no sound; only silence lay over the fields and woods and marsh."

The town described does not actually exist. "I know of no community that has experienced all the misfortunes," writes Miss Carson, "yet every one of these disasters has actually happened somewhere, and many real communities have already suffered a substantial number of them."

What has silenced the voice of spring in countless places, Miss Carson contends, is indiscriminate blanket spraying of vast areas from airplanes with potent chemicals, and similar misuses of insecticides and herbicides.

The beginnings of the devastation so graphically condemned by Miss Carson were a by-product of World War II. In experiments with agents intended for chemical warfare, it was found that some of the compounds were deadly to insects. After the war, chemical manufacturers, drug companies, agricultural schools, and government agencies started actively to develop and to promote the use of killers designed to exterminate various types of insects and undesirable plant growths. Handed these new weapons, the forester sprayed to protect his trees, the cranberry picker to protect his bogs, the cotton planter to save his cotton from the boll weevil, and so on down a long procession of farmers and gardeners—with little or no understanding of or concern for the consequences.

For thousands of years, man had fought to control pests—insects, rodents, weeds, bacteria, and other forms. Until World War II, the chief pesticides were arsenic, nicotine, and vegetable derivatives lethal to cold-blooded animals. The organic chemicals added to the plant growers' arsenal in the postwar period included the chlorinated hydrocarbons, such as DDT, and the organo-phosphorus substances, of which parathion is a common example. As a direct result, states Miss Carson:

> For the first time in the history of the world, every human being is now subjected to contact with dangerous chemicals, from the moment of conception until death. In the less than two decades of their use, the synthetic pesticides have been so thoroughly distributed throughout the animate and inanimate world that they occur virtually everywhere. They have been recovered from most of the major river systems and even from streams of groundwater flowing unseen through the earth. Residues of these chemicals linger in soil to which they may have been applied a dozen years before. They have entered and lodged in the bodies of fish, birds, reptiles, and domestic and wild animals so universally that scientists carrying on animal experiments find it almost impossible to locate subjects free from such contamination. They have been found in fish in remote mountain lakes, in earthworms burrowing in soil, in the eggs of birds—and in man himself. For these chemicals are now stored in the bodies of the vast majority of human beings, regardless of age. They occur in the mother's milk, and probably in the tissues of the unborn child.

(pp. 260-62)

Miss Carson continually stresses the perils to man himself from the widespread use or misuse of pesticides. If the chemicals are deadly to animal and plant life, can man with impunity eat contaminated meats and vegetables? A few human victims had already died in convulsions from exposure to certain highly concentrated pesticides, the author points out, and she fears that many others will eventually die of cancer, leukemia, hepatitis, or other dread diseases possibly caused by pesticides. Lethal poisons spread across the land, are blown into farm homes, settle on food, and pollute tanks and ponds. Emphysema, a serious lung disorder, unheard of until recent years, is becoming common in country areas, and respiratory illnesses are increasing by leaps and bounds in orchard and berry country. Because of birth-to-death exposure to dangerous chemicals, there is a progressive buildup of poison in our bodies, and the cumulative effect may well be disastrous. Many common insecticides for household use are highly toxic.

An exclamation point was added to Miss Carson's warnings when, two years after the appearance of *Silent Spring,* she herself died of cancer.

The basic fallacy overlooked by those who make extensive use of pesticides, Rachel Carson holds, is that they are upsetting the balance of nature. A vital fact which they ignore is that all life is one life, that the countless species of animals and plants and the soil, water, and air they live on are all intimately interconnected and interdependent. The ancient network of living things, in which each animal and plant depended upon every other one, has been upset by man, who is continually engaged in molding the environment to his own advantage. He must be supreme in nature, the human egotist believes, and the changes he makes

are often sudden and profound—and frequently irreversible. Too often, man has looked upon himself as opposed to nature, not as a part of her, and in his efforts to subdue, he has ravished and destroyed.

One of the frightening ways in which nature fights back is to produce new and more dangerous pests. Chemicals have quickly killed off the weak and feeble among the creatures attacked, but permanent control over the survivors is not gained. A thorough spraying may kill 90 per cent of a particular species. The hardier members, however, are resistant to the spray and survive; when they reproduce, most of their offspring inherit the immunity. Furthermore, the survivors often reproduce in fantastic numbers. To combat the new superpests, the chemists develop ever more poisonous sprays, thereby increasing the danger to all living things, including man. Thus, Miss Carson concludes, in upsetting the balance of nature, we are fighting a losing battle: "As crude a weapon as the cave man's club, the chemical barrage has been hurled against the fabric of life—a fabric on one hand delicate and destructible, on the other miraculously tough and resilient, and capable of striking back in unexpected ways." (pp. 264-65)

As could have been anticipated, the multi-million-dollar chemical industry, so vigorously attacked by Miss Carson, reacted violently. She had claimed that the industry's introduction of more and more chemicals was often based on profit rather than need. The Carson campaign was characterized by one commentator as "the most massive indictment of an entire industrial complex since the days of Ida Tarbell." The great corporations involved—mainly the major oil companies and their affiliates, the petrochemical companies—the economic entomologists, officials of the U. S. Department of Agriculture, and agricultural research workers generally quite predictably did not submit tamely to the scathing criticisms aimed at them.

A spokesman for the chemical industry, Dr. Robert White-Stevens of the American Cyanamid Company, issued a blast stating that "the book's major claims . . . are gross distortions of the actual facts, completely unsupported by scientific, experimental evidence, and general practical experience in the field." Miss Carson was accused of unfairness, prejudice, and hysteria, and the image of a crackpot was built up by her enemies, who chose to ignore her long career as a professional biologist, her sixteen years' experience with the Fish and Wildlife Service, and other accomplishments.

Departing from personalities, the critics asserted that chemical herbicides and insecticides have become necessary to man's survival. Without them, in a short time there would be no more marketable fruit or vegetable crops. If chemical pesticides were discontinued, they added, the agricultural areas of the world would soon be ravaged by hordes of grasshoppers, weevils, and other insect invaders. Chemical sprays make possible the huge food crops that farmers can now grow. Lacking them, surplus food would vanish, whole populations would starve, rivers and fields would be choked with weeds, and certain diseases would get out of control. Thus, the commercial interests and their spokesmen among the scientists presented a picture as one-sided and scary as anything in *Silent Spring.*

A telling argument used by pesticide supporters is that such chemicals have virtually eradicated many diseases. Mosquitoes, lice, ticks, fleas, and other insects are carriers of malaria, yellow fever, sleeping sickness, typhus, and other scourges. Malaria, which was formerly widely prevalent, has been practically stamped out in the United States and a number of other countries through the use of insecticides.

In short, maintain the proponents of pesticides, man has no choice except to upset the balance of nature. Otherwise, the insects will eventually inherit the earth.

Propaganda is not expected to give both sides of an argument, and *Silent Spring* is a fiercely passionate tract—emotional, dramatic, sensational in many respects. Nevertheless, Miss Carson concedes that farm chemicals have a place. "It is not my contention," she writes, "that chemical insecticides must never be used. I do contend that we have put poisonous and biologically potent chemicals indiscriminately into the hands of persons largely or wholly ignorant of their potentials for harm."

Miss Carson offers various constructive alternatives to the use of chemical pesticides. She feels that in many cases biological controls would be safer than chemical controls. The use of such natural controls has been limited; only about one hundred insect predators have been successfully introduced into the United States. Other alternates to insecticides are parasites, resistant crop varieties, sterilization of male insects by radiation, chemical sterilants, sex lures and physical attractants, such as light, to draw insects into traps. (pp. 266-67)

This is Miss Carson's vital solution: that insects, pests, and undesirable growths may be controlled by encouraging their enemies—a proposal offered at the beginning of the nineteenth century by Charles Darwin's grandfather, Erasmus. Ragweed causing hay fever can be fought, writes Miss Carson, by maintaining the dense shrubs and ferns that help to crowd it out; fight crabgrass by providing better soil for high-quality lawn grass; "fight insects by seeking to turn the strength of the species against itself," instead of by the careless, unrestrained use of chemicals. "As matters stand now," asserts Miss Carson, "we are in little better position than the guests of the Borgias." (pp. 267-68)

In a front-page obituary, the *New York Times* called Rachel Carson "one of the most influential women of her time." Senator Abraham Ribicoff, former U. S. Secretary of Health, Education, and Welfare, summed up her career by stating: "This gentle lady, more than any other person of her time, aroused people everywhere to be concerned with one of the most significant problems of mid-20th century life—man's contamination of his environment." Stewart L. Udall, Secretary of the Interior, one of Miss Carson's warmest admirers and supporters, added: "In the success of *Silent Spring* was the hope that those who truly care about the land have a fighting chance to 'inherit' the earth. That the pen of one so unassuming should have such an impact on national events was remarkable, and a heartening sign to conservationists everywhere." (p. 268)

Robert B. Downs, "Upsetting the Balance of

Nature: Rachel Carson's 'Silent Spring'," *in his* Books That Changed America, *The Macmillan Company, 1970, pp. 260-68.*

Paul Brooks

[*Brooks, former editor-in-chief and vice-president of Houghton Mifflin, was a personal friend of Carson's. In the following excerpt taken from his biography of Carson, he discusses her philosophy of life and theory of writing.*]

[In her writing], Rachel Carson was at once a daring adventurer and a meticulous craftsman: the stonemason who never lost sight of the cathedral. A modest person, she was bold enough to choose as the subject for her first major work nothing less than the sea itself. How she dealt with it is suggested in a letter she wrote five years after publication of *The Sea around Us.*

> The writer must never attempt to impose himself upon his subject. He must not try to mold it according to what he believes his readers or editors want to read. His initial task is to come to know his subject intimately, to understand its every aspect, to let it fill his mind. Then at some turning point the subject takes command and the true act of creation begins . . . The discipline of the writer is to learn to be still and listen to what his subject has to tell him.

The establishment of the proper relationship between author and subject, she felt, was where "the real agony of writing is experienced. At best, one can achieve it only sometimes, and in those moments one knows that something important has happened."

Rachel Carson never published any formal statement about the writer's art. But here and there in her correspondence one finds such comments. Particularly revealing, in respect to her own life and work, is her reply to a fan letter from a college girl with whom she obviously felt a special rapport—a girl who had found her only real childhood happiness in her love of nature, and who was hoping to combine a writing and a scientific career: . . .

> A writer's occupation is one of the loneliest in the world, even if the loneliness is only an inner solitude and isolation, for that he must have at times if he is to be truly creative. And so I believe only the person who knows and is not afraid of loneliness should aspire to be a writer. But there are also rewards that are rich and peculiarly satisfying—as, for example, a letter such as yours . . .

> Given the initial talent . . . writing is largely a matter of application and hard work, of writing and rewriting endlessly until you are satisfied that you have said what you want to say as clearly and simply as possible. For me, that usually means many, many revisions. If you write what you yourself sincerely think and feel and are interested in, the chances are very high that you will interest other people as well.

As she pointed out in her speech accepting the National Book Award [for *The Sea around Us*], there is no such thing as a separate literature of science, since after all the aim of science is to discover and illuminate the truth, which is also the aim of all true literature. She was opposed to "scientific books for young people, in which the author feels he has to write down to a supposed level of comprehension. I feel that if the author has something to say, and says it clearly, an intelligent reader of almost any age will understand him." While maintaining the highest professional standards, she wrote for the general public, and she avoided technical jargon. "My relation to technical scientific writing has been that of one who understands the language but does not use it." She was quite properly furious (though always polite) with editors who undertook to rewrite selections from her work. "It is my firm position, and one that I have stated before, that I will not knowingly permit any editor of any anthology to take liberties with my text." Or as she wrote with amazing restraint to the director of a university "reading laboratory" who had watered down a passage from **The Sea around Us** for eighth grade use: "I have, I confess, rather strong and definite prejudice against altering an author's words when excerpts from his writings are reprinted. A quotation, in my probably old-fashioned view, should be a quotation." (pp. 1-3)

[As a writer, Carson] used words to reveal the poetry—which is to say the essential truth and meaning—at the core of any scientific fact. She sought the knowledge that is essential to appreciate the extent of the unknown. She never worried lest the scientific discipline in which she was trained would dull her pen; *mutatis mutandis,* she was not ashamed of her emotional response to the forces of nature. When a friend confessed to being deeply moved by the "heart-stopping sight" of a flight of wildfowl above the spruces on the Maine coast, she replied:

> Don't ever dream I wondered at your tears. I've had the same response too often—perhaps always when alone. (I suppose there is a certain inhibition in the presence of anyone else . . .) The experience I relate in **Under the Sea-Wind** about the young mullet pouring through that tide race to the sea is one that comes to mind . . . I didn't tell it as a personal experience, but it was—I stood knee-deep in that racing water and at times could scarcely see those darting, silver bits of life for my tears.

Though she had the broad view of the ecologist who studies the infinitely complex web of relationships between living things and their environment, she did not concern herself exclusively with the great impersonal forces of nature. She felt a spiritual as well as physical closeness to the individual creatures about whom she wrote: a sense of identification that is an essential element in her literary style. (One thinks of Henry Thoreau, who felt wiser in all respects for knowing that there was a minnow in the brook: "Methinks I have need even of his sympathy, and to be his fellow in a degree.") (pp. 7-8)

Though she would probably have recoiled at the term "nun of nature" that has sometimes been applied to her, her attitude toward the natural world was that of a deeply religious person. When an elderly fundamentalist accused her of ignoring God and the Bible in writing **The Sea around Us,** she took the trouble to reply to him at length.

> It is true that I accept the theory of evolution as the most logical one that has ever been put forward to explain the development of living creatures on this earth. As far as I am concerned, however, there is absolutely no conflict between a belief in evolution and a belief in God as the creator. Believing as I do in evolution, I merely believe that is the method by which God created, and is still creating, life on earth. And it is a method so marvelously conceived that to study it in detail is to increase—and certainly never to diminish—one's reverence and awe both for the Creator and the process.

(She put the matter more succinctly on another occasion, when her mother reminded her that the Bible tells us God created the world. Yes, Rachel replied, and General Motors created her Oldsmobile, but *how* is the question.)

With the coming of the atomic age, Rachel felt that certain deep convictions she had cherished since childhood were being threatened. This realization had a direct effect on her writing career. Following the success of **The Sea around Us** and **The Edge of the Sea,** she had hoped to write a book on the origins of Life and the relation of Life to the physical environment. But, as she herself recognized, she was mentally blocked by an unwillingness to accept some of the implications of the scientific revolution that had occurred during the previous decade.

> Some of the thoughts that came were so unattractive to me that I rejected them completely, for the old ideas die hard, especially when they are emotionally as well as intellectually dear to one. It was pleasant to believe, for example, that much of Nature was forever beyond the tampering reach of man: he might level the forests and dam the streams, but the clouds and the rain and the wind were God's . . . It was comforting to suppose that the stream of life would flow on through time in whatever course that God had appointed for it—without interference by one of the drops of the stream, man. And to suppose that, however the physical environment might mold Life, that Life could never assume the power to change drastically—or even destroy—the physical world.

> These beliefs have almost been part of me for as long as I have thought about such things. To have them even vaguely threatened was so shocking that, as I have said, I shut my mind—refused to acknowledge what I couldn't help seeing. But that does no good, and I have now opened my eyes and my mind. I may not like what I see, but it does no good to ignore it, and it's worse than useless to go repeating the old "eternal verities" that are no more eternal than the hills of the poets. So it seems time someone wrote of Life in the light of the truth as it now appears to us.

(pp. 9-10)

. . . . .

In looking back across Rachel Carson's life work, it is im-

The writer must never attempt to impose himself upon his subject. He must not try to mold it according to what he believes his readers or editors want to read. His initial task is to come to know his subject intimately, to understand its every aspect, to let it fill his mind. Then at some turning point the subject takes command and the true act of creation begins . . . The discipline of the writer is to learn to be still and listen to what his subject has to tell him.

—Rachel Carson

portant, I think, not to allow the smoke of battle that lay over the *Silent Spring* controversy to obscure the sunlight that shone through all her writing, even when she was facing up to the "ugly facts" of man's destruction of the world she loved. Not long after *The Sea around Us* was published, she gave a talk which contained, in its concluding remarks, "A statement of something I believe in very deeply." Much of the statement was to appear in *The Sense of Wonder.*

A Statement of Belief

A large part of my life . . . has been concerned with some of the beauties and mysteries of this earth about us, and with the even greater mysteries of the life that inhabits it. No one can dwell long among such subjects without thinking rather deep thoughts, without asking himself searching and often unanswerable questions, and without achieving a certain philosophy.

There is one quality that characterizes all of us who deal with the sciences of the earth and its life—we are never bored. We can't be. There is always something new to be investigated. Every mystery solved brings us to the threshold of a greater one.

(pp. 323-24)

The pleasures, . . . the values of contact with the natural world are not reserved for the scientists. They are available to anyone who will place himself under the influence of a lonely mountain top—or the sea—or the stillness of a forest; or who will stop to think about so small a thing as the mystery of a growing seed.

I am not afraid of being thought a sentimentalist when I say that I believe natural beauty has a necessary place in the spiritual development of any individual or any society. I believe that whenever we destroy beauty, or whenever we substitute something man-made and artificial for a natural feature of the earth, we have retarded some part of man's spiritual growth . . .

We see the destructive trend on a national scale in proposals to invade the national parks with commercial schemes such as the building of power dams. The parks were placed in trust for all the people, to preserve for them just such recreational and spiritual values as I have mentioned. Is it the right of this, our generation, in its selfish materialism, to destroy these things because we are blinded by the dollar sign? Beauty—and all the values that derive from beauty—are not measured and evaluated in terms of the dollar.

Years ago I discovered in the writings of the British naturalist Richard Jefferies a few lines that so impressed themselves upon my mind that I have never forgotten them.

> The exceeding beauty of the earth, in her splendor of life, yields a new thought with every petal. The hours when the mind is absorbed by beauty are the only hours when we really live. All else is illusion, or mere endurance.

Those lines are, in a way, a statement of the creed I have lived by . . . I have had the privilege of receiving many letters from people who, like myself, have been steadied and reassured by contemplating the long history of the earth and sea, and the deeper meanings of the world of nature . . . In contemplating "the exceeding beauty of the earth" these people have found calmness and courage. For there is symbolic as well as actual beauty in the migration of birds; in the ebb and flow of the tides; in the folded bud ready for the spring. There is something infinitely healing in these repeated refrains of nature—the assurance that dawn comes after night, and spring after the winter.

(pp. 325-26)

No better epitaph could be written for Rachel Carson than the final passage in *The Edge of the Sea* [below], which she also had wished to be read at her funeral service. (p. 327)

[The Enduring Sea]

On all these shores there are echoes of past and future: of the flow of time, obliterating yet containing all that has gone before; of the sea's eternal rhythms—the tides, the beat of surf, the pressing rivers of the currents—shaping, changing, dominating; of the stream of life, flowing as inexorably as any ocean current, from past to unknown future. For as the shore configuration changes in the flow of time, the pattern of life changes, never static, never quite the same from year to year. Whenever the sea builds a new coast, waves of living creatures surge against it, seeking a foothold, establishing their colonies. And so we come to perceive life as a force as tangible as any of the physical realities of the sea, a force strong and purposeful, as incapable of being crushed or diverted from its ends as the rising tide.

Contemplating the teeming life of the shore, we have an uneasy sense of the communication of some universal truth that lies just beyond our grasp. What is the message signaled by the hordes of diatoms, flashing their microscopic lights in the night sea? What truth is expressed by the legions of the barnacles, whitening the rocks with their habitations, each small creature within finding the necessities of its existence in the sweep of the surf? And what is the meaning of so tiny a being as the transparent wisp of protoplasm that is a sea lace, existing for some reason inscrutable to us—a reason that demands its presence by the trillion amid the rocks and weeds of the shore? The meaning haunts and ever eludes us, and in its very pursuit we approach the ultimate mystery of Life itself.

(pp. 328-29)

Paul Brooks, in his The House of Life: Rachel Carson at Work; with Selections from Her Writings Published and Unpublished, *Houghton Mifflin Company, 1972, 350 p.*

Geoffrey Norman

[In the late 1950s, Rachel Carson was] a best-selling author of a trilogy about the sea, **The Sea around Us, Under the Sea-Wind,** and **The Edge of the Sea.** Her books were serialized by *The New Yorker* and had earned her a vast following and many correspondents, all of whom she was careful to answer. One of them wrote to ask for her help in stopping the spraying over a private bird sanctuary near Cape Cod. Carson made some inquiries, and as she learned more she became more alarmed. That was the beginning of a labor that was to result in her book **Silent Spring,** which led to action that saved the birds and energized millions to work and campaign and vote for an enduring cause that, for lack of a better name, is called "the environmental movement." (pp. 472, 474)

Her methods were simple enough. She read the available documents and corresponded with experts. Then, she went through several drafts, revising until she was satisfied with the flow of the prose.

The book that her efforts resulted in was about the spraying and what it did to the birds and other creatures. But that does not begin to describe its scope or account for its impact. One might just as well say that Darwin wrote about turtles and the Pacific islands where they were found.

What Carson did in **Silent Spring** was to introduce to the general imagination the concept of ecology: the way the natural world fit together, the pieces so tightly and inextricably bound that you could not isolate cause and effect. The consequences of any action rippled through the whole system, affecting everything and sometimes even changing the system itself. So when we poisoned gypsy moths with massive sprayings of DDT, we were, ultimately, poisoning ourselves.

The book opened with a parable that described a landscape from which the birds and fish had vanished and where people died of mysterious ailments. It is, on rereading, the weakest portion of the book. But you can understand why it was necessary when you recall that in 1962

people needed to be shocked. They thought pesticides were safe, if they thought about them at all.

From that first chapter, she went on to explain that life on the planet had been changing for millions of years, that such change was slow and organic and inevitable. But now there was something different, a new force at work. Man had made it possible to alter the environment suddenly and drastically, with unforeseen and possibly disastrous consequences.

After sounding the alarm and stating her thesis in the first two chapters, she described the poisons that we were encountering—DDT was showing up even in the fatty tissues of Eskimo who lived in areas where the stuff had never been sprayed. She used diagrams to show the molecular structure of the chlorinated hydrocarbons and made the distinctions between these new poisons and the older ones.

The book went on to detail the effects of these poisons on the environment. Not surprisingly, the most affecting chapter was on the birds. The book's title was inspired by some lines in Keats and an imagined spring when no birds returned.

There was information—data on every page. There was nothing half-baked or mystical about the book. More than fifty pages of sources were cited. But the science and information came filtered through her intelligence and shaped by her graceful writing style. On almost every page there was a gem that owed more to her vision than the research of any laboratory scientist. The best passages are, in fact, lyrical.

> Some 10,000 acres of sagelands were sprayed by the [United States Forest] Service, yielding to pressure of cattlemen for more grasslands. The sage was killed, as intended. But so was the green, life-giving ribbon of willows that traced its way across these plains, following the meandering streams. Moose had lived in these willow thickets, for willow is to the moose what sage is to the antelope. Beaver had lived there, too, feeding on the willows, felling them and making a strong dam across the tiny stream. Through the labor of the beavers, a lake backed up. Trout in the mountain streams seldom were more than six inches long; in the lake they thrived so prodigiously that many grew to five pounds. Waterfowl were attracted to the lake, also. Merely because of the presence of the willows and the beavers that depended on them, the region was an attractive recreational area with excellent fishing and hunting.

> But with the "improvement" instituted by the Forest Service, the willows went the way of the sagebrush, killed by the same impartial spray. . . . The moose were gone and so were the beaver. Their principal dam had gone out for want of attention by its skilled architects, and the lake had drained away. None of the large trout were left. None could live in the tiny creek that remained, threading its way through a bare, hot land where no shade remained. The living world was shattered.

(pp. 474, 476)

Today, [William] Shawn says of the book, "Before *Silent Spring,* nobody talked about the environment and ecology. It was all new to us when she wrote it. There were people who wrote about conservation and there were naturalists. But *Silent Spring* was something new. Rachel Carson was the first one to write things this way." (p. 476)

Geoffrey Norman, "The Flight of Rachel Carson," in Esquire, Vol. 100, No. 6, December, 1983, pp. 472, 474, 476, 478-79.

Carol B. Gartner

It is characteristic of the imbalance in Carson's reputation that although many have praised her as a scientist who wrote like a poet, she is not recognized as a significant literary figure, much less given her place in the pantheon of American writers with Henry David Thoreau.

From her earliest occasional writing, through the four major books, to her latest speeches, Carson's work is of a piece in substance, artistry, and underlying philosophy. But even beyond this, her life and work together formed an artistic whole. Preparation, dedication, and her sense of vocation as an artist interlocked with her sense of mission as a moral and social person. (pp. 122-23)

As naturalist and writer, she is a literary descendant of Thoreau. In personal terms, although they shared a certain reclusiveness, her life seems the opposite of his. Thoreau claimed to have lived the life he "might have writ," even though he did commit many careful words to paper. Carson's life was in her work, except for the part she devoted to her family.

If one keynote of the artistic personality is an overweening belief in the worth of one's art, then Carson was an artist not only in the quality of her work, but in the living of her life. Like all those who choose to be artists rather than pursue easier or more acceptable careers, she had tremendous faith in the importance of her mission and the value of her contributions. Her friend and colleague Shirley Briggs says Carson had "big ideas she wanted people to understand." Accepting their medal in 1952, she told The John Burroughs Society, "In justice not only to ourselves but to the public we ought to develop a more confident and assured attitude toward the role and the value of nature literature." (p. 123)

People have put Rachel Carson into many categories—among them, poet, scientist, conservationist—but these were not separate identities for her. Just as the concept of ecological interrelationships was a cornerstone of her philosophy, so her organizing principle was integration: of interests and activities, occupation and recreation, science and poetry, subject and structure, facts and message. Paul Brooks reports that Carson found his suggestion that she expand her *Holiday* magazine article "into a small book, aimed specifically at saving the rapidly disappearing remnant of unspoiled shoreline. . . . 'an appealing idea, as giving me a chance to *do* something.' "

"I myself am convinced," she told an audience in 1952,

that there has never been a greater need than

there is today for the reporter and interpreter of the natural world. Mankind has . . . sought to insulate himself, in his cities of steel and concrete, from the realities of earth and water and the growing seed. Intoxicated with a sense of his own power, he seems to be going farther and farther into more experiments for the destruction of himself and his world.

There is certainly no single remedy for this condition and I am offering no panacea. But it seems reasonable to believe—and I do believe—that the more clearly we can focus our attention on the wonders and realities of the universe about us the less taste we shall have for the destruction of our race.

She saw her obligation as helping others see and understand. Shirley Briggs writes that "a foray along the shore or through the spruce woods" with Carson "was always high adventure. Those of us who had the joy of sharing some of these expeditions . . . learned much about the creatures and plants we found, but most of all, we glimpsed a new way of seeing our world." A century earlier, Thoreau had written in his journal, "The question is not what you look at, but what you see." We, as readers, can still share Carson's adventures, and learn to see.

Carson's major books form changing patterns of pairs. The first, *Under the Sea-Wind,* and the second, *The Sea around Us,* focus on the oceans, while the third, *The Edge of the Sea,* and the fourth, *Silent Spring,* concentrate on the land.

The movement from *Under the Sea-Wind* to *The Sea around Us* follows the progression of learning experiences Carson describes in *The Sense of Wonder,* first the emotional, then the intellectual response, with the first preparing the way for the second. In both books, Carson intended to convey information. In *Under the Sea-Wind,* facts are integrated into the narratives and thus more limited, but Carson carefully patterned the content of the stories to allow logical coverage of the material. Each story carries us further into the sea until we have reached the deepest parts and learned about the most complex migrations. In *The Sea around Us,* the goal of providing information is central, so that orderly presentation of the material determines the form, and geographical coverage is more comprehensive.

From *The Edge of the Sea* to *Silent Spring,* Carson similarly expands both subject matter and geographical coverage, moving from shore areas to the whole of the land, as she moves from an ecological presentation to the dangers of ecological dislocation.

Under the Sea-Wind and *The Edge of the Sea* live on as delightful, informative reading. There is little to become dated and no overt message, although the hints and murmurs are clearly there. These books are literary in character, with her first book taking the narrative approach and her third following the lines of the familiar essay. The first excels in verve and beauty.

The second and fourth books are cosmic in approach, designed to change a reader's perceptions of the world. Filled with facts and emphasizing the latest research, they are highly subject to becoming dated, but Carson's perspective creates a framework for further knowledge. While *The Sea around Us* is thoroughly objective exposition, leavened with erudite yet intriguing references to history, literature, and myth, *Silent Spring* is an argumentative documentary, thrusting forward facts and interpretations.

In poetic effect, *Under the Sea-Wind* is the highest point on the incline, with the next two books sacrificing some loveliness to the cause of instruction, although the balance remains tilted to the artistic. With its concentration of unpleasant facts, *Silent Spring* is at the lowest point of Carson's poetic writing, yet is still a book of spare beauty with passages of lyrical brilliance. (pp. 124-26)

Although she perfected the scientific approach, [Carson] shared themes, preoccupations and literary approaches with naturalist writers of all periods. Nature writers generally use their literary skills to blend information into universal experiences, often working through sense impressions. They seek to awaken wonder, and recognize the need for reverence and love, as well as understanding, stressing the universal urge to live, and the complex web of ecological interrelationships.

Contemporary nature writers increasingly emphasize the impact of human beings on nature. [In *Green Treasury*], Edwin Way Teale, an important naturalist-writer himself, sees growing interest in "the whole ecological interrelationship of living things," in which "Man, too, is a part of the fabric of nature." Contemporary nature writing as a whole has a tone of deepening forboding, with increasing melancholy and pessimism joining the responses of wonder, joy, kinship, and sympathy.

Like Thoreau and later writers such as critic Joseph Wood Krutch and humorist E. B. White, Carson, in both method and ideas, belongs not only to the line of nature literature, but also to the broader literary tradition. She joins nineteenth-century transcendentalists such as Emerson and Thoreau in the belief that nature provides its own symbols. In her major books, there are the sea symbols, ranging from the structure of a shell to the rhythm of the tides. She points out land symbols—migrating birds, seasonal changes—in such works as *The Sense of Wonder* and a brief piece for *This Week* magazine called **"The Land around Us."** (pp. 127-28)

[There is also a] close resemblance between Carson's ideas in *The Sea around Us* and those of eighteenth-century English writers. The same ideas reappear in other books, particularly *The Edge of the Sea.* There are remarkable similarities between the eighteenth-century concept of "plenitude," the idea that a diverse multitude of living creatures fills every niche in the ascending "chain of being" leading from the lowest animal forms to the angels, and Carson's celebration of the abundance and variety of life and the strength of the life force.

Like eighteenth-century writers and philosophers, Carson believed that human beings can understand only a part of the total plan. In both *The Edge of the Sea* and *The Sense of Wonder,* she stresses the importance of our appreciating

the mystery and wonder of nature. She shares also a strong sense of the brevity of human tenancy of the earth.

In all her books, Carson seeks to undo the common idea that all things on earth were created for the benefit of human beings. Alexander Pope disparaged the same popular notion in the eighteenth century when he wrote:

> Know, Nature's children shall divide her care;
> The fur that warms a monarch warm'd a bear.
> While Man exclaims, "See all things for my use!"
> "See man for mine!" replies a pamper'd goose.
>
> (p. 128)

Carson differs from most nature writers in the solidity of her scientific base. When she generalizes, she bases her statements directly on specific facts or personal explorations. She always integrates the beauty of her medium and her literary techniques with the scenes or situations that call them forth, avoiding abstract rhapsodies and emotional tangents.

U.S. Secretary of the Interior Stewart Udall's tribute to Rachel Carson, a month after her death, shows, in the attributes he praised and the order he imposed on them, how successfully Carson joined science and literature, nature writing and poetry. She combined "the scientist's eye and the poet's sense," Udall writes.

> And the lyric tone of her prose, the insights she drew from her research, her clear commitment to nature's scheme of things made her a memorable teacher. There was always, there to admire in her work, the effortless way with which she bridged the gap between science and the humanities.

Carson's own statements frequently give us insight into her values. Reading her comment that "Poets often have a perception that gives their words the validity of science," we realize that for her, science carried the most weight. She clarified her approach in a statement for *Twentieth Century Authors.* "As a writer, my interest is divided between the presentation of facts and the interpretation of their underlying significance, with emphasis, I think, toward the latter."

As for style, she always screened her writing for "passages where disharmonies of sound might distract attention from the thought." Critically reviewing a less careful author, she complains, "Often it is difficult to hear what the author is saying because of the tumult of verbs at war with their subjects, and of 'sentences' that are only a confused tangle of phrases lacking sometimes a subject, sometimes a predicate."

Value, for Carson, was not measured by number of facts. She criticized one writer who "managed to compress 5,000 years of undersea history" into a book of only moderate size, concluding that "the very multiplicity of facts and the terse style in which they are presented are somewhat detrimental to the reading qualities of the book."

In two glowing book reviews, Carson suggests her own goals. Calling attention to Gilbert Klingel's awareness of all the senses and his rich imagery and evocative descriptions [in *The Bay*], Carson praises his "ability to describe the life of a limited area in terms that invest it not only with fascination but with rich meaning." Above all, "the universal themes of the slow unfolding of earth history and of the ceaseless, incomprehensible struggle of life to survive and to perpetuate itself . . . flow from a solid foundation of carefully observed fact."

[In a review of *A Land,* Carson asserts that] Jacquetta Hawkes achieves the "happy union of scientist and creative artist." "And out of the materials of these sciences her richly creative mind has evoked an image of 'an entity, the land of Britain, in which past and present, nature, man, and art appear all in one piece.' Such a book leaves the reader vastly richer not only in information but in understanding. It is always a joy to come in contact with a mind at once informed with scientific fact and leavened with imagination and intuitive understanding." She tells us to read Hawkes's book both for facts and for "deeper significance in interpreting the relation of man to his environment." We know she wants us to read her own books the same way. (pp. 131-33)

"No writer can stand still," Carson told the American Association of University Women in 1956. "Each task completed carries its own obligation to go on to something new." When she died, she left many projects uncompleted—the **"Help Your Child to Wonder"** [article, reprinted as *The Sense of Wonder*]; the important book on man and the environment, the war against unwise use of pesticides.

Nonetheless, the four books she wrote, and the scattering of pamphlets and articles, are a substantial accomplishment. A *New York Times* editorial eloquently testifies to Carson's place in history.

> She was a biologist, not a crusader, but the power of her knowledge and the beauty of her language combined to make Rachel Carson one of the most influential women of our time.
>
> For years warnings had been sounded about the lethal effects on wildlife—and possibly on human life—of the indiscriminate use of poisonous chemical sprays. But it was not until the publication of Miss Carson's *Silent Spring* in 1962 that the entire nation was alerted to the hazards to man and nature caused by pesticides.

Silent Spring began as an exposé of the dangers of pesticides but came close to becoming the major ecological work Carson had wanted to write. As in all her work, style and structure relate organically to the particular subject, but *Silent Spring* is nonetheless an extension of the motifs and themes of earlier books. When Douglas Costle, as Administrator of the United States Environmental Protection Agency, declared that Rachel Carson "sounded the alarm about environmental dangers," he credited not *Silent Spring* alone, but "her unique, empathetic presentation of the workings of nature in *Under the Sea-Wind, The Sea around Us, The Edge of the Sea,* and finally *Silent Spring*." (pp. 133-34)

[Carson's] claim to a place in literature as well as history rests on all her books, each an individually realized achievement representing a different kind of writing, all

testifying that she possessed what William Beebe considered the *"ideal* equipment for a naturalist writer of literary natural history":

> Supreme enthusiasm, tempered with infinite patience and a complete devotion to truth; the broadest possible education; keen eyes, ears, and nose; the finest instruments; opportunity for observation; thorough training in laboratory technique; comprehension of known facts and theories, and the habit of giving full credit for these in the proper place; awareness of what is not known; ability to put oneself in the subject's place; interpretation and integration of observations; a sense of humor; facility in writing; an eternal sense of humbleness and wonder.

This is Rachel Carson.

Under the Sea-Wind best shows her empathy with the creatures of the sea and the literary flair and abundant grace with which she spins her stories. *The Sea around Us,* as [Henry Hill Collins, Jr.] rhapsodized, "introduced thousands of people to the fascination of one of the most familiar but least-known areas on the surface of the globe—the ocean. It also introduced thousands of people to some extraordinarily beautiful nature writing." It is a thorough treatise on the geology, history, biology, ecology, and economics of the sea, and more, but Carson's "supreme enthusiasm," and all the other attributes Beebe lists, make it the masterpiece it is.

In *The Edge of the Sea* and *The Sense of Wonder,* Carson is relaxed and openly philosophical. She speaks to us directly so that we share delightful educational explorations, learning not only what nature means to Carson but what it can mean for us and for the children who explore with us. Reading these two books, we nestle in valleys below Carson's impressive literary peaks, but no visit to the coast is the same after *The Edge of the Sea,* and no woodland stroll or moonlit wanderings on the beach fail to remind us of our "sense of wonder." (pp. 134-35)

Henry David Thoreau is credited with making the nature essay a literary form. Rachel Carson has done the same for the science book. Her work is not yet recognized as the beginning of a new literary tradition, but its influence may already have affected the best recent science books for the general public.

Carson's example is hard to follow. It takes major talent to turn science into poetry. But when science writers pay attention to the craft of their writing, treating it as literary art, when they seek the broad perspective as well as the accurate statement, science writing can become literature. Each of Carson's books seems so distinct from the others that it is difficult to see them as representing a single departure in tradition, but it is their common strengths in form, tone, perspective, and style that make them so readable, and thus so effective as both science and literature.

When we look closely at Carson's subtle layers of meaning, when we measure her aesthetic effect and philosophical impact, we know that Rachel Carson is a preeminent writer of nonfiction. We know that she belongs not only in history, but in literary history as well. With seeming ease and fluent grace, her books fulfill the classic aims of literature, to teach and to delight. (pp. 135-36)

> Carol B. Gartner, in her Rachel Carson, *Frederick Ungar Publishing Co., 1983, 161 p.*

Vera L. Norwood

> She sweeps with many-colored Brooms—
> And leaves the Shreds behind—
> Oh Housewife in the Evening West—
> Come back, and dust the Pond!

> [Emily Dickinson, "Poem 219," 1891]

Emily Dickinson offers a succinct vision of woman's relationship with the natural landscape as one of housewife to home—one in which the poetic and the practical coexist. Although seemingly in keeping with gentle, domestic relationships with nature, in which the environment outside the home is experienced as a safe, tamed-garden version of the interior life Victorian women supposedly led, Dickinson's poem leads us to contemplate our definitions of female roles and the natural world, and the metaphors we use to understand our relationship to the world. As with most Dickinson poems, the image contains both text and subtext. The traditional role of Victorian women as household managers is subverted when the housewife inadvertently creates "dust" in her cleaning, and the leavings of her efforts enrich the world. Just as the image liberates women, it also liberates nature by suggesting that imperfection is as beautiful as perfection.

As natural historian Carolyn Merchant has suggested, such metaphorical connections between women and nature have informed both the environmental movements and the feminist movements of this century. The strength of these connections rests on the image of earth as our "home." Environmentalists take many of their principles from the science of ecology, the meaning of which derives from the Greek *oikos*, or house. Merchant argues, "The connection between the Earth and the house has historically been mediated by women." She notes that many feminists find the image of earth as a female space to be a powerful one, and she argues that defining nature as organic "home" leads to concepts of interrelatedness, equal value to all parts, and increased sense of community. She cites biologist Rachel Carson as crucial to the shift away from a mechanistic worldview and toward an understanding of the organic home suggested by Dickinson's poem. Merchant comments further that the science of ecology and the feminist movement share a similar ethic characterized by an affinity with the concept of nature as home.

The connotations of earth as a house, however, are not necessarily the same as those of the earth as home. In his history of developments in scientific ecology, [*Nature's Economy: The Roots of Ecology*], Donald Worster explains that "oeconomy" was a term used to describe the knowledge later dubbed ecology. By the eighteenth century the phrase "oeconomy of nature" connoted "the rational ordering of all material resources in an interacting whole. God was seen both as the Supreme Economist who had designed the earth household and as the housekeeper who kept it functioning productively. Thus the study of 'ecology' . . . was in its very origins imbued with a political and economic as well as Christian view of nature: the earth was perceived as a world that must be somehow managed for maximum output." Worster sees contemporary scientific ecology continuing to fulfill this economic, efficiency-, and production-oriented, managerial approach to nature.

So, when Carson speaks of the earth as a house, we must be careful to note whether by house she means organic home, economic household, or some combination of both. Dickinson's poem suggests that, more often than not, home values and household values are intertwined in our daily relationships with the natural world. Consequently, her poetry resists the sort of pigeonholing that simplifies the complexity of her response to the world. Carson's work reflects a similarly complex view of the world in which neither the organic home metaphor nor the economic household metaphor alone describes our natural environment.

Both Carolyn Merchant and Donald Worster credit Carson's work with inaugurating recent environmental movements, but both also locate her writing squarely in the organic tradition that sees nature as home—with all the connotations, both for nature and women, that such a metaphor has. These historians are not alone in their assessment. Most commentators on Carson's works have tended to focus on her "nature writing," the pieces that celebrate the wonders of the natural world, and have ignored or trivialized the works that take a more economic, household-oriented approach, such as the materials she prepared for the U.S. government or much of *The Sea around Us.* Such work has been studied only to the extent that it is considered of the same "literary quality" as her books; it has even been dismissed as evidencing an "enforced emphasis on utility."

Carson, like Emily Dickinson, was much more in touch with the complexities of her world than such categorizing of her work indicates. Indeed, the metaphors of organic home and economic household reside in constant tension within all her work, even while Carson maintains that nature does not really fit into the conceptual boxes these metaphors supply. In fact, human beings encounter the world most often as trespassers, alienated from both the organic home and the economic household. Recognizing this failure of human pattern making to describe the natural world, Carson confronts the epistemological hubris involved in all naming and human pattern making. These issues are first raised in her classic nature books—*Under the Sea Wind* (1941), *The Sea around Us* (1951), *The Edge of the Sea* (1955). These works, which shaped Carson's reputation as a nature writer and popularizer of ecology, are the pieces in which she struggled with the philosophical implications of standard literary conventions for describing nature.

In the late 1950s, the focus of Carson's concern shifted from the epistemological inadequacy of our understanding of nature to the consequences of such limited knowledge. She concludes by suggesting new norms for our relationship with the environment. This shift in emphasis changes her usage of the metaphors as she investigates the negative facets of nature as home/household—the harm that the human nurturer and manager can inadvertently do. *Silent Spring* details this shadowy side of our dealings with nature. In this work, Carson evinces an understanding of the limits of human pattern making that suggests connections between her work and the then-emerging philosophical critique of positivism and objectivism, particularly Thomas Kuhn's conception of science as "paradigm" governed. Carson realizes that paradigm shift occurs only when people are *taught* to see nature in new ways, so her last work emphasizes pedagogy; in *The Sense of Wonder* she offers a program for teaching children (and their parents) how to see nature as a system of processes rather than static conditions.

Thus, I discuss the growing complexity in Carson's nature writing, her movement from philosophical to normative issues, and the connections of her work not only to the ecology movements of the sixties and seventies but also to major developments in the twentieth century in philosophy, particularly the philosophy of science. My analysis suggests not only a new reading of Rachel Carson's work but characterizes her as a major voice within contemporary discussions of gender and science as well. How women respond to the natural world, its meaning in their symbolic constructions of reality, and their own sense of responsibility to the environment at various times and among different cultures are matters of wide debate among scholars in such fields as history, literature, and anthropology. Important to this work is an understanding of the ways in which women use symbolic language—language sometimes perceived to spring from their socially derived roles—to relate to nature. I argue that Carson makes a strong contribution to rethinking and reshaping narrow constructions of nature and human relationships with nature implicit in symbolic language. In so doing, she also participates in a tradition reaching back at least to the poet Emily Dickinson and forward to Nobel Prize-winning biologist Barbara McClintock, a tradition celebrating not narrow, "domesticated" nature but the expanding conceptions of nature as home and family to include appreciation and respect for the uncontrollable, unknown—even the never-to-be-known—aspects of the world.

Under the Sea Wind is Rachel Carson's first book. Influenced by well-known nature writers like Henry Beston and Henry Williamson, the book is a series of classic tales about the migrations of birds and fish over the span of a year. Carson identifies with the animals described and personifies them with names and human emotions. *The Sea around Us* established Carson as a natural history writer of the first order. The book was widely reviewed, quite popular, and earned a number of prizes. *The Sea around Us* catalogs most of what was understood about the world's oceans by the early 1950s, including what use humankind might make of the resources in the sea. Carson's third book, *The Edge of the Sea,* results from Carson's field research along the eastern U.S. coastline. Meant to be a guide or handbook, it became, instead, Carson's meditation on the interrelatedness of land and sea life. The book melds her perspectives in *Under the Sea Wind* and

The Sea around Us, treating both the animal life cycles and the geology of the coast.

All three early works contain metaphoric uses of nature as home and as household. They also, however, often contradict those metaphors. Since the depiction of nature as home is the most common interpretation of Carson's work, I begin there. "Home" in this context means that there is a family feeling for the physical and biophysical landscape; it evokes the image of nature as our "mother," advocates an identification with other creatures, and promotes a unification of self and nature—that sense of being organically (as if by blood) related to the natural world—all of which leads to a reverence and respect for all the materials of one's home.

In Carson's communities of creatures, nature is described as a mother creating a home for her children. These communities live on "homeplaces" in a natural landscape, homeplaces that can even be constructed by animals who provide shelter for other animals. Human structures also provide homeplaces for nature's flora and fauna, even to the extent that human landscapes of death become homes for life. For example, in *Under the Sea Wind* Carson vividly describes the killing efficiency of gill nets; later she offers her readers some relief from that horror by describing the gill net as homeplace:

> Tonight no fish would have tried to pass through the net, for all its meshes were hung with tiny warning lamps. Luminous protozoa and water flies and amphipods clung to the net twine in the dark sea, and the pulse of the ocean stirred from their bodies countless sparks of light. It was as though all the myriad lesser fry of the sea—the plants small as dust motes and the animals tinier than a sand grain—drifting from birth to death in an ocean of infinite size and endless fluidity, seized upon the meshes of the gill net as the firm reality in their uneasy world. . . . The gill net glowed as though it had life of itself. . . . The light lured many small creatures to rise from deep water and gather on the meshes of the gill net, where they rested all that night in the dark, wide sea.

These are comforting images that offer an organic niche for humans in nature. By showing how the natural landscape might absorb the artificial structure, they defuse human destructiveness. Nature's ability to overcome human carelessness is a crucial concept for Carson, one she ultimately acknowledges to be false, but one to which she, nevertheless, was drawn throughout her life.

The glowing gill net also reminds one that home can be a haven from the pressures of a harshly competitive world. Carson's first three books provide a litany of natural and artificial places becoming havens, particularly for babies. Carson's presentation of herself as a privileged visitor allowed to enter a unique and private world is important to this concept of nature as haven. For example, she describes a favorite tide pool as a place of gentleness and beauty eked out of an otherwise uncaring geological world. Such a stance speaks directly to the protective atmosphere of home, including our natural home, as an organic, magical, life-affirming place.

That said, we often come to the end of what *is* said about Rachel Carson's nature writing. For most of her critics, her love of nature is the backdrop and explanation for the intensity of feeling in *Silent Spring.* That she also mentions scientific developments in our knowledge of the sea, or "sneaks" in educational information about the oceans, or discusses the technicalities of the fishing industry is secondary to her reverent picture of nature as home. But there is another side to Carson's home metaphor, one fed not by her reading of classic nature writers but by her training as a scientist. Charles Darwin is not often mentioned as a source for Carson's writing, but she draws on him frequently in *The Sea around Us.* Both *The Sea around Us* and *The Edge of the Sea* reflect scientific ecological concepts that came out of the merger in the early twentieth century of biology and geology. Much of Carson's college training in biology must have been grounded in Frederic Clements's climax theories. Charles Elton, who first described food chains and wrote about the ecology of land animals, provides the fundamental web of interconnections behind *Silent Spring.*

As Donald Worster notes in *Nature's Economy,* the primary implication of the "well-managed household" is an economic one. Worster traces a convincing history of the connections between science and industrial society over three centuries, based on an economic ideal of progress that culminates in the mid-twentieth century in a "New Ecology." The New Ecology begins with Charles Elton's food chains. Animals and plants are categorized as producers, consumers, reducers, and decomposers: "These labels emphasized the nutritional interdependence that binds species together—the corporateness of survival—and they became the cues from which ecology would increasingly take an economic direction." Although the New Ecology resulted in a decreased interest in Darwinian competitive struggles, Worster is careful to show how new scientific breakthroughs arose from earlier tendencies to regard nature as a factory of sorts and humans (rather than God) as supreme managers.

Rachel Carson learned science and wrote her early books in the midst of the changing vision of nature Worster delineates. Thus her well-managed household looks both back to Darwin and forward to what Worster calls "pacified" nature. Further, in describing nature as an economic household, Carson, as she had done in describing it as a home, looks at the metaphor both as descriptive of the biophysical environment we see around us and as revelatory of our place within that environment.

Although all three books offer fulsome examples of the interplay, in the natural world, between competition and "corporateness," *Under the Sea Wind* offers a particularly illustrative case of the natural world and man's impact on that world—a dramatization of men hunting mullet. Initially Carson evokes the high drama of the battles between men and their prey, the uncertainties of the chase on both sides, but she concludes with the image of a well-regulated, cooperative household. Men discard mullet "too small to sell, too small to eat"; the sea carefully "laps" up some of these for "the hunters of the tide lines," the ghost crabs and sand hoppers who then come out to clean up the debris: "for in the sea, nothing is lost. One dies, another lives, as the precious elements of life are passed on and on in endless chains." Significantly, men have not altered the balance of life here as many "mullet [pass] unmolested through the inlet and [run] westward and southward along the coast."

In sum, Carson's work reveals a much more conflicted and complicated approach to nature than her reputation gives her credit for. Donald Worster's placement of Carson in the "arcadian" tradition—assuming identification with the natural world as the proper human response—is a classic example of the general tendency to emphasize only her reverence for nature. Carson, however, understands the economic imperatives too well to render only the solution offered by arcadia. A brief story from [*Under the Sea Wind*] epitomizes the tensions in her work, revealing how each of us continually balances the organic home and economic household meanings we find in nature. The story tells of a failed catch seen through the eyes of a young fisherman so new to the occupation that he is still filled with an "unslakable curiosity" about life under the sea's surface. He has family feeling for life in the sea: "It seemed to him incongruous that a creature that had made a go of life in the sea . . . should at last come to death on the deck of a mackerel seiner." Nevertheless, he is stuck with the economics of the household, with the inalterable fact of his own need to consume: "It was only later, when they had finished the long, wet task of repiling the 1200-foot length of seine in the boat, their hour's heavy work wasted, that he realized what it meant that the mackerel had sounded." Thus Carson alternates between a vision of nature as revered, respected homeplace, to be approached with an almost religious curiosity and as a household existing primarily for production, consumption, cooperation, and management.

More often than not, however, Carson is struck by the degree to which the natural world does not function as home *or* household for its human children. Finding herself and her fellows to be outsiders, trespassers in a world that is distinctly "other," she declares both nuturing and managerial responses to nature doomed to miss the point. The occasions when she fails to find herself at home in nature, paradoxically, constitute the high points of her experience. Similarly, the occasions when the economic metaphor shatters against the unwillingness of the natural world to "produce" meaning provide her most telling critiques of human limitations and lead her to doubt all "naming," all artificial boxes into which nature has been "fit." In this context, Carson becomes more than a nature writer; she raises fundamental questions about how human knowledge is constructed, questions that reveal the epistemological hubris underlying much human understanding. These questions prompt her later normative work in *Silent Spring* and *The Sense of Wonder.*

The first paragraph of *Under the Sea Wind* begins with a metaphor questioning easy assumptions about categories—in this case distinctions we normally make between land and ocean: "Both water and sand were the color of steel overlaid with the sheen of silver, so that it was hard to say where water ended and land began." The images suggest that the places where ocean meets land will not always conform to visions of a warm, life-giving mother from which all life sprang; this ocean is also cold, borderless, impermanent, and harsh with its living inhabitants. Such uneasiness about the exigencies of the ocean expressed in the opening paragraph of her first nature book flow through all three books. Carson constantly points out the risks in an environment that requires enormous waste of life. She notes [in *The Edge of the Sea*], for example, the thousands of young who die in the ocean for lack of a fortuitous piece of driftwood or buoy to make into a homeplace. Her concern is only increased by the tenuous security of these places—so easily destroyed by storms or tides. What are we to make of the mole crab, who lives but one year, dying at the end of the summer, leaving just one generation to tenant the household? Or of the sea cucumber spewing forth its internal organs when threatened? Looking at such a world, Carson can only note how strange it appears to human observers, how deficient we are in comprehending its reason.

Carson's writings are filled with allusions to the separation between humans and nature. In the most mundane examples, human beings are trespassers, physical intruders. In *Under the Sea Wind* the appearance of fishermen "alarms" a heron, sends shore birds scurrying toward the sea, sets the terns to flight "like hundreds of scraps of paper flung to the wind," and lands a ghost crab into the jaws of a channel bass. On a wider scale, the arrival of people in the delicate ecology of islands [as examined in *The Sea around Us*] "abruptly changes," "exterminates," "ruins," and "snaps the slender thread of life" for many species. Further, Carson laments that in important ways humans literally cannot see nature, and she constantly points out the physical limitations of our ability to grasp the world we so blithely call "home." Looking at a tidepool, she remarks [in *The Edge of the Sea*], "The human imperfection of my vision . . . prevented me from seeing those microscopic hordes that . . . seemed to me the most powerful beings in the pool."

Humans need mediating symbols (literal and figurative) in their attempts to make the natural world comprehensible. Technology, for example, symbolizes literally the need for some intervening device to aid our limited faculties. *The Sea around Us* is as much about such devices as about the sea itself: "Moving in fascination over the deep sea he could not enter, [man] found ways to probe its depths, he let down nets to capture its life, he invented mechanical eyes and ears that could recreate for his senses a world long lost." A specific example of such technology is the development of wave recorders, allowing us to "read" the language of waves that warns us of storms—an ability, Carson notes, that technology has reclaimed from the skills of earlier peoples. While such technologies allow for better readings of nature, they do not necessarily lead to an imperial dominance. We can now measure waves, but they still "may engulf lighthouses, shatter buildings, and hurl stones through lighthouse windows anywhere from 100 to 300 feet above the sea." Thus technology may help humans cope with their limitations, but it does not harness nature.

Figurative symbols, the meanings we give to natural phenomena, are undercut in similar fashion. A chapter on ocean seasons in *The Sea around Us* is an impressive exercise in the creation and destruction of simile and metaphor, ultimately pointing out the inadequacy of symbolic language. Carson first compares spring on the land and in the sea: "In the sea, as on land, spring is a time for the renewal of life." Much of the description depends on the economic household metaphor. She stresses the efficiency of the process of winter survival in the sea and the recreation of food chains as smaller life forms begin to multiply in the spring warmth. Agricultural images multiply as she describes the ocean's "hills" and "valleys," the plankton "grasslands," and "grazing" fish. These images continue to arise throughout the chapter, but a new set, stressing the "strangeness" of the seascape, also appears. Suddenly we are confronted with repulsive and nonproductive processes:

> The diatoms become more and more scarce, and with them the other simple plants. Still there are brief explosions of one or another form, when in a sudden orgy of cell division it comes to claim whole areas of the sea for its own. So, for a time each spring, the waters may become blotched with brown, jellylike masses, and the fishermen's nets come up dripping a brown slime and containing no fish.

The creatures of this place are not like land creatures but are of another world; they glow and their phosphorescence causes "fishes, squids, or dolphins to fill the water with racing flames and to clothe themselves in a ghostly radiance."

Natural metaphors no longer suffice. As the seascape becomes increasingly problematic, Carson resorts to descriptions of sea surfaces glowing "with sheets of cold fire" and fish pouring "through the water like molten metal." Finally, the ocean is neither home nor household but an ominous place lit by a tiny plant "that contains a poison of strange and terrible virulence." It is a place whose meaning must be decoded—in this case by the Indians of the Pacific coast who warn illiterate inlanders of the dangers the ocean poses.

Carson's aim here is not simply to write natural history; having evoked and discarded various figurative meanings given to the sea, she also then questions the adequacy of our pattern-making minds:

> Man, in his vanity, subconsciously attributes a human origin to any light not of moon or stars or sun. Lights on the shore, lights moving over the water, mean lights kindled and controlled by other men, serving purposes understandable to the human mind. Yet here are lights that flash and fade away, lights that come and go for reasons meaningless to man, lights that have been doing this very thing over the eons of time in which there were no men to stir in vague disquiet.

Showing such a need to find meaning or make patterns out of natural phenomena afflicts us all, she concludes with quotations from Charles Darwin and Joseph Conrad on anarchy in the autumn sea and death in the winter sea, respectively, using Darwin's and Conrad's figures to set up her own closing affirmation of life: "The lifelessness, the hopelessness, the despair of the winter sea are an illusion. Everywhere are the assurances that the cycle has come to the full, containing the means of its own renewal." In this essay on seasons of the sea she measures the ability of language, even in its most flexible expression in figures, to adequately provide a symbolic match to the protean environment. It is only as we see our similes and metaphors constantly giving way before change that we approach an understanding of nature.

Rachel Carson's questioning of the correspondence between human patterns and the natural world results from her own experiences with epistemological hubris. In fact, it is when she fails to find expected patterns that she has her most meaningful experiences. In the first chapter of **The Edge of the Sea** Carson explains why the shore continually attracts her. The two most important qualities of that place for her are a "sense of remoteness" and its fascination as "a world apart." To experience these qualities, she seeks that place of constant change that has always troubled her—the tide line—not during the day, but at night, to find "a different world, in which the very darkness that hides the distractions of daylight brings into sharper focus the elemental realities."

Humans seem to be one of the distractions. For Carson, the blackness of the night is "the darkness of an older world, before Man." In this nonhuman place, with the aid of the intrusive beam of a flashlight, she "surprises" (or trespasses on) a small ghost crab. The crab seems to be the only life on the beach. The night, the individual crab, the alien seascape all conspire to deny her a comfortable sense of identification with the world she sees. This disjunction with nature elicits an epiphany:

> I have seen hundreds of ghost crabs in other settings, but suddenly I was filled with the odd sensation that for the first time I knew the creature in its own world—that I understood, as never before, the essence of its being. In that moment time was suspended; the world to which I belonged did not exist and I might have been an onlooker from outer space.

This is not the identification with animal life so commonly attributed to Carson but, rather, a recognition of the impossibility of such identification. Nor is she engaged here in finding transcendent meaning in nature by moving outside her own skin, forgetting herself; she removes human culture but not the consciousness necessary for recognizing nature's "otherness."

The symbolic meaning she gains from such experiences is bound up in process rather than utility, either emotional or economic. The ghost crab experience obliterates the sense of community that can make us feel too much at "home" in the natural world, too able to understand, identify, or control. The crab becomes a symbol of life—"the spectacle of life in all its varied manifestations. . . . Underlying the beauty of the spectacle there is [elusive] meaning . . . that haunts us, that sends us again and again into the natural world where the key to the riddle is hidden." This grasp of the "elusive," "tantalizing," "ob-

scure," "inscrutable" meanings of nature, coupled with her understanding of the very human need to make patterns, is the basic source of the trespasser images. For Carson, one of the most important aspects of human interaction with nature is the realization that the protean quality of the natural world cannot be caught by our pattern-hungry minds but that it is our "nature" continually to seek the pattern. In these early books, this fact provides a sort of delicious frustration for her. Aiming to describe both beautifully and accurately the sea- and landscapes, she builds some of her most evocative prose out of foiled attempts at symbolization and categorization.

By the late 1950s Carson becomes less intrigued by this recognition; knowing that much human destruction results from not understanding nature's protean quality, Carson becomes increasingly concerned about the havoc human trespassers wreak. Faced with the crises of pollution and the nuclear age, her writing increasingly critiques human "nature," delineating our limited knowledge rather than celebrating nature's lessons. Rachel Carson always saw humans as trespassers and breakers, but only post-World War II American industrialization educated her to the massive threat this antagonistic character created for the "other" world, the nonhuman world. When she understands this, her writing takes a polemic turn. The three visions of human and nature interacting—as family in a home, as manager in a household, and as trespasser in an alien world—continue to appear in her writing, but they are depicted with a malevolent facet, introducing the reader to the destructive interactions that take place when homemakers and household managers become sick or corrupted. Recognizing the extent of the malady, Carson's writing shifts to a new, action-oriented concern for "right" understanding, the correct relationship between humans and the rest of the natural world.

The Sea around Us concludes with an upbeat vision of humans' "acquisition" of the resources of the ocean. When Carson revised the book ten years later in 1961, she added a preface that outlined the most recent achievements of science and technology in increasing our knowledge of the sea. Some of the most interesting discoveries pointed to the profuse interconnections between sea and land, fostering a concomitant change in our image of the deep sea from a place of relative stability to an environment of dynamic movement.

Carson particularly feared the growing use of the oceans as radioactive dumps, and she explained how the dynamic sea may distribute radioactive contaminants through the movement of currents and the action of food chains. Carson was outraged by those who act on insufficient knowledge and forget the ghost crab's lesson: we are limited in our ability ever to comprehend truly the protean land- and seascapes in which we live. Thus, the preface ends on an ominous note that questions the notion of nature as home or household: "It is a curious situation that the sea, from which life first arose, should now be threatened by the activities of one form of that life. But the sea, though changed in a sinister way, will continue to exist; the threat is rather to life itself." The sea is no beloved mother, nourishing life, passively accepting, absorbing and redirecting the changes her children go through; neither is the sea an endless factory of resources (or, in this case, storage places). It is "other" than humankind and as such may return our trespasses back on us in totally unexpected ways.

The sea is not the only natural terrain offering unpleasant surprises for human development. Although Carson sometimes uses the disjunction between humans as land creatures and the sea to develop that outsider persona, she finds a similar lack of connection between humans and all the nonhuman natural world. *Silent Spring,* the book following her revised *The Sea around Us,* offers stunning descriptions of the unpleasant surprises nature contains for twentieth-century household managers and homemakers. The book begins with an arcadian fable in which a group of settlers has developed the "middle-landscape," the American dream of home in nature, but the dream has soured: "Some evil spell had settled on the community: mysterious maladies swept the flocks of chickens; the cattle and sheep sickened and died. Everywhere there was a shadow of death." As she lists the various deaths, Carson constructs the lifeless landscape she foretold in the preface to *The Sea around Us.* Limited in their understanding of the ecosystem, the settlers have no idea what is bringing the end to life. Carson argues that they have done it themselves in the attempt to "improve" on their home, to increase the comfort of their middle landscape. In this example, Carson uses both home and household metaphors to emphasize the settlers' attitudes of care toward their natural home and their management approach toward the environment. But her ultimate explanation of the community's demise is that, despite their good intentions, they are unable to see or conceptualize the complex intricacies of their ecosystem. The ecological concept against which home and household metaphors are tested is the landscape's resistance to life, the idea that nature requires waste, impurity, accommodation, and seeming inefficiency in order to thrive. With this understanding as a constant backdrop, Carson redefines the household management and home care metaphors.

Those acting on the notion of earth as a household modeled on industrial economics do not even understand good management, according to Carson. In *Silent Spring* she takes up the burden of their education by redefining productivity and efficiency. Basically, she questions the value of progress toward ultimate goals, as well as the managerial ethos informing most 1950s' discussions of how to improve production in nature. Her analyses of "progress" in scientists' attempts to control the gypsy moth and the fire ant are examples of her manipulation of the economic household metaphor. For both of these pests, new insecticides were hailed as offering the opportunity to create a perfect environment—one with no "noxious" insects. Expensive and technologically demanding campaigns using these insecticides, however, destroyed or contaminated crops and other agricultural products such as milk and honey, made no change in the gypsy moth population, and led to an increase in the fire ant population. Further, Carson argues that less "sophisticated" methods, not requiring large-scale management techniques, are not only more successful at control but are also less expensive. Thus, Carson shows no sympathy for development that assumes

a passive landscape, a landscape incapable of responding (in often surprising ways) to human intentions. That is the lesson she offers to household managers. Our ability to know how efficiency and productivity are best served in our interactions with the landscape is limited by our ignorance of the complex, interconnected economies disrupted by any intrusion.

Just as Carson in *Silent Spring* both employs and questions the economic approach to nature, she also manipulates reverent, homeplace figures of nature. Those who attempt to identify human nature with the natural world are warned that "home" is in fact no haven from a harsh world. The interconnectedness of all life becomes sinister as we come to understand the webs of death interwoven with the webs of life. Throughout *Silent Spring* Carson emphasizes nature's complex system of checks and balances, which limits as well as nurtures species. Although humankind's interference, in the form of technological manipulations, may change the movers, the shift to regain balance continues, affecting not only the offending insects in the examples above but the whole chain of life and death. From this perspective "home" becomes a place of nightmares.

In the early books, Carson offers fascinating glimpses of developing embryonic life, of the growth and survival of animals in that resistant natural world, and of the lives of animal babies. In *Silent Spring* she continues the theme but considers the ominous possibilities natural processes contain. For example, Carson uses robins, those common harbingers of spring, to show how insecticides work in food chains. Using to her advantage her readers' family feelings toward these yard and garden friends, she leads us through the technical processes by which insecticides affect cell formation as she describes a robin's nest with its "complement of blue-green eggs" lying cold, "the fires of life that flickered for a few days now extinguished." Carson explains that radiation, insecticides, and pesticides interfere with the availability of ATP (adenosine triphosphate, a crucial energy "battery" for cell division) in embryos; she then relates this phenomenon to human life, to our membership in the robin family: "There is no reason to suppose these disastrous events are confined to birds. ATP is the universal currency of energy, and the metabolic cycles that produce it turn to the same purpose in birds and bacteria, in men and mice." A litany of the genetic implications of combined, long-term contact with radiation and chemical poisons concludes the chapter. Thus, using images of common, valued animal life, Carson delineates the consequences of human interference in nature for all life. In this scenario of nature as home we are indeed members of a family, and the death we bring is visited as well on all the family members. Carson does not deny the metaphor of earth as home but, as she does for the economic household metaphor, cautions against interpreting its meaning too simplistically.

In the final analysis, *Silent Spring* really is not about nature; rather, it is a close look at the limitations of human trespassing on nature. The problem Carson pursues throughout the book is that "nature has introduced great variety into the landscape, but man has displayed a pas-

sion for simplifying it." *Silent Spring* begins with a people
too "single-minded" to understand the effects of their own
actions. For example, our sense of the destructive potential of poisons pales when packages of deadly weed killer
are illustrated with "a happy family scene, father and son
smilingly preparing to apply the chemical to the lawn,
small children tumbling over the grass with a dog." The
real difficulty with such symbols, the underlying assumption that makes them too simplistic, is that they describe
only what the chemical creations seem to mean to humans—a better life, increased comfort in our present
"home." Such exploitation of the home and household
metaphors allows those who use the chemicals to avoid
moral responsibility, to justify their activities by basing
them on biophysical "laws" that imply humans are only
fighting to survive and, in keeping with post-Darwinian
ecology, are participating in natural processes of biological succession by helping to "improve" the environment.

Paradoxically, Carson found in our role as trespassers an
escape from the seemingly inevitable image of humans as
carriers of death and destruction. We are trespassers in
large part because of our self-consciousness, our pattern-
making minds; we may be of nature, but that observing
awareness, a function of culture, also separates us from the
environment. The case Carson ultimately makes for gen-
tler dealings with the environment rests on distinctions
she makes between nature and culture. Discussing the use
of nonselective poisons, she comments that such substances poison

> all life . . . the cat beloved of some family, the
> farmer's cattle, the rabbit in the field, and the
> horned lark out of the sky. These creatures are
> innocent of any harm to man. Indeed, by their
> very existence they and their fellows make his
> life more pleasant. Yet he rewards them with a
> death that is not only sudden but horrible. . . .
> By acquiescing in an act that can cause such suf-
> fering to a living creature, who among us is not
> diminished as a human being?

That we do see patterns in the ecosystem is thus a curse
and a blessing; we are condemned to feel like eternal outsiders to our household/home, but we are also gifted with
a curiosity and comprehension apparently available to no
other creature. Unfortunately, Carson could not find this
gift adequately developed in the American culture of her
time.

While most commentators feel *Silent Spring* ends on an
upbeat note, with Carson's much-discussed case for reliance on and development of natural controls, in fact her
last statement is a less than hopeful analysis of the current
state of scientific culture:

> The "control of nature" is a phrase conceived in
> arrogance, born of the Neanderthal age of biolo-
> gy and philosophy, when it was supposed that
> nature exists for the convenience of man. The
> concepts and practices of applied entomology
> for the most part date from that Stone Age of
> science. It is our alarming misfortune that so
> primitive a science has armed itself with the
> most modern and terrible weapons, and that in

turning them against the insects it has also
turned them against the earth.

Silent Spring ends with an image of failed evolution. The
twentieth century merely added new forms of technology
to the imperial philosophy that has not changed and continues to operate. *Silent Spring* concludes on this negative
note in part because the change in research that Carson
prescribes can come about only through what Kuhn
would call a "paradigm shift" in the way Americans view
the environment. Lack of adequate symbolism, not lack
of knowledge, is the issue; we continue to look for simplicity and regularity instead of recognizing that nature cannot
be conceptually tamed through metaphor. Whether we define nature as a loved home or as an economic household
is moot; either metaphor leads to a comfortable and misleading sense of familiarity. We need a paradigm that acknowledges flux and surprise as well as regularity and stasis.

The only way to effect such a change is to teach the next
generation adequate seeing. [In *Silent Spring*] Carson has
a specific sort of vision in mind: "We see with an understanding eye only if we have walked in the garden at night
and here and there with a flashlight have glimpsed the
mantis stealthily creeping upon her prey. . . . Then we
begin to feel something of that relentlessly pressing force
by which nature controls her own." This statement echoes
the earlier images of the beach walker trying to understand the tantalizing meaning of the ghost crab or the observer marveling at millions of diatoms flashing in the
ocean. Experiencing the natural world as resistant to
human pattern making changes the paradigms, moves us
beyond Neanderthal philosophies.

Near the end of her life, Carson turned to this image of
tantalized observer. She hoped to expand **"The Sense of
Wonder,"** an essay she wrote in 1956, into a book for parents that would help them encourage an appreciation of
nature in their children. The text of the essay, and a set
of complementary photographs, was published as a book
shortly after her death. "Wonderment" means a continuing surprise and curiosity about the environment. As
might be expected, the quintessential time and place for
such an experience in Rachel Carson's world is on a beach
at night; so *The Sense of Wonder* begins with Carson and
her nephew, Roger, standing "one stormy autumn
night . . . out there, just at the edge of where-we-couldn't-
see." Immediately following, we see them searching the
beach with a flashlight for "those sand-colored, fleet-
legged beings," ghost crabs. Throughout she emphasizes
the need to move away from comfortable, assumed visions
of the environment and to see it as new, astounding, unusual.

Building off the comment, "How can I possibly teach my
child about nature—why, I don't even know one bird from
another," Carson argues that adequate seeing and feeling
are more important than the ability to label and categorize
the environment. What she hopes to build in the next generation is a grasp of natural processes, not static landscapes. So *The Sense of Wonder* is process oriented:
"There is symbolic as well as actual beauty in the migration of the birds, the ebb and flow of the tides, the folded

bud ready for the spring. There is something infinitely healing in the repeated refrains of nature—the assurance that dawn comes after night, and spring after the winter." That she is not describing any mechanical, knowable environment in nothing such "refrains" is made clear by the conjoining, concluding vision of two people—both in their ninth decade of life—who maintain an infinite curiosity about the changing meanings of these rhythms.

Carson recognizes the extent to which burgeoning scientific knowledge displaces the lay person from viable, confident experiences of nature. *The Sense of Wonder* ends with an absolute assertion of the availability of the environment to anyone "who will place himself under the influence of earth, sea and sky." Carson's voice in all her books—her persona, if you will—is unequivocally allied with the nonspecialist. The most sophisticated instruments of technology we ever hear of her using are a flashlight, a magnifying glass, and (infrequently) a microscope. With all her appreciation of the technologies that "open" the natural world to our understanding, she is extremely cautious of supporting our tendency to go too far "into an artificial world of [our] own creation." It is impossible to find her speaking with a voice of superior authority; always her experiences are available to the general reader. In *Silent Spring,* the book most dependent on establishing a correct reading of the scientific findings, the true authority comes from people whose daily lives place them at the mercy of science.

Her commitment to writing for the general public should not, however, minimize the extent of her epistemological sophistication and the thematic connections between her work and important developments in the philosophy of science. Early in her career, Carson came to recognize the hubris implicit in imagining nature as our home or household, but she also seemed to grasp how pervasive such metaphors were in her culture. Their use in her writing gave her a verbal arsenal with which to attack positivism. In this she joined philosophers of science and critical theorists in a central intellectual movement of the fifties, sixties, and seventies.

Carson's comment in *Silent Spring*—which was published the same year Thomas Kuhn's *The Structure of Scientific Revolutions* appeared—that "nature has introduced great variety into the landscape, but man has displayed a passion for simplifying it" provides a fitting coda to Kuhn's landmark study of how paradigms develop and how they are changed. She would agree, too, with Kuhn's caution about the meaning of progress in our search for patterns that fit nature:

We are all deeply accustomed to seeing science as the one enterprise that draws constantly nearer to some goal set by nature in advance. . . . Does it really help to imagine that there is some one full, objective, true account of nature and that the proper measure of scientific achievement is the extent to which it brings us closer to that ultimate goal? If we can learn to substitute evolution-from-what-we-do-know for evolution-toward-what-we-wish-to-know, a number of vexing problems may vanish in the process.

What makes Rachel Carson more than a nature writer or popularizer of environmental consciousness is her own commitment to just the sort of evolution Kuhn describes and her mission to educate her readers to seek such a science. Carson's place as a liminal individual, able to deconstruct traditional frames of reference and offer new visions, is the result of her lifelong fascination with what Kuhn calls "progress toward no goal." This fascination is the source of her searches along the beach at night for encounters with the mysteries of life. For Carson, such mysteries were not necessarily interesting only to the extent that they could be solved; rather, they proved the value of the search itself.

One of Carson's least appreciated contributions is to have made available to a general readership new ideas about the nature of knowledge, ideas that have led to significant changes in our perspectives on science and the relationship between self and the surrounding environment. Furthermore, her work in this area reveals strong connections to other women's beliefs about appropriate human relationships with nature. Like Emily Dickinson before her and Barbara McClintock after, Carson displays a "feeling for the organism" much different from that which has dominated modern science since Francis Bacon. Rather than espousing a vision of nature's otherness as nasty and uncontrollable, she is "tantalized" by the alien, the mysterious. Rather than seeing in the "wild" an obligation to control and tame, she delights in the unharnessable quality of nature. Finally, rather than using images of home and household to set limits on the environment, she uses such metaphors to explode limits. Emily Dickinson played with common, domestic metaphors to plumb the wild within and about her; just so, Carson uses similar images to draw her readers out of preconceived notions and into the mysteries of nature. (pp. 740-59)

Vera L. Norwood, "The Nature of Knowing: Rachel Carson and the American Environment," in Signs, Vol. 12, No. 4, Summer, 1987, pp. 740-60.

Jung Chang
1952-

Chinese nonfiction writer.

The following entry focuses on Chang's *Wild Swans: Three Daughters of China.*

INTRODUCTION

Wild Swans: Three Daughters of China, the first English-language memoir by a child of high-ranking officials in communist China, chronicles the eventful lives of Chang, her mother, and her maternal grandmother. Reflecting twentieth-century China's tumultuous history, the narrative begins with Chang's description of her grandmother's experiences as the concubine of a powerful warlord and her eventual escape from his household. Chang continues with the story of her mother who, as a student, joined the communist movement and married a zealous guerrilla leader then fighting with Mao Tsetung in the civil war between the communists and the Koumintang. While Chang's parents rose to powerful positions within the communist government, the advent in the 1960s of the Cultural Revolution and Mao's brutal "re-education" campaigns resulted in their repeated denunciation and imprisonment. Finally, Chang recounts how the Cultural Revolution thrust her as an adolescent into the surreal world of the Red Guard, a group of young militants fanatically dedicated to Mao who ruthlessly persecuted those less faithful to the party leader. Ultimately disillusioned by the violence of the Red Guard and her later enforced "re-education" as a farm and factory worker, Chang left China in 1978 for Great Britain, where she continues to live. Although some critics questioned the efficacy of Chang's personal approach to China's complex history, most praised *Wild Swans* for its illuminating and moving portrait of the suffering and resiliency of the Chinese people. Edward Behr commented: "Jung Chang vividly evokes China's sights, sounds, and smells to create what must be one of the grimmest and most perceptive accounts of growing up . . . in the maelstrom that has swept China since the 1920s."

PRINCIPAL WORKS

Mme Sun Yat-sen [with Jon Hallidy] (nonfiction) 1986
Wild Swans: Three Daughters of China (nonfiction) 1991

CRITICISM

Judith Shapiro

When her mother was in detention in 1968, 14-year-old Jung Chang took her little brother by the hand and they walked back and forth in front of the gate of the cinema where she was being held, calling "Mother" as they scanned the windows for a glimpse of her. They later learned that at the sound of their voices, "she dug her nails into her palms to stop her tears from falling." The guards told her that if she would denounce her husband and confess to being a Kuomintang spy, she could see them immediately. If not, she might not get out of the building alive. She remained silent.

Such powerful material is routine in *Wild Swans,* Jung Chang's autobiographical epic of three generations of Chinese women. Her grandmother was sold to a warlord as a concubine; after his death she escaped in order to avoid being sent into a brothel. Jung Chang's mother was active in the communist underground. She made a "revolutionary" marriage to a man so principled that he made her walk 2,000 miles from Manchuria to Sichuan and showed little remorse when she suffered a miscarriage; after the revolution she became a high-ranking cadre, and was repeatedly denounced and incarcerated. Jung Chang herself, born in 1952 soon after "Liberation," was by turns a leftist intoxicated by Maoism, a peasant laborer, an utterly untrained barefoot doctor and a similarly unskilled electrical worker. She became a privileged "worker-peasant-soldier" college student in 1973 and, in 1982, she won a rare opportunity to study abroad, at York University, England, where she earned a doctorate in linguistics. She never went back.

But *Wild Swans* is far more than a story of three women. The other family members, particularly Jung Chang's high-ranking and puritanical father, who was eventually driven insane and "persecuted to death," are also vividly and sympathetically evoked. Nor does Jung Chang confine her tale to her immediate family; the memoir is a skillful interweaving of political history, hearsay and her own experience.

Jung Chang's political awakening closely parallels the pattern chronicled in other memoirs by members of China's "lost" generation. Youthful Maoist enthusiasm slipped into increasing confusion as persecution spread to family members and respected teachers, and her exile among the peasants threw communist braggadocio into question; she became utterly disillusioned as the regime's perfidy gradually became known and the country fell into economic paralysis and anarchy. Still, so deeply instilled was her adulation of Mao that only in the early 1970s did Jung Chang realize that the Great Helmsman was behind the senseless destruction of lives and waste of talent.

The main difference between *Wild Swans* and other such accounts is that the tale reaches back to "old China" (through interviews with Jung Chang's grandmother and mother and creative historical reconstruction). The portrayal of the bloody civil war and utter corruption of the Kuomintang vividly dramatizes the hope that the idealistic and simple-styled communists held out for China. In this context, *Wild Swans* appears not so much a record of the recent political tragedy of life under Chinese communism as an expression of a far lengthier and multi-causal tragedy of the Chinese people, whose best efforts to save themselves seem irredeemably to have failed.

Wild Swans is also the first memoir in English from a child of high-ranking cadres, and is probably the best account we have of the power struggles on the provincial level during the Cultural Revolution. As important leaders in Sichuan province, Jung Chang's parents were directly involved in many of the events that shook China's highest reaches, and they were primary targets in regional struggles, perhaps less for their lifestyles or political beliefs than for the fact that they were more devoted to principle than most, and were unwilling to wield the tactics of power and betrayal that saved a few others their hides.

Although *Wild Swans* contains few revelations, it is an unfailingly gripping tale of abuse and suffering, broken by moving accounts of family loyalty in the face of tremendous pressure. Jung Chang graces her memoir with an evocative, fluent prose style, and a keen recollection of

physical details like plants, smells and the architectural features of the elite schools she attended and adored. The library, for example, "was encircled on both floors by loggias, and the outside of these was enclosed by a row of gorgeously painted seats which were shaped like wings. I had a favorite corner in these 'wing seats' (*fei-lai-yt*) where I used to sit for hours reading, occasionally stretching my arm out to touch the fanshaped leaves of a rare ginkgo tree."

No matter how many tales of contemporary China one has heard, most accounts contain some particularly creative invention of torture or some particularly cruel "persecution to death" that shocks afresh. *Wild Swans* is full of such details.

We read of people eating human hearts in revenge, fathers eating their own babies in hunger, resale of concubines, suicides for love, for honor, for political reasons—there are suicide pacts, persecutions to death through humiliation; death through lack of medical treatment and egregious accident. If there remains the slightest doubt about the tragic quality of life in the China of this century, this memoir should put it definitively to rest.

Like most Chinese who have suffered and witnessed similar wrongs, Jung Chang never explodes into outrage. She offers few reflections on this massive sacrifice of human life and talent, or suggestions of hope for China's future. Either there are none to be made, or Jung Chang is not interested in Chinese intellectuals' endless debate on how to diagnose their bitterly beloved and perhaps terminally ill motherland.

For the Western reader, Jung Chang's straightforward prose may seem the more poignant for its restraint. But the Chinese people may wish to ask themselves whether their absence of outrage is a factor in their inability to realize a political system that fosters respect for human dignity or the right to make life choices without political interference.

> *Judith Shapiro, "Concubines and Cadres," in* Book World—The Washington Post, *September 8, 1991, p. 6.*

John Maxwell Hamilton

Nearly 20 years ago I met Ida Pruitt and read her book, *A Daughter of Han.* Pruitt, whose experience in China went back so far that she vividly remembered the Boxer Rebellion at the turn of the century, thought of the country in epic terms. Her book captured that in a fascinating way, by putting on paper the oral autographical account of a single Chinese working woman she knew. That simple story taught me more China than a pile of formal political histories.

Now comes Jung Chang's *Wild Swans,* which is three times as good, if for no other reason than it tells the story of three fascinating daughters of China.

Here is a young girl who becomes the concubine of a northern Chinese warlord; her daughter, whose despair over inequities propels her into the Chinese Communist party; and the granddaughter, Jung Chang herself, who suffers with her family through the violent Cultural Revolution, replete with petty loyalties and brutality that warlords and emperors would have understood.

Jung Chang fills in the necessary historical background as the saga unfolds. But the strength of her book lies in the lives of individual family members, which illuminate central truths about China in this century.

One of those truths has to do with women. Chinese society has traditionally relegated them to secondary roles. And grand histories of the country typically overlook the inner resolve and resourcefulness of women like Jung Chang's grandmother.

The warlord who set her up in a prison-home in her Manchurian hometown did not visit again during the six years after their honeymoon. When he later brought her and her daughter into his household, she fashioned an escape and never came back. After the warlord died, she married a kind elderly doctor with whom she endured the Japanese occupation. He gave her the name Wild Swan.

It is easy to see why Jung Chang's talented mother gravitated toward the Communists, with their slogans that "women hold up half the sky." One has to remember the popular Chinese enthusiasm that once existed for the Red revolution and its leaders. Under Mao Tse-Tung, Jung Chang shrewdly writes, "China became a power to be reckoned with in the world, and many Chinese stopped feeling ashamed and humiliated at being Chinese."

Jung Chang's mother married a man who joined Mao's revolutionary guerrilla movement in 1940. He rose swiftly in Communist ranks and was one of the top two dozen or so officials in Sichuan after the revolution. One sign of his status was the close proximity of the family apartment to the stepmother of Deng Xiaoping, today's de facto Chinese head of state.

Jung Chang's mother held responsible leadership positions in local government. Both she and her husband were high-minded and dedicated to creating a better country.

Not that Jung Chang's mother was always happy with her lot. Her scrupulous husband went out of his way to ensure she received no special favors. She had a miscarriage after he would not allow her to go back to her quarters one evening in an official car inappropriate for her rank.

The Cultural Revolution supremely tested his iron will and her resilience. Mao tore the country apart in the name of restoring the revolutionary spirit that brought him to power. Factions fought each other bitterly. Officials like Jung Chang's parents, who lost their jobs, were publicly humiliated and tortured.

Unlike many senior officials, her father refused to fake a confession to avoid harassment. When local leaders offered to put him back in a powerful position if he cooperated, he refused again. He thought they were unworthy of the Communist Party. Though broken mentally and spiritually, he might have lived through a heart attack in 1975 at age 54, but the local doctor would not attend him.

Jung Chang, a teenager during the Cultural Revolution,

effectively stopped going to school along with her peers, made an obligatory pilgrimage to Beijing and worked in the countryside. She abhorred much of the experience and did not denounce her family as many young people did.

Yet, remarkably, she did not blame Mao for the calamities that befell her or her parents until the very end. The Great Helmsman, as he was reverently called, had that powerful a hold on the people.

Revolutionary fervor had begun to work against the Communists in the 1950s, when Mao urged people to melt down pots and pans to make inferior steel. Local leaders would promise unrealistically high levels of agricultural production and, to fill quotas to the state, left local farmers without adequate food for themselves. Senior Communist leaders, who prided themselves on being in touch with the people, often learned too late of troubles in the countryside.

As Jung Chang shows, the Communist Party became a new imperial class in spite of itself. For all the talk about equality, children were judged on the revolutionary pedigree of their parents. Even parents as principled as Jung Chang's father could not prevent such favoritism.

Tribulation and injustice are strong themes in this book. But the author reveals enduring family bonds: to her grandmother, who lives through the first years of the Cultural Revolution and plays a stabilizing role in the tormented family, and to her mother, who goes over the heads of vindictive local authorities and personally asks premier Chou En-lai in Beijing to help her husband.

Jung Chang also finds rays of humor in the dark moments. Her brother, she notes, made a small fortune selling images of capitalist-hater Mao. The eagerness of urban youth to help peasants was not always appreciated. "We sometimes had to grab their bundles from them forcibly because some country women thought we were thieves."

The only shortcoming of this personal history is that it ends too soon. Jung Chang tells us how she won a scholarship to study in England in the late 1970s. A brief note says she was "the first person from the People's Republic of China to receive a doctorate from a British university" and that she now works in England. But why did she stay; what does her mother think; what does her expatriate status say about China?

A brief epilogue points to uncertainty about the future: "In political meetings today, people openly criticize Party leaders by name. The course of liberalization is irreversible. Yet Mao's face still stares down on Tiananmen Square."

Ida Pruitt, who died before the evils of the Cultural Revolution seeped into western consciousness, admired the Communists. But her ultimate interest was in ordinary Chinese. Pruitt's book, alas, is virtually forgotten. Fortunately, we now have Jung Chang's magnificent epic to illuminate the human side of 20th Century Chinese history.

John Maxwell Hamilton, "China's Human Side," in Chicago Tribune—Books, *September 15, 1991, p. 4.*

Edward Behr

This real-life saga of a Chinese family over three generations contains more domestic drama than "Dynasty," more violence than any film noir, more heart-rending tragedy than *Little Dorrit* and more ironic twists and turns and villains on the make than any Balzacian fresco.

[*Wild Swans*] is the tale of Jung Chang's grandmother, the beautiful Yu-fang, "sold" as a concubine to a Chinese warlord in 1924 at the age of 15; of her high-spirited mother, Bao Quin, who worked underground for the communists while still a schoolgirl in "Manchukuo" at the close of World War II; and finally of herself, ex-Red Guard, ex-"barefoot doctor" and secret Mao-hater, educated in the best schools for the privileged children of high-ranking communists and now, in her 30s, living and teaching in London.

Drawing from her memories and those of surviving family members, Jung Chang vividly evokes China's sights, sounds and smells to create what must be one of the grimmest, yet most perceptive accounts of growing up middleclass in the maelstrom that has swept China since the 1920s. Almost casually, Jung Chang introduces us to a world where personal insecurity, sudden ruin and the possibility of torture and violent death are as perfunctorily taken for granted as tomorrow's thunderstorm.

The story begins in Manchuria. Probably the most nightmarish Chinese province to grow up in, it had been invaded and pillaged by the Japanese, the Russians, the Kuomintang, and finally by Chinese communists taking revenge on real and imagined "collaborators." Bao Quin was one of the neatly dressed schoolgirls chosen to hand bouquets to Pu Yi, the emperor of Manchukuo (the puppet state created by the Japanese) and previously China's "last emperor."

Even though most of Bao Quin's friends were from families opposed to Pu Yi and loyal to China's National People's Party, the Kuomintang, and even though Bao Quin herself had fought heroically against the Japanese from the age of 16 on, she eventually became suspect to China's grotesque party cadres, conspiracy theorists who were perennially searching for "quotas" of "rightists" and traitors in their midst.

Early in *Wild Swans* is a clinical description of the way "grand-mother" Yu-fang's feet were bound, when she was a baby girl, to indulge the erotic fantasies of her future lord and master. It is impossible not to see, in this gratuitous and excruciating example of human cruelty, a microcosm of China's own propensity for self-inflicted wounds: the absence of any rule of law, the fatalistic attitude toward corruption, the acceptance of religious and social conventions that turned concubines into slaves and harpies (and compelled Manchu wives to rise at 3 a.m. to prepare different entrees for each of their family's segregated groups), the observance of arbitrary customs sanctified only by time—and, later, the most costly self-inflicted injury of all: China's enthusiastic surrender to Maoism, grafted onto the ancient evils and leading, over the next four decades, to more than 50 million deaths.

The period covered by Jung Chang already has been the subject of many first-rate academic studies, but there never has been a book like this. Here, family and political histories interweave. In the years before the Japanese occupation, Yu-fang becomes a virtual prisoner of her warlord "husband" (an ally of the notorious "Christian general") who keeps her in a gilded cage under the constant surveillance of predatory servants ready to do anything to gain his favor. She shares his bed for six days, then he disappears without trace for six years, only to return without warning or explanation to father her child.

Summoned with her baby daughter to join his household at the time of the warlord's death, she finds his palace in an uproar, with rival wives and concubines all plotting intrigues against each other, and planning escapes, at considerable risk. But family life, even after her remarriage to a saintly doctor, proves just as terrifying: The doctor's concubines, and sons by a previous marriage, gang up on her, forcing her and her husband to abandon all their worldly goods and leave town.

Almost casually, Jung Chang introduces us to a world where personal insecurity, sudden ruin and the possibility of torture and violent death are as perfunctorily taken for granted as tomorrow's thunderstorm.

—Edward Behr

Yu-fang's own father is a male chauvinist of almost mind-boggling proportion, selling her to the warlord in the first place not only to improve the status of the family but also to buy himself more concubines. A popular Chinese dictum was that all women had "long hair and short intelligence," but the lives of these these three generations of women are powerful evidence to the contrary: They were resourceful, immensely brave and, above all, survivors.

Not many men in their lives, in contrast, passed muster. Even the author's father, Yang Yu, the epitome of young, principled communist probity, is at times insufferably smug, indifferent to his wife's feelings, comfort or dignity in his abject need to conform to rigid narrow-minded Party rules. Significantly, Yu-fang originally voices her disapproval when her daughter starts dating him not because he is a communist, but because he is an official, and "there is no official who is not corrupt."

Jung Chang's parents were exceptional for their probity. During the "Great Leap Forward," her father almost starved to death rather than use his cadre's prerogatives and privileged food supplies. Her mother, Bao Quin, was both predator and victim: Even as she hunted down "capitalists" and profiteers in her husband's Sichuan district, she was undergoing constant interrogation about her "Manchukuo" past—confined, at night, to a detention camp and completely cut off from her family for six months before her final rehabilitation. Later, her parents became high-ranking Party members in Chengdu; Jung Chang gives us a fascinating glimpse of their lives of vice-regal, "country club" splendor inside a highly segregated, luxurious compound, accessible only to the tiny, highly stratified local Communist elite.

Nemesis comes with the "Cultural Revolution." Suicidally appealing to Mao himself to stop the insane movement, her father promptly is incarcerated and tortured. He goes mad, while her mother is locked up, beaten and humiliated, dressed up in a "dunce cap" and exhibited to jeering crowds of Red Guards. Both are victims, not just of youthful Red Guard hooligans but also of an abominable couple of Maoist functionaries, the Tings, who side with the Red Guards to reinforce their local prerogatives, and prove as evil, and as ruthless, as any pre-revolutionary warlords.

Both the author and her parents emerge from the "cultrev" completely broken, their lives in ruins, sustained only by their love for each other. In 1978, fulfilling a long-prepared plan, Jung Chang, a brilliant English student, leaves China for good on a coveted scholarship.

Perhaps this massive book's only failing—and it is a minor one—is its attempt to chronicle the Cultural Revolution both as history and as personal experience: A whole body of "Red Guard" literature (and Nien Cheng's *Life and Death in Shanghai*) has familiarized us with those horrendous years, and I impatiently scanned the pages dealing with the "tick-tock" leading up to the cultrev. I was eager to return to the town of Chengdu, to Jung Chang and her amazing family. (pp. 2, 8)

> Edward Behr, "Middle-Class in a Maoist Maelstrom," in Los Angeles Times Book Review, *September 15, 1991, pp. 2, 8.*

Carolyn See

If you care at all about the history of China in the 20th Century—or even if you don't, come to think of it—**Wild Swans** is riveting. It's blindingly good: a mad adventure story, a fairy tale of courage, a tall tale of atrocities and incidentally a meditation on how men will never understand women and vice versa.

Jung Chang chooses to tell the story of contemporary China through three exemplary lives: her grandmother's, her mother's and her own. Her grandmother was just at the last of the generation of Chinese girls to endure the horror of bound feet; she was second concubine to a fierce warlord, but had the unheard-of nerve to defy him. She ran away in the dark of night, carrying her baby with her. Then she wreaked havoc in a respectable family by marrying an elderly Manchu doctor (and had to endure, among a thousand other misfortunes, the *unbinding* of her feet).

By the time Jung's mother was an adolescent, China and Manchukuo were torn by civil war—Chiang Kaishek and Mao Ze-dong jockeying for power in a land wasted by corruption and already occupied by the Japanese army. That young girl fearlessly worked alongside the Kuomintang for a while: defying authorities, standing up for herself, refusing to marry, going to school, delivering secret messages, generally living the life of a modern hell raiser. Then, as a young Communist, she met an appealing gentleman Communist, fell in love, got married against her mother's wishes and then *walked a thousand miles* to be with her husband in their new home, while he drove there in a Jeep. By that time, after she'd almost drowned, and pitched off of high cliffs, and suffered a miscarriage and almost died, she was one irritated young Communist.

But stop! Imagine the speed of history here! From baby selling and abductions and bound feet and warlords to Chiang and his decadent cronies, to the caves of Ya'Nan, to a couple that strangely mirrors some American marriages. Jung's father always put the party before her mother, Jung Chang reports. His idealism was his sweetest quality and his most horrid fault.

Jung Chang was one of five children. Her father, because of his unquenchable idealism, rose fairly high in the party, in the province of Sichuan. Jung grew up with some privilege. Except that Mao began—as we might say in the West—going through some changes. He encouraged intellectuals to speak their minds. (Remember 'Let a hundred flowers blossom'?) Then he killed off or imprisoned the intellectuals. He got it into his head that steel was the key to the country's modernization (right about here the author loses her cool objective style for a chapter or two) and turned the whole population to smelting and melting down metal, which in turn led to the Great Famine of the early 1960s, in which millions starved to death.

Sure, we've read about these things—in Ross Terrill's *The White-Boned Demon,* Roger Garside's *Coming Alive* and all the fine works of Orville Schell, and even in popular fiction such as Monica Highland's *110 Shanghai Road.* But here all this history is both seen from the inside and filtered through an astonishingly lucid and chilly intelligence.

By the time Jung approached her own adolescence, Mao, beginning to distrust his own party—or perhaps because he had possessed a cosmic mean streak all along—unleashed the Cultural Revolution, in which children were encouraged to denounce their parents and teachers and students and peasants were exhorted to denounce any official (or any friend or neighbor) who might have done them wrong. After years of suppression and thought control, Jung tells us, the whole population was ripe to explode, and it did.

Again, all of this is seen from the inside. Ironically, Jung's mother, because she had been willing all along to bend the rules, suffers least. Her father, because of his blind and naive beliefs in the party, is the one who suffers most.

Jung and her siblings are packed off to the countryside while the entire nation convulses, dithers and slumps into lethargy, and millions of old scores are settled. It's unbelievable! Except that it's totally believable. All of us, for instance, have worked at jobs in which mediocrity is rewarded and merit punished. (But here merit isn't punished by kneeling in ground glass for four hours!)

The astonishing irony is that, like wonderful children who spring from a dysfunctional family, three out of four of

Jung's siblings have, like her, succeeded splendidly in the West; they're in constant touch with their beloved mother, and they got out. Did they turn out so wonderfully in spite of the terror of their Chinese lives, or perhaps because of it?

This is calm and measured history, but it reads like a best-seller. You can't, as they say, put it down.

> *Carolyn See, "Women of Courage in a Turbulent China," in* Newsday, *September 26, 1991.*

Anne Collier

You may feel you've read enough about the vicissitudes of 20th-century China—the subjugation of women with foot binding, the Japanese occupation of Manchuria, the "Great Leap Forward," the violence of the Red Guards. But in Jung Chang's book, you'll actually want to read about them again because you'll want to know how Yu-fang, Bao Qin, Chang herself, and their family fared through it all.

This is a cohesive, richly detailed personal account covering most of a century—from grandmother Yu-fang as a young woman to granddaughter Jung Chang at the same age. It's a century in China we in the West will want to know about, because among its great tragedies and tumultuousness are indicators of what comes next for China— the last significant holdout still languishing under communism and reactionary, aged leaders.

Wild Swans helps us understand the impact of this century's events on Chinese people we can relate to: educated, principled, loving people who learn how to fend for themselves. What we can't relate to is what they and their compatriots are confronted with by a capricious, often virulent, leadership. But through Chang's skill in making her family members familiar to us, they become a constant as events swirl around them. Mao's maneuverings can be measured through their eyes.

Bao Qin, Chang's mother, was a loyal Communist Party member and—ironically, but typically—one of its millions of victims. Born of a "lily footed" (having bound feet) concubine (Chang's grandmother, Yu-fang) and a warlord-general in 1931, Bao Qin's adolescent years saw Chinese tradition upended and a brutal Japanese occupation defeated.

She agitated against the Japanese as a student leader; risked her life as an agent for the Communist underground in Manchuria; married a young veteran of the Red Army's Long March; suffered a miscarriage on her own "long march" to her husband's ancestral home of Yibin 1,000 miles southwest on the Yangtze River; had four children; was imprisoned for months under suspicion of being a "hidden counterrevolutionary"; nursed her husband through a violent mental breakdown; was "sent down" during the Cultural Revolution to a remote labor camp; and was finally rehabilitated in 1971—all by the age of 40.

Although Jung Chang wasn't old enough to be fully aware of many of those events in her mother's life, or hardly any in her grandmother's, she covers it all in the kind of color-ful detail that reads like a novel. One wonders how she achieved such detail. Yet, despite her direct involvement in the story (Chang herself was a Red Guard) and first-hand experience of many of her parents' struggles, Chang has also managed to get some scholarly distance from it all. She has given these lives, including her own, well-researched historical context.

After Tiananmen Square, and with all that's happened in Europe and the Middle East, the world has become exasperated with China and, partly because of that, has to a degree lost interest. But interest needs to be maintained and public pressure applied to help another ossified leadership over the threshold of political reform. Books like Jung Chang's do their part to help us understand the conditions from which China's people need to be freed.

> *Anne Collier, "Family History During a Tumultuous Chinese Century," in* The Christian Science Monitor, *October 4, 1991, p. 13.*

Susan Brownmiller

Mao Zedong was dead and the Gang of Four had been toppled when a young woman from Chengdu in Sichuan Providence made use of a small opening to the West to study English abroad on a Government scholarship that took her to Britain in the fall of 1978. Her given name had been Erhong Second Wild Swan—and she was the second daughter born to a family of high Communist officials. More than a decade earlier, on the eve of the Cultural Revolution, she had prudently changed it, on her father's suggestion, to Jung—Martial Affairs. In the Sichuanese dialect, Er-hong could be taken for "faded red," signifying, in those perilous times, a dangerous lack of revolutionary ardor. She had learned before puberty that nuances mattered.

Jung Chang now lives in London and returns to her homeland for family visits. She has put her English studies to commendable use in a quirky, ambitious, occasionally amateurish but thoroughly engrossing memoir. *Wild Swans: Three Daughters of China* is her family's story over three-quarters of a century of turbulent change. The sprawling canvas is held together schematically by narrative accounts of her maternal grandmother, who was a concubine to a warlord in the 1920's; her mother, who chose a radically different life for herself in the 1940's as a Communist organizer married to a zealous functionary higher up on the party ladder; and Jung Chang's own peripatetic adventures, before her departure, as a Red Guard, peasant and factory worker.

By keeping her focus on three generations of female kin and their practical adaptations to the shifting winds of political power, Ms. Chang gives us a rare opportunity to follow the evolution of some remarkable women who not only reflected their times, but who also acted upon them in order to change their individual destiny. On the minus side, her macro-micro approach to historic events, a formula pioneered in nonfiction by Alex Haley in *Roots,* is marked by chronological lapses that are likely to frustrate a reader with a limited knowledge of the tortuous ideological campaigns inside the Chinese Communist Party.

Ms. Chang is riveting in her description of a strenuous six-month journey through five mountain passes undertaken by a group of party veterans and their wives during the war against the Kuomintang in 1949. As a senior officer, her father rode in a jeep. Her mother, 18 years old and pregnant, walked the distance with a bedroll on her back.

Ms. Chang writes:

> Could he not let her travel in his jeep occasionally? He said he could not, because it would be taken as favoritism since my mother was not entitled to a car. He felt he had to fight against the age-old Chinese tradition of nepotism. Furthermore, my mother was supposed to experience hardship. . . . She was only a young student. If other people thought she was being pampered she would be in trouble. "It's for your own good," he added, reminding her that her application for full Party membership was pending. "You have a choice: you can either get into the car, or get into the Party, but not both."

She reports that her mother "slogged on" and suffered a miscarriage.

Three years later, the Korean War makes a cameo appearance as the author's mother, now a middle-level functionary, exhorts her grandmother to donate her jewelry to a fund to buy fighter planes. In return for a certificate commending her patriotic zeal, Ms. Chang's grandmother, an indomitable, stylish figure hobbled by bound feet, reluctantly parts with her hard-won hoard, retaining a couple of bracelets, a pair of gold earrings and a gold ring. This scene would play brilliantly on "Masterpiece Theater," where world-shaking conflicts are seen through their impact on mom, pop and the kids.

Even more problematic than Ms. Chang's quirky historical ellipses is the role of her moody, authoritarian father, who fairly dominates the last two-thirds of the book despite her intention to concentrate on the women. Chang Shou-yu joined the Communist guerrillas at their base camp in Yanan in 1940 as an idealistic middle-class youth who loved classical Chinese poetry almost as much as he believed in the party. He was also a man of punctilious personal habits whose pride in his moral incorruptibility found expression in rigid adherence to hierarchical party discipline and the politically correct line. Ms. Chang offers few explanations for her father's long, slow slide from ruthless idealist to cautious, unquestioning bureaucrat, except to cast blame on those even higher up who effectively silenced all voices of opposition in the infamous purges of the 1957 "anti-rightist" campaign. She was his favorite child, and she loved him deeply.

Most of her own story takes place in Sichuan, where she was born in 1952. The second of five children, she was given to a wet nurse who lived with her in a protected cocoon-like Government compound. Jung Chang was a precocious 3-year-old nicknamed "Little Diplomat" when her mother was placed in detention for six months in a campaign to rout out "hidden counter-revolutionaries." Her unbending father, worried as usual about correctness, did not visit her mother during this time.

When she was 6 years old, Mao Zedong selected the city of Chengdu as the kickoff point for the Great Leap Forward. Her parents hurled themselves into the new campaign, her father as deputy head of public affairs for the entire province, her rehabilitated mother as a supervisor of 800 city employees, with hours that were no less demanding. Their children were boarded in nursery schools until their grandmother arrived to take over the household duties. These were Jung Chang's happiest years.

Among her memories were the roaring backyard furnaces that consumed the family's woks and iron bedsprings as the mobilizing slogan "Everybody, Make Steel!" blared from loudspeakers and was blazoned on banners and posters. The sooty fires were not permitted to die, nor were Chengdu's sparrow's permitted to rest. Mao's anti-sparrow campaign, initiated to save precious grain during a terrible famine, called out the community to frighten the scavenging birds by banging pots and pans day and night. It did not seem to matter that the backyard steel was of unusable quality, that the figures on grain production were outrageous lies or that the sparrows returned; a new campaign was already in place. One day eating at home was abolished in favor of communal canteens. She was admonished to clean her plate with tales of the poor, unfortunate children in capitalist countries who had nothing to eat.

Everything in her familiar world turned upside down when Mao unleashed the Cultural Revolution in 1966. Chengdu was wracked by factional fighting of such intensity that it verged on civil war. She joined the Red Guards in her school, along with other children of high Govern-

---

An excerpt from *Wild Swans*

Mrs. Shau slapped my father hard. The crowd barked at him indignantly, although a few tried to hide their giggles. Then they pulled out his books and threw them into huge jute sacks they had brought with them. When all the bags were full, they carried them downstairs, telling my father they were going to burn them on the grounds of the department the next day after a denunciation meeting against him. They ordered him to watch the bonfire "to be taught a lesson." In the meantime, they said, he must burn the rest of his collection.

When I came home that afternoon, I found my father in the kitchen. He had lit a fire in the big cement sink, and was hurling his books into the flames.

This was the first time in my life I had seen him weeping. It was agonized, broken, and wild, the weeping of a man who was not used to shedding tears. Every now and then, in fits of violent sobs, he stamped his feet on the floor and banged his head against the wall.

I was so frightened that for some time I did not dare to do anything to comfort him. Eventually I put my arms around him and held him from the back, but I did not know what to say. He did not utter a word either. My father had spent every spare penny on his books. They were his life. After the bonfire, I could tell that something had happened to his mind.

ment officials, and made a pilgrimage to Beijing to see the Great Helmsman. Later she was sent to the countryside to learn from the peasants. Her parents' odyssey was harder—they were both put in detention camps for their alleged sins as "capitalist-raiders."

Broken by the experience, her father suffered a mental breakdown and died at the age of 54. Her pragmatic mother emerged from the ordeal by mastering a new set of rules. She became an adept user of the system called "going through the back door" that had taken hold in the leadership vacuum. It was she who pulled the necessary strings to get her daughter's Government scholarship approved.

Jung Chang ends her story as she boards the plane that will take her to London. She reports in a brief epilogue that eventually her three younger brothers joined her in exile. Her mother and older sister remain in Chengdu. (pp. 14-15)

> Susan Brownmiller, "When Nuances Meant Life or Death," in The New York Times Book Review, October 13, 1991, pp. 14-15.

Jung Chang [Interview with Simon & Shuster]

[The following interview was issued by Chang's publisher as part of a press release.]

[Interviewer]: **Wild Swans** *is such an intense personal story—one that spans practically the entire history of 20th century China. What prompted you to write this incredible story?*

[Chang]: In 1988, my mother, who lives in Sichuan, China, came to England to visit me. For the first time ever, she told me the stories of her life and that of my grandmother. Under Mao, it would have been too dangerous for her to talk, even to me. We talked for hours and days and months. When she returned to China, I began to think back over my own past. I felt I had to write this book. I felt I had something worthwhile to say. I've called my book **Wild Swans,** because both my mother's name and my original name contain the Chinese character for "Wild Swans."

Tell us about the process of writing the book. How did you begin to put all the pieces of your family's life together? How did you go about organizing such vast quantities of information? Was there much research involved?

To begin with, I translated and wrote down the stories told by my mother. They were really great stories, and a lot. My mother has an extraordinary memory. And she had been under interrogation many times in her life when she had to go over every detail of her life for her interrogators. At one time the team investigating her consisted of fifteen people.

My own life I remembered very clearly. Apart from memory, I had written a lot of poems over the years which helped me recall both events and my feelings. I also wrote to my friends in China and asked them to let me have the letters I had written to them in the past; and they gave big bundles of them to me.

My brothers and sister filled out the stories of their lives. Then, in spring, 1989, I returned to China to do research. I travelled across China visiting the main places in the book with my mother, from Manchuria to Lulong at the foot of the Great Wall to the mountains of Sichuan. I met many relatives and family friends and my father's fellow guerrilla fighters for the first time, and they were eager to talk to me. I was lucky. It was the Chinese spring, just weeks before the massacre in Tiananmen Square. I came back to my computer with a wealth of details.

I took care to make sure that the book is very detailed. The process of tracing and ensuring the accuracy of the details continuously brought forth new information which would open up new dimensions in the book. I kept discovering new stories until the very last minute. For instance, I had not been aware of my father's conversation with my brother Jin-ming in his labour camp, during which he said, "If I die like this, don't believe in the Communist Party anymore", until January of this year when Jin-ming told me the story after he came to the West.

There was painstaking research in the libraries on the background to make sure the historical events, the national figures, and the dates were absolutely right. In fact, information about the career of General Xue, my grandfather, such as his role in toppling one president of China and putting another president in office, came out of libraries and the British official archives. In doing the research, my experience in working on my Ph.D. at York University in England helped a lot. The stories were checked over and over again, with my mother through our voluminous correspondence between London and China, with my siblings, and with many other sources. I went to Taiwan and interviewed senior people in the Kuomintang to cross-check the facts.

It must have been an incredible shock to hear stories from your mother of your family's history. Has your relationship with your mother changed since she shared the details of her life and your grandmother's life?

There are many things I had not known about my grandmother, my mother, and my father. I was deeply moved by what they had been through, and by how they had grappled with the superhuman dilemmas in conditions of unbelievable flux. Writing the book has made me understand them much better and love them much more. My mother could feel this. In one of her letters to me, she said this made her very happy.

What specific things about China and the Chinese people would you like the American public to learn from **Wild Swans?**

I want people to see what the Chinese have been put through this century, how much they have suffered. And also how they have fought, tenaciously and courageously, against impossible odds.

It seems to me that China has been remote to the Western public and the Chinese seen as mysterious and inscrutable. I would like people to think, after reading my book, "Ah, now at last I have a visceral understanding of what life in China has been like this century. The place may be like Mars, but I have finally understood the Martians. They are people just like us! They have the same reactions and emotions as us; I can identify with them. I wonder what I would be like if I were put in their situation?"

Your book is an incredible testament to the spirit, strength and endurance of Chinese women. Do you feel there is something in the character of Chinese women that has helped them to stand up to years of injustice and suffering?

There are good and bad women in any culture and race. Neither weakness nor strength is unique to any nation. It is just that in China, centuries of horrible injustice against women have forced them to be extra strong. They have to be to survive. There have been books about the strength of Chinese women, but mainly I want to show the world how they FIGHT, for their family, for their children, for a better society, as well as for themselves. I want my readers to see how women in China never stop trying to take their lives into their own hands.

In the 1970s, it suddenly became fashionable for foreigners to visit China. What do think were some of the myths and misconceptions the outside world had of China?

The biggest misconception, for me, is how Mao has been viewed. Few, if any, are willing to compare him with Hitler or Stalin. Mao caused no less deaths or suffering. I hope my book, and particularly the story of my own transformation from worshipping Mao—indeed, I was ready to die for him—to challenging him, gives people an idea what Mao was really like.

Many Westerners who came to China in the 1970s went back with eulogies of Mao and the regime. I used to be furious reading them in the special Chinese newspaper which carried foreign news. I used to say to my friends: "this is like telling the Jews how wonderful Hitler is!" I did not realize that perhaps it was difficult for foreigners to get truthful information. Many Westerners took the obligatory lies which the Chinese had to tell them at face value. They could not conceive of the kind of fear in which the Chinese lived, which produced smiles on people's faces when they were in extreme pain. They did not know that the abiding characteristic of Mao's years in power was simply, fear. But then, many of them did not want to know the reality. They were manipulated, but they colluded with this manipulation.

Mao's talk of turning the Chinese into selfless "new men" was highly deceptive. People did not realize that, while it was true that Mao wanted the Chinese selfless, he only wanted them to be so in order to get them to submit themselves totally to him. He wanted a nation with no thoughts of its own, the largest population in the world merely to be an instrument of his power. Some Westerners thought that the Chinese were uniform and lacking in individuality. But they did not realize that deviating even a millimeter from the line laid down by Mao could unleash unimaginable disasters, not only for oneself, but for one's whole family, relatives and friends.

Many foreigners were impressed by the "moral cleanli-

ness" of the society: a discarded sock would follow its owner a thousand miles from Peking to Canton, cleaned and folded and placed in his hotel room. The Westerners did not realize that they were under such close surveillance that anyone who stole from them was bound to be caught; and taking even a handkerchief from a foreigner was likely to be punished by death.

One other misconception was to regard Communist China as an egalitarian or even classless society. Nothing could be further from the truth, as I hope my book shows. When I first came to England in 1978, one of the first things that struck me was how incredibly classless England was, compared to China.

Are you more optimistic about the way things are in China today? With communism breaking down all over the world, do you feel that the Chinese people will have additional freedoms or even a chance at democracy?

Yes, I am optimistic. China today is already an altogether different place from the one I remember. Between 1983 and 1989, I went back to visit my mother every year, and each time I was overwhelmed by the dramatic diminution of the one thing that had most characterized life under Mao: fear. After the Tiananmen massacre in 1989, fear made a tentative comeback, but without the all-pervasive and crushing force of the Maoist days. Communication with the outside world has become part of everyday life. Major world events, including the revolutions and upheavals in Eastern Europe and the Soviet Union, are reported fairly accurately in the Chinese media.

One very important change from the Maoist days has been getting rid of the "hostage system". Under Mao, a writer could jeopardize the lives of his or her family, relatives and friends—and even readers. Now it is different. I feel fairly confident that my mother, who still lives in China, will not suffer retribution because of my writing this book. I am certain that the course of liberalization is irreversible, and democracy will come, sooner or later. I hope it will be a peaceful process. I hope my book shows that we Chinese have had more than our fair share of violent revolutions, and they seem to have produced more disasters than improvements.

What were your first impressions of the West when you came over? Were you surprised to find it so different from what you were told when you were growing up? What have you done since you came to England in 1978?

In a way, coming to England was like landing on Mars. Up till then, I had only seen one Western film and read a few contemporary Western books. I had never spoken to a single foreigner except for some sailors to whom we had been allowed some brief supervised conversations as students of English. I had never heard of Marilyn Monroe or Mick Jagger. When we arrived at London airport, I nearly walked into a men's toilet because I had no idea that the picture on the door wearing trousers was supposed to be a man. For many years in China, women were not allowed to wear skirts.

I was not a bit surprised that the West was not what Party propaganda said it was like. I did not expect it to be. When

I was small, if we did not eat up our food, our nursery teachers would say, "Think of all the starving children in the capitalist countries!" But by the time I left China, I had totally rejected my indoctrination.

I did not have preconceptions about the West. I was full of curiosity and was eager to find out, to embrace surprises and to be delighted by them. My first years of living in the West were a whirlwind of fresh experiences. I sought all chances to try out everything and to taste all that had so far been denied me. This was not easy. In those years, we were under strict control. Unable to suppress my longings to break out of this invisible prison, I led a dangerous life of secret endeavors. I had many adventures, all the time feeling torn between the burning desire for the undreamt of fun and new experiences, and the gnawing fear, even paranoia, of the Chinese embassy. As far as I knew, I was the first of my wave of mainland Chinese to go into a cinema, a pub—which was thought to be an indecent place with naked women gyrating—and many other places.

Soon, I was the first to go out on my own, and possessed, secretly, an English boyfriend. One day he took me dancing. All evening, I was terrified by the number of men who kept looking at me. I was convinced they were spies sent by my embassy. When I insisted on leaving my friend smiled and said, "They are no more spies than I am. They are just men!" My paranoia was such that I took to wearing heavy make-up for the first time in my life, in the belief that this would be a satisfactory disguise.

After a year in London studying English, I got a scholarship from York University, UK, where I did a doctorate in Linguistics between 1979-1982. Because I was among the first group to come out of China on academic merit, I became the first person from Communist China to earn a Ph.D. from a British university. Immediately afterwards, I worked as a consultant in London for a big TV series on China, first screened in America in 1985 on PBS. I have written for Cambridge University Press, Linguaphone, Harrap's and Penguin/Viking. Since 1986, I have been teaching at the School of Oriental and African Studies, London University. I supervise a course for the British Foreign Office to train diplomats before they are stationed in China. I have been involved in many Anglo-Chinese projects. I am a frequent China commentator on British television and the BBC World Service.

I have made London my home, and married Jon Halliday, an Englishman. I do not consider myself an exile, because an exile is someone who yearns to go back to their native land when the political system changes. I choose to live in London as an American might do. My husband is here. My work is here. My friends are here.

> *Jung Chang, in an interview published as a release in* News from Simon & Schuster, *1991.*

Naomi Bliven

In *Wild Swans: Three Daughters of China* Jung Chang, who teaches at London University, recounts her grandmother's life, her mother's, and her own and so tells the history of modern China as its victims lived it. Her family chronicle resembles a popular novel that stars strong, beautiful women and provides cameo roles for famous men, like Zhou Enlai. But *Wild Swans* is no romance. It's a story, at once grim and appealing, about the survival of a Chinese family through a century of disaster. Ms. Chang takes us all over China, and into all sorts of institutions, from the harem to the gulag; wherever she goes, her adroitness in explaining Chinese customs and expectations operates as local coloring always should—it heightens our awareness of the human in the parochial.

Her book begins in Manchuria, where her grandmother Yu-fang was born in 1909. Yu-fang was a beauty, and the most valuable asset of her father, an ambitious small-town policeman whose career was stalled by the collapse of the Manchu empire, in 1911. Her feet were bound, and her father saw to it that she learned music, drawing, and embroidery, and, when she was fifteen, made his fortune by selling her to a warlord as a concubine. Yu-fang's daughter, the author's mother, De-hong, was born in 1931. The warlord's childless wife took De-hong to raise as her own, but while the master lay on his deathbed Yu-fang kidnapped her baby and escaped. A few years later, she married a sixty-five-year-old widower, Dr. Xia. His grown children resented their beautiful young ex-concubine stepmother, so the Doctor gave them all his property, moved to another, bigger Manchurian town with Yu-fang and De-hong, and started all over again.

Dr. Xia is this story's Sarastro—a noble, wise, and kindly patriarch. His benevolence, combined with his professional success, should have assured his family's happiness. But the warlords' violent, unstable rule over Manchuria was succeeded by the Japanese occupation—a reign of terror that extended even to little schoolgirls like De-hong. Dr. Xia was an authentic humanitarian: his family risked their lives giving what help they could to victims of the Japanese, and after the war they also helped Japanese fleeing massacre, Communists hiding from the Kuomintang, and Kuomintang members persecuted by the Communists. Foot-binding had left Yu-fang crippled and in constant pain, but she hobbled through her days working for others with peppery good nature.

Yu-fang accepted the tradition that a woman showed her love by agreeing with her menfolk; De-hong insisted on thinking for herself. Like her parents, she had greeted the Kuomintang forces as liberators when they arrived, in 1945, but their ineffectuality at everything except corruption disillusioned her, and she risked her life again by joining the Communist underground. She met the author's father, Shou-yu Chang, after his Communist guerrilla unit helped capture their town, in 1948; they were married the following year. He was ten years older than De-hong and came from Sichuan, where his father's textile factory had been bankrupted by the warlords' extortions during the worldwide Great Depression of the nineteen-thirties. Shou-yu had spent several years roaming (and starving) at the bottom of Chinese society before he joined the Communist Party, in 1938; he made his way to Mao's army in Yan'an in 1940. In his certitude, Shou-yu may remind you of Bazarov in *Fathers and Sons,* though the young Communist was even surer of his purpose than Turgenev's young nihilist. In 1949 the Changs were transferred to Sichuan, and, in time, Shou-yu became deputy director of the Public Affairs Department for the province, overseeing culture and propaganda, and his wife became the head of the Public Affairs Department of the Eastern District of Chengdu, the provincial capital. Shou-yu insisted that his family avoid even the appearance of favoritism or privilege; when Yu-fang came to visit her pregnant daughter, Shou-yu shipped her back to Manchuria, because De-hong's rank in the civil service did not entitle her to have a parent living with her. After De-hong was promoted, in 1951, her parents came to stay. The Doctor died in 1952, but Yu-fang lived until 1970—long enough to tell her grandchildren stories, give them hugs, and, except when Communist policy made everybody eat in public canteens, cook them goodies.

The Changs had five children—the author's older sister, Jung herself (she was born in 1952), and three younger brothers. Their childhood was punctuated by incomprehensible separations; when Jung was only three, she and the other children were sent to government nurseries while her mother was being detained and investigated as a "hidden counterrevolutionary." Ms. Chang recalls spells of "tranquil and loving" family life after her mother was cleared, when she lived in what she later realized was a "privileged cocoon"—privileged, at least, in contrast to the seven million Sichuanese who starved to death in the famine caused by Mao's Great Leap Forward, of 1958-61. But Mao's next campaign, the Great Proletarian Cultural Revolution, which began in the mid-sixties, scattered the Chang family and shattered Shou-yu physically and psychologically.

Ms. Chang's mother and father never discussed their convictions or their difficulties with their children. The young people learned only years later how long their parents had been struggling to obey the Communist Party's commands—to betray their own judgments, deny realities they observed, and substitute Party orders for conscience. During the Cultural Revolution, they at last gave up trying to turn themselves into Party hacks. In 1966, as the denunciations and violence spread, Shou-yu wrote to Mao to protest the persecution of innocent people. Jung Chang later discovered that, when De-hong reminded him that their children would suffer if the parents were stigmatized as "capitalist roaders," he asked, "What about the children of the victims?"

Though their parents were vilified, beaten, jailed, and finally sent to penal colonies, Ms. Chang and the other children unthinkingly embraced the cult of Mao. They joined the Red Guards, and invaded the homes of "class enemies" exactly as Red Guard posses had invaded *their* home. (Those posses had made her father burn his books.) Ms. Chang explains that she was able to retain her faith both in her parents' goodness and in Mao's leadership by convincing herself that evil counsellors were misleading the Chairman. The Chang parents knew Party bigwigs, but the author only once glimpsed Chairman Mao, during a Red Guard pilgrimage to Beijing: she was standing among a hysterically cheering crowd when his car drove past their ranks. Mao seems to have been a man whose

greatest happiness was hating, but his personality didn't infect all the Chinese people. The Chang youngsters, each living out his own picaresque novel as China disintegrated, encountered very little hostility. When the middle brother joined a tough street gang, its members treated him as a kind of mascot, and Ms. Chang herself, during the months when she worked in a factory, found the same kind of goodnatured acceptance. The children were appalled to discover how poor, and how poorly educated, most Chinese were, for until their parents' downfall they had lived in an apparatchiks' compound, and had been taught in school how lucky they were compared with the children in capitalist countries, who had to leave school to support their parents. (Ms. Chang is a good describer of landscapes and cityscapes as well as of people, and the impression I get from travelling with her and her relatives across the century and the nation is that China isn't a poor country but, rather, a rich country pauperized by hundreds of years of misgovernment.) After the schools were closed, the children were sent to work in peasant communes, and there they saw the direst poverty of all. But the hard life hadn't made the peasants hard people: when Ms. Chang's sister married, in 1970, their gifts—"a handful of dried noodles, a pound of soybeans, and a few eggs, wrapped carefully in red straw paper and tied with straw in a fancy knot"—represented real sacrifices.

De-hong was released from penal camp and rehabilitated by a Communist Party tribunal in 1971; Shou-yu was freed in 1972 but died before he could be rehabilitated. The author's portrait of her father is full of insight and delicacy. At the height of his power, he was worshipped by the Sichuanese for his incorruptibility. But the reader finds this paragon an unsympathetic human being: he was harsh to his wife and children as well as to his Sichuanese clan. His wife's accusation "You are a good Communist, but a rotten husband!" is something of an understatement. Our feelings change only after Shou-yu, toward the end of his life, apologizes for his devotion to the Party at the expense of his family, and confides to his sons that he doubts whether his life of dedication has really helped build a better China. Even then, though, he finds himself unable to compromise his principles: when the author asks him to put in a word with his friends on the enrollment committee to help her get into the university in Sichuan, he refuses, saying, "It would not be fair to people with no power." We come to know Shou-yu as a daughter knows a parent, and in the end we see him as a tragic archetype— an idealist whose ideal betrays him. Luckily for the Changs, De-hong was more realistic. She worked the bureaucracy on behalf of her children and on behalf of the children of anyone who asked her help. Ms. Chang was admitted to the university, and resumed the study of English she had begun in middle school; in 1978, she won a scholarship to Great Britain, where she received a doctorate in linguistics, and has lived there ever since.

Though the settings in Chang's book are exotic, the people aren't strange. Before the First World War, the list of ladylike accomplishments was the same in Manchuria as in Massachusetts, and the Chengdu street gang knew exactly what a street gang is supposed to do without ever having seen *West Side Story*. The author's oldest brother, who became a physicist, was the same kind of child as my physicist brother. In traditional Asian patriarchal extended families, as in our own, a rich widower's grown children find ways to express their resentment at their father's remarriage; and many a Western mother has shared Yu-fang's dismay when, like De-hong, her daughter decides to marry without a traditional ceremony, feast, gown, and trousseau. The aspirations of the successive generations of women in this book parallel those of the same generations of Western women: Yu-fang, born in 1909, wanted to become a respected wife and mother; her daughter, born in 1931, hoped for a career but felt she ought to choose a nurturing profession and, since circumstances prevented her from studying medicine, turned her political job into social work; the author, born in 1952, took it for granted that women had jobs, and became a scholar.

It isn't that the Changs became "modern" and less Chinese. They're both. Dr. Xia practiced traditional Chinese medicine, but the family also used Western medicine. They didn't stop reading Chinese literature after they began reading Western books: they recognized trans- or supranational realities in the doings of Emma Bovary and Jo March, just as, reading Ms. Chang, we recognize small human crises (a first meeting between mother-and-daughter-in-law) and small human pleasures (a family Sunday in the park). The author's own candor and sense of humor keep everything in proportion. She never whines, preaches, argues, or makes public-policy recommendations. She just tells stories. Of course, we feel how suffocating it is to live in a country where it isn't possible to tell a policeman or a soldier to go away or a bureaucrat to mind his own business, and we observe that the retrograde tyrannies in this book all find ways to belittle or exploit women.

Misgovernment and the oppression of women aren't the only—or even the main—themes. *Wild Swans* is a narrative exploration of one of human-kind's few benign irrationalities—mother love. While Dr. Xia appreciated Shou-yu's nobility of character, Yu-fang objected to almost everything about her daughter's marriage; yet, though De-hong disappointed her, Yu-fang kept on loving her. De-hong took her mother's ineradicable devotion as her due, the way we used to take fresh air and clean water, and then duplicated her mother's devotion with her own children. As Ms. Chang follows her grandmother, her mother, and her brothers and sister through the decades, we see mother love's variety, nuance, and stubbornness—how it survives separation, coexists with disapproval or incomprehension, and evokes wholly unself-conscious self-sacrifice, even (or especially) on behalf of rebellious or defiant children.

Yu-fang died, her last illness undiagnosed and untreated, while her daughter was in prison during the Cultural Revolution; in her final hours, she hallucinated that she, like her daughter, had been the victim of a denunciation meeting. De-hong fared better—she's retired on a pension—but all her children except her elder daughter now live in the West. Mother love doesn't reward mothers, but it empowers children. In Ms. Chang's family, it imparted the courage and good temper that distinguish her book and outlast regimes. (pp. 95-8)

Naomi Bliven, "Good Women of Sichuan," in The New Yorker, *Vol. LXVII, No. 51, February 10, 1992, pp. 95-8.*

Jonathan Mirsky

Wild Swans is one of the most intimate studies of persecution, suffering, and fear in Mao's time, before and after his triumph in 1949, and one of the finest. Born in 1952, the daughter of high-ranking Party officials, Jung Chang participated and suffered in the Cultural Revolution before coming to Britain in 1978. She took her doctorate in linguistics at York University, and now teaches in London at the School of Oriental and African Studies.

Wild Swans: Three Daughters of China is Jung Chang's history of her grandmother, her mother, and herself, beginning in 1909, when the empire still existed and her grandmother was born, and moving through the Nationalist and Communist years to 1978, two years after Mao's death, when Jung Chang left China, although she didn't know it, forever.

In 1924, when her grandmother was fifteen, she became one of the concubines of General Xue Zhi-heng, chief of police of the shaky government in Peking. He was aroused by her tiny bound feet as she knelt before the Buddha in a Manchurian temple where she had been carefully positioned by her ambitious father to attract the general's attention.

After an opulent "wedding" ceremony (he already had a wife and other concubines) the general spent three days with his new acquisition before leaving—for six years. His teen-age concubine had already been told by her father that "in Peking they say, 'When General Xue stamps his foot, the whole city shakes,' " but as the general was leaving her he gave her a little pep talk about fidelity. Another one of his concubines, he said, had betrayed him with a male servant. So he dripped raw alcohol into a gag stuffed in her mouth.

> "Of course I could not give her the pleasure of dying speedily. For a woman to betray her husband is the vilest thing possible," he said. . . .
> "All I did with the lover was to have him shot," he added casually. My grandmother never knew whether or not all this had really happened, but at the age of fifteen she was suitably petrified.

When she was twenty-four, she fled on horseback in the dead of night from the general's house, which she was visiting while he was dying, and, with the infant who would become Jung Chang's mother, took shelter in the house of Dr. Xia, a kindly, sixty-three-year-old Manchu. Three years later she had a nervous breakdown and the doctor "was the first man she had ever met to whom she could say what she really felt, and she poured out her grief and hopes to him." They fell in love and married, over objections by his children so violent that one of them shot himself dead. They were a devoted couple, but had no children. "Years later," Jung Chang says, "my grandmother told my mother, somewhat mysteriously, that through *qi-gong* [a traditional quasi-medical practice involving pressure by the hands] Dr. Xia developed a technique which enabled him to have an orgasm without ejaculating."

Dr. Xia's envious children did not dare to openly insult his young wife, but her little girl was made to suffer. She sought comfort from Dr. Xia's coachman, who taught her to skate and told her stories about his past life as a hunter in the forests of northern Manchuria. Bears were fierce "and one should avoid them at all costs. If you did happen to meet one, you must stand still until it lowered its head. This was because the bear has a lock of hair on his forehead which falls over his eyes and blinds him when he drops his head."

After the defeat of Japan in 1945 Manchuria became a battleground in the civil war between the Nationalists and the Communists, and Jung Chang's fourteen-year-old mother De-hong (*de* means virtue, *hong* means wild swan), a bold, idealistic, and intensely patriotic school girl disgusted by the corruption of Chiang Kai-shek's forces, became increasingly involved with the Communist underground in Jinzhou, a key city in the struggle. Her first task was distributing Mao Zedong's *On Coalition Government,* which had to be hidden inside grain stalks and green peppers. De-hong was risking her liberty and even her life—at one point she was arrested by the Nationalists, and before she was released was shown prisoners being horribly tortured. She was placed before a firing squad which executed the man next to De-hong but spared her. Her willingness to sacrifice herself for the Party is bitterly ironic when one considers how savagely she and her family were to suffer at its hands.

Here lies the central tragedy of **Wild Swans,** a story of dashed idealism, and of suffering, endurance, and courage. The tragedy lies in the Chang family's dogged faith in Mao and the Party despite considerable early evidence of their true nature. Or indeed because the Changs, like many others, half perceived that nature and it terrified them. What we see in **Wild Swans** is that much of the Party's support depended on simple dread.

This can be understood from Jung Chang's father's early years in the Party and the first months of his marriage. In 1948, when she was seventeen, De-hong, who by now was well known to the Party as a daring and reliable supporter, met Chang Shou-yu, an already important regional Communist official, ten years older than herself. He was from Yibin, in Sichuan province 1,200 miles away, the son of a well-off textile manufacturer bankrupted during the worldwide Great Depression. After a poor and wandering childhood, during which he acquired the love of books he would pass on to his daughter, he joined the Party when he was seventeen. By 1940 he had made his way to Yanan, Mao's guerrilla headquarters.

His daughter says her father loved Yanan, which like the Americans who visited it during the war he compared to Kuomintang-controlled China and found it to be "a paradise of fairness." Self-educated but brilliant, the young man from the provinces amazed his big-city comrades by placing first in the entrance examinations for the presti-

gious Academy of Marxist-Leninist Studies, where, when he was barely twenty, he became the youngest research fellow. It was in this Academy that fear turned the upright and idealistic Chang Shou-yu into the still upright but rigid and unyielding Communist who loved Jung Chang's mother but blighted her life; thirty years later he would implore her forgiveness.

Jung Chang recalls that in 1942 Mao asked for open criticism of the Party's failures, as he was to do again in the late Fifties after the Hundred Flowers. The effect was the same as in 1957: having, as he put it, "charmed the snakes from their holes," Mao proceeded to punish his critics, who included leading intellectuals, such as the woman novelist Ding Ling. Some of the young research fellows, including Chang Shou-yu, had publicly called for individual expression and attacked the elite's personal corruption. "Mao did not like what he saw, and turned his campaign into a witch-hunt," says Jung Chang. Her father was accused by one of Yanan's top ideologues, Ai Si-qi, of having "committed a very naive mistake," and in what was an augury of decades of campaigns against intellectuals, Chang and his friends were subjected to months of group attack and self-criticism. They were charged with no less than causing chaos in Yanan and weakening Party discipline, "which could damage the great cause of saving China from the Japanese—and from poverty and injustice."

This *zheng-feng,* or rectification campaign, came to a climax at the Yanan Forum on Literature and Art in 1942, at which Mao laid down once and for all the rules for China's artists and writers to which they have been compelled, with more or less severity, to adhere ever since; it could be said that almost nothing worthwhile was written again.

Although what happened to Jung Chang's father was a tiny side show in this mighty upheaval, his ordeal, which is not crudely described by the metaphor of brainwashing, was significant for understanding the rest of his life: it "turned him into a convert. . . . He regarded his harsh treatment as not only justified, but even a noble experience—soul-cleansing for the mission to save China."

Jung Chang doesn't fully explain what happened to her father, although her description of him and the rest of his life helps us to understand him. She mentions that the young dissidents at the Academy were led by a young writer called Wang Shi-wei. She says little about him, except that he was accused of being a Trotskyist and a spy. But Wang, the author of an essay called "The Wild Lily," which was attacked as "a poisonous weed," was the only one of the Yanan victims actually put on trial and, in 1947, when Mao was forced out of Yanan by Chiang Kai-shek's forces, he was shot. As the Chinese expert Laszlo Ladany puts it, the Yanan purge "created a pattern which China was to find difficult to get rid of. . . . It culminated in the Cultural Revolution. . . . Mao made a number of fanatical converts who from their earliest days had only known one way of governing the Party and the country: namely the way Mao dealt with the Rectification campaign in the 1940s."

From then on Mao and his disciples tended to treat their critics like enemies. They terrified them, first by casting them out of the inner circle, which meant the victims suddenly became powerless, forcing them into detention or manual labor and, on occasion, shooting them. This should not be confused with Stalinism, which depended on one man, with enormous power, killing old comrades, singly or in great numbers, and eradicating religious and ethnic groups. Mao, by contrast, was a master at provoking the group, whether it was the Politburo or a cell in a primary school, into humiliating the people designated as legitimate targets. Although it was always possible that one could be executed, the prevailing fear among China's Party members and intellectuals, until the mass killing of the Cultural Revolution, was of being isolated from *guanxi*—the Chinese web of alliances that protects individuals and their families. Avoiding this fate was a major preoccupation of Party life and is a core theme of *Wild Swans.*

Eventually rehabilitated after his disgrace, around the time he met his seventeen-year-old future wife in 1948, Jung Chang's father had become a famous guerrilla leader in Manchuria. They were instantly attracted to each other—she by his cultivation and cultural interests, his fine appearance, his habit of brushing his teeth each day, and his use of a clean handkerchief; he by her beauty, daring, and political maturity. And now for the first time De-hong encountered Party coercion and total control. "For those who had 'joined the revolution,' the Party functioned as the family head." After securing Party approval to get married, the couple were literally on the point of climbing into their honeymoon bed when a Party representative arrived to take De-hong away "because of her family connections." Two weeks later they were again given permission to marry. But "revolutionaries" were supposed to spend every night in their offices. De-hong used to sneak over a wall to her husband's quarters and return at dawn. They were discovered. Each had to make a self-criticism. De-hong could not see "what harm [it] could do the revolution if she spent the night with her husband." To her dismay he admonished her: "A revolution needs steel-like discipline. You have to obey the Party even if you do not understand it or agree with it."

The reason for such insensitivity on the part of this unusually intelligent man, who deeply loved his wife and later his children, emerged fully in 1949. The young couple were ordered to travel, mostly by foot, over one thousand miles back to Sichuan, Wang's native province, where by 1966 he would be one of the top officials. It was a grueling ordeal for De-hong, who although she didn't know it was suffering the first pains of a miscarriage. Her husband's rank meant he could travel by jeep. Although she was vomiting continuously he refused to carry even her bedroll because that would be nepotism (as opposed to the elitism which permitted him use of a car) and told her, "You have a choice: you can either get into the car, or get into the Party, but not both."

Jung Chang is somewhat sympathetic to this on the grounds that the peasants would expect officials to be tough, and that her father had proved himself as a guerrilla fighter, but it seems to me that her father was frightened of criticism and its consequence—ostracism. It was regarded as disgraceful for a revolutionary to cry, Jung Chang says, and one night when her mother was weeping with pain her husband hurriedly clapped his hand over her mouth. Through her tears she heard him—the man who years before at Yunan had felt the blowtorch of Party discipline—whispering into her ear: "Don't cry out loud! If people hear you, you will be criticized." Later when she miscarried, and demanded a divorce, he apologized to her and washed her blood-soaked clothes, an unusual act for a Chinese man, Jung Chang observes. But when De-hong complained that "she could never please the revolution," and might as well go home, he warned her, "That will be interpreted as meaning you are afraid of hardship. You will be regarded as a deserter and you will have no future. . . . Once you were 'with the revolution' you could never leave."

Before long, when De-hong heard Mao proclaiming the victory of the revolution she scolded herself for her suffering—"trivial compared to the great cause of saving China." But soon, and for the rest of her life, she realized "that my father's first loyalty was to the revolution, and she was bitterly disappointed." Six years later, in 1955, when De-hong was in detention for six months while her "class background" once again came under minute scrutiny, her husband—one of the top twenty Party officials in a province of well over seventy million people—never visited or telephoned. "As he saw it, to comfort my mother would imply some kind of distrust of the Party." In 1957 De-hong told him, " 'You are a good Communist, but a rotten husband!' My father nodded. He said he knew."

In Chengdu, the provincial capital, because of her father's extremely high rank (her mother's was much lower, although she too had considerable power), Jung Chang grew up in a luxurious walled compound, surrounded by the squalor of the masses. Served by guards, chefs, and chauffeurs, she was entitled to see special movies and plays provided to the Party elite, and attended a "key school," founded in 141 BC, for which she had passed the entrance exam with perfect marks in Chinese and mathematics. (Her "class background" had helped too, although her father cautioned her not to count on it.) She belonged, in short, to a group of "high officials' children" (*gao-ganzi-di*), who had "an air which identified them unmistakably as members of an elite group, exuding an awareness of powerful backing and untouchability," and because her father advised against close contact with such children, Jung Chang had few other friends and found that it was nearly impossible to form relationships with ordinary people. So sheltered was this life that between 1959 and 1961 when, according to Jung Chang, China's great famine killed 30 million people, 7 million in Sichuan alone, or "10 percent of the entire population of a rich province" in which people were kidnapping and killing children for food, she knew nothing about the disaster—or "in fact, anything that might sow a grain of doubt in me about the regime, or Mao. My parents, like virtually every parent in China, never said anything unorthodox to their children."

And here, as is so often the case in *Wild Swans,* Jung

Chang provides us with part of the explanation for the success of the Mao cult. She observed that many Chinese believed that the Chairman had ended the civil war brought peace and stability to China, and restored it as a great country in foreign eyes. The almost complete lack of information in China made it impossible to distinguish between Mao's successes and failures—like the disastrous Great Leap and the ensuing famine—or even to compare his achievements with those of other Communist leaders. (Except, very quietly, within the inner circle: already in 1958, when the Great Leap was in full swing, her father had seen Marshal Ho Lung, one of China's greatest military figures, point at Deng Xiaoping, and murmur, "It really should be him on the throne.") According to a popular song, "Father is close, Mother is close, but neither is as close as Chairman Mao." But "fear was never absent in the building up of Mao's cult," which meant, as Jung Chang notes, that even thinking was dangerous.

All this was taking place long before the Cultural Revolution, and by 1961 Jung Chang's father was cracking under the strain. Although she did not know there was a famine Jung Chang hardly saw her father between 1959 and 1961 as he inspected its ravages. Her parents, working "right in the center of the misinformation machine," were racked with guilt, and before long her father collapsed, "no longer the assured puritan of yesteryear." When he came under attack during the Cultural Revolution this collapse was characterized, accurately, his daughter dryly remarks, as "the waning of his revolutionary will."

The last part of *Wild Swans* describes the Chang family's agony during the Cultural Revolution. It is the most harrowing and extended account I have read of the years between 1966 and 1976, and the most analytical. During much of this period Jung Chang, who was only fourteen in 1966 when the grim decade began, watched with fear and shame the wrecking of her beloved school by its own students and saw her even more beloved teachers being beaten and humiliated. The deputy headmaster cuts his throat. Her parents, although disillusioned, still said nothing to their children. "The situation was so complex and confusing that they could not understand it themselves." Mao, she says, wanted total obedience, and to secure it, "he needed terror—an intense terror that would block all other considerations and crush all other fears." All this was accompanied by a propaganda machine, with no rival sources of information, creating a picture of an all wise and good Mao for whose works even foreigners clamored.

But even when we take into account admiration for Mao's achievements, and the efforts of the gigantic cultmachine, outsiders are often puzzled that Mao was able so easily and quickly to persuade large numbers of Chinese to do awful things to each other. Fear of the consequences of noncompliance, as I have already observed, was a very big reason. Jung Chang, whose book is in large measure her attempt to make sense of what at the time felt like chaos, looks at the nature of Chinese society itself. "In China," she says, "there were virtually no safety valves for ordinary people." No football, few genuine demonstrations, no redress, no politics.

Jung Chang believed that when Mao launched

his call to "seize power," he found a huge constituency of people who wanted to take revenge on somebody. Although power was dangerous, it was more desirable than powerlessness, particularly to people who had never had it. Now it looked to the general public as if Mao was saying that power was up for grabs.

She notes, too, that the chance for "privilege, awe, and fawning," when combined with the fear of what would happen to anyone suddenly designated as a target, could have deadly consequences. Especially so in a country so violent that Jung Chang's father, a decent man, sympathized with a subordinate who had beaten to death a bandit chief and eaten his heart, because the bandit was not "an innocent person but a murderer, and a cruel one at that."

Yet even as the Cultural Revolution began destroying her protected world, separating her from her brothers and sisters, crushing her parents and driving her father insane, Jung Chang remained "incapable of rational thinking in those days." No one forced her to join the Red Guards, she admits—of which she became a timid and shrinking member:

> I was keen to do so. . . . They were Mao's creations, and Mao was beyond contemplation. . . . So, at the very time the Cultural Revolution had brought disaster on my family, I became a Red Guard.

By now her father, who had been personally attacked by Madame Mao, was being paraded around Chengdu in a truck with a placard hung from a thin wire which ate into his neck. He appeared not to care: "In his insanity, his mind seemed to be detached from his body." "What had turned people into monsters?" Jung Chang asked herself. She admits that previously, when people had been tormented, she had doubted their innocence, but she knew her parents were guiltless. (Innocence and guilt must be understood in Maoist terms.) She actively hated the government but thought of Mao as "the idol, the god, the inspiration. The purpose of my life had been formulated in his name. A couple of years before, I would happily have died for him. Although his magic power had vanished from inside me, he was still sacred and undoubtable." This sounds as if his magic still remained potent.

Jung Chang, whose book is in large measure her attempt to make sense of what at the time felt like chaos, looks at the nature of Chinese society itself.

—*Jonathan Mirsky*

In 1969 the Chang family was split up and sent off to the countryside. "Mao intended me to spend the rest of my life as a peasant," Jung Chang says succinctly. Although some Westerners imagined "education through labor" to be politically progressive, all Chinese, Jung Chang maintains, "knew that hard labor, particularly in the countryside, was always punishment. It was noticeable that none of Mao's henchmen, the members of the newly established Revolutionary Committees, army officers—and very few of their children—had to do it." One of her observations of the efficiency of the "down to the countryside movement" is new to me: fifteen million young Chinese were forced to take part in what she rightly describes as "one of the largest population movements in history." During a period of great turmoil, each was provided with sneakers, water can, flashlight, clothes, and bedding, all specially manufactured because they were not available in shops in such vast numbers.

The—astoundingly—still idealistic Jung Chang believed she was going to "a mountain of blossoms with a golden river at my feet," and indeed what she describes as the tempestuous beauty of mountains, snow, and flowers stunned her. But when she arrived at the village where she was expected to settle down as a peasant, like thousands of other urban Maoists, she saw at last how the revolution had failed the rural people of China, 80 percent of the population, to whom these students were the same as foreigners. "Everything at Ningnan was done manually, the way it had been for at least 2,000 years. . . . The peasants were too short of food to be able to afford any for horses or donkeys." The sheltered city girls, who had never cooked a meal in their lives, now had to walk for thirty minutes into the mountains, carrying empty water barrels which weighed ninety pounds when filled for the return trip. Foraging for firewood took four hours every day. Jung Chang had believed that the more one became like a peasant the better one was. With this "blind belief " gone she developed a skin rash, which lasted for three years but vanished each time she left the countryside.

Like her unhappy mother years before, when Dr. Xia's old coachman told her how to deal with bears, she heard a marvelous animal story:

> The wolves were very clever, the locals told the new arrivals. When one got into a pigsty, it would gently scratch and lick the pig, particularly behind its ears, to get the animal into a kind of pleasurable trance, so that it would not make a noise. Then the wolf would lightly bite the pig on one ear and lead it out of the sty, all the time rubbing its body with its fluffy tail. The pig would still be dreaming of being caressed by a lover when the wolf pounced.

At home in Chengdu, her ancient grandmother died, imagining she had been harassed by Maoists. Really, Jung Chang says, "she was finally killed by the accumulation of anguish." Her granddaughter remembers her as, "a great character—vivacious, talented, and immensely capable." But the ex-concubine had experienced little happiness. "How could the revolution be good, I asked myself, when it brought such human destruction, for nothing?" And still—she was not eighteen—"No matter how much I hated the Cultural Revolution, to doubt Mao still did not enter my mind."

She managed to take leave of her village to spend three months with her father in what she describes as a gulag

holding thousands of former officials. Although much aged, he was no longer insane. And he was full of remorse. He sent his wife a telegram: "Please accept my apologies that come a lifetime too late. It is for my guilt toward you that I am happy for any punishment. I have not been a decent husband. Please get well and give me another chance." A year later he told Jung Chang's brother that he had joined the Party to build a fair society. "But what good has it done for the people? If I die like this, don't believe in the Communist Party anymore."

In 1974, only two years before Mao's death and the end of the Cultural Revolution, Jung Chang, gripped by rage and hopelessness, "still did not condemn him [Mao] explicitly, even in my mind. It was so difficult to destroy a god." But in the fall of that year, now a student at Sichuan University, and as idealistically unquestioning about the West as she had been about Mao. She read in *Newsweek* that Madame Mao was Mao's "eyes, ears, and voice." Suddenly—because it was a foreign publication and therefore must be telling the truth—she "experienced the thrill of challenging Mao openly in my mind for the first time."

Chang Shou-yu died in 1975. His daughter wept for days for her father's wasted life, his betrayal by a cause to which he had given himself since he was a boy. Even after death his ordeal continued: he had been offered the chance to blame his "deviationism" on his insanity, but he condemned Mao by name, thus losing the chance for political rehabilitation. His wife understood that if his official memorial valediction mentioned these deviations her husband's descendants would be doomed "for generation after generation." It would be the final casting out. By pulling every string she managed to procure an innocuous statement, and saved her children from the political cold.

In words which will not endear her to the Chairman's old comrades who are still running China, Jung Chang hands down a terrible judgment: Mao, she says,

> had managed to turn the people into the ultimate weapon of dictatorship. That was why under him there was no real equivalent of the KGB in China. There was no need. In bringing out and nourishing the worst in people, Mao had created a moral wasteland and a land of hatred. . . . The greatest horror of the Cultural Revolution . . . was carried out by the population collectively.

In 1989 the protesters in Tiananmen Square were trying to do something about Mao's moral wasteland. The ceaseless assurances from Mao's elderly henchmen, who are forcing every student in China to study the Chairman's Thoughts, that the Peking massacre prevented another Cultural Revolution, are a particularly vicious example of the Big Lie. (pp. 6-10)

Jonathan Mirsky, "Literature of the Wounded," in The New York Review of Books, *Vol. XXXIX, No. 5, March 5, 1992, pp. 6-10.*

Katherine Dunn

1945-

(Full name Katherine Karen Dunn) American novelist.

The following entry provides an overview of Dunn's career through her 1989 novel, *Geek Love*.

INTRODUCTION

Dunn is the author of satirical works that delineate bizarre and often grotesque events and characters. In her successful third novel, *Geek Love,* and earlier works, Dunn portrays the lives of outsiders from the perspective of the alienated individual, inverting conventional contemporary values and evoking unusual portraits of the dark side of human nature. Deeply affected by photos of World War II Nazi concentration camps that she saw as a child and the mass suicide at Jonestown, Guyana, that occurred when she was an adult, Dunn has focused on the violent and the macabre in her writing in what she maintains is an attempt to confront the evil impulses underlying the perpetration of such horrors.

Dunn was born in Garden City, Kansas. Her father left the family before Dunn turned two years old, and she spent her childhood traveling with her mother, stepfather, and two brothers throughout the western United States. When Dunn was thirteen, the family settled in Tigard, Oregon. At an early age Dunn had ambitions of becoming a writer and was the only child in her family to earn a high school diploma. After graduating she wandered around the United States and at eighteen was jailed in Missouri for check fraud. Following her release she attended Portland State College (now University) and Reed College and was awarded a writing grant, which she used to travel. While living in Boston, Dunn wrote her first novel, *Attic.* She then traveled to Greece and completed *Truck.* After spending time in Ireland Dunn moved back to the United States and held various jobs, including waitress, bartender, and children's radio personality, while writing novels and short stories. Dunn did not submit these works to a publisher until she completed the novel *Geek Love,* twenty years after the release of *Truck.*

In *Attic* Dunn juxtaposes the events of a young woman's prison experiences with dream and fantasy sequences, incorporating autobiographical content into the work: the narrator, Katherine, runs away from her home in Oregon and ends up in a Missouri jail after trying to pass bad checks. Commentators have compared Dunn's treatment of the abhorrent aspects of prison to that of French novelist and playwright Jean Genet; like Genet's works, *Attic* presents a nonchronological, semi-autobiographical narrative that features exotic imagery and metaphors, slang, and scatological language. Dunn's second work, *Truck,* is a stream-of-consciousness novel concerning the adven-

tures of a teenage runaway named Dutch. Characterized by a discursive style, the work nevertheless realistically portrays Dutch's struggle to gain independence from the dictates of her parents and adult society.

During the two-decade hiatus from publishing that followed *Truck,* Dunn studied grammar and incorporated revision into her writing process, something that she admits she did not do with her first two books. The result was a more structured narrative in her next novel, *Geek Love.* Dunn attributes the inspiration of *Geek Love* to visiting a botanical garden, where she had the notion that children could be genetically engineered to fit the wishes of their parents. The narrator, Olympia, is an albino hunchbacked dwarf—one of four offspring born to Al and Lil Binewski, whose experiments with various drugs during Lil's pregnancies helped breed deformed children to serve as attractions in their traveling freak show, the Binewski Fabulon. Throughout the novel Olympia and the rest of the Binewskis insist on their superiority over those whom they derisively term the "norms," inverting standard conceptions of normality and abnormality. In order to make the bizarre events of the story believable, Dunn employs strict logic, elaborate details, and Olympia's insider point of view to convince the reader that such absurdities as a family of genetically designed freaks could exist. The plot eventually centers on the eldest child, Arturo, or Aqua Boy, who was born with flippers in place of limbs. Through manipulative tactics Arturo inspires the formation of a cult, called Arturism, wherein followers submit to the systematic removal of their digits and limbs and ultimately are left with only a torso and a head. In tandem with this primary story, which is told through long flashback sequences, Olympia narrates her present predicament: the rescue of her beautiful daughter from Mary Lick, a frozen-food heiress intent on disfiguring attractive women so they will be left to pursue intellectual interests without the interference of men. Olympia recounts in her characteristically farcical tone the gruesome events that transpire as both plots come to violent climaxes.

Critics have faulted Dunn's early novels for their obscurity and generally have concurred that in all her works plot takes precedence over thematic content. However, despite such criticism nearly all commentators have praised her narrative tone, evocative language, and vivid imagination. In reviewing *Geek Love* Matthew Giunti has written that "the first half of the book, in which Dunn establishes the world of her Fabulon in Olympia's elegiac and ironic tones, is her triumph: alternately clear-eyed and fanciful, precise and hyperbolic."

PRINCIPAL WORKS

NOVELS

Attic 1970
Truck 1971
Geek Love 1989

CRITICISM

Elizabeth Dalton

> Seven miles away and twelve stories up Sister Blendina turns up a black ace and the eyes begin to move and grow. At that point I try to slip out of Dogsbody the back way but it's a close fit and they're too fast for me. The uniform takes one long fast step that puts him behind me. That gives the eyes time to become metal rings opened wide and moving in quickly each one closing with a hard click around one of my thighs an inch below the crotch. My stomach drops and would fall but it catches on my crotch and is saved.

The action may not be very clear in this passage from *Attic*, but one thing is incontestably going on: a contemporary novel is being written by a young writer. The attempt to reproduce the confusion and simultaneity of experience as it happens, the somewhat factitious energy, the surreal imagery all make for a turned-on contemporary idiom that bears some resemblance, if not scrutinized too closely, to formal innovation.

The narrator—a young girl named, like the author of this first novel, Katherine Dunn—is getting arrested in this first scene for trying to cash a bad check. The rest of the novel takes place in jail, in a bizarre female world of prostitutes and petty thieves. The rather undifferentiated style works well here, making the characters, with their fights and intrigues and grotesque romances, as garish and fragmentary as images in a bad dream. Unfortunately, we don't get very much of this, or of anything but the narrator. Her life in jail is interleaved apparently at random with dreams, fantasies, scenes from childhood, with all sorts of experiences whose only connection seems to be the fact that they all happened to the same person.

The narrator is a fan of [Jean] Genet, and there are signs of his influence in these attempts to achieve an apotheosis through filth and pain.

—Elizabeth Dalton

What holds the material together psychologically, if not literarily, is a pervasive theme of humiliation and shame, involving the girl's obsession with her genitals and with the toilet, which plays a really remarkable role in the book. A great deal of the action takes place near or on the toilet, often before an audience: the novel includes a character who drowns herself in the toilet, a Mass held in a public toilet, even an ode to the toilet.

The spectators in the scenes of public shame link them with the childhood memories of the mother, who was obsessed with the little girl's sexuality, constantly accusing her of "monkeying with herself," inspecting her genitals, and so on. The later fascination with exposure and humiliation suggests an attempt to re-create the experience with the mother, to keep alive the terrible intimacy with her through shame.

There are a number of fantastic elaborations on the excremental and sexual themes. The weirdest of them concerns a specially designed merry-go-round with horses luridly equipped, some for little boys and others for little girls; at the end of this sequence the merry-go-round runs wild and one of the children is raped. In another fantasy, perhaps the coyest and most repulsive of them, a friendly dragon supports the inhabitants of an entire village with the products of his magical metabolism, excreting peanut clusters and lemonade, taffy and marshmallow cream instead of the usual substances. In a later chapter of this fantasy, all these good things undergo a drastic reverse metamorphosis, indicating the narrator's increasing despair, her inability to transform or disguise the painful materials of her experience. At the end of the book, evidently to provide the climax of horror, is a nightmare vision of childbirth in which an old woman pulls a squirming red lump from the heroine's body and then proceeds to eat it.

What is most striking about these episodes, particularly the earlier ones, is their childish character. Locked up in the hopeless lesbian world of the prison, the narrator regresses to fantasy, to an infantile preoccupation with the mother, with food, and with the mysterious openings and functions of her own body. The language of the sexual and scatological passages is often a kind of baby talk, and the sentences have the breathless rhythms and flattened-out syntax of the small child's speech. The vision in *Attic* is that of a sad and quite nasty little girl, staring in fascination at what half frightens and repels her.

It is a stifling, self-enclosed world, and it has the power of its pathology; but the writer fails somehow to find the means in language or structure to a more integrated response than the narrator's own primitive excitement and disgust.

The fantasies are in some sense an attempt to do this, to make art out of life by going life one better, by creating actively in the imagination a horror even more spectacular than what was passively experienced. The narrator is a fan of Genet, and there are signs of his influence in these attempts to achieve an apotheosis through filth and pain. Unfortunately, however, one cannot produce the authentic scent of a *fleur du mal* at will.

In the very extremity of the images there is something effortful and contrived that leaves the reader's emotions quite untouched and makes the fantasies seem ultimately silly and embarrassing rather than macabre. One can't dispute the author's right to her *donnée;* art can be made out of obsession if the obsession is submitted to some ordering principle other than its own. In *Attic,* however, the only principle at work seems to be the monotonous and dreary power of the repetition compulsion. (pp. 32-3)

> Elizabeth Dalton, *"A Great Deal of the Action Takes Place near the Toilet," in* The New York Times Book Review, *June 21, 1970, pp. 32-3.*

John Leonard

Attic refers to the mind of the young girl who tells her story in the first person in Katherine Dunn's first novel. (*Attic* may also refer to Athenian simplicity, purity and refinement, in which case an altogether different interpretation of the novel is in order, perhaps it's a parable about what prisons do to the human spirit.) This attic-mind is cluttered up with so many trunks full of so many traumas that a battalion of psychiatrists with vacuum cleaners couldn't clean it up. The girl to whom the mind belongs remains nameless throughout the book except in one flashback during which her mother shouts "Katherine" at her in anger . . . suggesting one more complication.

Katherine, if that is her name, suffered a mother so terrified of sex, and so zealous in the prosecution of all its tentative forms, that the daughter grows up wanting to be "a male homosexual" to make everything easier. She is, moreover, afraid to go to the bathroom. She runs away from home (in Oregon) and ends up (in Missouri) trying to cash a bad check she received as part of a traveling gang of magazine salesmen. She is thrown into jail, where she remembers, dreams, fantasizes and is brutalized.

Miss Dunn will have to get by on language, which she manipulates superbly, instead of plot, which she mutilates with cruel gleefulness. But she does get by. Her stroboscopic prose is so various, so perception-bending, that the reader must simply swim in it. Thus childhood is suggested by, "When doorknobs were still high and people usually knees . . . " A lawyer is " . . . heavy and comes far out in front of himself so even if our bellies touched his head would be far away . . . His shoes are dark as mirrors and rings on his fat fingers that don't even need to bend any more . . . "

Such swimming in words creates its own sort of credibility. One knows the prison is real; one is ultimately willing to listen to a Genet-like celebration of evil (a form of "purity," that other Attic intruding) and to accept self-criticism ("I've decided that there is no lucidity of vision, only consistency of distortion"). One will even entertain the suggestion of a one-to-one relationship between the young girl and the Mother of Jesus. For a while, anyway, while the language floods the mind.

> John Leonard, *"Sisterhood," in* The New York Times, *July 1, 1970, p. 43.*

William O'Rourke

Attic, . . . a first novel, presents a case of precocity that you can detect by its interesting spots. Miss Dunn uses her own name for her narrator which manufactures that oxymoron, the fictional memoir. A young girl college dropout ("Don't you see I'm gifted! . . . I mean I write poetry and things. . . . This magazine selling is just a joke because I ran away from college") is lost in a "dank and Independence November," locked in the Jackson County, Mo. jail for many months for passing a bad check. Miss Dunn is slumming. She has a knack for withholding and implying, the stuff of dreams. Though *Attic* is written in the first person, it reads like third, so little do we get of herself.

"Miss Dunn" is given the chance to call a lawyer and she calls the time instead. A recorded voice. Hers seems less alive. Very spaced out. While she is selling magazines to indigents in the Ozarks (with a detached heartlessness similar to a member of the Spahn Movie Ranch family) she sees in a hovel a "heart-shaped satin pillow from the greatest show on earth." Advertisement euphemisms replace nouns. A spare-parts imagination. Her scatological musings are as primitive as her cell's plumbing. "I never thought of other people wiping different." In the novel's penultimate sentence she is still worried about flushing a toilet and what for a few pages was interesting observation has long before revealed itself as complete obsession. The only thing she tries to come to grips with is her own carnality. After a dream of "pretending," it "makes me sick to remember in the daylight—shuddering hungry all through me and I lean my face against the cold steel and close my eyes until it goes away." Some of the description has a lewd eagerness to it, but it is pin-up girl forthrightness, eyes staring dumbly into the camera; behind the deadpan there is boastfulness. "I feel trapped in my own history—memory is such an aggressive thing—I have two lives—this still one in the cell where nothing changes and that eats at me—not what happened but what I can remember—there should be somewhere it turns off—" There sure should be; *Attic* is definitely a one-night stand.

> *William O'Rourke, in a review of "Attic," in* The Nation, *New York, Vol. 211, No. 5, August 31, 1970, p. 157.*

Sara Blackburn

Truck takes us inside the head of Jean "Dutch" Gillis, a fifteen-year-old girl from Portland, Oregon, who looks like a boy and wants to be free. It's not that she hates her parents, who are nice but in another world, but she hates high school and its absurd phoniness, and she hates sex roles, and she hates the world that assumes she'll probably grow up and marry a gas station attendant and live desperately ever after, dead like everyone else she knows. Everyone else but Heydorf, for one, her friend and maybe-boyfriend ("They think I'm his kid brother"), who tolerates her because he thinks she's smart, doesn't have to perform sexually with her, and exploits her for her skill at shoplifting and getting money for him. She loves being with Heydorf, and after elaborately scheming (selling cleverly ripped-off goods to an ever-greedy market of buyers), she secretly accumulates the money and provisions to run away and truck down to L.A. to join him, free and on the bum.

> And I'm trucking along with my junk hanging on me and it's too late and I'm glad. I didn't have to worry about going through with it. It's done and I'm free. Now just be careful and it's all open. The world. I'll be king. If they don't catch me first, I'll be king.

Their adventures and survival take up the rest of the novel, which is set mostly on a deserted California beach, before a surprising ending intervenes.

Katherine Dunn, whose first novel was *Attic,* has written a beautiful book here, and an important one. Dutch is funny, sad, and smart, but, as she is presented, in her own stream-of-consciousness perceptions about her life and the trip she takes, she is insistently, almost overwhelmingly, real. It is probably too much to hope that parents frozen into losing wars with their teen-aged kids will read this novel, but they'd do well to do so. Because what it charts, and with enormous skill and authenticity, is the desperation of being young and treated as a non-person in a frightened, locked-in society threatened beyond measure by the idea of real freedom; the terribly few alternatives that are available to make that freedom real; and the tough road of maintaining it, along with the ease with which security can be peddled as happiness. And though Dutch is unique, her story is a modern classic, not only because of how well Katherine Dunn knows her and conveys her, but because what Dutch says about how she feels and what she wants—and what she refuses to want—comprises an inside story about the people who are kids today in America.

> *Sara Blackburn, "The Threat of Freedom," in* Book World—The Washington Post, *August 15, 1971, p. 2.*

The New Yorker

Huck Finn's busy ghost [in *Truck*] invests a fifteen-year-old Oregon girl named Dutch Gillis. Dutch, who does not narrate in a vernacular so much as in a kind of typewriter solipsism, is supposed to look physically like a nine-year-old boy and to have an aversion to all but the basest reality. There being nothing baser than her cloddish friend Heydorf, she runs away with him to a deserted California beach. Here, strangely, the novel comes alive, and a convincing reckoning ensues. This book dwells constantly on much of all kinds, but Miss Dunn seems to enjoy messing in it.

> *A review of "Truck," in* The New Yorker, *Vol. XLVII, No. 32, September 25, 1971, p. 140.*

Sonja Bolle

One has only to open Katherine Dunn's new book, *Geek Love* . . . to know that somewhere in this lady's background there was a storyteller extraordinaire.

"My mother is Irish," Dunn tells [Sonja Bolle]. "And she couldn't come back from the grocery store without telling a story. She did all the voices, and acted it all out. She painted a bit, too, though she had to use whatever was around as a canvas. Whatever she did, she was always an artist. She used to tell me that man differs from animals in that he makes something. And if you're going to make something, she said, why not make it beautiful?"

Publishers Weekly's review called *Geek Love* (or The Geek, as Dunn affectionately calls her creation) "terrifying," "shocking" and "bizarre." It is all of these. And it's not just garden-variety repulsion. The terror induced by the characters in the traveling carnival, Binewski's Fabulon, is of the wake-up-in-the-middle-of-the-night-screaming variety.

How does Dunn square the horror and the beauty? "I've been accused all my life of being preoccupied with the bizarre, the macabre, the violent," she admits. "But they are actual parts of the world I see. The writers I like most tend to confront the aspect of life they're dealing with," she adds, citing Gabriel García Márquez and Günter Grass.

"The things most destructive to you are the things you must confront," she explains. "Otherwise, they'll come up on you with a two-by-four and whack you over the head when you're not looking."

Dunn recalls her horror and fascination with two events that had enormous emotional impact on her. "When I was about five years old, I came across a *Life* magazine with photos from the concentration camps. Those pictures were scarred into my corneas and they'll be there till I croak. My thought was, *I'll* be a victim. My mother, my brothers, we're all in danger. Later that turned into a defensive fury: Why didn't they fight back? Then later still, you discover that you're no longer just aware of the victim's point of view; you discover in yourself the capacity to be the perpetrator as well."

The second event was the Jonestown mass suicide. She was waitressing in Portland, and one of her customers came in with the newspaper. "I was a grown woman with a seven-year-old son," she recalls, "and I could see a mother squirting poison down her child's throat." These images, she says, "will come at me again and again if I don't confront them." So she writes.

Although Dunn reads widely and spins theories on literature, art and culture, she calls her background "standard American blue collar of the itchy-footed variety." She begins her life story with a typically epic flourish: "I was born on the day the U.N. treaty was signed—October 24, 1945."

Dunn's family worked as sharecroppers and migrant farm workers. Growing up without roots, she says, left her with an identity as an outsider, a self-image that she considered both abhorrent and fascinating. "We would come into town, the whole lot of us in the De Soto with a mattress tied on top, and people would look at us askance. We knew they were right to watch us carefully to make sure we wouldn't steal anything, because we had no investment in that community. And they knew we didn't care."

Dunn calls her family's roving a "standard Western American life," particularly common in the period after the war. "It wasn't bad. I don't want to give the impression it was an unusually hard life." Her mother kept things going. "That woman," Dunn says, "could make pie out of two saltines and a raisin, and frequently she did."

The desire to write came early for Dunn. "I always knew and I always told everyone"—she says in a small, so-there! little girl's voice—" 'I'm going to be a writer.' That, of course, in between being a trapeze artist and a cowboy and an anthropologist and a marine biologist. But I always thought that all those other ambitions were in service to writing."

When Dunn was 13, the family settled in Tigard, Ore. Her stepfather pumped gas, and eventually saved enough to buy his own gas station. From then on, hers was a "pretty regular" life. She was the only one of her siblings who graduated from high school—her brothers saw to it. But her wild streak prevented Dunn from being a model student.

One of her less savory adventures, soon after her 18th birthday, landed her in jail in Independence, Mo., for cashing a bad check. The experience persuaded her to do something constructive, so she returned to Oregon and enrolled in Portland State University, transferring, after a year, to Reed College, where she won a writing grant. Cash in hand, she took off to travel with her boyfriend. "I didn't sit down to write, of course, until I'd run out of money."

In a Boston rooming house "on the wrong side of Beacon Hill," Dunn wrote her first book (*Attic*) in the same dismal room that her heroine would inhabit almost 20 years later in *Geek Love.* She worked three jobs, going off in the same dress every day, "because it was all that I had." In the mornings, she read proofs at a typesetter's. Her afternoons were spent as companion to an invalid. "She was paralyzed, but she was a very witty woman," Dunn recalls. "My job was to entice her to eat by making her orna-mental snacks. She loved to discuss literature, and I learned a lot from her."

That stint finished,

> I would race home and watch Bobby Kennedy progressing across the country on TV. Then I went off to an assembly line at a candy factory. I was a Sugar Daddy wrapper. I always had a notebook with me, and every time I had a break, I would scribble a few lines. The factory was great, because I didn't have to think or respond to people. I thought out a lot of the scenes there, and I did a lot of writing in the restroom.

Her boyfriend turned out to be the line to a publisher. His mother knew Charlotte Zolotow, the children's book editor at Harper & Row, who was persuaded to have a look at the manuscript, and then passed it on to Harper & Row editor David Segal. Meanwhile, Dunn had been saving money so that she and her boyfriend could go to Europe. "I was getting impatient to leave, so I called up the guy in the fiction department, and told him: 'I handed in my manuscript two weeks ago, and I haven't heard from you. I'm leaving the country. I need an answer.' And he said, 'I want to publish it.' " That was the end of the 1960s, and "publishers were having one of those 'my author is younger than your author' competitions," Dunn says modestly. "So I think they were delighted to find someone who was willing to turn in 200 pages of seemingly connected language."

Upon the publication of *Attic* in 1969, Dunn underwent her first author interview—with disastrous results. The article appeared in *Life* magazine on her birthday. "I had just gotten a job as a bill collector with the phone company by lying to them about my work history," recalls Dunn.

> I said I'd been a governess on a farm in North Dakota for the past six years. When the magazine came out, I went in to work feeling pretty cock-a-hoop, and someone said, 'The boss wants to see you.' I went into his office, and there's the boss, sitting behind an acre of oak with a gas-chamber green carpet, and nothing on the desk but *Life* magazine open to the story about me, including the felony conviction. He's just tapping the desk with a pencil. He fired me, and I went back to my little hotel room. The funny thing is, I think he felt sorry for me because I couldn't have a career with the phone company.

She sold her second novel, *Truck,* to Harper & Row on the strength of a thumbnail sketch, and left for Europe (with the same boyfriend) to live on the advance. *Truck,* published in 1970, was written in a barn on the island of Karpathos in Greece. Then she became pregnant, and they decided to go to Ireland to have the baby.

"It was in Dublin that I had my revelation that I didn't know how to write," she recalls. She gave herself 10 years to learn, and began to study grammar books and to set herself all sorts of laborious exercises in Latinates and Anglo-Saxon roots.

Eventually she found her way back to Portland, where she did a lot of "hash-slinging and booze-slinging" to support herself and her son, Eli. For a time, she was the voice of

Red Ryder, a popular children's cartoon character, on a Saturday morning radio program in Portland called *Gremlin Time.* Red Ryder read aloud—everything from Kafka to Raymond Chandler, Lewis Carroll to Ray Bradbury. "I still run into people who say, 'That voice . . . I know that voice . . . you were Red Ryder on the radio.' "

In 1979, Dunn discovered boxing; she was instantly hooked when she saw her first fight. She now writes regularly on boxing, as an AP correspondent and columnist for a black community newspaper. She also contributes a weekly column to Portland's alternative newspaper, answering questions from readers on "any subject except cooking."

For 10 years, however, she was writing short stories and novels that never left the drawer. Then one day, on one of her customary marathon walks to the experimental rose garden above Portland, *Geek Love* was born, out of a fit of anger at her son. "I'd been keeping up on genetic research, and I was sitting there thinking I could have designed a better kid. I had a sudden vision of designer kids with little Calvin Klein labels on the napes of their necks."

What she had learned in the hiatus years was the rewrite. "In the old days, first draft was what went out. I thought rewriting meant copying it over in a clearer hand," she says. "But by now, I had learned to separate the writing process into two sections, two totally separate states of mind. The first is absolutely automatic writing, with no concern for structure, or flow, or style . . . and then," she says, pinching her lips and glaring over her spectacles, becoming the Grammarian from the Black Lagoon, "Miss Grundy comes along in the second installment." She goes back to being the lady journalist behind the big, fashionable glasses. "And that's a very long, involved process."

On the day [Sonja Bolle] meets her, Dunn has just received word from her agent, Richard Pine, that Knopf has agreed to buy her next novel. Pointing out the window toward the Willamette River, she says, "My next book takes place under that bridge." Set in the boxing world, the book has already prompted one columnist to dub her "Jane Austen in boxer trunks." It concerns a serial murderer, and is titled *The Cut Man.* In boxing terminology, the "cut man" is responsible for stopping a boxer's cuts from bleeding in between rounds; he is regarded almost as a sorcerer.

Dunn terms her interest in violence "purely professional." She actually thinks of herself as an inveterate romantic. "I have little affinity for Percy Bysshe and the boys. I mean, the standard definition of a romantic is someone who looks at donkey shit and sees fairy castles. But my definition is when you look at that donkey shit and truly see it—with the maggots, the smell, the globular forms—when you know it truly for what it is and find it beautiful—that's a romantic."

Dunn maintains, however, that hers is not a grim view. "I think of what I write as life affirming," she says. "It's a peek over the edge, but it's worth it." (pp. 66-7)

Sonja Bolle, "Katherine Dunn," in Publishers Weekly, *Vol. 236, No. 9, March 10, 1989, pp. 66-7.*

Stephen Dobyns

One of writing's many pleasures comes from seeing just how much you can get away with. How Kafka must have guffawed when he hit upon the idea of transforming Gregor Samsa into a gigantic insect. Similarly, Katherine Dunn must have experienced a happy moment when she decided to have her novel narrated by a bald albino hunchback dwarf by the name of Olympia Binewski, later known as McGurk.

The difference, perhaps, is that it is necessary that Gregor Samsa be changed into a bug: it is integral to the story. This is not so clear in the case of Ms. Dunn, who is the author of two earlier novels, *Attic* and *Truck.* When the extravagance is not integral, then it functions as spectacle. In *Geek Love* there is a lot of spectacle.

The book centers around Binewski's Fabulon, a carnival run by Aloysius Binewski and his wife, Crystal Lil, whose attractions include their own children, born as freaks owing to their parents' careful experimentation "with illicit and prescription drugs, insecticides, and eventually radioisotopes." Remember, this is basically a comic novel about love, betrayal and power.

First to be born is Arturo, or Aqua Boy, who has flippers instead of arms and legs. Next are the beautiful Siamese twins Electra and Iphigenia: two bodies above the waist, one body below. Next is the narrator, the hunchback dwarf Olympia.

> I was born three years after my sisters. My father spared no expense in these experiments. My mother had been liberally dosed with cocaine, amphetamines, and arsenic during her ovulation and throughout her pregnancy with me. It was a disappointment when I emerged with such commonplace deformities.

The youngest is Fortunato, nicknamed Chick. Although he looks like a "norm," Chick has amazing telekinetic powers which prove him to be his parents' masterpiece. Finally come the failures, the freaks who didn't make it and are preserved in alcohol in a 50-foot trailer called the Chute, which the curious can visit for a buck. These include Janus, perfect apart from a second head emerging from the base of his spine, and the Lizard Girl, who is green and has a long tail. "We had such hopes for her," Crystal Lil sighs. Janus died at birth, but the Lizard Girl died mysteriously at 7 months.

And this becomes the rub. Arturo or Aqua Boy or Arty wants to be boss freak. He killed the Lizard Girl and others as well. He is smart and cruel and he takes over the show. Arturo has great charismatic powers and eventually he creates a religious cult whose thousands of followers are not freaks. And so Arturo, with the help of a sinister nurse and the telekinetic powers of his little brother, obliges them. For a fee of course. At first the faithful—called Arturans or "the Admitted"—lose their fingers and toes, then bits of their arms and legs, then all their limbs and at last they are lobotomized in one of Arturo's rest homes.

The trouble is that Arturo cannot stand to share the limelight. He is jealous of the Siamese twins' musical act. He is jealous of his little brother. And so he manipulates and bullies and even murders to maintain his power.

> That geekiness—the comic exploration of the peculiar as an end in itself—is what gives *Geek Love* its main success: that and Ms. Dunn's tremendous imagination.
>
> —*Stephen Dobyns*

The story is told some years after it happens, when everyone is dead except the narrator and Crystal Lil, who live in a rooming house in Portland, Ore. Also in the rooming house is Olympia's daughter, Miranda, fathered by her own Uncle Arturo. An art student, Miranda was raised in an orphanage and has no idea that Olympia is her mother. She is beautiful, talented and perfect except for a scrawny tail that makes her the hit of the topless bar, the Glass House, where she works as a stripper.

Unfortunately, Miranda has attracted the attention of the peculiar Mary Lick, an immensely rich and oversized lady whose passion is to seek out beautiful, talented women and persuade them with large sums of money to become ugly, so ugly that men will leave them alone, which allows them to develop their intellectual and creative potential and achieve fulfilling, albeit celibate, lives. Mary Lick then spends her evenings watching the films of these uglifying operations and has a rollicking time.

Well, this is a pretty big piece of machinery to set in motion: twin plots galloping toward conclusions the reader knows will have to be violent, not to say cataclysmic. Along the way are dozens of peculiar characters, complicated passions and antipathies, buckets of jokes, a hugely imagined world that often seems to be propelled forward like a boulder rolling down a hill. And of course there are the geeks, those happy people who earn their livings by biting the heads off chickens. Late in the book the twins give birth to a monster baby, a 26-pound boy by the name of Mumpo who sets about trying to devour his mothers. Ms. Dunn's relationship with her novel partly resembles the twins' relationship with Mumpo. One wonders who's boss.

This takes us back to our original question. It is necessary that Gregor Samsa be changed into a bug, but is it necessary that all these people be freaks, geeks and apparent escapees from old Dick Tracy comic strips? The plot, once the spectacle is stripped away, is fairly conventional; while the characters, once free of their humps, fins, tails and general geekiness, tend toward specific types. The language, although wonderfully descriptive, is tied to the linguistic limitations of the narrator and is not interesting by itself. Nor is there much philosophizing about the nature of beauty and what it is to be a freak. There are attempts in that direction, but this is a big hungry plot and it needs

to be fed constantly with extravagant events that are gobbled up like so many salted nuts.

Without the spectacle, the novel is undistinguished, but that spectacle becomes part of the novel's reason for being. America's sentimental attachment to geeks is the dark side of its sentimental attachment to Mom and apple pie. That geekiness—the comic exploration of the peculiar as an end in itself—is what gives *Geek Love* its main success: that and Ms. Dunn's tremendous imagination. But the novel's sprawling quality is not an asset. The book is too long and too much exists for its own sake. It is not heartening to see a novelist pushed around by her own book. She needed to slap it back, put a gun to its head, make it walk a straight line, make it go on a diet. (pp. 11-12)

> Stephen Dobyns, "Hoping for Something Worse," in The New York Times Book Review, *April 2, 1989, pp. 11-12.*

James Idema

Near the end of Tod Browning's movie *Freaks* (1932), a band of sideshow pinheads, dwarfs and limbless torsos wreak vengeance on a normal woman who has betrayed one of them. The scene is a grotesque nightmare. A somewhat similar scene brings Katharine Dunn's unrelentingly bizarre new novel to a climax, although it is preceded in *Geek Love* by so many other grotesque moments that by then some readers may be more relieved than horrified.

Strictly defined, geeks are carnival performers who bite the heads off chickens. The book has some of these, but the title obviously refers to the more generic usage: Geeks are freaks of all kinds.

The viewpoints of *Freaks* and this novel at first seem opposed. Where the film exploited images of physical deformity for their potential to shock the audience, the novel immerses the reader in the lives of abnormal people in order to call into question concepts of who and what is normal.

In the book, freaks see themselves as "special" people. They rejoice in their specialness and are contemptuous of "norms." Nevertheless, what drew viewers to the movie is what surely will attract readers to the book: the undeniable fascination of freaks.

Those same readers, however, may balk at the novel's outrageous premise. Its narrator is a bald, albino, hunchback dwarf named Olympia Binewski. Meet the Binewskis and read how they grew.

Some years back, Al Binewski recognized the age-old appeal of human deformity when he hit upon his plan to revive Binewski's Carnival Fabulon, a traveling circus that had seen better days.

> The show was burdened with an aging lion that repeatedly broke expensive dentures by gnawing the bars of his cage; demands for cost-of-living increases from the fat lady, whose food supply was written into her contract; and the midnight defection of an entire family of animal eroticists,

taking their donkey, goat, and Great Dane with them.

Al's plan was based on sound marketing strategy. It would give the people what they wanted. Al would breed his own freak show.

In his bride, Lil, an aerialist who had been forced to give up her career after a fall, Al had a willing and eager partner. Both were of old Yankee stock, self-determination and independence ingrained in their makeup and financial security high on their list of life objectives.

" 'What greater gift could you offer your children than an inherent ability to earn a living just by being themselves,' Lil often said."

To achieve their goal, the resourceful pair experimented with prescription and illicit drugs, insecticides and eventually radioisotopes. And in a few years they produced, in fairly close order, a boy born with flippers instead of arms and legs; Siamese twin girls, joined at the waist and sharing one set of hips and legs; the dwarf girl, Olympia, and a boy—who at first appears normal, to everyone's disappointment, but then turns out to be telekinetic.

In varying degrees, the children all had their roles in bringing in the carnival's paying customers. Electra and Iphigenia, the Siamese twins, played four-handed piano. Olympia was a barker for the show. And for just an extra dollar the curious could ogle the results of unsuccessful experiments, six of which floated in formaldehyde in a special exhibition, the Binewski family shrine. Leona, "The Lizard Girl," her tail "as thick as a leg where it sprouted from her spine," and two-headed Janus, with his "four sets of miniscule eyelashes," were particular favorites.

Readers tempted to bail out after this cozy nuclear family is introduced are urged to persevere. Once under way, Olympia's narration will keep you turning the pages. Like all good yarns, it advances energetically and with vivid imagery. You may shake your head at appalling revelations, but you'll find yourself laughing, too, because part of this ghastly story's pleasure is in the narrative voice itself: its unflappable, ironic, at times farcical tone and its determinedly unliterary and casually ribald style. Yet while that voice mocks conventional values and attitudes, it reveals here and there the narrator's sensitivity to the fact that she is not just a freak but a freak by design.

But Olympia harbors little resentment about her extraordinary plight. In fact, she wishes she were even more special. Maybe two heads, she muses, or a tail. "My father and mother designed me this way," she explains. "They achieved greater originality in some of their other projects." And she loves her family, especially her older brother, known as Arturo the Aqua Boy.

Arty, as his family called him, graduated quickly from mere performer—as a tike he swam naked in a huge aquarium and made fish eyes at the crowd—to the carnival's star attraction, before he discovered he had evangelical powers. People were drawn to him, wanted to be like him, and a grisly cult called Arturism swept the country.

"I get glimpses of the horrors of normalcy," said Arty to an inquiring journalist. "Each of these innocents on the streets is engulfed by a terror of their own ordinariness. They would do anything to be unique."

What some thousands of them did was submit—for large fees—to the gradual removal of their limbs by the carnival's resident surgeon, starting with the fingers and toes. Known variously as the Blessed or the Admitted, they lived in various stages of amputation in a special compound, separated from the carnival camp by an electric fence and manned sentry posts. At least they were done with the horrors of normalcy.

Olympia's narration moves in two time-frames. In the first, the Binewski family saga unfolds in lengthy flashbacks that gradually explain Olympia's immediate crisis, which is dealt with in the second time-frame, the here and now. This involves her daughter, Miranda, who was born with the tail her mother never had.

Now a beautiful young woman, Miranda must be rescued from a fate worse than death. She is being stalked by a Miss Lick, who embodies the ultimate evil of normals. Miss Lick wants to help deformed people become normal, to find happiness through—irony of ironies—surgery.

No fair revealing how this perverse but riveting story plays out, except to warn that the ending seems as gruesome as the novelist could make it. Whether *Geek Love* succeeds as the dark allegory on the human condition the author obviously intends will depend on whether readers tolerate the horrors she limns so matter-of-factly. (pp. 7, 11)

> *James Idema, "A Disturbing, Freakish Novel on the 'Joys' of Deformity," in* Chicago Tribune—Books, *April 9, 1989, pp. 7, 11.*

Donna Minkowitz

Al and Lil are impresario parents. Because middle-class family values are what they hold dear, they get the brilliant idea of breeding their own capital: wildly deformed, carnival-attraction children who give a refreshing new meaning to the phrase "nest egg." Arty has no arms and legs, but crowds go crazy for his flippers. Iphy and Elly (Iphigenia and Electra) are Siamese twins who play the piano with the two hands they have between them. Olympia, the narrator, is a hunchbacked, albino dwarf. As my mother might have said, what's not to like? The children earn their own upkeep and more besides.

In Katherine Dunn's *Geek Love,* these parent entrepreneurs produce the children they want by "experimenting with illicit and prescription drugs, insecticides, and eventually radioisotopes." When Lil gives birth to kids who just don't make it in the special-effects department, they get abandoned or worse. Apple's only deformity was mental retardation (not enough of a crowd-pleaser), so Lil preserved her in formaldehyde along with the stillborns. The child died mysteriously when "a pillow fell on her face," and her surviving siblings strongly suspect Al. Chick, another baby born without apparent physical abnormalities, was about to be left behind in a gas station when his parents realized he had marketable telekinetic skills.

As if origins like these weren't enough to make a child feel like a worthless piece of unlovable dogshit, Olympia and Chick are relentlessly schooled in their own deficiencies by older brother Arty, who succeeds in getting the affection-starved pair to hate themselves as much as they love him. Chick cuts up the meat for Arty's sandwiches telekinetically, even though it makes him sick because he can hear the dead cow "talk to him about it . . . as he slices her." Arty requires this sacrifice from his five-year-old "slave-dog" because he likes to feel that people will go the distance for him. Oly becomes Arty's accomplice in the rape and forced childbearing of her sisters (big brother has Chick use his powers to prevent an abortion) because Arty's made her feel she's such a useless scuzzball she's beyond redemption.

In short, *Geek Love* is a merciless satire on the family and the atrocities committed in its name. I've hardly ever read a more enjoyable family narrative. Unfortunately, the nuclear family isn't all Dunn's interested in bashing. Her caricature of a murderously antimale, anti-pleasure lesbian demonstrates how satire can also serve the status quo. Olympia, who is straight, has an opportunity to learn moral courage for the first time in her life by resisting the bloodthirsty Miss Lick, who is threatening the rambunctious heterosexuality of her daughter.

Lick, a frozen-dinner heiress, pays beautiful gals incredible sums of money to become hideous-looking through surgery, so that men won't put their things in them. In some cases her arrangements make penetration literally impossible: Jessica H. gets her vagina "closed" and her clitoris and breasts removed, but the girl is still so beautiful that "if I could think of a way to seal her asshole, I'd do it. And maybe stitch her mouth shut and feed her with a tube going in under her chin." Lick reasons that "if I let her walk from her room to the can, three men would climb out of the light sockets on the way and find holes in her to cram their dicks into." With invisible cameras, Lick shoots before, during, and after shots of the women's disfigurement, so she can drool over the footage on home video. It's not just a cheap thrill: she thinks a ban on fucking is essential for women's emancipation.

Now, I agree that political crusades against penetration (or other forms of consensual sex) should be opposed with vehemence and even mockery, but using this bugbear to characterize the only lesbian (and only feminist) in the book is like casting the only nonwhite person in a novel as an evil African obsessed with performing clitoridectomies.

In a book in which the main theme is deliberate disfigurement, Dunn portrays lesbianism as a birth defect that makes its bearers psychopaths. Supposedly disabled by her lust for girls, Miss Lick desires nothing more intensely than to disable others. To close off their bodies from experiencing too much pleasure from penises, yet! (A well-known preoccupation of lesbians.) For all the wit and chutzpah with which Dunn savages the nuclear family, for all the attention she devotes to freaks, *Geek Love* is ultimately on the side of normalcy, meaning "normal" bodies and "normal" desires. The psychotic, literally killjoy lesbian is eventually burnt to death by Oly. At a time when les-

bians and gay men are getting assaulted (and even slain) with record frequency on the streets of New York and Portland, Oregon (Dunn's city), it's hard to find this humorous, even though other parts of her erratically subversive novel made me howl with glee. Why couldn't she have stuck to really funny things—like, for instance, the notion that male-dominated, rod-happy families are just what America's benighted children need? (pp. 50-1)

Donna Minkowitz, "Freak Show," in The Village Voice, *Vol. 34, No. 17, April 25, 1989, pp. 50-1.*

Faren Miller

Geek Love by Katherine Dunn has a lurid black on orange cover, an unsettling title, and an even more unsettling subject: a carnival family that breeds its own freaks. Repellent? Disgusting? Remarkably, it is not. Or rather, the grotesque material becomes both beautiful and moving in the hands of a talented writer. Dunn might be describing her own motivations as a writer when she has the narrator's daughter, a medical artist, present her reason for wishing to draw a naked dwarf:

> The first year I went to LoPrinzi's gym and did a series on a body builder. Technical, illustrative, and predictable. Last year I went to the medical school and did a flayed, emaciated cadaver. Classic and totally predictable. I've got to show more than a technician's skills this time. I've got to rock them. I've got to yank their hearts out.

Unbeknownst to the artist Miranda, the albino hunchback dwarf she will draw is her own mother. The story of Olympia Binewski's secret maternal love and her daughter's strange peril frames the equally perverse, magnificent, funny, and tender chronicle of the Binewski Fabulon freak show, its rise and fall.

Normal standards and behavior turn inside-out in the Binewski *menage.* In a scene much quoted by reviewers, the family nearly rejects a new, apparently normal baby, until newborn Fortunato displays his own weird talent.

Olympia herself, not considered freakish enough to be one of the Fabulon's pampered main attractions, is the loving heart of the book. Love may not keep the Fabulon from disaster, but it does transform the material of lurid horror into something far rarer. Horror fans should not expect the standard thrills and chills of the genre; non-fans should set aside their instinctual repulsion long enough to read a chapter or two—and be hooked by Dunn's audacious power. (pp. 15, 17)

Faren Miller, in a review of "Geek Love," in Locus, *Vol. 22, No. 6, June, 1989, pp. 15, 17, 56.*

Matthew Giunti

To readers starved for a serious novel unafraid of using plot's full range of devices, *Geek Love* will be solace and revelation. The story begins as the five Binewski children,

My characters' stories are exactly the same as everyone else's. . . . [*Geek Love* is] essentially any family's story. Every one of us is walking around with a hunchback albino dwarf somewhere inside. . . . Too often people know their hunchback, but they never become fond of it. If you step into my book, maybe you can recognize something, see part of your own life from a different angle. The book works if it helps shed clichés about who we are and how we live.

—*Katherine Dunn, in* **People Weekly,** *April 17, 1989.*

Arty, Elly, Iphy, Olympia and Baby Chick, gather around Papa Al to hear a revered family tale of their parents' courtship. Mama Crystal Lil interrupts and editorializes as she knits. It's as cozy a tableau of American family life as a Rockwell magazine cover—only Papa's story is about how Mama became the geek in his traveling carnival, and all five children are carnival freaks.

Trumpeted by Knopf as this season's fiction "sleeper," Dunn's book doesn't disappoint as a "ripping good yarn." Dunn—a virtual unknown who published two novels in the late '60s—is a writer of prodigious narrative gifts and bottomless invention. Her tale of the rise and fall of a family of freaks is fascinating and repellent, funny and touching, charming and tasteless, realistic and ridiculous, but never dull. (p. 664)

The book is already being compared to Kafka's *Metamorphosis,* and given Dunn's ability to engage the reader in an outlandish situation through sensual evocation and sheer imaginative conviction, the comparison is apt. But a better antecedent is Nathanael West's *Day of the Locust.* West was equally interested in surface grotesquerie, although his perspective was that of the empty masses who might flock to Hollywood or Arturism. Dunn takes the insider's view—what West's walking wounded were running toward. But in place of the surreality found in Kafka or West, Dunn substitutes a relentless logic. She'll begin with a preposterous conceit and work out its mundane, practical details to a startling degree, until you find yourself saying, Yes, this is *exactly* what it would be like to have flippers instead of limbs, or to be a Siamese twin, or to train a powerfully telekinetic infant.

At the same time, Dunn has an instinct for those experiences that are universal, for the aspects of human existence that have to be endured or mastered whether one is a hunchbacked, albino, dwarf or normal child. Discovering the fallibility of one's parents or suffering the indignities of puberty makes geeks of us all. The first half of the book, in which Dunn establishes the world of her Fabulon in Olympia's elegiac and ironic tones, is her triumph: alternately clear-eyed and fanciful, precise and hyperbolic.

But the book's strong point is also its downfall; as the plot's momentum builds, all of Dunn's energy is spent stoking the engine of her outlandish tale. Murder follows mutilation, and incident after incident is paraded across the page, each one more outrageous than the last. One is forced to ask, what does it all mean, anyway? Are Al's efforts to "design" his family a monstrous satire on present-day obsessions with programming children for the fast track? Is freakishness a metaphor for a celebrity-mad culture in which it is possible to be famous just for being famous? Is the type of self-mutilation engaged in by the Arturans a comment on contemporary cults like Jonestown? Does the novel mean any of these things, or anything at all?

The book does seem to make a statement about learning to accept oneself warts and all, about the liberating qualities of daring to be different and the awful price of unquestioning conformity. Dunn has stated, "Every one of us is walking around with an albino dwarf somewhere inside. . . . Too often people know their hunchback, but they never become fond of it." But for a book built on the premise that freakishness has its own beauty, Dunn still gets a lot of mileage out of lingering descriptions of physical deformity, mutilation and various grotesqueries. An occasional reflection on the value of physical beauty in a superficial society might have helped clear Dunn of charges that she wants to have it both ways: one hand beckons us to gape at her assembled monstrosities, while the other one wags a finger at our queasy fascination. (pp. 664-65)

Matthew Giunti, in a review of "Geek Love," in The Christian Century, *Vol. 106, No. 21, July 5-12, 1989, pp. 664-65.*

Roz Kaveney

Sometimes, overwriting is necessary: Katherine Dunn's tendency to the purple and the dandyish, her dealing out to her characters of idiolects involving lovers'-knots of syntax, is the only correlative which could get us past the superficially genial nightmare of her plot [in *Geek Love*]— we are so busy disapproving of stylistic excess that we are lulled into accepting her redefinition of the boundaries of taste. There is an implicit parallel between this set of priorities and that which makes us more capable of taking for granted the grossest of moral deformities, while straining at even minor physical variations from an assumed norm; here, too, Dunn is engaged in tricking us into a stock response, and then mocking us as crass gawkers.

This is a novel in which ordinary people are seen on the other side of the bars. The Binewskis are a family of dedicated circus performers—dedicated from before birth. Their mother Lil was in her time the most stylish of geeks, that is to say, the pseudo-savage or pseudo-lunatic who bites off the heads of chickens; she moved on to taking chemicals when pregnant in the hope of having profitably deformed children. This appalling idea is only the throwaway premiss of a novel which takes us through the interacting lives of the limbless and megalomaniac Arturo, the bitchy, piano-playing Siamese twins and high-class whores, Electra and Iphigenia, the psychokinetic Fortunato, and Olympia, the rather too sweet-natured hunchbacked albino dwarf heroine and narrator.

Most of the main body of the novel concerns the murderous jealousies of these five, avid for each other's attention and the love of their rather bland parents; a rather too extended subplot details the religious cult of surgically acquired limblessness which Arturo starts out of a mixture of greed and vindictive spite. Dunn works out a set of horridly witty *grand guignol* variations which continue marginally past the point where we cease to be fascinated and repelled by them and move through acceptance to mere jadedness. When almost everything goes up in smoke, we do not weep long over the ashes.

This applies to an even greater extent to the framing narrative, in which a slightly older Olympia keeps benevolent watch over her unknowing artist-daughter Miranda, beautiful in possession of a long tail. Miranda has become the potential prey of the sinister, asexual tycoon Miss Lick, who, partly through a perversion of feminism, mostly as an exercise of power, pays intelligent women fortunes to deprive themselves of the attributes which make them attractive to men. Olympia's intervention is predictable: after her brother's exploration of this sort of thing, she has had enough.

So, alas, by this stage have we. To tell essentially the same story twice is not so much to risk as to g·arantee diminishing returns; Miranda is nowhere near as vulnerable or attractive a character as her doomed aunts, and the process by which an older and wiser Olympia wins the trust of Miss Lick is too cold-blooded to be as interesting as her attempts to moderate the viciousness of the brother she selflessly loves.

It is not entirely clear, then, that this book's accomplishment, as opposed to its ambitions, entirely justifies its treatment of human pain as a literary game; if you take these risks, your failure is more likely to be censured. There is a mordant wit to most of the scenes and situations which is in the end rather more likely to be the road forward for Katherine Dunn than her exploitation of distress; she is too darkly funny to stay content with this slightly long-winded video nasty.

> *Roz Kaveney, "Grossed Out," in* The Times Literary Supplement, *No. 4510, September 8, 1989, p. 968.*

Carl Solomon

When I first noticed advance copies of [*Geek Love*] in bookstores, I thought it said "Greek Love" and assumed it was the usual folderol about pederasty. A closer look made me think back to 1940 and Tyrone Power playing the carnival geek in *Nightmare Alley*. This is closer. This is a fully realized masterpiece about geeks and freaks: the ultimate carnival novel, but updated beyond all other cultural material on its subject. Let the Grand Old Lady of this carny group explain the basic theme:

> Mama often said that fat folks went out of style because every tenth ass on the street now was

wider than the one in the tent. Folks could see it free on any block. Giants were also out of work owing, according to Mama, to basketball and the drugs they fed to babies to make them tall enough to play the game.

> It goes in streaks. But some things never go out of fashion. Hunger artists, fat folks, giants, and dog acts come and go but *real* freaks never lose their appeal.

The blood and gore exploited herein stamps this work at least as a *Titus Andronicus* of horror and shock. Its use of the modern cult theme evokes memories of the real Jonestown and the fiction of John Irving and beyond. It has already been called by one reviewer "a snuff film made legitimate by a reputable publishing house."

It assumes the form of a chronicle of her family's history by "Olympia Binewski McGurk," a bald, albino, hunchbacked dwarf and is, if nothing else, a cultural landmark. Cultural history is irreversible, and this novel, compared by Knopf to *Frankenstein* is another step down the path that the modern novel must traverse.

On its own terms, though, within its world of armless, flippered, telekinetic characters (Arty, the Aqua Boy; Miranda with a vestigial tail, etc.) it tells its tale of love, anguish, and pathos much as a "normal" novel (a novel about "normals") does and carries the reader along to a smash climax at a frantic pace—a firestorm destroying most of the bedeviled freaks. The symbol of its oddity is illustrated in the book's colophon: the usual Knopf greyhound, but here shown with a fifth leg.

The author's biography seems part of the package: the child of a chronic runaway and a migrant worker, she is boxing correspondent for Associated Press and has served time for passing a bad check.

A valid point of criticism, however, could be made of the novel's Irvingesque striving after bizarre shock effects and the concomitant sacrifice of any serious or compassionate treatment of its subject: freaks. They are undoubtedly worthy of such treatment, but Dunn's unfeeling, surreal approach is more traditional in twentieth-century American fiction.

Part of the "fun," of course, arises from accommodating sexual passion to the complexities of physical abnormality and disfigurement. Prosthetic problems involving amputees of various kinds with Siamese twins, and hints of worse. Also conception produced by telekinetic concentration. These pages constitute an unprecedented parade of oddity and horror.

Sadistic sequences involve, for example, the amputation of all four of a horse's feet. I can't recall an author lopping off limbs with greater gusto since Nathanael West in *A Cool Million*. I can't recall sadder characters since those in Andy Warhol's movie, *Trash*.

> *Carl Solomon, "Sad Characters," in* The American Book Review, *Vol. 11, No. 6, January-February, 1990, p. 28.*

FURTHER READING

Hayles, N. Katherine. "Postmodern Parataxis: Embodied Texts, Weightless Information." *American Literary History* 2, No. 3 (Fall 1990): 394-421.

> Dense analysis of similarities between postmodern liter-ature and genetic engineering, exploring "the resonances that develop between the registers of natural language, molecular language, and cultural context." Hayles as-serts: "*Geek Love,* starting from the abnormal, uses the gritty specificities of deformed bodies to constitute a nar-rative that brings pressure to bear on the presuppositions of normality."

Koenis, Rhoda. Review of *Geek Love,* by Katherine Dunn. *New York* 22, No. 12 (20 March 1989): 82-3.

Brief negative appraisal in which the critic states that *Geek Love* is the only book "I have walked out on" and relegates it "to connoisseurs of pathology."

Stone, Gene. "Novelist Katherine Dunn Admits Her *Geek Love* Is Stranger Than Most Fiction—But Aren't We All." *People Weekly* 31, No. 15 (17 April 1989): 127-28.

Biographical summary.

Young, Elizabeth J. "Delights of Decadence." *New States-man and Society* 3, No. 127 (16 November 1990): 38.

Praises Dunn for her outrageous delineation of deformi-ty, her "exploration of personality, love and pain," and the "wonderfully detailed neo-realism of her style" in *Geek Love.*

Additional coverage of Dunn's life and career is contained in the following source published by Gale Research: *Contemporary Authors,* **Vols. 33-36, rev. ed.**

Bret Easton Ellis
American Psycho

Ellis is an American novelist, born in 1964.

The following entry presents commentary on Ellis's novel *American Psycho* and the controversy surrounding this work. For further discussion of Ellis's life and works, see *CLC,* Vol. 39.

INTRODUCTION

Ellis is the author of *Less than Zero* and *The Rules of Attraction,* novels that depict a violent subculture of white youths who are desensitized by drugs, promiscuity, and the video revolution and whose depraved activities reflect the moral and spiritual deterioration of American society. These works have provoked debate between reviewers who have praised them as trenchant social commentary and those who have berated them as sensational exploitations of popular culture. Ellis's third novel, *American Psycho,* has generated a controversy beyond the scope of these previous disputes and has intensified his reputation as an author of shockingly graphic fiction.

American Psycho is the story of Patrick Bateman, a wealthy twenty-six-year-old investment banker who describes his materialistic lifestyle and obsession with appearances in a flat, dispassionate narrative rife with references to fashionable brand names and designer labels. In the same detached voice, he also recounts, in gruesome detail, a series of brutal murders he has committed, indicating no motive or remorse for his actions. The novel first generated controversy when Ellis's publisher, Simon & Schuster, withdrew from its agreement to publish *American Psycho,* citing the explicit and disturbing nature of its violent scenes. Although the work was immediately acquired by Vintage Books, a division of Random House, the novel has remained the focus of debate concerning such issues as the rights and responsibilities of publishing companies to publish or censor controversial material, the limits of artistic freedom, and the standards for judging a work's artistic merit.

Most critics who have interpreted *American Psycho* as an indictment of contemporary American culture have asserted that Patrick Bateman symbolizes the greed and inhumanity of the American upper class, while many of his victims represent voiceless and disadvantaged groups of society. Fay Weldon observed: "Those who are killed don't rate—they are the powerless, the poor, the wretched, the sick in mind, the sellers of flesh for money: their own and other people's." Although few critics have questioned the novel's thematic intent, opinions concerning its artistic worth have varied. Many reviewers have charged that Ellis's grotesque descriptions of brutality lack a moral context or psychological explanation and are therefore

both offensive and dangerous, while others have praised Ellis's willingness to explore the depravity underlying the materialism of the 1980s. Norman Mailer commented: "Is Bateman the monster or Bret Easton Ellis? . . . The book is disturbing in a way to remind us that attempts to create art can be as intolerable as foul manners. One finishes with an uneasy impulse not to answer the question but to bury it. Of course, the question can come back to haunt us. A novel has been written that is bound to rest in unhallowed ground if it is executed without serious trial."

CRITICISM

Anna Quindlen

[*In the following excerpt, Quindlen questions the decision of Simon and Schuster to cancel publication of* American Psycho.]

There were so many opportunities to reject Bret Easton Ellis's novel *American Psycho.*

There was the moment when the manuscript first landed on the editor's desk at Simon & Schuster, its pages filled with Armani ties, silk-satin pumps, severed heads, nail guns, kir royales, Bottega Veneta briefcases, mutilated corpses, microwave cannibalism and fabulous stereo equipment.

There was the day when its editor gave excerpts from the most violent chapters to the editorial board, or the weeks when women at Simon & Schuster first read the novel and were appalled by its graphic descriptions of sexual torture murders.

But over the last year one of America's great publishing houses had accepted, edited, and paid a reported $300,000 for the book about a fictional Wall Street serial killer, Harvard grad Pat Bateman, Ted Bundy by way of mergers and acquisitions.

American Psycho survived the revulsion of many of the people involved in its publication.

But in a world in which people have told me it's a horrible book through they haven't read it, a world in which appearance is worth two of reality, it was derailed by bad publicity.

[Early in November, 1990], Richard E. Snyder, the chairman of Simon & Schuster, announced he was canceling *American Psycho,* although the publishing house was to ship the book to stores soon. After slash-and-burn stories appeared in *Time* and *Spy* magazines, Mr. Snyder finally read the book that everyone was talking about, and decided it was in poor taste.

Mr. Ellis's agent, who is also my own, found another prestigious publisher in a nanosecond, and there's betting that the book will sell on controversy alone. This isn't Faulkner, folks. Much of *American Psycho* is of the tiresome enfant terrible school of fiction, heavy with name brands. All the clothes are expensive, all the fish is prepared rare and no one asks for vodka when they can ask for Absolut.

As an epitaph for the 80's, [*American Psycho*] has a repellent reality. The people are hateful, the violence nauseating, the sex graphic and impersonal.

—Anna Quindlen

But there's more than that here, and that's why two groups of respected editors, the ones who had it and the ones who have it now, wanted this book. Pat Bateman lives in a world so full of artifice and surface, so empty of any emotion, that one moment he's dismembering a woman and the next he's complaining about a bad table in this week's hot restaurant. He keeps warning people he wants to kill them, but the noise level in the clubs is so

high and the discourse at meals so vapid that no one hears. He doesn't need morals; he has money instead.

As an epitaph for the 80's, this has a repellent reality. The people are hateful, the violence nauseating, the sex graphic and impersonal. Is it heartening to read novels in which men and women treat one another with affection and respect, and kindness is the overweening emotion? Yes. Does that reflect the world? Hardly. The eternal question about violence in art is whether it simply reflects our worst behavior, or inspires it. We are so terrified of inspiration that sometimes we are moved to suppression. But reflection is essential because it often leads to thought, and occasionally to understanding.

That is why we publish troubling books. A publisher who makes safe decisions has abdicated. He is, according to a quip repeated often last week, not a publisher, but a printer.

Writers feared the conglomerization of publishing. They believed the day would come when men who know little about books—"but I know what I like!"—would make publishing decisions guided by profits and press coverage. Robert K. Massie, president of the Authors Guild, called the cancellation "a black day," adding, "It's a day the guild has been predicting would come since giant corporations started buying distinguished American publishing houses."

Book publishing has always been a balance between commerce and art. Sometimes a publisher publishes a book because it is wildly commercial, sometimes because it promises to be a master work, mostly because it falls somewhere in between. These decisions are subjective. When an editor reads a manuscript, finds it revolting and without artistic redemption, and rejects it, that is an exercise in taste. Some might have rejected *American Psycho* on those grounds when it was first submitted.

There was only one reason to reject it now, this late in the game.

That reason is cowardice.

Anna Quindlen, "Publish or Perish," in The New York Times, *Section 4, November 18, 1990, p. 17.*

Lorrie Moore

[*In the following excerpt, Moore defends Simon and Schuster's last-minute rejection of* American Psycho.]

It appears that the Authors Guild and certain publishers have rallied around Bret Easton Ellis's novel *American Psycho,* equating its late cancellation by Simon & Schuster with an act of censorship. Up until then, the book seemed destined to arrive at its publication date with so many daggers in its back that even the most savage book reviewer might have been predisposed to pity. . . .

But now that the misnomer of censorship has been applied to what was a botched rejection of a book, the literary public is off and away on a not particularly helpful discussion. If for reasons of taste a publisher exercises its freedom not to publish a book, even if it does so stupidly and at the last minute, how can this be compared to government intervention in the arts?

To be sure, we live in a time when the National Endowment for the Arts is rescinding funds for art with certain kinds of sexual and political content, and the First Amendment has never seemed so bullied. But if issues of literary censorship have taught us anything, surely it is that, astonishingly, words still have power. And so the word censorship should not be flapped about loosely, lest we get disoriented and lose the real battles against the thing itself.

As for sexual violence in art, American audiences sit passively in front of films and TV that serve up violence against women as entertainment. The highly acclaimed series "Twin Peaks" depicts the killing and dismembering of women as a goofy kind of vandalism—as if the murder of a woman were the equivalent of whimsically trashing a Buick. It is a chic nihilist's extension of the TV commercial, whether for a beer or a sports car or an after-shave, that equates women with objects. On the same show, however, violence against men is the violence of soldier against soldier, a chore performed usually with the quick firing of a gun.

It is violence against women that is estheticized, playfully prolonged, eroticized, made to serve as the dramatic engine of the story. David Lynch, the creator of "Twin Peaks," presents the graphic story of mutilated high school girls with a glint in his eye that, I am told, is satire.

A novel like *American Psycho* will probably prove not to be anything new. Perhaps it is only new, or sort of new, as literature. As a writing teacher, I have seen, over the last decade, more than one student short story that featured hacked-up women—almost always written by 20-year-old boys. Lately, however, I have been seeing even more of these kinds of stories. It's like David Lynch, the boys say now. It's getting to the truth, the difficult, hidden core, they say. Or else: It's like David Lynch; it's deliberately false, stylized, absurd. Get it?

What these boys have written, though they refuse to know it, is pornography. They have never seen a hacked-up woman. They don't know what they're talking about. A reader feels their belabored attempt to create this knowledge for themselves on the page, and what the writing becomes is not only inauthentic but motivated by its own inauthenticity: pornography. Not literature that shocks.

We tend to leave the protest against violent misogyny and its complicitous depictions to radical feminists and the fundamentalist right; too often, then, efforts at legislation ensue. If a work of art depicting sexual violence also fails at eloquence, authority and intelligence, if it seems faked and masturbatory, how is it that ordinary women, in a national climate where women are raped and murdered daily, do not cry out? Certainly readers or publishers should be able to do as much, or at least to dissociate themselves from such works as a way of exercising their freedom of speech. Why equate objection with censorship?

Perhaps these feelings are most uncomfortable for women

writers, who have the rights and freedoms of their profession to protect and consider, even if their profession does not reciprocate. A writer knows that a good novel, whether it's about Humbert Humbert of Nabokov's *Lolita,* or Huckleberry Finn, will always contain, at the very least, a troubled scrap of authorial sympathy for its protagonist. Perhaps there is such a scrap of sympathy in *American Psycho,* and that is what some have found so alarming. Or perhaps *American Psycho* is just not a good novel.

It should go without saying that writers may write what they want—even if it turns out to be pornography. Heading for danger zones or forbidden psychic places is what authors do. But perhaps we all should be better braced for the discussion afterward. Bone up on vocabulary. To call a muffed rejection by a publisher censorship is to give political stature to the thousands of manuscripts that are rejected by publishers everyday.

We live in a country where we probably don't know what our censored books are, and where what we consider censored books become best sellers, even as they're still being called "censored." That is what's so amusing, so cute, so strange about America.

> Lorrie Moore, "Trashing Women, Trashing Books," in The New York Times, Section A, December 5, 1990, p. 27.

Roger Rosenblatt

[*Below, Rosenblatt negatively assesses* American Psycho *and encourages readers to ignore the book.*]

As a tale of contemporary foolishness, the story of the pre-publication, de-publication and re-publication of Bret Easton Ellis's novel *American Psycho* has just about everything. You might call it "delicious," unless you have read Mr. Ellis's novel.

Simon & Schuster was about to ship *American Psycho* to the bookstores when the novel's moronic and sadistic contents were revealed in *Time* and *Spy* magazines. The articles caught the attention of Richard E. Snyder, the chairman of Simon & Schuster, and Martin Davis, the chairman of Paramount Communications, which owns Simon & Schuster. Either Mr. Snyder or Mr. Davis, or both, decided that they did not want to publish Mr. Ellis's novel after all. An 11th-hour judgment at the top became a slap at Robert Asahina, the b␣␣k's editor, and Charles Hayward, the president of Simon & Schuster's adult trade books division, who had accepted the novel. It also created a cause of sorts taken up by various voices in the book world.

Was Simon & Schuster acting cowardly or sensibly, if late? Was the mega-company Paramount exercising improper authority over its book enterprise? Should something like *American Psycho* be published by anyone any time anyway?

The last question was immediately answered by Sonny Mehta, the head of Vintage Books and Alfred A. Knopf, who rescued *American Psycho* on its fall from Simon & Schuster, assuming, reasonably, that the revolting publicity would bode well for sales. Or perhaps Mr. Mehta actually liked the book. That's something to consider, too.

So, what is *American Psycho?* Why are people saying such awful things about it? And what may we learn from this tale of our times?

American Psycho is the journal Dorian Gray would have written had he been a high school sophomore. But that is unfair to sophomores. So pointless, so themeless, so everythingless is this novel, except in stupefying details about expensive clothing, food and bath products, that were it not the most loathsome offering of the season, it certainly would be the funniest.

Several times, in the middle of some childishly gruesome description of torture or dismemberment, I found myself chuckling with revulsion. Mr. Ellis quotes from "Notes From the Underground" in one of his epigraphs. I wondered: could this fellow really think that he, like Dostoyevsky, was being shockingly critical of the amorality of modern urban life? Why, yes! The rake.

Parental discretion is advised for the following paragraphs, but I have to give you a direct idea of the nonsense here.

Patrick Bateman (Batman? Norman Bates? Who cares?) is a Harvard graduate, 26 years old, is single, lives on Manhattan's Upper West Side, nurtures his appearance obsessively, frequents health clubs by day and restaurants by night and, in his spare time, plucks out the eyes of street beggars, slits the throats of children and does things to the bodies of women not unlike things that Mr. Ellis does to prose. (p. 3)

A designer serial killer, Bateman knows from Tumi leather attaché cases and wool-and-silk suits by Ermenegildo Zegna and wing tip shoes from Fratelli Rossetti and Mario Valentino Persian gloves and carambola sorbet and Ettore Sottsass push-button phones and business cards with "Silian Rail lettering." (In case you can't tell, I'm out of my depth here.) He does have a way about him: "Oh, honey. The things I could do to your eyes with a coat hanger." He also drinks his own urine.

But his true inner satisfaction comes when he has a woman in his clutches and can entertain her with a nail gun or a power drill or Mace, or can cut off her head or chop off her arms or bite off her breasts or dispatch a starving rat up her vagina.

The context of these high jinks is young, wealthy, hair-slicked-back, narcissistic, decadent New York, of which, one only assumes, Mr. Ellis disapproves. It's a bit hard to tell what Mr. Ellis intends exactly, because he languishes so comfortably in the swamp he purports to condemn. Perhaps this is the tormenting ambivalence of his "twenty-something" generation, which he defined in *The Times*'s Arts and Leisure section of Dec. 2 [1991]. He wrote: "We are clueless yet wizened." Yes, that must be it.

Of course, you will be stunned to learn that the book goes nowhere. Characters do not exist, therefore do not develop. Bateman has no motivation for his madness—though there is one telling reference to his displeasure with a Wal-

dorf salad. (My guess would be the urine.) No plot intrudes upon the pages. Bateman is never brought to justice, suggesting that even justice was bored. Nor is Mr. Ellis.

The novel may not be much as fiction or as social criticism, but its publishing history shows what a glorious nut box people can get in when they lose sight of what writing is supposed to be. Mr. Ellis got the process going with his lame and unhealthy imagination. The product of that imagination was then urged forward by his editors, who either did not read the book—a sin not unknown in a publishing era when it is more important to acquire a book than to edit it—or worse, did read the book and felt that it had something.

It does. What *American Psycho* has is the most comprehensive lists of baffling luxury items to be found outside airplane gift catalogues. I do not exaggerate when I say that in his way Mr. Ellis may be the most knowledgeable author in all of American literature. Whatever Melville knew about whaling, whatever Mark Twain knew about rivers are mere amateur stammerings compared with what Mr. Ellis knows about shampoo alone.

The *Time* and *Spy* articles caught the worthlessness of the book, and thus subsequently did Mr. Snyder and Mr. Davis. Quite rightly, they stopped the book cold. What then should follow as the night the day? Cries of "censorship," naturally, from the Authors Guild and other best-intentioned sorts who are understandably oversensitive to censorship threats these days in an atmosphere poisoned by the malevolent ignorance of Jesse Helms and the cowardice of Congress and the National Endowment for the Arts.

Even Helms & Company aren't wielding censorship. You remember censorship. Censorship is when a government burns your manuscript, smashes your presses and throws you in jail. When an artist is unable to get a government grant, it may be inconvenient, but censorship it ain't.

If a publishing house is not entitled to withdraw its own book, who is? As for the timing of Simon & Schuster's decision, better late than never.

Which brings us to the other cry of the misguided good guys. There was a loud to-do over whether Mr. Snyder acted on his own or on orders from Mr. Davis. The implication was that Big Corporation America (Paramount) is polluting the literary arts. Big Corporation America is rarely criticized by us writers when it deals out huge advances, only when it has something to say about what or how it wants to publish. When we sign our contracts, publishing is a business. When they are broken, it's an art.

The only person who polluted *American Psycho* (such a title) was Mr. Ellis. Let's say that the word to snuff the book did come from Martin Davis. Is Mr. Davis stripped of his responsibility to assert moral judgment simply because he owns the shop?

If Mr. Davis and Mr. Snyder went wrong, it was in waiting to find God in *Time* and *Spy,* and in paying too little attention to the book they were about to loose upon the world in the first place. They cannot be expected to read everything they put out, but they sure can be expected to remind their editors what goes and what doesn't.

Enter Mr. Mehta and Vintage Books, clearly as hungry for a killing as Patrick Bateman. The folks at Vintage seem to me to be the special scoundrels of our tale, whether they are being cynical and avaricious or merely tasteless and avaricious. Either way, they must have a mighty low opinion of the public's ability to distinguish between art that is meaningfully sensationalistic and junk. No one argues that a publishing house hasn't the right to print what it wants. We fight for that right. But not everything is a right. At some point, someone in authority somewhere has to look at Mr. Ellis's rat and call the exterminator. (Will the Vintage people read that last sentence and reach for their copies of *Ulysses* and *Tropic of Cancer?* Or will they be honest enough to admit: "O.K. There's no civil liberties issue here. But there's plenty of dough"? You make the call.)

Finally, we come to ourselves, the muses of the story. It is our dough, after all, that everyone had in mind all along—Mr. Ellis, Simon & Schuster, Vintage Books. They saw us as lowlife and proceeded accordingly. Pause for introspection. Shall we prove them wrong? It would be sweet revenge if we refused to buy this book. Thumb through it, for the sake of normal prurience, but don't buy it.

That nonact would give a nice ending to our tale. It would say that we are disgusted with the gratuitous degradation of human life, of women in particular. It would show that we can tell real books from the fakes. It would give the raspberry to the culture hustlers who, to their shame, will not say no to obvious rot. Standards, anyone? (pp. 3, 16)

> Roger Rosenblatt, "Snuff This Book! Will Bret Easton Ellis Get Away with Murder?" in The New York Times Book Review, *December 16, 1990, pp. 3, 16.*

John N. Berry III

[*Berry is Editor-in-Chief of* Library Journal. *In the following editorial he discusses the concept of publishing "taste" and "standards" in relation to* American Psycho.]

Be skeptical when "standards," "taste," or a newly invented "responsibility" of publishers is invoked to challenge a book. Those were the reasons given most by a few New York literary and publishing industry insiders as they haughtily attacked *American Psycho* and its author Bret Easton Ellis. The attack came in the wake of Simon & Schuster's cancellation of plans to publish the book, and the quick decision by Knopf's Sonny Mehta to publish it as a Vintage paperback. . . .

Those attacks would have been more convincing if mainstream publishing hadn't replaced editorial judgment with bean counting years ago. Now the "mainstream" overflows with the likes of Stephen King, Danielle Steel, Jackie Collins, Judith Krantz, and Sidney Sheldon. . . .

In a more honest attack, the Los Angeles Chapter of the

> **Ellis on contemporary popular culture:**
>
> Since contemporary subversiveness is all on the surface popular culture doesn't, it can't, jolt us in ways it did previous generations. We're basically unshockable. And so culture doesn't play the same role in our lives that it did for previous generations: to liberate, break boundaries, show the unshowable.
>
> There has always been a fascination with the shocking and macabre in popular culture, from Mary Shelley's Frankenstein myth to the movie *I Was a Teen-Age Werewolf,* but this [twentysomething] generation has been wooed with visions of violence, both fictive and real, since childhood.
>
> If violence in films, literature and in some heavy metal and rap music is so extreme that it verges on the baroque, it may reflect the need to be terrified in a time when the sharpness of horror-film tricks seems blunted by repetition on the nightly news. But this audience *isn't* horrified by the endless slaughter, which is presented within the context of fantasy (*Robocop, Total Recall, Die Hard 2*) and the realm of the everyday.
>
> Bret Easton Ellis, in "The Twentysomethings
> Adrift in a Pop Landscape," The New York
> Times, 2 December 1990.

National Organization for Women expressed very real fear and unmuted outrage. "People are becoming less and less sensitive to what is brutal," said L.A. NOW spokesperson Tammy Bruce. "It is part of a vicious circle of misogyny that shows up in our lives every day. It leads to people on juries who don't find a rapist guilty because they see it every day. It's not just the perpetrator; the juries are desensitized." Bruce was convincing, if you agree with her that the book is nothing but hard-core pornography.

Whether or not *American Psycho* was written to shock and offend—as it does—it is clearly a serious work. It has already commanded more attention and attack than critique and that creates a difficult trap for librarians.

The publication of *American Psycho* is not the occasion for haughty posturing about standards and taste. There is no guidance for book selectors in snobbish appeals to "what is acceptable in mainstream publishing." If "taste" were a valid measure, rather than accept a "standard" set by Paramount (parent of S. & S.), why not one by Knopf, a publisher of obvious "taste," whose Sonny Mehta has an enviable track record of great books and better-than-average best sellers.

Where were the "boundaries of what is acceptable in mainstream publishing," and "standards" when we needed them? The gray sameness of the formula books that pour forth from that "mainstream" is the result of pandering to that "debased popular taste." That "taste" is measured by the numbers on the bottom line. . . .

American Psycho is a special case. That may be why it must be in libraries: to set the record straight, to allow readers to get by the posturing of offended literati to decide for themselves.

Book publishing needs *courage* much more than "taste" and "standards." Mainstream publishing needs the courage to risk books that break out of the boundaries that have trapped it in an intellectually bankrupt pursuit of best sellers that only occasionally, and usually accidently, brings great literature to libraries and readers.

> John N. Berry III, " 'American Psycho' Is Not the Problem," in Library Journal, *Vol. 116, No. 1, January, 1991, p. 6.*

Merle Rubin

[*In the following excerpt, Rubin discusses the graphic violence depicted in* American Psycho.]

Simon and Schuster's eleventh-hour decision last November to cancel the January publication of Bret Easton Ellis's third novel, **American Psycho,** drew accusations of corporate censorship in some literary circles. But among some feminists and others who are alarmed by escalating violence in American society, the decision was welcomed as a sign that the arts industry might do something to stem the rising tide of gratuitous hate and aggression, particularly against women.

The outcry from the Authors Guild on Ellis's behalf proved needless, and the relief felt by feminists was likewise premature: The book was instantly picked up by Sonny Mehta of Alfred Knopf for March publication as a Vintage paperback original. Tammy Bruce, coordinator of the Los Angeles chapter of the National Organization for Women, is continuing the drive against the book by proposing a boycott of Random House (parent company of Vintage and Knopf). (p. 78)

Some feminists condemn the book as a manual on how to torture and dismember women. To say that **American Psycho** is misogynistic, however, is a little like saying that nerve gas is unhealthy. Or, as Ellis himself remarks in a publicity release put out by his erstwhile publisher, Simon and Schuster, "Just when readers think they can't take any more violence . . . more is presented—and their response to this is what intrigues me."

In Ellis's book, graphic descriptions of increasingly gruesome violence (tongues, eyes, nipples, and intestines torn out, acid poured in orifices, a victim skinned alive, bodies dismembered, cooked, and made into meat loaf, and much more) alternate with scenes of equally excruciating vacuity in which the antihero, one Wall Street yuppie named Patrick Bateman, obsesses over the brand names of clothing, accessories, and mineral water while meeting his equally vacuous, interchangeable-seeming friends at trendy New York clubs and restaurants.

Apart from being denounced as "faggots" by the novel's deranged narrator, gay men get off pretty lightly here. One character, a salesman at Barney's who is infatuated with the fashionably turned-out yuppie butcher, claims he wants to die if he can't have him. (He doesn't realize he's a killer.) Bateman does not oblige either his love wish or his death wish. Following what is reputedly a not uncommon heterosexual male fantasy, Bateman prefers coercing women to have sex with each other before going on in his

own inimitable style to stab, mutilate, and electrocute them.

Ellis would doubtless claim that this book, like its predecessors (***Less Than Zero, The Rules of Attraction***), illustrates the connection between vacuousness and violence. But somehow, one feels that what we're seeing here is less the story of a man driven to violence by his own vacuity than the desperation of an author driven to writing about violence by *his* own vacuity. One doesn't have to agree with the feminist contention that Ellis is exploiting, even relishing, these brutal crimes to be disturbed by the sheer level of violence described in such extravagant detail.

When it comes to the question of where we draw the line between what is acceptable and what is not, the traditional response of liberals and libertarians—and of most artists, gay and straight alike—has been to err on the side of freedom of expression. Certainly, from formal acts of book banning (the fate of works like Radclyffe Hall's *The Well of Loneliness,* officially verboten for 28 years) to the de facto silencing effect of publishers unwilling or afraid to handle books treating gay themes, the excessive conservatism of American publishers has long been a serious concern to gays and lesbians.

But gays and lesbians are also among the most frequent victims of violent behavior, which may well be fostered by prevailing cultural attitudes about force, domination, sexuality, masculinity, femininity, and effeminacy. The temptation to join the feminist campaign to change cultural attitudes is a strong one.

To begin with, a publisher's decision not to print a book is not in itself censorship. The process goes on all the time. Publishers reject books that they consider too avantgarde or too old-fashioned, insufficiently commercial, or insufficiently "literary." Publishers are entirely free to exercise their taste (good or bad) and their business judgment (sound or foolish). Whether one cites the daunting tale of some truly original artist unable to find a publisher or the sad story of someone like the British novelist Barbara Pym (abandoned by publishers in the middle of her career for being insufficiently trendy), there are plenty of reasons to bemoan the crassness and insensitivity of the industry.

From this perspective, Simon and Schuster's decision not to go ahead with Ellis's novel should probably be welcomed as a rare instance of corporate responsibility. The firm might well have rejected the book as tasteless in the first place but for the belief that something so shocking would surely sell (Ellis was paid a $300,000 advance). Similarly, the protests, threatened boycott, and other tactics employed by the book's foes fall within the realm of exercising one's marketplace options, not the realm of state-imposed censorship.

Pressuring a manufacturer to refrain from producing harmful products is a time-honored consumerist approach. But pressure cuts two ways, as demonstrated by fundamentalist groups that threaten to boycott sponsors of television shows that depict gays and lesbians as normal human beings. In a large, pluralistic society, there may even be something to be said for pitting all these pressures against one another as checks and balances. But there is undoubtedly a chilling effect that comes with so much informal monitoring. In the long run, it may well be safer and more challenging to change our cultural environment by expressing our own views than by trying to police the expression of antipathetic ones.

But having taken the necessary and, I think, inevitable stand on behalf of freedom of expression, it's hard to work oneself up into a fever of indignation over the rights of untalented authors to be "as nasty as they wanna be." Nor can one feel all that alarmed about the Bill of Rights, when freedom of expression is threatened by nothing more severe than a proposed boycott.

In fact, what is most depressing about this whole affair is that a major publisher wanted to print the book in the first place and that another snapped it up within a day of it being canceled. It only goes to illustrate the sorry truth of George Bernard Shaw's acerbic observation, "It is clear that a novel cannot be too bad to be worth publishing." (pp. 78-9)

> *Merle Rubin, "Ellis in Blunderland," in* The
> Advocate, *January 29, 1991, pp. 78-9.*

Mim Udovitch

[*In the essay excerpted below, Udovitch suggests that* American Psycho *is the product of a writer who is compelled to express a weighty theme concerning contemporary society, yet lacks the literary skill or talent with which to communicate his perceptions effectively.*]

The real scandal surrounding the publication of **American Psycho,** Bret Easton Ellis's tale of a yuppie psychopath on the loose against a backdrop of nouvelle cuisine, is not that its graphic sexually violent passages are somehow too dangerous or tasteless to be allowed the light of day, but that a book as obvious as this one should be so widely misunderstood. Every line, paragraph, chapter, and train of thought proceeds ineluctably on parallel tracks, past the same scenery, to a single destination of social indictment. If you miss one by, say, knowing nothing about music, or designer clothing, you can barely avoid being run over by another. Where Ellis's previous works were marred by the monotony of a one-conceit-for-one-theme tradition, this book seeks to help build a strong argument 12 ways, with the result that if **American Psycho**'s impact is not less than zero, it is pitifully less than the sum of its parts.

Even the epigraphs, some not-very-arcane quotations from [Dostoyevsky's] *Notes From Underground,* Miss Manners, and Talking Heads, dealing with the barbarism and angst that underly civilization and its decay, function as a kind of closed caption for the thematically challenged. Some of the book's prepublication critics have had an unfair little field day pitting **American Psycho** against *Notes From Underground.* The novel is really much more like an inverted social pyramid of *Les Misérables,* a book to which it refers (as a musical) with greater frequency: as virtuous in principle as it is tedious in practice, and far, far too long.

The frenzied tilting at windmills undertaken by the book's detractors constitutes a much more telling and complex

metaphor of the modern moral order than the book's symbolism—the indifferent oppressor revealed as de facto murderer—approaches in its wildest moments. The campaigns launched against the book by its numerous opponents are barely disguised manipulations and distortions of morality for subjective amoral reasons, including, but not limited to: power, ego, money, attention. And the shame of the whole sorry enterprise is that the novel itself—flawed, boring, and so ambitious that it would have been a mammoth undertaking for a far more accomplished author than Ellis—is neither entirely defensible nor dismissable on its own mixed demerits. (p. 65)

Public objections to **American Psycho** took two forms, primarily political (the biblioclastic characterization of the work, by Tammy Bruce, president of the L.A. Chapter of NOW, as "a how-to novel on the torture and dismemberment of women") and primarily literary (Roger Rosenblatt's *Times Book Review* assessment [*The New York Times Book Review,* December 16, 1990, pp. 3, 16.] of the novel's "pointless" and "themeless" nature); both approaches were founded in part on fallacies and ignorance. The NOW statement, almost certainly sincerely motivated, is also misguided, a pure lucid syllogism. Its major premise (that sexual violence requires a manual), its minor premise (that **American Psycho** is such a manual), and its conclusion (that publication would thus promote as well as reflect real acts of violence against women) are all demonstrably false.

To fully endorse the first premise would be to believe that individual acts of sexual violence are not, in fact, a where-there's-a-will-there's-a-way proposition, but can be learned from a text; that a rapist manqué might therefore wander on the waterfront with the knowledge that he could have been a dismemberer, if only he'd had the tuition. To justify the second would be to imply that Ellis's amorality play condones the acts it describes, when they are clearly, indeed crudely, condemned on both literal and allegorical levels, not to mention being so flatly written that they are hardly memorable, let alone shocking. Some of the scenes of rape and dismemberment are positively childish: Look Ma, no hands. And the conclusion is thus as dubious—and to the extent that it siphons off energy that could be better employed against real rather than imagined misogyny, destructive—as any of the numerous parallel, puritanical assaults on pornography and the arts that so often proceed from the same faulty reasoning on the Jesse Helms-Andrea-Dworkin continuum.

Though severe literary criticism of **American Psycho** is quite justified, its most high-profile proponents (Rosenblatt in the *Times,* and Norman Mailer in *Vanity Fair* [March 1991, Vol. 54, pp. 154-59, 220-21.]) were similarly, though less passionately, misdirected. Rosenblatt, who apparently viewed this assignment as a chance to showcase his madcap wit—no mean feat, given the *Times* stylebook—undermined his own semivalid arguments by his bone ignorance of the subject. "Batman? Norman Bates? Who cares?" he queried parenthetically regarding the resonance of the American psycho's name. If he had troubled to familiarize himself with Ellis's work, he would know that Patrick Bateman is so named for the simple reason that he first appears, nonmurderously, in Ellis's second novel, *The Rules of Attraction,* as the older brother of one of the book's protagonists, Sean Bateman (who, incidentally, practices reciprocity by dropping into *American Psycho* for dinner).

Mailer, in a largely thoughtful and eloquent essay, was in error when he stated that *American Psycho* contained "not one, not two, but twenty or thirty scenes of unmitigated torture." In fact, the 399-page novel includes 10 passages describing torture or murder, plus two graphic but torture-free sex scenes, and a smattering of cursory allusions to those and other instances of human carnage, hardly an insignificant disparity in view of the relevance of the book's violence to the controversy. Mailer also loses his footing on more subjective grounds and ends up facedown in a charitable but intentional fallacy when he attributes the book's failure to its telling the reader "no more about Bateman's need to dismember others than we know about the inner workings in the mind of a wooden-faced actor who swings a broadax in an exploitation film." While it is true that if the book did set out to ask, "Psycho killer, qu'est-ce que c'est," it would indeed be answering "fa fa fa fa fa fa fa fa fa fa," its lack of insight into its characters is emphatically intentional. These characters can identify each other's Armani suspenders at 500 paces, but are constantly confusing one another's names, Ellis's hamfisted way of letting the reader know that psycho killers don't kill people; capitalist excesses kill people. This is a good old-fashioned Beckettesque anti-novel, with all the attendant no-frills—flat characters, monotonously detailed surface description, no plot to speak of, and endless repetitions. And if the absence of god had wanted Ellis to have round characters, the absence of god would have given them personalities.

The "faceless" nature of Patrick Bateman's mother and brother, which Mailer decries, is due to the fact that references to both are literary rather than American psychoanalytic: the chapter describing Bateman's visit with his mother is a barely altered quotation from Ellis's debut, *Less Than Zero.* Bateman's psychopathology is cultural, not personal, as Ellis makes unsubtly plain by equipping him with external homicidal influences in the form of an affinity for the legends of Ed Gein, John Wayne Gacy, Ted Bundy, *The Toolbox Murders, The Texas Chainsaw Massacre,* the power drill scene from *Body Double,* and Donald Trump, rather than the internal motivations of rage, anguish, conflict, and despair.

Though the disputed passages are cold and dull, they are technically capable of shocking the squeamish:

> I can already tell that it's going to be a characteristically useless, senseless death, but then I'm used to the horror. It seems distilled, even now it fails to upset or bother me. I'm not mourning, and to prove it to myself, after a minute or two of watching the rat move under her lower belly, making sure the girl is still conscious, shaking her head in pain, her eyes wide with terror and confusion, I used a chain saw and in a matter of seconds cut the girl in two with it. The whirring teeth go through skin and muscle and sinew and bone so fast that she stays alive long enough to watch me pull her legs away from her body—her actual thighs, what's left of her mutilated vagina—and hold them up in front of me, spouting blood, like trophies almost. Her eyes stay open for a minute, desperate and unfocused, then close, and finally, before she dies, I force a knife uselessly up her nose until it slides out of the flesh on her forehead, and then I hack the bone off her chin. . . .

And yet this stuff is so arid that a reader who, like this critic, had nightmares after seeing *Ghostbusters* might well remain unmoved.

Despite the gory detail, the sex and gender values of this book are not libertine, but profoundly conservative, the antithesis of the casual bisexuality and blurry, meaningless couplings in his first two books. Ellis is postulating a sexually repressive, ethnically oppressive American Psychosis, conveyed above by virulent misogyny, and conveyed elsewhere by the high-fiving, alcoholic homophobia of the many male-bonding passages. Where punk and its corollaries use graphic sex and violence to explore the potential of the impermissible, this book attempts to employ them to portray the reality of the permissible. Ask not what you intend to do about *American Psycho*'s violent content, ask what *American Psycho*'s violent content is intended to do for you.

Unfortunately, its high-blown aims aside, the book is unbearably bad, more to be pitied than censored, but it is also a far more serious (and less compelling) text than the critical focus on blood and guts gives it credit for. Unlike Ellis's previous work, it seeks to explode rather than perpetuate the myth of isolationist privilege that enjoys such high regard among the would-be isolationist privileged. The compulsive, lustful descriptions of designer wares are *American Psycho*'s real pornography, in the value-laden sense of the word.

These characters can identify each other's Armani suspenders at 500 paces, but are constantly confusing one another's names, Ellis's hamfisted way of letting the reader know that psycho killers don't kill people; capitalist excesses kill people.

—Mim Udovitch

The hip, passive characters of his first two books have evolved into unhip, actively destructive creeps, who have to pay to get into clubs, have trouble scoring good drugs, and make a habit of taunting beggars with a dollar that they whisk away at the last minute. Bateman himself is dismissive of Ellis's earlier work (" . . . she's talking about a new novel she's been reading by some young author—its cover, I've seen, slathered with neon; its subject, lofty suffering"). And who's to blame him? Where those works were in the stuck-in-the-mud stage of existentialism, this one is up and *engagé.* And unlike the essentially naturalistic tone of his earlier work, this book is stratospherically unreal and self-consciously literary. It contains numerous references to Ellis's own oeuvre and that of such vintage contemporaries he believes play in the *American Psycho* League: Tama Janowitz, Jay McInerney, and Tom Wolfe, who while not usually lumped with his juniors in the socialite realist genre, actually deserves to be if you think about it for a New York Is Decaying minute.

These references include the incorporation of characters (Stash from *Slaves of New York,* Alison Poole from *Story of My Life,* a mention of McCoy from *Bonfire of the Vanities,* and a whole raftload of figures from Ellis's own *The Rules of Attraction* and/or *Less Than Zero*); entities (Patrick Bateman and his young co-arbitrageurs work at Pierce & Pierce, which was Sherman McCoy's investment firm, refer to cocaine as Bolivian Marching Powder, the name given it by *Bright Lights, Big City*'s narrator, and sundry characters have attended Camden College, Ellis's standard nom du Bennington); plus the fusion of several slightly altered scenes or jokes from *Less Than Zero* and *The Rules of Attraction* with *American Psycho*'s sprawling narrative. In addition to these clearly intentional double-dealings, the ghost of Wolfe's style haunts a phrase or several ("my rabbit has been cut to look . . . just . . . like . . . a . . . star!" and the phonetic rendering of a speech defect—" 'Accent on the last syllable.' Akthent on thee latht thyllable"—are both . . . just . . . like . . . *Bonfire of the Vanities*!).

Whether these last are intentional or simply "My Sweet Lord" syndrome is difficult to say, since Ellis's style is just as likely to contain abrupt, sporadic lashings of Salinger's propensity for italicizing various spoken syllables, or for that matter the endlessly shallow, conjunction-laden sentences of Ernest Hemingway and Danielle Steele. But at the very least, those references of which one can be sure combine to announce that Ellis means *American Psycho* to be a definitive edition, if not a sort of prose Edda of the Bret pack, the product of a thoughtful writer, not just a purveyor of pieces of slaughtered meat. And besides, they provide a nice dose of that good old-fashioned Brechtian alienation effect to keep the Beckett stuff company.

And, hey, how about that topic, which happens to be nothing less than a satiric look at economic and social contributions to the cruelty of the human condition? *American Psycho* relates the indifference of the mostly male ruling class to the plight of the unempowered other. The independently wealthy Bateman savors killing women, but he's not above taking out blacks, Asians, homosexuals, dogs, and children, plus a fellow yuppie here and there for the allegorical hostile takeover. He refers to "niggers," "zipperheads," "faggots," "dumb bitches," and "hardbodies," as well as supporting apartheid and categorizing a beggar as a "member of the genetic underclass." These prejudices are combined with an obsessive, material interest in personal luxuries (characters are inevitably introduced with a laundry—or maybe dry-cleaning—list of designer apparel and accessories) to add up to a negligence so extreme and inexcusable that it amounts to murder, a premise that is both inarguable and simplistic whether its

author is Bret Easton Ellis or Sinéad O'Connor. How can he possibly know Karl Marx when he is only 27?

The book's truly irredeemable drawback is that laudable as Ellis's great lurch forwards is in thematic terms, he remains an amateurish formalist and a downright lousy stylist. Both *American Psycho*'s first phrase ("ABANDON ALL HOPE YE WHO ENTER HERE is scrawled in blood red lettering on the side of the Chemical Bank . . . ") and its last (" . . . above one of the doors covered by red velvet drapes in Harry's is a sign and on the sign in letters that match the drapes' color are the words THIS IS NOT AN EXIT") are so hackneyed you start with not wanting to go on and end up sorry that you did. The author, as well as his characters, is all too fluent in the President's American, and the effects are so labored you want to unionize them. They conspire to make not so much points as blunt instruments. Any reader tenacious enough to breach the denouement, a linking of Reagan's harmless appearance and inner evil with that of Patrick Bateman, will long since have been beaten senseless.

For example, on first noticing that the book's opening pages attribute "Be My Baby" to the Crystals rather than the Ronettes, one might be inclined to suppose that this book has benefited from the research assistance of Albert Goldman. Then, as you plow along finding correct citations for "The Lion Sleeps Tonight" (the Tokens) and "Lightnin' Strikes" (Lou Christie), but incorrectly attributed references to "Then He Kissed Me" (the Ronettes, rather than the Crystals) and "Dancing in the Street" (the Shirelles rather than the Vandellas), you begin to think that this is an author who can make distinctions between guys who sing falsetto, but not girl groups, a theory that falls apart when you see Brooklyn Bridge's "The Worst That Could Happen" attributed to Frankie Valli. By the time you reach an unmistakably intentional error ("You Can't Always Get What You Want" by the Beatles), and the hodgepodge of fact and error coalesces into the Signpost Back Behind, announcing: SLOW UNRELIABLE NARRATOR WORKING, there's no pay-off, since you will have been very obtuse indeed if you have not already deduced this information from other internal evidence.

Ellis is postulating a sexually repressive, ethnically oppressive American Psychosis, conveyed above by virulent misogyny, and conveyed elsewhere by the high-fiving, alcoholic homophobia of the many male-bonding passages.

—*Mim Udovitch*

Our old pal, the unreliable N., is put to more ambiguous use in the numerous ignored or misunderstood confessions and indications of psychopathology Bateman ascribes to himself: "I say, staring at her, quite clearly but muffled by 'Pump Up the Volume' and the crowd, 'You are a fucking ugly bitch I want to stab to death and play around with your blood,' but I'm smiling." But like the initially almost amusing fashionable food descriptions ("free range squid," "marlin chili," "watermelon-brittle tart," and "quail sashimi with grilled brioche and the baby soft shell crabs with grape jelly"), these appear, to wax Maileresque, not once, or twice, but 20 or 30 times until you want to run shrieking up Sixth Avenue wearing a blackened-peanut-butter-and-mango-salsa sandwich board reading: I GET IT, ALREADY. Repetitious is as repetitious does, and the hallowed aesthetic reproduction of boredom notwithstanding, this stuff is so relentless it's like *Pale Fire*, the Mars Blackmon remix. But wait. There's more! *American Psycho* also devotes three disparate chapters to overtly shoddy encomiums, dripping with irony and historical error, to pop musical lightweights Phil Collins, Whitney Houston, and Huey Lewis. And the characters converse on topics ranging from the etiquette of business clothing to bottled water to vacationing in the Bahamas, using the "found" dialogue of advertisements and travel brochures. Do ya know what these chapters are getting at? Do ya know? Do ya know? Do ya know?

To be scrupulously fair, there are some sweet and imaginative touches in *American Psycho* that Ellis's earlier work would not have implied him capable of. "The Patty Winters Show," the morning program to which Bateman's addicted, has several topics that are briefly successful fictional bits: "Talking animals were the topic of this morning's 'Patty Winters Show'. An octopus was floating in a makeshift aquarium with a microphone attached to one of its tentacles and it kept asking—or so its 'trainer,' who is positive that mollusks have vocal cords, assured us—for 'cheese.' I watched, vaguely transfixed, until I started to sob." "On 'The Patty Winters Show' this morning a Cheerio sat in a very small chair and was interviewed for close to an hour."

These instances are not wholly exceptional, there are not one, or two, but 20 or 30 others, but they are embedded in a very long text that is generally so awkward you sometimes want to grade it more than you want to read it. Ellis is a little freer with a cliché than can be justified on received depersonalization grounds. Twice, Patrick Bateman, crying out in psychopathic triumph, does not scream like a steam whistle, a siren, or a New Kids fan splashed with Donnie Wahlberg's sweat, but like a banshee. When mundane objects or events provoke in him feelings of anxiety, he is on five separate occasions filled with "a nameless dread," when in fact, unless you wish to give it a beard and call it BOB for reasons of dramatic efficacy, dread does a good enough job of naming itself. And bitchen irony abounds—having already murdered a beggar, Bateman misses a private Armani sale and reflects that "the world is more often than not a bad and cruel place"; the phrase "Silence Equals Death" is misperceived by a female character as "Silkience Equals Death," and by Bateman as "Science Equals Death." Ellis is frequently undone by this kind of near-aphasiac bad ear for nuance, a perceptual flaw that was also apparent in his simpleminded critical assessment of the movies, TV shows, and music he cited in his Arts & Leisure essay on his generation's cultural fatigue.

That this book, an unappetizing hash of poorly learned Warhol and Marx, is itself in as sorry a state as the culture it seeks to scorn should not be used as a springboard to continue criticizing it on other than its own terms. Ellis, who has in just three books been hailed, nailed, and assailed, is obviously possessed by so great a need to ascribe blame for the feelings he sees his generation as not having that no wind, no rain, no rumors that Joe McGinniss really wrote *Less Than Zero* or allegations of misogyny, unpleasant as they must be, can stop him.

Crying all the way to the bank on the road you've paved with your poorly articulated intentions is probably a truly dreadful way to end up spending your time, and it's hard to imagine that any writer would court it. The sense of desperation imparted by *American Psycho* is that of an author sincerely compelled to say something he hasn't the means or talent to express, and you'd have to be as callous as his characters not to feel that this is a sadly self-defeating volume. The real greed and exploitation inherent to the controversy would be better blamed on the agents and editors who did not advise Ellis to shelve this project for 10 years or until he grew up, whichever came first. (pp. 65-6)

Mim Udovitch, "Intentional Phalluses," in The Village Voice, *Vol. XXXVI, No. 12, February 25, 1991, pp. 65-6.*

Jonathan Yardley

[*Excerpted below is Yardley's scathing review of* American Psycho.]

No, there are no surprises in *American Psycho*. The novel that Simon and Schuster belatedly rejected last fall on grounds of "taste" turns out upon opportunistic publication by Vintage to be exactly what all the rumors had indicated: a contemptible piece of pornography, the literary equivalent of a snuff flick. Its concluding 150 pages can only be described as repulsive, a bloodbath serving no purpose save that of morbidity, titillation and sensation; *American Psycho* is a loathsome book.

It is also, and in the end this matters most, a bad book. It demonstrates conclusively that although the career of Bret Easton Ellis may be on the rise in terms of notoriety and remuneration, in literary terms it is a burnout case. Whatever latent talent some of us discerned in his first novel, *Less Than Zero*, took its leave in *The Rules of Attraction* and now is shown by *American Psycho* to be beyond hope of recovery.

There is within it not a single redeeming quality. Ellis is capable of putting together a competent sentence and his ear for conversation is not entirely insensitive, but his prose here is flat and his dialogue is self-indulgently pointless, not to mention interminable. His "style," if that is the word for it, consists primarily of endless recitations of brand names as well as unrelated clauses connected in a wearying succession of non sequiturs. When the brand names and the non sequiturs meet in a single sentence, as usually they do, the result can be numbing:

It was cool this morning but seems warmer after

I leave the office and I'm wearing a six-button double-breasted chalk-striped suit by Ralph Lauren with a spread-collar pencil-striped Sea Island cotton shirt with French cuffs, also by Polo, and I remove the clothes, gratefully, in the air-conditioned locker room, then slip into a pair of crow-black cotton and Lycra shorts with a white waistband and side stripes and a cotton and Lycra tank top, both by Wilkes, which can be folded so tightly that I can actually carry them in my briefcase.

Ellis wants us to believe that passages such as this, of which the novel contains scores, are meant to underscore the blind, obsessive consumerism of its antiheroic narrator, Patrick Bateman, but in truth they are part of the author's own strategy of desperation; since he has nothing to say, he fills his pages with familiar brand names and inane chatter. Apart from Bateman, not a single one of his characters is interesting, distinctive or sympathetic; all dissolve into a blur of mere names that, like the brand names, are both interchangeable and indistinguishable.

This isn't to say that Bateman is interesting or sympathetic, only that he alone among the members of this large cast is recognizable; at least he has an identity, a claim that can be made for none of the men with whom he exchanges macho Wall Street chatter or the women whom he violates and murders. If this is intended to be a metaphor for the emptiness of all these people, so be it; what Ellis fails to understand is that the book is every bit as empty and infantile as they are.

Again, he would have us believe otherwise. *American Psycho* is loaded with clumsy devices designed to underscore the Major Themes with which it allegedly is preoccupied. "I AM HUNGRY AND HOMELESS PLEASE HELP ME": So reads the "sloppy cardboard sign" held by a homeless man, one of many who crop up periodically to serve in unimaginative contrast to Bateman and his hedonistic friends. Similarly, the hit Broadway show *Les Miserables* is a recurrent leitmotif designed to serve parallel purposes: "A torn playbill from *Les Miserables* tumbles down the cracked, urine-stained sidewalk," thus reminding us that the unfortunate people of any city's streets are mere objects of amusement and exploitation for the privileged few.

Ellis wants to have it both ways: to join the reader in looking down his nose at these shallow young habitues of New York's cafe society while at the same time exploiting prurient interest in their doings. To put it as charitably as possible, the sneer is considerably less persuasive than the prurience; *American Psycho* is a surpassingly cynical novel, a rip-off of territory already claimed by Tom Wolfe in *The Bonfire of the Vanities* and by the New York tabloids in their coverage of Robert Chambers and the preppy murder case.

As to Bateman's murders, the first woman victim meets her fate on Page 245. She has been preceded by one homeless man, a Wall Street competitor of Bateman's and a couple of dogs; many other women follow, as well as a 5-year-old boy whom Bateman executes on a whim during a visit to the zoo. All of these encounters are described in thoroughly gratuitous detail and with what gives every evidence of being a fair amount of relish; Ellis seems to have enjoyed his labors every bit as much as Bateman does his murders, decapitations, disembowelments and other amusements.

All of which are meant to be metaphors for what the book's jacket copy sententiously calls "the insanity of violence in our time or any other," but probably not even Bret Easton Ellis really believes that. Beneath its very thin veneer of thematic posturing *American Psycho* is pure trash, as scummy and mean as anything it depicts: a dirty book by a dirty writer. Of course Ellis has every right to write it, and Vintage every right to publish it. But the rest of us have every right not to read it; as one who did so out of duty, and who feels thoroughly soiled by the experience, I can only urge—no, pray—that everyone else refuse to do so by choice. (pp. B1, B3)

> *Jonathan Yardley, " 'American Psycho': Essence of Trash," in* The Washington Post, *February 27, 1991, pp. B1, B3.*

Norman Mailer

[*Mailer is a prominent American novelist who has explored themes of sex, drugs, and violence in such works as* The Naked and the Dead *and* The Deer Park. *In the essay excerpted below, he considers the artistic merit of* American Psycho.]

"The Communists," says someone at a literary party, "at least had the decency to pack it in after seventy years. Capitalism is going to last seven hundred, and before it's done, there will be nothing left."

If there is reality to *American Psycho,* by Bret Easton Ellis—if, that is, the book offers any insight into a spiritual plague—then capitalism is not likely to approach its septicentennial, for this novel reverses the values of *The Bonfire of the Vanities.* Where *Bonfire* owed some part of its success to the reassurance it offered the rich—"You may be silly," Wolfe was saying in effect, "but, brother, the people down at the bottom are unspeakably worse"— Ellis's novel inverts the equation. I cannot recall a piece of fiction by an American writer which depicts so odious a ruling class—worse, a young ruling class of Wall Street princelings ready, presumably, by the next century to manage the mighty if surrealistic levers of our economy. Nowhere in American literature can one point to an inhumanity of the moneyed upon the afflicted equal to the following description. . . . :

> The bum's not listening. He's crying so hard he's incapable of a coherent answer. I put the bill slowly back into the other pocket of my Luciano Soprani jacket and with the other hand stop petting the dog and reach into the other pocket. The bum stops sobbing abruptly and sits up, looking for the fiver or, I presume, his bottle of Thunderbird. I reach out and touch his face gently, once more with compassion and whisper, "Do you know what a fucking loser you are?" He starts nodding helplessly and I pull out a long thin knife with a serrated edge and being very careful

not to kill the bum push maybe half-an-inch of the blade into his right eye, flicking the handle up, instantly popping the retina and blinding him.

The bum is too surprised to say anything. He only opens his mouth in shock and moves a grubby, mittened hand slowly up to his face. I yank his pants down and in the passing head-lights of a taxi can make out his flabby black thighs, rashed because of constant urinating in his pant-suit, the stench of shit rises quickly into my face and breathing through my mouth, on my haunches, I start stabbing him below the stomach, lightly, in the dense matted patch of pubic hair. This sobers him up somewhat and in-stinctively he tries to cover himself with his hands and the dog starts barking, yipping really, furiously, but it doesn't attack, and I keep stab-bing at the bum now in between his fingers, stab-bing the back of his hands. His eye, burst open, hangs out of its socket and runs down his face and he keeps blinking which causes what's left of it inside the wound to pour out, like red, veiny egg yolk.

(pp. 154, 156)

Obviously, we have a radioactive pile on our hands. Can-celed by Simon and Schuster two months before publica-tion at an immediate cost to the publisher of a $300,000 advance, picked up almost at once by Vintage Books, and commented upon all over the media map. . . .

The Sunday *New York Times Book Review* took the un-precedented step of printing a review, months in advance, on December 16. In the form of an editorial titled "Snuff This Book! Will Bret Easton Ellis Get Away with Mur-der?" it is by Roger Rosenblatt, a "columnist for Life mag-azine and an essayist for 'The MacNeil/Lehrer Newshour,'" who writes in a style to remind one of the critical bastinadoes with which *Time* magazine used to flog the ingenuous asses of talented young writers forty years ago.

> *American Psycho* is the journal Dorian Gray would have written had he been a high school sophomore. But that is unfair to sophomores. So pointless, so themeless, so everythingless is this novel, except in stupefying details about expen-sive clothing, food and bath products, that were it not the most loathsome offering of the season, it certainly would be the funniest.

(p. 157)

The indictment becomes more personal in *Spy,* December 1990, by a young—I assume he is young—man who calls himself Todd Stiles:

> [Ellis] couldn't actually write a book that would earn attention on its merits, so he chose a course that will inevitably cause controversy and get him lots of press and allow him to pontificate, kind of like the novelist and critic Leo Tolstoi, on the question What is Art? *I am purposely ex-aggerating the way yuppie men treat women. That's the point,* he will say. *I meant to convey the madness of the consumerist eighties.* Not much could be more sickening than the mis-ogynistic barbarism of this novel, but almost as

repellent will be Ellis's callow cynicism as he jus-tifies it.

In fact, Ellis has given a few indications that he is ready to justify it. For the "Arts & Leisure" section of the Sun-day *Times,* December 2, 1990, he wrote a piece called "The Twentysomethings, Adrift in a Pop Landscape."

> We're basically unshockable. . . . This genera-tion has been wooed with visions of violence, both fictive and real, since childhood.

> If violence in films, literature and in some heavy-metal and rap music is so extreme . . . it may reflect the need to be terrified in a time when the sharpness of horror-film tricks seems blunted by repetition on the nightly news.

It is obvious. Ellis wants to break through steel walls. He will set out to shock the unshockable. And *Spy* writer Todd Stiles is right—we are face-to-face once more with the old curmudgeon "novelist and critic Leo Tolstoi" (who not so long ago used to be known as Tolstoy). We have to ask the question once more: What is art? The clue presented by Bret Easton Ellis is his odd remark on "the need to be terrified."

Let me take us through my reading of the book, even though the manuscript I read was close to 200,000 words; the Vintage edition is bound to be shorter, for the novel is needlessly long—in fact, the first fifty pages are close to unendurable. There is no violence yet, certainly not if the signature of violence is blood, but the brain receives a myr-iad of dull returns. No one who enters the book has fea-tures, only clothing. We will learn in a while that we are in the mind of our serial killer, Patrick Bateman, but from the second page on, we are assaulted by such sentences as this: "Price is wearing a six-button wool-and-silk suit by Ermenegildo Zegna, a cotton shirt with French cuffs by Ike Behar, a Ralph Lauren silk tie, and leather wing-tips by Fratelli Rosetti." On page 5, "Courtney opens the door and she's wearing a Krizia cream silk blouse, a Krizia rust tweed skirt and silk satin D'Orsay pumps from Manolo Blahnik."

By page 12, Price is "lying on a late 18th century French Aubusson carpet drinking espresso from a cerelane coffee cup on the floor of Evelyn's room. I'm lying on Evelyn's bed holding a tapestry pillow from Jenny B. Goode nurs-ing a cranberry and Absolut."

Bateman's apartment has "a long, white down-filled sofa and a 30 inch digital TV set from Toshiba; it's a high-contrast highly defined model . . . a high-tech tube com-bination from NEC with a picture-in-picture digital effects system (plus freeze-frame); the audio includes built-in MTS and a five watt-per-channel on-board amp." We progress through Super Hi-Band Beta units, three-week eight-event timers, four hurricane halogen lamps, a "glass-top coffee table with oak legs by Turchin," "crystal ash-trays from Fortunoff," a Wurlitzer jukebox, a black ebony Baldwin concert grand, a desk and magazine rack by Gio Ponti, and on to the bathroom, which presents twenty-two name products in its inventory. One has to keep reminding oneself that on reading Beckett for the first time it was hard not to bellow with fury at the monotony of the language. We are being asphyxiated with state-of-the-art commodities.

[*American Psycho*] is boring and it is intolerable—these are the worst and dullest characters a talented author has put before us in a long time, but we cannot get around to quitting. The work is obsessive.

——*Norman Mailer*

Ditto the victuals. Every trendy restaurant that has succeeded in warping the parameters of the human palate is visited by the Wall Street yuppies of this book. For tens of thousands of words, we make our way through "cold corn chowder lemon bisque with peanuts and dill . . . swordfish meatloaf with kiwi mustard."

Themes will alternate in small variations. We pass from meetings at the office (where business is never transacted) to free-weight workouts in the gym, to Nell's, to taxi rides, to more descriptions of clothing, furnishings, accessories, cosmetics, to conference calls to expedite restaurant reservations, to acquaintances who keep mistaking each other's names, to video rentals and TV shows. We are almost a third of the way through an unending primer on the artifacts of life in New York, a species of dream where one is inhaling not quite enough air and the narrative never stirs because there is no narrative. New York life in these pages is circular, one's errands footsteps in the caged route of the prison bull pen. Bateman is living in a hell where no hell is external to ourselves and so all of existence is hell. The advertisements have emerged like sewer creatures from the greed-holes of the urban cosmos. One reads on addicted to a vice that offers no pleasure whatsoever. One would like to throw the book away. It is boring and it is intolerable—these are the worst and dullest characters a talented author has put before us in a long time, but we cannot get around to quitting. The work is obsessive—the question cannot be answered, at least not yet: Is *American Psycho* with or without art? One has to keep reading to find out. The novel is not written so well that the art becomes palpable, declares itself against all odds, but then, it is not written so badly that one can reject it with clear conscience. For the first third of its narrativeless narrative it gives off a mood not dissimilar to living through an unrelenting August in New York when the sky is never clear and rain never comes.

Then the murders begin. They are not dramatic. They are episodic. Bateman kills man, woman, child, or dog, and disposes of the body by any variety of casual means. He has penetrated to the core of indifference in New York. Humor commences; movie audiences will laugh with all the hysteria in their plumbing as Bateman puts a body in a sleeping bag, drags it past his doorman, heaves it into a cab, stops at a tenement apartment he keeps as his pri-

vate boneyard, hefts it up four flights of stairs, and drops the cadaver in a bathtub full of lime. Smaller body parts are allowed to molder in the other apartment with the concert grand and the ashtrays from Fortunoff. To visitors, he explains away the close air by suggesting that he cannot find just where the rat has died. He gets blood on his clothing and brings this soiled package to a Chinese laundry. A few days later, he will curse them out for failing to clean his suit immaculately. The proprietors know the immutable spots are blood, but who is to debate the point? If you argue with a stranger in New York, he may kill you.

So, Bateman's murders are episodic: Nothing follows from them. His life goes on. He works out in the gym with dedication, he orders shad roe and pickled rabbit's kidney with cilantro mousse, he consumes bottles of Cristal with friends, and in discos he scores cocaine. Over one summer, he has an idyll in the Hamptons with Evelyn, the girl he may marry, and succeeds in restraining himself from murdering her; he masturbates over porny videos, he tells a friend in the middle of an acrimonious meal that if friend does not button his lip, he will be obliged to splatter friend's blood all over the blonde bitch at the next table, and, of course, the speech is heard but not taken in. Not over all that restaurant gabble, not in all that designer din. When tension builds, Bateman kills in the same state of loneliness with which he masturbates; for relief, he hires two escort girls and tortures them to death before going off to the office next morning to instruct his secretary on who he will be available to on the telephone, and who not.

The murders begin to take their place with the carambola sorbet, the Quilted Giraffe, the Casio QD-150 Quick-Dialer, the Manolo Blahnik shoes, the baby soft-shell crabs with grape jelly. Not differentiated in their prose from all the other descriptions, an odd aesthetic terror is on the loose. The destruction of the beggar is small beer by now. A boy who strays a short distance from his mother at the Central Park Zoo is killed without a backward look. A starving rat is indeed introduced into the vagina of a half-slaughtered woman. Is Bateman the monster or Bret Easton Ellis? At best, what is to be said of such an imagination? The book is disturbing in a way to remind us that attempts to create art can be as intolerable as foul manners. One finishes with an uneasy impulse not to answer the question but to bury it. Of course, the question can come back to haunt us. A novel has been written that is bound to rest in unhallowed ground if it is executed without serious trial.

So the question returns, what is art? What can be so important about art that we may have to put up with a book like this? And the answer leads us to the notion that without serious art the universe is doomed.

These are large sentiments, but then, we live in a world which, by spiritual measure, if we could measure it, might be worse than any of the worlds preceding it. Atrocities, injustice, and the rape of nature have always been with us, but they used to be accompanied by whole architectures of faith that gave some vision to our sense of horror at what we are. Most of us could believe in Catholicism, or Marxism, or Baptism, or science, or the American family, or Allah, or Utopia, or trade-unionism, or the synagogue, or the goodness of the American president. By now, we all know that some indefinable piece of the whole is not amenable to analysis, reason, legislative manipulation, committees, expertise, precedent, hard-earned rule of thumb, or even effective political corruption. We sense all too clearly that the old methods no longer suffice, if they ever did. The colloquies of the managers (which can be heard on any given TV night and twice on Sunday morning) are now a restricted ideology, a jargon that does not come close to covering our experience, particularly our spiritual experience—our suspicion that the lashings have broken loose in the hold.

In such a world, art becomes the remaining link to the unknown. We are far beyond those eras when the English could enjoy the spoils of child labor during the week and read Jane Austen on the weekend. Art is no longer the great love who is wise, witty, strengthening, tender, wholesomely passionate, secure, life-giving—no, Jane Austen is no longer among us to offer a good deal more than she will disrupt, nor can Tolstoy still provide us (at least in the early and middle work) with some illusion that life is well proportioned and one cannot cheat it, no, we are far beyond that moral universe—art has now become our need to be terrified. We live in the fear that we are destroying the universe, even as we mine deeper into its secrets. So art may be needed now to provide us with just those fearful insights that the uneasy complacencies of our leaders do their best to avoid. It is art that has to take the leap into all the truths that our media society is insulated against. Since the stakes are higher, art may be more important to us now than ever before.

We live in the fear that we are destroying the universe, even as we mine deeper into its secrets. So art may be needed now to provide us with just those fearful insights that the uneasy complacencies of our leaders do their best to avoid. It is art that has to take the leap into all the truths that our media society is insulated against.

—*Norman Mailer*

Splendid, you may say, but where is *American Psycho* in all this? Is the claim being advanced that it is art?

I am going to try an answer on these lines: Art serves us best precisely at that point where it can shift our sense of what is possible, when we now know more than we knew before, when we feel we have—by some manner of leap—encountered the truth. That, by the logic of art, is always worth the pain. If, then, our lives are dominated by our fears, the fear of violence dominates our lives. Yet we know next to nothing about violence, no matter how much of it we look at and live with. Violence in movies tells us nothing. We know it is special effects.

All the more valuable then might be a novel about a serial killer, provided we could learn something we did not know before. Fiction can serve as our reconnaissance into all those jungles and up those precipices of human behavior that psychiatry, history, theology, and sociology are too intellectually encumbered to try. Fiction is indeed supposed to bring it back alive—all that forbidden and/or unavailable experience. Fiction can conceive of a woman's or a man's last thoughts where medicine would offer a terminal sedative. So Ellis's novel cannot be disqualified solely by a bare description of its contents, no matter how hideous are the extracts. The good is the enemy of the great, and good taste is certainly the most entrenched foe of literature. Ellis has an implicit literary right, obtained by the achievements of every important and adventurous novelist before him, to write on any subject, but the more he risks, the more he must bring back or he will leach out the only capital we have, which is our literary freedom.

We have to take, then, the measure of this book of horrors. It has a thesis: *American Psycho* is saying that the eighties were spiritually disgusting and the author's presentation is the crystallization of such horror. When an entire new class thrives on the ability to make money out of the manipulation of money, and becomes altogether obsessed with the surface of things—that is, with luxury commodities, food, and appearance—then, in effect, says Ellis, we have entered a period of the absolute manipulation of humans by humans: the objective correlative of total manipulation is coldcock murder. Murder is now a lumbermill where humans can be treated with the same lack of respect as trees. (And scream commensurately—Bateman's main tools of dispatch are knives, chain saws, nail guns.)

Such a massive thesis does not sit well on underdeveloped legs—nothing less than a great novel can support a great, if monstrous, thesis. A good novel with too major a theme can only be crushed by the weight of what it is carrying. The test of *American Psycho* is whether we can ever believe the tale. Of course, it is a black comedy—that all-purpose cop-out!—but even black comedies demand an internal logic. If we can accept the idea that the political air turned flatulent after eight years with the hornpipe wheezes of the Pied Piper, we must also entertain the thesis that the unbridled manipulations of the money-decade subverted the young sufficiently to produce wholly aimless lives for a generation of Wall Street yuppies. But was it crowned by the ultimate expression of all these meaningless lives—one total monster, a Patrick Bateman? Can he emerge entirely out of no more than vapidity, cupidity, and social meaningless? It does not matter whether a man like him does, in fact, exist; for all we know there might be a crew of Patrick Batemans at large in New York right now.

The demand is not that Bateman be factual, but that he be acceptable as fiction. Do we read these pages believing that the same man who makes his rounds of restaurants and pretends to work in an office, this feverish snob with a presence so ordinary that most of his casual acquaintances keep mistaking him at parties and discos for other yuppies who look somewhat like him, can also be the most demented killer ever to appear in the pages of a serious

American novel? The mundane activity and the supersensational are required to meet.

Bret Easton Ellis enters into acute difficulties with this bicameral demand. He is a writer whose sense of style is built on the literary conviction (self-serving for many a limited talent) that there must not be one false note. In consequence, there are often not enough notes. Even with writers as splendidly precise as Donald Barthelme, as resonant with recollected sorrow as Raymond Carver, or as fine-edged as Ann Beattie, there are often not enough notes. A book can survive as a classic even when it offers much too little—*The Great Gatsby* is the prime example forever—but then, Fitzgerald was writing about the slowest murders of them all, social exclusion, whereas Ellis believes he is close enough to Dostoyevsky's ground to quote him in the epigraph. Since we are going to have a monstrous book with a monstrous thesis, the author must rise to the occasion by having a murderer with enough inner life for us to comprehend him. We pay a terrible price for reading about intimate violence—our fears are stirred, and buried savageries we do not wish to meet again in ourselves stir uneasily in the tombs to which we have consigned them. We cannot go out on such a trip unless we believe we will end up knowing more about extreme acts of violence, know a little more, that is, of the real inner life of the murderer.

Bateman, however, remains a cipher. His mother and brother appear briefly in the book and are, like all the other characters, faceless—we are less close to Bateman's roots than to his meals. Exeter and Harvard are named as parts of his past but in the manner of Manolo Blahnik and Ermenegildo Zegna—names in a serial sequence. Bateman is driven, we gather, but we never learn from what. It is not enough to ascribe it to the vast social rip-off of the eighties. The abstract ought to meet the particular. In these pages, however, the murders begin to read like a pornographic description of sex. Bateman is empty of inner reaction and no hang-ups occur. It may be less simple to kill humans and dispose of them than is presented here, even as real sex has more turns than the soulless high-energy pump-outs of the pornographic. Bateman, as presented, is soulless, and because we cannot begin to feel some instant of pity for him, so the writing about his acts of violence is obliged to become more hideous externally and more affectless within until we cease believing that Ellis is taking any brave leap into truths that are not his own—which happens to be one of the transcendent demands of great fiction. No, he is merely working out some ugly little corners of himself.

Of course, no one could write if art were entirely selfless. Some of the worst in us has also to be smuggled out or we would use up our substance before any book was done. All the same, a line is always in place between art and therapy. Half of the outrage against this book is going to come from our suspicion that Ellis is not creating Bateman so much as he is cleaning out pest nests in himself. No reader ever forgives a writer who uses him for therapy.

If the extracts of **American Psycho** are horrendous, therefore, when taken out of context, that is Ellis's fault. They are, for the most part, simply not written well enough. If one is embarked on a novel that hopes to shake American society to the core, one has to have something new to say about the outer limits of the deranged—one cannot simply keep piling on more and more acts of machicolated butchery.

[The] greater horror, the real intellectual damage this novel may cause is that it will reinforce Hannah Arendt's thesis on the banality of evil. It is the banality of Patrick Bateman that creates his hold over the reader and gives this ugly work its force.

—Norman Mailer

The suspicion creeps in that much of what the author knows about violence does not come from his imagination (which in a great writer can need no more than the suspicion of real experience to give us the whole beast), but out of what he has picked up from *Son* and *Grandson of Texas Chainsaw Massacre* and the rest of the filmic Jukes and Kallikaks. We are being given horror-shop plastic. We won't know anything about extreme acts of violence (which we do seek to know if for no less good reason than to explain the nature of humankind in the wake of the Holocaust) until some author makes such acts intimately believable, that is, believable not as acts of description (for that is easy enough) but as intimate personal states so intimate that we enter them. That is why we are likely never to know: where is the author ready to bear the onus of suggesting that he or she truly understands the inner logic of violence?

To create a character intimately, particularly in the first person, is to convince the reader that the author is the character. In extreme violence, it becomes more comfortable to approach from outside, as Bret Easton Ellis either chose to do, or could do no better. The failure of this book, which promises to rise occasionally to the level of the very good (when it desperately needs to be great), is that by the end we know no more about Bateman's need to dismember others than we know about the inner workings in the mind of a wooden-faced actor who swings a broadax in an exploitation film. It's grunts all the way down. So, the first novel to come along in years that takes on deep and Dostoyevskian themes is written by only a half-competent and narcissistic young pen.

Nonetheless, he is showing older authors where the hands have come to on the clock. So one may have to answer the question: What would you do if you happened to find yourself the unhappy publisher who discovered this book on his list two months before publication?

I am not sure of the answer. The move that appeals most in retrospect is to have delayed publication long enough to send the manuscript to ten or twelve of the most respected novelists in America *for an emergency reading.*

Presumably, a number would respond. If a majority were clearly on the side of publication, I would feel the sanction to go ahead. To my knowledge, that possibility was never contemplated. A pity. Literature is a guild, and in a crisis, it would be good if the artisan as well as the merchants could be there to ponder the decision.

This is, of course, fanciful. No corporate publisher would ever call on an author, not even his favorite author, on such a matter, and perhaps it is just as well. A lot of serious literary talent could have passed through a crisis of conscience. How to vote on such a book? The costs of saying "Yes, you must publish" are fearful. The reaction of certain women's groups to **American Psycho** has been full of unmitigated outrage.

Indeed, an extract from one of the most hideous passages in the novel was read aloud by Tammy Bruce, president of the Los Angeles chapter of the National Organization for Women, on a telephone hot line. The work is described as a "how-to novel on the torture and dismemberment of women . . . bringing torture of women and the mutilation deaths of women into an art form. We are here to say that we will not be silent victims anymore."

While it is certainly true that the fears women have of male violence are not going to find any alleviation in this work, nonetheless I dare to suspect that the book will have a counter-effect to these dread-filled expectations. The female victims in **American Psycho** are tortured so hideously that men with the liveliest hostility toward women will, if still sane, draw back in horror. "Is that the logical extension of my impulse to inflict cruelty?" such men will have to ask themselves, even as after World War II millions of habitual anti-Semites drew back in similar horror from the mirror of unrestrained anti-Semitism that the Nazis had offered the world.

No, the greater horror, the real intellectual damage this novel may cause is that it will reinforce Hannah Arendt's thesis on the banality of evil. It is the banality of Patrick Bateman that creates his hold over the reader and gives this ugly work its force. For if Hannah Arendt is correct, and evil is banal, then that is vastly worse than the opposed possibility that evil is satanic. The extension of Arendt's thesis is that we are absurd, and God and the Devil do not wage war with each other over the human outcome. I would rather believe that the Holocaust was the worst defeat God ever suffered at the hands of the Devil. That thought offers more life than to assume that many of us are nothing but dangerous, distorted, and no damn good.

So I cannot forgive Bret Easton Ellis. If I, in effect, defend the author by treating him at this length, it is because he has forced us to look at intolerable material, and so few novels try for that much anymore. On this basis, if I had been one of the authors consulted by a publisher, I would have had to say, yes, publish the book, it not only is repellent but will repel more crimes than it will excite. This is not necessarily the function of literature, but it is an obvious factor here.

What a deranging work! It is too much of a void, humanly speaking, to be termed evil, but it does raise the ante so high that one can no longer measure the size of the bet.

Blind gambling is a hollow activity and this novel spins into the center of that empty space. (pp. 157-59, 220-21)

Norman Mailer, "Children of the Pied Piper," in Vanity Fair, *Vol. 54, No. 3, March, 1991, pp. 154-59, 220-21.*

Peter Plagens

[In the following excerpt, Plagens discusses the plot of American Psycho *and addresses accusations that the book's depiction of violence is misogynistic and potentially dangerous.]*

"Kimball is utterly unaware of how truly vacant I am," says Patrick Bateman, the young investment banker who moonlights as a serial killer in Bret Easton Ellis's third and latest novel, **American Psycho.** By page 275, unfortunately, the reader is way ahead of the private detective who appears only briefly and fecklessly. And way ahead of Bateman, too, who doesn't know when to quit—either killing or talking about himself. The older brother of Sean Bateman, a lead in Ellis's second book, **The Rules of Attraction** (who is in turn a college friend of Clay, the poor-little-rich-boy protagonist of Ellis's 1985 debut, **Less Than Zero**), Patrick Bateman is less a real character than a grotesque nouvelle cuisine meal ordered repeatedly by practically everyone in **American Psycho.** Let's see, I'll start with the Harvard man and some bland investment-banker sauce, then a main course of alienation (overdone, please), followed by sexual psychosis topped with whipped murder. Beverage? Bitter social satire, no sugar.

For a guy who continuously spills his guts—and a lot of other people's—Bateman is pretty much a blank. At the office, he frets about "the Ransom account" and "the Fisher account," but his tasks are revealed with all the detail of Darrin's job at the ad agency in the old "Bewitched" sitcom. He hangs around with his buddies McDermott, Price and Van Patten, who prattle about the right brands of booze, suits and accessories. Nothing these moneyed Slaves of the Universe worry so much about requires any education, real taste or life experience; it's all overpriced consumer hardware that any 26-year-old with a platinum American Express card can enjoy. Deep down, in fact, Bateman is a rube: he rents the tape of *Body Double* about 40 times instead of just buying the damned thing, and he's happy with his video club because it lets him check out as many tapes as he wants as long as he spends two grand a year on it.

But Bateman has a big kink: his amalgamated desires for consumer perfection—ostensibly fired to a fever pitch by New York in the Reagan '80s—are turning him into a bloodthirsty maniac. The pleasures promised by price tags turn ugly everywhere before his eyes. He is constantly and profoundly disappointed. "[As] inconspicuously as possible I try to peer over the counter to check out what kind of shoes she's wearing, but maddeningly they're only sneakers—*not* K-Swiss, *not* Tretorn, *not* Reebok, just cheap ones." Even his athletic coitus is rendered interruptus for lack of the right (water-soluble, that is) spermicide. Although Bateman fantasizes slicing up female acquaintances, his first kill (knife to the eyeballs) is a male bum.

But he soon starts dispatching women in ways that make chain sawing gentle by comparison (crucifixion by nail gun, breasts exploded by jumper cables, starving rat inserted vaginally). At the height of his derangement, he parades naked around his apartment sexually attached to a severed head.

Bateman is a sloppy murderer and a bad housekeeper, so it's especially odd that none of his handiwork hits the papers, not even the sensation-seeking *New York Post* (which Ellis repeatedly mentions). No cops come sniffing around, only one of the victims is ever missed and Bateman himself hardly skips a lunch date. His confession that "My appearances in the office the last month or so have been sporadic to say the least" carries no hint of pending unemployment, and his bottoming out—sleeping under his bed, drinking his own urine and Fed Exing the shriveled heart of one of his victims to her mother—turns out to be temporary. For anything besides another murder to happen (we experience a mere 20 of them) would, of course, require a plot, something Ellis has not yet been able to deliver. As in his first two novels, he merely winds up a clock of circumstance and lets entropy of the soul run it down.

American Psycho is more, however, than an exercise in extreme sexual violence. The jolting gore is surrounded by an almost trance-inducing mantra of brand names; every character, right to the bitter end of the book when the point has been made a hundred times over, is introduced, item by item, by his or her designer clothes and accouterments. ("Russell was wearing a two-button wool sport coat by Redaelli, a cotton shirt by Hackert, a silk tie by Richel, pleated wool trousers by Krizia Uomo and leather Cole-Haan shoes.") Bateman's disease, Ellis contends, is our disease: we want it all, we want it now and we really don't care who's hurt in the getting.

We Americans are still haunted by the paradox Tocqueville pointed out 150 years ago: democracy and mercantilism mean that anybody with a fat wallet can live like royalty, but never the real kind whose lineage assures the throne. (When a girlfriend calls him Honey, Bateman reacts: "King, I'm thinking. King, Evelyn, I want you to call me King.") So we build hierarchies of the right clothes, the right clubs, the right electronics, only to have them crushed by the next wave of nouveau riche poseurs with a line of credit at Citibank. In the jockeying for position, people lose their humanity and become mix 'n' matches of jackets, watches, skirts and suits. To underline the situation's hopelessness, Ellis concludes *American Psycho* with the sight of a sign: THIS IS NOT AN EXIT.

In the hands of a near-great writer, *American Psycho* might work, but Ellis is only passable good. He admits anachronisms like "tipsy," "Jeez" and "Yikes!" and his recurring references to what's featured on "The Patty Winters Show" is a lame steal from Jay McInerney's "Coma Baby" headlines in *Bright Lights, Big City*. In place of setup, Ellis pulls retroactive fact out of a hat when he needs it (". . . I carry the body up four flights of stairs until we're at the unit I own in the abandoned building"). The book seems barely edited once, let alone twice.

American Psycho stands accused, however, of being not only mediocre, but base, misogynous and dangerous. Its defenders invoke what might be called the Masters and Johnson law: better to know these things than not to know them, and fiction is our best probe into the dark side of the human condition. Although the novel will not likely cause any real deaths (unless chanting *Giorgio Armani* can kill), it does up the ante. Disembowelment will soon be *de rigueur*. . . . The climate of fiction grows steadily darker, its texture much coarser. Those who argue that equally shocking violence goes all the way back through *Beowulf* to the Bible should try savoring: "Most of her chest is indistinguishable from her neck, which looks like ground-up meat, her stomach resembles the eggplant and goat cheese lasagna at Il Marlibro or some other kind of dog food, the dominant colors red and white and brown." When asked if he knows of a more graphic book, Ellis told *Newsweek,* "Maybe there hasn't been."

Although the content ("She was too ugly to rape") of *American Psycho* is—and should be—incontestably objectionable to women, its cultural politics are worse. In the current issue of *Vanity Fair,* Norman Mailer (whose *An American Dream,* with its unapprehended wife-murderer Stephen Richards Rojack, somewhat presaged Ellis's novel a generation ago) gives Ellis a light pat on the head for trying his hand at a serious social critique. Mailer's essay and Ellis's book both assume that the fictional dismemberment of women is, in the end, men's business. The best that women can do in the cause of literary catharsis is to serve as brutalized bodies in novels, or as boycotting banshees in real life. Ellis, of course, is not actually Bateman, but on the back cover of *American Psycho* the author's photograph is posed and lighted quite like "Bateman's" on the front, and it's next to a boldface résumé of the banker, not the author. So when Bateman says, near the end of the book, "My pain is constant and sharp and I do not hope for a better world for anyone. In fact I want my pain to be inflicted on others," we would be well advised to start listening for other, less nihilistic voices in American fiction. (pp. 58-9)

> *Peter Plagens, "Confessions of a Serial Killer,"* in Newsweek, *Vol. CXVII, No. 9, March 4, 1991, pp. 58-9.*

Roger Cohen

As his novel *American Psycho* arrives in stores and death threats are delivered suggesting he should be dismembered like the victims of the book's fictional killer, Bret Easton Ellis seems dismayed that his work has sparked the biggest literary brouhaha since Salman Rushdie's *Satanic Verses.*

"I had no idea the novel would provoke the reception it's gotten, and I still don't quite get it," he said last week in his first interview since Simon & Schuster abruptly canceled the book's publication three months ago and it was resold to Vintage. "But then I was not trying to add members to my fan club. You do not write a novel for praise, or thinking of your audience. You write for yourself, you work out between you and your pen the things that intrigue you."

For Mr. Ellis, 26 years old, those intriguing things were

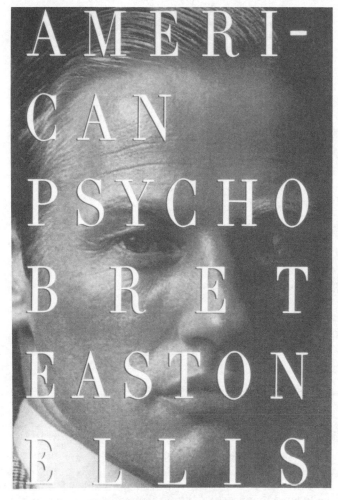

Dust jacket for American Psycho.

the obsessions of an affluent group of rootless young executives schooled by day in Wall Street greed and seeking by night to use the easy money of the late 1980's for the instant enactment of every fantasy.

In this world—relentlessly depicted in mind-numbing description of designer clothes, menus and furniture—Mr. Ellis chose to place a murderous madman, Patrick Bateman, because, the author says, "it seemed apt that this man would be working on Wall Street at that time."

Bateman, the narrator of *American Psycho* (which has been published as a trade paperback), is indeed as ruthless and amoral as the worst manipulators of 1980's Wall Street. He is a psychopath. He believes almost everybody is in love with him but he cannot feel, let alone love. He gets very upset when he cannot recognize the designer of a pair of socks. He knows a Gianni Versace suit at 50 yards.

Yet he is utterly untroubled by the most outlandish violence, described in hideous detail. He gouges out a homeless man's eyes, he axes off a business acquaintance's head while the poor fellow is "in midsentence." He does abominable things to women, including slicing out a tongue and

nailing limbs to the floor: then he kills them and, occasionally, cooks up the remains.

"During the years I worked on the book, I did not know how violent it would become," said Mr. Ellis.

> But it seemed clear to me that Bateman would describe these acts of brutality in the same numbing, excessive detail and flat tone that he recounts everything else—his clothing, his meals, his workouts at the gym. It seemed to me that he would not avoid telling the reader what he does when he murders people. For me, it was an esthetic choice that made sense.

The author, whose first novel, *Less Than Zero,* made him one of the hot young writers of the 1980's, along with Jay McInerney and Tama Janowitz, went on:

> I was writing about a society in which the surface became the only thing. Everything was surface—food, clothes—that is what defined people. So I wrote a book that is all surface action: no narrative, no characters to latch onto, flat, endlessly repetitive. I used comedy to get at the absolute banality of the violence of a perverse decade. Look, it's a very *annoying* book. But that is how as a writer I took in those years.

Critics, however, have generally dismissed any such serious intent.

Mr. Ellis shrugged off the torrent of criticism. "This is a work of fiction and should speak for itself," he said. "But clearly there are metaphors here. Bateman's actions and especially his *reactions* to what he does symbolize, at least to me, how desensitized our culture has become toward violence."

Several women's groups, however, contend that Bateman merely reveals Mr. Ellis's own misogyny. The Los Angeles Chapter of the National Organization for Women has called for a boycott of *American Psycho,* as well as of all books published by Vintage and its hard-cover counterpart, Alfred A. Knopf, whose publisher, Sonny Mehta, bought the novel.

"We will press this boycott very hard," said Tammy Bruce, the president of the Los Angeles chapter. "This is not art. Mr. Ellis is a confused, sick young man with a deep hatred of women who will do anything for a fast buck. And Mr. Mehta is worse. Ellis could have gone on writing until he choked on his own vomit if Vintage had not agreed to publish this misogynistic garbage."

Mr. Ellis said he had received 13 anonymous death threats, including several with photographs of him in which his eyes have been poked out or an axe drawn through his face. "It's a little dismaying," he commented.

He went on: "Bateman is a misogynist. In fact, he's beyond that, he is just barbarous. But I would think most Americans learn in junior high to differentiate between the writer and the character he is writing about. People seem to insist I'm a monster. But Bateman is the monster, I am not on the side of that creep."

Still, the possible confusion between author and fictional hero has been so extreme that as a precaution, Mr. Ellis is not going on a promotional tour. This is very unusual for a new book by a best-selling novelist. Moreover, Vintage, which paid an undisclosed sum for the book, is not doing any advertising.

"We are trying to publish in as quiet and dignified a way as we can," said Mr. Mehta, who has himself received abusive letters and telephone calls. He added, "Bret inadvertently offended a certain feminist sensibility in a book that is ugly but that captures a seedy and scummy aspect of our time."

For much of a two-hour interview, Mr. Ellis appeared disturbed above all that so many have questioned the seriousness of his intent in the 400-page book he worked on for more than three years.

"There seems to be a notion that when you are writing about someone killing and torturing people, especially women, you have to do it in a very earnest and politically correct way," he said. "But the murder sequences are so over the top, so baroque in their violence, it seems hard to take them in a literal context. And there are dozens more hints that direct the reader toward the realization that for all the book's surface reality, it is still satirical, semi-comic and—dare I say it?—playful in a way."

There are hints, among them the nonsensical impunity with which Bateman acts and the fact that one of his victims appears to come alive again despite being decapitated.

In the vision of the book that Mr. Ellis outlined, Bateman appears as the protagonist of a modern-day picaresque romp: an extremely black comedy, with Bateman as a one-dimensional, first-person narrative vehicle through which the author offers a frightening incarnation of the frivolous violence he sees at the heart of late 1980's Manhattan culture.

"Look at sex in the 80's," Mr. Ellis said.

> It was frightening, laced with danger, impersonal, something to be bought, negotiated. And when people, like those in my book, are so obsessed with the surface sheen of life, sex cannot be any more than that. How do you square something as organic and primitive as sex with an obsession with appearance, money and status? It can no longer be the satisfying outgrowth of a relationship.

Indeed, toward the end of the book Bateman declares bluntly that "sex is mathematics." He goes on: "Love cannot be trusted. Surface, surface, surface was all that anyone found meaning in . . . this was civilization as I saw it, colossal and jagged."

Turning to Simon & Schuster's decision to cancel his book (after having paid the author a $300,000 advance) on the grounds of taste, Mr. Ellis said he was distressed partly because Paramount Communications, the parent company of the publisher, puts out "squalid and extremely violent" movies like *Friday the 13th.* But there was also something deeper:

> When you're at a publishing house, you expect your publisher to understand what you do. You

do not expect them to be so timid about what the press or others might say about a work they have bought, printed and are about to ship. That strikes me as a definite betrayal of an article of faith in publishing.

Mr. Ellis added that two top editors at Simon & Schuster—Robert Asahina and Charles E. Hayward—called him to express their mortification over the decision. Mr. Asahina, the editorial director of the company's Summit imprint and Mr. Ellis's former editor, said: "I expressed regret to Bret. I am a great admirer of his."

Mr. Hayward, the president of the Simon & Schuster trade book division, declined to comment.

Mr. Ellis said that he found the outcry particularly dismaying at a time when serial killers are a recurring theme in popular culture.

"I guess you walk a very thin line when you try to write about a serial killer in a very satirical way," he said. "There's this new sensitivity. You cannot risk offending anyone." (p. C13, C18)

> Roger Cohen, "Bret Easton Ellis Answers Critics of 'American Psycho'," in The New York Times, *March 6, 1991, pp. C13, C18.*

Christopher Lehmann-Haupt

[*In the excerpt below, Lehmann-Haupt argues that* American Psycho *is an artistic failure due to its presentation of graphic violence without a moral context.*]

One approaches with a fair degree of awe a novel that has inspired the reaction that Bret Easton Ellis's **American Psycho** has done. To have provoked a publisher to reject a finished manuscript without demanding the return of a substantial advance; to have prompted hate mail and death threats; to have aroused a women's organization to call for a boycott of the book's new publisher—why, it's as if **American Psycho** had returned us to some bygone age when books were still a matter of life and death instead of something to distract us on a flight between JFK and LAX.

And **American Psycho** rewards one's expectations in its uniquely perverse way. Despite the lack of ironic distance between his own voice and that of his psychopathic narrator, Mr. Ellis clearly does not want or expect the reader to identify with Patrick Bateman.

For all the viscera and gore he spills, this Wall Street monster is not a flesh-and-blood character, nor is it a realistic world that his demented narrative creates. There are too many devices that transform it into a lifeless abstraction. There are the relentless fashion notes that identify the designer of every stitch of clothing nearly every character wears. There are the mechanically repetitive references to the musical *Les Misérables* and a television program called "The Patty Winters Show," whose interview subjects grow steadily more grotesque as the book progresses.

And there is the endless jumble of elegant objects, lavish menus, expensive restaurants, chic nightclubs, platinum Amex cards, adulterated drugs and empty small talk, as if no one in Mr. Ellis's world had the faintest sense of scale or proportion.

As for the notorious sex and mutilation scenes: the relentless and horrifying energy that seems to have gone into their creation betrays the mind not of a leering sensualist or a cynical pornographer but rather of a cartoonist trying to animate *Tales From the Crypt,* the comic book of the 1950's that tried in its clumsy way to make black humor of human physicality.

Since the people involved are unreal and the physiology of what is done to them impossible, it is not so difficult to conceive of their scenes as a Tom and Jerry cartoon with human body parts. An authorial mind that can build a construction out of a rat, a Habitrail and a female torso has gone far beyond the casual degradation of women into an expression of sadistic rage as an abstract end in itself.

What Mr. Ellis is evidently trying to say is that Patrick Bateman lives in a morally flat world in which clothes have more value than skin, objects are worth more than bones, and the human soul is something to be sought with knives and hatchets and drills.

That is the true outrage of *American Psycho,* not its violence to women, men, blacks, Jews, Chinese, Japanese, homosexuals, homeless people, rats and dogs . . . but its violence to an organic idea of art.

—Christopher Lehmann-Haupt

Patrick says as much himself in one of the novel's few moving scenes, when his secretary, Jean, mistakes him for someone worth her love, and Patrick in response is seized with a vision of his life that could well be a description of Mr. Ellis's novel:

> . . .where there was nature and earth, life and water, I saw a desert landscape that was unending, resembling some sort of crater, so devoid of reason and light and spirit that the mind could not grasp it on any sort of conscious level and if you came close the mind would reel backward, unable to take it in.

Patrick concludes:

> Nothing was affirmative, the term "generosity of spirit" applied to nothing, was a cliché, was some kind of bad joke. Sex is mathematics. Individuality no longer an issue. What does intelligence signify? Define reason. Desire— meaningless. Intellect is not a cure. Justice is dead. Fear, recrimination, innocence, sympathy, guilt, waste, failure, grief, were things, emotions, that no one really felt anymore. Reflection is useless, the world is senseless. Evil is its only permanence. God is not alive. Love cannot be trusted. Surface, surface, surface was all that anyone

found meaning in . . . this was civilization as I saw it, colossal and jagged. . . .

The trouble with *American Psycho* is, of course, that you can't create a meaningless world out of meaninglessness. Surface, surface, surface can not serve to define substance. For meaninglessness to cohere, it needs a context of meaning. *American Psycho* is built out of meaninglessness except for a couple of outrageously comic-satirical scenes, the best of them an episode in which Patrick explains to the woman who wants to marry him that he can't stand the burden of a commitment because he has this little problem with mass murder, and she fails to hear what he is saying in her desire to pin him down.

You get the feeling that Mr. Ellis began writing his novel with a single huge emotion of outrage, and that he never in his three years of working on it paused to modulate that emotion or to ask if it was helping to construct an imaginary world. How else could he have written scenes so flat and tedious that the reader wants to scream? Surely not with profit or exploitation in mind. If so, commercialism has never before produced anything so boring.

The idea that technique has meaning begins in the classroom. Only a student of modern literature could have conceived the idea that putting together what he saw as symbols of the Reagan 1980's would constitute an artistic statement about the 1980's. That is the true outrage of *American Psycho,* not its violence to women, men, blacks, Jews, Chinese, Japanese, homosexuals, homeless people, rats and dogs (all of whom Patrick Bateman succeeds in insulting to one degree or another), but its violence to an organic idea of art. It is significant that Thomas Harris's novel *The Silence of the Lambs* depicts far more degrading treatment of women than *American Psycho* does, and yet no one is complaining, despite the current success of *Lambs* as a film. That is because the killer's psychopathology is given a moral framework.

American Psycho lacks such a moral framework. Mr. Ellis teases us near the end into believing that Patrick Bateman may finally be brought to justice. But he isn't; at the book's close, he is still at large. The author is saying that today such monstrous criminality is indistinguishable from the general behavior of society. But Mr. Ellis's true offense is to imply that the human mind has grown so corrupt that it can no longer distinguish between form and content. He has proved himself mistaken in that assumption by writing a book whose very confusion of form and content has caused it to fail, and for that offense and no other does one have cause to excoriate *American Psycho.*

> *Christopher Lehmann-Haupt, " 'Psycho': Whither Death without Life?" in* The New York Times, *March 11, 1991, p. C18.*

Henry Bean

[*Below, Bean praises* American Psycho *as an insightful commentary on American society.*]

It is the mid-1980s, the boom years for young traders and investment bankers. Our narrator is Patrick Bateman, 26, handsome, Harvard BA, MBA, a Wall Street scion who wears (a limitless wardrobe of designer fashions), eats ("pilot fish with tulips and cinnamon"), buys (quantities of top-end audio/visual equipment) and boffs ("blond, big . . . ," every one of them). In short, he has, does and is everything the children of Reagan were promised they could have, do and be. True, he's sort of alienated and also commits serial murders, some of which he describes in disturbing detail, but, hey, in deregulation you live with the bumps. Let the marketplace take care of it.

What's rarely said in all the furor over this novel is that it's a satire, a hilarious, repulsive, boring, seductive, deadpan satire of what we now call—as if it were something in the past—the Age of Reagan.

The miracle of Bret Easton Ellis is that without a plot, without much in the way of characters and with a throwaway nonstyle that renders the luxurious, the erotic and the grotesque in the same uninflected drone, a prose that is pure exchange value, he nevertheless makes it virtually impossible to stop reading.

He's able to do this, in part, because he knows so well what we want. His endless lists of brand names, chic restaurants and thoroughly accessible hardbodies is the stuff of our fantasy life—the lower floors, perhaps, but we spend a lot of time there. The book satisfies those desires, in fantasy, at least, and keeps satisfying them until our cup runneth over and we're sickened by what we want and we go on wanting it anyway.

Balanced again this seductiveness is the fact that Ellis is, first and last, a moralist. Under cover of his laconic voice, every word in his three novels to date springs from grieving outrage at our spiritual condition. That impulse is more measured here, more withheld than in *Less Than Zero* (1985) or *The Rules of Attraction* (1987), and the restraint turns the adolescent complaint of the earlier books into the maturer satire of this one. But in all of Ellis' work, the force comes from this pairing of seduction and disgust, pandering and judgment.

Which makes it hard to understand how this book has become such a scandal. Compared to other literary renegades, from Sade on, who by now occupy an accepted place in the modernist canon, Ellis seems almost a choir boy.

Maybe that's his problem. Ferocious monsters, gore dripping from their grinning jaws, amuse us. They tickle our own too-bridled lusts, and we're flattered when they ask us, in William Burroughs' famous line, "Wouldn't you?" But a melancholy fiend like Bateman is a party pooper. He gets us all worked up, then sermonizes.

American Psycho has been called a sadistic book, and that's true if we mean sadism toward the reader. Like the pre-*Scarface* Brian DePalma, Ellis shoves our faces into our own appetites, forcing us to see how much we'll swallow (including gross implausibilities) just to get off. We forgive him because he always implicates himself; he isn't looking down on the venality of mortals, he's here in the glitzy gutter with us.

The loudest attacks have accused the novel of misogyny, exploitation of and unremitting violence toward women.

Yet of the 18 people (not to mention assorted animals) tortured and murdered by the narrator, eight are women, nine are men, and one is a small boy; of the book's 400 pages, fewer than 40 are devoted to these events. In the other 360, Ellis is unusually attentive to daily instances of racism, anti-Semitism, homophobia. And he repeatedly mocks the perfunctory sexism of his upper-class males. Here is one of them summing up the irrelevance of personality in selecting a girlfriend:

"A good personality," Reeves begins, "consists of a chick who has a little hardbody and who will satisfy all sexual demands without being too slutty about things and who will essentially keep her dumb . . . mouth *shut*."

It is true that some of the torture and dismemberment, especially of the women, is performed with particular zeal. Much rage is expended therein. But hatred of women being so prevalent in our world, it must surely be an appropriate subject for fiction. (One can imagine NOW [The National Organization for Women] demanding such books instead of boycotting them.) And it is difficult to conceive of anybody reading these passages without being moved to disgust, grief and finally pity.

Yes, Bateman commits these acts with relish, but it is a mechanical obedience to a compulsion. They bring him no more joy than the rest of his miserable life. He is not a creature of Sade, Lautreamont or Genet, someone whose crimes are a revolt against a repressive order, a thrust toward freedom. Bateman's freedom is his curse; he can do anything, therefore life is meaningless. Behind his crimes is the attempt to call down on himself the curse of a God whom he fears has ceased to exist. But of course the project is futile. He sins and no one cares. It almost seems that no one knows.

> Ellis is, first and last, a moralist. Under cover of his laconic voice, every word in his three novels to date springs from grieving outrage at our spiritual condition.
>
> —*Henry Bean*

Toward the end of the novel, Bateman is surprised that a couple of bodies he's left lying around haven't turned up in the newspapers. Neither, we realize, have any of the others. A private detective comes looking for a missing person and, in a hilarious scene, Bateman does his best to give himself away, but the detective wanders off and isn't heard from again. The police never show up. Strangest of all, a friend mentions that he's just had dinner in London with a Wall Street colleague whom Bateman had supposedly dissolved in lime (while Bateman smoked a cigar and listened to his Walkman).

What are we to make of this? That the friend, who keeps confusing Bateman with someone named Davis, has likewise confused his London dinner date with Bateman's victim, who himself addressed Bateman as Marcus Halberstam? (These guys are interchangeable; Bateman's crime could be any of theirs.) That Bateman is similarly confused about whom he has killed? Or is it possible that the murders themselves never occurred?

In the midst of one dismemberment, his mouth crammed with the "bluish rope" of a young woman's intestine, "Wheel of Fortune" blaring in the background on a giant television, Bateman remarks: "This is my reality. Everything outside this is like a movie I once saw."

But to the reader, even this "reality" feels like a movie. The most gruesome scenes have the deliberate inauthenticity, the stock horror of slasher movies. It is those films (which he compulsively rents from video stores) that are Bateman's real touchstones, not murder but the fantasy and representation of murder.

Once we begin to doubt the reality of the crimes, questions arise about other scenes: An interlude in East Hampton feels more dreamed than lived (though with bits of nightmare creeping in); a chase through the city practically has the shadow of a boom in it; one sex scene is thoroughly convincing, a comic horror show of spermicides and receptacle tips, while others are parodies of cheap pornography.

The novel subtly and relentlessly undercuts its own authority, and because Bateman, unlike, say, Nabokov's unreliable narrators, does not hint at a "truth" beyond his own delusions, *American Psycho* becomes a wonderfully unstable account. The most persuasive details are combined with unlikely incidents until we're not only unsure what's real, we begin to doubt the existence of reality itself.

Ellis makes this uncertainty into a philosophical condition, and though that is a brilliant way to describe the social and historical moment, it undercuts everything else in the book. Worse, it invites the suspicion that the author is covering up a graver problem: his inability to imagine the mind of his murderer.

Observing a woman who loves him trying to fathom his peculiar behavior, Bateman remarks: "[S]he is searching for a rational analysis of who I am, which is, of course, an impossibility: There . . . is . . . no . . . key." But that's a facile out. Too often the book omits exactly those moments—particularly the transitions from sex to violence—which would give if not an explanation at least the sense of felt experience. It never touches the inner logic that would turn the rage that is inside all of us into murderous frenzy.

But few works are capable of that: *Crime and Punishment,* some of Patricia Highsmith, Immamura's film *Vengeance Is Mine.*

What Ellis fully understands is the politics of social irresponsibility, that electoral strategy initiated by Richard Nixon but which has reached full flower in the Reagan-Bush years. *American Psycho* tells of the greed and soullessness to which we have all yielded in our way and that leads inexorably to gratuitous murder, to murder as our final expression of disgust and plea for judgment.

That the novel cannot fully explain this is only to say that it fails at a great thing. Ambition alone sets it apart from most contemporary fiction. Prudes, squares and feminist commissars aside, the rest of us should applaud Bret Easton Ellis for setting out in this noble and dangerous direction; his only fault is that he did not go far enough. (pp. 1, 5)

Henry Bean, "Slayground," in Los Angeles Times Book Review, *March 17, 1991, pp. 1, 5.*

A feminist interpretation of violence in *American Psycho*:

The problem with what Ellis has done can be understood only through [Andrea] Dworkins' and Catherine MacKinnon's interpretation of violent pornography: that it is a violation not of obscenity standards, but of women's civil rights, insofar as it results in conditioning male sexual response to female suffering or degradation.

Under that definition alone can we understand what is so troubling about his six or seven notorious scenes. Ellis consistently and skilfully pairs scenes that are often (to this reader) very arousing, with scenes of carnage that follow as a consequence of that eroticism. The transition is so swift that the violence enters the reader while she is in a state of heightened erotic receptiveness; there has been a powerful moment of conditioning. That is the one authentic reason that Ellis has been—and should be, only with greater consciousness—held accountable for having done other than merely written a story; he has consciously committed an act.

Naomi Wolf, in "The Animals Speak," New Statesmen & Society, 12 April 1991.

Bret Easton Ellis [Interview with Robert Love]

[*Love*]: *Though they have usually waited until your books were published, the critics have never been very kind to you. Are you affected by published criticism?*

[Ellis]: The critics have never made any major impression on me. I remember the first review of *Less Than Zero;* someone from Simon and Schuster called me up at college. They said, "Oh, the first reviews came out." And I was thrilled. I thought: "Oh, my God. I am being reviewed. I am going to pore over this review, I'm going to xerox it, I'm going to frame it, and I'm going to probably read it more than I've ever read anything else in my life." I read it—it wasn't a bad review—it was okay. And it was one of the most distinctly anti-climactic experiences I've ever had.

Why?

I had thought that the response of the critics—like the response from anybody—was really important. In the end I found that it's really not so important. You write for yourself. It's between you and the typewriter. There was nothing I learned from any of these critics. I mean, do most critics' taste extend beyond the hopelessly middle-brow? If you're a writer and you write because you hope the critics will be kind to you, then you're demented.

I think a lot of writers in their twenties expect that. They desperately want to be liked. And you can sense it in their books. They don't want to offend. They don't want to write anything messy or crazy. They don't want to deal with anything in a raw way, even if that means fumbling. A lot of writers I know want to write something that will be respected—that will play with the press. And most of their books, even the good ones, are just too concerned with appearances—with, for the lack of a better word, ass kissing. It's very polite and charming. A lot of it is sensitive. There was a quote from a critic on the back of a book from someone my age that said, "As light and as airy as a soufflé."

And you've obviously decided to cut against that grain.

And a lot of people would say that it's not worth it. A lot of people would say prose must be pitch perfect. That novels must have traditional narrative structure—that characters must change. You would think that most writers in their twenties would want to fool around a little bit—would want to be a little experimental—would want to write something a little bit subversive, even if it means risking failure.

*How long did it take you to write **American Psycho?***

I started the book in the fall of 1986, before I did the re-write on *Rules of Attraction.* I finished what I thought was the final draft in December of 1989.

Did it change shape over that time?

The books I've written so far have been completely thought-out before the actual writing begins. I do an out-line, which takes me three or four months, that incorpo-rates every scene. I work that way because the books are basically conceptual. I don't see them as novels in the proper sense. I get a character I want to write about; and I prefer, so far, to have these characters narrate. The char-acter's voice sets up the structure of the book, and even the length of the book. And that holds true for *American Psycho.* I wanted to write a book from the viewpoint of someone who kills people. I wanted to set it in New York. Fine. From just that I knew what the language of the book was going to be like, what the structure of the book was going to be like and even, to a degree, what its length was going to be. When all those problems are solved within the outline, then I start writing.

Did you know from the outset that the book was going to be so graphically violent?

With *American Psycho* it was very clear to me when I started writing that this was going to be a character who was so obsessed with appearances that he was going to tell the reader in minute, numbing detail about everything he owns, everything he wears, everything he eats. And that sense of detail spilled over into the murders. It seemed to me dishonest not to present those sequences in the same fashion that the narrator, Patrick Bateman, would de-scribe a plate of food at a restaurant, the interior of his apartment or the clothes everyone in a room is wearing. It seemed a logical extension of his voice.

So did this character take on a life of his own?

Well, every character takes on a life of its own. Especially if he's narrating the book. You become the medium. They place themselves in your head, and you become their voice. Some writers may scoff at this idea, but I didn't make a lot of the aesthetic choices in this book. With a character like Bateman, someone who's very far away from my life, I believe that you become 100 percent that person when you're writing. When I was writing this book, I became that man for hours at a time. I don't see how else you can do it.

Were you ever surprised by the choices Bateman was mak-ing?

Oh, constantly, but I have to say that was also true about writing *Less Than Zero*—which is undeniably closer to my life than this book is. Yeah, one of the things that keeps you going is being surprised by what your charac-ters say and do and how they decide to act.

Your character displays an incredible vocabulary of barbar-ity and viciousness. How did you feel when you were writing the torture and murder scenes?

They were incredibly upsetting to write, the hardest scenes I've ever had to write—for obvious reasons. Yet at the same time, I knew they had to be there. I knew that it was correct to have them there. So that made it a little less dif-ficult than, say, if I thought that *maybe* they didn't need to be there or *maybe* they didn't need to be this long. These scenes were probably more upsetting to write because I had to keep writing *I* all the time. *I* do this. *I* did that. That does a number on you psychologically that I can't quite describe. I don't think I could tell you how I felt after writ-ing those scenes. I cried a few times. For some reason, I hate admitting that, but it's true. I know I'm never going to write anything like that again. Not that it ever was in my system in the first place, but I probably got rid of those demons.

*In his piece about **American Psycho** in* Vanity Fair, *Nor-man Mailer criticized you for just that: chasing demons from your soul, or what's worse, using the reader for thera-py.*

I wouldn't disagree. But he was commenting in a disap-proving sense: that maybe this is not the way to go about it. I disagree with that. I think in some ways it was cathar-tic to write this book, and whether one likes to hear it or not, you can't help but work out demons when you're writing—even if you're writing a light comedy, airy as a soufflé.

Were you working out some kind of rage against women?

No. I don't think that played a part in it at all. And even the fact that I'd have to tell someone that no, I'm not a misogynist, is the kind of statement that automatically makes people perk their ears up and go, "Oh, really?"

But do you think there's a natural animosity between men and women?

Actually, I do think that. But I'm much more sympathetic to the female side. I saw my parents go through a very long, torturous divorce—it went on for eight years—where it seemed to me that the woman does not have the upper hand, or even a hand that's barely fair, in a case like that. And I've seen my sisters—I've got two younger sisters—I've seen both of them mistreated by various boyfriends at various times.

Since this book is, however, written from the point of view of the perpetrator, I think it would be hard for some women to believe you.

I would have to say I don't care what some women think or feel about this book, and I would have to say I don't care whether they find it offensive or not. That's not my problem, and I don't feel any responsibility toward women or the women's movement or NOW [The National Organization for Women] to write what they consider a socially acceptable book. What I'm doing is not that political, and they're turning it into something that is political. So my message to women who are offended by this book is: "Sorry, guys, read another book. Buy Alice Walker if it makes you feel better. Buy Amy Tan. I don't care what you read." But this book, for whatever reasons, should be allowed to be published, and people should have the choice of whether to read it or not to read it, to buy it or not to buy it, to like it or not to like it. I'm not going to sit at my typewriter and compose something only so it will not offend a woman's sensibility, and any writer who does that is a wimp. Who do they want me to be? Alan Alda?

Some of the scenes in the book are funny in a sly, dark and perverse way. The names of restaurants and the food they serve are grotesque and humorous. Bateman works for a firm called Pierce and Pierce. Do you feel that a lot of the people who are criticizing the book just don't get it?

Most of them haven't even read it, and those who have, I think, have missed it in a big way. The immense detail, the ridiculous minutiae, it gets to a point where it's so over the top that—well, you can have either of two reactions. Either you find it so numbing you skip it, which I don't think is a bad thing to do, or you find it funny. But at the same time, I wanted the violence to work on another level, to be upsetting, too. I don't care if a lot of people find that mixture of gallows humor and real harsh violence interesting, but that is something that was conscious.

Bateman knows so much about clothing. A lot of his descriptions read like fashion credits from GQ.

Many of them are. *GQ* was inordinately helpful in costuming the characters in the book. They should have gotten credit.

Then there are the endless specifications on his electronics, as well.

From various stereo magazines.

Bateman seems to be made from magazines.

A mixture of *GQ* and *Stereo Review* and *Fangoria* . . . and *Vanity Fair*.

In the book, Patrick Bateman has a favorite movie, Brian

De Palma's Body Double, *which he's rented thirty-seven times. I'm assuming that you saw it. Were you shocked by its violence?*

Yes, I was shocked. But I wasn't offended. People like those in the NOW coalition can't seem to divide the two things: being shocked and being offended. People seem to think that shock equals outrage—that if something shocks you, then you should be outraged by it. Being shocked by cultural, what's the word, *artifacts?*—movies, poems, songs, photography—more often than not can be a healthy, liberating experience.

Do you think that you could say to a member of NOW that **American Psycho** *is going to provide a healthy, liberating experience?*

I am not saying that reading my book is going to be a healthy, liberating experience for anyone. That's for a reader to decide. I'm saying that within our culture that when you are presented with material like that, more often than not, it widens your perceptions.

What NOW is about to perpetrate—this boycott of Random House—is harmful: It's intolerance being masked by this new sensitivity. They're treating people, and I think women especially, like infants by not giving them the choice to read this material on their own and make up their minds.

Are you shocked by the response the book has gotten even before it has been published?

I'm confused by it, but I think it's basically a joke. To put it as simply as possible: The acts described in the book are truly, indisputably vile. The book itself is not. Patrick Bateman is a monster. I am not. The outrage that has been expressed is totally disconnected from what this book is about. And if anything, it reflects the intolerance of our culture to deal with anything that falls outside the acceptable. (pp. 46, 49)

Not that this book is a loving little thing, but I don't think any book deserves this sort of advance negative scrutiny, no matter what the subject matter is. And I think the indignation and the hostility that the press expressed just seems far more intolerable than what this book is about.

This has obviously been a rough time. Have your friends and colleagues been supportive?

Actually, most people in publishing have been very supportive whether they've liked the book or not, so it has not been that rough a time. The worst aspect of this whole fiasco is that it puts the writer—it puts me—in the position of having to defend my work. A writer should never have to do that. I would never ask a writer or a songwriter or a poet why they wrote something. When people ask, "Why did you write this?" it automatically connotes a negative; that you've done something wrong or that you've been a bad boy. That's what has upset me the most.

Some people have said that you deliberately set out to write something this controversial—that your second book didn't sell very well, and you needed to create a public tempest to revive your career.

Well, that's a very complimentary suggestion—that I have the hindsight, plus the prowess, to actually do that. I started writing this book a year before *Rules of Attraction* was published. When my editor first saw the book and we talked about it, it was clear to us that this was a fairly dark, not very commercial novel.

I had never heard from my editor, from my agent or from anyone else that this was going to be a controversial novel. And I definitely had no idea that it would be attacked to the degree that it has been. So it's very flattering for people to assume that I could carry this whole thing off: have my publisher cancel the book a month before publication and have the National Organization for Women threaten to boycott my new publisher.

Let me stand in the place of the feminist critics: "Fine, you're an artist, you write for yourself. But did you have to go into such graphic detail, having Bateman put a rat up a woman's vagina, cut off a victim's breasts and cook them in the frying pan? The awfulness of those descriptions! Can you understand how women feel about reading that?" How do you respond to that?

I would respond with this question: "Would it be as upsetting to you, would you be as outraged by this book, if Patrick Bateman were a gay serial killer?" The fact that I even have to ask that question is offensive to me in the first place. But would it offend you if he committed the same actions on young men? If they were mutilated, tortured in the same manner, would you be boycotting this publisher? Well, Patrick Bateman is not gay. He attacks women—he has rage against women. His descriptions of the murders fit into his language—fit into how he narrates the book.

From my point of view, though, I don't know if we're that shocked or that upset by viewing murder or killing in this culture anymore. Perhaps we've witnessed so much of it that we've become numb to it, that when we do see it, it means little or it means nothing, and we turn the channel or get in line for the next movie, or we turn the page of the newspaper. It seemed to me that I had to really get the point across—if not to an audience, at least to myself while writing this book—that these murders *are* painful, that they're terrible, that they're messy, that they're as ugly as possible. That seemed important to me to describe in the book.

When I was writing this book, the last thing that occurred to me was women would be protesting it. I thought maybe serial killers would protest the book, but I had no idea that women would be protesting it. What's so offensive to me about NOW and about Tammy Bruce, who I think is getting on this little bandwagon for her own publicity reasons, is that there's this sense, unspoken—well actually, not unspoken—that I *advocate* this type of behavior. That's what this boycott and what this rage seems to indicate—that for some reason Bret Easton Ellis thinks that not only is this a good thing that Patrick Bateman is doing but he advocates it.

I saw Gloria Steinem on *Larry King,* and she was saying, "I hope Mr. Ellis realizes that when this book comes out and women are killed and tortured in the same fashion as is described in *American Psycho,* I hope he understands that he must take responsibility for this." If for some reason a deranged mind gets hold of this book and reads it and does commit a terrible act of violence against a woman—or a man . . . how does that affect my role as a writer? Do we not express ourselves the way we want because a very small, tiny, minuscule percentage of people might get the wrong idea? I mean, then why don't we start banning *Catcher in the Rye* because Mark Chapman shot John Lennon?

You're not the first novelist to write about serial killers. Today the movie The Silence of the Lambs *opens in New York. Thomas Harris wrote the book that this movie is based on, as well as one called* Red Dragon. . . .

I've read both the books.

Why do you think so much criticism, then, has been directed at you?

The obvious reason is that the violence in *American Psycho* is much more graphic than, say, the violence in *Silence of the Lambs.* I don't remember sequences in that book where he describes killing or skinning the women a lot. See! Again it all comes back to . . . when I say a sentence like that, it makes me *cringe.* The fact that I have to comment on how much skinning goes on in one book as compared with how much goes on in another book is ridiculous. I think it's because in this book it's unflinchingly described and in the other books it's alluded to.

So you made an artistic choice.

Yes, and now as a reader, you can reject that choice—and that's fine. But I don't think you should call for banning other people's books because of it.

Let's consider another point. Harris's books seem to be situated in a universe of good and evil. There are cops vigorously working the side of good, an equal resistance to the twisted desires of the killers. In **American Psycho,** *Pat Bateman is a devil working in a moral void. In the book, no one cares, no one even notices. You present this material—as you did in* **Less Than Zero**—*without anchoring it morally. There's no resolution; we don't get to understand Bateman or his rages.*

If at the end of this book Patrick Bateman was caught, jailed and executed, would the outrage still be there? I don't know. I can't say that this book is autobiographical in any sense of the word—but it does in some way reflect my outlook on what the Eighties seemed to symbolize for me. It's very basic. The Eighties seemed to me to be a very ugly decade, and this was what I came away with. And it's an ugly book.

Bateman works on Wall Street. It sounds like you're making a specific point about the rampant consumerism and greed of the last decade.

Yeah, but that's my outlook on these times. I know it's kind of rigidly nihilistic. That question about good and evil and how people need to be soothed—it seems more than ever right now that people want that. That there's this *spiritual*—for lack of a better word—malaise that people want coated with something. They don't want to know . . .

That evil can go unpunished.

Yeah. In so many movies and books, evil *does* go punished. The bad guys almost certainly always lose. But if something comes out where that does not happen, people take offense.

Did you do a great deal of research on serial killers?

I did so much research on this book. I read criminology textbooks. I read every pulp and true-life crime book I could get my hands on. I read every book about Ted Bundy. Actually, it was a really lousy year for reading. It was terrible. I read about murders that no one's ever heard of that are just completely appalling—what serial killers can and do inflict on their victims. I think it might have been an aesthetic choice of mine to up the ante a little bit in the book, but not by much.

The police reports about Gainesville [the Florida serial murders that remain unsolved]—a lot of that stuff is even creepier and more horrible than what Patrick Bateman does in this book. There is a level of human savagery and cruelty that is undeniable. If we can't reflect it in our culture, if we're intolerant of it, what does that mean? Does it mean that we don't want to see it in art because there's so much of it in real life? That we want entertainment instead? We want outcome, we want resolution. Do we want evil diminished in art because we don't always get that in our everyday life?

Do you believe in God?

Are you asking me if I was raised in a religious family or if I go to church? I was raised an agnostic. I don't know—I hate to fly, I have a fear of flying. That means either that I have no faith in air-traffic controllers or that I've done something really bad, and this is God's way of getting at me. Maybe I'm caught in the middle. . . . But no, I don't believe in God. That's such a strange thing to admit in an interview.

In Vanity Fair, *Norman Mailer stated that his problem with the book was that you indeed upped the ante in terms of graphic descriptions of intimate violence in a work of art, but you didn't bring back the interior life of Pat Bateman. He remains a cipher. Mailer wrote: "Ellis wants to break through steel walls. He will set out to shock the unshockable." But in the end he couldn't defend the book. In fact, he said he could not forgive you.*

All I can say is that it was a choice that I thought was inappropriate for this book. I don't think you can explain someone like Patrick Bateman—at least not within the context of a novel where the character is talking to you, narrating to you—without cheating. I didn't want to—and I didn't want Bateman to literally verbalize: "I was mistreated by my parents when I was younger, and that is why. . . . I was rejected by women when I was in my teens, and this is why I do this." Maybe an unspoken explanation is maybe what Mailer was looking for. Again what you have here are two writers disagreeing on their takes on a novel. To me there is no reasoning. To me this creature just exists.

There's a way of thinking about good writing that says if

you're going to take your reader through such a terrible experience, then you want to provide something that makes it comprehensible, that keeps it from being a joy ride.

That's an interesting word. I don't look at this book as a joy ride through evil. That's hard for me to understand. But now, because of what the press has done with this book, maybe there are people who will buy it to experience a kind of sick thrill from those passages. While I was writing, it did not occur to me that the reader would hope for an epiphany that would explain it all away—that would make it "worthwhile."

I agree with a lot of what Mailer wrote. I think it is, in many ways, an unendurable book. A lot of it is probably intolerable. It's violent. It's boring. I think some of it's sick. But I also think, to me, it accurately reflects my take on that scene and that time.

Simon and Schuster dropped the book because it offended the taste of the CEO of the company. Within days, Sonny Mehta of Random House announced that he would publish it. Did you face further resistance at your new publisher?

Though it was the best of circumstances that Random House bought it, and I think they're a publisher who deep down understands the book and who believes in it, I was also disheartened to find that they were a little frightened by it and that they expected cuts to be made that I wasn't aware of when I accepted them as the publisher. That was very, very upsetting. I felt the book had already been edited and did not need—or would benefit from—second opinions.

Were you again asked to cut the violent scenes?

Yes.

Did you?

No. There were maybe one or two trims that were made that were for purely aesthetic reasons and not political or moral reasons. The editing process at Random House, even though in the end I had pretty much free rein, still was a battle of sorts that I didn't expect and I felt was kind of unwarranted.

The comments on some of the other sequences were on target and were actually helpful. What was so strange was that they were trying to use the same reasoning for the violent sequences. And I'm talking about three or four violent sequences that they not only wanted trimmed but they wanted excised from the manuscript.

I really believed that they had to stay in. And without them a lot of the book would have been meaningless. So, overall I'm grateful that Sonny's my publisher, and I will probably stay with him. In fact, I know I'll stay with him for the next book. But the editing process of this one was, to put it mildly, shaky. And I think that's just because of the whole circus that followed this book into Vintage. I don't think it was Vintage's fault, I just think the reputation of the book had preceded it.

What shocks you these days?

I'm shocked that Vanilla Ice sells 7 million copies of a record. I'm *shocked* by it. It shocks me more than the fact that we're in a war with Saddam Hussein right now, because the war that's going on right now seemed predictable. It seemed like this was going to happen. I'll end up sounding like such an old curmudgeon if I go on on this. What's the thing that everyone complains about? The mediocrity of the culture—of popular culture and people's blind acceptance of it. How can you not be shocked by the public's overwhelming acceptance of a movie like *Total Recall* or *Die Hard 2*? The things that are accepted in popular culture constantly shock me. But then I'm stuck in this position: What do you do when you're part of it?

Are you working on another novel?

Yes, I'm writing a book about a homeless man who finds the true meaning of Thanksgiving. I want to write the sequel to *Watership Down.* I want to write what a critic is going to call "a big, warm hug of a book." I want to write a book that boils with love. I want to write a book about the environment. I want to write the most politically correct book I can think of. (pp. 49-51)

Bret Easton Ellis and Robert Love, in an interview in Rolling Stone, *No. 601, April 4, 1991, pp. 45-6, 49-51.*

Fay Weldon

[*Weldon is an English novelist and dramatist whose works often explore feminist issues. In the excerpt below, she considers Ellis's reflection of contemporary values in* American Psycho *and defends the work's artistic merit.*]

Shall we consider New York, 1991? New York today, every city in the world tomorrow: "Abandon Hope All Ye Who Enter Here" scrawled in blood-red lettering on the wall of a fine upstanding branch of the Chemical Bank? "Fear," scribbled likewise, on the McDonald's on 4th and 7th Avenue? In the newspapers, on the radio, on TV, snippets of murders and mayhem, of beggars and brutality.

Let's enjoy the dirt. Film and record posters revealing more, yet more, as if we couldn't get enough, don't get enough. Screaming women and crazed men (the paraphernalia of blood, sex, bondage and violence) looking down from the billboards. Look up, not at the stars but at a tortured, torturing humanity. Not just life but the imagination slipping, so far as we can see, out of control, into chaos.

Shall we now consider the society hostesses of Manhattan who continue to ask Bret Easton Ellis to parties? Ellis has been heard of, as has his novel, *American Psycho.* And his novel's cannibal murderer. That's what counts. A little excitement, a little thrill. If only Ellis's work was autobiographical. Okay for him to eat people's brains; I don't suppose he'll do it amongst the canapes. And if he did, is life really so much worse than death? Do come in, smart Mr. Bret Easton Ellis, serial killer! It's the year of the serial killing, isn't it? Aren't the films of the year about serial killers: murder for the fun of it? And we all clap and cheer. Me too, me too.

Money, restaurants, designer labels, smart clothes, *things*:

That's all we've got, we smart young things, to cheer us up. And nobody is shocked. Nothing shocks. We are stunned; we are brutalized. Only the military, who haven't got to this stage yet, seems able, with its clean-lined, elegant weapons of death, its promise of purity, and a neat, swift finality, to return us our dignity and our hope.

All very well for Norman Mailer to have complained that *American Psycho*'s "legitimate theme" needs "a greater writer than Bret Easton Ellis" to do it properly, but I reckon Ellis has done it properly; he's done it proud. His first book, *Less Than Zero,* was about the wealthy young of California, and what one flowery-powery generation has done to the next: If there's no love, only sex, the only good thing about sex is death; finality.

This man Bret Easton Ellis is a very, very good writer. He gets us to a 'T.' And we can't stand it. It's our problem, not his. *American Psycho* is a beautifully controlled, careful, important novel that revolves about its own nasty bits. Brilliant. (pp. C1, C4)

All you sweet people who have gotten upset because Bret Easton Ellis, in a novel devoted almost entirely to the obsessive consolations offered by a society, itself in the grip of a psychotic fit of sado-masochism scattered throughout a novel delineating why the serial killer kills, actually describes the detail of the killings: Why have you got so squeamish all of a sudden?

Of all the things you ought to censor—should have censored because we now live in a world so terrible, so full of "Abandon Hope" scrawled blood-red on our city walls, someone has to start crying, "Enough"—why pick on wretched, brilliant Bret Easton Ellis?

I'll tell you why. It's because there's always been someone in the other books to play lip service to respectability; to the myth that the world we now live in is still capable of affect. The serial killer gets discovered, punished, stopped. There are people around to throw up their hands in horror, who can still distinguish between what is psychotic and what is not. Justice is done. There is remorse.

Not in *American Psycho.* And we hate him for saying it. In *American Psycho,* nobody cares. Slaughtered bodies lie undiscovered. The city has fallen apart. Nobody takes much notice. The police have other things to do. Those who are killed don't rate—they are the powerless, the poor, the wretched, the sick in mind, the sellers of flesh for money: their own and other people's. The tides of the city wash over them, erase their traces. The landlady, seeing her blood-spattered walls, is vexed because she needs to re-let quick. She doesn't want a fuss, she wants her rent. Docilely, our anti-hero of the '90s (pray God), our hero of the '80s (young, unscrupulous, talented, highly-motivated, highly skilled, an asset to society), cleans up the walls, able to respond to this desire at least. Nowhere else can he find a response. Whatever he does, there is no affect.

So what do we cry? Ban the book! Disgusting! Pervert! Let's ask Ellis to our party, let's watch him. After that we'll take ourselves off to the cinema, watch a few flayed bodies; work ourselves in with *Nightmare on Elm Street.*

The books and the films don't create society, I promise you. They reflect it.

Our yuppie hero kills an abandoned dog, slices it with a knife, walks on. No one cares. Women get their kicks from bondage. Yuppie goes too far, the women get to bleed a bit, but they get paid. That's enough for them. The whole world's into bondage. So he goes further. What are the odds? Not a nice book, not at all, this portrait of psychotic America, psychotic us. Just enough to touch a dulled nerve or two, get an article or so written.

Picador, which is publishing **American Psycho** in Great Britain, is keeping the price high, so one hears, to keep the dreaded thing out of the hands of those who might use scenes of torture and cannibalism as a tool for self-titillation, and then escalate to the real thing, the way people escalate (or so they say) from dope to heroin. Such dreadful, unliterary people, Picador seems to assume, are poor, uneducated. Too abashed to go into a proper bookshop where the hardbacks sell. Can't afford the hardback anyway.

Well, that's hopeful of Picador. Publishers are nice folk. They see a world in which wealth and education will stop people from being mass murderers and perverts. Perhaps they're right. I reckon they're publishing it because it's a good book, this buzzer of a book. A seminal book.

The feminists—that's me too—see Ellis's book as anti-women. So it is. So's the world, increasingly. Dead women, the stuff of fiction. It's anti-dog too, and anti-beggar and anti-child. Women, in Ellis's book, just seem to queue up to be murdered, the way young men joining the army queue up to murder. I reckon if we can ban **American Psycho** as anti-women, and perhaps we should, a whole lot of anti-men books could be banned too. Let's ban Norman Mailer. Incitement to murder the male. Incitement to war, the other pornography.

Look, I didn't want you to actually read Ellis's book. I did it for you. I expect you have enough trouble with your own fantasies of revenge, as you wonder whether you're brave enough to walk down your street late at night. The book is upsetting all right. Just don't insult a novel without reading it first, that's all I ask.

I wouldn't go to the stake for it as I would for Salman Rushdie's right to publish *The Satanic Verses*. **American Psycho** is a novel written out of the American tradition—the novelist's function is to keep a running tag on the progress of the culture; and he's done it brilliantly, but others are doing it too. And anyway no one is suggesting that Bret Easton Ellis should be killed, eaten alive, for writing it. Or not yet. *The Satanic Verses* comes more out of a European tradition; its function not just to collate the world, but make sense of it: move it on a little further towards civilization. Not much, but all we've got. God knows it's an uphill struggle. (p. C4)

> *Fay Weldon, "Now You're Squeamish?" in* The Washington Post, *April 28, 1991, pp. C1, C4.*

> The real issue [surrounding *American Psycho*] is our increasingly degraded and brutal popular culture. The fact that our rape and murder rates are triple those of other Western nations has a lot to do with the violent images and fantasies flooding our culture.
>
> —*John Leo, 1990.*

Richard Corliss

[In the following excerpt, Corliss discusses the motif of film and video in American Psycho.*]*

Patrick Bateman, vidkid for the Nineties. This 26-year-old is rich: Tom Cruise lives in the penthouse of his Upper West Side apartment. Patrick's suave and handsome: "pure prep perfection," a friend admiringly says. He's successful: a high-paying job at Pierce & Pierce (Sherman McCoy's old company) pads his inherited wealth. And he kills people: insatiably, sadistically, randomly—or almost. One afternoon he watches a juggler, then moves on "in search of a less dorky target. Though if he'd been a mime, odds are he'd already be dead." Patrick has standards.

He is mad, of course. Mad enough that he sees the Manhattan homeless everywhere, shouldering their way into his dangerous gaze, in person or in the posters for *Les Misérables* that trail him like implacable Javert. Mad enough to punctuate his apologia with essays on pallid pop stars like Genesis and Huey Lewis. Indeed, he is so mad that there is every good reason to believe that all the killings and many of the characters exist only in his pretty-ugly head. The one male friend he kills is reliably reported to have been seen in London. But then, nearly everyone in **American Psycho** mistakes nearly everyone for nearly everyone else.

Patrick is also video-mad. His only compulsive cultural interest is "The Patty Winters Show," a morning talkfest he tapes religiously. Patty's subjects include: real-life Rambos, UFOs that kill, toddler murderers, Nazis who juggle grapefruit, "Has Patrick Swayze become cynical or not?," people over 700 pounds (What Can We Do About Them?), how your pet can become a movie star, a boy who fell in love with a box of soap, human dairies, men who've been raped by women, Ted Bundy's letters to his fiancée, people with half their brains removed, an interview with Bigfoot ("I found him surprisingly articulate and charming"), orgies for 8-year-olds, fourth-grade girls who trade sex for crack, and "Doormen from Nell's—Where Are They Now?".

Life bustles for a vidiot like Patrick. No time for a business lunch, a dinner date, even a capricious homicide: he's got to watch "a movie about five lesbians and ten vibrators" on his 31-inch Panasonic TV set and his Toshiba VCR, and then "I've got to return some videotapes." At his neighborhood store, VideoVisions, he realizes that "there are too many couples in line for me to rent *She-Male Reformatory* or *Ginger's Cunt* without some sense of awkwardness or discomfort," but notes that an acquaintance is taking out *Friday the 13th: Part VII* plus a documentary on abortions. Patrick asks the counter girl if the store stocks any Jami Gertz movies (the film version of Ellis' *Less Than Zero* would be one), then opts for *Body Double,* which he has rented 37 times previously, "because I want to watch it again tonight even though I know I won't have enough time to masturbate over the scene where the woman is getting drilled to death by a power drill since I have a date with Courtney at seven-thirty at Café Luxembourg."

By now it should be obvious what Ellis is up to. But for a moment let's strip *American Psycho* of its satirical style, as most reviewers have, and tell you, . . . where to find the good (i.e., bad, violent, repellent, newsmaking) parts in the Vintage Paperback edition. Browsers take note. Page 131: Patrick attacks derelict and attendant dog. Page 165: He eviscerates sharpei and dog's owner. Page 180: He stabs Asian delivery boy. Page 207: He brutalizes his friend Alison. Page 213: He beats up a beggarwoman because the sign she is holding misspells *disabled.* ("She was too ugly to rape.") Page 217: He axes his friend Paul. Page 245: He nail-guns and Maces his friend Bethany. Page 289: He butchers his friend Elizabeth and uses jumper cables and pliers on a callgirl, Christie. Page 298: He kills a child at the zoo. Page 303: He Maces and skins two prostitutes, Torri and Tiffany. Page 327: A girl and a rat. Page 345: Another victim, whose body he dismembers, cooks, and attempts to eat. Page 348: He shoots a street minstrel.

Disgusting, you must think. But justified, I hope you'll agree. For beneath and within the lurid toolbox murders, *American Psycho* is black humor, intended and achieved. It's a comic monologue, an updated, X-rated gloss on Robert Browning's "My Last Duchess," except that Patrick's victims aren't hung in stairway portraits, they're left to rot in a dead friend's apartment. It's Peter Greenaway Guignol, but more so. It's a morality play disguised as a snuff movie. Ellis' tone is the same as Patrick's: uninflected rage. The difference is that the author is appalled at the society—one desensitized by Hollywood and The Movies, one based on indifference, snobbery, sex, greed, envy, lies, drugs, and videotape—in whose dead heart his protagonist can flourish. Patrick's heinous shallowness, faithfully reproduced in the prose, is the book's point; the tedium is the message. The most daring and perverse thing about the book is its trust that the reader will get it. You have to look for the fury behind the facetious façade.

[This] is a book of lists: videos, hi-tech possessions, interchangeable victims. There's hardly a simile in the 399 pages. Ellis' prose is stripped of metaphor, because Patrick is too self-absorbed to bother thinking how anything might be like something else. The problem is that the book's savagers have condemned Ellis as a sleaze merchant just because he is faithful to Patrick's point of view. They don't think Randy Newman really hates blacks and short people—why should they assume Ellis approves of the satanic creep he has created? This is concept comedy,

pitched in some hitherto uncharted territory between Albert Brooks and Lenny Bruce.

The model for Patrick could be Robert Chambers, the preppie murderer. Over dinner (pizza for two, $90), Patrick blithely confides, "Some friends of his, well, mainly *me,* are trying to remount his defense." It's possible Ellis read about Chambers, figured the guy sounded like a character out of *Less Than Zero,* and decided to blend the Chambers character and the Ellis style into a spectacular literary gamble—an affront not only to his critics but to the upper-yuppie class of which Patrick is only the most atrocious specimen. They are as deaf to Patrick's atrocities, which he confesses to anyone who won't listen, as he is to his victims' cries. They show an utter lack of interest in understanding Patrick's decidedly offbeat avocation. They are as obsessed as he with designer clothes, the Zagat restaurant ratings, and their social superiority to the world's *misérables.* "I'm left with one comforting thought," Patrick muses toward the end: "I'm rich—millions are not." The book's last line of dialogue is an ego mantra of the Young Republican generation: "yup yup yup yup yup yup. . . . "

Most of all, *American Psycho* is movie-bred: *American Gigolo* out of *Psycho.* Patrick's patron saints might be Richard Gere and Ed Gein. Gere for the haberdashery. And Gein, the mass murderer on whom Robert Bloch modeled Norman Bates, because when he saw a pretty girl he wondered "what her head would look like on a stick." Patrick, orphaned from empathy but a dauphin of home movies, merely wonders what a head would look like through a lens: "As usual, in an attempt to understand these girls I'm filming their deaths." This ethnographer of carnage could host his own "America's Sickest Home Videos" show. But what he really wants is to direct. Life is one of his movies: "Pan down to the *Post* . . . a slow dissolve . . . from my POV. . . . Like a smash cut from a horror movie—a jump zoom—Luis Carruthers appears." His life is the camera that kills.

Because the book's murder passages are as rancid as any in mainstream American fiction, and because the first person narration doesn't allow for an authorial overview to explain and condemn Patrick's crimes, the book can be expected to shock some readers. We can only advise them not to read it. They or their neighbors can go out and rent a nice antiseptic video, something like *Blond, Hot, Dead* (which gets thumbs up from Patrick) that fastidiously avoids the wild thrill of artistic ambition pulsing just under the bland, diseased surface of *American Psycho.*

Which is soon, we hear, to be a major motion picture. If somebody manages to do justice to the project—Paul Schrader is an obvious candidate—do see it in a real movie theater, a place as dark and majestic as Patrick Bateman's mind and Bret Easton Ellis' Black Bible. (pp. 55-6)

Richard Corliss, in a review of "American Psycho," in Film Comment, *Vol. 27, No. 3, May-June, 1991, pp. 55-6.*

Terry Teachout

[In the following review, Teachout faults several aspects of American Psycho, *particularly its lack of a moral landscape in which to place the protagonist's actions.]*

Bret Easton Ellis, it seems, was puzzled by the universally unfavorable reception of his third novel, **American Psycho.** Small wonder. Ellis's all-too-obvious purpose was to write a scathing satire of Eighties materialism that was politically correct in every possible way. Patrick Bateman, the narrator of **American Psycho,** is a Wall Street yuppie who watches pornographic video-cassettes, calls blacks "niggers" and homosexuals "faggots," and gets his after-hours jollies by killing and dismembering people. Though most of his victims are women, Bateman is an equal-opportunity psychopath, for he also butchers an aging homosexual, a homeless man, and a dog. (The dog is a particularly nice touch.) Much to his surprise, Ellis ran afoul of the feminist wing of sensitivity fascism, and subsequently received the same treatment in the popular press that Bateman's girlfriends receive in **American Psycho.** Moral: In the Nineties, you can never be pure enough.

At first, I actually felt a mild twinge of theoretical sympathy for Ellis, in much the same way that a soft-hearted member of the National Association of Scholars might pity an Ivy League leftist who inadvertently ran afoul of the PC police and suddenly discovered that his old friends wouldn't return his calls.

This sympathy lasted exactly as long as it took me to get through the first half-dozen pages of **American Psycho.** Every bad thing you've read about it is an understatement. It's ineptly written. It's sophomoric. It is, in the truest sense of the word, obscene. And the main charge of the feminists is right on the mark: Ellis describes the bestial acts committed by his cardboard hero in a way that is positively lascivious. One would hate to be his next date.

It would take more space than the task deserves to catalogue all of Ellis's myriad ineptnesses, but I'm especially struck by the utter incredibility of the events he describes. Though Patrick Bateman chops up one or two women, cabbies, and sushi delivery boys every week, his leisure-time activities attract little attention from the New York Police Department. And though he does his dirty work in a pair of Manhattan apartments, nobody ever hears any screaming and nobody ever smells anything funny.

Bateman himself is equally preposterous. A devoted "thirtysomething" fan who thinks Whitney Houston is "the most exciting and original black jazz voice of her generation," he is obsessed with upscale creature comforts (more products are identified by brand on an average page of **American Psycho** than in any chapter of *The Bonfire of the Vanities*) and with safe sex (I suspect Ellis thought this a positively Swiftian stroke of irony). A graduate of Exeter and Harvard, he displays a poster of Oliver North in his West Side apartment, and prefers *not* to blow away his girl friends with Soviet-made automatic weapons. Anyone who knows anything about serial killers knows that all of this is perfect nonsense. They are weak, nondescript, maladjusted loners who kill women in order to satisfy their twisted sexual longings, not Masters of the Universe with a taste for human flesh.

Bret Easton Ellis would presumably argue that **American Psycho,** being a satire on the Reagan era, need not be overly literal. But having chosen to write his book in an ultra-naturalistic style, Ellis is stuck with the conventions of naturalism, which include a certain amount of surface plausibility, of which **American Psycho** has none whatsoever. In any case, Ellis undercuts his satirical intent by asserting (through the medium of an epigraph drawn from, of all people, Dostoyevsky) that "such persons . . . not only exist in our society, but indeed must exist, considering the circumstances under which our society has generally been formed." Sorry, but no sale. Manhattan may be crawling with serial killers, but I find it highly unlikely that any of them are doubling as investment bankers.

It isn't hard to see why Ellis chose a serial killer as his subject. Serial murder is a theme of enormous literary potential, just as the psychopath is one of the great untapped character types. Its power is suggested by a number of purely popular novels about serial killers that are genuinely compelling, including Jim Thompson's *The Killer inside Me* and the novels of Thomas Harris, creator of Dr. Hannibal Lecter, America's hottest anti-hero. Harris's books are exceptionally interesting in this connection. Though they make no pretense to literary seriousness, *Red Dragon* and *The Silence of the Lambs* take seriously an issue that **American Psycho** ignores altogether: the question of evil. In *The Silence of the Lambs,* Dr. Lecter, a psychiatrist who kills and eats his patients when they become boring, refuses to allow his captors to explain him away with therapeutic clichés. "You can't reduce me to a set of influences," he says to Clarice Starling, the FBI trainee who asks him to fill out a questionnaire. "You've given up good and evil for behaviorism, Officer Starling. You've got everybody in moral dignity pants—nothing is ever anybody's fault. Look at me, Officer Starling. Can you stand to say I'm evil?"

By contrast, there is no moment in **American Psycho** where Bret Easton Ellis, who claims to be a serious artist, exhibits the workings of an adult moral imagination. It is as if he knows nothing of good and evil. If so, it wouldn't be surprising. Where, after all, would a novelist born in 1964, raised in Los Angeles, and educated at Bennington College have picked up such quaint bourgeois prejudices? No doubt Ellis spent his undergraduate years steeped in the modish brand of academic nihilism that goes by the name of "deconstruction," a school of criticism in which works of art are verbally hacked to pieces in order to prove that nothing means anything. He seems to have learned his lessons well, if a bit too literally. (pp. 45-6)

Terry Teachout, "Applied Deconstruction," in National Review, *New York, Vol. XLIII, June 24, 1991, pp. 45-6.*

Carol Iannone

[In the following essay, Iannone summarizes the critical reception of American Psycho *and discusses the work as a reflection of "Reaganite America."]*

[*American Psycho*] has received widespread critical condemnation, even from Norman Mailer, reigning champion of extreme experience and the author of a novel, *An American Dream,* that may have received tribute in the title of Ellis's book.

What accounted for this unusual behavior? After all, only a few months earlier, during the uproar over government funding of the photographs of Robert Mapplethorpe, we had all been instructed on the artist's absolute right to express himself freely in whatsoever manner he wished. If we did not like Mapplethorpe's photographs, we did not have to look at them, did we? One might have expected that this attitude of each-to-his-own would apply even more to a book, with its contents between closed covers, than to an exhibit mounted on the walls of a big-city museum. Yet suddenly the doctrine of absolute aesthetic freedom was taking a beating. "Standards, anyone?" Roger Rosenblatt asked at the end of his piece in the New York *Times Book Review* [16 December 1990, pp. 3, 16.], apparently undeterred by fear of the automatic retort that had for so long followed even the tentative pronunciation of so much as the first syllable of that word: *Whose* standards? Who is to decide?

Granted, there was some confusion among Ellis's critics about whether his book was offensive on moral or on aesthetic grounds. Half the time it was denounced for what was in it, the other half for how badly it was done. Tammy Bruce, president of the Los Angeles chapter of the National Organization for Women (NOW), asserted, "This is not art." But if it were, would "those" scenes be acceptable to her, or did she mean to suggest that such depictions could not, by definition, be art?

In the meantime, Ellis himself was playing all sides of the question. In a Sunday New York *Times* piece [2 December 1990, Section 2, pp. 1, 37] that appeared some months before his novel was published, he remarked that American society in general, and his own twentysomething generation in particular, were "basically unshockable"—hence the need to render an extreme portrayal of violence. Indeed, the indifference of society to the moral nihilism of the young was a set theme in his much-acclaimed first novel, *Less Than Zero* (1985), which concerns a group of young and overprivileged Los Angelenos spinning aimlessly in a void of utter permissiveness.

As often happens with artists who set out to shock society, however, when society started to register the presumably hoped-for shock waves Ellis ran for cover. The reaction to his book, he orated, "reflects the intolerance of our culture to deal with anything that falls outside the acceptable." The twist in this case was that the "culture" being intolerant of him consisted not just of the stereotypical Yahoos of the Right, always to be counted on to censor all that is daring and progressive and bold, but, as Ellis specifically complained, the "politically correct" crowd as well, with its peculiar sensitivity on the topic of women. Still another twist—a real complication, this—was that in many ways *American Psycho* is quite PC itself.

The novel's anti-hero, twenty-six-year-old Patrick Bateman, the character who commits the horrible murders described by Ellis in such grisly detail, is, in fact, an example of one of the most reviled figures of our age, the 1980's Wall Street yuppie. Moreover, he is clearly meant to embody Reaganite America gone amok, from the portrait of Oliver North that hangs in his bedroom to his ruthless treatment of the pathetic homeless people who approach him, Dickenslike, as he leaves a restaurant after a three-figure meal. Although he is supposed to be a broker, we never see him broker anything, which is evidently part of the point; his six-figure salary from Pierce & Pierce is no more earned by him than is his large family inheritance.

Patrick spends most of his time tending to his appearance; his morning toilette makes the lazy hedonists of *Les Liaisons Dangereuses* seem like bustling careerists by comparison. Between facials, massages, manicures, and picking designer clothes to wear to restaurants where he and those who pass for his friends and colleagues scream at each other uncomprehendingly over the din, he is one un-busy boy. While all of this is described in ludicrously overdone detail, it does represent an attempt by Ellis to convey something about the psychopathology that drives Patrick to hideous acts of sexual torture and humiliation, murder, even cannibalism. As Mailer, whose piece appeared in the March [1991] *Vanity Fair,* ponderously interprets it: "*American Psycho* is saying that the 80's were spiritually disgusting and the author's presentation is the crystallization of such horror."

With this thesis, of course, Mailer and the rest of the "politically correct" crowd could hardly agree more. Nevertheless, it was not enough to save Ellis from their disapprobation. There are perhaps two reasons for this: first, Ellis goes so far with the yuppie stuff that his novel is always threatening to turn into a satire not of Reaganite America but of people who hold such clichés about Reaganite America; and second, even a reader convinced that Ronald Reagan is the fount and focus of evil in the world may be hard put to add power-tool torture and sexual murder to his many crimes. Thus Alfred Kazin, a critic whose denunciations of Reagan and the Reagan era have rarely been equaled in their hysteria, protested in his review of *American Psycho*: "But really, Mr. Ellis goes too far. . . . [It] is finally difficult to be as indignant as he is about Patrick's poster of Oliver North, the *ninety* dollars gentlefolk pay for a pizza, or his cruelty to homeless people with dixie cup in hand." Mailer for his part does his best to "entertain the thesis that the unbridled manipulations of the money-decade subverted the young sufficiently to produce wholly aimless lives for a generation of Wall Street yuppies." But then he pulls back: "But was it crowned by the ultimate expression of all these meaningless lives—one total monster, a Patrick Bateman? Can he emerge entirely out of no more than vapidity, cupidity, and social meaninglessness?"

This astonishing admission—that there may be worse evils than those allegedly produced by Ronald Reagan—is followed by Mailer's almost Aristotelian analysis of the problem presented by Ellis's minute descriptions of horror. While he does not retract his own long-held insistence that the artist must be allowed—indeed encouraged—to explore forbidden territory, it does occur to Mailer that when a writer goes as far as Ellis, he ought to bring something back from the abyss:

> Since we are going to have a monstrous book with a monstrous thesis, the author must rise to the occasion by having a murderer with enough inner life for us to comprehend him. We pay a terrible price for reading about intimate violence—our fears are stirred, and buried savageries we do not wish to meet again in ourselves stir uneasily in the tombs to which we have consigned them. . . . If one is embarked on a novel that hopes to shake American society to the core, one has to have something new to say about the outer limits of the deranged—one cannot simply keep piling on more and more acts of machicolated butchery.

We should remember these points in future literary controversies. Suddenly, it seems, "standards" are not so impossibly difficult to invoke or define; suddenly, the encounter with the extreme in literature can have a corrupting effect on readers; suddenly, freedom of expression is not an absolute.

Mailer is certainly right that the brutal scenes in *American Psycho* are gratuitous, coarsening, horrific, absolutely unjustified. But if Ronald Reagan did not produce Patrick Bateman/*American Psycho,* what did? This novel, says Mailer, shows us "where the hands have come to on the clock." Where is that? An answer begins to peep obliquely out of Mailer's own ramblings on *American Psycho,* which, he worries, ends by making evil look banal rather than satanic. "For if Hannah Arendt is correct," he comments,

> and evil is banal, then that is vastly worse than the opposed possibility that evil is satanic. The extension of Arendt's thesis is that we are absurd, and God and the Devil do not wage war with each other over the human outcome. I would rather believe that the Holocaust was the worst defeat God ever suffered at the hands of the Devil. That thought offers more life than to assume that many of us are nothing but dangerous, distorted, and no damn good.

This may seem odd coming from the mother of all literary bad boys, yet it is true in a qualified but measurable way that over the decades Mailer's own flirtations with the abyss, with the void, with the forbidden, *have* been contingent upon some sense of a traditional moral universe as backdrop, whereas for Ellis such a backdrop seems to have all but completely collapsed. Why and how it collapsed is suggested in an epigraph by Miss Manners (Judith Martin) he has placed at the beginning of his novel:

> One of the places we went wrong was the naturalistic Rousseauean movement of the 60's in which people said, "Why can't you just say what's on your mind?" In civilization there have to be some restraints. If we followed every impulse, we'd be killing one another.

In one way or another, then, Ellis seems to have absorbed a sense of our age as one in which a deluded permissiveness has badly misread human nature and the contingencies surrounding the human condition. In this light, his caricature of Reaganite America becomes a mere epiphenomenon of a deeper cultural holocaust. Indeed, when Patrick Bateman speaks his mind, he invokes not the culture of Reagan, which for better or worse is only the culture of middle-class America, but rather a phantasmagoric, quintessentially post-modernist landscape from which all traditional structures, values, truths, have been eliminated:

> . . . where there was nature and earth, life and water, I saw a desert landscape that was unending, resembling some sort of crater, so devoid of reason and light and spirit that the mind could not grasp it on any sort of conscious level and if you came close the mind would reel backward, unable to take it in. It was a vision so clear and real and vital to me that in its purity it was almost abstract. This was what I could understand, this was how I lived my life, what I constructed my movement around, how I dealt with the tangible. This was the geography around which my reality revolved: it did not occur to me, *ever,* that people were good or that a man was capable of change or that the world could be a better place through one's taking pleasure in a feeling or a look or a gesture, of receiving another person's love or kindness. . . .

In the end, Patrick is trying to be stopped, hoping to be found out, literally screaming his confession at people who simply cannot take it in, who are, as the novel repeatedly emphasizes, obtusely unaware even that crimes have been committed, let alone being ready to place him under the slightest suspicion. In a deconstructed world of jagged surfaces, devoid of hierarchies of meaning, there are no depths to cry out of, and none to receive the cry.

I am not suggesting that Ellis really means to say all this. In fact, the catastrophic inclusion of the now famous offensive scenes reveals a staggering aesthetic and moral immaturity that turns the novel into an example of the very disease it purports to diagnose. But just so, we should make no mistake as to what we are witnessing: a novel that both seeks to portray and at the same time is itself a manifestation of extreme cultural breakdown. As such it inadvertently forces a number of politically incorrect truths on our attention—that civilization does not cause barbarism, it controls it; that the weakening of civilized restraints does not mean the flowering of the individual but the rise of savagery; that when we deny the moral law, people will just go farther to hit bottom, to feel, if only negatively, the boundaries of their humanity.

In the meantime, Ellis's critics, despite all their new-found moral indignation—and welcome as that is—are still missing the point, refusing to see the connection between what they denounce in him and the cultural values they themselves usually celebrate and defend. As for Ellis himself, he is getting what he called for (which is not what he wanted): a boundary, a barrier, a point at which people will fight back. But alas for all of us that it has had to go so far. (pp. 52-4)

Carol Iannone, "PC & the Ellis Affair," in Commentary, *Vol. 92, No. 1, July, 1991, pp. 52-4.*

Alberto Manguel

[In the essay excerpted below, Manguel compares American Psycho *to several literary works that employ themes of horror as illustrations of aesthetic or philosophical ideas.]*

American Psycho follows the daily routine of one Patrick Bateman, New York businessman, young, rich, and psychotic. For endless pages, Bateman sits and talks to his acquaintances (he has no friends) about brand names—of food, of clothes, of gadgets, of anything consumable—after which, without ever changing from Bateman to Mr. Hyde, he takes up murder. Though he also murders dogs, vagrants, and children, Bateman's victims are usually women whom he slowly tortures and then dismembers and devours in scenes written by Ellis in clumsy detail. Of course, *American Psycho* is not an isolated example. Books of this kind exist—usually under the graphic label of "splatter punk" (in the axe-murder tradition) or "hardcore thrillers" (descendants of Mickey Spillane)—but most of the time they are presented to the public in lurid covers that make no attempt to conceal the sort of story they are offering.

The packaging of *American Psycho* is a curious affair. The cover shows a photo from a German edition of *Vogue,* the face of a Robert Redford lookalike. The epigraphs quote Dostoevsky (*Notes from Underground*) regarding the need to portray in fiction certain characters who "exist in our society"; Miss Manners on restraint ("If we followed every impulse, we'd be killing one another"); and the rock group Talking Heads ("And as things fell apart / Nobody paid much attention"). The first line in the book is Dante's motto for the gates of Hell: "Abandon all hope ye who enter here." In fact everything is set up in such a way as to make the reader believe that the story that follows is of a literary nature: contemporary and ironic (cover and Miss Manners quote), hip (Talking Heads), serious and philosophical (Dostoevsky and Dante).

The next 128 pages (the first brutal scene begins on page 129) are agonizing for anyone not accustomed to reading fashion advertising:

> He's wearing a linen suit by Canali Milano, a cotton shirt by Ike Behar, a silk tie by Bill Blass and cap-toed leather lace-ups from Brooks Brothers. I'm wearing a lightweight linen suit with pleated trousers, a cotton shirt, a dotted silk tie, all by Valentino Couture, and perforated cap-toe leather shoes by Allen-Edmonds.

This may be meant to be read as social satire; it cannot be, because Ellis's prose does nothing except copy the model it is supposed to deride. I have found greater amusement in flicking through the Owen Sound phone book.

When the gruesome scenes do occur, Ellis uses the brand-name-dropping to remind the reader that the "satiric mode" has not been abandoned. The stomach of a slaughtered woman is compared to "the eggplant and goat cheese lasagna at Il Marlibro"; the screams of a tortured woman are smothered in a Ralph Lauren camel-hair coat; the horrors are filmed with a "Sony palm-sized Handycam." Women, the main target of Bateman's frenzies, are treated much like the brand-name goods that make up his life and his language. But the point is lost in the grotesqueness of the accounts and in Ellis's awkward, flat prose. I cannot conceive of anyone's being able to call this sort of writing "witty," but that is how the publishers' catalogue describes it. "*American Psycho,*" reads the blurb, "is an explosive novel which brilliantly exposes American culture today in a witty but dangerously alarming way." Alarming? Indeed. But this quality comes not from the writing but from the fact that publishers of literary works have chosen to include an example of violent pornography in their lists. In however many ways I have tried to read this book, the feebleness of its style, its meagre vocabulary, the poor craft with which the author constructs both dialogue and description disallow any approach except that of the pornographer. By this I mean that unless you, as a reader, are titillated by the scenes of violence, the only other reaction you can expect is one of horror: not intellectual terror, which compels you to question the universe, but physical horror—a revulsion not of the senses but of the gut, like that produced by shoving a finger down one's throat. Ann Radcliffe, author of one of the earliest gothic novels, cleverly distinguished between terror, which dilates the soul and excites an intense activity in all our senses, and horror, which contracts them, freezes them, somehow destroys them. *American Psycho* is a novel of pornographic horror.

The literatures of both terror and horror are as old as our imagination. As a species, we don't want contentment, we shy away from appeasement, we are less interested in the bud than in the worm. Death and the suffering unto death have been among our most treasured readings since the first babblings of literature. It is as if, confident in the magical powers of the word, we have always expected a writer to bring to life on the page our worst nightmares, to be the geographer of an undiscovered country, to allow us through rhyme and reason vicariously to experience that which we thought unthinkable.

For centuries, the writer has been, like Virgil and Dante, a guide through the foulest corners of the human imagination: voyages to the underworld in the literature of Greece and Rome, illustrated with frightful portraits of Hell's ghostly inhabitants; hagiography in the Middle Ages, full of detailed accounts of the tortures suffered by the martyred saints; tragedies in the Elizabethan and Jacobean eras, in which infanticide, cannibalism, and rape are commonplace; the gothic novel in the eighteenth and nineteenth centuries, with its vampirism and necrophilia. There is no doubt that horror has been part of our literary tradition. But it wasn't until 1773, with two essays published in London by J. and A. L. Aikin, that literary terror received scholarly recognition in its own right. "On the Pleasure derived from Objects of Terror" and "Enquiry into those kinds of Distress which excite agreeable sensations" sought to explain and affirm the proliferation of ruins, corpses, dark shadows, and foul creatures that had invaded the fiction and poetry of Romantic Europe, but in fact lent aesthetic validity to all its illustrious predecessors. And about the same time a German, Friedrich von Hardenberg, better known as Novalis, made a bold discovery about the cruel appeal of terror: "It is startling," he wrote, "that the veritable source of cruelty should be desire."

But what desire? Another contemporary, Donatien Alphonse François, Marquis de Sade, provided a possible answer: the desire to refuse civilization, to become a "child of nature," to embrace the natural order. "Cruelty," wrote de Sade, "far from being a vice, is the earliest sentiment wrought in us by Nature; the infant breaks his rattle, bites his nurse's teat, strangles his pet bird, long before he has attained the age of reason." A son of the French Revolution, de Sade replaces the God of Abraham ("the idea of God is the only mistake I cannot forgive my fellow men") not with the Goddess Reason but with nature—another, more savage deity. Nature hurls us blindly in a vertiginous progress from birth to death, establishing an order in which we are but parts of an atrocious machine that ultimately destroys us. Human passions are, for de Sade, nothing but "the means employed by Nature to fulfil its designs." His monstrous sexual inventions appear as mechanical and unemotional devices meticulously described. Roland Barthes, in a controversial essay, denies that de Sade is erotic because "eroticism can only be defined by a language that is perpetually allusive," and suggests that this quest for the explicit natural order, even within the debauchery, dominates the entire Sadean oeuvre.

De Sade had his protagonists seek the terrors of cruelty through a desire for natural order. Others, such as Poe, Kafka, and the surrealists, sought disorder, taking things apart in the hope of revealing universal mysteries, like children dissecting a clockwork toy. Cruelty—for instance the eye sliced with a razor in the archetypal surrealist film, *Un Chien andalou*—is born from the voluptuous desire for anarchy.

These frameworks, these contexts, these notions that allow us to read depictions of horrific acts as illustrations of aesthetic or philosophical theories, are absent from Ellis's book. In de Sade, in Poe, in hundreds of other writers, there are sections that, read on their own (the equivalent of what we, in school, used to call "the dirty bits"), can be either titillating or revolting, or both, depending on our inclinations, but which, as part of a whole, acquire a different meaning. When Ovid's Marsyas is flayed alive in the *Metamorphoses*; when Lucan's witch in *The Civil Wars* bites the tongue of the corpse she has been kissing; when Lady Macbeth speaks of plucking her nipple from her baby's boneless gums and dashing the brains out; when Kafka's prisoner in "The Penal Colony" is slowly tortured to death by a needle that engraves on his body the unuttered nature of his crime; when Winston in Orwell's *1984* is threatened with rats that will attack his eyes and shouts "Do it to Julia! . . . Tear her face off, strip her to the bones!"; when Dr. Noyes rapes his daughter-in-law with a unicorn's horn in Findley's *Not Wanted on the Voyage*: even though it may be possible for a reader to find pornography in the descriptions by ignoring the contexts, those contexts do exist. They colour the violence, give it meaning, allow for redemption, help understanding. Violence, and the glimpse it gives us of Hell, is the starting point Yeats perhaps had in mind when he wrote in "The Circus Animals' Desertion," his poem on the sources of inspiration: "I must lie down where all the ladders start, / In the foul rag-and-bone shop of the heart."

The rag-and-bone shop is a reality and different writers have visited it with more or less talent. Many fail, but lack of talent is not a criminal offence and badly written books will always be with us to test our charity. As regards publishers and false advertising, the peddling of one book under the cover of another is nothing but an ethical crime, and it is for such occasions that we are lumbered with a conscience. It is we, the readers, who, I believe, have the final responsibility. The most astounding aspect of language is its versatility: it can be babble, it can be invective, it can be prayer, it can be joke, it can be fable. It can be revelation and exalt us, or it can be pornography and immure us. And it can't hurt to remember that every time we choose a book for bedtime, we're also picking our way through intimations of Heaven and promises of Hell. (pp. 46-7, 49)

Alberto Manguel, "Designer Porn," in Saturday Night, *Vol. 106, No. 6, July-August, 1991, pp. 46-7, 49.*

FURTHER READING

Adler, Jerry; McGuigan, Cathleen; and Crichton, Sarah. "The Killing of a Gory Novel: But Ellis's *American Psycho* Rises Again." *Newsweek* CXVI, No. 22 (26 November 1990): 85.

> Considers the ethical questions surrounding the decision of Vintage Books to publish *American Psycho*.

Baker, John F. "Publisher Responsibility and Bret Easton Ellis." *Publishers Weekly* 237, No. 48 (30 November 1990): 7.

> Editorial by the editor-in-chief of *Publishers Weekly* arguing that Simon & Schuster's decision to cancel the publication of *American Psycho* was an example of responsible publishing rather than censorship.

Bernstein, Richard. "*American Psycho,* Going So Far That Many Say It's Too Far." *The New York Times* (10 December 1990): C13, C18.

> Compares the impact of violence depicted in *American Psycho* with that in several contemporary films.

Gardner, Marilyn. "Their Keepers." *The Christian Science Monitor* 83, No. 78 (19 March 1991): 13.

> Discusses the role of violence in art and criticizes the failure of *American Psycho* to evoke an emotional response from readers.

Hoban, Phoebe. " 'Psycho' Drama." *New York* 23, No. 49 (17 December 1990): 32-7.

> Detailed explanation of the corporate decisions behind the cancellation and later publication of *American Psycho*.

Iyer, Pico. "Are Men Really So Bad?" *Time* 137, No. 16 (22 April 1991): 94.

> Argues that the pervasive images of male violence in

American Psycho and the media are harmful to men as well as women.

James, Caryne. "Now Starring, Killers for the Chiller 90's." *The New York Times* (10 March 1991): Sec. 2, pp. 1, 20-1.
> Discusses artistic reflections of a violent world in several contemporary films and literary works, including *American Psycho.*

Kennedy, Pagan. "Generation Gaffe." *The Nation* 252, No. 12 (1 April 1991): 426-28.
> Considers each of Ellis's works, asserting that none of his novels have merited the level of critical attention they have received.

Kimball, Roger. "Much Less Than Zero." *The Wall Street Journal* (6 March 1991): A7.
> Rejects Ellis's assertion that *American Psycho* is a work of social criticism.

McDowell, Edwin. "Vintage Buys Violent Book Dropped by Simon & Schuster." *The New York Times* (17 November 1990): A13.
> Discusses the acquisition of *American Psycho* by Vintage Books following its cancellation by Simon & Schuster.

Motion, Andrew. "American Psicko." *Observer,* No. 10410 (21 April 1991): 61.
> Negative review of *American Psycho* criticizing the work as "boring" and "disgusting."

Reuter, Madalynne. "Vintage *American Psycho* Has Only Minor Changes from S. & S. Version." *Publishers Weekly* 238, No. 12 (8 March 1991): 6.
> Describes minor editorial changes in *American Psycho* preceding its publication by Vintage Books and discusses the opinions of several American booksellers regarding the ethics of selling the work.

Sheppard, R. Z. "A Revolting Development." *Time* 136, No. 18 (29 October 1990): 100.
> Negative review of *American Psycho* anticipating the controversy concerning its graphic depiction of violence.

Will, George F. "Slamming the Doors." *Newsweek* CXVII, No. 12 (25 March 1991): 65-6.
> Faults Ellis for capitalizing on America's market for violent entertainment.

Additional coverage of Ellis's life and career is contained in the following sources published by Gale Research: *Authors and Artists for Young Adults,* Vol. 2; *Contemporary Authors,* Vols. 118, 123; and *Contemporary Literary Criticism,* Vol. 39.

Ursula K. Le Guin

The *Earthsea* Cycle

(Born Ursula Kroeber in 1929) American novelist, short story writer, nonfiction writer, critic, editor, poet, dramatist, and author of children's books.

The following entry focuses on the four novels in Le Guin's *Earthsea* Cycle: *A Wizard of Earthsea* (1967), *The Tombs of Atuan* (1971), *The Farthest Shore* (1972), and *Tehanu: The Last Book of Earthsea* (1980). For further information on Le Guin's life and career, see *CLC,* Vols. 8, 13, 22, and 45.

INTRODUCTION

Le Guin's *Earthsea* Cycle is considered a major achievement in fantasy literature, comparable in stature to such popular works as J. R. R. Tolkien's *Lord of the Rings* and C. S. Lewis' "Chronicles of Narnia." Earthsea encompasses an imaginary archipelago with diverse societies where the use of magic has a profound effect on life. Le Guin meticulously details the islands and peoples of Earthsea as well the customs, laws, and ethical choices associated with the use of magic. The protagonists of the *Earthsea* books undertake quests that become physical and psychological journeys for self-knowledge and objects of power; as they encounter formidable adversaries, the protagonists confront their personal fears and social responsibilities. Dennis J. O'Brien stated that the strength of Le Guin's *Earthsea* books "is to make us feel the spiritual struggle between a world to be summoned and a world of nameless power."

The *Earthsea* Cycle originally comprised a trilogy of novels published between 1967 and 1972. Each of these books won a major award in the field of children's literature. Like fantasy works by Tolkien and Lewis, the *Earthsea* Cycle appeals to young readers by providing a series of suspenseful adventures and magical events in an otherworldly setting while developing themes relating to good versus evil and coming-of-age. Elements of symbolism, allegory, myth, Jungian psychology, and Taoism, and Le Guin's exploration of the nature and power of language, broaden the appeal of the works for adult readers and scholars. In addition, the fourth installment of the *Earthsea* Cycle, *Tehanu: The Last Book of Earthsea,* published eighteen years after completion of the trilogy, reflects Le Guin's interest in feminist issues and has been read as a feminist critique of the male-dominated fantasy genre.

A Wizard of Earthsea, which won the *Boston Globe/Horn Book* Award for children's literature, introduces Ged, a primary character in the *Earthsea* Cycle, as a child who displays a talent for performing magic. Ged is later admitted as an apprentice into the prestigious College of the Isle of Roke, where he is instructed in wizardry and the value of disciplining his powers. However, spurred by pride

when challenged by another apprentice, Ged performs an ill-considered feat that sets loose a malevolent force which almost kills him and threatens evil upon the world of Earthsea. Ged's quest to locate and overcome this shadowy force forms the plot of the novel. On one level Ged's quest dramatizes the psychological theories of Carl Jung that pertain to adolescent encounters with the unconscious, as the shadow represents fears Ged must confront in his passage from childhood to maturity. On another level the quest is informed with Taoist tenets concerning the need to balance opposing forces in order to achieve harmony. Ged's action upsets the precarious equilibrium between good and evil that helps order the world of Earthsea. The nature of language and artistry are other themes introduced in this book that recur throughout the *Earthsea* Cycle. An example of the former theme occurs when Ged learns that to have control over any creature one must know its secret name; an example of the latter is Ged's gradual understanding of the power of his magic.

The story of Ged's maturation in *A Wizard of Earthsea* is complemented by a feminine coming-of-age tale in the second book of the *Earthsea* Cycle, *The Tombs of Atuan,* a Newbery Medal Honor Book. This work focuses on

Tenar, High Priestess of the Nameless Ones, who complacently accepts her role as mistress of labyrinthine tombs for an authoritarian society. Tenar gains greater self-knowledge during her encounters with Ged, who invades the tombs in an attempt to retrieve an object of power. As Tenar recognizes her limited social possibilities, her sexuality, and the responsibilities associated with freedom, she struggles to break free from roles imposed on her by society.

In *The Farthest Shore,* which won the National Book Award for Children's Literature, Le Guin utilizes a mythic archetype—the prince who passes a series of tests before becoming king. An immature prince is guided by Ged, now a respected wizard, through a series of heroic adventures that require courage and self-control. In one episode an old enemy of Ged has convinced a society that they have achieved immortality, an illusion that proves stronger than sorcery. Ged and the prince undertake a quest to dispel this illusion and to discover the source of a blight that is spreading over Earthsea.

Tehanu examines myth and heroic fantasy from a feminist perspective, creating what Michael Dirda described as "a woman's world, a realm of socially imposed weakness and of male stupidity, of child abuse and evil with a human face." The simple domestic life of Tenar, who had relinquished use of her powers to become a farmer's wife, undergoes sudden change as she cares for a horribly abused, abandoned child and the aging Ged, who has lost his powers. These acts of benevolence place her in jeopardy, which she braves with traditional feminine values and magic. Robin McKinley stated that "[the] astonishing clear-sightedness of *Tehanu* is in its recognition of the necessary and life-giving contributions of female magic—sometimes disguised as domesticity." Critics generally agree that *Tehanu* represents a satisfying conclusion to the *Earthsea* Cycle because it develops themes and characters while maintaining a sence of unity and introduces feminist values that reflect changes in Le Guin's personal outlook. Le Guin explained: "My *Earthsea* trilogy is part of [the male tradition of fantasy]—that is why I had to write this fourth volume. Because I changed. I had to show the other side."

REVIEWS OF THE *EARTHSEA* BOOKS

Theodore Sturgeon

A Wizard of Earthsea is that increasingly rare delight, a "journey" story, which ever since Homer sang the *Odyssey* (and probably before) has had its own special magic. Take me to a strange country and lead me over the mountains and across the seas, never knowing what monsters, what men, what adventures I might encounter, and you have me well hooked. The planet Earthsea is a strange country indeed, where real magic, with harsh disciplines and real self-consistency, exists and operates, and where the trained sorcerer (who must be gifted before he can be trained) is treated with respect, for he has vital functions.

Here again is the one impossible thing you are asked to believe, and the author makes you believe it. And in addition to being a simple journey story, *Wizard* is a fable—that is to say, an analogy with a moral you can comprehend and use. When the young wizard's pride is stung, he makes a terrible mistake—terrible in its truest, terror-full, terrifying sense; and for that he has to pay off. How he does it, and the nature and name of the dreadful force he must confront and overcome, is the story and its high moral. (p. 41)

Theodore Sturgeon, "Memento Mori—Et. Seq.," in National Review, New York, Vol. XXIII, January 12, 1971, pp. 39, 41.

The Times Literary Supplement

Any quick list of the outstanding books for the young of the past forty years or so will reveal that almost all have drawn on the extra dimension of magic or fantasy—Tolkien, White, Lewis, Pearce, Garner, Hoban and the rest. The numbers are not so many, though. It should also be remembered that most of the vast mass of quickly forgotten tales have been rashly drawn from the same dangerous sources, by authors not realizing the limitations and subtleties as well as the obvious pantomime powers of the supernatural. To find one novel a year to join the first group noted above is as much or more than one may expect, but there seems little doubt that *A Wizard of Earthsea* is the likeliest candidate that we have had for some time: if a book as remarkable as this turns up in the next twelve months we shall be fortunate indeed.

The story tells of Ged, a bronzesmith's son on a mountainous island, who when still very young shows a natural gift towards wizardry. His aunt, a witch in a small way, begins to teach him this and that, starting with the core of all magic, that, to have power over any creature or thing, you must first know its secret name.

> This was [his] first step on the way he was to follow all his life, the way of magery, the way that led him at last to hunt a shadow over land and sea to the lightless coasts of death's kingdom.

But, ignorant how to use what he has learnt, he almost destroys himself by raising a mist to keep off raiders, and lies paralysed and spent. The great Mage of the region, Ogion of Re Albi, hears of the boy, restores him, names him with his secret name, and invites him to be his disciple. Yet even with this wise Master, whom he loves, Ged is impatient and rebellious and almost wrecks himself once again by peering into the Mage's book and studying the most proscribed of all runes, that of raising the dead.

So, with a letter of entry from Ogion, he goes on to the College of the Isle of Roke, in the Inmost Sea, where nine Mages, under an Archmage, teach every branch of their art. Here Ged thrives—until, at the midsummer festival, he is goaded by his one rival into a duel of skills. The forbidden page of Ogion's book rises in his mind, and he uses it to summon up from the unknown dark the Queen Elfarron, dead a thousand years. But something else besides the sad, faint glimmering lady slides out of the crack—a shapeless thing, which fights to enter Ged's body.

Ged lives, for the Archmage himself comes to save him, but he is scarred and changed. He takes small posts on humble islands, looking always for what he has loosed into the world, afraid to encounter it, afraid to lose its tracks. It is his old master who counsels him at last to turn pursuer, but it is his own plan to meet the thing at sea. The sea has "storms and monsters, but no evil powers; evil is of earth".

The notable section on the work of the College of Roke may owe something in impetus to *The Sword in the Stone;* but it is doubtful if a more convincing and comprehensive account of a sorcerer's training exists anywhere in fiction outside the *Earthsea* chapters. The boding journey through the vast bleak snow-filled empty plain to the Castle of the Terrenon Stone—most ancient and most evil—may recall, in a quick flicker of the mind, Childe Roland's journey to Browning's nameless Tower. The *gebbeth* itself, appearing on this very plain, or, no less horribly, in Ged's boat on a lonely sea, may be a cousin to the shapeless creature in Edwin Muir's poem "The Combat"—or, even, to Stevenson's Mr. Hyde.

Yet these may as well be parallels as borrowings. And what comes out of them all is a new quest-story, an original allegory. Curiously, while there is almost nothing local or datable in its machinery, yet every piece of mage-advice seems immediate and topical. (Most learning, skills and crafts that come our way are, after all, a form of wizardry.) One finds in *Earthsea* none of the private and scratchy hates and theological quiddities that even a marvellous yarn cannot cover over in the stories of C. S. Lewis. The matter of the true and secret Name which every creature and thing possesses goes back into the furthest reaches of myth. (Was it not by his secret Name that Egypt's Ra first held then lost his power?) But it is as valid today as ever it was; need one point to its uses in the fields of advertising and politics? The advice to change the role of pursuer and pursued: to look for the fear instead of running away from it, is again wholly sound. Nor is the warning against using magic needlessly, and without considering its results (which may disturb the world's Equilibrium), a dictum merely for fairy tales.

There are many memorable passages—not only the great midsummer scene when Ged raises the *gebbeth,* nor the final engagement, with its brilliant resolution, on the fixed waves of the sea. Ged's defeat of the great dragon of Pendor, not by butchery but by counter-moves of power, should be added to every dragon-anthology. And there are lighter passages, such as the riddling interviews with the Master Doorkeeper, when the boy arrives, and later, when he leaves. But the book is more than a sum of its parts. An image used by Ged himself about a boat he takes on one of his expeditions comes to mind. Was it "illusion" that made it watertight? he was asked. Partly (he replies),

> because I am uneasy seeing the sea through great holes in my boat, so I patched them for the looks of the thing. But the strength of the boat was not illusion . . . but made with another kind of art,

a binding spell. The wood was bound as one whole, one entire thing, a boat.

The book has this kind of wholeness.

An excerpt from *A Wizard of Earthsea*

At [his] studies Ged was apt, and within a month was bettering lads who had been a year at Roke before him. Especially the tricks of illusion came to him so easily that it seemed he had been born knowing them and needed only to be reminded. The Master Hand was a gentle and lighthearted old man, who had endless delight in the wit and beauty of the crafts he taught; Ged soon felt no awe of him, but asked him for this spell and that spell, and always the Master smiled and showed him what he wanted. But one day, having it in mind to put Jasper to shame at last, Ged said to the Master Hand in the Court of Seeming, "Sir, all these charms are much the same; knowing one, you know them all. And as soon as the spell-weaving ceases, the illusion vanishes. Now if I make a pebble into a diamond—" and he did so with a word and a flick of his wrist—"what must I do to make that diamond remain diamond? How is the changing-spell locked, and made to last?"

The Master Hand looked at the jewel that glittered on Ged's palm, bright as the prize of a dragon's hoard. The old Master murmured one word, *"Tolk,"* and there lay the pebble, no jewel but a rough grey bit of rock. The Master took it and held it out on his own hand. "This is a rock; *tolk* in the True Speech," he said, looking mildly up at Ged now. "A bit of the stone of which Roke Isle is made, a little bit of the dry land on which men live. It is itself. It is part of the world. By the Illusion-Change you can make it look like a diamond—or a flower or a fly or an eye or a flame—" The rock flickered from shape to shape as he named them, and returned to rock. "But that is mere seeming. Illusion fools the beholder's senses; it makes him see and hear and feel that the thing is changed. But it does not change the thing. To change this rock into a jewel, you must change its true name. And to do that, my son, even to so small a scrap of the world, is to change the world. It can be done. Indeed it can be done. It is the art of the Master Changer, and you will learn it, when you are ready to learn it. But you must not change one thing, one pebble, one grain of sand, until you know what good and evil will follow on that act. The world is in balance, in Equilibrium. A wizard's power of Changing and of Summoning can shake the balance of the world. It is dangerous, that power. It is most perilous. It must follow knowledge, and serve need. To light a candle is to cast a shadow . . . . "

He looked down at the pebble again. "A rock is a good thing, too, you know," he said, speaking less gravely. "If the Isles of Earthsea were all made of diamond, we'd lead a hard life here. Enjoy illusions, lad, and let the rocks be rocks." He smiled, but Ged left dissatisfied. Press a mage for his secrets and he would always talk, like Ogion, about balance, and danger, and the dark. But surely a wizard, one who had gone past these childish tricks of illusion to the true arts of Summoning and Change, was powerful enough to do what he pleased, and balance the world as seemed best to him, and drive back darkness with his own light.

"The Making of a Mage," in The Times Literary Supplement, *No. 3605, April 2, 1971, p. 383.*

The Times Literary Supplement

A book as formidable as *A Wizard of Earthsea* might well raise doubts about any work that follows. Could the feat be managed a second time, without pastiche or self-imitation? But Earthsea has many regions and, indeed, *The Tombs of Atuan* (named as an Honor Book for the Newbery Medal) again has its own completeness. Though it keeps to a more restricted theme, it is very clearly out of the same imagination; its value comes from the same qualities. One is a total realization of place, time, customs, laws of behaviour, of magic too; the Atuan detail is as unerring as that of the youthful Brontës' imaginary countries. And though, in the areas of the supernatural, the author's eerie force is hard to match, her human creatures—and even wizards and priestesses are mortals first and last—hold the foreground interest; they change and grow, and this change directs the plot.

Ritual and responsibility are the opposing poles of the new book, and ritual holds together the "Place", in a desert region—a lonely group of temples and dwellings in the shadow of nine black stones, each some twenty feet high.

> Once the eye saw them it kept returning to them. They stood there full of meaning, and yet there was no saying what they meant. . . . These nine stones were the Tombs of Atuan. They had stood there, it was said, since the time of the first men, since Earthsea was created. . . . They were the tombs of those who ruled before the world of men came to be, the ones not named, and she who served them had no name.

The girl Tenar is marked out as an infant to be High Priestess of the Nameless Ones. It was her chance to be born when the last one died; the age-old rule of appointment, though many village mothers (like Tenar's) would try to conceal the birth. We see her, at the age of six, perfectly trained, go through the rites that turn her into Arha, the Eaten One (her soul being eaten by her Masters) and follow her through austere years of duties, ceremonials, and a special education; she must re-learn, as it were, what she knew "before she died". At 15, haughty, bored, but still unquestioning, she comes into her full powers: she must impose the ultimate dreadful penalties (for treason and sacrilege); hers alone are the mysterious keys to all the unknown doors; only she may explore the great dark city that lies underneath the tombs, with its dust and dread, and evil prisons, and rooms of untold treasure, and the vast frightful labyrinth. This underworld, where all paths must be learnt by number and touch, for no light is allowed, becomes her refuge: the only kind of journey that she knows.

But someone does enter the unenterable: the wizard Ged, seeking the utmost treasure, the broken half of an ancient silver ring. It has nine runes, he tells her:

> The other eight are known to Mages: Pirr that protects from madness and from wind and fire. Ges that gives endurance and so on. But the bro-

ken rune was the one that bound the hands. It was the Bond-Rune, the sign of dominion, the sign of peace . . . Since it was lost there have been no great kings in Havnor.

For the girl's first sense of outrage has given way to an unwonted pity; as his strength, and magic, ebb, and he lies near death, lost in the maze, she brings him her own meagre food, and hides him (by a route so secret and so terrible that even she has never dared to use it) in the room where the ultimate treasures are supposed to lie. But by contravening the laws by which she lives, she destroys all that she owns, her authority. The old powers are not dead, the wizard tells her, in the magnificent escape chapter, but they are not for humans to worship. She must take on the greater burden of freedom, which is heavier than the old one of belief. "It is not a gift given, but a choice made, and the choice may be a hard one. The road goes upwards towards the light; but the laden traveller may never reach the end of it." If the book could flag it is here, as they make their troubled way through the hills and dunes, but there is a solution and a path: it satisfies, and it is not commonplace.

"Earthsea Revisited," in The Times Literary Supplement, *No. 3661, April 28, 1972, p. 484.*

The Times Literary Supplement

Opinions may always differ on whether *A Wizard of Earthsea* or its current sequel, *The Farthest Shore,* is the greater book. (Strictly, this is the third of the Earthsea books, but the second, *The Tombs of Atuan,* branches off in its theme.) There are some who value Looking-glass more than Wonderland *Alice, The Princess and Curdie* more than *The Princess and the Goblin,* later Nesbit or C. S. Lewis even than earlier—and perhaps in every case for similar reasons. But few will dispute that both Le Guin books are cut from the same cloth, offer the same heady range of scene and plan, pose and meet no less audacious problems, in no less seductive style.

In *The Farthest Shore* a young prince, Arran of Enlad, of Earthsea's oldest and noblest line, is sent by his father to seek advice at Roke, the centre of magic learning. A creeping blight is affecting the land; even wizardry has no power. But Ged the Archmage, now a man in his middle years, already knows of this sickness, affecting every kind of life and craft and magic skill through the south and west of the Archipelago. The ill must be traced to its source, and he sets out with the boy. To Arran, courtly and brave, but sheltered, this is at first the summit of his desire.

Still, even youthful loyalty wavers as the journey grows more dreadful. Why is the mage so sparing of his magery? Which is the leader, which the led? "It is your fear I follow", his master tells him. "We must go on. We must go all the way. We must come to the place where the springs run dry, the place to which your mortal terror draws you." There are marvellous episodes: a sojourn with the Children of the Open Sea, raft-dwellers, "stalk-thin and angular, great-eyed like strange dark herons and cranes", untouched by the ways and maladies of the land. There is a bitter climb over cold black mountains, and a flight at last on the back of the oldest living dragon in the world, a creature who turns to the princeling a look of "profound and mild hilarity". But the great Le Guin climax is with the dead, re-risen sorcerer, who has used the forbidden spells to tamper with life and death and has opened a hole in the world. The living who fear to end are lured by his promises; as for the dead—

> they must climb over the wall of stones when I bid them, all the souls, the lords, the mages, the proud women; back and forth from life to death, at my command. All must come to me, the living and the dead, I who died and live!

But his triumph is also his torment.

At its very simplest level the book is a major adventure yarn: heroic, anguished, desperate, noble, demanding to the uttermost. (What would yesterday's boy readers have made of it?) But the wounds and scars don't come from the usual battlefields. Though swords are drawn, the contests are really of wit and will, on the open sea, or mountain peak, in slave-rowers' galley or drug-den, or underground, in the face of deepest horror. The author does not even resort to that hallowed and useful convention of fairy tale, which comfortably packs all evil into non-human creatures, cyclops, troll, or beast. When she deals with ultimates—the greatest mage, the farthest edge of the world (and this is a major element in Le Guin)—she carries total belief. She writes as if she were herself a graduate of the College of Roke—if girls had entrance there. Unlike Kingsley, Macdonald, Kipling, C. S. Lewis, she does not take any overt political or theological stance. Indeed her own voice (again, compare that crotchety set of geniuses) does not seem to be heard at all. But the ideas are inescapably there, intrinsic to the whole, and with sure contemporary relevance. The disturbance in Earthsea's equilibrium comes from human greed allied to ill-used human knowledge (or sorcery). Earthsea is not the only place with a secret name for every thing or being; with a choice in the personal road that every one must take.

> *"A Hole in the World," in* The Times Literary Supplement, *No. 3709, April 6, 1973, p. 379.*

Dennis J. O'Brien

The Earthsea Trilogy by Ursula K. LeGuin presents a world of realized magic. It is easy enough to wheel in the mechanisms of magic—charms and spells, sorcerers and dragons—it is another thing to make us believe in such a world. Ursula LeGuin's special gift is making magic real and important. The arch-mage Sparrowhawk's power rests on a world view that we still dimly perceive and would wish to validate. The secret of magic in Earthsea lies in names. Dragons who speak in the old tongues know the true names of things, and the art of the mage lies in the names which give power. The world view of Earthsea is pre-modern, a world in which the powers of the earth could be *summoned*. To name a thing is only sensible if there lies deep down a core of spirit that can be called upon as we summon the person by invoking a proper name. In archaic and even classical cultures the world was full of gods, spirits, daimons, muses who dwelt in sea and air, in sex and science. The arts and commerce both high and low lived in and through the invocation of these spirits. The world was there to be summoned by a name.

The journey to modernity can be seen as the loss of names, the inability to summon any spirit at the core of the things and events. The old *powers* are still there, but they are now regarded as nameless, impersonal forces which master us and resist being called by name. In the second (and to my mind, best) of the volumes in the Trilogy, *The Tombs of Atuan,* the basic conflict is between the mage and the priestess of The Nameless Ones who dwell in eternal darkness. The strength of Ursula LeGuin's writing is to make us feel the spiritual struggle between a world to be summoned and a world of nameless power. In that dimension it is more than fairy tale and fantasy.

> *Dennis J. O'Brien, in a review of "The Earthsea Trilogy," in* Commonweal, *Vol. CIV, No. 25, December 9, 1977, p. 797.*

Michael Dirda

Perhaps no modern work of fantasy has been more honored and loved than Ursula Le Guin's Earthsea trilogy. Though marketed as young-adult novels, *A Wizard of Earthsea* (1968), *The Tombs of Atuan* (1971) and *The Farthest Shore* (1972) are as deeply imagined, as finely wrought, as grown-up as any fiction of our time. They deserve that highest of all accolades: Everyone should read them. *Tehanu: The Last Book of Earthsea* unexpectedly turns the trilogy into a tetralogy; though less sheerly exciting than the earlier books, it may be the most moving of them all.

The earlier novels describe the life of Sparrowhawk, whose secret name is Ged, from youth to maturity, each installment in the sequence focusing on a particular moment of crisis. In *A Wizard of Earthsea,* for instance, young Ged must master his dark half, so as to pass from childhood to maturity. The other two books deal with—what else?—sex and death. Archetypal imagery predominates—light and dark, labyrinths, night journeys. The prose is grave and elevated, a style of moral seriousness to match these soundings into the soul's journey through life, the voice that of the chronicler or mythmaker: "But in the Deed of Ged nothing is told of that voyage nor of Ged's meeting with the shadow, before ever he sailed the Dragon's Run unscathed, or brought back the Ring of Erreth-Akbe from the Tombs of Atuan to Havnor, or came at last to Roke once more, as Archmage of all the islands of the world."

At the conclusion of *The Farthest Shore,* Ged journeys to the land of the dead, battles his greatest enemy and heals a crack in the world's fabric. In so doing, he uses up all his mage-power. He returns to the wizards' stronghold at Roke clinging to the back of the ancient dragon Kalessin, bestows a blessing on the young companion who will become king, and then vanishes into the mists of legend.

Or does he? This is where *Tehanu* begins. A mage no longer, Ged is a broken, emptied vessel, another poor guy who's lost his job after 30 years and doesn't know what to do with himself or what remains of his life. All he can think to do is go back to his childhood home on the island of Gont. But what becomes of a hero, a superman once he's grown old and lost his power?

In Tennyson's poem the old Ulysses sails off into the sunset, to certain death, proclaiming heroic verse: "To strive, to seek, to find, and not to yield." But Ged feels nothing of this, only shame and fearfulness. His particular powerlessness Le Guin naturally associates with the general condition of women. As a result, *Tehanu* enlarges its focus to take up again the story of Tenar, once priestess of the Tombs of Atuan, but now a middle-aged farmer's widow who has put all magery behind her and chosen the classic path to happiness: To live unknown.

An artist who has lost his power, a woman who has refused any: Together they shape *Tehanu* into a study of two people coming to terms with age, weakness, mortality. (pp. 1, 9)

Throughout the earlier *Earthsea* books Le Guin emphasized the importance of balance, of integrating shadow and self, of trust; she examined the nature of power and how it shapes us, seducing us to its own ends. These same themes reappear in *Tehanu,* but with a darker, more realistic edge. We are done with journeying and boys' adventures. This is a woman's world, a realm of socially imposed weakness and of male stupidity, of child abuse and evil with a human face. It is also a tale, not of an individual hero, battling to save himself or his realm, but of a family in the making, trying to live quietly, coming to terms with what abides after much is taken. It is consequently meditative, somber, even talky.

As such, *Tehanu* may be a little too autumnal for many young people. It is in fact a kind of pastoral, almost a woman's novel like *Cranford,* where most of the characters are women: the naughty old witch Aunty Moss (right out of Frost's "Witch of Coos"), the kind-hearted Lark, the bright as a button Apple, the envious crone Ivy. All, though, are finally "good" where most of the men prove wanting at best and usually actively malevolent. And for all its quietness, *Tehanu* builds to a climax of almost pornographic horror, nearly too shocking for its supposedly young adult pages.

Yet, maybe because it is a fantasy, all comes right in the end. Therru turns out to be much more than a burned little girl: As Ogion said on his deathbed, "They will fear her." But then sharp readers will have suspected as much, those who remember that Odin paid for wisdom with an eye, that dragons, the wisest of beasts, live in fire, and that wholeness embodies a balance of light and dark. The least shall be made great.

Some critics feel that in recent books Le Guin's writing has grown windy and soft, too feminist, too mythic, too preachy. Certainly this book is pointedly feminist and the motivation of its male villains a little fuzzy. But make no mistake. Le Guin can still stand your hair on end with her sentences. At one point Ged and Tenar balance on the edge of a stony cliff high above the sea, awaiting almost certain death. Made mute by a spell, Tenar unexpectedly points up to the sky. Her enemies mumble something about an albatross. Then Tenar "laughed aloud.

"In the gulfs of light, from the doorway of the sky, the dragon flew, fire trailing behind the coiling, mailed body. Tenar spoke then."

" 'Kalessin!' she cried, and then turned, seizing Ged's arm, pulling him down on the rock, as the roar of fire went over them, the rattle of mail and the hiss of wind in upraised wings, the clash of the talons like scytheblades on the rock."

At the end of *Tehanu* a new world seems dawning, and there is obviously much more to tell, especially of Therru. But we can guess her future, as well as Ged's and Tenar's. Still, it would be wonderful if this were not in fact our last visit to Earthsea. (p. 9)

Michael Dirda, "The Twilight of an Age of Magic," in Book World—The Washington Post, *February 25, 1990, pp. 1, 9.*

Robin McKinley

[*Tehanu: The Last Book of Earthsea*] is a story of loss, of the unfairness of fate and of people's carelessness and cruelty to one another and to their world. And yet it is also a story of joy, of finding brightness behind the shadow, of learning to *look.*

Tehanu is a major novel by a major novelist. It is deceptively short, and written in a deceptively simple style. It is also another tale of Earthsea, the realm made famous by Ursula K. LeGuin's early trilogy, which began with *The Wizard of Earthsea.* The second volume, *The Tombs of Atuan,* was a 1972 Newbery Honor Book, and the third, *The Farthest Shore,* won the 1973 National Book Award for Children's Books. Those prizes explain why the new novel is being published as a children's book and, as here, reviewed as such. But this label, and the publicity sheet that came with the book, declaring that *Tehanu* addresses "issues of aging, feminism and child abuse," are doing the novel no favors. Ursula LeGuin is an important figure in American letters, so *Tehanu* has a much better chance of finding its audience than a similar one by a lesser-known, or more genre-bound, author. But the excellence it contains transcends the glib, false packaging of "children's book" or "sociological novel."

It isn't that *Tehanu* is not about aging, feminism and child abuse; it is just that saying this is like saying that *Bleak House* is about judicial corruption and *Tess of the D'Urbervilles* is about postal error. *Tehanu* is a novel rich in the ways of humanity. Some of that richness works within the genre of fantasy, for here there be dragons, and Ms. LeGuin's dragons are some of the best in literature.

But the characters here are not on fire with the grand, world-threatening passions that we are accustomed to in much traditional fantasy. By those standards *Tehanu* is unbearably sad. It requires a certain quietness of mind—a quietness the wizard Ogion would approve of—to recognize and appreciate the subtler world-threatening passion here.

The very best thing about this novel is its sense of growth, of distance traveled as well as time passed. The *Earthsea* trilogy is deservedly considered a classic. Ursula LeGuin shows courage in writing a sequel to an accomplished series that demonstrated the full but traditional intellectual and magical gifts of wizards who were always male. The astonishing clearsightedness of *Tehanu* is in its recognition of the necessary and life-giving contributions of female magic—sometimes disguised as domesticity. This book would be admirable and evocative by itself, but it has the advantage of the resonance it gains from the three that went before, and our memories of them. *Tehanu* isn't a children's book. Young readers of the Earthsea trilogy should be obliged to wait a decade or two before they read it. Adults may read the quartet as a finished work.

> *Robin McKinley, "The Woman Wizard's Triumph," in* The New York Times Book Review, *May 20, 1990, p. 38.*

Meredith Tax

Therru, a little girl crippled by the sadism of her father and his friends, is the center of [*Tehanu: The Last Book of Earthsea*]. One of Therru's eyes is blind, one hand has been burned into a claw, and half her face is a hard mask of scars. "They raped her and beat her and burned her; these things happen, my lord," says Tenar, who takes care of her. "These things happen to children." It could be a story from Child Abuse Hotel or Crack House Street. It could be the story of Lisa Steinberg.

But it isn't. Because, suddenly, there are dragons. And they make all the difference. *Tehanu: The Last Book of Earthsea* is about child abuse, but it is also about the common heritage and uncertain borderline between humans and dragons. It is about power: male power and what happens when it's lost; female power and how no one knows what it is; and the mysterious, fragile power of Therru, the burnt child.

And it is a children's book. People in this country are rather strict about the boundary between children's and adult's literature, but I have never felt completely at home on either side of that divide. I read most kinds of novels, classic, modernist, realistic, science fiction, "young adult," detective stories, depending on my mood. Why eat a steak if what you really want is a peach? When I feel anxious, sad, or needy, when I long for a world simpler and cleaner than my own, where the individual's ability to affect events is a given, responsibility is clear, and morality is more important than success, then I read fantasy. These qualities are, of course, found in religious literature as well; the end of *Tehanu*, in fact, reminds me of that moment in Milton's *Samson Agonistes* when the hero's torment turns suddenly, out of all reason, to power and transcendence.

Milton? Aren't we getting a bit grand for "kiddielit," as it is called in the trade?

Don't be fooled by marketing categories. The *Earthsea* books are children's literature like the *Odyssey* and *Beowulf* are children's literature. Composed sparely, shaped by narratives so basic they must be inscribed upon our cells, they read as if they were not written but found, dug out like jewels from rock.

Each tale in the *Earthsea* trilogy is an extended metaphor. *A Wizard of Earthsea,* concerning young Ged's flight from, then pursuit of the Shadow he has arrogantly called up from the netherworld, is about overcoming childish grandiosity, accepting one's mortality along with one's strength. *The Tombs of Atuan* tells of Ged's rescue of Tenar, and her efforts to escape the dark goddesses she has been raised to serve—the struggle to emerge from the darkness of childhood fears and irrationality, to learn to think clearly, to find the light of civilization and friendship. *The Farthest Shore* is the tale of Ged's fight against a monstrous, immensely powerful egoist willing to send everyone in the world to death that he might live forever. The battle is so grueling Ged loses his own powers in winning it, but he also finds and tests the young king who will bring order to the world.

The Farthest Shore, published in 1972, was supposed to be the end of the series. Now there's *Tehanu,* which takes up where the last book left off, but is a different kettle of fish entirely. The first Earthsea books are linear, gestural, full of action; this one is talky and abrupt, doubling back on itself, full of unresolved menace, without closure. Its heroes wait, hide, and flee; they have no power to fight. The first three books lay out the answer to the problem of evil with some confidence (lack of balance); this one asks, like Gertrude Stein on her deathbed, "What is the question?"

The answer to the missing question has already been revealed. Since Ged has lost his powers, the wizards who keep balance in the universe need a new Archmage. One of them has a vision, "a woman on Gont," the small island where Tenar and Therru live. But what does the vision mean? A woman cannot be Archmage; this would be a contradiction in terms. What can the question be to which the answer is a woman?

Tehanu is a feminist deconstruction of heroic fantasy, Le Guin's critique of a younger, simpler self, who, as she told me recently, took as her model Tolkien, the great breakthrough writer who legitimized the form, "though he was heir to a long, purely male tradition of heroic adventure fantasy. My Earthsea trilogy is part of this male tradition—that is why I had to write this fourth volume. Because I changed. I had to show the other side."

Feminism has made heroic fantasy—and a number of other classical literary modes, not to mention social relations—impossible, without developing alternative modes to put in their place. Like the worker in Brecht's poem who asked, "Who built the seven gates of Thebes?" Le Guin asks, by implication, who did the dishes for all those feasts in Tolkien? And how can any of us—even men who share housework—be heroes when we have to spend so much time caring for house and children? And without heroes, how can evil be defeated?

So many questions. Some feminist writers try to substitute female knights in armor for male, but that doesn't work for me. What works is books that ask questions of myth, like Christa Wolf's *Cassandra,* Leslie Marmon Silko's

Ceremony, and the fiction of Ursula Le Guin. Le Guin is a prophet unhonored in her own country. Oh, she is honored (one Horn Book Award, one Newbery Medal, three Hugos, one National Book Award for Children's Literature), but as a writer of genre books—the ones you find under "Science Fiction" or "Children" instead of "Literature."

Le Guin disdains such boundaries. "I am always trying to break down walls," she says. She writes science fiction, fantasy, *New Yorker* stories, young adult books, poetry, and essays. Almost all her work is political. This fact has not been noticed too much by the people in charge of standards—you know, the guys who set the value of books, the literary equivalent of the Federal Reserve system. Of course, they think the political novel is dead anyhow, and they aren't about to recognize one that pops up in the wrong part of the bookstore. They expect political writing to be set in the real world, and Le Guin's is set in a universe of possibility. . . .

[In *Tehanu*] one has the sense of an evil growing stronger, of a good barely able to defeat it. Who is there to stand against the dark but Ged, a wizard who has lost his power, and Tenar, a woman who gave hers up to marry and have kids? It is no accident that the central symbol of *Tehanu* is a burned, abused child.

But this is fantasy, so there are dragons. And in Le Guin's dragons, as in Tolkien's, lies much of the satisfaction of her universe. There is also the homespun American purity of her language. For, as she says in one of her essays, in fantasy, style is everything:

> There is no borrowed reality of history, or current events, or just plain folks at home in Peyton Place. There is no comfortable matrix of the commonplace to substitute for the imagination, to provide ready-made emotional response, and to disguise flaws and failures of creation. There is only a construct built in a void, with every joint and seam and nail exposed. . . . Where the act of speech is the act of creation. The only voice that speaks there is the creator's voice. And every word counts.

Kid stuff? Sure, if all adults need are stories of mundane cleverness and failure, small loves and missed connections. Children's literature, sure, if children are the only ones who need stories that remind us of the firelight flickering on the walls of the cave.

> Meredith Tax, "Fantasy Island," in The Village Voice, Vol. XXXV, No. 44, October 30, 1990, p. 75.

John Clute

Ursula Le Guin's *A Wizard in Earthsea* first appeared in 1968 from a small Californian publishing house. The story, which traced the life of the Archmage Ged from birth to early manhood, seemed from the first as polished and word-perfect a tale for older children as could be imagined. Nor did its sequels, *The Tombs of Atuan* (1971) and *The Farthest Shore* (1972), diminish in the slightest one's sense of Le Guin's achievement.

An excerpt from *Tehanu: The Last Book of Earthsea*

She was combing the black goat for the fine underwool that she would spin and take to a weaver to make into cloth, the silky "fleecefell" of Gont Island. The old black goat had been combed a thousand times, and liked it, leaning into the dig and pull of the wire comb-teeth. The grey-black combings grew into a soft, dirty cloud, which Tenar at last stuffed into a net bag; she worked some burrs out of the fringes of the goat's ears by way of thanks, and slapped her barrel flank companionably. "Bah!" the goat said, and trotted off. Tenar let herself out of the fenced pasture and came around in front of the house, glancing over the meadow to make sure Therru was still playing there.

Moss had shown the child how to weave grass baskets, and clumsy as her crippled hand was, she had begun to get the trick of it. She sat there in the meadow grass with her work on her lap, but she was not working. She was watching Sparrowhawk.

He stood a good way off, nearer the cliff's edge. His back was turned, and he did not know anyone was watching him, for he was watching a bird, a young kestrel; and she in turn was watching some small prey she had glimpsed in the grass. She hung beating her wings, wanting to flush the vole or mouse, to panic it into a rush to its nest. The man stood, as intent, as hungry, gazing at the bird. Slowly he lifted his right hand, holding the forearm level, and he seemed to speak, though the wind bore his words away. The kestrel veered, crying her high, harsh, keening cry, and shot up and off toward the forests.

The man lowered his arm and stood still, watching the bird. The child and the woman were still. Only the bird flew, went free.

"He came to me once as a falcon, a pilgrim falcon," Ogion had said, by the fire, on a winter day. He had been telling her of the spells of Changing, of transformations, of the mage Bordger who had become a bear. "He flew to me, to my wrist, out of the north and west. I brought him in by the fire here. He could not speak. Because I knew him, I was able to help him, he could put off the falcon, and be a man again. But there was always some hawk in him. They called him Sparrowhawk in his village because the wild hawks would come to him, at his word. Who are we? What is it to be a man? Before he had his name, before he had knowledge, before he had power, the hawk was in him, and the man, and the mage, and more—he was what we cannot name. And so are we all."

The girl sitting at the hearth, gazing at the fire, listening, saw the hawk; saw the man; saw the birds come to him, come at his word, at his naming them, come beating their wings to hold his arm with their fierce talons; saw herself the hawk, the wild bird.

Nor, again, did it seem, after she moved on to other things, that she had left the *Earthsea* trilogy incomplete. Like any "High Fantasy" saga of more than sensational interest—like, for instance, Tolkien's *Lord of the Rings,* which Le Guin's sequence emulates in small—the *Earthsea* books are at heart tales of ontology, quests for the true meaning of the roots of the world. In language almost any child over ten will comprehend, the three tales also work as a song of praise.

Ged the Sparrowhawk's progress from wild boy to Archmage of all Earthsea is an epic of contemplation, a progress from uncontrolled action to the immobility of the sage. In the first volume, Ged learns that his every act jostles the Equilibrium which governs the plenitude of Earthsea, whose archipelagos and sheltering seas are a ravishing dream of the Earthly paradise. In the second, he and a young girl, Tenar of Atuan, re-forge a ring whose wholeness will enable the kingdoms of the world themselves to re-unite after aeons, in imitation of the Long Dance of Being. In the third, some final and profoundly unChristian lessons are taught: that time is a cycle, that death is inevitable, and that the Long Dance, which occurs at the shortest day of the year, is performed over the abyss. In the end, having given up his power, Ged retires to his home island, to contemplate (we guess) things in themselves.

None of this seems undeliberate, or lacking in wholeness, and *Tehanu: The last book of Earthsea* comes therefore as a kind of shock. This is clearly deliberate. The first half of *Tehanu* is a forcible—and at times decidedly bad-tempered—deconstruction of its predecessors. It is a statement that the wholeness of the trilogy is an artefact and an imposition, because the order which expresses that wholeness is inherently male. That the centre of the world no longer holds is evident enough, and social dissolution threatens; but for Tenar of Atuan, now middle-aged and a widow, as a "mere" woman, there is nothing new in a world gone blind and deaf. Earthsea has always been a man's world, as defined in the harsh, abstractly rational cadences of the father's tongue; and has always been blind and deaf to the weave and shuttle of women's talk. So Tenar must dodge and hide; she must protect her ward, Therru, whom men have ravaged. Ged (who is nothing like the Ged of the trilogy) sulks because he is powerless, but comes at last to Tenar's bed, where she teaches him what wizards cannot know. We now learn that the absence of females of power from the trilogy derives, not from conventions of storytelling to which Le Guin adhered and which the reader therefore did not notice, but from the fact that wizards cannot have sex. Finally, young Therru, whose scarred face has seemed from the first dragon-like, saves Tenar and Ged from the last of the death-denying wizards, and herself turns out to be the new shaper of Earthsea.

Tehanu ends, therefore, in a sudden flush of the old magic. But most of it, told deliberately in the chuntering rhythms of the disfranchised women of Gont, has a slightly sour effect on the reader. It is not that Le Guin is wrong in her analysis of power, of the "dance of masks" which makes up man's world, or that it is inappropriate to create tales in which women live whole. But in the end one resents the corrosiveness of *Tehanu,* for in telling this particular tale Le Guin has chosen to punish her own readers for having loved other books she herself wrote.

John Clute, "Deconstructing Paradise," in
The Times Literary Supplement, *No. 4578,*
December 28, 1990-January 3, 1991, p. 1409.

Tom Easten

Ursula K. Le Guin is renowned for her novels both of science fiction and of fantasy. Among the latter is a trilogy of so much charm and depth and insight, that even though it was marketed as "children's" fiction, it found no such limits among its readers. That trilogy comprised *A Wizard of Earthsea, The Tombs of Atuan,* and *The Farthest Shore,* and it has been compared to the works of Tolkien and Lewis.

Like Tolkien, Le Guin wound up being badgered for a sequel. Eventually—when she realized that there really was more of the tale to tell—she succumbed. The result is *Tehanu.* The protagonist is Goha, a woman who was once the Tenar whom the wizard Ged (once known as Sparrowhawk) rescued from darkness in *The Tombs of Atuan.* After her rescue, she stayed and studied lore awhile with Ged's one-time mentor Ogion before retreating to the countryside to marry a farmer and raise a family.

Now the farmer is dead. The family is grown and gone. Goha has only the waif Therru, hideously scarred both physically and mentally when her father and his friend raped her and beat her and threw her in the fire. And now Ogion summons her to his deathbed.

Before Ogion dies, he utters certain portentous words about Therru. After, a dragon arrives bearing a disempowered wizard, no longer Ged, only Sparrowhawk, whom Goha must nurse back to health and then send off before the new king's men, searching for Ged to honor him in their way, can find him. There is a rumor of a woman who has all the potencies of dragons. There is conflict between the forces of love, justice, and fairness on one side, and those of hate, greed, and tyranny on the other. There is a hint of utopian androgyny, the idea that age can bring nurturance and aggression (femininity and masculinity, if you like) into better balance in both men and women. To see that same combination in youth is rare; when it appears, it seems the mark of extreme wisdom.

I dare not say much more about the story for fear of spoiling your enjoyment. Much of *Tehanu* is built of small events, homey material, hearth and garden and petty encounters. Yet the small is touched by the large to the extent that the reader feels a part of something grand. This book and its three predecessors form a whole to cherish.

But is it really a whole? Is the "Earthsea Cycle" really over? Le Guin has said it is, but she said as much before. And as *Tehanu* closes, there is obviously room for more. Perhaps in time Le Guin will see fit to give us all another gift.

Tom Easten, in a review of "Tehanu," in Analog Science Fiction/Science Fact, *Vol. CXI, No. 13, November, 1991, p. 166.*

LE GUIN ON *EARTHSEA*

Ursula K. Le Guin

All my life I have written, and all my life I have (without

conscious decision) avoided reading how-to-write things. The Shorter Oxford Dictionary and Follett's and Fowler's manuals of usage are my entire arsenal of tools. However, in reading and teaching and talking with other writers one does arrive at a certain consciousness of technique. The most different technique from my own, the one that starts from the point farthest removed, is just this one of preliminary plans and lists and descriptions. The technique of keeping a notebook and describing all the characters in it before the story is begun: how much William weighs and where he went to school and how his hair is cut and what his dominant traits are.

I do have notebooks, in which I worry at plot ideas as if they were old bones, growling and snarling and frequently burying them and digging them up again. Also, during the writing of a piece, I often make notes concerning a character, particularly if its a novel. My memory is very poor, and if there's something I just noticed about the character, but this is not the right point to put it into the book, then I make a note for future reference. Something like:

W. d not appr H's ing.—Repr!!

Then I lose the note.

But I don't write out descriptions beforehand, and would indeed feel ridiculous, even ashamed, to do so. If the character isn't so clear to me that I know all *that* about him, what am I doing writing about him? What right have I to describe what William did when Helen bit his knee, if I don't even know what he looks like, and his past, and his psyche, inside and out, as well as I know myself? Because after all he is myself. Part of myself.

If William is a character worthy of being written about, then he exists. He exists, inside my head to be sure, but in his own right, with his own vitality. All I have to do is look at him. I don't plan him, compose him of bits and pieces, inventory him. I find him.

There he is, and Helen is biting his knee, and he says with a little cough, "I really don't think this is relevant, Helen." What else, being William, could he say?

This attitude toward action, creation, is evidently a basic one, the same root from which the interest in the *I Ching* and Taoist philosophy evident in most of my books arises. The Taoist world is orderly, not chaotic, but its order is not one imposed by man or by a personal or humane deity. The true laws—ethical and aesthetic, as surely as scientific—are not imposed from above by any authority, but exist in things and are to be found—discovered.

[This] . . . anti-ideological, pragmatic technique applies to places, as well as people. I did not deliberately invent Earthsea. I did not think "Hey wow—islands are archetypes and archipelagoes are superarchetypes and let's build us an archipelago!" I am not an engineer, but an explorer. I discovered Earthsea.

Plans are likely to be made, if well made, inclusively; discoveries are made bit by bit. Planning negates time. Discovery is a temporal process. It may take years and years. People are still exploring Antarctica.

The history of the discovery of Earthsea is something like this:

In 1964 I wrote a story called **"The Word of Unbinding"** about a wizard. Cele Goldsmith Lalli bought it for *Fantastic*. (Cele Lalli gave me and a lot of other people their start in SF; she was one of the most sensitive and audacious editors the field has ever had.) I don't recall now whether the fact is made much of in the story, but it was perfectly clear in my mind that it took place on an island, one among many islands. I did not give much attention to the setting, as it was (as William would say) not relevant; and developed only such rules of magic as were germane to the very small point the very minor story made.

Soon after, I wrote a story, **"The Rule of Names,"** in which both the islands and the rules of magic were considerably more developed (Cele published it too). This story was lighthearted (the other one was glum), and I had fun playing around a bit with the scenery, and with the old island ladies drinking rushwash tea, and so on. It was set on an island called Sattins, which I knew to be one of an outlying group east of the main archipelago. The main character, a dragon known first as Mr. Underhill and then, when his nature is revealed, by his true name Yevaud, came from a westerly isle called Pendor.

I did not much bother with all the islands that I knew lay between Sattins and Pendor, and north and south of them. They weren't involved. I had the distinct feeling, however, that the island of **"Word of Unbinding"** lay up north of Pendor. I am not now sure which island it actually is, that one I first landed on. Later voyages of discovery have so complicated the map that the first landfall, like that of the Norsemen in the New World, is hard to pin down for certain. Sattins, however, is on the map, high in the East Reach between Yore and Vemish.

Along in 1965 or 1966 I wrote a longish story about a prince who travels down through the archipelago from its central island, Havnor, in search of the Ultimate. He goes southwest out into the open sea, beyond all islands, and finds there a people who live on rafts all their lives long. He ties his boat to a raft and settles down with them, content with this as the Ultimate, until he realizes that out past the farthest journey of the drifting raft-colony there are sea-people, living in the sea itself. He joins them. I think the implication was that (not being a merman) he'll wear out eventually, and sink, and find the ultimate Ultimate. This story wasn't submitted for publication as it never worked itself out at all well; but I felt strongly that the basic image—the raft-colony—was a lulu, and would find itself its home somewhere eventually. It did, in the last of the Earthsea books, *The Farthest Shore.*

I explored Earthsea no further until 1967, when the publisher of Parnassus Press, Herman Schein, asked me if I'd like to try writing a book for him. He wanted something for older kids; till then Parnassus had been mainly a young-juvenile publisher, putting out the handsomest and best-made picture books in America. He gave me complete freedom as to subject and approach. Nobody until then had ever asked me to write anything; I had just done so, relentlessly. To be asked to do it was a great boon. The exhilaration carried me over my apprehensions about writing "for young people," something I had never seriously tried. For some weeks or months I let my imagination go groping around in search of what was wanted, in the dark. It stumbled over the Islands, and the magic employed there. Serious consideration of magic, and of writing for kids, combined to make me wonder about wizards. Wizards are usually elderly or ageless Gandalfs, quite rightly and archetypically. But what were they before they had white beards? How did they learn what is obviously an erudite and dangerous art? Are there colleges for young wizards? And so on.

The story of the book is essentially a voyage, a pattern in the form of a long spiral. I began to see the places where the young wizard would go. Eventually I drew a map. Now that I knew where everything was, now was the time for cartography. Of course a great deal of it only appeared above water, as it were, in drawing the map.

Three small islands are named for my children, their baby-names; one gets a little jovial and irresponsible, given the freedom to create a world out of nothing at all. (Power corrupts.) None of the other names "means" anything that I know of, though their sound is more or less meaningful to me.

People often ask how I think of names in fantasies, and again I have to answer that I find them, that I hear them. This is an important subject in this context. From that first story on, *naming* has been the essence of the art-magic as practiced in Earthsea. For me, as for the wizards, to know the name of an island or a character is to know the island or the person. Usually the name comes of itself, but sometimes one must be very careful: as I was with the protagonist, whose true name is Ged. I worked (in collaboration with a wizard named Ogion) for a long time trying to "listen for" his name, and making certain it really was his name. This all sounds very mystical and indeed there are aspects of it I do not understand, but it is a pragmatic business too, since if the name had been wrong the character would have been wrong—misbegotten, misunderstood.

A man who read the ms. for Parnassus thought "Ged" was meant to suggest "God." That shook me badly. I considered changing the name in case there were other such ingenious minds waiting to pounce. But I couldn't do so. The fellow's name was Ged and no two ways about it.

It isn't pronounced Jed, by the way. That sounds like a mountain moonshiner to me. I thought the analogy with "get", would make it clear, but a lot of people have asked. One place I do exert deliberate control in name-inventing is in the area of pronounceability. I try to spell them so they don't look formidable (unless, like Kurremkarmerruk, they're meant to look formidable), and they can be pronounced either with the English or the Italian vowels. I don't care which.

Much the same holds for the bits of invented languages in the text of the trilogy.

There are words, like rushwash tea, for which I can offer no explanation. They simply drink rushwash tea there; that's what it's called, like lapsang soochong or Lipton's

here. Rushwash is a Hardic word, of course. If you press me, I will explain that it comes from the rushwash bush, which grows both wild and cultivated everywhere south of Enlad, and bears a small round leaf which when dried and steeped yields a pleasant brownish tea. I did not know this before I wrote the foregoing sentence. Or did I know it, and simply never thought about it? What's in a name? A lot, that's what.

There are more formal examples of foreign languages in the trilogy; in *The Farthest Shore* there are several whole sentences in the Language of the Making, as dragons will not speak anything else. These arrived, spelling (formidable) and all, and I wrote them down without question. No use trying to make a lexicon of Hardic or of the True Speech; there's not enough in the books. It's not like Tolkien, who in one sense wrote *The Lord of the Rings* to give his invented languages somebody to speak them. That is lovely, that is the Creator Spirit working absolutely unhindered—making the word flesh. But Tolkien is a linguist, as well as a creator.

(In other books I have taken the invented languages further. I knew enough Karhidish, when I was writing *The Left Hand of Darkness,* to write a couple of short poems in it. I couldn't do so now. I made no methodical lexicon or grammar, only a word list for my own reference.)

I said that to know the true name is to know the thing, for me, and for the wizards. This implies a good deal about the "meaning" of the trilogy, and about me. The trilogy is, in one aspect, about the artist. The artist as magician. The Trickster. Prospero. That is the only truly allegorical aspect it has of which I am conscious. If there are other allegories in it please don't tell me: I hate allegories. A is "really" B, and a hawk is "really" a handsaw—bah. Humbug. Any creation, primary or secondary, with any vitality to it, can "really" be a dozen mutually exclusive things at once, before breakfast.

Wizardry is artistry. The trilogy is then, in this sense, about art, the creative experience, the creative process. There is always this circularity in fantasy. The snake devours its tail. Dreams must explain themselves. . . . (pp. 38-43)

Most of my letters about the Earthsea books from American readers are from people between sixteen and twenty-five. The English who write me tend to be, as well as I can guess, over thirty, and more predominantly male. (Several of them are Anglican clergymen. As a congenital non-Christian I find this a little startling; but the letters are terrific.) One might interpret this age difference to mean that the English are more childish than the Americans, but I see it the other way. The English readers are grownup enough not to be defensive about being grownup.

The most childish thing about *A Wizard of Earthsea,* I expect, is its subject: coming of age.

Coming of age is a process that took me many years; I finished it, so far as I ever will, at about age thirty-one; and so I feel rather deeply about it. So do most adolescents. It's their main occupation, in fact.

The subject of *The Tombs of Atuan* is, if I had to put it

in one word, sex. There's a lot of symbolism in the book, most of which I did not, of course, analyze consciously while writing; the symbols can all be read as sexual. More exactly, you could call it a feminine coming of age. Birth, rebirth, destruction, freedom are the themes.

The Farthest Shore is about death. That's why it is a less well built, less sound and complete book than the others. They were about things I had already lived through and survived. *The Farthest Shore* is about the thing you do not live through and survive. It seemed an absolutely suitable subject to me for young readers, since in a way one can say that the hour when a child realizes, not that death exists—children are intensely aware of death—but that he/she, personally, is mortal, will die, is the hour when childhood ends, and the new life begins. Coming of age again, but in a larger context.

In any case I had little choice about the subject. Ged, who was always very strong-minded, always saying things that surprised me and doing things he wasn't supposed to do, took over completely in this book. He was determined to show me how his life must end, and why. I tried to keep up with him, but he was always ahead. I rewrote the book more times than I want to remember, trying to keep him under some kind of control. I thought it was all done when it was printed here, but the English edition differs in three long passages from the earlier American one: my editor at Gollancz said, "Ged is talking too much," and she was quite right, and I shut him up three times, much to the improvement of the whole. If you insist upon discovering instead of planning, this kind of trouble is inevitable. It is a most uneconomical way to write. The book is still the most imperfect of the three, but it is the one I like best. It is the end of the trilogy, but it is the dream I have not stopped dreaming. (pp. 45-6)

> *Ursula K. Le Guin, "Dreams Must Explain Themselves," in her* The Language of the Night: Essays of Fantasy and Science Fiction, *1979. Reprint by Berkley Books, 1982, pp. 37-46.*

SCHOLARLY STUDIES OF THE *EARTHSEA* CYCLE

George Edgar Slusser

[*A small portion of this essay appears in* CLC, *Vol. 13*].

In her essay, **"Dreams Must Explain Themselves"** (1973), Le Guin tells us her mage is an artist—the [*Earthsea*] trilogy is an artist-novel. Traditionally, the artist is the most private of heroes; the struggle to create is primarily a struggle with self, with one's own powers and the need to control them and their consequences. The scientists and "observers" of [her] earlier novels occupy an intermediate position between men of action and the artist. But in Le Guin the pull is always toward action. . . . Ged is a loner. *A Wizard of Earthsea* tells the story of a private battle; the two books which follow show the hero moving toward companionship and collaboration. The quest in *The Farthest Shore,* though undertaken in the same secretive, un-

assuming spirit as always, has profound public implications. The artist no longer travels alone; and the one he takes with him is not another mage, but a young prince, trained not in the arts, but with the sword. (p. 34)

In **"Dreams Must Explain Themselves,"** Le Guin describes the thematic progression of the three Earthsea novels. *Wizard* deals with the hero's "coming of age." It is a novel of initiation and apprenticeship. The subject of *The Tombs of Atuan* is "sex"; it relates a "feminine coming of age." In broader terms, its theme is love. The third novel, *Farthest,* is about death, "a coming of age again," says Le Guin, "but in a larger context." This is the hero's last and greatest adventure. First an apprentice, then a master, Ged-grown-old now takes a new apprentice with him, thus completing the epic chain. The adventure is also, in a way, a return. Young Ged became a man by accepting and absorbing the shadow of his own death. Now he goes to fight a man who has refused death, who has been possessed by his shadow.

The central theme of all these novels is the nature of human evil. . . . Ged is both an ideal hero in an idealized world order, and an everyman. His powers seem exceptional, and yet he wins his greatest battles with means we all possess. *Earthsea,* in its sharp, limited vision, explores in depth the question of individual responsibility. To deny death is to turn from life. But worse still is to project an anti-shadow, abstracting personal fear into a general virtue, and making fear of death into a quest for eternal life.

The image of the shadow dominates *Wizard*. . . . Like all of Le Guin's heroes, Ged is an alien, an orphan in the spiritual sense, ignored by his insensitive parent. Like the odd ones of myth and fairy tale, this child of innate gifts is sired by ordinary people. The "mage born" is adopted by the wizard Ogion and made his apprentice. But in his godgiven gift lie the dangers of pride and ambition, and to these Ged succumbs. His attempt to raise the dead, to prove his power through an unnatural act, looses the terrible shadow upon him. He had been warned by Ogion that danger surrounds power as shadow surrounds light. Like all men, Ged must learn his limitations the hard way, and bear the consequences of his act. These consequences, fortunately, also have their limits; if it were not so, the balance would have long since failed. Young Ged is foolish, not wicked; but he releases a force which nonetheless seeks to possess him, to turn him into an instrument of evil. The novel narrates his struggle with the shadow—first his attempts to flee, then his resolve to hunt it down, and finally his confrontation and victory.

But what is the nature of Ged's struggle? The enemy is a shadow, part of the hero himself, something from within. And, yet, Ged moves in a world where things seem to be working against him, leading him to ruin. He is pursued by a hostile destiny. It is the young witch girl on Gont who, daring Ged, first suggests raising the dead. This leads him to read the fatal runes in Ogion's book. Jasper again dares him—and this time he raises the dead, and releases the shadow with it. Then there is the mysterious messenger who directs him to Osskil, where the shadow nearly takes his life. These figures exist—we see and hear them. But as "antagonists," they too are shadows, of Ged's own mind. He comes close at one point to believing in fate. This is more than illusion; Ged is fooling himself. For in seeking "causes" outside of himself, he avoids the look within. His own pride and fear have invested neutral shapes with purpose and hostile will in an attempt to cast the weight of responsibility onto something beyond him. In the final episode on the open sea, the man is alone with his shadow. Before he finally absorbs it, it changes shape. What passes before him is his own life. One of the shapes is Jasper; but he also sees his father, and Pechvarry his friend. The shadow is formed of his own acts and choices, and in accepting it, he accepts responsibility for them. For he, not Jasper or any other man or force, must bear the blame for what he does.

At first reading, the mood cast by *Wizard* is strange and dream-like; we seem to fluctuate between objective reality and the hero's mind. The shadow is loosed into a very real world—an Archmage dies sealing the breach—but is gradually drawn back towards Ged. The hero's adversaries are sometimes phantoms of his own creation, and sometimes real powers, like the dragons and the Lord of Terrenon. Behind this fluctuation lies a carefully controlled pattern. The traditional novel of apprenticeship shows the hero first learning, then doing. But Ged is the sorcerer's apprentice—he does before he learns, and his first deed is misbegotten. For this mistake he is not sequestered; instead he becomes a mage, and is sent forth, master of his craft, but still ignorant of its implications. Again and again, life forces him to act first and learn later. Confronting the problem of action, he comes to see a deeper truth: to do great deeds, one must be whole oneself. And one is whole only by knowing one's limits. (pp. 34-7)

[What] is the nature of evil in *Wizard?* What does the symbolism of darkness signify? Earthsea contains many "dark powers"—the Stone of Terrenon, the dragons. But these are primeval, inhuman powers; beside them and over them man has built up civilization. The use of the Old Speech, for instance, binds a man to truth, but dragons can twist true words to false ends, because this language is theirs. These truenamers are fundamentally indifferent to man, they are unman. In order to exist, man must strike a balance with them. They cannot be conquered, but they must be contained: Ged names and fixes the dragon, and the stone is sealed in the fortress. They must not be served, because, in seeking to rule these forces, man enslaves himself to them—he consents to darkness. In the same way, Ged, wishing to rule over death by his conjuring, consents to it, and so becomes its prey.

But just what is this "shadow" he releases? Does it represent Death, a figure that walks among us; or is it a figure of his mind, the "shadow of his own death"? Ged flees the shadow, and it nearly claims him. Is he the victim of his own fears? The Otak dies to remind us that the struggle is not entirely in the mind. Ged pursues the shadow, and runs aground, nearly perishing. Finally, he stops running or searching; he knows that neither can escape their fate. When they have finally come to the time and the place destined for their last meeting, then they will meet. This other is Death, but the hero does not meet it here. But what does he encounter on the sand inside the ocean? The place is nowhere if not in the mind. And the act is inconclusive in terms of conquest or defeat: Ged neither loses nor wins, but in naming the shadow of his death with his own name, he makes himself whole again as a man. The evil here is neither death nor the darkness; it is rather Ged's refusal to grant these things their rightful place in the balance of nature. Only the whole man, who has accepted death, is free to serve the powers of life. Yet for all of this, Le Guin does not intend death to lose its sting or its reality. The ambiguity of the shadow is purposeful, for it reminds us that the mind is not everything. Death is, as Ged affirms in a moment of gloom, more than fear or a misunderstanding of life. It is a power as well, perhaps the only one that has any real hold on man.

It is significant that the struggle with the shadow is not mentioned in the epic poem celebrating the mage's life, whereas the journey to the tombs is. The first merely lays the foundation for deeds, the second is the true public act. In *Tombs,* Ged goes to the Kargad lands, home of the savage blond barbarians who raid Gont in the earlier novel, to recover the lost half of the ring of Erreth-Akbe from the tombs. As long as the ring remains divided, Earthsea will know neither unity nor peace.

Ged goes seeking neither fame nor fortune. His goal is a quest for knowledge. The two halves of the ring joined together form the "lost rune." To know the "true name" of a thing in Earthsea is to know its essence; so it is here. The true nature of unity is no longer understood because its sign is lost. This loss occurred long ago, when the attempts of the mage Erreth-Akbe to unify the world were defeated, and Earthsea slipped back into faction and darkness. This is no Christian fall which will end in a redemption. Ged follows Erreth as another man of wisdom and moral courage who attempts to bring harmony to a world. The tension between making and unmaking is constant and ongoing; man's continuing responsibility is to oppose the forces of disorder. The task is neverending, and utterly necessary. Against the permanence of chaos, mankind forms chains: the task passes from Estraven to Ai, from Erreth to Ged. (pp. 37-9)

The ring has been broken in two; one half was scattered to the winds, the other buried in the tombs. The world seems permanently in the grip of fear and greed. A false unity has been imposed on men by laws and priests. True harmony, in Le Guin, comes only from the gift freely given. The half of the ring in the world was thought buried at the ends of the earth—on a nameless sandbar along with the pair of royal siblings—and yet it returns. Ged is accidentally shipwrecked on the island in *Wizard.* Though rendered a near-savage from isolation, the woman nonetheless reaches out to mankind, and gives Ged the fragment. A chain of gifts begins which leads the hero to Selidor in the extreme west, where the dragon reveals to him the meaning of the object, then back to Atuan in the farthest east where, in the bowels of the tombs, the priestess Tenar gives him with the other half of the ring his greatest gift—his life.

At the heart of the public deed, we find a very private experience. The real drama is not Ged's, but Tenar's. She is faced with the same ordeal that Ged faced in *Wizard*—the coming of age. But she has no Ogion to guide her, and no school of wizardry to teach her. Her world is one that has sunk into ignorance and perversion. The proper balance of light and darkness, death and life, has been upset. Tenar is a person of great natural strength and imagination, but the priestesses guide her to darkness and denial of life. All feelings are repressed; her mind has nothing open to it but the dark labyrinth beneath the tombs. Ged's initiation began with water to life and a name. Tenar's name is taken from her in a grotesque ceremony in which the proper relationship between life and death is willfully inverted. A figure in white wields the sword of sacrifice, while one in black stays the hand at the last minute, and claims Tenar for the darkness. Thus, ironically, she becomes "the reborn"—her name is replaced by that of the "immortal" priestess Ahra. But this is eternal death, not life; the living are entombed, "eaten," swallowed by darkness: the dead become their master. In the case of the young child Tenar, it is Blake's "marriage hearse," the corruption of life at its source.

Le Guin on *Tehanu:*

Tehanu starts at the end of *The Farthest Shore*. There's no gap in time between the books, though there was a huge gap in *my* life. That in itself was a bit of an enchantment for me—like I was being carried around on dragons. It's strange to go back that way and yet be a different person, carrying the story on. . . .

I was able to write it because I had changed, but of course a book changes you as you write it. That's why I write books. It was tremendously free—the experience of writing it really was like flying.

Ursula Le Guin, in Locus: The Newspaper of the Science Fiction Field, *January 1990.*

Ged is taken prisoner in the tombs. Tenar, the master of prisoners, holds him, and yet is fascinated by the presence of life in her dark domain. She will not yield him up to the God-King's priestess and death. Through their mutual contacts she comes, gradually, to see she is the one imprisoned, and not Ged. This mage shows her the marvels of the wide world beyond, but she claims superiority over him in the knowledge of her domain: "You know everything, wizard. But I know one thing—the one true thing!" Tenar is an intrepid explorer. She has gone farther than anyone else in the labyrinth, and now she pursues Ged with the same intellectual passion—she would know. It is only because her mind is great that she can make the breakthrough. Suddenly, she realizes Ged has gone farther than she even in her own realm of darkness. Seeing the scars on his face, she sees that "he knew death better than she did, even death." Their relationship is not only inverted, it changes levels as well. What was prisoner and jailer now becomes pupil and teacher. Ged knows one more thing—her name—and he gives it back to her. Only now, in accepting this gift, is she truly reborn. It is fruit from the tree of knowledge, for with her name the undying one

must accept her mortality. The burden of life, she will discover, is a heavy one.

Once more, freedom comes only through acceptance of limitation. This is symbolized by the ring itself. Unlike the chains of the tombs, this "ring" is an armband which, in being joined and bound together, will free mankind. Tenar calls Ged a thief when she first meets him. But, just as the first half of the ring was freely given, this one must be too. It is Tenar who ultimately gives Ged both the ring and his freedom. In the tombs, literally, there is freedom only in joining. Tenar is surprised that Ged's magic seems powerless there. He must use it to keep from succumbing to darkness. But fighting the inner battle, he has not the strength to take the ring and return. Neither person alone, in fact, has the power to return to the light. Their only hope lies in the bond of mutual trust. The Ged who had lost faith in himself in *Wizard* was saved by a friend's kindness. Now Ged gives Tenar her name and life; in return, she gives him back water and life: "It was not the water alone that saved me. It was the strength of the hands that gave it." The union of these two is that of minds reaching out across the void. The result is a flood of light: from Ged's staff and hands a "white radiance" shows the walls of the great vault to be diamonds. Their opposite (the image runs through this novel and the next) is the spider, self-sufficient, weaving his futile web out of himself in dry, dark places.

Once again, darkness is emptiness, a negative thing with the power neither to make nor unmake. The tomb merely contains Ged and Tenar; it collapses of its own accord when they leave. Evil occurs only when men serve this darkness, and there are many degrees of evil in *Tombs.* (pp. 39-41)

In a sense the last Earthsea novel, *Farthest Shore,* again plays out the struggle of *Wizard,* but this time on a different level, and in what appears a much more perilous and imperilled universe. Through the earlier novel there runs a deeper faith in the balance of things—it will right itself eventually, no matter what. Even if Ged had succumbed, and become an instrument of darkness, Vetch was still there to sink the boat. Ged had no intention of going to Iffish, his friend's home; a fortunate "chance" simply took him there. In *The Farthest Shore,* however, such checks and balances seem to have failed. A great wizard has yielded to the darkness, and his actions menace the equilibrium in Earthsea. To some extent, this wizard is again Ged's shadow, since Ged is largely responsible for the man's actions. Out of anger and vanity, Ged had once challenged a renegade mage named Cob, who had debased the summoning of the dead to a carnival trick, and dragged him to the wall that separates the land of the living from that of the dead. "Oh, a lesson you taught me, indeed," Cob later tells Ged, "but not the one you meant to teach! There I said to myself: 'I have seen death now, and I will not accept it.'"

Cob begins turning people from the natural rhythm of things by offering them eternal life. Against this irrational lure, knowledge is impotent—there must be power as well. The rune of peace has been procured, but the world remains divided. Without a central authority, a king on the throne, men and islands fall easy prey to him who would be Anti-King. The new leader will be young prince Arren, who comes to Roke and agrees to go with Ged to seek out the source of this evil.

Their journey takes them south, then west to land's end. At first, the object of their search is vague: it is a "break," a "breech." They seek a place, then a person, and eventually realize that what they are looking for is ultimately in themselves. Evil, in *Farthest Shore,* is more than ever "a web we men weave." The Anti-King is present in each man's mind, and their journey is that of each man to his death. But at the same time, it is also a journey through a series of real lands, people, and things; ultimately, it is a journey to Cob—an evildoer is destroyed, the breach in the universe is healed. The devastation is not only in their minds; real people are ravaged, leaders turn aside from duty, their lands fall to waste. More purposefully than ever, allegory functions here on several levels; the result is almost Dantesque. Symbolic levels are not only beautifully woven together, but firmly rooted in a concrete world which at every moment claims a reality of its own. (pp. 42-3)

The physical journey may be read as a projection of Arren's fears, doubts and hopes. The trip south ends in a deadpoint—a slack sail and a paralyzed will. All along there is, significantly, little wind from Ged's magic. Arren in fact begins to doubt his power: what use is it? What can an old man and a boy do alone? *Farthest Shore* reflects Le Guin's interest in dreams. Arren dreams again and again—always visions of promise which end in chaos and darkness. The silk fields of Lorbanery become entangling spider webs. He hears the call to "come" during the seance with the drugged wizard Hare, and plunges deep into darkness. Later Roke itself falls victim to the same blight: students and masters begin to doubt their magic, recourse to crystal balls yield visions of unmaking, the Master Summoner loses himself in darkness. Arren becomes totally twisted around: he believes Ged is seeking death, and allies himself with the madman Sopli in the boat, whose madness is fear of death, water, and life itself. After the attack by the savages which wounds Ged, he himself is caught in the web of inaction; reality becomes a dream: "I could think of nothing, except that there was a way of not dying for me, if I could find it." Yet he cannot move, and life flows from him as from a broken scab.

The turning point is their rescue by the raft people, who beyond all land have built life and community over the abyss of the sea. Arren first believes this world a dream; but it is real, and the Long Dance is danced here as in all other lands of Earthsea; its people know joy and death. Here the young man learns that to refuse death is to refuse life—their relation is easy to see on the rafts, but is the same everywhere. More importantly, Ged shows him that no one is immune to this evil: "What is a good man . . . one who has no darkness in him? Look a little farther. Look into yourself! Did you not hear a voice say 'Come'? Did you not follow?" Arren is now freed to act; when the singers fail at the Long Dance, he can complete the song. But for him there is more to achieving selfhood than there was for young Ged. He is to be the king; the evil must be

rooted out of the kingdom before he can rule. All nature comes to his aid, as helpful now as it was recalcitrant before. The dragon flies before them as their guide, and magewind fills the sails. The ancient powers join with men to combat the ultimate perversion. As with the tombs of Atuan, but on a vaster scale, the land of the dead is part of the balance. Cob has violated it. (pp. 43-4)

[Cob's tragedy] is one of profound error; his "eternal life" is a colossal lie, and he is the first to be duped by it. This lie comes close to destroying mankind. It is not, however, an alien lure; it is man's deepest temptation.

Wisdom can heal the breach, but physical strength alone can make the return journey—Ged must rely on Arren to help him cross the Mountains of Pain and return to life. The young man, who failed Ged once before, now sets his will, and they escape back to the ocean shore, to water and life. To refuse death was to refuse life; in *Wizard,* here, the acceptance of death becomes a thirst for life. In his final voyage to the underworld, Arren, like the young Ged before him, learns what it is to be a man: "Only to man is given the gift of knowing he will die . . . Would you have the sea grow still and the tides cease to save one wave, yourself?"

The thrust of this epic is not simply "pre-Christian"; it is quite un-Christian, un-Western, in its naturalism, its reverence for the balance of life, and its refusal of transcendental values. The story is Arren's—his deed, like Ged's, is the acceptance of his own limits, his achievement of self-hood. He meets victory for the first time standing "alone, unpraised, at the end of the world." His victory is the act of closing his hand over a piece of dark stone from the Mountains of Pain. He thus accepts pain, and yet encapsulates it, enclosing it in warm life. Neither Ged nor Arren retreat from life in order to find it. Ged's "making" is the control of natural powers. More significantly, his successor is not a mage, but a king; the sword he wields may only be in the service of life, but it is nonetheless a sword. Power has become more and more necessary to the world of Earthsea. In this shift of focus from artist to ruler, Le Guin affirms the primacy of the social realm. (pp. 45-6)

George Edgar Slusser, in his The Farthest Shores of Ursula K. Le Guin, *Borgo Press, 1976, 60 p.*

T. A. Shippey

"There is a desire in you to see dragons," remarks one character in Ursula Le Guin's *Earthsea* trilogy to another, and he seems to speak for and about many modern readers and writers. But however great their desire, all modern people, apart from very young children, have dragons classified irrevocably as fictional/fantastic, along with wizards, runes, spells, and much else. The writer of fantasy in the present day, then, does not have the Chaucerian freedom, and is always faced with the problem of hurdling conceptual barriers. He knows that magic, in particular, cannot be assumed, but will have to be *explained,* even defended from the scepticism now intrinsic in the word's Modern English meaning. (pp. 148-49)

[The] creation of relevance from what appears to careless readers as unbridled fantasy is embodied as well as anywhere in modern literature by Ursula K. Le Guin's trilogy of books, *A Wizard of Earthsea, The Tombs of Atuan, The Farthest Shore:* and significantly enough it is based on a semantic point. The archipelago-world of the trilogy (we never find out where or when it is) is devoid of science, but based on magic. Mrs. Le Guin identifies the workers of magic reasonably indifferently as wizards or witches or sorcerers, but there is one term she does not use, and that the commonest of all in Modern English: a worker of magic is never described as a "magician." The reason, of course, is that this term has a familiar current sense, deprecatory if not pejorative, "a practitioner of legerdemain." The word has been much affected by the rise of "scientist"; it contains strong suggestions that magic is no more than a "pretended art," as the *O.E.D.* so firmly insists—an affair of rabbits up sleeves and deceptive mirrors. A "magician," then, is barely superior to a "conjurer" or a "juggler." Mrs. Le Guin accordingly, makes consistent use of the base-form from which "magic" itself is derived, "mage," from Latin *magus;* and from it she creates a series of compounds not recorded in the *O.E.D.* at all, "Archmage," "magelight," "magewind," "magery" etc. The point may seem a trivial one, and yet is close to the trilogy's thematic centre. The continuous and consistent use of words *not* familiar to the modern reader reminds him to suspend his judgement: his ideas, like his vocabulary, may be inadequate, or wrong.

This, indeed, is the basic point repeated through the first half of the first book in the sequence, *A Wizard of Earthsea.* Definitions of magic are repeatedly implied, or stated, and then turned down or disproved: the definitions bear a close resemblance to those current in our world. "You thought," says one of the characters to the hero, Ged, "that a mage is one who can do anything. So I thought, once. So did we all." The idea is immediately reproved as boyish, dangerous, the opposite of the truth (which is that a mage does only what he must); nevertheless we recognise it immediately, familiar as we all are with such phrases as "it works like magic," which imply that magic is effortless, unlimited. The magic of Earthsea, though, is given moral boundaries; in an earlier scene it was given intellectual ones. There Ged, still a boy and only just exposed to magic, finds himself facing a piratic invasion with the men of his village. In this situation he naturally wishes for some blasting stroke of magic, and rummages in his spells for one that might give him some advantage. "But need alone is not enough to set power free," the author reminds us: "there must be knowledge." The maxim gains added point by being a total reversal of a standard and familiar modern theory of magic, the anthropological one, stated most clearly by B. Malinowski [in "Magic, Science, and Religion"], that magic is in essence a cathartic activity, called forth by stress, and working in so far as it produces confidence. "Science is founded on the conviction that experience, effort, and reason are valid; magic on the belief that hope cannot fail nor desire deceive." But Ged understands perfectly well the difference between desire and fulfilment, hope and fact. He is, in short, not the self-deluding savage whom Malinowski regards as the appropriate and natural practitioner of magic.

Ged is in fact at all times rather precisely placed within a framework of anthropological theory. For Malinowski's "cathartic" notion is not the only influential modern explanation of magic. Even more widespread were the "intellectualist" theories of Herbert Spencer, E. B. Tylor, Sir James Frazer, and others, by which magic was, as it were, a crude and mistaken first step in the evolution of man towards science and the nineteenth century, a "monstrous farrago" indeed, but nevertheless one based on observation and classification, if not experiment: something closer to science than to religion (so Frazer argued [in *The Golden Bough*]) because based on the assumption that the universe ran on "immutable laws." It may seem that the magic of Earthsea can be reduced to a kind of unfamiliar technology in this way, since it depends on knowledge and has severe limits to its power, but that too would be wrong. For the very first thing that Mrs. Le Guin does in the trilogy is to show us one way in which magic differs profoundly from science: it all depends on who does it! Ged, as a boy, overhears his aunt saying a magic rhyme to call her goat. He repeats it, ignorantly and by rote—and calls *all* his goats, calls them so strongly that they crowd round him as if compressed. His aunt frees him, promises to teach him, but at the same time puts a spell of silence and secrecy on him. Ged cannot speak, indeed, when she tests him; but he laughs. And at this his aunt is afraid, to see the beginnings of strength in one so young. All this, evidently, is not like our experience of science. A light turns on, an engine starts, regardless of who is at the switch; but spells are not the same. A mage, then, is knowledgeable, like a scientist; but his knowledge needs to be combined with personal genius, a quality we tend to ascribe to artists. And unlike both, his skill (or art, or science) has some close relationship with an awareness of ethics—something we expect, not of a priest perhaps, but of a saint.

It is the oscillation between concepts of this kind (and they are all familiar ones, even if readers do not feel a need to voice them consciously) which draws one on into *A Wizard of Earthsea,* searching for conclusions, and the book is evidently a *Bildungsroman,* a story of a sorcerer's apprenticeship, where one's attention is simultaneously on the growth of personal maturity, as one would normally expect, but also on the acquisition of technique. Once again, the basic processes of magic in Earthsea depend on a concept brought to prominence by early modern anthropology: what one might call the "Rumpelstiltzkin" theory. This is, that every person, place, or thing possesses a true name distinct from its name in ordinary human language; and that knowing the true name, the *significant,* gives the mage power over the thing itself, the *signifié.* The theory behind this simple statement is expressed in many ways and at some length all the way through *A Wizard of Earthsea.* One of Ged's first lessons from the mage Ogion (a lesson whose inner meaning he fails to understand, equating it with mere rote-learning) is on the names of plants. Later, and better educated, he spends much time at the Wizards' School of Roke learning lists of names, and nothing more, from the Master Namer, Kurremkarmerruk. Even at the end of the book he is still explaining the ramifications of the theory to casual acquaintances (and more relevantly, of course, to us). A key point, for instance, is the distinction between magical illusion and magical reality; it is relatively easy for a mage to *appear* to take another shape, or to make people see stones as diamonds, chicken-bones as owls, and so on. But to make this appearance real is another matter. Magic food and water do not really solve problems of provisioning, for though they may satisfy eye and taste, they provide neither energy nor refreshment. That is because the thing transformed retains its real identity, which is its name. . . . Sir James Frazer opened his chapter on "Tabooed Words" by saying firmly if carelessly that the reason why "the savage" thought there was a real bond between *significant* and *signifié* was that he was "unable to discriminate clearly between words and things." The statement is an echo of Bacon's remark, so close to the development of self-consciously scientific attitudes, that the "first distemper of learning" comes when men "study words and not matter," a remark rapidly hardened into a simple opposition between words and things. Sir Francis probably believed in the truth of *Genesis* 2:19-20, which would give him pause; but Sir James had no real doubt but that things were always superior to words. What Mrs. Le Guin is clearly suggesting, though, is that this promotion of the thing above the word has philosophical links with materialism, industrialisation, the notion that, to modern men [according to C. S. Lewis], "Nature is a machine to be worked, and taken to bits if it won't work as he pleases." In her imagined world, the devotion to the word rather than the thing is bound up with an attitude of respect for all parts of creation (even rocks), and a wary reluctance to operate on any of them without a total awareness of their distinct and individual nature. To the Master Namer even waves, even drops of water, are separate, and not to be lumped together as "sea"; for the mage's art depends on seeing things as they are, and not as they are wanted. It is not anthropocentric.

Mrs. Le Guin puts this over more fully and more attractively than analytic criticism can hope to, and, as has been said, it is for much of the time the explanations of technique, limitation, and underlying belief-structure which hold the attention of even young readers. The questions remain: "Where does the background stop and the story start? What is the story really *about?*" By asking these one sees that the semantics and the explanations and the detailed apprenticeship of Ged are all necessary preparations to allow the author to approach a theme which cannot be outranked in importance by those of the least "escapist" of "mainstream" fictions, and which can perhaps nowadays only be expressed in fantasy: matters, indeed, of life and death. (pp. 149-52)

[The] temptation which runs as a thread through the account of Ged's apprenticeship is to act, to exploit his power, to reject the wise passivity of the true mage. He shows this from his first appearance, when he calls the goats, not because he wants them, but to *make them come;* his instinct is fostered by the witch-wife who is his first teacher; and it leads him to repeated acts of mastery when he attempts to summon the dead (to please a girl), and *does* do so (to outdo a rival). This instinct is not entirely selfish, for he acts several times for others' benefit, saving his village from the pirates, saving his later "parishoners"

from the threat of a dragon. But it *is* always dangerous, exposing Ged three times to bouts of catalepsy, and furthermore inhibiting his development and causing him to be sent away twice (affectionately enough) from his mentors at Re Albi and at Roke. It is dangerous not just because it breaks the rules of magery, including the often-mentioned but dimly-defined concept of Equilibrium, but because light and speech draw their opposites, shadow and silence: which are, quite overtly, terms for death. In seeking to preserve and aggrandise himself (and others) Ged draws up his own extinction. The point is made clearly enough when Ged (like the Sorcerer's Apprentice) reads his master's book for a necromantic spell, discovers a shadow watching him, and is saved only by his master's return; and again when (like Marlowe's Dr. Faustus) he calls up the spirit of the most beautiful woman known to history, to show his power, and—unlike Dr. Faustus, though in line with the severer morality of Earthsea—calls with it a shadow-beast, which savages him and pursues him ever after. In a way, though, the most powerful scene of the book is a relatively incidental one when Ged, from pure disinterested affection, breaks the first rule of magic healing and tries to bring back the dying son of his friend from the land of the dead. This "undiscovered country" is visited spiritually, but conceived physically, and its almost casually undramatic nature makes a stronger impact than any charnel-scene. . . . Ged turns back up the dark hillside and climbs slowly to the top, where he finds the "low wall of stones" (why "low"? we wonder) which marks the boundary between life and death. And there he finds the shadow-beast waiting. Nevertheless, it is not that which is frightening, but the land of the dead itself, with the little boy running uncatchably downhill into it: a conception lonelier and less humanised than the Styx which Aeneas crosses with his golden bough, and yet closer to Classical images than to the familiar Christian ones of Heaven and Hell.

It may be said that the fear of this dim place underlies the whole of the *Earthsea* trilogy, to be faced directly in the last book. But the land of the dead also acts as an ultimate support for the structure of ideas already outlined. Ged's temptation is to use his power; it is a particularly great temptation to use it to summon the dead or bring back the dying; he rationalises it by wishing to "drive back darkness with his own light." And yet the respect for separate existences within the totality of existence, which is inherent in magic dependent on knowing the names of things, resists the diminution of others which comes from prolongation of the self, extension of life. One might say that the darkness has rights too. So the nature of his own art is against Ged, and his attempts to break Equilibrium with his own light only call forth a new shadow. The shadow, as has been said, appears in the "Sorcerer's Apprentice" scene, becomes tangible and ferocious in the "Dr. Faustus" scene. The questions that agitate Ged and the reader from then till the end of the book are: "What is it? Has it a name?"

On this last point opinions are divided. Archmage Gensher says it has no name. Ogion, the dragon of Pendor, and the sorceress of Osskil, all insist that it has. Their disagreement is one of philosophy, not of fact. For Mrs. Le Guin is evidently no Manichaean; her powers of darkness are essentially negative (shadow, silence, not-being) rather than having a real existence that is simply malign. It follows that the shadow-beast, being absence rather than presence, should be nameless. But Ogion says "*All* things have a name." The puzzle is resolved in the only possible compromise when Ged, after being hunted by the beast and then turning to hunt it instead, catches up with it in the desolate waters beyond the easternmost island. As he catches up, the water turns to land; evidently, to the dry land, the "dark slopes beneath unmoving stars," which we have seen before as the land of the dead. Here man and shadow fight, *and fuse;* the land turns back to sea; for each has spoken the other's name simultaneously, and the names are the same, "Ged." The shadow, then, is equal and opposite to the man who casts it; it does have a name, but not one of its own. And the scene rounds off the definitions of magic, the debate over names, the running opposition of death and life. . . . The key words are perhaps *his* and *empty.* The first tells us that Ged's call to resist death would, in the end, not be selfless but self-preserving; the beast was born of fear. The second reminds us that—since the sky *is* empty, hiding no divinity—the fear is justified, but has to be accepted as Ged accepts and fuses with his shadow. Yet the emptiness that frames his mortality also enhances it. *He* is the bright hawk, of the last image, for his use-name is "Sparrowhawk." The story then makes a clear final point, needing almost no critical exegesis. What should be realised further and more consciously, however, is first that this point about the nature of existence is in harmony with the earlier discussion of the nature of magic, with its restrained if not submissive philosophy; and second that all the philosophical implications of *A Wizard of Earthsea* exist in defiance of twentieth-century orthodoxys, whether semantic, scientific, or religious. It is an achievement to have created such a radical critique and alternative, and one so unsentimentally attractive.

One final way in which the book may be considered is indeed *as* an alternative, one might say a parody or anti-myth if the words did not sound inappropriately aggressive. Ged's re-enactment of the scene of Helen and Dr. Faustus has already been noted, as has his return from the land of the dead, reminiscent of the *Aeneid* in its difficulty—*hoc opus, hic labor est,* as the Sybil says (VI, 129)—though different in being done without a golden bough. To these one might add the final scene. For one of Sir James Frazer's great achievements in *The Golden Bough* was to create a myth of wasteland and fertility rite and king who must die, a myth mighty yet, as one can see just from book-titles. The regenerative aspect of that myth, as Miss Jessie Weston restated it, was the "freeing of the waters," the clearing of the dry springs. In Ged's sudden return from the dry land of the dead to the open sea, we have a version of it; yet it is typical that with the "glory of daylight" that is restored to him comes "the bitter cold of winter and the bitter taste of salt." The weakness of Sir James's myth was that it asked us to accept a cyclic process as rebirth; and Mrs. Le Guin knows the limits of such consolation. More positively, there is another aspect in which *The Golden Bough* is rejected by *A Wizard of Earthsea.* Sir James entitled his third volume—which contains the discussion of names—"Taboo and the Perils of

the Soul"; and his account of true- and use-names was accordingly entirely about psychic dangers and the universal mistrust of savages. But Ged and his companions, once again, are no savages, for all their habits of nomenclature. Repeatedly in the book we have moving scenes where characters, instead of concealing their names as is normal and advisable, *reveal* them to each other in gestures of trust and affection. Vetch saves Ged at a black moment by this gift; at Roke the Master Doorkeeper tells his name to all graduands, in a mildly comic *rite de passage.* And that is the final impression that Earthsea gives: a world surrounded by the ocean in space and by the dry land of the dead in time, but still bright, warm, and fearless, removed from both the insecure exploitativeness of modernity and the meaningless murderousness of Frazerian antiquity. It offers a goal rather than an escape. (pp. 152-55)

[The movement of the first two books of the trilogy is] on the whole downwards, into a deepening gloom, and towards us, towards familiarity. It is continued and even accelerated in the last book, *The Farthest Shore,* which describes what things are like when the magic starts to run out. Earthsea begins to resemble America in the aftermath of Vietnam: exhausted, distrustful, uncertain. This is conveyed in a series of interviews with wizards who have lost their power, and who try, not to seek help, but to justify themselves to Ged, now grown old, and his young companion Arren. The first one they meet is a woman, once an illusionist, who has turned instead to being a saleswoman and employing in that trade the more familiar arts of distraction and hyperbole. She has, in short, become a conjuror and defends herself dourly: "You can puzzle a man's mind with the flashing of mirrors, and with words, and with other tricks I won't tell you. . . . But it was tricks, fooleries. . . . So I turned to this trade, and maybe all the silks aren't silks nor all the fleeces Gontish, but all the same they'll wear—they'll wear!' They're real, and not mere lies and air . . . " She has a point even a business-ethic; but her equation of magic with mumbo-jumbo has robbed the world of beauty. She distinguishes herself sharply, furthermore, from the drug-takers who now for the first time appear in Earthsea, but when Ged speaks to one of these he insists similarly that eating *hazia* helps you because "you forget the names, you let the forms of things go, you go straight to the reality." There is something ominous about the "reality" both speakers oppose to "names" and "words"; one remembers the subjection of "words" to "matter" discussed earlier. The point is sharpened by a third experience on the silk isle of Lorbanery, where the inhabitants insist that magic has never existed, and that things are the same as ever, but where the workmanship has become notoriously "shoddy," economics is rearing its ugly head, and a "generation-gap" appears to have been invented. In the end even the innocent Raft-folk who never touch inhabited islands are affected, as their chanters fail to carry through the ritual dance of Sun return; their forgetting the old songs represents the breach of tradition, the failure of authority, which has been, in some sense, the inheritance of the Western world since the mid-nineteenth century. Earthsea, in a word, has grown secularised; and we recognise the condition.

The root of the process is told us many times, and is entirely predictable from the two preceding books. It is the fear of death, the voice that cries (so Ged puts it) *"let the world rot so long as I can live!"* But the fear of death has been on or near Ged since the first few pages of *A Wizard of Earthsea.* The new if related factor in *The Farthest Shore* is more precisely the hope of life. A wizard has arisen who is able, for the first time, to go through the land of the dead and out the other side, to return to the world after his own death. His example, and the promise it offers, give those who know of it a new hope; but their preoccupation with that hope makes them fear the future more and love the present less, while their wish to preserve themselves is inherently destructive of the Equilibrium through which name-magic works. Besides, the breach that the wizard has made is imagined as a hole through which the magic of the living world runs out, so that the change affects even the ignorant.

There is, to a modern reader, something almost blasphemous in these statements about the dangers of eternal life. In the final confrontation near the exit from the dead land, the reborn wizard boasts:

> I had the courage to die, to find what you cowards could never find—the way back from death. I opened the door that had been shut since the beginning of time. . . . Alone of all men in all time I am Lord of the Two Lands.

Opener of gates, conqueror of death, promiser of life—one can hardly avoid thinking of Christ, the One who Harrowed Hell. Probably one has been thinking of Him since the dark lord first appeared, holding out "a tiny flame no larger than a pearl, held it out to Arren, offering life." And yet in Earthsea the one who brings the promise is a destroyer; the Christian of *Pilgrim's Progress,* who flees from his family with his hands over his ears, shouting "Life, life, eternal life!," now reappears as the wizards who abandon their trade and turn the world to shoddiness and gloom. The gifts of magic and of religion could hardly be more fiercely opposed. Yet the weakening of magic in Earthsea resembles the weakening of religion here. For there is a consistent image which underlies *The Farthest Shore,* and which seems to be taken from another book about the failure (and reattainment) of belief, Dostoyevsky's *Crime and Punishment.* (pp. 158-60)

In both works faith (whether in magic and Equilibrium or in Christianity and eternal life) is wrecked by doubt, a parallel which ought to clear Mrs. Le Guin of the charge of wilful blasphemy. She is implying, not that Christianity leads to morbidity, but rather that the present inability of many to believe in any supernatural power lays them open to fear and selfishness and a greedy clutching at hope which spoils even the present life that one can be sure of. Her striking presentation of the land of the dead, so alien to either Christian or Classical concepts, seems also to have a root in the great lapse of faith of the late nineteenth century. For in *The Farthest Shore* Ged and Arren have actually to pass through this country, and see it as a strange analogue of the land of the living: people, streets, houses, markets, movement—but no emotion. Arren saw "the mother and child who had died together, and they were in the dark land together; but the child did not run,

nor did it cry, and the mother did not hold it, nor even look at it. And those who had died for love passed each other in the streets." The last sentence offers no eternal cure for the pathos of parting we so often see in Earthsea. (p. 161)

[The *Earthsea*] books clearly aim at having some of the qualities of parable as well as of narrative, and that the parables are repeatedly summed up by statements within the books themselves. Mages appear to think in contrasts. "To light a candle is to cast a shadow," says one; "to speak, one must be silent," says another; "There must be darkness to see the stars," says Ged, "the dance is always danced . . . above the terrible abyss." In their gnomic and metaphorical quality such remarks are alien to modern speech; and yet they turn out to be distinctively modern when properly understood, the last one for example relying strongly on our rediscovery of the importance of social ritual (the dance), and our new awareness of the extent of time and space (the abyss). A reader may start on *A Wizard of Earthsea* for its spells and dragons and medieval, or rather pre-medieval trappings; he would be imperceptive, however, if he failed to realise before long—however dim the realisation—that he was reading not just a parable, but a parable for our times.

It is tempting to lead on and declare that Mrs. Le Guin is a "mythopoeic" writer (an adjective many critics find easy to apply to fantasy in general). The truth, though, seems to be that she is at least as much of an iconoclast, a myth-breaker not a myth-maker. She rejects resurrection and eternal life; she refutes "cathartic" and "intellectualist" versions of anthropology alike; her relationship with Sir James Frazer in particular is one of correction too grave for parody, and extending to "The Perils of the Soul" and "The Magic Art" and even "The Evolution of Kings," his sub-titles all alike. As was said at the start, she demands of us that we reconsider even our basic vocabulary, with insistent redefinitions of "magic," "soul," "name," "alive," and many other semantic fields and lexical items. One might end by remarking that novelty is blended with familiarity even in the myth which underlies the history of Earthsea itself, the oldest song of *The Creation of Éa* which is sung by Ged's companions in at least two critical moments. "Only in silence the word," it goes, "only in dark the light. . . . " By the end of the trilogy we realise that this is more than just a rephrasing of our own "Genesis" as given by St. John. Mrs. Le Guin takes "In the beginning was the Word" more seriously and more literally than do many modern theologians; but her respect for ancient texts includes no great regard for the mythic structures that have been built on them. (pp. 162-63)

> *T. A. Shippey, "The Magic Art and the Evolution of Words: Ursula Le Guin's Earthsea Trilogy," in* Mosaic, *Vol. X, No. 2, Winter, 1977, pp. 147-63.*

Raymond H. Thompson

In an article entitled **"The Child and the Shadow,"** Ursula K. Le Guin argues that the universal appeal of fantasy

Map of the Island of Gont—"a land famous for wizards."

stems from the archetypal patterns which are such vital ingredients of the form, imparting to it vitality as well as enduring fascination. She goes on to discuss these patterns in terms of the psychology of Carl Gustav Jung, whom she describes as "the psychologist whose ideas on art are the most meaningful to most artists." Such an approach to fantasy is clearly valuable, but nowhere more so than in dealing with Le Guin's own work in the field, where the Jungian shadow looms very large indeed. (p. 189)

In both *A Wizard of Earthsea* and *The Tombs of Atuan,* Ged's quest follows the basic pattern of the monomyth outlined by Joseph Campbell in *The Hero with a Thousand Faces.* This quest involves the voluntary journey to the Otherworld (the dark sand eventually reached at the edge of the world in the first novel, the Tomb in the second); an encounter with a shadow presence or barrier that guards the passage (first encounter with the Shadow of Gont, the Red Rock door); a combination of testing and assistance by ambivalent powers (the Shadow which functions as both guide and opponent, Arha/Tenar); ultimate triumph represented by illumination and freedom in which the powers become friendly (reconciliation with the Shadow) or by bride-theft and flight, in which they remain hostile (union with Tenar, established by a bond of mutual trust and love and symbolized by the joining of the two halves of The Ring of Erreth-Akbe, followed by escape through the earthquake-shaken Labyrinth); return to freedom leaving the transcendental powers behind (return to Iffish, return to Havnor); bearing the boon that restores the world (acceptance of the Shadow, Tenar, and the

Ring). Yet in both books this quest is well integrated with the central subject: in *A Wizard of Earthsea* Ged's quest is the external analogue of his growth to maturity, and it remains firmly subordinated to the focus on the coming-of-age of Tenar in *The Tombs of Atuan.*

In *The Farthest Shore,* however, Ged's quest increasingly dominates the story, so that interest shifts from Arren, his young companion, to the Archmage himself. The first half of the book focuses on Arren's growth and development; he is a youth full of promise but untried, so that he must learn to recognize his own limitations before he can accompany Ged on the final perilous descent into the realm of the dead. The second half of the novel, by contrast, focuses on Ged's confrontation with Cob, the "Lord of the Two Lands," and once again the journey he undertakes follows the pattern of the monomyth: Ged enters the realm of the dead, whose entrance is guarded by Cob; he penetrates to its very heart, the black hole that sucks the light out of the world; he seals it, then returns to the living world, which has been saved by his deed.

This division of interest can be partially justified, however, by scrutinizing the relationship of the two central characters to the figure of the shadow. In *Aion* Jung notes that what he calls the "shadow" cast by the conscious mind of the individual contains the hidden, repressed, and unfavorable aspects of the personality. The traits of the shadow appear in Cob, whose preoccupation with self would destroy the entire world; this selfishness manifests itself most strikingly in the qualities of vanity, despair, and fear of death: "Very strange was the mixture of despair and vindictiveness, terror and vanity, in his words and voice." However, the shadow only embodies the negative traits that are actually part of one's own personality, as Le Guin reminds us in **"The Child and the Shadow"**: "Unadmitted to consciousness, the shadow is projected outward, onto others. There's nothing wrong with me—it's *them.* I'm not a monster, other people are monsters." According to Jung in *Aion,* this process offers the most stubborn resistance to moral control, since the projections are not recognized as such; the cause of the problem "appears to lie, beyond all possibility of doubt, in the other person." Like the shadow creature in *A Wizard of Earthsea,* Cob serves to mirror the faults of the hero. In *The Farthest Shore,* Ged's act of vanity lies in his past, during his punishment of Cob for raising the spirits of the dead: "I was possessed by anger and by vanity," he admits to Arren. However, when repressed the shadow merely waxes stronger, and so Cob's power expands to threaten the entire world of Earthsea, affecting first the more remote reaches, but inexorably moving closer to Roke itself which, as the center where magic is the subject of disciplined intellectual study, can be equated with the conscious self. For as Jung explains in *Aion,* "One cannot dispose of facts by declaring them unreal. The projection-making factor, for instance, has undeniable reality. Anyone who insists on denying it becomes identical with it, which is not only dubious in itself but a positive danger to the well-being of the individual." Nevertheless, though he has not left pride entirely behind him, Ged has grown in wisdom since his rebuke to Cob, as can be seen during his rescue of Arren from the slave-traders, for he refuses to punish them. Moreover, though we can perceive the traces of Ged's pride, we can discern little of either despair or fear of death in the Archmage; nor does the author choose to recall events from his youth which might have helped. Instead she provides Ged with a young companion who functions as his alter ego.

At the outset of the story Ged is reminded, "You have always gone alone. Why, now, companioned?" He responds, "I have never needed help before. . . . And I have found a fit companion." What Arren has to offer are love and devotion to duty, which mirror Ged's own great virtues, but they must be tempered by stern tests before they can be put to the ultimate trial. In the course of these tests, Arren succumbs not only to vanity, but, even more obviously, to despair and the fear of death, the traits possessed by the shadow of selfishness. Initially Arren's pride is but a spur to his sense of responsibility. When asked if he takes pride in his lineage, Arren wins Ged's approval by responding, "Yes, I take pride in it—because it makes me a prince; it is a responsibility, a thing that must be lived up to." However, his pride rebels when he is made to feel useless to Ged's quest: "He was merely dragged along on it, useless as a child. But he was not a child." And when Ged lies grievously wounded in the boat, he gives way to the inactivity of despair and the fear of death: "I was afraid of death. . . . I could think of nothing, except that there was—there was a way of not dying for me, if I could find it. . . . And I did nothing, nothing, but try to hide from the horror of dying." Typically, Arren projects the selfish traits of pride and despair on another, namely Ged, whom he blames for bringing about this situation: "In his pride, his overweening pride as Archmage, he feared lest they might gain [eternal life] . . . he would die himself, to prevent them from eternal life." Yet even in this darkest moment commitment remains. Though parched with thirst, the youth saves what water remains in the boat for Ged, never even contemplating taking any for himself, and his first thought after rescue by the raft-folk is for his companion. Consequently, he is able to recognize and to confess his fault, thus earning the right to accompany the Archmage on the most perilous stage of their journey: "He had learned his own weakness, also, and by it had learned to measure his strength; and he knew that he was strong. But what use was strength, if he had no gift, nothing to offer, still, to his lord but his service and his steady love?"

Nevertheless, Arren, the alter ego, has been valuable for his weakness as well as his strength, for it has served as a link to the shadow. As Ged points out to his young companion, the Lord of the Two Lands speaks "in your own voice." The traits of the shadow lie within us. To confront them we must approach our weakness: "You are my guide—the child I sent before me into the dark. It is your fear I follow." However, the guide for the next stage of the journey is the dragon Orm Embar, the traditional animal messenger. In "The Phenomenology of the Spirit in Fairy Tales," Jung identifies the animal as one form of the Spirit archetype, which also appears as the Wise Old Man. As such it shares "on the one hand in the daemonically superhuman and on the other in the bestially subhuman." Both aspects exist in the dragons of Earthsea, which are treacherous and greedy yet possessed of an age-old wisdom and power. In **"The Child and the Shadow,"** Le Guin observes,

"It is the animal within us, the primitive, the dark brother, the shadow soul, who is the guide," and Ged and Arren rejoice that he has come: "This time we will not go astray, I think." Orm Embar does indeed lead them to their quarry and in his role as the animal helper intervenes to save Ged, albeit at the cost of his own life. He is not the first animal to save Ged's life: when he lies spirit-lost in *A Wizard of Earthsea,* Ged is recalled to consciousness by his little otak acting with instinctive wisdom. The otak, too, is slain by the shadow, for though guides may assist along the way, the final confrontation must take place between ego and shadow alone, as Le Guin reminds us in **"The Child and the Shadow";** "When you have followed animal instincts far enough, then they must be sacrificed so that the true self, the whole person, may step forth from the body of the animal, reborn."

Orm Embar's sacrifice defeats the shadow power that guards the entrance to the kingdom of the dead, and so Ged and Arren, ego and alter ego, venture down to the heart of this land for their final confrontation with the shadow. The links between all three are reinforced when they meet at the Dry River: "Arren thought, with a little dread but not much, 'We have come too far.' . . . Speaking his thought, Ged said, 'You have come to far to turn back,' . . . A voice in the darkness said, 'You have come too far.'" Arren's answer provides the clue to the final confrontation. Orm Embar has shown the way: to conquer the crippling shadow of selfishness one must be willing to make the ultimate sacrifice of one's own life. And this is what Ged does. To close the black hole that is sucking all the light out of the world, he expends all his power and vitality until there remains "no more light in Ged's yew staff, or in his face. . . . 'It is done,' he said. 'It is all gone'," words that echo those of Christ when he sacrificed himself on the Cross. At the black hole Arren proves himself by rejecting Cob's offer of immortality, and now, despite his own exhaustion, he helps the Archmage return to the world, even crawling "back to the dark" to drag his companion to safety with the last of his strength. This self-sacrifice reflects Ged's own. Nevertheless, Ged's return is more spiritual than real. The deed done, Ged slips out of sight, borne off by Kalessin, the oldest dragon, perhaps to attend Arren's coronation before sailing on a final journey westward over the sea, perhaps to wander in the solitude and silence of the forests of the mountain, where "He rules a greater kingdom."

Ged's death is necessary. In the first place, only by actually undergoing willingly the experience of death can the fear of it be finally overcome. Thus alone can the shadow's power be broken. Yet the shadow's power is both a part of Ged's wizardry and a vital ingredient in the essential tension between light and dark that creates the Balance. Consequently, when Ged releases Cob's anguished spirit into death, he himself must follow if the "Equilibrium of things" is to be preserved. When the Archmage seals the black hole with the words "Be thou made whole," he heals not only a divided and chaotic world but also his own fragmented personality. Ged and Cob must fade in order that Arren can be reborn as Lebannen, the young King of All the Isles. Cob remains among the shadows of the dead, but Ged must return to the surface, for he, like Erreth-Akbe, "is the earth and sunlight, the leaves of trees, the eagle's flight. He is alive. And all who ever died, live."

Yet the pattern of Ged and Arren as ego and alter ego confronting Cob and shadow is not the only one in the novel, and herein lies a structural problem. While Arren serves as Ged's alter ego, Ged's function in relation to Arren is that of the Wise Old Man, who, as Jung points out in "Phenomenology,"

> represents knowledge, reflection, insight, wisdom, cleverness, and intuition on the one hand, and on the other, moral qualities such as good will and readiness to help, which makes his 'spiritual' character sufficiently plain . . . what is more, he even tests the moral qualities of others and makes his gifts dependent on this test.

Arren's experiences in the first part of the book constitute just such a test of moral qualities, necessary before he can win the gift of self-knowledge which Ged possesses. Yet just as all archetypes have a positive side, they also have a negative side, such as that embodied in "the wicked magician who, from sheer egoism, does evil for evil's sake," and this role is assigned to Cob. To develop the personality, one must listen to the voice of wisdom (Ged's influence) but avoid being possessed by it to the point where one takes on delusions of grandeur (Cob's influence). As a result, it is necessary for Arren to accept Ged's guidance yet preserve and develop his own judgment if he is to achieve kingship. As in the story of King Arthur and Merlin, the sage must depart so that the hero can reach maturity. This pattern, too, requires Ged's death. From the point of view of structure, the problem is that Le Guin has not completely integrated the two patterns of Ged and Arren as ego and alter ego confronting Cob as Shadow on one hand, on the other of Arren as ego developing his personality under the combined guidance and threat of the positive and negative sides of the Wise Old Man or Spirit archetype (Ged and Cob). Yet it is essential for several important reasons that Le Guin initiate Arren's journey through life before Ged's draws to a close.

First, as Ged explains, "In life is death. In death is rebirth. What then is life without death?" To coin an image suggested by the title, as one wave breaks on the farthest shore and recedes, so another rises to take its place. This philosophical need to initiate the new cycle before the old one completes its turn requires a rising young hero coming into his powers, as well as an aging champion expending his in one last titanic struggle.

The struggle to death that imposes the need for a new hero to replace the old one is demanded by developments within this novel and within the Earthsea trilogy as a whole. Each book moves progressively closer to the experience of death. In *A Wizard of Earthsea,* Ged's journey follows the pattern of the monomyth with its descent to the Otherworld, ending on the shores of death's kingdom; in *The Tombs of Atuan,* Ged and Tenar descend into the Tombs wherein lie the bones of the dead; in *The Farthest Shore,* Ged and Arren enter the actual realm of the dead. The deepening levels of the descent are necessitated by the widening awareness of the shadow's range: Ged must deal first with his own personal shadow, then the shadow of another individual, and finally the collective shadow of all mankind.

Moreover, there is another development within the trilogy as a whole that requires the second pattern with Ged as the Wise Old Man, and that is the progression toward a quaternity, identified by Jung as a symbol of wholeness. Jung writes, "The integration of the shadow . . . marks the first stage in the analytic process. . . . The recognition of anima or animus gives rise, in a way, to a triad, one-third of which is transcendent: the masculine subject, the opposing feminine subject, and the transcendent anima. With a woman the situation is reversed. The missing fourth element that would make the triad a quaternity is, in a man, the archetype of the Wise Old Man." Integration of the shadow is accomplished in *A Wizard of Earthsea;* both the male and female triads appear in *The Tombs of Atuan* as Ged-Arha-Tenar and Arha/Tenar-The Nameless Ones-Ged; Ged functions as the Wise Old Man in relation to Arren in *The Farthest Shore.* This steady movement toward unity concludes with the crowning of a king to rule over all the isles.

This approach is not intended to deny that the characters serve other, non-Jungian functions. It would be surprising were a writer of Le Guin's ability to limit herself thus. Like Ahar/Tenar in *The Tombs of Atuan,* Arren provides the story with a point of view that is particularly valuable for younger readers. What I hope I have demonstrated, however, is how an appreciation of the Jungian patterns in Le Guin's work can help us understand the structural problems in *The Farthest Shore.* The concept of linking Arren and Ged as ego and alter ego in the struggle against the shadow is a fine one that promises to integrate Ged into the action, yet keep the focus on the young Arren, whose character is growing and developing toward maturity. Unfortunately, for the reasons outlined, Ged finally does need to depart. Such a hero deserves a fitting exit, and Le Guin certainly rises to the occasion. Just as in *Beowulf* the self-sacrifice of the aged hero-king overshadows the courage and loyalty of young Wiglaf, so inevitably Ged's last great act of self-sacrifice overshadows the impressive achievement of Arren, who carries him out of death's kingdom to the farthest shore that lies beyond. As pointed out earlier, Le Guin is well aware of the effect caused by her imaginative involvement with Ged, who "took over completely in this book." However, despite its structural flaws, *The Farthest Shore* remains the author's favorite book, and few would choose to see Ged's heroic struggle against Cob and his magnificent flight home on Kalessin, the Eldest Dragon, in any way reduced in the interests of neater structure. The passing of the hero enriches as well as diminishes the world it leaves behind. (pp. 189-95)

> *Raymond H. Thompson, "Jungian Patterns in Ursula K. Le Guin's 'The Farthest Shore',"* in Aspects of Fantasy, *edited by William Coyle, Greenwood Press, 1986, pp. 189-195.*

Elizabeth Cummins

The impetus for the *Earthsea* series was Le Guin's invitation in 1967 from Herbert Schein, publisher of Parnassus

Press, to write a book for an adolescent audience. That audience, Le Guin explains in her essay **"Dreams Must Explain Themselves"** (1973), led to her choosing the main theme of coming of age and the genre of fantasy. "Coming of age," she writes, "is a process that took me many years; I finished it, so far as I ever will, at about age thirty-one; and so I feel rather deeply about it. So do most adolescents. It's their main occupation, in fact." In the trilogy Le Guin narrates the coming-of-age process as a journey into the self. In the same essay she says, "Fantasy is the medium best suited to a description of that journey, its perils and rewards. The events of a voyage into the unconscious are not describable in the language of rational daily life: only the symbolic language of the deeper psyche will fit them without trivializing them." (p. 22)

Fantasy, in other words, like myth and dream, assumes the existence of a world of being beyond or underneath perceived, empirical reality; and it reproduces that other world by means of symbol and literary archetype. Wizards, shadows, dragons, a labyrinth, ring, dragon, and sword are some of the symbols and archetypes that reverberate with ethical, emotional, and aesthetic meaning in Le Guin's fantasy trilogy.

These archetypes and symbols can carry such meaning because, as she relates in her essay **"The Child and the Shadow"** (1975), "we all have the same general tendencies and configurations in our psyche." The idea of shared psychic roots is based on Carl Gustav Jung's psychology. Jung argued that beyond the conscious mind there lay two other mental activities—the individual unconscious, which is unique to each person, and the collective unconscious, which is shared by all people. The symbols and archetypes that are common to myths throughout the world are the manifestations of the collective unconscious. The myths were stories that connected the unconscious and the conscious, stories that used symbols and images to connect the desires and fears and hopes and creativity of the unconscious to the conscious mind.

Such a connection is made during that journey into the unconscious which is part of the adolescent's coming of age. Le Guin believes that a primary characteristic of such a journey is that it is "not only a psychic one, but a moral one," one that "contain[s] a very strong, striking moral dialectic" between the potential for good and for evil within the self. The goal of this psychic and moral journey is, in Le Guin's words, the hope that the journeyer "will be less inclined, perhaps, either to give up in despair or to deny what he sees, when he must face the evil that is done in the world, and the injustices and grief and suffering that we all must bear." (pp.23-4)

Le Guin first used Earthsea as a fictional setting in two short stories published in 1964, **"The Word of Unbinding"** and **"The Rule of Names,"** and in an unpublished story written in 1965 or 1966. Earthsea is an archipelago populated by people, wizards, and dragons; it is a place where magic works. Although Earthsea is a kingdom, its islands are separated and different enough in resources and climate that each has a sense of independence and an awareness that some independence must be sacrificed to make a unified kingdom. Beyond this dynamic relationship between individual island and aggregate kingdom is the dynamism of natural forces suggested in the archipelago's name, Earthsea. The balance of the powers of the physical landscape is a manifestation of still another level of balanced forces, a cosmic balance which the people of Earthsea call the Equilibrium. They speak of the world as being "in balance"; the act of creation is described as a "balancing of the dark and the light"; and they look to the Archmage, the highest ranking wizard to "watch the Equilibrium."

A world, then, is not just the tangible elements of place, nature, humankind, culture; it is also a process, a creative relationship among all things that exist—physical and spiritual, natural and human. Le Guin's concept of a world exhibits ideas compatible with those of both twentieth-century anthropologists and twentieth-century physicists. Much of her father's early field work among Native Americans in California revealed stories that stress an intimate relationship between nature and human society. This relationship has also been expressed by Werner Heisenberg, who asserted that in modern physics "there appears above all the network of relationships between men and nature, of the connections through which we as physical beings are dependent parts of nature and at the same time, as human beings, make them the object of our thought and actions." This "network of relationships" is a metaphor Le Guin suggests in her choice of earth and sea as the world of her fantasy trilogy.

The principle of balanced powers, the recognition that every act affects self, society, world, and cosmos, is both a physical and a moral principle of Le Guin's fantasy world. The people of Earthsea honor the Equilibrium in their dances, songs, and rituals performed at the winter and summer solstices when the sun appears to change direction. They believe that their participation assists the movements of the cosmos and ensures the sun's return. The people with magic powers, from archmage to village witch, can directly influence the Equilibrium if they know the "true" name of that which they wish to change. Naming is the key to magic; to know the true name of anything is to know its essence and thus be able to control it. Humans honor the acquisition of names. When each girl or boy reaches puberty, part of the passage ceremony is being given a true name, which is told only to the most trusted friends. The creative power of naming in wizardry is analogous to the creative power of word use in the art of fiction.

A wizard like Earthsea's protagonist Ged spends his life learning the words and spells, which can affect the balance, and learning the consequences of acting. (pp.25-7)

During the thirty or forty years covered by the trilogy Earthsea is a world which is out of balance. The kingdom has not had a king for some eight hundred years; disrespect for the mages, for the principle of balanced powers, and for the kingdom itself has grown on certain islands. The new king, it has been prophesied, will be he *"who has crossed the dark land living and come to the far shores of the day."*

The world Le Guin discovered in her imagination is appropriate for the three subjects she wished to explore. This is not to suggest that she methodically worked out the details of the world to fit the themes she wanted to discuss. Given her insistence that in order to create fiction the writer also journeys into the unconscious, one can say only that the world, characters, and themes are all interwoven. The concept of the Equilibrium dramatizes the significance of the individual's coming of age, for knowledge of the self and of the potential to do good or evil is essential for protecting the delicate balance of cosmos, kingdom, and community—hence three coming-of-age stories. To restore balance to the kingdom requires a lengthy tale of a great hero—hence Ged's story from youth to old age. The power by which magicians can affect the world is activated by words—hence the magician doubles as the creative and transforming artist. (pp. 27-8)

Coming-of-Age Stories

Each of the three novels presents the process of coming of age for a different character, in a different context, and with different results. In *A Wizard of Earthsea* Ged must learn to discipline his innate power of magic and understand the need for discipline. His psychological journey is mirrored in his physical journey from the heart of Earthsea out to its western and eastern edges. In *The Tombs of Atuan* the young priestess Tenar must break free of the role imposed on her by her society and join the larger human community of Earthsea. Her trapped self is mirrored in the walled-in religious center where she lives. In *The Farthest Shore* the young prince Arren must achieve the courage, self-reliance, and self-knowledge to become the first king of Earthsea in eight hundred years. Arren's psychological journey is also a physical journey; he sails from the heart of Earthsea west into the uncharted sea and then enters the land of the dead.

A Wizard of Earthsea is, of the three novels, the most complete account of coming of age as a journey into the self; its protagonist is one of the kingdom's greatest wizards. So private is this journey it is not included in the public celebration of his life, the *Deed of Ged*. In his journey from adolescence to adulthood Ged acquires psychological and moral knowledge about his innate power of wizardry. The journey is intensified when, motivated by pride, he uses his powers to call up a spirit from the dead; the resulting crisis affects Ged and the safety of those who associate with him. For the straight-forward narrative of Ged's life, from about age seven to nineteen, Le Guin uses an omniscient point of view. This allows her to use the opening and closing paragraphs of the novel to establish a context for Ged's maturation. The reader learns not only that Ged's quest is successful, but that he eventually achieves the highest mage's rank, Archmage of Earthsea. *A Wizard of Earthsea* is in the tradition of the apprenticeship novel (*Bildungsroman*), which traces the development of a young person's awareness of self, society, and nature. Particularly the novel is a male *Bildungsroman,* for Ged achieves a socially sanctioned and acclaimed role. (pp.30-1)

At the School for Wizards on Roke, Ged learns of the nature and ethics of power. He is warned by Master Hand:

But you must not change one thing, one pebble, one grain of sand, until you know what good and evil will follow on that act. The world is in balance, in Equilibrium. A wizard's power of Changing and of Summoning can shake the balance of the world. It is dangerous, that power. It is most perilous. It must follow knowledge, and serve need. To light a candle is to cast a shadow.

Such warnings do not speak as loudly to Ged as his own inner voice of pride does; he thinks, "But surely a wizard . . . was powerful enough to do what he pleased, and balance the world as seemed best to him, and drive back darkness with his own light."

To light a candle is to cast a shadow" is a metaphor for the idea that opposites are actually complementary. To explain fantasy's frequent use of light and darkness as symbols of good and evil, Le Guin uses the yang-yin symbol, an ancient Chinese pictograph of the integration of opposites. (pp. 32-3)

The yang-yin symbol is common to Taoism (the only religion Le Guin has admitted to) and other ancient Chinese philosophies. Yin and yang are the primal forces out of whose interaction arises the world of being. The symbol expresses the operations of Tao, the inexhaustible, self-creating principle of the universe. As the two halves appear to be in unstable balance, the symbol expresses the Taoist belief that all existence is in a state of change, flux, and transformation. But the symbol also suggests unity because both are held within the circle's boundary and in each is contained the germ of the other. All existence, from the cosmic to the personal, is seen as consisting of complementary opposites, such as being and becoming, duration and creation, essence and change, male and female.

In Western thought light and dark are often regarded as symbols of the dualistic, warring powers of good and evil. Such dualism suggests that the world consists of hierarchical relationships and that self and other (defined as that which is different; e.g., in culture, race, sex, religion) is always a relationship of competition and power.

Ged misuses his power in the duel with Jasper because he is more interested in demonstrating his personal power than he is in respecting the interrelationship of light and darkness. Not fully understanding what he sought nor the effect of his powers, Ged allowed his conscious mind to call up Elfarren while his unconscious mind simultaneously attracted the shadow. The shadow, a common image in fairy tales, is a literary archetype for that integral part of the self which the immature individual tries to deny. So important is one's confrontation with the shadow to the process of growing up that Jung, Le Guin notes in **"The Child and the Shadow,"** identified it as the guide for the journey into the self. The shadow is "all the qualities and tendencies within us which have been repressed, denied, or not used." The shadow symbolizes Ged's unrecognized pride, desire for power and control, and fear of his own death.

Although the shadow is Ged's personal adversary, its emergence and disappearance have far-reaching consequences. The remaining two-thirds of the novel tells the story of Ged's quest to avoid the shadow and then to find and name it. The episodes test his wizardry and initiate him into his socially approved role as one of Earthsea's greatest mages. Specifically, Ged's initiation includes knowledge of the trust and betrayal in human society; of evil and death; of the wisdom and power of nature; and of his own arrogance, denial, fear, and despair. (pp. 33-5)

The novel ends with the successful completion of Ged's journey into himself and his attainment of adulthood. Ged's journey, which can be traced on Le Guin's map of Earthsea in the novel, is in the pattern of an unclosed circle or spiral. The pattern, seen in other Le Guin novels, suggests that a journey into the self does not end with the return to the beginning place. The successful completion of the journey means the hero has been changed. Further, the unfinished circle, coming at the end of the novel, suggests that one's life is a series of changes or transformations. Thus, although the novel began as a single volume and has a sense of an ending, its image of the open circle suggests the possibility of further narratives.

In *The Tombs of Atuan* Le Guin examines the coming-of-age story under different circumstances. The protagonist is a young woman, Tenar, and she lives on the margin rather than at the center of Earthsea. Second, unlike Ged, whose development was a result of his own choices, Tenar has had an identity forced upon her just as surely as her black clothing has been woven and put upon her. Further, Tenar's acts and eventual quest are more public than Ged's. Ged's quest was private, a confrontation with the realities of his psyche. Tenar's decisions, however, have immediate sociopolitical consequences. *A Wizard of Earthsea* focused on the journey inward to knowledge of the self; *The Tombs of Atuan* focuses on the journey outward to knowledge of the relationship between self and human community.

Le Guin again uses the omniscient point of view for the narrative, but she lets *A Wizard of Earthsea* establish the context for the second novel. Ged appears as a character midway in the novel; the crisis is caused by the threat to the Equilibrium's balance by the Dark Powers and the threat to Earthsea's political harmony by the Kargad Empire.

Both of these powers are preventing Tenar's normal psychological development into selfhood and womanhood. This active opposition to Tenar's coming of age places Le Guin's novel in the tradition of the female *Bildungsroman.* Annis Pratt, in her study *Archetypal Patterns in Women's Fiction,* writes of this tradition:

> The novel of development portrays a world in which the young woman hero is destined for disappointment. The vitality and hopefulness characterizing the adolescent hero's attitude toward her future here meet and conflict with the expectations and dictates of the surrounding society. Every element of her desired world—freedom to come and go, allegiance to nature, meaningful work, exercise of the intellect, and use of her own erotic capabilities—inevitably clashes with patriarchal norms.

What the adolescent needs for her development into an adult is not what society needs her to have. The adolescent woman experiences, Pratt writes, a "collision between the hero's evolving self and society's imposed identity." *The Tombs of Atuan* and other similar stories use images of suffocation, entrapment, and madness to portray the woman's plight. By contrast, the male *Bildungsroman* usually shows the adolescent achieving the characteristics of an adult which are those society needs him to have, as illustrated in *A Wizard of Earthsea.* By setting Tenar's struggle in the Kargad Empire, Le Guin can portray Tenar's rebellion against the patriarchal empire and then have her escape into a different society where she will have the freedom to define herself and to learn to choose and act responsibly. (pp.38-41)

Le Guin once wrote that the subject of *The Tombs of Atuan* was sex, by which she apparently meant not only the physical maturity but also the recognition of and potential for intimate interaction with that which is different. [In *Love and Will*] Rollo May identified such maturation as *eros;* his definition is helpful in describing what Tenar must learn:

> a desiring, longing, a forever reaching out, seeking to expand . . . the drive toward union with significant other persons in our world in relation to whom we discover our own self-fulfillment. Eros is the yearning in man which leads him to dedicate himself to seeking *arête,* the noble and good life.

The Place mirrors female experience in Kargish society. Ostensibly protected by its walls and guards and eunuchs, the women are actually imprisoned. Ostensibly honored by their society, they are actually punished by being isolated, perhaps a reflection of the male fear of the female principle. Ostensibly powerful in their roles as religious leaders, they are actually functionaries who have internalized male standards and enforce them. The women have become their own prison guards, figuratively speaking. Kossil is the epitome of the woman who is imprisoned and imprisoning; she is cruel, hateful, unable to nurture anyone, obsessed with the desire for power.

The labyrinth symbolizes the women's imprisonment. Deep underground, changeless and dark, it is a closed circle; one door leads in but not out, and the other door leads in and then out into the Temple of the Nameless Ones. It is a tomb for the meaningful lives these women might have led and for the kind of society Kargad could have become. The labyrinth also symbolizes Arha, the dark side of Tenar's self; her passage into adulthood must involve a confrontation with the light just as traumatic as was Ged's confrontation with the dark. The extent of her darkness is evident in her thinking of the labyrinth as a "safe" place and in her choosing to spend hours exploring it. She becomes a good priestess by choosing to repress rather than to explore her self. Although there are many hints that Arha is not completely satisfied with her life at the Place, it is not until she must deal with her first political prisoners that she begins the self-struggle toward rebirth. (pp. 42-4)

The coming-of-age story which Le Guin tells in *The Far-*

thest Shore is more like Ged's than Tenar's. Not only is the adolescent again a male, but the process is symbolized by a spiral journey out to distant islands, across open sea, and back to the Inner Lands. Furthermore, Arren is not trapped in an identity as Tenar was. However, like Tenar he has no wizardly powers; his power, he must discover, is the ability to lead and to govern.

The novel presents yet a third variation of the coming-of-age narrative; it is the story of the hero who is tested before he becomes king. The adolescent hero, Arren, born into the oldest royal house, has the potential to become the king for which the people of Earthsea have been waiting eight hundred years. The sequence of events is close to the paradigm of the testing of the mythic hero. For example, using the Greek stories Northrop Frye lists seven features of the paradigm: "Mysterious birth, oracular prophecies about the future contortions of the plot, foster parents, adventures which involve capture by pirates, narrow escapes from death, recognition of the true identity of the hero and his eventual marriage with the heroine." Le Guin includes all but the first and the last in her account of several months in Arren's life.

Of greater importance, however, are two other differences between this novel and the previous two. First, the consequences of the characters' actions are shown in the largest political context. In the novel the Dark Mage has broken the Equilibrium, is turning all of Earthsea into a wasteland, and has challenged the authority of both Roke and Havnor. Second, the success of this quest depends on the bond relationship of Ged and Arren. Arren and Ged begin and end a long journey together; and Arren moves from a naïve, unquestioned fealty to Ged, through despair and alienation from him, to a mature acceptance of himself and Ged. The final act of fealty is that which Ged swears to Arren, the long-awaited King of Earthsea.

Although Le Guin shows Arren's courage and heroism, as one would expect in a traditional account of the testing of the hero-king, she examines in detail the process by which these traits are acquired. To discuss the stages of Arren's transformation the language of anthropology is especially helpful. Noting analogues in literature and myth and history, Victor Turner has projected the three stages of the initiation rites in African tribes into all social situations of transition. These three stages are "separation, margin (or *limen*, signifying 'threshold' in Latin), and aggregation." He briefly defines them as follows:

> The first phase (of separation) comprises symbolic behavior signifying the detachment of the individual or group either from an earlier fixed point in the social structure, from a set of cultural conditions (a "state"), or from both. During the intervening "liminal" period, the characteristics of the ritual subject (the "passenger") are ambiguous; he passes through a cultural realm that has few or none of the attributes of the past or coming state. In the third phase (reaggregation or reincorporation), the passage is consummated. The ritual subject, individual or corporate, is in a relatively stable state once more and, by virtue of this . . . he is expected to behave in accordance with certain customary norms and ethical standards binding on incumbents of social position in a system of such positions.

In the opening three chapters Le Guin shows that Arren and Ged are aware that they are considering a significant separation from homeland, known associates, and social roles. Arren offers to accompany Ged, and Ged chooses him as a "fit companion," acknowledging that he "never needed help before." Arren's initial concern is that he will fail Ged. Upon leaving Roke in Ged's sailboat *Lookfar,* they begin "an unsafe journey to an unknown end" by entering liminality, the second phase of the physical and psychological journey.

On their journey, cut off from associates and the need to function in their customary roles, Arren has only Ged as a representative of human community. The social bond, the most elemental feature which makes human society possible, is what Turner calls *communitas,* a "communion of equal individuals," a bonding outside of the structured sociopolitical system. Arren's coming of age is a journey toward both understanding the bond of trust and fealty with the other and understanding himself, for unless he "turns clear round" and looks at the very desires he tries to repress, he cannot have a mature, honest relationship with the other.

Arren tries to repress his desire for immortality. Like Tenar, however, his dreams and nightmares pressure him toward self-awareness. Just as Tenar dreamed of suffocating when she felt the pressure to be Arha, so Arren dreams of being chained or being wrapped in cobwebs when he feels the pressure to deny the dark side of himself. That Arren is tempted by the desire for immortality is first revealed in Hort Town. While Ged tries to stay with Hare in his trance, Arren suddenly breaks through to that which Hare seeks: "There, in the vast, dry darkness, there one stood beckoning. *Come,* he said, the tall lord of shadows. In his hand he held a tiny flame no larger than a pearl, held it out to Arren, offering life. Slowly Arren took one step toward him, following."

This step is as much a step into adulthood as was the step Arren took to get into Ged's boat and begin the journey. No longer functioning as the dependent child to father-Ged, he steps out toward something he wants. It is a step toward that which he must admit and confront, the dark side of himself, his potential for evil—in this case his desire for something which violates nature.

When Arren represses thoughts of his desires, his dreams are affected. Although the dreams foreshadow his experience in the land of death, they also suggest Arren's powerlessness as long as he continues to deny his own potential for evil. The fear and repression are intensified by Sopli's presence; his fears of death and desire for immortality echo Arren's inmost thoughts. When Ged is wounded, Arren is so overcome with the presence and fear of death that he cannot think or act. Unwilling to examine himself, he blames Ged for all that has happened; despairing, he sees Ged with "no power left in him, no wizardry, no strength, not even youth, nothing." Having denied his own potential for evil, he has essentially been fostering and believing in a false self; when it crumbles, there is nothing for Arren to get hold of to help him solve the problems. He is without hope.

Rescued from near death by the raft people, Arren recovers as he reestablishes the bond of trust and love with Ged and as he thinks critically about the social bond of the raft people. Arren confronts his dishonesty about himself and about his bond with the other when he courageously confesses to Ged the depths of his despair. The ensuing conversation is similar to those between Ogion and Ged when Ogion told Ged he must look into himself, and between Ged and Tenar when Ged told her what her name was. In all three psychological healing begins when the problem and solution can be named, when the admission of weakness becomes strength. The society of the raft people challenges the idea of a commitment to the larger society of Earthsea. In contrast to the chief's refusal to accept any responsibility for that larger society, Arren includes the raft people in his commitment, as indicated when he sings in the dawn and celebrates the creation of all of Earthsea.

In addition to this new knowledge about himself and society Arren also learns more about his participation in the Equilibrium. This interdependence of nature and humans is represented in the reciprocal relationship of dragon and man. In Earthsea, instead of suggesting the destructiveness of nature, Le Guin's dragon suggests the ancient, wise, enigmatic aspect of nature which will always be different from human life but affected by it.

Arren's experiences in the land of the dead strengthen his commitments. He encounters the dead who have lost themselves and the *communitas* bond with others. Void of reason, feeling, and the art of making anything, they are the shells of people once living; Arren has thus come to knowledge of the death he feared, and it no longer frightens him. Arren also discerns that Cob has lost his selfhood and *communitas*. Unable to experience love, he exists in isolation and alienation; existence has been reduced to the struggle for power. Symbolically, Cob's eye sockets are empty; he has sacrificed his self ("I"), his ability to see the power of light, his ability to see the natural environment and human community. Rejecting Cob's offer of immortality, Arren leads Ged to Cob so that Ged can restore the wholeness of the world.

Arren continues to be the leader as he chooses their way out to the shores of light. Crossing the mountains of pain symbolizes Arren's acceptance of pain and mortality as elements of the personal, social, and cosmic life he has come to understand. Their return to Roke on the back of the oldest dragon is dramatic, partly because this cooperation between human and nonhuman symbolizes the balance of apparent opposites that Ged and Arren have restored to Earthsea which makes possible the Equilibrium, the kingdom of Earthsea, and the integrated self. Ged kneels to Arren, acknowledging his acceptance of him as the next king of Earthsea and symbolizing the irrevocable changes which occurred for both of them in liminality.

Life Story of the Wizard

Each volume of the Earthsea trilogy tells a different story about the coming-of-age process. When viewed together, the completed trilogy provides Ged's life history, which is both a story of the epic hero who successfully deals with the forces that threaten the Equilibrium and the kingdom and a story of the epic hero as creative artist.

Each of the novels recounts a quest at a different stage in Ged's life. As a youth he hunted down the shadow which he released into the world; as a mature wizard he searched for the missing half of the Ring of Erreth-Akbe whose Bond-Rune ensures the king's successful reign; and as an old man he tracked Cob, who opened a hole in the world and returned from the dead. (pp.49-56)

Le Guin has emphasized the psychological qualities of the story in her selection of the key events of Ged's life to narrate. The reader learns, for example, that Ged's most famous deeds are not featured in the three novels. Instead of focusing on the public deeds, the deeds that ensured his sociopolitical role in external society, Le Guin examines the deeds which show Ged's inner struggles and psychological growth. After all, as Ged tells Arren in *The Farthest Shore,* heroes are "the ones who seek to be themselves."

As the life story of a wizard, the trilogy is also a story of the efficacy of art. (p.57)

The magic of Earthsea, sometimes called "artmagic," depends, as does fiction, on the user's genius and knowledge of language. Like the work of art, the magic transforms reality. (p.58)

Just as the life of the epic hero is developed in stages from youth to old age, so the trilogy also depicts the life of the artist-wizard progressively from youth to maturity. In *A Wizard of Earthsea* Ged becomes aware of his innate power and learns from his masters, as an artist learns from mentors, how to discipline it. Discipline of the imagination, Le Guin has written, "does not mean to repress it, but to train it—to encourage it to grow, and act, and be fruitful." Like Ged, the artist must have a fully developed knowledge of the self and will, in fact, find the journey into the self a creative connection between the conscious and the collective unconscious. Le Guin writes: "To reach the others, the artist goes into himself. Using reason, he deliberately enters the irrational. The farther he goes into himself, the closer he comes to the other." Ged learns to resist the easy roads to knowledge and power, the route of a Faustus or a formula novelist who barters away power or talent.

The artist-wizard, once sure of his talent, begins a lifelong search for names, the "right words," by which he exercises his power. "For me," Le Guin wrote, "as for the wizards, to know the name of an island or a character is to know the island or the person. Usually the name comes of itself, but sometimes one must be very careful: as I was with the protagonist, whose true name is Ged." In general, the power of language for the writer comes from the idea that if a thing can be named (be it an object, a theory, a tool, a psychological trait), then its existence can be dealt with, can be made a part of the reader's experience. The threat of the dragons of Pendor is solved when Ged can call Yevaud by its name; the threat of the shadow, of all that Ged fears and represses, is absolved into an acknowledged part of himself when he can name it, Ged. More specifically, in Le Guin's philosophy of life, the power of naming also lies in its ability to honor the thing which is being named. (pp.58-9)

A Wizard of Earthsea can be regarded as depicting the artist in apprenticeship, and *The Tombs of Atuan* depicts the mature artist confronting a hostile audience and gradually transforming that person's perception of reality. What Ged tells Tenar about the world outside the Place and the Kargad Empire is, to her, fiction in the sense that it is a very different world and one which she has never experienced. Her hostility toward his art is based on her false education and on fear. She is a disbeliever and sneers at his art as mere illusion. Le Guin wrote of such a hostile audience in "Why Are Americans Afraid of Dragons?" where she identified the "hardworking, over-thirty American male" in business as one who dismisses fiction, especially fantasy, because he has learned to repress his imagination. Ged assists Tenar by showing her beauty, joy, and light; he assists her by the words which reveal a larger, more humane world and by the word for her other self, Tenar.

The Farthest Shore depicts the artist toward the end of his life, assisting an entire country in dealing with a crisis of language. His action for the prince, the kingborn, is the same as that for Tenar; he gives assistance, offers stories of another kind of existence and a different system of values, and then allows the young prince to choose. All of Earthsea is threatened by the disbelief in artmagic; wizards are forgetting the true names of things and are losing their own true names, dragons lose the power of speech. The artist in his old age is the only one who can reestablish balance because, as Ged says of himself, "I desire nothing beyond my art." He is not vulnerable to temptation.

Ged's belief that there is no escape from death is carried to its logical extension when he retires at the end of *The Farthest Shore.* Powerful as artistry is, it cannot provide a permanent escape to another world. Artist and reader alike must also deal with the consensus reality which surrounds them and with the limits of time and power. No artist's power is permanent, and one who is tempted to believe that it is goes the way of Cob or Faustus. No artist's role as aesthetic and moral guide for the people is permanent. An artist, Le Guin suggests in this novel, may uphold the standards when the ruling powers are deficient, but such is not the permanent role of the artist. Le Guin is conscious of her own lapses into didacticism, i.e., when the message overpowers the story, when the artist begins "to preach" rather than allowing people the freedom they need to be transformed. So the trilogy ends with news of the coronation of Arren as King of Earthsea, and the reader's attention is focused on the social realm. Ged retires, satisfied and fulfilled. Given the difficulty with which he has learned the lesson of turning clear around, of always seeking to connect with his roots in his actions, the ending is—like all of his quest journeys—an open circle. He returns to his beginning, to Roke and to the life of contemplation which he had rejected as a young man. But he returns as a changed man. The creative process has also transformed the artist. (pp.60-2)

Elizabeth Cummins, in her Understanding

Ursula K. Le Guin, *University of South Carolina Press, 1990, 216 p.*

FURTHER READING

Bittner, James W. *Approaches to the Fiction of Ursula K. Le Guin.* Ann Arbor: UMI Research Press, 1984, 161 p.
Emphasizes complementarity among Le Guin's works and incorporates discussion of the *Earthsea Trilogy* within the context of Le Guin's career.

Bucknall, Barbara J. *Ursula K. Le Guin.* New York: Ungar Publishing Co., 1981, 175 p.
Thorough discussion of Le Guin's works through 1980, including a chapter that focuses on such topics as Taoism and the coming-of-age theme as developed in the *Earthsea Trilogy.*

Cameron, Eleanor. "High Fantasy: *A Wizard of Earthsea.*" *Horn Book Magazine* 47 (April 1971): 129-38.
Laudatory review that places *A Wizard of Earthsea* in the category of "high fantasy," which includes entertaining fantasy works that offer poignant observations relevant to the real world.

De Bolt, Joe, ed. *Ursula K. Le Guin: Voyager to Inner Lands and to Outer Space.* Port Washington, N.Y.: Kennikat Press, 1979, 221 p.
Collection of essays on Le Guin's work that includes three pieces on the *Earthsea Trilogy:* "Four Letters about Le Guin," by Rollin A. Lasseter; " 'But Dragons Have Keen Ears:' On Hearing 'Earthsea' with Recollections of *Beowulf,*" by John R. Pfeiffer; and "The Earthsea Trilogy: Ethical Fantasy for Children," by Francis J. Molson.

Extrapolation, Special Issue: Ursula K. LeGuin 21, No. 3 (Fall 1980).
Includes four essays on the *Earthsea Trilogy:* "Shadows in Earthsea: Le Guin's use of a Jungian archetype," by Edgar C. Bailey, Jr.; "Taoist Magic in the *Earthsea Trilogy,*" by Robert Galbreath; "On a Far Shore: The Myth of Earthsea," by Brian Attebery; and "A Time to Live and a Time to Die: Cyclical Renewal in the *Earthsea Trilogy,*" by Thomas J. Remington.

Harris, Mason. "The Psychology of Power in Tolkein's *The Lord of the Rings,* Orwell's *1984* and Le Guin's *A Wizard of Earthsea.*" *Mythlore* 55 (Autumn 1988): 46-56.
Examines the drive for absolute power as a common theme in twentieth-century fantasy literature.

Kottner, Ann E. "New Worlds for Women." *The Women's Review of Books* VII, Nos. 10-11 (July 1990): 40.
Positive review of *Tehanu* and the *Earthsea* cycle.

Olander, Joseph D., and Greenberg, Martin Harry, eds. *Ursula K. LeGuin.* New York: Taplinger Publishing Co., 1979, 258 p.
Collection of essays on Le Guin's work that includes two pieces on the *Earthsea Trilogy:* "Words of Binding: Patterns of Integration in the *Earthsea Trilogy,*" by John H.

Crow and Richard D. Erlich, and "Mythic Reversals: The Evolution of the Shadow Motif," by Sneja Gunew.

New Yorker LXVI, No. 23 (23 July 1990): 88.
    Brief, laudatory review of *Tehanu.*

Selinger, Bernard. *Le Guin and Identity in Contemporary Fiction.* Ann Arbor: UMI Research Press, 1988, 183 p.
    Detailed study of Le Guin's major novels. Offers a psychoanalytic reading of *A Wizard of Earthsea.*

Slethaug, Gordon E. "The Paradoxical Double in Le Guin's *A Wizard of Earthsea.*" *Extrapolation* 27, No. 4 (Winter 1986): 326-33.
    Reading of *A Wizard of Earthsea* based on Jungian theories of personality.

Spivack, Charlotte. *Ursula K. Le Guin.* Boston: Twayne Publishers, 1984, 182 p.
    Comprehensive discussion of Le Guin's life and work. Includes a chapter on the *Earthsea Trilogy.*

Additional coverage of Le Guin's life and career is contained in the following sources published by Gale Research: *Authors in the News,* Vol. 1; *Children's Literature Review,* Vol. 3; *Concise Dictionary of Literary Biography, 1968-1988; Contemporary Authors,* Vols. 21-24, rev. ed.; *Contemporary Authors New Revision Series,* Vols. 9, 32; *Contemporary Literary Criticism,* Vols. 8, 13, 22, 45; *Dictionary of Literary Biography,* Vols. 8, 52; *Major 20th-Century Writers;* and *Something About the Author,* Vols. 4, 52.

Elmore Leonard

1925-

(Full name Elmore John Leonard, Jr.) American novelist, short story writer, and screenwriter.

The following entry covers Leonard's work from 1985 to 1991. For further information on his life and career, see *CLC*, Vols. 28 and 34.

INTRODUCTION

The author of such best-selling novels as *Stick* and *Glitz,* Leonard has been lauded as one of the finest contemporary crime writers in the United States. His gritty accounts of urban life feature the exploits of lower-class characters trying to make fast money and are often set in the locales of southern Florida and Detroit. Although he began writing during the early 1950s, he did not receive widespread attention until the 1980s. Since then he has enjoyed a broad and loyal readership. The film adaptations of his novels *Mr. Majestyk, Fifty-two Pickup,* and *Stick* have further enhanced his popularity. Biographer David Geherin noted: "Leonard's fiction represents a major achievement in crime writing. . . . In their artistry, originality, and impact, Leonard's novels deserve a permanent place beside those of [Dashiell] Hammett and [Raymond] Chandler on the shelf marked simply Outstanding American Fiction."

Leonard was born in New Orleans and grew up in Detroit. During the 1950s, while working as an advertising copywriter, he began writing western stories for pulp magazines and eventually published several western novels, of which *Hombre* is the best known. Also during this period he sold the film rights to his western short stories "3:10 to Yuma" and "The Tall T," thus beginning a long and lucrative relationship with the Hollywood film industry. By the early 1960s, however, public interest in westerns had waned, and Leonard turned to writing mystery and suspense novels, the first of which, *The Big Bounce,* was rejected eighty-four times before being published in 1969. Discouraged by this apparent lack of interest in his suspense fiction, Leonard returned to writing westerns but abandoned the genre again after the film rights to *The Big Bounce* sold for $50,000. He published several crime novels in the years that followed, including *Fifty-two Pickup, Cat Chaser,* and *Unknown Man, No. 89,* but did not achieve major success until the publication of *Stick* in 1983. Favorable reviews by respected critics in the *New York Times* and the *Washington Post* fueled interest in *Stick,* and in 1985 the novel was made into a film directed by and starring Burt Reynolds. Although Leonard disavowed the film, citing Reynolds's refusal to remain faithful to the plot and tone of the original work, it solidified his status as a talented and bankable crime writer.

Critic Michael Kernan has observed that the typical Leonard novel is distinguished by "guns, a killing or two or three, fights and chases and sex. Tight, clean prose, ear-perfect whip-smart dialogue. And just beneath the surface, an acute sense of the ridiculous." Many of these elements can be seen in *Glitz.* In this work, Miami cop Vincent Mora travels to Puerto Rico to recover from a bullet wound and meets Teddy Magyk, a murderer and rapist whom he once put in prison. Their cat-and-mouse chase leads them to Atlantic City, where they tangle with mobsters and drug dealers before their final confrontation. Like many of Leonard's books, *Glitz* has been praised for its memorable characters, sharp dialogue, and suspenseful plot. Other recent works by Leonard provide variations on these characteristics. *Bandits* follows the adventures of Jack Delaney, an ex-hotel thief who is persuaded by an ex-nun to steal five million dollars from a Contra leader in order to help the Sandinistas in Nicaragua. In *Touch,* a former seminarian who heals the sick and exhibits stigmata tries to free himself from the influence of con men and unscrupulous religious leaders who want to exploit his powers. *Killshot* revolves around a working-class couple who, after witnessing a murder, must elude a hit-man and a psychopath. Leonard's most recent works, *Get Shorty*

and *Maximum Bob,* continue in this vein. *Get Shorty* centers on Chili Palmer, a small-time hoodlum who becomes involved with movie producers, actors, and the mafia, while *Maximum Bob* revolves around Bob Gibbs, a bigoted judge known for his tough prison sentences, who becomes the target of several assassins.

While he is often compared to crime writers Ross Macdonald, Chandler, and Hammett, Leonard acknowledges Ernest Hemingway, John Steinbeck, and John O'Hara as his literary influences. The lean prose style of these authors is evident in such works as *Killshot, Touch,* and *Glitz.* Leonard has been praised particularly for his ability to capture the nuances and rhythms of conversation. *Time* magazine called Leonard "Dickens from Detroit" because of his strong character portrayals and realistic dialogue. Minimizing narration and description, Leonard allows his characters' conversations to tell the story. Of Leonard's writing technique, Diane K. Shah observed: "There appears to be no narrator at all: as if a bunch of honest, hard-working guys and a parade of deadbeats had run into each other in Detroit or South Florida and begun talking; as if, by chance, this Elmore Leonard, lurking in the shadows, had turned on his tape recorder, getting it all."

PRINCIPAL WORKS

NOVELS

The Bounty Hunters   1953
The Law at Randado   1954
Escape from 5 Shadows   1956
Last Stand at Saber River   1957; also published as *Lawless River,* 1959; and *Stand on the Saber,* 1960
Hombre   1961
The Big Bounce   1969; revised edition, 1989
The Moonshine War   1969
Valdez Is Coming   1970
Forty Lashes Less One   1972
Fifty-two Pickup   1974
Mr. Majestyk   1974
Swag   1976; also published as *Ryan's Rules,* 1976
The Hunted   1977
Unknown Man, No. 89   1977
The Switch   1978
Gunsights   1979
City Primeval: High Noon in Detroit   1980
Gold Coast   1980; revised edition, 1985
Split Images   1981
Cat Chaser   1982
LaBrava   1983
Stick   1983
Glitz   1985
Bandits   1987
Touch   1987
Freaky Deaky   1988
Killshot   1989
Get Shorty   1990
Maximum Bob   1991

SCREENPLAYS

Joe Kidd   1972

High Noon, Part 2: The Return of Will Kane   1980
Desperado   1987
*The Rosary Murders   [with Fred Walton]   1987

*Based on the novel by William X. Kienzle.

CRITICISM

J. D. Reed

For 20 years, he has watched the creators of Lew Archer and Travis McGee pick up all the applause and critical esteem. No longer. At 58, after 24 novels in 32 years, Elmore Leonard has finally won it all: money, raves and, this month, an Edgar—the Mystery Writers of America version of the Oscar. No more is he the hard-cover talent with the paperback rep. (p. 84)

The lateness of the awards is understandable. After all, Leonard has never featured blue-jawed heroes, hair-trigger comebacks and estrous groupies. Instead he has specialized in strangely principled con men, jailbirds and hustlers who need to score a few bucks or a few points without committing Murder One in the process. The label "glamorous" adheres to none of them.

Detroit Policeman Raymond Cruz of *City Primeval* (1980), for instance, is mistaken for a high school shop teacher by a girl he tries to pick up in a bar. Ernest Stickley Jr. is a dour Oklahoma hick who, in *Swag* (1976), conducts a doomed 100-day armed-robbery career. Resurfacing in *Stick,* seven years and a prison stretch later, he has scarcely improved; he worships Actor Warren Oates and thinks disco is dynamite. But, like all of Leonard's main men, deep down he is as incorrodable as a zinc bar and as heady as the stuff on top of it.

Although the author is a master of the unexpected, violence is not his specialty. Leonard's principal virtues are a Panasonic ear and an infallible sense of character. His narrative tone is that of the man across the airplane aisle who has a good story to tell, if only he could trust you. Grammar is irrelevant; sentences seem to have been delivered, not written: "At approximately 1:30 a.m. he saw the Silver Mark VI traveling south on John R at a high rate of speed with a black Buick like nailed to its tail." His humor is stag: "When the girls would say do-it-to-me, do-it-to-me, he would think, What do you think I'm doing?" or Vegas: "Listen, when I was a kid, the neighborhood I grew up in? It was so dirty I'd sit out in the sun for two hours and get a nice stain." But it is terse, credible and consistent with the speakers, odious or otherwise.

Leonard's world splashes across a crowded Dickensian canvas where social strata collide, and the gravedigger waits by the charnel house. In this underworld, usually located in downtown Detroit or Miami's coke country, thugs and pushers are unappealing, malignant—and instantly recognizable. All one needs to know of Hit Man

Eddie Moke in *Stick,* for instance, is that he changed his image from heavy metal to urban cowboy but still looked "like he mainlined cement." Paco Boza, a Cuban street junkie of *La Brava,* tools around South Miami Beach in a stolen Eastern Airlines wheelchair "because he didn't like to walk and because he thought it was cool." Cornell Lewis, a black ex-con houseman for a high roller in *Stick,* explains his boss: "What the man likes is to rub up against danger without getting any on him. Make him feel like the macho man . . . See, he sits there at the club with his rich friends? Say, oh yeah, I go right in the cage with 'em. They don't hurt me none."

Pursuing his prototypes, the author has gone into the same cage, hanging around ethnic and inner-city bars, courtrooms and squad rooms. These days, however, he is content to stay at a 200-year-old writing table in the large and comfortable study of his Birmingham, Mich., home 15 miles and financial light-years from the Detroit streets he portrays. Even so, the man who made close to $1 million last year from film deals and literary rights has not let success alter his owlish image. Let others compose on word processors, Leonard still writes in longhand and revises on a reconditioned portable. "People tell me I can afford a Mercedes, but I don't want one," he insists. He has no desire to move to New York or Beverly Hills: "I'd be calling up producers or talking away my books."

Leonard began by writing Apache-and-cavalry stories for pulps like *Dime Western* while working in an advertising agency: "I'd get up early, write, then go crank out zingy copy for Chevrolet trucks." By 1967 he had sold his novel *Hombre* to Hollywood and was liberated from office routine. One divorce, five children and 20 novels later, he arrived at his pared-down adrenal style. By now, he feels, he deserves the signed photograph of Hemingway that decorates his study. Says he: "I learned to write from *For Whom the Bell Tolls.*" But, he concedes, "my attitude's different. I see humor everywhere. The fact is, I'm probably closer to Richard Pryor." The accuracy of his work comes from dogged research. *Glitz,* the novel in progress, is set in Atlantic City. Before he went there himself, Leonard's assistant, Detroit Film Writer Gregg Sutter, had collected interviews with dealers and policemen and delivered 180 sequential photographs of the entire town. The American speech that lends authenticity to every page comes from every source: "I'll be watching a prison documentary on TV and some guy will say, 'Right from Jump Street I ran a number on 'em, man.' That goes into the novel."

Leonard seldom reads crime fiction, preferring short-story writers like Raymond Carver and Bobbie Ann Mason. Now that his children are grown, he and his second wife Joan live a regulated life. He generally writes from 9:30 a.m. to 6 p.m. without a lunch break. He will finish *Glitz* in a month, and is already "casting" the next one. Says the hottest thriller writer in the U.S.: "I just like to be left alone and write my stories. Why should I change what I do?" No reason in the world, say his 3 million readers. (pp. 84, 86)

J. D. Reed, "A Dickens from Detroit," in

Time, *New York, Vol. 123, No. 22, May 28, 1984, pp. 84, 86.*

Gary Giddins

It happens like clockwork. Every 10 or 15 years, a writer of genre fiction is discovered by a certified intellectual, and the rest of us—starved for sex and violence rendered with metaphors and snappy dialogue—race to the trough. Remember when Eudora Welty did the trick for Ross Macdonald, and how delighted you were to discover a sensitive detective who knew almost as many metaphors for ennui as he did femmes fatales with murderous and/or incestuous pasts, racing around California restoring the moral order? Remember how surprised, and then disappointed, you were a year later when you realized that he kept writing the same book over and over, with only the metaphors changed to protect the ennui? Last year it was Elmore Leonard's turn, thanks to *LaBrava,* which deserved the enthusiasm it garnered and set the stage for *Glitz* to be a best-seller.

Having read only two of his 19 novels, my disappointment with *Glitz* is strictly relative. Once again Leonard has engineered a thriller that delivers beefy characterizations, macho competence, bimbos aplenty, and stomach-turning violence, all at a whizzing velocity; but it seems almost rote after *LaBrava,* which moved the *Times* to calibrate his talent: "Leonard gives us as much serious fun per word as anyone around." I'm less convinced this time of the seriousness, though *Glitz* may please the anything-for-kicks *Christian Science Monitor,* which was inspired to formulate a biblical injunctive: "Leonard knows that providing entertainment is the novelist's first commandment." All told, the reviewers—according to the heavy-breathing jacket copy—have compared him to Dickens, George V. Higgins, Macdonald, Dostoyevski, Hammett, Chandler, and Balzac. What book critics won't do for a little amusement! In any case, *Glitz* is not "Elmore Leonard's best," and stylish mannerisms that were kind of fun in one book are just mannerisms when they're done to death.

Leonard can be a stunning craftsman—what he does well he does very well. His supporting characters, though often stock types (especially the women), are splendidly drawn and he never loses sight of them. A scene as funny as the one that introduces a former Miss Oklahoma named LaDonna, who has a phobia about Italian restaurants because she's afraid of accidentally getting shot in one, virtually ensures her return to the narrative. (Dickens!) Leonard's sense of place suggests the scrutiny of a careful researcher: his portrait of Atlantic City as a rotting resort festering with mobsters, done over in plastic glitz to attract busloads of tourists who come to have fun but never smile, is ornate and convincing, as is the Puerto Rican scenery—decaying barrios, the main stem, rain forests—he sketches. (Balzac!) He has an uncanny capacity, reminiscent of the more perverse if less craftsmanlike Jim Thompson, to get into the skull of utterly monstrous psychopaths who can rationalize every extreme of antisocial behavior—even murder and necrophilia. (Dostoyevski!)

Leonard's empathy for villains is frightening—they are

more energetic, determined, and colorful than his heroes, who tend to be rather sentimental. A far cry from Hammett and Chandler, whose errant knights almost always get the best parts. Leonard's psychos scare the hell out of you in *LaBrava;* they even walk away with some of the better movies based on his stories—*The Tall T, 3:10 to Yuma, Mr. Majestyk.* Yet the scumbag villain in *Glitz,* the murderer-rapist-necrophiliac Teddy Magyk, so outclasses the hero cop, Vincent Mora, in eliciting the novelist's best conceits that the story's moral equilibrium is fatally skewed. What's more, the suspense mechanism is occasionally derailed by Mora's slowness in recognizing facts long since handed over to the reader. For a veteran Miami-based cop, he's incredibly naive about the 20-year-old prostitute who takes a job as a casino "hostess." When she dives 18 floors from a highrise balcony, wearing only panties in which an envelope with his name and address is tucked, he takes half the novel to realize what the reader already knows, and probably could have guessed if the novelist hadn't spilled the beans.

Leonard's dialogue usually crackles. Yet the very gimmicks that seem startlingly right in moderation wear thin when they're used on every character. His favorite tricks include sentences that start in medias res ("You asking me for?" means "What are you asking me for?"); sentences without conjunctions ("You two're the perfect combination I ever saw one"); strangely misspelled words ("homasexyul"); and—worst of all—strangely parsed phrases ("that's all you got a do"). Instead of racing along with the repartee, you begin to wonder how the pronunciation of "want a argue" differs from "wanta argue," and whether either is as accurate as "wanna argue?"

Leonard's classiest technique is the way he shifts the point of view between major and minor, active and passive characters. The opening scenes with Teddy and a cabdriver are riveting because you don't yet know which of them will dictate the action. Leonard effortlessly inhabits the perceptions of every soul he brings on stage (Gogol!). But as the loose ends of the mystery are tied up, the story suddenly switches to a *Dirty Harry* mode—the scales of justice are balanced in favor of the bad guys, so what's an honest cop to do. The animated supporting players fade away, the inevitable confrontation is set up, and the unsurprising conclusion is all ashes to the taste (Byron!), like a Charles Bronson movie. Since the evidence of two novels seems to suggest that Leonard's true gift is for penetrating the workaday delirium of crazed megalomaniacs (Shakespeare!), perhaps his most impressive bid for seriousness will come with a story set entirely in the muck. The hell with sexy heroes and movie sales.

> *Gary Giddins, in a review of "Glitz," in VLS, No. 32, February, 1985, p. 4.*

Stephen King

How good is this novel? Probably the most convincing thing I can say on the subject is that it cost me money. After finishing *Glitz,* I went out to the bookstore at my local mall and bought everything by Elmore Leonard I could find—the stuff I didn't already own, that is.

The fact that I *do* own four novels by Mr. Leonard and had read none of them might tell you something about the block I've had about him before this. Three of my four unread Leonards were sent to me a couple of years ago by a writer I respect—"You'll like these," the laconic note attached said. I put them on the shelf in my summer home, where they remain. Last year Mr. Leonard's publishers sent me galleys of *LaBrava,* presumably for a blurb. I put it on the shelf where it remained until last night. I picked it up and started it as soon as I finished *Glitz.* I think the reason I had to be *paid* to start reading Mr. Leonard was that I never read a review that said he was a hack or that he was writing trash. And that was not because he wasn't being reviewed; he was.

My favorite crime novelist—often imitated but never duplicated—is Jim Thompson. Thompson was rarely reviewed, but when he was he was excoriated. I was in fact originally attracted to him by a review that called *Cropper's Cabin* "unbearably repulsive." I immediately wanted to read that book, figuring anyone with enough energy to get a reviewer to call his work unbearably repulsive must have something going for him. Well, *Cropper's Cabin* was pretty repulsive, all right, but it was *nothing* compared to *The Killer Inside Me.* But both of those books—Thompson's whole *oeuvre,* in fact—were also really good.

How does this bear on my Elmore Leonard block? Simple. I figured if so many critics liked him, he was probably a bore.

Mr. Leonard is far from boring, critical kudos or no. You can put *Glitz* on the same shelf with your John D. MacDonalds, your Raymond Chandlers, your Dashiell Hammetts. In it, Mr. Leonard moves from low comedy to high action to a couple of surprisingly tender love scenes with a pro's unobtrusive ease and the impeccable rhythms of a born entertainer. He isn't out front, orating at the top of his lungs (another one of the things I was afraid of when I read all those glowing reviews); he's behind the scenes where he belongs, moving the props around and keeping the story on a constant roll. This is the kind of book that if you get up to see if there are any chocolate chip cookies left, you take it with you so you won't miss anything.

It *is* a good story, too. I have to emphasize that, because in the crime-suspense genre, the good writers have not always told the best stories—there are Raymond Chandler novels I *still* haven't figured out, and I've read those babies to rags. Same with Ross MacDonald (only with MacDonald you *did* know one thing: somewhere along the line, two people who were related to each other but didn't know it were going to end up in the sack together). It doesn't always matter, particularly with Chandler; the classy, sassy power of the prose is enough to carry you along.

Finding a rational tale as well as that cheeky prose in *Glitz* was something of a bonus—but hey, I'll take it, I'll take it. I'll even tell you a little bit of the story, but not enough to spoil it—as far as I am concerned, there's too much on the dust jacket already.

Glitz is about a Miami cop named Vincent who takes a rest cure in Puerto Rico after being shot by a speed-freak. Two things happen to him in San Juan: He meets and half falls in love with a prostitute named Iris, and he is observed by Teddy Magyk, one of popular fiction's really great crazies. It seems Vincent put Teddy away, and Teddy still remembers. Boy, does he.

Fade out sunny San Juan; fade in the Boardwalk and glitzy false-fronted casinos of Atlantic City. I could tell you why the scene shifts, but, as a former President observed in one of his more thoughtful moments, that would be wrong. Suffice it to say that there's a murder, and Vincent gets involved with an array of casino men, women and gangsters as a result.

My favorite among Mr. Leonard's casino men is Jackie Garbo, who has an office decorated with autographed pictures of Vegas-Atlantic City celebs. He refers to them as dear friends, as in "my dear friend Johnny Carson" and "my dear friend Joan Rivers." My favorite gangster is Ricky the Zit, who once killed a man by chopping his spine open with a cleaver. My favorite woman—and the book's best supporting character—is LaDonna Holly Padgett, a one-time Miss America contestant who lost the big brass ring but who *was* picked as Miss Congeniality. Now she lives with Jackie Garbo, drinks a lot of what she calls "bloodies" and has developed a phobia about Italian restaurants. "You know what I'm scared the most of?" she asks Vincent. "We're having dinner at Angeloni's or one of those places and somebody comes in with a machine gun to kill one of those guys like you see in the paper? You see 'em lying on the floor with blood all over? . . . I think about it, I get petrified."

All of this comes to a smashing and satisfying conclusion. It's fun, all right, but Mr. Leonard's view of the fervid Atlantic City gambling world goes a step beyond both mere fun and the Arthur Hailey sort of "this is how it works" subtext. He is not a cynic—his view of his characters is sympathetic and sometimes almost loving—but the picture he draws of the Boardwalk dream-machine is fairly acrid: "Two thousand [tour buses] a day came into the city, dropped the suckers off for six hours to lose their paychecks, their Social Security in the slots and haul them back up to Elizabeth, Newark, Jersey City, Philly, Allentown. Bring some more loads back tomorrow—like the Jews in the boxcars, only they kept these folks alive with bright lights and loud music and jackpot payoffs that sounded like fire alarms." That sound fairly acrid to you? I thought so too.

Time magazine has called Mr. Leonard a "Dickens from Detroit." I haven't read enough of him yet (give me a month or so) to agree, but his wit, his range of effective character portrayal and his almost eerily exact ear for the tones and nuances of dialogue suggest Dickens to me. Although it's only February, I'll venture a guess—*Glitz* may be the best crime novel of the year. Even if it's not, I'm sorry it took me so long to catch up to Mr. Leonard.

> *Stephen King, "What Went Down When Magyk Went Up," in* The New York Times Book Review, *February 10, 1985, p. 7.*

John Sutherland

Genre fiction is as competitive as prize-fighting. The current champion of thriller writers in America is Elmore 'Dutch' Leonard. With the imminent release of the film *Stick* (a much-hyped but somewhat limp adaptation directed by and starring Burt Reynolds) he should make number one here, too. Leonard's eminence ties in with the emergence of Miami as the new crime fashion centre of the United States. Styles have changed. Chicago was speakeasies and gangs; Las Vegas high-rolling casinos; New York, the five Mafia families. Miami crime has no roots in long-standing urban deprivation, minority ethnic solidarity, or the anomalies of state gambling laws. It was created by a series of rapid influxes of people, capital and contraband all cooked in the Sun Belt's year-round summer. First came the monied retirees, who triggered off the real-estate boom. . . . Secondly, the mind-boggling sums of money generated by middle-class America's insatiable appetite for prohibited cocaine. Thirdly, the invasion by criminal classes educated in villainy outside the US—in Cuba, Haiti and Colombia. Fidel Castro's exporting his entire population of moral incorrigibles from Mariel in 1980 topped off the anti-social mixture nicely.

Miami crime is above all stylish: a compound of fluorescent tones, salsa rhythms and what Leonard calls 'glitzy crap'. This glitz was the leading feature of Brian De Palma's remake of *Scarface,* with its play on luminous surfaces in which blood, neon and Miami sunsets finally merge into a single crimson garishness. The same glitz features in the TV hit, *Miami Vice.* Mafiosi are usually portrayed as dressing like funeral mutes. The Miami vicious, by contrast, strut in gold chains, flaring silk and sharp disco fashions. Fashion (as determined by prime-time TV) also dictates the choice of weaponry. The point is made with Leonard's usual few words in *LaBrava:*

> 'Any pistol you want,' Javier said, 'wholesale price to a Marielito. Machine-gun one-third off, MAC-10 cost you eight hundred.'
>
> 'Something small,' Cundo Rey said.
>
> 'You want a snubbie. This one, .38 Special, two-inch barrel. Same kind the Charlie's Angels use.'
>
> 'Yea?'
>
> 'Also Barney Miller.'
>
> 'Wrap it up,' Cundo Rey said.

It's not a pitch one can imagine working with Don Corleone.

Mario Puzo's *The Godfather,* like Howard Hawk's original *Scarface,* was steeped in age-old moral patterns and conventions, and clan loyalties. Traditional crime fiction is consolingly dutiful to moral truisms: either that crime does not pay, or that (as in the necessary sequel, *Godfather II*) it pays only at the cost of one's finer being. There is no such consolation in Elmore Leonard's vision of Miami outlawry. The ubiquitous Marielito, for instance, is a cold-eyed loner, conscienceless and very successful. In *Stick,* the type is represented by Nestor Soto, who for routine disciplinary reasons requires blood sacrifice (in the form of an employee to murder) from a fellow dealer who unwittingly exposes him to a Federal bust. In *LaBrava,* the principal murderer (there are at least three others among the main characters) is another Marielito, Cundo Rey. Cundo commits his crimes in the dark: but three nights a week under the spotlights he is a go-go dancer, in leopard skin jockstrap, for women's strip joints (one of the less highminded products of the liberation movement). Cundo murdered a Russian adviser in Cuba for his LaCoste shirt; murdered the American captain who brought him to Florida for 'complaining'. And once landed, and a new American himself, he continues murdering with no more compunction than he dances. Both are natural to him. The novel is inward with this reptile, but he is beyond understanding: a force of evil which can only be propitiated or (with a great deal of luck) exterminated.

Wholesale extermination would be an Augean task. The likes of Cundo Rey are a majority in Leonard's world. He portrays an America weltering in its crime. There is no battle, because the bad guys have won. In Raymond Chandler's novels, the mean streets were patrolled if not policed by crusaders upholding impeccable private moralities ('shop-soiled Galahad' is how the ironic Marlowe describes himself). Alfred Harbage once calculated that seven out of ten people in Shakespeare's plays are good. In Chandler, the ratio is less favourable but must run about seventy-thirty, bad over good. For Elmore Leonard, one good man a novel is par. And even his upstanding types are not the kind who win citizen-of-the-month awards. In *Stick,* the hero is an ex-con, just released from serving seven-to-ten for armed robbery. He does not solve, uncover or avenge crime. He merely happens to be around and puts things right as neutrally as one might straighten a crooked picture.

As Leonard's *homme moyen sensuel,* Stick expresses a cool, exhausted tolerance of a crime wave become tidal. Submerged in it, the means of survival is, as Stick puts it, 'not to react to things'. Or if absolutely required to react, the approved style is laid-back to the point of lethargy. Take, for instance, a standard thriller episode where Stick is obliged to deal with a drunken hoodlum, terrorising the local citizenry. Traditionally, heroic fists fly and bad guys fall, conveniently stunned. Stick, by contrast, ambles on the scene with a rusty two-gallon gasoline can:

> Stick walked over to the buffet table. He placed a glass on the edge, unscrewed the cap on the gooseneck spout of the gasoline can and raised it carefully to pour . . . Stick paused, almost smiled. Then he emptied the glass with an up-and-down toss of the hand, wetting the front of Cecil's shirt and the fly of his trousers. There was a sound from the guests, an intake of breath, but no one moved. They stared in silence . . . Stick raised his left hand, flicked on a lighter and held it inches from Cecil's chest. 'Your bag's packed,' Stick said, looking at him over the flame. 'You want to leave or you want to argue?'

The merest flick of a thumb replaces righteous assault and battery. And the final twist is that the gasoline can actually contained water. 'Where was I going to get gasoline? Drive all the way over to the Amoco station?'

Although Penguin publicity labels him 'America's new No 1 writer', Leonard has been around a long time. He served his apprenticeship doing Westerns. (This is a background he shares with his near rival in the thriller, Brian Garfield, author of *Death Wish*). Leonard wrote the book and screenplay for what has been solemnly judged—by the Western writers' association—one of the 20 best works ever in the genre, **Hombre.** The film was directed by Martin Ritt, and starred Paul Newman, with Richard Boone taking the acting honours as the psychopathic adversary. **Hombre** is patently a remake of *Stagecoach.* But whereas John Ford's passengers were a cross-sectional mixture of the good, the bad and the redeemable, Leonard's coachload are all crooks or degenerates, different only in their anti-social specialisms. A possible exception is the hero, the 'man' of the title. He has been brought up by Indians, and is returning to civilisation reluctantly to claim an inheritance he does not want. He is drawn into saving his fellow passengers against his better instincts, which tell him to cut loose and look after himself. His instincts are correct. 'Hey, hombre, what ees your name?' his Mexican killer asks, and is unanswered. The name is unimportant and the hero's sacrifice worthless. He shouldn't have bothered.

Another successful film adaptation of Leonard's Western fiction was *3:10 to Yuma* (1957), a jaundiced homage to *High Noon.* Leonard's heroes are not reluctant from motives of becoming modesty, but because of the pointlessness of heroic effort in the face of the odds against it. In *LaBrava,* the name-belied hero used once to be in the IRS and the FBI, agencies devoted to keeping America clean and lawful. He has turned in his badges and when the story begins has been for three years a free-lance photographer in Miami, snapping away at the bizarre sights around him. He no longer attempts to control things; he merely observes and takes his cut.

> She said, 'Maury, who's Joseph LaBrava?'
>
> 'It was LaBrava took the shot of the guy being thrown off the overpass . . . He looks up, sees the three guys and gets out his telephoto lens. Listen, he got off two shots before they even picked the guy up. Then he got 'em, they're holding the guy up in the air and he got the one of the guy falling, arms and legs out like he's flying, the one that was in *Newsweek* and all the papers.'
>
> 'He must've done all right.'
>
> 'Cleared about twelve grand so far, the one shot.'

The language is that of police enforcement: 'he got off two shots . . . then he got'em.' But the crime is neither prevented, interrupted nor punished. It's merely profitably witnessed from a safe distance.

In the usual way of Leonard's narratives, LaBrava gets sucked into the action by a momentary dropping of the guard, 'reacting to things' when an intelligent survivor shouldn't. Coincidence brings him together with a 50-year-old movie-star, whose screen image as a bad-beautiful girl he had loved when he was a 12-year-old cinemagoer. This pubescent passion was apparently the last real feeling LaBrava experienced, and it returns to betray him. His affair with the star (called 'Jean Shaw' and a compound of Veronica Lake, Bette Davis and Loretta Young) revives dangerous nostalgia for Hollywood's clear-cut moralities:

> 'And I remember—I don't know if it was that picture or another one—you shot the bad guy. He looks at the blood on his hand, looks down at his shirt. He still can't believe it. But I don't remember what it was about. I can't think who the detective was either, I mean in *Obituary*. It wasn't Robert Mitchum, was it?'
> She shook her head, thoughtfully. 'I'm not sure myself who was in it.'

In fact, LaBrava is in it. For obscure motives (to do with nostalgias of her own), the star has chosen to replay the movie by setting up an elaborate plot to heist $600,000. Inevitably, she shoots the bad guy and is turned in by LaBrava, pulled back from retirement.

LaBrava has been much applauded, and won the 1983 Edgar Allan Poe award. But it seems to me one of Leonard's weaker performances. If he has a fault, it is a tendency to overcomplicate his plots and lose narrative clarity. Unless one is very alert to detail and nuances of dialogue, it's difficult to work out what's going on—though the portrayal of Miami wild life is very entertaining. *Glitz* is more disciplined. It opens with the hero, Lieutenant Vincent Mora of the Miami police, being mugged off-duty on the way out from the supermarket: 'Vincent turned his head to look at the guy and there was a moment when he could have taken him and did consider it, hit the guy as hard as he could. But Vincent was carrying a sack of groceries. He wasn't going to drop a half gallon of Gallo Hearty Burgundy, a bottle of prune juice and a jar of Ragu on the sidewalk.' So he tells the mugger he's a cop, and is promptly shot right through the Hearty Burgundy. He returns fire, and gets his man. It's the first time Mora has killed, and once out of intensive care, he goes on vacation to Puerto Rico to recover his nerve. Here, he's hunted down by a vindictive psychopath, Teddy Magyk, whom he put away a few years before. A string of consequent murders draws Mora to Atlantic City (another new vice capital) and back, finally, to the intensive-care ward. In this most recent novel, Leonard's vision has darkened to pitch-black. Now it seems that even the Miami Police Force can't run far or fast enough to escape the bad guys.

It's not chancing one's critical arm to predict that for the next few years Elmore Leonard will be the hottest crime writer in the Anglo-American market. He deserves fame. His novels are slick efforts in a demanding genre, and he has exploited a new location, Miami, with trail-blazing verve. But, not to be heavy-handed, Leonard's fiction has its grim significance. Just as the mass of well-thinking Britons have at last accepted that there is nothing to be done about unemployment, so, apparently, America's remorseless crime statistics have had their effect. Epidemic violent crime is now accepted as an ineradicable social fact. In its popularity, Leonard's fiction answers to a widely-held sense of hopelessness about the bad guys. You can't beat them. You can't pen them up in ghettos any

more. And however low you keep your profile, they're probably going to get you in the end.

John Sutherland, "No. 1 Writer," in London Review of Books, *Vol. 7, No. 15, September 5, 1985, p. 16.*

Michael Wood

Sam Spade and Philip Marlowe were tough in their time, but recent American crime fiction tends to make them look like kindly nannies, mere bleeding hearts. The mean streets have got meaner since Chandler wrote about them, and the same goes for the bars, brothels, clubs, diners, gaols, resort hotels, apartment blocks, tycoons' residencies and police precincts. Ross Macdonald's Lew Archer became a designed anachronism in his later career, weary, wise, straight, the man with the divorce and the beat-up Porsche, the guy who's seen it all—except, it turns out, that he hasn't seen the half of it. Even the old locations, Los Angeles and New York, seem tame and faded, almost genteel. The real meanness is on the streets of Detroit, Miami, Atlantic City, countless little mid-western towns with names like Sagamore. The streets of San Francisco are just picturesque.

The new meanness says a lot about the social landscape, of course; about the fears it inspires and the dreams people have of the ways to survive in it. It has much to do with the amount of money to be made from drugs; with the mingling of politics and crime since Watergate, particularly Cuban politics in exile; with terrifying quantities of random and lethal craziness on the streets; with the sort of impatience with the law's delays which prompts Clint Eastwood and Charles Bronson movies. Yet Chandler's formula still serves us well, if not as a prescription, then as a pattern, a tune inviting variations. "Down these mean streets a man must go who is not himself mean . . . ". If he is mean, he will need another claim on our interest, some sleazy charm or rabid pathology or a heart of gold hidden in the meanness. If he is not mean he will need, these days, some kind of safeguard against his own implausibility.

For what is both dated and attractive in Chandler's vision is not the crime in it—he names hold-ups, liquor rackets, the numbers, the mafia, crooked mayors, corrupt and political judges, dodgy lawyers, stupid juries, gangsters who "rule nations and almost rule cities"—but the quiet outrage it contains. Chandler is talking tough, but he thinks he is exaggerating, and expects us to feel this, and to feel surprised. We have run out of surprise, we are all tough guys now, at least in our imagined knowledge of the world. Consequently, Chandler's antidote, his unmean man, seems hopelessly romantic. He is "neither tarnished nor afraid . . . a complete man and a common man and yet an unusual man . . . a man of honour. . . . He must be the best man in his world and a good enough man for any world . . . ".

Elmore Leonard's characters are usually tarnished and afraid, but pretty good at surviving. In his recent work Leonard seems to be evolving a new, hardened version of Chandler's hero, a man who is tough, even a killer, when his choices are confined, but not mean; a man who can be very mean indeed when he wants but remains honourable, a better man than most worlds deserve. This is not an easy figure to draw convincingly, and it is a measure of Leonard's considerable talent that he brings it off. Leonard has been much praised in the United States, and sells hugely, deservedly so. Eight of his novels are now newly published or republished in Britain, and another is apparently on the way. Some of them are recent—*Cat Chaser,* 1982, *Stick* and *LaBrava* 1983, *Glitz,* 1985—while others go back to 1974 and 1976.

Leonard has been writing novels and screenplays, thrillers and westerns since 1967. He was born in 1925, served in the US Navy and worked in advertising. The writing of westerns may have helped him on his way to his laconic dialogue, all slang and silences, endlessly oblique. In *Glitz,* a cop in Atlantic City gets shot at while in bed with a girl, and gives chase:

> 'I ran outside in my underwear, got my gun, I'm coming back in and a drunk is standing there on the sidewalk looking at me, weaving. You know what he said?'
>
> 'Atlantic City, three o'clock in the morning,' Dixie said, 'Resorts International across the street, he told you don't do it, it ain't worth it. Think of your wife and kids.'
>
> 'He said, "You should a bet your underwear. You never know when your luck'll change." '

But blossoms of rhetoric also flourish in this packed prose. The cop who was shot at arranges for one mafioso, on the basis of misleading information, to kill another, to the delight of most of the population. The cop says, modestly, "Wonderful things can happen when you plant seeds of distrust in a garden of assholes." His friend says, "Wait, I want to write that down." Leonard's characters, good and bad, say things like, "What's your game?" or "You'll be all right, kid", not because they talk like that but because they have always wanted to talk like a movie. When a Latin type does a bit of heavy breathing he does it in full-dress cliché, squinting eyes and lines around his nostrils. "This was to indicate", the man watching him assumes, "nerves of ice banking the Latin fire inside."

The fast, self-aware language reflects a fast and crowded world, a world so full of things and people and action that it makes almost any other thriller kingdom seem underpopulated. All the cars are dated and named, the Camaro, the Nova, the yellow 1977 Olds; all the guns and the drinks identified, every last frill and cocktail lounge furnishing noted. The effect is not that of a documentary, although, without doubt, the details are right, but of a baroque profusion, a world full of glittering, pointless toys—dangerous toys, or toys for dangerous people. We know how Colombian cocaine money is laundered, how casinos are monitored, how gambling managers lose their licences; who sleeps on which waterbed, and what the girls round the pool do for a living when they are not falling into bed with the guys round the pool. Above all we know, or gradually learn, who is double-crossing whom, since that is what this world is largely about. Some readers have felt that Leonard's plots are too complicated, a form of writer-

ly self-indulgence. I think not, partly because I don't think a plot *can* be too complicated (I treasure the, no doubt apocryphal, story of Chandler, during the filming of *The Big Sleep,* unable to explain his plot to Howard Hawks), and partly because this complication is Leonard's great subject.

All these novels portray people, central or marginal, heroes or hangers-on, who are watching for an angle, trying to find their fortune in other people's messes. Of any situation they do not ask, Is it good or bad, is it safe or dangerous?, but, How will it play, what's my next move? They are not all blackmailers, but none of them can resist the thought of their cut, their piece of the action that as yet is only a handful of compromising cards waiting to be shuffled and dealt. The good guys stay at the thought, but even they have the thought. One character is asked to sit back and permit the killing of his mistress's bilious husband (former police chief in the Dominican Republic, famous for sewing people's eyelids to their eyebrows and shining harsh light on them), and then he can just walk off into the sunset with his girl. "Moran actually saw a picture of a red sunset, sky-red night . . . ". Another good guy roughs up an Italian mobster who has been gathering protection money and finds himself with $12,000 on his hands. He can't keep it and he can't return it, and he doesn't want, yet, to hand it in to the police. So he uses it as a deposit in a fancy hotel, which is happy to provide any kind of complimentary service (room, drinks, credit, transport, girls) for such a nice rich man.

What all this angle-seeking means is that Leonard's fiction is full of losers, people who think they are smart and aren't. His survivors are sometimes a little smarter, sometimes just lucky, sometimes ruthless. In *Swag* two rather forlorn robbers get deeper and deeper into double-cross trouble—there is a grim comedy in the scene where one of the robbers is held up by casual muggers and finds himself, desperate, having to shoot them both—but manage against the odds to keep afloat. *Cat Chaser* has an ex-cop and an ex-actor and a Dominican pimp all trying to get their hands on the same stack of money, and pretending to collaborate, while George Moran, the novel's good guy, tries to keep true love going amid all the roughing up and conspiracy. There are one or two of Leonard's rare false notes here ("all that longing they could now release", "They talked . . . and were at ease with each other in silence"). Tenderness he can't do. But loyalty and courage he can, and straightness when everything else looks bent. George feels sorry for the losers around him: he sees their game but lets them play until they play too rough. The death of Rafi, the Dominican pimp, horrifies George and is peculiarly and quietly scaring, in a novel full of gunshots and crazy Cubans trying to take away a fellow's manhood with the garden shears. Rafi, who can't swim, is simply pushed into a pool and left; a loser who lacked a very simple survival skill. What was he doing in a realm of sharks? When George kills the scheming ex-cop, not to save his life, but to save his girl's money—or not even the money, but just the principle that you don't have to give things to people who think they are tougher than you are—the effect is shocking but feels right. George is not Chandler's hero, but he is ours. He has broken out of the prison of meekness, he has done it for the girl, he has not turned into a thug, and he will probably serve time for manslaughter.

Glitz seems to me the most complex and risky of these novels. It has many threads of plot, and some strange, understated motivations which hover between the not quite plausible and the genuinely incomprehensible—just where we find so much actual behaviour, in fact, but where novelists are reluctant to go. Vincent Mora, a Miami Beach cop who has been wounded, convalesces in San Juan, Puerto Rico, and meets a psychopath he put away for seven years in the Florida State penitentiary. We see the psychopath from inside, follow the horrors of his thought without comment, the sheer levity in them making the horror really quite extreme. He tips a drugged girl from a high balcony to her death and assesses her fall as if it were a competition dive: "Nice execution, but 'ey, she didn't keep her feet together." He is out to get Vincent, but not before tormenting him; Vincent wants to know who killed the girl, although Atlantic City is not his beat, and we are soon in the thick of cocaine, illegal gambling, murder, protection, a whirl of fear and vice which makes Miami, as Vincent thinks, look like a retirement home.

But Vincent, like George, stays straight, and what makes him credible, a man of honour in a world that is not even dishonoured because it has forgotten what honour is, is the fact that he has company—not much but some; decency is rare but not extinct, or alive only in our hero. That, and the fact that most people in the novel can't fathom him at all. He won't take bribes, won't arrange for the psychopath to die in an "accident"—even though he knows this charming type has killed three people in three weeks. Vincent's theory is that if you scare people enough you won't have to kill them. This theory works for much of the book, but it didn't stop him from getting wounded in the first place, and it gets him into near terminal trouble at the end. This is what thrillers are always telling us, this is the smart, sad belief they offer, although not often with the swish and flair of Elmore Leonard: that a man who's good enough for any world is ready for the next world.

Michael Wood, "Down These Meaner Streets," in The Times Literary Supplement, *No. 4366, December 5, 1986, p. 1370.*

Walker Percy

The question here is, Why is Elmore Leonard so good? He is. He is as good as the blurbs say: "The greatest crime writer of our time, perhaps ever," "Can't put it down," and so on. It's true enough. But how does he do it? Because it looks like he's thrown away the rules of a noble genre. He doesn't stick to the same guy or the same place. I had thought Raymond Chandler wrote the book when he set down Philip Marlowe in Los Angeles, in his lonesome house up Laurel Canyon, stoic and pure-hearted amid the low life of Sunset Boulevard and the bad cops of Bay City, a tough Galahad pitted against some very sleazy barbarians.

But look at what Mr. Leonard is doing. Here he is now in New Orleans. I haven't read many of his books, but, as I recall, he's taken on Detroit, Miami Beach, Bal Harbour,

Jerusalem, with a different cop or a different tough guy in each place. His New Orleans is done up with meticulous accuracy. The restaurants, streets, bars, hotels are just right—especially a lovely neighborhood restaurant, Mandina's, which tourists have never heard of, and even the funeral home across the street. One imagines Mr. Leonard moving into a city for a couple of weeks, yet doing his research as exhaustively as John Gunther doing another "Inside" book. Yet Mr. Leonard's New Orleans lacks the authenticity of Chandler's L.A., which works for Marlowe—and for us—as his very soul's terrain.

I've often wondered why some good crime writer, local or otherwise, hasn't taken up with New Orleans, what with its special raffishness, its peculiar flavor of bonhomie and a slightly suspect charm. It's got the backdrop: Mafia types and the French Quarter downtown, enough decayed aristocrats uptown, lonesome anonymous suburbs like Gentilly, a greater ethnic mix than Marseilles. There are no ranker patios anywhere. Yet I can't recall a good novel in this genre and only one second-rate television series, "Bourbon Street Beat."

Does Elmore Leonard do the job in *Bandits*? The early signs are not auspicious. His hero is an ex-con, a jewel thief turned mortician. The female lead? A good-looking ex-nun just back from Nicaragua where she took care of lepers until the contras hacked them up with machetes. *Lepers?*

The ex-nun wants to smuggle a young Nicaraguan woman—who contracted leprosy and whom her lover, a Somoza-type colonel, is trying to kill for honor's sake and because he thinks she might have given him leprosy—out of Carville, a leprosarium in Louisiana. He is also raising millions from rich Americans to take back to the contras. The ex-jewel thief and his tough ex-con ex-cop friend are out to steal the money that the ex-nun wants so she can help the lepers and the Sandinistas.

H'm.

When she was a nun, the woman believed in touching people. Why did she quit her vocation? Because, she says, "I was burnt out." "What does that mean?" her ex-jewel-thief boyfriend asks. "I was touching without feeling," she explains.

Oh my. What has Mr. Leonard got himself into this time? Nicaraguan politics and a gun-toting ex-nun who touches without feeling? Is it going to be standard Leonard crime and punishment flavored by gumbo and laced with bad contras and good Sandinistas?

But wait. Things are not so simple. Who should show up but a Miskito Indian who is working for the contras and who shoots people in the head with his 9-millimeter Beretta. He's a Miskito, and we know, don't we, what the Sandinistas did to the Miskitos.

A preposterous business this, but we keep turning the pages. Why?

Here's one reason. Here's Jack Delaney, ex-con mortician, talking to his tough ex-con ex-cop friend, Roy, who's tending bar. Mr. Leonard has got the bar just right. We know what the bar looks like, what street it looks out on. Jack is telling Roy about the $5 million they can take from the colonel. Roy is mixing a drink, not paying attention. He ventures a remark. "Delaney, you know what broads do when they get sick? I've never seen it to fail, they throw up in the washbasin. They don't throw up in the toilet, like you're supposed to."

This gets your attention. What's Roy up to?

Jack is telling him about stealing the $5 million from the contras and serving humanity at the same time. Roy is unimpressed by serving humanity. He tells about the humanity he serves at the bar.

> Guy comes in, looks around, he whispers to me, "You got any absinthe?" He says, "They don't have none at the Old Absinthe House. They tell me it's against the law to serve it." I say how do I know, to this little . . . fella, you're not a cop? He shows me he's from Fort Wayne, Indiana. I glance around the bar, get out a clear bottle I make up that's got Pernod in it and a piece of deadwood with a caterpillar stuck on it. [He] drinks five of 'em at five bills a shot. Serve humanity, I serve 'em any . . . thing they want.

Mr. Leonard has got my attention.

You begin to notice his prose, the way he moves people around. People get shot in dependent clauses. Franklin de Dios is the Miskito Indian. " 'I said I quit,' Franklin said, and shot him."

The snap and crackle of the dialogue is something to hear. Mr. Leonard's ear is sharp and accurate: "Jack put on a reasonably stupid grin for Wally Scales and slipped a little bit of West Feliciana Parish into his sound. 'Well, I can't say it was enjoyable, but I come through it, yes sir.' " Sure enough, folks in West Feliciana Parish, which is next door to where I'm writing, could say that.

Franklin drives a Chrysler Fifth Avenue. A black New Orleanian can't figure him out—he looks Indian but he's got nappy hair. "Man, I look at you close I thought you were a brother. You know what I'm saying? I thought you were black." "Yes, one part of me," Franklin says. "The rest Miskito."

Here's an item for the next doctoral thesis on Mr. Leonard: he often drops the word "if" in dialogue—and uses hardly any conjunctions. "I had a tire iron we could find out in ten minutes." This sentence could use an "if" and a comma and would be worse for it.

Yes, Mr. Leonard knows what he's doing. In the end he senses that Nicaragua and the gun-toting ex-nun may not be working out here. He backs off. Says Roy, mystified: "I want to know, for my own information, which are the good guys and which are the bad guys." Jack doesn't know either. Mr. Leonard's instincts are good. Nicaraguan politics, it turns out, may be a bit too heavy to be carried by the graceful pas de deux of Mr. Leonard's good guys and bad guys. For this reason, *Bandits* is not quite of a piece, like *Glitz*.

But it will do. Mr. Leonard has got his usual diverting cast of grifters and creeps up his sleeve and action as Byzantine

as ever Chandler himself thought up. In fact, reading it, I felt like William Faulkner when he was writing the

---

An excerpt from *Maximum Bob*

There he was now, and to look at him he appeared harmless. About five-seven with a solemn, bony face, dark hair combed flat to his head. Maybe too dark, Kathy thought. He dyed it. A little guy in judicial robes that looked too big for him. Round-shouldered in a way that made him seem purposeful crossing to the bench. His bailiff, Robbie, a sheriff's deputy in a uniform sport coat, told everyone to rise. Kathy glanced around. There weren't more than a dozen spectators, friends or relatives of offenders sitting in the front row, the ones in state blue.

Everyone remained standing as Judge Bob Gibbs looked over his court, his gaze moving from the public defender, a young guy Kathy didn't know, to a county deputy removing Dale Crowe's handcuffs. Now he was looking this way, where Kathy stood at the prosecution table with Marialena Reyes.

He said, "*Buenos dias,* ladies. I see we have the Latinas versus the Anglos today. Good luck, boys. You're gonna need it."

The young public defender smiled. Dale Crowe, standing next to him now, didn't smile. The judge turned as his court clerk, Mary Ellen, handed him a case folder. He glanced at it and then looked toward the court reporter relaxed behind his steno machine. "You want this one in English, don't you, Marty?"

Marty said, "Yes sir," without moving, as deadpan about it as the judge.

Looking this way again, Gibbs said, "Ladies, is that okay with you? We take it slow and talk Southern? Else I don't think it would be fair to the defense."

Marialena Reyes smiled and said, for the people of the state of Florida, "I would prefer it, Your Honor."

"Ms. Bacar, is it okay with you?"

The little bigot with his solemn face and dyed hair stared at her, waiting.

Kathy said, "It's Baker, Judge."

"Excuse me?"

"My name is Baker, not Bacar."

Gibbs looked down at the case file and up again.

"It was Bacar though, huh, before you changed it?"

"It was always Baker," Kathy said.

Let him figure it out.

Elmore Leonard, in his Maximum Bob, *Delacorte, 1991.*

---

screenplay for the film version of Chandler's novel *The Big Sleep*. The story is that he had to call up Chandler to find out what was going on. Chandler wasn't sure.

Yes, it will do.

Walker Percy, "There's a Contra in My Gumbo," in The New York Times Book Review, *January 4, 1987, p. 7.*

Clancy Sigal

Elmore Leonard has saved my sanity more than once. Ever since I chanced upon a copy of *Stick*—his novel about a Detroit-based ex-convict—at an airport bookstand, I never go abroad without at least one of his 14 books. Especially on transatlantic flights, when my anxieties are literally sky high, Leonard's stories of small-time American hoodlums so absorb me that time passes almost effortlessly. Yet the world he invites us into can hardly be called 'escapist'.

For example, his latest crime thriller almost stopped me cold on the first page, where the hero Jack Delaney's brother-in-law is 'prepping' a corpse for disposal at a New Orleans funeral parlour. Jack 'kept his eyes on Leo, who was squirting Dis-Spray, a disinfectant, into all of the guy's orifices, his nostrils, his mouth, his ears, all of his dark openings.' Try THAT at 30,000 feet. Clearly, Leonard is out to test the stomachs and patience of loyal fans like me—the first time I recall him trying to shock us in such grisly detail. But *Bandits* is also a 'first' in other ways, including political comment, interlaced with suggestions of religious sentiment, almost wholly absent from his past work. What overt sex was to Raymond Chandler—an embarrassing block—'commitment' may be to Leonard.

Among US crime writers I'm not sure where Elmore Leonard fits in. He's less romantic than Chandler, less interested in justice or fair play than Hammett. The greatest similarity probably is with America's poet laureate of losers, Nelson Algren, whose Frankie Machine (*The Man with the Golden Arm*) and Dove Linkhorn (*A Walk on the Wild Side*), would instantly recognise Leonard's downbeat protagonists as blood cousins. Algren and Leonard start from essentially the same premise: normal middle-class life is bullshit; existential reality begins at your lowest point—in Leonard's case usually in prison. A character's having 'done time' is the normal equivalent of an Oxbridge education. Even Leonard's few police heroes—in *Glitz* and *Cat Chaser*—are virtually indistinguishable from his low-life hoods. The important thing is street wisdom. As Roy, Jack Delaney's corrupt cop buddy in *Bandits* says, 'You have to get down there in the sewer with the assholes and talk to 'em man to man.'

Women don't often have a big role to play in Leonard novels, except—most successfully, in *La Brava*—as wily villainesses in the mould of Brigid O'Shaughnessy in *The Maltese Falcon.* I can see why. Like so many tough-guy writers, Leonard is both scared by, and soft on, dames. *Bandits'* Sister Lucy, a leper-nursing but (of course) sexy nun, tends to bring the racy action almost to a halt whenever she's in shot. (Leonard, who has written many pot-

boiling westerns, including successful screenplays for movies like *3.10 to Yuma,* possibly owes his largest debt not to literary predecessors but to Forties Hollywood film noir.) Depending on how you like your nuns, she's either attractively dedicated or a total weirdo, turned on in equal parts by causes and religious exaltation. The first time she makes love to Jack Delaney it's because she sees a bit of St Francis of Assisi in him. I hope to God that the author doesn't, because in all other ways he's the classic Elmore Leonard anti-hero.

Naturally, Jack has served time at the super-tough Angola State Farm, for cat-burgling hotel rooms. 'He had felt alive going into all those . . . rooms, to score but also to be doing it . . . ' This difference, between the deadness of conventional life and the vitality to be found only outside the law, is crucial to understanding, and possibly even identifying with, Leonard's men. Once Jack broke into a room only to find another thief there: his instant decision was to 'play it, see where it goes' by chatting with the intruder instead of slugging him. Now, after four years' parole-penance as assistant undertaker at the funeral home, Jack is bored by his 9-to-5 routine. Sister Lucy, rich oil man's daughter but lately devoted to the Sandinistas of Nicaragua where she too has 'done time' among the lepers, lures him into a five-million-dollar scam.

Before the car chases and bloodletting are over, Jack finds himself in a typically ambiguous Elmore Leonard trap. He is sexually, perhaps even spiritually, drawn to Sister Lucy and the possibility of a more exciting life for himself even—or especially—if it involves crime. But, in this cat's cradle of Contra killers, CIA agents, IRA gunrunners, crooked detectives, ex-cons and Latin American mercenaries, 'which were the good guys and which were the bad guys?' Jack's instincts are to stay small-time, low-profile, sceptical of large issues and the disguised con artists who push them. But he really wants to please Sister Lucy even if it means joining her criminal crusade to steal money from the murderous Somoza hireling, Colonel Diaz, and give it to Contra victims.

Although Leonard has (gingerly) touched upon politics before, *Bandits* is a departure from his usual neutral stance. The pleasure in this new novel comes not only from his superbly off-the-wall dialogue ('It perturbs me off', Roy irritably tells Jack), tight characterisation and fluid narrative, but from participating in Leonard's experiment with sexual and other politics. Like Jack Delaney, I'm suspicious of the effects of big ideas on little people— but what the hell, life is too boring to stay in a rut, right?

Clancy Sigal, "Which Are the Bad Guys?" in The Listener, *Vol. 117, No. 3006, April 9, 1987, p. 28.*

Andrew Greeley

Juvenal is a stigmatic. He reads minds. He heals the sick and then bleeds with the five wounds of Jesus. Does he really heal them? He thinks he does. Is he a saint? He's not sure. Probably not. Will his amazing powers get him into trouble in a world in which nothing seems sacred? Is the pope Catholic?

A sometime Franciscan brother, Juvenal (né Charlie Lawson) was eased out of the order because he cured too many natives in Brazil. He has taken refuge in a Catholic center for alcoholics where he minds his own business until a rogue's gallery of crooks tries to exploit him.

One is tempted to look again at the name of the author. Is this Elmore "Dutch" Leonard, the author of fabulous scam stories with vivid street dialogue and wry, slightly bent characters, the author of **Glitz** and **Stick** and **Cat Chaser**? You bet your life it is. Then why is he messing around with religion? Bad enough that there were an ex-nun and some liberation theologians in **Bandits.** Why a putative saint? Has Dutch, to use his own argot, got religion or something?

The author's personal religious life is his own business and no one else's. It suffices to say that it would be difficult though not impossible for a man who lacked faith to turn out as delicate and as subtle a work as **Touch**—skeptical yet accepting of an open universe in which wondrous events may occur even if they usually don't. More to the point, Leonard knows that there is only one area of human behavior more open to scams than religion, and that is sanctity. So **Touch** is alive with scams and alive, too, with the usual Dutch treat of kinky dialogue and kinkier characters. The book may be about a saint, but it is quintessential Leonard, a slim volume which provides page for page as much delight to Dutch addicts as any of his other books. Maybe a little more.

The principal scamsters are a crooked fundamentalist minister, a right-wing Catholic layman and a Donahue-like TV interviewer. Aided by a topless dancer whose boy Juvie cured, a reporter hungry for news, a Franciscan priest whose bowels were ruined in the jungle and other assorted Dutch-like characters, the bad guys close in on Juvie. His only ally is a tart- (to be euphemistic) tongued, hip young woman named Lynn who fakes alcoholism to check the miracle worker for the minister, is fascinated by the saint, and then falls in love with the man.

Unlike other Dutch heroes, Juvie (the nickname is the young woman's) cannot defend himself with his weapons or his fists. On his side he has only goodness. And we know what that's worth against scamsters, don't we? The final war in heaven between Juvie and Lynn and those who would exploit his powers is pure joy. I won't even give a hint about what happens and you'll never guess till the end.

The love affair between Juvie and Lynn is elegant and touching, the woman of the world who is an innocent and the innocent young man who knows more of the world's evil than she can ever imagine. They love each other with a simple, passionate yet—one must use the word—sweet intensity that makes their story the most appealing of all the appealing loves which are to be found in Leonard's books.

The post-Vatican II Catholic atmosphere has the right "feel," something which one could not say about many more self-consciously Catholic writers like Mary Gordon, who either do not know or have forgotten what it was (and is) like inside the Catholic community.

But does Elmore Leonard *really* believe in miracles? If you pick up the book expecting that in the end he will provide a purely natural explanation for Juvie's powers, you will be greatly disappointed—and you might have misunderstood the difference between ideology and storytelling. Leonard brings onstage a Jesuit theologian from Detroit University to present the church's traditional suspicion of such phenomena and offer the raw materials of a purely natural explanation. He leaves it to the reader, however, to decide why Juvenal heals and why he bleeds. He also seems to suggest that these are, as the extra-terrestrial says to Woody Allen in *Stardust Memories,* "wrong questions!"

Two final comments: in an introduction (in which he warns against "mystifying" interpretations of the story) Leonard notes wryly that **Touch** had been accepted and paid for by a publisher (Bantam, though he doesn't say so) which could not find a marketing angle for it and returned the rights to him after two years. Small wonder: the New York best-seller world is ill-equipped to deal with saints and miracles and even religion. I suspect the so-called book-reviewing fraternity will be similarly put off.

They will be as wrong as the decisionmakers at Bantam. With a modest shrug, Leonard ends his introduction by saying that "friends of mine who read a lot think it's my best book." They're right. (pp. 1-2)

Andrew Greeley, "Elmore Leonard's Miracle in Detroit," in Book World—The Washington Post, *August 23, 1987, pp. 1-2.*

Rhoda Koenig

The villains of Elmore Leonard's **Freaky Deaky** have an almost supernatural awfulness about them; they might be the stars of a horror film called *They Came From the Sixties: The Things That Would Not Die.* Twenty years ago, Robin Abbott and Skip Gibbs were into high times, protesting the fascist-imperialist state and ripping off the capitalist pigs. Reunited in Detroit, they reminisce about the days of acid and roses: " 'Man, we let it rip, didn't we? Dope, sex, and rock and roll. Old Mao and Karl Marx tried to keep up but didn't stand a chance against Jimi Hendrix, man, the Doors, the Dead, Big Brother and Janis.' " Skip tenderly recalls the first time he saw his old flame: " 'You had on a tank top and you were holding up a poster that said, real big, F-- THE DRAFT, waving it at the cops. I kept looking at you, your little nips showing in that thin material, your hair real long down your back. I said to myself, I think I'll score me some of that.' " After several such pages, you may decide that one of the less objectionable features of this pair is that they plant bombs.

Though Skip and Robin's diction has been subject to cryogenics, their motivations have moved with the times. Robin wants revenge against Mark Ricks and his wealthy brother, Woody, who turned them in to the FBI, but, more important, she wants to score her some of Woody's millions. One obstacle in her path is Donnell Lewis, a former Black Panther reduced to being chauffeur, chaperon, and nurse to the alcoholic, addle-brained Woody; another is Chris Mankowski, a detective who turns up to investigate a charge of sexual assault lodged against Woody by one of his party guests and gets on to the scent of manipulation and murder.

For all the high-intensity emotions and action, *Freaky Deaky* is a rather weightless affair. Most of it is dialogue, easy to read but not too demanding of the reader's attention—your eye slides down the page unimpeded by any narration to create pacing and suspense. It is perfectly functional but in no way memorable, as all but one of the characters never rise above stereotypes or have any inner lives (unless one counts such passages as Robin's musing, "What she needed was a release, an upper that wasn't dope. A guy who could lighten her mood. Not Skip, he was basically a downer. . . . She liked Skip, but he always had b.o. Which used to be okay, but not now. Having b.o. was no longer in").

The weightlessness is emotional and moral too. From the first, Chris has his eye on Greta, the girl who cries rape under somewhat dubious circumstances, and later becomes her lover; yet, when he interviews the fat, slobbering Woody, we sense none of his indignation or disgust. And when Woody offers Greta a $25,000 payoff, she blandly accepts it as compensation for her pain and suffering, and Chris doesn't object. Without any redeeming stylistic value, any hard-edged, glittering cynicism, this lack of distance between debauchee and victim collapses our reaction into a shrug and a "So what?"

The one character Leonard seems engaged and amused by is the desperately scheming, déclassé Donnell. Once a revolutionary stud, he now cleans up Woody's bed and bathroom after nights of overindulgence and makes sure he doesn't choke on his Chinese-takeout meals, all the while reminding the enormous baby of his employee's usefulness and utter devotion. Scenes in which a grossly obvious con artist fails to sucker a supremely gullible pigeon are always funny, and the almost vaudevillian routine Leonard has contrived for the two is no exception. While Woody, more forgetful than most humans outside the Oval Office, keeps getting distracted from making a new will, Donnell has to beat back his rage and frustration and cajole him with gentle suggestions: " 'Go through the alphabet. *A . . . B . . . C . . . D.* Anybody you like start with *D,* Mr. Woody?' " Yet not all of Donnell's Panther claws have been pulled. When the law starts to intrude on his scam, he gets right on the phone and arranges for the persistent detective to lose the use of a leg.

What perplexed me most about *Freaky Deaky* was not any kink in the plot but the cover blurb calling Leonard "the greatest crime writer of our time, perhaps ever." Where's the gritty sense of place one gets from, just to name the two Boston boys, Robert B. Parker and George V. Higgins? Where's the deft wit of Dashiell Hammett or the lurid quasi-poetry and anguished loss of honor of Raymond Chandler (unless we let the Brits have him)? This is a book a lot of people will be taking on vacation, but I can't imagine too many of them bringing it home.

Rhoda Koenig, in a review of "Freaky Deaky," in New York *Magazine, Vol. 21, No. 18, May 2, 1988, p. 86.*

Andrew Vachss

Readers are consumers. Consumers are critics. Some critics are only enamored of their own discoveries, equating growing popularity with a dulling of the edge. The neighborhood restaurant that serves the best French onion soup in town is worthy of raves when those critics first introduce it to their friends, but it does a fast fade when there is a wait for a table because of the crowds. It happens to writers, too.

For years, Elmore Leonard's work was discussed in the hushed, reverent tones reserved for literary celebrities. Then came *Glitz,* the publisher's dream, the "breakthrough book." Now Leonard writes Best Sellers, and the popular line is that his older stuff was better. *Killshot* is Leonard's answer.

For this book, Leonard steps into the ring with what got him there. No high-concept plots, no glitz. Parallel narratives in the same time zone, all in the third person. Nothing filtered, nothing interactive. Whatever his characters say is their truth. No complex interior monologues, no introspection—what they do is what they think.

Leonard's realism is his own brand. If a hitman getting his instructions from a mob boss over the phone seems strange to you, if the hitman taking a used Cadillac instead of cash seems off-center, if a federal marshal turns out to be a bully and a rapist, that's just the way it is. Things happen, you know?

Leonard has his own take on crime and criminals. His characters may kill for cash, but they're not "professional" in any sense of the word. They're chronics—small-time, small-minded losers. Richie, the grinning sociopath who kills when he gets upset. Armand, a.k.a. the Blackbird, an Indian hitman who kills when he gets paid. Ferris, the U.S. marshal, who threatens the people he is paid to protect. You never know why, and you never care.

This is a deliberate choice, a matter of style. When Leonard tells us about Wayne and Carmen, an ironworker and his real-estate saleswoman wife, we get a wealth of detail, a richness of texture. The good people are human, and we do care about them. The laconic, slightly downbeat style opens just enough to let the reader's empathy loose.

The plot? Armand is on his way to the place of his birth when Richie decides to steal his car at gunpoint. Armand quickly turns the tables with his own gun. Richie just as quickly proposes that Armand join him in an extortion scheme involving a real estate broker. They form an instant partnership and retreat to the cottage occupied by Richie's girlfriend, a middle-aged ex-prison guard who makes all their meals in a microwave and dreams of traveling to Graceland to commune with the spirit of Elvis.

When Armand and Richie visit the broker, Wayne is there with his wife, Carmen. There's a fight, Wayne wins, and Armand and Richie retreat. The cops come. Turns out Richie and Armand are real bad guys, and Wayne and Carmen are in real danger. Time for the Witness Protection Program, which finds the couple a safehouse in another state.

Turns out Richie himself was in the Program. Seems he stabbed his own cellmate during a prison stretch and then successfully blamed it on the inmate who had ordered the hit. So he knows how it all works. (How Richie pulled this off is a mystery indeed—he says he was told to either kill his cellmate or be killed himself, but instead of informing he commits the murder and then turns rat.)

Richie and Armand find out Carmen is coming home soon to be with her sickly mother, while Wayne has taken a job out of town. Meanwhile, the federal marshal responsible for the couple's safety has announced his own plans for a sexual attack on Carmen, and he's heading for the safehouse. Things happen.

The cops are no match for the evil loose in the world, so the solid citizens have to reach deep inside themselves for the strength to do what has to be done. What's different here is that when it comes down to the crunch, Carmen has to carry the weight all by herself—carry it or be crushed by it.

For those who see Leonard's work as a parabolic curve, peaking, perhaps, at *City Primeval,* this book is a step back up the mountain. *Killshot* lacks the plotting of *Unknown Man No. 89,* and its portrait of amoral menace isn't up to *City Primeval* but any long-time fan will feel right at home.

Elmore Leonard hasn't left his fight in the gym. He's lost a little something off the jab, and his footwork isn't as dazzling as it once was. Sometimes it seems as if he's fighting on instinct, working well within himself, setting a comfortable pace, not taking chances. There'll be no first round TKO here, but the old master still packs the equalizer. It's called Narrative Force, and Leonard has more of it than most writers do at their absolute peak. (pp. 1, 4)

> *Andrew Vachss, "Back in Top Form: Tough, Honest Elmore Leonard," in* Chicago Tribune—Books, *April 9, 1989, pp. 1, 4.*

David Geherin

Novelist Walker Percy spoke for many readers and critics alike when in his review of *Bandits* in the *New York Times Book Review* he concluded: "[Leonard] is as good as the blurbs say." But Percy was also one of the few to ask the key question: "Why is Elmore Leonard so good?" Attention has often centered on Leonard's long-overdue rise to popular and critical acclaim after decades of obscurity. However, little effort has been made to explain the reasons behind the artistic excellence of his work. In large part this is due to the seeming artlessness of his novels. As Donald Westlake put it, "He's so good, you don't notice what he's up to." But seeming artlessness is not artlessness. Fiction, no matter how natural it appears, is created, and in Leonard's case, created by an artist with rare gifts.

Leonard's literary excellence is the result of artistic genius coupled with an approach to writing that can be expressed in three main tenets: (1) Get It Right; (2) Let It Happen; (3) Be Natural.

1. GET IT RIGHT: For Leonard this means doing research.

Research has played an essential role in his fiction since his earliest westerns. Often the purpose of the research is simply to gather specific information: how do the local police investigate a killing? how does a drug dealer launder money? how does a casino surveillance system work? how do you make a bomb? Research of this type enhances the realism of the fiction by insuring authenticity down to the smallest detail.

Leonard is not the sort of writer (like James Michener, for example) who does an enormous amount of research and then tries to incorporate as much of it as possible into his novel. He uses only what is appropriate, and what he uses he works in very unobtrusively. The factual information is never allowed to impede the flow of the story. A reader of *Bandits,* for example, won't be given every detail about how to conduct an embalming (which, based on his eye-witness research, Leonard could give); but because Jack Delaney is a mortician's assistant, the reader will be given enough details to convince him of the authenticity of the scenes of him at work.

What Leonard's research does for *him* is even more valuable: it provides him a clear picture in his own mind of his main characters. He will often develop an entire history of a character before beginning to write. His characters then become as lifelike to him as real people. Even if much of this background information is never included in the novel, it nonetheless gives Leonard a vivid feel for his characters. An illustration of how real his characters are to him is that he was prompted to write *Stick* when a glance at the calendar reminded him that Ernest Stickley, whom he had used seven years earlier in *Swag,* was due to be released from prison and he wondered what he was up to now.

In this process of familiarization, names are very important. "I love names. I can't get a character to talk until he has the right name," Leonard admits. (He also has a liking for certain names: there are multiple Ryans, Majestyks, Moons, Rendas, and Lewises in his novels.) *Bandits*'s Jack Delaney, for example, began as Frank Matisse, but for the first hundred pages or so he wouldn't talk very much. When Leonard changed his name to Jack Matisse, he opened up a little. When he finally became Jack Delaney, he came fully to life.

More important than getting the name right is getting the character's sound right. If there is any one quality that sets Leonard's novels apart from the works of most other contemporary writers, it is this, his remarkable ability to capture the sounds of his characters.

Leonard is a great listener. He possesses what one critic [J. D. Reed] calls a "Panasonic ear" capable of recording the exact sounds he hears. Leonard doesn't use a tape recorder. When he listens, he isn't listening for specific dialogue but for rhythms of speech and cadences of sound. He has a particular liking for a certain sound. "It's the sound of savvy people, or people who *think* they're savvy and talk that way. To me, they're so much more interesting than educated people. . . . I guess I'm still a kid on the corner of Woodward Avenue listening to my friends, who were all blue-collar kids."

Leonard is also a great transcriber. He is able to reproduce on the page what he hears so exactly, so true to life, that his writing sounds not so much written but, in the words of one critic, "as if it had been wiretapped." He even fooled the Detroit police who were the subjects of the profile he wrote for the *Detroit News*. "They swore all the lines in it were tape-recorded," Leonard said, "which none of it was." What he relied on was his ability to get their sound exactly right. Though he sometimes uses specific lines he picks up from TV or that are given to him by his wife and others, almost all his dialogue is made up. It just sounds real.

The range of sounds he captures is impressive. He is a true virtuoso of voices. Whether it's a black man from Detroit, a Moskito Indian from Nicaragua, a redneck from the Florida swamps, an ex-beauty queen from Oklahoma, a Marielito boat-lifter, a revolutionary from Ireland, or even Ronald Reagan himself, Leonard creates a distinct voice. He only uses words—be they racist, obscene, or ungrammatical—that are appropriate to the specific character. Also, he follows the rules of grammar his characters do. A line like the following—"You mean like Sea World, they put on the porpoise show, a guy rides a killer whale, Shamu?"—may not follow the rules of proper syntax, but that's exactly how some people really talk. What Raymond Chandler said about Dashiell Hammett applies just as well to Leonard: "He put these people down on paper as they were, and he made them talk and think in the language they customarily used for these purposes."

Leonard does much more than simply mimic dialects. Getting the sound right enables him to expose the way his characters think. Once they open their mouths, they open their minds to us. Leonard prefers using multiple points of view rather than limiting himself to first-person narration (which he used only once, in *Hombre*). This frees him to employ a variety of sounds as well as a variety of interior monologues. He uses these monologues to express a character's thoughts in his or her distinctive language. Leonard never has to describe his characters; they reveal themselves.

Much has been made of the Elmore Leonard sound: tough, deadpan, funny. But the term "Elmore Leonard sound" is a misnomer. It's never his voice one hears, only the sounds of his characters. Leonard is a skilled ventriloquist whose own lips never move. He always remains in character, maintaining the sounds of his characters throughout the entire novel. There are similar voices in some of his novels simply because there are certain types of characters he enjoys using: cops, ex-cons, smooth-talking con artists, guys trying to sound tough. But there are always distinctive new voices to give a fresh sound to each book.

Leonard's uncanny ability to impersonate so many different characters demands great empathy on his part. He finds it helps to imagine all his characters, good and bad, as human beings; his heavies have to face many of the same problems (what to wear, when to eat, how to get along with their wives or mothers) that his good guys do. "The only premise I begin with is that my characters are human beings," Leonard says, "and I'm going to treat

them honestly, despite their inclinations—not approving of those who commit criminal acts—but rather accepting the fact impersonally, without making moral judgments." One reason his bad guys are so convincing is that they are treated with such understanding.

Leonard's good guys and bad guys are just ordinary people. His antagonists sometimes have good qualities; his protagonists, who are no storybook heroes, are sometimes even criminals themselves. By alternating point of view between the hero and the villain as he often does, Leonard further narrows the distinction between the two. Because there is no controlling authorial voice in the novel, both points of view arc given equal time, so to speak. This has the effect of forcing the reader to relate to both on a common human level. Leonard doesn't expect the reader to overlook the actions of his bad guys; but demonstrating that it is real people who perform such awful deeds contributes to the potent realism of his fiction.

2. LET IT HAPPEN: Once Leonard begins writing his book, he switches to an entirely different approach. Instead of depending on research, he now relies on instinct. To borrow a phrase uttered by several of his characters, Leonard's philosophy of composition can be described as "letting it happen." As intimately as he knows his various characters, he never knows in advance what they'll do. Once he begins a book, he lets them "tell" him what will happen next.

"I hate to plot," Leonard concedes. He used to plot out his books very carefully; in fact, some of his early novels were based on detailed screenplay treatments he had first written. Now he no longer worries about plot. He knows one will take shape once he creates interesting characters and comes up with a situation that forces them to rub against each other. (He also concedes it is useful to have a gun somewhere in his story. "I don't have any desire to fire guns," he says, "but they come in handy in a book.")

Leonard likes unpredictable characters; an unplotted story affords him a greater opportunity to take advantage of such characters. Also, not plotting his books in advance insures that the action will be natural and unforced. In many instances, Leonard doesn't know what will happen more than a scene or two ahead. Usually he doesn't even know how his novel will end until he is almost finished writing it. (The ending of *Bandits* didn't occur to him until three days before he completed the novel.) He figures that if he's curious about what will happen next, the reader will be too. What is surprising to him will then likely also be surprising to the reader.

Leonard's admission that his plots are improvised as he goes along may seem odd coming from a writer whose novels are often hailed as models of invention. But just as he fooled the Detroit police into thinking their dialogue was tape-recorded, Leonard fools many into assuming his clever plots are worked out in advance. One reviewer [Neil Johnson in *New York Times Book Review*, Nov. 27, 1983], for example, praised the denouement in *LaBrava* for "plausibly [resolving] an ironic plot that was fully thought through before either writer or reader began." In truth, the ending was suggested to him at the last moment by his wife, and the plot, as usual, developed only as the novel was being written.

Because he is not tied down to any continuing character or specific type of novel, Leonard has no preconceived notions as to the direction his story must take. This allows him the freedom to take advantage of the unforeseen, to proceed in an unplanned direction. His improvisational plots are also perfectly suited to his protagonists, who often stumble into unexpected situations and get sucked into the action. In addition, Leonard's openness allows for the emergence of so many "sleeper" characters, people like Walter Kouza, Jiggs Scully, Jackie Garbo, etc., who weren't planned as major characters but who sprang to life on the page and demanded a larger role.

"If I were a half-decent narrative writer, " Leonard admits, "I wouldn't adopt the storytelling method that I do." His method of compensating for his narrative deficiency is to devote all his attention to his characters, who then take over the task of storytelling for him. As soon as he hears their voices clearly, interesting things begin to happen to propel the story along. Aside from an occasional slackness at the beginning (e.g., *Cat Chaser*) or in the middle of a novel (e.g., *Bandits*), his technique usually produces a well-paced novel with plenty of surprises and satisfying twists.

Despite the unplanned method of their composition, Leonard's novels are far from shapeless. Though he begins without a definite plot in mind, Leonard takes great care in the organization of individual scenes, rearranging them to achieve the best pace and rhythm and the most effective balance between action and exposition. If there is too much exposition in one scene, he will break it up by intercutting it with another scene. *Freaky Deaky* originally opened with the reunion scene between Robin and Skip in which they talk about the good old days. Sensing that this was too much exposition at the beginning of the novel, Leonard shifted scenes in order to begin with Chris Mankowski's last day on the job. Now action precedes exposition.

Leonard also takes care in shaping individual scenes. Many of his scenes end with a punch line, a zinger that puts a finishing touch on the preceding action or dialogue. He also takes care to get the right perspective for each scene, often rewriting from a different perspective to achieve better effect. As an experienced writer of screenplays, Leonard knows the importance of moving a story scene by scene. Few do it better than he does.

3. BE NATURAL: A corollary to his philosophy of "letting it happen" is "let it happen naturally." Leonard avoids situations that are artificial, contrived or clichéd. His readers will not get what convention dictates but what develops naturally out of the characters and the situation. He was inspired to write *Hombre*, for example, because of his impatience with all those "white flag" situations he was used to seeing on TV, where gunfighters followed the rules of polite gentlemen. In his novel, after John Russell's opponent approaches waving the white flag of surrender, Russell shoots him in the back as he walks away. One gets the sense that this is exactly how such a scene would be played out in real life.

Leonard's novels have such a natural quality about them because he rigorously avoids stereotypes and clichés. In his books personal confrontations between characters don't always result in fisticuffs or gunplay, as they invariably do in the works of lesser writers who lazily depend on formula. Leonard likes to avoid the expected. He also likes the unexpected when it comes to violence in his books. In *Bandits,* for example, Franklin de Dios walks up behind Jerry Boylan and shoots him in the head while he's standing at a urinal. His action is shocking simply because it is so surprising. And so realistic.

Leonard also avoids anything gimmicky in his prose. A writer like himself who takes such care to eliminate his own voice from his novels isn't going to do anything showy to draw attention to his writing. In *The Switch* a character comments on a local TV sportscaster's hokey attempt to sound like W. C. Fields reporting a Detroit Tiger victory: "Why don't they just say it, without all that cute shit?" he asks. Leonard's writing never contains any "cute shit." No clever images, no fancy descriptions, no flowery language. Some of his characters (e.g., Barry Stam in *Stick* or Jackie Garbo in *Glitz*) might try hard to be cute, but that's because of who *they* are. Leonard himself is never cute, never showboaty.

Maurice Zola's assessment of Joe LaBrava's photography expresses this quality of Leonard's prose: "He's not pretentious like a lot of 'em. . . . You don't see any bullshit here. He shoots barefaced fact. He's got the feel and he makes *you* feel it." Later in that novel, Joe LaBrava quotes from a newspaper review of his photographs: "The aesthetic sub-text of his work is the systematic exposure of artistic pretension." This is exactly what the *Village Voice* reviewer said about Leonard's work. LaBrava's put-down, "I thought I was just taking pictures" is not so much a repudiation of the critic's statement about Leonard's avoidance of pretense than a comment on the pretentious way he said it.

Leonard's artistic success isn't a matter simply of doing a little research and following a few rules of composition. If it were that easy, anybody could write as well as he does. It takes genius to do it as well as Leonard. It also takes a particular kind of genius to create humor as effectively as he does. Juvenal, the stigmatic hero of *Touch,* says that "being serious doesn't mean you have to be solemn." Leonard's novels are about serious matters—murder, kidnapping, extortion, robbery—but their presentation is often exhilaratingly funny.

Leonard's characters are the primary source of humor. Their actions aren't ordinarily comic, but their words (and often their unspoken comments about what others say) frequently are. Leonard's novels abound with snappy one-liners ("I spent most of my dough on booze, broads and boats and the rest I wasted"; "Jerry wasn't the brightest guy I ever married"; "If bullshit was worth anything, Jack, you'd have the fertilizer market sewed up") and brilliant exchanges between characters:

"How come you broke the guy's arm?"

"I didn't mean to. He raised it to protect his head."

Or,

"You never said a kind word about mama in your life."

"I couldn't think of any."

Or,

"I read in the paper that in the U.S., I think it was just this country, a woman is beaten or physically abused something like every eighteen seconds."

Roy said, "You wouldn't think that many women get out of line, would you?"

Some of the biggest laughs come from the monologues of his great talkers, characters like Walter Kouza, Jiggs Scully, or Jackie Garbo. Leonard uses monologues far more sparingly than George V. Higgins. He resists the temptation to let his talkers go on too long and upset the balance of the novel. But when he has a character with the gift of gab, he knows how to use him to great effect.

The key to Leonard's humor is that the comic lines are usually spoken by characters who aren't intentionally funny. With a few notable exceptions like Barry Stam in *Stick,* Leonard's characters don't try to be funny. They just are, in a deadpan manner. One reason Leonard disliked the film version of *Stick* was that the actors paused after their lines for a laugh, or smirked as they delivered the lines. For best effect, his lines must be read straight, for they are spoken by characters who aren't aware that what they say is humorous. However, because of their attitudes and distinct speech mannerisms, what they say often makes one laugh.

Leonard currently enjoys a reputation as America's greatest living crime writer. And deservedly so. While it may be going a bit too far to claim, as [Fred Lutz] did, that "Leonard very well may be, strictly in terms of literature, one of the most meaningful and important writers working today," he has no peer when it comes to writing uncompromisingly realistic novels about crime and criminals.

Leonard is characteristically modest in describing his artistic aims: "My purpose is to entertain and tell a story," he declares simply. But as a proven master of storytelling, he has a genuine talent for keeping the reader hungrily turning the pages while offering him great entertainment along the way. But like many others who write realistic crime fiction, Leonard is more than a mere entertainer; he's also a social historian.

His crime novels paint a colorful portrait of an often overlooked segment of American life (perhaps more correctly, American lowlife). His subject isn't life among the rich and famous, or as it is lived behind the well-tended front lawns of suburbia. He's staked out as his territory the shadowy borderline between the cops and the crooks. His characters are usually simple people—jewel thieves and chauffeurs, blackmailers and process servers, con artists and morticians' assistants—who must work for a living.

It's just that in his books, many of these individuals pursue occupations that take them outside the law. Out of such characters Leonard has created a series of novels noted for their drama, excitement, humor, thrills, and plain human interest.

Some have attempted to explain Leonard's popularity in terms of the rising crime rate in America. Roger Kaplan in *Commentary* [May 1985] argued that "Leonard's popularity . . . has increased as the Hobbesian view of society that his novels project has gained adherents." John Sutherland, in the *London Review of Books* [Sept. 5, 1985], voiced a similar notion: "In its popularity, Leonard's fiction answers to a widely-held sense of hopelessness about the bad guys. You can't beat them."

But the fact is that his novels would likely be just as popular (and certainly just as good) if there were no crime in them at all. The success of his work isn't due to any increase in crime in America but rather to his ability to make his criminals come alive. Though his characters are frequently involved in crime, his primary focus is always on the person instead of the crime. A specific crime only serves to bring out the features of an individual—greed, revenge, a hankering for excitement—that make that person so fascinating to read about.

Choosing Leonard's best novel is difficult (Peter S. Prescott argues that "the margin of difference between Leonard's better and lesser works would admit, with difficulty, a butterfly's wing"). The overall excellence and consistent quality of his fiction is impressive. The novels since *City Primeval* are particularly rich in texture, colorful setting, and vivid characterization, and they contain some of the most entertaining dialogue in the business. The best of these—*Split Images, Cat Chaser, Stick, LaBrava, Glitz, Freaky Deaky*—are among the finest crime novels ever written.

Leonard's fiction represents a major achievement in crime writing. Though his novels do not belong to the Dashiell Hammett—Raymond Chandler school of hard-boiled writing, they do belong on the same shelf with the works of those two other giants. For the sake of convenience, novels by all three writers are usually shelved in the mystery sections of bookstores and public libraries. The fact is, however, in their artistry, originality, and impact, Leonard's novels deserve a permanent place beside those of Hammett and Chandler on the shelf marked simply Outstanding American Fiction. (pp. 126-36)

> *David Geherin, in his* Elmore Leonard, Continuum, *1989, 158 p.*

Whitney Balliett

Book by book (he publishes almost one a year), the tireless and ingenious genre novelist Elmore Leonard is painting an intimate, precise, funny, frightening, and irresistible mural of the American underworld. This mural is peopled with thieves, embezzlers, kidnappers, loan sharks, drug dealers, rapists, and killers, but there is no camp in it and no caricature. Leonard, laughing just loud enough to let us know that he has everything in perspective, slowly reveals his characters as the fools and clowns they are; inevitably, they go too far and are destroyed. This usually happens somewhere near the end of his books, and before it does we hear, see, and even smell these people. Leonard treats them with the understanding and the detailed attention that Jane Austen gives her Darcys and Emma Woodhouses. They have heritages and pedigrees. We learn where they came from and how they think and communicate—occasionally on a frequency we can barely understand. We learn how, for instance, a man graduates with a master's in business administration from the University of Michigan, teaches accounting, is fired for running a part-time abortion service (ten per cent of the fee), embezzles from a chain of dress shops, and, slipping gradually sidewise, ends up seven years after his graduation as a blackmailer and killer. But Leonard never lectures or preaches or points a finger at his figures or at society; evil suborns evil in his books, then self-destructs. At the center of this turbulence are his wondrous heroes, who survive, no matter how badly scarred. The heroes include ex-cons, a California melon grower, a Miami cop, the owner of a Detroit machine-tool company, the wife of an ironworker, an ex-marine and Pompano Beach-motel owner, an ex-Secret Service agent turned Walker Evans-type photographer, and, in his newest book, *Get Shorty* a reformed loan shark who works his way into the movie business.

Get Shorty is not red-tomato Leonard. Its plot within a plot—the loan shark, Chili Palmer, uses the story we are reading as his first script idea—moves at a surprisingly slow speed, and there is little of the tension that made *Killshot* and *Glitz* almost unbearable. The best thing to do when Leonard falters—he did recently in *Bandits* and *Freaky Deaky,* too—is to reread *Mr. Majestyk,* or *LaBrava,* or *The Hunted,* or even one of the lesser-known Leonards, such as the marvellous *52 Pick-Up,* first published in 1974 and now available in paperback. It tells how the middle-aged owner of a machine-tool shop, Harry Mitchell, is blackmailed by three men: the Michigan-business-school graduate, a fat alcoholic who runs a "modelling" agency, and a drug addict and thief. (One afternoon, as a lark, the thief and his girl, who is got up in a blond wig and dark glasses, hijack a Detroit Gray Line sightseeing bus, strip the thirty-six passengers of their money and jewelry, and net over four thousand dollars.) Mitchell, a Second World War ace, is an honorable, conscientious gent with an attractive wife and two children, but he has taken up with a girl just a year older than his daughter. She turns out to be working with the blackmailers, who repeatedly film Mitchell and the girl. They show Mitchell the films and demand a hundred and five thousand dollars. Then they kill the girl, using Mitchell's licensed .38 Smith & Wesson, which they have stolen from his house. Mitchell refuses to buckle; slowly piecing things together, he figures out who the blackmailers are and begins closing in on *them.* The addict shoots the alcoholic, and the Michigan graduate shoots the addict and is then blown up by Mitchell in a stolen truck in which he expects to pick up the fifty-two-thousand-dollar payment Mitchell has promised him. Along the way, Leonard gives us the credo by which his heroes live: Mitchell "felt his confidence coming back and, with it, the beginning of an urge to get up and do something. That was the essence of the

good feeling: to be able to remain calm and relax while he was keyed up and confident. Never panic. Never run. Face whatever had to be faced. Be practical, reasonable, up to a point. And if reason doesn't work, get up and kick it in the teeth."

Leonard did not get his due until the early eighties, after he had published twenty books. (The earliest are creditable Westerns, written mostly in the fifties and sixties, and already full of recognizable Leonard figures.) He has a brilliant ear—he is as good as George Higgins was in his first books, and makes Chandler and Cain sound Victorian—and his prose, which is often a curious echo of his dialogue, is wasteless and limber. He is a master of narrative (he can make a story walk or run at will), and his plots are as intricate as Wilkie Collins'. He is a poet of the vernacular, who almost never uses metaphors or similes. When he does, it's a beauty: "Chili's gaze moved from Ronnie the fool to Bo Catlett the dude, the man composed, elbows on the chair arms, his fingertips touching to form a tan-skinned church, a ruby ring for a stained-glass window." Leonard takes great care with his locales—among them are Detroit, New Orleans, Los Angeles, Atlantic City, and Florida. He is particularly good on the east coast of Florida, and that strange, spooky city Miami jumps off the page. So do his throwaway social bits. This one is from *Cat Chaser* (1982): "Jerry was a retired insurance salesman, sixty-seven, who cocked his golf cap to one side, slapped his broken blood vessels with Old Spice and went after lonely widows who'd invite him up to their condominiums for dinner, happy to cook for somebody again, have some fun."

Leonard's strongest books make you stand up and sit down a lot during their tight moments, but *Get Shorty,* despite its occasional white-knuckle passages, belongs to that vast vinegary canon known as the Hollywood novel. There is a crafty, movie-wise Roger Corman producer named Harry Zimm, whose reputation rests on pictures called "Slime Creatures" and "Grotesque, Part Two." There is a sharp, tough, needling female big-studio producer and an equally sharp retired actress, who became famous for her screams in Harry's pictures. Best of all is the portrait Leonard gives us of a seven-million-dollar-a-picture star named Michael Weir. (Leonard's names are perfect. They make the characters they are attached to reverberate in just the right way.) Weir is a fine actor, a De Niro or a William Hurt, but he's spoiled, indecisive, and empty-headed. He is having dinner in a Hollywood restaurant with Harry and Chili Palmer:

> Then Michael had to look at the menu for a while, Harry willing to bet anything he wouldn't order from it. It was an unwritten rule in Hollywood, actors never ordered straight from the menu; they'd think of something they had to have that wasn't on it, or they'd tell exactly how they wanted the entrée prepared, the way their mother back in Queens used to fix it. The seven-million-dollar actor in the jacket a bum wouldn't wear told the headwaiter he felt like an omelet, hesitant about it, almost apologetic. Could he have a cheese omelet with shallots, but with the shallots only slightly browned? The headwaiter said yes, of course. Then could he have some

kind of light tomato sauce over it with just a hint of garlic but, please, no oregano? Of course. And fresh peas in the tomato sauce? Harry wanted to tell him, Michael, you can have any fucking thing you want. You want boiled goat? They'll send out for it if they don't have one. Jesus, what you had to go through with actors. The ideal situation would be if you could make movies without them.

Leonard likes little inside jokes. When Chili Palmer first meets the smooth, deadly black dude Bo Catlett, he asks him if he is related to the great swing drummer Sid Catlett. Bo, looking dreamy, says, "Big Sid, huh? No, I'm from another tribe." Chances are that Bo, born around the time of Catlett's death, in 1951, would never have heard of him. Leonard wants us to know that *he* has, though. (pp. 106-07)

Whitney Balliett, "Elmore Leonard in Hollywood," in The New Yorker, *Vol. LXVI, No. 29, September 3, 1990, pp. 106-07.*

Nick Kimberley

From the heroic prolixity of *The Law at Randado* and *Last Stand at Saber River* to the guttural bark of *Stick, Swag* and *Glitz,* the titles of Elmore Leonard's novels write their own chapter in the life-story of American fiction.

The long titles belong to the Westerns with which Leonard began his publishing career in the early Fifties. The one-worders belong to thrillers with which he has established himself as one of the most viscerally exciting novelists in America today.

When Leonard started writing, the Western novel, like the Western movie, was an ailing genre, although it has never quite been killed off, as Cormac McCarthy demonstrated in 1985 with his astonishing Wild West allegory *Blood Meridian.* If Leonard never aspired to the mythic beauty of McCarthy's novel, he was still an efficient, alert writer of Westerns. His men bore the scars of their flawed manhoods, his women were tough and independent, his native Americans were proud.

Still, the market for this fiction was waning, and Leonard has not been ashamed of being a writer in the marketplace. In the Sixties, he belatedly made the switch from Western wilderness to urban jungle. The crucial year seems to have been 1969, a year in which he published (but not necessarily wrote) a Western, *Valdez is Coming;* a transitional piece of period mayhem, *The Moonshine War,* set in the Thirties; and an utterly contemporary thriller, *The Big Bounce.*

To an extent, Leonard's contemporary thrillers borrow generic devices from his Westerns, a fact he wrily acknowledged in the subtitle of his 1980 novel *City Primeval: High Noon in Detroit.* Leonard's characters transformed themselves from tough, decent loners battling against the Frontier to tough, decent loners battling against the City Primeval. The violence of the land, which generates so much of the tension in Westerns, has been supplanted by the violence of uncontrollable psychotics, whose capacity for maiming and murder threatens the equipoise of the more or less balanced heroes.

Not that Leonard's heroes are straight-ahead good guys. Chili in *Get Shorty* is a case in point. He's a likeable enough sort of chap, works hard and does not gladly suffer fools. But his job is to make sure that people who borrow money from his none too scrupulous bosses don't welsh on their debts. When people find out what he does, they assume that his method of collection is to break a few bones, shoot a few bullets. But that assumption is his greatest weapon—that, and the ability to say, 'Look at me' and sound as if he means business.

Chili, then, is not a wholesome fellow. He comes from Brooklyn but lives in Miami, one of Leonard's favoured locations (the other is Detroit) and ends up working in Hollywood, a place Leonard knows a lot about, having sold film rights to most of his novels—Westerns and thrillers—and written a few screenplays. In pursuit of his trade in Tinseltown, he runs up against colourful and occasionally frightening villainy, gets drawn into engaging and unlikely plotting, but never loses track of his purpose: to get the money.

In outline, Leonard's plots always seem routine. What matters is the skill with which he assembles his gallery of deeply flawed human beings, the ease with which they talk dirty and influence people, the messy scrapes they get themselves into. And through it all runs a rich vein of humour—Leonard likes his characters, even when they have a Smith & Wesson .38 in their hands. At the risk of making him sound worthy, he tackles those potentially deadening issues of class, race and gender with a wit that few supposedly more serious writers can manage. Instead of being dilemmas to be addressed, that triad generates confrontation and action, the base ingredients of the thriller.

Of course, there are problems. I don't share the point of view that sees Leonard's work as a reflection of the decay of the social dimension in American life, but it is certainly true that the infallible ability of his heroes (not always men) to put things right can be wearing. It was not ever thus. In what critical literature may come to see as Leonard's middle period—say, 1975-85—the novels were more ambiguous, unresolved, their moral ground a quagmire rather than a rock. And Leonard is now so sure of his skill, and of his readers, that he can present pages of dialogue as if they were just a script. Of course, this is a wry joke on Chili's changed perceptions now that he's in Hollywood, but, while dialogue is the crucial medium of the novel, it can't be reduced to the level of screenplay.

Perhaps now that he has critical acclaim Leonard leavens the toughness of his earlier thrillers with a touch of ironic self-consciousness. That's what *serious* novelists do—the dustjacket of *Get Shorty* quotes one critic's view that Leonard has 'completed the transition from thriller-writer to novelist'. If that's the case, I hope he has a return ticket. Genuine thriller-writers are thin on the ground. (pp. 30-1)

Nick Kimberley, "Thrill Seekers," in The Listener, *Vol. 124, No. 3185, October 4, 1990, pp. 30-1.*

Elmore Leonard [Interview with Jean W. Ross]

[*Ross*]: *The desire to write books survived the years of working for an ad agency, when you had to get up at five in the morning to devote two hours a day to fiction, and later the years after you quit the agency to write full-time but had to take on free-lance commercial work to pay the bills. Was doing the fiction then always a pleasure on some level, despite the pain?*

[Leonard]: No, it wasn't a pleasure *yet,* and I wasn't sure that it was ever going to be anything but work, which I don't consider it now. It was hard. I had an idea what kind of sound I wanted, and I pretty much had it in my westerns, in the fifties. But I hadn't yet discovered what I think you might call my most natural sound, which is a little more easygoing and laid back. I was more serious then. I hadn't yet discovered that if I didn't try to write, it would come out better.

I was determined, for some reasons, to tell stories, to write stories and novels—I'm not sure why: I've just always liked stories. And I liked movies. I chose westerns in the fifties as a genre in which to learn because I liked western movies a lot. I don't think I was too depressed in that early sixties period when I had to give up writing, because I really hadn't, in my mind, said, OK, I'm giving it up; I won't be able to write again. It was just that I was busy making a living, and I was doing something new and different for me, and interesting— freelancing, running my own ad agency, in a way, since it was a one-man shop. That was all kind of exciting. But I still couldn't wait, really, for an opportunity to have enough money at one time to get back into a book, and finally the sale of *Hombre* to Fox for a movie gave me that chance.

Do you think writing the ad copy and doing the commercial filmscripts for Encyclopaedia Britannica helped in some way with the fiction writing?

No, not at all, because I had sold at least a dozen short stories before I ever got a job as a writer in advertising. And I knew, as I said, what kind of sound I wanted, kind of a lean, deadpan delivery. I knew that from having studied Hemingway in the early fifties.

Everybody who reads your books agrees that you're a master of dialogue, and you've said that you spend a lot of time just listening to people talk. What sort of process does the talk undergo between what you hear and what the reader finally gets on the printed page?

It's very seldom a phrase or a sentence; it's more just the rhythms of speech. Sometimes it's an expression. Yesterday I was talking to a guy on the phone that I hadn't seen in a long time, and he referred to martinis as "see-throughs." I'd never heard that expression before. My wife had. He said something like, "If you have three or four of those see-throughs, they'll get you in trouble." And I can hear one of my characters using that same expression. Every once in a while something like that will come along. The same friend used to refer to certain people as "chickenfat," which I used in one of my books. I'll pick up something like that. And there's a certain attitude that the character has who uses a word like chickenfat.

Peter Prescott said in his Newsweek *cover story about you that you don't begin with a plot, but rather "with a situation and a handful of characters." How do you go about developing those characters to the point of beginning to write their story?*

I do spend some time with the characters. I may very well write down a character's background, or the way the character talks. Or, for example, in *Bandits,* the way Lucy Nichols referred to her father. Her attitude about her father I put into dialogue in a notebook, trying to get her style, what she was like. I did the same thing with Jack Delaney. I have to get their names right before they'll talk. That's a very big part of them. Jack Delaney was originally Frank Matisse, and he didn't come off the way I wanted him to. He acted older. I *saw* him as older, even though I don't see characters clearly. He was older, and he just wasn't outgoing enough. I had already started to write him. I changed his name to Jack Matisse, and he opened up a little bit; then Jack Delaney, and I had him, the guy I wanted.

Have you ever tried to create a character that just didn't work out?

No. Usually it's the name. If I get the name right, the character will talk. The best kind of character, though, is the one who isn't planned but just kind of comes forth—a character who was going to be minor, let's say a second- or third-string heavy—and he gets into his scene. The Miskito Indian is that character in *Bandits.* In *Freaky Deaky* Donnell Lewis was going to be, not a minor character, but a very menacing character; he was going to be The Heavy. But in the scene where I introduced him, I liked him. I was doing the scene from the point of view of the main character. He sees this black guy in a chauffeur's uniform, and he likes him. I had a lot of fun with Donnell, and I saw the opportunity to do that very early on, though he wasn't planned that way at all.

Do you ever get ideas from real stories in the news, the kind of grim things we read or hear about once or twice a week now?

I make reference to things that are in the paper. In *Bandits,* for example, the two Contra money-raisers are watching the Ferdinand Marcos home movies on television, with Imelda Marcos singing to her husband at his birthday party. Then they're distracted by something and when they look back they think it's more of the home movies, but it's "Wheel of Fortune" going on. In the book that I just finished, there's a reference to whether Elvis Presley is still alive, whether he's coming back—which interests some people, especially my kind of characters.

You manage to get some of your research done by employing an assistant. How does that process work? And does it ever cause problems, having somebody else do that part of the work for you?

On the contrary. My researcher works for a film company in town that does automotive-comparison slide films and movies. He does a lot of computer work for them. But he has an understanding with them that he'll do my work first, because he likes it. So anytime I need anything at all, he'll get it immediately. In the case of the book that I just finished in April, I'd been curious about Cape Girardeau, Missouri. That's a port town on the Mississippi; what's a cape doing there? He was going down to Nashville to see George Jones, one of his favorite performers. So I said, "Go on over to Cape Girardeau and take a look at it. Find out what it's like." He came back with pictures, and what caught my eye was this floodwall that runs three or four thousand yards along the Mississippi River. It looks like a prison wall. That got me started on a way to use Cape Girardeau in that book.

You developed steady and diligent work habits early on, maybe by necessity. Do you give yourself a break between books?

Yeah. I'm between books right now, and I'm reading.

What do you like to read?

I'm reading *Character: America's Search for Leadership,* by Gail Sheehy. It's profiles of those people who were prominent most recently in the presidential campaigns. Since I've finished that last book I've read Jim Harrison's *Dalva,* Gabriel Garcia Marquez's *Love in the Time of Cholera,* William Boyd's *The New Confessions,* Doris Lessing's *The Fifth Child,* and a new book by Glendon Swarthout that's coming out in the fall, called *The Homesman,* a wonderful story.

Women sometimes get treated pretty roughly in your books, and there's a growing concern about the violence done to women in current fiction. Do you have any thoughts about it? Do you see it as a sexist approach on the part of male writers?

I treat women now as persons. I don't think of them as women per se, in the sense of saying, I need a woman in this book, or I need a girlfriend for this guy. I try and flesh them out as people as well as I can, just as I do the men. In my newest book, the one I just finished, a woman is the main character. I started with a husband and wife who get involved in the Federal Witness Protection program. He's an ironworker, and he was going to be the main character—he's a very macho kind of guy. She sells real estate. They've been married for twenty years. She takes over; she becomes the main character, and I was very happy to see it happen.

You have a lot of female readers, haven't you?

I do; in fact I would say that most of the letters I get are from women.

An important part of publisher Donald Fine's campaign to promote your work was getting the attention of reviewers. Do you think crime and mystery fiction is getting to be less categorized and better treated by reviewers generally?

I would say so. And I've been asked that enough to think it must be a fact. When I was on "Today" with Ed McBain, we were asked what we thought was the reason for the resurgence of the popularity of crime fiction. We probably kind of looked blank, because we didn't know that it ever *wasn't* popular. And there are so many books that deal with crime that aren't considered crime novels on the bestseller list.

It's too bad there's as much categorization as there is. You've noted before that your own books aren't mysteries, though they're sometimes put in that category.

They're definitely not mysteries in the classic sense of being puzzles. They're certainly not whodunits. The reader knows everything that's going on—very often more than the main character.

The movie version of **Stick,** *one of several you've done a screenplay for, was a major disappointment for you, on top of some earlier disappointments. Will you stay involved in the movies made from your books?*

To some extent I will. *Glitz* is being produced right now as an NBC movie. I did three drafts of a script for it as a feature, the last one with Sidney Lumet, but Lorimar then decided it would cost too much money to make it that way. It would probably cost fifteen or sixteen million dollars, and they didn't think it would gross enough. Their rule-of-thumb is that you have to gross three times the production cost to make a profit, and they didn't think it would do that, at least at that time. So it was rewritten for television. I'm not sure when it will be on. Jimmy Smits from "L.A. Law" is the star. *Freaky Deaky* has been optioned by Richard Brooks, who made "In Cold Blood" and "Looking for Mr. Goodbar." He'll write the screenplay himself.

Have you played with the idea of producing movies on your own so that you could have control over your original stories?

I did play with the idea, and I got involved in it with a screenplay I did back about eight years ago. "The Hunted," from the 1977 book. I got together with a friend of mine who's a local film producer to raise the money to produce it independently. RKO had been out of the picture business about twenty-five years at that time, and they were talking about coming back in, so we made a deal with them. Then it was a question of our coming up with the actors, and they disagreed with us. There was quite a lot of disagreement. Finally they just broke the contract, and that was that. I wasted some time doing it, and I had no business, really, getting involved to the degree that I did. What I do is write, and that's what I should stick to. I don't know of any writer who has control of his material when it goes to the movies. There aren't even that many directors who have final cut, and that's the whole thing.

Do you think the crime and detective shows on television cut down the market for books, or are there two separate audiences involved?

It certainly hurt the sale of western fiction when there were about thirty western series on prime-time television. But I don't think it hurts the crime and detective books. So many more people are interested in police and crime stories than in westerns. The stories are so much more sensational on television, for the most part, with the car chases and the explosions, which you don't get in the books.

Has the popularity that started building in the mid-eighties brought many more readers to the older books?

Definitely. All my titles, including the westerns, are now in print. The thing is that there are reviewers who will say, "I like his older stuff better, his paperbacks." For some reason these reviewers think I started out doing original paperbacks, which I didn't; even my first westerns were hardcover, from Houghton Mifflin. Out of twenty-six books, twenty-seven counting the new one, I'd say maybe seven or eight were original paperbacks. But since *Glitz*, in 1985, they have picked up the ones that were written in the late seventies and early eighties in paperback, because that's the only form in which they're available, and they think that these books were original paperbacks. One reviewer in particular felt that's what I should be writing—"those paperbacks," kind of well worn, with corners turned down and coffee stains on the covers. The thing is, those reviewers weren't reading me in the late seventies; they only read me after *Glitz*. Where were they when I needed them?

Is there something you'd like to write about, or some kind of book you'd like to do, that's completely unlike anything you've done before?

No. I don't know what I'm going to do next, ever. I'm thinking of the next one right now, and I think it'll be set in Hollywood, but the same kinds of situations will develop as far as the good-versus-evil theme goes. There will be crime involved.

You seem so comfortable with that kind of story. Your books read like the work of somebody who has a good time writing them.

Well, I do. That's what I didn't have before I finally developed the way I write best, most efficiently, the kind of attitude I have to have when I sit down to write. John D. MacDonald said you have to write a million words before you have a sense of knowing what you're doing. I certainly agree with that. It takes about ten years.

Success was a much longer time coming to you than it should have been. Now that you've got it, what's the best part of it?

I never thought I was unsuccessful, because everything I wrote sold; and practically everything—all my books except two—sold to the movies. And though I did have to write screenplays and I did need those movie sales to support my novel writing, perhaps more than ninety percent of writers are in that boat. I didn't see anything unusual in that. I didn't think that what I was writing was bestseller material; I didn't write the big book, I'm not writing *literature*—it's commercial fiction. It's to entertain. I felt that I didn't write well enough or poorly enough to get that big bestseller. And I was kind of surprised when it did hit the list.

Do you like the public attention that's come with it?

Notoriety was never my goal. But to be received well by people I respect—yeah, that's a goal. To get the kind of response that I'm getting from respected reviewers, and letters from people thanking me for a good time—that's really satisfying. (pp. 284-87)

Elmore Leonard and Jean W. Ross, in an in- *terview in* Contemporary Authors New Revision Series, *Vol. 28, Gale Research Inc., 1990, pp. 284-87.*

James W. Hall

Early on in *Maximum Bob,* Elmore Leonard's latest, an alligator mysteriously appears in Judge Bob Gibbs's backyard. While the reptile is roaming around in the dark, Leonard gives us a glimpse of things from the gator's point of view. "The wind rose and with it came a scent she recognized as something she liked she had smelled before sometime in her life and had eaten. After several more minutes she began to move in a sluggish sort of way as though half asleep, not entirely upright on her legs, brushing the grass with her tail."

What the gator smells is Pokey, the beloved dog of the judge's wife, Leanne. And we quickly learn that the judge himself secretly ordered the alligator to be delivered to his yard because his wife is deeply frightened of the beasts. He wants to drive Leanne away because she has become an embarrassment to him, what with her multiple personalities and all, particularly that tendency of hers to speak in the voice of a Georgia slave girl named Wanda.

It's a very strange interlude, going into the gator's mind like that. An odd and risky moment, even for Elmore Leonard, who is used to dipping into some pretty exotic minds, capturing speech patterns with amazing authenticity. Strange and risky, yet, I for one, come away totally convinced that this is how an alligator thinks. The very words it uses. And if it doesn't think this way, then by god it should. Such is Leonard's magic.

"Maximum" Bob Gibbs is a politically incorrect circuit court judge in Palm Beach County, known far and wide as a hanging judge, one tough nut. In his long career he's made a whole lot of enemies, so many in fact that several of them may be trying to kill him at once. Take a number, get in line.

Once the gator has successfully freed the judge of his wife, Gibbs casts his sexually harrassing eye on Kathy Baker, a probation officer in his court. Kathy is a tough-as-she-needs-to-be lady, and not at all the easy mark the judge imagines. Still, Gibbs finagles her into going home with him one night, and just as Kathy is fending off his advances, someone takes a shot at him. It's both a scary and an hilarious moment. For as one assassin is lining up his shot at the judge, he is almost killed by the errant bullet of a second assassin who fires from the other direction.

As it turns out, Baker just happens to be the probation officer for the human reptiles behind one of these murder attempts. It's a cast of bad guys as colorful and convincing as any Leonard has given us in a while. There's Tommy Vasco, a crack-loving dermatologist who is under Community Control, and is forced to wear an electronic anklet that keeps him penned in his sumptuous estate where he is waited on by his homosexual houseboy Hector. The hitman whom Dr. Tommy has hired to murder Judge Gibbs is Elvin Crowe, an ex-con redneck with a love for cowboy paraphernalia, Cadillacs and 20-year-old polyester suits.

While it's true that Elvin has blood brothers in some of Leonard's other novels, he is nevertheless an original and frightening permutation of the breed.

The book is set in Palm Beach, but it's not *that* Palm Beach. As close as we get to beachfront compounds is the estate of Dr. Tommy, probably the only skin doctor in America who spends most of his daylight hours nude sunbathing. Judge Gibbs and most of the other characters live a long way from the Trumps and Kennedys and the Vascos. They haunt the western edge of the county, "a different *world,* the Glades, bottomland America with a smell of muck and fish and half a million acres of sugarcane off on the left side of the road there."

Like all of Leonard's novels, *Maximum Bob* takes us for a ride up and down the social register, from alligators and alligator poachers to doctors and judges. And as we've come to expect, while the social distance is great, the moral distance between these people is minimal. Almost everyone here is wallowing in one form of muck or another.

As Elvin Crowe is trying to pick the right time and place to execute the judge, he hangs out with his nephew, Dale Crowe, who has only a few days left before he must depart for prison. To prepare Dale, Elvin shares with him a number of his observations about prison life. For one thing, he says, "There ain't no more real convicts since this crack [expletive] come about. Convicts, they'd sit around talking about jobs, banks they'd held up, argue about how to blow a safe. Now you got *in*mates instead of cons and these guys are crazy. All they think about is getting dope and getting laid, looking to see who they can turn."

This indeed is one of the great pleasures of *Maximum Bob,* this voyage through the heart of the heart of the judicial system. Guided by the major players themselves, we witness the inner workings of a probation session, snoop into judges' chambers, and into a judge's mind and temperament. We also get a fine and funny lesson in New Age nuttiness from Leanne. We learn about crystals and auras and psychic scraping. We take side trips to tourist shows at Weeki Watchi Springs, learn how the mermaids breathe and smile underwater. And Elvin leads us on a special tour through the sugarcane ghetto of Belle Glade, and the mean back streets of Delray Beach.

As Elvin meanders, Kathy Baker is falling in love with Gary Hammond, the laconic cop who is investigating the attempt on the judge's life. Gary is one of Leonard's calm, true-grit tough guys. Those sensible people who are often stranded dead center in the killing zone of these novels. A nice guy, worthy of Kathy's love, hero material. Trouble is, you're never quite sure if he's mean enough or quick enough on the draw to handle the Elvin Crowes of this world.

As Elvin and Kathy and Gary spiral in closer and closer to the inevitable confrontation, the pace and pulse quicken. One of the reasons Leonard's novels are so compelling, so often tense and disquieting, is that the good folks, his Kathys and Garys, don't always prevail. You just never know who's going to get it, and who's going to get away with it. There are no easy answers, no moral certainties, no simple white-hat victories. As Elvin says, "That was the difference between a book and real life. In a book, the one who was supposed to be the bad guy always got killed in the end." Not so in LeonardWorld. For often, as at the conclusion of *Maximum Bob,* some of the reptiles slither off to bite another day.

Year after year, book after book, Leonard has been sketching in the details of this quirky, dangerous world and evolving its moral structure. Detailing the fine print of his own brand of toughness. In *Maximum Bob* it is Kathy Baker's bend-but-don't break gristle that's the model. In fact, more and more in his recent novels it is the women who triumph. Women who can look the bad guys or the pompous judges square in the eyes and pull the trigger when they have to.

So, yes, it's another wonderful book from Leonard. Another right-on, perfect pitch novel, with wide social scope, comic genius, page-burning storytelling magic, and juicy characters who wrench your heart and gut. In fact, Elmore Leonard has been blurring the distinction between entertainment and literary fiction for so many years now that maybe it's time to stop calling him a major crime novelist, and just admit it: The guy's a for-real major novelist. Because, if you stack them up book after book, Leonard has already laid claim to terrain as rich and true as any that our best writers have discovered. And the ore he mines from that rough soil is 24-carat stuff. What's most amazing about him is, he seems to be just hitting his stride. (pp. 1-2)

James W. Hall, "Alligators and Other Reptiles," in Book World—The Washington Post, *July 14, 1991, pp. 1-2.*

FURTHER READING

Broun, Heywood Hale. "Elmore Leonard's Contra Caper." *The Washington Post Book World* XVI, No. 52 (28 December 1986): 3.
    Discusses *Bandits* as "an old-fashioned moral tale."

Campbell, Don G. "Stix Dix Fix Nix." *Los Angeles Times Book Review* (23 April 1989): 14.
    Praises the realistic dialogue and characters in *Killshot,* concluding that "*Killshot* is a riveting page-turner, a hare-and-hounds chase through the bleak suburbs of Detroit and the seamy riverfront dives of Cape Girardeau."

Ephron, Nora. "The Shylock Is the Good Guy." *The New York Times Book Review* (29 July 1990): 1, 28.
    Reviews *Get Shorty,* praising Leonard's writing style and technique.

Kaplan, Roger. "Hard Guys & Heroes." *Commentary* 79, No. 5 (May 1985): 64, 66-7.
    Review of *Glitz* in which the critic asserts that the novel "is mediocre. . . . As with all Leonard's books, there is no real plot, . . . attempts at humor are rare, the conver-

sation is notable for its vulgarity, and the characters are detestable to the point of caricature."

Locke, Richard. "A Motor City Thriller." *The Wall Street Journal* CCXI, No. 105 (31 May 1988): 22.
> Reviews *Freaky Deaky,* assessing Leonard as a mystery writer.

Lupica, Mike. "St. Elmore's Fire." *Esquire* 107, No. 4 (April 1987): 169-74.
> Profile of Leonard in which he discusses his crime novels, his writing process, and his sources of inspiration.

Prescott, Peter S. "Making a Killing." *Newsweek* CV, No. 16 (22 April 1985): 62-4, 67.
> Cover story on Leonard that recounts his success as a crime novelist and screenwriter.

Rule, Philip C. Review of *Touch,* by Elmore Leonard. *Los Angeles Times Book Review* (30 August 1987): 2, 8.
> Favorably reviews *Touch,* characterizing the work as a "classy mystery."

Additional coverage of Leonard's life and career is contained in the following sources published by Gale Research: *Authors in the News,* Vol. 1; *Bestsellers 89,* Vol. 1; *Bestsellers 90,* Vol. 4; *Contemporary Authors,* Vols. 81-84; *Contemporary Authors New Revision Series,* Vols. 12, 28; *Contemporary Literary Criticism,* Vols. 28, 34; and *Major 20th-Century Writers.*

Audre Lorde

1934-

(Full name Audre Geraldine Lorde; also wrote under the pseudonym Rey Domini) American poet, essayist, autobiographer, and nonfiction writer.

This entry focuses on Lorde's career from 1979 through 1991. For further information on her life and works, see *CLC,* Vol. 18.

INTRODUCTION

Lorde's poetry evokes images of African culture, candidly depicts racial intolerance and urban blight, and emphasizes pride and anti-victimization among African-American women. Describing herself as a "black lesbian feminist mother lover poet," Lorde blends elements of history and mythology to create a poetic idiom that celebrates the differences between social groups as dynamic and liberating rather than as threats to self-identity. Lorde also advocates poetry as a means to address the conflicts that lead to cultural separatism and to alleviate the pain of emotional isolation and displacement. Believing it her moral responsibility to address the concerns of women, Lorde has stated that she writes "for [those] women for whom a voice has not yet existed, or whose voices have been silenced."

Lorde was born in New York City to West Indian immigrants. After graduating from high school, during which she published her first poem, Lorde attended Hunter College where she earned a bachelor's degree in library science. During this time she supported herself by intermittently working as a medical clerk, x-ray technician, ghost writer, and factory worker. Lorde received her master's degree from Columbia University and in 1966 became head librarian at Town School Library in New York City, where library patrons knew her as the "librarian who wrote." In 1968—a year she considers a turning point in her life—Lorde received a National Endowment for the Arts grant, became a poet-in-residence at Tougaloo College in Mississippi, and published her first collection of poetry, *The First Cities.* In this volume, Lorde employs nature imagery to explore the mutability of love and human consciousness. Calling *The First Cities* a "quiet, introspective book," Dudley Randall asserted that "[Lorde] does not wave a black flag, but her blackness is there, implicit, in the bone." Her second volume, *Cables to Rage,* is considered more confrontational and pessimistic due to Lorde's emerging social concerns and her exploration of guilt and betrayal. This collection is also notable for the poem "Martha," in which Lorde reveals her homosexuality for the first time: "yes Martha we have loved each other and yes I hope we still can / no Martha / I do not know if we shall ever sleep in each other's arms again."

Lorde's *From a Land Where Other People Live* was nominated for a National Book Award for poetry in 1973. In this collection, which is considered more universal in conception than the author's earlier volumes, Lorde confronts racial oppression, worldwide injustice, and her identity as an African-American woman. *The New York Head Shop and Museum,* often described as Lorde's most political and radical work, depicts images of a decaying New York City and the hardships of poverty and urban decay: "There is nothing beautiful left in the streets of this city. / I have come to believe in death and renewal by fire." *Coal,* Lorde's next volume, was the first of her collections to be released by a major publisher, thus exposing her to a broader readership. Comprising poems from *The First Cities* and *Cables to Rage* as well as newly published verse, *Coal* demonstrates Lorde's increasing mastery of figurative language. Throughout the collection, for example, coal is a unifying metaphor through which Lorde celebrates her blackness: "I am black because I came from the / earth's insides / Take my word for jewel in your / open light."

The Black Unicorn is widely considered Lorde's most poetically mature work. In this volume Lorde utilizes symbols and mythology associated with the African goddess Seboulisa to integrate themes of motherhood, black pride, courage, and spiritual rejuvenation. Abandoning the tight free verse for which she was previously noted, Lorde employs loose rhythmic forms associated with African oral traditions and American blues music. In *Our Dead behind Us* she speculates on the history of womankind as she travels to such diverse locales as Grenada, Germany, and the Transvaal in South Africa. The poem "Call," for example, invokes images of Rosa Parks, Winnie Mandela, and Fannie Lou Hammer to create a metaphorical bond between Africa and women of African ancestry.

The Cancer Journals, Lorde's first work of nonfiction, chronicles the author's experience with breast cancer and her feelings of hopelessness and despair as she underwent a radical mastectomy. A collection of journal entries, speeches, and conversations with friends, this volume traces Lorde's initial grief, her eventual acceptance of her condition, and her apparent recovery. Praised for her honest and revealing account of her illness, Lorde stated she wanted "to write a piece of meaning words on cancer as it affects my life and my consciousness as a woman." *Zami: A New Spelling of My Name,* Lorde's second prose work, is what the author describes as a "biomythography," or a work in which she combines elements of history, biography, and mythology. Although considered a work of fiction, *Zami* incorporates numerous events from Lorde's youth in New York City. *Sister Outsider: Essays and Speeches* includes addresses and essays written between 1976 and 1983 and elucidates Lorde's development as a poet and a feminist. In "Learning from the 60s," for example, Lorde explores how the call for cohesion among members of the feminist movement contributed to racial, sexual, and ideological intolerance.

Lorde learned in the late 1980s that her cancer had metastasized to her liver. Instead of undergoing a biopsy, she chose a holistic treatment combining homeopathy, meditation, and self-hypnosis. She is currently in remission. In *A Burst of Light,* a collection of essays in which she openly contemplates her own death, Lorde parallels her fight for life with black South Africa's struggle for equality and the lesbian community's fight against discrimination. Lorde's continuing focus on social issues despite her serious illness reflects her aims as a poet: "I feel I have a duty to speak the truth as I see it and to share not just my triumphs, not just the things that felt good, but the pain, the intense, often unmitigating pain. . . . But I think what is really necessary is to see how much of this pain I can feel, how much of this truth I can see and still live unblinded."

PRINCIPAL WORKS

POETRY

The First Cities   1968
Cables to Rage   1970
From a Land Where Other People Live   1973
The New York Head Shop and Museum   1974
Between Our Selves   1976
Coal   1976
The Black Unicorn   1978

Chosen Poems: Old and New   1982
Our Dead behind Us   1986

OTHER

The Cancer Journals   (journal)   1980
Zami: A New Spelling of My Name   (novel)   1982
Sister Outsider: Essays and Speeches   (essays)   1984
A Burst of Light   (essays)   1988

CRITICISM

Andrea Benton Rushing

I can think of few poems by Afro-American women which reflect Africa. Early on there are Margaret Danner's poems *Impressions of African Art Forms* and younger poets of the Black Arts Movement of the 1960's have sometimes written about how it feels to be in Africa. In **The Black Unicorn,** Lorde dares something else: she uses African mythology and folklore as the symbolic ground for a dozen or so poems, includes a glossary of African names at the end of the book, has a bibliography, and has—as jacket illustration—a headdress which represents the spirit *Tji-Wara* or *Chi-Wara,* who is said to have introduced agriculture to the Bambara People.

As early as **"The Wings of Orisha"** in *From the Land Where Other People Live,* Lorde alerted us to her interest in African ideas, and her essay **"Scratching the Surface: Some Notes to Barriers on Women and Loving"** (*The Black Scholar,* April 1978) gives the reader insight into her use of African history and culture in **The Black Unicorn.** In substantiating her contention that "black women have always bonded together," she cites the close, involved and complex relationship between co-wives, the Amazon warriors of ancient Dahomey, and West African market women's associations. In **The Black Unicorn,** Lorde has not succumbed to nostalgia or exoticism; instead, she has attempted to find the sources of Afro-American women's resilience and glory in the cultures from which our ancestors came, setting aside both Anglo-American ideas about white women as dumb blondes, sex objects, castrating Moms, angels, and bitches and the stereotypes of Afro-American women as tragic mulattoes, hotblooded exotics, and black matriarchs. The wisest and most beautiful thing about this new book of poems is its creative use of African sources. In building the Yoruba and Dan religious traditions, Lorde has created a truer vision/version of our selves and has provided a useful corrective for those excesses of 1960's cultural nationalism which urged women into polygamous and deferential relationships to men.

In **"The Winds of Orisha"** Lorde mentions Mother Yemanja, Oshun, Shango, and Oya. Yemanja, re-appears in **The Black Unicorn** along with Mawulisa (creator of the universe and mother of all other "Vodu"); Seboulisa, "the Mother of us all"—a local representation of Mawulisa;

and Yaa Asantewa, an Ashanti queen mother who led her people in several successful wars against the British in the nineteenth century. Lorde highlights not only the divinity of Earth Mother but also women's warrior strength. The word "warrior" occurs several times in these poems: the famous Afro-American woman mentioned is a controversial contemporary warrior, Assata Shakur/Joann Chesimard whom Lorde, as myth-maker, presents as a new kind of hero.

> Assata my sister warrior
> Joan of Arc and Yaa Asantewa
> embrace
> at the back of your cell.

Reading the poems in this section is not easy, but as Lorde herself warned us **"Good Mirrors Are Not Cheap,"** and the effort of re-reading and re-thinking a poem like **"Coniagui Women"** with its allusions to the belief and rituals of an African culture,

> The Coniagui women
> wear their flesh like war
> bear children who have eight days
> to choose their mothers

and **"125th Street and Abomey"** which juxtaposes Harlem street life with Dahomey,

> Seboulisa mother goddess
> . . . .
> see me now
> your severed daughter
> laughing our name into echo . . .

is richly rewarding.

There is no simple way to explore the poems in this volume. Steve Henderson's excellent framework in *Understanding the New Black Poetry* is tangential here because Lorde does not evoke Afro-American music and rarely (though her diction is often colloquial) employs specifically Afro-American speech. Instead, she employs her characteristic blend of black and feminist themes and perspectives. She not only touches on most of the themes of black women's fiction that Mary Helen Washington includes in *Black-Eyed Susans* but charts unexplored territory as well. A candid reviewer points out her early interest and favorites (knowing that poems become ours with use—like recipes, and clothes, and homes) and urges readers to search out their own favorites. For those who expect feminists to hate men, I recommend **"Eulogy for Alvin Frost."** For the wit and wonder of growing up, **"Hanging Fire."** For an evocation of the seamlessness of Afro-American versions of sacred and secular, **"About Religion."** And for a resonant look at love, **"Walking Our Boundaries."**

I have three regrets about *The Black Unicorn.* First, though the title has the wit of paradox (unicorns are imagined as white), evokes a Dudley Randall poem, and may ironically conjure up virgins who are supposed to be more likely to catch unicorns than anyone else, it unfortunately leads away from the African mythology of the first section and the colloquial tone of much of the rest of the book. Second, abbreviated versions of the definitions in the glossary placed *with* the poems in which African terms occur would have been a great help. Third, though the jacket

notes say the poems are "nourished in an oral tradition," I do not sense that in reading the text and would be thrilled to hear Lorde do them in her lush and vibrant voice.

Audre Lorde is a brilliant and unique voice in the orchestra of black women poets and, while no poem in this volume touches me with the power of **"Coal," "Black Mother Woman,"** or **"Father, Son, and Holy Ghost,"** it has authority, wit, and incandescence of its own. (pp. 114-16)

Andrea Benton Rushing, "A Creative Use of African Sources," in Obsidian: Black Literature in Review, *Vol. 5, No. 3, Winter, 1979, pp. 114-16.*

R. B. Stepto

Audre Lorde's seventh volume of poems, *The Black Unicorn,* is a big, rich book of some sixty-seven poems. . . . Perhaps a full dozen—an incredibly high percentage—of these poems are searingly strong and unforgettable. Those readers who recall the clear light and promise of early Lorde poems such as **"The Woman Thing"** and **"Bloodbirth,"** and recall as well the great shape and energy of certain mid-1970s poems including **"To My Daughter the Junkie on a Train," "Cables to Rage,"** and **"Blackstudies,"** will find in *The Black Unicorn* new poems which reconfirm Lorde's talent while reseeding gardens and fields traversed before. There are other poems which do not so much reseed as repeople, and these new persons, names, ghosts, lovers, voices—these new I's, we's, real and imagined kin—give us something fresh, beyond the cycle of Lorde's previously recorded seasons and solstices.

While *The Black Unicorn* is unquestionably a personal triumph for Lorde in terms of the development of her canon, it is also an event in contemporary letters. This is a bold claim but one worth making precisely because, as we see in the first nine poems, Lorde appears to be the only North American poet other than Jay Wright who is sufficiently immersed in West African religion, culture, and art (and blessed with poetic talent!) to reach beyond a kind of middling poem that merely quantifies "blackness" through offhand reference to African gods and traditions. What Lorde and Wright share, beyond their abilities to create a fresh, New World Art out of ancient Old World lore, is a voice or an *idea* of a voice that is essentially African in that it is communal, historiographical, archival, and prophetic *as well as* personal in ways that we commonly associate with the African *griot, dyēli,* and tellers of *nganos* and other oral tales. However, while Wright's voice may be said to embody what is masculine in various West African cultures and cosmologies, Lorde's voice is decidedly and magnificently feminine. The goal of *The Black Unicorn* is then to present this fresh and powerful voice, and to explore the modulations within that voice between feminine and feminist timbres. As the volume unfolds, this exploration charts history and geography as well as voice, and with the confluence of these patterns the volume takes shape and Lorde's particular envisioning of a black transatlantic tradition is accessible.

All this begins, as suggested before, in the first nine poems in which we encounter the legendary women and goddesses—the sisters and especially the mothers—who inaugurate Lorde's genealogy of timbres and visages. In poems such as **"From the House of Yemanjá," "Dahomey,"** and **"125th Street and Abomey,"** mothers including Yemanjá (goddess of oceans, mother of the other *Orisha* or Yoruba goddesses and gods) and Seboulisa ("The goddess of Abomey—'The Mother of us all' ") appears, often in new renderings of the legends that surround them:

> My mother has two faces and a frying pot
> where she cooked up her daughters
> into girls
> before she fixed our dinner.
> My mother has two faces
> and a broken pot
> where she hid out a perfect daughter
> who was not me
> I am the sun and moon and forever hungry
> for her eyes

Much of this would be little more than mere reference of the sort alluded to before were the poems not galvanized and bound by the persona's unrelenting quest for freedom, voice, and women kin. At the beginning of the quest, the persona is a black unicorn, a protean figure who, in one manifestation, is a Dahomean woman with attached phallus dancing the part of Eshu-Elegba (Yemanjá's messenger son of many tongues) in religious ritual. At the end, she is a "severed daughter"—"severed" in that she is in a new but tethered geography (**"125th Street and Abomey"**) and has cut away an imposed ritual tongue—who has found a voice of her own that can utter "Whatever language is needed" (a skill allowed before only to Yemanjá's *son*) and can even laugh.

> Half earth and time splits us apart
> like struck rock,
> A piece lives elegant stories
> too simply put
> while a dream on the edge of summer
> of brown rain in nim trees
> snail shells from the dooryard
> of King Toffah
> bring me where my blood moves
> Seboulisa mother goddess with one breast
> eaten away by worms of sorrow and loss
> see me now
> your severed daughter
> laughing our name into echo
> all the world shall remember.

As we move from the first set of poems about black mothers, daughters, and sisters—women who can "wear flesh like war," conjoin "dying cloth," and "mock Eshu's iron quiver"—to those which come in the remaining three sections, there is a subtle shift in poetic form that appears to signal, in turn, a shift in focus from acquisition of voice to that of art. In the first set, in stanzas such as

> The black unicorn is restless
> the black unicorn is unrelenting
> the black unicorn is not
> free.

and

> Mother I need

> mother I need
> mother I need your blackness now
> as the august earth needs rain.

Lorde makes effective use of the principle of repetition that is at the heart of oral composition in all "preliterate" cultures, and at the heart as well of such conspicuous Afro-American art forms as the blues. (Indeed, each of the stanzas just presented may be said to be a modified but identifiable blues verse.) In the remaining sections of the volume, repetition and other devices which are, in this context, referents in written art to oral forms, are largely forsaken in favor of the kind of taut free verse Lorde usually employs. What is fascinating about this, as suggested before, is that while the declarative voice forged in the first group of poems remains, that voice speaks less of discovering language and of moving, perhaps, from speech to laughter, and more of poems—of written art readily assuming the posture of a healing force.

This is true even of the poems about social unrest and injustice. In **"Chain,"** for example, a poem prompted by a news item describing two teenage girls who had borne children by their natural fathers, there is the cry,

> Oh write me a poem mother
> here, over my flesh
> get your words upon me
> as he got his child upon me

Similarly, in **"Eulogy for Alvin Frost"** we find,

> I am tired of writing memorials to black men
> whom I was on the brink of knowing
> . . . .
> Dear Danny who does not know me
> I am
> writing to you for your father
> whom I barely knew
> except at meetings where he was
> distinguished
> by his genuine laughter
> and his kind bright words

In the final section, **"Power"** begins with yet another suggested distinction between poetry and speech,

> The difference between poetry and rhetoric
> is being
> ready to kill
> yourself
> instead of your children.

and ends with a very particular statement of confession and self-instruction,

> I have not been able to touch the destruction
>   within me.
> But unless I learn to use
> the difference between poetry and rhetoric
> my power too will run corrupt as poisonous
>   mold
> or lie limp and useless as an unconnected wire.

As the latent sexuality in the final line suggests, the shift in *The Black Unicorn* in poetic concern from acquisition of voice to that of art concerns as well the articulation of a homosexual love that was only barely alluded to before in the many figurations of tongue as women-warriors' sword and speech. Indeed, the pulsing love poems, in which tongue finally becomes most explicitly an erotic tool and goal—

> I am tempted
> to take you apart
> and reconstruct your orifices
> your tongue your truths your fleshy altars
> into my own forgotten image
>
> ("Fog Report")

—and in which sex and art most explicitly meet—

> I do not even know
> who looks like you
> of all the sisters who come to me
> at nightfall
> we touch each other in secret places
> draw old signs and stories
> upon each other's back and proofread
> each other's ancient copy.

—consummate the volume in a rich if not altogether unexpected manner.

Whether or not the subject at hand is love, children under assault, people in prison, childhood "wars," or the quest for a certain rare literacy, the poet in *The Black Unicorn* steadily pursues (and defines in that pursuit) a viable heroic posture and voice for womankind. The success of the volume may be seen in the fact that when the poet declares in the final poem,

> I will eat the last signs of my weakness
> remove the scars of old childhood wars
> and dare to enter the forest whistling

we believe her. In this period between renaissance and/or revolutions, Lorde's verse may need promotion in order to sell, but that doesn't mean that the verse is thin or insignificant. *The Black Unicorn* offers contemporary poetry of a high order, and in doing so may be a smoldering renaissance and revolution unto itself. (pp. 315-20)

> *R. B. Stepto, "The Phenomenal Woman and the Severed Daughter," in* Parnassus: Poetry in Review, *Vol. 8, No. 1, 1979, pp. 312-20.*

Lorde on the source of her poetic inspiration:

I am Black, Woman, and Poet—all three are facts outside the realm of choice. My eyes have a part in my seeing; my breath is in my breathing; and all that I am in who I am. All who I love are of my people; it is not simple. I was not born on a farm or in a forest but in the centre of the largest city in the world—a member of the human race hemmed in by stone and away from earth and sunlight. But what is in my blood and kin of richness, of brown earth and noon sun and the strength to love them, comes the roundabout way from Africa through sun islands, to a stony coast; and these are the gifts through which I sing, through which I see.

> *Audre Lorde, in a statement written for the poetry anthology* Sixes and Sevens, *Breman, 1963.*

Rosemary Daniell

Carriacou is an actual West Indian island as well as the isle of Audre Lorde's imagination; Zami is "a Carriacou name for women who work together as friends and lovers." And while the publisher's claim that in *Zami: A New Spelling of My Name* Miss Lorde "creates a new form, biomythography, combining elements of history, biography and myth," is a bit pretentious, the book is, actually, an excellent and evocative autobiography.

Indeed, among the elements that make the book so good are its personal honesty and lack of pretentiousness, characteristics that shine through the writing, bespeaking the evolution of a strong and remarkable character. The reader quickly grows to love the sturdy little black girl—daughter of parents immigrated to New York from Grenada before she was born—who is tongue-tied, unable to see without her glasses; who forces herself to stay awake half an hour after her parentally-imposed bedtime in order to listen to the stories nightly serialized by her two older sisters; who, in her loneliness, dreams of having a "little female person" all her own; yet who yearns for the magical moments of privacy disallowed by a stern mother who, considering solitude a social perversion, insists that Audre's bedroom door remain open except when she is studying, constantly studying.

With her, we experience the pain of her gradual recognition of racism (something from which her powerful mother seeks for years to protect her); the suicide of a teen-age best friend for whom she has been able to do nothing. With her, we leave the rigid confines of home—a Washington Heights apartment—at 17 to become marginally self-supporting; to endure (at times) hunger, an abortion and Christmas alone. We share her growing awareness of her attraction toward her own sex; her first affairs with women; a longed-for trip alone to Mexico at 19-feeling-like-35, on one of those journeys that serve as routes for psychic discovery; and life as a "gay-girl" in the Greenwich Village of the 50's. We live with her through her first primary love relationship and its excruciating conclusion; and, finally, an affair with a black Southern woman—Afrekete—whose sensuality and independence equal her own; it is a relationship that becomes metaphor for her conciliation with her own reality, and with the world.

Throughout, her experiences are painted with exquisite imagery. Indeed, her West Indian heritage shows through most clearly in her use of word pictures that are sensual, steamy, at times near-tropical, evoking the colors, smells—repeatedly, the smells—shapes, textures that are her life. Her attention to detail is exacting whether she's describing a supper of hot tamales and cold milk in Mexico City or an evening of bar-hopping in the West Village of two decades ago. Her use of language is often imaginative but uncontrived, as in her description of her first lover, Ginger, as having "high putchy cheeks" or her reference, in one of the many meals deliciously detailed in the book, to "chopped onions quailed in margarine."

Yet Miss Lorde is at her best when her images become—as they often do—metaphors for states of being: A torn stocking caught in the wind on the side of a tenement building becomes symbol of her terror when, as a small child, she hangs by one hand from the window of her apartment, only to be saved by her mother's timely return home. Or the day she has begun her first menstrual period: Left alone by her usually ever-present mother in the kitchen, she crushes with mortar and pestle the garlic, onions and celery leaves that will season the meat for dinner; as she pounds—and pounds and pounds—she becomes carried away, the scents from the ground herbs mixing with her own. And her membership at Hunter High School in what she calls The Branded, The Lunatic Fringe, is really her wider membership in that part of the population made up of artists, blacks, women and homosexuals.

Despite her obvious poet's ease with symbol, metaphor, image, her references to herself as poet—a vocation held since childhood—are unemphatic: ". . . sometimes there was food cooked, sometimes there was not. Sometimes there was a poem, and sometimes there was not. And always, on weekends, there were the bars," she writes, describing life with her lover Muriel. And while her downplaying of her commitment to poetry may be partly an attempt to avoid widening the distance between the reader and herself, there is the sense, in *Chosen Poems* as in *Zami,* of a writer who has other, more pressing concerns—such as cooking a meal, making a living, or simply living out the life style that for many homosexuals is an avocation in itself. It is as though the life on the streets was so rich that it left little time for meticulous literary stitching up in some West Village or Staten Island tower . . . ; she is distant from Sylvia Plath or Anne Sexton who, out of isolation, even alienation, made language scream; or Cynthia McDonald and Marilyn Hacker, with their intricate linguistic embroideries. This imperative immediacy sometimes gives Miss Lorde's poems an undeveloped, abstract air, leaving one wishing for the exacting detail of her prose, the evocation of the undeniable, concrete world made fully tangible in *Zami.*

At the same time, Miss Lorde's poems are refreshingly removed from the pale frozen works of many poets, who appear immobilized by the image of themselves as poet. Instead, she is a poet of her time, her place, her people, and unlike poets whose works fall apart when fused by conviction, she is at her best in her most political pieces:

> I inherited Jackson, Mississippi.
> For my majority it gave me Emmett Till
> his 15 years puffed out like bruises
> on plump boy-cheeks
> his only Mississippi summer
> whistling a 21 gun salute to Dixie
> as a white girl passed him in the street
> and he was baptized my son forever
> in the midnight waters of the Pearl.

So she writes in **"Afterimages,"** a poem in which her empathy extends finally even to the white woman who has caused Emmett Till's terrible death. In the more recent poems in this volume, which draws from works written over 30 years, she employs increasing imagistic skills; yet even some of the earlier poems—such as **"Martha,"** a long piece about a woman hospitalized and fighting for her life—are strong enough to give a reader the kind of gut-level jolt Emily Dickinson deemed the most reliable judgment of a poem.

To read both these volumes is to feel, at least for a few hours, that one has lived, not merely intellectualized, Audre Lorde's life. Throughout each, one is aware of the author's growth toward an unusual autonomy. For readers who begin with *Zami, Chosen Poems* will serve as recognizable markers for that journey and since the autobiography concludes in 1960, an extension into present-tense awareness. Her works will be important to those truly interested in growing up sensitive, intelligent and aware in the second half of the twentieth century in America. (pp. 12, 29)

> *Rosemary Daniell, "The Poet Who Found Her Own Way," in* The New York Times Book Review, *December 19, 1982, pp. 12, 29.*

Mary J. Carruthers

[Audre Lorde has] produced a large body of poetry over an appreciable length of time. In her recent poems, including some in *Coal,* she has come to see in the bonding of women an image both of home and of a new world. *The Black Unicorn* (an image which richly summarizes the self-image of the poet) specifically develops the image of woman-bonding as a necessary start to the end of all forms of oppression. She writes in **"Between Our Selves"** of the selling into slavery of her pregnant great-grandmother:

> Under the sun on the shores of Elmina
> a black man sold the woman who carried
> my grandmother in her belly
> he was paid with bright yellow coin
> that shone in the evening sun
> and in the faces of her sons and daughters.
> When I see that brother behind my eyes
> his irises are bloodless and without color
> his tongue clicks like yellow coins
> tossed up on this shore
> where we share the same corner
> of an alien and corrupted heaven
> and whenever I try to eat
> the words
> of easy blackness as salvation
> I taste the color
> of my grandmother's first betrayal.
>
> I do not believe
> our wants
> have made all our lies
> holy.

In this "alien and corrupted heaven," Lorde speaks of loneliness and homelessness, fragmentation and lies, contrasted often to a vision of a new world which is also home. The odyssey theme is Lesbian—women together can figure forth home, the lover is the bridge, as in **"Bridge through My Window,"** from *Coal:*

> In curve scooped out and necklaced with light
> burst pearls stream down my out-stretched arms
>   to earth.
> Oh bridge my sister bless me before I sleep
> the wild air is lengthening
> and I am tried beyond strength or bearing

over water.

Love, we are both shorelines
a left country
where time suffices
and the right land
where pearls roll into earth and spring up day.
Joined, our bodies have passage into one
without merging
as this slim necklace is anchored into night.

And while the we conspires
to make secret its two eyes
we search the other shore
for some crossing home.

The poem incorporates the prevalent image of remnant survivors in an alien country seeking to get home through their bond, which is both home, "the right land," and passage home.

In creating her version of the Lesbian myth, Lorde draws upon Dahomeian religious myths, which are matriarchal in character, and ritual, in which women figure prominently. This mythic system provides a society of women, and it operates in Lorde's poetry much as the Greek myths do in Broumas', as a remembrance, an archaelogy. For example, in **"125th Street and Abomey,"** she invokes the mother-goddess:

Head bent, walking through snow
I see you Seboulisa
printed inside the back of my head
like marks of the newly wrapped akai
that kept my sleep fruitful in Dahomey
and I poured on the red earth in your honor
those ancient parts of me
most precious and least needed
my well-guarded past
the energy-eating secrets
I surrender to you as libation . . .
give me the woman strength
of tongue in this cold season. . . .

Seboulisa mother goddess with one breast
eaten away by worms of sorrow and loss
see me now
your severed daughter
laughing our name into echo
all the world shall remember.

Her myth is also apocalyptic, as, for example, in these lines from **"The Women of Dan Dance with Swords in Their Hands to Mark the Time When They were Warriors"**:

I come like a woman
who I am
spreading out through nights
laughter and promise
and dark heat
warming whatever I touch
that is living
consuming
only
what is already dead.

More so than her white fellows, Lorde takes violence as a central, dominant theme for her poetry. Seboulisa, the Dahomeian goddess, cut off one breast so that she might

fight more easily, but violence is not always seen as so productive. Lorde's poetry is haunted by the images of the "children who become junk": the heroin-drugged girl of **"My Daughter the Junkie on a Train,"** Donald DeFreeze, ten-year-old Clifford Glover who was shot by a white cop, the teenager in the poem **"Power"** who succumbs to "rhetoric" and rapes and murders an 85-year-old white woman "who is somebody's mother," the women who are "stones in my heart" because "you do not value your own / self / nor me."

But violence is the prerequisite for rebirth, the apocalypse necessary to create a new earth. Lorde often uses the Lazarus figure (seen as a woman) set free by an act of violence that bears her to a new and truer being. In **"Martha,"** a poem from *Coal,* she meditates upon a former lover nearly killed in a car accident and her long recovery:

No one you were can come so close
to death without dying
into another Martha.
I await you
as we all await her
fearing her honesty
fearing
we may neither love nor dismiss
Martha with the dross burned away,
fearing
condemnation from the essential.

You cannot get closer to death than this Martha
the nearest you've come to living yourself.

It is instructive to compare this poem with Plath's "Lady Lazarus," a poem which ends with a terrible, avenging, disembodied self-image ("Out of the ash / I rise with my red hair / And I eat men like air"). Martha is more herself, more essentially embodied through violence and death than she was before: "Martha with the dross burned away." The experience of violence passes through death to peace discovered in an integrated self. It is a necessary part of healing, not merely cataclysmic but truly apocalyptic. . . . (pp. 316-20)

For Lorde . . . the most important virtue—imaged by the female bond—is integrity: alienation and secrecy are reborn as the power of wholeness. The final poem of *The Black Unicorn,* **"Solstice,"** expresses this process eloquently:

My skin is tightening
soon I shall shed it
like a monitor lizard
like remembered comfort
at the new moon's rising
I will eat the last signs of my weakness
remove the scars of old childhood wars
and dare to enter the forest whistling
like a snake that has fed the chameleon
for changes
I shall be forever.

May I never remember reasons
for my spirit's safety
may I never forget
the warning of my woman's flesh
weeping at the new moon
may I never lose

that terror
that keeps me brave
May I owe nothing
that I cannot repay.

Yet integrity is not isolation. Because it is constructed through sharing and bonding, through seeing the selves in others, recognizing and recovering them, it leads to a truly civilized and social vision of being. Lorde . . . never withdraws. Her African archaeology is firmly attached in Harlem, where it transforms and redeems. Because her muses are so intensely familiar and intimate (even when cloaked in the myth of a distant Dahomeian goddess), she can present her poetic faces whole, the myth and the life, the self and civility. . . . (pp. 320-21)

> Mary J. Carruthers, "The Re-Vision of the Muse: Adrienne Rich, Audre Lorde, Judy Grahn, Olga Broumas," in The Hudson Review, Vol. XXXVI, No. 2, Summer, 1983, pp. 293-322.

Valerie Miner

Vision. Visibility. Sight. Hindsight. Insight. Second Sight. This is the metaphorical spectrum of Audre Lorde's bright new prose work *Zami.*

Zami is a Carriacou name for women who work together as friends and lovers. This "biomythography"—which blends past and present, dreams and premonitions—describes the varied women who shaped Audre Lorde's life. As the daughter of West Indian immigrants, she traces passionate umbilical ties back to Carriacou, the island of her mother's birth. Lorde felt her way along the streets of New York to become a noted poet and English professor at Hunter College. Her story is a marvellous excursion into the imagination of hope.

Unlike so many early literary memoirs or conventional *Kunstlerromans, Zami* does not fetishize the isolated artist as individual seeker. Rather Lorde describes the lives of many other women to highlight and underline her own experience. She is explicit about the racism and homophobia she suffered. This social consciousness adds heart and power to an autobiography which moves with the subtle drama of good fiction.

Sight—being seen, being able to see—is the line of suspense on which the story is drawn. As a child, Lorde was almost blind. Finally she got her glasses, which separated her from the other kids. As the youngest daughter of exhausted parents, she was often overlooked. As the black student of white nuns, she was easily discriminated against. Her mother "protected" her from racial prejudice by trying to ignore it, by insisting, for instance, that the white people who spat on young Audre did so at random, by accident. Other people denied her color, like the man, who after serving her breakfast for seven years, expressed amazement that she had won a Negro scholarship. Also, as a lesbian, she met many people who knew and did not want to know her identity. Often Lorde felt that part of her was hidden to everyone else in the world. Ultimately what made her fully visible—and *Zami* proves she is now

a flaming presence—was her own uncanny sight and her powerful gift to communicate what she saw.

> At home, my mother said, "Remember to be sisters in the presence of strangers." She meant white people, like the woman who tried to make me get up and give her my seat on the Number 4 bus, and who smelled like cleaning fluid. At St. Catherine's, they said, "Be sisters in the presence of strangers," and they meant non-catholics. In high school, the girls said, "Be sisters in the presence of strangers," and they meant men. My friends said, "Be sisters in the presence of strangers," and they meant squares.
>
> But in high school, my real sisters were strangers; my teachers were racists; and my friends were that color I was never supposed to trust.

Zami takes readers from Lorde's childhood to her twenties. We see the poet discovering her own intelligence, finding the voice to write, hacking at grubby jobs to make her way through school, going to Connecticut to work as an X-ray technician (a poignant section for those who have read *The Cancer Journals* and know that she would later have a mastectomy), spending time in Mexico, observing McCarthyism and the early Civil Rights Movement, dancing and drinking in the gay-girl bars in the 1950s. The momentum is so intense that it's hard to believe at the end of the book that we've only travelled the first half of Lorde's life.

Always this is more than one woman's story. It is a eulogy and benediction for the women who helped Lorde to see and to grow visible: her taciturn mother; her two sisters; her first playmate, Toni; her teenage friend Gennie who commits suicide; her first woman lover Ginger; the pickled and pungent expatriate Eudora; her Communist roommate Rhea; her tender-mad partner Muriel and, finally, Afrekete, who shines her light on what it means to be a loving, proud, black lesbian.

Lorde's language is graceful and sensuous. Her honesty is uncompromising without being rigid. Boldly, she describes a physical attraction for her mother, concluding the book with the line, "There [in Carriacou] it is said that the desire to lie with other women is a drive from the mother's blood." The scenes between Lorde and her lovers are gorgeous. *Zami*'s vitality heightens all the senses, but particularly the sense of smell—the aromas of sex, food, flowers and New York City itself.

The narrative is fairly straightforward chronologically, but illumined by momentary flashbacks and flashforwards. Lorde creates her own "Manual of Style" to redress traditional visibility, using capital letters for "Black," "Colored," "Negro," and lowercase for "white," "american," "catholic."

The epilogue is a spirited coda, drawing together the women who have enlightened her, "Their names, selves, faces feed me like corn before labor. I live each of them as a piece of me, and I choose these words with the same grave concern with which I choose to push speech into poetry, the mattering core, the forward vision of all of our lives."

Valerie Miner, in a review of "Zami: A New Spelling of My Name," in The American Book Review, *Vol. 5, No. 6, September-October, 1983, p. 12.*

Lorde on poetry and women:

For women . . . poetry is not a luxury. It is a vital necessity of our existence. It forms the quality of the light within which we predicate our hopes and dreams toward survival and change, first made into language, then into idea, then into more tangible action. Poetry is the way we help give name to the nameless so it can be thought. The farthest external horizons of our hopes and fears are cobbled by our poems, carved from the rock experiences of our daily lives.

Audre Lorde, in her "Poems Are Not Luxuries," *published in* Claims for Poetry, *University of Michigan Press, 1982.*

Audre Lorde [Interview with Claudia Tate]

[*In the following interview, published in Tate's* Black Women Writers at Work *(1983), Lorde discusses the meaning and development of her work, her political ideology, and the relationship between feminism and literature.*]

[*Tate*]: *How does your openness about being a black lesbian feminist direct your work and, more importantly, your life?*

[Lorde]: When you narrow your definition to what is convenient, or what is fashionable, or what is expected, what happens is dishonesty by silence. It is putting all of your eggs into one basket. That's not where all of your energy comes from.

Black writers, of whatever quality, who step outside the pale of what black writers are supposed to write about, or who black writers are supposed to be, are condemned to silences in black literary circles that are as total and as destructive as any imposed by racism. This is particularly true for black women writers who have refused to be delineated by male-establishment models of femininity, and who have dealt with their sexuality as an accepted part of their identity. For instance, where are the women writers of the Harlem Renaissance being taught? Why did it take so long for Zora Neale Hurston to be reprinted?

Now, when you have a literary community oppressed by silence from the outside, as black writers are in America, and you have this kind of tacit insistence upon some unilateral definition of what "blackness" is, then you are painfully and effectively silencing some of our most dynamic and creative talents, for all change and progress from within require the recognition of differences among ourselves.

When you are a member of an out-group, and you challenge others with whom you share this outsider position to examine some aspect of their lives that distorts differences between you, then there can be a great deal of pain.

In other words, when people of a group share an oppression, there are certain strengths that they build together. But there are also certain vulnerabilities. For instance, talking about racism to the women's movement results in "Huh, don't bother us with that. Look, we're all sisters, please don't rock the boat." Talking to the black community about sexism results in pretty much the same thing. You get a "Wait, wait . . . wait a minute: we're all black together. Don't rock the boat." In our work and in our living, we must recognize that difference is a reason for celebration and growth, rather than a reason for destruction.

We should see difference as a dialogue, the same way we deal with symbol and image, in literary study. "Imaging" is the process of developing a dialectic, a tension between opposites that illuminates the differences and similarities between things in apparent opposition. It is the same way with people. We need to use these differences in constructive ways, creative ways, rather than in ways to justify our destroying each other.

With respect to myself specifically, I feel that not to be open about any of the different "people" within my identity, particularly the "mes" who are challenged by a status quo, is to invite myself and other women, by my example, to live a lie. In other words, I would be giving in to a myth of sameness which I think can destroy us.

I'm not into living lies, no matter how comfortable they may be. I really feel that I'm too old for both abstractions and games, and I will not shut off any of my essential sources of power, control, and knowledge. I learned to speak the truth by accepting many parts of myself and making them serve one another. This power fuels my life and my work. (pp. 100-02)

Have your critics attempted to stereotype your work?

Critics have always wanted to cast me in a particular role from the time my first poem was published when I was fifteen years old. My English teachers at Hunter High School said that a particular poem was much too romantic. It was a love poem about my first love affair with a boy, and they didn't want to print it in the school paper, which is why I sent it to *Seventeen* magazine.

It's easier to deal with a poet, certainly with a black woman poet, when you categorize her, narrow her down so that she can fulfill your expectations, so she's socially acceptable and not too disturbing, not too discordant. I cannot be categorized. That has been both my weakness and my strength. It has been my weakness because my independence has cost me a lot of support. But you see, it has also been my strength because it has given me a vantage point and the power to go on. I don't know how I would have lived through the difficulties I have survived and continued to produce, if I had not felt that all of who I am is what fulfills me and fulfills the vision I have of the world, and of the future.

For whom do you write? What is your responsibility to your audience?

I write for myself and my children and for as many people as possible who can read me, who need to hear what I have to say—who need to use what I know. When I say myself,

I mean not only the Audre who inhabits my body but all those feisty, incorrigible black women who insist on standing up and saying "*I am* and you cannot wipe me out, no matter how irritating I am, how much you fear what I might represent." I write for these women for whom a voice has not yet existed, or whose voices have been silenced. I don't have the only voice or all of their voices, but they are a part of my voice, and I am a part of theirs.

My responsibility is to speak the truth as I feel it, and to attempt to speak it with as much precision and beauty as possible. I think of my responsibility in terms of women because there are many voices for men. There are very few voices for women and particularly very few voices for black women, speaking from the center of consciousness, from the *I am* out to the *we are* and then out to the *we can*.

My mother used to say: "Island women make good wives; whatever happens they've seen worse." Well, I feel that as black women we have been through all kinds of catastrophe. We've survived, and with style.

I feel I have a duty to speak the truth as I see it and to share not just my triumphs, not just the things that felt good, but the pain, the intense, often unmitigating pain. It is important to share how I know survival is survival and not just a walk through the rain. For example, I have a duty to share what it feels like at three o'clock in the morning when you know "they" could cut you down emotionally in the street and grin in your face. And "they" are your own people. To share what it means to look into another sister's eyes and have her look away and choose someone you know she hates because it's expedient. To know that I, at times, have been a coward, or less than myself, or oppressive to other women, and to know that I can change. All of that anxiety, pain, defeat must be shared. We need to talk about what feels good. We talk about what we think is settled. We never seem to talk about the ongoing problems. We need to share our mistakes in the same way we share our victories because that's the only way learning occurs. In other words, we have survived the pain, the problems, the failures, so what we need to do is use this suffering and learn from it. We must remember and comfort ourselves with that fact that survival is, in itself, a victory.

I never thought I would live to be forty, and I feel, "Hey, I really did it!" I am stronger for confronting the hard issue of breast cancer, of mortality, dying. It is hard, extremely hard, but very strengthening to remember I could be silent my whole life long and then be dead, flat out, and never have said or done what I wanted to do, what I needed to do because of pain or fear. . . . If I wait to be assured I'm right before I speak, I would be sending little cryptic messages on the Ouiji board, complaints from the other side.

I really feel if what I have to say is wrong, then there will be some woman who will stand up and say Audre Lorde was in error. But my words will be there, something for her to bounce off of, something to incite thought, activity.

I write not only for my peers but for those who will come after me, to say I was there, and I passed on, and you will pass on, too. But you're here now, so do it. I believe very strongly in survival and teaching. I feel that is my work.

This is so important that it bears repeating. I write for those women who do not speak, for those who do not have a voice because they/we were so terrified, because we are taught to respect fear more than ourselves. We've been taught that silence would save us, but it won't. We *must* learn to respect ourselves and our needs more than the fear of our differences, and we must learn to share ourselves with each other.

Is writing a way of growing, understanding?

Yes. I think writing and teaching, child-rearing, digging rocks (which is one of my favorite pastimes), all of the things I do are very much a part of my work. They flow in and out of each other, help to nourish each other. That's what the whole question of survival and teaching means. That we keep our experience afloat long enough, that we share what we know, so that other people can build upon our experience. There are many ways of doing that in all aspects of our lives. So teaching for me is in many respects identical to writing. Both become ways of exploring what I need for survival. They are survival techniques. Because as I write, as I teach, I am answering those questions that are primary for my own survival, and I am exploring the response to these questions with other people; this is what teaching is. I think that this is the only way that real learning occurs. Learning does not happen in some detached way of dealing with a text alone, but from becoming so involved in the process that you can see how it might illuminate your life, and then how you can share that illumination.

When did you start to write?

I looked around when I was a young woman and there was no one saying what I wanted and needed to hear. I felt totally alienated, disoriented, crazy. I thought that there's got to be somebody else who feels as I do.

I was very inarticulate as a youngster. I couldn't speak. I didn't speak until I was five, in fact, not really until I started reading and writing poetry. I used to speak in poetry. I would read poems, and I would memorize them. People would say, "Well, what do you think, Audre? What happened to you yesterday?" And I would recite a poem and somewhere in that poem there would be a line or a feeling I was sharing. In other words, I literally communicated through poetry. And when I couldn't find the poems to express the things I was feeling, that's when I started writing poetry. That was when I was twelve or thirteen.

Do black male and female writers dramatize characters and themes in distinctly different ways? Gayl Jones replied to this question by saying she thought one distinction has to do with the kinds of events men and women select to depict in literature. She thinks black women writers tend to select particular and personal events rather than those which are generally considered to be representative.

I think that's true. This reflects a difference between men and women in general. Black men have come to believe to their detriment that you have no validity unless you're "global," as opposed to personal. Yet, our *real power* comes from the personal; our real insights about living come from that deep knowledge within us that arises from our feelings. Our thoughts are shaped by our tutoring. As black people, we have not been tutored for our benefit, but more often than not, for our detriment. We were tutored to function in a structure that already existed but that does not function for our good. Our feelings are our most genuine paths to knowledge. They are chaotic, sometimes painful, sometimes contradictory, but they come from deep within us. And we must key into those feelings and begin to extrapolate from them, examine them for new ways of understanding our experiences. This is how new visions begin, how we begin to posit a future nourished by the past. This is what I mean by matter following energy, and energy following feeling. Our visions begin with our desires.

Men have been taught to deal only with what they understand. This is what they respect. They know that somewhere feeling and knowledge are important, so they keep women around to do their feeling for them, like ants do aphids.

I don't think these differences between men and women are rigidly defined with respect to gender, though the Western input has been to divide these differences into male and female *characteristics*. We all have the ability to feel deeply and to move upon our feelings and see where they lead us. Men in general have suppressed that capacity, so they keep women around to do that for them. Until men begin to develop that capacity within themselves, they will always be at a loss and will always need to victimize women.

The message I have for black men is that it is to their detriment to follow this pattern. Too many black men do precisely that, which results in violence along sexual lines. This violence terrifies me. It is a painful truth which is almost unbearable. As I say in a new poem, it is "a pain almost beyond bearing" because it gives birth to the kind of hostility that will destroy us.

To change the focus, though ever so slightly. Writing by black Americans has traditionally dramatized black people's humanity. Black male writers tend to cry out in rage in order to convince their readers that they too feel, whereas black women writers tend to dramatize the pain, the love. They don't seem to need to intellectualize this capacity to feel, but focus on describing the feeling itself.

It's one thing to talk about feeling. It's another to feel. Yes, love is often pain. But I think what is really necessary is to see how much of this pain I can use, how much of this truth I can see and still live unblinded. That is an essential question that we must all ask ourselves. There is some point at which pain becomes an end in itself, and we must let it go. On the other hand, we must not be afraid of pain, and we must not subject ourselves to pain as an end in itself. We must not celebrate victimization because there are other ways of being black.

There is a very thin but a very definite line between these two responses to pain. And I would like to see this line more carefully drawn in some of the works by black women writers. I am particularly aware of the two re-

sponses in my own work. And I find I must remember that the pain is not its own reason for being. It is a part of living. And the only kind of pain that is intolerable is pain that is wasteful, pain from which we do not learn. And I think that we must learn to distinguish between the two.

How do you integrate social protest and art in your work?

I see protest as a genuine means of encouraging someone to feel the inconsistencies, the horror of the lives we are living. Social protest is saying that we do not have to live this way. If we feel deeply, and we encourage ourselves and others to feel deeply, we will find the germ of our answers to bring about change. Because once we recognize what it is we are feeling, once we recognize we can feel deeply, love deeply, can feel joy, then we will demand that all parts of our lives produce that kind of joy. And when they do not, we will ask, "Why don't they?" And it is the asking that will lead us inevitably toward change.

So the question of social protest and art is inseparable for me. I can't say it is an either-or proposition. Art for art's sake doesn't really exist for me. What I saw was wrong, and I had to speak up. I loved poetry, and I loved words. But what was beautiful had to serve the purpose of changing my life, or I would have died. If I cannot air this pain and alter it, I will surely die of it. That's the beginning of social protest.

How has your work evolved in terms of interest and craft? Let's look at the love poetry, for instance, which dominated your early work [**The First Cities** *and* **New York Head Shop**] *and which appears in* **The Black Unicorn**.

Everyone has a first-love poem that comes out of that first love. Everybody has it, and it's so wonderful and new and great. But when you've been writing love poems after thirty years, the later poems are the ones that really hit the nitty gritty, that meet your boundaries. They witness what you've been through. Those are the real love poems. And I love them because they say, "Hey! We define ourselves as lovers, as people who love each other all over again; we become new again." These poems insist that you can't separate loving from fighting, from dying, from hurting, but love is triumphant. It is powerful and strong, and I feel I grow a great deal in all of my emotions, especially in the capacity to love.

Your love poetry seems not only to celebrate the personal experience of love but also love as a human concept, a theme embracing all of life, a theme which appears more and more emphatically in your later work. Particularly interesting, for instance, are the lesbian love poems [*"**Letter for Jan**" and "**Walking Our Boundaries**"*]. *It didn't seem to make much difference whether the poems depicted a relationship between two women, two men, or a man and a woman. . . . The poems do not celebrate the people but the love.*

When you love, you love. It only depends on how you do it, how committed you are, how many mistakes you make. . . . But I do believe that the love expressed between women is particular and powerful because we have had to love ourselves in order to live; love has been our means of survival. And having been in love with both men and women, I want to resist the temptation to gloss over the differences.

I am frequently jarred by my sometimes unconscious attempt to identify the sex of the person addressed in the poem. Since I associate the speaker's voice with you, and since I'm not always conscious that you are a lesbian, the jarring occurs when I realize the object of affection is likewise a woman. I'm certain this disturbance originates in how society defines love in terms of heterosexuality. So if we are to see love as a "universal" concept, society pressures us to see it as heterosexual.

Yes, we're supposed to see "universal" love as heterosexual. What I insist upon in my work is that there is no such thing as universal love in literature. There is *this* love in *this* poem. The poem happens when I, Audre Lorde, poet, deal with the particular instead of the "UNIVERSAL." My power as a person, as a poet, comes from who I am. I am a particular person. The relationships I have had, in which people kept me alive, helped sustain me, were sustained by me, were particular relationships. They help give me my particular identity, which is the source of my energy. Not to deal with my life in my art is to cut out the fount of my strength.

I love to write love poems. I love loving. And to put it into another framework, that is, other than poetry, I wrote a paper entitled **"The Uses of the Erotic,"** where I examine the whole question of loving as a manifestation, love as a source of tremendous power. Women have been taught to suspect the erotic urge, the place that is uniquely female. So, just as we tend to reject our blackness because it has been termed inferior, as women we tend to reject our capacity for feeling, our ability to love, to touch the erotic, because it has been devalued. But it is within this that lies so much of our power, our ability to posit, our vision. Because once we know how deeply we can feel, we begin to demand from all of our life pursuits that they be in accordance with these feelings. And when they don't we must raise the question why do I feel constantly suicidal, for instance? What's wrong? Is it me, or is it what I am doing? We begin to need to answer such questions. But we cannot when we have no image of joy, no vision of what we are capable of. After the killing is over. When you live without the sunlight, you don't know what it is to relish the bright light or even to have too much of it. Once you have light, then you can measure its intensity. So too with joy. (pp. 103-10)

Would you describe your writing process?

I keep a journal and write in it fairly regularly. I get a lot of my poems out of it. It's like the raw material for my poems. Sometimes I'm blessed with a poem that comes in the form of a poem, but other times I've worked for two years on a poem.

For me, there are two very basic and different processes for revising my poetry. One is recognizing that a poem has not yet become itself. In other words, I mean that the feeling, the truth that the poem is anchored in is somehow not clearly clarified inside of me, and as a result it lacks something. Then it has to be re-felt. Then there's the other process which is easier. The poem is itself, but it has rough edges that need to be refined. That kind of revision involves picking the image that is more potent or tailoring it so that it carries the feeling. That's an easier kind of rewriting and re-feeling.

My journal entries focus on things I feel: feelings that sometimes have no place, no beginning, no end; phrases I hear in passing; something that looks good to me; sometimes just observations of the world.

I went through a period once when I felt like I was dying. I wasn't writing any poetry, and I felt that if I couldn't write I would split. I was recording in my journal, but no poems came. I know now that this period was a transition in my life.

The next year, I went back to my journal, and here were these incredible poems that I could almost lift out of it. Many of them are in **The Black Unicorn.** "**Harriet**" is one of them; "**Sequelae**" and "**The Litany for Survival**" are others. These poems came right out of the journal. But I didn't see them as poems then.

"**Power**" was in the journal too. It is a poem written about Clifford Glover, the ten-year-old black boy shot by a cop who was acquitted by a jury on which a black woman sat. In fact, the day I heard on the radio that O'Shea had been acquitted, I was going across town on 88th Street [New York City] and I had to pull over. A kind of fury rose up in me—the sky turned red. I felt so sick. I felt as if I would drive the car into a wall, into the next person I saw. So I pulled over. I took out my journal just to air some of my fury, to get it out of my fingertips. Those expressed feelings are that poem. That was just how "**Power**" was written.

A transition has to occur before you can make poetry out of your journal entries.

There is a gap between the journal and my poetry. I write this stuff in my journal, and sometimes I cannot even read my journals because there is so much pain and rage in them. I'll put it away in a drawer, and six months, a year or so later, I'll pick up the journal, and there will be the seeds of poems. The journal entries somehow have to be assimilated into my living; only then can I deal with what I have written down.

Art is not living. It is the use of living. The artist has the ability to take the living and use it in a certain way and produce art.

Does Afro-American literature possess particular characteristics?

Afro-American literature is certainly part of an African tradition. African tradition deals with life as an experience to be lived. In many respects, it is much like the Eastern philosophies in that we see ourselves as a part of a life force; we are joined, for instance, to the air, to the earth. We are part of the whole-life process. We live in accordance with, in a kind of correspondence with the rest of the world as a whole. And therefore living becomes an experience, rather than a problem, no matter how bad or how painful it may be. Change will rise endemically from the experience fully lived and responded to.

I feel this very much in African writing. And as a consequence, I have learned a great deal from Achebe, Tutuola, Ekwensi, from Flora Nwapa and Ama Ata Aido. Leslie Lacy, a black American who lived temporarily in Ghana, writes about experiencing this transcendence in his book *The Rise and Fall of a Proper Negro.*

It's not a turning away from pain, error, but seeing these things as part of living, and learning from them. This characteristic is particularly African, and it is transposed into the best of Afro-American literature. In addition, we have the legends of our struggle and survival in the New World.

This transcendence appears in Ellison, a little bit in Baldwin. And it is present very much so in Toni Morrison's *Sula,* which is a most wonderful piece of fiction. And I don't care if she won a prize for *The Song of Solomon. Sula* is a totally incredible book. It made me light up inside like a Christmas tree. I particularly identified with the book because of the female-outsider idea. That book is one long poem. Sula is the ultimate black female of our time, trapped in her power and her pain. Alice Walker uses that quality in *The Color Purple,* another wonderful novel of living as power.

The recent writing by many black women seems to explore human concerns somewhat differently than do the men. These women refuse to blame racism alone for every negative aspect of black life. They are examining the nature of what passes between black women and black men—the power principles. Men tend to respond defensively to the writing of black women by labeling them as the "darklings" of the literary establishment. Goodness knows, the critics, especially black male critics, had a field day with Ntozake Shange's For Colored Girls Who Have Considered Suicide When the Rainbow is Enuf. *And they are getting started on Alice Walker's* The Color Purple. *But there are cruel black men, just as there are kind black men. Can't we try to alter that cruelty by focusing on it?*

Let me read an excerpt from a piece in *The Black Scholar* for you, which I wrote a while back:

> As I have said elsewhere, it is not the destiny of black America to repeat white America's mistakes. But we will, if we mistake the trappings of success in a sick society for the signs of a meaningful life. If black men continue to do so, defining "femininity" in its archaic European terms, this augurs ill for our survival as a people, let alone our survival as individuals. Freedom and future for blacks do not mean absorbing the dominant white male disease. . . .
>
> As black people, we cannot begin our dialogue by denying the oppressive nature of male privilege. And if black males choose to assume that privilege, for whatever reason, raping, brutalizing and killing women, then we cannot ignore black male oppression. One oppression does not justify another.

It's infuriating. Misguided black men. And meanwhile they are killing us in the streets. Is that the nature of nationhood?

I find this divisiveness to be oppressive and very persistent.

It's been going on for a long time. It didn't start with Ntozake. It's been coming more and more to the forefront now. If you ask any of the black women writers over thirty whom you're interviewing, if she's honest, she will tell you. You know there's as much a black literary mafia in this country as there is a white literary mafia. They control who gets exposure. If you don't toe the line, then you're not published; your works are not distributed. At the same time, as black women, of course, we do not want to be used against black men by a system that means both of us ill.

Do you think that had it not been for the women's movement black women would still be struggling to achieve their voice in the literary establishment?

Without a doubt. Black women writers have been around a long time, and they have suffered consistent inattention. Despite this reality, you hear from various sources that black women really have "it." We're getting jobs; we're getting this and that, supposedly. Yet we still constitute the lowest economic group in America. Meanwhile those of us who do not fit into the "establishment" have not been allowed a voice, and it was only with the advent of the women's movement—even though black women are in disagreement with many aspects of the women's movement—that black women began to demand a voice, as women and as blacks. I think any of us who are honest have to say this. As Barbara Smith says, "All the women were white and all the blacks were men, but some of us are still brave." Her book on black women's studies [*Some of Us Are Brave*], which she edited along with Gloria Hull and Patricia Bell Scott, is the first one on the subject.

Are you at a turning point in your career, your life?

I think I have deepened and broadened my understanding of the true difficulty of my work. Twenty years ago when I said we needed to understand each other I had not really perfected a consciousness concerning how important differences are in our lives. But that is a theme which recurs in my life and in my work. I have become more powerful because I have refused to settle for the myth of sorry sameness, that myth of easy sameness. My life's work continues to be survival and teaching. As I said before, teaching is also learning; teach what you need to learn. If we do this deeply, then it is most effective. I have, for example, deepened the questions that I follow, and so I have also deepened the ways I teach and learn.

The work I did on the erotic was very, very important. It opened up for me a whole area of connections in the absence of codified knowledge, or in the absence of some other clear choice. The erotic has been a real guide for me. And learning as a discipline is identical to learning how to reach through feeling the essence of how and where the erotic originates, to posit what it is based upon. This process of feeling and therefore knowing has been very, very constructive for me.

I believe in the erotic and I believe in it as an enlightening force within our lives as women. I have become clearer about the distinctions between the erotic and other apparently similar forces. We tend to think of the erotic as an easy, tantalizing sexual arousal. I speak of the erotic as the deepest life force, a force which moves us toward living in a fundamental way. And when I say living I mean it as that force which moves us toward what will accomplish real positive change.

When I speak of a future that I work for, I speak of a future in which all of us can learn, a future which we want for our children. I posit that future to be led by my visions, my dreams, and my knowledge of life. It is that knowledge which I call the erotic, and I think we must develop it within ourselves. I think so much of our living and our consciousness has been formed by death or by non-living. This is what allows us to tolerate so much of what is vile around us. When I speak of "the good," I speak of living; I speak of the erotic in all forms. They are all one. So in that sense I believe in the erotic as an illuminating principle in our lives.

You've just finished a new work.

Yes. *Zami: A New Spelling of My Name* was just published. It's a biomythography, which is really fiction. It has the elements of biography and history of myth. In other words, it's fiction built from many sources. This is one way of expanding our vision.

I'm very excited about this book. As you know, it's been a long time coming. Now that it's out, it'll do its work. Whatever its faults, whatever its glories, it's there.

You might call *Zami* a novel. I don't like to call it that. Writing *Zami* was a lifeline through the cancer experience. As I said in *The Cancer Journals,* I couldn't believe that what I was fighting I would fight alone and only for myself. I couldn't believe that there wasn't something there that somebody could use at some other point because I know that I could have used some other woman's words, whatever she had to say. Just to know that someone had been there before me would have been very important, but there was nothing. Writing *The Cancer Journals* gave me the strength and power to examine that experience, to put down into words what I was feeling. It was my belief that if this work were useful to just one woman, it was worth doing.

What can you share with the younger generation of black women writers and writers in general?

Not to be afraid of difference. To be real, tough, loving. And to recognize each other. I can tell them not to be afraid to feel and not to be afraid to write about it. Even if you are afraid, do it anyway because we learn to work when we are tired, so we can learn to work when we are afraid. Silence never brought us anything. Survive and teach; that's what we've got to do and to do it with joy. (p. 111-16)

> *Audre Lorde and Claudia Tate, in an interview in* Black Women Writers at Work, *edited by Claudia Tate, Continuum, 1983, pp. 100-16.*

Barbara Christian

Lorde's essays [in *Sister Outsider: Essays and Speeches*] date from 1976 to the present. For much of her writing life, she has exclusively published poetry. She tells us in her interview with Adrienne Rich (included in *Sister Outsider*) that she couldn't write prose for many years because "communicating deep feeling in linear solid blocks of print felt arcane, a method beyond [her]." Although the fifteen essays in *Sister Outsider* cover only these last seven years, they, along with *Zami* (1983), her first published book of prose, trace important concepts in Lorde's development as a black feminist thinker—primarily her intense concern with repression as a means of control, which is reflected in her emphasis on the erotic and her analysis of the concept of difference.

Some of these deeply felt concepts are compressed in the poem, "Sister Outsider," after which this volume is named. The poem appeared in Lorde's *The Black Unicorn* (1978) which uses as one of its central motifs the ancient wisdom of the women of Dahomey. Throughout the collection of essays, Lorde probes this ancient wisdom. Many of her essays flow from the last lines of her poem:

> now
> your light shines very brightly
> but I want you
> to know
> your darkness also
> rich
> and beyond fear

Whether Lorde is writing about her trip to Grenada (her mother's homeland) or to Russia; whether she is analyzing the sexism and homophobia among black women and men, the racism ingrained in white women, the sexism, racism, homophobia of American society; or whether she is asserting the importance of the transformation of silence into language and action, her words are guided by that ancient tradition which cherishes the "darkness" of feelings as well as the "light" of ideas.

In the first essay she'd written in twenty years, Lorde uses the interaction of light and dark imagery to illuminate her affirmation that **"Poetry is not a Luxury."** In a sense this essay is her bridge between her writing of poetry and of prose. Insisting that "the woman's place of power within each of us is neither white nor surface; it is dark, it is ancient, and it is deep," she also emphasizes that poetry is "the quality of light within which we predicate our hopes and dreams toward survival and change, first made into language, then into idea, then into more tangible action." The thrust of this critical essay is Lorde's belief that we must combine the ancient, non-European cherishing of the power of feeling with the European concept that ideas will make us free. And that women have the possibility of this fusion because we still have some respect for that darkness within. Her axiom, "The white fathers told us, 'I think, therefore I am.' The Black Mother within each of us—the poet—whispers in our dreams, 'I feel, therefore I can be free'," is examined in other essays, in **"The Uses of Anger,"** and in her provocative essay, **"Uses of the Erotic, The Erotic as Power."**

This essay, for me, is one of Lorde's most significant statements, even as it is one of her most difficult to summarize—partly because it is written in such distilled language, partly because the erotic in this society has been so confused with sex that anyone who uses the word, in its root sense, is in danger of being misunderstood. Yet Lorde uses our persistent misunderstanding of the word, and therefore our loss of an important source of power, to make essential distinctions between the pornographic and the erotic. In so doing she addresses one of the dilemmas of humanity: how do people get to the point where they not only recognize their own oppression but will initiate the changes necessary to free themselves?

In defining the erotic, Lorde goes back to the Greek word, *eros,* "the personification of love in all of its aspects—born of Chaos and personifying power and harmony." Each part of this definition is critical to her discussion of the uses of the erotic: the trusting of self, the Chaos not fully understood but from which creativity and harmony spring, the power that the passion for life has to move us towards action. And in discussing its uses for women, she places this definition in sharp focus. For women are the ones who have been trivialized as "feeling" beings who cannot "think," even as society gives us the charge of feeling for men. As a result, Lorde asserts, we have come "to distrust that power from which rises our deepest nonrational knowledge," which is our basis for demanding from life all that we know it can be. Out of touch with that disturbing Chaos, from which creativity and satisfaction come, we need not be controlled by external forces, we maintain our own repression. But if we are responsible to ourselves in the deepest sense, in our work, in our pleasures, in our struggles, "our acts against oppression become integral with self, motivated and empowered from within."

Her articulation of the power of the erotic is also connected to the other critical concept that characterizes her thought: difference as a dynamic force. For Lorde, the erotic is the source of that "sharing of joy" which provides a deep connection between persons who are, necessarily, different. Thus the erotic is one means by which difference among people can become a source of creative dialogue, rather than a threat.

Difference is, for Lorde, a given in any human situation. What she articulates in essays like **"Scratching the Surface, Some Notes on Barriers to Women and Loving,"** or in **"Age, Race, Class and Sex: Women Redefining Difference,"** is that racism, sexism, classism, ageism, homophobia, all stem from the same source—"an inability to recognize the notion of difference as a dynamic human force which is enriching rather than threatening to the defined self." And what she analyzes in essays like **"The Master's Tools Will Never Dismantle the Master's House,"** or in **"Learning from the 60s"** is how movements like the Black Movement, the Women's Movement, which spring from society's intolerance of difference, tend to be just as intolerant of differences among their own constituents. The result is not only the weakening of the movement, once so many are excluded from the inner sanctums, but the loss of the creative function of difference as a source of new ideas, new visions. Thus if "women" are defined as white, heterosexual, young women whose class position enables them to see certain aspects of life as the only ones that demand change, then what is lost is the knowledge of women of color, of older women, of poor women, of lesbian

women. If we succumb to the master's most effective tool, the pitting of people against one another by using the threat of difference, we can never dismantle the master's house. Lorde warns that "in our world, divide and conquer must become define and empower."

Lorde, however, is not so naive as to see the path she advocates as an easy one. It means, as she writes in her poem **"Among Ourselves,"** that we must "stop killing / the other / in ourselves / the self that we hate in others." It therefore means the exposure of self, and the recognition of the terror we have for a particular difference. It means to struggle with those with whom we might have much in common, with whom we might have differences. Such a stance means that most of us must give up something, whether it is class privilege or self-absorption. (p. 6)

As a black, lesbian, feminist, poet, mother, Lorde has, in her own life, had to search long and hard for *her* people. In responding to each of these audiences, in which a part of her identity lies, she refuses to give up her differences. In fact she uses them, as woman to man, black to white, lesbian to heterosexual, as a means of conducting creative dialogue. She asserts that "the results of woman-hating in the Black communities are tragedies which diminish all Black People" and that the black man's use of the label "lesbian" as a threat is an attempt to rule by fear. She reminds white women who fear the anger of black women that "anger between peers births courage, not destruction, and the discomfort and sense of loss it often causes is not fatal but a sign of growth." In **"Eye to Eye,"** she acknowledges the anger that black women direct toward each other, as well as our history of bonding, in a society which tells us we are wrong at every turn.

In discussing our condition she reminds black women who attack lesbianism as anti-black of "the sisterhood of work and play and power" that is a part of our African tradition, and of how we have been taught to see each other as "heartless competitors for the scarce male, the all important prize that could legitimize our existence." This "dehumanization of the denial of self," she asserts, "is no less lethal than the dehumanization of racism to which it is so closely allied." And underlying all of Lorde's attempts to hold creative dialogue with the many parts of her self is her recognition that the good in this society is tragically defined in terms of profit rather than in terms of the human being.

Lorde's essays are always directed toward the deepening of self, even as she analyzes the ways in which society attempts to dehumanize it. In showing the connections between sexism, racism, ageism, homophobia, classism, even as she insists on the creative differences among those persons they affect, she stresses the need to share the joy and pain of living, through language. In speaking, in breaking the silence about what each of us actually experiences, what we think, in voicing even our disagreements, we bridge the differences between us. Like Jordan's and Walker's essays, Lorde's collection "broadens the joining."

Sister Outsider is another indication of the depth of analysis that black women writers are contributing to feminist thought. It is an analysis that stresses the connections between people and criticizes a stance of easy separatism. As people who have been excluded, because we are black, woman, poor, lesbian, not correct in some way, black women writers carefully search for the sources of real connections. Particularly when Lorde's collection of essays is seen within this growing body of feminist thought, her assertion that difference is a dynamic force is a powerful one for those of us who are serious about recreating our world. (p. 7)

> *Barbara Christian, "Dynamics of Difference," in* The Women's Review of Books, *Vol. I, No. 11, August, 1984, pp. 6-7.*

Kate Walter

Hey, hey, ho, ho, patriarchy's got to go! That's the gist of *Sister Outsider,* Audre Lorde's collection of 15 essays and speeches from the past eight years. I suspect most readers already know the politics of this erudite black lesbian feminist poet: the more you resemble her target of white, male, thin, young, heterosexual, Christian, and financially secure, the more you'll squirm under her verbal guns. One might question whether guilt-tripping is the best way to encourage social change, but when she lets rip, it's hard to argue. And men aren't the only ones at fault; **"Age, Race, Class, and Sex: Women Redefining Difference"** warns that ignoring racial differences is the most serious threat to the women's movement. She blames this bias on white European patriarchal conditioning.

Feminists who believe they've rehashed the anti-patriarchal thing ad infinitum might have trouble with Lorde's hypothesis, but I'm in her corner here, and I wonder whether those other folks aren't straight middle-class white feminists who've opted for what Lorde calls the "range of pretended choices and rewards for identifying with patriarchial power and its tools." I wonder if they live in the same world as me. If you're black, gay, or left-wing, it's easier to identify with Lorde because we can never join the patriarchy, even if we're tempted. How can men and women get beyond the repercussions of our upbringing? According to Lorde, we must use our racial, cultural, sexual differences as a springboard for creative growth. That sounds terrific, except it's not clear how we're supposed to go about it.

Sister Outsider includes Lorde's reflections as a lesbian mother ("The question of separatism is by no means simple. I'm thankful that one of my children is male, since that helps to keep me honest.") and a recap of her battle with cancer. **"Scratching the Surface: Some Notes on Barriers to Women and Loving"** reminds us that lesbian-baiting is used to obscure the real issues of racism and sexism; she tackles the problem of horizontal infighting— black women viewing other black women as competitors, black men threatened by the bonding of black women; black and white women squabbling over who is more oppressed. **"Sexism: An American Disease in Blackface"** urges black men to turn their rage against the capitalist system, rather than toward their black sisters. Lorde, an American of Grenadian descent, zings it to Reagan and

the CIA in **"Grenada Revisited: An Interim Report";** she believes the invasion last October was a test to see whether black Americans would fire on other blacks. The essay ends on a hopeful note: Lorde describes Grenadians as resilient, an adjective that also applies to this survivor who refuses to be silent about what needs to be changed. The provocative ideas of *Sister Outsider* will unsettle some readers, but that's just what Lorde intends.

> *Kate Walter, "Outside In," in* The Village Voice, *Vol. XXIX, No. 6, September 4, 1984, p. 52.*

Jerome Brooks

Audre Lorde has been writing now for more than twenty years, and the turbulent events of the past two decades find eloquent voice in her poetry. What is remarkable, however, as one looks back over her work so far is the powerful personal voice of her own struggles with life. Although she is decidedly political and has enjoyed an extremely engaged and active life, the world is seen in her poetry mainly through the conflicts and confrontation of her coming to terms with herself or with very private pain. Indeed, the words anger and rage come up time and again in her poetry, but the key word is pain. And for her pain is private and intimate. When she writes of her personal suffering, the writing is almost clinically precise, original, and direct.

A central poem in this regard, and one of her finest, is **"Father, Son, and Holy Ghost,"** about the death of her father. It is central also to an understanding of the mind of Audre Lorde. It is appropriately not about his death, but about the young daughter's experience of his absence. The poet cannot bear to visit his grave, so massive and vital a presence was he while alive. His presence was intellectual and moral in nature: "he lived still judgments on familiar things." His physical stature invaded the very details of the house. Although the poet has never seen his grave, there is an imagining of its daily routine, visited each day by a "different woman," and a man "who loved but one" thus being cared for each day by a different woman arouses an unacknowledged jealousy in the bereaved daughter. The jealous grief finds solace in the lively memory that he "died / knowing a January 15 that year me."

This poem of 1960 thus established the three central themes and motifs of Lorde's life and the pattern of her poetry: her preoccupation with the male principle and the issue of power; her profound quest for love; and the commitment to intellectual and moral clarity about "familiar things."

It should be noted that the image of her mother in Lorde's poetry is also a dominant one, but of a different order. The mother, for example, in **"Black Mother Woman,"** is a spirit to be exorcised, for there is nothing gentle and maternal in her memory. The daughter must fend through a thicket of anger and fury to find "the core of love." From her mother, she has acquired a "squadron of conflicting rebellions," elsewhere described as a conflict between racial values. The daughter's identity is achieved through standing apart from, against the mother.

The poetry is, then, a prolonged spiritual effort to reach the father, to be transformed into him, and to be his likeness, more son than daughter. This preoccupation with the male principle and with power is a tribute to the father's legacy. And this concern in turn is at the root of those disconcerting, wild, surrealist images that characterize much of her poetry. One has a feeling often of toughness and determination, of anger, in many of the poems. These are the ghosts of the father.

She speaks of herself as warrior, and she longs for "victories over men, over women, over my selves." In *The Black Unicorn,* the contact with Africa is the contact with the father who is revealed in a wealth of mythological symbols. "It was in Abomey that I felt / the full blood of my father's wars / and where I found my mother Seboulisa." But the poet herself identifies with Eshu, who is both male principle and prankster. The women while working on fabric openly scorn his "iron quiver / standing erect and flamingly familiar / in their door-yard," while the men create the poetry of war into tapestries. The poet is inspired by this warlike company to wear two drums on her head and "to sharpen the knives of my tongue." The fundamental image of the unicorn indicates that the poet is aware that Africa is for her a fatherland, a phallic terrain. It serves this function all the more clearly in that there is an easy passage in this mythic terrain between male and female, between parent and child. This confusion is her favorite trickery. Mawulisa (Mawu and Lisa), for example, is both male and female, or, if you prefer, both parent and son. In a particularly witty passage in **"The Winds of Orisha,"** she reminds us that in Greek legend, Tiresias took five hundred years to become a woman "until nut-like she went to sleep in a bottle." The poet takes heart from this transformation: "Tiresias took 500 years to grow into a woman / so do not despair of your sons."

These symbols are an incantation of the spirit of the father, a quest for his power. Lorde's quest is not for power for its own sake. Nor is it a self-serving quest, but a search for power at the service of a tremendous social anger. Lorde's poetry of anger is perhaps her best-known work and the source of much of her East Coast following, though, in my judgment, it does not always represent her finest work. What I will call her social poetry is sometimes marred by what she herself calls an "avid insistence on detail," or what I would rather term a Whitmanesque democratic litany of events. This litany is redeemed, however, by the internalization of facts through haunting imagery, as in the poem called simply **"Power,"** where the streets of New York become "a desert of raw gunshot wounds" and the poet's dream is disturbed by the "shattered black / face off the edge of my sleep." Her ability to hold event up to her relentlessly clinical analysis often leads to a perception of human character that is, perhaps, the ultimate justification for art. In the same poem, for instance, speaking of the jury that acquitted the policeman who shot down a ten-year-old boy, she singles out for rebuke the "one black woman who said / 'They convinced me' meaning / they had dragged her 4'10" black woman's frame / over the hot coals of four centuries of white male approval / until she let go the first real power she ever had. . . . "

This rage (a favorite word and the title of one of her volumes) is especially apparent in the new poems of her latest book, *Chosen Poems—Old and New* (1982), where, for instance, she reflects on a brief sojourn she spent many years ago in Jackson, Mississippi. The death of Emmett Till in the Pearl River becomes a christening at which the poet becomes his sponsor and he becomes her "son forever." The poet seems to be acknowledging in this poem, **"Afterimages,"** that residence in the South had a deeply transforming effect on her political and poetic awareness. She has a maternal feeling for all outsiders, especially, the young Blacks of New York; I am thinking particularly of the young girl nodding on the subway whom she addresses as her daughter. These are the images by which "A woman measures her life's damage."

In recent years Lorde's militancy has been directed toward sexual oppression, as in the poem **"Need: A Choral of Black Women's Voices."** Arranged as a funeral antiphonal between the ghosts of two Black women and the chorus or congregation of all the living, the most moving part of the poem is the vehement denunciation of Black men whose spurious "need" spells destruction: "Who ever learns to love me / from the mouth of my enemies / walks the edge of my world / like a phantom in a crimson cloak." One may safely question the sweeping nature of this accusation, but the juxtaposition of love and enmity and the vulgarity of the TV phantom are hard to fault.

Lorde's anger is directed not only to popular political issues but to what may be called the slight cruelties and injustices of everyday life. But what is perhaps important to insist on is the relation between the two preoccupying militances of her poetry, namely, sexual and racial oppression. In an essay entitled **"Scratching the Surface"** (*Black Scholar,* 1978), she argues for the inclusion of all Black peoples in the struggle against oppression and for the exclusion of none. She is particularly exercised by the assumption of the larger Black community that those who fight the sexual oppressor are only tepidly devoted to fighting the racial oppressor. These are "kitchen wars," she says, which detract from everyone's genuine self-interest. The root of all social-sexual discrimination, she argues, whether racism, sexism, heterosexism, or homophobia, is the assumption of superiority and the will to power. She seems to be calling for the inclusion of the outsider, or arguing for the outsider as insider in American society. This inclusion is, I think, the meaning of another favorite word, empowering. I need not point out that this, too, is a religious term, and investiture of the daughter with the father's powerful mantle and approval. In **"Who Said It Was Simple,"** she talks about the many roots of anger and the many branches of liberation:

> But I who am bound by my mirror
> as well as my bed
> see causes in colour
> as well as sex
>
> and sit here wondering
> which me will survive
> all these liberations.

For all her militancy, however, there is another side to Audre Lorde and another style in her poetry. She is a woman capable of very deep and quiet love and her poetry here becomes almost traditional in form. It is here above all that her powerful poetic instinct finds fulfillment. Her method here is not the re-creation of event in searing detail and surrealist image. She is at her best in exquisite and economical narrative that is luminous with insight. In these poems the symbolism grows out of, is integral to, the event, and awareness or wisdom is gently released from the form. Here, too, she is freer to be herself and is not limited by political strictures. The subject of her narrative poetry is all-embracing.

"Walking Our Boundaries" is one of her great poems. Elizabeth Janeway, in her chapter on women writers in *The Harvard Guide to Contemporary American Writing,* speaks of Black women writers as survivors, and this is certainly a great poem of survival. It is written after Lorde's bout with cancer and close encounter with death, and the poem catches the sense of wonder at being alive in a small garden that she owns with her friend and at the survival of their love. There is a sureness of tone, a mastery of both sound and symbol, and an infusion of the word pain that takes place in the opening lines:

> This first bright day has broken
> the back of winter
> We rise from war
> To walk across the earth
> around our house
> both stunned that sun can shine so brightly
> after all our pain

The balance of the poem is prefigured by the effortless and natural alliteration of these lines. The ravages of winter reflect last winter's pain. The friends are both "half-afraid there will be no tight buds started / on our ancient apple tree." The symbolism of the scene is illuminated in an excellent line: "it does not pay to cherish symbols / when the substance / lies so close at hand." A light affectionate touch on the shoulder, reaching back to the opening lines of the poem, breaks the back of the spiritual winter of suffering. The sense is clear in spite of the momentary lapse of image in "dead leaves waiting to be burned / to life." The final stanza yields a triumph of the human will over physical decay: "the siding has come loose in spots / our footsteps hold this place together." It is a nearly perfect poem, reminiscent of Robert Frost in its method and mood.

This is her characteristic method in poems of love, beautiful narration, symbolism matched with deep feeling. **"Brother Alvin,"** for instance, tells of a childhood schoolmate who missed a lot of classes between Halloween and Thanksgiving and then just before Christmas disappeared. Their mutual dependence is recalled, and the definitive separation after all these years is symbolic of the final one; the search for him becomes a fascination with the magic that will unlock the mystery of all separations. In **"Eulogy for Alvin Frost,"** the untimely death of someone loved and admired, though not long enough to become friends, is lamented. This Alvin, a cherished acquaintance, evokes the earlier childhood schoolmate of the same name, and stands for all Black men lost too soon, "all the black substance poured into earth / before earth is ready to bear." The poem is in four movements, the narration being the

middle movements. A kind of prologue introduces the narrative, which is followed by a simple maternal address by the poet to the survivor's son, Danny, a moving poem in its own right.

Occasionally, as in **"Poem for a Poet,"** an image will trigger the event and become intertwined with it. Sitting in her car in a Greenwich Village street, her mind wanders to North Carolina and the happy memories of Randall Jarrell. The car suddenly becomes his coffin, and she says with childlike affection, "How come being so cool / you weren't also a little bit black." Silent homage is later paid to him in a line from **"Story Books on a Kitchen Table,"** inspired by the opening of "The Death of the Ball Turret Gunner": "Out of her womb of pain my mother spat me."

Invariably the poetry in this mode is a way of reaching out to the memory of the father and capturing his love. These poems have a tone, a unity between event and symbol and feeling, that is very satisfying. They are the most neglected poems of this insufficiently known poet and the works which her vast feminist following is likely to overlook. But they are the most attractive side of a complex woman. She is more like her mother than she knows: powerful and fierce. Yet she much resembles the father: exceedingly thoughtful and kind.

Another kind of narrative poem is a result of the poet's sojourn in West Africa, where she obviously did a great deal of research into Yoruba mythology, particularly as it occurs in Nigeria and Dahomey, present-day Benin. These ancient myths brought a wealth of insight and psychological maturity to the poet. And the work of this period is extremely African in its sense and texture, yet is imbued with the themes and concerns of Audre Lorde. **"Coniagui Women,"** for example, tells the story of how the warrior women wean their sons and force them into becoming men. The last lines are forceful in their directness and economy: " 'Let us sleep in your bed' they whisper / 'Let us sleep in your bed' / but she has mothered before them. She closes her door. / They become men." From Africa she learned how to see the symbol residing in the event and to leave it embedded there like a jewel. In a very Wallace Stevens-like short poem entitled **"A Rock Thrown into the Water Does Not Fear the Cold,"** the snails consume a snake at twilight, "Their white extended bodies / gently sucking / take sweetness from the stiffening shape / as darkness overtakes them." The poem has found a surprisingly new image of sexual submission and human development.

A major preoccupation of this poet, indeed, is how really to become her father's daughter, how to acquire the wisdom to find one's way in the world, how to emulate "his judgment on familiar things." Like a great teacher, she is able to sense the confusion in the minds of both young and old, the terror in not being able to do the arithmetic of life. The fourteen-year-old girl in **"Hanging Fire"** worries about her ashy knees and the fact that she has nothing to wear, that her boyfriend secretly sucks his thumb, and that she might die before she grows up. All the while, the person who once held all the secrets of life now hides them and herself: "and momma's in the bedroom / with the door closed." Equally, in **"Litany For Survival,"** those adults who live on the margins of life, "on the constant edges of decision," are filled with another kind of daily fear, "like bread in our children's mouths." These, in a devastating line, have learned "to be afraid with our mother's milk." The system, "the heavy-footed," did not wish them to survive. And thus they are afraid of life itself:

> And when the sun rises we are afraid
> it might not remain
> when the sun sets we are afraid
> it might not rise in the morning
> when our stomachs are full we are afraid
> of indigestion
> when our stomachs are empty we are afraid
> we may never eat again
> when we are loved we are afraid
> love will vanish
> when we are alone we are afraid
> love will never return
> and when we speak we are afraid
> our words will not be heard
> nor welcomed
> but when we are silent
> we are still afraid.

For such as these the poet offers the comfort that their plight is understood. The real comfort, however, comes from the courage to give a name to the enemy's weapons and purpose: "So it is better to speak / remembering / we were never meant to survive."

This courage is sometimes humorously turned inward, as in **"Chorus,"** where Lorde comes to terms at last with her light-skinned mother while finding herself humming Mozart, who was, she suddenly remembers, "a white dude."

It would be impossible to conclude this aspect of Audre Lorde's writing without mentioning a brave little book called **The Cancer Journals.** It is really a pamphlet based upon a diary that she kept during a very traumatic experience with breast cancer from September 1978 to March 1979, an experience which culminated in radical mastectomy. For a beautiful woman proud of her appearance, it was a profoundly humiliating, sad event. The pamphlet consists of an introduction and three chapters. The introduction contains diary entries, very candid statements of fear for her life and her work, of occasional despair, of the support she found in many women friends. The first chapter is a short address Lorde gave at the annual convention of the Modern Language Association in 1977, at a time when she had just recovered from surgery which discovered a benign tumor of the breast. The theme is "The Transformation of Silence into Language and Action." The second chapter is subtitled "A Black Lesbian Feminist Experience." The subtitle, in my reading, is valid only to identify the author; beyond one discreet episode some twenty-five years earlier that took place in Mexico, it does not characterize what is in the text. The chapter is a very courageous description of all the emotions lived during and after the operation. Conversations with her friend Frances, with her brother-in-law, Henry, and with her mother are recorded. There is wild grief, as well as humor and love and finally acceptance. As usual, Lorde has done her research into the incidence and treatment of breast cancer, and her remarks are certainly of wider interest than the subtitle would indicate. For this is a problem that arouses vast human sympathy, that has touched many of us, men and women, intimately. The final chapter, in keeping with Lorde's fierce spirit, is on her decision not to wear a prosthesis, a decision, it must be added, that she does not suggest for others, but which she uses to expose some of the hypocrisies of the medical profession as well as the venal practices of an economic system that values profit more than the health and well-being of its people.

Lorde is a poet for whom writing is a serious moral responsibility. She came to poetic and personal awareness in the late fifties and early sixties, but has grown steadily since in both complexity of vision and clarity of purpose. She has worked very hard at her craft and we may expect to see more changes and growth in the years to come. As I have indicated, she has a devoted following in New York and the East Coast generally, but for the gravity of the issues she raises, for her luminous insight, meticulous research and skill, and for the breadth of her interests, she deserves a far wider audience. One can only hope that this valuable voice will survive all its liberations, and in so doing enlarge our own sense of freedom and capacity for life. (pp. 269-76)

> *Jerome Brooks, "In the Name of the Father: The Poetry of Audre Lorde," in* Black Women Writers (1950-1980): A Critical Evaluation, *edited by Mari Evans, Anchor Press/ Doubleday, 1984, pp. 269-76.*

Joan Martin

One of the most oft-quoted lines from Audre Lorde's poetry is from her anthology *Coal:* "I am Black because I come from the earth's inside / now take my word for jewel in the open light." Indeed, much of her poetry deals with the nature of the "word" as an entity unto itself. For Lorde, words "ring like late summer thunders / to sing without octave / and fade, having spoken the season." Words "explode / under silence / returning / to rot. . . . " Words are alternately Life, Death, Silence, Truth. And they are the natural tool of the poet.

Her themes cross continents, wind through city streets, lavish color and form over seasons, and echo songs of intimacy: visions of tender loves. Browsing through her several anthologies, we see Lorde as multipersona. She is favored companion to African gods. Defender of Black women suffering the injustice of white America. Child-woman seeking still a mother's love. Black mother agonizing the fated issue of her womb. Black lesbian feminist socialist. The "outsider." The "different." The Poet.

It is little wonder that her poetry, indeed all of her writing, rings with passion, sincerity, perception, and depth of feeling far beyond the many voices, bland and putrid, that today cry out "I am a poet!"

Audre Lorde is a rare creature, not because of political, racial, or sexual concerns. She is the Black Unicorn: magical and mysterious bearer of fantasy draped in truth and beauty. Like the Black female poets who came before her, she has known injustice, bitter betrayal, oppression and ostracism, disease, loneliness, and pain. And like the giants who preceded her, she has gathered these bitter threads and woven them into the precious fabric of truth and beauty that is the rightful realm of the poet.

Her duty as poet is to taste lustily of the experience of life and to translate that experience into an act of love. This love act—the poem—can then be shared and entered into by the rest of mankind.

The poetry that results from this process is a measure of the writer's mastery of the craft, as well as a reflection of the intensity of the life experience. Creator and craftsman, artist and technician, combine as one in the poet. Technique is striking; content is both familiar and new; and the message is relevant and timely. The experience becomes a vital part of one's own essence. Audre Lorde is such a poet.

Her world is big-city, urban, cosmopolitan, New York. And her view of this world molds her poetry more formidably than perhaps any other force in her life. The city is cold, impersonal, unfeeling. It is populated with people who do not so much "live" as they in fact seem to indulge in the "experience of life." They dabble. They touch at love, life, death, dope, family, God, religion. They engage in quick conversations, passing affairs, and matters requiring protest. There is an incessant sense of aloneness and alienation about this world. Yet, despite these seeming negatives, Lorde, like a benign Creator, drapes her people in love and paints them with an understanding and a tolerance that makes them real, touchable, even likable, for the reader.

The trick is honesty. Honesty. Honesty coupled with a sincere love and sense of admiration for her world and all things in it. Lorde's world is not a black-and-white one. Its colors are varied like the people and situations reflected. And Audre Lorde is not per se a "Black" poet. She is a woman poet who also happens to be Black. Though Lorde does not revel in the "Black experience," she certainly does not neglect it. Her writing deals with the pain of being a person of color in a white-dominated world, but it does not depend on racial protest for its survival. She deals with the problems of race as she does with the problems of love. They are a fact of life. One must accommodate one's life accordingly if one is to coexist with the situations at hand in relative peace. Her race-oriented poems, therefore, are quite striking when one encounters them. They are not contrived for effect. They are not written to prove a point. They present a conflict, explore it, and thrust it at the reader with all the viciousness and horror intrinsic to the fact of racism in America. The true artist does not need to belabor a situation. She needs only to present it in its strongest light.

A striking example of Lorde's biting attack on the race issue in America is in the poem **"The American Cancer Society Or There Is More Than One Way to Skin a Coon":**

> . . . the american cancer destroys
> By seductive and reluctant admission
> For instance

> Black women no longer give birth through their
>   ears
> And therefore must have A Monthly Need For
>   Iron:
> For instance
> Our Pearly teeth are *not* racially insured
> And therefore must be Gleemed For Fewer Cav-
>   ities:
> For instance
> Even though all astronauts are white
> Perhaps Black People *can* develop
> Some of those human attributes
> Requiring
> Dried dog food frozen coffee instant oatmeal
> Depilatories deodorants detergents
> And other assorted plastic.

> . . . this is the surest sign I know
> That the american cancer society is dying—
> It has started to dump its symbols onto Black
>   People
> Convincing proof that those symbols are now
>   useless
> And far more lethal than emphysema.

[*The New York Head Shop and Museum*]

The sarcasm here goes past the bitter stage; it is stronger than mere protest or rage. It is invective reminiscent of the most potent examples of Juvenalian satire which flourished in eighteenth-century English literature of which Dr. Samuel Johnson is still undisputed master. The castigation of white America's treatment of its darker brothers is total and complete. Lorde offers no hope and no possibility of redemption for either predator (white America) or prey (Black America). The poem is organically complete—opening with the certainty of death imprinted on Black people through the act of selling them cigarettes, and closing with the statement that the dumping of the useless plastic symbols of the world of white America onto Blacks is far more lethal than emphysema. The absorption of these artificial symbols by Blacks, however reluctantly offered, is the ultimate fact of death—not only of unsuspecting Blacks, but of the entire vapid, sterile American society.

On a more subtle but no less venomous level, Lorde addresses the race issue in America in **"The Brown Menace or Poem to the Survival of Roaches."** In the poem, roaches symbolically represent Black Americans who in turn represent the alter ego of white Americans. Lorde uses to great advantage the hideous aspects associated with the crawling pests, to amplify the ironic twist of the shared identity between Black and white. The poem cries out an ominous warning to all those who would attempt the destruction of Americans of color.

> I am you
> in your most deeply cherished nightmare
> scuttling through the painted cracks
> you create to admit me
> into your kitchens
> into your values at noon
> in your most secret places
> with hate
> you learn to honor me
> by imitation

as I alter—
through your greedy preoccupations
through your kitchen wars
and your poisonous refusal—
to survive.

[*The New York Head Shop and Museum*]

The final warning is implicit in the statement, "I am you / in your most deeply cherished nightmare. . . ." The thing hated and the creature exerting the hatred are one and the same. The incestuous love-hate relationship described by the narrator in the poem is the ultimate irony. Self-hatred, fear of the unknown, and a fear of that which is known is one's own self ring throughout the lines of this poem. The "brown menace" is everywhere and everyone. It is the face looking at itself in a mirror, being at once fascinated and repulsed by what it sees. And Lorde deftly introduces the forever forbidden sexual intimation. ". . . call me / roach and presumptuous / nightmare on your white pillow. . . ." And the irony builds as the metamorphosis continues: "with hate / you learn to honor me / by imitation / as I alter—." And the warning is repeated. If the roaches—the "brown menace"—are destroyed, those who persist in the destruction will simultaneously be destroyed: "and your poisonous refusal— / to survive." As in **"The American Cancer Society . . . ,"** Lorde offers neither hope nor means of redemption from fate. Hope exists only in the warning. This rather Beckettian twist of wry humor is the only humor to be found in the Lorde canon.

An equally powerful statement on the race problem can be found in the poem **"Blackstudies"** part IV:

> Their demon father rode me just before daylight
> I learned his tongue as he reached
> for my hands at dawn
> before he could touch the palms of my hands
> to devour my children
> I learned his language
> I ate him
> and left his bones mute in the noon sun.
> Now all the words in my legend come garbled
> except anguish.

[*The New York Head Shop and Museum*]

And indeed, "anguish" seems to be the only correct word for describing the peculiar situation nonwhites find themselves in in white America. Anguish or intense physical and emotional pain is the one constant in their lives. But if one is to live, reasons for living must be found in *this* life; if indeed Lorde believed the situation to be totally hopeless, there would be no reason for her to write or to function in any way as a creative artist. To find her reasons, we must examine her treatment of themes less volatile than race relations in America. One of Lorde's favorites, and indeed perhaps the most universal theme in all literature, is love. And Audre Lorde writes of love in a manner which is at once worldly and exquisitely personal.

Usually when one thinks of love, images of romantic involvement come to mind. Rarely does one consider the love that exists between a mother and a child, one friend for another, an individual's love for his/her family, or the love an artist holds solely for his/her art. And with the image of romantic love invariably comes the traditional image of a man and a woman: the personification of heterosexual love. Lorde does treat the theme of heterosexual love in some of her poems. However, the bulk of her poetry and her other writings deal with the various love relationships mentioned above, with special emphasis being placed on the romantic love shared between two women. Audre Lorde makes no secret of her sexual preference for women. More importantly, however, she makes it very clear that her sexual preference is her own business, and she offers no apologies for it, nor does she make any attempts at explanations. One's sexual life, as Lorde sees it, is one's own business: personal and self-chosen, as it should be. Yet, to fully appreciate the mature love poems, it will be necessary to examine first the sequence of events in the poet's life that played such a major role in molding her needs and choices as an adult.

Part of the charm of the beautiful love poems Lorde writes is the honesty inherent in each piece. There are the limitless highs and the abysmal lows that all love relationships are subject to. One doesn't have to profess heterosexuality, homosexuality, or asexuality to react to her poems. One reacts to the skill with which they are written, the intensity of the experiences, and the sincerity of the author. Anyone who has ever been in love can respond to the straightforward passion and pain sometimes one and the same, in Lorde's poems.

> One of Lorde's favorites, and indeed perhaps the most universal theme in all literature, is love. And Audre Lorde writes of love in a manner which is at once worldly and exquisitely personal.
>
> —*Joan Martin*

Without a doubt, the absence of love is treated with the same power and intensity as love secured. And it should come as no surprise that that love which by its absence has caused the most pain for the poet is that needed from her mother. The poem **"Story Books on a Kitchen Table"** is a bitter commentary on the author's seemingly loveless entrance into the world:

> Out of her womb of pain my mother spat me
> into her ill-fitting harness of despair
> into her deceits
> where anger re-conceived me
> pointed by her nightmare
> of who I was not
> becoming.

[*Coal*]

And the sequel to the legend of her birth is no more pleasant than its precursor. Witness the daughter, now grown, looking back on her childhood and seeing herself still as unwanted, undeserving, lonely, and alone, in the poem entitled **"From the House of Yemanja"**:

My mother had two faces and a frying pot
where she cooked up her daughters
into girls
. . . two faces
and a broken pot
where she hid out a perfect daughter
who was not me
. . .
Mother I need
mother I need
. . . I am
the sun and moon and forever hungry

[*The Black Unicorn*]

As in the race-oriented poems, there is the incredible presence of discordant images, self-hatred, bitter alienation, and the almost surrealistic sense of nonexistence by the poet. "Pointed by her nightmare / of who I was not / becoming." Here Lorde seems to be spiraling toward nonbeing—a state perhaps preferable to that of being "spat" out of her mother's womb, into an "ill-fitting harness of despair. . . ." Antithesis builds upon antithesis in **"From the House of Yemanja,"** where the mother has two faces, two daughters (one is perfect; the other is Audre Lorde), two pots, and the great curiosity: two women borne on the poet's back—"one dark and rich and hidden / in the ivory hungers of the other / mother / pale as a witch. . . ." Again and again the irony persists. The intimation of cannibalism on the part of the mother (cooking up the daughters) and the devouring of the dark rich woman by the "mother / pale as a witch" described as possessing "ivory hungers." One mother, two identities, split personalities—bringing Lorde "bread and terror" in her sleep. Yet, despite the reality of a tenuous identity on the part of both the mother and the daughter, the poet still cries in anguish, "Mother I need . . . I need your blackness now / as the august earth needs rain." And she offers perhaps the most poignant statement in the entire poem: "I am the sun and moon and forever hungry / for her eyes." The cry for the love of her mother is from the bowels. And though she sounds it like thunder in a summer storm, Lorde knows the awful truth that what she wants most from her mother can and will never be. "I am / the sun and moon and forever hungry / the sharpened edge / where day and night shall meet / and not be / one." Nothing else need be said. The antithesis stands. She is the edge where day and night shall meet but will never be one.

This poem, as do the others about Lorde's childhood relationship with her mother, ends in frustration which is total and complete. The poet is girl-child—hopeless, confused, loving, and not being loved in return. As a child, it is difficult to grasp the reasons why this fact should be. Yet, in her **"Ballad from Childhood,"** the poet makes a valiant attempt to analyze (as a child might) the "reasons why," and ultimately accepts them as being not only reasonable but wise. Note her use of the folk idiom in the italicized responses used as a refrain between the verses. This gives a strength, a credibility, to these responses that is as old as Black folk wisdom itself:

. . . Mommy may I plant a tree?

What the eyes don't see the heart don't hurt

But mommy look the seed has wings
my tree might call a bird that sings . . .

Watch the birds forget but the trap doesn't.

Please mommy do not beat me so!
yes I will learn to love the snow!
yes I want neither seed nor tree!
yes ice is quite enough for me!
who knows what trouble-leaves might grow!

I don't fatten frogs to feed snakes.

[*The New York Head Shop and Museum*]

In three lines, the mother totally destroys what little pleasure and joy the child might ever hope to find in her "land of ice and house of snow." The frigid imagery of the home and its surroundings stands in stark contrast to the tiny seedling that has the power to produce a tree and even call a "bird that sings." The house will have no life-producing tree and no music from bird or child. The beatings help effect Lorde's conclusion that "yes ice is quite enough for me!"

With this type of negative backdrop behind her own childhood memories, it is most surprising to read Lorde's poem **"Now That I Am Forever with Child."** Here is Audre Lorde speaking as mother of her own child.

How the days went
while you were blooming within me
. . . I thought
now her hands
are formed, and her hair
has started to curl
now her teeth are done
now she sneezes . . .
I bore you one morning just before spring . . .
my legs were towers between which
A new world was passing.

Since then
I can only distinguish
one thread within running hours
You, flowing through selves
toward You.

[*Coal*]

The poem needs no explanation. Audre Lorde as mother has only love for the life that springs from her body. Her child need never fear the harshness of growth without life around her. She will know warmth, and trees, and singing birds. She will have a mother's love. And it will come to her freely, without burden of guilt, and with full acceptance of her as herself. The tenderness and love the poet craved as a child was denied her. But this did not make Lorde bitter against her own children when circumstances changed her role from that of child to mother. She had learned to give love, even though she never quite learned how to acquire it. And as an adult woman, she learned to both give and receive the love and affection so vital to both physical and emotional survival. And the love a woman denied her as a child was given to her in abundance by many women when she became an adult. It is this mature love, this sexual love, this fulfilling love, that Lorde writes about with a fury and passion rarely achieved by contemporary writers—male or female. These are the poems where the poet as craftsperson and the poet as technician meet to create pure art.

"Bridge Through My Window" is an exquisite example of Audre Lorde's technique as a poet coupled with the intense sensuality of a woman in love.

> . . . Oh bridge my sister bless me before I sleep
> the wild air is lengthening
> and I am tried beyond strength or bearing
> over water.
>
> Love, we are both shorelines
> a left country
> where time suffices . . .
> and the right land
> where pearls roll into earth and spring up day.
> joined, our bodies have passage into one
> without merging
> as this slim necklace is anchored into night . . .
>
> > [*Coal*]

> Touching you I catch midnight
> as moon fires set in my throat
> I love you flesh into blossom
> I made you
> and take you made
> into me.
>
> > [*The Black Unicorn*]

"Woman" is a dream poem, both in statement and in effect. In it, the lover's body is metaphor for the giving earth, where Lorde seeks to reap an "endless harvest." Even the rocks offer unending joy in their beauty. Nothing common will come from such precious soil. Here again, the metaphor is utilized to maximum effect. And the result is nothing short of a breathtakingly beautiful poem.

> I dream of a place between your breasts
> to build my house like a haven
> where I plant crops
> in your body
> an endless harvest
> where the commonest rock
> is moonstone and ebony opal
> giving milk to all of my hungers
> and your night comes down upon me
> like a nurturing rain.
>
> > [*The Black Unicorn*]

As is true with every seemingly perfect landscape, rain must at some point fall in paradise. And so it is with Audre Lorde's love life. There must be clouds if one would cherish the rainbow. And Lorde writes as skillfully of her stormy love affairs as she does of those with quiet beauty. Note the merging of the various poetic techniques in the poem **"Fog Report."** Note also that though the situation is a negative and painful one for the poet, the passion intrinsic to her writing is as intense here as ever. The tone is somber, the mood grave. In using the first person pronoun "I" for the narrator, Lorde makes the poem both intensely personal and forces the reader's direct involvement. She creates the setting against which the action will take place and establishes the cast of characters. "In this misty place where hunger finds us / seeking direction / I am too close to you to be useful." The two lovers in this scenario are lost. One is distracted; the other is "often misled" by the "familiar comforts" of her lover. They know

each other by little intimate details: the shape of one's teeth is written into her lover's palm "like a second lifeline." "The smell of love" on the narrator's breath distracts her lover. Like mad King Lear, the narrator is found "wandering at the edge / of a cliff / beside nightmares of [her lover's] body." Lorde draws on the involvement of all five senses in this poem. We smell love, taste thighs, seek direction, feel the shape of teeth. And we are given teasing tidbits of alliteration: ". . . too close to you to be useful." Lorde ends the poem in brilliant fashion, combining simile, alliteration, metaphor, and personification into one unforgettable image:

> your tongue your truths your fleshy altars
> into my own forgotten image
> so when this fog lifts
> I could be sure to find you
> tethered like a goat
> in my heart's yard.
>
> > [*The Black Unicorn*]

But Lorde does not always brood over bitter loves with quite the same enchanting imagery she employs in **"Fog Report."** Her poem **"Parting"** is as tersely written as its title suggests.

> Belligerent and beautiful as a trapped ibis
> your lean hands are a sacrifice
> spoken three times
> before dawn
> there is blood in the morning egg
> that makes me turn and weep
> I see you
> weaving pain into garlands
> the shape of a noose
> while I grow
> weary
> of licking my heart
> for moisture
> cactus tongued.
>
> > [*The Black Unicorn*]

We are drawn into this rather dismal, disturbing scene like penitents before a high priest. Indeed, the language in this poem is reminiscent of that of a Lenten mass: "lean hands," "sacrifice," "before dawn," "three times" (Peter's denial of Christ, perhaps?), "pain," and "blood." There is no redemption for the lost love offered in this poem. Lorde once again has found herself in a totally loveless situation. But this time we know she will emerge victorious. Her other poems tell us it is so. And we know too that the emergence will make her stronger, more certain of herself, secure in the knowledge that she is able and always will be able, from now on, to find love. And her strength will come not just from lovers but from friends as well. And her circle of friends will be women like herself—artists, writers, musicians, women who love freely and without fear or guilt. And this knowledge will make Lorde strong enough to face the biggest challenge of her life: that of the possibility of death by cancer. The story lies within the pages of Lorde's first major prose piece, *The Cancer Journals.*

The Cancer Journals is an autobiographical work dealing with Audre Lorde's battle with cancer, her horror at discovering that she was being forced to face her own mortality head on, and the lessons she learned as a result of this most painful experience. She talks constantly of fear, anxiety, and strength. And strength is the substance of which she seems made. The opening statement of the Introduction addresses the problem immediately. "Each woman responds to the crisis that breast cancer brings to her life out of a whole pattern, which is the design of who she is and how her life has been lived. The weave of her every day existence is the training ground for how she handles crisis" (*The Cancer Journals*). She further states, "I am a post-mastectomy woman who believes our feelings need voice in order to be recognized, respected, and of use" (*The Cancer Journals*). And we hear her feelings voiced in a manner both eloquent and disturbingly prophetic. As in her poetry, Lorde states her truths with no holds barred in this short but powerful prose work. Her biggest fear beyond the loss of her breast and the possibility of imminent death is that she should die without having said the things she as a woman and an artist needed to say in order that her pain and subsequent loss might not have occurred in vain. In her own words, she says, "I had known the pain, and survived it. It only remained for me to give it voice, to share it for use, that the pain not be wasted." (*The Cancer Journals*) And like the love she lost as a child and learned to survive without, Lorde has taken the loss imposed on her by death-dealing breast cancer and survived with dignity and new strength. Her adamant refusal to wear a prosthesis after the removal of her breast is an example of that self-esteem we saw developing in the young child. It has emerged complete in Audre Lorde the woman. Note the following quote from the *Journals:*

> Prosthesis offers the empty comfort of "Nobody will know the difference." But it is that very difference which I wish to affirm, because I have lived it, and survived it, and wish to share that strength with other women. If we are to translate the silence surrounding breast cancer into language and action against this scourge, then the first step is that women with mastectomies must become visible to each other. For silence and invisibility go hand in hand with powerlessness. . . . Surrounded by other women day by day, all of whom appear to have two breasts, it is very difficult sometimes to remember that I AM NOT ALONE. Yet once I face death as a life process, what is there possibly left for me to fear?
>
> [*The Cancer Journals*]

Lorde's questions at the end of the above quote is rhetorical. She has not only faced death as a "life process," she has accepted it. And herein lies the source of her strength. She learned earlier not only to love but to *be* loved as well. And that knowledge gave her the ability to love herself. Loving oneself is not a selfish act. It is a necessary prelude to the act of loving another human being. From what we have learned of Audre Lorde through analyzing her poetry, we can see the clear progression from frightened unloved child to secure well-loved woman. And with this security of loving herself and being loved by others comes the strength which Lorde so handsomely displays in *The Cancer Journals.* She can indeed face death and physical loss (amputation) without succumbing, because she did

not have to face it as an empty woman. She was full with the love of family, friends, and lover. And she used her fears to teach other women some of the lessons she learned from her tragedy. Her feelings, by way of her poetry, her prose, and the many lectures she delivers across the country, are being voiced, "recognized, respected, and of use." Her book *The Cancer Journals* affords all women who wish to read it the opportunity to look at the life experience of one very brave woman who bared her wounds without shame, in order that we might gain some strength from sharing in her pain.

It has been mentioned that the one major element lacking in Audre Lorde's work is "humor." Perhaps the reason for this can be found in a statement in *The Cancer Journals* describing the poet's feelings about "happiness," since this would have a definite bearing on her use or nonuse of humor in her writings. She mentions in the *Journals* of having read a letter from a doctor in a medical magazine which stated that "no truly happy person gets cancer" (*The Cancer Journals*). After experiencing a bout of guilt raised by the doctor's statement, Lorde examined her own attitudes and arrived at the following conclusion:

> Was I wrong to be working so hard against the oppressions afflicting Women and Black people? Was I in error to be speaking out against our silent passivity and the cynicism of a mechanized and inhuman civilization that is destroying our earth and those who live upon it? Was I really fighting the spread of radiation, racism, womanslaughter, chemical invasion of our food, pollution of our environment, the abuse and psychic destruction of our young, merely to avoid dealing with my first and greatest responsibility—to be happy? In this disastrous time, when little girls are still being stitched shut between their legs, when victims of cancer are urged to court more cancer in order to be attractive to men, when 12 year old Black boys are shot down in the street at random by uniformed men who are cleared of any wrong-doing, when ancient and honorable citizens scavenge for food in garbage pails, and the growing answer to all this is media hype or surgical lobotomy; when daily gruesome murders of women from coast to coast no longer warrant mention in *The N.Y. Times,* when grants to teach retarded children are cut in favor of more billion dollar airplanes, when 900 people commit mass suicide rather than face life in america, and we are told it is the job of the poor to stem inflation; what depraved monster could possibly be always happy?
>
> [*The Cancer Journals*]

And after reading the above passionate retort, can any one of us condemn her for not believing in "happiness forever"? We too, would have to admit then to acceptance of the insanity we see happening daily around us. And so, we must assume that if in fact it is the job of the poet to feel with an intensity beyond that of the ordinary person, and to write with that same passion and intensity, Audre Lorde is doing her job. And she does it with a vengeance.

In both poetry and prose, we find certain elements that appear to characterize Lorde's style. Her language is most often formal, filled with very graphic concrete images.

Metaphors seem to abound in the poetry, and she creates them with an ease and grace that is rare in any literature. In her African poems, she employs a mythology that is a study unto itself. Yet, we can read the poems with enjoyment and understanding. Lorde utilizes a type of mini-epic formula in some of her poems. **"Coniagui Women"** is an excellent example of this device, as are some of the other African poems. For the most part, the tone throughout Lorde's works is somber, angry, bitter, didactic. The mood is invariably serious. Though we can perhaps understand the reasoning behind the lack of humor in the anthologies, it is difficult to digest large doses of very serious literature at a sitting. Some humor would not only relieve the tension of the demanding pieces, but it would heighten the impact of the stronger works. Lorde tends to have favorite images, and even favorite lines, which she repeats without serious backlash. In some cases, this use of repetition allows her the opportunity to create some rather startling and impressive effects. If one is not used to repetition of words and images by a professional writer, reading Audre Lorde's work for the first time can be a bit disconcerting. She makes up for the repetition, however, by the sheer power of the material and the manner in which she handles it. No subject seems to be foreign to Lorde. She is a versatile woman who displays her broad range of knowledge particularly in the poems. And she touches her audience in a way which is personal and lasting. This fact is skillfully conveyed in the poem entitled **"For Each of You"**:

> Be who you are and will be
> learn to cherish
> that boisterous Black Angel that drives you
> up one day and down another
> protecting the place where your power rises
> running like hot blood
> from the same source
> as your pain . . .
>
> . . . Each time you love
> love as deeply
> as if it were
> forever
> only nothing is
> eternal.
> Speak proudly to your children
> wherever you may find them
> tell them
> you are the offspring of slaves
> and your mother was
> a princess
> in darkness.

[*From a Land Where Other People Live*]

In this final message to Black people, Lorde again manages to take a fairly common theme (Black pride/Black power) and lift it to a new and startlingly beautiful level. It is her gift **"For Each of You."** It is powerful, simply stated, and honest. It is poetry.

This is only one theme of many employed in the Lorde canon. There are others. The mystical, powerful, flamboyant, haughty African gods. And there are the street-life people, and the lovers. Some nameless and faceless. Some too real to be tolerable. And the mosaic shines with the fervor and brightness of each contributor. Lorde's genius reaches its peak in **The Black Unicorn.** The symbolic creature which does not exist even in its traditional form is made more ironic and magical by becoming Black. And the Black Unicorn—Audre Lorde—is not free. Audre Lorde tells us it is so. (pp. 277-91)

> *Joan Martin, "The Unicorn Is Black: Audre Lorde in Retrospect," in* Black Women Writers (1950-1980): A Critical Evaluation, *edited by Mari Evans, Anchor Press/Doubleday, 1984, pp. 277-91.*

Joseph A. Brown, S.J.

With her latest volume of poetry, [**Our Dead Behind Us**], Audre Lorde once again invites the reader to the sacred kitchen table of Afro-American women word-artists, to be nourished by a tradition that has been simmering inside Lorde throughout her long and prophetic service to the world. And we readers must bring with us the proper ritual responses, also honed finely by generations of priestess/presiders—the grandmothers, mothers, aunts, sisters and lovers in the blood and of the spirit.

We are attentive, respectful, observing the forms. At times we can expect to be lectured, or questioned, or educated. At other times we need merely be present as the warrior women prepare some meal, seasoning the air with snatches of songs, stories, family (or neighborhood) gossip; or occasional signs of the spirit that admit us into their shadowed and doubting hearts.

Audre Lorde is talking to us, in **Our Dead Behind Us,** as she always has; her voice resonates just as surely and implacably as ever. The themes, the relationships, the quality of her details, even conversations with her previous poetry (the "Generation" series) are familiar and comfortable when recognized. But one can never be comforted by the words, the issues of Lorde's poetry.

Lorde has been journeying; **Our Dead Behind Us** lays out the world she has collected for our instruction and our shame. Shells, photographs, dried flowers, scraps of journals, postcards; bitter memories; clashes of the unexpected; rocks. Wherever Lorde has travelled, from Grenada to the Transvaal to Berlin to Brooklyn, she has made a promise: the black women, old and young, who have died, who will die, who resist death every day *will* be grieved. What Audre Lorde promised at the gravesites, in an act of embracing sisterhood, will be delivered upon her readers:

> I cannot recall the words of my first poem
> but I remember a promise
> I made my pen
> never to leave it
> lying
> in somebody else's blood.

("To The Poet Who Happens to Be Black and the Black Poet Who Happens to Be a Woman")

Throughout these poems, irony is transformed into harmony. The poet may *say,* **"There are No Honest Poems About Dead Women,"** and surround the poem so titled with one searing honesty after another. These are all honest poems, we may counter-understanding the poet's twist. But that is beside the point. There must be poems filled with rage and sharp edges and rock and fire; with commitments to spill no more blood on the altar of sacrifice. Lorde identifies herself with the victims *and* the resting stone:

> I am a Black woman stripped down
> and praying
> my whole life has been an altar
> worth its ending
> and I say Aido Hwedo is coming.
>
> ("Call")

The author's note to this poem says that Aido Hwedo is the "Rainbow Serpent; also a representation of all ancient divinities who must be worshipped but whose names and faces have been lost in time." When the book is finished, the response to this note is, "but of course the assertion is not true." Audre Lorde makes sure that our dead are *not* behind us. From the cover of the book to the last poem, the presence of the special divinities who inspire the poet is felt:

> and hanging on my office wall
> a snapshot of the last Dahomean Amazons
> taken the year I was born
> three old Black women in draped cloths
> holding hands.
>
> ("Beams")

Lorde plays the most elemental of poet-games, punning, with the word, "altar." And by doing so, she transforms the dead, these ancient Amazons, into the guides to the future of us all. "We cannot alter history / by ignoring it / nor the contradictions / who we are." She does *altar* history, by bearing upon her tongue the words of the dead, by carrying in her hands the photograph of the old ones, by declaring herself to be "a bleak heroism of words / that refuse / to be buried alive / with the liars." And the only true history is written nowhere "except in poems." The photograph of the Dahomean Amazons is super-imposed on a crowd of militant South Africans, creating the cover of this book. The dead are glaringly *before* us. Every name set down in one of these poems keeps these divinities—sacrificed by our deliverance—known to us, precisely.

Our Dead Behind Us is a book of contradictions, without hidden meanings, without ambiguities. For me, one of its loveliest poems celebrates the contradictions, elevates the calling of the poet and names Audre Lorde as the bearer of wisdom:

> When a mask breaks in Benin
> the dancer must fast
> make offerings
> as if a relative died.
> The mask cannot speak
> the dancer's tears
> are the tears of a weeping spirit.
>
> ("Wood Has No Mouth")

The Amazons can no longer speak, nor can Eleanor Bumpers; nor the brittle-boned Ethiopian girl. Audre Lorde has made her declaration of war, which is a declaration of Love: "I am going to keep telling this / if it kills me / and it might in ways I am / learning." In ways, we are *all* learning. Because she has kept at it and brings the dead to haunt us and coerce us and move us to change ourselves. Audre Lorde is the Rainbow Serpent she invokes: fire-tongued, the holy ghosts' linguist. (pp. 737-39)

> *Joseph A. Brown, S.J., "We Are Piecing Our Weapons Together," in* Callaloo, *Vol. 9, No. 4, Fall, 1986, pp. 737-39.*

[The] more poetry I wrote, the less I felt I could write prose. Someone would ask for a book review, or, when I worked at the library, for a précis about books—it wasn't that I didn't have the skills. I knew about sentences by that time. I knew how to construct a paragraph. But communicating deep feeling in linear, solid blocks of print felt arcane, a method beyond me.

—Audre Lorde, in an interview with Adrienne Rich, **Signs: Journal of Women in Culture and Society,** *1981.*

Alice H. G. Phillips

Audre Lorde begins her new collection, [*Our Dead behind Us*], as she did her old ones: militantly, this time in South Africa. Her black South African lover, whose teenage daughter has died as a result of police torture, sells the ticket to Durban that Lorde gives her, to buy guns and sulfa which she will carry back to her black "homeland". Present at the parting of the two women are all the murdered children of South Africa not mentioned in the *New York Times*. Barred from accompanying her, Lorde travels instead to Grenada (at least in imagination), Berlin, Florida, Tashkent, reporting on old atrocities and new outbreaks of oppression, and returns to her racially unsettled neighbourhood in Staten Island, across the water from Manhattan, to write poems about them.

For Lorde, all relationships, most situations and even typography have political implications that must be examined: her household in Staten Island, consisting of a black woman, a white woman and their children, is an outpost of social change in the heart of New York Ku Klux Klan territory . . . ; learning to swim and to write are acts of political self-expression; a routine drive over the Verrazano Bridge gives rise to a meditation on the exploitation of black labour and the need to destroy corrupt structures, tangible and intangible.

Unlike the youthful [Alice] Walker of *Once* and the slightly giddy [Ntozake] Shange of *Nappy Edges*, Lorde is a mature poet in full command of her craft; many of the poems here are classically austere, and even the more obviously message-ridden are tautly constructed. She ends as she began, with women arming themselves for a struggle, conscious of their historically inferior status but with examples of womanly strength behind and before them—female warriors who led their people into battle; Rosa Parks and Winnie Mandela; "she who scrubs the capitol toilets, listening". "On worn kitchen stools and tables / we are piecing our weapons together", Lorde chants in **"Call"**, and she calls on Aido Hwedo, the "Mother" and Rainbow Serpent, a compilation of all the ancient lost divinities, and asks, as a woman and poet, for knowledge, fluency and the right kind of power.

> *Alice H. G. Phillips, "Calling for the Right Kind of Power," in* The Times Literary Supplement, *No. 4437, April 15-21, 1988, p. 420.*

Gloria T. Hull

In Audre Lorde's poem **"A Meeting of Minds,"** a woman who "stands / in a crystal" is not permitted to dream ("the agent of control is / a zoning bee") or to speak ("her lips are wired to explode / at the slightest conversation"), although around her, "other women are chatting."

> the walls are written in honey
> in the dream
> she is not allowed
> to kiss her own mother
> the agent of control
> is   a white pencil
> that writes
> alone.

Denied access to her sleeping consciousness, this heroine cannot see her past or future, nor can she fully know and constitute herself. Prohibited conversation, she cannot connect with other women except in what feels like one-way visual separation, rendered even more cruel by her observing of their verbal sharing with each other around the honeyed walls. Crystal, a gem used by women for vision, protection, and the transmission of healing energy, becomes here cold, imprisoning stone whose properties only enhance her torment and isolation. Kissing her mother, her own and not a stepmother, would reinstate the first and most basic contact in a touch that embraces and validates the self. But even this simple bloodright/rite is not allowed.

As bad as the zoning bee and explosives undoubtedly are, Lorde's climactic and pointed placement of the "white pencil / that writes / alone" (note the spatial pause between "is" and "a white pencil") signals its overall importance. This pencil which signs the woman's ultimate alienation is, first of all, white and, second, self-contained and -propelled. Its color is the blank neutrality of the dominant world, and there is no visible agent-author to own its powerful interdictions. It has the deterministic force of Khayyam-FitzGerald's "moving finger" (which having writ, moves on), plus a disembodied horror impossible to efface.

Lorde has spent her entire career as a black lesbian feminist poet writing against this white, Western, phallocentric pencil. She has placed a colored pen within the woman's grasp and authorized her to inscribe her own law—an order that valorizes dreaming, speaking, and kissing the

mother and, above all, does not seek to hide its hand in a transparently cloaked objectivity. Honesty and responsibility—even in the midst of difficult saying—are premier goals and motivations. Lorde's poem **"Learning to Write"** begins with a question:

> Is the alphabet responsible
> for the book
> in which it is written
> that makes me peevish and nasty
> and wish I were dumb   again?

This present-tense outburst against someone's vexing use of language triggers a childhood memory of practicing the drawing of letters, and then concludes with a resolution obviously generated in response to what has irritated her:

> I am a bleak heroism of words
> that refuse
> to be buried alive
> with the liars.

Time and again she asserts her position, comparing her honesty (in **"A Question of Climate"**) to her "powerful breast stroke" / "a declaration of war" which she developed by being "dropped into the inevitable."

Identity is no meaningless accident. Thus, writing honestly requires acknowledging the particulars that construct the self. This seems to be the message of **"To the Poet Who Happens to Be Black/and the Black Poet Who/Happens to Be a Woman,"** a title that places sarcastic weight on the word *happens* and a heavy disapproval on those poets who discount their race and gender. Part one of the poem records her first birth "in the gut of Blackness / from between my mother's particular thighs." The second stanza recounts the first sister touch, a joyous woman birth which wrote into her body a "welcome home." Black and woman born, she survives all the attempts in part three of the poem to cancel her out "like an unpleasant appointment / postage due." The movement ends:

> I cannot recall the words of my first poem
> but I remember a promise
> I made my pen
> never to leave it
> lying
> in somebody else's blood.

There is always the pitfall of lying, which is accentuated in these lines by the obvious pun. Writing with the ink of her own precisely claimed blood keeps Lorde from using her pen—like a ghostly white pencil—to spill the blood of others.

Of course, saying honestly is not especially easy. Having worked through inner pressures and prohibitions, the poet still must face the unspeakable in experience and language. When "cadences of dead flesh / obscure the vowels," there can be "no honest poems about dead women." Likewise, in **"This Urn Contains Earth from/German Concentration Camps,"** Lorde contemplates the well-trimmed order of a West Berlin memorial, its

> Neatness
> wiping memories   payment
> from the air.

She contrasts this scene with a summer picnic, where "rough precisions of earth" marked her "rump" and a smashed water bug oozed eggs into a bowl of corn. It is this latter which is

> Earth
> not the unremarkable ash
> of fussy thin-boned infants
> and adolescent Jewish girls
> liming the Ravensbruck potatoes

This realization forces the sobering knowledge that

> careful and monsterless
> this urn makes nothing
> easy to say.

Here, by juxtaposing the abstract "mythization" of the Holocaust horror with concrete corporeality, Lorde makes her project clear. She is rescuing meaning from immateriality, from the sanitized wipeout of traditional history's magic pencil. Unburying the bones and rotting flesh of what has been covered up may not be pretty, but, for her, the unthinkable alternative is muteness, a condition she ascribes to bottles and wood and interdicted women encased in stone.

Lorde began her published work in 1968—twenty years ago—with *The First Cities.* When she arrived via five volumes of verse and a growing reputation at *Between Our Selves* (1976) and *The Black Unicorn* (1978), she had gone from merely writing poetry to casting wise and incantatory magic. A *Choice* reviewer put it quite sensitively when s/he wrote:

> Audre Lorde has always been a good poet. . . .
> But now, with the arrival of *The Black Unicorn,*
> these previous books [of hers] have an added
> value; for they show, in a unique way, how a
> black poet has changed over a decade, in re-
> sponse to the poetic styles and to her own deep-
> ening sensibilities. . . . As a woman, mother,
> teacher, lover, she has been a strong lyrical fig-
> ure in Afro-American Life. Now she has added
> another self—the spirit that has gone to Afri-
> ca. . . . Here is poetry that is rich, startling in
> its speed and fervor. The personal experience
> still startles her, as in her previous work, but the
> stark, ironic, almost taunting poems of her earli-
> er years have given place to words of acceptance
> and transcendence.

The Black Unicorn is a majestic voicing of statements and propositions whose applications are further worked out in her later book, *Our Dead Behind Us* (1986). Much of the struggle of defining and instating herself was done in the earlier volume, so that now she can simply put herself in motion, acting and being who she is. And because we know—and she knows that we know—where she is coming from, there is no need for her to repeat herself. At this hard-earned point, we can read Audre Lorde in her own light.

When Lorde names herself "sister outsider," she is claiming the extremes of a difficult identity. I think we tend to read the two terms with a diacritical slash between them—in an attempt to make some separate, though conjoining, space. But Lorde has placed herself on that line between the either/or and both/and of "sister outsider"—and then erased her chance for rest or mediation. However, the charged field between the two energies remains strong, constantly suggested by the frequency with which edges, lines, borders, margins, boundaries, and the like appear as significant figures in her work. One of the more striking uses begins her famous poem **"A Litany for Survival"**:

> For those of us who live at the shoreline
> standing upon the constant edges of decision
> crucial and alone

Those for whom she chants this survival song are outsiders who exist between their versions of life and the conflicting hegemonic scheme, who occupy the moment between a precarious present and a better future, "looking inward and outward / at once before and after." This margin, their place—if a space this untenable can be so concretely designated—is for marginal, that is, expendable beings. Lorde celebrates their "instant" and their "triumph," stating: "We were never meant to survive."

Two contiguous poems in *Our Dead Behind Us* further explore limits. After venturing past the easy spots where men catch proven trout in calm, knee-deep water, the speaker in **"Fishing the White Water"** confesses that she "never intended to press beyond / the sharp lines set as boundary." Yet she finds herself laboring in rapids back to back with her lover, choosing her partner's "dear face" over "the prism light makes / along my line." **"On the Edge"** contemplates relationship possibilities in terms of slicing blades and dangerous knives, leaving the speaker dreaming "I am precious rock / touching the edge of you."

Yet, it is not simply lines which attract Lorde. She is almost equally fascinated by what happens as they cross and recross, touch, and intersect with one another. Hence the "grids" and "crostics" of her poems (and also the bridges, which I do not discuss here). Her lover's face is "distorted into grids / of magnified complaint." Life in New York City forms "the complex / double-crostic of this moment's culture." A couple's two names become "a crostic for touch." These puzzling, intersecting lines that posit communication also attempt to pattern a map that can both locate and guide one through difficult geographies. Place is central in Lorde's work. Ethiopia, Berlin, Florida, Soho, and Vermont appear in her titles as a sampling of all the hot and troubled spots which engage her—Amsterdam Avenue, Mississippi, Grenville, Grenada, 830 Broadway, Santiago de Chile, Bleecker Street, Vieques, St. Georges, Johannesburg, White River Junction, Southampton, Maiden Lane, Pretoria, Alabama, Eau Claire, Tashkent, Gugeleto, and on and on—all place-names marking the wide area of her political and personal concerns. Lorde's vision encompasses the world, although she often approaches it from inside the woods, a garden, the next room, on a trail or a path to the deeper and broader meanings which glue the grid together. The bottom line is drawn clearly in the conclusion to **"Outlines"**:

> We have chosen each other
> and the edge of each other's battles
> the war is the same
> if we lose

someday women's blood will
congeal
upon a dead planet
if we win
there is no telling.

Lorde's seemingly essentialist definitions of herself as black/lesbian/mother/woman are not simple, fixed terms. Rather, they represent her ceaseless negotiations of a positionality from which she can speak. Almost as soon as she achieves a place of connection, she becomes uneasy at the comfortableness (which is, to her, a signal that something critical is being glossed over) and proceeds to rub athwart the smooth grain to find the roughness and the slant she needs to maintain her difference-defined, complexly constructed self. *Our Dead Behind Us* is constant motion, with poem after poem enacting a series of displacements. The geographical shifts are paralleled by temporal shifting in a "time-tension" which Mary J. Carruthers sees as characteristic of lesbian poetry: "the unspoken Lesbian past and the ineffable Lesbian future bearing continuously upon the present." The ubiquitous leave-takings are not surprising—**"Out to the Hard Road"** ("I never told you how much it hurt leaving"), **"Every Traveler Has One Vermont Poem"** ("Spikes of lavender aster under Route 91 / . . . I am a stranger / making a living choice"), **"Diaspora"** ("grenades held dry in a calabash / leaving"). Yet even more telling is the way Lorde brackets "home."

A poem with that title begins:

We arrived at my mother's island
to find your mother's name in the stone
we did not need   to go to the graveyard
for affirmation
our own genealogies
the language of childhood wars.

Ostensibly, these lines confirm a beautiful sisterhood between the two travelers which goes beyond the need for external documentation. And well it does—for none of the conventional "proof" of origin and kinship is forthcoming. At the outset, another mother's name occupies the space where the speaker expected to find her own matrilineage. Nor does proof come from the "two old dark women" in the second stanza who blessed them, greeting

Eh Dou-Dou you look *too* familiar
to you   to me
it no longer mattered.

Has this woman arrived at home, the place where her particular face is recognized?

"On My Way Out I Passed over You/and the Verrazano Bridge" is a mediated suspension between leave-taking and home. In fact, the poet is literally hanging in the midair of an airplane flight, "leaving   leaving." Beneath is water, sand, "silhouette houses sliding off the horizon," her and her lover's house, too, which "slips under these wings / shuttle between nightmare and the possible." The home which "drew us" because of space for a growing green garden now holds "anger" in a "landscape of trials," comparable to the way sulfur fuels burned in New Jersey have turned the Staten Island earth bright yellow. So what is to be done?

we live on the edge
of manufacturing
tomorrow or the unthinkable
made common as plantain-weed
by our act of not thinking
of taking
only what is given.

Their domestic conflict is encompassed by global pain and injustice which render home/place tenuous and terrifying for people all over the world—from Poland to Soweto, the Bay Street Women's Shelter, and the altars of El Salvador. Winnie Mandela's steps and her blood are slowing "in a banned and waterless living." Thus, when Lorde says

I am writing these words as a route map
an artifact for survival
a chronicle of buried treasure
a mourning
for this place we are about to be leaving

all of this madness is what she wants to put behind.

The penultimate movement of the poem telescopes ordinary, heroic women at war, some of them "burning their houses behind them" or being "driven out of Crossroads / perched on the corrugated walls of her uprooted life." This unkind history necessitates

            articulation
of want   without having
or even the promise of getting.

So permitted, the poet—returning to her immediate conversation with her lover—can

            dream of our coming together
encircled   driven
not only by love
but by lust for a working tomorrow
the flights of this journey
mapless   uncertain
and necessary as water.

Despite its long and torturous charting of this farewell gesture, the poem ends as it began, suspended in moving uncertainty. Home is continually deferred in a world which, as Matthew Arnold put it, "hath really neither joy, nor love, nor light, / nor certitude, nor peace, nor help for pain." Lorde herself had told us earlier, in *The Black Unicorn,* that

for the embattled
there is no place
that cannot be
home
nor is.

Lorde's inability to rest—in place, time, or consciousness—is reflected in a technique she frequently uses of playing meaning along lines that shift both backward and forward. In the first excerpt from **"Home"** quoted above, the clause "we did not need" stands as its own declarative, but it also modifies "stone" in a completion of "the stone we did not need," as well as begins the new sentence of "we did not need to go to the graveyard." The next phrase, "for affirmation," is likewise shared, as prepositional closure for the "graveyard" behind it and as introduction for the forwarding statement of "for affirmation, [we had] our own genealogies." The "to you to me" of the second quote is also doubly constructed. In the first **"On My Way Out"** passage, the reader pauses after "of manufacturing"—only to have to pick up the burden of the line to make an object of "tomorrow or the unthinkable," which then becomes the subject of "made common"—if one has not already read "we" as that phrase's nominative designation.

Lorde's seemingly essentialist definitions of herself as black/lesbian/mother/woman are not simple, fixed terms. Rather, they represent her ceaseless negotiations of a positionality from which she can speak. Almost as soon as she achieves a place of connection, she becomes uneasy at the comfortableness . . . and proceeds to rub athwart the smooth grain to find the roughness and the slant she needs to maintain her difference-defined, complexly constructed self.

—*Gloria T. Hull*

The poet is not (only) playing games; she is also writing political poetry. We need to think about the industrial pollution that neighbors us *and* the way we determine our future tomorrows. We need to realize that willfully not thinking makes both ourselves and the worst world we can imagine "common" (also meaning vulgar) and acceptable. Amitai F. Avi-ram has published a study of Lorde's use of this technique which in rhetoric is termed *apo koinou,* a Greek phrase meaning "in common." She has this to say about its thematic and formal functions in Lorde's poetry:

> *apo koinou* seems to be a controlling method in Audre Lorde's art. It enables her to suspend the ordinary pressures of sentence-closure, to reveal the suspect "nature" of such closure and its ideological consequences, and to reveal the hidden possibilities of meaning in words, especially in their ideological dimensions. It also enables her to form a new language that both criticizes reality and pursues the articulation of feeling as the satisfaction of a kind of erotic demand. In so doing, finally, *apo koinou* affords Lorde a technique for an alternative constitution of the subject in poetry as one that makes contact and has intense feelings in common with others, but preserves its ability to experience and to mean by observing its own differences in a world fraught with difference.
>
> [*Callaloo,* Winter 1986]

Employing this stratagem, she is pressing further

> the sharpened edge
> where day and night shall meet
> and not be
> one.

Lorde's tricky positionality—as exemplified by her rela-

tionship to home and poetic lines—also extends to community, which she likewise desires, but problematizes and finds problematic. An early poem, **"And What About the Children,"** alludes to the "dire predictions" and "grim speculations" that accompanied her interracial marriage and mixed-race offspring. She takes defiant comfort in the fact that if her son's head "is on straight,"

> he won't care
> about his
> hair
> nor give a damn
> whose wife
> I am.

"Between Ourselves" recalls her former habit of walking into a room seeking the "one or two black faces" which would reassure her that she was not alone; but

> now walking into rooms full of black faces
> that would destroy me for any difference
> where shall my eyes look?
> Once it was easy to know
> who were my people.

Caught during a women's rally between a racially deferent black counterman at Nedick's restaurant and a group of white companions discussing their problems with their maids, Lorde learns afresh that

> I who am bound by my mirror
> as well as my bed
> see causes in color
> as well as sex

In **"Scar,"** having "no sister no mother no children" is juxtaposed with what is "left": "only a tideless ocean of moonlit women / in all shades of loving."

These communal displacements are not so critically prominent in ***Our Dead Behind Us***—perhaps because, by now, they are so familiar. Instead, we find glyphs of female connection—the "large solid women" who "walk the parapets beside me"; the "corn woman bird girl sister" who "calls from the edge of a desert" telling her story of survival; the "Judith" and "Blanche" with whom she hangs out; the "warm pool / of dark women's faces" at a Gainesville, Florida, lecture. At this point, Lorde has achieved spiritual bonding with an ancestral and mythic past. The Amazons and warrior queens of Dahomey and the orisha of the Yoruba religious pantheon have given her a family that cannot fail:

> It was in Abomey that I felt
> the full blood of my fathers' wars
> and where I found my mother
> Seboulisa

Even on 125th Street in New York City,

> Head bent, walking through snow
> I see you Seboulisa
> printed inside the back of my head
> like marks of the newly wrapped akai [braids]
> that kept my sleep fruitful in Dahomey

The cover of ***Our Dead Behind Us*** consists of "a snapshot of the last Dahomean Amazons," "three old Black women in draped cloths," superimposed upon a sea of dark and passionate South Africans at a protest demonstration. This image projects Lorde's membership in a community of struggle which stretches from ancient to modern times. In **"Call"** she invokes "Oya Seboulisa Mawu Afrekete," "Rosa Parks and Fannie Lou Hamer / Assata Shakur and Yaa Asantewa / my mother and Winnie Mandela," speaking into exclusionary spaces a transcendent black woman power "released / from the prism of dreaming."

However uneasy her identity may be, it is imperative for Lorde that she read the world as a meaningful text and not as a series of interesting and elusive propositions. For her, to "read" is (1) to decipher—like the musician Prince—the signs of the times, (2) to decode—as the lesbian/gay community does—the submerged signification of the visible signs, and (3) to sound out clearly and "to your face" uncompromising truth as she sees it, in that foot-up, hands-on-hip loudness that is self-authorized black female jeremiad, sermon, and song. From the beginning, her vatic voice has defined her moral and didactic arena—in the same way that her presence claims its territory on the stage or in a photographic frame. She and Adrienne Rich, especially, have been criticized for their heavy seriousness. However, with so many dead behind her, Lorde is too busy pulling the bodies from bars and doorways, jungle tracks and trenches to find time for unrestricted poetic laughter. Her task is to foreground the carnage in a valiant effort to make such senseless dying truly a thing of the past.

From the first poem in her first book, **"Memorial II,"** Lorde has decried society's chewing up of young girl-women like **"Martha"** (in *Cables to Rage*) and **"Genevieve."** She begs, "Genevieve tell me where dead girls / Wander after their summer," and asks, in **"Suffer the Children,"** "But who shall dis-inter these girls / To love the women they were to become / Or read the legends written beneath their skin?" Their spirits still shadow her lines—as she yearns each spring "to braid the hair of a girl long dead" **("Beams"),** or as they reincarnate as the liminal "dark girls" of her haunted lyrics (for example, in **"Diaspora"**).

These readings are gentle, compared to the devastating fury that drives poems such as **"Equal Opportunity"** and **"For the Record."** In the latter, it is the poet herself who "counts" the big fleshy women like black grandmother Eleanor Bumpers who was brutally murdered by police while defending her home and then ignominiously carried out "dress torn up around her waist / uncovered." The next day Indira Gandhi, another sixty-seven-year-old "colored girl," is shot down in her garden, and the two women—who are now perhaps talking to each other—"weren't even sisters." The first poem is scathing satire of the black female "american deputy assistant secretary of defense / for Equal Opportunity" who preens in her crisp uniform and defends the department's "record / of equal opportunity for our women"—while United States troops invade Grenada, terrorizing "Imelda young Black in a tattered headcloth" whose empty cooking pots are overturned and garden trampled, whose husband was "buried without his legs," and who stands carefully before these trigger-nervous men asking for water for herself and her child. In **"Soho Cinema,"** she takes to task a well-off white woman for her complacently liberal nonresponse to the world's problems.

Irony blasts in these poems as explosively as it does, laughter-tinged, in **"A Question of *Essence*,"** where Lorde repeats that magazine's query, "Is Your Hair Still Political?" and quips "tell me / when it starts to burn." This is her kind of humor—piercing wit in the service of a serious cause. **"The Art of Response"** reads:

> The first answer was incorrect
> the second was
> sorry the third trimmed its toenails
> on the Vatican steps
> . . . .
> the sixth wrote a book about it
> the seventh
> argued a case before the Supreme Court
> against taxation on Girl Scout Cookies
> the eighth held a new conference
> while four Black babies
> and one other picketed New York City
> for a hospital bed to die in
> . . . .
> the thirteenth
> refused
> the fourteenth sold cocaine and
> shamrocks
> near a toilet in the Big Apple circus
> the fifteenth
> changed the question.

The cataloged responses are wildly comic, but the point is that the problem of how to live in this mad world—the unstated "question"—is usually posed in terms that make meaningful, efficacious response impossible; thus the only valid move is for one to change the "question." Similarly, the "some women" in **"Stations"** who love to wait at various spots "for life for a ring / in the June light for a touch / of the sun to heal them," for "their right / train in the wrong station," for love "to rise up," for visions, "that do not return / where they were not welcome," for themselves "around the next corner," are contrasted with the women in the final stanza who wait for something

> to change   and nothing
> does change
> so they change
> themselves.

Both **"Stations"** and **"The Art of Response"** carry a lilt and tone different from most of Lorde's work.

Her way is to paint social and political injustice in intimate and familiar forms. She "outlines" the difficulties faced by an interracial lesbian couple in a racist-sexist-homophobic culture "with not only our enemies' hands / raised against us": dog shit dumped on the front porch, brass wind chimes stolen, a burning cross ten blocks away, and the "despair offerings of the 8 A.M. News" reminding them that they are "still at war / and not with each other." This union is as charged with significance as the play of language and power which structures an exchange between the poet and an almost extinct Russian Chukwu woman in **"Political Relations."** Their warm words to each other must be spoken across the thin lips of dominance, white

Moscow girls who translated for them "smirking at each other."

"Sisters in Arms," the brilliant poem that begins *Our Dead Behind Us,* starts with:

> The edge of our bed was a wide grid
> where your fifteen-year-old daughter was hang-
>   ing
> gut-sprung on police wheels

Instantly, the poet and the black South African woman in bed beside her are catapulted through space and time into the embattled Western Reserve where the girl's body needs burying:

> so I bought you a ticket to Durban
> on my American Express
> and we lay together
> in the first light of a new season.

The "now" of the poem is the speaker clearing roughage from her autumn garden and reaching for "the taste of today" in embittering *New York Times* news stories that obscure the massacre of black children. Another shift occurs with "we were two Black women touching our flame / and we left our dead behind us / I hovered you rose the last ritual of healing." These lines show traces of the deep, joyous, authenticating eroticism Lorde describes in another of her poems as "the greed of a poet / or an empty woman / trying to touch / what matters."

These two women's loving is flecked with the cold and salt rage of death, the necessity of war: "Someday you will come to *my* country / and we will fight side by side?" When keys jingle, threatening, in "the door ajar," the poet's desperate reaching for "sweetness" "explodes like a pregnant belly," like the nine-year-old Joyce mentioned earlier who tried to crawl to her bleeding brother after being shot during a raid, "shitting through her [own] navel." The closing section of the poem looks backward on the grid to the only comfort in sight—a vision of warrior queen Mmanthatisi nursing her baby, then mapping the next day's battle as she

> dreams of Durban   sometimes
> visions the deep wry song of beach pebbles
> running after the sea

—in final lines whose rich referentiality links all the "Sisters" together in an enduring tradition of nurturance and hopeful struggle.

The oracular voice that powers—at different frequencies—Lorde's work can best be heard full force in the majestic orality of **"Call,"** a spiritual offering of praise and supplication that is chilling, especially when she reads it. Aido Hwedo is, a note tells us, "The Rainbow Serpent; also a representation of all ancient divinities who must be worshipped but whose names and faces have been lost in time." Stanza one summons this

> Holy ghost woman
> Stolen out of your name
> Rainbow Serpent
> whose faces have been forgotten
> Mother - loosen my tongue or adorn me
> with a lighter burden

Aido Hwedo is coming.

She invokes this deity in the name of herself and her sisters who, "on worn kitchen stools and tables," are piecing their "weapons together / scraps of different histories":

> Rainbow Serpent who must not go
> unspoken
> I have offered up the safety of separations
> sung the spirals of power
> and what fills the spaces
> before power unfolds or flounders
> in desirable nonessentials
> I am a Black woman   stripped down
> and praying
> my whole life has been an altar
> worth its ending
> and I say Aido Hwedo is coming.

She brings her best while asking for continuing power to do her work as a woman/poet. And she is blessed to become not only the collective voice of her sisters, but Aido Hwedo's fiery tongue, "the holy ghosts' linguist."

Critic Robert Stepto pronounced *The Black Unicorn* "an event in contemporary letters" because of its author's "voice or an *idea* of a voice that is essentially African in that it is communal, historiographical, archival, and prophetic *as well as* personal in ways that we commonly associate with the African *griot, dyēli,* and tellers of *nganos* and other oral tales." This voice holds in her later volume, which continues to "explore the modulations within that voice between feminine and feminist timbres" and also to chart "history and geography as well as voice" [*Parnassus,* 1979].

Lorde's moral and political vision combined with her demanding style make her difficult for many readers. Her aggressive exploration of her own alterity (she is a repository of "others" personified) is strategic defiance. Reviewing *Our Dead Behind Us* in the *Los Angeles Times* [December 1986], Ted C. Simmons even uses that word: "What further animates Lorde's work beyond this ore vein of contrapuntal interplay is her defiance. She seems to live defiance, thrive on it, delight in it. She is up-front, a feminist and militant, an activist juju-word woman."

Her stance impels commentators to approach her writings in terms of sympathy/guilt and the likeness/unlikeness of potential readers to the poet herself. A particularly exaggerated version of this tack occurs in the *Village Voice,* [in Kate Walker's September 1984 review of Lorde's] essay collection *Sister Outsider:* "the more you resemble her target of white, -male, -thin, -young, -heterosexual, Christian, and financially secure, the more you'll squirm under her verbal guns. . . . If you're black, gay, or left-wing, it's easier to identify with Lorde because we can never join the patriarchy, even if we're tempted." The same theme sounds in remarks such as the following about her poetry: "[*Chosen Poems—Old and New*] has an enormous appeal for those who share the author's feelings and would like to see their own feelings and experiences confirmed in print." "The *content* [of *Our Dead Behind Us*] is laudable; at least if you agree with her. But . . . there's more than a little of the disingenuous about her approach, which seems bent on instilling guilt in the reader as much as offering enlightenment." Those who squirm the most seem to be those who are most uncomfortable with their own privileged identities, and a great deal of the "guilt" is unacknowledged responsibility inappropriately reversed.

The wide divergence of opinion regarding the worth of Audre Lorde's poetry is striking. At one extreme rests the critic [Michael T. Siconolfi] who believes that, in ***The Black Unicorn,*** "ugliness predominates" and that "most of the poems are simply bad; they don't work as organic wholes and leave the reader surprised that a piece continues on the next page" [*Best Sellers,* January 1987]. The renowned Hayden Carruth begins his assessment of the book [*The Nation,* December 1978] with negative judgment and ends in a confusion of praise: "The truth is, I don't care much for her writing, which seems far too close to the commonplace. . . . Yet few poets are better equipped than Lorde to drive their passion through the gauzy softness of commonplace diction and prosody. One can't help being absorbed in it. Her best poems move me deeply."

Many critics pinpoint what they perceive to be her weaknesses, and credit their discoveries of beauty and strength: "If I have a complaint, it is that lines sometimes tend to be prosaic . . . yet the musicality and the self-assurance make it work as poetry" [Joan Larkin in *Ms.,* September 1974]. "Audre Lorde is a brilliant and honest poet, and while no poem in this volume touches me as the earlier Lorde poems do, ***The Black Unicorn*** should be read for its own wit, wisdom, and incandescence" [Andrea Benton Rushing in *Ms.,* January 1979]. Others are even more unstinting in their admiration. The *Library Journal's* reviewer consistently describes Lorde as "an excellent craftsman: her voice is lyrical and her eye is sharp" and pronounces her poems "hard-edged, compelling, and vital." Stepto concluded his discussion of Lorde with "***The Black Unicorn*** offers contemporary poetry of a high order, and in doing so may be a smoldering renaissance and revolution unto itself." Paula Giddings begins her review of ***Our Dead Behind Us:*** "Each new volume published by Audre Lorde confirms the fact that she is one of America's finest poets" [*Essence,* September 1986]. On the dust jacket of ***The Black Unicorn,*** Adrienne Rich elevates Lorde's "poems of elemental wildness and healing, nightmare and lucidity" which "blaze and pulse on the page, beneath the reader's eye."

Readers who—by whatever means of experience, empathy, imagination, or intelligence—are best able to approximate Lorde's own positionality most appreciate her work. For instance, it is clearly Siconolfi's ethnocentric ignorance of African traditions and their importance to Afro-Americans which leads him to arrogantly dismiss Lorde's "surprising" ("for a resident of Staten Island") "dragging in" of "a plethora of African mythology (a handy glossary is mercifully provided)" as a "purple Dashiki patch"— while black American critics Stepto and Andrea Rushing see this same material as a creative use of important African sources. Yet readers who also have "radically-situated subjectivities" still find themselves challenged by Lorde's poetry. Sandra Squire Fluck, a self-described "educator, poet/writer, and peace and social justice activist," writes

the following in her review of ***Our Dead Behind Us:*** "As uncomfortable as Lorde makes me feel here about the world situation, I do not have to relive my own righteous anger, brimming with angst and isolation, as it used to [be]. But I do have to accept Lorde on her terms, because she challenges me to see history her way as a Black lesbian woman." Only Lorde's recognition of "the limits of righteous anger" allows Fluck to "say yes" to her "without being threatened or overwhelmed" [*New Directions for Women,* January-February 1987]. As I write this, I recall that my own "Poem for Audre" of a few years ago begins with the words

> What you said
> keeps bothering me
> keeps needling, grinding
> like toothache
> or a bad conscience

Clearly, Lorde keeps her reader—as she does herself— unsettled.

Viewed stylistically, Lorde's poetry is not transparent. Understanding her texts requires attention, effort, energy, hard work. Even a sympathetic reviewer like Fahamisha Shariat admits that Lorde "may not be totally clear on a first, or even a second reading—sometimes her language approaches the surreal," but that "her poems are rich enough to send us back for new discoveries with each reading." ***Our Dead Behind Us*** is simpler in language and reference than ***Coal*** or ***The Black Unicorn,*** the poems less coded and more straightforward. Nevertheless, today's literary marketplace seems to be filled with customers looking for an easy "read" (usually fiction) and setting aside most of what cannot be conveniently discussed as narrative/narrativity.

Taking up Lorde reminds us of the still-unique nature of poetic discourse, the essence of which is a submerged textuality that, like Nietzsche's truth, remains an army of metaphors. Lorde's own poetry is basically a traditional kind of modernist free verse—laced with equivocation and, to use an old-fashioned concept, allegory. Only in her black Broadside Press-published books does she employ to any significant extent a recognizable ethnic idiom. Thus, who we hear with her foot up, specifying, does not sound to our ears like Zora, or Bessie, or, among the contemporaries, Sonia or Nikki, Pat or June.

Trying to read Lorde's more veiled texts can leave one foundering in her wake. These poems, I think, derive from a more vulnerable, unprocessed self, or from the poet's desire to keep some secrets partially hidden. **"Berlin Is Hard on Colored Girls"** comes across as a private joke about personal deprivation in a strange city and some kind of (dream?) encounter. Even read in the light of its two predecessors, **"Generation III"** remains densely impenetrable, except to suggest something emotionally strenuous related to mother-family and child-children. A handful of these private poems touches haltingly on Lorde's protracted fight with cancer and the idea of impending death— **"Mawu"** (which ends with the line "insisting / death is not a disease"), **"From the Cave"** perhaps, and **"Never to Dream of Spiders"** (with its glimpses of hospital surgery, recovery, a fiftieth birthday in 1984, and its concluding phrase, "a burst of light," which became the title for her second book about her health and illness).

Finally, Lorde's stylistic challenges are probably related to the manner in which she came into language/poetry. An inarticulate, left-handed child who had been forced to use her right hand, Lorde did not talk until she was five years old. Screaming in a four-year-old tantrum on the floor of the Harlem library (caused, I am sure, by the frustration of not being able to otherwise communicate), she was taken up by an impressive librarian who sat down and read her some stories. Audre knew instantly that that was "something I was going to do," and went on from there to read, then talk, then write—in that unusual order.

Words became for her "live entities." As a child she would take them "apart and fragment them like colors." She possessed a vocabulary which she had never heard spoken and did not know how to pronounce. These words such as *legend, frigate,* and *monster* "had an energy and power and I came to respect that power early. Pronouns, nouns, and verbs were citizens of different countries, who really got together to make a new world." During this period, she charmed away nightmares by choosing words which most terrified her and then "stripped them of anything but the sound—and put myself to sleep with the rhythms of them." This sense of words as sound full of both malevolent and joyful possibility is captured in her early poem **"Coal"** (which contains the lines, "how sound comes into a word, coloured / by who pays what for speaking").

Lorde's first language was, literally, poetry. When someone asked her "How do you feel?" "What do you think?" or any other direct question, she "would recite a poem, and somewhere in that poem would be the feeling, the vital piece of information. It might be a line. It might be an image. The poem was my response." Since she was hit if she stuttered, "writing was the next best thing." At this point, Audre was well on her way to becoming schizophrenic, living in "a totally separate world of words." She got "stoned on," retreated into poetry when life became too difficult. As miscellaneous poems no longer served to answer questions from herself and others, she began to write her own. These she did not commit to paper, but memorized and kept as a "long fund" in her head. Poems were "a secret way" of expressing feelings she was "still too afraid to deal with." She would know that she "finally had it" when she spoke her work aloud and it struck alive, became real.

Audre's bizarre mode of communication must surely have meant frequently tangential conversations, and certainly placed on her listeners the burden of having to "read" her words in order to connect her second-level discourse with the direct matter at hand. At any rate, her answer to "How do you feel?" or "Do you want to go to the store with me?" could rarely be a simple "fine" or a univocal yes or no.

In high school, she tried not to "think in poems." She saw in amazement how other people thought, "step by step," and "not in bubbles up from chaos that you had to anchor with words"—a kind of "nonverbal communication, beneath language" the value of which she had learned intuitively from her mother. After an early, pseudonymously published story, Lorde did not write another piece of prose until her 1977 essay **"Poetry Is Not a Luxury."** Even though she had begun to speak in full sentences when she was nineteen and had also acquired compositional skills, "communicating deep feeling in linear, solid blocks of print felt arcane, a method beyond me." She "could not focus on a thought long enough to have it from start to finish," but she could "ponder a poem for days." Lorde possessed an admirable, innate resistance to the phallogocentric "white pencil," to being, as she put it, "locked into the mouth of the dragon." She had seen the many errors committed in the name of "thought / thinking," and, furthermore, had formed some precious convictions about her own life that "defied thought." She seems always to have been seeking what she calls, in *Our Dead Behind Us,* "an emotional language / in which to abbreviate time."

Lorde had not connected words with a reality outside her individual head until she stood on a hill in Mexico one breathtaking morning, also when she was nineteen, and realized that she could "infuse words directly with what I was feeling," that "I didn't have to create the world I wrote about," that "words could tell." She found that the "trees" and "forest" she used to dream and fantasize about could indeed "be a reality" that words can "match" and "re-create." With this, Lorde had taken the final step of a journey that had begun when, extremely nearsighted and legally blind, she had put on her first pair of spectacles at four and saw that trees were not "green clouds."

This remarkable story inescapably suggests what the French poststructuralist critic Julia Kristeva posits about language and subjectivity—her locating of meaning in the unconscious, chaotic, preverbal, infant *chora,* in the rhythmic pulsing of semiotic sound, the drives and tides of a maternal body. According to Kristeva, this locus (which appears most strongly in poetry and which Kristeva even calls at one point poetic language) dynamically charges and interacts subversively with the symbolic, thetic world where rational, conceptual language and communication are situated. Lorde's is a living experience of that about which Kristeva theorizes.

Viewing Lorde's poetry in the light of Kristeva's theory reminds us that finding new, more provocative ways to discuss black women's poetry is a project that could claim more attention than is currently focused in that direction and, further, that these ways might well evolve from sensitive digging in the soil of diverse traditions. (pp. 150-72)

Gloria T. Hull, "Living on the Line: Audre Lorde and 'Our Dead Behind Us'," in Changing Our Own Words: Essays on Criticism, Theory, and Writing by Black Women, *edited by Cheryl A. Wall, Rutgers University Press, 1989, pp. 150-72.*

FURTHER READING

Annas, Pamela. "A Poetry of Survival: Unnaming and Re-naming in the Poetry of Audre Lorde, Pat Parker, Sylvia Plath, and Adrienne Rich." *Colby Library Quarterly* 18, No. 1 (March 1982): 9-25.

> Examines Lorde's "survival poetry," asserting that the relationship between poetry and feminism is complex, unique, and necessary because "a poem is a stage in the process of self-definition, a grounding and realizing of self-image."

Avi-ram, Amitai F. "*Apo Koinou* in Audre Lorde and the Moderns: Defining the Differences." *Callaloo* 9, No. 1 (Winter 1986): 192-208.

> Examines the elements of *Apo Koinou*—"a figure of speech . . . in which a single word or phrase is shared between two distinct, independent syntactic units"—evidenced in Lorde's poetry.

Hammond, Karla. "An Interview with Audre Lorde." *The American Poetry Review* 9, No. 2 (March-April 1980): 18-21.

> Lorde discusses her personal life, political ideology, and the repercussions of racism.

———. "Audre Lorde: Interview." *Denver Quarterly* 16, No. 1 (Spring 1981): 10-27.

> Lorde talks about trends in African-American literature and the development of her writing.

Rich, Adrienne. "An Interview with Audre Lorde." *Signs: Journal of Women in Culture and Society* 6, No. 4 (Summer 1981): 713-36.

> Lorde discusses her experiences in Mexico, her career as a teacher, and her views on feminism.

Additional coverage of Lorde's life and career is contained in the following sources published by Gale Research: *Black Literature Criticism; Black Writers; Contemporary Authors,* Vols. 25-28 rev. ed.; *Contemporary Authors New Revision Series,* Vols. 16, 26; *Contemporary Literary Criticism,* Vol. 18; *Dictionary of Literary Biography,* Vol. 41; and *Major 20th-Century Writers.*

Rohinton Mistry

1952-

Indian short story writer and novelist.

The following entry focuses on Mistry's career through 1991.

INTRODUCTION

Mistry has earned critical acclaim for his vivid depictions of Indian society. He particularly focuses on its Parsi, or Parsee, community, a small religious minority that traces its roots to Zoroastrianism and ancient Persia. By examining the Parsi culture through a combination of sympathy and criticism, Mistry analyzes the conflicts which arise among Parsi individuals both in Indian society, where they are often excluded by the predominant Hindu and Muslim populations, and in Western nations. He has been favorably compared to such Indian writers as V. S. Naipaul and R. K. Narayan, and has been recognized by Keith Garebian for providing "a microcosm of Indian Life, but, more particularly, . . . a microcosm of a highly defined sect that has managed to keep its own customs, language, and religion intact while becoming a vital part of the Indian scene."

Tales from Firozsha Baag, Mistry's first collection of short stories, largely focuses on problems of faith experienced by residents of a Bombay apartment complex known as Firozsha Baag. For example, the protagonist of "The Exercisers" defies his parents and their spiritual advisor by dating a woman who is not a Parsi, while Dualat of "Condolence Visit" shocks her neighbors by departing from religious custom and refusing to mourn her husband according to Parsi tradition. To suggest each character's mental anguish, Mistry incorporates elements of mysticism and surrealism in his stories: the lonely Parsi maid of "The Ghost of Firozsha Baag" has a sexual relationship with a spirit, while a mentally unbalanced woman imprisons her neighbor's child in a bird cage in "The Paying Guests." Some critics claimed that because protagonists of several stories in *Tales from Firozsha Baag* play such minor roles in other stories, the book's emotional impact was lessened; others, including Amin Malak, have praised Mistry's use of recurring characters, noting that they consequently appear to be "locked in a cycle of restrictive traditions, economic needs, racial and religious tensions, and inner psychological conflicts."

Mistry's first novel, *Such a Long Journey*, is also set in an apartment complex in Bombay. This book, for which Mistry won Canada's 1991 Governor General's Award, focuses on Gustad Noble, a middle-class Parsi bank teller and former member of India's upper class who becomes enmeshed in various domestic and political conflicts during the Bangladesh War of the early 1970s. While trying to cope with the death of his best friend, his daughter's illness, and his teenage son's rebelliousness, Gustad is duped

by an old friend into helping divert public funds into a savings account reserved for Indira Gandhi. Because the book has often been interpreted as an allegorical retelling of contemporary Indian history, some critics found Gustad an unconvincing vehicle for Mistry's views; others concurred with the opinion of John Clement Ball, who asserted: "In the finest tradition of the realistic Victorian novel, Mistry's book traces the moral growth of a complex and sympathetic character during challenging times."

PRINCIPAL WORKS

Tales from Firozsha Baag (short fiction) 1987; also
  published as *Swimming Lessons, and Other Stories
  from Firozsha Baag,* 1989
Such a Long Journey (novel) 1991

CRITICISM

Amin Malak

[In *Tales from Firozsha Baag*], an impressive collection of eleven stories, Rohinton Mistry sympathetically presents the vibrations of life in Firozsha Baag, a residential block in Bombay inhabited by middle-class families of Zoroastrians or Parsis, a tiny religious minority in India that traces its cultural identity and beliefs back to pre-Islamic Persia. Mistry's narrative strategy involves locating the stories within the building complex as well as interlinking them with characters who appear and reappear in more than one story. These characters seem locked in a cycle of restrictive traditions, economic needs, racial and religious tensions, and inner psychological conflicts.

The definition of the setting and the concentration on a limited number of characters with whom the readers readily become familiar give the stories coherence in both tone and structure. In a subtle and unpretentious style, Mistry presents his characters and incidents with fidelity and dexterity. The narrative retains a detached irony yet shows sympathetic affection for the characters as they face their daily concerns, petty worries, and social and religious tensions. Despite near-tragic circumstances, Mistry's characters survive and cherish hopes for better days. Following the models of psychological realism set by Chekhov and Joyce, Mistry reveals a knack for generating humour in the midst of tragedy. As he portrays the behaviour of individuals striving to retain their distinctive identity alongside the constricting edicts of a traditional community threatened by a hostilely changing world, Mistry adroitly blends tragedy with irony, cynicism with humour, scepticism with belief.

The discourse in the collection's later stories transcends irony toward a potent social message; the narrative also expands into the experiences of Indian emigrants in Canada. **"Squatter"** and **"Lend Me Your Light"** illustrate Mistry's work at its best. Complexly structured to accommodate the narrative's shifts between India and Canada, these two exceptional stories dramatize clashes between Oriental and Western cultures. In **"Squatter,"** Mistry uses the technique of story-within-story. Through the witty, sardonic Nariman, the storyteller, he narrates the comic tribulations of the Indian emigrant Sarosh who is transformed into Sid on arrival in Toronto. Among Sarosh's innumerable maladjustments is his perennial difficulty with the toilet seat:

> At the point where our story commences, Sarosh had been living in Toronto for ten years. We find him depressed and miserable, perched on top of the toilet, crouching on his haunches, feet planted firmly for balance upon the white plastic oval of the toilet seat.

> Daily for a decade had Sarosh suffered this position. Morning after morning, he had no choice but to climb up and simulate the squat of our Indian latrines. If he sat down, no amount of exertion could produce success.

As if anticipating his difficulties in his prospective land of promise, Sarosh's mother insightfully encapsulates the truth that every sensitive immigrant comes to embrace: "It is better to live in want among your family and friends,

who love you and care for you, than to be unhappy surrounded by vacuum cleaners and dishwashers and big shiny motor cars." Sarosh's tragi-comic ordeals with the toilet seat, and his symbolic inability to perform his normal bodily functions (a malady that baffles his Canadian physician), cannot be overcome until he takes off back to India.

Amusingly, the storyteller Nariman colours the sardonic tale to his enchanted young listeners from Firozsha Baag with a scathing comment on Canadian multicultural policy:

> The Multicultural Department is a Canadian invention. It is supposed to ensure that ethnic cultures are able to flourish, so that Canadian society will consist of a mosaic of cultures—that's their favourite word, mosaic—instead of one uniform mix, like the American melting pot. If you ask me, mosaic and melting pot are both nonsense, and ethnic is a polite way of saying bloody foreigner.

Retaining the story's ironic tone, Mistry closes with a parody of Othello's last speech. He lets Sarosh derisively sum up his immigrant experiences: just as Othello remained alien to the confusing values of Venice, Sarosh remains unfit for the dizzying world of Toronto:

> I pray you, in your stories. . . . When you shall these unlucky deeds relate, speak of me as I am; nothing extenuate, nor set down aught in malice: tell them that in Toronto once there lived a Parsi boy as best as he could. Set you down this; and say, besides, for some it was good and for some it was bad, but for me life in the land of milk and honey was just a pain in the posterior.

The implication of this acerbic treatment of the immigrant's experience may seem pernicious, yet the story's psychological thrust creates a humorous effect that counterbalances the cynicism. Moreover, the story closes with a humane scene of care and compassion involving the storyteller and his young audience.

Whereas humour prevails in **"Squatter,"** tragedy predominates in **"Lend Me Your Light,"** whose material possesses the expansiveness of a potential novel. Drawing on several layers of narrative structure and points of view, the story involves two friends: Jamshed, the spoiled upper-class malcontent who scorns India's backwardness and leaves for his American dreamland, and Percy, the idealistic middle-class enthusiast who chooses to devote his energies to help poor peasants against the exploitation of the village usurers. (As the story's epigraph suggests, Percy's project derives its inspiration from Rabindranath Tagore's humanist exhortation for the symbolic non-usurious lending of light pronounced in *Gitanjali*: "your lights are all lit—then where do you go with your lamp? My house is all dark and lonesome—lend me your light.") Between these contradictory attitudes stands the narrator, Percy's brother, who also leaves India for Canada, yet keeps his cultural identity as an Indian and maintains cordial but critical contacts with the Parsi community of Toronto. The conflicting visions in the narrator's mind are skilfully articulated in eye imagery and through the metaphorical use of the figure of Tiresias:

> But as I slept on my last night in Bombay a searing pain in my eye woke me up. It was one o'clock. I bathed my eyes and tried to get back to sleep. Half-jokingly, I saw myself as someone out of a Greek tragedy, guilty of the sin of hubris seeking emigration out of the land of my birth, and paying the price in burnt-out eyes: I, Tiresias, blind and throbbing between two lives, the one in Bombay and the other one to come in Toronto. . . .

The story thus offers two parallel levels of conflict: an external one between the pompous Jamshed and the idealist Percy, and its internalized version within the narrator between his roots and his new Western life style.

Mistry's critical but committed stance towards his cultural roots provides, as in Joyce's writings, infinite inspirational material. . . . The writer's sympathies preclude his condemning or disowning his culture in its entirety, and the humorous rendition of character and incident makes the criticism poignantly effective and lasting.

—Amin Malak

The story concludes tragically with the village usurers assassinating one of Percy's co-workers, leading to the collapse of the humanitarian project. Jamshed, of course, triumphs in his worldly wisdom. Once more, Mistry deploys his favourite Tiresian metaphor to close his narrative:

> Gradually, I discovered I'd brought back with me my entire burden of riddles and puzzles, unsolved. The whole sorry package was there, not lightened at all. The epiphany would have to wait for another time, another trip.
>
> I mused, I gave way to whimsy: I, Tiresias, throbbing between two lives, humbled by the ambiguities and dichotomies confronting me. . . .

Regardless of this ambivalence, the story's tone unequivocally favours the self-sacrificing Percy. Despite defeat, he is not giving up: the struggle continues.

Mistry's critical but committed stance towards his cultural roots provides, as in Joyce's writings, infinite inspirational material. Mistry's irony creates a fit vehicle to expose gently, sensitively, and truthfully a traditional community that still regards women as unclean, practises arranged marriages, and believes in magic, ritual, and superstition. The writer's sympathies preclude his condemning or disowning his culture in its entirety, and the humorous rendition of character and incident makes the criticism poignantly effective and lasting. What enriches the hu-

mour even further is that the narrative blends the comic with the heroic as the characters strive to survive and transcend their reality.

With the publication of *Tales From Firozsha Baag,* a collection that shows brilliance and promise, Canadian literature has gained a fresh and distinctive voice. Mistry, together with such talented writers as Michael Ondaatje, Joy Kogawa, and Neil Bissoondath, opens exciting new vistas that expand the Canadian imagination beyond familiar Anglo-European motifs towards Oriental and Third World dimensions. Rohinton Mistry is a writer to watch and welcome. (pp. 101-03)

> Amin Malak, *"Images of India,"* in Canadian Literature, *No. 119, Winter, 1988, pp. 101-03.*

Rohinton Mistry   (Interview with Geoff Hancock)

[Hancock]: Bharati Mukerjee has written that India's children in the new world are a mystery to her. Is this something that interests you?

[Mistry]: I'm sure it interests me. But I have not dealt with it in my work as much as I would like to. I'm still more concerned with the lives of those children in the old world. A time will come when I am content with examining their lives in the new world.

Bombay is a crucial place in your fiction. Does writing make your own origins clearer?

Place in fiction is as much a matter of chance or coincidence as place of birth, is it not? That's what I am stuck with and that's what I deal with.

Will the interface between the two experiences of Canada and India become more apparent in your work?

The novel I am writing is set entirely in Bombay. This may be disappointing to people who speculate the last story in *Firozsha Baag* will be the first story in the next book.

Why would they speculate that?

In *Tales From Firozsha Baag,* we have Kersi the narrator whose development we witness from childhood to teenager to young man in Canada. Many people see that story as autobiographical. The parents in that story say the book was very interesting to read, but they would like to learn more about how he lives in Canada. People who should know better see this as the author writing a book for his parents. But it's the narrator of the fiction who's speaking, not me. One interviewer even hoped my next book would be about my years working in a Canadian bank! I smiled politely at that, and gave him a 'who-knows' type of look.

You recently spent some time in Los Angeles where your wife was a school teacher. In your letters to me you said it was a grim experience, with inner city students bringing weapons to school. So far at least, the Canadian and American experiences are much different. (p. 144)

Your question hints at what do I think about the two different experiences of the Canadian Mosaic and the American Melting Pot. Multiculturalism and the Melting Pot. I haven't followed all the arguments for and against Multiculturalism. I used to think Multiculturalism was an invention of the politicians, to have a new portfolio, find ways to structure their time, win votes and so on. Lately, I understand that the people Multiculturalism is supposed to help are worried about it. It's become counterproductive, as they say in government offices.

Somebody said Multiculturalism creates Multi-Cul-de-Sacs. Dead Ends from which the ethnic community cannot participate, or be assimilated more fully into Canadian life. Others have said Multiculturalism is just a subtle form of racism. They point to the Melting Pot, where racism is out in the open. Or like the employer who says he can't give you a job because you lack 'Canadian experience—it's not the colour of your skin or the way you speak.' Some people say it's more pernicious because one can't really identify it.

However, I think I prefer Multiculturalism to the direct racism of the Melting Pot because I'd rather be alive and face the subtle discrimination. The overt racism of the Melting Pot often leads to a violent end. Here, I'm thinking of teenage gangs like the Dot Busters in New Jersey. The dot they refer to is the red dot that married Hindu women wear on their foreheads. Beating, maiming, and killing East Indians is what the Dot Busters do when they want a good time. The subtle racism denies people promotions or jobs they are qualified for and have a right to. I'd rather go without my promotion, but be alive to fight for it instead of being killed on the street some day. Finally, I wonder if there is any significantly greater amount of melting taking place in the Melting Pot than in Multiculturalism.

As a writer do you feel an obligation to speak for a sense of tribe, as Margaret Laurence described it? To articulate for those who can't articulate?

I don't think I have a message. One must write for the sake of writing, to create good literature. The other things follow in a very natural way. I grew up in Bombay. Now I am here. I'm a writer. I am determined to write good literature. That is my primary concern. But to write well, I must write about what I know best. In that way, I automatically speak for my 'tribe'.

Is that your obsession as a writer, to write well?

Yes, Is there anything else? If I could not write well, I'd be happier working in the bank. Something that is just a job.

You've done remarkably well in a short time. You won a prize with the first story you wrote, and the second. Within five years, you've been in all the major quarterlies, brought out a book with a major publisher, and been nominated for the Governor General's award for fiction. Is writing a gift you have?

Is it a gift? Or a fortuitous confluence of events? Is it because Multiculturalism is fashionable? I believe in the sin of hubris. It is not propitious to examine these things too closely. (pp. 145-46)

Do you have a sense of audience?

I suppose the world is my audience. At least, I wish it. But if you mean do I think of an audience when I write, no. The work is finished when I like it. Then I hope everyone else will too.

It seems it is very important to you to be exact in your description. Why is that?

I think it's something I owe to the place where I grew up. Honesty, truth, and accuracy is the least I owe to that place.

And what most?

Never to forget. The most and the least then combine. I don't want to forget anything about Bombay. The life, the places, the people.

Are criticisms and reviews of any interest to you?

In all modesty, I must admit that so far, I have only received positive reviews. I haven't felt the sting of a bad review. Having said this, I ask myself, should I believe all that reviewers say? If I say yes, then someday, I will have to believe a bad review as well. In the best of all possible worlds, there would be no reviewers and critics; there would only be writers and readers. All readers would read all that was written, and it would be good writing, since it's the best of all possible worlds! But silliness aside, I do admire criticism that reaches the exalted heights of T. S. Eliot, Cleanth Brooks, F. R. Leavis. Does criticism this fine serve the function of criticism? The criticism is itself art.

What do you think when your works are compared to V. S. Naipaul or R. K. Narayan?

It's hard to pin down this question of influence. How does one know when someone has been an influence? Does one start writing like someone? Or does one think like that writer? I suppose the writers one reads repeatedly influence one in some way that cannot be defined. If I had a magic lamp like Aladdin's, I still wouldn't want to write like someone else. I greatly admire Naipaul's books and have read most of them more than once. I like John Cheever. I've forgotten the number of times I've read James Joyce's *Dubliners*. My other favourites are Malamud, Nabokov, Isabel Allende, Jakov Lind, especially his stories, *Soul of Wood*. Turgenev, Chekhov, Muriel Spark, Lessing, Camus, Bellow, Heinrich Boll—my list goes on. (pp. 146-47)

Do you see yourself as a religious or political writer?

If politics or religion come into my work, they come in a secondary way.

Are folktales and myths important to you? To explain who your characters are? Their mix of good and evil and dreams?

How does a Parsi become the way he is? I don't need a myth or a fable to explain the Parsi to a reader. There are enough points of experience in common with all peoples around the world. Perhaps one basic myth is common to all of us.

Would you take this as far as Jungian archetypes?

I'm not familiar with Jung. The Parsi characters in my

stories, and their dreams, ambitions, and fears are as accessible to the Western reader as the Indian reader. The universalities of the story are sufficient. Again, with this idea of universality, I don't say to myself: 'This story needs three doses of universality and five doses of particularity.' When I start writing, it all just happens.

What makes a story universal?. . . . [What] is a story?

Don't take my word for it, but a story is drama, character, detail and entertainment. A story is boring for me when the words don't sing and when the ideas which the words try to convey don't fly.

Do you concern yourself with technical things?

When a story doesn't work, I try to see why. Then I consider things like active verbs, nouns, adverbs, the lyrical quality of the prose. Then I read the story aloud to see where it jars and where it flows. (pp. 147-48)

Do you see yourself as a traditional or experimental writer?

Both, perhaps. Every time one brings words together to make a sentence, one is experimenting. I suppose I am a traditional writer. I am not trying to break new ground or pioneer new techniques.

Are you attracted to the work of Salman Rushdie, also from Bombay: his use of magic realism, hyperbolic situations, pushing language to extremes?

Magic realism is fascinating to me, though I've not been tempted to try it. (p. 148)

Who or what are the antagonists for your characters? The old ways under siege, the desire for someplace else, old religions and superstitions, tension between youth and age?

All these are in my tales. But there is also something larger which oppresses the characters. Why death? Why must we struggle with life and die? My characters worry about these things. I don't know if it comes out in my stories.

Is faith not enough? In Hindu India, the characters would say it was karma.

But my characters are outside Hindu India. And because of the history of the Zoroastrian religion, it does not provide a solid anchor like Hinduism or Judaism or Islam. The religion was lost, then recouped in questionable ways. There is no complete book written by the Prophet that survives. Only fragments exist from 5,000 B.C. Everything else has been built upon by priests. So a tradition developed which is often the cause of much controversy. Religion for my characters is insubstantial and provides very few answers.

You returned to Bombay recently. Was it exciting, shocking?

None of those things, a picture formed in my mind of what it would be like when I visited again. Yet some part of me hoped I was wrong. I found sadly that this picture was right. Bombay had no magic transformation. Everything continued in the same way. Only slightly more intense. More people live on the streets. More corruption and bribery and red tape. Four or five years ago, we hoped for a lot when Rajiv Gandhi came on the scene. That optimism

has evaporated. It all seemed very bleak. Bleak was the picture I created when I was here. That's exactly the way it is.

Does that make you pessimistic as a writer?

No. There are still those amazing moments of hope, those sparks. Those moments that make me feel despite all the misery and sorrow, that life is still good and must go on. My wife and I were on a train to north India. We stopped at a station around one A.M. There was the absolute chaos that is normal in an Indian railway station. Tickets were double sold for the same seats. People rushed the compartments to take over already occupied seats. The scene seemed one of hostility. We were going through the Punjab. On the train were Sikhs, Muslims and Hindus. We expected dire consequences. But within minutes, everything calmed down. People in the compartments shared food with the newcomers, total strangers with whom minutes earlier they had been desperately arguing and ready for hand-to-hand combat over the reserved seats.

Could you elaborate on something you said, that the most appalling things in life are the most promising for a writer?

That makes me sound ghoulish. Waiting for something horrible to happen. Reporters call it a slow day when there are no catastrophes. But what horror is human nature most capable of? That can be used as a point of departure. Could a writer have imagined the Holocaust? I suppose Thomas Mann in *The Magic Mountain* foreshadowed the darkness that Europe was going to plunge into. But he didn't imagine this official machinery for eliminating a whole race. Could a writer have imagined something so horrific? But now, it's something writers have to deal with.

The novel you're writing is set during the months of the Bangladesh war in 1971. Is it, therefore, much darker in tone than your short stories?

The war between India and Pakistan, leading to the liberation of Bangladesh, lasted only thirteen days. Preceding that, were months of guerilla warfare and the genocide of two million Bengalese by the Pakistan army. But the novel is not about the war. It is set in Bombay, more than a thousand miles away from the horror. I won't give away the story. This horrible war impinges on this family in Bombay in a most peculiar manner and it creates strange currents in their life. We hear about the war through newspapers and the radio. The horror is once removed.

Is Kersi, the narrator of **Tales From Firozsha Baag,** *your alter-ego? Is he a character we may see more of?*

No, he isn't.

Through Kersi, you examine the nature of story telling. Is that the essence of fiction for you, to be receptive to story telling?

I suppose we are all listeners. Some of us like to tell stories. Do all people wish they could tell stories? I wonder. I sometimes think there is a latent desire in all of us to be story-tellers. In the best of all possible worlds, all of us would be story-tellers and listeners. (pp. 148-50)

Rohinton Mistry and Geoff Hancock, in an in-

terview in The Canadian Fiction Magazine, *No. 65, 1989, pp. 143-50.*

Michiko Kakutani

[In one story in *Swimming Lessons, and Other Stories from Firozsha Baag*], a group of neighborhood boys in Bombay clusters around Nariman, the local storyteller, to listen to his latest tale. Jehangu, the would-be intellectual of the group, declares that "unpredictability was the brush" Nariman used to paint his stories with, "and ambiguity the palette he mixed his colours in."

> Jehangu said that Nariman sometimes told a funny incident in a very serious way, or expressed a significant matter in a light and playful manner. And these were only two rough divisions, in between were lots of subtle gradations of tone and texture. Which then, was the funny story and which the serious? Their opinions were divided, but ultimately, said Jehangu, "it was up to the listener to decide."

The same description might well be applied to these tales by Rohinton Mistry, a young writer who has already won considerable acclaim abroad. Having left India in 1975 to live in Canada, Mr. Mistry has created in this volume, a world and a time—presumably, as one highly autobiographical story implies, the lost world of his own childhood in Bombay. As in R. K. Narayan's Malgudi books, the volume is informed by a tone of gentle compassion for seemingly insignificant lives, and as in Mr. Narayan's work, the stories interconnect to give us a portrait of a minutely detailed fictional place—in this case, the apartment complex of *Firozsha Baag.*

In other respects, *Swimming Lessons* has more in common with Joyce's *Dubliners*: not only do the stories all deal with a fading middle class—both its suffocating atmosphere of pettiness and its shabby decencies are chronicled by an author who has already left it behind—but they also tend to pivot around incidents that reveal to the characters some unforeseen truth about their lives.

In **"One Sunday,"** a young cricket player named Kersi, who has become pals with the local handyman, is called upon to catch a thief who has stolen money from a neighbor—a thief who turns out to be his old friend. In **"Auspicious Occasion,"** an aging sourpuss named Rustomji finds that an accident on the way to the local temple (a man spits on him from a bus) has focused all his anxieties and abruptly shattered his life's self-satisfied facade. And in **"The Collectors,"** a doctor, disappointed by his own progeny's boorish behavior, takes on a neighbor's child as his surrogate son—only to suffer feelings of betrayal and disappointment after a prized stamp from his collection mysteriously disappears and the boy fails to clear his name.

As we are initiated into the day-to-day rhythms of this ingrown Parsi community (the weekly religious rituals performed by the devout, as well as the daily squabbles and exchanges that take place between neighbors), we slowly get to know all the building's residents: the local curmudgeon, who secretly covets his wife's cleaning woman, the fat Najamaj, who ingratiates herself with others by giving

them access to her precious refrigerator; Jacqueline, a superstitious maid, whose sexual fantasies produce a real-life ghost, and a couple who sublet a room in an apartment and soon succeed in making life miserable for everyone in Firozsha Baag. As the stories span a decade or so, we see the older residents deal with death and illness, the younger ones grow up and move away.

Caught on the margins of a changing culture that embraces everything from arranged marriages to Mercedes-Benzes, many of the characters in *Swimming Lessons* feel torn between tradition and modernity, the old rituals of piety and self-abnegation, and the new imperatives of ambition and self-fulfillment. A woman named Daulat, whose husband has just died, frets over a busybody neighbor's insistence that she follow every last religious ritual to the letter, and she surreptitiously proceeds with her own agenda, confident that her husband's soul will nonetheless be saved. A teen-ager similarly chafes under his parents' insistence that he consult a holy man about his new-found romance. But while he worries that such a consultation will cause his girlfriend to dismiss him as a shallow fool, he ends up succumbing to his parents' wishes—with predictably unhappy results.

In the case of another young man—the cricket player Kersi, whom we met in an earlier story—the conflicts between the old and the new open out into a larger question of cultural loyalties. Having left his family and friends to live in Toronto, he finds himself torn between a nostalgic loyalty for India and an eagerness to escape its suffocating poverty, its backwardness and provincialism. A trip home to visit his family, however, does not clarify matters, as Kersi hopes; he returns to Canada, as confused as before.

It is in [**"Swimming Lessons"**] that Kersi is revealed as a kind of fictional surrogate for the author, and we are made to understand the evolution of the book we hold in our hands.

As Kersi's parents read his collection, his mother says "he must be so unhappy" there in Canada, "all his stories are about Bombay, he remembers every little thing about his childhood, he is thinking about it all the time even though he is ten thousand miles away." His father disagrees. "He said it did not mean that he was unhappy, all writers worked in the same way, they used their memories and experiences and made stories out of them, changing some things, adding some, imagining some; all writers were very good at remembering details of their lives."

> *Michiko Kakutani, "Tales from a Bombay Apartment Complex," in* The New York Times, *February 3, 1989, p. C32.*

Janette Turner Hospital

In writing a series of interlinked tales, which have a cumulative and reverberative effect, Mistry is following a pattern received from both his Indian and Canadian literary milieus. R. K. Narayan wrote tales that intermesh and map out life in the South Indian village of Malgudi, and Alice Munro continues to embroider the rich tapestry of a small Ontario town. One is frequently reminded of both authors in reading *Swimming Lessons* as Mistry, with the meticulousness of an archeologist uncovering a civilization shard by shard, reveals the microcosm of Firozsha Baag, an apartment complex in Bombay.

Firozsha Baag's residents, mostly Parsi, but also Hindu and Muslim, represent middle-class Bombay, or rather the *professional* middle class (accountants, lawyers, doctors) who live in more or less genteel poverty. By the final story, we *know* Firozsha Baag. We know its leaking plumbing and peeling paint, its aged cars, the apartment that has the refrigerator (shared by many) and the one with the telephone (shared by all.) We know marital secrets, family triumphs, generational conflicts. We know the families and their servants and their relatives, including the sons and daughters who've emigrated to New York or Toronto, and who remain no less tied to Firozsha Baag for that. In fact, as one deliciously satirical story makes clear, neither distance nor time nor even a legal chance of passport can free the roving sons and daughters of Firozsha Baag from their past. As a Toronto counselor for Immigration Problems comments about certain symptoms of culture shock: "Some of us thought these problems were linked to retention of original citizenship. But this was a false lead."

The liveliest stories are the early ones, when the children who will later emigrate are still playing cricket in the compound, and teasing the old *ayah* who sees ghosts, and hiding under the slatted steps with voyeuristic intentions when the teen-age girls go upstairs. The tiny details that make up life in Bombay are exquisitely evoked: the constant chewing and spitting of betel juice that covers the ground (and in one story, a freshly laundered white *lungi*) with what appear to be splats of blood; the way the city water supply is turned off at 6 a.m. during the hot, dry season, so that a household has to be up at 5 a.m. to fill all available vessels with water; the way people are far more intimately connected with the processes of aging and bodily frailty and dying than is the case any more in North America.

There are weaknesses in the stories, moments when the reader is conscious that this is a first collection from a young writer. Mistry is imitative of Indian novelist Anita Desai in his depiction of sudden and grotesque incursions of violence into the community, but he has a habit of predictably and rather portentiously foreshadowing these events (a splat of betel juice on white cloth prefigures a murder; a rat bludgeoned with a cricket bat precedes the bludgeoning of a starving servant) and in general there is a tendency toward heavy-handed symbolism.

In *Swimming Lessons,* which charts most closely the cultural displacement of the young Parsi in Toronto, I was forcibly struck by the narrator's blind spot, an unintentional one, I suspect, on the author's part. The swimmer alludes (without comment, and hence powerfully) to racist gestures and remarks made by others in the locker room; but he himself frequently makes extremely sexist observations about women and seems unaware of the parallel insult. In both cases, with derogatory impact, a human being is reduced to caricature and bodily stereotype.

On the other hand, there are cultural nuances in Bombay that Mistry conveys with the skill of a master. He evokes, with sharp eye and gentle wit, the secret eroticism of a puritan culture: the innocent voyeurism of married men (who covertly watch their unencumbered-by-underwear washerwomen at work) and the fantasies of widowed women (an old *ayah* is molested by a most affectionate ghost). He conveys sparsely and powerfully the tug of war between compassion and the survival instinct: "Rustomji too would have liked to feel sorrow and compassion. But he was afraid. He had decided long ago that this was no country for sorrow or compassion or pity—these were worthless and, at best, inappropriate."

As for the Firozsha Baag people who now live in Toronto and New York, I feel that Mistry's significant stories about those displaced lives are yet to come, and that they will be worth waiting for. (pp. 2, 11)

> *Janette Turner Hospital, "Living in Toronto, Dreaming of Bombay," in* Los Angeles Times Book Review, *March 5, 1989, pp. 2, 11.*

Hope Cooke

Rohinton Mistry's 11 intersecting short stories in *Swimming Lessons* center on the Parsi inhabitants of Firozsha Baag, a walled-in lower-middle-class housing complex in Bombay. In this first book, Mr. Mistry, a young Indian writer now living in Toronto, treats the apartment block with such microscopic intensity that it makes the imaginary village of R. K. Narayan—an author to whom Mr. Mistry has been compared—seem like a vast metropolis. Skillfully interwoven into stories about the apartment inhabitants' domestic strivings are fearsome glints of the outside world: communal strife, dowry murders, color prejudice.

Compression is the book's genius and a perfect mode for describing the compressed lives of the tenants—all Parsi (a tiny minority in India) except for a handful of servants. The tales, which unfold over a span of years covering the childhood and adolescence of one of the characters—who, we come to realize, is the author—are narrated by several of the block's motley dwellers.

Mr. Mistry's ability through antic humor and compassion to make the repellent—or, at the very least, sad—story material of Firozsha Baag life-affirming, even ebullient, is astonishing given the horrifyingly stunted lives he depicts. In part, the author's success at leaving the reader with a sense of community and of life's bounty, in the face of all evidence to the contrary, comes from his facility in creating a feeling of flow and unfolding. The densely packed hive that is Firozsha Baag has a pulse that belies the trapped lives of its individuals.

The stories all turn on excruciating situations made vivid by Mr. Mistry's use of locking imagery. The characters are throttled by their immediate surroundings and foreclosed futures. Constipation is an almost manic concern. In the opening story, **"Auspicious Occasion,"** the curmudgeonly protagonist can't defecate and is doused by a broken overhead toilet tank. When he tries to reach the Parsi temple through narrow, dangerous streets, he is forced to flee home by a non-Parsi street crowd that threatens him with violence. A long shaggy dog story in the tale titled **"Squatter"** hinges on the inability of a former Firozsha Baag resident to evacuate in a Western-style toilet and his warning, based on this experience, to the young of the apartment block not to immigrate west.

Locks, insistent realities, become almost surreal in these stories. In **"The Paying Guests"** a newborn baby is imprisoned in a parrot cage. In **"One Sunday"** an odd-job handyman (from outside the Parsi community) is horribly beaten by an apartment mob for allegedly stealing from a tenant with 17 padlocked cupboards. In **"The Collectors"** a stamp hobbyist (his stamps are wrapped in cellophane, stored in tins in cupboards) dies on a journey and his decomposing corpse, locked in the trunk of a car, is carried home on a two-day trip across the desert. The Firozsha Baag youngster who inherits the albums allows them to rot in a trunk under his bed.

The stultifying lives of the Firozsha Baag inhabitants are punctuated and heightened by raucous, largely repressed sexual yearnings, and by violence, generally mitigated by slapstick—organized children's games feature the stoning of cats; a crazy tenant intimidates her landlady by daily littering her doorstep with feces and filth; a teen-ager's phallic cricket bat is used for squashing rats, and then a man. Only occasionally are life-enhancing acts possible, as when in the masterly story **"Condolence Visit"** a widow defies custom and gives away her dead husband's enshrined puggree (ceremonial hat) to a young man who needs it for his wedding.

In the last story, **"Swimming Lessons,"** set in Toronto, one of two pieces to move away from the apartment complex, Mr. Mistry steps out of frame to comment on his artistic patterning of life's material, both past and future. Articulating the problem of creating metaphors to describe his new Canadian experience in writing (as well as the more basic necessity for him to invent a new life), he notes his authorial need to shape and redeem. He uses his Toronto apartment house to evoke Firozsha Baag, implying that the violent break of his immigration has in some way been healed, made more of a circular process. He also uses the Canadian cycle of seasons as a metaphor for change softened by the comfort of continuity. Inevitability is transformed into a life force.

> *Hope Cooke, "Beehive in Bombay," in* The New York Times Book Review, *March 5, 1989, p. 26.*

Keith Garebian

Indian fiction in English has long passed out of its nostalgic and nationalistic phases although its truths, as V. S. Naipaul has frequently complained, have tended to be rehearsals of old myths—perennial answers to perennial questions. But with the advent of such excellent writers as Salman Rushdie and Anita Desai, the province of Indo-Anglian fiction has acquired a sophistication based more on technical accomplishment than on sociological or thematic stakes. With *Midnight's Children* and *Shame,* Rushdie redrew the Indian literary map (as the *New York Times*

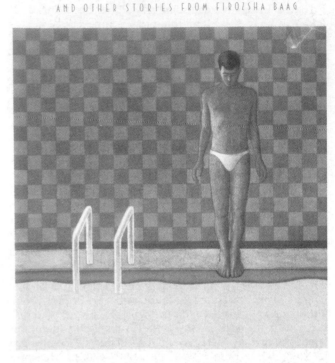

Dust jacket for the American printing of Tales from Firozsha Baag.

asserted), showing on the one hand, a marvelous epic sense and feeling for contemporary history, and on the other, a robust, baroque style which, while buoyantly in the tradition of Grass, Borges, and Marquez, never lost sight of its debt to earlier literary masters such as Sterne and Dickens. Desai proved with her most recent novel, *In Custody,* that she could more than rival R. K. Narayan in satire, while telling a more piquant truth about human comic agony. (p. 25)

The past year, however, has belonged to the expert Ruth Prawer Jhabvala and two relative newcomers, Vikram Seth and Rohinton Mistry. (p. 25)

[In *Tales from Firozsha Baag*], Rohinton Mistry, who emigrated to Canada from Bombay in 1975, has given Indo-Anglian literature its first significant collection of short fiction that expresses the Parsi sensibility. Mistry's apartment complex of Firozsha Baag is but a microcosm of Indian Life, but, more particularly, (as a Parsi colony) it is a microcosm of a highly defined sect that has managed to keep its own customs, language, and religion intact while becoming a vital part of the Indian scene. Parsi orthodoxy (that encompasses religion, language, food, and dress) demarcates this sect from the non-Parsis, who are blessed with a "resilient ingenuity" for making their squalid lives bearable. The narrator in the first tale, **"Auspicious Occasion,"** divides the "clean" Parsi world from the "unclean" one of "uneducated, filthy, ignorant barbarians," but there is never any final doubt that Rustomji the curmudgeon (who is full of abuse and vituperation because of a leaking lavatory) is ever anything but Indian himself, part of a continuing pattern of existence in which he is a plaintive but inextricable component.

Mistry indulges in no special pleading for his fellow Parsis. As his narrator (obviously an autobiographical projection) shows, he does not seek to appeal to the vanity of his Parsi community. **"Swimming Lessons"** is one of two stories that contain explicitly Canadian references and setting. Its narrator is a budding writer in Canada who builds his tales out of his memories of the characters and incidents of Firozsha Baag. The title connects his Canadian swimming lessons with images of beach water from an Indian childhood, but the symbolism, meant to suggest purification and regeneration, is left ambiguous because of the unusual circumstances of the narrator's aquatic experience. However, his writing upsets his parents in India, because his stories do not commemorate the nobler side of Parsis. His father, observing that the son's Parsi families are poor or middle-class, desires something more positive—some testament to "the great Tatas and their contribution to the steel industry, or Sir Dinshaw Petit in the textile industry who made Bombay the Manchester of the East, or Dadbhai Naoroji in the freedom movement, where he was the first to use the word *swawraj,* and the first to be elected to the British Parliament where he carried on his campaign."

But it is precisely this refusal to romanticize or apotheosize that distinguishes Mistry's book. The historical legend of the Parsis—their descent from Cyrus the Greatland the magnificent Persian Empire, and their flight from Islamic persecution in the 7th century—is a background datum. Mistry's preoccupation is with the commonplace emotions, habits, and rituals that define quotidian community life. The Parsi characters run the gamut from the pernicious to the merely eccentric, from the violent to the benevolent, and the charm of Mistry's writing lies in the skill with which he conjures up their anxieties and projects the vicissitudes of their fates with a freshness quite beyond the ravages of time. Like Nariman the storyteller who hypnotizes the boys of the Baag with his awesome tales of Parsi heroes, Mistry paints stories with the brush of unpredictability. Unlike Nariman, he eschews hyperbole (although there is exaggeration in **"The Paying Guests,"** where Khorshedbai's madness is trumped up), and sometimes tells a funny incident in a very serious way, or expresses a significant matter in a playful manner (as in **"Squatter"**).

What to some Western readers might seem to be an ingenious display of the exotic is really a credible picture of the teemingly bizarre in Bombay. Mistry's most outstanding feature is his accuracy with dialogue and speech, whether it is the abusive, hybrid cursing of Rustomji (*"Arre,* you sisterfucking *shatis,* what are you laughing for? Have you

no shame? *Saala chootia* spat *paan* on my *dugli* and you think that is fun?"), the Mangalorean rhythms of the servant Jaakaylee ("O it pains in my old shoulders, grinding this *masala,* but they will never buy the automatic machine. Very rich people, my *bai-seth.*"), the sly, trickster slang of Eric D'Souza, the pervert at St. Zavier's Boy School ("C'mon man, what you scared for, I'll flick. You just show me and go away."), or the *kitsch*-flecked archness of the narrator in **"Swimming Lessons"** ("The sea of Chaupatty was fated to endure the finales of life's everyday functions."). In short, Mistry's is a *tour de force* first collection, on a higher order than V. S. Naipaul's first collection, *Miguel Street.* (pp. 25-6)

Keith Garebian, "In the Aftermath of Empire: Identities in the Commonwealth of Literature," in The Canadian Forum, Vol. LXVIII, No. 780, April, 1989, pp. 25-33.

Lucasta Miller

Can you criticise a novel for its lack of sincerity? It might be philosophically dodgy: novelists, after all, take on many disguises, and always speak from behind one mask or another. But there must be some way of distinguishing between the gimmicky, pussy-footing prose of so many contemporary novels and something more substantial.

Rohinton Mistry's first novel is definitely something more substantial. Set in Bombay during the birth-throes of Bangladesh, **Such a Long Journey** is primarily a novel about people. Although it evokes a sense of place, it has nothing of the travel writer's superficial "sights, sounds, and smells of the Subcontinent" about it. And although it attempts to illuminate a particular political and religious culture, there's nothing didactic in its tone. Place and politics are refracted through the experiences of one family, who are individuals, not merely representatives of their society.

Gustad Noble is a very ordinary man. Middle-aged and middle class, he has a wife, three children, and a longstanding job in a bank. The events of his life are personal and domestic: his father's bankruptcy, a road accident that left him with a limp, the academic success of his elder son Sohrab, squabbles with his neighbours, the illness of his daughter, the death of a friend. But when an old friend and neighbour asks a favour, he becomes unwillingly caught up in the convoluted corruption of the Congress Party. For Gustad, political intrigue isn't a question of glamour, greed, or ideological zeal, but a doubt-inducing twist in a relationship.

He discovers that even his control over his own little world is limited, that fate offers no explanations, and that there's no God to dole out easy rewards and punishments. Irritated more and more each day by the passers-by who keep using the wall outside his block of flats as a public urinal, he's touchingly pleased with himself when he dreams up the solution and persuades a pavement artist to paint a mural featuring the gods and saints of every conceivable religion. The wall becomes a focus of celebration, the embodiment of Gustad's own belief, springing from a sort of humanistic theism, that all religions are equal. But the municipality sends out an arbitrary order to knock down the wall, and a riot ensues.

Yet for all the violence and confusion that Gustad encounters, he never gives in to despair. With a central character so sympathetic, and with such genuine emotional depth, **Such a Long Journey** is both utterly unpretentious and brilliantly perceptive. To call it "written from the heart" would give slightly the wrong impression, implying some sort of artless, impassioned naivety. It's far more mature than that, but still the sort of novel in which characters come before style-consciousness. Its style, as a result, is fluent, pithy and unclogged by artifice.

> Lucasta Miller, "Heart Land," in New Statesman & Society, *Vol. 4, No. 143, March 22, 1991, p. 46.*

Lee Lemon on Mistry's fiction:

The most surprising thing about Mistry's stories is their vitality. The literary short story can be a rather lethargic form in which few characters do little until the end where, if the writer is up to it, the protagonist's major epiphany is described in delicately purple prose. Mistry's stories burst with life. They are as crowded and as noisy and as bustling as the apartment complex in which they are set. One gets a feeling of living in a world in which people rub shoulders with each other, know too much and understand too little about their neighbors, and struggle valiantly simply to keep their positions.

> Lee Lemon, in Prairie Schooner, *Spring 1990.*

Richard Eder

Could Charles Dickens write today and not be Tom Wolfe? If you think that the author of *Bonfire of the Vanities* is a latter-day Dickens, of course, the question doesn't stand. If you think that he has a clever feel for present-day social ironies and little for the humans who inhabit them, clothes and manners apart, then it does stand.

The answer is no; not in our time and our place. On the other hand, it may be yes, elsewhere; in parts of what we call the Third World. A dramatic (perhaps stagy), heart-rending (perhaps sentimental), rich-hued (perhaps showy) realism seems to work when history lets it legitimately express the aroused, churning individual—clearly and roundly seen—tumbled up with an aroused, churning society—also clearly and roundly seen.

It works with **Such a Long Journey** by the Indian writer Rohinton Mistry. Its story of a middle-class Parsi family in Bombay, struggling to maintain its hope and values in a rising tide of poverty and corruption, is authentically Dickensian. It can be garish and contrived, and indulgent and self-indulgent in the marshaling of its story, but its major characters and some of its minor ones are unforgettable and deeply and broadly moving. That is, as they individually move us, their world moves and cracks around them.

One of the major characters is an apartment house. The Khodadad Building lies around a courtyard; respectable but not lavish when it was put up; decaying now, though still struggling to be respectable. A cinder-block wall sets it off from the human swamp of the streets, but the set-off is illusory. Passersby relieve themselves against it; the stench and the mosquitoes seep into the unscreened windows above.

The Khodadad residents—the police inspector who cycles to and from work; an old man who leans from his window to argue with God over the local and national news; Tehmul, a brain-damaged young man who sees himself as the building's watcher and news-bearer; Miss Kutpitia, who has the only telephone—are a panoramic background. They are picturesque, comic, touching, but they are not random vignettes. Rohinton uses them as a context for his story of India versus Gustad Noble and his family.

Gustad is noble, in fact, and terribly plagued. Son of a prosperous bookseller, his memories are of culture and dignity, if not wealth. His present is all indignity and struggle. A bank clerk, poorly paid, he is cramped into his Khodadad apartment with his wife Dilnavaz, his half-grown sons, Sohrab and Darius, and his little daughter Roshan.

Home is tenderness, fury and a continual struggle, not just to get by but to get by with a spark of hope and pleasure. At the start, Gustad has brought home a live chicken. Feed it for two days, have it slaughtered, and it will taste like chickens used to taste and not like the store-bought frozen ones. So he tells his protesting wife. She has been up since 5 a.m. collecting water in tubs because it is shut off most of the day. She has been haggling with the milk-seller over his wretchedly watered milk. She struggles all day with dirt and bugs and stench.

The chicken is fed and killed—Roshan is in tears, having fallen in love with it—and served at dinner to Dinshawji, their friend and Gustad's fellow bank clerk. But it never gets eaten. There is a terrible quarrel beforehand between Gustad and Sohrab, his eldest, and nobody has any appetite.

Gustad wants Sohrab to go to the technical college, for which he has qualified. Sohrab refuses; he wants to stay with his friends and study liberal arts. Gustad has been all over town collecting scholarship applications. Sohrab throws them away. Dilnavaz retrieves them.

Sohrab is Gustad's hope that the future will have some of the same luster as he remembers from the past. He can accept present drudgery and hardship if it will bridge the two, just as he accepted being crippled after a street car hit him while he was rescuing Sohrab—then a baby—who had fallen onto the tracks.

If Sohrab is Gustad's beacon—and his despair when it flickers—another is his friendship with Maj. Jimmy Bilimoria. "Major Uncle" was a hero from the early days of independence and virtually a godfather to the entire family. The hope he represented was not personal so much as national. Major Uncle stood for the dream of what India might be. When he disappeared without a farewell, mortally offending Gustad, the injury abated when word trick-led out that he had joined the country's intelligence ser-vice. Surely he was fighting nobly against the Pakistanis in what was to become Bangladesh.

So, when Gustad receives a message from Major Uncle telling him secretly—and illegally—to deposit a huge amount of money, bit by bit, in his bank, he accepts it as a patriotic mission and enlists his friend Dinshawji to help him.

It turns out to be a corrupt swindle. The money is appro-priated for the personal use of Prime Minister Indira Gan-dhi and her family. Major Uncle is part-victim, part-accomplice. Gustad and Dinshawji are victims, not so much materially—they manage to extricate themselves, though Dinshawji dies from cancer and stress—as in their belief.

It is a melancholy story of betrayed hope—personal and national—and sometimes, in its twists and turns, it is a forced and melodramatic one. The strength of Mistry's novel is not in its big story but in its many small ones. It is in the daily struggles, victories and defeats of Gustad, his family and his friends.

Above all, it is in the vividness of the characters and of their lives. There is Dilnavaz, loving and skeptical, su-premely rational in the face of Gustad's flights, yet capable of trying out a whole set of spells to restore peace in the family.

There is the instructor in the spells, the prim and reserved Miss Kutpitia, upstairs. With a little extra money, she does good in strictly measured doses, and refuses to la-ment her great past grief: the death of a cherished nephew. "Tears have all been cried long ago, not one drop remain-ing," she says, dragging her eyelids down with her forefin-gers. "See, totally dry."

There is the grotesque yet human Pehmul. He falls in love with Roshan's doll, steals it and has sex with it; but Mistry lets us see this as pure yearning as well as deformity. There is Sohrab, stiff-necked and rebellious, yet full of love for his father. There is Dinshawji, who conceals his fatal can-cer and sadness with ebullient clowning. It is a kind of no-bility. "Let me tell you it's more difficult to be a jovial per-son all the time than to be a quiet sickly one," he tells Gustad not long before he dies.

Finally, of course, there is Gustad; choleric, undaunted, battling despair and consumed with tenderness. Mistry has made a memorable character, and has allowed him one shining victory.

Gustad notices a pavement artist whose specialty is reli-gious pictures. He persuades him to come to the Khoda-dad and decorate its wall with 300 feet of images of Hindu and Christian deities and saints. Not only do the passersby desist from using it as a latrine, out of respect, but some of them attach flowers and incense to it. Instead of reek-ing, the wall perfumes. It is comic and joyful.

And when the city bulldozes the wall—all miracles are frail in Bombay—the author gives a last word to the artist.

Picking up his crayons, he prepares to move on. Where will he go, asks the dejected Gustad?

"Where does not matter, sir. In a world where roadside latrines become temples and shrines, and temples and shrines become dust and ruin, does it matter where?"

Richard Eder, "Curried Dickens," in Los An-geles Times Book Review, *April 21, 1991, p. 3.*

David Ray

Rohinton Mistry won critical acclaim two years ago with a short story collection about the Parsee communities of Bombay and Toronto. Though uneven, the tales in **Swim-ming Lessons and Other Stories from Firozsha Baag** in-clude some marvelously entertaining scenes, in which Mr. Mistry vividly evokes both the texture of life in modern India and the experience of Indian immigrants in Canada. His descriptions of daily life are exact and convincing. His angry portrait of the damaging vestiges of the caste sys-tem, "oozing the stench of bigotry," is compelling.

Such a Long Journey again involves us with Bombay's Parsee community. The year is 1971, and Mr. Mistry's bank clerk hero, Gustad Noble, is beset by family and fi-nancial problems as well as conflicts at work. He gets drawn by a friend into a plot involving the diversion of Government funds. Gustad does not at first know that his friend, Jimmy, is in fact a member of the Indian version of the Central Intelligence Agency. Nor does he realize how deeply corruption has come to dominate the Govern-ment. Gustad assumes that he is involved in an effort by Indira Gandhi, the Prime Minister, to support anti-Pakistan guerrillas. But the scheme is actually rooted in personal greed, compromising many and stretching, ulti-mately, back to Gandhi herself.

Mr. Mistry catches the unsettling effects on everyday life of the many upheavals afflicting India in the 1960's and 1970's: sporadic riots, social unrest, border conflicts with China and a rapidly deteriorating situation with Pakistan, culminating in war. Seemingly his intention is to inter-weave, in Graham Greene fashion, the threads of Gustad's personal life and his deepening, unwitting involvement in espionage. In the background, we can almost hear the strumming of the "*Third Man*" Theme."

The insurgents Gustad thinks he is helping to support de-clare their independence from Pakistan, renaming the province of East Pakistan the Republic of Bangladesh. The violence following that declaration is immediate and appalling. Refugees streaming over the border from the would-be nation bring with them "tales of terror and bes-tiality, of torture and killings and mutilations."

Such a Long Journey traces, in convincing detail, Gustad's painful loss of innocence about his Government and his efforts in a chaotic time to sort out his responsibili-ties to his country and his family. Dying, Jimmy reveals to Gustad the true nature of the plot into which he has in-nocently been drawn. Indira Gandhi, Jimmy insists, is ex-ploiting the threat of war with Pakistan to cover the diver-sion of the funds supposedly earmarked for insurgents in

Bangladesh into purely personal projects. Using the police and espionage agencies to spy on "opposition parties, ministers," even, according to Jimmy, "spying on her own cabinet," the Prime Minister has all of the Government "in her pocket." The liberation of Bangladesh is simply another issue capable of being manipulated for political gain. Jimmy wonders: "What hope for the country? With such crooked leaders?" and Gustad can only despairingly agree.

While the events leading up to the creation of Bangladesh, and the details of Indian political life, are fascinating, *Such a Long Journey* is more than a recapitulation of a particularly disheartening and violent moment in India's recent history as experienced by a kind of contemporary everyman. As in his stories, Mr. Mistry manages to convey a vivid picture of India; his portrait of the monsoon, for instance, is marvelous. His sharp, affectionate sketches of Indian family life, and of life in Bombay's crowded precincts, are fascinating. He has a gift for erotic satire. And both in a subplot involving a simple-minded character and in his sketches of Bombay's red-light district, Mr. Mistry demonstrates a deft command of the kind of intensified,

magic realism we are familiar with from the works of Gabriel García Márquez.

But despite his decency, and despite the extraordinary nature of his discoveries about the abuse of power in India, Gustad is not a convincing figure. He never seems more than a kind of standard suffering drudge, a bepuzzled gull drawn into a world he does not understand. Many of the novel's passionate political concerns seem warmed over. It is often unclear what tone Mr. Mistry is reaching for. While he is clearly capable of trenchant, fierce political satire, *Such a Long Journey* only occasionally reaches the comic heights scaled by the stories in *Swimming Lessons.* The novel frequently poses a problem for all but the polyglot reader. Words from several Indian languages are dropped in liberally. Some passages are veritable pastiches of two or more languages. A glossary would have been welcome. None the less, Rohinton Mistry's is a strong voice, and a welcome one.

David Ray, "Under Her Thumb and in Her Pocket," in The New York Times Book Review, *July 7, 1991, p. 13.*

Mark Strand

1934-

American poet, short story writer, editor, translator, author of children's books, and art critic.

The following entry contains criticism of works published throughout Strand's career, with particular emphasis on his 1990 collection *The Continuous Life* and the reissue of his *Selected Poems*. For further information on Strand's life and career, see *CLC,* Vols. 6, 18, and 41.

INTRODUCTION

Strand, along with his contemporary, Charles Simic, is credited with introducing a variety of tones and attitudes from Latin American and European verse to American poetry during the 1960s. Listing his formative influences as Franz Kafka, Elizabeth Bishop, and such practitioners of Latin American surrealism as Pablo Neruda and César Vallejo, Strand often focuses on what Irvin Ehrenpreis referred to as the "elusiveness of self." Although some reviewers have characterized Strand's early verse as solipsistic, most have consistently praised the clarity and dynamism of his language and the imaginative depth of his poetry. Robert Pinsky asserted that Strand's characteristically "short lines and . . . short, spare sentences provide an elegantly terse vehicle for [his] impetuous, exciting imagination: a busy fountain of mysteries, brooding formulae and images, disciplined by the curt, declarative form."

In his first book, *Sleeping with One Eye Open,* Strand uses tightly controlled verse, surreal imagery, and an apprehensive aura to explore the difficulties and contradictions of self-definition. Poet A. R. Ammons commented that in the volume's better poems, "a fuzzy, peripheral, half-realized terror seems about to take shape. The tension is that if the terror materializes, becomes specific, the poet will be run out of the house of himself." Strand's ensuing collections, *Reasons for Moving* and *Darker,* reveal a similar element of anxiety but make playful use of black humor as the poet struggles to recognize and reconcile conflicting notions of self. In *The Story of Our Lives,* Strand departs from the abbreviated lines and solipsistic focus of his earlier poetry to explore the world outside the speaker's consciousness, particularly that of his childhood and present life. Critics have especially praised Strand's "Elegy for My Father (Robert Strand 1908-68)," a frequently anthologized poem that describes the death of the father and the son's consequent awareness of his own mortality. David Kirby commented that this tribute comprises a "magnificent poem, one of the great elegies of the English language."

In *The Late Hour,* Strand returns to the self-reflexive minimalism of his earliest verse while retaining the focus on childhood evident in *The Story of Our Lives.* Despite their emphasis on loneliness, the poems in this volume are less self-obsessed and more optimistic in their valuation of love than his previous works. *The Continuous Life,* Strand's first poetry collection in ten years, includes serious and satiric poems written primarily in iambic meter on topics ranging from philosophy to the art of translation. While some reviewers have faulted the poems in *The Continuous Life* as derivative of the works of Wallace Stevens, W. H. Auden, and other poets, most consider them a valid extension of Strand's verse style, which many believed to be in danger of stagnation. George Bradley commented: "Astonishingly, Mark Strand has found a voice again, and it is a richly rewarding one. After a decade's moratorium during what might have been the prime of his career, he has now returned to print with perhaps his most impressive work to date."

In addition to writing poetry, Strand has also edited numerous anthologies of work by other poets and has translated the poetry of such authors as Rafael Alberti, Carlos Drummond de Andrade, and Jorge Luis Borges. In 1990 Strand succeeded Robert Penn Warren as the Poet Laureate of the United States Library of Congress.

PRINCIPAL WORKS

POETRY

Sleeping with One Eye Open   1964
Reasons for Moving   1968
Darker: Poems   1970
The Sargeantville Notebook   1973
The Story of Our Lives   1973
Elegy for My Father   1978
The Late Hour   1978
The Monument   1978
Selected Poems   1980
The Continuous Life   1990

CHILDREN'S BOOKS

The Planet of Lost Things   1982
The Night Book   1985
Rembrandt Takes a Walk   1986

OTHER

Art of the Real: Nine American Figurative Painters   (art criticism)   1983
Mr. and Mrs. Baby, and Other Stories   (short stories) 1985
William Bailey   (art criticism)   1987

CRITICISM

Sven Birkerts

In an essay titled **"Hopper: The Loneliness Factor,"** Mark Strand (who once studied to be a painter) submits several of Edward Hopper's canvases to a searching formal analysis and locates what he believes to be the source of their unsettling power. The artist, he finds, constructed many of his paintings around the dominant shape of an isosceles trapezoid, thus introducing a "nonexistent vanishing point." The works refuse, that is, to resolve their tensions within their own perimeters; the viewer can enter, but cannot settle.

That Strand should have chosen Hopper for a subject is fitting. He, too, creates at the core of his poetry a disquiet that is somehow more profound than what the lines themselves seem to warrant. It is an effect that deepens as one reads through the oeuvre, until it becomes unbearable and the poems must be set aside. And yet the source of the unease—the vanishing point, if you will—is impossible to pin down; it is off the page. The New Critics, with their insistence on the independent, artifact quality of the finished poem, would have deemed such an observation heretical; but I would be fascinated to read a New Critical explication of this man's work.

Over the past three decades Strand has perfected a chill-inducing poetry of nothingness. The poems are not about life—the inscrutable forward-moving, time-contending process—but about the emptying out of life. They are, taken together, a place of night sounds, where the wind keeps moving because it has no place to stop, and where the self thinks about itself thinking and finds that its thoughts, like the wind, have nothing to adhere to. This poet's art is to make an impression of nothing out of something, out of the ciphers and the signifiers of our shared reality. The making itself is so skillful that the words all but vanish into their signifying. In the wake of the reading, one feels that one has connected not with the poem, but with something anterior to its making—anterior, even, to its maker. The focus lies elsewhere and the elsewhere is nowhere. A vanishing act.

Strand, who is the Poet Laureate at the Library of Congress, is unique among poets in that he has not grown or changed very much over the course of his career. This is not a slight. The point is that his vision—a vision of how things are beyond or outside the clutter of self-making—is not the sort that admits of great modification. In Strand, nothingness and absence are *termini*, not points of origin. The poet's ongoing preoccupation has resulted in a deepening through reiteration. His **Selected Poems,** which includes work from 1964 to 1980, shows how change and development are severely constrained by the nature of the vision, but his new collection, **The Continuous Life,** his first in a decade, suggests that his attitude may be evolving toward accommodation.

In attempting to isolate Strand's distinctive approach, one could do worse than cite the opening stanza of the well-known **"Keeping Things Whole"** from **Sleeping With One Eye Open** (1964):

> In a field
> I am the absence
> of field.
> This is
> always the case.
> Wherever I am
> I am what is missing.

While many of Strand's other poems have more specific (though still generic) settings, these lines distill his metaphysics, a kind of reversed Cartesianism wherein to be is not to be and thinking throws existing into question. The diction, here as elsewhere, is assertively neutral. The rhythms are even, unemphatic—anything more expressive would serve as a subliminal signal of the life force—and the main agency of formal control is the line break, which Strand deploys with a cool de Stijl composure.

Though they differ in their conceits and approaches, the poems of the first three books, including also **Reasons For Moving** (1968) and **Darker** (1970), are of a piece. The imaginings are nocturnal, and the visual alphabet, as here in **"The Dress,"** is drawn from the place of dreams:

> Lie down on the bright hill
> with the moon's hand on your cheek,
> your flesh deep in the white folds of your dress,
> and you will not hear the passionate mole
> extending the length of his darkness,
> or the owl arranging all of the night,
> which is his wisdom, or the poem
> filling your pillow with its blue feathers.

> But if you step out of your dress and move into
>   the shade,
> the mole will find you, so will the owl, and so
>   will the poem,
> and you will fall into another darkness, one you
>   will find
> yourself making and remaking until it is perfect.

If this short poem, with its oneiric logic, its mysterious primal images, seems familiar, it is perhaps because the early Strand (along with the more folkloric Charles Simic) exerted a tremendous influence on younger poets during the 1970s and early 1980s. The Strand procedure became a full-blown strain in American poetry, which for a period was a dark and dreamy place populated with creatures of the night. There are surface similarities, moreover, with the so-called "deep image" poetry that Robert Bly was proselytizing at about the same time.

And yet the differences must be promptly underscored. In Bly's poetics, the deep images are the avenue to a psychic plenitude; in Strand, they are tokens of a force that cares nothing for us. His dark places are not hoards of ancient energies but terrifying zones abutting on the void. As Strand wrote in his early poem **"Violent Storm"**: "Already now the lights / That shared our wakefulness are dimming / And the dark brushes against our eyes." No myths or imaginings are proof against the contact.

For Strand, it is thus: we have been hurled into being and there is no immanent or transcendent ground for the self. Yet we possess, in uneasy wakefulness, a capacity to perceive and to reflect. This is our curse, for it cuts us off from the serene unknowingness of the rest of the natural world. The traditional recourse has been religion—to believe that we are not held simply within ourselves, but, in some fashion, within the love (or purpose) of a higher being. But there is no hint of this in Strand, not anywhere. He has rigorously pruned from his lines anything that could suggest a telos, or a redemption of pain and isolation. His figures are at large in space; they move about in time—time afflicts them—but they never progress *to* anything.

As might be expected, where there is no higher power or entity, there will flourish the imagining of the Other—that neutral psychic echo that is the not-self. Strand's poetry posits this other at every turn. Indeed, it is a small step, if a step at all, from "Wherever I am / I am what is missing" to the querying in the last stanza of **"My Life By Somebody Else"**:

> Why do you never come? Must I have you by
>   being
> somebody else? Must I write *My Life* by some-
>   body else?
> *My Death* by somebody else? Are you listening?
> Somebody else has arrived. Somebody else is
>   writing.

With the publication in 1973 of *The Story of Our Lives,* Strand made what was for him a significant departure, leaving behind the short poems, so distinctive in their polished austerity, to explore the rhetorical and narrative possibilities of the long poem. The book opens with the powerful **"Elegy for My Father,"** a poem in six sections. Strand's lines are loose, often repetitive, but they press at

their subject with a mounting urgency. In the absence of any argument or metaphysics, the sheer perseverance of address is impressive. Strand succeeds by varying the pitch and approach, moving from the affectless pronouncements of the first section:

> The hands were yours, the arms were yours,
> But you were not there.
> The eyes were yours, but they were closed and
>   would not open.

to a more urgent reimagining of the process of dying in section three:

> You put your watch to your ear.
> You felt yourself slipping.
> You lay on the bed.
> You folded your arms over your chest and you
>   dreamed of the world without you.

to the final section, which achieves an impersonal, even elemental perspective, integrating the loss into the rhythm of seasonal passage:

> It is winter and the new year.
> Nobody knows you.
> Away from the stars, from the rain of light,
> You lie under the weather of stones.

The elegy manifests rather overtly the influences of Spanish and South American poets. Strand freely adopts the surreal particularizations favored by Neruda and Vallejo ("The years, the hours, that would not find you / Turned in the wrists of other.") and the recursive repetitions of Carlos Drummond de Andrade, whom Strand has translated.

In this same collection we also find the long tour-de-force narratives **"The Story of Our Lives"** and **"The Untelling,"** both of which pit narration against itself, showing how the memory tape can be played backward, undoing the causal chain until, as Eliot wrote, "What might have been and what has been / Point to one end, which is always present." In Strand's version, the real and the possible commingle in the perpetual present of art. He ends **"The Untelling,"** a sequence in which the speaker is a writer wrestling with what might be either a memory or an imagined event, by putting the tail inside the snake's mouth; the writer begins the poem that we have, presumably, been reading. We read:

> He turned and walked to the house.
> He went to the room
> that looked out on the lawn.
> He sat and began to write:
>   THE UNTELLING
>   *To the Woman in the Yellow Dress*

While the conceit of these longer poems is interesting, the line-by-line progress is often tedious, without much to savor in the poetry itself.

Strand may have recognized the problematic aspects of narration (which are bound to be aggravated a hundredfold for a writer who cares little for telling). In any event, with *The Late Hour,* published in 1978, he returned to doing what he does best—the short, visually structured lyric. Where these efforts differ from his earlier work is in their greater preoccupation with his own native terrain (Strand was born on Prince Edward Island) and with childhood. To the bleak movement toward nothing that characterizes adulthood, he opposes the undivided time of childhood. He turns his staring eye upon the past and, as here in the final stanzas of **"Where Are the Waters of Childhood?,"** works his way back past all ruin and change:

> Keep going back, back to the field, flat and
>   sealed in mist.
> On the other side, a man and a woman are wait-
>   ing;
> they have come back, your mother before she
>   was gray,
> your father before he was white.
>
> Now look at the North West Arm, how it glows
>   a deep cerulean blue.
> See the light on the grass, the one leaf burning,
>   the cloud
> that flares. You're almost there, in a moment
>   your parents
> will disappear, leaving you under the light of a
>   vanished star,
> under the dark of a star newly born. Now is the
>   time.
>
> Now you invent the boat of your flesh and set it
>   upon the waters
> and drift in the gradual swell, in the laboring
>   salt.
> Now you look down. The waters of childhood
>   are there.

This retrogressive probing is no mere idiosyncrasy; it is a very natural compulsion in a man who faces a world that is without apparent purpose. Projecting any act or initiative forward into the future only bares its ultimate futility. Perhaps, then, there is some clue to be found in origins. But as **"Where Are the Waters of Childhood?"** suggests, this starting point, this original potency, remains a sealed enigma.

Reading Strand, we are apt to realize just how much most other poetry—most other writing—makes an assumption of a telos, is premised on a confidence in events tending toward meaningful ends. But in this poet's world, as in the worlds of Beckett and Kafka, there is no place to which movement leads, except extinction. We get, in the static *nature morte* compositions and the various untellings, a sense of the present that bears little relation to the present that most of us experience. It is a kind of duration grounded in nothingness.

Strand's new collection, **The Continuous Life,** is thus aptly titled. And the best poems in the book, like the lovely— and terrifying—**"A.M.,"** express the familiar Strand recognitions with a classical rigor:

> Another day has come,
> Another fabulous escape from the damages of
>   night,
> so even the gulls, in the ragged circle of their
>   flight,
> Above the sea's long lanes that flash and fall,
>   scream
> Their approval. How well the sun's rays probe
> The rotting carcass of a skate, how well

> They show the worms and swarming flies at
>   work,
> How well they shine upon the fatal sprawl
> Of everything on earth. How well they love us
>   all.

This is a passage that can stand side by side with the best of Baudelaire. In the final couplet a near-masochistic glee tinges the implicit neutrality of the high-altitude vantage. And while the poet has not changed his fundamental perception, there is a subtle new suggestion of openness. Ambiguous and stern as the final words are, they also make a place for the reader. The sheer beauty of the saying redeems some part of the dread.

Alas, too many of the other pieces in the book fall flat. Strand has a penchant, to me mysterious, for a self-conscious and silly kind of black humor, a penchant that finds it apotheosis in the 1985 prose collection *Mr. and Mrs. Baby.* In a lengthy piece titled **"Translation,"** for example, Strand fills page after page with this sort of thing:

> I was in the bathtub when Jorge Luis Borges
> stumbled in the door. "Borges, be careful," I
> yelled. "The floor is slippery and you are blind."
> Then, soaping my chest, I said, "Borges, have
> you ever considered what is implicit in phrase
> like 'I translate Apollinaire into English' or 'I
> translate de la Mare into French' " . . .

But these worked-up whimsies and bits of ventriloquism are, mercifully, redeemed by a handful of poems that must be ranked with Strand's very finest. The reader who knows the work will remark a certain shift. While the void has by no means receded or become less voidlike, the poet's own angle of regard seems to have altered. The scenarios, as the passage from **"A.M."** might attest, are no longer calculated to be unsettling. Their enlarged—one might say Lucretian—perspective suggests a growing acceptance by the poet of what he perceives to be the nature of things.

In the poem **"Fiction,"** to cite another instance, Strand projects himself as a God-like figure pondering the sealed fates of characters in novels, and then turns to consider the very different situation of the self in a Godless universe. As the final lines bring about a fusion of fiction and life, they also carry a hard-won note of solace:

> The war that raged for years will come to a close
> And so will everything else, except for a pres-
>   ence
> Hard to define, a trace, like the scent of grass
> After a night of rain or the remains of a voice
> That lets us know without spelling it out
> Not to despair; if the end is come, it too will pass.

Similar ambiguity flashes up at the end of **"Always,"** which might stand as the signature poem of our laureate, a poet enraptured by the void but also, increasingly, by the plenum that insists on filling it:

> Always so late in the day
> In their rumpled clothes, sitting
> Around a table lit by a single bulb,
> The great forgetters were hard at work.
> They tilted their heads to one side, closing their
>   eyes.
> Then a house disappeared, and a man in his yard

With all his flowers in a row.
The great forgetters wrinkled their brows.
Then Florida went and San Francisco
Where tugs and barges leave
Small gleaming scars across the Bay.
One of the great forgetters struck a match.
Gone were the harps of beaded lights
That vault the rivers of New York.
Another filled his glass
And that was it for crowds at evening
Under sulphur yellow streetlamps coming on.
And afterwards Bulgaria was gone, and then
  Japan.
"Where will it stop?" one of them said.
"Such difficult work, pursuing the fate
Of everything known," said another.
"Down to the last stone," said a third,
"And only the cold zero of perfection
Left for the imagination." And gone
Were North and South America,
And gone as well the moon.
Another yawned, another gazed at the window:
No grass, no trees . . .
The blaze of promise everywhere.

(pp. 36-8)

Sven Birkerts, "The Art of Absence," in The
New Republic, *Vol. 203, No. 25, December 17,
1990, pp. 36-8.*

David Kirby

When a poet selects one poem to lend its title to an entire
collection, the reader may well wonder what is being announced: is the title poem intended to serve as a sort of
manifesto of the poet's beliefs, or does it posit a ground
from which the other poems in the collection grow, or is
it simply the poet's notion of his own best poem, the one
that will make the reader want to read all the others? [The
title poem of *Sleeping with One Eye Open*] is not the most
accomplished poem in this collection, and neither its tone
nor its subject lends itself to manifesto-making. Instead,
this title poem introduces in succinct detail a speaker
whose voice can be heard throughout this collection and
also throughout Strand's later works, intoning the poems
that define him.

It is a moonlit, windy night, he writes, "my night to be rat-
tled, / saddled / With spooks." This speaker feels "dead,"
"forgotten," "moon handled": the moon is a "half-moon /
(Half man, / Half dark)," and the speaker mirrors it since
he is asleep yet has one eye open. At once substantial and
nonexistent, both the speaker and his cosmos recall Paul
Valéry's observation [in *Analects,* 1970] that God made
the world from nothing, yet the nothing shows through.
Even the moonlight, traditionally beautiful and romantic
in poetry, is here "fishy," its white the sickly white of
death, of Moby-Dick's awful whiteness, of Pap Finn's pal-
lor. Early in the collection (**"Sleeping with One Eye
Open"** is the second poem in the book), alone in his bed
and hoping, as the last line says, that "nothing, nothing
will happen," the speaker dreams the rest of the poems in
the collection.

The traditional antidote to loneliness is companionship, of

course, and in **"The Whole Story"** the setting is as pregnant with potential as the one in **"Sleeping with One Eye
Open"** is sterile: the speaker is on a train, there is someone
with him, and there is a fire outside the window. In the
process of discussing the fire with his companion, however, the speaker begins to suspect that he likes fires perhaps
a little too much and is therefore indulging a passive pyro-
mania, just as he questions the intentions of his companion, who may be either someone else who "loves a good
fire" or else a fireman in disguise and therefore an enemy.
In the end, he is not even sure whether the fire exists at
all or if he made it up.

Hence the unreliability of the speaker's world—of the
speaker himself, actually, since the world is clearly a product of his own imaginings. Even in the promisingly titled
"Taking a Walk with You," the speaker announces in the
first lines that the countryside lacks "the wit and depth /
That inform our dreams' / Bright landscapes." No one
can honestly say we are at home on this earth, which was
not planned "with us in mind." Speaker and companion
live unsettled lives, stay in places only long enough to find
they don't really belong, and in the end walk off—"As if
to say, / We are not here, / We've always been away."

However, two poems in *Sleeping with One Eye Open* operate as companion pieces to show that it is neither this
speaker nor his interlocutors who are inadequate; rather,
it is the relations between people that are either shabby or
tortuous. In **"The Tunnel,"** a faceless, motionless man
watches the speaker's house unceasingly and drives him
to a frenzied, ludicrous attempt at escape, through a tunnel dug by hand from his own basement to a neighbor's
yard. Yet when the speaker emerges, there is, if not the
faceless man, at least someone who watches him still.
Tired and vulnerable, the speaker feels menaced, though
there is nothing in his vicinity that seems especially menacing. **"Poem"** also details the interaction of torturer and
tortured, and here the menace *is* literal: a villain slips into
the speaker's bedroom and begins slowly to cut him to
pieces with a pair of nail clippers. His cruelty tires him,
however, and when the speaker tells this reluctant sadist
that he has done enough and can go home, he departs
thankfully. These oversized, nightmarish actions (tunnel-
ing, death by nail clippers) illustrate the grotesquerie of relations between people who seem to be more or less inof-
fensive on their own.

Several of these poems deal with large groups of people in
search of a collective memory, people uncomfortable with
or dismayed by their present environs and therefore ripe
for nostalgia. One such group realizes that a time is coming **"When the Vacation Is Over for Good,"** for already
the air is heavy, the wind dumb, the cities ashy, the clouds
aglow. A wonderful time has passed. Still able to pun in
their penultimate moment, the people realize they have
just lived through "summer / At its most august." The destruction certainly sounds like a nuclear one, but no one
seems to know, and there is no promise of a new Adam
and Eve. These people grasp for certainty, and fail. The
poem rhymes loosely in *a b c a* quatrains as the people try,
fail, try, and fail again. (Here, as elsewhere, Strand wears
techniques lightly as his dramatis personae lurch in and

out of certainty, now taking a definite stand, now retreating into either a studied ambivalence or a state that is even more equivocal.)

A **"Violent Storm"** doesn't disturb those who inhabit the "commodious rooms of dreams," though it does trouble the wide-awake ones who, like the couple in **"Taking a Walk with You,"** are unsure and ill at ease in this world. Like that couple, these speakers are continually moving on, always describing the familiar, including the "last resorts" they once frequented yet inexplicably left. Bewildered, pun-prone (we may be dying, but there's no need to be morbid about it), these erstwhile vacationers confirm the reader's suspicion that, if the sleeping world is a world of dreams, the waking one is a low-grade nightmare punctuated by occasional bursts of unwitting insight and throwaway humor. Typically, Strand's speakers, singly or together, straddle both worlds; that is to say, they sleep with one eye open.

Generally, these speakers are of an indeterminate age, old enough to know something about the world, too young to be at peace with it. Certainly, age itself is no panacea for anxiety; the **"Old People on the Nursing Home Porch"** differ from characters in other poems in that they have ceased pointless roving, at least physically, though they can be seen

> moving back
> And forth over the dullness
> Of the past, covering ground
> They did not know was there.

So whereas the people in other poems are too involved with the Saint Vitus' dance of ordinary life to know where they are, the old ones can at least see where they have been, though where they have been is nowhere.

Eventually, this inchoate world cries out for organization. It is not an especially frightening or even gloomy place—it is one that can even be viewed with wise-cracking humor, as we have seen—yet it is an unsettling one. "Truth has bounds. Error none," wrote William Blake, and there seem to be no limits to this quasi-metaphysical, quasi-emotional fog. One poem, **"Keeping Things Whole,"** seems to feature the confident alter ego of the title poem's fretful semisleeper. This spiritual athlete finds a positive reason for all that Strandian motion. He is what is not: "In a field / I am the absence / of field," and so on. To walk through the world is to make it coherent and to create in it a balancing point for our thoughts about the world and about ourselves, though not a fixed balancing point, as in geometry, but a moving one, as in calculus. This speaker has clearly made a separate peace, however, for whereas "we all have reasons / for moving," a line that cannot but bring to mind the goalless shufflers of other Strand poems, he alone says "I move / to keep things whole." This accomplished fellow is not smug, precisely, but, given the context in which he appears, he seems indifferent to and perhaps even disdainful of the plight of the benighted multitude, and almost certainly because he is so unlike them.

Indeed, **"Keeping Things Whole"** itself is a major departure from what might be called typical early Strand. This is mysticism with both feet on the ground, and as such it

recalls Theodore Roethke's "Open House," another poem that offers a physical solution to a metaphysical difficulty ("Myself is what I wear: / I keep the spirit spare"). **"Keeping Things Whole"** also brings to mind Wallace Stevens's "Anecdote of the Jar," in which nature rises up around a manmade object and loses its wildness, just as here a man brings order out of chaos simply by placing himself at the center of it. So, although it is one of the most beautiful and intellectually satisfying of Strand's shorter poems, **"Keeping Things Whole"** is too much like the poetry of other writers to provide a satisfying response to problems unique to Strand's speakers.

In this sense, a more gratifying work is the prose poem **"Make Believe Ballroom Time"**; appropriately placed late in the collection (it is the third-to-last work), it leaves the reader with a sharply drawn portrait of the unsettled self that is typical of the early poetry. As do other poems in *Sleeping with One Eye Open,* this one posits the coexistence of two worlds, a platonic world as well as the fallen one in which ordinary people live. The main character seems a transitional figure, since his suit is both drab and expensive, his speech simultaneously uninflected and precise. In the middle of a party, he gets up and begins to dance, disturbing the other guests, who would rather talk. The speaker realizes that the dancer hears a music inaudible to the others, though, and envies him. The dancer does not look backward, as do the people in **"When the Vacation Is Over for Good"** and **"Violent Storm"** and **"Old People on the Nursing Home Porch**; he looks beyond, to the land of beauty. The speaker would like to dance to that music too, but he can't, stuck as he is where the book began, half-man, half-dark, neither completely in this world nor out of it.

Many poems in Strand's first book show an uneasy preoccupation with self, and the vehicle used to express that preoccupation is often a dream state in which the speaker is divided between two worlds and can locate himself comfortably in neither. The poems in *Reasons for Moving* (1968) are generally longer, more supple, more subtly crafted than those in *Sleeping with One Eye Open*; they suggest a poet's growing ease with his craft. At the same time, however, the basic themes are treated in the poems with a growing unease that the reader feels more intensely than before—as his skill increases, so does the poet's power to disturb.

"The Kite" is a poem of extraordinary lyrical beauty in which a kite's soaring progress over farms and trees and water is framed by "the wonderful crack and drum" of a distant thunderstorm. In the chilly air, watchers blow on their hands, name the birds that fly by, ponder the "small / White roses" of a first snowfall. In a nearby house, a man is sleeping in a chair and dreaming—in fact, he is dreaming the kite, the landscape, the cold air, and the watchers as well, and as the poem ends, the dreamer begins to wake. It is hard not to feel a spasm of irritation at this blameless dreamer, at least on the watchers' behalf, because he gives them such a palpable and satisfying life in the first part of the poem and then takes it away when his dream is over. The dreamer is just sleeping and waking like the rest of us, however; if the fault is anywhere, it is in the watchers for thinking that life can be consistently satisfying.

Many of Strand's poems seem to be assaults on what he calls "the myth of comfort." That phrase is used in **"The Door,"** another poem about dreaming and waking. But whereas **"The Kite"** deals with a single episode, **"The Door"** is a perpetually self-repeating nightmare. There is shrieking, a "mad voice," a body turning to dust, people jumping from jetliners, a murderous surgeon. The poem's last words are, "This is where you come in," making it a never-ending horror movie in which one is not a spectator but a participant. As in **"The Kite,"** there is a contrast between two worlds, the one that is dreamed and the one in which the dreaming occurs, but in **"The Door"** the beautiful real world is served up mockingly at the end, taunting the poor character who runs through the falling leaves to the nightmare-house and stops with his hand on the door. The reader knows he will go in; he always does.

Given the appeal of things Gothic to many readers, there is a delicious pleasure, if not to uncomfortably personal poems like **"The Kite"** and **"The Door,"** at least to more cinematic poems like **"The Fast Bus"** and **"The Ghost Ship,"** which elevate the two-world idea to big-screen status. In **"The Fast Bus,"** the speaker is leaving a sleeping Rio de Janeiro on a death bus, watching the ghosts of bathers rising from the surf as he passes, their eyes burning like stars. The speaker is as anxious as he is in any other early Strand poem, but there are distractions: a wolfish driver, a seductive woman with a garden in her eyes, "where rows of dull, / white tombstones crowd the air / and people stand, / waving goodbye." Frightened, the speaker looks back, but the city he is leaving isn't Rio, perhaps fittingly—at a midpoint between two worlds, with the next world invisible, the world we knew may very well be revealed as different from the way we thought it when we lived there. Certainly the worlds of **"The Ghost Ship"** contain mysteries their inhabitants can't see; the living can't see the death ship as it moves through their city, just as the dead are oblivious to the living. Each world mirrors the incompleteness of the other, and there is no mutual recognition.

All of these poems about two worlds eventually return to the anxiety of the divided self. *Schizophrenia* is too clinical a term for critical purposes, but Strand's early speakers do seem split between their emotions and their reason, unfocused, uncentered, out of sync with their surroundings because they are ill at ease with themselves. Survivors (but barely) in the post-comfort era, these thoughtful, miserable people are doubly distraught because they know themselves to be the authors of their own misery.

Perhaps the most revealing poem in *Reasons for Moving* is **"The Mailman,"** in which a weeping courier arrives at midnight to beg the speaker's pardon for the letter he is about to deliver. The exact contents of the letter are never disclosed, but the reader can guess at their nature when he learns that the speaker has written to himself and is composing more letters in the same vein, saying, "You shall live / by inflicting pain. / You shall forgive." In fact, the mailman may be the speaker himself: for a profession-

al, he keeps very odd hours, and his handwringing is quite familiar.

"The Accident" has the same kind of interplay between a speaker and another character. This poem begins, "A train runs over me," and with that out of the way, deals mainly with the solicitude of the engineer, who says he is innocent, relates his life story, returns home, is startled by someone with a flashlight, and returns guiltily to carry the speaker to his own house. Just as the speaker in **"The Mailman"** is both pain-inflicting and forgiving, to others and to himself, so this engineer is simultaneously hurtful and helpful to someone with whom he is unusually intimate, someone who he may, in fact, be.

The longest poem (120 lines) in *Reasons for Moving,* one fittingly titled **"The Man in the Mirror,"** is a one-way conversation in which the speaker addresses his unresponsive reflection. Though bored by his own windiness ("How long will this take?"), the speaker is keen on addressing his alter ego's betrayal point by point. For betrayal it is. The self has split off from the self in a kind of mitosis that halves life instead of doubling it:

> One day you turned away
> and left me here
> to founder in the stillness of your wake.

The connection between the two halves of the divided self is real, though it is only visual, and if the speaker in **"The Man in the Mirror"** is afraid that the other will disappear, he is equally fearful, as he says in the last line, that the other will stay. As in so many early poems by Strand, the last stop is limbo: there is a partial world on each side of the mirror, and the self, too, is halved.

Poetry is not programmatic, of course, and not every poem in these early books is devoted to the war of the selves or the almost identical idea of the self divided between two worlds. Most of the rest of Strand's poems, however, at least remind the reader how individuals are cut off, preoccupied with their own internal struggles.

"The Babies," for example, with its altruistic refrain, "let us save the babies," seems to have a disposition uncharacteristically charitable. The technique belies the message, however. The lines are staccato, repetitious; after a while, they bespeak a sense of futility with which the reader is already familiar. When the speaker discusses what he and a female companion should wear as they rush off to save the babies (who are apparently being turned into unblinking robots in a warehouse downtown), somehow one doubts his dedication. And when he says, "let us not wait for tomorrow," one is certain that he will.

Perhaps this couple is like the one in **"The Marriage,"** who are brought together in marriage and procreation by the wind and then parted the same way. As they drift apart, it is the wind they think fondly of, not each other. The wind is a familiar feature in Strand's poetry: in such poems as **"Sleeping with One Eye Open"** and **"Violent Storm"** (*Sleeping*) as well as **"The Accident," "The Man in the Tree,"** and **"The Man in the Mirror"** (*Reasons*), the wind is a force, like chance itself, for pulling people apart or bringing them together. In several of these poems a speaker is listening unhappily to the wind outside, and no wonder: windless, these characters are either left in morbid isolation or stuck in dead-end relationships, whereas the force of the wind can lift them out of their present misery and carry them toward a future that may be happier or that will at least be different.

This is not to say that personal initiative is entirely discounted in these poems. Far from it: sensing that ordinary life is not going to deliver what it promises, one speaker seeks, not a suntan so as to be attractive to others, but a **"Moontan"** so he can be invisible. The catch is that, as the speaker realizes, there is no such thing as a moontan.

Similarly, the efforts at self-redemption in **"What to Think of "** are equally filled with false promise. The character here organizes his world, a lush jungle paradise, simply by walking through it, like the speaker in **"Keeping Things Whole"** (*Sleeping*), though the last lines suggest it is all a fantasy. When told that butterflies fill the air "like the cold confetti of paradise," the reader realizes that none of this is real but is instead a studio shot complete with cheap effects—in other words, success is intoxicating, but temporary. And the speaker in **"The Dirty Hand"** knows that washing is pointless (the water itself is putrid, the soap is bad), but this knowledge has not stopped him from washing, scrubbing, and polishing, dreaming that the object of his attention will turn to diamond or crystal or simply "a plain white hand." In the end, though, he throws in the towel, so to speak: much as the people in **"The Marriage"** and the other wind poems wait for their lives to be changed by chance, so this speaker counts on time and hope ("and its intricate workings") to bring him another, better hand.

In a manner both self-reflexive and explicit, poets sometimes turn to poetry as a way out. Since individual poems can be redemptive or at least cathartic, poems about poetry as panacea are not uncommon. **"The Man in the Tree"** begins as a poem in the cathartic mode; in it there are two people who are not connecting, the speaker (the man in the tree) and another. What makes this poem different from such initially similar poems as **"Taking a Walk with You"** and **"The Whole Story"** (*Sleeping*) is that catharsis is never achieved because the poem invalidates itself, ending: "The poem that has stolen these words from my mouth / may not be this poem." Evident here is a self-disgust different from that in **"The Dirty Hand."** Here, poetry itself is tested, and it fails. But that may be because it is the speaker's own poem that is being judged, and why should we expect this speaker to be happier with his poetry than he is with any other aspect of his being?

In **"Eating Poetry,"** one of Strand's most joyful, amusing, and widely anthologized poems, poetry is regarded altogether differently, perhaps because it is the poetry of others, and presumably the great poetry of the past, that is being considered. The speaker in **"Eating Poetry"** is doing just what the title says: "Ink runs from the corner of my mouth," he writes, and "there is no happiness like mine." Of course, "the librarian does not believe what she sees"; to her, the speaker is a dog like other dogs, a threat. But the poetry he eats renews him and makes him whole:

> I am a new man.
> I snarl at her and bark.

> I romp with joy in the bookish dark.

Poetry does not seem to be effectual in **"The Man in the Tree"**; after all, it is the speaker's own poetry and thus another manifestation of his unsatisfactory introspection. Here, the poetry of others is good for this speaker because it takes him out of himself. With **"Eating Poetry,"** the speaker realizes that poetry may be not merely a vehicle for expressing his difficulties but also a means of ameliorating them.

Genuine solutions are arrived at slowly, however; it will take quite a few poems before this idea is fully realized.

Strand's third collection [**Darker** (1970)] illustrates one of the complexities of reading someone's poetry thematically and chronologically. We have seen in the first two books both the expression of certain morbid concerns and the dawning of possible remedies to them. It would make sense to expect a lessening of the morbidity and a corresponding increase in self-awareness in this next book, but poetry doesn't necessarily work that way. For one thing, a book published in 1970 might contain poems more thematically appropriate to the 1964 and 1968 volumes yet excluded from them for one reason or another. Also, the poetic mind seldom moves forward or backward in a steadfast manner. Easy decisions are come by easily, but when the mind is working at the very highest level, it backs and fills, takes quantum leaps as well as snails' paces, goes over old ground and crosses new frontiers, often without knowing it. So both anxiety and enlightenment are present in *Darker.* The title may be deceptive, however; the proportion of dark to light is changing, and without knowing it, Strand's persona is on the verge of an important realization: that the poetry, which has seemed merely an eloquent expression of his disquiet, is actually a means of remedying it.

Some of these poems would not seem out of place in *Sleeping with One Eye Open* and *Reasons for Moving.* For example, **"The Prediction"** describes a young woman who not only foresees a bleak future but can't even connect satisfactorily with the present: her husband will die, her children will leave her, and all she can think of is the wind erasing her present life and carrying her on to something unknown, as in other Strand poems. **"My Life by Somebody Else"** recalls **"The Man in the Mirror"** (*Reasons*), and similar poems, in which an alter ego is chided for neither completing the halved speaker nor quitting the field so the speaker can become whole again on his own.

In both of these poems, however, it is important to notice that the act of writing figures prominently. More often than not in poetry self-expression is seen as a healthy thing, and in **"The Man in the Tree"** and **"Eating Poetry"** (*Reasons*) in particular, Strand's speaker seems to be at least considering the possibility that poetry (his own or others') will save him. Later in Strand's career, writing becomes virtually a lifesaving necessity, but that idea has its origins in these earlier poems.

Indeed, the most disconcerting poems in *Darker* are those in which the attitude is one of total resignation; even the low-energy act of writing requires more effort than the characters can make. **"Elegy 1969,"** for example, says,

"You slave away into your old age / and nothing you do adds up to much"; therefore "you are quick to confess your failure and to postpone / collective joy to the next century." And **"The Way It Is"** is one of those bad-neighbor poems by Strand in which the villains are not monsters but the people down the hall, people who, just by being themselves, wound the speaker so deeply that he seems to be dying. Ultimately, there is more death than life in the affectless world of this poem: "the dead / shall inherit the dead."

These two poems represent uncharacteristic low points, however. In **"Nostalgia,"** there is the stasis of time not passing, but that is a far cry from the stasis of resignation and death. Moreover, like many Strand poems, this one has a beauty that belies its sorrow: "On the beach the sadness of gramophones / deepens the ocean's folding and falling." And if **"Coming to This"** is another poem in which a relationship has failed, leaving the couple with both "no place to go, no reason to remain," **"Courtship"** supplies the comic antidote by having the male character first boasting of the size of his penis and then, having shocked the girl he loves, saying he is almost a girl himself, that he has no penis at all, that he wants to be the one who bears the children, and so on.

Comedy only takes Strand's speaker so far in his quest to escape from his anxiety, however; ever ready to joke, his jokes are but field bandages on his psychic wounds and no substitute for real treatment. The kidder emerges again in **"Not Dying,"** where he makes light of old age by insisting he is still the boy his mother used to kiss, but this poem describes a strategy that will not work for very long—a boy is a fine thing to be, but postponing adult life, even such life as Strand's speaker suffers, is not only impractical but perhaps not even desirable.

Another strategy tested is that of seeking darkness and invisibility. Reminiscent of **"Moontan"** (*Reasons*), **"The Sleep"** describes a speaker who will disappear into a darkness that fits him like a skin, never to emerge from it; and **"Seven Poems"** posits the existence of a dark world and then a still darker one into which we can escape from the too-bright world we live in.

Blackness is silence, though, and Strand's speaker can't keep quiet; at moments he seems near catatonia, but before long he is nervous and chatty again. At times, he is downright forceful. Sometimes his effort pays off: in **"The Hill,"** the speaker is walking away from everything—the grass, the trees, the hours, the years. This is a poem about a strenuous escape from the world. It works, but not easily. It doesn't really work, in other words, since the escaped speaker is burdened by his memory of the struggle.

Besides, the problem is self, not the world. **"The Remains"** also has a rather muscular metaphysics; as in **"The Hill,"** the speaker is working overtime and getting rid of everything, though to little avail, for "I empty myself of my life and my life remains." The opposite tack is no good, either; a relative of the doomed prince in **"What to Think of "** (*Reasons*), the greedy fellow in **"The One Song"** says, "I long for more," even though he admits that "more is less."

More than one poem in *Darker* suggests that the best ac-tion is no action at all. For "the good life gives no warning": "It weathers the climates of despair" (or the "weather of hell," as Strand wrote in **"The Way It Is"**) and "appears, on foot, unrecognized, offering nothing, / and you are there." In poems like **"When the Vacation Is Over for Good"** and **"Old People on the Nursing Home Porch"** (*Sleeping*), the fact that our present lives are unknowable is disturbing, but in **"The Good Life"** and **"Black Maps"** the reader is told that we needn't understand our lives but simply live them—all maps are black and "your house is not marked / on any of them," but "you are there."

Ultimately, though, it is not where a Strand speaker is in the world that is important so much as where he is in himself. Each of us suffers from "the sickness of self," as a wife in **"My Life"** says to a husband whose "life is small / and getting smaller." It is better to desert that sick self altogether. "Slowly I dance out of the burning house of my head," says the speaker in **"The Dance"**; each of us has one foot in the grave, yet "who isn't borne again and again into heaven?." And a sustainedly joyful and Whitmanesque poem called **"From a Litany"** begins, "There is an open field I lie down in a hole I once dug and I praise the sky [*sic*]." Each of the twenty-seven remaining lines starts with "I praise . . . "; by the end of this outward-looking poem, the reader is sure that the "hole I once dug" refers to the self the Strand speaker has wallowed in for so long but has now escaped from.

The remaining poems in *Darker* make it clear that the self cannot be joked away or neutralized temporarily or ignored. Instead—and here the reader gets a glimpse of what is to come in Strand's poetic program—the self must be dissolved. The last lines of **"The Dress"** say,

> if you step out of your dress and move into the
>   shade,
> the mole will find you, so will the owl, and so
>   will the poem,
> and you will fall into another darkness, one you
>   will find
> yourself making and remaking until it is perfect.

These lines contain familiar elements: moving away from the self; moving into darkness; allowing nature to organize itself around one; poetry; strenuous effort. Whereas each of these has been a stopgap measure in the speaker's attempt to quell his anxiety, together in this one poem they create a state that is "perfect."

Other poems comment on different aspects of this successful program of self-dissolution. **"Letter,"** for example, might be taken as a response to the ethnocentric mysticism of Theodore Roethke and Wallace Stevens that is echoed in **"Keeping Things Whole"** (*Sleeping*). Whereas the earlier poem saw the world organizing itself around the speaker, this one proposes that the world will seek its own beneficial order if we simply get out of its way: for example, people drop pens, others pick them up, and that's how letters are written.

> How things fall to others!
> The self no longer belonging to me, but asleep
> in a stranger's shadow, now clothing
> the stranger.

This is a more assured Strand, no longer borrowing the proven yet temporary solutions of his distinguished predecessors. **"The Hill"** speaks of vigorous movement away from the self; **"The Dress"** and **"Letter"** recommend a simple discarding. Similarly, **"Tomorrow"** observes that if your best friends desert you, don't run after them—wait, because it wasn't something you did or said ("the house of breath collapsing / around your voice, your voice burning, are nothing to worry about"), and "tomorrow they will come back and you / will invent an ending that comes out right." Let the anxious put their effort into quiet invention, then, not grand and futile gestures.

For a poet, invention means more poetry. The Strand speaker, however, has been through a lot; he has despaired, exalted, and in his search for a cure for his own morbidity, he has stopped at every way station between despair and exaltation. The old poetics will no longer suffice; the speaker requires **"The New Poetry Handbook."**

There have been fleeting references to poetry earlier and an extended paean to its power in **"Eating Poetry"** (*Reasons*), but now a true anatomy is conducted. Here, poetry is treated in greater detail, with greater seriousness and awe. **"The New Poetry Handbook"** argues that poetry can have the same presence in our lives that a person can: "If a man lives with two poems, he shall be unfaithful to one," and "if a man conceives of a poem, he shall have one less child." More than that, though, poetry is magical beyond the limits of mere biology, even to the point of bringing on Old Testament-style plagues if treated scornfully: "if a man publicly denounces poetry, his shoes will fill with urine."

Ultimately, poetry is good for the poet. As the last line of **"The New Poetry Handbook"** says, "if a man finishes a poem, he shall bathe in the blank wake of his passion and be kissed by white paper." Poetry can save you, in other words, but you must treat it with respect, neither clutching it too tightly nor letting it slip from your grasp. The poet must handle the poem the way Ishmael handles Queequeg in chapter 49 of *Moby-Dick,* where the two mariners are joined by a "monkey-rope" that is meant to save Queequeg's life but that could drag Ishmael into the unforgiving ocean.

What makes this **"The New Poetry Handbook"** is that whereas the old poetics sought fulfillment in the well-crafted poem as an extension of the self, the new poetics looks toward both a poem and a poet that are "blank" and "white." The new poet is no imperialist, no prince of Paraguay as in **"What to Think Of "** (*Reasons*). Handling his materials deftly yet lightly, he uses poetry to escape rather than extend the self.

"The New Poetry Handbook" figures as a manifesto of sorts, placed at the beginning of *Darker* after the poet had reviewed his other sundry grapplings with the problem of self. Strand is now saying that poetry can be curative as well as expressive, and from this point on in his work poetry will figure not only as a medium but also as a subject. (pp. 9-26)

David Kirby, in his Mark Strand and the

Poet's Place in Contemporary Culture, *University of Missouri Press, 1990, 89 p.*

Strand on the function of form in poetry:

I believe that all poetry is formal in that it exists within limits, limits that are either inherited by tradition or limits that language itself imposes. These limits exist in turn within the limits of the individual poet's conception of what is or is not a poem. For if the would-be poet has no idea of what a poem is, then he has no standard for determining or qualifying his actions as a poet, i.e., his poems. Form, it should be remembered, is a word that has several meanings, some of which are near opposites. For instance, form has to do with the structure or outward appearance of something but it also has to do with its essence. In discussions of poetry it is a powerful word for just that reason; structure and essence seem to come together, as do the disposition of words and their meanings.

> *Mark Strand, in his "Notes on the Craft of Poetry," 1978, published in* Claims for Poetry, *edited by Donald Hall, University of Michigan Press, 1982.*

Michael Dirda

Late last year Strand brought out *The Continuous Life* and *Selected Poems,* a brace of books that any poetry reader should want. Austere, philosophical, playful, a Strand poem generally offers an unruffled surface of calm, like a philosophical argument or an Anglican prayer, but with a lot of action underneath. The poems possess a deceptive simplicity that at first tantalizes and then lingers. Consider the very human opening stanza of **"Not Dying"**:

> These wrinkles are nothing.
> These gray hairs are nothing.
> This stomach which sags
> with old food, these bruised
> and swollen ankles,
> my darkening brain,
> they are nothing.
> I am the same boy
> my mother used to kiss.

That was first published some 20 years ago. As it happens though, Strand's new book shows him writing at his absolute peak. *The Continuous Life* offers so many different kinds of work—prose poems, imitations, acts of homage (to Kafka, Virgil, Chekhov, Borges), philosophical investigations, witty grotesques—that it almost seems like an anthology of half a dozen poets. Consider the Rilkean ring of "Our masters are gone and if they returned / Who among us would hear them . . . "; or the Barthelme-like humor of **"From a Lost Diary"** ("I had not begun the great journey I was to undertake. I did not feel like it"); or **"The Couple,"** which adopts a mock-ballad measure à la Auden's "Miss Gee" and recounts the tragically brief love affair of Jane and a bored Princeton professor.

Strand writes with mastery in any style he chooses. Listen to the grave majesty of **"Cento Virgilianus"**:

> And so, passing under the dome of the great sky,
> Driven by storms and heavy seas, we came,
> Wondering on what shore of the world
> We were cast up . . .

But this same guy can also make you laugh out loud, as in his trio of **"Grotesques"**:

> It was the middle of the night.
> The beauty parlors were closed and the pale
> moon
> Raced above the water towers.
> "Franz," screamed the woman, "take the corpse
> outside;
> It's impossible to think in here."

These are terrific poems. Mark Strand's not the poet laureate for nothing. (pp. 6-7)

> *Michael Dirda, "The Sublime and the Surreal," in* Book World—The Washington Post, *March 3, 1991, pp. 6-7.*

Alfred Corn

Mark Strand, who was recently appointed Poet Laureate of the United States, has now brought out, after a decade without a book, *The Continuous Life* as well as a *Selected Poems* taken from his first five collections. A quarter of a century ago, in his first book, Mr. Strand said, "I am always amazed at / how easily satisfied / some people are." One form of dissatisfaction for him is a continuous revision of how he writes. Latin American surrealism, Elizabeth Bishop and Kafka were formative influences on him, and behind them the darker strain in American consciousness that produced artists like Hawthorne, Poe and Dickinson. In his early books—filled with dread and tombstones and women problematic to the poet—he poured an edgy brilliance into litanies to nothingness that make ordinary happiness seem rather sappy. He approached his theme from several angles, expanded his vision and refined his expressive means from book to book. There were also frequent excursions into an ironic, wincing comedy somewhere between Beckett and Grand Guignol. In his previous book, *The Late Hour* some of the intransigence softened, and glimmerings of consolation appeared.

The Continuous Life doesn't strike me so much as a capstone of Mr. Strand's career as one more turning in his development. The poems are cast in long, fairly regular iambic lines, and the level of diction has risen. A first-person plural is used in a number of the poems, implying more than private perspectives. This is a poetry written, as it were, in the shadow of high mountains, and touched with their grandeur:

> For us, too, there was a wish to possess
> Something beyond the world we knew, beyond
> ourselves,
> Beyond our power to imagine, something never-
> theless
> In which we might see ourselves. . . .

As that poem, **"The Idea,"** progresses, a cabin appears in the frozen reaches imagined by the narrator as a counterpart to his state of mind:

> And we stood before it, amazed at its being
> there,
> And would have gone forward and opened the
> door,
> And stepped into the glow and warmed our-
> selves there,
> But that it was ours by not being ours,
> And should remain empty. That was the idea.

Readers of Wallace Stevens will be reminded of the deserted cabin on the beach in "The Auroras of Autumn," and the refrain of "Farewell to an Idea," which makes an elegy of that poem. Mr. Strand's last sentence is a pun, making a colloquial phrase Platonic, visionary. What's usually called negative transcendence is presented here with a light touch.

In **"Orpheus Alone"** Mr. Strand for the first time uses a figure from Greek mythology to base a poem on. Three of Orpheus' songs are described, the third in high-Romantic terms and with its own, I suppose, Orphic power—a sort of sublime "review" of a poem, in a poem:

> it came in a language
> Untouched by pity, in lines, lavish and dark,
> Where death is reborn and sent into the world
> as a gift,
> So the future, with no voice of its own, nor hope
> Of ever becoming more than it will be, might
> mourn.

It comes as something of a surprise that there are also satiric prose narratives and comic verse here, with titles like **"Grotesques," "Translation"** and **"The Continental College of Beauty,"** which, to a degree, muffle the impact of the serious poems. Yet they make Mr. Strand seem less like a visionary to be approached reverentially. He can be seen as susceptible to human weaknesses like impatience and scorn. And some of the wisecracks made me laugh, which is always welcome. (p. 26)

> *Alfred Corn, "Plural Perspectives, Heightened Perceptions," in* The New York Times Book Review, *March 24, 1991, pp. 26-7.*

Henri Cole

Mark Strand is a poet of mood, of integrated fragments, of twilit landscape, and of longing. In his poems the reticent among us are illuminated by the sun's golden rays and given sudden visionary articulations of the sublime. "The things that we build or grow or do are so little when compared to the things that we suggest or believe or desire," Stevens wrote in his *Letters,* his own poems, like those of Strand, reaching for the unnameable. And in an era when narrative is king, there is dissent on these pages. "Negative narratives," Strand calls his poems for their refusal "to begin because beginning is meaningless in an infinite universe. . . ." And so they also refuse to end, leading narrative poetry by the ear out of the Parnassian Academy. "What we call narrative is simply submission to the predicate's insufferable claims on the future; it furthers continuance, blooms into another predicate," Strand maintains in his prose poem **"Narrative Poetry,"** whose surreal humor does not defeat its message.

It has been ten years since Strand's *Selected Poems,* which has been reissued by Knopf simultaneously with *The Continuous Life,* a new volume like none other in the English language today. The poems are singularly idiosyncratic and searching. Strand, the urbane stoic, returns an elemental poet, his home overlooking a valley, where the trees seem continually awash with wind beneath an expansive scarlet sky, the setting for consciousness of the most prophetic sort. The poems are difficult to excerpt, for their ethereal, cumulative effect, but here are concluding lines of **"Luminism"**:

> The evening dimmed and darkened
> Until the western rim of the sky took on
> The purple look of a bruise, and everyone stood
> And said what a great sunset it had been. This
>   was a while ago,
> And it was remarkable, but something else happened then—
> A cry, almost beyond our hearing, rose and rose,
> As if across time, to touch us as nothing else
>   would,
> And so lightly we might live out our lives and
>   not know.
> I had no idea what it meant until now.

The two fixed points of man's life are the self and God; both are darknesses, one leading to another. In a Strand poem, the sun tumbling beyond the horizon, burnishing us as it falls, would seem an earthly embodiment of this passage—the sun's eternal brightness as much an emblem for "the continuous life" as the moon is of the ruinous void. We remember Valéry's dictum: "Man's deepest glances are those that go out to the void. They converge beyond the All." Such is the confident plunge of **"Luminism."**

The unknown or unsayable lingers continuously at the edge of Strand's poems, and it is this craving for the unknown that gives his poetry its *raison d'être.* The cry that we hear from "across time" at the end of **"Luminism,"** like Stevens's bird-cry in "Not Ideas About the Thing but the Thing Itself" brings a kind of "new knowledge of reality," to borrow from Stevens again. Reality is a sobering thing on these pages, however, and is largely spent recovering from "the damages of night," or by extension, escaping the inevitability of death. Assuming the mask of Gregor Samsa in **"Two Letters,"** also a prose poem, Strand asks, "with death always imminent, do we not keep hoping to be reborn? This is the human condition. We are citizens of one world only when we apply to the next; we are perpetual exiles, living on the outside of what is possible. . . ."

In his monograph on the contemporary American painter William Bailey, Mark Strand praises Bailey's still lifes for their "hiddenness," for their "calm, aristocratic denial of access." In a like fashion, the palette and composition of *The Continuous Life* is stately and reticent, striking us with its "majestic self-interest." The poems are classical in their postures, converging before us with Aristotelian clarity, even serenity, in spite of the mournful landscapes they often evoke, where always "the fair" is "turning

foul," and there are "high-pitched wails of women," "worms and swarming flies," a sky "stained with a reddish haze," and "somebody's limbs / scattered among the matted, mildewed leaves"—so much darkness that in his poem **"Se la vita e sventura . . . ?"** Strand asks,

> Where was it written
> That the world, because it was merciful after all,
>   would part
> To make room for the blurred shape of the murderer
> Fleeing the scene, while the victim, who had already
> Slipped to his knees, would feel the heat of his
>   whole being pass
> Into a brief, translucent cloud unravelling as it
>   was formed?

The interrogative itself is part of Strand's philosophical or meditative pattern of composition, his poems often maintaining a three-fold structure: a pastorally descriptive preludium, an intermediate colloquy or questioning, and a final elusive resolution—his brushwork smooth and unselfconscious throughout.

The humor here, often black, reveals itself in a poem like **"The Couple,"** one of three **"Grotesques"** and a perfect ballad recounting the fatal meeting on a subway platform of Jane and Mr. Right. Eros having guided them blindly onto the subway tracks, the poem ends,

> Just as they reach the utmost
>   Peak of their endeavor,
> An empty downtown local
>   Separates them forever.
>
> An empty downtown local
>   Screams through the grimy air,
> A couple dies in the subway;
>   Couples die everywhere.

Or there is also the Borges-like parable poem, **"Translation,"** which attempts to define the true nature of translation ("Wouldn't it be best to think of translation as a transaction between individual idioms, between, say, the Italian of D'Annunzio and the English of Auden?" Strand asks earnestly).

Among the most memorable poems in this book, and there are many, are **"The Idea," "Velocity Meadows," "A.M.," "Cento Virgilianus," "Orpheus Alone," "Luminism," "Life in the Valley," "The Continuous Life," "Se la vita e sventura . . . ?," "The Midnight Club,"** and **"The End"**—the last being a straightforward coda to his book's chief theme, though the five letters that give us DEATH are scarce in this collection:

> Not every man knows what he shall sing at the
>   end,
> Watching the pier as the ship sails away, or what
>   it will seem like
> When he's held by the sea's roar, motionless,
>   there at the end,
> Or what he shall hope for once it is clear that
>   he'll never go back.

Instead, Strand's is a more distant, stalwart voice, trembling now and again, perhaps, but as dignified and upright as a cenotaph. (pp. 54-7)

Henri Cole, in a review of "The Continuous Life," in Poetry, *Vol. LLVIII, No. 1, April, 1991, pp. 54-7.*

Dennis Sampson

Pretension and disdain reach through Mark Strand's first book in ten years, *The Continuous Life,* an accumulation of curious poems and prose poems by one of our better-known writers. It was John Ciardi who commented that after craft had been mastered, failures in the writing were failures of character; and Strand, who has written some fine things, especially when composing at length, as in **"The Story of Our Lives"** and **"The Untelling,"** appears to have reached a point at which criticism of individual lines no longer seems to him to be necessary.

> And though it was brief, and slight, and nothing
> To have been held onto so long, I remember it,
> As if it had come from within, one of the scenes
> The mind sets for itself, night after night, only
> To part from, quickly and without warning.
>
> **"Luminism"**

This and most of the poems in this volume are at the mercy of a posture which rarely allows engaging speech and undermines any effort to argue imaginatively. Descriptions of landscape and seascape sound like Hemingway:

> A frieze of clouds lowered a shadow over the
> town,
> And driving wind flattened the meadows that
> swept
> Beyond the olive trees and banks of hollyhock
> and rose.
> The air smelled sweet, and a girl was waving a
> stick
> At some crows so far away they looked like flies.
>
> **"Velocity Meadows"**

Like Charles Wright, Strand glides from forgettable image to image without any apparent wish to test himself, mimicking Auden in **"Grotesques,"** Stevens in **"The End,"** Donald Justice in **"Life in the Valley"** for reasons that become obvious after a time: the subject of Mark Strand's life no longer seems accessible to him in his poetry. For this reason, too many poems seem written in jest as an exercise in creative writing, aping gestures, say, of Stevens in "Lunar Paraphrase":

> Not every man knows what he shall sing in the
> end,
> Watching the pier as the ship sails away, or what
> it will seem like
> When he's held by the sea's roar, motionless,
> there in the end,
> Or what he shall hope for once it is clear that
> he'll never go back.
>
> **"The End"**

Donald Justice can do this because he makes it authentic. Strand can't. There is dumbfoundingly little underneath these elegantly embroidered garments, "a blown husk that

is finished" perhaps, or worse, a mocking and satisfied and complacent self. (pp. 336-37)

Dennis Sampson, in a review of "The Continuous Life," in The Hudson Review, *Vol. XLIV, No. 2, Summer, 1991, pp. 336-37.*

Strand on the value of criticism:

Criticism, when practiced in the grandest possible terms, can be exhilarating; especially if one figures into those terms. The journalistic criticism is very often demeaning and tends to make the writer feel somewhat diminished in his enterprise. What I've rarely felt in a piece of journalistic criticism is that my work has been understood. On the other hand, more lengthy, academic pieces have made me feel that I've done much more than I in fact intended, and made me feel rather good as a result. Let me say this, in addition, that criticism, whether small or grand, has never influenced me to write in a particular way or to abandon a particular mode of working. I mean, even if I feel that critic is much smarter than I am, and some of them are very much smarter *than* I am, I just feel that I must do what I do.

Mark Strand, in "Is This the Future?: A Forum," in Quarterly West, *1986.*

George Bradley

Mr. Strand's first five books of poetry cultivated an aesthetic of deliberate extremity. The lines were typically short, the volumes thin, the hope afforded slim. Some ten years ago, the work ceased altogether, and although Mr. Strand's silence was cause for regret, it was difficult for a reader familiar with his work to feel much surprise. The poet had made his mark, so to speak, by sawing off the psychological limb on which he was sitting, by painting himself into a corner, by climbing into a coffin and pulling down the lid.

The casket was a cocoon. Astonishingly, Mark Strand has found a voice again, and it is a richly rewarding one. After a decade's moratorium during what might have been the prime of his career, he has now returned to print with perhaps his most impressive work to date. Against long odds, [*The Continuous Life*] justifies his long absence, for Strand's poetry has been transformed. His line is more fluid now, dignified and yet unstrained. His diction is now informed by the greatest practitioners of English verse—Milton, Blake, Coleridge, Stevens, Whitman—and many of his new poems allude to these very authors, albeit obliquely and unobtrusively. In the past, Strand's work has been minimalist, surreal, quasi-theoretical. The new work is quasi-neoclassical.

It is possible that Mr. Strand's metamorphosis reflects not only the poet's personal development, but a larger development in our culture as well. Perhaps a latinate neoclassicism reminiscent of the eighteenth century is becoming what this poet terms "the dominant idiom of the period." *The Continuous Life* does in fact include a *cento Virgili-*

anus (a late classical form in which lines from Virgil's work are reassembled into an independent macaronic), but the prevailing spirit here is more Greek than Latin. Strand asks the same question Socrates did: "What can we know?"

"Very pretty," said one well-known critic to me in reference to Strand's new poems, "but they're not really *about* anything." That assessment won't entirely do, though. The new poems are about the role of language and the possibility of meaning, about limits of all sorts. They are about the poet's advance into old age, about his departure from the packed frenzy of New York City to the largeness and emptiness of Utah. But "very pretty" they are. This is literally a luminous book, filled with descriptions of the spectacular light effects of our western desert. The lines are lit, sometimes with the crepuscular radiance of Whitman's "Crossing Brooklyn Ferry," sometimes with the fiery "darkness visible" of Milton's Pandemonium.

Finally, this is an ambitious book. Strand has "immortal longings." Though the poet contemplates the acceptance and serenity he hopes can be achieved with the passing years, he simultaneously strives to recapitulate the past and speak to the future. In a powerful poem called **"Orpheus Alone,"** Mr. Strand gives us a parable of the poet's mission cast in terms of poetry's primary myth. Strand's Orpheus first confronts his mortality, then succeeds in reimagining his world, and at last bequeaths his conception, even as he dies, to a future that will be dependent upon him. What better applause than to close with the poet's own words, as he transmits his vision of heaven and hell, of earth, to succeeding ages:

> . . . in a language
> Untouched by pity, in lines, lavish and dark,
> Where death is reborn and sent into the world
>   as a gift,
> So the future, with no voice of its own, nor hope
> Of ever becoming more than it will be, might
>   mourn.

(pp. 564-65)

George Bradley, "Lush and Lean," in Partisan Review, *Vol. LVIII, No. 3, Summer, 1991, pp. 562-65.*

Jane Candia Coleman

Years ago, as a fledgling poet, I stumbled on a horrifying, nearly overwhelming fact: that there were thoughts, visions, happenings for which I, as poet, had no words. I was so frustrated by this that I mentioned it to a musician friend, asking if he had experienced something similar with music. He looked at me sadly and lifted his hands in despair. "All the time," was his answer.

Thus my introduction to the tragedy that must be dealt with by all artists, a tragedy to which Mark Strand, Poet Laureate of the United States, Professor of English at the University of Utah, author of seven books of poetry and numerous works of fiction and non-fiction, is certainly no stranger.

With the publication of his new collection, *The Continu-*

ous Life and the reissue of *Selected Poems,* the reader has a comprehensive view of Strand's growth—as a poet and as a human in the twentieth century—and of his solutions to the problems inherent in both.

In his book, *Mark Strand and the Poet's Place in Contemporary Culture,* David Kirby makes the point that the early Strand, in his attempt to "recreate the poem" and bring it under the control of language began by "jettisoning himself." An in-depth reading of *Selected Poems* shows that this is not quite true.

Mark Strand is not a poet for Everyone. His is not work that will be set to music or sung on the streets. The cursory reader will be bewildered, lost. But the reader who delves, who meets the poet halfway, will be rewarded by glimpses of a different world, that changeable one of dreams and the elusive beauty that haunts us all.

—Jane Candia Coleman

Strand, the poet, the questioner, the wrestler with the invisible, even as a young man could write in **"Keeping Things Whole,"** "In a field / I am the absence of field . . . / Wherever I am I am what is missing . . . / We all have reasons / for moving. I move / To keep things whole."

This is certainly not removal of self but the poet as an integral, almost god-like part of the universe, attempting to write the mystical, the unsayable from the inside out, battling with a world that may (or may not, always Strand's stance) exist except in the experience of the seer.

This is the poet who could write in the poem **"The New Poetry Handbook,"** a series of aphorisms ending with number 21: "If a man finishes a poem, / He shall bathe in the blank wake of his passion / And be kissed by white paper."

Again, not denial of existence of self but the tragedy of the attempt to write something that turns to nothing simply through the fact of its imprisonment in language.

Language is the poet's only tool, all that he has, and it is language—and all the poetic techniques from simile and metaphor to rhythms and startling portrayals of the ordinary turned surreal—that Strand manipulates, turning and twisting, viewing from all points in his desire for the truth.

Moving from [the selected works] to *The Continuous Life* gives the diligent reader remarkable insight into the art of writing poetry, a favorite theme of Strand's. Here, too, we see the mature poet pushing language to its limits, bending sentences and stanzas to his will. These are formidable poems, clear and precise, and they demand close attention.

"Orpheus Alone," perhaps the finest poem in the book

and, to my mind, one of Strand's finest poems to date, gives us Orpheus—poet, singer, lover—mourning his loss, "Taking off to wander the hills / Outside of town, where he stayed until he had shaken / The image of love and put in its place the world / As he wished it would be, urging its shape and measure / Into speech of such newness that the world was swayed . . . " and, "The voice of light / Had come forth from the body of fire, and each thing / Rose from its depths and shone as it never had. / And that was the second great poem, / Which no one recalls anymore. The third and greatest / Came into the world as the world, out of the unsayable / Invisible source of all longing to be / It came in a language / Untouched by pity, in lines, lavish and dark, / Where death is reborn and sent into the world as a gift, / So the future, with no voice of its own, nor hope / Of ever becoming more than it will be, might mourn."

The poet's duty, then, is to write the world, to define it, inventing language as he goes, making something "out of the unsayable," whether or not it is forgotten. A hopeless proposition? Perhaps. Perhaps not. Poets since Cassandra have stood outside the pale, listening, singing, reaching out to an uncaring, unheeding audience.

Mark Strand is not a poet for Everyone. His is not work that will be set to music or sung on the streets. The cursory reader will be bewildered, lost. But the reader who delves, who meets the poet halfway, will be rewarded by glimpses of a different world, that changeable one of dreams and the elusive beauty that haunts us all. (pp. 178-79)

Jane Candia Coleman, in a review of "The Continuous Life," in Western American Literature, *Vol. XXVI, No. 2, Summer, 1991, pp. 178-79.*

FURTHER READING

Jackson, Richard. "Charles Simic and Mark Strand: The Presence of Absence." *Contemporary Literature* 21, No. 1 (Winter 1980): 136-45.

Relates poems by Simic and Strand to ideas expressed by such philosophic thinkers as Martin Heidegger, Jacques Lacan, Jacques Derrida, and Paul Ricoeur.

Strand, Mark. "Slow Down for Poetry." *The New York Times Book Review* (15 September 1991): 1, 36-7.

Previously published essay addressing the difficulties experienced by readers of fiction in comprehending poetry.

Additional coverage of Strand's life and career is contained in the following sources published by Gale Research: *Contemporary Authors,* **Vols. 21-24, rev. ed.;** *Contemporary Literary Criticism,* **Vols. 6, 18, 41;** *Dictionary of Literary Biography,* **Vol. 41; and** *Something about the Author,* **Vol. 41.**

Peter Taylor

1917-

(Full name Peter Hillsman Taylor) American short story writer, novelist, and dramatist.

The following entry covers Taylor's works through 1991. For further information on Taylor's life and career, see *CLC*, Vols. 1, 4, 18, 37, 44, and 50.

INTRODUCTION

Taylor is considered one of the most celebrated figures in contemporary American fiction, both for his highly accomplished short stories and for his Pulitzer Prize-winning novel, *A Summons to Memphis*. His works are concerned exclusively with the lives of upper middle-class Southerners from the 1930s to the early 1950s, a time when the industrialization and urbanization of the "New South" began to erode the foundations of the genteel agrarian white society. Although Taylor's fiction is focused on a specific region, his work is often praised for its universal relevance.

Taylor was born in Trenton, a small town in northwest Tennessee, to an upper middle-class family that had been involved in state politics for several generations. When Taylor was seven years old, his family moved to Nashville and subsequently to St. Louis and Memphis. This experience of displacement from a small town to urban centers and the attendant confrontation between an older and more modern milieu are cited by commentators as sources of much of Taylor's fiction. A more immediate influence on Taylor's artistic and intellectual development was his university education. Taylor is closely identified with the Southern Renaissance or Agrarian movement that his respective mentors at Vanderbilt University and Kenyon College, Allen Tate and John Crowe Ransom, helped to develop in the 1920s and 1930s. The Agrarians were a group of writers dedicated to preserving what they perceived as the southern way of life. Concerned with social and political issues as well as literature, they attacked northern industrialism and sought to preserve the southern agricultural economy. Tate and Ransom later became prominent figures among the New Critics, who practiced close readings of poetry and insisted that criticism should be based on a study of the structure and texture of a given poem, not on its content. From his association with these critics, as well as his friendship with the poets Randall Jarrell and Robert Lowell, Taylor acquired an appreciation for the clarity and precision of poetry that is reflected in his stories.

In his first collection, *A Long Fourth, and Other Stories,* Taylor established the themes and milieu that he has continued to explore throughout his career. The title story, which is regarded as one of Taylor's best, delineates the

changing values of a society and dramatizes the suffering of those unable to reconcile themselves to social change. The narrative centers on a prosperous Nashville woman and her attempts to plan a memorable weekend for her son, a New Yorker, who will visit her before joining the army. Several circumstances undermine her preparations, revealing the manners and traditions that once provided order in her world to be powerless rituals of a lifestyle that no longer exists. The trauma of social change is also central to *A Summons to Memphis*. The narrator of the novel, Phillip Carver, is shaped by the events of his youth in Tennessee during the 1930s and 1940s. He recalls how his self-absorbed father moved his family from genteel Nashville to a rougher environment in Memphis, a change so dramatic it affected all family members except the father. Phillip becomes emotionally disturbed, his mother withdraws from her formerly active life, and his sisters become embittered spinsters who seek revenge upon their father. Taylor's skill at evoking tragedy from this scenario is a frequent subject of critical commentary. Typical of his style in both his short stories and *A Summons to Memphis* is the gradual unfolding of a narrative in an indirect, ruminative fashion, using little action or dialogue. Through an accumulation of finely observed details that evoke the manners and morals of a particular era, Taylor builds tension and discloses his characters' personalities.

It was not until the mid 1980s that Taylor earned the widespread recognition many critics thought his fiction had long deserved. *The Old Forest, and Other Stories,* a retrospective collection of Taylor's stories from the late 1930s to the 1980s, sparked new interest in his work and won the PEN/Faulkner award for fiction in 1986. That same year, Taylor won the Pulitzer Prize for *A Summons to Memphis.* Critics consistently praise Taylor's meticulous recreation of a world that, through his richly detailed descriptions of social manners and customs, becomes uniquely his own. Several commentators have observed that although Taylor's works are set in a particular time and place, their concern with perennial questions of morality and human nature transcend the restrictions of period fiction. As J. D. McClatchy has commented: "The South is his setting, but Taylor could as well be writing about any society in transition."

PRINCIPAL WORKS

NOVELS

A Woman of Means 1950
A Summons to Memphis 1986

SHORT FICTION

A Long Fourth, and Other Stories 1948
The Widows of Thornton 1954
Happy Families Are All Alike 1959
Miss Lenora When Last Seen, and Fifteen Other Stories
  1963
The Collected Stories of Peter Taylor 1969
In the Miro District, and Other Stories 1977
The Road, and Other Modern Stories 1979
The Old Forest, and Other Stories 1985

PLAYS

Tennessee Day in St. Louis 1956
A Stand in the Mountains [first publication] 1971
Presences: Seven Dramatic Pieces [first publication]
  1973

CRITICISM

Andrew Lytle

[*Lytle is an American fiction writer, historian, biographer, and critic. In the following excerpt, he comments on the demise of the family as it is presented in Taylor's drama* Tennessee Day in St. Louis.]

Mr. Taylor is the only American writer, and indeed to my knowledge the only writer in English, whose subject is the dislocation and slow destruction of the family as an institution. He has fixed upon the one fact central to the social

revolution going on in this country; how far it involves the rest of the western world is not immediately relevant. It is relevant that Mr. Taylor is a Southern writer, or better still from the border state of Tennessee, which gives him a distinct perspective upon the historical situation, and defines the aesthetic distance of his point of view. Nowhere else in this country is the family as a social unit so clearly defined as in the South. Its large "connections" amplifying the individual family life, the geographic accident which allowed the family in this greater sense (it was the community) to extend itself in a mild climate and alluvial soils where the physical barriers were not too severe, and slavery too, gave the family a more clear definition of its function as not only an institution but *the* institution of Southern life. So it was elsewhere in the country but never quite so clearly evident. In the succeeding wests the constant movement impaired its stability. In New England, at least in the coastal areas, there was always the sea to intervene, keeping its mind colonial and spiritually dependent upon England, holding up a distant image and not the immediate one of a constant scene such as land allows. Both the sea and land are feminine images, but the sea takes only men; and so the communion between husband and wife is disrupted. When you think of woman in New England's past, witch-hunting comes to mind; in the South, and the matriarch shows herself. Land keeps the family intact. Husband, wife, children, the old, middle and young generations, all serve it and are kept by it, according to their various needs and capacities. The parts of the family make a whole by their diversity. The military defeat of the South, which was total in the sense of its structural overthrow and the acceptance of this, gives the writer a ground of comparison for the changes this defeat brought about. Most Southern writers of necessity must be aware of this. None has so clearly made fine stories out of it as has Mr. Taylor. However, he merely implies the more stable situation of the family on the land in dealing with its predicament in town and city. *Exiled at home* might best describe Mr. Taylor's earlier stories. In **Tennessee Day in St. Louis** the exile is actual, as it is in most of the stories in **The Widows of Thornton.**

Families from other parts of the country, when they move, identify themselves most readily with their new surroundings. The Southern family, like Lot's wife, turns back its head. The Tolliver household is the archetype of such a family. There are no heroes. The actors are all decent human beings caught in the situation of trying to maintain in absentia manners and mores which do not express their economic habits. The house has for its self-invited guest a former Senator who will be the speaker at the annual Tennessee day in St. Louis. It is also the birthday of Lanny, the youngest son of the house, as well as the anniversary of the parents, James and Helen. The family, as the curtain rises, discovers itself at a moment when both its public and private ceremonies happen upon the same day. Formerly, at "home," this would have seemed a happy occasion to combine the rituals of hospitality, birth, and the public thing. But the play opens in a different way. The *ficelles* describe a conflict between the public and the private ritual. The Senator has taken over the whole lower floor of the house, "evicting" the family while he memorizes his speech. But he has not been able to have it alone.

Auntie Bet and Flo Dear, a rich old maid and her companion, defy the Senator by remaining downstairs working at a puzzle. They all have one thing in common: they are all self-invited. The ladies, however, have made themselves a part of the household; yet they feel insecure; the Senator, a temporary guest as they once were, threatens their place. The "connections," instead of working at and adding to the common occasion, jealously and selfishly find themselves at odds, if in the most civil fashion.

This competition between the public and private thing descends to a conflict within the privacy itself upon the entrance of James, the head of the house. He comes in as if he were intruding in his own home and hides his gift for Lanny, even locks it up. The reason given is that the Senator must not be made to feel his intrusion at such a time, and so the birthday is concealed. This is certainly a strain of manners, but it is more than that. If the Senator's kinship were true in the old sense, there would be no need for a guilty suppression of a private celebration. The guilt lies in the fact that there is nothing to be private about. The family is a husk, committed to keeping up the appearance of what a family is. The meaning of this shows in the father's gift, golf clubs which he loves and his son hates, as he does all games, preferring history and literature. The gift should represent love for the child in the occasion: it represents instead self-love and appearance. With ruthless insistence the family holds to this.

The family in a Christian society has only one function, to operate as a family and perpetuate itself through its children. Each member is called upon to deny much of his individual nature in the service of the whole, and this service sustains the common love and life. But the service must rest upon domestic laws, the principal one of disciplining children and servants, if there be servants. This discipline is entirely lacking in the Tolliver house. Love becomes selfish, self-indulgent, and destructive; that is, irresponsible. William, Helen's brother, invites himself to the house, lives in it without paying his part; but the essential truth about William is that he rebelled against the family and its discipline back in Tennessee, because that discipline seemed harsh. It seemed harsh because the family had lost its meaning for itself and the South. Lanny quotes the old Senator to Lucy: " . . . there is no new South; there is only the old South resurrected with the print of the nails in her hands." Lucy supports her parents but flees their poverty. The Senator, who is more nearly the protagonist, came to manhood during Reconstruction, and has a historic perspective upon the situation. He suffered more immediately the family's dislocation, because he had been brought up in the real thing. He comes to St. Louis to sponge on the exiles, "to enjoy all the familiar patterns . . . without any of the responsibility," where the kin are not too close for comfort. His self-indulgence is food and drink and comfort. All the actors recognize in moments of insight what is wrong, but they usually see the failure in others. To their own shortcomings they are blind or fatally committed. It is their need for family life which makes them see; it is the self-indulgence and self-interest which makes this insight blurred.

The Senator, as he gulps his host's whiskey (Jack Daniels, Tennessee whiskey), compares St. Louis families of Tennessee extraction to the colony of Virginians who, caught by the Civil War in Paris, became the favorites of the French Court. But James Tolliver is more realistic: he replies that the men came to St. Louis of their own free will to make money in shoes, banking and insurance. But James refuses to understand the full meaning of this in terms of the ex-Tennesseans' plight in that border city with the Southern face. What he fails to understand is that these business men have substituted the means for the end, that is, money, not as a part of the family's economy, but as the *end* itself Money, not the *res publica,* nor the American Union, is now the common American dream, as earlier the Union, an abstraction, had supplanted the concrete image of the King with its long history and religious implications. These successive changes in the nature of the state up to the Civil War had merely altered the meaning of the family. In the play the family itself has disintegrated, or is far along in ruin.

Money is got through competition. The Tolliver family has exchanged love for this competition. The controlling symbols for this are the games which fill the vacuum left by love. Helen, the wife and mother, is the priestess who orders all the play. She will allow no disobedience in this, lest the husk show its emptiness. William with unconscious irony describing in part himself says that gamblers are nervous, senseless sort of men who know they have nothing and ought to want something. He is about to take all his money and flee west, which he considers something new, fleeing west or making more money, just as he is deluded into thinking he can be "outside history." The Senator treats gambling with religious veneration, for it is not only skill, all that it is to William, but also luck: a small abstraction of life itself. "Luck is the most marvellous thing in the world, and no man knows whether or not he is lucky til he's seen his last day." With his historical perspective the Senator in this compares the present moment, where the family is the microcosm of the material society, with only competition and skill left, to the past where the family was an organism out of which man came with a richer sense of the mystery and possibilities of life, not consciously seeking security but seeking out of the only security possible, a stable society, the larger meaning of life.

The irony in the action which Francis Fergusson describes as lying below the plot is just this: that the family must keep up the appearance of amity and love and service, for that is all that is left to disguise their plight, which is selfishness and self-indulgence. All of the threats to the surface calm of the week-end take place: William flees with his money, abandoning his mistress, who breaks off her association with the family; the Senator affronts his audience by talking about old times, reminding them, we presume, of the parts they would like to forget; Lanny attempts suicide; Jim is going away to meet Nancy's people in Tennessee and ask for her hand (jumping from the frying pan into the fire). Any one of these incidents should mar the appearance of things; and yet they happen without in any crucial way disturbing the necessary fixation on appearance. The Tennessee Society is entertained in the front part of the house, while the birthday and anniversary take place in the back room; the meaningless gifts are exchanged; Lanny's birthday cake is brought in all aflame. His father admonishes him to blow the candles out, lest he set the house afire: that is, keep up the appearance or we are lost. Appearance is now the only salvation in a society which the Senator in the speech he never delivers defines as "The most frightful of all spectacles, the strength of civilization without its mercy. . . . It was artfully contrived by Augustus, that, in the enjoyment of plenty, the Romans should lose the memory of freedom."

But with all the changes and reversals which take place and resolve the plot it is clear that even the appearance of the old family will go. The Senator, in his speech to Lanny, makes this plain. Lanny has hoped by seeing the Senator and talking with him to discover direct and authoritative connection with the past, "as if it were day before yesterday." But there will be by any sensible reckoning of history a thousand years between the Senator's generation and the world Lanny will grow up in. This is the Senator's final warning to the boy, whose eagerness to know himself in terms of his past has forced the Senator to confront in himself his plight, which stands for the plight of all. As the curtain falls, we see that the appearance of family is doomed. Lanny sees it, and his insight is the beginning of manhood. "Give me time. Give me time," he says in the closing lines, not the time which his mother has killed with her games but time to find himself in the reality of the situation which will be his in the brave new servile world.

Mr. Taylor's play is a fine performance. The well-done intricacies of the plot I have left for the reader to find for himself in the pleasure of reading the play, or that better experience of seeing it done on the stage: for no matter how good the dialogue a play must be seen. And this is a cause for wonder in Mr. Taylor's change from fiction to the drama. The drama is only the scene and depends upon the accidents of extraneous and numerous aids, such as actors whom God made and not the author. Fiction as an art is more responsible to control in its entirety, and the best of actors can never supplant the pictorial or panoramic effects which summarize and prepare for the scene. Mr. Ransom, in replying to someone who asked him why he had given up the writing of poetry, said "It's a free country." After reading this play, one wonders again how free it is; or certainly how free the fiction writer as artist is to employ his time in a more restricted art form. One sees the Muse frown slightly, not turn away, for surely she understands Mr. Taylor's true devotion. (pp. 115-20)

> *Andrew Lytle, "The Displaced Family," in*
> The Sewanee Review, *Vol. LXVI, No. 1, Winter, 1958, pp. 115-31.*

Walter Sullivan

[*Sullivan is an American educator, novelist, short story writer, and critic. In the following excerpt, he discusses the milieu of southern upper middle-class society on which Taylor's work is focused.*]

Few writers have staked out for themselves more narrowly defined domains than Peter Taylor. His place is middle and west Tennessee, and when a story or play is set in St. Louis or Detroit, the foreign ambience enhances the sense of southern custom. Taylor's southerners in exile remain what they are: second- and third-generation Tennessee agrarians who have made an urban progress in the world. His time is the decade of the thirties, and he is such a master of anachronism that whatever the stated date of a story may be, the attitudes and actions and details recreate the uneasy last decade of the hegemony of the southern gentry. His people are the well connected and well-to-do; the middle-class and poor and black characters who appear in his work are defined by their relationships to the wealthy. Think of the unfortunate Miss Bluemeyer in **"The Death of a Kinsman,"** or of Jesse in **"A Friend and Protector,"** or of the girls of the Memphis "demimonde" in **"The Old Forest."**

Social distinctions are nowhere made more important than in *A Stand in the Mountains.* The Weavers, rich and prominent, come from Louisville to Owl Mountain for the summers; the Campbells, poor and graceless, live in the coves and eke out a living working for people such as the Weavers. But nothing can be so neat. Louisa Weaver and Thelma Campbell are matriarchs of the two parties, but their relationship has been complicated by the marriage of Louisa's son Harry to Thelma's granddaughter Lucille. This union, entered into by Harry to protest his mother's inveterate snobbishness, has incurred for both parties more misery than it has cured. Harry's brother Zack rebels against his mother's values by claiming poetry as his vocation, moving to Italy, and becoming the lover of a woman whom Louisa once tried to present to Louisville society. The action here, the most violent of which takes place offstage, is grim and only partially redeemed; and in his preface Taylor tells us why.

> All of the heroes and heroines in my play suffer in some degree from the emptiness of the old roles they are playing, and their suffering is increased whenever they try to make some sense out of their roles. No doubt all human beings are punished for accepting preconceived notions of their identity and of their relationship to other human beings. . . . And yet, how can anyone escape these preconceptions? In fact, the person who will always be punished most severely is he who . . . at once rejects these preconceptions and tries to continue to live amongst those who are suffering daily for their acceptance of that which he is rejecting.

Better then to escape as Zack did; but like Georgia, his mistress, who earlier has run from Louisa, he cannot stay away. They apparently return to Owl Mountain to flaunt their independence, but they become embroiled once more in all from which they thought they had freed themselves. Even to do nothing is to come off second best. Will Weaver, Louisa's brother-in-law, has refused throughout her long widowhood to pursue his love for her or even to utter it. He is an undistinguished historian who has grown old writing unread books about the Indians who once lived around Owl Mountain, but his history is as empty as Zack's poetry, and his work has been his life. At the other social level things are no better. Lucille is equally as miserable in marriage as Harry, and this connecting of the two families has compromised Thelma's social position: being an in-law of the Weavers, she is no longer hired by the summer people to do domestic work.

The strains of these relationships are exacerbated by Louisa's having moved from one social role to another. The daughter of a west Tennessee preacher, she was translated to Louisville and riches as the second wife of a much older man. Since his death she has relived her life through surrogates, cousins fetched out of the country to be given debuts and conducted toward acceptable marriages. Georgia fled Louisville before the process was completed. She and Zack and Harry urge Mina, another of Louisa's Tennessee cousins, to leave before her time begins, but Mina remains loyal to Louisa.

In most of Peter Taylor's work the characters, their attitudes, and their social intercourse with one another constitute, to a great extent, the story. Typically, in *A Stand in the Mountains,* the big action occurs offstage. Mina is in love with Harry; Zack is in love with Mina; Harry is in love with Georgia; but a chaste embrace is the most we see. Near the beginning Harry shoots his wife—he claims it was an accident; and near the end he kills Lucille and her grandmother and his two children and himself. Perhaps Taylor needs to shed this much blood to command our attention. In **"The Old Forest,"** in what is almost an aside, the narrator tells of losing his two brothers in the Korean war, his mother and father in a fire, and two of his children in accidents. By ordinary standards any one of these events would be more dramatic and more moving than the search for the narrator's missing girl friend and his fiancée's verbal exploration of caste and class in Memphis. But Taylor creates his characters so well and delves into their psyches so thoroughly that sometimes only bursts of violence will restore our awareness of a larger world beyond.

When *A Stand in the Mountains* ends, everything is in the grip of change. Georgia and Zack are returning to Italy, forced back into the aimless pattern of their itinerant life. They know now that they do not love each other very much and that their relationship and their artistic puttering travesty proper concepts of family and vocation—and are at best no less ridiculous than Will's feckless scholarship and Louisa's social conniving. Indeed Louisa will not return to Louisville: she and Will and Mina will remain until the modern world catches up with them, which will not be very long.

As Taylor points out frequently in his work, his aristocrats are the last Agrarians. They left their ruined plantations after the Civil War to engage in business or a profession in the city. They brought with them the old manners and customs, the country sense of family—or "connection" as they would put it; as we are told in **"The Old Forest,"** what they brought from the old order "made them both better and worse than business men elsewhere." Their wives and daughters shared their values and were also better and worse and happier and unhappier than their contemporaries who broke with the past. Taylor's people know who they are; they know how they are supposed to behave; and so at the outset of their lives they have answers to the two questions that most vex the rest of the modern world. They need not search for their identities or enter into endless engagements over what is right or wrong in a given situation. But the past, any mundane past, is imperfect, and freedom is not to be found in its service. Bound by what they believe in, Taylor's characters take their stands and await their defeats.

At the end of the Civil War, Lee was urged to lead the remnants of his army into the Virginia mountains where, his advisors believed, he might hold out for however long it took the Federals to grow weary of the fight. This is the source of the title of Taylor's play. It is evident that Lee made the sensible choice in laying down his arms, but it is less certain how the last survivors of his tradition should bear themselves at the end of their losing battles. The incursion of the interstate into the country where the Indians once roamed will violate all that Will has lived for; but he has no choice in the matter, and he might as well wait on the sacred ground for this disaster to happen. After the blood that Harry has spilled, Louisa never again can guide debutantes through a Louisville season. So she must stay with Will, and Mina will stay with her. This is right. Given the failures and dislocations of contemporary life, where would they go and what end would they seek that would be better than the conclusion they are now heirs to? We can consider this question as, at the end of the play, dialogue stops and the lights fade, leaving the stage in symbolic silence and darkness.

Taylor's plays gloss his stories in that they are more straightforward and less complicated than his fiction. Take for example **"A Long Fourth"** (1948), which appears in *The Old Forest.* Harriet Wilson, matriarch and protagonist, is one of the most fatuous figures in literature. She is a caricature of everything that is or ever has been wrong with the South: a snob whose head would be empty without the prejudices that reside there. Her patronizing affection for her black cook is no more than skin-deep, and while the world engages or prepares to engage in war, her thoughts are confined to domestic niceties in general and specifically to Son's visit and the party she is going to give for him and Ann.

Yet, in the ambience that Taylor provides for her, Harriet is no worse than anybody else. Sweetheart, her husband, is willing to drift with history, a devoted adherent to the status quo. The daughters, Helena and Kate, comprehend the moral poverty of the way of life to which they were born: they complain about the narrowness of their mother's vision, but, as ineffectual as their father, they protest the vicissitudes of life by smoking and, on occasion, drinking too much. Son and Ann are liberated from the past, but their lives are rooted in clichés different from but no more valid than those which guide Harriet. And Son, who claims, at least tacitly, to have outgrown the unjust attitudes of his childhood, toys with Ann's affection and exposes her to humiliation, which his sisters are glad to furnish out of boredom or malice or both.

Think of the roles the characters fill in terms of Taylor's statement of intentions in his preface to *A Stand in the Mountains.* Harriet is wrong and does suffer because she tries to fulfill herself in the position to which she was born. But Son, who has broken the old fetters, is worse; and between him and his parents the sisters sulk, alienated from their own tradition, but ignorant of any other direction their lives might follow. Ann is a southerner too, and because she has made an almost complete break with her heritage, she is the most unhappy character in the story. What she has tried to suppress in her life of the mind is the one quality that Harriet has in abundance, however misdirected: a capacity for love. Consequently, though by this I do not mean to imply simple cause-and-effect, her rejection of her role has been a part of her undoing.

What I have said so far makes Taylor's work appear to be formulaic, which is neither my intention nor the case. **"A Long Fourth"** achieves its force not only from the relationships of its individual characters but from the relationships of different groups of people. The initial conflict of the story is joined when Mattie, the black cook, claims the right to compare her affection for her nephew B. T. to Harriet's attachment to Son and to make them equal in their common destiny of having been drafted. Harriet's reprimand of Mattie over this point embarrasses the reader: clearly Harriet is not only insensitive but wrong. Yet the case is not as simple as Ann would make it when she suggests that Sweetheart help B. T. buy a farm. There is no evidence that B. T. wants a farm: he appears to be happy living in his cabin behind the Wilsons' house, getting drunk on Saturday night and bringing home dissolute women. Those most in need of reforming sometimes do not want to be reformed, and not everyone has ambition. In this story blacks and whites are locked together not so much in mutual dependence but—as we have seen in a thousand other southern stories and novels—in mutual doom.

The whole story is seen in the context of a war that would leave the world in spiritual and cultural disorder from which it has yet to recover. The point is not to assert that the old order was particularly good, but to ask whether what replaced it is necessarily better. To take such a cautionary view of life is salutary because it is accurate. I do not want to suggest that Peter Taylor's stories are reactionary or gloomy: they are neither. But fiction seeks to tell the truth, and one truth is that we move from one set of morally skewed and unjust conventions to another, and we seem to learn more from and to comprehend ourselves more fully in images of the past than of the present— which is to repeat a truism that applies to all of the best southern writing. Taylor is the youngest and chronologically the last of the writers of the southern renascence, born, like St. Paul, too late, but nonetheless allowed to see the old South's twilight, the crepuscular moment when the old social values stood balanced against the new, though on a scale reduced from that of Warren or Faulkner. Still his vision is complete and achieves, I think, its fullest fruition in *A Woman of Means* (1950).

In this novella, as in most of Taylor's other work, the past defines the present; but Gerald Dudley, a widower with a twelve-year-old son, does not typify Taylor's business and professional men. When the narrative begins, he is a salesman, afire with ambition; and, except for a few sentimental memories which he is willing to keep, he is eager to shed his country ways and forget his country background. He is humiliated when his date reprimands him for wearing brown shoes with his tuxedo, and although he permits Quint to spend summers on a Tennessee farm with his grandmother, he lays down rules governing what Quint should be allowed to do and see. He will not hear Mrs. Lovell's argument that it is good for children to be raised in the country. Yet what but an affection for his own rural past would prompt him to tell Quint to take off his shoes and walk in the wet grass "so you can remember what it feels like"?

Gerald becomes an executive in the hardware company for which he works, moves to St. Louis, and marries the woman of means; but because she is city-bred and cosmopolitan, a divorcée schooled in the ways of the world, he is never comfortable with her. He loves her, to be sure, and loves her daughters by her previous marriage; but he never understands them—never really trusts them. They are women and therefore mysterious; but, more than this, they have no knowledge of the social conventions that well-bred Memphis and Nashville girls would have been taught from the cradle. For all three women the sense of family, so important in the South, has been distorted: Ann has been made skittish and possessive by the failure of her first marriage. The girls are loyal to their own father as well as to their mother and stepfather, and because they are independently wealthy, they are ultimately beyond their mother's control. When Laura, home from school in the East, fails to treat Gerald with the courtesy he thinks is due him, relationships begin to disintegrate.

Laura's offense is about as small as it could be, a matter of manners exquisitely defined, but Gerald's southern sensibilities are offended; and when the girls return for Christmas, he refuses to attend their parties, claiming the urgency of business. Indeed his business is in trouble, and readers who find patterns of southern behavior incomprehensible can see in Gerald's impending dismissal as president of his company sufficient motivation for his coldness to the girls. Believe what you will about the ghosts of agrarian custom—they nevertheless haunt Gerald and drive his life and finally help to rob Ann of her sanity. In his stiff insistence that the family must live on his reduced pay, she discovers another kind of masculine betrayal.

They must, Gerald tells Ann, leave the grand house her father built for her and move into an apartment that he can afford. Quint will be withdrawn from St. Louis Country Day and enrolled in a public school. According to Gerald's code, for him and Quint to be supported by a woman is not proper. But what of Ann? For Gerald to return to the life he lived before he and Ann were married is one thing, but she has never known this life, which her past makes unsupportable. She cannot go with him, but she cannot endure the thought of losing him and Quint. She begins her plunge into incurable mental illness, the first and enduring symptom of which is that she claims falsely that she is pregnant. She fantasizes that she will have a boy to replace Quint.

Yet the situation is still more complicated. In this confrontation be-between tradition and modernity that drives Ann insane, no one is blameless. Early in the action Ann wonders aloud to Quint whether Gerald might have married her for her money. In a world where values are predominantly materialistic, such a question is bound to arise and to remain a shadowy presence. The code under which Gerald lives was developed, in part, to allay such suspicions. As cruel as Gerald's decision not to live on Ann's money seems, it must be balanced against Laura's concern with her own beauty and Bess's engagement to a band leader and the general indifference of the girls and their father—and to a certain extent Ann—toward the forms that in Gerald's view define civilized society.

The key to a proper reading of this story is Quint. He is the narrator, less an actor in the main thrust of the story than an innocent observer who comes to knowledge at the end. Captivated by the warmth of his new family, who in the beginning feel genuine affection for one another, he drifts away from the traditions that rule his father's life without realizing that he is changing. Or perhaps he is induced into a change of heart by the love and need of his stepmother. She says that she has always wanted a son, and she is not convinced that a son might not have saved her first marriage. Quint returns her love and at times shares her mystification at his father's behavior.

At the end, when Ann is to go to a sanitarium in Connecticut to be near the girls who are moving east, and the house is to be torn down and sold piecemeal, Quint's allegiance has been claimed by the modern dispensation. While his father and Bess discuss her planned marriage and blame each other for what has happened to Ann, Quint reads over and over the newspaper account of Lindbergh's successful flight across the Atlantic. In the future Quint will live once more in a boardinghouse with his father; perhaps he will visit his grandmother on the farm, but this will not touch him. From the start, it is now clear, Quint has belonged more than he realized to his stepmother and to the culture out of which she derived; but nevertheless he knows by the novel's end that the agrarian age has ended, and his eyes are on a future that will be increasingly technological.

A Summons to Memphis takes Taylor farther from his home base than he usually allows himself to travel. Philip Carver, his narrator, though originally from Nashville and Memphis, now lives in New York; and Philip's father, George, an octogenarian when the novel begins, is spiritually adrift because he was betrayed forty years earlier by his best friend, Lewis Shackleford. When Shackleford's firm, for which George Carver works, fails, Carver moves his family from Nashville to Memphis. His wife immediately takes to her bed and withdraws from society. Carver, with little apparent motive beyond his bitterness toward Shackleford, frustrates in succession the marriage plans of his two daughters and his son, causing the daughters to remain spinsters and the son to leave the South. Now a widower, George Carver intends to remarry, and Philip Carver is called to Memphis to help prevent the old man's wedding as he earlier prevented theirs.

Philip Carver is not a typical Taylor character. His translation to a job in publishing and a Manhattan flat shared with a Jewish woman from Cleveland seems to have dulled his personality. Making a reluctant passage home, he is uncertain until his plane lands whether he will help his sisters or his father. Since George is at the airport to meet

him, he decides he will "stand up" with George; but the intended bride has left Memphis, having been subverted by the sisters. The next family crisis and the next summons to Memphis come when George, having made up his differences with Lewis Shackleford, wants to pay him an extended visit. This time Philip sides with his sisters, but the sudden death of Shackleford renders any loyalty or action supererogatory.

A Summons to Memphis gives the impression of being at once old and unfinished, as if it were written in the early seventies—when the main action takes place—and resurrected now without revision. The book is loosely constructed, often repetitive; and one of the characters, Philip's brother who has died in World War II, is too little a human being, too much a symbol. An editor should have repaired these defects. Of more importance are the uncertainty of George's motives and Philip's fecklessness. Compared to Son in **"A Long Fourth,"** another southern expatriate, Philip seems flat; but Son and Philip exist in different worlds. In 1939 the agrarian South was doomed, but it lived in the manners and affections of Sweetheart and other business and professional men of Memphis and Nashville. It was shared by their wives and children. By the seventies the last survivors of the old dispensation are dead or too old to continue the struggle, and southern custom endures only in such private confrontations as those Taylor delineates here.

Yet the novel embodies a public dimension in an irony that Taylor has not exploited previously. The lives of all the Carvers are distorted by the failure of Lewis Shackleford's business, but it was his success, and the success of others like him, that eradicated the influence of southern agrarianism. Shackleford's character is based on Rogers Caldwell, and Taylor follows his prototype faithfully. In 1917 Caldwell founded the first investment banking firm in the South. When his financial empire collapsed in 1930, he barely escaped prison. But, like Lewis Shackleford, by the end of his life Caldwell was considered a financial genius; and invitations to his Saturday luncheons were prized by Nashville businessmen. His ambition became the common ambition, as the agrarian twilight faded into darkness. What is left by the seventies is remnants—manners privately practiced, standards privately held.

In *A Summons to Memphis* the demise of southern society is seen in the flamboyant dress and suggestive conversation of the aging Carver sisters, in George's dates with young women and his visits to discos, in Philip's alienation from home and tradition. He and his girlfriend from Cleveland see their parents as part of the graying of America, the geriatric crisis that concerns us all. And when Philip's boyhood friend suggests that he give his collection of rare books to a Memphis university, he can only laugh. For him there is no more Memphis, no more family, no more South. Thus the story Peter Taylor has been telling all his writing life reaches its proper end.

Like any other writer Peter Taylor has his weaknesses. Much of his work is written in the first person, and he does not always resist the temptation to self-indulgence that this point of view presents. **"The Old Forest,"** successful though it is, is too long: the narrator is allowed to express too many opinions, to go on at too great length about the social situation out of which the story develops. He is tedious at times. In other stories—I think of **"Porte Cochère"** and **"Promise of Rain"**—characters seem directed more by moods and inherent disposition than by motivation. The social conventions that inform most of his fiction are of scant use to him in the wartime setting of **"Promise of Rain,"** and they become too rarefied to support significant action in **"Porte Cochère."**

Peter Taylor's canvas is small—not because his usual form is the short story but because he lacks the range of, for instance, V. S. Pritchett, who can spin tales about undertakers or antique dealers or lords of the manor with equal authority and grace. But as Taylor has often said, a writer is as good as his best work; and the Peter Taylor of *A Woman of Means* and many of his stories is very good indeed. (pp. 309-17)

> *Walter Sullivan, "The Last Agrarian: Peter Taylor Early and Late," in* The Sewanee Review, *Vol. XCV, No. 2, Spring, 1987, pp. 308-17.*

David Robinson

[In the following excerpt, Robinson interprets "Venus, Cupid, Folly, and Time" as an analysis of southern values and culture.]

If Taylor's reputation grows beyond that of an accomplished regionalist . . . it will not be because he abandoned that sense of place fundamental to all fiction. "One place comprehended can make us understand other places better," Eudora Welty wrote. "Exactness," "concreteness," and "solidity . . . achieved in a story correspond to the intensity of feeling in the author's mind and to the very turn of his heart; but there lies the secret of our confidence in him." Taylor's delineations of Tennessee manners and mores do give the reader such confidence, but his achievement is marked less by the realized portrait of a culture than by the dramatizations of that culture understanding itself. Both the experience and the reflected consciousness of the experience count heavily in the best of Taylor's stories.

One of Taylor's most precise social dissections, and one of his most enthralling psychological analyses, is **"Venus, Cupid, Folly and Time,"** from his 1969 *Collected Stories.* The accumulating suspense of this story is sustained by the gradual stripping away of the layers of social form to reveal its psychological underpinnings; the resonance of this story lies in the way that Taylor persuades us of the interconnections of the social world and the psychological. The recounting of the story of Louisa and Alfred Dorset's last party in **"Venus, Cupid, Folly and Time"** charts the moment at which a personal, psychic crisis and a crisis of the social order coalesce, typifying Taylor's fundamental strength, the weaving of psychological portraiture and precise social analysis into a narrative of submerged tension and building suspense. The heart of his enterprise is to dissect those moments, rare and difficult to discern, in which an eruption in the ground of a tightly ordered society can be linked to a psychic fault. In Chatham, Tennessee, the social order has found a curious manifestation in the parties that the Dorsets, an aging and unmarried brother and sister, give annually for the select youth of the town. The most unlikely "social arbiters," the Dorsets are held in mild disgust by the social powers of the town, that is, the women of Chatham. Yet the Dorsets' role as electors of the town's "best" youth is never questioned until the night the Meriwether children find themselves among the elect, and set in motion the Dorsets' downfall.

The personal oddities of the Dorsets are striking, especially to their conservative neighbors in the West Vesey Place neighborhood. They are seen at various times in Chatham stores with "the cuff of a pajama top or the hem of a hitched-up nightgown showing from underneath their ordinary daytime clothes." That Alfred Dorset wore his sweater "stuffed down inside his trousers with his shirt tails," that he washed his car in "a pair of skin-tight coveralls . . . faded almost to flesh color," that his sister came outside "clad in a faded flannel bathrobe," are all grounds for a certain revulsion which the Dorsets generate in their neighbors, particularly the women. "There was, in fact," the narrator tells us, "nothing about Mr. Dorset that was not offensive to the women." Actually the Dorsets are mirrors in which the community focuses what is essentially its own self-revulsion against the repressed sexuality that is the foundation of its ordered life. At one point Tom Bascomb, who later plays a more central role in the Dorsets' social downfall than any woman in the community, reported seeing Miss Louisa "pushing a carpet sweeper about one of the downstairs rooms without a stitch of clothes on." Tom's description of how she "dropped down in any easy chair and crossed her spindly, blue-veined, old legs and sat there completely naked" epitomizes the fascinated disgust with which Chatham observes the Dorsets, finding in them a convenient objectification of what the people of Chatham cannot entirely suppress in their own sexual and psychological unconscious.

In their own version of themselves, the Dorsets are sexless beings. As bachelor and spinster, they "have given up everything for each other." But are they sexless? Although the story offers no confirmation of an incestuous relationship, the unarticulated suspicion of incest hovers over the Dorsets, and is enough to account for the curious identification of the Dorsets with offensive sexuality. Nonetheless, the Dorsets have maintained an odd connection with the youth, and therefore the social heart, of Chatham. Their annual party for adolescents functions as something of an imprimatur of caste.

> For a Chatham girl to have to explain, a few years later, why she never went to a party at the Dorsets' was like having to explain why she had never been a debutante. For a boy it was like having to explain why he had not gone up East to school or even why his father hadn't belonged to the Chatham Racquet Club.

The Dorsets have thus been capable of transforming their social ostracism into a capacity for social dictation. They display the sense of possessing a natural social superiority, of belonging to an aristocracy that not only elevates them above ordinary residents of Chatham, but allows them to recognize and receive initiates into their class. "Why, *we* know nice children when we see them," Miss Louisa says as her final party is broken up, in a protest which attempts to preserve the illusion under which she and her brother have lived. Superficially they are asexual, having renounced both world and flesh to preserve the purity of their devotion to an ideal of innocence. Yet behind the Dorsets' superficial innocence lurks an obsession with sexuality (the extent of conscious subterfuge on their part remaining debatable) which manifests itself unmistakably at their annual parties. Despite their general acceptance as social arbiters, and their nostalgia for the preadolescent past, it is the fascinating whiff of decadence which accounts for the Dorsets' hold over their young guests. The parties live as much in Chatham legend as anywhere else. "Before our turn to go ever came round, we had for years been hearing what it was like from older boys and girls. Afterward, we continued to hear about it from those who followed us." The Dorsets themselves are the fuel for much of this legend, for they cast their dowdiness dramatically aside this one evening. When Miss Louisa greets the guests, it is "her astonishing attire" that is "the most violent shock of the whole evening." A gown, new every year, "perfectly fitted to her spare and scrawny figure," long, newly-dyed hair, dark rouge, suntan powder—these comprise her transformation, making her not merely a sexual, but a threateningly sexual, figure. Mr. Alfred, "in a nattily tailored tuxedo," and unusually well-groomed for the evening, almost matches his sister's transformation. The parents who send their children, and "never pretended to understand what went on at the Dorsets' house," could sense the air of the sexually forbidding which imbued the parties. These parties "are not very nice affairs to be sending your children to," says Ned and Emily's father as the children prepare to leave. He is met by his wife's "but we *can't* keep them away." Tacitly conceding his wife's sense of the social necessities, he replies, "it's just that they are growing up faster than we realize."

There is nothing overtly wrong with the parties, which combine "light refreshments (fruit Jello, English tea biscuits, lime punch)," and a tour of the house. More particularly, the guests listen to a version of the Dorsets' life story, and see a series of curious decorations arranged to accentuate certain works of art. Yet the fascination of their parties is that they function as metaphors for the end of sexual innocence, holding an innocent vehicle and a corrupt tenor in uneasy but imaginatively fertile suspension. Despite the sexual ambience of the parties, the Dorsets are in fact trying to project an image of youthful innocence to their guests. While the party is laden with sexual symbolism, it is also textured so that the Dorsets can display before this captive audience their own version of their innocent sacrifice. This enactment of self-justification is of primary importance to them. Their protestation of innocence takes the form "of an almost continuous dialogue" in which they explain their reaction in their teens to the death of their parents. Forced to struggle against "wicked in-laws" who wanted to sell their house, and "marry them off to 'just anyone,'" they were eventually disinherited by their grandparents, and further threatened by "a procession of 'young nobodies'" hoping to steal one of the two in marriage. The Dorsets dealt with the trauma of their loss by retreating into mutual self-possession, finding their

relation as siblings, and their family home, a haven from threatening change. They have attempted to freeze their emotions at preadolescence, and the parties bring before them fresh images of the innocent youths they have tried to remain. "Ah, the happy time," they say to the young guests, "was when we were *your* age!" For them, the party is a pantomime of return, a vicarious recovery of both their youth and their social place.

But at the parties the Dorsets also create an environment, notably through the art works in their house, in which sexuality looms as a beckoning, threatening force. "A strange perfume pervaded the atmosphere of the house," which contributed to the impact of a series of visual displays in which masses of paper flowers conceal partially illuminated replicas of works of art. Three are mentioned in the story—Rodin's "The Kiss," "an antique plaque of Leda and the Swan," and "a tiny color print of Bronzino's 'Venus, Cupid, Folly and Time.'" Each has a sexual subject matter, and their method of display, partially concealed, yet illuminated with odd and compelling shafts of light, seems consonant with the ambiguous sexual identity of the Dorsets. The displays seem to function as traps set to capture the maturing sexual curiosity of the young guests. The children, warned beforehand about the works of art by previous guests, "stood in painful dread of that moment when Miss Dorset or her brother might catch us staring at any one of their pictures or sculptures." The children are at least mature enough to understand that they should attempt to maintain a facade of innocence in the face of this seeming corruption. "We had been warned, time and again, that . . . she or he would reach out and touch the other's elbow and indicate, with a nod or just the trace of a smile, some guest whose glance had strayed among the flowers." The children wander through this maze of sexual signals, compelled on the one hand by their fascination with the Dorsets, but equally repelled by what appear to be their attempts to implicate them in a suspected corruption.

The central symbol of the party ritual, and the evening's high point, is the dance Alfred and Louisa perform. They dance in a dimly lit room with "grace" and "perfect harmony in all their movements." After the dance we see Mr. Dorset "with his bow tie hanging limply on his damp shirtfront," hair askew, and "streaked with perspiration." This pantomimed sexual intercourse, the most direct suggestion of incest in the party, is followed by the most desperate plea of innocence. It is then that the Dorsets call the age of their guests "the happy time" and urge them to enjoy their freedom.

> With many a wink and blush and giggle and shake of the forefinger—and of course standing before the whole party—they each would remind the other of his or her naughty behavior in some old-fashioned parlor game or of certain silly flirtations which they had long ago caught each other in.

The Dorsets feel they have conquered the "naughtiness" that sexual maturity represents by insulating themselves from the adult world through their sibling relationship. They repress their sexual identities only partially, however, and their attempt to freeze themselves at preadolescence causes the lingering suspicion of incest even while they attempt to parade their innocence. Despite this ironic result, it seems reasonable to conclude that however emotionally crippled, the Dorsets are not incestuous. Although the effect is the reverse of what they intend, the whole point of their parties seems to be to provide them with a forum from which to protest their innocence, an innocence which they equate with presexuality. Even the suggestive pictures, which seem to be the means by which the corrupt attempt to entrap the innocent, are better understood as the Dorsets' attempt to assure themselves of their own purity. If they can prove to themselves that even these young people have a sexual consciousness and curiosity, then their own incompletely repressed sexual natures seem somehow validated. The pictures and the children's reaction to them are further assurance which the Dorsets need of the legitimacy of their own condition.

As a portrait of the workings of social pressures and social selections in a small Tennessee city, and of the curious psychology underpinning them, **"Venus, Cupid, Folly and Time"** firmly achieves the regionalist's objective. Without slighting this achievement, I would argue that the story only begins with this grounding. Through its parallel focus on the adolescents who finally disturb the Dorsets' drama, it also becomes a work with the critical force and artistic sympathy which marks fiction of major stature. The story's narrator, drawn from the same class and sharing much the same experience as the Meriwethers themselves, cannot treat them with the same interested but distanced objectivity with which he handles the Dorsets. As a result, the reader is drawn into their situation with an engagement surpassing the curiosity which the Dorsets generate.

The children plan a prank through which the Dorsets' social pretensions will be mocked. They bring Tom Bascomb to the party posing as Ned, with Ned himself later joining the group unbeknownst to the Dorsets. The harmlessness of the gesture is belied only by the fact that the Dorsets take pride in inviting only the "best" children to their party, fortifying their sense of self-worth by an imagined capacity to know such superior individuals intuitively. And, by common assent, Tom Bascomb is not such an individual. It is here that the socio-economic basis for the Dorsets' social arbitration becomes clearest. Tom has the paper route for the prestigious West Vesey Place neighborhood, and his family lives "in an apartment house on a wide thoroughfare known as Division Boulevard." As the narrator explains, "all of us in West Vesey had our Tom Bascombs." Each of the privileged children, that is, maintained some contact with an outsider, some friend from a lower economic class by whom they could both measure their own elevation and simultaneously feel a sense of connection to the larger world beyond their neighborhood. Tom's being anointed as one of the chosen would forever put the lie to the Dorsets' claims to be natural social arbiters. The difficulty with the Meriwether childrens' plan is that Tom plays his assigned role too well. He pushes the plan into forbidden ground, shaking the delicate psychological balance of the Dorsets—and of Ned and Emily. If his job is to shatter illusions, he does it with a relish, and while his work of destruction centers on the

Dorsets, it also pulls Ned and Emily in as well. Their own innocence is the unintended victim of the trick they have conceived.

While the prank is an important gesture of freedom for Ned and Emily, for Tom it is an opportunity to mock a group from which he has been excluded. But freedom has been the compensation for his exclusion, a freedom which Ned and Emily covet. The question as Taylor presents it here is not only who belongs and who does not, but the psychological cost of belonging—or of breaking free. So when Ned and Emily freeze at the sound of Mr. Dorset at the doorbell, Tom "looked at Emily's flushed face and saw her batting her eyes like a nervous monkey." A "crooked smile played upon his lips." Tom's Hawthornean smile signals his capacity to be a predator on innocence—both the false or unnatural innocence of the Dorsets and the real innocence of Ned and Emily. Taylor thus interweaves a narrative of initiation into his analysis of the social structure of Chatham. We first glimpse this in Emily's reaction as she walks with Tom to Mr. Dorset's car.

> And with her every step toward the car the skirt of her long taffeta gown whispered her own name to her: *Emily . . .Emily.* She heard it distinctly, and yet the name sounded unfamiliar. Once during this unreal walk from house to car she glanced at the mysterious boy, Tom Bascomb, longing to ask him—if only with her eyes—for some reassurance that she was really she.

The causes of Emily's crisis of identity and the motivation for Tom's crooked smile are related, as the reader fully understands later when the children's plan is enacted. "The moment Miss Louisa Dorset's back was turned Tom Bascomb slipped his arm gently about Emily's little waist and began kissing her all over her pretty face. It was almost as if he were kissing away tears." Those tears signify Emily's grief as she crosses a threshold into adulthood. This final part of the plan had been conceived as a trick to suggest mockingly the Dorsets' suspected incest. In it, Emily enacts a role which has in part freed her from the restraints she would ordinarily have had. Through playing this part she is freed, but frighteningly so, from the innocent self of her youth.

In the odd triangle which emerges at the Dorset's party, Ned is also deeply affected. Although he had helped to plan the trick, even Tom's kissing Emily, he "found himself not quite able to join in the fun." After "an explosion of giggles filled the room," we are told, Ned "would look up just in time to see Tom Bascomb's cheek against Emily's or his arm about her waist." Ned's increasing discomfort arises from his seeing Tom as himself. There has been a symbolic exchange of identities. The suggestion of incest which was meant to shock the Dorsets backfires, reminding Ned of his own sexual subconscious. After each burst of laughter, Ned looks at the Dorsets, who exchange "half suppressed smiles" which last "precisely as long as the giggling continued." But their expressions become "solemn" when they see him. Ned represents the other to them, a threatening outsider who does not conform to the order of the social world as they conceive it. But in his growing uneasiness with Tom and Emily's sexual displays, he comes to be an accusing reminder of an identity that the Dorsets have tried unsuccessfully to suppress. The prank has forced Ned into an acknowledgment of his own sexual identity, and his sudden recognition of his and his sister's sexuality casts a shadow over their relationship. This sexual awareness will inevitably color their relationship. That is the chief tragedy of the story, but its prelude is the tragedy of the Dorsets, who are forced by Ned to confront their own sexual identities.

Tom and Emily extend their mockery of the Dorsets by squeezing themselves "into a little niche . . . in front of the Rodin statuary," where Tom kisses her "lightly first on the lobe of one ear and then on the tip of her nose." Emily remains "rigid and pale as the plaster sculpture behind her and with just the faintest smile on her lips." Ned sees this, and also sees the Dorsets seeing it: "gazing quite openly at Tom and Emily and frankly grinning at the spectacle." The surface grin of the Dorsets signifies the surface innocence that their self-conception as children has produced. But they look at the scene as if into a mirror, only subconsciously recognizing themselves there. Their grin also signifies their submerged recognition of desires they have had to suppress in order to maintain their innocent sibling relationship. They see in Tom and Emily's pose an act of potential self-expression that is fascinating but inadmissible.

For Ned, whose sexual awareness has been made acute by the pantomime that he has helped to create, the Dorsets are a distorted model or self-image which he must reject for his own survival. The Dorsets are thus a dark self-image for Ned, and he is painfully unable to suppress that identity. His self-confrontation takes the form of confronting them: " 'Don't you *know*?' he wailed, as if in great physical pain. 'Can't you *tell*? Can't you see who they *are*? They're *brother* and *sister*!' " Ned's outburst is of course not a part of the original plan. It turns mockery and subtle satire into open confrontation. He is met first with stunned silence, while the Dorsets "continued to wear their grins like masks," making it impossible to "tell how they were taking it all." But the masks fall, and we realize that Ned's outbreak, whatever cost it had for him, is also searing for the Dorsets. "Miss Louisa's face, still wearing the grin, began turning all the queer colors of her paper flowers. Then the grin vanished from her lips and her mouth fell open and every bit of color went out of her face." This shock becomes rage as the Dorsets turn on Ned: "What we know is that you are not one of us. . . . What are you doing here among these nice children?"

The phrase "nice children" punctuates this moment of emotional crisis with wry humor, but in the terms of the symbolic identities which have developed in the evening, the question is pertinent. When the Dorsets go on to ask "Who is he, children?" Ned confirms their sense that he is an "intruder." "Who *am* I? Why, I am Tom Bascomb . . . I am Tom Bascomb, your paper boy!" This is, of course, in line with the plan of the evening, but it has a deeper significance for Ned, because it signifies the turn in his relationship with Emily. If he has seen a dim reflection of himself in watching Tom kiss Emily during the

party, he now breaks from that self. "To the real Tom Bascomb," the narrator tells us, "it had seemed that Ned honestly believed what he had been saying."

Ned does flee from the party, but in an interesting twist to the story's action, he flees *up* the stairs into the second story of the Dorsets' house. The entire house is densely symbolic territory, and to penetrate the second story is to enter further than anyone ever has into the Dorsets' psychological secrets. Mr. Dorset pursues Ned up the stairs, and finally corners him and locks him in a room. Through all this chaos, which is fundamentally serious but punctuated with a certain humor (we are given a glimpse of Miss Dorset trying to serve lime punch while she waits for a policeman to come drag away her presumed paperboy), Emily remains mysteriously passive. She "was still standing in the little niche among the flowers" seemingly "oblivious to all that was going on while she stood there." Tom's report that "her mind didn't seem to be on any of the present excitement" does not trivialize those events, but rather underlines the profound impact of the entire encounter. Emily, like Ned, has been rushed into a maturity for which she was not perhaps prepared. Tom's reaction is the more dramatic, but Emily's abstracted withdrawal bespeaks as profound a change.

The story is one of lost illusions, and the Dorsets are the first victims. They have taken Tom to be the "nice" boy, and Ned to be the intruder, and when Ned's parents arrive, they are forced to recognize their mistake. Emily tells her father that Ned is locked upstairs, but Miss Louisa insists that the boy upstairs is an intruder. "*We* know nice children when we see them," she insists. This insistence becomes a plea as Miss Louisa begins to realize the implications of her mistake. " 'We knew from the beginning that that boy upstairs didn't belong amongst us,' she said. 'Dear neighbors, it isn't just the money, you know, that makes the difference.' " This article of faith is echoed by her brother: "People *are* different. It isn't something you can put your finger on, but it isn't the money." But as they find, it is the money, or the presumption of money, that has guided their choice of "nice" children. That false sense of an ability to make social discriminations on some vague basis of personal superiority is exposed in their mistaking Tom for Ned. When Mr. Meriwether finally finds Ned upstairs and confirms the Dorsets' mistake, the party ends, and with it the Dorsets' position as social arbiters. They are broken, retreating into an almost complete isolation from their neighbors.

The narrator's final attention, however, is devoted to Ned and Emily, the real protagonists of the story. Their tragedy, not that of the Dorsets, reverberates as the story ends. The narrator reports that "nowadays" (well over two decades since the events of the party) "Emily and Ned are pretty indifferent to each other's existence." That indifference seems to have arisen the night of the party, at least according to Ned's wife, who has heard the story repeatedly, and has developed a horrified fascination for Chatham as it once was. That older Chatham is inseparable from the Dorsets. As she understands, the party "marked the end of their childhood intimacy and the beginning of a shyness, a reserve, even an animosity between them." If freed from the social structure represented and enforced by the Dorsets' parties, Ned and Emily have paid a price for that freedom. The prolonged, artificial, and ultimately corrupt innocence of the Dorsets paralleled Ned and Emily's own presexual innocence. The shattering of the Dorset's self-conception similarly paralleled their own sudden confrontation with sexual maturity. By feigning to be the Dorsets' secret selves, Ned and Emily unnaturally forced a buried self of their own into momentary consciousness. The reaction to that self cost them their sibling relationship. The resonance of loss in the story is theirs.

But as we listen to the narrator's final ruminations, one other loss impresses us. In fact, the narrator seems more profoundly melancholic over this loss than over the fate of the Dorsets or even the Meriwethers. It is the loss of Chatham, the fading of the community as it once was. It is really only in the final pages of the story that the narrator ceases to be a quasi-authorial voice, and emerges as a character from whom the readers must establish some distance. The status of these parties as part of the communal consciousness of Chatham has allowed the narrator to assume a near omniscient point-of-view, relying on the texture of legend, tradition, and gossip which is the town's shared knowledge. But as the narrative continues, his personal stake in the social structure of Chatham becomes clearer. It is at least arguable that for him, the parallel tragedies of the Dorsets and the Meriwethers have been the scaffolding for the social tragedy of Chatham itself. This is not a case of mere nostalgia; the narrator has not lost his sense of estrangement from the social ritual which the story has so thoroughly exposed. But there is in his tone the bitterness of a man unable to let go even of something he finds stifling and threatening. To find loss in freedom, to cling even to that which you know to be destructive—this is the tragedy not only of the narrator but of the South.

This final sense of loss can be discerned when the narrator tells of his attempt to explain Chatham to Ned's wife, an outsider. While her interest extends only to the Dorsets, he insists that Chatham's story extends back to the Revolutionary War, when Chatham was "one of the first English-speaking settlements west of the Alleghenies." It was out of this context of migration and rootlessness that Chatham's social hierarchy developed. Families who had stopped "for a generation or two to put down roots in Pennsylvania or Virginia or Massachusetts" felt that this was an important distinction, and tried to enforce it on the social world of Chatham. But what appears to be the narrator's explanation, however flimsy, for social hierarchy, does not apply to Alfred and Louisa Dorset's ancestors. "They were an obscure mercantile family [from the English midlands] who came to invest in a new Western city." The distinction between investing and putting down roots is crucial; the Dorsets were wholly mercenary—and wholly rootless—leaving Chatham as soon as they had made their fortune there. But it was their mercenary success which made their social place. Having become "rich beyond any dreams" within two generations in Chatham, their lineage was irrelevant. "For half a century they were looked upon, if any family ever was, as our first family." These facts amplify the significance of Louisa Dorset's last

plea: "Dear neighbors, it isn't just the money, you know, that makes the difference." Alfred and Louisa Dorset, abandoned when the rest of their family left Chatham, are abandoned with the social distinctions which money has made, but without the money itself.

This historical background demonstrates the fundamental emptiness of the superficially dense social world that the narrator has known. He makes Ned's wife hear the whole story out of his own need to purge himself through truth. He knows the emptiness of Chatham social discriminations: "If the distinction was false, it mattered all the more and it was all the more necessary to make it." And he knows even more deeply that this emptiness casts a shadow over his own life. The Dorsets, all except Alfred and Louisa, had left Chatham, proving their final lack of social connectedness. But the Dorsets' leaving, ironically, had cast the same estranging light on those who stayed, pretending, with Alfred and Louisa, that "it isn't just the money." The narrator admits that "despite our families of Massachusetts and Virginia, we were all more like the Dorsets—those Dorsets who left Chatham—than we were *un*like them." These structures of social exclusiveness are nothing more than expedients to power, without the authority that a genuine communal bond might give. As expedients to power, they are poor substitutes for the raw wealth of the Dorsets. The Dorsets' (the ones who left Chatham) "spirit was just a little closer to being the very essence of Chatham than ours was," the narrator says. The most revealing admission follows: "The obvious difference was that we had to stay on here and pretend that our life had a meaning which it did not."

Only here do we fully understand that in their extraordinary strangeness, Alfred and Louisa Dorset mirrored not only Ned and Emily, but all their neighbors in West Vesey Place. Even as we can surmise that Ned and Emily recognized something of themselves in the Dorsets, so we can understand that the whole social group of which they were a part also dimly saw themselves in the Dorsets. They paid them homage and made them social arbiters because in so doing they tacitly honored themselves. It took only one outsider, Tom Bascomb, to bring down this house of cards. The narrator is one, and presumably one of many, who still feel the aftershocks of the collapse.

Taylor has structured **"Venus, Cupid, Folly and Time"** so that the social tragedy as personally experienced by the narrator frames the underlying pathos of the Dorsets and of the Meriwether children. The narrator's portrayal of a class of people, in which he surely includes himself, who pretend that "life had a meaning which it did not," grounds his story in a deeply personal base, even as Taylor is engaged in a penetrating social analysis. In leaving Chatham the Dorsets are catalysts of a wholly typical kind: "They were city people, and they were Americans. They knew that what they had in Chatham they could buy more of in other places. For them Chatham was an investment that had paid off." One need not listen to this voice too closely to discern the bitterness in it—not a bitterness that can be focused into a specific anger, but a bitterness that ultimately turns inward, to silence. As surely as Alfred and Louisa Dorset were abandoned, so was the narrator, and so by implication was the whole class of which he was a part. This portrayal of the demise of a class does indeed establish the regional credentials of the story, and of its author. But it is one credential among others, one of several extended radii of significance, whose ultimate subject, in the words of our greatest regionalist, is the problem "of the human heart in conflict with itself." (pp. 282-94)

David Robinson, "Tennessee, Taylor, the Critics, and Time," in The Southern Review, *Louisiana State University, Vol. 23, No. 2, April, 1987, pp. 281-94.*

Lamar York

[*In the following essay, York analyzes the relationship between the old and the young in Taylor's "Promise of Rain," "The Scoutmaster," "The Gift of the Prodigal," and "In the Miro District."*]

Peter Taylor's stories are leisurely to read because they are about simply being a family, rather than about some of the more exceptional things that families do. Yet they have a dramatic intensity, and it seems to come mainly from the retelling of a single moment, or event, in a family's life. Among the most interesting of these moments is one that might be called an initiation scene, or recognition by a parent that a child is about to leave the family for a life beyond it.

Yet these are not stories about coming of age in the usual sense, in which an adolescent first becomes aware of himself as an adult, usually physically and, specifically, sexually. Peter Taylor's characters, even the young ones, are too sophisticated to be revealed at the moment of their sexual awakening. The reader senses that these young people have been awake to the world for some time. Moreover, they have been far too well brought up to discuss aspects of the rites of passage at the dinner table, which is where they are often seen in these stories. There is nevertheless a recognizably distinct group of stories which, though not initiation stories in the usual sense, are about the moment in a family's life when a young member takes on a new role, and one that usually is to be outside the family.

What is most distinct about these stories is that Taylor does not describe the effects of the leave-taking on the young initiate, but rather the reaction of a parent, usually the father. It might, in fact, be said that the father-son relationship at the moment of the leave-taking is among the most intense relationships described in Taylor's stories.

The main stories in which the father-son relationship is the focal point of the narration include **"The Gift of the Prodigal," "Promise of Rain," "The Scoutmaster," "The Captain's Son,"** and **"In the Miro District."** These are initiation stories in that they tell about the new directions young men take in life, but the most absorbing change in characterization in these is apt to happen to the father rather than to the son. Because Taylor's concern is the family's character, it is not the activities of the boys that matter so much as it is the impact that boys' decisions

have on their families. Taylor's men are often more interested in their role as father to a boy undergoing the rites of passage than they are in their role as husband in the rites of married life. Their lives as husbands are stable and predictable, but their lives as fathers are volatile, which gives these stories their vitality.

The Thornton and Chatham of Taylor's stories are not a country of the young but of the established. Yet without the evolving lives of their children, these characters would be more or less static. Within the father-son relationship the father seems always to be involved in trying to explain himself, his actions, or some adult way of looking at family matters, to his son. But the change brought about by a son's initiation into the wider concerns of his place in the world is shown by the only one who can—a parent. The child doesn't necessarily realize any change, much less judge the significance of internal family affairs. But the father knows he is himself changed by these encounters.

In terms of the age of the son, the most nearly literal initiation story is **"Promise of Rain."** Mr. Perkins remembers gently reprimanding Hugh Robert for wearing his knickers unbuckled and asking him why all the kids at school wear them that way. The others do so to feel important, Hugh tells his father, but " 'I didn't get any kick out of it. I don't blame them too much, though. Those guys don't have much to make them feel important.' " Even in this most traditional of Taylor's initiation stories it is still the father who is shown to be the one who changes, pained as he is over these expressions of his son's rites of initiation. "I had to bite my tongue," he says, "to keep from asking the boy what he had to make him feel important. But I let it go at that, because I saw what he was getting at. I realized I was supposed to feel pretty cheap for having criticized the people he went to school with." With times slow at the family business, only his growing son keeps Mr. Perkins from becoming static. This father owns a finance company, and the health of his business depends on the health of the city's economy generally. "It did something for me," he says, "to get out and look at the town, to see how it had stopped building and growing. The feeling I got from it was that Time itself had stopped and was actually waiting for me instead of passing me by and leaving me behind just when I was in my prime."

But prime, for Peter Taylor's fathers, comes at the discretion, or lack of it, of their sons. And though the sons are unaware of how their fathers are to be changed by a son's actions, fathers, as Mr. Perkins acknowledges, know that change is in store for them, and they try, usually futilely, to prepare for it: "during high school, when we mentioned college to him, he only laughed at the idea. . . . it made me realize how soon he might be gone from us to wherever he had in mind going."

It is seldom important in these stories to know what happens to anyone outside the moments he spends with his family. Hugh Robert Perkins, who becomes a theatrical director in New York, is among the few about whose later lives any clues are offered. But the events that lead up to a son's going away are important, especially to the father. These events hinge upon a "promise of rain," rain that will prevent the radio broadcast of a baseball game and offer as a substitute a recording which Hugh Robert has made at school under the direction of his drama teacher. The broadcast of the recording will be a pivotal event in Hugh's life, but his father is slow to recognize how important it is to him: "I found I was pitting my hopes against his," he confesses. "I was, at least, until I saw how awfully worked up the boy was. Then I tried my best to hope with him. But I don't think I ever before had such mixed feelings about so small a thing as whether or not a ball game would be rained out."

The baseball game is rained out, but the bad weather produces such static on the radio that it almost drowns out the recording. Though the father is now attuned to the inner life of his son, he still misreads the boy: "Poor boy had endured his uncertainty, had for days been pinning his hopes on the chance of rain, and now had to hear himself drowned out by the static on our old radio. I thought it might be more than flesh and blood could bear. I thought that at any moment he might spring up and begin kicking that radio to bits." But only now can this father begin to see how incorrectly he has read his son's emotions. Hugh's back has been to the family as he looked directly at the radio, but when the reading is over, he turns to the family: ". . . Hugh was on his feet and facing us with a broad grin of satisfaction. I saw at once that for him there had been no static. . . . And I felt as strongly then as I feel it now that that was the real moment of Hugh's departure from our midst." Hugh bounds out of the house to join his friends, and though his father learns that "he wasn't really going to leave us for some time yet," he also learns something of how his son will take his leave: ". . . I knew it wouldn't be a matter of a letter on the breakfast table when he did go, because it couldn't any longer be a matter of a boy running away from home." Then this father imaginatively joins his son on the journey that the boy is about to undertake: "I felt certain that this afternoon he had seen his way ahead clear, and I imagined that I could see it with him."

Finally, after Mr. Perkins assesses the events of the afternoon, he records the epiphany that Peter Taylor's fathers experience in the initiation rites their sons undergo:

> I had a strange experience that afternoon. I was fifty, but suddenly I felt very young again. As I wandered through the house I kept thinking of how everything must look to Hugh, of what his life was going to be like, and of just what he would be like when he got to be my age. It all seemed very clear to me, and I understood how right it was for him. And because it seemed so clear I realized the time had come when I could forgive my son the difference there had always been between our two natures. I was fifty, but I had just discovered what it means to see the world through another man's eyes. It is a discovery you are lucky to make at any age, and one that is no less marvelous whether you make it at fifty or fifteen. Because it is only then that the world, as you have seen it through your own eyes, will begin to tell you things about yourself.

"The Scoutmaster" offers several variations on Taylor's unusual approach to the initiation theme. The narrator is a boy, the youngest member of the family, but it is not his or his brother's rite of passage their father endures, but their older sister's, Virginia Ann. Moreover, the parental reaction is not just that of the parents, but of two other adults, surrogate parents, Uncle Jake, their father's brother, and Aunt Grace, their mother's sister. At the very beginning of the story the narrator remembers their father, like most fathers, being critical of his daughter's use of faddish slang: ". . . he would say that he could not bear to hear her using [a certain faddish] expression, though he said he didn't know why he could not. 'I can't abide it,' he would say. 'That's all there is to it.' " The boy also remembers Uncle Jake coming at once to her defense, "asking Father very gently why he was so 'hard on' Virginia Ann and asking if he didn't know that all 'modern girls' were like that."

Yet the question of which adult's view of this daughter's growing up the story will present is not settled. To Father, his brother Jake, who "had had a motherless daughter to raise and to nurse through a fatal illness at the age of nineteen," would be "old-fashioned . . . because just raising a child did that for one," yet Uncle Jake is the one who can see that "customs change. Everything changes." Even in Aunt Grace, who left them after six weeks to go to her new job in Birmingham, the young narrator sees a parental role: "She was not the utterly useless if wonderfully ornamental member of the family. . . . I was surely on the verge of finding some marvelous function for her personality. (I would have said my mother's function was Motherhood, and my father's, Fatherhood.) I was about to find the reason why there should be one member of a boy's family who was wise or old-fashioned enough to sit with Mother and Father and discuss the things they could not abide in Virginia Ann and yet who was foolish or newfangled enough to enjoy the very things that Virginia Ann called 'the last word;' " his speculations, however, are interrupted when the taxi in which he and his brother are accompanying Aunt Grace to the train station arrives at the station.

But it is finally Uncle Jake who best exemplifies the parental surrogate's role. He challenges the children's father just by his looks. While their father is Taylor's characteristically domestic man, "who had no real life but in his office and in our house," Uncle Jake "had lived outdoors so much with his hunting and fishing and his other activities with the Boy Scouts that his skin was considerably rougher than Father's." The narrator remembers Uncle Jake's large hands and "how much softer to the touch they were than one could imagine from their rough appearance." Jake praises the children's parents to them, declaring " 'I don't know any other parents these days who live as much for their children as yours do. It's always looked to me like they each learned secrets of happiness from their parents that none of the rest of us did. . . . You children are their whole life, and you ought to remember that.' " And it is Jake, because he is the Scoutmaster, who takes both boys to the Scout meeting, where he comes into his own, "losing himself in the role of the eternal Scoutmaster." The young narrator sees his uncle become something far beyond the affable kinsman he has seen at home in the role of peacemaker between Virginia Ann and their father. Once again, the metamorphosis of an adult, rather than of a child, takes place, but this time of an uncle, not a father:

> To the exclusion of all the world Uncle Jake was now become a Scoutmaster. I felt myself deserted by the last human soul to whom I could turn. . . . He stood before us like a gigantic replica of all the little boys on the benches, half ridiculous and half frightening to me in his girlish khaki middy and with his trousers disappearing beneath heavy three-quarter woolen socks.

More importantly, this boy, undergoing this rite in place of his sister, the real initiate in this story, gets to hear the lament that most Taylor fathers make to themselves but do not share aloud with their sons or daughters:

> In that cold, bare, bright room he was saying that it was our great misfortune to have been born in these latter days when the morals and manners of the country had been corrupted, born in a time when we could see upon the members of our own families—upon our own sisters and brothers and uncles and aunts—the effects of our failure to cling to the teachings and ways of our forefathers. And he was saying that it was our duty and great privilege . . . to preserve those honorable things which were left from the golden days when a race of noble gentlemen and gracious ladies inhabited the land of the South. He was saying that we must preserve them until one day we might stand with young men from all over the nation to demand a return to the old ways and the old teachings everywhere.

"The Gift of the Prodigal" involves not only a much older than usual son, but also a father who seems to experience much more of the pain of a son's immaturity than most of Peter Taylor's fathers. Ricky, the son, seems at first to have more in common with Absalom than with the Prodigal Son. Yet at the end of the story the reader is reminded that, like his biblical namesake, Ricky undergoes his initiation rites out of sight of his father, then returns home, but only when he is beyond the change of initiation. Meanwhile, Ricky's father is the character most dramatically moved by this son's return home.

This father's compulsion to take on his son's pain begins in the knowledge that whatever Ricky has come home for this morning, it will be less traumatic ultimately for his son than for himself; Ricky always comes home for help, but not in suffering or repentance. For Rick, this trip home, his father muses, "must be like going to see any other old fellow who might happen to be his boss and who is ailing and is staying away from the office for a few days." Ricky's father, narrating this story, readily accepts the inevitability of his son's trip home for help and recognizes his own inevitable role in this domestic drama, for he knows that "there would be no other solution to [Rick's] problem but to see his old man."

The narrator does not allow disaffection to help him stay aloof from his son's problems, knowing, as he knows this son realizes, "that it is not, after all, such a one-sided business, the business between us." So, fully reconciled to the inevitability of the pain it will cause, this father plunges into whatever new escapade Ricky has brought to lay be-

fore him, for "it seems [Ricky's problem] was all there ever was. I forget my pains and my pills, and the canceled golf game, and the meaningless mail that morning. I find I can scarcely sit still in my chair for wanting Ricky to get on with it."

So another Peter Taylor father is transfixed by the relationship with a son, a son who causes pain, whose growing up, or, in this case, inability to grow up, changes life for a father from a static routine to a full, willing involvement. He is at once drawn completely into his son's life, "listening not merely with fixed attention but with my whole being. . . . I hear him beginning. I am listening. I am listening gratefully to all he will tell me about himself, about any life that is not my own."

The father suffers change as a result of his son's youthful peccadilloes. Ricky's father, long a widower, now with a settled existence, except for the possibility of vicarious involvement through Ricky, is ready for the most dramatic experience Peter Taylor's characters undergo, as father accepts pain over ennui: ". . . Ricky begins. . . . it is all anyone in the world can give me now—perhaps the most anyone has ever been able to give a man like me." Now that Cary, his wife, is dead, the father finds his mind occupied with Ricky, though perhaps Ricky has always been on his mind more than his wife.

A paradigm of the most predictable circumstances in the usual initiation story is presented in **"In the Miro District."** Yet this story, too, has Taylor's ironic twist of the usual circumstances. Though Taylor, more clearly than in his other stories, gives the emerging adolescent the right age and situation for initiation to occur, here again initiation is as much a phenomenon for a parent as it is for a child; here again the older generation becomes protagonist by changing most dramatically. Even Taylor's young initiate understands that this event in their lives is more "for my grandfather, of course, whose story this is meant to be—more than mine." The young man in this story recognizes, too, that whatever change, whether it's called "initiation" or something else, has occurred, it occurred in his grandfather's life, and not in his own. He knows that he is as yet a young man without an identity:

> Whatever else his behavior that day meant, it meant that the more bad things I did and the worse they were, then the better he would think he understood me and the more alike he would think we were. But I knew there was yet something I could do that would show him how different we were and that until I had made him grasp that, I would not begin to discover what, since I wasn't and couldn't be like him, I *was* like. Or if, merely as a result of being born when I was and where I was, at the very tail end of something, I was like nothing else at all, only incomparably without a character of my own.

Grandfather and grandson realize that their relationship with each other has changed, as neither will "ever [be] quite the same—not the same with each other and probably not the same within themselves. Whatever their old relationship had been, it was over forever." But well beyond such philosophical considerations of an adolescent, the older man changes, in actual, palpable ways. He leaves off wearing his old gabardine coat and his broad-brimmed hats. He grows a beard, resumes attending Confederate veterans' reunions, and allows himself to be promoted in rank among his fellow veterans, all of which he had earlier rejected. He even begins to tell war stories. His grandson's behavior, as the boy tries to grow up, alters the old man in ways more immediately visible than any change in the young man. Though **"In the Miro District"** starts out as a traditional initiation story, it reminds the reader that in Peter Taylor's world initiation is not a boy's story, but an adult's.

But initiation, like all Taylor's themes, is a family matter. Taylor's families generally enjoy social status and economic independence, but what makes them the people they are is the family they belong to. So it does not matter which family member serves as the instrument of an adolescent's initiation, as long as it is a member of the family. And in the eighteen-year-old narrator's world of Nashville's Miro District, the young are taught by their grandfathers:

> This ancient and well-established practice of pairing off young with old so relentlessly and so exclusively had, I think—or *has*—as one of its results in Nashville the marvel that men over fifty whom one meets there nowadays are likely to seem much too old-fashioned to be believed in almost—much too stiff in their manner to be taken seriously at all. They seem to be putting on an act. It is as if they are trying to *be* their grandfathers. . . . To hear them talk, one would actually suppose none of them ever had a father. One gets the impression that they only had elegant grandfathers, born before 1860.

Even in Peter Taylor's reminiscence of the world of youth in the early part of this century, initiation is clearly the role of grandparents, to the extent that "in that quaint Tennessee world I grew up in . . . an old graybeard and a towheaded little boy . . . were expected to be more companionable even than fathers and sons are told today they ought to be."

Initiation in Peter Taylor's stories is a circumstance mainly of youth and age, freeing the generation between them from the responsibilities of overseeing the rites of passage. The Manley parents are "living their busy, genteel, contented life" without "the slightest conception of what that old man my grandfather was like. Or of what that boy, their son, was like either." But perhaps initiation is made even easier in this genteel family because of the role played by the middle generation, the parents of the growing boy; on the day he and his grandfather "part company," the boy delineates the role of the actual parent as he realizes that his "parents, somehow, . . . would forever be a wall between us, and that once any people turned away from what he was, as they had done, then that—whatever it was he was—was lost to them and to their children and their children's children forever."

But though initiation is a pulling away from family, it is also a reminder that the rites of passage are an important way of holding families together, of making the idea of family continue to work. Such a reflection is true even for an adolescent protagonist of **"In the Miro District,"** who

knows he will not lose sight of "a picture that comes into my mind almost every day that I live," the picture of "one of those other grandfathers out walking with a little grandson along West End Avenue," it being "apparent at once that the two of them were made of the same clay or at least that their mutual aim in life was to make it appear to the world that they were."

"In the Miro District" has some overtones of a more traditional approach to the initiation theme than Peter Taylor usually takes. In this story, the final acting out of the rites of passage begins in tumult, as one might expect in the most customary version of initiation. Grandfather Manley comes upon the boy during a rebellious drinking scene, and the boy believes "that this was the beginning of my freedom from him." Soon after—"hardly six weeks later"—while the boy's parents are out of town, the grandfather discovers him and three other boys, each with a girl, "in the four bedrooms on the second floor of my parents' house in Acklen Park." The punishment he receives is traditional; his grandfather canes him. The boy thinks, probably on behalf of a great many Taylor adolescents awaiting the firm hand of discipline, "At last he had struck me! That was what I thought to myself. At last we might begin to understand one another and make known our real feelings, each about the other." Yet this story, too, leaves the adolescent reflecting that only he understands what has happened, thinking, after he has spent most of the weekend at home with a girl, that this grandfather "might be morally correct about everything else in the world, but he was not morally correct about love between a man and a woman," which is no doubt the very way every adolescent has ever felt during his own growing up. But the character who changes, as is characteristic of Peter Taylor's stories, is the grandfather. The young narrator observes all the changes in his grandfather's behavior, and thus knows that a new time in his own life has come.

Peter Taylor's stories of initiation are not like the usual stories of initiation, which consist of little boys confronting their first sexual experiences, or little girls confronting menses for the first time. The Taylor characters who seem to be the initiates are not even boys, but grown men. Hugh Robert of **"A Promise of Rain,"** now a New York theater director, and the Manley grandson in **"In the Miro District"** are the only two initiates we even know as boys. The rest of the initiations take place long after the usual time of rites of passage in a child's life, because Taylor is describing a much more complicated initiation than the visceral and physical wrench of leaving adolescence to become an adult. He is describing, rather, the kind of life and society these young protagonists will inherit. He is not describing the adults they must become, but the world of family in which they must become adults.

Taylor's is a world where generations, rather than genders, do battle. His world is inhabited by a middle-aged generation of people who do not say things they will regret later, because they are very much in control of their emotions. These are people who avoid speaking in maxims, proverbs, and old wives' tales. They are folk, but gentle folk, not hill folk. They accomplish conversation through the indirectness of metaphor and story. They never say, simply and directly, "You're wrong." These people do not make excessive use of nouns of direct address, even at home. Their narrators may call them by their Christian names, but they seldom call each other by their Christian names. They never call each other by pet names of endearment. In Peter Taylor's stories "Mother" and "Father" are still proper nouns, and not titles of familiarity.

Peter Taylor's stories offer instruction in how to recognize the "good people" of the society that his young men are being initiated into. Good people have Anglo-Saxon names, belong to clubs, know all their kinfolks, whom they take trips to see; they live in large houses with wide halls and they are always at home when these stories take place. Their stories do not necessarily take place in any particular room in the house. But if it is in a particular room, it is usually the breakfast room, or the sun porch, and not the kitchen, or the bathroom, or the bedroom. We easily imagine their entrances into family settings and conversations through wide doors, just off spacious halls.

Southerners were probably the last people in America to continue the ritual of eating breakfast, and Peter Taylor's people are the last Southerners to eat both heartily and leisurely every morning. Dining is, in fact, what these people do best, and it is at the table that their young sons learn to face the world at large, and the extended family in particular, in which they will live. Yet the closest their table conversations come to confrontation is the rhetorical question. This is a world in which too many direct questions would be abrupt, even casual, to the point of disrespectfulness of privacy. Even "polite offers to fetch something" ("The Captain's Son,") are offered in the expectation that they will be declined. It is a kind of familiarity meant to breed, not contempt, or even casualness, but ritual and civility. These are not old-fashioned people because their stories took place long ago, in a simpler age. They would be old-fashioned in any generation.

Peter Taylor does not fall back on the romantic stereotypes of little boys and grotesque old men in order to prove that kin counts. His people are seldom ancients and never infants. They are middle-aged or adolescent, bordering on middle-age. They are not ruined by any Industrial Revolution. They are the people who came to town before the war for an agrarian South was lost to mercantilism. They are the people Southerners would have been if they had won their fight to lose the Revolutionary War. In the eyes of the rest of the nation they would likely have been the stereotypical Southerners if the South had won its war for independence.

Peter Taylor's stories are about the failure of these people to communicate their real feelings. The one relationship not sufficiently ritualized as to rule out the possibility for actual communication is that of father and son. But when these fathers pass on lessons to their sons, it is not old men dreaming dreams, urging their young sons to see visions. At his kindest, Peter Taylor describes Southerners with a bittersweet prose reminiscent of the verse of A. E. Housman. At his most direct, he describes Southerners who live at the very end of an old social order, and who are not participating in the creation of any new order to take its place. Taylor's stories of father and son attempt to show the

break-up of "the general nature of this world where [we] must pass [our] days" ("A Long Fourth"). But while the rituals of family community are on the one hand comforting, they are on the other hand isolating and deindividualizing, and do not show these young initiates any views of the larger world they might influence.

For the most part, Peter Taylor's men are not active, only contemplative, even to the point of indolence. They all stay home. They are "this strange kind of man who would come in from work at four-thirty in the afternoon, disappear above stairs to change from a dark double-breasted suit to a plaid jacket and gray trousers, and then reappear and settle down to a long evening, without ever mentioning the work that had kept [them] all day." In this setting Taylor treats the reader to the sad spectacle of men trying to pass the torch to their sons, when these men don't themselves bear torches. They bear titles, like "doctor," "lawyer," or "teacher," though they might even all be writers. We see them only at home, engaged in the pleasantries and crises there. The most dramatic experience they encounter is the retelling of the stories of their sons' leave-taking. (pp. 309-22)

Lamar York, "Peter Taylor's Version of Initiation," in The Mississippi Quarterly, *Vol. XL, No. 3, Summer, 1987, pp. 309-22.*

Allen Tate on Taylor:

I was Peter's first college English teacher, but I found I could not teach him anything so I asked him to leave the class after about two weeks. The simple truth is that he did not need to know anything I could teach him. He had a perfection of style at the age of 18 that I envied.

I do not think he owes very much to anybody. If the South has produced a Chekhov, he is Peter Taylor. Literary theories or other abstractions do not blur his vision.

Allen Tate, in an essay in Shenandoah, *Winter, 1977.*

Simone Vauthier

[*In the following essay, Vauthier argues that the stylistic and structural complexity of Taylor's stories conveys a greater meaning than their regional subjects and realistic narrative technique suggest.*]

From the beginning the stories of Peter Taylor have had a following of devotees—some of them recruited among the best literary minds of the period — and criticism has generally underlined the writer's craftsmanship. Nevertheless negative responses to his work have been heard now and then. Reviewing *The Collected Stories,* Barbara Raskin considered Taylor's "Southern-fried realism", with its "insipid, if not insidious, situations" ultimately "mind-deadening", while Christopher Ricks regarded the stories as "slices of life", adding that "sliced life often has the vapidity of sliced bread". Although those are dissenting voices, they are worth quoting insofar as they point to the hazards of reading "realistic" fiction: even when it is avowedly concerned with the surfaces and objects of everyday life, fiction is a "trope", as Catherine Kerbrat-Orecchioni has observed, the two levels of which must be perceived and maintained in the mind: "le récepteur d'un trope doit à la fois partager l'illusion (que constitue le sens littéral), et n'en être pas dupe (savoir que le vrai sens est ailleurs")".

Assuredly Peter Taylors's stories are set in precisely realized settings which are frequently Southern. They create life-like characters, often middle- or upper-middle-class, often rooted in, or coming from the mid-South, confronting carefully detailed domestic dilemmas and family crises, or recollecting vividly a small-town past while involved in the changes of city life. Thus they undoubtedly have a strong referential dimension. Yet their meticulous precision, their "solidity of specification", is never simply mimetic, as the best Taylor critics have not failed to see; rather it becomes a way of expanding their faithfulness to a limited range of life into a larger and less definable truth. A way of achieving what Barthes called "the indirect language of literature": "nommer en détail les choses afin de ne pas nommer leur sens dernier et tenir cependant sans cesse ce sens menaçant, désigner le monde comme un répertoire de signes dont on ne dit pas ce qu'ils signifient"; for as Barthes points out, "le sens de l'objet tremble toujours, non celui du concept; d'où la vocation concrète de l'écriture littéraire".

A little-examined story, **"First Heat"**, provides a good example of this "concrete vocation of literary writing", as practiced by Peter Taylor, and of how it works towards an "indirect language" which makes a feast of a slice of life.

In **"First Heat"**, the anonymous protagonist, a youngish State Senator, has just come back from the Senate, where in voting an amendment to a waterways bill he has reneged on his word to a political ally. He is waiting in his hotel room for his wife to join him before they both go to the Governor's reception, and is mulling over his political gesture. The drama is all internal: even the bill, the external event that has caused all the turmoil, is not itself, "of any great import", in the mind of the protagonist (and we have no reason seriously to doubt his word on this point). What matters to him is the reality of his betrayal, and the dread of his wife's judgment. But when she finally arrives, her eyes are "understanding and forgiving" and there is nothing to do but go on with the ordinary moves of life.

This is, one might say, bread thinly sliced: public pressures and marital tensions which are the basis for the psychological realism of the story (and common themes of Peter Taylor's work), are restricted to a time-span of a few hours, located within a single setting—which at first glance might seem to contribute to the slightness of the story. There are a few flashbacks which evoke the times when the protagonist discussed his choice of a political career with his wife or was warned against it by father and friends, as well as one or two backward glances at moments in his youth, but they do not greatly expand the potential time of the story.

Similarly, such retrospects imply a heterotopic (Greimas) space but do not always introduce the locus in with the remembered episode took place. And when time is handled in less traditional fashion through several anticipations, such departures do not appear as narratorial playing with time-sequences, for they are motivated by the protagonist's mental habits. The illusion is that *he* anticipates or projects real or imaginary events—pictures, for instance, his wife surprising a prostitute in his room. Just as these vivid flights of fancy seem to define him, so does, conversely, the relative spatial imprecision of the décor of his daydreams.

When all is said however, the very *thinness* of the slice becomes arresting, susceptible of generating meaning above and beyond that of the represented scenes. The vagueness of the heterotopic space, for example, does not simply provide information, as I have just indicated, about the nature of the character's imagination (literal level), it also highlights, by an effect of parallelism, the impersonal bareness of the hotel room with its few accessories, thereby suggesting its symbolic relevance (figurative level): the topic space in which the character's transformation is enacted becomes a metaphoric *huis-clos* where he confronts only versions of the self—including his wife.

Furthermore, the narrator's stringent limitation of story-time to an interval of waiting between two public performances structures two of the text's major oppositions, between the public and the private worlds, the public and private selves; in that sense, the time-gap is equivalent to the identity crisis which the character goes through. Besides, the gap, while emphasizing stasis, the suspension of the self in potentiality, permits in fact the articulation of a passage, as though empty time were the prerequisite, and a symbol for the (attempted) emergence of the self and its ensuing disappearance. In short, the caesura may be seen as engendering the many splits in both story and narration but also as signifying them.

The narration, of course, itself originates in a series of disjunctions and conjunctions. The primary disjunction separates the narrating agency which is undramatized and the narrated character. However the distance between the two is often blurred for two reasons. First, the narrator readily reports the thoughts of the protagonist in indirect style or in free indirect style so that there is a conflation of two voices, which are all the more difficult to distinguish because both are educated and gentlemanly. When, in addition, the character rehearses thoughts which echo those of other people—his wife's, the *doxa's*—there is a fading of voices: "In politics the ends were what mattered, had to matter. In politics that was the only absolute. If you were loyal to other men, you were apt to betray your constituency. Or did he have it all backward? No, he had it right, he was quite sure." In this passage various *paroles* merge then are disjoined as the character gropes for a meaning that vacillates. Ironically his voice comes to the foreground only to betray the extent to which he is spoken through by the collective *parole* rather than truly speaking. Secondly, although the dominant focalizer is external, identified with the narrator, nevertheless, since he perceives the character either from without or from within, presents his outer gestures or his inner life, it follows that the focalized character himself becomes an internal focalizer. The character is seen by the external focalizer as himself seeing. Numerous verbs of perception usually introduce or justify the changes in focalization while building an isotopy of sight: "he glanced backward and saw", "his eyes lighting on the mirror", "taking in the different views he had of the body", "he observed features that . . . ", "he could see", etc. In his overwrought state, however, the character's sight turns visionary; he can "see beneath the skin", "as though his eyes were equipped with X-rays". Through the relayed focalization, the narration can therefore *naturalize* aberrant perceptions while exploiting the hallucinatory power they generate.

In short, the Senator's being the so-called "central consciousness" of the story facilitates the reader's construction of the literal level, but the discrepancy between the narrator-focalizer and the focalized/focalizing character promotes, along with other features of the narration, awareness of the narrator's mediation and of the tropological level of the story.

Interestingly, even at the literal level, the protagonist is involved in a quest which mirrors that of the reader. For he is also trying to find the meaning, not of a printed text, but of a series of signs—his own acts, his own body responses, his wife's voice. The metaphor of *reading* even surfaces in the text: "He read the eyes as he had not been able to read the voice on the telephone." In the space-time of the story he is engaged in two strands of actions, which the narration braids together, now joining, now disjoining them: on the one hand, the protagonist broods over his voting and apprehends his wife's reactions, on the other, he has to cope with, and he worries about, an alarming flow of perspiration. In neither case does he quite know how to interpret what he is involved in.

From the start, he realizes that his voting the amendment "which Nat Haley had said would be ruinous" is a betrayal and he feels guilt. "He could hear his own voice in the Senate Chamber that afternoon. Not his words, just his *guilty* voice" (emphasis mine). Waiting for his wife who must have heard the news and must "know who betrayed whom" he attempts to find the self-justification which will enable him to face her. But what all his agonized pondering succeeds in is making the structure of the betrayal more problematic: whom or what has he betrayed? "not his country or his family. And not God knew, his constituents". He must return to the question: "who, then was he betraying?". Far from being simply a way of rationalizing his disloyalty to Nat Haley, who is, after all, "the damndest kind of double dealer", this is a truly important question, but the protagonist can never answer it. (Even if the reader senses in the ungrammaticality of the query—the *who* which confuses subject and object of the act of betrayal—the possibility of a hypothesis of his/her own). Uncertain of his values and of his self, the protagonist circles around a problem which he cannot name, shifting from one position to another. Now questioning, as parents and friends warned him he would, whether he is really made for politics, now seeing in the incident a confirmation that he *is*: "wasn't this merely his baptism—in betrayal?". The

interrogative statement contains a semantic echo of the metaphor inscribed in the polysemic title, **"First Heat"**, and develops one of its meanings: insofar as baptism initiates the baptized into a new life, it seems that the "first heat" has been successful and may have qualified the Senator for the political *race*. The utterance, of course, is more explicit than the title, not only by reason of its place in the narrative and of its direct association with the character: it has both an oxymoric quality and generalizing potentialities since it presents betrayal as a metonym of political life, which the phrase "first heat" lacks.

To regard his experience as a baptism in betrayal redeems it in the mind of the character all the more clearly because thus he can set it within an ethical frame which he has already considered—and discussed with his wife: "they had agreed that one's political morality could not always coincide with one's private morality". However, he is not certain, in this case, on which side loyalties rested. "If you were loyal to other men, you were apt to betray your constituency. Or did he have it all backward?" Nor can he rest assured in a knowledge that has been handed down to him: "They had read that (the non-coincidence of political and private morality) somewhere, hadn't they? At any rate, one had to be prepared to face up to that morality . . .". In spite of all this rationalizing, he is so little ready to "face up to that morality"—and to his wife, the embodiment of his conscience, that he engages in thoughts of private immorality. If he had a woman come up to his room, how "sinful—how clearly sinful—he would know himself to be". And the thought being here father to the wish, he indulges in a full-scale fantasy, narrated in the present: "There the two of them are, in bed. But suddenly there comes a knock on the door! He will have to hide her. His wife is out there in the passage". The satisfaction is not in fantasized sexual gratification (note how the comma, at the beginning of the daydream, makes the bed almost an after-thought) but in the necessity to "hide the creature" who "will have to stand naked", in the closet while he and his wife dress for the reception. Secrecy, however, is only one aspect of the scenario, the end of which should be discovery of the shameful secret, as is revealed in the final episode.

On his wife's arrival, the protagonist, in his panic at the idea of facing her, resorts again to the fantasy. "Oh, if only, if only—if only there were a woman, herself covered with sweat, and still—still panting, for him to hide. What an innocent, simple thing it would be". (His evaluation of this imaginary adultery has passed from "clearly sinful" to "innocent"). However, when his wife enters the room, she does not offer him what he dreaded *and* needed—condemnation, or even disapprobation. "But if only the mouth and eyes would not forgive, not yet. He wanted their censure, first". So he elaborates another version, less imaginary and more symbolic, of the fantasy, as she pauses before opening the closet and looks back at him:

> Suddenly he understood the kind of sympathy she felt for him. Is it the lady or the tiger? Her hesitation seemed to say. If only, she seemed to say with him, if only it *were* the lady, naked and clutching her bundle of clothing to her bosom.

This time he assumes that his wife shares his wish for the discovery of a plain (and private) form of betrayal. He also translates his private fantasy into the dynamic intertextual structure of a well-known limerick. This resort to intertextuality enables him at once to dramatize and symbolize what he feels is the problem:

> But he knew of course, as did she, it would be the tiger, the tiger whose teeth they had drawn beforehand, whose claws they had filed with their talk about the difference between things private and things political. The tiger was that very difference, that very discrepancy, and the worst of it was that they could never admit to each other again that the discrepancy existed.

The protagonist has managed to rise to a *figurative reading* of his predicament. The difference between the public and private morality which he saw as creative of freedom and power (riding on the declawed tiger) is now perceived as destructive (the tiger eventually swallows the lady). The character then anticipates the events to follow, and his reported projection of the future concludes on these words:

> And after a while the tuxedo and the evening gown would leave the hotel room together and go down the elevator to the lobby and ride in a cab across town to the governor's mansion (. . .) But when the reception was over and the gown and the tuxedo came down the steps from the mansion; got into another taxi and rode back across town to their empty hotel room, who was it that would be in them then? Who?

The story ends on these questions. Again, if we take it that these are his reported thoughts, the character expresses, though the symbolism of clothes and the limerick polarities of inside/outside, what he cannot articulate conceptually, his awareness of the destructiveness of his/their role-playing, his sense of a loss of identity. This is his dark epiphany, which culminates in the anguish of the final questions.

Such a struggle to come to terms with his betrayal is accompanied with, and bound to, his coping with his exceptional perspiration. If the liminal sentence, "He turned up the air conditioning and lay across the bed, wearing only his jockey shorts" seems to relate the phenomenon to the outside climatic conditions (thereby generating a first literal interpretation of the title), it soon becomes clear that this sweating, which the text repeatedly describes in vivid detail, must have other causes. And the sufferer, while again and again taking steps to dry himself, attempts—in vain—to account for the "sickening sweat". "Perhaps it was the extra sleeping pill he took last night". "Perhaps he was ill, really ill!". Such physical explanations do not convince him. Nor does long contemplation of his body in a mirror shed much light on the problem. Yet in one rumination, he comes to a sort of negative conclusion: "Ah, if only his body *had* been his great care and concern in life—his problem. And no doubt that's what his sweating meant! He *wished* it were only a bodily ill!". But he does not go any further. And although he observes the chronological link between the "charges" of sweat and his thinking about his political act or about his wife, he does not try to analyse the connection, however close to it he

may come, as in the following example: "Yes, and this time the sweat came before the thought—just a little before the thought this time. The thought of what he had done and left undone concerning the amendment, said and left unsaid concerning the amendment, (. . .) all thought of *that* seemed something secondary and consequential to the sweat". Later, even the chronology, important as it seems to him, will elude him. He cannot remember whether he pulled off his clothes because of the sweat: "it seemed to him almost that the sweat began *after* he had stripped off his clothes". Towards the end, he shows a greater awareness that the perspiring is a symptom of something mental. His wife having just announced herself on the hotel phone, he begins dressing hastily:

> She must not find him undressed, this way. It would seem too odd. And if he should begin the sweating again, he was lost, he told himself. He would have to try to ignore it, but she would notice, and she would know . . .

But what there is to know never surfaces in the narration, or rather it disappears in the blankness of the three dots . . . Whatever it is, let me insist, cannot be the fact of his "betrayal"; she has already heard the news, has already told her husband that she was "sure he had good reasons". What there is to know is something which the protagonist cannot name.

To put it succinctly, the character has not been able to produce a reading of his bodily symptom. His failure to do so, needless to say, in no way detracts from his psychological credibility, rather the contrary in an age when the unity of the self is no longer taken for granted. Nevertheless, as it casts some doubts on his overall interpretation of the crisis and moreover creates an obvious specific gap, such failure is one more incentive for us to go beyond the primary, literal construction of the character.

Willingly yielding to the referential illusion, we have treated the fictional character as a subject in his own right. It is now time to take a closer look at him as a figure of discourse.

There are of course several ways in which one could go beyond the literal level. Pursuing, on our own account and with more critical tools, the process of naming in which the character fumblingly engages only to stop short, would of course be a possibility. For Barthes, the process of naming connotations is "l'activité même du lecteur: lire c'est lutter pour nommer, c'est faire subir aux phrases du texte une transformation sémantique (. . .). Lire, comprendre, thématiser (du moins le texte classique) c'est de la sorte reculer de nom en nom à partir de la butée signifiante". A reader of **"First Heat"** so inclined could slide from name to name, until s/he reaches a psychoanalytic totalization of the text. This procedure however would tend to foreground the psychological realism of the story, which by now should be evident, at the expense of the patterns of discourse out of which, together with whatever referential and intratextual material is available to us, we create the figure. I will therefore follow another path—or rather, since space is limited, take a series of short cuts through the story, in an attempt less to *figure out* the protagonist than to see how he is *figured in*.

To distinguish between the character as the *subject,* which his being "the center of consciousness" leads us to construct, and the character as the *object* of fictional discourse, is to be made aware of the discrepancy of the two.

While the character, as a subject of his quest for making sense of his experience, tries to face himself and his wife, throughout the narrative there builds up quite a different pattern of evasion. For example, even the moment when he looks at himself in the mirror comes about accidentally as a result of his trying to avoid self-perception. It is when he "turns away" from "the wet shadow of himself that his perspiration ha(s) left on the bed" that he is suddenly confronted with his image in the "large rectangular mirror above the dresser" and the mirror in the bathroom door; even so his first response is to "hurl" his wadded towel at the door and the offending image. Only then does he realize that "the body interested him as never before" and he observes it carefully. But the contemplation ends with what may be considered another way of eluding a real self-confrontation when he can "see beyond the skin and under the flesh to the veins and tendons and the ropelike muscles, the heart and lungs" etc. "Had it been a dream? A vision?"—the subject does not know and does not care, but the two words carry semes of 'unreality'. Moreover if the subject "experience(s) momentary relief", the object of the reader's perception may well appear on the way to an ominous depersonalization: it was as though he "had looked beyond all that which particularized him and made his body and life meaningful, human". I will come back to this in a moment.

The isotopy of "hiding", which prevails throughout, powerfully contributes to what I call the pattern of evasion. To quote but a few examples:

"He began drying himself—and hiding himself ",

"Catching a glimpse of himself in the mirror, he blushed bashfully and began pulling on his trousers to cover his naked legs".

"He will have to hide the creature". (The satisfaction provided by the woman scenario lies to some extent in the hiding of the *corpus delicti.*)

"But if only there were something besides his body, something else tangible to hide."

As this last example illustrates, "hiding" doubly belongs to the pattern of evasion since it semantically implies putting out of sight and contextually involves a displacement: something tangible is (to be) hidden in order to hide something intangible, (i.e. not material or . . . already hidden).

The pattern of evasion may also be deciphered at the lexical, syntactical and figurative levels. In his flight of fancy, the character achieves "the great satisfaction" of sinfulness, yet he is presented as rising only to a series of synecdochical euphemisms, "hotel creatures", "the creature", "the woman". When imagining himself caught in *flagrante delicto,* he can only picture the woman "covered with sweat and still—still panting", the dash marking his hesitation to use the word "panting" which yet seems a mild enough selection among the qualifiers which might have been used. The recurrence of the structure "if only"

(in one instance repeated three times in a row) underlines the character's propensity to replace the actual with the imaginary. (Similarly, resort to the present and future tenses turns the first evocation of the woman into an almost hallucinatory avoidance of the present moment). The questions and oscillations between opposed points of view which implement the character's quest for truth become, though their very frequency, a sort of intellectual mannerism, which, the reader suspects, is a way of evading conclusions. The conspicuous use of synecdoches and metonymies in the narration of the protagonist's confrontation with his wife points to the nature of their meeting. Take the following comparison in which the character's and the narrator's voices are fused, "It was as though only a pair of blue eyes—bodiless, even lidless—hung there in the open doorway, suspended by invisible wires from the lintel". The arresting synecdoche, together with the hyperbole "bodiless, even lidless", which indicates his wrought-up state, also suggests how ruthlessly selective and egocentric is his perception of his wife, reduced to this part of her which can offer him a message to "read". In like fashion, the statement "but if only the mouth and the eyes would not forgive, not yet" both fragments and depersonalizes the wife's image. The discourse keeps showing that the protagonist does not face a person but a set of attributes signifying attitudes towards him. To this extent, he avoids a truly interpersonal encounter and seeks only a self-image. Similarly, in the last sentences, the metonymies "the tuxedo and the gown" forcefully underline that the characters have shrunk into their roles and their marriage into a social front. "And there was no denying that when the tuxedo and the evening gown got out of the taxi and went up the steps and then moved slowly along in the receiving line, *he and she, for better* or *worse,* would be inside them" (italics mine). Even though here again it is difficult to decide where the figures originate, those last images contribute to the stereographic effects which the narration creates in many ways, allowing for a double vision of the character.

Moreover, whereas the subject is attempting to repair his self-image, the discourse, for its part, keeps fragmenting the object. Doubles proliferate and perhaps nowhere more clearly than in the one passage when the subject looks at himself in the mirror. Then he experiences a moment of reprieve in a narcissistic contemplation of a body that has changed but is still recognizably the same: "it was—almost—a young man's body still (. . .) it was only a little heavier around the hips than it had once been, and the arm muscles were really better developed than when he was twenty". But the narration keeps presenting us with doubles. There is the "wet shadow of himself " on the bed, a mention which is duplicated by "his silhouette on the sheet", a "silhouette" being itself often defined in terms of "shadow". The character recalls that "as late as his college days he had sometimes shadow-boxed before mirrors". The room is equipped with two large mirrors so that character and reader are presented with two reflections. "But as he turned away from his silhouette on the sheet, there he was, in all his nakedness, in the large rectangular mirror above the dresser. And there he was in the mirror on the open bathroom door". The first sentence juxtaposes and contrasts two images, one a shadowy trace, the other, as it seems, the self itself, "there he was". An illusion revealed by the no less sudden emergence of yet another reflection. Space itself is textually doubled in the implicit opposition between a "here" and a "there" and redoubled in the appearance of another "there", while the repetition of the verbal syntagm "there he was" is itself a textual mirroring effect.

The subject has a fugitive feeling of meeting a double: "For a moment, it was like meeting someone from the past, someone he had almost forgotten—an old friend and old enemy". But what he looks at is "the body in the door mirror and in the large mirror oven the dresser", and "the body in the two mirrors", "the body in the mirrors": such insistence signals the discrepancy between the subject's vision and the text's construction of its object. (It also directs attention to the fact that the character's observation is extremely selective: he eliminates not only the face but the head—and, though he can take in different views, the back.) The subject is conscious of the uniqueness of his body, confident at this point in a certain permanence of his self through time. But with the use of the article instead of the possessive, the narration separates body and self as in "*the* body interested him as never before" (emphasis mine), and the description splits off parts of the narrated body. Finally what we are presented with is a ghostly appearance, an anonymous anatomical representation. Though the character is aware of what joins the different parts, the tendons, "every bone and joint of the skeleton", the picture is anatomical in the etymological sense of the word (derived from *anatomia*: a cutting up), as it shows "*the* heart and lungs, *the* liver, *the* intestines, *the* testicles", etc. Thus the scene ends with one more double, which brings the doubling and splitting off the object almost to the point of dematerialization. The subject, as I have said, takes comfort in the vision bathed in a supernatural light. "Was that the ultimate nakedness? Why, it could just as well have been old Nat Haley's insides he had seen. And he did relax now". He has escaped, it would seem, the limits of his troublesome identity and found a sort of commonalty with Nat Haley, the "double-dealer" he betrayed. But the image of the X-ray picture introduces connotations of disease and the comparison with *old* Nat Haley is also a reminder that what men have in common, beyond and through physiology, is mortality. To the reader, the anatomical vision of the subject may therefore function as a modern allegory of Father Death or of temporality. And the desire to see beyond "the covering skin", to see one's inside as if it were outside—which cannot tell the subject anything about his self—may perhaps tell us something about the regressive impulses of the character.

Doubling also occurs at other levels. If repetition is the law of all narratives, **"First Heat"** makes capital of the law. The confinement of the protagonist within a restricted locus with few objects to manipulate, and his obsessive character naturalize the repetition of gestures—removing clothes, drying himself, getting up or lying down on the bed, throwing his underwear at the ceiling or a wadded towel at the door. (In this last example the repetition is emphasized in the discourse by the recurrence of the verbs "wad" and "hurl" and a comment: "he wadded up the towel just as he had the jockey shorts, and hurled it at the door"). But no matter how motivated, the doubling process remains a striking feature of the narration, which draws attention away from the character to the discourse itself and its tropological possibilities.

Mulling over his betrayal, the subject perceives himself caught between public and private morality and although he is dimly aware that his sweating is not "a bodily ill", he wishes it were. Thus he attempts to cope with his problem by relying on binary oppositions, private/public, mind/body, inside/outside.

The narration, of course, also relies on such oppositions. The bi-isotopy nakedness/clothing, for instance, governs the narrative. Diachronically, the transformation of the protagonist is rendered by having him naked in the first part of the story and facing his wife "fully clothed" at the end. What the character does with his clothes, removing them, hurling his wet underwear at the ceiling, pulling them on again, is the basic stuff of the outward action. But the opposition naked/clothed which seems so obvious becomes at moments less clear-cut. It is not only that the associations of nakedness and clothing vary, although undoubtedly they do. Stripping off his clothes, the character seems to get rid of the constraints of the social world in the search for lost purity; clothes then are negatively and nakedness positively connoted. But when he pulls them on again at the end, he is seeking the protection of clothes against his wife and the outside world so that the connotations are reversed. Then the negative suggestions are renewed in the last sentence, which questions whether it is the lady inside the tiger-like clothes. More curiously, there are degrees in nakedness: sweating makes the protagonist "feel more utterly, thoroughly naked than he had ever before felt in his entire life". There are differences in the nature of nakedness. After the X-ray vision, "it seemed to him now that he was not naked at all, or that this was not the nakedness he had sought when he removed his clothes." There is a nakedness of the body and a nakedness of the mind, and there even may be one beyond those: having "seen beyond mere nakedness of body and spirit", the character wonders: "Was that the ultimate nakedness?". The context therefore redefines "nakedness" differently and a word that normally applies to objects of the visible world is used metaphorically to refer to the intangible world. But what is indeed the ultimate nakedness? We are typically in the situation described by Barthes: "Le monde est désigné comme un répertoire de signes dont on ne dit pas ce qu'ils signifient".

Similarly, the opposition public/private is both asserted and undercut. This is evident even in the minor case of places. The hotel room is at once not-public and not-private. A home is a private place but in the Senator's there are private loci within the privacy of the house: the Senator's wife "still knock(s) on door to his study, on the door to the bathroom, even on the door to their bedroom". More importantly, the whole movement of the story denies the public-versus-private opposition inasmuch as a political move affects the protagonist's relationship to his wife, first to the extent that he dreads facing her, then to the extent that their marriage which, if not very intimate was a close partnership, will be changed. As the character anticipates things, the tuxedo and the gown will still be able to function in the public world but what has happened to the selves within the clothes is dubious. Of course, the most striking single piece of evidence that there is an interference between "things private and things political" is the "sickening sweat".

This constitutes a crossing of the bi-isotopy of the somatic and the psychic, which is here associated with the major isotopies of the narration. The "damnable perspiration" is a language of the body (the private, the inside) which manifests *outside* the character's inner perturbation which itself is causally and metonymically linked to a public, outside event and to a private meeting to come. This language, expressing non-verbally something which the subject's psyche represses, is part of the dialectic between the hidden and the revealed in the action and contradicts the very notion of boundaries which the narration at once implements and undercuts.

The narration, while building on marked systems of oppositions, also operates equally marked conjunctions and conflations. The polysemy of the title is a first instance. It encapsulates various semantic possibilities that are later deployed—temperature, qualifying contest, pressure resulting in strain or tension, sexual excitement. The treatment of the perspiration motif offers another interesting example of the conjunctions which the discourse operates. The motif is a fictional (and aesthetic) expansion of well-known idioms, a colloquial idiom "all of a sweat", and an informal one, "in a cold sweat" (in fact the character's sweat is "like ice water on his skin"); as such, it builds up the theme of anxiety and guilt at the same time as it contributes to the development of the thematic polarity of hiding/exhibiting—all themes strongly linked to the protagonist. But the perspiration motif is also associated with the protagonist's imaginary partner in marital unfaithfulness. As he listens for his wife's footsteps, he thinks, "Oh, (. . .) if only there were a woman, *herself* covered with sweat" (italics mine); in the context "sweat" immediately connotes sexual activity but, mediately through the comparison implied in *herself,* it conjoins the woman and the protagonist, not diegetically in sexual intercourse but semantically and symbolically in whatever the sweat is a symbol of. Whereas the subject uses the fantasy of the woman to cover the guilt of his betrayal by displacing it, the narration uncovers the displacement by placing both the character and the fantasized woman in the isotopic field of sweat.

Such a connexion reactivates the isotopy of sexuality which reading tends to background since, even when present in the woman scenario, sexuality is perceived as a mask. If in the reading experience, we now feel called upon to foreground it, we shall remember that the description of the body in the mirror, following the gaze of the character, slides metonymically along a sexual axis: "the modest island of dark hair on the chest, which narrowed into a peninsula pointing down below the navel and over the slightly rounded belly, almost joining the pubic hair above the too-innocent-looking penis". The signs of the character's maleness are however suspiciously "modest". Some features of his body are almost feminine (e.g. "the

hairless arms" contrasting, to be sure, with the "muscular calves", the "stooped" shoulders). Furthermore the metaphorical deployment of the limerick in the text, which ironically turns "the woman" into "the lady", also involves a more remarkable transformation. Is it the lady or the tiger in the closet? wonders the wife. "But he knew of course, as did she, it would be the tiger . . .". What does that make of him, if not the lady who thought she could ride the tiger but ended "inside"? Once more the narration, whether reporting the character's thoughts or not, blurs the binary oppositions on which he relies.

In those conditions, the reader is tempted to draw other conclusions than those the subject reaches. If at a primary level, the personal sexual fantasy seems a displacement for political betrayal, at a secondary level, it is the political betrayal *and* its displacement which appear as a further metaphorico-metonymic displacement for a guilt which is itself darkly related to sexuality. To sum it up very baldly, whereas he seems to substitute for a conflict between ego and the outside world a conflict between Ego and Superego (clearly represented by his wife), there are hints that the conflict may be between Ego and Id. Or we may feel that his rationalizing disregards his desire to be "seen", censured and then forgiven, by another body, by the eyes and mouth of an all-knowing yet all-forgiving figure, which may seem to us very close to a Mother image. (An hypothesis strengthened by the need of the character to tidy up his room and himself before his wife arrives.) At any rate, the subject's recognition that talk of the difference between "things private and things political" could not succeed in declawing the tiger, that the tiger is that "very discrepancy", may well seem to us to evade the fact that his body denied the discrepancy. Should we then say that to trust in the discrepancy, and make it into a code of behaviour is destructive—as is also the refusal to admit the difference—because the self is the interface of the public and the private worlds?

When all is said, such interpretations fail to satisfy us. Something still eludes us—which is often the case with Peter Taylor whose best stories manage to be at once pellucid as realistic representations and somehow tantalizingly opaque as fictional tropes.

In **"First Heat"**, the elusiveness is perhaps what the story finally is about. The character's epiphany, his recognition of his relation to the tiger of reality, is also ultimately a vanishing of the self, (and with it, of the possibility of meaningful interpersonal relationships). "But when the reception was over and the gown and the tuxedo (. . .) rode back across town to their empty hotel room, who was it that would be in them? Who?". Who is there beneath the clothes, the roles, the words (which are the words of the Other as instanced in that very question)? Everything seems to point to absence. Earlier in the mirror, a partial self-image dissolves into the "vision" of a skeleton. There is no woman to hide in the closet, no secret to protect in the locked attaché-case.

But "empty" as the subject may feel and the hotel room may be, nevertheless there is always something *going on:* the play, light or anguished, with mirror reflections and appearances, the antics of nakedness and the ludicrous donning of clothes to keep together a fragmented self, the endless splitting-off in search of an imaginary unity, the dread and the desire to be seen, condemned *and* forgiven by the Other. The comedy of life. Life as comedy.

The comedy implicates us. To the extent that the nameless fictional character represents the "divided subject", he is of course our image. Even as readers we also go through the same splitting off as he does. Though the narration requires us to fill gaps and to see connexions between the different perspectives which are the text's isotopies, it also compels us to experience discontinuity: description of a body can only proceed metonymically and selectively, whether it mimics a fictional observer's self-fragmentation or not. Writing/reading the body can only be writing/reading a mind's response to the body pictured in the signs on the page, can only be writing/reading in the gap. Yet we are looking for principles of coherence, constructing a unified meaning out of a "repertory of signs". (And what is this essay if not an attempt to fixate, as it were, what I know the fictional trope keeps suspended?) Furthermore, as Wolfgang Iser has noted [in his *The Act of Reading: A Theory of Aesthetic Response*], "(t)he ability to perceive oneself during the process of participation is an essential quality of the aesthetic experience; the observer finds himself in a strange, halfway position; he is involved and watches himself being involved."

Although we may reach a more comprehensive view of the fictional situation, if only because we include the character's deciphering as one more series of signs, the text's directions are all we have. There is no truth "hidden" in the text. Even to say that the story fictionalizes, i.e. is a trope for, a fairly contemporary conception of the Subject as inescapably split is only to make the self a theater of illusions and deceptions. But of course, there remains the fascination of this our mirror reflection as it emerges/vanishes in the narrative. The terror of "Who" is left in the drama of identities reverses into the thrill of playing a game which at the same time addresses the human condition. Trying to ride the textual tiger, too, is dangerous business, yet if one must fail to remain outside and in control of the text's significance, the smile, as one returns from the trip through **"First Heat"**, is not simply on the face of the tiger. (pp. 73-91)

> *Simone Vauthier, "Trying to Ride the Tiger, a Reading of 'First Heat'," in* Journal of the Short Story in English, *No. 9, Autumn, 1987, pp. 73-91.*

Philip Hanson

[*In the following essay, Hanson reconsiders the importance of regionalism in Taylor's writing, focusing on "The Captain's Son."*]

When W. F. Cash asserts [in his *The Mind of the South*] that "this word 'agrarian' is an extremely loose one," he might just as correctly have been talking about the words "Southern" or "regionalism." Too often applying these monolithic labels to Peter Taylor's fiction has resulted in blurring or glossing over the fine regional distinctions his fiction struggles to maintain. Taylor almost seems to have had this problem in mind when he had the narrator of the

---

> **Taylor on *A Summons to Memphis*:**
>
> [*A Summons to Memphis* is] about a family in Nashville that moved to Memphis, and the children all are at an age when the changes are ruinous to them almost, or it seems so to the narrator. It's from Nashville to Memphis they move, and I use those two cities to mean different things in the story. Then, of course, a lot of it is autobiographical, all stories are, but it doesn't matter. To make material over into a story, none of the characters can remain the characters they were in life and it's not making judgments on anybody, I hope.
>
> It's a story concerned with old people in our society and what becomes of them. It's about an old man whose children try to prevent his marrying again when he's eighty, and it's not because of the money really, and it's not because of the grandchildren. There are no grandchildren, there is no land. I say at one point in it that Memphis is a land-oriented city, that everybody owns some land, that's partly the thing that people ought to be keeping for the children, but it's none of those reasons. But then what is it? That's the mystery of the story—Why are they doing this? But then the story wanders about back into their past life and how he behaved in certain moments, and so on. It was a great satisfaction to me to write it, and I want to see if I can write another that long.
>
> *Peter Taylor, in an interview in* Journal of the Short Story in English, *Autumn, 1987.*

---

title story in his collection, **In the Miro District and Other Stories,** go to great lengths to clarify fine distinctions between certain regions in Tennessee:

> The world I am speaking of isn't the hard-bitten, monkey-trial world of East Tennessee that everybody knows about, but a gentler world in Middle Tennessee and more particularly the little region around Nashville which was known fifty years ago as the Nashville Basin and which in still earlier times, to the first settlers—our ancestors—was known somewhat romantically perhaps, and ironically, and incorrectly even, as the Miro District.

In a recent interview Taylor expanded on the importance of context in his work when he said of his fiction, "The real poetry emerges in the coincidence between the context and the character." One can only allow the poetry "to emerge" in Taylor's fiction by treating the context (or in some cases multiple contexts), in one of his stories with the same sensitivity with which Taylor presents it. While many of Taylor's stories would serve to illustrate this point, I have chosen to discuss **"The Captain's Son"** because to blur the regional distinctions in that story is seriously to misread it.

The opening paragraphs of **"The Captain's Son"** would seem to argue against what I have been asserting. The narrator carefully explains how "a young man of good family," whether he be from Nashville or Memphis, "for whom something has gone wrong," will often leave his home city and take up residence in the other city in order to escape association with what has "gone wrong" or, depending on the circumstances, to avoid embarrassing his family in their home city. The narrator take pains to establish that at one level it makes no difference which city the "immigrant" comes from. He says, "it is an old story with us in Tennessee." As the story unfolds, however, it becomes clear that the narrator's account of the interchangeableness of Memphis and Nashville refers to a shared code that the two central families, due to subtle differences in their backgrounds, will finally react to differently.

Looking back over an unspecified period of years on incidents that occurred during his late teen-age years, the unnamed narrator sets out to examine how the larger code played a role in the tragic outcome of his sister Lila's marriage to Tolliver Campbell. The narrator associates the Campbell family with Memphis and plantation Mississippi and his own family with the more progressive city of Nashville. Part of the problem for the narrator's family is that they do not take history seriously enough. He tells us, "At our house we tended to laugh at anything that was far in the past or far in the future. We were more or less taught to." This helps explain the somewhat negative light the family sees Tolliver in. The narrator says Tolliver "was what we in Nashville used to think of as the perfect Memphis type. Yet he was not really born in Memphis. He was raised and educated out there but he was born on a cotton plantation fifty miles below Memphis—in Mississippi, which as anybody in Nashville will tell you, is actually worse."

At various points in the story, the narator will expand on the suggestion that it is worse to have been born on a cotton plantation in Mississippi. Gradually it will become clear to the narrator that what he took to be laughable regional differences will ultimately account for an unbridgeable gap between the two families. Shortly after Lila and Tolliver are married, the narrator's father, for reasons the narrator does not at first comprehend, maneuvers them into moving in with the family. Tolliver's behavior there, specifically his refusal to take on a career, disturbs Lila's parents. That Tolliver Campbell had no occupation provokes Lila's mother to complain, "that might be how you did things on a Mississippi plantation, but not in Nashville." Rather than seeking some outside occupation, Tolliver behaves "like a teen-ager lounging around the house in the summertime." He spends his afternoons playing tennis or bridge or reading the newspaper or playing solitaire. We are told, "His smile seemed to say, 'Isn't this great, our life in this house?' "

A better sense of Taylor's reading of Tolliver's origins can be gained by looking at historical documents describing traditional plantation life of a sort that Tolliver's grandparents, and perhaps even his parents, would have known. A transplanted New Yorker, John Anthony Quitman became a plantation owner near Natchez, Mississippi. In a letter, Quitman described what plantation life for a very wealthy plantation owner was like:

> We hunt, ride, fish, pay many visits, play chess, read or lounge until dinner . . . In two hours afterward everybody—white and black—has disappeared . . . The ladies retire to their appartments, and the gentlemen on sofas, settees, benches, hammocks, and often, gipsy fashion, on the grass under the spreading oaks. Here, too, in fine weather, the tea-table is always set before sunset, and then, until bedtime, we stroll, sing, play whist, or croquet. It is an indolent, yet charming life, and one quits thinking and takes to dreaming.

Cash, who traces this plantation life back to a particularly hardcore version of the individualistic "frontier" life of the very early South, asserts that "the plantation tended to find its center in itself: to be an independent social unit, a self-contained and largely self-sufficient little world of its own." Of the mind-set that Cash believes characterizes the plantation owner Cash says, "Everywhere and invariably his fundamental attitude is purely personal—and purely self-asserting."

Tolliver's version of what the narrator calls the "Deep South Planter life" makes a successful marriage with Lila impossible. The narrator's language illustrates the depth of the chasm between the two families when he refers to Tolliver's "life of leisure, supported by the labor of others or maintained by an unearned income" as "an immoral sort of existence." Conversely the lives of the narrator's parents have been framed by qualified compromise, adaptation, and, at times, hypersensitivity to the opinions of others. Their differences with the Campbells can also partly be explained by subtle differences in the histories of Memphis and Nashville. Surveying the situation of the post-Civil War South in the late 1870s, C. Vann Woodward points out [in his *Origins of the New South, 1877-1918*] the widespread sense of economic ruin and a failure to adapt to the changing times. Along with Montgomery, Vicksburg, and New Orleans, Woodward cities Memphis as one of the cities paralyzed by "economic blight." As exceptions to the malaise of the times, however, Woodward mentions "Atlanta, Nashville, and Richmond." Though by the mid-1880s Memphis had begun to be transformed by the Southern Industrial Revolution, its history leaves a lingering sense of a city more intractable, less adaptable, than Nashville.

The narrator reveals a similar sense of Memphis when he tries to explain the differences his parents perceive between themselves and the Campbells. When Lila and Tolliver first meet they find "their chief connection" is an old family quarrel. The families are presented as differing in terms of how seriously they take the memory of the old quarrel. The narrator observes that it was "a quarrel which our two families had once had and which Tolliver, being from Memphis, still took quite seriously. For that's the way people are out at Memphis. They tend to take themselves . . . too seriously." Understanding Tolliver's Memphis intractability enables one to posit an explanation for the senior Campbells' uncontrollable alcoholism and for Tolliver's own failure to succeed as a member of the Governor's staff, a job secured for him by Lila's father, as well as for his sexual failures with Lila.

Tolliver's desire to take on the role of a second son to the narrator's parents represents his wish to resist having to enter an adult world that demands flexibility, adaptation, and occasional compromise. The narrator's parents are equally desirous of Tolliver taking on some kind of occupation because they feel his idleness will look bad to out-siders (at a time when economic times are hard and any display of easy living would be in poor taste). Having tried and failed to maneuver Tolliver into the adult world, Lila's father finally makes Tolliver an offer he cannot refuse by appealing to a higher code, one operative among both Mississippi planters' descendents and "sensible, representative" citizens of Nashville. Lila's father, who has arranged for Tolliver to have a position on the Governor's staff, tells Tolliver, "As your father-in-law I ask you to accept the Governor's appointment." Tolliver acquiesces and the results are disasterous. Shortly after accepting the post, he resigns. The narrator, whom for the only time in the story Tolliver calls "Brother"—as a kind of appeal to the narrator's own innocence—says that "He just wasn't cut out, he said, for the kind of work required of somebody on a governor's staff. He said not an hour of the day passed without your having to tell a big lie or do something else that went against the grain." Like his parents, Tolliver proves incapable of adapting to the inflexible world associated with Nashville.

If, as I have been arguing, history informs Taylor's fiction, in terms of enabling readers to distinguish between some of the subtle shades with which Taylor paints his contexts, I believe that his fiction can also inform our sense of history. At the very least, **"The Captain's Son"** provides us with an interpretation of history to which we can react. The narrator's presentation of Tolliver's intractability—he either must hide from life by refusing to live as an adult or he must obliterate the pain of compromise by drugging himself into near insensibility with alcohol—provides one interpretation of the plight of one sort of resistive agrarian. Rather than define agrarianism—something this story does not set out to do—Taylor dramatizes the plight of the agrarian whose independence and personal integrity are threatened by the changing world. Tolliver's efforts to avoid partaking of the rites of passage that lead to this world result in his refusal to consummate his marriage to Lila and later to his effort to escape into alcoholism.

However, I do not mean to suggest that **"The Captain's Son"** is a one-sided critique of intractable Mississippi planter types. The narrator's parents, "representative" of "the old social values in Nashville," with their constant concern for appearances, are examined just as minutely. Their relationship, as well as that of the Campbells, with alcohol mirrors Tennessee history in which the temperance issue was long a central and divisive subject in Tennessee politics. A statue erected to Edward Ward Carmack on the south side of the state capitol building speaks of the depth of temperance feeling that once existed in Tennessee. Carmack was an early champion, and martyr, of the temperance movement in Tennessee. [In his *Prohibition and Politics*] Paul E. Isaac points out the irony of a tunnel erected just below the statue which was dedicated to Len Motlow and his son, "distillers of Jack Daniel whisky." Carmack, it is worth noting, running on a temperance platform, once posed a threat to Peter Taylor's grandfather Robert Taylor's gubernatorial campaign, which helps one apprehend how personal and regional history meet in this story. The narrator of **"The Captain's Son"** interrupts his narrative at one point to give an ac-count of how his parents behaved during prohibition. He says when the Eighteenth Amendment was enacted "no liquor was served in our house." His father "even gave up his toddy before dinner. The only liquor kept in the house was kept under lock and key." When the Eighteenth Amendment was repealed, he says, "Father brought forth his bottle of bourbon and renewed his old habit of a single toddy before dinner."

However, the apparently admirable conduct of the narrator's parents goes beyond respect for the law. Their advanced views partly result from an overly sensitive desire to maintain an appearance of acceptable behavior. They do not entertain during the Depression because "it would look bad to be dressing up and giving parties." For the same reason they do not want wealthy Tolliver staying at home day after day. The extremities to which their concern over what their Nashville peers might think are revealed when it becomes apparent that marriage to Tolliver has turned Lila into a helpless alcoholic. The problem leaves the family two alternatives: they can get a doctor for Lila or they can conceal her problem from their neighbors. Put another way, they can try to cure Lila or they can protect her reputation. They opt for protecting reputation. To keep Lila quiet, at one point, her mother gives Lila a drink.

By giving **"The Captain's Son"** the elements of a *bildungsroman*,—the narrator describes his own loss of innocence through observing his parents handling of Tolliver and Lila, which parallels the loss of innocence experienced by Lila and Tolliver—Taylor puts the narrator in the reader's place. The lengths the narrator goes to to unblur the regional differences between the two families reflects his concern for locating himself in relation to the external world, mirroring one of the reasons we turn to fiction. The narrator nearly falls into alcoholism himself as he approaches despair over what he has seen. Newly enrolled at a university, he fails two of his examinations. At one point he says, "I embraced almost any opportunity that summer that might help me interpret for myself what was going on at home." Moving away from home, his father's maneuvering Tolliver and Lila to move to Memphis, and just the passage of time enable him to gain a perspective on what has happened. He sees that the victim of a failure to adapt, Tolliver, and the victim who was unequipped to refuse to adapt, Lila, have been ruined. Tolliver and Lila, he says, might just have "the bad luck to live forever."

The narrator has gained this perspective by a kind of anthropological examination of his subjects, that is, by looking carefully at their regional origins and subtle cultural differences. The kind of care with which the narrator examines what has happened allows him to perceive the significance of subtle differences between regions and genealogies. Hopefully the reader will come to similar conclusions so that the monolithic term, regionalism, will cease to be an all-encompassing, generally applicable label. This frees the fiction to be analyzed on its own terms, with its subleties intact, rather than treating it as a specimen that always supports some more general idea. Once, in an interview granted in 1973, Peter Taylor responded to a question about *The New Yorker's* interest in his work by saying he believed that Harold Ross, then the magazine's editor, was interested in "pieces concerned with regional differences." It comes as no surprise that twenty years earlier when Taylor offered a description of his interest in some of the characters in his fiction, he called it "anthropological." (pp. 93-9)

Philip Hanson, "Reconsidering Regionalism in Peter Taylor's Fiction," in Journal of the Short Story in English, *No. 9, Autumn, 1987, pp. 93-9.*

FURTHER READING

Bibliography

Griffin, Carl H. "Peter Taylor." In *Andrew Little, Walker Percy, Peter Taylor: A Reference Guide,* edited by Victor Kramer, Patricia Bailey, Carol G. Dana, and Carl H. Griffin, pp. 187-243. Boston: G. K. Hall & Co., 1983.
> Comprehensive bibliography. Lists secondary writings chronologically by year.

Wright, Stuart T. *Peter Taylor: A Descriptive Bibliography, 1934-1987.* Charlottesville: The University of Virginia, 1988, 228 p.
> Annotated bibliography of works by and about Taylor.

Criticism

Baumbach, Jonathan. "Peter Taylor." In *Moderns and Contemporaries: Nine Masters of the Short Story,* edited by Jonathan Baumbach and Arthur Edelstein, pp. 343-44. New York: Random House, 1968.
> Critical introduction to "Venus, Cupid, Folly, and Time" and "Two Pilgrims."

Eisinger, Chester E. "The Conservative Imagination." In *Fiction of the Forties,* pp. 146-230. Chicago: The University of Chicago Press, 1963.
> Examines Taylor's *A Long Fourth, and Other Stories* and *A Woman of Means.*

Griffith, Albert J. *Peter Taylor.* Rev. ed. New York: Twayne Publishers, 1990, 192 p.
> Biographical and critical study.

Holman, David Marion. "Peter Taylor." In *The History of Southern Literature,* edited by Louis D. Rubin, Jr., pp. 494-96. Baton Rouge: Louisiana State University Press, 1985.
> Divides Taylor's writings into two categories: "The first group . . . might be termed modern tales of manners; the second consists of psychological tales in the tradition of the southern grotesque."

Matthews, Jack. "Peter Taylor's Most Recent Fiction." *The Kenyon Review* 8, No. 1 (Winter 1986): 118-19.
> Favorable review of *The Old Forest, and Other Stories.*

Miller, Karl. "Memphis Blues." *London Review of Books* 7, No. 15 (5 September 1985): 15.
> Review of *The Old Forest, and Other Stories* in which

Miller praises Taylor's skill in portraying southern upper middle-class society.

Peden, William. "Metropolis, Village, and Suburbia: The Short Fiction of Manners." In his *The American Short Story: Continuity and Change, 1940-1975,* pp. 30-68. Boston: Houghton Mifflin Company, 1975.
> Discusses the major recurrent themes of Taylor's short story collections *The Widows of Thornton, Happy Families Are All Alike, Miss Leonora When Last Seen* and *A Long Fourth, and Other Stories.*

Pinkerton, Jan. "The Vagaries of Taste and Peter Taylor's 'A Spinster's Tale'." *Kansas Quarterly* 9, No. 2 (Spring 1977): 81-5.
> Examines "A Spinster's Tale" in order to demonstrate how critical evaluations of literary works are determined by their subject matter and author's reputation.

Robinson, Clayton. "Peter Taylor." In *Literature of Tennessee,* edited by Ray Willbanks, pp. 149-61. n.p.: Mercer University Press, 1984.
> Overview of Taylor as a short story writer, novelist, and dramatist. Robinson praises Taylor's early fiction but expresses disappointment at his later dramas and short stories.

Robison, James Curry, ed. *Peter Taylor: A Study of the Short Fiction.* Boston: Twayne Publishers, 1988, 183 p.
> Includes a lengthy critical study by Robison and previously published essays and reminiscences by writers such as Robert Penn Warren and Allen Tate.

Towers, Robert. "A Master of the Miniature Novel." *The New York Times Book Review* (17 February 1985): 1, 26.
> Review of *The Old Forest, and Other Stories,* praising Taylor for "an exactitude of observation and loving attention to the minutiae of class behavior that characterizes so much of our best writing in the realist mode."

Voss, Arthur. "Peter Taylor." In his *The American Short Story: A Critical Survey,* pp. 352-53. Norman: University of Oklahoma Press, 1973.
> Outlines Taylor's works and themes.

Walker, Jeffrey. "1945-1956: Post-World War II Manners and Mores." In *The American Short Story: 1945-1980,* edited by Gordon Weaver, pp. 16-18. Boston: Twayne Publishers, 1983.
> Focuses on Taylor's first two collections of stories, *A Long Fourth, and Other Stories* and *The Widows of Thornton.*

Walkiewicz, E. P. "1957-1969: Toward Diversity of Form." In *The American Short Story: 1945-1980,* edited by Gordon Weaver, pp. 44-6. Boston: Twayne Publishers, 1983.
> Examines "Taylor's fondness for the supernatural, the slightly surreal, and the grotesque."

Williamson, Alan. "Identity and the Wider Eros: A Reading of Peter Taylor's Stories." *Shenandoah* 30, No. 1 (Fall 1978): 71-84.
> Explores the concepts of identity and eroticism as exemplified in Taylor's stories.

Young, Thomas Daniel. "The Contemporary Scene." In his *Tennessee Writers,* pp. 77-111. Knoxville: University of Tennessee Press, 1981.
> Outlines the major subjects and themes of Taylor's writ-

ings and presents "A Long Fourth" as an illustration of
the characteristic issues found in Taylor's short stories.

**Additional coverage of Taylor's life and career is contained in the following sources
published by Gale Research:** *Contemporary Authors,* **Vols. 15-16, rev ed.;** *Contemporary
Authors New Revision Series,* **Vol. 9;** *Contemporary Literary Criticism,* **Vols. 1, 4, 18, 37,
44, 50;** *Dictionary of Literary Biography Yearbook, 1981;* **and** *Major 20th-Century
Writers.*

William Trevor

1928-

(Full name William Trevor Cox) Irish short story writer, novelist, and dramatist.

The following entry covers Trevor's works from 1983 to 1991. For further information on his life and career see *CLC*, Vols. 7, 9, 14, and 25.

INTRODUCTION

Trevor is acknowledged as one of Great Britain's finest contemporary short story writers. Often compared to James Joyce and Frank O'Connor, he skillfully blends humor and pathos to portray the lives of people living on the fringe of society. While many of his early works are set in England, his most recent fiction incorporates the history and social milieu of his native Ireland. In such works as the novel *The Old Boys* and the short fiction collection *The Ballroom of Romance, and Other Stories,* Trevor explores the importance of personal and national history as he focuses on lonely individuals burdened by the past. Critic Jane Smiley observed that in Trevor's works "only the shallow characters manage to escape the implications of the past, and there are no compensations either; not even wisdom is a comfort. But his vision is too spacious to be cruel. . . . A master of literary craft who sees things whole, William Trevor is one of the foremost writers now writing in English."

Born in County Cork to Protestant parents, Trevor moved frequently while growing up and attended thirteen different schools before entering St. Columba's College in Dublin in 1942. "That constant moving has always left me a bit of an outsider and a loner," Trevor has recalled. "I never think of a home in Ireland, but of Ireland as a whole being home." In 1952 he left Ireland to accept a position teaching art in England, where he currently resides. While he was in his mid-thirties, he abandoned a successful career as a sculptor to pursue writing full-time. His first novel, *A Standard of Behaviour,* the story of a young man who loses his fiancée to an old schoolmate, was generally dismissed as pretentious and overly self-conscious. Trevor's second novel, *The Old Boys,* which concerns a group of elderly men whose return to their English public school rekindles former hostilities, proved significantly more successful, receiving the Hawthornden Prize for literature in 1964. In the years that followed, Trevor produced several plays, including *Going Home, Marriages,* and *Scenes from an Album,* as well as the short story collections *The Day We Got Drunk on Cake, and Other Stories, Angels at the Ritz, and Other Stories,* and *Old School Ties.* One story in particular—"The Ballroom of Romance"—established Trevor's reputation as a talented short fiction writer, inspiring comparisons to works by Evelyn Waugh, Graham Greene, and Muriel Spark. Focusing on a young woman

who decides to marry an alcoholic bachelor rather than live alone, this story also became a popular television play. Although he has published several successful novels since *The Old Boys,* including *Fools of Fortune* and *The Silence in the Garden,* Trevor considers the short story to be his principal genre. "I'm a short story writer who writes novels when he can't get them into short stories." Trevor's most recent short fiction collections, *The News from Ireland, and Other Stories, Family Sins, and Other Stories,* and *Two Lives: Reading Turgenev; My House in Umbria,* continue to generate popular and critical acclaim.

In his works Trevor typically focuses on eccentric individuals isolated from mainstream society. For example, in "The General's Day" a retired British army officer living in a shabby apartment falls victim to his housekeeper who exploits his loneliness and steals from him. The protagonist of "The Original Sins of Edward Tripp" also leads a secluded life with his half-crazed sister. Many of Trevor's characters are also imprisoned by the past, such as the title character of the short story "In Love with Ariadne" who cannot bear the shame of her father's suicide and rumors of his pedophilia. As a result, she enters the convent, refusing a future with a man who loves her. Other Trevor characters, dissatisfied with their present lives, relive the past. In "Virgins," a story published in *The News from Ireland,* two women who are unhappy in their marriages recall their youth when they fell in love with the same man, while the protagonist of *My House in Umbria* confuses memories from her past with the present.

Trevor's recent fiction incorporates the history and political turmoils of Ireland with his thematic concerns. *Fools of Fortune, Beyond the Pale, and Other Stories,* and *The News from Ireland* address more directly the troubles in Ireland and its tenuous relationship with England. For instance, in the title story of *Beyond the Pale,* English tourists are exposed to terrorist violence while staying at an isolated resort in Northern Ireland. While initially rationalizing the event, the vacationers eventually confront their own roles in perpetuating the Anglo-Irish conflict. The novel *Fools of Fortune* links the importance of history—both personal and national—in shaping individual destiny. Set in Ireland during the Anglo-Irish War, *Fools of Fortune* focuses on a young man who avenges the murder of his family by killing the British soldier responsible for their deaths. However, his guilt impels him to abandon his English lover and escape to Italy, where he is tormented by memories from his past.

While some critics have praised Trevor's emphasis upon the past, others have found his subject matter tiresome. Anatole Broyard lamented: "Too many of Trevor's characters are haunted by the past. After a while, when I grew tired of them, they reminded me of the sort of people who sentimentalize in attics. Although nothing demands deftness so much as nostalgia, Mr. Trevor is sometimes content just to shamble around it." Despite the often bleak tone of his work, Trevor is lauded for his compassionate characterizations. Robert Towers especially appreciated Trevor's sympathetic portrayal of misfits as "real" people, without resorting to condescension or caricature. In such stories as "A Husband's Return" and "Kathleen's Field" the protagonists are portrayed as honorable people who sacrifice their happiness to hide a family secret or shame. Trevor's restrained writing style and subtle humor have also received favorable attention. Michael Heyward observed: "[Trevor] is a master of nuance, of the flick of the wrist that seems to disclose everything. His sense of pace and timing, of the balance between dialogue and description, is flawless. The humor in his work is dark and unforgiving, though he also knows how to be simply funny. . . . He may write in an unassuming style, but whoever tackles his work in quantity becomes aware of an accumulating richness."

PRINCIPAL WORKS

SHORT FICTION

The Day We Got Drunk on Cake, and Other Stories　1967
The Ballroom of Romance, and Other Stories　1972
Angels at the Ritz, and Other Stories　1975
Old School Ties　(short stories and memoirs)　1976
Lovers of Their Time, and Other Stories　1978
The Distant Past, and Other Stories　1979
Beyond the Pale, and Other Stories　1981

The Stories of William Trevor　1983
The News from Ireland, and Other Stories　1986
Nights at the Alexandra　(novella)　1987
Family Sins, and Other Stories　1990
Two Lives: Reading Turgenev; My House in Umbria　(novellas)　1991

NOVELS

A Standard of Behaviour　1958
The Old Boys　1964
The Boarding House　1965
The Love Department　1966
Mrs. Eckdorf in O'Neill's Hotel　1969
Miss Gomez and the Brethren　1971
Elizabeth Alone　1973
The Children of Dynmouth　1976
Other People's Worlds　1980
Fools of Fortune　1983
The Silence in the Garden　1988

PLAYS

*The Old Boys　1971
Going Home　1972
The Fifty-Seventh Saturday　1973
A Perfect Relationship　1973
Marriages　1974
Scenes from an Album　1981

OTHER

A Writer's Ireland: Landscape in Literature　(nonfiction)　1984

*Adapted from Trevor's novel *The Old Boys.*

CRITICISM

Robert Towers

It has taken a while, but William Trevor's reputation as a major literary presence in the English-speaking world should by now be secure in this country. **The Old Boys,** his harshly comic novel of willful and perverse old age, got this Anglo-Irish writer off to a good start nearly 20 years ago. Since then seven novels and five collections of short stories have appeared—a record of productivity that few American writers of comparable quality have been able to emulate.

To coincide with the publication of his eighth novel, **Fools of Fortune,** Penguin has brought out **The Stories of William Trevor,** a fat paperback that contains all the stories from the previous collections. Readers are now in a position to take a longish view of the accomplishment of a master of short fiction who (like V. S. Pritchett, his only rival in England) has never settled for an easy formula. As for **Fools of Fortune,** which signals an abrupt shift into a more extended time-scheme and a more romantic mode than Mr. Trevor has hitherto attempted, opinion will, I predict, be divided between those who welcome the innovations and those who find them less than congenial to the author's temperament and craft.

Like Mr. Pritchett, Mr. Trevor in his early stories shows a robust appetite for the eccentric and the isolated, for prurient adolescents (**"An Evening with John Joe Dempsey"**), for half-cracked bachelors living with their crazy sisters (**"The Original Sins of Edward Tripp"**), for the seedy, the mother-dominated and the weird. The tone ranges from a clear-eyed and unsentimental sympathy to the kind of gleeful misanthropy that characterizes the novels of the same period. With commendable firmness and dispatch, Mr. Trevor sets his wryly observed scenes, often juxtaposing highly contrasting styles of speech and ways of life for comic effect. Here is a passage from **"The General's Day,"** a story whose elderly central figure could well have been one of the Old Boys in the novel of that name or one of the obstreperous inhabitants of Mr. Trevor's second novel, *The Boarding House*:

> The brown café, called 'The Cuppa,' was . . . bustling with mid-morning traffic. Old men and their wives sat listening to the talk about them, exchanging by the way a hard comment on their fellows. Middle-aged women, outsize in linen dresses, were huddled three or four to a table, their great legs battling for room in inadequate space, their feet hot and unhappy in unwise shoes. Mothers passed unsuitable edibles towards the searching mouths of their young. Men with girls sipped at the pale creamy coffee, thinking only of the girls. Crumbs were everywhere. . . .
>
> The General entered, surveyed the scene with distaste, and sat at a table already occupied by a youth engrossed in a weekly magazine. The youth, a fat bespotted lad, looked up and immediately grinned. General Suffolk replied in kind, stretching the flesh of his face to display his teeth in a smile . . . , for the pair were old friends.
>
> "Good morning, Basil. And how is youth and vigor today?"
>
> "Oh well, not so bad, General. My mum is in the family way again."
>
> "A cause for joy," murmured General Suffolk, ordering coffee with Devonshire cream and the fruit pie he favoured. "Your mother is a great one for babies, is she not?"
>
> "My dad says the same. He don't understand it neither. Worried, is Dad. Anyone can see that."
>
> "I see."
>
> "Well, it's a bit fishy, General. Dad's not the man to be careless. It's just about as fishy as hell."
>
> "Basil, your mother needs all the support she can get in a time like this. Talk about fishiness is scarcely going to help her in her ordeal."

But for all the humor, the lonely, impoverished old man's plight is not a happy one, and Mr. Trevor is characteristi-

cally objective in exposing its bleakness. Again and again, in both the stories and the novels, decent folk are victimized by moral monsters notable for their inventiveness and tenacity. In the General's case, it is Mrs. Hinch, his daily help, who exploits him, planning "for his absence a number of trunk calls on his telephone, a leisurely bath, and the imbibing of as much South African sherry as she considered discreet" and finally robbing him when he is drunk and sexually desperate.

In **"The Penthouse Apartment"** a janitor drunkenly wreaks havoc in a fancy living room set up to be photographed for a chic magazine—and then successfully manages to put the blame on an elderly spinster and her little dog. In most of this early work, Mr. Trevor's comic briskness and the energy with which he invests his villains do much to mitigate any depressing effect that the regular defeat or disappointment of the innocent might otherwise produce.

Drawing upon the dual nature of his heritage and experience, Mr. Trevor evenhandedly locates his stories in London, in rural England (where he now lives) and in provincial Ireland (where he was born and raised). One of the most touching of his Irish stories is **"The Ballroom of Romance,"** for which his second collection was named. It centers upon Bridie, an Irish farm woman in her 30's who resignedly looks after her crippled old father. Bridie goes to a dance hall on Saturday nights, attends mass on Sundays and favors a road-mender named Dano Ryan who plays the drums in the dance-hall band. But Dano, though kind, is not attracted to her, and the only amorous attention Bridie gets comes from a drunken bachelor, Bowser Egan, who presses kisses on her after the dances.

Bridie's choice is a discouraging one:

> She rode through the night [on her bicycle] as on Saturday nights for years she had ridden and never would ride again because she'd reached a certain age. She would wait now and in time Bowser Egan would seek her out because his mother would have died. Her father would probably have died also by then. She would marry Bowser Egan because it would be lonesome being by herself in the farmhouse.

Such a bald conclusion conveys little sense of the story's richness of texture or of the humor with which Bridie's relationships with the other women at the dance hall—at once friends, rivals and horrid examples—are sketched.

Repeatedly, Mr. Trevor's characters, ill equipped for the circumstances of their present lives, succumb to the ashen pleasures of living in the past. A number of them see ghosts. It is a tribute to Mr. Trevor's craftsmanship as well as his humanity that he can portray such a population of leftovers and losers with shrewdness, empathy and a delight in their particularity while neatly sidestepping the twin dangers of condescension and caricature. His special note of friendly objectivity derives in part from his technique as a story-writer: Unlike many of his contemporaries, he is a fearless and unabashed narrator who not only tells his readers what they need to know about the characters and their situations but also feels free to enter the minds of each of them whenever he chooses. In this respect, he belongs to a race of storytellers who ignore the limiting prescriptions of Henry James—and do so without any diminution of the dramatic impact of the work.

Since the mid-1970's there has been, I think, a subtle change of tone in the stories. The harsh comedy—the gleeful misanthropy—is less in evidence, as is the stance of impartiality; in the later work one can guess rather clearly where the author's sympathies lie. There has been an extension of his subject matter as well. In recent years Mr. Trevor has developed a series of stories that cast a cool, if judgmental, eye upon the mores (and especially the "wilting" marriages) of a set of prosperous Britons of indeterminate class who inhabit the outer suburbs of London. In these, he will remind some readers of his equally prolific American contemporary John Updike.

The series is announced by a piece called **"Angels at the Ritz,"** which depicts with delicacy and pathos the (incomplete) resistance of a couple to being drawn into a mate-swapping game in which, at the end of a Saturday night party, the husbands throw their car keys on the carpet and the wives, blindfolded, pick them up. Another well-known story in the series is **"Torridge"** (it appeared in *The New Yorker*), in which a fatuous reunion of former schoolmates, their wives and teen-age children is disrupted by the appearance of an often ridiculed "old boy" who boldly proclaims his homosexuality and then devastatingly spills the beans about what really went on at the school.

Still another extension of Mr. Trevor's range can be observed in the recent pieces that deal with the renewal of the "troubles" in Ireland, particularly as experienced by the Anglo-Irish long resident in the country or, in the remarkable story called **"Beyond the Pale,"** by English visitors at a posh hotel on the Irish coast. Violence, terrorism, melodrama—these are new elements in the work of a writer who had hitherto tended to subordinate the political to the personal. Occasionally their presence produces a sense of strain, a feeling that the materials have been unduly coerced for the sake of a shattering impact. But, in general, the level of performance remains exceptionally high, and the latest stories provide an exhilarating conclusion to the collection as a whole.

Mr. Trevor's novels have been for the most part short, compact, highly saturated works that explore the consequences of a single event or situation: a campaign for the presidency of an Old Boys' association, the death of the owner of a boarding house, or (in his fine seventh novel, ***Other People's Worlds***) the brief, unconsummated marriage of a middle-aged widow to a psychopath. His new book is also short, but it has the scope of a much longer work, containing as it does a complex action and spanning some 65 years from 1918 to the present.

The lurid and sorrowful events of Irish history beat like a muffled drum through the pages of ***Fools of Fortune.*** The narrator of the first extended section is Willie Quinton, born into a family of Anglo-Irish, Protestant gentry who have lived for generations in a Georgian house called Kilneagh in County Cork. Addressing the beloved woman, Marianne, whose destiny he shares, Willie begins his story with a nostalgic evocation of the house and the quaintly provincial life that his family led there until the end of World War I, when Willie was 8.

> I wish that somehow you might have shared my childhood, for I would love to remember you in the scarlet drawing room, so fragrant in summer with the scent of roses, warmed in winter by the wood Tim Paddy gathered. Arithmetic and grammar books were laid out every morning on an oval table, red ink in one glass, black in the other.

We meet Willie's affectionate father and strong, gentle mother, his two high-spirited sisters, his mildly eccentric aunts, his tutor (a defrocked Catholic priest) and the handful of Irish retainers that keep the household going.

Over the white marble mantel is a portrait that symbolizes the complex ties between England and Ireland—a major theme in the novel. The subject is Willie's great-grandmother, Anna Woodcombe Quinton, an English aristocrat who, having married into Ireland, becomes a local heroine during the famine of 1846. Willie's mother, we learn, is the second Woodcombe to marry a Quinton, and Willie's own Marianne is her niece. It is Marianne who says that "when you looked at the map England and Ireland seemed like lovers."

The idyll, of course, is set up to be shattered. Willie's father, despite ancestry and claws, identifies with the cause of Irish freedom and is visited by the revolutionist Michael Collins. A spy for the British is hanged (without the Quintons' participation or knowledge) on the grounds of Kilneagh, and in retaliation a band of Black and Tans, led by a Sergeant Rudkin, descend on Kilneagh, burning the house and killing Willie's father, his sisters, two menservants and the family dogs. Willie's mother never recovers from this atrocity; moving to Cork with her son, she becomes an alcoholic recluse and eventually kills herself. Violence exacts its toll from one generation to the next. Now it is Willie's turn.

The second major narrator is the English cousin, Marianne, with whom Willie falls in love while still in his teens. Returning to Ireland at the time of Mrs. Quinton's suicide, Marianne slips into Willie's bedroom in an effort to console the grief-stricken boy. Realizing later that she is pregnant, she journeys to Ireland a third time, only to discover that Willie has mysteriously disappeared and that no one will reveal his whereabouts. Here the story takes a fantastic turn. For the next 50 years Marianne waits at Kilneagh for the fugitive's return; meanwhile, she has given birth to a fey child, Imelda, who, in her eventual madness, becomes an object of holy awe for the local population.

All of this constitutes a vast amount of plot for a short novel to absorb. In fact, Mr. Trevor does little to make his story credible in terms of realistic fiction. The tragic events—the atrocity at Kilneagh, the acts of vengeance, the years of wandering and waiting, etc.—take place mainly offstage, so to speak, and seem like happenings in some ancient chronicle or myth. The principal characters, too, exist as figures in a romantic saga in which a concern for psychological *verismo* would seem out of place. Nothing prepares the reader for Mrs. Quinton's alcoholism, no matter how terrible the shock she endured. Or for the chaste and inexperienced Marianne's visit to Willie's bed. Or for the sudden transformation of a normal, if bereaved, schoolboy into what Willie becomes. These seem as arbitrary as the drinking of a love potion in *Tristan und Isolde.*

If Mr. Trevor had decided to flesh out his story in his usual way, with the scenic richness and the shrewdness of insight to which he has accustomed us, *Fools of Fortune* would perforce have been—at a minimum—half again as long. Instead, as if deciding to put his strongest gifts as a writer into escrow, he allows his novel to slip into a kind of Celtic twilight, hovering somewhere between dream and reality—as do the fantasies of the mad Imelda, to whom the legend of Cuchulain, the burning of Kilneagh and the lines from "The Lake Isle of Innisfree" seem all of a piece. The celebration of a love that can endure 50 years of separation does not strike me as ample compensation for all that has been omitted.

Having voiced my disappointment, I must add that *Fools of Fortune* is immensely readable and that it contains sections—the evocation of the old life at Kilneagh, an extended and often funny account of Willie and his cronies at boarding school—that are in Mr. Trevor's most skilled and generous vein. One can sympathize with his evident wish to loosen his form, to reach out for grand and tragic themes while concluding (on the basis of this one brave effort) that compact subjects, lending themselves to concentrated treatment, remain the most congenial to his talents. (pp. 1, 22, 24)

> Robert Towers, "Gleeful Misanthropy," in The New York Times Book Review, October 2, 1983, pp. 1, 22, 24.

Ann Hulbert

Heir to the Hibernian sense of history as a nightmare, William Trevor barely seems to sleep. Instead, he writes, all the time. For nearly two decades now he has produced a novel or a collection of short stories almost every year. His pen has never been the slightest bit jittery, however. It flows quickly, but with a fine-edged moral clarity. [Now] Penguin has published an omnibus edition of all of Trevor's stories (five collections' worth) [entitled *The Stories of William Trevor*] to accompany his new novel, *Fools of Fortune,* his ninth. Decorated with prizes in Ireland, where he was born, and in England, where he now lives, he is at last acquiring renown in this country.

Together, the thick volume of stories and the slender novel call attention to Trevor's central preoccupation: the wages of history, on both a public and private scale. Few of his characters are spared an uneasy sense of the past weighing on the present, looming over the future. The places they live are none too promising—wayside spots in England and Ireland, more often seedy than scenic—but it's the passage of time that seems to pose the most trouble.

In Trevor's earlier stories, the past in question is personal—the span of a lifetime, often a long one. Elderly characters are featured in his first collection, *The Day We Got Drunk on Cake.* In **"The General's Day,"** the 78-year-old General is feeling a little muddled even before he gets sur-

passingly sloshed, as he does in the course of his Saturday stroll—soon enough it's a roll—through the village.

> The General walked on, his thoughts rambling. He thought of the past; of specific days, of moments of shame and pride in his life. The past was his hunting ground; from it came his pleasure and a good deal of everything else. Yet he was not proof against the moment he lived in. The present could snarl at him; could drown his memories so completely that when they surfaced they were like the burnt tips of matches floating on a puddle, finished and done with. He walked through the summery day, puzzled that all this should be so.

The General has plenty of company in his puzzlement. Trevor's briskly paced stories generally center on characters who are slightly, or greatly, off-balance—easy victims not only of cooler, unkind types but also of their own delusions or uncomfortable insights. Trevor's prose, by contrast, is clear and confident, and the disparity gives a comic edge to even his bleakest stories.

And many of them are bleak. The present often snarls at Trevor's Protestant families living in what has become Catholic Ireland, at lonely women and confused husbands, at unhappy children and retirees in both England and Ireland. Their memories of better days tend to be elusive, unsettling rather than inspiring. The brazen romanticism of Trevor's titles for his first three collections—*The Day We Got Drunk on Cake, The Ballroom of Romance,* and *Angels at the Ritz*—betrays the irony characteristic of his nostalgia. That dizzying day with cake "would slide away like all the other days," lasting in memory "only as a flash on the brittle surface of nothing," the narrator of the title story laments. Those angels have long since fallen away from truth and into illusions, both comic and tragic.

Some fall further than others. Polly in **"Angels at the Ritz,"** one of the best stories, is among Trevor's sturdier characters. Surrounded by suburban pretense and middle-aged silliness, she hasn't succumbed—except to "middle-aged calmness," which she half-regrets. Malcolmson, a dismal divorced father in **"Access to the Children,"** has fallen further, solacing himself with ever fonder memories and fantasies the lower he gets. Each Sunday, after seeing his children, he "drank to the day that was to come, when the error he had made would be wiped away, when the marriage would continue. 'Ridiculous,' he said, 'Of course it is.'" Even Trevor's children feel a sense of loss; the young narrator of **"Mr. McNamara,"** another outstanding story, can no longer remember his dead father except with bitterness, having discovered a lie at the heart of the man's life. His own history, the boy feels, has been forever warped: ". . . I, who had taken his place, must now continue his deception, and keep the secret of his lies and his hypocrisy."

In Trevor's two most recent story collections, as well as in his new novel, history happens on a larger scale, and his imagination flourishes on the more expansive terrain. The time Trevor treats is an entire violent century: years of tension and outbreaks of trouble between England and Ireland, as well as two world wars. Here, as in his earlier stories, memory is an ambivalent power. As a child Matilda, the narrator of **"Matilda's England"** in *Lovers of Their Time,* listens to an old widow's recollections of World War I. On top of that dark inheritance, she accumulates her own memories of the next war and finally goes mad. In the title story of *Beyond the Pale,* Cynthia too is overwhelmed by history's legacy as she sits in an Irish hotel and listens to a man's tale of a childhood sweetheart turned terrorist. "Evil breeds evil in a mysterious way," she rants, more ravaged than enlightened by the appalling insight.

But there is another, transcendent, truth that time teaches and that some of Trevor's luckier characters learn. In **"Autumn Sunshine,"** also in *Beyond the Pale,* an Irish rector passes it on in a sermon "in which he tried to make the point that one horror should not fuel another, that passing time contained its own forgiveness." That merciful lesson is more powerful coming from Attracta in *Lovers of Their Time,* who discovers that her Protestant parents were accidentally killed by the same people who are her steadfast friends years later. "The years had turned the truth around," she attempts to explain to the children she teaches, small witnesses to too much violence.

Willie Quinton, the hero of *Fools of Fortune,* also knows the horrors of history up close—closer than any of Trevor's characters ever have. Endeavoring a more encompassing and emblematic treatment of the themes familiar from his recent stories, Trevor invests an Anglo-Irish family saga—three generations of Quinton travails—with almost allegorical significance. In this novel memory confronts a nightmare of history that has assumed mythic proportions.

The novel begins, however, on a more familiar and modest familial scale. The first half of *Fools of Fortune* is devoted to Willie Quinton's reminiscence of his childhood first at Kilneagh, the homestead of his Irish Protestant family over generations; then in a bleak apartment in Cork; and then in boarding school. Those days are a distant past for the man who is recalling them now, many years and ordeals later. The nostalgia that suffuses his account is the morally regenerative, rather than the escapist, kind—steady and clear, not blurred, moving by virtue of its understated exactness. Willie sees that past truly, free of either retrospective sweetness or bitterness.

Back then there were questions as well as comforts in life at Kilneagh with his tranquil Irish father, resolute English mother, two younger sisters, and loyal household staff. Willie basked in the slow provincial way of life he was born to. Yet he also wondered about two less predictable paths, love and politics, as he watched the servants' flirtations and observed revolutionary leader Michael Collins's visitations to his father. And unpredictable they certainly prove to be: one day Willie's father and sister are killed and Kilneagh burned by Black and Tan soldiers on a mission of revenge as crudely unjust as it is carefully calculated. After a sad span of years, Willie's love for his English cousin Marianne, which promises to be his salvation, is unexpectedly shattered by yet more violence.

It's here that Trevor's narrative also takes an unexpected turn, away from reminiscence and toward mystery and myth. Except for one more brief tale from Willie, the rest of the novel is told first by Marianne, who returns to Ireland pregnant with Willie's baby, only to find that he has disappeared; then from the perspective of their fey child, Imelda. Next to Willie's tragic ordeal, Marianne's trials seem Gothic, more a product of scene than of history. She has no past for us, only an arduous present, settling into the charred remains of Kilneagh to await Willie's return and to ruminate on his fate, often with bitterness. Their daughter Imelda dwells on her father's story with childish, then crazed, intensity. Obsessively piecing together fragments of the events before her birth, the child goes mad—a transformation Trevor daringly, and successfully, depicts, his prose still spare as he weaves myth with realism.

But if Trevor's prose is equal to his more expansive saga, his plot does not prove to be. Throughout the short novel, the narrative has been elliptical, leaping, usually with grace, among characters and in time. At the end, however, Trevor takes a transcendent step that is too large, moving beyond history and into a realm of fantasy that seems to reduce, rather than to redeem, his characters and their circumstances. Imelda's visions of fire and screaming children are replaced by idyllic images of old Kilneagh and evenings full of the linnet's wings. Revered among the local people, she radiates a calm born of her sense that "tranquility was there, no matter how death came"—a saintly shadow of her former self. Fortune deals equally sweetly with Willie and Marianne, for whom solace seems to come too easily. "They are aware that there is a miracle in this end," Trevor writes, in "the mercy of their daughter's quiet world in which there is no ugliness."

In fact, however, the miracle of this novel is not in its end—in Imelda's saintly vision, in which a transcendent truth has turned time around. The real miracle unfolds in Trevor's beginning—in Willie's humane memory, in which time has turned the mundane truth around. His recollection of his past, all its mystery and madness preserved, is far from a mere flash on the brittle surface of nothing. It is a light that might guide toward a more merciful future. (pp. 37-9)

Ann Hulbert, "A Long Story," in The New Republic, *Vol. 189, No. 22, November 28, 1983, pp. 37-9.*

Bernard McCabe

William Trevor is a wonderfully skilled storyteller, with a sharp eye for physical detail and a sharp ear for patterns of speech. He can encapsulate a character with miraculous speed, his invention seems inexhaustible and he offers an almost Dickensian range of faces and voices. He is also prolific. *Fools of Fortune* is his ninth novel to appear in the last twenty years; many of his plays have appeared on stage and television; *The Stories of William Trevor* brings together no fewer than sixty of his published short stories.

Trevor, unlike John McGahern, Edna O'Brien, Benedict Kiely, Bernard MacLaverty and Brian Friel, comes from the other side of the Irish fence, the Protestant side, or at least a corner of it—the world of Anglo-Irish gentlefolk who live in the Big House, or know the people there, who educate their sons in English or Anglo-Irish public schools and at Oxbridge or Trinity College, Dublin. It is a world that is almost gone. Like Elizabeth Bowen before him, Trevor moved to England long ago, and now lives there permanently. But he writes with fluent ease and apparently equal sympathy about both countries, both religions and all classes—especially well about the odd minglings that occur between them.

His topics are familiar enough. He deals with ordinary, domestic emotions, though with a heavy emphasis on the darker feelings, especially the deceptions and self-deceptions lurking in human relationships. Love is undermined by anxiety or fear. Sudden death comes to happy, stable families. Sudden disastrous unmaskings and revelations occur in unhappy, unstable families. There is a lot of loneliness, a lot of sexual inadequacy and sexual dishonesty. He is especially expert at evoking casual malignity, effectively dramatizing human evil without resorting to any of William Golding's elaborate mumbo jumbo. Trevor stays with the real. His careful observation of people and places—a bleak pub in bleakest South London, a hotel in the dreariest of small Irish market towns or the flabby luxury of the London middle class, "the fallen," as he calls them in one story—makes Trevor an old-fashioned realist.

The stories, though, are also full of fantasy. But it is the fantasy of real people behaving in the fantastic way that real people do. So the darkest tales tend to have a comic underlining. What begins as comedy will suddenly draw us up short, close to tragedy. **"The Penthouse Apartment,"** a knockabout farce with a drunken Irish janitor, an innocent *au pair* girl and a nervous spinster together wreaking minor havoc on a vulgarly expensive flat in London, suddenly changes key. We find we are really reading about how a lonely old woman's peace of mind is being irrevocably destroyed. The outrageous janitor, the man responsible for this destruction, is, with his effortless lies and anarchic resourcefulness, a favorite Trevor type, a comic rogue who battens on and arbitrarily destroys vulnerable people. Such figures turn up in many stories and in several novels, in *The Love Department* and *Other People's Worlds,* for example, and, in a sinister, psychopathic form, in *The Children of Dynmouth.*

A crueller version of **"The Penthouse Apartment"** comes in a later story, **"Broken Homes,"** in which a doctrinaire social worker arranges group therapy for a gang of teenagers by having them redecorate the apartment of a lonely old woman. She is defenseless before them as, drunk and drugged, they savagely destroy her modest possessions and her way of life.

For Trevor, real life is full of such fantastic black humor. In **"A Complicated Nature,"** a withdrawn bachelor is persuaded by a married woman from the apartment upstairs to help her reclothe the naked body of her afternoon lover, who has apparently died in action. **"In at the Birth"** presents a childless couple who keep an aging man in their upstairs nursery, fully equipped with playpen, outsize cradle, even a baby-sitter. When he dies they find another "baby." In **"The Hotel of the Idle Moon,"** a predatory pair simply moves in and takes over an old couple's quiet home. In

each case, the victim's inherent vulnerability is caught and exposed.

Not all of these stories come off. Trevor's odd, arresting sense of humor insists on those absurd specificities of human intercourse that interfere with potentially solemn or tragic moments. At his best he can convey a deep sense of the pathos of ordinary lives, yet the insistent high jinks in some stories tend to obscure or defuse compassion. One is then aware of a very cold artist's eye. But Trevor can achieve the utmost delicacy of both irony and feeling: in **"Another Christmas,"** about the breakdown of an old friendship stemming from a "wrong" political remark; in **"Being Stolen From,"** about a lonely middle-aged Irishwoman in London being pressured to return her small adopted child to its natural mother; and especially in **"Teresa's Wedding,"** a truly Chekhovian picture of a pregnant girl's forced marriage in an Irish small town. Each of these stories, by the way, is told largely from the woman's point of view. That kind of understanding self-projection is one of Trevor's great strengths. It shows itself most convincingly in his fine novel *Elizabeth Alone.*

In his most recent stories Trevor seeks to extend his range beyond the small parochialisms of the heart. Strainings and awkwardnesses result. **"The Bedroom Eyes of Mrs. Vansittart,"** for example, a rather silly and nasty story about sexual blackmail with a fancy new locale, Cap Ferrat, is a pointless parody of Somerset Maugham. Much more interesting are **"Beyond the Pale"** and the trilogy **"Matilda's England."** In **"Beyond the Pale"** Trevor confronts contemporary Anglo-Irish politics for the first time head-on. Four English bridge-playing old friends find that their annual visit to an idyllically serene, English-run hotel in a quiet corner of Northern Ireland is shattered by the sudden intrusion of political violence—a suicide following a vengeful murder. Three of the four, ruthlessly self-indulgent, treat the affair as a minor inconvenience, but the fourth, one of Trevor's recurrent half-crazed wise women, delivers a hysterical sermonette comprising a thumbnail history of Ireland's long oppression by England and a denunciation of their own corrupt lives and sleazy sexual practices. Clearly Trevor wants to link, in intensifying ways, the moral and psychological violence that this group visits upon itself to the larger horrors of Irish-English politics, where comparable malignities and victimizations prevail. But the revelation scene has too much work to do and seems stiff and strained.

There's a larger objection. Trevor is properly repelled by the cold-hearted violence that political dissension can produce, and is wonderfully good at depicting its immediate human impact. But that is all he does; the heart of the story remains the private misery of private violence. If you step into the complex world where private and public acts intermingle (Conrad's world, Malraux's, sometimes Graham Greene's), decent outrage at atrocities is fair enough but does not go far enough. (pp. 574-76)

The three short stories that make up **"Matilda's England"** are about the impact of other English wars. Matilda has grown up on a farm on an estate in southern England. As a child she is made to suffer vicariously the trauma visited on a woman whose idyllic life in the estate's manor house has been shattered by World War I. Matilda's own happy childhood is similarly destroyed by the deaths of her beloved father and brother in World War II. She conjoins the two disasters in her tormented mind and works a crazy vengeance on the new rich family that has taken over the estate. She ends up living there herself, alone in the collapsing house: in her madness she is avenging herself on history, too, by denying it. This strange story is closely followed by **"Attracta,"** a horrifyingly graphic tale of I.R.A. vengeance against the English in Northern Ireland. Vengeance is Trevor's obsession.

Fools of Fortune addresses Ireland's political violence at full length. Like **"Matilda's England,"** it is about a child's vulnerability, about an idyllic world destroyed and, more insistently than ever, about revenge. In 1918, 8-year-old Willie Quinton lives in Kilneagh, a big house in County Cork. His father is an Irish Protestant mill owner, his mother an elegant English-woman. Distant cousins live at Woodcombe, a "stately home" in Southern England. The ordered way of life at Kilneagh is richly evoked: custom and ceremony, innocence and beauty. Willie loves his parents, his two charming sisters, his eccentric great-aunts and especially Father Kilgarriff, a gentle ex-priest whose lessons on Ireland's turbulent history preach nonviolence. Life for Willie moves quietly and happily.

Then disaster strikes. The Quintons, although Protestant, have supported Irish nationalism for generations, and Willie's father befriends Michael Collins, the Sinn Fein leader in the Anglo-Irish war just getting under way. Then one of his millworkers, thought to be an informer, is found hanged, with his tongue cut out. In reprisal for this grisly act of vengeance, the Black and Tans (British mercenaries notorious for their atrocities) burn down Kilneagh. Willie's father dies trying vainly to save his two young daughters from the flames. A whole way of life is suddenly destroyed; Willie and his mother survive to live in frowsty lodgings in Cork City, and Mrs. Quinton, overcome by these events, becomes an alcoholic. Willie grows up warily and miserably.

Marianne, a distant cousin from the English Woodcombe connection, comes to visit and the two young people fall awkwardly in love. For one night they sleep together in the surviving wing of burnt-out Kilneagh. Willie returns to Cork to find that his mother has cut her wrists and died. He disappears. Marianne returns to Kilneagh pregnant, and stays on there with her baby, Imelda. Then we learn that the absent Willie has sought out the Englishman responsible for destroying his family, has worked *his* revenge by savagely stabbing him to death and has fled to Italy where he will spend most of a lifetime in exile.

The novel concludes with Willie in old age coming quietly back to Kilneagh to end his days with Marianne. A final twist: their sensitive daughter Imelda accidently learns in childhood the history of her family, her grandfather's terrible death, her grandmother's suicide, her father's murderous revenge. This knowledge drives her insane. Now middle-aged, she, like Matilda, has become a sort of holy fool who can see into the idyllic past. She is much respected by the local people, who believe she is "gifted" and bring the afflicted to her.

This dramatic, not to say melodramatic, tale is told, as ever, crisply and freshly. The house-burning is stunning in its impact; Willie and Marianne's hesitant lovemaking and the slow decline of Mrs. Quinton bring out all of Trevor's delicate observation. And the book jacket suggests that we read *Fools of Fortune* straight, as a powerful account of lives ruined by history, of fools destroyed by fortune.

It is not that simple. Trevor, characteristically, sounds some discordant notes. In a long central episode, for example, Willie goes to one of Trevor's awful public schools, and one night he sees a former teacher—"I was sacked for sodomy"—climb a ladder and carefully make water over the sleeping form of a fellow teacher who many years before had turned him in. Again, the key has changed; but this vengeful pissing surely parodies at length the whole novel's preoccupation with revenge, or at least defuses its impact in a familiar disturbing way.

The final chapter creates similar problems. It's a scene of general reconciliation, of a world gone beyond vengeance. But Trevor, who deftly changes style and tone throughout the novel, here chooses to write in an amalgam of romantic early Yeatsian wistfulness (the evening is full of the linnet's wings), lofty piety in a *Book of Common Prayer* mode (O Lord now lettest Thou Thy servant) and—no doubt to anchor us back into the real, to assure us that real people have led these fantastic lives—a flat everyday prose featuring trams, the laundry and chicken stew. Some strange narrative games are being played. The reunion of the aged star-crossed lovers ("Pleasanter to be here, he reflects, than seeing out his days in the Ospedale Geriatrico. . . . The skin of his hairless head feels tight, like a shell") surely parodies the happy endings of romantic novels.

As in some of the short stories, one is left with a sense of uncertainty. Trevor, as I have suggested, has been working to expand his range. *Fools of Fortune,* like **"Matilda's England"** and **"Beyond the Pale,"** clearly proposes some big allegorical meanings—violence and vengeance are to be lived out and Anglo-Irish relations to survive in the mystically peaceful person of Imelda—or something on those lines. Trevor is adept as ever in exploring his preferred personal themes, but in confronting these larger issues he seems to be uneasily working against his own imagination, which really hasn't much to say about them. He therefore retreats, covering his tracks with his old tricks, like one of his own outrageous janitors. The truth is he is much better off, if he would be content to stay there, in his uniquely observed microcosms of eccentric human encounters. (pp. 576-77)

Bernard McCabe, "Irish Outrage," in The Nation, *New York, Vol. 237, No. 18, December 3, 1983, pp. 574-77.*

Steve Connelly

William Trevor's *A Writer's Ireland* readily accommodates itself either to the coffee table or the scholar's library. It is simultaneously comely and enlightening, entertaining and instructive. Trevor establishes tone and method at once, offering apt quotations from Giraldus Cambrensis followed by his own concise and witty commentary:

> [Giraldus's] topographical map can have been
> nothing like the symbol of freedom with which,
> centuries later, the early Irish Free State re-
> placed a royal profile on its postage stamps. As
> a glimmer of nostalgia, the symbol still twinkles
> for the exile in bars all over the world: four prov-
> inces in different colors, green and red, yellow
> and blue, on the label of Paddy Whiskey.

Trevor is a master of the resonant fact, the informational nugget which accretes meaning through implication. Thomas MacDonagh noted that to the Irish "the half-said thing is dearest," and Trevor echoes him: "The art of the glimpse," he observes, is what "delights the Irish sensibility and the Irish mind." The art of the glimpse is inherent not only in Trevor's subject but also in his method.

Trevor announces immediately that this book "is not an academic investigation of either Irish literature or the inspiration of Irish landscape," but "is a writer's journey, a tour of places which other writers have felt affection for also, or have known excitement or alarm in." In spite of this disclaimer, he manages in under 200 pages to convey more effectively a sense of those two major Irish resources—literature and landscape—than have shelves of literary scholarship and ceaseless volumes of lavish Irish landscape books. To be sure, this is not an academic investigation, but it most certainly provides a rapid, insightful history of Irish literature. And though Trevor may not have intended it, his excellent text in combination with judiciously selected illustrations does impart an appreciation of the inspiration of Irish landscape rarely achieved by works attempting to do so.

That Trevor's survey of Irish literature is broadly chronological is reflected in his chapter titles: "The Distant Past," "The Gentle Years," "England's Ireland: The Anglo-Irish World," "The Uneasy 19th Century," "The Infant Nation," "The Road to Brightcity." However, he frequently and effectively doubles back to underscore the continuity of Ireland's literary heritage. He begins his chapter on the Anglo-Irish world, for example, by noting that "political complications" ensnare surveys of Irish literature after 1170—that, indeed, Ireland's landscape and literature mirror her history right up to the present. Putting an aspect of history in the context of the whole view— one of his numerous virtues—Trevor declares that "the Reformation was a stumbling block" because of the "Irish instinct for the mystery of faith, for the supernatural, for the excitement of yet another complex epic" which informs the national character. Ireland's cultural heritage includes a "need to believe, to accept with pleasure awe the mysterious and the wonderful," and this need has shaped literature and politics from the days of the earliest epics to the present.

Not only does Trevor's insight into continuity and the whole view qualify a strict chronological presentation, so too do the repeated references to two particular books: Giraldus Cambrensis's *The History and Topography of Ireland* and Mr. and Mrs. S. C. Hall's *Ireland: Its Scenery, Character*. . . . Giraldus merits extra attention "because

in a sense he led the way" as the first to document his appreciation of the Irish landscape. In the process, he also qualified as Ireland's first fiction writer"—"his credulity was part of his storyteller's genius"—with reports of such phenomena as a talking cross, a stone which daily bled sufficient wine for saying Mass, a man who was part ox, an island fatal to women.

The Halls were prototypes, reflecting "the developing tourist attitude to a country that was, above all else, 'picturesque.' " They wrote the archetypal Irish travel book, the many descendents of which even today echo their views—for good or ill. One wonders whether Trevor intended a small measure of revenge against those who presented the shattered monuments of Ireland's tragic history as "picturesque" when he used these lines from the Halls as caption for a contemporary photograph of a Belfast wall thoroughly blemished with political graffiti:

> The cleanly and bustling appearance of Belfast
> is decidedly un-national. That it is in Ireland,
> but not of it, is a remark ever on the lips of visi-
> tors from the south or west.

Such adept juxtaposition generates pith throughout the book, as when Trevor describes Cúchulainn as "a kind of Old Testament Christ, mystically born, a mixture of gentleness and extreme ferocity." There is pith, too, in such concentrated passages as his one-paragraph summary of the importance of trees to Irish history, literature, and landscape—from the ancient Celts to Seamus Heaney—or in his perceptive explanation of how the well-upholstered 19th-century novel came to bypass Ireland and of the consequences for Irish literature.

Indeed, any appreciation of *A Writer's Ireland* must border on display, for small gems sparkle throughout: "O'Brien's Dublin was somewhere to float away from, on stout or wine or as many balls of malt as the constitution could support," or "Many Irish writers subsequently adopted the O'Flaherty model and with some notable exceptions the short story in Ireland has ever since been in a hurry." Trevor moves so smoothly from close-up to overview that the reader barely has time to fully enjoy one jewel before Trevor has suggested its appeal and moved on to another class altogether. Yet, he strings them together masterfully. A discussion of Máirtín O'Cadhain's version of "a very familiar Irish tale" is suddenly an illumination of the modern landscape:

> Ó Cadhain's Brightcity glimmers all over the
> country now, as inevitably it must. . . . Beyond
> the fluorescent shopping-centres and wastelands
> of grey cement, motorcycles scramble through
> heather and boglands, over scree and rock-face.

Trevor follows this observation with a seeming paradox that "nothing can destroy the Ireland of its writers" or "the story of history, or saints and scholars who have left behind their voices." As if to comfort the reader he has only moments before "saddened," Trevor again surveys the echoes of history, of saints, scholars, and writers in the modern landscape, suggesting reassurance in the fact that even those things which change remain the same:

> Higgeldy-Piggeldy the travelling people are scat-

tered all over untidy Ireland, another aspect of its landscape as travelling people have always been. All around them there's more litter than in the past, more plastic bags that rain cannot destroy.

Trevor's eye for the piquant detail, the allusive particular, makes *A Writer's Ireland* captivating reading. It is definitely "a writer's landscape." Indeed, it calls to mind James Plunkett's *The Gems She Wore,* both for the high quality of its writing and its combination of the best aspects of a number of genres: literary anthology, literary survey, travel book, cultural history, coffee table volume, commonplace book. It is all of these things, and above all it is a superb exposition of the centrality of Ireland's landscape to its history and literature. The book's illustrations are magnificent, but more important, they are integral. Text and illustrations mutually reinforce one another. For example, Trevor quotes a passage from Elizabeth Bowen's *A Love Story* which begins, "Mist lay over the estuary." On the facing page is an evocative photograph of the estuary of the River Lee, overhung with mist. Similarly, a ruined cottage has this caption from William Allingham's *Tenants at Will:* "Mere shattered walls, and doors with useless latch / And firesides buried under fallen thatch." Happily, Trevor has chosen his illustrations carefully and with purpose; the result is a unity of text and picture rare in landscape books. William Trevor's *A Writer's Ireland* is a book with truly extensive appeal. It is difficult to imagine a reader who could not find a great deal to enjoy, whether it be Trevor's fine writing, his wit, the beautiful illustrations, or the numerous insights into Ireland and her people. (pp. 144-47)

> *Steve Connelly, in a review of "A Writer's Ireland: Landscape in Literature," in Éirc-Ireland, Vol. XX, No. 2, Summer, 1985, pp. 144-47.*

Elizabeth Spencer

Ten novels, six story collections and numerous dramatic writings have already come to us from William Trevor, and in this [*The News from Ireland, and Other Stories*] his seventh book of short fiction he proves once more that he is best when writing about his native land. Born in County Cork and educated in Dublin, he now lives in Devon. That England has been his home for a long time can be surmised from the quantity of fiction he has written about the English—country English, village English, London English, the English abroad. Mr. Trevor is a sturdy writer of clear and satisfying prose, who knows how to seek out the fictionally viable character and how to catch the pulse beat in a relationship or the secret strain within a heart. Yet his English stories seem strangely "produced," planned instead of crying to be written. It is the news from Ireland that, wander where he will, he is always returning to give voice to—and these are the stories with flow and power.

"**The News From Ireland**" may seem a curious title to give to the splendid initial story in this collection; we think of "news" as being of the present, while the action here takes place in 1847, during the Irish potato famine. For its grasp

of a historical moment, penetration of character and dramatic force, this story, less than 40 pages long, comes close to creating the resonant effect of a full novel. The setting is a mansion recently inherited by a distant relative of the Pulvertaft family, who has come to Ireland from England with his household. Sadly run down, the estate is about to pass back "into the clay it came from," but now it is Mr. Pulvertaft's "responsibility," and he goes about its restoration with devoted English thoroughness. He hires an estate manager for the grounds; for his children, he brings a governess from England, Anna Maria Heddoe.

Inside the elegant mansion, the three marriageable daughters are thinking of suitors and trips abroad, learning piano and French and gathering for music at tea time. Outside, workmen, weak from lack of food, are falling in their tracks; beggars are waiting before the church; soup is being distributed at the lodge gates; bloated, poisoned corpses are being piled into common graves. Fogarty, the butler, poor and Irish, grows fascinated with the governess, and singles her out for something like persecution. He is a curious study in motivation: he holds to the odd belief that nothing should have been done to redeem this property, that it should have passed back to nature to feed the common good. He thinks Anna Maria should know sinister things because, unlike the Pulvertafts, she can feel them. She is the one he can terrify—and he does. Through Fogarty, the "news" comes in upon her from the stricken outside to the privileged world within. And because of it, she will never be the same.

In his 1983 novel, *Fools of Fortune,* Mr. Trevor wrote about another time of turmoil in Ireland—when the English sent the Black and Tans to "quell civil disobedience"—as background for a story that reads like a family's passionate memories of its own unjust doom. "**The News From Ireland**" draws on this same source of feeling, as if on actual memory, it being, one feels, part of a tribal memory, where events have been stored from being told many times over. (One frequently finds the same quality in the writing of Southerners about the South.)

What about the other stories in this book? The English stories show us restrained and discouraged characters, unable to live richly experienced lives. In "**On the Zattere**," a father and daughter traveling in Venice have little to say to each other or to anyone else. The father is a widower; the daughter has lost her lover of 16 years. Both are trying to "make the best of it." The Irish stories, like "**Virgins**," "**Music**" and "**The Wedding in the Garden**," do indeed create a sense of strongly felt reality, and so engage the reader; but in these stories, too, one finds the sense of disaffection with life that marks this volume as a whole.

Mr. Trevor is a writer not given to easy solutions. Good. Still, after many downbeat endings, one begins to long for the bounce and the honest earthiness of other Irish writers.

From one story ("**The Property of Colette Nervi**") however-er, gleams of light do come through. A crippled Irish girl, living above her parents' small shop at a remote country crossroads, watches the people who travel from afar to seek out "a ring of standing stones that predated history."

One day a handsome French couple show up in a shining sports car. Obviously lovers, they pass before the girl's eyes in minute detail, distracting her from the Wild West romances she all but feeds on. A purse is lost. Years later it shows up as the property of the man who owned the pasture where the stones are, and when the girl marries him, the necklace found in the purse, warm with that day's images, is hidden below the neck of her wedding dress.

One does wish at the end of this worthy book that a few more French couples had passed through it, leaving favors of love.

Elizabeth Spencer, "French Lessons While the Neighbors Starve," in The New York Times Book Review, June 8, 1986, p. 14.

Veronica Geng

An Irishman who has spent his adult life in England, a Protestant born in southern Ireland a dozen years after the Easter Uprising (his birthplace of Mitchelstown then the heart of IRA rebel country), William Trevor has been writing for over 20 years about fanaticism. Or, more accurately, fanaticisms: he treats his subject not as an exotic phenomenon limited to a few "trouble spots," but as a commonplace mental habit taking as many forms as there are people who feel powerlessness or loss. Even when he deals explicitly with political violence (not often), he writes of its repercussions in the lives of people at some remove from it. He writes of a parentless Protestant girl, knowing only tolerance (as he did) in a Catholic town, and the embittered Protestant neighbor who tells her a baffling story of her parents' being "destroyed like pests" in an ambush meant for the Black and Tans.

Usually Trevor sounds more like this: "Quigley had seen her, he said, a week before her husband died, hitting her husband with a length of wire because he would not oblige her with his attentions." Seemingly particular to the point of eccentricity, this sentence actually contains the basic elements of Trevor's fiction: the mock-scrupulous "he said" immediately trampled by the detail of the report; inattention that triggers a cycle of pain and retaliation, and ultra-attention that elaborates an alleged fact into an interpretive scenario hard to swallow.

Whether the reader is meant to swallow it depends. Trevor's characters range from artless country servant-girls to a London antiques dealer with a racket; from West Indian immigrants to Riviera expatriates to a rural Irish clergyman whose daughter brings home a cockney parlor-Provo loaded for bear. Among them are hardened obsessives and sudden converts of every stripe, thrown up against zealous skeptics, rational minds out of their depth, and people who just don't want to hear about it. And they all spout stories: gossip, delusory extrapolations, highly colored public and private histories, and numerous failed drafts—frustrated attempts to arrange what they know in a way that sounds plausible. They use the words "truth" and "lie" more often than George Orwell.

"Fact" is a word that especially gives Trevor the willies. One of his stories begins, "For years, ever since she'd listened to Liz Jones telling the class the full facts of life, Eleanor had been puzzled by the form the facts apparently took when different people were involved." Even his plainest use of the word has a gingerly spin on it ("He was not a particularly clean man, and this was a fact he now thought about"), and his characters' arrangements of facts tend to go off like explosive devices:

> Barbara held out hairs that had been wrenched from the head of a boy called Bridle. She had found them in a wastepaper basket; Bridle had said they were his and had shown her the place they'd come from. She returned the hairs to a plastic bag that once had contained stockings. The hairs would be photographed, Barbara said, they would appear on the front page of a Sunday newspaper. . . . Milton Grange, turreted, baronial, part ivy-clad, would be examined by Sunday readers as a torture chamber.

The shakiest logic flowers with the most precise details. "*In vino veritas,*" says a tipsy woman who, unhappy and neglected herself, is seized with sympathetic insight into the nature of a wimpy stranger at a party. "I daresay you're a pervert . . . , [a] chap who likes to dress himself out as a children's nurse and go with women in chauffeur's garb. . . . You are a homosexual." Others then act on the reality the fiction has acquired. "Heads turned. . . . He had been heard to cry that he was not a homosexual, and people had wished to see for themselves."

Trevor is a satirist of mental contortions. He's not a descriptive writer but an analytical one—an analyst of misunderstandings. He can write so touchingly of children's believing minds that when a boy comes to wonder "why my father was being described as a decent man," you're shocked to see the thought born in cold print. He can also write of people incapable of such a spontaneous thought, bogus to the core, like the man who fatuously calls himself "helpless in an emergency" and is proved all too correct when his mental processes are exposed: "He wondered if she might be Jewish, which would account for her emotional condition." The dynamics are the same—a cycle of ignorance and intolerance, as ritualized as a P. G. Wodehouse farce. Trevor once wrote an appreciation of Wodehouse, and it applies somewhat to himself:

> . . . his people insist on coming to life. They do so in sudden spasms or by acting out of character. . . . It all looks like a carnival of eccentricity in which anything can happen and often does. But there are rules, . . . the well-kept rules of a one-man band.

Trevor draws too much from life to be a one-man band, but he draws always to fit his scheme. His rules are a satirist's, technical and moral. He's a theme-and-variations artist, with one theme.

"The News from Ireland," the long title story of Trevor's new collection, is his primal story. From it has flowed all his earlier fiction—five volumes of stories, twice as many novels—and he's needed 20 years to be able to write it.

It takes place in Ireland in 1847-48, during the Great Famine, on an estate recently inherited by an English family named Pulvertaft, whose ancestor was granted the land by Elizabeth I. They now think of it as "home"; but the Irish Protestant butler, Fogarty, thinks of them as still "the Pulvertafts of Ipswich," wishing "he might speak the truth as it appears to him: that . . . they perpetrate theft without being thieves. He . . . has nothing against them beyond the fact that they did not stay where they were."

Mr. Pulvertaft is having a road built around the estate, employing local men whose families are starving; from the village comes a rumor that peasant parents have taken to the priest a child with the stigmata on its hands and feet. These two responses to emergency, one seeming practical and the other transcendental, are interpreted by different members of the household: the road as an act of charity, a nice route for a picnic drive, a continuation of the work of the Mad Dean Swift (said to have helped plan the original landscaping), and a "useless folly" that "leads nowhere and only insults the pride of the men who built it"; the child's wounds as a miracle, a superstition, an analogy to poor people eating their babies "like in the South Seas," and a fraud.

Trevor enters all these points of view, with conviction and satire gently fluctuating. Between them he scatters sparse facts, like crumbs: a damp cloth laid over a fruitcake, ice broken so birds may drink. The story tightens into a struggle between Fogarty and Miss Heddoe, the imported English governess. Heddoe believes in the road *and* the stigmata. Even when told the baby has died, its marks inflicted by the parents, she can't dismiss "what the people who were closer to the event took to be a miracle." But Fogarty hates her for being the "voice of reason" that dismisses as "drunk," "insane," and "ridiculous" the only thing *he* believes in:

> If the estate had continued in its honest decline, if these Pulvertafts had not arrived, the people outside the walls would have travelled here from miles around. They would have eaten the wild raspberries and the apples from the trees, the peaches that still thrived on the brick-lined walls, the grapes and plums and greengages, the blackberries and mulberries. They would have fished the lake and snared the rabbits on Bright Purple Hill. There is pheasant and woodcock grown tame in the old man's time. There was his little herd of cows they might have had. I am not putting forth an argument, miss; I am not a humanitarian; I am only telling you.

This is a dream of the "ghost republic," as Conor Cruise O'Brien called it in a recent article in the *New York Review of Books:* "undying, or undead, as an ideal—. . . a republic of the whole island of Ireland, totally separate from Britain, . . . an ever-unrealized republic, for which heroes and martyrs died." Trevor prefers the less secular term "Paradise." In an earlier story, he had a wealthy widow die, willing the "Paradise" of her house and gardens to an institute "for the study of rare grasses." The butler, gripped by an idea, a devious speculative tale of medical negligence, turns into "some creature out of which a devil of hell had come," bullying the other servants into a blackmail plot whereby the doctor will "lose" the death certificate so they can bury the dead employer in the garden and live there forever. The doctor, stolidly hearing him out,

concludes that "it seemed cruelly fitting that the loss of so much should wreak such damage in pleasant, harmless people."

This is one of the few times it's tempting to accept a character's voice as Trevor's own. In his only nonfiction book, *A Writer's Ireland: Landscape and Literature* (1984), treating Ireland as a place virtually brought into being by the interplay between physical facts and various fictions imposed on them, he came maybe as close as he can to explaining his role in his own stories:

> [The commentator] Giraldus of Wales visited Ireland for the first time in 1183. . . . He was not always accurate—indeed, so often the opposite that he might be dubbed . . . Ireland's first fiction writer. But usually, in his claims, he was simply quoting what others had told him, for his credulity was part of his storyteller's genius. . . .
>
> The cocks of Ireland, so Giraldus says, crow differently from other cocks. . . . Near Wicklow there lived a man who "had all the parts of the human body except the extremities, which were those of an ox." . . . In Dublin there was a cross which spoke.
>
> "The island is rich in pastures and meadows, honey and milk, and wine, but not vineyards. Bede, however, . . . says that it is not altogether without vineyards. On the other hand Solinus says that it has no bees."

If Trevor loves Wodehouse for his rules, he loves Giraldus for having no rules, for his "credulity." Trevor will listen to any damn thing—and not just listen, but deeply entertain it. This is what humanizes his satirist's strictness. He writes often about people who so abhor a lie that they can't hear the truth a lie may contain. Such people create a deadly silence. In one of his many stories set in prep schools (a natural breeding ground for oppressive and defensive simulations), a boy calling himself a "pocket Hamlet" insists his father murdered his mother to marry her sister; and a young Horatio, worried for his friend's mental state, tries confiding in a schoolmaster, Mr. Pinshow:

> "Do not lie, boy. I know a lie. I feel a lie on its utterance. Likewise, do not exaggerate."
>
> I knew then that it was going to be useless. It had been a mistake to come to Pinshow. . . . I said nothing, hoping he would not press me.
>
> "I see," he said.

Pinshow fills with his own fantasies the vacuum he's created, causing events to realign sadly with their Shakespearean source.

Fanaticism is fantasy turned aggressive. It's not always clear where Trevor's characters cross that line. He exercises our capacity to listen, to tolerate, to seek out the places where forgiveness might break the cycle. To do this, to invite us to entertain what these people say, I think he needs to remain entertaining—to give us his funny, beautiful, horrifying details. This isn't a question of seriousness; **"The News from Ireland"** contains his blackest joke, when the estate manager says of the peasants starved by the English Corn Laws, "Fraud is grist to their mill."

"Virgins," the richest of the other stories in the new book, is perhaps drawn from Trevor's teenage memories of Ireland during World War II—compared to England, a place of nourishment and safety. An Irish schoolgirl and her visiting English friend, in an idyll of movie-going and food, both get crushes on a sophisticated, sickly neighbor, Ralph de Courcy, whose deceit causes them to deceive each other: a high-comedy take on the all-seeing, saintly invalids of literature. Most of these other stories, though, are thinner, their pleasures cooler and more abstract. A handbag stolen from an Italian tourist pays for a poor couple's fraudulent marriage; a mother obsessed with completing her dead husband's scholarly work—"an investigation into how, over centuries, the meanings of words had altered"—gives her daughter "the vengeful urge to destroy. . . ." Some stories occur in Italy, where Trevor has lived for periods since (he told an interviewer a few years ago) he thought it would refresh him to be "a stranger," "not to know a language." But maybe his optimum distance from home is the width of the Irish Sea. Or maybe, if everything you write is in a way the news from Ireland, you grow sickened at taking pleasure in writing about it—weary of it all, as the people who live there are.

Yet these are still the best stories around. And in two recent ones in the *New Yorker,* there's renewed joy in detail, and a familial emotion. The latest, **"Kathleen's Field,"** is about a daughter sold by her family, everyone touched by guilt—all for an extra piece of land. The land is pictured as "the morning sun lingered on the heart of it . . . , the curving shape of it like a tea cloth thrown over a bush to dry." That small map can make you cry.

Trevor's characters crave credibility, legitimacy. (He's written several times about illegitimate children.) The implication of all his work is that no child, pervert, maniac, or fanatic, no one "confused," "silly," "senile," or "away in the head," should be dismissed as illegitimate, cut off from family or history. Trevor is a democrat without illusions, and each of his characters another precinct heard from. (pp. 28-30)

> *Veronica Geng, "Geographer of Delusions," in* The New Republic, *Vol. 195, No. 23, June 9, 1986, pp. 28-30.*

Robert Towers

The Anglo-Irishman William Trevor writes in a tradition of storytelling that is seldom encountered in America today. He takes for granted the importance of the historical and social setting in which he places his characters and takes pains to render it plausibly. He know that class distinctions matter, even when they are not emphasized. He imagines a past for his characters that is more than merely personal or familial, a past that bears down continuously on their present behavior. As a result, his short stories, like those of V. S. Pritchett, often have the weight and density of miniature novels. William Faulkner once wrote such stories in this country; Peter Taylor—another southerner—continues almost alone to do so today.

> **Trevor on the process of writing:**
>
> I think in an awful lot of what I write, there are no heroes and no villains. It's always circumstance and fate which catch you in the end; much more something to be aware of.
>
> I mine stories like a coal miner. And I may start with a character that I'm not so fond of, and end up being fond of the person. It is that little journey, I think, that makes the story for the fiction writer an essential journey—it takes it out of you. Writing fiction *should* take it out of you, make you old before your time.
>
> *Trevor, in an interview with Gail Caldwell, reprinted in* The Writer, *October, 1990.*

The most novellike of the stories in Trevor's impressive new collection [*The News from Ireland, and Other Stories*] is the title story itself, which is actually set in the past. **"The News from Ireland"** takes place in 1847 and 1848, when for two consecutive years the Irish potato crop has rotted in the ground. An English gentleman, Mr. Pulvertaft, has inherited the decayed estate of a distant relative in Ireland and is now busy "improving" it in the best tradition of his class. Along with the estate, the Pulvertafts have also inherited a butler, Fogarty, and a cook, Miss Fogarty, who regard their new employers with a skeptical—and, in the case of the butler, a disapproving—eye. Fogarty would like to see the estate sink back into the clay from which it came. The Pulvertafts have also hired an English estate manager—a brusque, one-armed ex-military man named Erskine—and they have imported an English governess, Miss Heddoe ("a young woman of principle and sensibility") to take charge of the youngest of their four children. Fogarty watches Miss Heddoe's response to Ireland with an obsessive curiosity.

Inside the estate, the conventions and entertainments of a well-conducted Victorian household are genially maintained. Outside, the famine is devouring its tens of thousands. The Pulvertafts, who are well-intentioned people, do what they can: soup is dispensed at the gatehouse to the starving women and children, and Mr. Pulvertaft has ordered a road to be built on the estate—a road leading nowhere—to give employment to men weakened by hunger.

Such is the situation when the sinister Fogarty tells Miss Heddoe (whose diaries and letters he has been secretly reading) that a newborn baby in the neighborhood has the marks of the stigmata. Reactions to this report vary greatly: the local peasantry regard the event as a miracle sent from heaven in a time of distress; the impressionable Miss Heddoe is moved; the Pulvertafts and Mr. Erskine see it as one more instance of benighted Catholic superstition; and Fogarty, when the baby soon dies, maintains that the marks were inflicted by the parents, who had already lost their other children to the famine. Time passes and complications ensue, among them a possible match between the governess and Mr. Erskine.

Trevor deftly constructs his complex story from the diaries of Miss Heddoe, from conversations between Fogarty and his sister, and from passages of direct narration, infusing them with the atmosphere of the period. Here is a section of Miss Heddoe's diary that reminds me of scenes from Charlotte Brontë or the early Trollope; she is reporting the Pulvertafts' discussion of the new road:

> "Now, what could be nicer," he [Mr. Pulvertaft] resumed, "than a picnic of lunch by the lake, then a drive through the silver birches, another pause by the abbey, . . . and home by Bright Purple Hill? This road, Miss Heddoe, has become my pride."
>
> I smiled and nodded, acknowledging this attention in silence. I knew that there was more to the road than that: its construction was an act of charity, a way of employing the men for miles around. . . . In years to come the road would stand as a memorial to this awful time, and Mr. Pulvertaft's magnanimity would be recalled with gratitude.
>
> "Might copper beech trees mark the route?" suggested Adelaide, her dumpling countenance freshened by the excitement this thought induced. . . .
>
> "Beech trees indeed! Quite splendid!" enthused Mr. Pulvertaft. "And in future Pulvertaft generations they shall arch a roof, shading our road when need be. Yes, indeed there must be copper beech trees."
>
> The maids had left the drawing room and returned now with lamps. They fastened the shutters and drew the curtains over. The velvets and silks changed colour in the lamplight, the faces of the portraits became as they truly were, the faces of ghosts.

Yet while **"The News from Ireland"** is the longest piece in the collection, it is still a short story, less than forty pages. The impression of Victorian amplitude is essentially *trompe l'oeil,* created by a master of foreshortening.

The other stories have contemporary settings—Ireland, England, or Italy—and the present situation is always conditioned by the characters' past, a past made explicit by dramatized scenes or extended flashbacks. In **"Virgins,"** two middle-aged, married women have trouble recognizing each other when they meet in the "wasp-striped" cathedral in Siena. One, Laura, is English; the other, Margaretta, is Irish. Decades before, they had become the closest of schoolgirl friends when Laura was sent to Ireland for safety and nourishment during the war. The scenes from the past are wonderfully done as Trevor evokes the delight the girls take in each other and their excitement in visiting Ralph de Courcy, the invalid son of local gentry, with whom they both fall secretly and rapturously in love. Cut off from active life by a rheumatic heart, Ralph de Courcy shamelessly indulges himself by toying with the affections of both girls, writing love letters to each of them before dying, as predicted, at an early age. Their jealous love for Ralph leads to a break between the two girls. Now, meeting in Italy years later, the two women realize that their lives might have been significantly different if

their friendship had continued, a friendship which "in its time went deeper than the marriages they have mentioned." But they are strangers now. At the very end Trevor allows himself a summation unthinkable to contemporary practitioners of the open-ended story, one that links his story, without strain or falseness, to that ancient theme: the vanity of human wishes.

> Regret passes without words between them; they smile a shrugging smile. If vain Ralph de Courcy had chosen their girlish passion as a memorial to himself he might have chosen as well this rendezvous for their middle age, a waspish cathedral to reflect a waspish triumph. Yet his triumph seems hollow now, robbed by time of its drama and the heady confusions of an accidental cruelty. Death's hostage he had been, a ghost who'd offered them a sleight of hand because he hadn't the strength for love. They only smile again before they part.

Trevor enjoys the boldness of a non-autobiographical imagination. He is free to enter the mind and inhabit the body of a well-to-do Irish widow of fifty-nine in **"Bodily Secrets."** Mrs. O'Neill's body—once her delight—is now repellent to her: "Flesh hung loosely, marked with pink imprints of straps or elastic. If she slimmed herself to the bone there would be scrawny, empty skin, loops and pockets, hollows-as-ugly as the bulges." Lonely but unwilling to expose such a body, she defies her grown children by knowingly marrying a closet homosexual (and a Protestant to boot!) who, unlike her other suitors, can be counted on not to enter her bedroom and "stake his claim there."

Trevor slips with similar ease into the false cheeriness of an English widower, and into the bitterness of his disillusioned daughter in **"On the Zattere,"** and in **"Lunch in Winter"** into the boozy consciousness of a much-married ex-chorus girl with an eye for young Italian waiters. While the use of a single point of view—whether in the first or the third person—has become almost a fixed canon in the contemporary short story, Trevor does not hesitate to "get behind," in Henry James's phrase, a number of disparate characters in the same piece. Yet this freedom of movement does not create diffuseness, as it can so easily do in unskilled hands; rather, it adds to our impression of a novelistic breadth and variety. Even when confined to three or four characters, Trevor's stories seem thickly populated.

Not all the pieces that make up *The News from Ireland* are first-rate. **"Two More Gallants"** is little more than an anecdotal byproduct of one of the stories in Joyce's *Dubliners.* Another, **"Music,"** reads like a compendium of dull and familiar details of Irish provincial life. But admirers of Trevor's novels—particularly *The Old Boys*—and his earlier collections of stories will find four or five pieces here that stand with the very best work that this splendid writer has produced. (pp. 32-3)

Robert Towers, "Good News," in The New York Review of Books, *Vol. XXXIII, No. 11, June 26, 1986, pp. 32-3, 35.*

Michael Ponsford

"Nobody tells the truth," says Mrs. Fitch in one of William Trevor's earliest short stories, **"Raymond Bamber and Mrs. Fitch,"** [in *The Stories of William Trevor*]. She is speaking rather drunkenly at a cocktail party—a typical Trevor setting—to Raymond Bamber, who has been relating the mundane events of his past year, the most remarkable of which has been the death of his old nanny. A shy man, as he describes himself, Raymond is unprepared for the way in which Mrs. Fitch is about to deny her own statement about truth and shatter the glib surface of the party. Indicating her elderly features, she tells Raymond that she is fifty-one but could be mistaken for sixty-five; his polite and gracious answer is immediately flung back at him:

> "You don't look fifty-one," said Raymond. "Not at all."
>
> "Are you mocking me?" cried Mrs. Fitch. "I do not look fifty-one. I've told you so. I've been mistaken for sixty-five."
>
> "I didn't mean that. I meant—"
>
> "You were telling a lie, as well you know. My husband is telling lies too."

She goes on to tell her reluctant and embarrassed listener about her unhappiness at her youthful-looking husband's persistent philandering and that she looks older than her years; as she does so, she is unable to resist adding some disconcerting insights into the character of Raymond himself. She justifies this rudeness by insisting on her truthfulness. "What I say is true," she remarks, and, when Raymond tries desperately to rid himself of this unpleasant company, "You are trying to avoid the truth." But Raymond thinks of the truth in very different terms as he reveals when Mrs. Fitch, in a brief respite, asks him about himself:

> "Actually, I've told you quite a bit, you know. One thing and another—"
>
> "You told me nothing except some nonsense about an old creature in Streatham. Who wants to hear that, for Christ's sake? Or is it relevant?"
>
> "Well, I mean, it's true, Mrs. Fitch."

Mrs. Fitch cannot find any truth in the inane chatter of cocktail parties, and her reply to Raymond is that their hostess, Mrs. Tamberley, had once referred to him as "a grinding bore." Mrs. Fitch finds truth in the revelation of the inner self, however unpleasant. "I cannot tell lies," she says; "I am a little the worse for wear . . . but I can still tell the truth"; and, as her husband finally leads her away, she claims "I've been telling him the truth." Her last words, *"In vino veritas,"* sum up her campaign.

William Trevor, who has emerged as one of the most significant—and one of the most prolific—contemporary writers, is almost as preoccupied with truth as is Mrs. Fitch. This is noted by Julian Gitzen in his astute survey of Trevor's fiction, both the stories and the novels, that was published in 1979 ["The Truth-Tellers of William Trevor," *Critique: Studies in Modern Fiction*]. Gitzen con-

tends that Trevor's characters invariably respond to an unpalatable truth in one of two ways: "some accept the truth, while others find illusion the only bearable remedy." Gitzen's emphasis, however, is on those characters who "display strength in accepting or reconciling themselves" to "unpleasant truths," finding that "Trevor repeatedly demonstrates that acceptance of truth requires resoluteness and the power of forgiveness."

But Trevor's world, I think, is darker than this emphasis allows. The short stories, whose narrow scope throws the features of Trevor's longer fiction into strong relief, can certainly depict characters who accept the truth, but the consequences of such an acceptance are never very welcome. Rather than accepting, the characters are more frequently forced to acknowledge a truth, but there are many others for whom the truth is elusive or for whom the discovery of truth can mean only unhappiness. To intensify this negative focus, Trevor chooses as his agents of truth characters who are somehow apart from the rest of society and whose conveying of truth can only pass on a sense of alienation. Trevor's characteristic perception of truth is two-fold: either the truth is ineffectual, or it effects only misery and despair. It is just as much the denial as the acceptance of truth that demands resoluteness.

Raymond Bamber demonstrates one kind of resoluteness—a deeply entrenched naivety, a blindness about society and about himself in particular: he is the perpetual ingenue. His analysis of Mrs. Fitch's behavior fails to countenance that she might, in fact, have been telling the truth; he is unable to convince another party-guest, Mrs. Grigson, however:

> "She has a reputation," said Mrs. Grigson, "for getting drunk and coming out with some awkward truths. I've heard it said."
>
> "Not the truth," Raymond corrected. "She says things about herself, you see, and pretends she's talking about another person."
>
> "What?" Said Mrs. Grigson.
>
> "Like maybe, you see, she was saying that she herself's a bore the way she goes on—well, Mrs. Fitch wouldn't say it just like that. What Mrs. Fitch would do is pretend some other person is the bore, the person she might be talking to. D'you see? She would transfer all her own qualities to the person she's talking to."

Raymond's self-delusion is a survival technique, a way to avoid becoming a sadder and wiser man. Mrs. Fitch is indeed rather like the Ancient Mariner, impelled to tell her tale if only to *convey* (in both senses of that word) her misery: "Oh yes! she said to Raymond, attempting to pass a bit of the unhappiness on. 'A grinding bore. Those were the words of Mrs. Tamberley'."

But Mrs. Fitch fails to convey this truth, and not only because of Raymond's self-delusion. She also fails because, in her drunkenness, she is unable to restrain her imagination, inventing further unpalatable "truths." As her husband escorts her from the party, she passes these on to him—within earshot of Raymond:

I was telling him what I am and what you are, and what the Tamberleys think about him. It has been home-truths corner here for the woman with an elderly face and for the chap who likes to dress himself out as a children's nurse and go with women in chauffeur's garb. Actually, my dear, he's a homosexual."

Of course, nothing could go further from the truth about the ineffectual, sexless Raymond Bamber. Hearing this falsehood about himself, he can easily dismiss all of Mrs. Fitch's statements as fabrications of a warped imagination.

Trevor's art, though it is concerned with the way in which a society is built on deceptions, treating this theme with some measure of comedy, is not exactly satirical: the truth never reforms manners or draws order out of society's chaos as it does in pure satire. For Trevor's sad-comic world is peopled not by reformers or malignants but by a variety of innocents, ingenues for whom the truth never dawns, like Raymond Bamber. But most are not so fortunate—or determined—in resisting the truth as Raymond, and far more numerous than the perceptual innocents are those for whom the acknowledgement of truth means alienation and the loss of stability. Trevor focusses on innocents (he has a particular fondness for stories about children) at their fall, being shocked into a world of deceit and lies, by a perpetrator of the truth; Trevor thus finds the exposure of hypocrisy and deception—the insistence on the truth—as an essentially destructive impulse. An encounter with truth can yield only misery, at best a bewildered frustration, at worst the madness of insight.

Characteristic of the pattern is **"Mr. McNamara,"** a story set in "ivy-clad Ireland" about a boy's progress to an unpleasant truth. The narrator is a thirteen-year-old whose father makes frequent trips to Dublin, trips that include a visit to Fleming's Hotel, where he talks with his friend, Mr. McNamara. The accounts of Mr. McNamara and his household that the boy hears are so vivid that even the death of his father cannot erase the picture of them:

> The house in Palmerston Road, with Mr. McNarmara's aunt drinking in an upstairs room, and the paper-thin Mrs. Matchette playing patience instead of being successful in the theatre, and Mr. Matchette with his squashed forehead, and Trixie O'Shea from Skibbereen, and the spaniel called Wolfe Tone: all of them remained quite vividly alive after my father's death, as part of our memory of him.

The narrator's inevitable curiosity about this aspect of his father eventually leads him to cut school to cycle to Dublin where he hopes to visit Mr. McNamara at Fleming's Hotel. The guest turns out to be another instance of *in vino veritas,* because the boy drinks rather more of the local beer than he can cope with. In his drunkenness, he learns from the landlord that the name of the woman who has attracted his curiosity all afternoon—he has already wondered whether she might be a prostitute—is McNamara. The awareness that his father had been involved in an affair is devastating to the boy, for this truth ironically engenders more deceit, passed on like an inheritance from father to son.

At Christmas, back with his family, he was still overwhelmed by the misery that truth brings:

> It was no consolation to me that he had tried to share with us a person he loved in a way that was different from the way he loved us. I could neither forgive nor understand. I felt only bitterness that I, who had taken his place, must now continue the deception, and keep the secret of his lies and his hypocrisy.

The uncovering of truth, then, merely complicates the deceit. The truth does not enlighten the narrator but precipitates his fall from innocence into experience. He has learned the bitter truth of the separation of appearance from reality.

Death in Trevor's stories is frequently a breeder of truth. A death can force a concealed truth to the surface, as in **"Mr. McNamara,"** or it can compel survivors to recognize a further truth about themselves and those around them. The theme is rich in possibilities for Gothic treatment, and several of the stories would fit a broad definition of Gothic—their hints of the horrific, their portrayal of a bizarre existence on the fringes of normal society. In **"The Original Sins of Edward Tripp,"** for example, it is an imagined death that causes the eruption of truth. Edward and Emily Tripp, a middle-aged brother and sister, have lived in the same house all their lives, first with their parents, but now alone together.

They intermittently enact a curious ritual, Emily in earnest, Edward playing a part. Emily imagines that some horror has occurred in their neighborhood and sends her brother to investigate. On this occasion, she imagines that their neighbor, Mrs. Mayben, has been murdered and tries to persuade Edward to enter Mrs. Mayben's home to confirm the fact. She has seen the murderer loitering. "Death has danced through Dunfarnham Avenue and I have seen it," she insists, "a man without socks or shirt, a man who shall fry in the deep fat of Hell. For you Edward, must put a finger on him." Emily is preoccupied with death: "We have buried our parents: we know about the deceased. They're everywhere, Edward. Everywhere."

Emily is mistaken about the fate of Mrs. Mayben, who invites Edward in when he calls at her home, having succumbed, as he always does, to Emily's insistence. But Edward has previously decided that Mrs. Mayben is the right person to hear his story: " 'I am going to tell you the truth,' explained Edward, 'as I have never told a soul in all my life. It is an ugly business, Mrs. Mayben'." So he tells the story of his cruelties to Emily in their childhood and of how his sister had consequently grown up with her strange imaginings. "My sister pretends, exacting her revenge," he explains. "God has told me, Mrs. Mayben, to play my part in her pretended fantasies. I owe her the right to punish me, I quite understand that."

But the comfort from Mrs. Mayben that Edward had anticipated is unforthcoming; she tells him that she cannot concern herself with his guilt and the sadness of their house. He returns home uncomforted, but later imagines the scene of his sister's death and the end of his punishment. In Heaven, he imagines, "she would smile as once she had smiled as a child, offering him her forgiveness while saying she was sorry too, and releasing him in sumptuous glory all the years of imprisoned truth."

The theme of madness and its relation to truth is taken up with even greater intensity in the later story, **"The Raising of Elvira Tremlett,"** another story set in a small Irish town. Again, the story concerns a child's discovery of an unpleasant truth. The youngest of five children, the narrator is treated with suspicion by his family—his brothers and sisters, his mother, his father, who drinks heavily, and his quiet uncle, who lives with them. Alienated within this household, the boy wanders into the Protestant church, where he is drawn to the monument of Elvira Tremlett, an English girl who had died locally in 1873.

The child's imagination brings this girl back into being as a part of his consciousness; she becomes his companion and confidante. Finally, however, she tells him the secret of his rejection: that he is actually not the child of his father, but of his uncle, to whom his mother had once turned when her husband had stayed out drinking too long. This knowledge works into the child, and his urge for impulse comfort is to complete the alienation from his family: "I wanted to go away, to escape from the truth we had both instinctively felt and had shared." His escape is eventually found in madness, haunted by the spectre of Elvira Tremlett, now grown elderly and haggard. He is finally sent away to the insane asylum where she, too, had once been sent and had died in her youth.

The juxtaposing of childhood innocence with an unpleasant deception of adulthood frequently forms the basis of Trevor's stories. Occasionally, the same character forms this antithesis, with Trevor portraying him both in childhood and in adulthood. Trevor shows a particular interest in the school environment, a microcosm of hidden lies and emerging truth. Perhaps the finest of the school stories is **"Torridge,"** in which—against a background of *bijous* and protectors, the boys' ritualized homosexual encounters—one pupil, R. A. J. Fisher, accidentally sends a note to Torridge, the butt of the school's jokes. The note had been intended for Arrowsmith whose disdain for Fisher apparently causes him to drop out of the school in embarrassment or despair. The truth of this episode emerges only three years later, when the now middle-aged Arrowsmith and his two school friends, Wiltshire and Mace-Hamilton, meet together (as they often do) with their families for dinner. A recurrent joke at these get-togethers has been the memory of Torridge, and Arrowsmith has sought to perpetrate the joke by inviting him that evening.

When Torridge arrives, however, the three friends, now slightly drunk, discover that he is not at all as they remember him, and an insight into Mace-Hamilton's reaction to Torridge introduces the theme of truth: "There was a suavity about him that made Mace-Hamilton uneasy. Because of what had been related to his wife and the other wives and their children he felt he'd been caught out in a lie, yet in fact that wasn't the case." But while Mace-Hamilton (like the others) has not actually lied to his family, he has omitted to tell the whole truth about his activities in school; Torridge is determined to let this truth—and another—be known.

To everybody's horror, he starts talking about the world of *bijous* and gay masters, including the chaplain, whose alleged homosexuality had been a school joke. Again, the distinction between the truth and falsehood becomes blurred: "It was somehow in keeping with the school's hypocrisy," the three friends think, "that God Harvey had had inclinations himself, that a rumor begun as an outrageous joke should have contained the truth." As Torridge continues with his truth-telling exercise, and the world of *bijous* becomes real to the families, other truths and deceptions come to mind, and doubts proliferate.

Mrs. Wiltshire recalls her reaction to her husband when she discovered that he'd been unfaithful to her with Mrs. Arrowsmith: "She had not told him that he had never succeeded in arousing in her the desire to make love: she had always assumed that to be a failing in herself, but now for some reason she was not so sure." More confusion haunts Arrowsmith's son, and his daughter realizes that "her parents' marriage was messy, messier than it had looked." But Torridge's final thrust is yet to come; he reveals that Fisher had not left the school but, after writing a note to Arrowsmith, had killed himself. Arrowsmith is astounded:

> "Note?" he said. "For me?"
>
> "Another note. Why d'you think he did himself in, Arrows?"
>
> Torridge smiled, at Arrowsmith and then around the table.
>
> "None of that's true," Wiltshire said.
>
> "As a matter of fact it is."

And so Torridge departs, his truth having been revealed. He leaves behind him friends and families now alienated from each other, wracked by bitterness and confusion.

Other stories about school life reinforce this idea of the destructive energy of truth. There are the convoluted lies that breed upon each other in **"A School Story"**; ultimately, there emerges one pupil so skilled at telling lies that they are taken for the truth by almost everybody. So convincing is Williams and so adept at manipulating the imagination of Markham concerning the death of his father and step-mother that he convinces everyone, including Markham himself, that Markham is their killer. In **"Nice Day at School,"** Eleanor's introduction to sexuality leads her to recognize, as Arrowsmith's daughter does, the unpleasant truth about her parents' marriage—their bitter, mutual imprisonment.

The truth is discovered too late in **"Mrs. Silly,"** in which Michael is humiliated by his mother's awkwardness in the public eye of his school. His shame forces him to acknowledge his father, rather than his mother, to his friends when his parents (who are divorced) both attend his confirmation. It is his imagined picture of her that leads to a truth that comes too late to provide comfort.

> He imagined his mother . . . sitting on the edge of the bed, probably having a cry. He imagined her bringing back to London the stuff she's bought for a picnic in her room. She'd never

refer to any of that, she'd never upbraid him for going to the Ernad for dinner when she'd wanted him to be with her. She'd consider it just that she should be punished. . . . In the dark, he whispered to her in his mind. He said he was sorry, he said he loved her better than anyone.

Here again, the failure of truth to assert itself causes an intimate relationship to break apart; again, the imagination creates an insight into the truth and allows the reader to see that it is not only Michael, the narrator, but also his mother who is unhappy and alone.

In **"O Fat White Woman,"** another school story, the truth is again ineffectual. The story centers on Mrs. Digby-Hunter, the wife of the headmaster of an unorthodox private school where most of the teaching is backed up by violence. Mrs. Digby-Hunter chooses to ignore this, and her concern with truth stretches only to the question of whether the maids have bathed. She considers them, at fifteen, "hardly the age at which to expect . . . truthfulness." Ironically, however, it is these girls who eventually force Mrs. Digby-Hunter to recognize the sadism that is rampant at the school and its consequences:

> "Your husband," said Dympna, "derives sexual pleasure from inflicting pain on children. So does Kelly. They are queer men."

> "Your husband," said Barbara," will be jailed. He'll go to prison with a sack over his head so that he won't have to see the disgust on people's faces. Isn't that true, Mrs. Digby-Hunter?"

These truths are too late, however, for a boy has already died. Yet, as so often happens in Trevor's fiction, one truth forces others to the surface by a spasm of the imagination. Curiously, Mrs. Digby-Hunter thinks of her husband's failure to make love to her on their wedding night (and ever since) and somehow connects this to the present tragedy. She sees both as a failure to confront the truth.

> She went on talking: you couldn't blame them for hating her, she said, for she might have prevented death and hadn't bothered herself. In a bedroom in Wales she should have wept, she said, or packed a suitcase and gone away.

Mrs. Digby-Hunter is typical of Trevor's characters in her determination to resist the truth. It is hardly surprising that his characters choose this line of defense, for the world they inhabit is a comically malignant one, and the truth, if allowed any chance to emerge, will then flourish and breed, multiplying manifold. And this proliferation of truth forces one to recognize more general truths about society that were only faintly discernible before—that marriages are loveless, that lovers and families are betrayed, that people are alienated and unhappy, clinging to the deceptions that will allow them to come to terms with their situation. It takes strength of will and the instincts of survival to resist these truths.

All of this might suggest that Trevor's interests are limited to apolitical human relationships, but this is not entirely the case. As an Irishman, he is naturally drawn to the political theme, the euphemistically-termed "Troubles" of Northern Ireland. Trevor's focus, however, is never broadly political, but concentrated on individuals whose lives are somehow touched by the endemic Irish violence.

In **"Another Christmas,"** Norah and Dermot, an Irish couple living in London, have traditionally entertained their friend and landlord, Mr. Joyce, each Christmas Day. But Norah does not expect Mr. Joyce to come this Christmas, for a few months earlier Dermot had spoken bluntly to him concerning the violence in Ulster after hearing of another bombing. "He couldn't understand the mentality of people like that, Mr. Joyce said yet again, killing just anyone, destroying life for no reason. . . . Then Dermot had added that they mustn't of course forget what the Catholics in the North had suffered." Norah tries to rescue this situation: "All that was in the past, she'd said hastily, in a rush, nothing in the past or the present or anywhere else could justify the killing of innocent people. Even so, Dermot had added, it didn't do to avoid the truth."

Unlike Dermot, Norah has the capacity to see that the truth has relative currency and a destructive potential. "Everyone knew that the Catholics in the North had suffered. . . . But you couldn't say it to an old man who had hardly been outside Fulham in his life. You couldn't say it because when you did it sounded like an excuse for murder." So she knows that Mr. Joyce is offended and will not visit that Christmas. Dermot cannot countenance this possibility and is unaware, too, that his blind faith in the truth is creating the failure of love. "She looked at him, pale and thin, with his priestly face. For the first time since he had asked her to marry him in the Tara Ballroom she did not love him."

Norah can now see only his cruelty, and she experiences the spasm of the imagination so frequently felt by Trevor's characters when they are confronted by a truth. "Their harmless elderly landlord might die in the course of that same year," she thinks, "a friendship he had valued lost, his last Christmas lonely." Dermot's insistence on the value of the truth has ensured a bleak future for him and Norah in which "she would feel ashamed of him, and of herself " for their Irishness.

The interaction of the Irish political situation with the relationship of individuals is even more intense in **"Beyond the Pale,"** a story which builds inexorably towards its climax of rage and released truth. Four middle-aged bridge-playing friends—Dekko, Cynthia and Strafe (a married couple), and the narrator, Milly, who is also Strafe's mistress—are holidaying in Ireland as they do every June. On one crucial day of the holiday, Cynthia decides to stay at the hotel while the others go into town. " 'Cynthia likes to mooch, you know,' Strafe pointed out, which of course is only the truth," remarks Milly.

Her phrase is very revealing about Trevor's art. "Only the truth" at once suggests how insignificant the truth can be—"petty," as Norah calls it in **"Another Christmas"**—as well as ironically foreshadowing Cynthia's later all-important encounter with the truth as victim and as agent. For, as the three friends return to the hotel, they find it in confusion, with Cynthia distraught and unintelligible. They learn that in their absence she had been confronted by another guest, an enigmatic man who had, it seems, conversed with her at length and had soon after fallen from the cliffs and drowned. They immediately assume that the man had propositioned Cynthia—that he "tried something on with her," as Strafe puts it.

But at tea-time, Cynthia rejoins the group and, and in a rather manic fashion, retells the story that the man had told her. It is a story of two childhood sweethearts who used to visit an idyllic place where the hotel now stands. The two, as they grew older, became lovers but eventually parted and lost contact when the girl moved to London. The man at length discovered what had become of his youthful lover; to his horror he learns that she has been making bombs for the republican campaign of violence in London. As Cynthia now sees, this relationship cannot escape the weight of Irish history where violence breeds violence, for the man had traveled to London and there found only bitterness in the girl. In desperation, he killed her and then returned to their childhood paradise to try to understand the sadness of their lost innocence. Here he had told his story to Cynthia and, then, killed himself.

Strafe, Dekko, and Milly are already discomfited by Cynthia's persistent and strident public story-telling, but the worst is yet to come. Cynthia, first of all, has learned a great truth about the Irish situation, as she makes clear to the waitress:

> Through honey-tinted glasses we love you and we love your island, Kitty. We love the lilt of your racy history, and we love your earls and heroes . . . How can we be blamed if we make neither head nor tail of anything. Kitty, your past and your present, those battles and Acts of Parliament? We people of Surrey: how can we know?

But secondly, her grasp of this truth and the sadness of the events she has witnessed has made her vulnerable to other truths which she now unleases. She points at Milly, exclaiming:

> That woman . . . is my husband's mistress, a fact I am supposed to be unaware of. . . . My husband is perverted in his sexual desires. His friend, who shared his schooldays, has never quite recovered from that time. I myself am a pathetic creature who has closed her eyes to a husband's infidelity and his mistress's viciousness. . . . I hardly exist.

Strafe's reply is a perfect echo of Wiltshire's to Torridge and as ineffectual: "None of that's true," he says, and then explodes in fury and hatred at his wife. Cynthia seems unperturbed but offers a new insight: "No-one cares, and on our journey home we shall all four be silent. Yet is the truth about ourselves at least a beginning?" But her rhetorical questioning points to an ambiguity. It is by no means clear that her insistence on truthfulness has gained anything. The group is certainly chastened, but it is also humiliated and fragmented.

The invalidity of truth underscores the bleakness of William Trevor's world. All the institutions upon which people depend to shape existence and give it meaning are illusory. Human relationships break and fail. Intimate friends, lovers even, have no real knowledge of each other's inner selves. It is because of their reluctance to face up to such a society that Trevor's characters inflict deceptions upon themselves and others; such blindnesses are a natural defense mechanism against a hostile existence. (pp. 75-86)

Michael Ponsford, "'Only the Truth': The Short Stories of William Trevor," in Éire-Ireland, *Vol. XXIII, No. 1, Spring, 1988, pp. 75-86.*

Trevor on his short fiction:

People always ask me how stories begin. They expect me to say, well, they begin by sitting in a place like this, because I'm known as quite an eavesdropper. But it's not as neat as that. It's an untidy, rather dirty business, and it's messy. And the manuscript looks like a manuscript *should* look: It's absolutely filthy, and often stained with coffee and wine and crossings-out—and not at all something to bring into the home!

And out of that chaos, you have to create order. The whole thing really is the order.

Trevor, in an interview with Gail Caldwell, reprinted in The Writer, *October, 1990.*

John Naughton

What is it about the Anglo-Irish that is so fascinating? Why does this faded caste of 'Protestants on horses'—living in decaying Georgian cubes, drawing rents from undrained land, pawning the silver to pay the butcher, despising (and yet totally dependent upon) the natives—exert such a mesmeric grip on British literary sensibilities? Is it just another manifestation of the Raj phenomenon, a preposterous upsurge of nostalgia for a vanished age? And why does remembrance of such ludicrous and often shameful past times often give rise to fine writing?

Like Mr Trevor's latest novel, which is about an Anglo-Irish family, the Rollestons, living out their closing years in a standard-issue 'Big House', Carriglas, on an island off the coast of County Cork. They came in Cromwell's bloody wake, expropriating the natives in the usual way. Yet by the time the novel opens, in the opening decade of this century, they have acquired the strangely beneficent nickname of 'the Famine Rollestons' for their kindness to the natives during the potato famine. During that catastrophe, they made work and organised relief, in sharp contrast to most of their caste. And when that wasn't enough, they waived rents, thereby losing title to their lands and sowing the seeds of their eventual decline.

The cast of characters is firmly in the tradition of Anglo-Irish literature. There is the Colonel, who is decent, upright and admirable, and who is killed in the Great War. There are his sons, John James and Lionel, who are sent to school in England, and wind up ineffectually leading lives of quiet desperation. There is a grandmother who is the last remaining embodiment of Rolleston virtues. There is a young daughter—Villana—who is mysteriously disappointed in love and winds up marrying an elderly solicitor. There are the usual old retainers, complete with dog carts and an abiding interest in thoroughbred horseflesh. There is Sarah, part-governess, part-factotum, part-companion. And there is the cook's illegitimate son Tom, whose father was killed by a Republican booby-trap intended for the Rollestons.

Sarah and Tom are the key figures. Being outsiders, they both see things in sharper relief, and provide Mr Trevor with the backbone of his narrative. She is the unmarried daughter of a clergyman relative. Her life, like that of many another spinster of that class and time, is one of duty and unrequited love, shaped by other people's greater claims. She keeps a dairy, fragments of which break through from time to time. She tells, as it were, the inside story—though she often feels excluded. 'I feel,' she writes, 'that I live in a cobweb of other people's lives and do not understand the cobweb's nature . . . '

Tom, who lives with his mother in the gatehouse, provides the link with the wider world. The links are partly literal—for he is the one who runs errands from the island to the mainland. But they are also partly metaphorical, in that the ordinary life of the community is seen refracted through Tom's character. His illegitimacy is perceived—as indeed it was in the Ireland of the period—as a contaminating stain, and many townsfolk react to him much as they might to a leper. He is an unforgettable and exquisitely-drawn character, stoic and innocent by turn, and endowed with the kind of staying power that the Rollestons lack.

The Silence in the Garden is a beautifully-crafted book, in which the secrets—petty as well as dark—of the Rollestons are slowly teased out. Although it was before my time, as they say, the period detail seems absolutely authentic, and the dialogue is very well done. The characters live and die in their peculiar ways, and one is left wondering—again—wherein lies the fascination of such tales? Perhaps it is because the history of the Anglo-Irish is really just a metaphor for a deep-seated worry that civilisation is a plant with exceedingly shallow roots. (pp. 25-6)

> *John Naughton, "The Irish Raj," in* The Listener, *Vol. 120, No. 3072, July 21, 1988, pp. 25-6.*

Julian Moynahan

Trevor has made his home in Devon, England, for some time, but in no sense has he put Ireland behind him. The key to his literary character is that he makes free with every aspect of the mixed traditions that produced him—Irish and English, Catholic and Protestant, religious and secular, urban and rural. A great onlooker and eavesdropper, he has said that an embracing curiosity is a good writer's first tool. That is not to suggest he is some sort of Anglo-Irish Studs Terkel. Trevor can be fiendishly clever in a purely literary sense. Take **"Beyond the Pale,"** the title story for his 1981 collection of short fiction. In a story

about two intertwined English couples on their annual vacation in a bijou hotel in the Glens of Antrim, Northern Ireland, Trevor, in a somewhat Jamesian way—that is to say, indirectly—encompasses the troubled politics of that region. But to call it Jamesian is misleading, for the story actually and deliberately rewrites the complex plotting of Ford Madox Ford's *The Good Soldier,* using the Northern Irish conflict of Protestant and Catholic as an analogue to Ford's theme of Reformation and Counter-Reformation. The story is a miracle of compression.

Trevor's first novel, *A Standard of Behaviour* (1958), covered the uncertainty and drift of early adulthood. In it, Trevor displayed an urban bohemia of exceptional seediness, inhabited by would-be artists and writers and patrolled by Circe-like hostesses, avid for the companionship of the aimless young. One is never sure whether the ambience is Irish or English, though a recollected school adventure of getting drunk with school servant girls points to Ireland. There is also comedy. A gentleman farmer, Uncle Ned, who is introduced beating a newborn calf, conducts hostilities against all his domestic animals on the ground that they are greedy, malignant, dumb, obstinate, and dirty. And there is the surprising suicide of an old school chum to undermine further the diffident narrator's confidence in what lies ahead. This little book owed something to early Waugh, something to *The Ginger Man,* and left its author free to proceed in almost any direction.

The direction Trevor took had already been laid out by Frank O'Connor in his study of the short story, called *The Lonely Voice.* O'Connor claimed that short fiction was best suited to portray isolated and lonely souls, those who by choice or fate had become marginal in their societies. Trevor's **"The General's Day,"** a disturbingly funny story about a retired World War II officer in his 70s in an English village, coming apart from lonesomeness (along with too many gins), demonstrated a mastery of the O'Connor formula, as did other early stories such as **"The Table"** and **"The Penthouse Apartment."** These latter show an intimate knowledge of London life; and all three display a mastery of dialogue. (Two of the stories were easily rescripted for broadcasting.)

Trevor's urbanity did not prevent him, however, from dealing easily with rural scenes. **"The Ballroom of Romance,"** the title story of his 1972 collection, is one of his greatest successes. It is about Bridie, the 39-year-old daughter of an Irish farmer, whose one night out, year in year out, is Saturday, which she spends at a rural dance hall. On this particular night, her forlorn hope of making a connection with the one decent unmarried man who comes there is finally disappointed.

Trevor does sometimes load the dice. One can feel of his situations what Matthew Arnold felt about his own early poems: that there is everything to be suffered and nothing to be done. Granted that the appealing Bridie is entrapped since the death of her mother, but did her father have to be a crippled leg amputee as well? The lonesomeness and hardship of Irish rural life in the 1970s is less convincing or typical than it would have seemed in the 1930s and '40s, when O'Connor was doing his best work.

Trevor is also not above occasional self-plagiarizing. **"In Isfahan,"** dating from a 1975 collection, describes an encounter between travelers in which a cold, possibly impotent Englishman rebuffs the advances of an Englishwoman unhappily married to an Indian businessman. Ten years later he published **"Cocktails at Doney's,"** set in Florence, in which an impotent-seeming Englishman rebuffs the advances of a beautiful, unsuitably married American woman. Trevor's fiction is full of emotionally blocked and frozen men, some of them closet homosexuals, a number of whom have not consummated even their marriages. This subject has its fascinations, but the repetition can be a little too much at times.

Trevor's first big success in the novel was with *The Old Boys* (1964), about the competition among ancient men to become president of the Old Boys Association of a 500-year-old public (that is, private) school. A leading candidate is Jaraby, a former school bully, who tyrannizes over his wife and has driven his 40-year-old son into a life of vagabondage and sociopathy. The wife is wonderful. Her desperate unhappiness in marriage has sharpened her wits and brought her to an independence of outlook that is virtually saintly, and which Jaraby, who is quite mad himself, mistakes for insanity. *The Old Boys* is a leading document in a lifelong struggle Trevor has been conducting against public schools for boys, for the callowness and cruelty of their class values, and for the brutal manner in which they distort the social and sexual development of their juvenile clients. He won't win, of course, for the simple reason that those English people devoted to public schools tend to regard all attacks as more tribute to the superiority of the system itself. Trevor's knockout story **"Torridge,"** from the 1970s, tells the same story—all on the theme of school romance and sex play, showing how these experiences, whether freely or involuntarily undergone, are left behind, and yet not left behind, in later life.

In the 1970s, *The Children of Dynmouth* (1976) stands out—a book that, though not exactly lovable, is impossible to forget. Set in a run-down Devon coastal resort during the days preceding Easter, it displays a number of maimed rites and shocking incidents designed, I believe, to show the failure of communal bonds not only in this particular town, but in Britain as a whole. Its principal characters include a hard-pressed vicar on whose doorstep arrive all the crazy, the neglected, and the superannuated people, while he must attend to his wife's severe depression over a recent stillbirth and the inspired mischief of their four-year-old twins. The town is being harried by Timothy Gedge, a latchkey child, now a 15-year-old village scourge and blackmailer.

This not-so-tiny Tim appears to represent the community's bad conscience incarnated as a youthful psychopath. Among his targets are Kate and Stephen, honorable and sensitive 12-year-olds whose respective mother and father have just married and gone off on a brief wedding trip. Timothy wants Stephen to believe that his mother, who accidentally fell from the cliff path to her death, was pushed by Stephen's father, an ornithologist who was having a clandestine affair with Kate's divorced mother. Gedge's other targets for blackmail include a tough whor-

ing pub keeper who occasionally makes out with Gedge's mother in the Dynmouth public lavatories, and Commander Abigail, a fondler of cub scouts who has lived chastely with his wife of 36 years without ever confessing to certain proclivities.

Gedge's weird characterization is something of a tour de force. But his remarkable success as a snooper, and the fact that nobody in town, not even the publican, can stand up to him strains belief. The book edges into parable, in the form of a debate between Kate, who thinks Gedge is possessed by devils, and the vicar, who believes the boy is just a neglected offspring trying to get attention, another twist on the British-Irish debate between a religion of magic and a religion of Anglican trimming.

The religious question aside, *The Children of Dynmouth* is successful in its picture of the curiously snakebitten and defeatist atmosphere of Britain during the mid-1970s, when the country seemed to have run out of luck. This was the era of stagflation, when pop, TV, and youth culture all seemed to go a little rotten at the same time, when Great Britain was called "the sick man of Europe." Naturally Kate and the Reverend couldn't know that governessy Margaret Thatcher was waiting in the wings, birch rod in hand, quite prepared to go at the Gedges of this society until they stopped making nuisances of themselves. Timothy's "eyes were the eyes of the battered except that no one had ever battered him." The decade to come would fix that.

During the 1980s Trevor got around to examining or meditating upon his Anglo-Irish roots. As well as the long story, *The News from Ireland* (1986), set during the great famine of 1847-48, he wrote *Fools of Fortune* (1982), a romantic epic about the destruction of a great house and the blighting of a great English and Irish family, the Quintons, in the era of the Anglo-Irish War (1918-21). It is the novel that really made Trevor's reputation among American readers. Its Gothic and Romance conventions draw on Faulkner's example in *Absalom! Absalom!,* and the Yeats of *Ancestral Houses* and *Purgatory,* who chose the Gothic mode to demonstrate how violence and beauty are woven together in an agrarian tradition centering upon great "aristocratic" houses. Early in the 19th century, the somewhat deranged Dublin clergyman Maturin, who wrote *Melmoth,* the greatest of Anglo-Irish Gothics, remarked that "Ireland is the country where the Gothic happens—daily." No subsequent Anglo-Irish writer who is any good, not even Beckett, has neglected to put that insight to work.

Yet Trevor's new novel, *The Silence in the Garden,* does try to cut back on melodrama, on grand gestures and appalling turns of fate. It covers the period 1904 to 1974, but focuses on 1931, the year when the island demesne of Carriglas, home of the Pollexfens, lost its lordly isolation. (A bridge replaced the small ferry as a link between Carriglas and the mainland village the Pollexfens formerly controlled as the landlords.) One notices that Trevor does not choose to write directly about the Northern Irish political troubles, which have racked both Ireland and Britain since 1969. Still, the intense moral scrutiny to which he subjects Anglo-Irish tradition, the tradition of those who have controlled most of the land, wealth, and political power in Ireland for several hundred years, inevitably reflects, though only indirectly, the new round of troubles in the North.

The guilt and violence are personalized, the arrogance and unfeelingness bred in a tradition of privilege are scaled down to small acts of delinquency: the Pollexfen children hunt after a tenant's child with an old shotgun during one long summer. It's hard to make as much of this as Trevor does when our daily newspapers tell us of children setting fire to homeless men in city parks or operating crack parlors. Indeed, this book seems somewhat under-imagined—an unusual complaint to bring against Trevor—and overfussy in the way it shuttles back and forth between various dates and events of the 70 years it covers. By 1931, the year the bridge was completed, the Anglo-Irish had already been marginalized in de Valera's new Ireland, though local populations were generally too polite to tell the surviving "quality" to their faces how little they mattered. Besides, 1931 was a year of appalling dullness in Ireland, as cultural parochialism took hold and memories of the great days of struggle following the 1916 Easter Rising were dimmed. Trevor, a writer too honest to pretend it was otherwise, is powerless to prevent the dullness from spreading through his book, like dank mist off a bog.

If the vein of Anglo-Irish big house romance is really worked out, as this last, sad effort suggests it is, what should this fine writer now be doing? With his ample gifts of irony, compassion, and wry humor, and with the scrupulous craft of a minor master, there is a simple solution: he should return to the ordinarily human beings around him, the overlooked lives of Thatcherite England, the new Ireland of technocrats, Eurocrats, and nervously emigrating educated young. It is Trevor's unique destiny to find his roots in neither one country nor the other but in both. And both countries need him now. (pp. 37-40)

> *Julian Moynahan, "Tales of Two Nations," in* The New Republic, *Vol. 200, No. 6, February 6, 1989, pp. 37-40.*

Joel Conarroe

Short fiction is alive and well and living all over the place. The past few months alone have seen the publication of several unusually impressive collections, including *Friend of My Youth* by Alice Munro, a Canadian who has established a reputation as one of the finest short-story writers anywhere, and "In a Father's Place," a first book by Christopher Tilghman, an American whose auspicious debut bodes well for the future. And now here is *Family Sins & Other Stories* by William Trevor, an Irishman living in England. (From Joyce on, it seems, gifted Irish writers have tended to distance themselves from the turf they then devote their lives to documenting.)

Made up of a dozen stories . . . Mr. Trevor's collection is a worthy successor to his last book, *The Silence in the Garden,* a nearly perfect short novel that was published here in 1988. A Chekhovian study of a country estate's gradual decline, that disturbing narrative confirmed its creator's celebrated imagination for disaster. As often

happens in his work, a shameful event, long hidden, is ultimately revealed: as children, the likely heirs of the estate had terrified a peasant child by hunting him with guns, as if he were a wild animal. This primitive behavior permanently shapes the lives of everyone involved. In Mr. Trevor's fictional landscapes, the past, however remote in time, is always palpably present.

In the stories in *Family Sins,* all of which are built around troubled domestic relationships, it is more typically the sins of the parents that are visited upon the children. **"In Love With Ariadne,"** for example, concerns a medical student who falls in love with a strange young woman who lives and works at his boardinghouse. Following their only walk together, with its promise of increased intimacy, she immediately retreats to a convent, unable, evidently, to escape the shame of her father's suicide, years earlier. And in **"Family Sins,"** a young man's life is permanently stifled by the violent death of his inebriated parents in a car crash. A young cousin, who bears the burden of an unspoken love for him, becomes the scapegoat for his alcoholic rage.

Unrequited or destructive love plays a central role in nearly all these bitter narratives, with results that range from the strewn corpses in one horrific story (**"Events at Drimaghleen"**) to the unarticulated hopelessness in several others. Two of the stories, portraying women as sexual and economic victims, are especially heartbreaking, without being maudlin. In **"Kathleen's Field,"** an innocent farm girl works, lonely and miserable, in the home of a merchant to whom she has been sent so that her debt-ridden father can buy a field he covets. Her gray-haired employer takes to standing close to her while furtively masturbating, and since she cannot mention his repellent abuse to anyone, her feeling of isolation acquires "an extra, vivid dimension." This ghastly parody of intimacy, she realizes intuitively, is probably the only "marriage" she will ever know: "Twelve years or maybe fourteen, she said to herself, lying awake in her bedroom: as long as that, or longer." One is reminded of Joyce's emotionally paralyzed Dubliners, helpless to extricate themselves from suffocating lives.

"A Husband's Return," another exercise in naturalism, is equally unrelieved in its depiction of undeserved penance. Here a young woman is stunned when her husband of several months runs off with Bernadette, her promiscuous sister, the family favorite. When the pregnant Bernadette dies, it is domestic, hard-working Maura who receives the brunt of the blame: "People would be sorry for her, but they would always say it was her foolishness that had dragged the family through disgrace, her fault for marrying a scoundrel. In the farmhouse and the neighbourhood that was the person she had become."

Mr. Trevor's obsession with injustice, his sense that no good life goes unpunished now and then puts the reader in the position of a somewhat reluctant voyeur, transfixed by the fascination of the abomination. In **"Honeymoon in Tramore,"** 33-year-old Davy emerges as a masculine counterpart of the inexperienced farm girl in **"Kathleen's Field."** On the day of his wedding to Kitty, whom he has long worshipped from afar and who has married him only because she is pregnant, any dreams of erotic bliss are quickly shattered. Kitty downs too many drinks, gossips with strangers about her sexual history, and then gets sick in the bedroom before passing out, having rewarded her new husband with not so much as a kiss. There is black humor here, just as there is, to a lesser degree, in **"A Trinity,"** a story about an accident-prone young couple who arrange to vacation in Venice but through a clerical error end up in Switzerland with a bus load of geriatrics. One learns to read any Trevor work braced for the worst.

A couple of these stories—**"Coffee With Oliver"** and **"Children of the Headmaster"**—lack the novelistic richness we have come to admire in the author's earlier collections. None of the new stories, moreover, quite match the full-textured brilliance of **"Beyond the Pale,"** the title piece of an earlier collection. Nevertheless, several of these carefully written tales, grim but filled with a dark beauty, are wonderfully resonant. They clearly add luster to Mr. Trevor's reputation as one of the major writers of the English-speaking world.

> Joel Conarroe, "No Good Life Goes Unpunished," in The New York Times Book Review, *June 3, 1990, p. 9.*

Michael Heyward

There can be few living writers of English with so sure a touch as William Trevor. He is a master of nuance, of the flick of the wrist that seems to disclose everything. His sense of pace and timing, of the balance between dialogue and description, is flawless. The humor in his work is dark and unforgiving, though he also knows how to be simply funny. His formal understanding of the story is traditional, but he tampers with structure and point of view. He hears the speech of his characters exactly. He never panders to the reader, yet his prose is direct, as supple and spare as a blade of grass. He is the kind of writer whose achievement we are inclined to underestimate because his work does not draw attention to itself and because the mysteries of his technique are not easily visible in the effects he creates. He may write in an unassuming style, but whoever tackles his work in quantity becomes aware of an accumulating richness.

Trevor was born in Ireland in 1928 but has lived in England for many years. He began his artistic life as a sculptor and took up writing only in his mid-thirties. For a late starter his fictional resources are immense, and his output since his first novel, **The Old Boys** (1964), has a kind of Victorian abundance about it; there's a new book every year or so. In an age of magical realism, of mannerisms hankering to invigorate the language, Trevor comes from another tradition of writing entirely; his literary ancestors include Chekhov, Joyce (in *Dubliners*), and Katherine Mansfield, who in their different ways all practiced an art intent on exposing the hidden codes of conduct and the subtleties of a confined world. With his disdain of show, his sharp eye, and his disabused outlook, his prose might be the equivalent in fiction of the poetry of Philip Larkin.

Trevor moves with ease between the novel and the story. The early novels and the stories are cut from the same

cloth, but later novels, such as **Fools of Fortune** (1983) or **The Silence in the Garden** (1988), dramatize a version of Anglo-Irish history that is passionate and fraught, haunted by a child's memory of the scent of sweet pea and rose, scarred by sectarian hatred and war. Their events take place across several generations, and the broad sweep of time is essential to Trevor's evocation of history as tragedy. These novels have the air of a lament for lost domain: the identification of writer with subject seems etched on their every page.

The stories in **Family Sins** are very different. By compressing his fiction into discrete entities, each a single concentrated movement, Trevor seems able to abstract himself from the predicaments that he explores. It is as if the constraints of the form permit a certain detached tone not as purely evident in the longer fiction. The sheer narrative strength of the stories suggests comparisons with Chekhov, but Trevor also calls to mind Joyce's potent image of the author as a godlike dandy, "paring his fingernails." For Trevor is a descendant of Flaubert, too, a realist who is also a satirist, a stylist who stares at his characters until they come clean.

Family Sins works much the same territory as Trevor's previous collections, though he no longer bothers with the metropolitan dandies he sent up in his earliest work. The stories are set on farms, in small-town pubs, country boarding schools, in both Ireland and England. Sometimes the locale is Europe—especially Italy—seen through a tourist's eyes. With the exception of the European figures, who are mostly misfits, the characters are defined by their ordinariness, the way they blend into their surroundings, a humdrum provincial world where everything, no matter how tawdry or tedious, has its niche, and where it seems that nothing can change. Without fuss, Trevor detonates whatever consolations this world might seem to offer, like a sniper picking off his target through the camouflage. The explosions the reader encounters along the way are caused when the characters brush against the truth.

In **"A Trinity,"** a couple are mistakenly sent on the wrong package holiday, to Switzerland instead of Venice. Their fury at the travel agency that made the error is inconsequential: what they fear most is the mockery of the old man with whom they live, who has underwritten their holiday while he stays at home. A benign arrangement is finally understood by the reader as a shocking denial of independence, and the social comedy that sustains the action of the story withers at the conclusion. "Their first holiday since their honeymoon was paid for by the elderly man they both called Uncle," the story begins, as though nothing could be more innocent or charming. The closing paragraph, with its perfect rhythms and exquisite progression, is pitiless in its scorn for these puny creatures of the writer's imagination, falling asleep together in the wrong hotel:

> In the darkness they did not say that their greed for his money was much the same as his greed for their obedience, that greed nourished the trinity they had become. They did not say that the money, and the freedom it promised, was the

galaxy in their lives, as his cruelty was the last pleasure in his. Scarcely aware that they held on to one another beneath the bedclothes, they heard his teasing little laugh while they were still awake and again when they slept.

Like many characters in Trevor's work, these are possessed by a despair they cannot themselves speak of. As the author speaks for them, the peculiar intensity of effect derives from the combination of intimacy and severity in his detailing of character. Pettiness, meanness, and persistent stupidity have had no better chronicler. There is nothing cathartic about these stories, never any hint of transcendence or release. No one escapes. Either nothing happens, or things get worse, or someone learns how terrible things were all the time. Experience is bitter, the stories say over and over, and knowledge is merely the loss of innocence. The stories project a Sisyphean horror of endless repetition, of seeing one's days stretch out ahead as if already known, already spent. In **"A Husband's Return,"** Maura Brigid, whose husband has run off with her sister, rejects his overtures to return and understands that "people would be sorry for her, but they would always say it was her foolishness that had dragged the family through disgrace, her fault for marrying a scoundrel. In the farmhouse and the neighborhood that was the person she had become." For so many of the characters in these stories, the future—which Trevor remorselessly projects—is already behind them.

That's not to say that Trevor's stories lack suspense. In his superbly modulated, taut style, he probes the situations he sets up until what we had taken for granted may simply dissolve. The more we know the less we know, though the diminishing reality that Trevor presents never quite reaches degree zero. In the small world his characters inhabit and depend on, nothing lacks significance, and the buildup of tension can be inexorable. Nowhere is the streak of fatalism characteristic of Trevor's fictional consciousness better demonstrated than in **"Events at Drimaghleen,"** a queasy thriller without a solution.

"Nothing as appalling had happened before at Drimaghleen," it opens, though without declaring what. Then the story introduces the McDowds, who "began the day as they always did" before discovering that their daughter Maureen has not been home the previous night. Her parents, "who did not say much to one another," drive to a neighboring farm, convinced that their daughter has eloped with Lancy Butler. "The little bitch," her father remarks on the way. The McDowds' second discovery of the morning is gruesome: the bodies of Maureen, Lancy, and his mother litter the farmyard, riddled with gunshot wounds.

A scenario is established by the local police: Mrs. Butler, always overprotective of her son, murdered Maureen in a fit of jealousy. Her son shot her, and turned the gun on himself. When two journalists from the city arrive, with money and questions, a different version emerges—it also fits the circumstantial evidence—and is published in an English Sunday newspaper: it was Maureen who held the shotgun that day, who slaughtered her lover and his mother before taking her own life. Her grieving parents understand that they have now lost more than everything, and the story finally becomes a somber meditation on journalistic ethics, though such a description betrays its resonant ambiguity and immense dramatic power. The closing tableau presents, in its quiet, painterly way, an indelible image of horror:

> . . . in the kitchen that looked different in Jeremiah Tyler's photograph Mrs. McDowd screamed. She sat at the blue-topped table with her lips drawn back from her teeth, one short shrill scream following fast upon another. Father Sallins did not again attempt to comfort her. McDowd remained by the window.

In **"The Third Party,"** a man who no longer loves his wife, Annabella, meets her lover, Lairdman, in a pub. The conversation that is supposed to "clear the air" before she leaves her husband in fact ends up preserving the status quo. Boland, the cuckold, knows after their prickly talk that Lairdman will not have Annabella, not because he humiliates Lairdman—and he does—but because Boland finally discloses his wife's most intimate secret. The mystery is not so much whether Boland can be believed but what imperative prevents him from surrendering his wife. The story is about the way in which nothing happens. Boland himself cannot fathom it, and is left standing alone in Donovan's public house "wondering why he hadn't been able to let Lairdman take her from him."

The secret of Trevor's fiction is that he grasps the terror of the commonplace. The gaze in his stories can seem merciless, not because he is indifferent to his characters but because the force of his inquiry erodes the masks that they themselves show the world. His observation never flinches. The couple in **"A Trinity"** could not have children for fear of disturbing the old man: "There'd been an error when first they'd lived with him; they'd had to spend a bit terminating it." McDowd scratches "at his gray, ragged hair, which was a way he had when he wished to disguise bewilderment." His wife notices the journalist from the city "wasn't seedy but you could see she was insincere from the way her mouth was. You could hear the insincerity when she spoke." In the final story, Kathleen, a serving girl in a pub, is tormented by her "master," who comes up close behind her as she works and touches her hair and clothes. She plays over in her mind what she cannot see: his "scarlet complexion" and "spiky gray hair," the "odor of cigarette smoke" on his clothes. The conviction is all in the detail, and the detail is always precise. For the duration of the story, the characters stand before us, exposed as if spotlit, and then they shrink back into the world in which they were born and in which they will die. (pp. 40-1)

Michael Heyward, "Domestic Terrors," in The New Republic, *Vol. 203, No. 14, October 1, 1990, pp. 40-1.*

Gregory A. Schirmer

In 1910, the year Virginia Woolf chose as the birthdate of the modern sensibility, E. M. Forster published his penultimate novel, *Howards End,* a book that carried on its title page the phrase "Only Connect," and that expressed throughout Forster's belief in the need for compassion and connection, for a willingness to transcend lines of class, economics, and cultural taste in a society that seemed to Forster to be splintering into dangerously disparate groups. A dozen years and one world war later, that trust in the efficacy of an essentially humanistic moral vision seemed, to many, bleakly irrelevant; in 1922, T. S. Eliot's *The Wasteland* appeared in the pages of *Criterion* magazine, and its attitude toward Forster's principle of "Only Connect" could not have been plainer. "On Margate Sands," Eliot wrote, "I can connect / nothing with nothing."

These two positions have served as starting points for much modern and post-modern literature. For William Trevor, an Anglo-Irishman whose eleven novels and six collections of short stories have earned him a respected position in contemporary English and Irish letters, the tension between Forster's "Only Connect" and Eliot's "I can connect / nothing with nothing" has provided the governing moral force of his work. And although Trevor's writing is frequently admired—and rightly so—for its precision of style, its sensitivity to nuance of character and setting, and its subtle sense of comic irony, Trevor has always worked inside the mainstream tradition of fiction written out of strong moral commitments, and it is ultimately the moral dimension of his work, the complex vision of contemporary life generated by both an advocacy of Forster's principle of compassion and connection and a counterpointing, realistic assessment of contemporary society as alienated and disconnected, that makes him a writer of considerable significance, on both sides of the Irish Sea and on both sides of the Atlantic.

When Trevor's work first started attracting the notice of reviewers, in the middle and late 1960s, he was usually labelled a satirist or black humorist, and seen as principally preoccupied with the underside of contemporary British society; his fiction was frequently compared to that of Evelyn Waugh, Kingsley Amis, Graham Greene, Muriel Spark, and Ivy Compton-Burnett. This view of Trevor as chiefly a chronicler of losers, an ironist working out of a vision of despair, has unfortunately tended to stick. It is, however, far too reductive to account for either the range of subject-matter in Trevor's writing or the breadth and complexity of his moral vision. Trevor has, for example, written at least as much about middle-class life in prosperous London suburbs as about lonely, alienated men and women wasting away in London bed-sitters or provincial Irish towns. He has written extensively about love and marriage, especially among the middle class, and some of his best work has to do with women and the elderly from various strata of society. His work encompasses both Irish and English life, and within the Irish tradition, he has written with equal authority about Protestant Ireland and Catholic Ireland. And he has frequently written out of a commitment to address some of the most pressing political and social issues of his day, especially in his native Ireland.

Trevor's ever-present irony also needs to be read not simply as an instrument for registering hopelessness and despair, but as a means of negotiating between Forster's "Only Connect" and Eliot's "I can connect / nothing with nothing," between an affirmation of the need for compassion and connection in contemporary society and a qualifying recognition of the full strength of the forces ranged against those values. This kind of irony requires distance, and much of the distance in Trevor's work is generated by his commitment to writing outside his own experience. "Personally," Trevor once said, "I . . . disagree with that awful advice that's always given to children: 'Write about what you know.' I'd say the opposite, in a way: 'You mustn't write about what you know. You must use your imagination.' " Trevor has written short stories that draw on his youth in provincial Ireland, and there are stories and parts of novels that owe something to his days in boarding-schools; but on the whole, very few traces of autobiography can be found in Trevor's fiction. It is no accident, for example, that his second and third novels, written when he was in his thirties, take as their principal focus the elderly. Nor is it an accident that Trevor has written more intimately about women than about men, nor that a number of his novels, like those of Dickens, rely on large canvasses with many characters from various walks of life. Trevor is, in fact, an admirer of Dickens, and even his view of Joyce, another strong influence on his work, reflects this bias; in Trevor's view, Joyce's greatest work, *Ulysses*—as distinct from the heavily autobiographical *A Portrait of the Artist as a Young Man*—stands squarely in the tradition of Dickens. "He worked very like Dickens," Trevor said in an interview. "He used lots and lots of acquaintances and turned them into characters in the book, but again like Dickens, he wrote at a distance."

In somewhat the manner of Joyce, Trevor also has deliberately written at a geographical distance. Having left Ireland for England as a young man, Trevor wrote his early novels and stories almost exclusively about the least familiar of the two countries he knew—England. What Trevor said once about Elizabeth Bowen, another twentieth-century Anglo-Irish writer who devoted the larger part of her energies to writing about her adopted as opposed to her native country, describes equally well Trevor's own position as an Irishman writing about England: "She came to know England well, but always wrote about the English from an angle which suggests a stranger on the edge of a circle of friends." In recent years, Trevor has increasingly written about Ireland, but only after he has become something of a stranger to it.

Not only has Trevor almost always written from this angle of exile, but also his life has been that of someone on the edge, of a spectator on the outside looking in. Born William Trevor Cox, in Mitchelstown, Co. Cork, Trevor had a childhood that was mobile to say the least. His father, James William Cox, was a bank official and the family moved frequently because of his work. Trevor once said that as a child he lived "like a middle-class gypsy" and: "We were always on the move. I found it impossible to make and keep friends because we were never in a single place for long enough. I have no roots." Between the time he started going to school and the time he entered Trinity College, Dublin, Trevor attended thirteen different schools, in provincial towns such as Skibbereen, Tipperary, Enniscorthy, Wexford, and Youghal. Moreover, a number of these schools were Catholic, and Trevor's family was Protestant. Trevor has written about the vagaries and varieties of his early education in his partly autobiographical collection of essays, *Old School Ties:*

> I attended many schools and for long periods of my childhood I attended no school at all, wandering the streets of provincial Irish towns untaught for months on end. Sometimes my brother and I were placed under the tutelage of a failed Christian Brother or a farmer's daughter who had passed the Intermediate Certificate Examination and would agree to come daily to the house. My mother found such figures in the same way as she found her endless string of maids, by driving out into the countryside and knocking on farmhouse doors.

The frequent moving from one provincial town to another stopped in 1941, when Trevor, at the age of thirteen, enrolled at Sandford Park School in Dublin. From there he went to St Columba's College, also in Dublin, in 1943, and then to Trinity College. He took his degree, in history, from Trinity in 1950, and then spent a year in Dublin and two years in Armagh, Northern Ireland, teaching at a school before moving to England. Trevor taught art in the Midlands of England from 1953 to 1955, and then moved to southwest England, where he devoted himself to sculpting, eventually earning a small reputation as a sculptor. In these years he also began writing, publishing his first novel, *A Standard of Behaviour,* in 1958. His second novel, *The Old Boys,* appeared in 1964, to considerable critical acclaim; a year later, he gave up a job in advertising that he had taken in 1960 to support his writing, and has since devoted himself fulltime to writing. He has continued to live in England, in the Devon countryside, with his wife Jane, whom he married in 1952. In recent years, he has divided his time between England, Ireland, and Italy, and, characteristically, has begun publishing some short stories with Italian settings. As he suggested in a recent interview, Trevor now finds himself in the position of feeling something of a stranger—the position he considers most advantageous for his writing—in several countries:

> The country [Ireland] did not fall into place until I'd been in exile. Things you take for granted you don't actually see when you're living there. Every minute in Florence, for instance, you have to come to terms with something strange. It's a strangeness I still feel in England. I'm still puzzled and curious here.

Trevor's tendency to court this feeling of strangeness, and to write about something only when he considers himself at a sufficient remove from it, has produced a body of writing extraordinarily broad in its range of interests. *A Standard of Behaviour* is set for the most part in Bohemian London, a reckless world of young, would-be artists and their circles of friends. This book may well contain some autobiographical elements drawn from Trevor's early years in England, when he was working to develop his writing and his sculpting, but this is an uncharacteristic novel, one which, moreover, Trevor has apparently tried to put behind him by regularly excluding it from lists of his published works. It is with *The Old Boys,* his second novel, that Trevor finds the style and voice—particularly

the precise, understated note of irony—that have become his trademarks. It is also with this book, not coincidentally, that Trevor begins writing outside his own experience. Having to do with various intrigues among a group of old boys from an English public school, this novel, which won the Hawthornden Prize for Literature in 1964, also evidences a sharp sense of satire, and so inspired reviewers to draw comparisons between Trevor and writers like Waugh and Amis. *The Boarding-House,* Trevor's next novel, published in 1965, is markedly Dickensian in its scope and diversity of character. Set in a slightly seedy suburban boarding-house, this novel also carries Trevor into fictional territory that he has made his own, the shabby underside of society, populated by petty criminals and con-artists, lonely single men and women, sexually deviant or inadequate characters—people, in general, whom love and compassion have passed by. Along with *The Old Boys, The Boarding-House* established Trevor as an urban writer, and in his fourth novel, *The Love Department* (1966), he continued to write about London, but this time with a sharply different focus. This novel marks the beginning of Trevor's interest in writing about the suburban middle class, and about love and marriage. Although it is as much a moral fable as a realistic novel, *The Love Department* explores the marriages and affairs of its middle-class couples with psychological authenticity. For Trevor, as this novel reveals, love and marriage are important barometers of human behavior, and his view of contemporary society as characterized by alienation and disconnection finds no more powerful objective correlative throughout his work than that of broken marriage and failed love.

As their titles indicate, Trevor's three middle novels—*Mrs Eckdorf in O'Neill's Hotel* (1969), *Miss Gomez and the Brethren* (1971), and *Elizabeth Alone* (1973)—are written primarily from a woman's point of view. They are also, to one degree or another, concerned with love and marriage. But these books dramatize more pointedly than do the earlier novels the tension between a humanistic faith in the principle of compassion and connection and an ironic, qualifying view of contemporary society as alienated and disconnected. The central protagonist of *Mrs Eckdorf in O'Neill's Hotel,* a photo-journalist on the run from two failed marriages who arrives in Dublin to investigate the supposedly scandalous past of a rundown hotel, brings to her work an obsessive vision of man's moral responsibility to his fellow man. In the end, however, the sordid world that Mrs Eckdorf tries to save—a world in which human relationships are seen not as matters of love or selfless connection but as vehicles of exploitation or deceit—overwhelms her; her moral views are ignored and she herself ends in madness. *Miss Gomez and the Brethren* follows somewhat the same pattern, but is an even bleaker novel. Set in an urban-renewal area of London, a wasteland that reflects perfectly the moral barrenness of most of its characters, this book tracks the failures and failings of a protagonist considerably more alienated than Mrs Eckdorf—a Jamaican and an orphan who comes to London as a young woman only to find herself an outcast because of her class, race, and gender. Like Mrs Eckdorf, Miss Gomez is inspired by a moral vision of man's need for connection and compassion, but also like Mrs Eckdorf, Miss Gomez is inspired by a moral vision of man's need for connection and compassion, but also like Mrs Eckdorf, Miss Gomez finds no one to listen to her. *Elizabeth Alone,* Trevor's seventh novel, is one of his most ambitious—it is a large book, with an extensive cast of characters embracing everything from the suburbs of the upper-middle classes to seedy city neighborhoods worked by con-artists and petty criminals—and certainly the most successful in terms of his efforts to write from a woman's point of view and about love and marriage. It is also a more affirmative novel than the two books that precede it; its protagonist, a well-to-do suburban widow, does come to understand—mainly through a series of relationships that brings her into contact with people from different classes and cultural backgrounds—the importance of compassion, and the book ends with more than a fleeting suggestion of her prospects for a sounder, healthier life.

Trevor has said that he is not a political writer—except in so far as his work is, in his words, "based on an objection to the intolerances and conventions that . . . society has generated"—but in his two later novels, *The Children of Dynmouth* (1976) and *Other People's Worlds* (1980), Trevor's view of the contemporary world as alienated and disconnected is manifested to a considerable degree in a depiction of the inherent moral wrongs of the class system. Timothy Gedge, the 15 year-old protagonist of *The Children of Dynmouth* (which won the Whitbread Literary Award in 1976), is portrayed pointedly as a victim of the class system, someone locked into a life of working-class drudgery and alienation from which there seems to be no escape. Unlike Pinkie in Graham Greene's *Brighton Rock*—and the comparison seems appropriate in part because *The Children of Dynmouth* is set in an English seaside town—Timothy is less an embodiment of evil as defined by a religious point of view than a victim of a society that has abandoned Forster's humanistic principle of connection. In *Other People's Worlds,* the ill-advised marriage of Julia Ferndale, a genteel woman used to a life of social privilege and bucolic tranquillity, to a man who turns out to be one of Trevor's most pathetic and sinister con-artists, plunges her into an unsettling but ultimately morally enlightening confrontation with an entire world of urban, lower-class life defined by chaos and despair.

Many of the formal qualities of Trevor's novels, including their frequent use of juxtaposition and parallelism, are particularly suited to the short story, and Trevor's work in this genre can hardly be overestimated. Falling somewhere between the radical experimentalism of high modernist writers and the more or less traditional methods of the realistic short story, Trevor's stories depend heavily on suggestion, irony, and cinematic juxtaposition. In thematic terms, they tend to be relatively bleak; characters in them rarely discover the means to overcome their feelings of alienation or the crippling illusions that they rely on to mask their inadequacies, and so there is little promise of moral redemption. Among the most effective of Trevor's stories in this vein are those that use the corruption or destruction of love—marriages ending in divorce or separation, love replaced by casual sexual relationships, romance worn down by time and circumstance—as an objective correlative. In Trevor's three latest collections, however— *Lovers of Their Time* (1978), *Beyond the Pale* (1981), and

The News from Ireland (1986)—his stories have increasingly been informed by political and social concerns, portraying characters caught in conflicts between private values such as love and family loyalites and the impersonal forces of history or political ideology.

Not surprisingly, some of the most powerful of Trevor's writing of this kind has to do, directly or indirectly, with the sectarian violence in contemporary Northern Ireland. Seamus Heaney once said that the literary artist confronted with political catastrophe must "deal with public crisis by making your own terrain take the color of it," and Trevor's fiction about the Ulster conflict places the violence and divisiveness squarely in the context of the broad moral vision that informs most of his work. His short stories having to do with Ulster tend to see the political and religious fanaticism that has fuelled much of the violence there as a product of the abandonment of humanistic values, but they also often see the conflict as an experience that forces individuals into taking moral stands inspired by a humanistic values, but they also often see the conflict as an experience that forces individuals into taking moral stands inspired by a humanistic belief in connection, into recognizing a moral obligation that extends, often at considerable cost to the individual, beyond private concerns and needs. This complex moral vision also informs Trevor's two most recent, and most insistently historical, novels, *Fools of Fortune* (which won the Whitbread Prize for Fiction in 1983) and *The Silence in the Garden* (1988). The central relationship in *Fools of Fortune,* between the son of an Anglo-Irish Protestant landowning family and his distant English cousin, is played out against a violent backdrop of historical and political events that eventually, and with tragic inevitability, destroy their love. At the same time, the novel also applauds the individual's willingness to act, at whatever cost to private needs and desires, in a way that recognizes a moral obligation larger than that to one other human being. The principal focus of *The Silence in the Garden* is the demise in the early decades of this century of a once prosperous Anglo-Irish Protestant family. But this subject-matter, despite its echoes of Yeats, is specifically in the service of Trevor's concern with the conflict between individual values and political ideology and fanaticism. This is a thoroughly tragic novel, one in which most of the characters are crushed under the unavoidable weight brought to bear on their lives by Ireland's long, violent past—*"a thread of carnage,"* as one character puts it, *"that was unbearable even to think about,"* and one that is still tragically visible in today's Northern Ireland.

Trevor has described himself as "the least experimental of writers," and he is working in a tradition that is arguably less given to experimentalism than is that of American or continental fiction. But British (and Irish) writing is more conscious of modernist and post-modernist departures from convention than is often assumed, and Trevor has absorbed into his essentially traditional fiction a number of techniques usually associated with modernist fiction and its various offspring. In large part, these techniques have in common a distrust of narrative omniscience, and so are crucial to the expression of Trevor's moral vision— one that constantly needs to qualify even its most tentative affirmations of compassion and connection with the recognition that the contemporary world is hostile ground for such values.

The most striking of these narrative strategies is the use of multiple centers of consciousness. Trevor's fiction tends to be constructed of many segments, each of which is associated with one character, or dominated by one character's perception. The result is a mosaic of different points of view, relying heavily on juxtaposition and parallelism. This technique is hardly new to the twentieth century—Dickens used it frequently—but Trevor is inheriting it less from Dickens than from modernist writers like Conrad, James, Woolf, and Joyce, for whom limited points of view embodied in formal terms a philosophical scepticism. More specifically, Trevor uses multiple centers of consciousness to shift back and forth between an interior view of a character and various exterior views, and therefore to negotiate between sympathy and irony, intimacy and distance, and, in larger terms, affirmation and qualification. At the same time, fictions constructed out of such fragments present narrative fabrics that themselves embody the idea of connection; Trevor's novels and stories are essentially networks of perceptions and attitudes, and the reader is forced to make connections between the various points—to enact, in the process of reading, the principle of connection.

The other technique that Trevor relies on consistently to create ironic, qualifying pressure in his fiction is the manipulation of narrative voice. Trevor's writing has more often than not been described as dominated by a cool, distant, largely unjudging narrative tone. In fact, narrators of this stripe appear in pure form only occasionally in Trevor's work; the bulk of Trevor's narration is strongly colored by individual characters, usually the center of consciousness in a given passage. This strategy enables Trevor to avoid, if not actually undermine, narrative omniscience at the same time that it enhances the effect of his use of multiple centers of consciousness. In this kind of fiction, characters tend to be defined by their own subjectivity, often embodied in the narrative voice that controls the sections in which they are the center of consciousness; by the views of others characters, revealed in part through the narrative voice that controls *their* sections; and, on occasion, by a relatively neutral narrator who sees things from a distant, supposedly objective point of view. This flexible narrative voice thereby helps establish and maintain those complex balances between interior and exterior views of characters—and thus between sympathy and irony, intimacy and distance—that are so crucial to the vision that informs Trevor's writing.

Given this use of multiple centers of consciousness and of a narrative voice that takes its tone from different characters, juxtaposition and parallelism are obviously important to Trevor's fiction. One of the most dramatic forms of juxtaposition that Trevor employs is that between an extremely intimate point of view and a distant, birds-eye point of view. These shifts from passages in which the narrative voice is closely identified with a given character to essentially panoramic perspectives—a technique that owes something to Virginia Woolf (especially *Mrs Dalloway*) and something to James Joyce (especially the

"Wandering Rocks" episode of *Ulysses*)—generate precisely the kind of ironic qualification that Trevor is almost always working for; the force of individual passions or attitudes is inevitably defused or undercut when seen from a perspective in which the individual appears relatively insignificant.

Trevor is not a metafictional writer. There are, however, a number of characters in his novels and stories who clearly are authorial figures. Not surprisingly, these characters tend to be driven by strong moral instincts, in some instances by an almost missionary-like zeal to make other people see the truth of their lives. Trevor is, after all, working in the mainstream of British fiction, and, as one critic of the British novel has put it, that genre "has always believed that the most important issues are moral issues, and that moral issues, whilst they may be difficult, are ultimately tractable." And yet, however tractable the issues may ultimately be, the authorial surrogates in Trevor's writing almost always fail in their ambition to act as moral agents. This, too, reflects Trevor's vision of both contemporary society and the contemporary artist. In his short story **"Beyond the Pale,"** a middle-aged Englishwoman named Cynthia, suddenly caught up in the terrorism of contemporary Irish politics, tries to make her English travelling companions, on holiday in Northern Ireland, see their connection to the destructive realities lying just beyond the false harbor of their seaside inn. Like so many of Trevor's authorial characters, Cynthia finds that her story, and its moral implications, are soundly ignored. And yet she believes, as does Trevor, that the truth must be told, that there is always the chance that it might make a difference. "No one cares," Cynthia tells herself after her tale has been told. "No one cares, and on our journey home we shall all four be silent. Yet is the truth about ourselves at least a beginning?" (pp. 1-11)

Gregory A. Schirmer, in his William Trevor: A Study of His Fiction, *Routledge, 1990, 180 p.*

Dean Flower

Almost any William Trevor story, sketched quickly, can suggest how powerful his basic conceptions are. A teacher ridicules a slow child, but he earnestly seeks her approval. When she refuses sympathy, he finds that the only response is to hurt her in return. His opportunity comes, horrifyingly, when she has a baby (**"Miss Smith,"** 1967). Everyone likes the mild husband and is shocked by the bitchy wife, who punishes him systematically with verbal nastiness and ill-concealed affairs. But what emerges is that she's surrendered her life to playing humiliation games in order to satisfy his monstrous masochism (**"The Bedroom Eyes of Mrs. Vansittart,"** 1981). A woman adopts a child at birth but eight years later the mother, now married and comfortable, wants the child back. Setting aside her own needs and rights, the adoptive mother succumbs to selfish arguments of others—and decides it would be best to give up the child (**"Being Stolen From,"** 1981). Even when all the artful telling of these stories is stripped away, Trevor's force remains. He has now published 84 stories in seven books since 1967 (not to mention ten novels), and his themes are the same: disillusionment, dispossession, deception, the anguish of those who are good, the humanness of those who are cruel, the awful intelligibility of evil, pain, and harm.

Take **"Kathleen's Field"** for example, the last of a dozen stories in Trevor's most recent collection, ***Family Sins.*** Kathleen Hagarty's father wants to buy a rich pasture, adjacent to his impoverished little farm in Ireland. The bank won't loan him money, and he can't raise enough by selling his prize bullocks. But the Shaughnessys are affluent, and want a slavey to keep house for them in town; they loan Hagarty the money in exchange for Kathleen. She is so plain, everybody knows she'll never marry. And besides, all the other children have moved away—except for the eldest male who will inherit a better farm and marry well if Kathleen sacrifices fourteen years of her life. Never mind that Mrs. Shaughnessy is critical and impatient and lazy, or that Mr. Shaughnessy finds a subtle way of tyrannizing Kathleen sexually. It's all for the good of the family. "You're a great girl," her father says, unaware that he's forced his daughter into a form of prostitution.

Trevor makes such powerful material work by systematic self-effacement. His techniques may seem old fashioned at first, permitting leisurely exposition and switching from one point of view to another. But soon you realize that no judgments come from the author, that the style conforms to each character, and objective-sounding information is really subjective, frequently verging on indirect discourse. Hagarty for example sits in the pub "with a bottle of stout to console him," telling himself that since he's already paid to have the bullocks penned, "he might as well take full advantage of it by delaying a little longer." Trevor's indebtedness to the James Joyce of *Dubliners* is especially apparent here; both are masters of the subjective third-person and the ironic nuances of indirect discourse. Here's a choice moment, from **"In Love with Ariadne,"** where Trevor shifts from direct to indirect:

> "If there's a man in Dublin that knows his bricks and mortar better than Ned Sheehy give me a gander at him."
>
> Barney said he didn't think he could supply the old woman with such a person, and she said that of course he couldn't. No flies on Ned Sheehy, she said, in spite of what you might think to look at him.

Joyce ends "Ivy Day in the Committee Room" with the exquisitely ironic anticlimax, "Mr. Crofton said that it was a very fine piece of writing"; Trevor ends **"Kathleen's Field"** with an equally crushing use of the device, "her mother would say again that a bargain was a bargain."

Sometimes Trevor will switch from direct to indirect discourse five or six times in a short scene. It's all so swiftly and compactly done you hardly notice the narrator's voice is absent. Trevor also switches quickly from one character's mind to another, untroubled by Jamesian conventions, yet the effect is never omniscience. In **"A Husband's Return"** the first four paragraphs convey four different minds, without any "author" there at all; in **"A Trinity"** the irritations of husband and wife interweave so inconspicuously we hear them both thinking and take neither side: "The trouble with Keith was, he always sounded confident, as though he knew something she didn't"; and then "[Keith] wished she'd leave the talking to him." Trevor also likes to intercut dialogue with remembrances. In **"The Third Party"** and **"August Saturday"** conversations go on in the present while the main character's attention keeps lapsing and escaping into the past. Eventually memory becomes the more powerful storyteller. Often too Trevor will embed a letter or fragments from a journal in a story so as to complicate and extend a seemingly simple point of view. What all these techniques have in common is the author's disappearance from the text. You never quite hear Trevor's own voice. Even stories that sound like autobiography—**"A Choice of Butchers"** (1972), **"Matilda's England"** (1978), ***Nights at the Alexandra*** (1987)— turn out to be just first-person fictions, about different Irish childhoods that may or may not resemble the author's. For decades now the dust jackets have informed us simply that Trevor was born in County Cork and "lives in Devon with his wife and two sons." His reticence is just about flawless.

I do not mean to suggest that Trevor never adopts a storyteller's expository "once upon a time" role. He often begins in this seemingly authoritative old mode, e.g., the first story in ***Family Sins:*** "Nothing as appalling had happened before at Drimaghleen; its people had never been as shocked." And he sometimes ends stories with a George Eliot-like summation (e.g., **"The Wedding in the Garden,"** 1986). But in these roles he reveals no trace of performative ego. Even when he's onstage he's off: the words are someone else's. One reviewer complained a few years ago that Trevor was prudish about sex, assuming from the opening words of **"Mulvihill's Memorial"** (1981) that the author had to be squeamish to describe details in a pornographic film with such dowdy language as "petticoat," "further underclothes," and "divested himself." In fact the description amusingly reflects the quaintly inhibited prurience of a middle-aged bachelor, Mulvihill himself. The only lapse in Trevor's rigorous self-effacement that I have ever found occurs in **"The Time of Year"** (1981) when a tall, awkward boy is said to give "the impression of an etiolated newt." It's an almost shocking intrusion.

The truth is that Trevor does not want to tell his own stories, he wants other people to tell theirs. Curiosity about others, he once said, impels him to write. He is fascinated by other people's worlds, especially by their ability to invent coercive fictions or to be victimized by them. Apparent in Trevor's earliest work (e.g., **"The Table,"** 1967), the theme has become noticeably darker in recent years. Ever since ***Other People's Worlds*** (1980), his novel about a pathological actor-liar-fantasizer and the swath of destruction he cuts in other lives, Trevor's fiction has emphasized that storytelling itself is dangerous. And everyone has a story to inflict on someone else. Each story in ***Family Sins*** involves someone's coercive narrative, some reductive and destructive fable. The first one, for example, **"Events at Drimaghleen"** describes the murder of a young woman, her boyfriend, and his mother, all violently shotgunned in a farmyard. The young woman's parents decide at once who killed whom and why, but along come two

English journalists, offering money and taking pictures, and they produce a dramatically different story, more plausible in some ways than the first, but blighting the lives of the parents. Trevor prevents us from determining what really happened; the two explanations are equally Procrustean, each useful (in a terrible way) and made to fit rather than true. That families and communities do this just as much as individuals is a truth Trevor has been telling for years.

The dangerous storyteller in **"Family Sins"** is Hubert, a school chum of the narrator's who invites him home for the weekend. Hubert's tales in the dormitory were funny (he ridiculed his grandfather) and glamorous (his father was a con man, his mother a barmaid; both were killed in a head-on collision). But at home Hubert's stories are exposed as manipulative and cruel, and pathetically self-deceiving. Even when disillusioned the narrator wants to believe it when Hubert claims he was born in the back row of a cinema. And Hubert's tale of his parents' collision—with a truck of a traveling zoo, and the escaping apes "chattered with delight"—reappears with peculiar force in the narrator's dream. There's a deep warning here about fictive truth. It jumps so easily from one mind to another, and seems to have happened there, in effect *has* happened, even though it didn't.

In **"Coffee with Oliver"** Trevor studies the systematic lies and deceptions by which a rather charming old Englishman in Florence manages to eke out his impoverished life. Oliver cadges and gyps and rationalizes, stealing a little something from everyone (including his dying mother), and always finds a neat justification for it. His solipsism is almost impeccable. Told entirely from his point of view, the story is both comic and savagely critical. Oliver knows exactly how to deal with others who wish to talk: "finding the interruption of his own narration discourteous, Oliver did not listen." He is of course so busy narrating his life into palatable form that he cannot listen to anyone else. Trevor has a seemingly endless supply of such bad listeners. They are usually male, frequently headmasters of boarding schools or businessmen, and they all have impervious egos.

"The Third Party" consists of two male narratives in competition. Lairdman has been having an affair with Boland's wife, so they meet in a bar to settle things. Lairdman wants to marry Annabella and Boland wants nothing more than to surrender her, but he can't resist "correcting" the story of her that Lairdman has in his head. He's also busy despising Lairdman, whom he remembers from boarding school days as a prig. Boland's idea of his wife is "that she can't help telling lies" and "actually disliked the truth." He doesn't see how his own storytelling—not hers—betrays him. He would end his unhappy marriage, he knows he should. But anger and pride will not release him from the "truth" he must tell. Trevor's stories say this again and again. Old injuries, old resentments and grievances harden into the fictions that rule our lives. We keep uttering them to ourselves and others not to find absolution or escape but to justify ourselves after all. To have the last word. To impose our truth no matter what.

When communities and nations do this, Trevor suggests,

the costs are even more unbearable. His two most recent novels, *Fools of Fortune* (1983) and *The Silence in the Garden* (1988), are clearly his best—most heartbreaking, most disturbing, most complex—because they address exactly the problem of coercive narrative and silenced truth. The news from Ireland, as Trevor's 1986 story about the potato famine suggests, hasn't essentially changed for 150 years; they're still rewriting the same old tales. But Trevor is exposing those old mechanisms in a way nobody has before. The finest story in *Family Sins*, **"In Love with Ariadne,"** dramatizes how a young woman in Dublin is tainted by her father's crime, shamed and stigmatized forever by the whispered story of his pedophilia. So powerful is that collusive narrative that Ariadne must internalize it. When the story's protagonist, a young medical student from the country, tries to woo her away with his own fictions, he finds not only that his efforts have driven her into a convent but that what attracted him in the first place was abnormal, the vestige of family sin: "what seemed like a marvel of strangeness in Ariadne was damage wrought by shame." Repelled by ordinary women, drawn by her very unreachability, he falls into the same web of shame. Thus ever so subtly and dangerously in Trevor's world do the sins of the fathers visit themselves upon the next generation. (pp. 686-90)

Dean Flower, "The Reticence of William Trevor," in The Hudson Review, *Vol. XLIII, No. 4, Winter, 1991, pp. 686-90.*

Julia O'Faolain

William Trevor's fictions swing between realism and the escape-hatch of fantasy and the process is symbiotic, for it is his characters' plausibility which earns credence for their excesses. Like real people, they can commit cartoonish follies without becoming cartoonish. Reality dogs them. Realism delivers them up to scrutiny and we like Peeping Toms, may even feel an uneasy shiver at its verisimilitude. Humour rarely distances his subjects for long. Just as we settle to the release of laughter, a twitch of the plot hauls them back in for another shock of recognition. They are apt to be close to the end of their tether and are often very like ourselves. Trevor's empathy finds poignancy in the plainest lives.

It is this generosity of vision which makes the publication of his twenty-first book an occasion for celebration. So does his feel for a reality spliced with dreams. He is a writer attuned to this secular age which is full of hype and hope, when many are tantalized and fantasy is not only an escape but also a coping mechanism. Some of his most moving narratives pivot on the way their dreams nerve people to snatch at a happiness beyond their means. Thus, in his 1960s tale, **"Lovers of Their Time",** a couple, who have nowhere to be alone, take to sneaking into an Edwardian bathroom in the Great Western Royal Hotel, where they make love in a tub whose Great Western spaciousness was not meant for their sort. Nemesis, to be sure, catches up. Beneath the fizz of farce is a desperation kept, precariously, at bay.

There is a fair bit of that in Ireland, where Trevor has lately been setting more stories, no doubt because of the way the past there acts on the present—one of his themes. Able, when he chooses, to make realism levitate, he can, by subverting it, show up the shiftiness and dangers of truth. The title story of a recent collection, *Family Sins,* does just that. At first it seems to be a tale from rural stock about a possessive mother turning a gun on the girl her son wants to marry. Sadly, when all seems over, the girl's parents accept their bereavement. They are small farmers, and wrenching a living from poor land leaves scant time for brooding. Then, a journalist from the city writes an article which destroys their self-respect. Baffled at seeing themselves described as "disadvantaged", they are shamed by innuendo about their dead daughter and by the shock of seeing their lives through alien eyes. Interestingly, the story counterpoints a classic one on the same theme. Frank O'Connor's "In the Train" shows villagers returning from perjuring themselves in court so as to shield a murderess whom they would now punish in their own way. There, the alien consciousness is recognized as inimical and outfaced. Half a century later, it is harder to resist. Writing, truthful or not, is an intrusion and it is typical of Trevor's seriousness that he should turn his scrutiny on his own craft. His latest book does this again.

Two Lives is the umbrella title for a brace of novellas which turn on a common theme: fantasy filtering into a woman's life to replace, and perhaps redeem it. The lives are harsh and the dream-doses powerful. Side-effects wreak havoc and the women end up a little mad. The question left simmering is whether this is a mercy. The first of the two, **"Reading Turgenev,"** belongs to the author's chronicle of Anglo-Irish decline. This time we are far from the Yeatsian glories of the great houses whose fall Trevor has dramatized with such panache in earlier books. Ordinary people too get trapped by history, and Mary Louise, whose blue eyes "had a child's wild innocence", belongs to a poor Protestant community whose "very life was eroded by the bleak economy of the times". The times are the 1950s and she, stuck on a lonely farm, yearns for the lights of the local town. Unable to find work, she settles for marriage with "the only well-to-do Protestant for miles around". Elmer Quarry owns the town drapery, is fourteen years older than she, "square-looking" and "attired invariably in a nondescript suit".

The stale vocabulary—"attired" rather than "dressed"—sets the tone. Elmer, in keeping with family custom, has given his best years to his shop before thinking of "the securing of the line". When he does, he invites Mary Louise to the cinema, without bothering to find out what is on. It is *The Flame and the Flesh:* elements with which he has not reckoned, and it is, he will find, "about a woman in Italy, with a number of men interested". The subdued term for erotic arousal has a ring of the counting-house is where his true passions lie.

Clearly, the marriage is a mistake which Trevor, persuasively, turns into a destiny. Detail after coercive detail is hammered home until the couple are helpless. The proposal made and—after a month—accepted, "Elmer passed his tongue over his lips, dried them with a handkerchief and announced that he was going to kiss her." He was "decent and reliable"; Miss Mullover, the schoolteacher and chorus, takes a "sanguine view".

What no one will know is that Elmer is also impotent. In rural communities, a woman caught in such a plight does not shame her man by trying to escape it. Their joint misery drives him to drink and her to seek out an invalid cousin who reads Turgenev to her, tells her he was in love with her as a boy, then dies. Their few trysts are in a graveyard where she will later yearn to lie with him. Memory will turn to fantasy and fiction become her refuge. Reading to her "had been her cousin's courtship, all he could manage, as much as she could accept". Now, rather than grapple with realities, she frightens her sour sisters-in-law and poor, soft stick of a husband by openly buying rat poison, then colouring their rissoles with green ink. Committed to an asylum for the mad, she is happy "in a refuge where her love affair could spread itself". From dream, to macabre prank, to possibly feigned madness: her shifts have the mutually reinforcing coherence of metaphor. Rooted in a helpless community, they allegorize its fate while Trevor's precision—the brand of ink used is Stephen's, as it would have been in those years—guarantees authenticity. Our last glimpse of her recalls a remark from a previous novel: "in Ireland it happens sometimes that the insane are taken to be saints of a kind". And indeed there is something devotional about her cult of her dead cousin. " 'I dress for him,' she says. 'I make up my face in our graveyard.' " The opium of the people has, it would seem, been privatized.

As often now with Trevor, he is reworking an old theme. In **"The Raising of Elvira Tremlett,"** an unhappy boy fantasizes about a dead girl and ends, with relief, in an asylum. A girl in *Fools of Fortune* becomes a saint "of a kind" and, in *Nights at the Alexandra,* another yearner retreats into the memory of someone dead. However, the last two of these have more buoyancy than **"Reading Turgenev"**, in which unalloyed realism is bleakly deterministic and lacks leavening. There was complexity and humour in *Fools of Fortune,* while in *Nights at the Alexandra* the redemptive memory was more magical, perhaps because its dream-source was a cinema whose romance and scarlet seats and "rosy gloom" offered a counterpose to the drabness outside. Turgenev's world provides a less effective contrast with provincial Ireland, since his very name evokes a parallel to it: a sluggish society full of tragic destinies. Moreover, *On the Eve,* the particular novel which Mary Louise keeps reading, is about a lover who dies.

Despite the shared theme, the second novella here is very different. Mrs Delahunty, narrator of *My House in Umbria,* is quite without roots, constructs her identity as she goes along, and possesses several aliases. She was born fifty-eight years ago in an English seaside town to parents who owned a Wall of Death around which her father rode a motorbike with her mother on the pillion. They sold their daughter forthwith to foster-parents whom she left on her sixteenth birthday because the man kept forcing himself on her in the back-yard shed. Later adventures led to a brothel in Africa where she made the money to buy a house in the Umbrian countryside, in which she and her dubious Irish factotum, Quinty, now take paying guests. Meanwhile, she writes money-making romances which improve greatly on life as she has known it. Boozy and big-hearted, she has the common touch.

On a trip to Milan, her train compartment is blown up by a bomb. Later, in hospital, she is a prey to "ugly" memories, which she tries to baffle by planning a new romance and wondering about those around her. A champion survivor, she now has fellow survivors to care for and invites three to her villa. One, Aimée, an eight-year-old American girl orphaned by the explosion, becomes the particular object of her concern, and no doubt stands in for the abused child of Mrs Delahunty's memories. Cared for by Doctor Innocenti, whose name echoes the one usually put on foundling hospitals in Italy, Aimée's mind is in a precarious state. So is Mrs Delahunty's. Her fantasies darken as she wonders who could have wanted to slip a bomb into the travellers' luggage. Ingenious explanations occur to her and she begins to see Aimée as an agent of redemption.

Back at the house, farce and oddity take over as Quinty, the con-man, imports into its genteel surroundings something of the brothel where he and Mrs Delahunty first met. Expecting to inherit from her, he seems a likelier bomber than the suspect on whom her fantasies have fixed. She has now begun to believe that she sees into the minds and pasts of other people and, as this conviction grows more compelling, the narrative we are reading becomes increasingly unreliable.

When Aimée's uncle, an American professor, whose speciality is ants, turns up to take her home with him, there are farcical scenes in which Mrs Delahunty pleads ardently with him not to do so. Unfortunately, her manner is that of the brothel, and the ant-expert is repelled. Eavesdropping on his telephone conversations, she comes to the conclusion that he lacks the warmth which Aimée needs. In one of these overheard conversations, he distresses her by describing her fiction as "trash". "Her imagination has consumed her,' he said. From his tone he could have been referring to an ant." Two years later, she learns that Aimée has been put in a home. Though her romances may be "trash"—and evidence is provided to show them to be pretty much that—her intuitions were right. Her unreliable fantasies contained a core of wisdom.

Trevor has frequently been praised for allowing life to present itself without preaching, but this time Mrs Delahunty sermonizes on his behalf. The preoccupations of these two novellas—the use and abuse of the imagination—are old concerns of his but they have not elicited his usual verve. The first is a grim threnody. Strangely for Trevor, the second is lacking in particularity: Umbria is picture-postcard, and Mrs Delahunty a bit of a rattle. Graceless though it may be to quarrel with a writer who has so often provided marvels of entertainment, he is not here at the top of his form.

Julia O'Faolain, "The Saving Touch of Fantasy," in The Times Literary Supplement, No. 4600, May 31, 1991, p. 21.

Anita Brookner

I find increasingly, as I read and re-read William Trevor, that the effect is terrifying. It is not that he writes ghost stories—nothing so simple, although his main work has to do with hauntings—but his calm voice, completely in control of his often sad or bizarre material, leads one quietly along logical paths to an outcome bordering on insanity. Small towns in Ireland are found to contain tragic lives which are rarely ascribed to familiar causes. Social or psychiatric explanations will simply fail to uncover what the novelist uncovers so well. And it is suggested that once lives have departed from what is understood as the norm they cannot be put back together again: the doctor's optimism will, disquietingly, be found to be misplaced.

The unravelled or unravelling destinies which he has made his specialty have a way of remaining disconnected. In his hands this sad business is exhilarating, even comic. Yet there is a dread at the heart of it, together with a suggestion of impotence which has led some critics to compare him with Chekhov. He is not like Chekhov; at the same time he is strikingly un-English. He is particularly unnerving when he is dealing with deluded widows or falsely jovial drinkers, characters who have not quite given up but whom fate has marked down. All this is recounted in a prose so measured that the reader is moved forward unresistingly: quirks and oddities of dialogue and detail make the progress even easier. He is fatally comfortable to read, yet his conclusions are bleak.

One of his more disturbing characters is Mrs Delahunty, the protagonist of ***My House in Umbria,*** the second of the two fine novels here on offer, and the superior of the two. We first meet Mrs Delahunty in her honorable retirement, hostess of a gracious house to which Umbrian hoteliers occasionally direct their superfluous guests. She is agreeably wealthy, having made her pile by writing romantic novels (marvellously done, and only faintly parodied: who would not want to read *Precious September, Flight to Enchantment, For Ever More, Behold My Heart?*). Mrs Delahunty was not always so well placed. She was the child of circus acrobats, was farmed out to a couple of seaside lodging-house keepers, was duly interfered with by her adoptive father, and went on to embrace various careers: assistant in a shoe shop, stewardess on the *S.S. Hamburg,* madame of an African brothel, and finally, after her brief but flourishing literary career, mistress of a handsome Italian property.

The grotesqueries, which William Trevor deals out with unfailing impartiality, do not disappear with Mrs Delahunty's youth. Now fat and given to drink, but queenly and well-dressed, Mrs Delahunty might have been allowed to go her own way had she not happened to be on the Rome express to Milan when a terrorist bomb explodes in her carriage, killing most of the occupants and landing her with the survivors, to whom she offers a home in her house in Umbria. The English general, the German boy who lost an arm, and the child who lost her parents take up residence with Mrs Delahunty. The child's uncle is sent for. His arrival is the signal for Mrs Delahunty's bizarre beginnings and fictional fantasies to take on an even more alarming volume. Her dreams become divinatory; she claims to understand everything. But she is not allowed to explain even part of them, and her attempts to do so are chillingly repulsed. She is left alone again, once more respected but even more deeply removed from what Trevor himself has called other people's worlds.

This is quite frightening and quite brilliant. The other novel, **Reading Turgenev,** is far less complex and perhaps a little disappointing, although its pellucid storytelling will be justly admired. A poor Irish girl, Mary Louise Dallon, marries a man she does not love in order to get away from her parents' farm. The bridegroom, Elmer Quarry, is a prosperous draper who could do with another hand in the shop and an heir to carry on the business. These almost 19th-century signifiers have much to do with the unfolding of the story of the loveless marriage, of the belated awakening, and of the romantic dream which costs Mary Louise her sanity. She falls in love with her cousin Robert, an invalid, who reads Turgenev to her. This cousin, indeed this branch of Mary Louise's family, whom we know quite intimately, is introduced carelessly into the narrative in a way which is not sufficiently Turgenevian, nor does the country churchyard in which the cousins meet quite serve as a parallel to Turgenev's infinitely splendid dust-whitened summer vistas. The value of the episode is to set off the mean-minded daily routine in the house above the shop, where Mary Louise eventually defies her husband's two sisters and retreats to the attic. Nobody is surprised when she is taken away. And yet romance has made her strong, strong enough at all events to outlast her tormentors.

There is a sing-song fairy-tale quality to this story which stayed disappointingly in my mind once I had finished it, yet the seemingly casual pace and the almost classical amplitude are impressive. Perhaps 19th-century classicism of the romantic kind—in the sense that Turgenev is both classic and romantic—is not to be recaptured in these fragmented times. Fictional distance is perhaps the next best thing. One feels that these novels will endure. And in every beautiful sentence there is not a word out of place.

Anita Brookner, "Enduring What Can't Be Mended," in The Spectator, *Vol. 266, No. 8499, June 1, 1991, p. 28.*

FURTHER READING

Craig, Patricia. "The Shape of Past Iniquities." *The Times Literary Supplement,* no. 4445 (10 June 1988): 643.
Admires Trevor's social insight, use of humor, and economical writing style in *The Silence in the Garden.*

———. "The Pressure of Events." *The Times Literary Supplement,* no. 4530 (26 January 1990): 87.
Examines three recurrent themes in Trevor's short fiction: domestic scandals, acrimony in marriages, and recollecting the past.

Dillon, Eilis. "A Literary Link to a Historic Landscape on the Emerald Isle." *Los Angeles Times Book Review* (11 March 1984): 4.
Favorably reviews *A Writer's Ireland: Landscape in Literature,* praising in particular the photographs included in the work.

Eder, Richard. Review of *The News from Ireland, and Other Stories,* by William Trevor. *Los Angeles Times Book Review* (4 May 1986): 3.
Praises Trevor's skills as a short story writer, citing "The News from Ireland" as one of his finest stories.

———. "Parable with an Audible *Ping!*" *Los Angeles Times Book Review* (20 May 1990): 3.
Explores how the keeping of family secrets irrevocably affects the lives of all the characters in *Family Sins.*

Gordon, Mary. "The Luck of the Irish." *The New York Review of Books* XXX, No. 20 (22 December 1983): 53-4.
Examines the influence of Trevor's middle-class, Irish Protestant background on his work.

Greig, Geordie. "Guarded Celebrant of the Human Condition." *The Sunday Times* (29 May 1988): 68-9.
Profiles Trevor, discussing his beginnings as a writer and his short story collection *The News from Ireland, and Other Stories.*

Kakutani, Michiko. "The Decisive Moments in Characters' Lives." *The New York Times* (11 May 1990): C-33.
Maintains that "Kathleen's Field" in *Family Sins* showcases Trevor's three major skills as a short story writer: "his intimate knowledge of his characters' inner lives, his ability to conjure up an entire world through a descriptive phrase or two, [and] his intuitive sense of a story's natural arc."

Morrison, Kristin. "The Family Sins of Social and Political Evils." *The Irish Literary Supplement* 10, No. 1 (Spring 1991): 20.
Thematic discussion of *Family Sins.*

Mosher, Howard Frank. "William Trevor: Pictures from an Irish Exhibition." *The Washington Post Book World* XVI, No. 21 (25 May 1986): 6.
Compares the stories in *The News from Ireland, and Other Stories* to those of James Joyce, concluding that "like Joyce before him, Trevor is entirely his own writer, with his own uncompromised vision of human limitations made accessible by a rare generosity toward his characters and their blighted lives."

Neustatter, Angela. "A Natural Curiosity." *The Sunday Times* (26 May 1991): 6-7.
Brief biography of Trevor.

Taliaferro, Frances. Review of *The Stories of William Trevor* and *Fools of Fortune,* by William Trevor. *Harper's* 267, No. 1601 (October 1983): 74-5.

> Argues that *Fools of Fortune* is Trevor's most romantic and lyrical work.

Yardley, Jonathan. "William Trevor and the Loss of Paradise." *The Washington Post Book World* XIII, No. 39 (25 September 1983): 3.

> Laudatory review of *Fools of Fortune,* praising its characters, theme, and plot.

Additional coverage of Trevor's life and career is contained in the following sources published by Gale Research: *Contemporary Authors,* Vols. 9-12, rev. ed.; *Contemporary Authors New Revision Series,* Vol. 4; *Contemporary Literary Criticism,* Vols. 7, 9, 14, and 25; *Dictionary of Literary Biography,* Vol. 14; and *Major 20th-Century Writers.*

Tennessee Williams
The Glass Menagerie

(Full name Thomas Lanier Williams) Born in 1911, Williams was an American playwright, short story writer, novelist, poet, scriptwriter, memoirist, and nonfiction writer. He died in 1983.

The following entry presents criticism on Williams's *The Glass Menagerie.* For further information on Williams's life and career, see *CLC,* Vols. 1, 2, 5, 7, 8, 11, 15, 19, 30, 39, and 45.

INTRODUCTION

Williams is considered one of the most important American playwrights since World War II. *The Glass Menagerie,* his first successful Broadway production and the winner of the New York Drama Critics Circle Award in 1944, established his reputation as an innovative dramatist whose expressionistic style and complex themes revolutionized the American theater. In this play, as in such later works as *A Streetcar Named Desire, Cat on a Hot Tin Roof,* and *The Night of the Iguana,* Williams combined lyrical, symbolic, and realistic elements to portray sensitive individuals struggling to survive in a brutal, unsympathetic world. Centering on the vulnerability and grace of its characters, *The Glass Menagerie* probes the fragile illusions that both sustain and entrap them. Richard Gilman asserted: "A drama of 'memory,' which transforms autobiography into lucid, objective art, [*The Glass Menagerie*] is small, domestic, deeply felt, its lyricism reigned in by perception, sentimentality tightened by insight, experiment anchored in sure classical techniques."

Williams wrote *The Glass Menagerie* while working as a screenwriter for Metro Goldwyn Mayer, a major Hollywood production studio. Based on his short story "Portrait of a Girl in Glass," the play was originally presented to MGM executives as a script outline entitled "The Gentleman Caller." It was rejected, however, as his previous story ideas had been, and Williams was eventually asked to leave the studio. He spent the remaining three months of his contract revising the play, which soon attracted the attention of Eddie Dowling, a successful Broadway actor who agreed to direct and perform in *The Glass Menagerie.* The production debuted in Chicago on December 26, 1943, starring Laurette Taylor, whom many critics regarded at that time as America's greatest stage actress. Laudatory reviews of the play and Taylor's performance aroused the interest of critics and theatergoers in New York City, where *The Glass Menagerie* opened to sold-out audiences the following March. S. Alan Chesler described the atmosphere surrounding *The Glass Menagerie* as "the excitement of experiencing the work of a new talent and very likely a landmark in the history of American drama." Two weeks after its arrival on Broadway, the play was

awarded the New York Drama Critics Circle Award. In 1945 Williams published what critics often refer to as the "reading" text of *The Glass Menagerie.* The most widely anthologized and reprinted version of the play, the reading text presents *The Glass Menagerie* as it appeared before rehearsals for the original production. Williams also published an "acting" text in 1948 that incorporates changes he made to the play during the rehearsal process. Critics generally agree that the revisions of dialogue and characterization contained in this version improved upon the reading text and should be considered in discussions of the play.

In writing *The Glass Menagerie* Williams drew extensively upon his own experiences and those of his family. The play revolves around Amanda Wingfield and her adult children, Tom and Laura, who live, as Williams's family had, in a dingy tenement in depression-era St. Louis. Williams's autobiographical protagonist, Tom, both narrates and participates in the action onstage. He advises the audience in his opening soliloquy that "the play is memory" and features characters who are aspects of his own consciousness, tinged by sentimentality. His retrospective commentary continues throughout the play and provides an ironic counterpoint to the unfolding events. A poet trapped in a tedious job at a shoe warehouse, Tom dreams of becoming a writer and escapes nightly to the movies, where he vicariously experiences the adventure he craves. Tom's sister, Laura, like Williams's sister who was diagnosed as a schizophrenic, is debilitated by shyness, forcing her to withdraw from reality and retreat into a fragile world of old phonograph records and glass animals. The matriarch, Amanda, possesses many personality traits that have been attributed to Williams's mother, Edwina Dankin Williams. A fading southern belle abandoned by her husband, a telephone man "who fell in love with long distances," Amanda clings to the past and memories of her genteel girlhood in Blue Mountain. Yet she also exhibits a fierce determination to overcome her grim circumstances, and often badgers her children about family responsibilities and planning for the future.

The dramatic action of *The Glass Menagerie* centers upon Amanda's attempt to obtain a secure future for her daughter, who Amanda knows cannot survive independently. When Laura's attempt to attend business school ends disastrously, Amanda acts on her final hope that a husband can be found who will provide for and protect her daughter. She pesters Tom to choose a suitable "gentleman caller" from among his coworkers, and, he eventually agrees to bring his friend Jim O'Connor to dinner. Delighted, Amanda immerses herself in plans for his visit, the prospect of a suitor for her daughter stirring memories of her own beaus in Blue Mountain. Laura, however, is terrified and becomes physically ill when Jim arrives. Described in Tom's narration as "an emissary from a world of reality," Jim is a spirited young man who believes in the power of self-improvement courses and the future of television. He is also the popular boy for whom Laura secretly pined in high school. Left alone with Laura after dinner, he gradually sets her at ease with his personable manner and eventually persuades her to dance. Their movement is awkward, however, and they bump against the table that supports Laura's glass unicorn, breaking its horn. The mood of the scene then shifts and what began as Jim's attempt to build Laura's self-confidence becomes an expression of genuine admiration, ending with a kiss. Apologizing, Jim explains that he is engaged and cannot call on Laura again. He leaves abruptly, taking the unicorn that Laura gives him as "a souvenir." Following Jim's departure, Amanda berates Tom for having cruelly betrayed his family. Tom storms out of the apartment, leaving Amanda alone to comfort Laura. The play concludes with a soliloquy by Tom in which he reveals that he never returned to the tenement and that he chose, as his father had, to wander the world. His final words are addressed to his sister and reveal his inability to assuage his guilt for having abandoned her.

Commentators agree that the primary theme of *The Glass Menagerie* is the conflict between illusion and reality. Amanda and Laura, considered among Williams most gentle creations, are the first of his many vulnerable characters to use fantasy to escape harsh reality, yet they do not rely on alcohol or sexual promiscuity to sustain their illusions as do such later Williams protagonists as Blanche Dubois of *A Streetcar Named Desire*. While Williams sym-

pathetically portrayed their needs, he also dramatized, in the words of Joseph K. Davis, "the tragedy of indulging in the kinds of behavior and thinking that negate the possibilities of living." This theme is explored at a more complex level through the character of Tom. As a participant in the play, he shares in the escapism of his mother and sister. Yet, as its narrator, he communicates the ambivalent attitude of one who has acted on his dreams. By confessing that he cannot forget his sister, Tom also admits that he cannot permanently escape from the unreal world in which his family lives.

As Williams exposed the falseness of the Wingfield's fantasies, he also condemned what he perceived as the illusions of American society. For example, the South of Amanda's dreams—distinguished by jonquils, gentleman callers, and negro servants—is an idealized popular fiction that thwarts progress in the region just as it prevents Amanda from developing as a person. Additionally, Jim's optimistic belief in America's capitalist system is subtly undercut by his lowly position at the warehouse despite his many achievements in high school. Finally, in his soliloquy on the "social background" of the play, Tom accuses the American middle class of "matriculating in a school for the blind" as social unrest and violence sweep through Europe, destined to explode as World War II.

Williams presented the themes of *The Glass Menagerie* through a complex blend of symbolism, realism, and expressionism. While some critics have objected to the pervasiveness of the play's symbols, most concur that they significantly enhance the meaning of the characters and the action. For example, Laura's unique yet fragile personality is symbolized by the delicate glass unicorn and Jim's high school nickname for her, "Blue Roses." Similarly, the photograph of Amanda's absent husband and the fire escape where the Wingfields find relief from the summer heat signify liberation from the stifling atmosphere of the apartment and the family. Williams drew on the realistic tradition in creating the setting and characters of *The Glass Menagerie,* yet he also used several experimental production techniques involving screens, lighting, and music to produce the sense of events recollected in memory. Most important, Williams infused the dialogue of his characters with a poetic lyricism that universalizes the emotions enacted on the stage. Judith J. Thompson observed that through "a profusion of symbolic references and a recurrent pattern of anticipation, momentary fulfillment, and ultimate despair, the meaning of the play is enlarged. It is not simply the story of one shy crippled girl, a neurotic mother, and a dreamer of a son, not the story of just one more broken family, but an analogue of modern man's alienation from God and isolation from his fellow man."

By writing *The Glass Menagerie,* Williams hoped to introduce "a new, plastic theater" that would "take the place of the exhausted theatre of realistic conventions." Critics have agreed that to a great extent he succeeded in his aspiration and have hailed *The Glass Menagerie* as a landmark in American drama. Along with Eugene O'Neill's *Long Day's Journey into Night* and Arthur Miller's *Death of a Salesman, The Glass Menagerie* is regarded as one of several works to have supplanted European sensibilities in the American theater, communicating universal themes through a distinctly American voice. *The Glass Menagerie*, through its union of transcendent lyricism and realistic family drama, remains one of his most revered works. Edmund A. Napieralski observed that the play "still holds audiences in the theatre as well as in the study. Unlike Laura whom Williams compares to glass with a 'momentary radiance, not actual, not lasting,' *The Glass Menagerie* enjoys a radiance that is both actual and indeed lasting."

PRINCIPAL WORKS

PLAYS

Cairo! Shanghai! Bombay! [with Bernice Dorothy Shapiro] 1935

Headlines 1936

The Magic Tower 1936

Candles to the Sun 1937

Fugitive Kind 1937

Battles of Angels 1940; also performed as *Orpheus Descending,* 1957

The Long Goodbye 1940

This Property Is Condemned 1942

You Touched Me! [with Donald Windham] 1943

The Glass Menagerie 1944

The Purification 1944

Stairs to the Roof 1945

Moony's Kid Don't Cry 1946

The Last of My Solid Gold Watches 1947

Portrait of a Madonna 1947

A Streetcar Named Desire 1947

Summer and Smoke 1947; also performed as *Eccentricities of a Nightingale,* 1964

American Blues: Five Short Plays [first publication] 1948

The Rose Tattoo 1950

Camino Real 1953

Cat on a Hot Tin Roof 1955

Something Unspoken 1955

Three Players of a Summer Game 1955

27 Wagons Full of Cotton 1955; also performed as *All in One,* 1955

Sweet Bird of Youth 1956

Period of Adjustment 1958

Suddenly Last Summer 1958

Talk to Me Like the Rain and Let Me Listen 1958

I Rise in Flame, Cried the Phoenix 1959

The Night of the Iguana 1959

The Milk Train Doesn't Stop Here Anymore 1962

The Gnädiges Fräulein 1966; also performed as *The Latter Days of a Celebrated Soubrette,* 1974

The Mutilated 1966

The Two-Character Play 1967; also performed as *Out Cry,* 1971

The Seven Descents of Myrtle 1968; also performed as *Kingdom of Earth,* 1975

Dragon Country [first publication] 1969

In the Bar of a Tokyo Hotel 1969

Confessional 1971; also performed as *Small Craft Warnings,* 1972

I Can't Imagine Tomorrow 1971

The Theatre of Tennessee Williams. 7 vols. 1971-76

The Red Devil Battery Sign 1976

This Is (An Entertainment) 1976

Vieux Carré 1977

Crève Coeur 1978; also performed as *A Lovely Sunday for Crève Coeur,* 1979

Tiger Tail 1978

Clothes for a Summer Hotel 1980

Some Problems for the Moose Lodge 1980; also performed as *A House Not Meant to Stand,* 1981

Will Mr. Merriweather Return from Memphis? 1980

Something Cloudy, Something Clear 1981

NOVELS

The Roman Spring of Mrs. Stone 1950

Moise and the World of Reason 1975

The Bag People 1982

POETRY

In the Winter of Cities 1956

Androgyne, Mon Amour 1967

SCREENPLAYS

The Gentleman Caller 1943

Baby Doll 1956

SHORT FICTION

One Arm, and Other Stories 1948

Hard Candy: A Book of Stories 1954

Three Players of a Summer Game, and Other Stories 1960

The Knightly Quest: A Novella and Four Short Stories 1966

Eight Mortal Ladies Possessed: A Book of Stories 1974

It Happened the Day the Sun Rose, and Other Stories 1982

OTHER

Memoirs (memoirs) 1975

Where I Live: Selected Essays (essays) 1978

CRITICISM

Joseph Wood Krutch

It is not often that a first play—indeed, it is not often that *any* play—gets such a reception as *The Glass Menagerie* got from audience and from press alike. After the final curtain had descended, the unfamiliar cry of "Author! Author!" rang through the auditorium, and next morning the reviewers staged what is commonly called a dance in the streets. Undoubtedly some of this enthusiasm was for the acting and the production, especially for the performance of Laurette Taylor, who got everything that was to be had from the character of the pitiful and terrible old woman who is the central figure. But undoubtedly the enthusiasm was also and in almost equal measure for the playwright, a young man named Tennessee Williams previously known chiefly to prize committees and to the editors of avant-garde magazines.

In his first Broadway play Mr. Williams has chosen to set forth a powerful and arresting, if somewhat abruptly truncated, situation in an elaborate and highly fanciful manner. The action begins with a pretentious and inflated speech delivered in front of a blank wall by Eddie Dowling, who is several times in the course of the play to step out of his role to act as a usually unnecessary "narrator." Then the lights behind the wall go on and we see into the dismal interior of a slum flat in St. Louis presided over by an ex-Southern belle long ago deserted by her irresponsible husband and now striving desperately to arrange some sort of future for her crippled, neurotic daughter and her restless son, about whose neck the two female millstones are hanging. In her dreams this mother, now shabby and old and fat, still relives the days when she led the cotillion at the Governor's Ball and entertained seventeen callers at one time. All her vocabulary, all her standards, all her plans are in the terms of that dead past. "Gentlemen callers," "widows well provided for," and "young men of character and promise" are the figures of the mythology from which she cannot escape. She is vulgar, nagging, and unreasonable. But she is also desperate, pathetic, and gallantly hopeless in a fight against overwhelming odds—altogether, at least as Miss Taylor plays her, unforgettable as well as almost unbearable. She finally induces her son to entice a "gentleman caller" from the warehouse where he works; the gentleman caller charms the sickly daughter, and then, at the end of his first and only visit, announces his approaching marriage to someone else. The son leaves the house forever to join the merchant marine. His mother runs out after him to denounce his desertion and to show that she nevertheless is strong enough to go on with the fight. Then the lights go out, and the narrator steps again to the front of the stage. That, he announces, is the end of all the author has to tell. The imagination of the audience must supply for itself the rest of the story.

I have already said that the central character is unforgettable, and I must add my opinion that the fact is due at least as much to the writing as it is to the acting. Moreover, nothing which I am about to say should be taken as denying the fact that *The Glass Menagerie* is a remarkable play and its author a man of extraordinary talent. But there is no use failing to mention that his weaknesses are as patent as his gifts, or that very good writing and very bad writing have seldom been as conspicuous in the script of one play. It has a hard, substantial core of shrewd observation and deft, economical characterization. But this hard core is enveloped in a fuzzy haze of pretentious, sentimental, pseudo-poetic verbiage which I can compare only to the gauze screens of various degrees of filmy opacity which are annoyingly raised and lowered during the course of the physical action in order to suggest memory, the pathos of distance, and I know not what else. How a man capable of writing as firm as is some of that in this play can on other occasions abandon himself to such descriptive passages as that in which a young man is described—in Oscar Wilde's worst style—as "like white china" is a mystery. Moreover,

the incongruity is almost as conspicuous between personages as it is between passages. The insubstantial, unconvincing wisp of a Little Nell [who is Laura] simply does not belong in the same world as the one her mother so solidly inhabits.

The limitations of a good writer are sometimes best passed over in silence. One accepts them, and one can do nothing else. But when defects are of a corrigible sort, when they seem the result of a sort of self-indulgence which is likely to grow and grow if encouraged or even tolerated, then they ought to be reprehended in some downright manner. And the defects of Mr. Williams's manner are defects of that sort. Probably he admires most in himself what is least admirable there. At the moment no doubt many agree with him. But they will not continue to do so for long. He is one of those writers who had best heed the advice: whenever you have written a line you like especially well, strike it out. (pp. 424-25)

Joseph Wood Krutch, in a review of "The Glass Menagerie," in The Nation, *New York, Vol. 160, No. 15, April 14, 1945, pp. 424-25.*

John Mason Brown

Recently I had the good fortune to see *The Glass Menagerie,* but the bad fortune to see it after reading the reviews and hearing ecstatic reports about it from Chicago. Although Tennessee Williams's fantasy is a play I would not have missed, I wish I had missed both the reviews and the advance reports. At least until later. I wish I had missed them because Mr. Williams's play was forced to live them down. It was compelled to struggle against them much as a joke, however good, is condemned to a harder hearing when introduced by some witless fellow who insists upon laughing first, and then saying, "Oh, that reminds me of a very funny story."

A play would have to be a masterpiece indeed to compete with what has been said about *The Glass Menagerie* both in Chicago and New York. Mr. Williams's script, I am afraid, is not that masterpiece.

It has its high, its shimmering virtues. It is blessed with imagination. It has its many lovely moments. It is the kind of play one is proud to have the theatre produce, and pleased to sit before even when disappointed in this scene or in that. In any season it would be uncommon; in this season it is outstanding. It is the work of a mind both original and sensitive. Although it follows trails blazed by Thornton Wilder and William Saroyan, it manages to walk down them with a gait of its own.

It is as promising a first play as has been seen hereabouts in many a year. As set and directed, its unusual merits are admirably preserved. (p. 34)

Mr. Williams's is a play of moods; a study in frustration. Its plot is nonexistent, at least so far as plotting is ordinarily understood. It is too close to the heart of life to bother about story-telling merely for the sake of telling a story. To attempt to suggest its qualities by outlining its actions would be as unfair to *The Glass Menagerie* as it would be to try to suggest the qualities, say, of *The Three Sisters* in terms of a synopsis. No one can deny that *The Three Sisters* is about three Russian women who want to go to Moscow and never get there. Yet to say this—and only this—is to omit the wit, wisdom, perception, and autumnal radiance which make Chekhov's play one of the wonders of the modern stage.

Mr. Williams bases his drama upon an incident rather than a plot. The only story he tells is how an impoverished Southern mother has her hopes dashed when she learns that the Gentleman Caller, who has at last come to see her crippled daughter, is already engaged. But Mr. Williams's interest does not stop with this story. His concern is what lies under the surface of events. He deals with those small happenings which can loom so large in the lives of unhappy people. He shows us the hopes such happenings can quicken, the memories they stir, the transformations they are able to effect, and the despair they often evoke.

His drama is projected as a memory, seen at moments not only through the actual gauzes provided by [the set designer], but in flashes through the thicker curtain of time itself. Mr. Williams's is the simplest kind of make-believe. The narrator he employs is the crippled girl's brother. The scenes we are invited to share are this brother's recollections. They are recalled to him when, as a merchant sailor in a foreign port, he sees objects in a store window which remind him of his sister's glass menagerie at home.

We move back in the sailor's life until we encounter the nagging and the dulness which drove him to seek the release of the sea. We learn of his hatred of the factory in which he worked; of his need for escape; of his incessant movie-going when (as Mr. Williams puts it), in the company of millions of other Americans sitting in darkened theatres in the pre-war years, he let a few Hollywood actors have all his adventures for him.

With this sailor brother we enter the poor home his memory has recreated. We inhale the honeysuckle of his mother's Southern recollections. We overhear her steady, soft-voiced scoldings, and understand her exasperation. We meet the crippled sister, too. She is a girl who lives in the dreams summoned by the music of her Victrola records and the small glass animals in her collection to which she has given her heart. This sister is painfully shy. She is denied life by the self-consciousness her braces have forced upon her. In an overstressed moment of symbolism, Mr. Williams insists that, because of her deformity, she is as out of place among her healthy contemporaries as is the glass unicorn in her menagerie among the commoner animals.

We learn how this girl blooms under the attentions of a happy extrovert who cannot marry her. We also eavesdrop on her when, at last, she consents to face the boy her brother has asked home from the factory for a humbler version of the *Alice Adams* dinner party. Above all, we understand the decision of the brother, being what he was, to go to sea.

Mr. Williams writes about his characters warmly, with a sympathy that is constant and yet probing. He knows how to etch them in line by line, so that before the evening is over we know them well. We are on intimate terms even

with the hard-drinking father who has deserted them and is represented only by a shoddy photograph on the wall. But, in spite of Mr. Williams's perceptions and the quality of his play, his writing lacks the impact of Clifford Odets's phrasing and the ultimate radiance of William Saroyan's feeling.

Full though his heart is, Mr. Williams's drama sometimes proves empty. I found that it lost my interest even while it held my admiration. Fascinated as I remained by the way in which its lines were spoken, it became difficult for me to keep my mind (in the second act) on every line that was being spoken. I was certain of my respect for the play in general, but increasingly aware of Mr. Williams's uncertainties.

Perhaps this was because, unlike Chekhov, Mr. Williams permits us to become uncomfortably conscious of how slight is the incident upon which he has based his play. Perhaps it is because his dialogue is not always active enough to compensate for the lack of action in his story. Perhaps it is because he allows us to know too much too early about all his characters except the charmingly written and played Gentleman Caller. . . . Or perhaps, as I have hinted, it is because the praise the play had won in advance had led me to expect that miracle which is every critic's hope. (pp. 34-5)

John Mason Brown, "Miss Taylor's Return,"
in The Saturday Review of Literature, *Vol.*
XVIII, No. 15, April 14, 1945, pp. 34-6.

Kappo Phelan

All sorts of things are going on on the stage of the Playhouse under [the title *The Glass Menagerie*] and I suspect it is to Tennessee Williams's advantage that his play is being wholly celebrated and bought as a performance. A mixture of symbolism (the title), naturalism (the body of the piece), and fantasy (a number of theatrical effects), the work presents a sure rigmarole to the audience simultaneously with large opportunities for bravura to the players. I can only imagine Mr. Williams's intention was to present a man, "Now," and his story, "The Past." (Quotations are taken from the time-sequence listed in the program.) However, what chiefly emerges is the story and it is this: a decayed and not quite genuine Southern Belle, deserted by her no-account husband and arrived in a back alley tenement in St. Louis, ceaselessly nags her weakling son (support of the family) to provide some opportunity for his crippled sister who, utterly repressed, lives only in the contemplation of her collection of glass animals. A "Gentleman Caller" is deviously procured, momentarily lifts the daughter into life and delight, and disappears into the arms of his own girl. The significance of the title (and the possible solution of the problem of the crippled daughter) will be an over-simplified incident during the "Caller's" visit when the horn of a glass unicorn is inadvertently broken and the animal is returned to the shelf with "the other horses." So much for "The Past." For the "Now," a new dimension is added to the work, or rather precedes it. The "Son" of the story is also its narrator, opens it, names it a "play of memory," and adjusts its purely theatrical devices such as cueing in the music, raising and dimming the lights. In this rôle, he is brilliantly assisted by the design of the setting which accentuates perfectly the real-dream skip in action. It having been projected in the body of the piece that this character wishes to escape to the Merchant Marine, evidently we are supposed to guess his escape before we can learn his identity, his primary clue as narrator being a pea jacket and woolen cap—and these accoutrements an afterthought on the part of the producers as the publicity pictures show. However, rejecting the gnawing smallness of this quibble, what the work proves is the impossibility of detailed characterization (even of such excellence as this author's) based on faulty documentation or no documentation at all. As studies in naturalism the four characters on view are to the life. I can imagine no spectator unable to identify them through experience. And they are as completely written as played. However, even though "as large as life and twice as natural," their circumstance (and I oppose this term to action) is extremely fancy indeed. We are asked to believe, for instance, in a sailor in the "Now" with no recognizable reference to the "Now" as we know it. His account of "The Past" would appear to be a story of American life during the years of depression, but this supposition is destroyed when (later in the "Now") we suddenly learn that the story's period is that of the Spanish Civil War at the same time as (note quote) "America was singing 'The World Is Waiting for the Sunrise' "! At this same date, the "Gentleman Caller" of the piece is made to speak convincingly of "getting into Radio on the ground floor," and there are instances of dialect, slang, and tunes which jump the situation all over yesterday in spite of the especial and familiar period the narration has fixed, or will do. If these items of complaint seem unduly fractional, it must be remembered that the method Mr. Williams has chosen for his main play depends wholly upon the fractional, upon the building of infinitesimal pieces of observation to create men and women. And it is his extreme astuteness in handling this method which breeds suspicion in his audience when he veers into false or no detail, into abstraction, into metaphysical extensions of theater presentation. In the last analysis, what he has accomplished is the creation of four walloping parts which, by virtue of his cast, results in an exhibition of the art of playing and no play. It seems to me the kindest comment on this phenomenon will be to call Mr. Williams a playwright *in transition* rather than an irresponsible artist, and the only conclusions we can offer him (or, in fact, that he offers us) are axiomatic: that a little logic is a silly thing; that random eclecticism in no way comprises poetry or drama; that projected forms are certainly to be explored before they are peopled. (pp. 16-17)

> *Kappo Phelan, in a review of "The Glass Menagerie," in* The Commonweal, *Vol. XLII, No. 1, April 20, 1945, pp. 16-17.*

Benjamin Nelson

The Glass Menagerie is the most consciously biographical of all Williams' dramas, and if the seven scenes which comprise this play are not literal representations of the St. Louis days in the early 1930s they nevertheless blend into an uncompromising emotional portrait of the tragic situation which was the author's home.

The story is simple. Tom Wingfield, a young man with dreams, is bound to his mother and sister because his father vanished one day and left them destitute. He realizes how much he is needed, and yet he knows that he must escape from them if he is ever to find himself. "His nature is not remorseless, but to escape from a trap he has to act without pity." The mother, Amanda, lives in two worlds: the pleasant dream of the past, Moon Lake Casino, Blue Mountain, the memory of seventeen gentleman callers in a single day, and the drab and demanding world of the present, with bills to pay, a son who is "a poet with a job in a warehouse," and a daughter who has refused to accept the harsh reality of her life and has withdrawn into the world of glass figurines she has collected "till she is like a piece of her own glass collection, too exquisitely fragile to move from the shelf." Concerned about her son, whom she does not understand, and who she feels must gather himself together and face his responsibilities, Amanda is much more distraught with her daughter who, she realizes, is helpless and lost. An attempt to instill confidence in her by sending her to secretarial school has been a dismal failure, and Amanda has only one last hope: to find a husband who will provide for her and somehow keep her from submerging entirely into a world of imagination.

At his mother's almost cajoling insistence, Tom finally brings home a gentleman caller, a young man named Jim O'Connor who works with him at the shoe corporation. The final two scenes of the play present the supper at the Wingfield home and the incipient relationship between Jim and Laura. For a brief, breathless moment Laura emerges from the glass menagerie, but while she is still swaying precariously on the threshold, Jim admits that he is already keeping company and is soon going to be married. As the world crashes, he departs, Amanda berates Tom for his apparent stupidity and then hastens to comfort her daughter who has finally enclosed herself in her illusions. And Tom Wingfield now breaks free and departs into the world from which Laura has made her final, irrevocable retreat.

Laura Wingfield, obviously created from the figure of Rose Williams, is the least successful portrait in this play. Too far removed from the world of her brother or mother, she never quite attains a lucid characterization. The girl in glass is a shadow girl whose dilemma motivates much of the thought and action of those around her, but who never emerges as a human being in her own right. She and her plight are too close to the author and rather than probe her experience he makes statements about it. He says, through the characters in his play, that she is beautiful, her beauty and fragility are anachronisms in our world, she will be destroyed, and this is a tragic thing. Rather than cope with her mental unbalance, he creates her with a limp and an inferiority complex to account, at least in part, for her extreme introversion. Otherwise we know very little about Laura, nor are we going to be enlightened during the course of the drama. In a play marked by its objectivity, she remains too subjective. She exists on the single dimension of sympathy.

But if the character of Laura is never fully realized, her plight is given luminous expression. For Williams, the beauty of the ideal is far too delicate to long survive in a world where beauty and delicacy have become little more than petty catchwords. The beauty and gentility of Laura and Rose only make them anachronisms who must either retreat into the ideal beauty of unreality or break in the face of the meaningless harshness of the world outside the glass menagerie. Their plight is symbolized in a poem Williams calls **"Lament for the Moths."**

> A plague has stricken the moths, the moths are dying,
> their bodies are flakes of bronze on the carpets lying.
> Enemies of the delicate everywhere
> have breathed a pestilent mist into the air.
>
> Lament for the velvety moths, for moths were lovely.
> Often their tender thoughts, for they thought of me,
> eased the neurotic ills that haunt the day.
> Now an invisible evil takes them away.
>
> I move through the shadowy rooms, I cannot be still,
> I must find where the treacherous killer is concealed.
> Feverishly I search and still they fall
> as fragile as ashes broken against a wall.
>
> Now that the plague has taken the moths away,
> who will be cooler than curtains against the day,
> who will come early and softly to ease my lot
> as I move through the shadowy rooms with a troubled heart?
>
> Give them, O mother of moths and mother of men,
> strength to enter the heavy world again,
> for delicate were the moths and badly wanted
> here in a world by mammoth figures haunted!

As in **You Touched Me!,** the attempt is made to lead the moth out of her cocoon, into the "heavy world," but this time the attempt is unsuccessful. The moth is much too fragile to fly in "a world by mammoth figures haunted," and the flame of life which glowed with such intensity in the romantic, semi-fantastic figures of Benjamin Murphy and Hadrian, is little more than a flicker in the person of Laura's gentleman caller.

Jim O'Connor is referred to by Tom Wingfield as "an emissary from a world of reality that we were somehow set apart from." Vibrant, simple and hearty, he seems to Tom and to his mother and sister, "the long delayed but always expected something that we live for." He alleviates Tom's intense embarrassment at the dinner table by easily carrying on a bantering discussion with Mrs. Wingfield. And alone with Laura after dinner he immediately begins to persuade her that her limp is only a minor disability, that she is beautiful and personable and need not fear anything. He jokes with her about their high school years—they had attended the same school—and good-naturedly boasts about his impending climb to success.

> I wish to be ready to go up right along with it.

Therefore I'm planning to get in on the ground floor. In fact I've already made the right connections and all that remains is for the industry itself to get under way!

> Full steam—
>
> *Knowledge—Zzzzzp! Money—Zzzzzzp!—Power!*
>
> That's the cycle democracy is built on!

Soon Laura is caught up in the warmth and confidence of the young man. To prove to her that her limp is no barrier he asks her to dance and as he takes her in his arms, "a fragile, unearthly prettiness has come out in Laura: she is like a piece of translucent glass touched by light. . . ." As they dance they inadvertantly break the glass unicorn which evokes Laura's comment:

> I'll just imagine he had an operation. The horn was removed to make him feel less—freakish! Now he will feel more at home with the other horses, the ones that don't have horns. . . .

In the ensuing kiss Laura comes closer than she ever has been to emerging into a new world; but like the translucent glass touched by light, her radiance is "a momentary radiance, not actual, not lasting." And Jim, so completely at ease and self-assured moments before, is unable to help her at the moment she needs him most. With his stammered confession that he is already engaged to a girl he awkwardly departs and leaves Laura to retreat into her glass world. Her brief joy is snuffed out and her loneliness is only intensified. It is obvious that she will never allow a Jim O'Connor to happen to her again.

To view Jim's embarrassed confession to Laura as the result of his realization that she may be falling in love with him is to see only one side of the situation. It is true that Jim has unwittingly aroused emotions in Laura with which he cannot cope. But it is similarly true that she has aroused emotions in him which have suddenly upset his life. On the surface Jim is the young man most likely to succeed. He has made the right connections, he is engaged, he is waiting for the inevitable thrust that will catapult him to success. He radiates confidence and his conversation is sprinkled with references to the marvelous opportunities which await the "go-getter." But Jim is not at all as confident as he would have Laura believe. Beneath the bravado and good-hearted bluster, Jim is afraid that democracy—the good old U.S.A.—may leave him behind:

> But just look around you and you will see lots of people as disappointed as you are. For instance, I hoped when I was going to high school that I would be further along at this time, six years later, than I am now—

Although he begins by attempting to convince Laura that she need not feel inferior, he soon betrays his own fear and insecurity. Six years have passed and he is still "planning to get in on the ground floor." Maybe he still will, but after six years with no appreciable progress he must struggle to quell the fear and doubt.

Laura is not the only person "awakened" in their moments together; Jim is awakened to a part of himself that he has not quite successfully suppressed: the unsure, uncertain, frightened Jim O'Connor. His reaction to Laura is that of a bewildered boy, needing tenderness and beauty, and seeing it for a moment in a strange girl. But he cannot accept Laura and preserve his wonderful dream of himself, and she in turn is much too ineffectual to make any positive gesture toward him. So they come together, for one instant, in their mutual need and Jim once more gains control. It's ridiculous, he convinces himself, I must be crazy; I'm engaged to Betty (wholesome part of the American Dream!) and the sooner I tell this odd girl the better. And so he tells Laura and they have suddenly passed in the twilight, each visibly shaken by this unexpected moment of truth.

The story of Laura and Jim is simple and poignant, but it is neither the sole nor the central conflict in the play. Laura's personal dilemma is part of a greater dilemma: the destruction—slow and remorseless—of a family. It is not a melodramatic destruction; there is no battle of angels above them. It is gradual, oblique and laced with pathos and humor, but it is the erosion of a family nonetheless; and the central protagonist of this drama is not Laura, but Amanda, her mother. Amanda Wingfield is

> a little woman of great but confused vitality clinging frantically to another time and place. Her characterization must be carefully created, not copied from type. She is not paranoiac, but her life is paranoia. There is much to admire in Amanda, and as much to love and pity as there is to laugh at. Certainly she has endurance and a kind of heroism, and though her foolishness makes her unwittingly cruel at times, there is tenderness in her slight person.

Amanda does cling frantically to the past, but she clings just as desperately to the present. She is attempting to hold two worlds together and realizes that both are crumbling beneath her fingers. The world of her youth has already vanished and her constant references to gentleman callers and jonquils are not only out of place in the dingy St. Louis apartment—they are agonizing. Her horribly dated clothing and her mannerisms also underscore her as a foolish old woman impossibly attempting to relive a wasted life. Puritanical and narrow minded, she is appalling in her unreasonable devotion to the past. At the same time she is shrewish, nagging and vulgar in her attempts to cope with the bleak reality of her environment. At one moment she enrages her son with her pretentions and her postures, in the next she prods him and goads him for his inability to be more than a dreamer in a situation where positive action is needed. She berates Tom with the statement that

> you are the only young man that I know who ignores the fact that the future becomes the present, the present the past, and the past turns into everlasting regret if you don't plan for it.

Amanda does not ignore these facts. She recognizes them all too well and attempts to flaunt them with her own special dreams. She knows that her existence and the existence of her son and daughter is a desperate struggle, and she accepts that struggle. It is this acceptance which elevates her stature above the cloying, often ignorant and embarrassing dowdy, and makes her the most vital and moving character in the play. For whatever Amanda is or

does, she possesses a fighting spirit and a stubborn gallantry in the face of overwhelming odds. And in Williams' words, "the most magnificent thing in all human nature is valor—and endurance." It is precisely this heroism and endurance which finally manifest themselves in Amanda and leave us with the impression of a truly valiant woman. This impression does not arise out of any particular word or action. Throughout the play she nags, scolds, dreams, plays the coquette and rages helplessly at her son. And yet, although nothing is said in her behalf, she emerges as a noble and strangely tender figure with a valor that abides alongside pettiness and a tenderness which is at once intertwined with insensitivity and cruelty. It is only at the conclusion when she realizes that her desperate plan for Laura has been crushingly defeated that the great strength and beauty of this woman emerges.

> The interior scene is played as though viewed through soundproof glass. Amanda appears to be making a comforting speech to Laura who is huddled upon the sofa. Now that we cannot hear the mother's voice, her silliness is gone and she has dignity and tragic beauty. Laura's dark hair hides her face until at the end of the speech she lifts it to smile at her mother.

Williams' portrait of Amanda is one of the most compelling and honest he has ever drawn. If it is not a factual likeness of the playwright's mother—he reports that she was aghast when she first viewed Laurette Taylor's performance—it is nevertheless an unerring emotional portrait drawn with amazing candor and with great objectivity. And the ambivalence in the relationship between the son and the mother is as poignant as it is terrifying.

In his story of the disintegration of a family and the desperate need for one member of that family to break free, Williams has presented a deeply moving play. For Amanda, as for Laura, and even for Jim to a lesser extent, life is finally overwhelming. Despite their gallantry, bluster, tenderness and rage, they are defeated. John Gassner, in a summary of the play [in his *A Treasury of the Theatre*, Vol. III], stated:

> In this delicate work Williams retains a highly objective attitude toward his picture of a life of failure. He locates his story in the context of the larger world, which demands a wideawake attitude toward a society that, ailing and torn with the conflict of a Second World War, challenges our intelligence and capacity for action. Although the play is written in a mood of tenderly rueful reminiscences, Williams exhibits much strength of mind and objectivity. Sympathize though he does with his failures, he recognizes that one cannot accept their quiescence and bumbling. . . . *The Glass Menagerie* is . . . a "mood." But it is a mood not mistaken by either the author or the Narrator (and they are actually the same person . . .) for the whole of reality. The author was attached to his characters to such a degree that he could make them move us deeply, but he was also detached enough to locate them in time, place and necessity.

Gassner's statement brings us to the fourth protagonist of *The Glass Menagerie,* Tom Wingfield, the son and narrator. Tom is caught in the web of his family and is fully aware of his plight. He knows that his job in the shoe company will stifle him and the anguish he feels in the presence of his mother will soon tear him apart. He knows that one day he will have to commit the cruelest act of his life: abandoning mother and sister. As Gassner noted, he may love and sympathize with these people but he cannot accept their failure. The world will not accept them and Tom must make his stand in the world, "for nowadays the world is lit by lightning. Blow out your candles, Laura—and so good bye. . . . " So Tom leaves "with a wide-awake attitude toward a society that . . . challenges our intelligence and capacity for action." He cuts the silver cord and like Paul Morel of *Sons and Lovers* walks out of the darkness toward the challenging and shimmering unknown.

But is Tom Wingfield's departure a positive effort on his part, or the final fraying of a bond which could no longer maintain itself? Tom, in the role of Narrator, speaks a good deal about truth and illusion and reality and dreams, but Tom, the protagonist in the story, possesses the romantic soul of a dreamer. Despite the perceptions he shows as Narrator he has as much trouble facing his situation as does his mother. In part, the play is his attempt to overcome his fears, but we are left with no assurance at the conclusion that he has succeeded. He is plainly disgusted with his mother for her poses and apparent refusal to cope with reality, and yet he, too, escapes daily from the oppression of his life by seeking the narcotism of the cinema. Before he makes his final departure Amanda accuses him of living in illusions:

> Go to the movies, go! Don't think about us, a mother deserted, an unmarried sister who's crippled and has no job! Don't let anything interfere with your selfish pleasure! Just go, go, go—to the movies!

Thus a mother who is accused by her son of living in illusions, makes the most harsh and realistic statement in the play when she berates the boy, who considers himself the realist, for being an ineffectual dreamer. The author of the play is here not the narrator. Williams turns a double-edged blade unmercifully, honestly and beautifully. When Tom leaves he escapes from a trap, a situation which is plainly unendurable, but there is nothing heroic or even positive and challenging in his departure. He is discharged from his position with the shoe company and he knows he can no longer remain home. His departure is little more than the snap of a twig in the wind.

Tom is a part of the dilemma of his family and he cannot break completely free. If the bond between him and his mother and sister has frayed, it nevertheless holds and will hold all his life. As he admits in retrospect, "Oh Laura, Laura, I tried to leave you behind me, but I am more faithful than I intended to be." Wherever he may go and whatever he may do, he will always be more faithful than he intended to be, to Amanda as well as Laura. In the final analysis, he is the fourth of a quartet caught in the ordinary and terrifying situation of attempting to exist in a world which gives them no sensible reason for existence.

The Glass Menagerie exhibits several of Williams' weak-nesses as well as his strengths as a playwright. The great strength of the play is of course the delicate, sympathetic, yet objective creation of meaningful people in a meaningful situation. Williams has caught a decisive and desperate moment in the lives of four individuals and given it illumination and a sense of deep meaning—no small feat for any writer.

His characterizations are not equally realized. He has been unable to create Laura on more than a single dimension, while Amanda is overwhelming in her multi-faceted delineation. On a more technical level the play manifests a doubt on the part of its author toward the power of the written word. As a backdrop for *The Glass Menagerie,* Williams originally wished to use a screen to register emotions and present images from the past, present and future. For example, when Jim O'Connor confesses to the family that he is going steady with another girl, the legend on the screen is to read, "THE SKY FALLS." Fortunately, Eddie Dowling [the first director of the play], deleted these touches of the poet from his production, but the play still abounds with a number of pretentious statements on the part of Tom as Narrator.

I assume that the final scene between Amanda and Laura is played in pantomime because Williams wished to portray Amanda's dignity through her gestures and her daughter's reaction, rather than through the mother's speech, which during the course of the drama has been either shrill, simpering or saucy. But in relegating this scene to background silence while Tom makes a self-conscious statement about drifting like a dead leaf "attempting to find in motion what was lost in space," he has substituted a painfully pretentious narration for what could have been an intense and luminous moment between the two women.

Again, on the credit side of the author, his play presents genuine situation, motivation and, as Joseph Wood Krutch has noted [in *The Nation,* 14 April 1945], "a hard substantial core of shrewd observation and deft, economical characterization." But Mr. Krutch also noted that "this hard core is enveloped in a fuzzy haze of pretentious, sentimental, pseudo-poetic verbiage." In *The Glass Menagerie,* the strained lyricism runs parallel with dialogue that is fresh, alive and highly characteristic, particularly in the speech of Amanda. This dialogue fortunately dominates the proceedings, but the excess of self-conscious "poetical" passages is quite apparent and is a fault of which Williams is to be guilty in much of his later work.

But the great weakness of *The Glass Menagerie* does not lie in its author's artistic or technical deficiencies. The weakness lies at the core of the play and evolves out of what is to become the playwright's hardening philosophical commitment. We can begin to comprehend this when we ask ourselves whether or not *The Glass Menagerie* is a tragedy. It presents a tragic situation and characters who, despite their moodiness and foolishness and self-deception, possess a sense of the tragic. With the possible exception of Laura, they are intensely genuine and the destruction of their dreams and aspirations bears the illusion of great importance. But the play is not a tragedy. The universe of *The Glass Menagerie* does not allow tragedy.

Everyone in the play is a failure and in the course of their drama they all perish a little. Amanda, the most heroic of the quartet, is pitiful but not tragic because from the outset she is doomed to failure despite her desperate struggle to right things. None of these people are given the opportunity to triumph against a fate which is as malignant as it is implacable. Their struggle is a rear-guard action against life, a continuous retreat. This retreat may be moving, pathetic, melodramatic or boisterous, but it is always a withdrawal. After all, what is the world outside the glass menagerie?

> There was only hot swing music and liquor, dance halls, bars and movies, and sex that hung in the gloom like a chandelier and flooded the world with brief, deceptive rainbows . . . all the world was waiting for bombardments!

The world outside the Wingfield apartment is a world of illusions, also, even more deceptive and destructive than those held by Amanda and Laura. It is the world of *Stairs to the Roof* and this time the escape is not to a new star but into the individual and personal illusions fostered by each of the characters as his private defense against destruction. Jim waits for the day when his "zzzzzp!" will at last disperse his fear and uncertainty; Laura creates her own sparkling, cold world which gives the illusion of warmth but is as eternal in its unreality as the glass from which it is composed; Amanda strikes out with all her power against her fate by clinging to the past as to a shield; and Tom, recognizing the plight of his family, can do no more than drift away from them, rudderless, frightened and never really as far from Amanda and Laura as he knows he should be.

Not one of these individuals can cope with his situation. They struggle and their hopes and the destruction of these hopes possess a sense of great importance because Williams has created genuine people in an intensely genuine situation, but they lack the completeness to truly cope with their dilemma. They are not responsible for what has happened to them and they are much too helpless to do more than delay the inevitable. And destruction is inevitable because it is implicit in the universe of Tennessee Williams.

> For the sins of the world are really only its partialities, and these are what sufferings must atone for. . . . The nature of man is full of such makeshift arrangements, devised by himself to cover his incompletion. He feels a part of himself to be like a missing wall or a room left unfurnished and he tries as well as he can to make up for it. The use of imagination, resorting to dreams or the loftier purpose of art, is a mask he devises to cover his incompletion. Or violence such as a war, between two men or among a number of nations, is also a blind and senseless compensation for that which is not yet formed in human nature. Then there is still another compensation. This one is found in the principle of atonement, the surrender of self to violent treatment by others with the idea of thereby cleansing one's self of his guilt.

This statement emanates from the core of Williams'

thought and is perhaps his most illuminating commentary about himself and his work. It represents a philosophy, or let us say an attitude toward man in his universe, which is to manifest itself in all his work. It is taken from his short story, **"Desire and the Black Masseur,"** which deals with the final compensation cited in the above quotation: purification through violence. In this tale, a man atones for what the author feels is a cosmic fragmentation and guilt by allowing—and actually furthering—his destruction by a cannibal. In **Battle of Angels** and **The Purification,** we find this same kind of violent cleansing.

The Glass Menagerie is a far cry from any of these works; it is the most non-violent drama written by Williams. Nevertheless it adheres to the belief set forth in the short story. The underlying belief in **The Glass Menagerie** is that there is very little, if any, reason for living. Man is by nature incomplete because his universe is fragmented. There is nothing to be done about this condition because nothing *can* be done about it. Human guilt becomes a corollary of universal guilt and man's life is an atonement for the human condition. In each character in **The Glass Menagerie** there is a part "like a missing wall or a room left unfurnished and he tries as well as he can to make up for it." The mask devised by Laura and Amanda and Tom and Jim is "the use of imagination, resorting to dreams." The Wingfields are broken, fragmented people because "the sins of the world are really only its partialities." They are really not at all responsible for their condition, and thus are in no way able to cope with it. They are trapped in a determined universe. Without some kind of responsibility on the part of the protagonist there is opportunity neither for tragic elevation nor tragic fall. The Wingfields were doomed the moment they were born. At best their struggles will allow them to survive . . . for a time. They will never be allowed to triumph. Thus their struggles, their hopes and even their eventual destruction can never move far beyond pathos. The beauty and magic of **The Glass Menagerie** is that this pathos is genuine, objective and deeply moving. (pp. 97-112)

> *Benjamin Nelson, in his* Tennessee Williams: The Man and His Work, *Ivan Obolensky, Inc., 1961, 304 p.*

Nancy M. Tischler

The six-months contract Audrey Wood had wangled for her client with M.G.M. on the basis of his one-acters and **Battle of Angels,** proved to be considerably more profitable for Williams than for his boss and the studio. Although the author had expected to work on the best-selling novel *The Sun Is My Undoing,* the studio immediately set him to work on the scenario for *Marriage Is a Private Affair,* a bit of fluff that eventually starred Lana Turner. Williams has since established a mental block about the picture, refusing to remember its title. "I always thought of it as *The Celluloid Brassière,*" he says. The dialogue he wrote was brilliant, he recalls, but not suitable for the story or the star. When his scenario was rejected, he was assigned to another picture starring Margaret O'Brien. His refusal to perform this chore was prefaced by a violently candid evaluation of child actors. He said such prodigies made him vomit. (p. 91)

Williams on the connection between Laura and his sister:

[My family] moved to St. Louis when I was about thirteen. . . . We took an old house that just had windows at the front and back. My sister, who was a year older than I was, had a sad little shadowy room that looked out on an alley, so we painted it white for her, and she collected a lot of little glass animals and put them on the white shelves to brighten things up. It's something you remember. Especially if you're a playwright.

Tennessee Williams in "The Celluloid Brassière," The New Yorker, April 14, 1945.

After his abortive attempts at writing movie scripts, he offered the film industry an idea of his own which he felt worthy of development. He had worked out the synopsis for a film he referred to as *The Gentleman Caller.* In introducing the outline to his superior at M.G.M., he announced, "This will run three times as long as *Gone With the Wind.* Shortly thereafter, his boss advised him to draw his pay-check quietly each week for the remainder of his contract—three and a half months—and to stay away from the office. Delighted, Williams sat out the remaining period of his $250-a-week contract on the beach at Santa Monica writing *The Gentleman Caller,* which he renamed *The Glass Menagerie.*

His life was happier now than it had been in some years. He had a good salary, a good idea for a play, and as good health as he ever allows himself to admit. Since he is never happier than when working, the arrangement was ideal. A short story that grew out of this period, **"The Mattress in the Tomato Patch,"** describes his solidly contented landlady, the tanned athletes who roamed the beach and the house, and the richness of the sun-worshipping life— symbolized by the lushness of a bowlful of ripe tomatoes on his desk. Seldom have characters received such benevolent treatment at the hands of Tennessee Williams as in the work of that Santa Monica period—this earthy short story and the gentle play about his frightened sister.

When his contract was up he moved to Provincetown where he finished the play and sent it to his agent. Rather apologetically, he spoke of it to friends as "another of those old uncommercial plays of mine." Paul Moor records that "Miss Wood, much affected by the delicate story, tried to think of a producer who would be sympathetic to it and not botch it. For three weeks it did not leave her office; the fact that Williams never murmured about this apparent inactivity is a sample of his regard for Miss Wood. . . . Finally she remembered Eddie Dowling's touching production of Paul Vincent Carroll's *Shadow and Substance,* and sent it to him. No other producer

ever had a chance at it. Dowling bought it, literally overnight."

Never a good critic of his own work, Williams later looked back at both *Battle of Angels* and *The Glass Menagerie* and said of the first, "That play was, of course, a much better play than this one. The thing is, you can't mix up sex and religion, as I did in *Battle of Angels,* but you can always write safely about mothers." He had worked so hard on the complex plot for his first Broadway play that the simple story of the second made it appear inferior. Authors seldom perceive that difficulty in composition bears little relation to the merit of the finished product. The troublesome play is like a maimed or difficult child that one loves all the more for the trouble he causes. To anyone but the writer himself, the fact that *The Glass Menagerie* was so easy to write suggests something of its truth, its naturalness, and its artistry. (pp. 92-3)

[The play's] simple story, turning on a dinner party given by a Southern family for an outsider whom they hope to match with their unmarried daughter and the character revelations that occur in its course, constitutes Tennessee Williams' most fragile and lovely play.

In some ways, *The Glass Menagerie* is a variation of the battle-of-angels theme. Tom expresses the same need to escape the nailed-up coffin of his restricted existence that Val expresses in the earlier play; but Tom seems to be more conscious of a corresponding loss that such freedom implies. He rejects the possessive love of his family because he can accept it only by shouldering the responsibility and accepting the imprisonment that go with it. The rejection of this relationship gives him pain, however, as his proposed desertion of Myra apparently did not give Val. This is a more realistic evaluation of human needs and yearnings. The characters also are more realistic. Although Tom and the others in *The Glass Menagerie* may represent attitudes toward life, none are personified abstractions. There is no Jabe to represent death [as in *The Battle of Angels*]. A subtler type of characterization combined with a simpler, less melodramatic story yields a far more artistic product.

One of the chief characters is sketched only by implication. The father of the Wingfield family hovers over the scene, although he never appears on stage at all. An enlarged photograph of him, which the spotlight occasionally illuminates, reminds us of his part in the formation of the dramatic situation. It is the picture of a handsome young man in a doughboy's cap. Though deeply hurt by his desertion, Amanda considers her erstwhile husband the embodiment of romance, associating him with that time in her life when the house in Blue Mountain was filled with gentleman callers and jonquils. (Blue Mountain is Mr. Williams' poetic name for Clarksdale, the standard symbol in his plays for romantic, happy youth.) Not having seen her husband growing old and ugly enables her to preserve her romantic image of him. That the father does not appear directly in the play suggests that Tennessee Williams could not view him with sufficient objectivity to portray him. The photograph apparently represents the standard view the outside world caught of [William's own father], the gay, soldierly C. C. Williams, whom his son hated so much that the sweetness would have gone out of the play if he had been included.

To Tom Wingfield, on the other hand, his father represents escape. He says of him, in the narrator's preface to the story, "He was a telephone man who fell in love with long distances; he gave up his job with the telephone company and skipped the light fantastic out of town." Then follows a hinted admiration of his romantic disappearance: "The last we heard of him was a picture post-card from Mazatlan, on the Pacific coast of Mexico, containing a message of two words—'Hello—Good-bye!' and no address." Tom's interest in his father's wanderlust, at the beginning of the play, prepares us for Tom's departure at its end. The picture itself, an enlarged photograph of Tom's own face, further emphasizes the similarities of their natures. Thus, while the father still personifies love to the romantic memory of the middle-aged Amanda, he symbolizes another kind of romance to his son—the romance of escape and adventure.

In discarding the real father's part, Tennessee Williams found it necessary to endow the mother with some masculine practicality, thus giving Amanda Wingfield an exceedingly complex personality. Like Myra of *Battle of Angels,* she has her past to recall and her present to endure. One had Moon Lake and love in the vineyard, the other Blue Mountain and gentleman callers. Amanda is, obviously, far more the lady, the Southern aristocrat, than the more voluptuous Myra. The only way Amanda can live with ugly reality is to retreat into her memories; there is no sexual solution for her. Her clothes, her speech, and her ideals for her children declare her belief in the past and her rejection of the present. As the author says of Amanda, "She is not paranoiac, but her life is paranoia."

The feature of this woman, which makes her a more admirable character than the later Blanche of *Streetcar* is the anomalous element of practicality encased in her romantic girlishness. Although she has approached much of her life unrealistically, her plans for her children and her understanding of their shortcomings are grimly realistic. Even when refusing to admit it, she knows Laura will never marry. She then tries to find Laura a protective corner of the business world. When this fails, she rallies for the valiant but hopeless attempt to marry the girl off. This second failure, we feel, is less tragic for the daughter than for the mother.

Here we see the quality that Williams suggests from the beginning as the key to her character—her heroism. This, rather than her romantic turn, is her attraction. At the end of the play, when Tom has left, Amanda bends over Laura, huddled upon the sofa, to comfort her. By then, the audience realizes that Amanda herself is in greater need of this sympathy than the quietly resigned Laura. "Now that we cannot hear the mother's speech," says Williams, "her silliness is gone and she has dignity and tragic beauty."

We see this heroism in Amanda in her relations with Tom as well as with the more delicate and more romantic Laura. Although Tom understands the personality of his mother better than any other character in the story, he is more visionary and irresponsible than she is. He cannot see or accept the necessities of their life. Because of this and her previous experience with a romantic husband, she discourages Tom's attempts at a poetic or a nautical career. She returns the D. H. Lawrence novel to the library and nags at him whenever he escapes to a movie. She prods him to take an interest in practical things, like Jim's night classes in electro-dynamics. Here, as with her daughter, she is doomed to failure. Consequently, her final line is, "Go, then! Then go to the moon—you selfish dreamer!" Amanda is better able to speak these words with understanding because she shares his yearnings. Her dream has been smashed by reality, but has not been forgotten.

Tom is a poet who is desperately unhappy in his warehouse job, and, as yet, frustrated in his poetry. Since Tennessee Williams knows something of this not-very-tender trap, he speaks with feeling about the afflictions of the machine age. Believing that many, like himself, are poetic rather than mechanistic, he considers surrender to the machine a perversion of man's nature. His escape, heartless though it may seem, is a "necessary and wholesome measure of self-preservation" (as John Gassner expresses it).

Laura, like [William's sister] Rose, obviously can't escape into movies, alcohol, or literature; she simply isn't that violent or decisive. Her retreat is into a world of glass and music. Her father's old phonograph records provide her with escape that the unfamiliar new tunes can't provide. In the short story out of which the play grew, **"Portrait of a Girl in Glass,"** Tom occasionally brings new records to his sister, but she seldom cares for them because they remind her too much of "the noisy tragedies in Death Valley or the speed-drills at the business college." Her collection of glass absorbs her time. She spends hours polishing the tiny animals that are as delicate and fragile as she.

Unable to adapt to the modern scene of electro-dynamics, she lives in a world of candlelight and fantasy. The encounter with the machine age is brief and useless. Laura could no more learn to type than Tom could ever come to like his job. Yet, unlike Tom, Laura seems not to feel the ugliness and entombment of their lives. Incapable of his violence, she never steps into the world for fear it would be impossible to bear. She merely stands at the brink and catches what she can of its beauty without becoming a part of it—a lovely picture of the simple Rose, who all through her brother's life has represented to him everything good and beautiful, soft and gentle.

Laura's early surrender is explained at the opening of the play by an allusion to an illness in childhood which left her crippled, one leg slightly shorter than the other and held in a brace (a physical parallel to Rose's mental affliction). The author explains, "Stemming from this, Laura's separation increases till she is like a piece of her own glass collection, too exquisitely fragile to move from the shelf."

Her mother is both Laura's disease and her brace. It is Amanda's forcefulness that allows Laura to walk at all, but it is also Amanda's example that discourages Laura from walking naturally. At one point, Laura puts on her mother's old coat, which of course is a poor fit for her, an action symbolic of her vague efforts at imitating a personality so alien to her powers and her own nature. She knows that she is like the unicorn or the blue rose, wrong for real life. Laura cannot see that Amanda exaggerates this wrongness by her impossibly romantic dreams. When Laura entered her high-school classes late, the sound of the brace on her leg seemed to her like claps of thunder. She thinks her affliction is dreadful because Amanda thinks it is. This flaw, a symbol of the crippling of a sensitive person thrust into a world unwilling to make allowances for sensitivity, becomes the cause of her separation from reality.

This play, unique among Williams' dramas, combines poetic and unrealistic techniques with grim naturalism to achieve a gossamer effect of compassion, fragility, and frustration, typical of Tennessee Williams at his most sensitive and natural best.

—Nancy M. Tischler

For Tennessee Williams, his sister became a symbol of the sensitive and the outcast, for their sensitivity invariably subjects them to mutilation. It is no accident that Laura's story appears in the collection of early fiction, eventually published under the title *One Arm.* Every important character in the book—the college students, the vagrant poet, the sallow little masochist, the perverted artist, the consumptive factory worker, the one-armed male prostitute, and the girl with her glass menagerie, can be destroyed at a touch. All, like Laura, are crippled in some way. The radiance of such people is like a "piece of translucent glass touched by light, given a momentary radiance, not actual, not lasting."

Laura contrasts with the normal, middle-class, realistic Jim, with whom she falls dreamily in love. Their views show their complete diversity. For example, when they discuss her favorite animal, the unicorn, Laura thinks of him as intrinsically different from his companions, while Jim sees him simply as a horse with a horn. In the same way, Jim sees the defect in Laura's leg as only unfortunately incidental to her normal body, while Laura feels that the flaw transforms her whole being. Jim can sympathize with Laura's world of glass and candlelight for this evening, but his real interests are in the modern mechanical world of self-improvement. He is the only character in the play who goes out of the house into a normal world of "reality." Tom emphasizes this in the opening and closing lines of the play; he is an emissary from another world; he does not belong to the Wingfield world of dreams and fears and unexpressed desires.

Jim is not an especially effective character study because Williams can feel little sympathy with such a substantial and placid citizen. Yet he is a kindly reminder of the reasonable, normal human pattern, like the men Williams had met at the shoe factory—clean-living, honest, sweet-natured, materialistic, eager American businessmen. The gently satirical portrait bears no relationship to the later, bitter portraits of C. C. Williams.

Since it is characteristic of Amanda, more than of the others, to long for everything Jim represents, he is for her an archetype of the "long delayed but always expected something we live for." Unintentionally, Jim breaks up the Wingfield dreams. We suspect that his entrance into the household is part of a recurring pattern. Every contact with the real world has shattered Amanda's unrealistic hopes over the years.

The setting of *The Glass Menagerie* was interesting in its symbolism and technical experimentation. Moving from the deep South to St. Louis for his story, Williams retains the memory of the South, as a haunting presence under the superimposed Midwestern setting. The audience, never seeing the gracious mansion that was the scene of Amanda's girlhood, feels its remembered glory and its contrast to the mean present. Awareness of the past is always an element in Williams' plays. His characters live beyond the fleeting moments of the drama—back into a glowing past and shrinking from a terrifying future. For both Amanda and the later Blanche of *Streetcar,* the South forms an image of youth, love, purity, all of the ideals that have crumbled along with the mansions and the family fortunes.

Since the setting in *Menagerie* is that of a memory play, Tennessee Williams could feel free in its staging. His theory of expressionism is propounded in the introductory production notes, which are, in fact, directly applied in the play. His concept of the "new, plastic theatre" was probably influenced by Erwin Piscator, a German director who had helped him at the New School Seminar. He suggests that in *The Glass Menagerie*'s "considerably delicate or tenuous material, atmospheric touches and subtleties of direction play a particularly important part." Williams justifies such unconventional techniques as expressionism or impressionism on the basis that their subjectivity provides a "closer approach to truth." No playwright should use such devices in an effort to avoid the "responsibility of dealing with reality, or interpreting experience." But he believes that the new drama has followed the other arts in recognizing that realism is not the key to reality.

"The straight realistic play with its genuine frigidaire and authentic ice-cubes, its characters that speak exactly as its audience speaks," he says, "corresponds to the academic landscape and has the same virtue of photographic likeness." Then, with unique optimism regarding current artistic tastes, he continues, "Everyone should know nowadays the unimportance of the photographic in art: that truth, life, or reality is an organic thing which the poetic imagination can represent or suggest, in essence, only through transformation, through changing into other forms than those which were merely present in appearance." The philosophy expressed here is in accord with the nineteenth century romantics and their followers in this century. The expressionistic concepts propounded in this preface have proved so effective in Tennessee Williams' work that set-designers have usually chosen to use expressionistic even when realistic settings are called for in Williams' manuscripts. Williams has a poet's weakness for symbols, and this modern technique frees his hand for scattering them about the stage. Their use to reflect, emphasize, and contrast with the meanings of the actions and the words has become a trademark of the Williams play.

The Glass Menagerie projected symbolic elements in line with Williams' newly enunciated theory. To reinforce the spoken word the author recommends the use of a screen device. A legend or image projected on the screen for the duration of the scene emphasizes the most important phrase. For example, in the scene where Jim remembers that Laura is the girl who was stricken with pleurosis, whom he mistakenly nicknamed "Blue Roses," the legend on the screen accents the peculiarity of the name, and the audience, along with Laura, is made more keenly aware that although blue is beautiful, it is wrong for roses. Eddie Dowling, [the play's first director], considered this device superfluous and omitted it from the stage production, and wisely so. (pp. 95-103)

Williams' expressionist theory also leads him to another variation from strictly realistic drama. The lighting changes with the mood. The stage is as dim as the participants' lives. Shafts of light flicker onto selected areas or actors, "sometimes in contradiction to what is the apparent center." When Tom and Amanda are quarreling, the light on them is low red, while Laura stands in a pool of light of that "peculiar pristine clarity such as light used in early religious portraits of saints or madonnas." The tone, strength, and occurrence of the lights have the power of emotional emphasis. In a technique reminiscent of Chekhov's, Williams heightens the emotional truths of the scenes and the reality of the internal action through unusual external effects.

The musical accompaniment of *The Glass Menagerie* is another element of Tennessee Williams' expressionism that characterizes his dramas. The theme is a tune called "The Glass Menagerie," composed by Paul Bowles. It is "like circus music, not when you are on the grounds or in the immediate vicinity of the parade, but when you are at some distance and very likely thinking of something else. . . . It expresses the surface vivacity of life and the underlying strain of immutable and inexpressible sorrow." The music becomes Laura's symbol: of this world which is like a circus for her—heard from a safe distance; and of her retreat into a world of music as well as of glass.

The depiction of the Wingfields' apartment also follows the dicta of expressionism. The ugly uniformity of the tenements depresses Tom and makes him frantic to escape. The place is described as "one of those vast hive-like conglomerations of cellular living-units that flower as warty growths in overcrowded urban centers of lower middle-class populations." They are, says the temporarily socially conscious author, "symptomatic of the impulse of this largest and fundamentally enslaved section of American society to avoid fluidity and differentiation and to exist and function as one interfused mass of automatism." Of the characters in the play, only Tom seems aware of this grotesque uniformity; and since the whole story takes place in his memory, he would naturally exaggerate the dismal reality he sees.

On both sides of the building, dark, narrow alleys run into "murky canyons of tangled clotheslines, garbage cans and sinister lattice-work of neighboring fire escapes." The meaning of these alleys is clear if the reader recalls Tom's picture of "Death Valley," where cats were trapped and killed by a vicious dog. The predicament becomes a symbol of his factory work, murderous to his creative imagination. For Laura, the alley represents the ugly world from which she retreats to gaze into her tiny glass figures. For Amanda, too, the alley is the world of her present hopeless poverty and confusion from which she retreats into her make-believe world of memory and pretence. Inside the apartment, where she tries to create an illusion of gentility, her husband's portrait grins at her futile efforts.

The apartment is entered by a fire escape, "a structure whose name is a touch of accidental poetic truth, for all those huge buildings are always burning with the slow and implacable fires of human desperation." On this fire escape, Tom Wingfield seeks liberation from his private hell. It is no mere coincidence that this play's solution (like those of *Battle of Angels* and *Stairs to the Roof*) centers around the stairway. Stairs are the tangible sign of man's change in levels of reality.

It would seem that every item of the setting is symbolic—even the Paradise Dance Hall, across the alley. There sexual gratification provides the cliff-dwellers of the neighborhood a temporary paradise. In their moments of closeness, they achieve the escape that Tom finds in his movies and poetry.

The story, characterization, and setting of this play combine to form a "static" drama, a technique Williams has used in other plays, including the rewrite of *Battle of Angels.* Action is softened by this "patina" of time and distance; framed in memory, it becomes more artistic. The interest of this play depends on neither incident nor situation. Unlike most of Williams' other works that are charged with sensationalism and sex, this story holds the audience by the revelation of quiet and ordinary truths. This play, unique among Williams' dramas, combines poetic and unrealistic techniques with grim naturalism to achieve a gossamer effect of compassion, fragility, and frustration, typical of Tennessee Williams at his most sensitive and natural best. The play is his most effective poetic work. (pp. 103-05)

> *Nancy M. Tischler, in her* Tennessee Williams: Rebellious Puritan, *The Citadel Press, 1961, 319 p.*

Roger B. Stein

In an interview with *Newsweek* in the spring of 1960, Tennessee Williams made an announcement which was bound to be of interest to widespread audiences and critics of the drama alike. He declared that he was "through with what have been called my 'black' plays," that from then on his plays would be free from their earlier accent on the bestiality of man. While not denying that bestiality still existed, Williams declared, "I want to pass the rest of my life believing in other things. For years I was too preoccupied with the destructive impulses. From now on I want to be concerned with the kinder aspects of life" [*Newsweek,* 27 June 1960]. The sweeping quality of the remark was almost Tolstoyan in its rejection of Williams' earlier vision. By contrast to the violence and blackness of the earlier plays, the newer vision seemed to be one of sweetness and light. Williams' last phrase alone reverberates with William Dean Howells' injunction seventy years ago that our novelists "concern themselves with the more smiling aspects of life, which are the more American" [*Criticism and Fiction*].

The turn in Williams' career should not have come as a complete shock (even putting aside the question of psychoanalysis). In the foreword to *Sweet Bird of Youth* several years ago, Williams marveled at his audiences' capacity to accept the violence which he was dealing out to them, and by this time violence—of rape, castration, and cannibalism—had become the hallmark of the Williams mode, his way of resolving, or avoiding the real resolution of, the conflicts between his lonely, haunted characters. In that same foreword Williams tried to indicate that violence was not his only dramatic weapon. He divided his dramas into two groups: the violent plays, those which emphasize man's bestiality, and the non-violent plays. Among the latter he included both *The Glass Menagerie* and the then uncompleted *Period of Adjustment,* because neither depends for its moral justification upon the Aristotelian idea that violence is purged by its poetic representation on a stage and neither play offers us violence as the way to "the release from the sense of meaninglessness and death," which Williams understands to be the object of a work of tragic intention.

The grouping is useful in showing Williams' earlier uneasiness with violence as his sole dramatic technique. Reaching back to his earliest successful drama, Williams grasped again at an approach built not upon the reduction of dramatic situation and motivation to a series of overcharged, sexually violent and symbolically loaded confrontations, where "release" comes from explosion, but upon a quieter pattern of lonely human beings who fail in a variety of ways to make contact with one another and with their universe.

Then, to strengthen one's conviction that Williams was searching for a way out of the pattern of violence which had become his trademark, the 1961 Broadway season gave us *The Night of the Iguana.* Despite the hints of violent action offstage and the explosive personality of its central character, the exminister Shannon, the new play offers us through its most sympathetic character Hannah Jelkes an ideal of endurance, of quiet strength facing the pain and loneliness of human existence. Her plea at the third act curtain is "Oh God! Can't we stop now? Finally? Please let us. It's so quiet here, now."

The attenuated nature of her cry suggests several observations regarding Williams' work. In the first place, the mood of the play is muffled and elegiac, reminding one, as several critics have noted, of *The Glass Menagerie.* Actually the similarity extends beyond mood to Williams' approach to the problem of the loneliness of defeated souls, his particular area of sensitivity and compassion as playwright. Furthermore, it may be noted that Hannah's cry is framed not solely in human terms, but in terms of man's relation to a God-centered universe. The importance of this has been largely overlooked by Williams' critics heretofore and certainly in their examination of *The Glass Menagerie.*

Finally, both Hannah's speech and *The Night of the Iguana* as a whole help to put *Period of Adjustment* into its very special place in the canon of Williams' work as a deviation from the pattern of his development, a deviation comparable in many ways to that nostalgic comedy, *Ah! Wilderness,* in the career of Eugene O'Neill. For though *Period of Adjustment* is, with *The Glass Menagerie* and *The Night of the Iguana,* a non-violent play, unlike them it is subtitled "A Serious Comedy," and whatever Williams may mean by "serious," it is clearly comic in its underlying belief in the essential health of society once certain adjustments have been made. This is not to say that the break with his earlier work is complete. Certainly *Period of Adjustment* bears the imprint of the earlier Williams: the concern with homosexuality behind Ralph's fear for his son; the heavy-handed and overinsistent symbolism of the Bates's home being built on a "high point over a cavern"; the parody of the American dream through the spoofing about longhorns and the wild West; and perhaps most important, Williams' tendency to see human conflict too exclusively in sexual terms, whether successfully resolved here, as it was in *The Rose Tattoo,* problematic, as in *Cat on a Hot Tin Roof,* or unresolved and leading to catastrophe, as in *Suddenly Last Summer.* Yet these similarities should not blind us to the more basic shift which occurred and which is implied in the very title of the play. What set this play off from his earlier work, both "violent" and "non-violent," and from *The Night of the Iguana* was Williams' apparent belief that the lives of four individuals, the well-being of middle-class America, and even the happiness of the Christmas season could be preserved if one was only willing to go through a little "period of adjustment."

Williams' vision in *The Glass Menagerie* of 1945, by contrast, was not one of successful adjustment but of failure, the failure of any manipulation to piece together the fragmented lives of human beings. The essentially sanguine view of the "kinder aspects" which he adopted in 1960, that a little tinkering would set all to rights, was a real if perhaps temporary departure not only from the violent plays but from *The Glass Menagerie*'s searching and poetic vision of catastrophe.

When *The Glass Menagerie* first appeared, it was hailed as a major dramatic event (Williams himself later spoke of the play's favorable reception as "The Catastrophe of Success"). In 1948 John Gassner dubbed Williams the "dramatist of frustration" because Williams had captured with such skill the truncated lives of his characters, caught in a world of their own illusions and unable to break out. Gassner was inclined to see the frustration as that of individuals, though he suggested briefly that the sketched background of the play was social. But the power of *The*

Glass Menagerie is even greater than earlier critics have suggested. The full measure of its intensity has yet to be taken, and the contrast between the comic premise of *Period of Adjustment* and the note of endurance in *The Night of the Iguana* is one more reason why we should turn back to his early and perhaps his greatest play to examine not just the surface of frustration but the fullness of its catastrophic vision, a vision not only of individuals who fail to communicate with one another, nor of a society temporarily adrift in a depression, but of man abandoned in the universe.

The means which Williams has used to give form to this vision are symbolic rather than literal. His play about the man who came to dinner and failed to satisfy the expectations of two neurotic women depends not so much upon plot or characterization as upon an undercurrent of allusion, the range of secondary associations which, instead of being in the foreground of dramatic action, serve as a background of ironic commentary on the essentially static surface of this "memory play."

Williams has often asserted, sometimes at rather too great length, that he is the poet in the theater. Again and again he has stressed the inadequacy of the literal significance of words to convey meaning. In his early one-act verse drama, *The Purification,* the son says that "Truth is sometimes alluded to in music. / But words are too loosely woven to catch it in. . . . " In the afterword to *Camino Real* he went so far as to condemn "words on paper, . . . thoughts and ideas of an author, those shabby things snatched off basement counters at Gimbel's," and to insist that it was the natural symbol for which he was really reaching. In *The Glass Menagerie* this problem is expressed in the poignant interview between Tom and his mother, when Amanda says and Tom agrees that "There's so many things in my heart that I cannot describe to you!" Like his dramatic forebear Chekhov, Williams is constantly faced with the yawning gap between his characters' feelings and their ability to verbalize. In Williams' work this gap often threatens to become an abyss into which the play itself collapses. His critics have been quick to point out when the playwright has substituted strident symbolism for effective dramatic situation. The awkwardness of the screen device proposed for *The Glass Menagerie,* Val's snakeskin jacket and Lady's speech about fig trees and Christmas decorations in *Orpheus Descending,* perhaps the iguana itself in the title of his latest play, and the generally cluttered quality of *Camino Real* come immediately to mind as cases where Williams has failed to develop and then rely upon the dramatic situation and leans upon allusion to carry the meaning rather than dramatic conflict.

The particular excellence of *The Glass Menagerie,* by contrast, is that Williams was able at this one point to sustain both a credible dramatic situation of the anticipation and appearance of the Gentleman Caller at the same time that he developed with extraordinary skill the secondary level of allusion which gives to the drama its full symbolic significance. The pattern of allusion, the tightness of poetic texture, transforms the pathetic story of the Wingfield family into a calamity of immense proportions.

The structure of the play helped Williams to move away from realistic drama and too great a dependence upon only the literal significance of word or action. His development of *The Glass Menagerie* as a "memory play," organized around Tom's remembrances of things past, gave Williams the freedom to develop the "new plastic theatre" of which he spoke in the author's production notes to be published versions of the play. Lighting, music, and the device of the narrator who is both a commentator on and a part of the series of tableaux which he presents in his search for the meaning of the past all contribute to the play's fluidity, a quality and metaphor which one critic sees as central to Williams' art.

If we move from the play's poet, Tom, to the question of the play's poetry, certainly the clearest and most obvious organizing image is the glass menagerie itself, which embodies the fragility of Laura's world, registers so sensitively any changes in lighting, and stands in vivid contrast to the harshness of the outside world, the so-called world of reality which can shatter it so easily. Dramatically the glass menagerie is the focus of much of the action of the play in much the same way that the garret is the focus of Ibsen's *Wild Duck.* Like the wild duck, the menagerie is almost too strident a symbol. Williams is almost too insistent at times on the parallel between Laura and her menagerie, between the glass unicorn's losing its horn and Jim's impotence when he tries to bring Laura into the "real world." But again like Ibsen, Williams does not hang the entire play upon his title symbol; instead he gives to the play as a whole a poetic texture and a wealth of ironic allusion.

This comes out clearly in his handling of Tom, the narrator, struggling poet, and embryonic Tennessee Williams, whose role has a value far exceeding the range of autobiographical reference which was undoubtedly its starting point. The world of literature is developed through more than the convention of the narrator alone. The play's numerous literary allusions serve both to give a sense of specific detail to the evanescent tableaux-scenes and to reinforce central dramatic issues.

Tom, the poet in the warehouse, is "Shakespeare" to Jim, the Gentleman Caller. Jim realizes dimly that his friend is that strange creature, the artist, set apart from his fellow men. In the Acting Version Williams inserted a few lines during which Amanda tries to adjust the lamp for Tom while he is writing. She chides him: "I know that Milton was blind, but that's not what made him a genius." Like the Shakespeare reference, this is Amanda's recognition of Tom's difference from other men and as such establishes one character's attitude toward another. It also underscores our sense of Amanda's well-meaning meddling in Tom's privacy. Furthermore it works ironically, for it should suggest to the audience Milton's sonnet on his blindness and add to our sense of the conflict between Tom's desire to escape from home and the warehouse and Amanda's belief that "they also serve who only stand and wait." And beyond this, there exists the even broader contrast, inherent in the Milton image, of sight and blindness, of light and darkness. This pattern of imagery is as important to *The Glass Menagerie* as it is to Ibsen's *Wild Duck,* where the conflict between illusion and reality is shaped in terms of visual imagery, of motion toward and away from light of various kinds.

Such an expansion of the range of reference of a single image is neither accidental on the author's part nor implanted there by the critic. It is part of the very texture of the play. The conflict between Tom and his mother is developed in a variety of ways and the world of literature is one battleground. Amanda is outraged at Tom's reading of D. H. Lawrence. When he makes a Lawrencian speech about man's being by instinct "a lover, a hunter, a fighter," she retorts that instinct "belongs to animals! Christian adults don't want it!" (though it should be noted that she is not beyond stuffing Laura's bosom with "Gay Deceivers" before the Gentleman Caller appears). The barrier to literary communication works both ways. Tom sees the heroines of Amanda's "literary world" of the *Homemaker's Companion* in Lawrencian terms—"bodies as powerful as Etruscan sculpture"—but the appeal of this magazine to Amanda and those to whom she sells subscriptions is not the passion, but the fantasy world of romance of the horsy set on Long Island, a northern version of the fantasy South of her youth. Where Tom opposes the grim actuality of tenement life here by an appeal to the pagan and the primitive, Amanda sells the deceptive view of romance of Bessie May Harper, who "never lets you down" and "always leaves you with such an uplift." The heroines of Bessie May Harper are everything that Amanda hoped to be and that Laura is not, and even the magazine's title is ironic, for Amanda has failed as a homemaker and Laura will never be one.

In the Library Edition of the play, Amanda ranks Bessie May's latest effort with *Gone With the Wind,* compounding the irony. The universal desirability of the romantic Scarlett O'Hara makes Laura seem all the more neglected, and the fantasy of rebuilding Tara ironically underlines Amanda's loss of her Blue Mountain girlhood. Furthermore, Amanda Wingfield is not alone in the nostalgic backward glance to a lost Eden, a fantasy South that existed only in the American imagination. It is not coincidental that Margaret Mitchell's Southern romance should have been a best seller during the depression years. While the allusion to *Gone With the Wind* clearly sets Amanda apart from her son, it also broadens the context of Amanda's escape from reality. This escape was one which most Americans seemed to want to share, and thus her delusion takes on a larger social significance. Finally one may note that the title image itself of *Gone With the Wind* underlines the evanescent quality of this dream and all of the Wingfields' illusions. As such, it points directly to the last line of the play and Tom's injunction to "Blow out your candles, Laura."

On the level of plot, this widening circle of reference enhances the credibility of the dramatic situation. Given Amanda's sham version of idealized love and a fantasy past, how could the Gentleman Caller's visit be other than a failure? Despite Amanda's dress which is "historical almost," despite the attempt to live in the nineteenth century when the electric power goes off, Jim is not Rhett Butler but an "emissary from a world of reality," as Tom calls him, an engaged twentieth-century man on vacation. The flickering candlelight of Jim's scene with Laura is not enough to sustain the illusion; at the end of their scene this illusion collapses and we are left in darkness.

Williams weaves numerous patterns of imagery skillfully within the play. Many converge upon this last scene, and with a care he has not matched since, he directs all of the separate objects and fleeting images toward the central concerns of the drama. After Tom has announced the imminent visit of the Gentleman Caller, he tries to warn Amanda not to expect too much. He urges her to face the fact that Laura is crippled. Amanda refuses, not only explicitly but also implicitly when she turns thereafter and asks Laura to make a wish on the moon, "A little silver slipper of a moon." The image suggests at once romance, reflected soft light, and (ironically) Laura's limp. The slipper itself foreshadows the later dancing scene between Laura and Jim. At this point Jim destroys the illusion by knocking against the glass menagerie. In the Library Edition there is a further verbal irony in this scene, when Jim kisses Laura, retreats, and then brands himself a "stumblejohn." The gesture of love which she needs so desperately does not heal the crippled Laura and release her from her bondage to her illusions. It shatters her. All the kiss seems to have done is to pass on to Jim, momentarily, Laura's crippled condition. As the ironic use of imagery helps to make clear, the failure of vision at the end of the play is everybody's failure. Even Tom, who thought he was being helpful by bringing Jim home, has illusions which blind him and doom the visit of the Gentleman Caller to failure. Tom can only escape, leaving Laura and Amanda to withdraw even further into their private worlds.

But *The Glass Menagerie* is built upon more than the poignant plot of illusion and frustration in the lives of little people. Williams has given the drama further significance by deepening the losses of individuals and pointing to social and even spiritual catastrophe. The time of the play is 1939, as the narrative frame makes explicit both at the beginning and the end. The life of illusion is not confined to the Wingfields alone. As Tom says, "the huge middle class of America was matriculating in a school for the blind." What he calls the "social background" of the play has tremendous importance. The international backdrop is Guernica and the song America sings is "The World is Waiting for the Sunrise," for the sober truth is that America is still in the depression and on the brink of war. The note of social disaster runs throughout the drama, fixing the lives of individuals against the larger canvas.

Amanda's anxieties are in large part economic and there is money behind many of her illusions: her mythical suitors were all wealthy men; she hopes to make money by selling subscriptions to the fantasy world of *The Homemaker's Companion;* she computes the money Tom would save by giving up smoking. When Tom complains of the grimness of life in the shoe factory, she replies, "Try and you will SUCCEED!" If this is another of Amanda's illusions, it is one shared by her fellow Americans, for "try and you will succeed" is the traditional motto of the American dream of success, the theme of confident self-reliance canonized in the romances of Horatio Alger.

It is not Amanda, however, but Jim, the emissary from reality, who is the chief spokesman for the American dream. To Jim the warehouse is not a prison but a rung on the ladder toward success. He believes in self-improvement through education, and the lecture on self-confidence which he reads to Laura is part of the equipment of the future executive. Jim is a booster in the American tradition. He is awed by the fortune made in chewing gum and rhapsodizes on the theme of the future material progress of America: "All that remains is for the industry to get itself under way! Full steam—*Knowledge*—Zzzzzp! *Money*—Zzzzzp! *Power!* That's the cycle democracy is built on!"

Yet when the strident theme of success is superimposed upon the lives of the characters, the social irony emerges. Father was not the successful businessman, but a telephone man who "fell in love with long distances." Tom, the substitute father, refuses to pay the light bill, plunges his family into darkness, and then runs out, and Amanda sells subscriptions and brassieres only at the loss of her dignity. Jim's own dream of success seems to have reached its peak in high school. (Williams later explored this theme more fully in *Cat on a Hot Tin Roof*). The trek upward through the depression years is disappointing, but the indomitable optimist is not discouraged.

The experience of the 1930s did not turn Williams into a proletarian writer or social realist, but it did open up for him a darker vision of American life which he suggests to his audience but which is denied to his characters, still "matriculating in a school for the blind": a belief that the American dream itself is a sham and a failure. In his essay "The Catastrophe of Success," Williams said that "the Cinderella story is our favorite national myth, the cornerstone of the film industry if not of the Democracy itself." The social catastrophe inherent in *The Glass Menagerie* lies precisely in the fact that Laura is *not* Cinderella: the silver slipper does not fit finally, and Jim is not Prince Charming but one of the innumerable Americans who would soon be moving overseas in troop ships. As Tom says at the end, "for nowadays the world is lit by lightning! Blow out your candles, Laura—and so goodbye. . . ." The world which had been waiting for the sunrise burst with bombardments instead, and the lives of the Wingfields at the end are absorbed in the larger social tragedy.

Williams goes even further than this, however. The end of the play involves more than just the snuffing out of Laura's hope; it is even more than social tragedy. It is a *Götterdämmerung.* For the candles and the lightning which close the play have appeared together before. We are told by Amanda that the candelabrum "used to be on the altar at the church of the Heavenly Rest. It was melted a little out of shape when the church burnt down. Lightning struck it one spring." Amanda's comment opens up another whole dimension of the play, and points to a catastrophe which readers of *The Glass Menagerie* and Williams' dramas in general have hitherto neglected.

Williams said in 1948 that the dominating premise of his work was "the need for understanding and tenderness and fortitude among individuals trapped by circumstance." To read this statement exclusively in naturalistic terms, how-ever, is to miss much of the force of Williams' dramas. Williams is the grandson of an Episcopal rector in whose house he spent his early years. He is also the inheritor of a Southern religious tradition which includes writers like Faulkner and Robert Penn Warren. Again and again in his plays he comes back to the world of Christian symbolism to describe his individuals "trapped by circumstance." What so often makes the trap horrifying is his recognition, explicit or implicit, that there is no release from it in a world to come. Christian imagery becomes a means of denying Christian belief. In its quieter forms the combination produces cosmic irony; in its most violent manifestations, grotesque parody. (pp. 141-49)

The religious overtones of *The Glass Menagerie* are . . . pervasive. Though they never obscure the literal line of the story or seem self-conscious, as they do in some of the later plays, these overtones add a dimension to the play which reaches beyond individual pathos and social tragedy. Williams' stage directions clearly indicate his intention. As with Hannah in *The Night of the Iguana,* he tells us that the lighting for Laura should resemble that "used in early religious portraits of female saints or madonnas." The scene where Tom tells his mother that a Gentleman Caller will appear Williams entitles "Annunciation." The dressing of Laura for the Caller's appearance should be "devout and ritualistic." During her scene with Jim she is lit "inwardly with altar candles," and when Jim withdraws after kissing her Williams informs us that the "holy candles in the altar of Laura's face have been snuffed out. There is a look of almost infinite desolation."

Those overtones extend beyond Williams' hints to the director and become a crucial part of the fabric of dramatic action. The first scene in both the Acting Version and the Library Edition of the play opens on this note. In the former, Amanda narrates her "funny experience" of being denied a seat in the Episcopal church because she has not rented a pew. The idea of the Wingfields' exclusion from Christian ceremony is established thus at the outset, and it is underlined by the ensuing talk of digesting food, mastication, and salivary glands. In the Wingfield apartment, eating is an animal process only; it lacks ritual significance. The Library Edition opens with Amanda's call to Tom, "We can't say grace until you come to the table," and then moves on to the question of digestion. The lines are different, but their import is the same. When the Gentleman Caller comes, the scene is repeated, only this time it is Laura whose absence holds up "grace."

Amanda, who condemns instinct and urges Tom to think in terms of the mind and spirit, as "Christian adults" do, is often characterized in Christian terms. Her music, in the Library Edition, is "Ave Maria." As a girl she could only cook angel food cake. She urges Laura, "Possess your soul in patience," and then speaks of her dress for the dinner scene as "resurrected" from a trunk. Her constant refrain to Tom is "Rise an' Shine," and she sells subscriptions to her friends by waking them early in the morning and then sympathizing with them as "Christian martyrs." Laura is afraid to tell her mother she has left the business school because "when you're disappointed, you get that awful suffering look on your face, like the picture of Jesus' mother in the museum!"

The next picture Laura mentions is the one of Jim in the yearbook; though the context seems secular enough at this point—Jim is a high school hero—his religious function emerges later on. In the "Annunciation" scene, when Amanda learns that the Gentleman Caller's name is O'Connor, she says, "that, of course, means fish—tomorrow is Friday!" The remark functions not only literally, since Jim is Irish Catholic, but also figuratively, for the fish is the traditional symbol of Christ. In a very real sense both Amanda and Laura are searching for a Savior who will come to help them, to save them, to give their drab lives meaning.

Tom is unable to play this role himself. Though he appears as the angel of the Annunciation, he denies the world of belief and in a bitter speech to his mother calls himself "El Diablo." With him Christian terms appear only as imprecations: "what in Christ's name" or "that God damn Rise and Shine." When Tom returns home drunk one night, he tells Laura of a stage show he has seen which is shot through with Christian symbolism, none of which he perceives. Here the magician, Malvolio, whose name suggests bad will, dislike, or even hate, plays the role of the modern Christ. He performs the miracle of turning water into wine and then goes on to blasphemy by turning the wine into

---

Williams's mother on Amanda Wingfield:

Someone mentioned to Tom the opposite receptions given *Angels* and *Menagerie* and he explained this by saying, "You can't mix sex and religion . . . but you can always write safely about mothers."

To which I say, "Ah, can you, Tom?"

Over the years both subtly and not so subtly, I have often been reminded that the character of Amanda was rooted in me, and this is not generally meant as a compliment. The critics have described Amanda in such inelegant words as "an old witch riding a broomstick," "a raddled belle of the old South, sunk deep in frustration," "the scuffed, rundown slipper that outlived the ball," "a simple, sanely insane, horrible Mother, pathetic and terribly human and terribly real" and "a bit of a scold, a bit of a snob." . . .

Tom has contradicted himself when asked if the play were based on his life. Once he told a reporter it was a "memory play," adding, "My mother and sister will never forgive me for that." Another time he said, "It was derived from years of living." Then again, he denied it was autobiographical, calling it "a dream or fantasy play. The gentleman caller is meant to be the symbol of the world and its attitude toward the unrealistic dreamers who are three characters of the play."

I think it is high time the ghost of Amanda was laid. I am *not* Amanda. I'm sure if Tom stops to think, he realizes I am not. The only resemblance I have to Amanda is that we both like jonquils.

Edwina Dankin Williams in her Remember Me to Tom, *1963.*

---

beer and then whiskey. He also produces his proper symbol, the fish, but it is gold-fish, as if stained by modern materialism. Most important, perhaps, he escapes from a nailed coffin. But Tom reads the symbolism of this trick in personal terms only. When Laura tries to keep him from awakening Amanda, Tom retorts:

> Goody goody! Pay 'er back for all those "Rise an' Shine's." You know it don't take much intelligence to get yourself into a nailed-up coffin, Laura. But who in hell ever got himself out of one without removing one nail?

The illumination of the father's photograph at this point suggests one answer to this question, but the pattern of Christian imagery in the drama, especially when reinforced here by the "Rise an' Shine" refrain, should suggest to us another answer—the resurrection itself—which Tom's rejection of Christian belief prevents him from seeing.

It remains therefore for Jim to come as the Savior to this Friday night supper. The air of expectancy is great, with the ritualistic dressing of Laura, the tension, and the oppressive heat. Jim's arrival is marked by the coming of rain, but the hopes of fertility and renewal which this might suggest are soon dashed. Laura's attempt to come to the dinner table is a failure, signaled by a clap of thunder, and Tom's muttered grace, "For these and all thy mercies, God's Holy Name be praised," is bitterly ironic, mocked by what follows. The only paradise within reach is Paradise Dance Hall, with its "Waste Land" mood of slow and sensuous rhythms and couples kissing behind ashpits and telephone poles, "the compensation for lives that passed . . . without any change or adventure," as Tom remarks. The failure of electric power after dinner—previsioning the blackout of the world—leads to Amanda's joking question, "Where was Moses when the lights went off?" This suggests another savior who would lead his people from the desert into the promised land, but the answer to her question is "In the dark."

Jim's attempt to play the modern savior is an abysmal failure. In the after-dinner scene, he offers Laura the sacrament—wine and "life-savers," in this case—and a Dale Carnegie version of the Sermon on the Mount—self-help rather than divine help—but to no avail. At the end of the play Laura and Amanda are, as the joke bitterly reminds us, "in the dark," and Tom's last lines announce the final failure, the infinite desolation: "For nowadays the world is lit by lightning. Blow out your candles, Laura—and so goodbye. . . . "

Here as elsewhere in his plays Williams draws upon his frightened characters' preference for soft candlelight to harsh daylight or electric bulbs, not only because it serves him dramaturgically to establish his conception of a new plastic theater where evanescent characters and images flicker across the stage momentarily, but also because his characters so often want to withdraw from the blinding light of reality into the softer world of illusion. At the end of *The Glass Menagerie,* however, the blackout is even more catastrophic, for it not only develops the Laura of Tom's memory and serves as another reminder of the blackout of war which shrouds the world: it is also the denial of any final "Rise an' Shine" for these frail creatures. The church has been struck by lightning, and all hope of resurrection has been lost in this damned universe where belief turns into metaphor, where man seems abandoned by his God, and where the echoes of prayer are heard only in blasphemy or irony. The bleakness of Williams' vision in *The Glass Menagerie* is complete. If Tom is released finally, it is in the words of Job, "And I only am escaped alone to tell thee." It is as the author's surrogate, as writer and chronicler of catastrophe, that he emerges at the end. (pp. 150-53)

> Roger B. Stein, " 'The Glass Menagerie' Revisited: Catastrophe without Violence," in Western Humanities Review, *Vol. XVIII, No. 2, Spring, 1964, pp. 141-53.*

Lester A. Beaurline

"Not even daring to stretch her small hands out!—nobody, not even the rain, has such small hands." Tennessee Williams scrawled these words from e. e. cummings at the top of the last page of *The Glass Menagerie* sometime after finishing the one-act play that was to grow into his first successful work. The quotation suggests the gentle, elegiac tone that he tried to attain, and since the last half of the passage survived as the play's epigraph, it apparently expressed Williams' later feelings too. The fragile pathos of Laura Wingfield's life was Williams' original inspiration in his short story, **"Portrait of a Girl in Glass,"** and theater audiences continue to respond to the basic human appeal of the play.

In **"Portrait"** the narrator feels compassion for Laura, who "made no positive motion toward the world but stood at the edge of the water, so to speak, with feet that anticipated too much cold to move." In this early story we can already recognize Williams' other trademarks: the theme of Tom's flight from "a dead but beautiful past into a live but ugly and meaningless present," the images of leaves torn from their branches, the hundreds of little transparent pieces of glass, the tired old music of the dead past, and the emotional undercurrent of sexual passion roaring through the entire story. These themes, I suppose, show Williams' kinship with D. H. Lawrence; and Tom, no doubt, suggests the figure of Paul Morrell or Aaron Sisson. But the later revisions show Williams' real talents as a playwright, none of which he inherits from Lawrence: his breadth of sympathy, his sense of humor, his brilliant dialogue, and his talent for building highly charged dramatic scenes.

Evidence survives for at least four stages in the composition of *The Glass Menagerie:* (1) The sixteen page story entitled **"Portrait of a Girl in Glass"** (written before 1943 and published in *One Arm and Other Stories,* 1948), where attention is on Laura, the narrator's sister.

(2) A sixty page one-act play in five scenes, of which twenty-one pages survive in the C. Waller Barrett Library at the University of Virginia. It is clear from the existing fragments that Williams had the main lines of his play

firmly in hand at this stage. Here the clash between Tom and Amanda, the painful relationship between Amanda and Laura, and the contrast between Jim and Tom have become as important as Laura herself. This script was probably written before Williams went to California to work on a movie script in 1943 and before he worked up a synopsis for a film named *The Gentleman Caller.*

(3) A 105-page play manuscript, now in the C. Waller Barrett Library at the University of Virginia. This complex document contains ten kinds of paper, is written on at least six different typewriters, and has four different kinds of handwritten pencil or ink revisions. It may represent about eight to ten layers of revision, but for the sake of clarity, I will refer to only the final stage of the third version: the manuscript as it stood when Williams sent it off to his agent in the fall of 1943. He called this the "reading version," and it is very close to the Random House edition, published in 1945 and reprinted by New Directions in 1949. However, this printed edition (which unfortunately has gotten into the college anthologies) contains several errors and a few alterations. The long version of the manuscript is in seven scenes and is a development and expansion of episodes in the one-act version. At this stage the major emphasis in the play is on memory, Tom's memory. It is a play about growing up as Tom must recognize the fatal choice between Laura's glass animals and Jim's gross materialism.

(4) The acting version, published by the Dramatists Play Service in 1948 (and revised again sometime in the mid-fifties). This purports to be "a faithful indication of the way the play was produced in New York and on the road" by the original company. Many changes have been made in the stage directions and details of the dialogue. One new scene was added, and over 1100 verbal changes appear in the dialogue alone. I think that Williams is now finished with the play and that the fourth version represents his final intentions. Therefore a responsible editor of an anthology should *not* reprint the old "reading version," and a critic ignores the acting version at his peril.

Changes in Tom's last speech epitomize all the revision in the play, so it is worth examining a long passage that closes the **"Girl in Glass."**

> Not very long after that I lost my job at the warehouse. I was fired for writing a poem on the lid of a shoe-box. I left Saint Louis and took to moving around. The cities swept about me like dead leaves, leaves that were brightly colored but torn away from the branches. My nature changed. I grew to be firm and sufficient.
>
> In five years' time I had nearly forgotten home. I had to forget it, I couldn't carry it with me. But once in a while, usually in a strange town before I have found companions, the shell of deliberate hardness is broken through. A door comes softly and irresistibly open. I hear the tired old music my unknown father left in the place he abandoned as faithlessly as I. I see the faint and sorrowful radiance of the glass, hundreds of little transparent pieces of it in very delicate colors. I hold my breath, for if my sister's face appears among them—the night is hers!

In the second draft (the one-act version), Williams heightened Tom's emotional tension between his necessary cruelty and his affection for the ones he is hurting. His cruel side comes out when he says, "Then I escaped. Without a word of goodbye, I descended the steps of the fire-escape for the last time." The incestuous implications of the speech become more explicit: "In five years time I have nearly forgotten home. But there are nights when memory is stronger. I cannot hold my shoulder to the door, the door comes softly but irresistably open. . . . I hold my breath. I reach for a cigarette. I buy a drink, I speak to the nearest stranger. For if that vision goes on growing clearer, the mist will divide upon my sister's face, watching gently and daring to ask for nothing. Then it's too much: my manhood is undone and the night is hers. . . . " (pp. 142-44)

In the third version, the speech is more integrated with the scene. Amanda had just shouted at him, "Go then! Then go to the moon!—you selfish dreamer." So Tom begins his epilogue with "I didn't go to the moon. I went much further—for time is the longest distance between two places." (We should recall that Amanda had asked Laura to wish on the moon before the gentleman caller came.) Another unifying detail was added at the end. Laura, in pantomime, blows out the candles, which like the moon have come to suggest her hopes, the romantic half-light, similar to the glow that came across the alley from the Paradise Ballroom. She had already blown out her candles in the second version, but in the third, Tom says, "anything that can blow your candles out! (*Laura bends over the candles*) Blow out your candles, Laura!—for nowadays the world is lit by lightning! Blow out your candles, Laura,—and so goodbye. . . . (*She blows the candles out. The scene dissolves.*)" So the dialogue and action reinforce each other.

Also in the third version Tom gives a more concrete impression of the memory of his sister. He suggests a little dramatic scene where he is no longer in a bedroom with his shoulder to the door. Perhaps the lines from e. e. cummings stimulated an impression of out-of-doors rather than a bedroom. Tom says,

> Perhaps I am walking along a street at night, in some strange city, before I have found companions. I pass the lighted window of a shop where perfume is sold. The window is filled with pieces of colored glass, tiny transparent bottles in delicate colors, like bits of a shattered rainbow.
>
> Then all at once my sister touches my shoulder. I turn around and look into her eyes. . . .
>
> Oh, Laura, Laura, I tried to leave you behind me, but I am more faithful than I intended to be!

The fourth or acting version emphasizes Tom's maturity and cruelty even more; now Tom leaves out all mention of his being fired from his job at the warehouse. The impression is that he voluntarily left home—to join the merchant marine. His costume, on stage, has become a pea jacket and a watch-cap, again combining the dialogue and the spectacle.

Joining the merchant marine represents his escape into freedom, his escape from a box; and the second and third versions for the whole play show the regular growth of this theme. To draw the light away from the relations of Tom and Laura and towards an inevitable clash between Tom and Amanda, Williams wrote a long argument into the early scenes. Amanda accuses Tom of being selfish, not caring for his poor sister, and Tom replies vehemently. The first half of this passage is, as many other speeches in the manuscript, in loose blank verse, which the printed texts obscure.

> Listen! You think I'm *crazy* about the *warehouse?*
>
> You think I'm in love with the Continental Shoemakers?
>
> You think I want to spend fifty-five *years* down there in that—*celotex interior!* with— *flourescent—tubes?!*
>
> Look! I'd rather somebody picked up a crow-bar and battered out my brains—than go back mornings! I GO! Everytime you come in yelling that God damn 'Rise and Shine! Rise and Shine!' I say to myself, 'How *lucky dead* people are!'

As J. L. Styan [in his *Elements of Drama*] observed, good dramatic speech has had a "specific pressure put on it"; it is economical because it functions in several ways at the same time. This speech not only furthers the action, but it characterizes Tom, the frustrated poet, who sees his work and his home as a box where he endures a living death, surrounded by phoniness and clichés. But the audience is also aware of Amanda's reaction, because we have just seen how she suffers, in her comitragic telephone conversations, while she tries to sell magazines in order to put her daughter through business college. Meantime Laura spends her days walking in the park or polishing her glass. Neither does Williams let us forget Laura during the big argument. In the third version, a spotlight shines upon her tense body; in the fourth version, she stands in the living room, at the door of the dining room, overhearing the whole exchange. Thus she is between the audience and the action in the dining room.

Then before Tom storms out of the apartment, he flings his coat across the room, "*It strikes against the shelf of Laura's glass collection, there is a tinkle of shattering glass. Laura cries out as if wounded.*" This stage business is an obvious parallel with the accident that occurs in the next act at the end of Laura and Jim's dance, when the little glass unicorn is broken, just before Jim reveals that he is engaged to marry. He can never call on Laura again.

Scene four, the only new scene that was written for the acting version (but printed in the Random House edition and absent from the Barrett MS) also emphasizes the choice that Tom has between death and escape. Tom has come home from the movies, where he gets his adventure, and he describes the magician in the stage show.

> But the wonderfullest trick of all was the coffin trick. We nailed him into a coffin and he got out of the coffin without removing one nail. There is a trick that would come in handy for me—get out of this 2 by 4 situation. . . . You know it

don't take much intelligence to get yourself into a nailed-up coffin, Laura. But who in hell ever got himself out of one without removing one nail? (*As an answer, the father's grinning photograph lights up.*)

There are a hundred ways that the body of the play depicts Tom's awareness of the essential hopelessness of the Wingfield family and the essential deadness of their beautiful memories. I will not explain how each detail came into the script; two more examples will have to suffice. One of the greatest moments in modern theater occurs when Amanda comes on stage to greet Laura's gentleman caller. Nobody says a word for a few seconds; everyone's eyes are fixed on Amanda's dress—the old ball dress that she wore when she led the cotillion years ago. Before age had yellowed this dress she had twice won the cakewalk, and she had worn it to the Governor's ball in Jackson. The dress, at this moment, suggests the utter futility of Amanda's efforts to find a husband for her daughter. She defeats her own purposes; she cannot resist pretending that the gentleman caller has come to call on her, just as seventeen of them came one afternoon on Blue Mountain. Tom is shocked and embarrassed. The grotesque sight leaves Jim speechless, and he is a young man proud of his high-school training in public speaking. Meanwhile Laura lies in her bedroom, sick with fear.

Mr. Williams did not achieve such a theatrical triumph by writing with his guts or by pouring out his uncontrolled libido. In the short story, he tried to make Laura pathetic by dressing her in one of her mother's old gowns, and Tom is momentarily surprised by her appearance when she opens the door. In the one-act version, Amanda's memories of Blue Mountain are written into the script, and Laura is furnished with a new dress, but now she is lame. By the third version (possibly in the second, too, but I cannot be sure because the relevant pages of the second version do not survive), Amanda wears the old dress and becomes a coquette. In the fourth version, Williams softens the effect slightly and adds a little more to the irony by a brief exchange between Tom and his mother. At the peak of Tom's embarrassment, after the pregnant pause, he says:

Mother, you look so pretty.

AMANDA. You know, that's the first compliment you ever paid me. I wish you'd look pleasant when you're about to say something pleasant, so I could expect it.

Then Amanda swings into her girlish chatter. These last additions seem to assure the audience that Tom is genuinely shocked but that he is trying to cover up his feelings. At the same time the audience has to have evidence that Amanda is not completely out of her mind. She can still recognize a hollow compliment, and she can return the jibe.

By typical use of his dramatic talents, Williams makes the audience conscious of several characters' feelings at the same time, like a juggler keeping four balls in the air. Each revision puts another ball in the air or increases the specific pressure. We are never allowed to forget the tension between Tom and his mother, and the scene strongly sug-

gests that Laura's anxiety and withdrawal may have been caused by her aggressive mother. The final image of Amanda in the Epilogue is that of a comforter and protector of Laura. She is dignified and tragic. But she is most vividly depicted in the middle of the play as a vigorous, silly, and pathetic old woman. Fearing that her daughter might become an old maid, she arranges the visit of a gentleman caller. Yet, she cannot resist the temptation to smother her daughter and relive her Blue Mountain days; she vicariously seduces the man herself. She has to keep bringing the dead but beautiful past into the present; Tom must go into the ugly but live future. He must break out of the coffin and leave his sister behind in darkness.

The transmutations of Jim O'Connor illustrate Mr. Williams' talent for depicting minor characters. At the start, Jim had a warm masculine nature; he was a potential lover and a Lawrencian hero.

Jim was a big red-haired Irishman who had the scrubbed and polished look of well-kept chinaware. His big square hands seemed to have a direct and very innocent hunger for touching friends. He was always clapping them on your arms or shoulders and they burned through the cloth of your shirt like plates taken out of an oven.

In the one-act version, Jim becomes slightly hollow when he tries to persuade Tom to study public speaking. Then, in the reading version, Jim assimilates some of the play's nostalgic tone when he becomes an ex-high-school hero. The distracting homosexual suggestions disappear, and now Tom was "valuable to him as someone who could remember his former glory, who had seen him win basketball games and the silver cup in debating." On the edge of failure, Jim seems to put on his hearty good nature. He is more often named the "gentleman caller" than Jim O'Connor, a detail that helps to transform him into an idea in the head of Amanda, just as Laura becomes an image of "Blue-roses" in his mind. Also in the reading version Jim first talks enthusiastically about the world of the present and future—the world that Amanda and Laura cannot enter. When he should be romancing with Laura, he orates on the Wrigley Building, the Century of Progress, and the future of television. "I wish to be ready to go up right along with it. Therefore I'm planning to get in on the ground floor. In fact I've already made the right connections and all that remains is for the industry itself to get under way! Full steam—(*His eyes are starry.*) *Knowledge—Zzzzzp! Money—Zzzzzp!—Power!* That's the cycle democracy is built on!" He clumsily breaks Laura's unicorn, and he awkwardly kisses her.

Jim finally impresses us as a dehumanized figure, an unromantic voice of power and cliché; his sex appeal has been carefully removed, and his insensitive words, and power of positive thinking take its place. Consequently, with every change he suits Laura less and less, and he embodies Tom's "celotex interior" more and more. In the finished play, Amanda's mental projection of the old-fashioned gentleman caller reveals him to be Tom's brute reality.

Other important changes are found in the stage directions, especially the visual images and printed legends that Williams experimented with and rejected—wisely, I think. One legend, "A Souvenir," survives in the fragments of the one-act play (at the beginning of what was eventually scene viii), and the earliest forms of the reading version show an attempted use of a blackboard on which Tom wrote in chalk such things as *"Blue Roses"* (scene ii), *"Campaign"* (scene iii), and *"Où sont les Neiges d'antan"* (scene i). The completed reading version projected these legends by means of the much discussed "screen device," possibly conceived in the film synopsis that preceded the reading version. Williams said, "The legend or image upon the screen will strengthen the effect of what is merely allusion [*sic*] in the writing and allow the primary point to be made more simply and lightly than if the entire responsibility were on the spoken lines" (New Directions edition, 1949). The real weakness of the device lies in the author's anxiousness and small confidence in his audience. "In an episodic play, such as this, the basic structure or narrative line may be observed from the audience; the effect may seem fragmentary rather than architectural. This may not be the fault of the play so much as a lack of attention in the audience." And I suspect that if the screen device has ever been tried, it distracted the audience from the actors, just as the lighting can distract unless it is used sparingly. Father's lighted picture seems to work once or twice, but I doubt if similar mechanical marvels add to the unified effect. At any rate, Williams says he does not regret the omission of the screen device in the first New York production, because he saw that Laurette Taylor's powerful performance "made it suitable to have the utmost simplicity in physical production." [Production designer] Jo Melziner's two scrims no doubt also helped persuade him. An air of unreality is one thing but pretentious pointing out of meaning is another.

Williams' most successful revisions of stage directions unobtrusively change the story's matter-of-fact tone into memory. The narrator of the story becomes the presenter of the play, and significant stage properties appear in the big scene: the blasted candelabra from the altar of the Church of the Heavenly Rest, the ice cream, fruit punch, and macaroons. In the reading version the ice cream was replaced with dandelion wine (for a mock communion?), and Amanda "baptizes" herself with lemonade—all of which contributes to the vague religious impression of the scene. No one explicitly defines the meaning of these symbols, but they quietly suggest that the events represent Laura's pitiful initiation rites; this is as close as she will ever come to the altar of love, because Jim is no Savior. She must blow her candles out. The empty ceremony is over. (pp. 144-49)

> *Lester A. Beaurline, " 'The Glass Menagerie':*
> *From Story to Play," in* Modern Drama, *Vol.*
> *VIII, No. 2, September, 1965, pp. 142-49.*

James L. Rowland

Tennessee Williams' first successful play, *The Glass Menagerie,* has become one of the most popular dramas of the first half of this century and is produced more frequently than any other play in high schools, colleges, and community theatre groups. It has also been revived year after year on Broadway, and it had special revivals in honor of its tenth and twentieth anniversaries. It has been widely anthologized and has been included in many high school and college literature courses.

Despite this popularity, the astonishing fact remains that there are really two plays, not one, and that those who read the play are reading not merely a different *Glass Menagerie,* but, I believe, a distinctly inferior one. The problem is significant not only for this play, but for the general question arising in the reading of all dramatic literature: Which version is correct, which version represents the author's final intention?

The problem is nearly as complicated as any study of a Shakespearean folio, and confusion and error are abundant in the record. The first question is: What version are we talking about? For simplicity's sake, let us designate two—the so-called "reading version," found in most anthologies and copyrighted in 1945, and the so-called "acting version," seldom reprinted except through the Dramatists Play Service and copyrighted in 1948.

A background of the development of the play has been outlined by Lester A. Beaurline [in *Modern Drama,* September 1965], who traces its growth from a short story and loses it somewhere in the fog of "revised again sometime in the mid-fifties." In short, there was an unpublished version copyrighted (as an unpublished play) in 1945; in that same year a copyrighted, published version appeared: the "reading version" found in most anthologies. This version is distinguished immediately by the elaborate introduction of the characters, and by the intricate "magic lantern" stage business, which the author's introduction tells the reader was never used. Williams explains further that the only important difference between the reading and the acting versions of the play is the omission of the screen device, a statement which I find impossible to accept. In 1948 the "acting version," produced in 1945, was copyrighted and published. I am concerned here with the confusion caused by the existence of two published versions of the play, and the significant reasons for believing that only one of them, the "acting version," should be regarded as representing the real *Glass Menagerie.*

This confusion has infected criticism. Signi Lenea Falk refers to the *Glass Menagerie* as "a memory play, a series of seven sharply remembered scenes," and a conversation is quoted from the "reading version" of the play. However, Falk's note for this discussion actually refers to the "acting version." (pp. 331-32)

More important, however, is the question of which play should we read as the author's final intention. The "acting version" is my choice, not because it is a later version, but because the characters are more fully developed, and more understandable. Beaurline states that there are more than "1100 verbal changes." The count is probably accurate; yet it is the significance of the changes I wish to discuss. Beaurline presents a few examples of changes that were made in Tom. In this study I shall use Amanda in order to show the transition the play makes from its "reading" to its "acting version," for it is my belief that she is the character in the drama to whom the other participants react. Changes made in Amanda often necessitate changes in the other characters. (p. 332)

The first revision appears on the first page. In the "reading version" Amanda, under the heading characters, is described as,

Amanda Wingfield (the mother)

A little woman of great but confused vitality clinging frantically to another time and place. Her characterization must be carefully created, not copied from type. She is not paranoiac, but her life is paranoia. There is much to admire in Amanda, and as much to love and pity as there is to laugh at. Certainly she has endurance and a kind of heroism, and though her foolishness makes her unwittingly cruel at times, there is tenderness in her slight person.

In the "acting version" all that is listed under characters is "The Mother." The above description, at first viewing, seems like a necessary explanation. As one compares these two versions, however, it becomes evident that Williams, through revision and expansion of Amanda's lines in the "acting version," took care of the extensive introduction within the play. The production notes for the "reading version" are also long and detailed. By the time the "acting version" was published, most of these had been eliminated. Nearly all of Williams' suggested production techniques and devices were cut out by directors.

The changes continue at the very start of the drama. In scene I of the "reading version" Amanda calls Tom and explains, "We can't say grace until you come to the table!" This speech is omitted in the "acting version." Here Amanda opens with a comment on the Northern versus the Southern Episcopalians. She has recently been to church and was refused a seat because a woman told her that the pew was rented. Williams has changed an innocent religious activity into a social comment on the North and the state of a church in that area. The rest of this speech is nearly the same, yet Amanda is not as dictatorial in the "acting version." A few lines further, her reaction to Tom's leaving the table is more harsh in the "acting version" than it is in the "reading version." In the "reading version" the passage reads, "[lightly]. Temperament like a Metropolitan star! You're not excused from the table." In the "acting version" it reads, "Temperament like a Metropolitan star! You're not excused from this table." The direction "lightly" is dropped and "the" is changed to the more immediate "this." Thus in the first scene Amanda does not seem to be part of a dream world, but rather a part of a here-and-now world. When Laura offers to get the coffee, Amanda answers: "No, sister, no, sister—you be the lady this time and I'll be the darky" ("reading version"). The revised line reads, "No, no, no, no. You sit down. I'm going to be the colored boy today and you're going to be the lady" ("acting version"). The two important changes in this line are the change from the order "No sister" to the lighter "No, no, no, no," and the use of the more socially acceptable term "colored boy." The next line, "Resume your seat, little sister—I want you to stay fresh and pretty—for the gentlemen callers" ("reading version"), changes to "Resume your seat. Re-

sume your seat. You keep yourself fresh and pretty for the gentlemen callers" ("acting version"). Again an order has been changed to a lighter, more conversational command.

In the remainder of scene I only three more changes are of major importance. Amanda again uses colored boy rather than darky. Thus a socially acceptable term is again substituted for a southern one. In the "reading version" a spotlight is placed on Amanda during her speech about her youth and her gentlemen callers. This light is not used in the "acting version," and thus a more realistic, less dreamlike atmosphere is produced. A single spotlight is occasionally used in the "acting version." In this case it is an important omission, for as we have observed, this scene, in the "acting version," seems to bring Amanda into the real world, the world of St. Louis, not the dream world, the world of her youth in the South. The other important change in Amanda, which is noticeable throughout the first scene, is that her speeches are more conversational in the "acting version." She is a participant in the action, and not a dreamy bystander.

In scene II the conversational tone observed in scene I continues to develop in the "acting version." Amanda enters the apartment and finds Laura at the typewriter after learning that Laura has not been attending business school. The "reading version" opens with "Hello, Mother, I was—!" and Amanda replies, "Deception? Deception?" The "acting version" opens with,

LAURA. Hello, Mother, I was just.

AMANDA. I know. You were just practicing your typing, I suppose.

LAURA. Yes.

AMANDA. Deception, deception, deception!

In the "acting version" a realistic conversation is created, for Amanda is sure that Laura is deceiving her. In her next speech Amanda changes "forever" ("reading version") to "the rest of my entire life" ("acting version"), again a more realistic and less dreamlike statement. A more conversational tone has continued to develop when "I thought you were an adult; it seems that I was mistaken" ("reading version") is changed to "I was under the impression that you were an adult, but evidently I was very much mistaken" ("acting version"). This tone is present in many more speeches of scene II in the "acting version." When Amanda tells Laura about her visit to the Rubicam's Business College in the "acting version," we find that Laura really did get sick to her stomach and that the college did call her home "every day," neither of which happens in the "reading version." When Laura starts to play the victrola she is told not to in the "acting version." In the "reading version" she must know she is not to play it by Amanda's facial action. When Amanda asks Laura where she has been going when she should have been at the school, Amanda is much more understanding in the "acting version" than in the "reading version." A few lines further Amanda says, "You did all this to deceive me, just for deception? Why?" ("reading version"). In the "acting version" three more whys are added, and again the tone is softened. This tone of sympathy, yet more concern, continues. In the "reading version" Amanda says, "So what are we going to do the rest of our lives? Stay home and watch the parades go by?" This is changed to, "So what are we going to do now, honey, the rest of our lives? Just sit down in the house and watch the parades go by." ("acting version")

Later in scene II when Laura and Amanda have discussed the boy Laura knew in school, Amanda decides that Laura might marry. Amanda says, "Girls that aren't cut out for business careers usually wind up married to some nice man. Sister, that's just what you'll do!" ("reading version"). In the "acting version" Amanda explains, "That's all right honey, that's all right. It doesn't matter. Little girls who aren't cut out for business careers sometimes end up married to very nice young men. And I'm just going to see that you do that, too!" The differences in the above speeches again point out, quite well, the differences in the development of Amanda that I have tried to suggest. The "reading version" gives Laura and Tom a stage companion. The "acting version" gives them a mother. Three lines later, the end of scene II, Laura says that she is a cripple. In the "reading version" Amanda's attitude is matter-of-fact. In the "acting version" she is more understanding, more human, more full of and worthy of love.

At the beginning of scene III we find Amanda talking on the telephone, attempting to sell magazine subscriptions to lady acquaintances. Money is needed so that she can launch her campaign to obtain a husband for Laura. There are many changes in the conversation between Amanda and Ida Scott. In the "reading version" we find Amanda's speech less emotional and pitiful. She does not receive any sympathy from Ida. In the "acting version" Amanda is sweeter, more concerned, more compromising, and thus more hurt when the woman hangs up on her. These changes can be shown by a look at one line, the last, of this conversation, "I think she's hung up!" ("reading version"), which is changed to "Why, that woman! Do you know what she did? She hung up on me" ("acting version"). In the "acting version" we see Amanda as an emotional and thus hurt and insulted individual, not just a line of explanation in a play.

At this point the "reading version" dims out. In the "acting version" we find Amanda giving Tom a health lesson concerning his eyes and posture. After an excess of Amanda's concern, Tom explodes and swears at her. The "reading version" begins action at this point. The difference between the "reading version" and the "acting version" is just a few lines, yet we see another example of Amanda's love and concern for her children, and Tom's reaction to her overbearing love. Also a smooth transition is made from one part of the scene to another without an artificial dimming of the lights.

Tom and Amanda's conversation in scene III includes an argument about a novel. The speeches are not changed importantly. What is important is Tom's reaction. When Amanda calls a novel by D. H. Lawrence "horrible" and something for people with "diseased minds," Tom laughs at her "wildly" and then "still more wildly" ("reading version"). This is not his reaction in the "acting version," where he merely listens to her speech. It is here that we can see the necessity of the additional lines included in scene III, mentioned above. Amanda loves Tom and Tom knows it, and this mutual love is much different from the cold and mocking nature of the characters in the "reading version."

Later in this scene we again find that Amanda's and Tom's lines are more realistic, more emotional, yet more lifelike. When Tom explains that he does not care for his job, Amanda reacts as follows, "What right have you got to jeopardize your job? Jeopardize the security of us all? How do you think we'd manage if you were—" ("reading version"). In the "acting version" this speech is changed very little, but the changes are important and help explain the change in Amanda. She says, "How dare you jeopardize your job? Jeopardize our security? How do you think we'd manage?" It is now "How dare you" and "our," and the speech is finished and more normal and thus not part of a dream world. As a result of the argument Tom calls Amanda an "ugly-babbling old-witch." He then throws his coat and breaks the glass collection. Laura screams. In the "reading version" we are told "[*But Amanda is still stunned and stupefied by the "ugly-witch" so that she barely notices this occurrence. Now she recovers her speech.*] [*In an awful voice*]. I won't speak to you—until you apologize!" What is important here is the use of a written explanation for Amanda's reaction to Tom's insults. In the "acting version" the explanation is omitted. Reaction is expressed, much more naturally, when Amanda says "[*in an awful voice*]. I'll never speak to you again as long as you live unless you apologize to me." Again Williams has learned to do within the "acting version" of the play that which he had to do outside of the play in the "reading version."

As scene IV opens we find Tom trying to enter the apartment in a state of drunkenness. He drops his key, and Laura lets him in. After a brief discussion about what Tom has been doing, Laura succeeds in persuading him to go to bed. In the "reading version" the scene dims out at this point, and a dreamlike state is again the vehicle for movement from one part of a scene to another. In the "acting version" a more pronounced break is made, for the play moves on to scene V. This is a very slight change, yet a feeling that a real night has passed is created by the scene division in the "acting version." In the "reading version" we are left, and rightly so, with the feeling that this is all part of one action, a feeling that is not the desired reaction in the "acting version."

Amanda has only five more changes in the remainder of scene IV of the "reading version," scene V of the "acting version." The first four changes again show Amanda's lines as more conversational and Amanda as more gentle, more loving and understanding, more realistic. Only one of these changes warrants a close inspection. Tom has apologized to Amanda, and she "sobbingly" has forgiven him and has explained how much she worries about her children. She has told Tom to try harder, and he says that he does try hard. In the "reading version" Amanda then says:

> [*with great enthusiasm*]. Try and you will SUCCEED! [*the notion makes her breathless*]. Why,

you—you're just full of natural endowments! Both of my children—they're unusual children! Don't you think I know it? I'm so—proud! Happy and—feel I've—so much to be thankful for but—Promise me one thing, Son!

The above speech seems to be something a mother might say under such circumstances. But note how much more warmly, how much more affectionately, the same lines can be penned:

> [*with great enthusiasm*]. That's all right! You just keep on trying and you're bound to succeed. Why, you're—you're just full of natural endowments! Both my children are—they're very precious children and I've got an awful lot to be thankful for; you just must promise me one thing.

Amanda's lines in the "reading version" now seem more naturally a part of a Horatio Alger novel or a Dale Carnegie speech. Amanda's lines in the "acting version" are those of a sensitive, frail, emotional woman.

The last change made in scene IV of the "reading version" is at the end. This is a second telephone conversation concerning magazine subscriptions, this time with an Ella Cartwright. There are changes in the first part of the conversation. One finds, again, a more conversational tone to Amanda's language, and she is sweeter and more pitiful in the "acting version." The important change, however, and this change does fit and follow well the changes in tone, appears in the "acting version" as an addition to the conversation. Scene IV of the "reading version" ends with the telephone conversation unfinished. In the "acting version" the call is continued and finished, and in doing so Williams again makes Amanda more human, more sensitive, more pitiful, and more worthy of our sympathy. The end of the conversation is as follows:

> You, you have? You have read it? Well, how do you think it turns out? Oh, no. Bessie Mae Harper never lets you down. Oh, of course we have to have complications. You have to have complications—oh you can't have a story without them—but Bessie Mae Harper always leaves you with such an uplift—What's the matter, Ella? You sound so mad. Oh, because it's seven o'clock in the morning. Oh, Ella, I forgot that you never got up until nine. I forgot that anybody in the world was allowed to sleep as late as that. I can't say any more than I'm sorry, can I? Oh, you will? You're going to take that subscription from me anyhow? Well, bless you, Ella, bless you, bless you, bless you.

Poor Amanda, she so badly wants to sell a subscription, yet she does not remember that all people don't have to "rise and shine" at six o'clock. We can almost see her on her knees, and because her apology is sincere and warrants sympathy she receives it from Ella, and she receives it from us.

From scene V of the "reading version" to scene VI of the "acting version" many minor changes are made in the position of the lines within the scenes and in the meaning of the lines, due to word changes. In the "reading version" the scene opens with Amanda. Ten lines later we find Tom's speech that opens the scene in the "acting version." This rearrangement removes an awkward break in the action of the "reading version" and creates a smoothly moving scene in the "acting version."

In all of the word changes in Amanda's lines, we find her, again, more conversational, more human, and more realistic. It is in this scene that Tom tells her that they shall have a gentleman caller. In the "reading version" Amanda's and Tom's conversation about the caller, Jim, is tight, stiff, unnatural, and unloving—unloving because Amanda reacts very harshly to Tom's withholding of information. In the "acting version" Tom and Amanda have a light and fun-filled interplay on the subject of, if, when, and why Jim shall come. Even their discussion of Laura and her handicaps has lost some of its bite. Other minor changes are as follows. All of her silver, monogrammed table linen, fresh curtains, a new sofa, and chintz covers ("reading version") become three pieces of silver, that old lace tablecloth, no change of curtains, a bright piece of cretonne for the daybed, and a bright cover for the chair ("acting version").

Thus we see a more humble and practical Amanda in a more depressing and realistic world. The long-gone father is mentioned several times by Amanda in the "reading version," only once in the "acting version." Again we see Amanda in a less dream-filled world. Near the end of scene V of the "reading version," Tom gets up to leave and Amanda says, "[*sharply*]. Where are you going?" Tom replies he is going to the movies. Amanda's response is critical ("reading version"). These lines are not included in the "acting version," and again we see a more understanding, a more realistic Amanda.

This brings us to the end of Part I in the "reading version." Scenes VI and VII are located in Part II. This division appears only in the introductory comment and does not mean a change of acts. Thus the "reading version," even with a curtain between scenes V and VI, remains a one-act play. In the "acting version" an act division is made, and as the curtain rises we look in on act II scene VII.

Scene VII of the "acting version" again presents us with several examples of tone changes in Amanda's lines. Two examples show this change in a dramatic manner, for both Laura and Tom have a new line, a line that is a result of love for and understanding of their mother. As the scene opens Laura and Amanda are preparing for the gentleman caller. When Amanda tells Laura she must wear "Gay Deceivers," she says:

> LAURA. I won't wear them!
>
> AMANDA. You will!
>
> LAURA. Why should I?
>
> AMANDA. Because to be painfully honest, your chest is flat.
>
> ("reading version")

Note how this same conversation is changed in the "acting version."

> LAURA. I won't wear them!

AMANDA. Of course you'll wear them.

LAURA. Why should I?

AMANDA. Well, to tell you the truth, honey, you're just a little bit flat-chested.

("acting version")

We now see Amanda as an understanding, loving mother, this time in relation to Laura. Amanda then leaves the stage to dress. Her lines in the "reading version" continue to be harsh and arrogant. When she comes out with her dress on in the "reading version," Laura makes no comment. In the "acting version" the understanding, loving Amanda continues to talk to Laura as she dresses. When she enters the living room, Laura says "Oh, Mother, how lovely!"

Later in this scene when Jim has arrived and Amanda comes into the room where Jim and Tom have been talking, Tom makes no comment on her appearance in the "reading version." In scene VII of the "acting version" when Amanda enters, Tom says, "Mother, you look so pretty." These may seem like minor changes, and in the number of words they are. In the overall reaction to and the understood meaning of the play, they are worth paragraphs. In two lines of nine words, Tom and Laura have displayed their love and understanding of Amanda.

As the last scene opens, we see that dinner has been completed. In the "reading version" this is scene VII, in the "acting version" this is act II scene VIII. There is a noticeable difference in Amanda's treatment of Jim in these two versions. Amanda is much less formal in the "acting version." This is suitable to Amanda's new character in the "acting version," for she is now more relaxed with and less formal toward her children and their life. In the "acting version" we find a woman who has accepted more readily her situation in life. The "reading version" is a play that seems to exist in a more dreamlike world. The "acting version" is still a memory play, but it takes place in more realistic surroundings and with more realistic stage devices— the lack of a screen, difference in music, and difference in lighting. Amanda herself has become more realistic. Scene VIII of the "acting version" is a perfect example of this change. In the "reading version" when the lights go out, the conversation is as follows:

AMANDA. Where was Moses when the lights went out? Ha-Ha-Do you know the answer to that one, Mr. O'Connor?

JIM. No, Ma'am, what's the answer?

AMANDA. In the dark!

("reading version")

In the "acting version" the question remains the same. Jim's reply changes to, "No, Ma'am, what's the answer to that one?" Amanda then says, "Well, I heard one answer but it wasn't very nice. I thought you might know another one."

We see Amanda only once more, and this is at the end of the play. There is little change in her lines or in any of the final lines. We discover that Jim is engaged. We see that Tom must leave in the "acting version" as he leaves in the

"reading version," and Laura and Amanda are left to fare for themselves. What then is the difference between the 1945 "reading version" and the 1948 "acting version"? The difference is that in the "acting version" we see an understanding and loving mother, we see Amanda as a person who truly suffers, and her suffering is such that others have pity for her. We can see that Laura loves Amanda in the "acting version" for Amanda is not as matter-of-fact toward her problems and her defects. When Laura suffers, Amanda suffers also. We know that Tom loves Amanda, for Tom knows that she only wishes him the best. He knows that she is at least trying to understand him and trying to do what is best for Laura, whom he loves so deeply. Therefore, the final scene has changed, for Amanda, Tom, and Laura have all changed. When Tom leaves, we know he leaves a mother that he loves, a mother who loves him. In the "reading version" Tom leaves, and we are glad. In the "acting version" Tom leaves, and we understand, and we are glad, yet we weep, for we know that he would not leave if it were possible for him to stay.

Earlier in this study an opening description of Amanda that is used in the "reading version" was quoted. Now that we have seen how Amanda changes from the "reading" to the "acting version," it is easy to see why this introduction was not included in the "acting version." In the "acting version" Amanda is all that she is supposed to be, for there is much to admire and there is as much to love and pity as there is to laugh at. At times she is tender, at times she is harsh, at times she is foolish. We do not have to be told this in the "acting version." We can see it for ourselves. We can see it in Amanda's lines, lines that are full of life and realism. In the "reading version" Amanda's traits are set forth in the beginning, and as we read the play we think of her in those terms. Thus we see a move from the artificial to the natural, from a weak to a strong Amanda, from a good play to a classic.

As Lester Beaurline explains, the "reading version" should not be reprinted in an anthology, and the "acting version" should not be ignored by a critic. The "acting version" should also not be ignored by the student of drama. Nor should it be ignored by the casual reader, for it is the play, the complete play, *The Glass Menagerie.* (pp. 332-40)

James L. Rowland, "Tennessee's Two Aman-das," in Research Studies, *Vol. 35, No. 4, December, 1967, pp. 331-40.*

Elmo Howell

[Williams frequently uses the South] as symbolic of an elusive grace—spiritual, if you will—uncommon in a technological society. His attitude is by no means consistent. More often than not, his Southern women are doxies or fallen ladies and his men the vulgar bullies of hillbilly origin like Boss Finley or Big Daddy of *Cat on a Hot Tin Roof.* But Williams enjoyed a great many years of childhood security in Mississippi, where he was born in the vicarage home of his grandfather in Columbus. Although he abhors Southern racism, he has an affinity with the aristocratic ideal, which he associates with the venerable figure of his grandfather, a gentleman of the old school and one of the strongest influences in his life.

Amanda Wingfield of *The Glass Menagerie,* a faded belle from Blue Mountain, Mississippi, with recollections of seventeen gentlemen callers in one afternoon, exults in her Southern past to make more bearable the St. Louis industrial slum where an unfortunate marriage has brought her. A garrulous and silly woman, she torments her son about his drinking and his movie-going and makes her daughter's life miserable because Laura, unable to cope with a physical infirmity and a natural shyness, seeks refuge in an imaginary world of a glass menagerie. Amanda's patter about the gentlemen callers begins as a tiresome joke; but in the course of the play by some obscure alchemy of which the author himself seems unaware, the Southern past confers on Amanda a tragic depth which her children do not share.

The Glass Menagerie is a product of Williams' own experience. When his family left Mississippi to live in St. Louis when he was about twelve, he remembered the rural South as "a wide spacious land that you can breathe in." Like Amanda, he prized his Southern associations. "My folks," he said, "were pioneer Tennesseans, mostly of a military and political disposition, some of them, such as Nollichucky Jack Sevier, having been famous Indian fighters when the South was being settled. I am also related to the late Senator John Sharp Williams, who was a famous silver-tongued orator of Mississippi." Above all, the quiet rectory life of his childhood in Columbus and then in Clarksdale (the Blue Mountain of his plays) is lodged in his memory and serves as a touchstone against which the tawdriness of urban life is measured. The moon over Garfinkel's delicatessen, the alley where cats fight and couples wander from the Paradise Dance Hall, the fire escape which reminds Amanda of her Southern verandah, the dark rooms where the sun never penetrates—all are painful images drawn from the stark contrast of two cultures.

Otto Reinert calls *The Glass Menagerie* a play "in the modern democratic tradition that assumes that serious drama can be made of the sufferings of small people." The play is indeed about small people. Tom Wingfield has his poetry and his dreams and eventually his escape, like his father. Laura is crippled, physically and emotionally. Amanda is stronger than either, but under the pressure of circumstance she also gives way to littleness, in her constant nagging and in impossible demands on her children. In what way, then, does the play rise above littleness? It is in Amanda Wingfield's memory, "seated predominantly in the heart," of her life before she came to an urban industrialized North, which Williams refers to as "the fundamentally enslaved section of American society." The tragic dimension of the play is centered in Amanda, for neither of her children is capable of seeing, as the mother sees, their starved present in the light of a larger past.

Amanda is an ordinary woman who is somehow transfigured by the memory of her early life in Mississippi and who tries to pass the influence on to her children. She exaggerates her glories, like the number of gentlemen callers, but the idea of a very different way of life is real, and this is enough to establish her as the dominant interest in the play. When she talks of Blue Mountain, her children patronize her and laugh behind her back. "I know what's coming," Tom says. "Yes. But let her tell it," Laura says. "She loves to tell it." And then Amanda simpers and capers in a mere burlesque of the high life she recalls as a Southern belle. Tom wants to know how she managed to entertain all those gentlemen callers. She knew the art of conversation, she says. A girl in those days needed more than a pretty face and figure, "although I wasn't slighted in either respect"; she had to know how to talk and to discuss significant things. "Never anything coarse or common or vulgar." Amanda's escape from the dreary present is different from Tom's and Laura's. They try to escape reality, but she in her own way is coming to grips with it, by trying to make a breadwinner out of Tom and by securing Laura's future with a career or marriage. "Both of my children—they're *unusual* children! Don't you think I know it? I'm so—proud!" The gentlemen callers are not designed to reflect her popularity so much as to suggest to her children the larger possibilities that life has to offer which they from limited experience are unable to see.

In spite of her silliness, the mother represents the fundamental decencies that Williams must have known in his Southern boyhood. She reacts with Victorian fervor when Tom brings home a book by D. H. Lawrence. "I cannot control the output of diseased minds and the people who cater to them, but I won't allow such filth brought into my house." When Tom mentions instinct, she picks up the word as if it were obscene. "It belongs properly to animals," she says; "Christians and adults have got away from it." She makes herself ridiculous in voicing the pruderies of the Bible Belt—that is the first impression of her; but as her character unfolds, her puritan reservations, like her affected Southern manners, become part of a larger nature that commands respect. The closing scene of Amanda comforting her daughter after Tom has left them and Laura's hopes have failed elevates the mind in terms of the mother's suffering and her acceptance of it. "Her silliness is gone," says the author, "and she has dignity and tragic beauty."

In the figure of Amanda, Tennessee Williams uses his Southern background to enforce a unity of effect where theme is imprecisely imagined. Mother, son, and daughter are all personal with the author and their sufferings deeply felt, but no one of them has a certain preeminence in the author's mind. Only in the mother, as the story progresses, does a definite meaning emerge. The gentlemen callers begin as a joke; Amanda herself is a joke, in the eyes of her children and of the generation which they represent; but Williams' concept of a very different way of life in his native South enables him to transmute the silly mother and her dreams into something which is noble and true. In its larger meaning, Amanda's tragedy becomes a parable of the inadequacy of modern life.

The Glass Menagerie suggests the wholesome use of a living tradition to the artist. Unlike his fellow Mississippians William Faulkner and Eudora Welty, Williams has no strong feeling for place. Like Tom Wingfield, he is a rover; and when he returns to Mississippi for a setting it is more often than not for exotic effect, not for cultural reasons, as in *The Rose Tatoo,* where he peoples a Gulf Coast town with Sicilians. But the placid environs of his boyhood fixed in his imagination an ideal which in his best moments lifts his drama above mere sensation. "Whoever you are," says Blanche DuBois to the attendant from the state institution, "I have always depended on the kindness of strangers." In spite of her weakness, Blanche is the noblest creation of *Streetcar* and the source of the tension, for she like Amanda recalls for Williams a certain beneficence in human relations which has all but disappeared. Williams' use of the South for shock value is gross and deliberate, but the part the South plays in shaping his moral vision is more impressive because it is unself-conscious. In the character of Amanda, *The Glass Menagerie* moves almost imperceptibly into mythic meaning. (pp. 84-9)

> *Elmo Howell, "The Function of Gentlemen Callers: A Note on Tennessee Williams' 'The Glass Menagerie',"* in Notes on Mississippi Writers, *Vol. 11, No. 3, Winter, 1970, pp. 83-90.*

Frank Durham

Modern American attempts at verse drama have, on the whole, produced a harvest of respectable failures—*vide* the ambitious but incongruously rhetorical and ornate plays of Maxwell Anderson and the mannered and rather coldly calculated pieces by T. S. Eliot. . . . One of the difficulties regarding the use of verse in the modern theatre, as Eliot and [Archibald] MacLeish point out, is the belief that the audience demands to see life as it is and that to such an audience poetry (or is it merely verse?) sounds "artificial." Eliot does say [in *On Poetry and Poets*] that there is a "peculiar range of sensibility [which] can be expressed by dramatic poetry, at its moments of greatest intensity," "a fringe of indefinite extent," beyond the capabilities of prose drama to express. However, it is the contention of this paper that, while American drama has increasingly sought to portray this "peculiar range of sensibility," the most successful means of doing so has not been verse. It has, instead, been best portrayed by a new, or seemingly new, poetic drama which eschews verse for an eclectic but organic union of both verbal and non-verbal elements of the theatre, which many critics have recognized and which Tennessee Williams, one of its major practitioners, calls "plastic theatre." *The Glass Menagerie* will serve as a prime example of the form.

It is, of course, no longer necessary to argue that verse need not be metrical, but certainly the comparative failures of both Anderson and Eliot can be attributed largely to their clinging to the idea that metre is an essential of poetic drama. In fact, Anderson employed a somewhat modified blank verse, which in itself throws up a barrier between the contemporary play and the contemporary audience's acceptance of it; for blank verse is firmly fixed in the theatre-going mind with Shakespeare and the raft of pallid pseudo-Shakespeareans. To use it on stage today is somewhat analogous to employing the Dickensian chronicle for a modern psychological novel. It reeks of the past—and of fustian. And Eliot's adherence to a three-stressed line with a caesura is somewhat reminiscent of Anglo-Saxon verse.

What we have developed in twentieth-century America is a type of poetic drama peculiarly relevant to our own time, a drama which maintains a speaking acquaintance with surface reality but which, through all the means at its disposal, probes into and bodies forth what Eliot calls that "peculiar range of sensibility," the inner truth, the often unutterable essences of human action and human emotion. As Alan Downer says [in *Fifty Years of American Drama, 1900-1950*]:

> Thus the true poet of the theater is not necessarily concerned in the least with the traditional forms and language of poetry, but with making all the elements at his disposal—plot, actor, action, stage, lighting, setting, music, speech—unite to serve as a vehicle for his theme, his vision, or his interpretation of man's fate.

And again:

> Properly handled, organically related to the action and purpose of the whole work, the devices of expressionism have permitted playwrights to penetrate beneath the surface of their situations, to reveal truths which realism by its nature tends to disguise. This penetration, this revelation of inner truth, brings the contemporary drama once more into a close relationship with the great repertory of the poetic drama of the past.

O'Neill was one of the first American playwrights to move thus beyond realism toward a new poetry of the theatre, but today its chief figure is Tennessee Williams.

In his "Author's Production Notes" to *The Glass Menagerie,* in which he discusses at length such "extra-literary" elements as music and lighting, Williams makes clear that he is consciously striving to write this new type of poetic drama. Calling the piece "a memory play" and saying that it is therefore to be produced "with unusual freedom of convention," he says:

> Because of its considerably delicate or tenuous material, atmospheric touches and subtleties of direction play a particularly important part. Expressionism and all other unconventional techniques in drama have only one valid aim, and that is a closer approach to truth. When a play employs unconventional techniques, it is not, or certainly shouldn't be, trying to escape its responsibility of dealing with reality, or interpreting experience, but is actually or should be attempting to find a closer approach, a more penetrating and vivid expression of things as they are. The straight realistic play with its genuine frigidaire and authentic ice-cubes, its characters that speak exactly as its audience speaks, corresponds to the academic landscape and has the same virtue of photographic likeness. Everyone should know nowadays the unimportance of the photographic in art: that truth, life, or reality is an organic thing which the poetic imagination can represent or suggest, in essence, only through transformation, through changing into other forms than those which merely present an appearance.

These remarks are not meant as a preface only to this particular play. They have to do with a conception of a new, plastic theatre which must take the place of the exhausted theatre of realistic conventions if the theatre is to resume vitality as a part of our culture.

Thus Williams is consciously ushering in a new period in drama and a form, as Esther Merle Jackson [in her *The Broken World of Tennessee Williams*] says, distinctively and consciously American, a popular art form embodying all levels of American culture and life and in its intentions definitely poetic: "The search for a concrete expressive form—a shape congruent with poetic vision—is a motif that appears throughout the work of Williams."

His realization of the need for "transformation" suggests Frost's idea: " . . . it is the height of poetry, the height of all thinking, the height of all poetic thinking, that attempts to say matter in terms of spirit and spirit in terms of matter." And, Frost continues, poetry (and thinking) is simply "saying one thing in terms of another" ["Education by Poetry"]. Elsewhere Frost maintains that "every poem is a new metaphor inside or it is nothing," and every poem is a symbol. Certainly in **The Glass Menagerie**, often called a "lyric play," Williams is employing this concept of "transformation," of the dominant metaphor and symbol. Tom, his narrator-character, begins by telling us: "I give you truth in the pleasant guise of illusion."

In **The Glass Menagerie** there are two dominant metaphors or symbols. The more obvious is, of course, glass, as the title itself implies. Laura's glass animals, especially the unicorn, which is broken, symbolize the tenuousness of her hold on reality, the ease with which her illusion may be shattered. Of her, Williams says. " . . . the lovely fragility of glass which is her image." This symbol is relevant to the other characters also, for their ability to exist at all in the world rests on illusions as easily destroyed as the unicorn. Without her belief in her romantic past and in Laura's ultimate wooing by the non-existent Gentleman Caller, Amanda, who is the strongest, would be unable to face the harsh struggle for survival, would lose that fierce strength which in her is both comic and tragically admirable. At the touch of truth, her world will shatter into a thousand irretrievable fragments. The Gentleman Caller, Jim O'Connor, is also sustained by two illusions, that of his great success and promise in high school and that of his future triumph based on the empty slogans of his television night course: "Because I believe in the future of television! I want to be ready to go right up along with it. . . . I'm planning to get in on the ground floor. Oh, I've already made the right connections. All that remains now is for the industry itself to get under way—full steam! You know, *knowledge*—zzzzppp! *Money*—zzzzzzpp! POWER! Wham! That's the cycle democracy is built on!" Jim himself, as Tom tells us, is the momentary and disappointing embodiment of Laura and Amanda's illusion— "But having a poet's weakness for symbols, I am using this character as a symbol—as the long-delayed but always expected something we live for." Tom, despising his job in the warehouse, escaping temporarily into the fantasy world of the movies, cherishes the ideal of the absconded father ("He was a telephone man who fell in love with long

distance. . . . ") and envies Malvolio the Magician, who, nailed inside a coffin, "got out without removing one nail." But in Tom's case glass is both fragile and everlasting, for his physical escape brings no real liberation. Though he travels widely, the trap still holds him:

> Perhaps it was a familiar bit of music. Perhaps it was only a piece of transparent glass. . . . Perhaps I am walking along a street at night, in some strange city, before I have found companions, and I pass the lighted window of a shop where perfume is sold. The window is filled with pieces of colored glass, tiny transparent bottles in delicate colors, like bits of a shattered rainbow. Then all at once my sister touches my shoulder. I turn around and look into her eyes.

While glass is the more obvious of the metaphors or symbols which govern the play—and it is, to me, the symbol of the theme—the motion picture serves as the symbol determining the over-all form of the play. Tom, the narrator, through whose consciousness we see the entire action, tells us at the start, "The play is memory. . . . Being a memory play, it is dimly lighted, it is sentimental, it is not realistic." Since it is Tom's memory and since Tom's escape from reality is the motion picture, Williams logically portrays Tom's memories in terms of the motion picture, the silent film even though dialogue is used. The structure and rhythmic flow of the scenes are like those of the motion picture. The screen device, generally omitted in production, resembles closely the use of subtitles on the silent screen, and Williams even employs simulated close-ups on several occasions, focusing his spotlight on individuals or objects, such as the father's photograph, much in the manner of the camera.

Once Tom's initial address to the audience establishes the entire play as memory, the action begins. The opening scene, that of Amanda and Laura in the dining room at the rear of the living room, commences as if it were what in motion pictures is called a long shot, for the two women are seen through a pair of scrim curtains which achieve the effect of both unreality and distance. First, the scrim representing the outside wall is raised, and Tom joins the women. Then Williams calls for the raising of the inner scrim, and the whole effect is like that of a camera dollying in for a closer shot. In the most widely published version, though not in the acting edition, Williams calls for subtitles and images to be projected "on a section of wall between the front-room and the dining-room," like those of the silent film. In such films a subtitle was often used at the beginning of a scene to tell the audience what to expect, sometimes to give the mood or thematic significance of the images to follow. When Laura and Amanda are revealed the subtitle is "OU SONT LES NEIGES." Williams says that the screen device was originally intended

> to give accent to certain values in each scene. Each scene contains a particular point (or several) which is structurally most important. In an episodic play, such as this, the basic structure or narrative line may be obscured from the audience; the effect may seem fragmentary rather than architectural. . . . The legend or image upon the screen will strengthen the effect of what is merely allusion in the writing and allow

the primary point to be made more simply and lightly than if the entire responsibility were on the spoken lines.

["Production Notes"]

In short, Williams is describing a structure remarkably close to that of the silent film—a series of short scenes, each making one or more points, with little or no transition between. The cumulative effect of these scenes, the relationships achieved by their juxtaposition and flow—these resemble what is in film called montage, originally associated with the work of Griffith and Eisenstein. Several critics have likened Williams' technique to that of the cinema and have used the term *montage* in their analyses of his structure.

In his comments on lighting and in his use of it in the play. Williams frequently suggests cinematic camera shots. He employs light, for example, for reaction close-ups. He says,

> Shafts of light are focused on selected areas or actors, sometimes in contradistinction to what is the apparent center. For instance, in the quarrel scene between Tom and Amanda, in which Laura has no active part, the clearest pool of light is on her figure. This is also true of the supper scene, when her silent figure on the sofa should remain the visual center.

In this way, the emphasis is not on the action itself but on a character's reaction to that action, the character highlighted as if in a close-up. And somewhat reminiscent of the diffused lighting Griffith used to employ to heighten the fragility of the young Lillian Gish or Mae Marsh, Williams calls for a special lighting of Laura: "The light upon Laura should be distinct from the others, having a peculiar pristine clarity such as the light used in early religious portraits of female saints or madonnas." He further says that throughout the production the light should suggest that in religious art, notably the work of El Greco, and that such lighting will make the use of the screen device more effective. The highlighting of the father's photograph has already been cited, and yet another outstanding example of the use of the cinematic close-up comes in Act I, Scene III, when Amanda tries to sell magazine subscriptions on the telephone. The light in the alley where Tom is fades out, *"and a head-spot falls on AMANDA, at phone in living-room."* The rest of the stage is dark, and Amanda stands alone in a circle of light revealing only her face. At the conclusion of her scene, *"Dining-room and living-room lights dim in. Reading lamp lights up at same time."* The close-up gives way to a longer shot of the whole room. Speaking generally of the lighting, Williams says: "A free, imaginative use of light can be of enormous value in giving a mobile, plastic quality to plays of a more or less static nature."

In the motion picture, both silent and sound, music has been a key element. For silent films whole scores were sometimes composed, for example, that played by the full orchestra which accompanied the initial road-showing of *The Big Parade* and *Ben Hur;* and for lesser films there was usually a music cue-sheet to guide the organist or pianist in his underlining of the mood or action of various

scenes. Throughout the Acting Edition of *The Glass Menagerie* there are many music cues, and Williams stresses the importance of music as an "extra-literary accent" in the production. He calls for a "single recurring tune, 'The Glass Menagerie,' " to supply "emotional emphasis to suitable passages," and the mood of memory is established at the outset by *"dance-hall music. . . Old popular music of, say, 1915-1920 period."* The music, in general, is dim, like music far away. "It seems . . . to continue almost interminably and it weaves in and out of your preoccupied consciousness." It should be both gay and sad, expressing the beauty and the fragility of glass. "Both of these ideas should be woven into the recurring tune, which dips in and out of the play as if it were carried on wind that changes." It serves, too, as a link between the narrator and his story and helps to join the episodic, cinematic scenes: "Between each episode it returns as reference to the emotion, nostalgia, which is the condition of the play. It is primarily Laura's music and therefore comes out most clearly when the play focuses upon her and the lovely fragility of glass which is her image." Thus, as in the film, music is employed for both mood and transition, evoking the atmosphere of memory and establishing relationships between the individual scenes, stressing the fluidity of the progress of an otherwise static plot. It is significant that the first dramatic version of the story Williams did was a motion picture script for Metro-Goldwyn-Mayer.

Other elements of the new non-verse poetic drama are also integral parts of the play. One of the most commented upon in the work of Williams is the symbol. In his preface to *Camino Real* Williams writes:

> I can't deny that I use a lot of those things called symbols, but being a self-defensive creature, I say that symbols are nothing but the natural speech of drama.

> We all have in our conscious and unconscious minds a great vocabulary of images, and I think all human communication is based on these images as are our dreams; and a symbol in a play has only one legitimate purpose, which is to say a thing more directly and simply and beautifully than it could be said in words.

Sometimes, it is true, Williams tends to overwhelm us with symbols, apparently for their own sake, but in *The Glass Menagerie* the symbols are employed effectively as organic elements in his poetic concept. A simple listing of them would include such obvious ones as the Paradise Dance Hall, the fire escape, the father's photograph, "Blue Roses," the idea of the Gentleman Caller, and many others. But the one most often discussed is the glass unicorn from Laura's little menagerie. Williams' use of it reveals him at his poetic best, for the unicorn not only stands for something else (or for several something elses) but is used dramatically to symbolize a change in relationships between two of the characters. Generally, the glass menagerie, including the unicorn, portrays Laura, her fragility, her delicacy, her beauty, her unworldliness, and at the same time the unicorn in particular symbolizes her life-maintaining illusion, her idealized concept of Jim, the high school hero. When Jim appears in person, and the audience sees him as a sadly commonplace and frustrated human being, Laura still retains her illusions about him. But when she entrusts the unicorn in his hands, she says, "Oh, be careful—if you breathe, it breaks!" And Jim says, "Unicorns, aren't they extinct in the modern world?" Then in the ecstasy of the dance he knocks the unicorn from the table and it breaks—loses its horn, the thing that made it different from the others. And Laura, foreshadowing her coming disillusionment with the discovery of Jim's engagement, says, "The horn was removed to make him feel less—freakish! . . . Now he will feel more at home with the other horses, the ones who don't have horns. . . ." Thus Jim, the unicorn, the unique hero, subsides into the normal, the ordinary, himself destroying the aura of distinctiveness which Laura gave him, destroying her illusion—and yet she seems to accept this catastrophe with resignation. The unicorn has vanished, yes; but she still has her glass menagerie and the escape offered by her ancient phonograph records. One illusion is gone, but her other means of escape, her other illusions, still offer protection from life's harsh realities. Here the use of the symbol is not static but dynamic, embodying and underlining a major alteration in relationships.

While Eliot clung to the idea that poetic drama should be in verse, his concept of the effect which dramatic verse should create is relevant to Williams' use of language. [In "Poetry and Drama"] Eliot says that audiences at a poetic, to him verse, drama

> expect poetry to be in rhythms which have lost touch with colloquial speech. What we have to do is to bring poetry into the world in which the audience lives and to which it returns when it leaves the theatre; not to transport the audience into some imaginary world totally unlike its own, an unreal world in which poetry is tolerated. What I should hope might be achieved, by a generation of dramatists having the benefit of our experience, is that the audience should find, at the moment of awareness that it is hearing poetry, that it is saying to itself: "*I* could talk poetry too!" Then we should not be transported into an artificial world; on the contrary, our own sordid, dreary daily world would be suddenly illuminated and transfigured.

It is just this, I believe, that Williams is able to accomplish and to do so without resorting to the dangerous artificialities of verse. He takes colloquial speech, often the colloquial speech of the South, and through a keen ear for its rhythms and patterns, its imagery and symbolism, lifts it to the level of poetry. It is *real* speech, but real speech intensified and heightened so that it not only evokes the pleasure of recognition but communicates the inexpressible, the very essence of character, emotion, and situation in a way traditionally associated with poetry.

The Glass Menagerie is filled with such passages, expressing a broad spectrum of the emotions—Tom's hilariously pathetic parodies of motion pictures and stage shows, Amanda's tragi-comic magazine sales talk, and many others. The oft-cited jonquil speech is perhaps the best known. It has the patterned construction of a poem, its rhythms capture the emotions of its speaker, it embodies the comic-pathetic ideal of the gracious past, and it relies on floral imagery to enhance its resonance as poetry. Awaiting the arrival of the Gentleman Caller, Amanda dresses herself in the old gown of her youthful triumphs in the lost Never-Never Land of the Delta:

> This is the dress in which I led the cotillion. Won the cakewalk twice at Sunset Hill, wore one spring to the Governor's ball in Jackson!
>
> See how I sashayed around the ballroom, Laura?
>
> [*She raises her skirt and does a mincing step around the room.*]
>
> I wore it on Sundays for my gentlemen callers! I had it on the day I met your father—
>
> I had malaria fever all that spring. The change of climate from East Tennessee to the Delta—weakened resistance—I had a little temperature all the time—not enough to be serious—just enough to make me restless and giddy!—Invitations poured in—parties all over the Delta!—"Stay in bed," said Mother, "you have fever!"—but I just wouldn't.—I took quinine but kept on going, going!—Evenings, dances!—Afternoons, long, long rides! Picnics—lovely!—So lovely, that country in May.—That was the spring I had the craze for jonquils. Jonquils became an absolute obsession. Mother said, "Honey, there's no more room for jonquils." And still I kept on bringing in more jonquils. Whenever, wherever I saw them, I'd say, "Stop! Stop! I see jonquils!" I made the young men help me gather the jonquils! It was a joke, Amanda and her jonquils! Finally there were no more vases to hold them, every available space was filled with jonquils! No vases to hold them? All right, I'll hold them myself! And then I—[*She stops in front of the picture.* MUSIC] met your father!
>
> Malaria fever and jonquils and then—this—boy. . . .

Tom's final speech is another "set-piece," with its rhythmic flow, its recurrent imagery, its colloquial tone heightened by both the freight of the emotion and the suggestion of a pattern.

It is not only in the somewhat extended speeches that the poetic qualities are evident; many of the dialogues are made up of brief exchanges with the repetitive rhythmic patterns, almost like refrains, of verse but avoiding the rigidity of metre. Tom's teasing announcement of the visit of the Gentleman Caller is an example:

> TOM. We are going to have one.
>
> AMANDA. *What?*
>
> TOM. A gentleman caller!
>
> AMANDA. You mean you have asked some nice young man to come over? . . .
>
> TOM. I've asked him to dinner.
>
> AMANDA. You really did?
>
> TOM. I did.

AMANDA. And did he—accept?

TOM. He did!

AMANDA. He did?

TOM. He did.

AMANDA. Well, isn't that lovely!

TOM. I thought you would be pleased.

AMANDA. It's definite, then?

TOM. Oh, very definite.

AMANDA. How soon?

TOM. Pretty soon.

AMANDA. How soon?

TOM. Very, very soon.

Here is approximately the give-and-take of traditional stichomythia retaining the quality of colloquialism.

Basic to the poetic qualities of Williams' language is his Southern origin, as several critics have noted. [In *Essays in the Modern Drama*] Marion Migid speaks of his long line, which achieves its most striking effects through a Steinian repetitiveness, through the use of unexpected archaisms, and the insertion of unexpected "literary" words and ironically elegant turns of phrase. It is a stylized rendering of Southern diction, which is more self-conscious, more evasive, but also more imaginative than Northern speech.

Miss Jackson repeats this idea, stressing the fact that the natural symbolism of Southern diction has produced "a highly developed iconography." "This Southern aesthetic," she says, "has provided for the drama of Williams a kind of basic linguistic structure comparable to that which appeared in elementary stages of Greek tragedy" [*The Broken World of Tennessee Williams*].

Modern studies of poetry have frequently developed the concept of the poet as a user of myth and a creator of new myths. Certainly in other plays, notably *Orpheus Descending, Suddenly Last Summer,* and *Camino Real,* underlying the action and characters are classical myths and pagan rituals. In his later plays especially, as Miss Jackson points out, Williams "has put together a kind of modern myth, a symbolic representation of the life of man in our time." She sees this myth as "synthetic," "composed, after the manner of cinematic montage, from the fragments of many ethical, philosophical, social, poetic, intellectual, and religious perspectives . . . the image of modern man caught between opposing logics—man in search of a means of reconciliation." In *The Glass Menagerie* Williams reaches out tentatively for the materials of this myth. Basic to it is the idea of man's alienation from the world around him, man still clinging to old values in an environment where they are no longer relevant. Certain archetypal Williams figures begin to take shape in the play: the poet-wanderer, later to acquire sexual elements from D. H. Lawrence; the fragile girl threatened with destruction and either escaping into a dream world of the past or being corrupted by the jungle world of the present;

the same girl in maturity, strong and defensive in her struggle against the present but finding sustenance through cherishing the ideal of lost grace and beauty. It is the myth of the alienated, the lost, seeking some sort of tenable posture in the present chaos. It is the source of the poet's vision. Williams himself says, "Personal lyricism is the outcry of prisoner to prisoner from the cell in solitary where each is confined for the duration of his life" ["**Person-To-Person**"].

One of the constants of lyric poetry, and of much other poetry as well, is its immediacy, its capturing of the moment, the intense moment of experience and insight. Man is in constant battle with Time the Destroyer, and poetry is one of his oldest means of achieving victory. In his use of time and in his attitude toward it, Williams is typically the poet. He says, "Snatching the eternal out of the desperately fleeting is the great magic of human existence" [*Perspectives on Drama*]. In most of his plays his characters fight against time, its attrition and its ravages, and time becomes a major symbol of the adversary, malignant and malevolent. Amanda and Laura seek to turn time back, to recapture a past which they have perhaps idealized out of all semblance to reality but the very search for which gives meaning to their lives. On the other hand, Tom looks forward, toward a future time as an escape, but when that future becomes his present, he finds himself a prisoner of the past.

In *The Glass Menagerie* time is used another way, an equally poetic one. Tom stands with us in the immediate present. At the start he wears a merchant seaman's outfit indicative of escape from the physical past, of his having left his mother and sister behind. But through his consciousness we are carried back in time to his life in the drab apartment before his escape, and we retrace with him events leading to his decision to leave. Within this train of memory there are two types of time, the generalized and the specific, and through the use of these two we are given a deeper insight into the lives and relationships of the Wingfields. The first scene in the apartment, the dinner scene, is an example of generalized time. It is not any one particular dinner but a kind of abstraction of all the dinners shared by the trio in their life of entrapment. Amanda's admonitory speeches are ones often repeated, her stories of the seventeen gentlemen callers are oft-told tales—and Tom's irritated responses are those he makes each and every time the stories are retold. Amanda's telephone call to Ida Scott, with its pathetic attempts at salesmanship, is not one specific call, but, as the isolating spotlight tells us, it is an action out of time and place, the essence of a repeated action rather than a unique event. There are also unique moments in the parade of Tom's memory, highlights with a significance of their own—the imaginative reconstruction of the visit of Jim (for Tom was not present during some of the dialogue with Laura), for example. Through this multiple use of time Williams embodies both the concrete, the particular, and the general, the typical, his images often achieving the force of what Eliot has called the objective correlative of abstract truth.

From one point of view, as in *Death of a Salesman, The Glass Menagerie* actually transfixes and holds up for insight a single, brief moment of Tom's consciousness, a moment in the present in which, like Proust, he recapitulates the past, a past inextricably intertwined with the present and the future, freezes this moment—the intense moment of poetic insight, of lyric intuition. And this is often what a poem does. Williams is himself well aware of what he is doing. He says:

> It is this continual rush of time, so violent that it appears to be screaming, that deprives our actual lives of so much dignity and meaning, and it is, perhaps more than anything else, the *arrest of time* which has taken place in a completed work of art that gives certain plays their feeling of depth and significance. . . . If the world of the play did not offer us this occasion to view its characters under that special condition of a *world without time,* then, indeed, the characters and occurrences of drama would become equally pointless, equally trivial, as corresponding meetings and happenings in life.

In such a timeless world, like that of Greek tragedy, man becomes aware of his potential nobility:

> The audience can sit back in a comforting dusk to watch a world which is flooded with light and in which emotion and action have a dimension and dignity that they would likewise have in real existence, if only the shattering intrusion of time could be locked out.
>
> [*Perspectives on Drama*]

By arresting time, by embodying in a single moment the past, the present, and the future, by making this frozen moment one of tremendous intensity permitting an insight otherwise impossible, Williams has made *The Glass Menagerie* a lyric drama.

In conclusion, by utilizing many of the elements of poetry and the non-verbal facilities of the theatre—controlling metaphors and symbols, "transformation," lighting, music, movement, patterned colloquial speech, mythic elements, and the arresting of time to permit insight into the particular and the general—and by organically shaping these through a poet's vision—Williams in *The Glass Menagerie* exemplifies twentieth-century American poetic drama, free of the anachronism of verse, a poetic drama peculiarly adapted to the complexities of the present. Linking Williams with Arthur Miller, Kenneth Tynan [in *The Modern American Theater*] says that both men, "committed to prose drama . . . have uncovered riches which make the English 'poetic revival' [of Eliot and Fry, for example] seem hollow, retrogressive, and—to use Cyril Connolly's coinage—praeterist." (pp. 3-15)

> *Frank Durham, "Tennessee Williams, Theatre Poet in Prose," in* South Atlantic Bulletin, *Vol. XXXVI, No. 2, March, 1971, pp. 3-16.*

Gerald Berkowitz

The Glass Menagerie is, as Tennessee Williams tells us, a "memory play," a play about the persistence and the haunting reality of memory. It is also, most readers would agree, a play about failures and outcasts, and the discovery

that they are not as freakish and absurd as we may first have thought. Indeed, this is the underlying message of all of Williams' work: that people who are very different from you and me are not really all that different from you and me, that the common bond of humanity we all share is stronger and more significant than the surface dissimilarities. What has, I believe, never been pointed out before is that Williams repeatedly uses a simple but subtle theatrical device—a trick of perspective, in a sense—to make this point. Observing this device at work in *The Glass Menagerie,* where it is most openly employed, will help to illuminate not only this play but also, by extension, such very different works as *A Streetcar Named Desire, The Night of the Iguana* and *The Milk Train Doesn't Stop Here Anymore.* And, as a bonus, it will offer a new understanding of *The Glass Menagerie*'s other theme, the persistence of memory.

The device I am referring to is that of giving each play a definite *locus,* a specific physical setting that is defined, theatrically or symbolically, as being separate and apart from the rest of the universe. Such a spot—an island in the Mediterranean, a mountaintop in Mexico, or the end of the trolley line in New Orleans—becomes the objective correlative for the suggestion that we are in another world, a separate reality with its own characteristics, standards and even physical laws. Finding ourselves in this new terrain, we are forced to drop our preconceived value judgments, particularly our notions of "normal" or "acceptable" behavior. The characters we encounter—at least those who seem to belong in this "other world"—are seen in their native habitat, and inevitably come to seem less freakish than they might otherwise have. Conversely, the more "normal" characters become the outsiders, the invaders and the misfits.

In short, the effect of this geographical symbolism is to forestall and counteract our instinctive prejudice against those who are "different." We may even go so far as to identify with the natives and reject the invaders, wishing that Blanche had not disrupted the Kowalski home, for example, or resenting Mae's intrusions into Brick and Maggie's bedroom. At the very least, though, we will be looking at all the characters in a new way and reevaluating our standards and judgments from a new perspective. And in *The Glass Menagerie* we will also gain a new understanding of Tom's dilemma as we realize that his haunting memories are the result of his leaving his native habitat to wander in the foreign land that is our everyday world.

The *locus* of *The Glass Menagerie* is the Wingfield apartment, defined by the play's language and events as someplace separate from the everyday real world. Approached or left only through a fire escape—"a structure whose name is a touch of accidental poetic truth"—and a back alley, it is literally on the far side of paradise—the Paradise Dance Hall. (One thinks in this context of *A Streetcar Named Desire,* set in the section of New Orleans called the Elysian Fields, which is a streetcar ride past the cemetery.) The ties between the Wingfield apartment and the outside world are minimal and tenuous: the electric power is cut off in the middle of the play, Amanda's telephone customers hang up on her, and Tom loses his key down the same holes in the fire escape that trip up Laura when she goes out. Even Tom's frame sequences emphasize the separateness of the apartment, in time as well as space; Tom stresses that the "distance" from here to there is greater than that from the earth to the moon. Moreover, Jim O'Connor, "the most realistic character in the play," becomes, as a result of this device, "an emissary from a world of reality that we were somehow set apart from."

The first effect of this device, as I suggested, is that we are introduced to the Wingfields in their native habitat; as we discover each aberration or peculiarity in their characters, we also discover that it is benign or even appropriate to their setting. Laura's pathological shyness does not stifle her at home; she is even able to overcome her fear of Jim when talking of her glass animals. Her lameness, which so embarrassed her in high school, becomes irrelevant when she is sitting in the apartment; Tom points out that "we don't even notice she's crippled any more." And even Jim can see that the girl he barely noticed in school takes on a special beauty in her proper setting.

Similarly, Amanda's demands on Tom become more than mere nagging when seen as expressions of an earnest sense of mutual responsibility—"In these trying times we live in, all that we have to cling to is—each other." Her attempts to manipulate Laura's life are not just fussy interference but expressions of love and concern:

> What is there left but dependency all our lives? I know so well what becomes of unmarried women who aren't prepared to occupy a position. I've seen such pitiful cases in the South— barely tolerated spinsters living upon the grudging patronage of sister's husband or brother's wife!—stuck away in some little mousetrap of a room—encouraged by one in-law to visit another—little birdlike women without any nest— eating the crust of humility all their life!
>
> Is that the future that we've mapped out for ourselves? I swear it's the only alternative I can think of! [*She pauses.*] It isn't a very pleasant alternative, is it? [*She pauses again.*] Of course— some girls do marry.

Even her attempts to preserve the myth of the old South lose their air of foolishness after a while, as Williams gives them an eloquence that cannot be resisted:

> This the dress in which I led the cotillion. Won the cakewalk twice at Sunset Hill, wore one Spring to the Governor's Ball in Jackson! See how I sashayed around the ballroom, Laura? [*She raises her skirt and does a mincing step around the room.*] I wore it on Sundays for my gentlemen callers! I had it on the day I met your father . . . I had malaria fever all that Spring. The change of climate from East Tennessee to the Delta—weakened resistance. I had a little temperature all the time—not enough to be serious—just enough to make me restless and giddy! Invitations poured in—parties all over the Delta! "Stay in bed," said Mother, "you have a fever!"—but I just wouldn't. I took quinine but kept on going, going! Evenings, dances! Afternoons, long, long, rides! Picnics—lovely! So lovely, that country in May—all lacy with dog-

wood, literally flooded with jonquils! That was the spring I had the craze for jonquils. Jonquils became an absolute obsession. Mother said, "Honey, there's no more room for jonquils." And still I kept on bringing in more jonquils. Whenever, wherever I saw them, I'd say, Stop! Stop! I see jonquils!" I made the young men help me gather the jonquils! It was a joke, Amanda and her jonquils. Finally there were no more vases to hold them, every available space was filled with jonquils. No vases to hold them? All right, I'll hold them myself! And then I—[*She stops in front of the picture. Music plays.*] met your father! Malaria fever and jonquils and then—this—boy . . .

It is the outsider who is the misfit in this world, as much a freak and failure as Amanda and Laura might seem in our world. It is Jim who is clumsy and destructive; it is he who breaks the glass unicorn. His dreams and values, as practical and "realistic" as they may be, sound shallower and more comical than Amanda's in this foreign terrain:

> My interest happens to lie in electro-dynamics. I'm taking a course in radio engineering at night school, Laura, on top of a fairly responsible job at the warehouse. I'm taking that course and studying public speaking . . . Because I believe in the future of television! [*turning his back to her.*] I wish to be ready to go up right along with it. Therefore I'm planning to get in on the ground floor. In fact I've already made the right connections and all that remains is for the industry itself to get under way! Full steam—[*His eyes are starry.*] Knowledge—Zzzzzp! *Money*— Zzzzzp!—*Power!* That's the cycle democracy is built on!

If Laura's symbol is the glass menagerie, Jim's is the pack of chewing gum, and his disquisitions on the art and etiquette of its use sound far more odd and foolish than Laura's fantasies about the animals' feelings. And it is Jim, ultimately, who is the play's foremost failure; he is, after all, not really the Gentleman Caller he is expected to be.

The point is not that Amanda is wise and Jim is foolish; it is that Amanda is not necessarily any more foolish than Jim just because she doesn't function well in our world— reversing their respective positions has proven that. Amanda is not more unrealistic and escapist than the habitues of the Paradise Dance Hall or the readers of *The Home-Makers Companion,* and her memories of the old South play the same role in her life as Jim's recollections of high school triumphs do in his. Laura's life with her glass animals is no more pathetic than the behavior of the millions who let movie stars have all their adventures for them, and Tom's fantasies of becoming a poet are no more absurd than Jim's talk of "planning to get in on the ground floor" in television.

The Wingfields, we learn, are driven by the same needs— for security, loyalty, a set of moral values, a sense of accomplishment (past, future or fantasized), and occasional escape—that we recognize in our "real" world. If the Wingfields are different from you and me it is not because they are inferior, but because they are foreign—because some basic metaphysical characteristics of their world make them unable to function in ours.

One source of the difference is the isolation itself. Just as the Wingfield apartment is all but cut off from the rest of the world, the mental and spiritual universe that Laura and Amanda inhabit is almost completely self-contained. Laura is almost literally unable to set foot in the outside world; after the fiasco of the business school she spends her days in the protection of a botanical hothouse, and when sent on an errand she trips and falls right outside the apartment door. Neither of them has any sense of Guernica or Berchtesgaden, or even of the "long distance" that lured Mr. Wingfield away. And neither can really deal directly with the "emissary from another world;" Amanda confuses him in her mind with the gentleman callers of her memories, and Laura becomes physically ill with panic.

But a more basic limitation of their world is that it is timeless. Within the walls of this apartment time does not pass, and therefore the things that the passage of time brings—change, growth and development—can not take place. Amanda is doomed to live in the past, and to relate to the present only in terms of the past. She not only creates the myth of the Gentleman Caller around Jim, but turns him into *her* Gentleman Caller, wearing her old dress and lapsing into her old flirtations. What future she can see is measured out in the short, abrupt bursts of a magazine serial, or merely a reflection of the past: Laura becoming a Southern old maid, or Tom following his father's example. Mr. Wingfield's picture hangs on the wall as if to deny the fact of his absence and, as Tom notes, his spirit does remain behind as the fifth character in the play. Laura also tends to live in the past, but more importantly she lives among her sterile, unchanging glass animals, where unicorns, "extinct in the modern world," still remain, and where any change (such as a broken horn) requires banishment. Laura's shyness represents an emotional and social immaturity, just as her small bust suggests a lack of physical development. It is certainly significant that Laura did not "take in the Century of Progress," because for her there is no such thing as progress. And the eternal changelessness of her world is demonstrated by the persistence of Tom's memory and by the fact of the play itself.

Tom is also a native of the Wingfield world. Though, of necessity, he functions in the outside world somewhat more effectively than his mother and sister, he is clearly not at home out there. He hates his job, neglects his duties to write poetry on the shoeboxes, fails to pay the electric bill, and retreats into the fantasies of movies and stage magicians. And, as the play itself demonstrates, he is as haunted and controlled by memories and the past as is Amanda.

And here, I suggest, is the key to Tom's tragedy, for he also has inclinations that distinguish him from his mother and sister. As a reader of Lawrence, as a believer in instinct, as an aspiring poet and adventurer, he feels the need to grow, change and create. For him the Wingfield apartment becomes a magician's coffin from which he must escape, even though it *is* his natural home. He tells us he had to move forward in time to get away, but the converse is also true: to be able to move forward, he must move away.

And so he is forced to leave home and, in the symbolic guise of a merchant seaman, wander in the foreign land that is the outside world. He tries to aclimatize himself to this new environment, and to convince himself that the world of Guernica, the Depression and the coming war is the only reality, but the persistence of his memory proves him wrong. Tom never fully realizes the significance of the ghosts that haunt him, but we must: they are flashes of his real world imposing themselves on a consciousness that, having committed itself to the life of an alien, must try to deny the validity of the haven it left behind:

> I would have stopped, but I was pursued by something. It always came upon me unawares, taking me altogether by surprise. Perhaps it was a familiar bit of music. Perhaps it was only a piece of transparent glass. Perhaps I am walking along a street at night, in some strange city, before I have found companions. I pass the lighted window of a shop where perfume is sold. The window is filled with pieces of colored glass, tiny transparent bottles in delicate colors, like bits of a shattered rainbow. Then all at once my sister touches my shoulder. I turn around and look into her eyes. Oh, Laura, Laura, I tried to leave you behind me, but I am more faithful than I intended to be! I reach for a cigarette, I cross the street, I run into the movies or a bar, I buy a drink, I speak to the nearest stranger—anything that can blow your candles out! . . . For nowadays the world is lit by lightning! Blow out your candles, Laura—and so goodbye . . .

I have perhaps schematized the effects of this division of realities too mechanically, but the theatrical and literary device is there in the play, and it offers a key to Williams' method and ideas. By defining these characters as aliens, he has paradoxically made them more accessible to our understanding. Since we are drawn into their world to view life from their perspective we are free to identify and sympathize rather than judge. If Amanda and Laura cannot function in our "real" world, we must celebrate their fortune in having a congenial island in which they can survive. If Tom is in some way superior for moving out and

---

Foster Hirsch on *The Glass Menagerie*:

A warm play, deeply personal and yet shrewdly shaped for popular appeal, *The Glass Menagerie* is a detour for Williams, a calm moment between the flamboyant melodrama of *Battle of Angels* and the highstrung combats of *Summer and Smoke* and *A Streetcar Named Desire*. *The Glass Menagerie* is a typical autobiographical play; yet it is clearly the work of a unique sensibility. All of the usual elements of a Williams play are here, but in no other drama has Williams written in the mellowed, autumnal tone of this American perennial.

Foster Hirsch in his A Portrait of the Artist: The Plays of Tennessee Williams, *1979.*

facing the challenge of the outside world, we must understand the terrible price he pays. A similar understanding is the goal of the other plays in which Williams uses this device. Brick and Maggie Pollit, Stanley and Stella Kowalski, and the Reverend T. Lawrence Shannon all share with the Wingfields the fate of being failures and grotesques who find the hospitable environment that is their natural home. And certainly Tennessee Williams, the poet of the lonely and afraid, cannot bring himself to criticize such rare and wonderful fortune. (pp. 150-53)

> *Gerald Berkowitz, "The 'Other World' of 'The Glass Menagerie',"* in Players: The Magazine of American Theatre, *Vol. 48, No. 4, April-May, 1973, pp. 150-53.*

Thomas L. King

Tennessee Williams' *The Glass Menagerie,* though it has achieved a firmly established position in the canon of American plays, is often distorted, if not misunderstood, by readers, directors, and audiences. The distortion results from an overemphasis on the scenes involving Laura and Amanda and their plight, so that the play becomes a sentimental tract on the trapped misery of two women in St. Louis. This leads to the neglect of Tom's soliloquies—speeches that can be ignored or discounted only at great peril, since they occupy such a prominent position in the play. When not largely ignored, they are in danger of being treated as nostalgic yearnings for a former time. But they are not sentimental excursions into the past, paralleling Amanda's, for while they contain sentiment and nostalgia, they also evince a pervasive humor and irony and, indeed, form and contain the entire play.

Judging from the reviews, the distortion of the play began with the original production. The reviews deal almost wholly with Laurette Taylor's performance, making Amanda seem to be the principal character, and nearly ignore the soliloquies. Even the passage of time has failed to correct this tendency, for many later writers also force the play out of focus by pushing Amanda forward. (p. 207)

The play, however, is not Amanda's. Amanda is a striking and a powerful character, but the play is Tom's. Tom opens the play and he closes it; he also opens the second act and two further scenes in the first act—his is the first word and the last. Indeed, Amanda, Laura, and the Gentleman Caller do not appear in the play at all as separate characters. In a sense, as Stark Young noted, Tom is the only character in the play, for we see not the characters but Tom's memory of them—Amanda and the rest are merely aspects of Tom's consciousness. Tom's St. Louis is not an objective one, but a solipsist's created by Tom, the artist-magician, and containing Amanda, Laura, and the Gentleman Caller. Tom is the Prospero of *The Glass Menagerie,* and its world is the world of Tom's mind even more than *Death of a Salesman*'s is the world of Willy Loman's mind. The play is warped and distorted when any influence gives Amanda, Laura, or the glass menagerie any undue prominence. If Amanda looms large, she looms large in Tom's mind, not in her own right; though

of course the image that finally dominates Tom's mind is that of Laura and the glass menagerie.

The full meaning of the scenes between the soliloquies lies not in themselves alone but also in the commentary provided by Tom standing outside the scenes and speaking with reasonable candor to the audience and reader. Moreover, the comment that the soliloquies make is not a sentimental one; that is, they are not only expressions of a wistful nostalgia for the lost, doomed world of Amanda, Laura, and the glass menagerie but also contain a good deal of irony and humor which work in the opposite direction. They reveal Tom as an artist figure whose utterances show how the artist creates, using the raw material of his own life.

The nature of the narrator's role as artist figure is indicated by Tom's behavior in the scenes. He protects himself from the savage in-fighting in the apartment by maintaining distance between himself and the pain of the situation through irony. For example, when he gets into a fight with Amanda in the third scene and launches into a long, ironic, and even humorous tirade—about how he "runs a string of cat-houses in the valley," how they call him "Killer, Killer Wingfield," how, on some occasions, he wears green whiskers—the irony is heavy and propels him out of the painful situation, out of the argument, and ultimately to the movies. Significantly, this scene begins with Tom writing, Tom the artist, and in it we see how the artistic sensibility turns a painful situation into "art" by using distance. In his verbal assault on his mother, Tom "creates" Killer Wingfield. Tom's ability to distance his experience, to protect himself from the debilitating atmosphere of the apartment makes him different from Laura. Laura does not have this refuge; she is unable to detach herself completely from the situation and she is destroyed by it. She does, of course, retreat to the glass menagerie and the Victrola, but this is the behavior of a severely disturbed woman. Her method of dealing with the situation, retreating into a "world of her own," does indeed, as Tom says, make her seem "just a little bit peculiar." (scene V). Tom's method is more acceptable; he makes art.

The kind of contrast that exists between Laura and Tom is illustrated by a comment Jung made about James Joyce and his daughter, Lucia. Lucia had had a history of severe mental problems and, in 1934, she was put under the care of Jung. Discussing his patient and her famous father in a letter, Jung wrote: "His [Joyce's] 'psychological' style is definitely schizophrenic, with the difference, however, that the ordinary patient cannot help himself talking and thinking in such a way, while Joyce willed it and moreover developed it with all his creative forces, which incidentally explains why he himself did not go over the border. But his daughter did, because she was not a genius like her father, but merely a victim of her disease." On another occasion Jung said that the father and daughter "were like two people going to the bottom of a river, one falling and the other diving" [*James Joyce*]. We see here a psychoanalyst's perception of the problem of artist and non-artist which is much the same as the problem of Tom and Laura. Tennessee Williams' real-life sister, Rose, has also suffered from mental disturbances.

That an author's early play should contain a highly auto-biographical character who shows the mechanism by which art is made out of the material of one's life is not particularly surprising, but it is a generally unnoted feature of *The Glass Menagerie* which is inextricably linked to the irony of the soliloquies. For the artist, irony is a device that protects him from the pain of his experience so that he may use it objectively in his art. . . . The artist needs his distance from the material of his art so that he may handle it objectively, and the soliloquies of *The Glass Menagerie,* in part, reveal the nature of that distance and how it is maintained.

Generally, each soliloquy oscillates between a sentimental memory of the past, which draws the narrator into it, and a wry irony which keeps him from being fully engulfed and controlled by it. This tension is found in all the soliloquies, though it is not always handled in the same way: sometimes the fond memory is predominant and sometimes the irony, but both are always present. At times, Tom seems almost deliberately to court disaster by creating for himself and the audience a memory so lovely and poignant that the pain of giving it up to return to reality is too much to bear, but return he does with mockery and a kind of wit that interrupts the witchery of memory just short of a withdrawn madness surrounded by soft music and a mind filled with "delicate rainbow colors." In short, Tom toys with the same madness in which his sister Laura is trapped but saves himself with irony.

The opening soliloquy begins on an ironic note. Tom says:

> Yes, I have tricks in my pocket, I have things up my sleeve. But I am the opposite of a stage magician. He gives you illusion that has the appearance of truth. I give you truth in the pleasant disguise of illusion.

These opening lines have a cocky tone—"I will trick you," Tom says, "I'll tell you that I'm going to trick you and I'll still do it even after you've been warned. Besides," he says with perhaps just a touch of derision, "you prefer trickery to the naked truth." Tom begins in the attitude of Whitman on the facing page of the first edition of *Leaves of Grass*—head thrown back, mocking, insolent, but not cruel.

Tom continues in the same mode by saying

> To begin with, I turn back time. I reverse it to that quaint period, the thirties, when the huge middle class of America was matriculating in a school for the blind. Their eyes had failed them, or they had failed their eyes, and so they were having their fingers pressed forcibly down on the fiery Braille alphabet of a dissolving economy.
>
> In Spain there was revolution. Here there was only shouting and confusion.
>
> In Spain there was Guernica. Here there were disturbances of labor, sometimes pretty violent, in otherwise peaceful cities such as Chicago, Cleveland, Saint Louis . . .

To this point in the speech, Tom's principal mode is ironic, but as he moves on, though the irony remains, a stronger element of sentiment, of poignant memory creeps in. He begins to speak of memory and to enumerate the characters in the play:

> The play is memory.
>
> Being a memory play, it is dimly lighted, it is sentimental, it is not realistic.
>
> In memory everything seems to happen to music. That explains the fiddle in the wings.
>
> I am the narrator of the play, and also a character in it.
>
> The other characters are my mother, Amanda, my sister, Laura, and a gentleman caller who appears in the final scenes.

The only break in this poignant mood is the phrase "that explains the fiddle in the wings"—an unfortunate phrase, but demonstrative of the tension, of the rhythmic swing back and forth between sweet nostalgia and bitter irony. The play may be sentimental rather than realistic, but "that explains the fiddle in the wings" breaks the sentiment.

Tom continues by saying:

> He [the gentleman caller] is the most realistic character in the play, being an emissary from a world of reality that we were somehow set apart from.
>
> But since I have a poet's weakness for symbols, I am using this character also as a symbol; he is the long delayed but always expected something that we live for.

With these words, the narrator drops his ironic detachment and enters into the mood of memory. The words can hardly be delivered but as in a reverie, in a deep reflection, the voice coming out of a man who, after frankly acknowledging the audience at the beginning of the speech, has now sunk far into himself so that the audience seems to overhear his thoughts. He then shakes off the mood with a return to irony and makes a kind of joke:

> There is a fifth character in the play who doesn't appear except in this larger-than-life-size photograph over the mantel.
>
> This is our father who left us a long time ago.
>
> He was a telephone man who fell in love with long distances; he gave up his job with the telephone company and skipped the light fantastic out of town . . .
>
> The last we heard of him was a picture post-card from Mazatlan, on the Pacific coast of Mexico, containing a message of two words—
>
> "Hello—Good-bye!" and no address.

There is humor here—not sentiment and not sentimental humor. Tom speaks fondly of his mother and sister and remembers their lost lives and the gentleman caller who symbolizes the loss and the failure, and we can imagine that his gaze becomes distant and withdrawn as he allows himself to be carried away into the memory, but then he remembers another member of the family, the father, and that hurts too much to give in to so he shakes off the reverie and returns once more to irony. The irony is no longer the playful irony of the interlocutor before the audience, but an irony which protects him from the painful memories of the past, that allows him to rise superior to the "father who left us" and to get a laugh from the audience, for the audience should and will chuckle at the end of the opening soliloquy as the light fades on Tom and he leaves his seaman's post. The chuckle may be good-natured, but the humor is not; it is gallows humor in which the condemned man asserts himself before a crowd in relation to which he is horribly disadvantaged by making it laugh. Tom is in control of his memory and already he is beginning to endeavor to work his trick by manipulating the audience's mood.

The opening soliloquy, then, reveals a number of elements that are to be important in the play: it establishes a tension between sentimental nostalgia and detached irony as well as a narrator who is to function as stage magician. The narrator disavows this, but we cannot take him at his word. He says that he is the opposite of a stage magician, but only because his truth looks like illusion rather than the other way round; he is still the magician who creates the play. He says that the play is sentimental rather than realistic, but that is a half truth, for while it contains large doses of sentiment, for the narrator at least, irony sometimes quenches the sentiment. Indeed, Irving Babbit's phrase describing romantic irony is appropriate here: "Hot baths of sentiment . . . followed by cold douches of irony" [*Rousseau and Romanticism*].

The dominant note of the second soliloquy, at the beginning of the third scene, is irony. In the first soliloquy, Tom has provided the audience with a poignant picture of Laura and Amanda cut off from the world "that we were somehow set apart from." In the second soliloquy, irony almost completely obliterates the poignance as we see Amanda at work trying to find a gentleman caller for Laura, a gentleman caller who is "like some archetype of the universal unconscious." Tom continues the irony as he says:

> She began to take logical steps in the planned direction.
>
> Late that winter and in the early spring—realizing that extra money would be needed to properly feather the nest and plume the bird—she conducted a vigorous campaign on the telephone, roping in subscribers to one of those magazines for matrons called *The Homemaker's Companion,* the type of journal that features the serialized sublimations of ladies of letters who think in terms of delicate cup-like breasts, slim, tapering waists, rich, creamy thighs, eyes like wood-smoke in autumn, fingers that soothe and caress like strains of music, bodies as powerful as Etruscan sculpture.

The mocking humor in this is revealed by the derisive alliteration, the hyperbolic language, and in the humorous, parodying evocation of all the clichés of these stories. The speech makes fun of the literary equivalents of Amanda's memories of gentleman callers in the mythical South. This is not to say that Amanda is savagely attacked with a kind

of Swiftian irony; nevertheless, the attack is there, though the irony is balanced somewhat by one irruption of the nostalgic, pitying mode of discourse when Tom says that even when the gentleman caller was not mentioned "his presence hung in mother's preoccupied look and in my sister's frightened, apologetic manner." The irony is also humorous and gets a laugh from audiences if it is performed as irony—especially at the end of the speech where, just as the first soliloquy breaks into a mild humor at the end, Tom humorously parodies the magazine stories.

The first soliloquy strikes a balance between irony and nostalgia, the second is primarily ironic, and the third is primarily nostalgic. The third soliloquy begins with the Paradise Dance Hall:

> Across the alley from us was the Paradise Dance Hall. On evenings in spring the windows and doors were open and the music came outdoors. Sometimes the lights were turned out except for a large glass sphere that hung from the ceiling. It would turn slowly about and filter the dusk with delicate rainbow colors.

Rainbow colors, in fact, fill much of the play: in the scene with Laura, late at night, after Tom has returned from the movies, the magic scarf he produces is rainbow-colored—this is one of the few scenes in which Tom and Laura relate tenderly to one another; the Paradise Dance Hall filters the dusk with "delicate rainbow colors"; sex hangs "in the gloom like a chandelier" and floods the world with "brief, deceptive rainbows"; and, in the last soliloquy, Tom says that he sometimes passes the window of a shop where perfume is sold—"The window is filled with pieces of colored glass, tiny transparent bottles in delicate colors like bits of a shattered rainbow." In the third soliloquy, the Paradise Dance Hall provides the rainbow colors that fill and transform the alley. The irony breaks through in only a few places: when Tom disrupts the mood of magic by pointing out that you could see the young couples "kissing behind ash-pits and telephone poles," and, as usual, at the end when he says, "All the world was waiting for bombardments."

All three soliloquies in the first act work together to help define its movement. The first soliloquy is fairly well balanced between nostalgia and irony. The detached irony of the second soliloquy foreshadows Tom's struggle to detach himself from his situation; after it Tom fights with his mother and leaves to go to the movies. The third soliloquy asserts the nostalgic mode, and the scene following this, in which Tom and Amanda talk of the gentleman caller, is a tender, loving one. We see a playful, warm scene between Tom and his mother out on the fire escape which shows how, in spite of their quarrels, Tom and Amanda could also have their warm, understanding moments. By the end of the first act, the audience should be taken in by Tom's trick, drawn into the rainbow-colored world and the pleasant memory of past times. The pain of Tom's memory has been repudiated in the second soliloquy with irony, and, after the fight, when Tom runs off to the movies, with the delicate nostalgia of the third soliloquy, flooding the stage with rainbow light. The trick is working—we begin to think that Tom and his mother will get along after all, that a gentleman caller will come to rescue them, but it remains a trick wrought by the magic of the rainbow which is broken, whose colors are "deceptive."

The second act begins with a soliloquy which, like the first, strikes something of a balance between irony and nostalgia. Tom begins with a description of Jim in language that indicates that he has a genuine kind of amazed liking for this Irish boy. Only gentle irony is present in the following words:

> In high school, Jim was a hero. He had tremendous Irish good nature and vitality with the scrubbed and polished look of white chinaware. He seemed to move in a continual spotlight. He was a star in basketball, captain of the debating club, president of the senior class and the glee club, and he sang the male lead in the annual light operas. He was always running or bounding, never just walking. He seemed always at the point of defeating the law of gravity.

Jim is made light of by the phrases "white chinaware" and "defeating the law of gravity," but the mockery is mild, though it becomes stronger as the speech continues:

> He was shooting with such velocity through his adolescence that you would logically expect him to arrive at nothing short of the White House by the time he was thirty. But Jim apparently ran into more interference after his graduation from Soldan. His speed had definitely slowed. Six years after he left high school he was holding a job that wasn't much better than mine.

The irony begins to break through even more strongly after these words, for Tom was "valuable to him as someone who could remember his former glory, who had seen him win basketball games and the silver cup in debating." And the irony even cuts against Tom: "He knew of my secret practice of retiring to a cabinet of the wash-room to work on poems whenever business was slack in the warehouse." A degree of bitterness begins to emerge when Tom says that, with the example of Jim, the other boys began to smile at him too, "as people smile at some oddly fashioned dog that trots across their path at some distance." The bitterness is quickly moderated, however, when Tom sympathetically remembers his sister in high school: "In high school Laura was as unobtrusive as Jim was astonishing." Finally, as always in these soliloquies, the speech ends with an ironic barb that can often draw a laugh from the audience. Tom says that when he asked Jim home to dinner "he grinned and said, 'You know, Shakespeare, I never thought of you as having folks!' He was about to discover that I did. . . ."

The culmination of all the soliloquies and of the tension between irony and nostalgia that is carefully developed in them, is in the final one. Tom's last speech contains just two touches of ironic detachment, but these are critical and are the foci on which this speech and, indeed, for Tom, the whole play turns. The speech begins with a touch of ironic humor. In the preceding scene, Amanda has told Tom to go to the moon. He begins his final speech with "I didn't go to the moon." This is a decidedly humorous line, indicating that Tom still has access to his detachment, but the audience is not laughing anymore, its de-

tachment has been broken down. The speech then quickly moves into a tone of lyric regret:

> I didn't go to the moon, I went much further— for time is the longest distance between two places—
>
> Not long after that I was fired for writing a poem on the lid of a shoe-box.
>
> I left Saint Louis. I descended the steps of this fire-escape for a last time and followed, from then on, in my father's footsteps, attempting to find in motion what was lost in space—
>
> I traveled around a great deal. The cities swept about me like dead leaves, leaves that were brightly colored but torn away from the branches.
>
> I would have stopped, but I was pursued by something.
>
> It always came upon me unawares, taking me altogether by surprise. Perhaps it was a familiar bit of music. Perhaps it was only a piece of transparent glass—
>
> Perhaps I am walking along a street at night, in some strange city, before I have found companions. I pass the lighted window of a shop where perfume is sold. The window is filled with pieces of colored glass, tiny transparent bottles in delicate colors, like bits of a shattered rainbow.
>
> Then all at once my sister touches my shoulder. I turn around and look into her eyes . . .
>
> Oh, Laura, Laura, I tried to leave you behind me, but I am more faithful than I intended to be!
>
> I reach for a cigarette, I cross the street, I run into the movies or a bar, I buy a drink, I speak to the nearest stranger—anything that can blow your candles out!
>
> —for nowadays the world is lit by lightning! Blow out your candles, Laura—and so good-bye.

The irony in this passage is no longer humorous. When Tom says "I didn't go to the moon," no one is laughing, and the final, ironic "and so good-bye" is not even potentially humorous. Tom seems to have been captured by the memory and the audience has almost certainly been captured, but Tom, in the end, still has his detachment. Laura's candles go out and Tom is relieved of his burden, uttering a final, flip farewell, but the audience has been more faithful than it intended to be; they are left behind, tricked by Tom who is free for the moment while they must face their grief, their cruelty, for they are the world that the Wingfields were somehow set apart from, they are the ones who shattered the rainbow.

The soliloquies, then, are of a piece: they all alternate between sentiment and irony, between mockery and nostalgic regret, and they all end with an ironic tag, which, in most cases, is potentially humorous. They show us the artist manipulating his audience, seeming to be manipulated himself to draw them in, but in the end resuming once more his detached stance. When Tom departs, the audience is left with Laura and Amanda alone before the dead, smoking candles, and Tom escapes into his artist's detachment having exorcized the pain with the creation of the play. This is the trick that Tom has in his pocket. (pp. 208-14)

> Thomas L. King, "Irony and Distance in 'The Glass Menagerie'," *in* Educational Theatre Journal, *Vol. XV, No. 2, May, 1973, pp. 207-14.*

Edmund A. Napieralski

The new dramatic criticism developing during the last decade has served to distinguish drama as a poetic mode from fiction and poetry and to bridge the gap between the text and the experience of drama. "Performability" is the keynote of this new criticism, which has provided fresh insights into the distinguishing qualities of the play in performance. In light of new critical values the work of playwrights like Tennessee Williams, whose "sense of theatre" Esther Merle Jackson says [in *The Broken World of Tennessee Williams*] has put him beyond the reaches of conventional criticism, deserves to be re-examined. A previously neglected feature of Williams' achievement in **The Glass Menagerie** lies in his use of dramatic metaphor, that is, a metaphor defined not only through the vehicle of language but through action, the mode that distinguishes drama from narrative. In **The Glass Menagerie** not language alone, but stage positions, gesture, activity, and movement define Amanda as the center of a metaphor that is the drama itself: Amanda not only dramatizes her own behavior and image of herself but also attempts to create roles for, to direct, prompt, and even costume the other characters in a drama of which she is author, producer, director, and leading lady. This dramatic metaphor, fashioned out of Amanda's experience and with the reluctant cooperation of Laura and Tom, gives depth to the dramatic illusion of **The Glass Menagerie** and gives the play its special power.

The setting of the play is perfectly suited to the work's use of drama as a metaphor since the Wingfield apartment appears as a stage on which Amanda can control the action. At the outset of the play, while Tom introduces the main characters, his family's circumstances, and the play as memory, a gauze curtain representing the outside wall of the apartment separates the audience from the interior. At the completion of his monologue, lighting permits the audience to see through the transparent wall of the building and through the transparent gauze portieres of the dining room arch. During this opening scene the gauze wall ascends and is not brought down again until the end of the play. This gauze curtain is not the theatre's curtain, the stage directions make clear, but the curtain that rises and falls on the action of the play's core or interior, that is, on Amanda's stage. The gauze portieres separating the dining room area from the living room also figure prominently in the play's action. For example, on several occasions Tom and Laura try to take refuge behind them to escape Amanda's control. At such times both characters behave like animals—sometimes fierce, sometimes fearful—in a menagerie. Worthy of note in the set, too, are the alleys

that flank the Wingfield apartment: these have the effect of isolating the location and thus enforcing the sense of confinement, the sense of a cage in which Tom and Laura are controlled. Amanda's actions and mode of behavior, however, do more than the set to define the metaphor of the drama.

In Scene I Amanda's voice is heard even before the lights go up and the outer wall is raised out of sight. When the scene is illuminated, Amanda, seated at the table with Tom and Laura, faces the audience while the other characters are in profile. Her first words to Tom are a command, or better, directions given by a tyrannical director to a recalcitrant actor. First she instructs him on table manners: "Honey, don't *push* with your *fingers*. . . . And chew—chew!" When Tom refuses her direction, Amanda proceeds to accuse him, ironically, of having a "Temperament like a Metropolitan star!" and once more reprimands him, this time for smoking too much. Tom, then, for the first time in the play retreats to the portieres. Amanda, apparently used to Tom's rejection of her advice, proceeds to demonstrate her propensity for pretense, for impersonation; as Laura attempts to rise to get the dessert, Amanda directs, "No sister, no sister—you be the lady this time and I'll be the darky." Amanda's words and behavior here foreshadow the more elaborate impersonation she will devise for the play's climax in the last scene. Then, despite the sarcasm of Tom and with Laura's forbearance, Amanda tells once more the story of her gentleman callers in Blue Mountain, this time through reverie taking the role of her younger self with "a pretty face and a graceful figure" and a "nimble wit." After the story she transfers her pretense to Laura as she directs her to prepare for her own gentleman callers. Just as her brother did earlier in the scene, Laura attempts to take refuge from her mother's painful charade, slipping *"in a fugitive manner through the half-open portieres,"* which she draws gently behind her. By the end of the first scene, then, Amanda has established the set as her stage, has assumed several roles, and has attempted to design a kind of scenario for two reluctant players whose gestures clearly evidence their own desire to escape Amanda's influence.

Scenes II and III continue to elaborate the dramatic metaphor as Amanda tries to shape the roles of Laura and Tom. In Scene II Amanda enters looking grim and hopeless after discovering that Laura has played truant from Rubicam's Business College. Williams' stage directions here make it clear that Amanda deliberately engages in *"a bit of acting."* Before speaking to Laura, who watches her nervously, Amanda *"slowly opens her purse and removes a dainty white handkerchief which she shakes out delicately and delicately touches to her lips and nostrils."* Amanda proceeds to re-enact for Laura's benefit the scene with the typing instructor, going so far even to quote the dialogue carefully. Laura, obviously shaken by her mother's accusations, explains how she spent the time her mother supposed her to be at school. When Amanda, continuing her dejected air, replies, "You did all this to deceive me, just for deception?" Laura calls attention to her mother's affected pose, a pose which is in effect another role for Amanda, the suffering Madonna: "Mother, when you're disappointed, you get that awful suffering look on your face, like the picture of Jesus' mother in the museum." Once Laura confesses, at her mother's prompting, to liking a high-school hero who called her "Blue Roses," Amanda becomes revived with the thought of a new plan—to get Laura married. Refusing to accept Laura's objection that she is crippled, Amanda effusively counsels her to "cultivate other things to make up for it," ironically recommending pretense or deception to one whom she had just berated for deception. It is clear throughout this scene that Amanda's pity and her fear of what the future may hold are directed more to herself than to Laura, that in effect she is here, as earlier and later in the play, priming Laura to assume the role of the young Amanda who reigned in the Delta.

In Scene III Amanda attempts to govern Tom as she governed Laura in the preceding scene. Her accusations of deception are now levelled at Tom, who bitterly resents Amanda's criticism of his reading D.H. Lawrence, his writing, his mediocre position at the warehouse, and his fondness for the movies. As in Scene II, Amanda's fear for herself obviously motivates her attack: "What right have you to jeopardize your job? Jeopardize the security of us all? How do you think we'd manage if you were—." But Tom cuts her off, pointing to his father's picture and threatening to leave as he did. One cannot avoid the suspicion here that just as Amanda tries to design Laura as a version of her younger self, she tries here and later in the play to design Tom as an idealized version of her deserting husband. Amanda's romantic conception of the past and her commitment to an idealized reincarnation of that past haunt the entire play. But Tom, unlike his delicate sister, struggles desperately to avoid his mother's despotic direction. Calling her an "ugly babbling old witch," he struggles to put on his coat to make an escape but tears the sleeve in the attempt and angrily hurls it across the room where it strikes Laura's glass collection, sending shattering glass to the floor. Laura, who has witnessed the bitter confrontation between mother and son cries, "My glass?—menagerie . . . ".

Although Laura does not explain until Scene VII that it is Amanda who has given the name "menagerie" to her glass collection, nowhere else in the play has the designation more appropriateness than it does here, coming as it does after Amanda's manipulation of Laura in Scene II and of Tom in this scene, to symbolize Amanda's relationship to her children. Amanda's choice of diction is significant because a menagerie is a place where animals are kept and trained, especially for exhibition. The action of the play defines Amanda not only as a producer of a drama but also as a proprietress of a menagerie—like the drama a means of exhibition—in which Laura and Tom are caged, trained, and displayed. And like the animals in a menagerie, Laura and Tom have attempted escape, not only by resorting to their own fantasies and illusions but even physically by retreating as they do several times to and behind the portieres, as if straining against the confines of their cage.

Amanda strengthens her position in the next two scenes, first by regaining control over Tom and second by carrying out her "plans and provisions" to secure a gentleman caller for Laura. At the beginning of Scene IV Tom, after a night of heavy drinking, returns home to tell Laura of his experience at the theatre where he witnessed a magician's escape from a coffin. The greater part of the scene, however, is given to Tom's reconciliation with Amanda. The following morning, Laura persuades Tom to apologize to their mother and, wearing her mother's old coat, leaves the apartment to run an errand. Tom does apologize and his mother, here too perhaps with a bit of acting, accepts the apology. Playing her martyred role skillfully and having apparently learned little from their recent quarrel, Amanda proceeds to coach Tom again, decrying his drinking, his movie-going, and finally his defense of man's instinct for adventure. Tom's modes of escape remind Amanda of her husband's desertion, and her speech implies once more that she is trying to mold Tom into an idealized form of his father. Also, in response to Tom's defense of man's instinct for adventure and freedom, Amanda retorts, "Don't quote instinct to me! Instinct is something that people have got away from! It belongs to animals!" Amanda is ironically unaware that such instinct belongs to animals in a menagerie as well. After the lecture Amanda reluctantly concedes to Tom's demand for independence, but only after his sister is provided for. When Tom asks what he can do about her, Amanda with irony again responds, "Overcome selfishness! Self, self is all you ever think of!" Then Amanda gives him instructions to find a gentleman caller for Laura. As he has done earlier in the play, Tom again tries to escape but so strong has Amanda's grip on his actions become that he is compelled to consent before he can tear himself away down the fire escape and into the alley.

The crux of Scene V lies in Tom's "annunciation" to Amanda that she will get, after all, her gentleman caller. Williams opens the scene, however, with actions that further amplify the metaphor of the drama. Amanda's first words are a direction to Tom to comb his hair. She explains her request by alluding to Tom's father: "There's only one respect in which I would like for you to emulate your father. . . . The care he always took of his appearance. He never allowed himself to look untidy." Amanda's reference here is of course to the actual husband, not to the idealized vision of him that unconsciously inspires her in her behavior with her son. Tom takes refuge on the fire escape, in consequence of his being reprimanded again for his smoking and lack of ambition, while Amanda turns to look at her husband's picture. Although the picture's presence on the set has provoked comment from the play's critics, no one has remarked on the curiousness of the deserter's picture enjoying so prominent a position in Amanda's living room. Amanda should certainly not want this painful reminder of her husband's infidelity, unless she believes that this image and her own past can somehow be redeemed in Tom and Laura. Amanda then follows Tom onto the fire escape and after complaining about the landing as a poor excuse for a porch, *"sits down gracefully and demurely as if she were settling into a swing on a Mississippi veranda."* In the slightest and apparently most unconscious gestures throughout the play, Amanda acts as if she were performing, pretending, fulfilling a role.

After Tom's announcement that the gentleman caller will

appear "on the scene" the following day, Amanda exhibits a bristling enthusiasm, a sparkling vivacity that contrasts sharply with the joylessness that has characterized her actions earlier in the play. Immediately she begins to conceive with frenetic zeal the setting for the grand performance to be given for the gentleman caller's benefit: "All my wedding silver has to be polished, the monogrammed table linen ought to be laundered! The windows have to be washed and fresh curtains put up. And how about clothes?" Although the limitations of time will force Amanda to forego new wallpaper, a new lamp and chintz covers will complete the set. Amanda's enthusiasm continues as she grills Tom on Jim O'Connor's qualifications. Gestures are significant here as Amanda brushes Tom's hair: Tom, the stage directions explain, submits *"grimly to the brush and the interrogation,"* as he has grimly submitted to Amanda's direction and control for the entire play; Amanda, on the other hand, behaves as if she were preparing an actor for his performance, or a performer for exhibition. Their interview ends with Tom's warning to his mother not to expect too much of Laura. Although Amanda's responses here are congruous with her refusal to accept the reality of her own and her children's situation throughout the play, more important as far as the dramatic metaphor is concerned is the form of her responses. As if she were a director, or prompter or script-girl, Amanda corrects her son's dialogue: when Tom contends that because of their love for Laura he and his mother have overlooked her being crippled and perhaps appearing peculiar to outsiders, Amanda counters with, "Don't say crippled. . . . Don't say peculiar." Not only Tom's behavior but even his lines should, as far as Amanda is concerned, conform to her conception of the script.

Scenes VI and VII present Amanda's full-scale production, her play within the play she has made of her life. Even though she will have an audience of only one in Jim O'Connor, it will be the most elaborate performance she has constructed. Now she will have the fullest opportunity to exercise the talent for improvisation that she has displayed in earlier scenes. For Scene VI the setting reflects the care Amanda has taken with her stage. After Tom's monologue that presents the facts of Jim's background and Tom's relationship to him, the lights go up to reveal Amanda dressing Laura. The stage directions make it clear that this activity enlarges the dramatic metaphor: "LAURA *stands in the middle with uplifted arms while* AMANDA *crouches before her, adjusting the hem of the new dress, devout and ritualistic."* Amanda is, in effect, costuming her character. Although Laura is a striking figure, fragile and unearthly as Williams describes her, her appearance here is less compelling than is Amanda's. She announces her "spectacular appearance" to Laura and then does indeed enter spectacularly with her *"girlish frock of yellowed voile with a blue silk sash,"* a bunch of violets and behavior that Williams calls feverish. Can there be any doubt that this is the leading lady, performing her *"mincing step around the room"* and in ecstatic reverie, recalling her jonquil summer on the Delta? Laura, then, discovers to her horror that the gentleman caller will be none other than Jim O'Connor, the high school hero she always admired from a distance. Terrified by the approach of Jim and Tom and by the ringing doorbell, Laura retreats to the portieres and to her victrola. The panic that grips her is only aggravated by Amanda's prompting, *"(very, very gaily)* Laura, that is your brother and Mr. O'Connor! Will you let them in, darling?" Laura does finally manage to follow her mother's direction, but then runs off once more behind the portieres. Amanda, on the other hand, suffers no stage fright and enters with *"gay laughter and chatter."* It is only fitting that the leading lady should make her appearance after the minor characters have set the action in motion, and there can be no doubt that Amanda is the leading lady. Amanda, *"coyly smiling, shaking her girlish ringlets,"* dominates the conversation for the remainder of the scene, and at the same time as demanding director or stage manager tries to cue the other performers to perform the scene as she would have it. But Laura, faint and trembling, is unable to perform on cue and Amanda is left at the end of the scene as hostess, for the moment at least actually assuming the role she wished to play only vicariously.

Scene VII presents the climax not only of Williams' play but of Amanda's as well. It may well be for Laura, as Williams says in the stage directions, "the climax of her secret life," but the events here have at least as much if not more import for Amanda's real life. At the beginning of the scene Amanda still dominates the action as the gay and charming hostess, becoming even more rhapsodic as she assures the gentleman caller, "why, Mr. O'Connor, nobody, *nobody's* given me this much entertainment in years—as you have!" Although much of the ensuing scene belongs to Laura and Jim, Amanda is never far off. She has designed the set, even furnished the lighting with the old candelabrum, and has carefully coached, directly and indirectly through her example, the minor characters in the production. Moreover, Laura refers to Amanda so often that she is virtually present even though she is out of sight in the kitchen with Tom. Amanda's presence is also actual, however, because of her off-stage laughter that incongruously punctuates the encounter of Laura and Jim. The first instance of this gay laughter occurs when she leaves them alone in the living room. Then, after Laura gradually relaxes in Jim's presence and they recall their high school days, Laura explains her glass collection. On three occasions here she refers to the glass as a "collection"; on the third occasion, at a point which represents about the middle of her scene with Jim, Amanda's *"peal of girlish laughter"* once more comes from the kitchen, and Laura goes on to explain, "Mother calls them a glass menagerie."

The moving incident with the unicorn that follows has often enough been explained and effectively apprehended by both critics and audiences: the delicate, translucent, and fragile unicorn loses its freakish horn and loses also, as Laura briefly does, its peculiarity, its uniqueness. For a precious instant Laura shuns fantasy and enters a natural, fresh, warm and human reality; for that rare moment Laura escapes her mother's menagerie. Her feelings are climaxed by Jim's kiss, a tender gesture cruelly contradicted by another of Amanda's peals of girlish laughter. Within minutes another laugh from Amanda prefaces Jim's apology to Laura and his revelation about his engagement to Betty. Laura is virtually silent for the remainder of the scene, but Amanda, unaware that her play is a dismal flop, enters brightly with lemonade and macaroons to celebrate what she believes is the gaiety of the occasion. The truth of the matter, nevertheless, is not enough to distract her from the demands of her role. The frustrated producer and actress assures her audience when he expresses his gratitude that "It really wasn't anything at all." To Jim's excuse that he cannot keep Betty waiting, Amanda calmly but ironically replies, "Yes, I know—The tyranny of women!" Even now, Amanda cannot give up prompting as she urges Laura to join with her in wishing Jim luck, happiness, and success. Laura's quiet "Yes," is the only line breaking her pathetic silence.

The following exchange between Amanda and Tom testifies that her own disappointment, her own failure as playwright and producer, rather than Laura's disappointment, motivates Amanda's harsh words to her son. Amanda's first concern, as has been evident from the beginning of the play, is herself. After condemning Tom for living in a dream, for manufacturing illusions, she cries, "Go to the movies, go! Don't think about us, a mother deserted, an unmarried sister who's crippled and has no job! Don't let anything interfere with your selfish pleasure!" Only Laura's scream as Tom plunges out on the fire escape and slams the door seems to startle Amanda into realizing that her daughter is there, that Laura has heard her mother's bitter and brutal words. The scene ends with Tom's monologue accompanied by an interior pantomime that features Amanda comforting Laura. Significantly, it is Amanda's movements that strike the audience and that obviously struck Williams too. The stage directions say little about Laura's appearance and gestures but about Amanda, Williams explains *"Now that we cannot hear the mother's speech, her silliness is gone and she has dignity and tragic beauty. . . . Amanda's gestures are slow and graceful, almost dancelike, as she comforts the daughter."* Although Amanda may not be tragic, she is nevertheless, as Benjamin Nelson contends [in his *Tennessee Williams: The Man and His Work*], heroic: while Laura never emerges as a human being in her own right and exists on a "single dimension of sympathy," Amanda engages in a desperate struggle to design the pattern of her family's existence and "leaves us with the impression of a truly valiant woman." Her past cannot be redeemed; Amanda cannot be reincarnated. But by designing a performance, by devising her own role and the roles of others in her production, Amanda has tried not only to redeem the past but to give form to the present and the future, to give shape to destiny.

The dramatic metaphor with Amanda at its center defines the structure of *The Glass Menagerie* and explains its special power as a dramatic work. Williams had no need to fear, as he explained in the production notes, that the audience would receive a fragmentary rather than architectural effect from the play. The effect would be fragmentary only if the audience were distracted by Tom and Laura. Practically speaking, such a distraction is unlikely since Amanda's presence is unmistakable in every scene. While Tom is absent from all of Scene II and Laura from most of Scenes IV and V, Amanda is always on the scene or close at hand. Even if the audience might be more ready to sympathize with Tom or Laura at points in the play,

it could not fail to sense even subliminally that Amanda is in control of the action. (pp 1-11)

As a structural element, as well as one which subtly affects the emotional response of the audience, the dramatic metaphor also serves to give the play a tight coherence. The relationship of the metaphor of the drama to the play's central symbol of the menagerie has already been explained in terms of performance and exhibition. Another strand in the play's fabric, moreover, the religious and vague archetypal allusions, can also be coordinated with the figures of the drama and the menagerie. The religious references are to the Blessed Mother, her Annunciation, and the arrival of the Savior; the archetypal allusions to emblematic characters and situations. Tom's calling the gentleman caller "some archetype of the universal unconscious" in Scene III is more obvious perhaps than the more oblique references to death and rebirth, to water and regeneration, and to initiation rites that appear in Scenes VI and VII. Since these religious and archetypal elements operate at a muted level of suggestion, they have less significance in themselves than they do in relation to the dramatic metaphor: both elements intimate rites, rituals, or ceremonies which involve performance and are, therefore, perfectly congruous with the central metaphor of the drama.

Williams' play is brilliant theatre because it uses the drama itself to intensify the illusion of virtual life. As in other literary works, the language of the play does serve to elucidate the metaphor. More important, however, in *The Glass Menagerie* the metaphor is defined primarily in terms of the distinctive poetic mode of drama—through gesture, movement, and action. The metaphor, then, is dramatic in the exclusive sense of that word. Even if Williams were not completely conscious of his design, his sense of theatre was great and inspiring enough to create the dramatic metaphor. No wonder, then, that the play, almost thirty years after its first production, still holds audiences in the theatre as well as in the study. Unlike Laura whom Williams compares to glass with a "momentary radiance, not actual, not lasting," *The Glass Menagerie* enjoys a radiance that is both actual and indeed lasting. (pp. 11-12)

> *Edmund A. Napieralski, "Tennessee Williams' 'The Glass Menagerie': The Dramatic Metaphor," in* The Southern Quarterly, *Vol. XVI, No. 1, October, 1977, pp. 1-12.*

Joseph K. Davis

The dramatic pattern Tennessee Williams worked out in *The Glass Menagerie*—and one which assured it not only initial but continuing theatrical success—manifests two significant features: (1) the dramatization of men and women by a display of their fragmented, tortured psychologies; and (2) the depiction of these characters against a haunting environment which is itself a condition of their alienation and unhappiness. This dramatic realization of what are essentially *landscapes of the dislocated mind* constitutes typical Williams theater. The pattern developed is one Williams consistently uses, though with refinements, in later plays.

In achieving what in the "Production Notes" he terms "a new, plastic theatre," Williams adapts to the stage a technique already familiar to modern art media, especially to fiction and film. The entire play is staged literally with an actor, Tom Wingfield, who is not only the principal character but who also supplies the point of view for both events and theme of the drama. The effect recalls a cinemagraphic montage, with simultaneous use of interrelated memories, scenes, symbols, and musical motifs. Tom's presentation is characterized, as he himself says, by "truth in the pleasant disguise of illusion." The story he stages is not simply an account of how an individual gifted with a poetic temperament is denied a useful, creative life because of a hostile environment and cruel family circumstances. And if Tom himself recalls similar modern individuals who search for self-expression, he is also concerned with reminiscences that quickly suggest much more than his own quest. Both as a major character and as a narrator he is unable to construct out of the materials he offers either a coherent or a personally satisfying explanation of reality. Nor is he able to establish with any confidence a genuine relationship with his family, his environment, or indeed with himself. The world of Tom Wingfield is clearly that of twilight, memory, and fantasy, from which images and shadows of the past loom threateningly over the present.

Tom's mode of dramatic presentation is clarified by a definition of two very different types of thinking. *Directed thinking* is logical in its verbal formulations and intentions, for it is causally linked with the external world by a more or less direct relationship with what it seeks to communicate. *Nondirected thinking* is spontaneously produced and unconsciously motivated. The former is occasionally referred to as progressive because it is oriented to reality and the demands of reality; the latter, as regressive because it is associated with formulations which have no apparently useful, sensible meanings (e.g., as in the materials of most day- and night-dreaming). Directed thinking seeks as its object adaption to reality and productions which reality esteems, while nondirected thinking turns away from reality and is concerned with a subjective content often bizarre and unacceptable to the normal modes of human consciousness. Tom's narrative throughout consists of nondirected thinking, a concept that may explain the entire play.

The function of Tom extends beyond any thematic intention to render inner experience or some quality of expressionistic reality. In its dramatic mode and theme, in fact, *The Glass Menagerie* portrays individuals not only fleeing from reality but also wishing to escape time and history. Each of the major characters is unable to accept and live with daily events; and each compensates for this failure by rejecting the present through wish-projections and fantasizing. Unable to live in the present, each character retreats into a time appropriate to his or her individual fantasy. Tom Wingfield cannot endure his home life or his job in the shoe factory and uses the motion pictures as a temporary means of escape. Seeing himself as a poet he even-

tually leaves home and hopes to find a life as an artist. His sister Laura tries to live in the present, but her crippled body and grim prospects in the secretarial school overcome her fragile sensibilities. She withdraws into the world of her glass animals, and so flees into a no-time of approaching mental collapse. The mother Amanda Wingfield cannot accept life in the St. Louis tenement and returns in fantasies to the past—an earlier period of gracious living on the plantation in Mississippi where, as she chooses to remember, she was surrounded by chivalric men of wealth and fashion who wanted to marry her. Each character is capable only of the briefest moments of realistic thinking; none can sustain anything like a vital relationship with another or with the facts of daily existence.

Not surprisingly, then, the dramatic structure of *The Glass Menagerie* cannot be worked out on the level of direct action. The present is avoided and actually repressed as too painful and monstrous to be faced and accepted. The landscape in which each of the three characters seeks refuge is one within his or her mind. Thus the entire play consists of an interplay of shadow and act—a structural movement which supports Williams' theme of flight from the present time and indeed from history.

Laura Wingfield is both the lyrical and the symbolical center of the play. Her shattered sensibility and delicate mental balance compel the only instance of genuine affection and compassion either Tom or Amanda shows in the drama. Unable to cope with her crippled body or the mechanical routine of the business school she briefly attends, she fabricates a nether-nether world out of the glass animals she collects. Quite literally they offer her the only security, intimacy, and permanence she can find in the brutal environment of her St. Louis tenement. Fragile and artistic, these glass figures, like Laura herself, suggest a world other than the one Williams depicts in the play. They symbolize all the artistry and beauty which to her, and perhaps to Williams, are missing in the secular-urban order of the modern era. In high school Laura attempted unsuccessfully to relate to a fellow student. Her secret beau turns out to be Jim O'Connor, the "gentleman caller" whom Tom brings to dinner. Once more Laura is betrayed, for Jim is already engaged to another girl. The idea of Jim as "savior" . . . provides a final cruel moment in the play. Laura withdraws completely from the present, defeated by the world around her; she moves into the no-time of her glass animals and thus suffers a devastating mental collapse. Williams offers no "saviors," it seems. Art and beauty are given no way to exist in the world of *The Glass Menagerie.*

In addition to his role as stage narrator, Tom Wingfield emerges as Williams' prototypical "fugitive"—a sensitive, modern individual who is artistic in impulse and temperament. Tom rejects both his present menial job at the warehouse and his mother and her professed recollections of a chivalric, heroic past in Mississippi. He can only project his life into the future by means of fantasies as a poet. Tom exemplifies, in fact, two related patterns Williams consistently employs in his plays: (1) a rejection of past and present—both the romanticized past of his southern men and women and the bourgeois everydayness of contemporary secular-urban life; and (2) the Orphean compulsion toward the deeply instinctive regions of sexuality and violence. These areas cluster around what William Barrett in *Irrational Man* terms the Oresteian "Furies," or feminine earth-spirits, who demand a place in a society that is increasingly rationalistic and organized to serve the machine. The older Promethean/Faustian lifestyle of post-Renaissance times, represented in *The Glass Menagerie* by the gallantry and heroic order of the South, no longer are viable. Indeed, Tom cannot accept either as real or as desirable the way of life Amanda challenges him to emulate. The brutal fact of the commercial-industrial state cancels any possible return to such behavior. Caught between past and present, therefore, Tom retreats into fantasies and at last flees the stifling apartment.

Only in instances of wish-projections of himself into the future as poet-artist can Tom relieve the terrible depression and anxieties of his deadly lifestyle in St. Louis. Using various literary allusions—Jim O'Connor, for example, calls Tom "Shakespeare"—Williams reinforces Tom's hope that by means of art he might in time escape the world he now lives in. As a further act of rebellion, he identifies with the father who deserted them some years earlier and so, thief-like in the night, at last flees. Yet this act occasions the Angst and guilt Tom clearly admits during his troubled narrative. Survival in today's world, Williams implies, is bought at the cost of these debilitating inner conflicts.

The second Williams theme Tom exemplifies is the Orphean plunge into the life of the body. At one point, Tom exclaims to his mother: "Man is by instinct a lover, a hunter, a fighter, and none of these instincts are given much play at the warehouse!" These activities are markedly predatory, but to Tom they belong to a side of human life repressed by the sterile organization of contemporary society. Yet they too must have a place in the full life of individuals; for if they are denied, they will rise in behavior that is ugly and violent. In *The Glass Menagerie* this theme is not treated in great detail; but in later plays it emerges with tremendous force and often with terrible consequences for Williams' men and women. So significant is it, in fact, that some clarification of it here is useful.

The Orphic theme, only foreshadowed in Tom's affirmation of man's beastlike aspects, points to several related emphases in Williams' plays. At one level it suggests the supernal power and role of art and artist. The legendary Orpheus, son of a divine Muse and a Thracian prince, was a master musician who rivaled the Olympians themselves. His lyre enchanted human beings and animals who heard it; it even saved Jason's mariners from despair and the bewitching songs of the Sirens. Orpheus, then, recalls the artist whose music calms and heals; for his incomparable songs purge the weariness and pain of life, uniting all who hear their ethereal melodies. At another level Orpheus alone dares the dark powers of the Underworld in search of his beloved Eurydice, taken from him by the sting of the poisonous viper. So beautiful is his music that the rulers of Hades agree to return her to him if he departs immediately and never looks back. Unfortunately he looks back too soon upon regaining the world above, and Eurydice,

still within the gloomy shadows, is lost forever. But in seeking her he has challenged the fearful depths and so is one who quests for the reunification of body (the animal, sexual body) and spirit (the cognitive, enlightened heights of thought). Orpheus attempts to bring nature and man into harmonic unification. Williams clearly introduces both of these characteristics into his dramas.

The outcome of events in *The Glass Menagerie* dramatizes the tragedy of indulging in the kinds of behavior and thinking that negate the possibilities of living fully and honestly in the present.

—*Joseph K. Davis*

This Orphean quest for unification of man's animal and intellectual dimensions through artistic means is a persistent dilemma in Williams' plays. Williams is never able to reconcile the split between man the artist and man the thinker. The body in its full, free life always becomes either a brutal punishment or an agent of tragedy. The Orphic dilemma, expressed by the ancient warning, soma sema (*the body, a tomb*), is one of the consistent mythopoeic themes in Williams' work. As the half-crazed Maeneds tear Orpheus to pieces, tossing his parts into the river Hebrus, so the heroes and often the heroines in Williams' plays must suffer dismemberment in their attempts to live the full life of the body.

If *The Glass Menagerie* only introduces Williams' Orphic dilemma, later works deal more or less consistently with it. *A Streetcar Named Desire* (1947), for example, rejects as dangerous and damaging the idea that individuals can live exclusively for unlimited self-indulgence, especially sexual gratifications. At the same time Williams recognizes that in attempting to seize their lives men and women experience definite limits. Each of us, after all, is not simply situated in this universe; and Williams undertakes specific explorations in his dramas of the 1950s of what moral order, if any, exists. In these plays he examines the terms whereby individuals may purposively act and thus the standards which can effectively measure their actions as creative or destructive. These plays reveal that Williams' investigations are undergirded by the conviction, never entirely absent from his work, that limits exist beyond which persons may not venture except at supreme risk and perhaps inevitable retribution.

That Williams came to such a view of human existence is seen in a growing preoccupation in the works of the 1950s and later with the problem of moral guilt and the violence which all too frequently this guilt generates. (pp. 192-97)

We may be entirely correct to say that for Williams man is finally a sinner and that through suffering he must expiate his sin and lose his guilt, but it is far too easy to pass over [his] complex dramatic presentations with such remarks.

It is more likely that Williams' dramatizations of the problem of guilt and moral ambiguity contain no successful way out. Indeed, his Orphean hero has necessarily become something of an Oresteian hero—a representative modern individual driven by self-admitted guilt and obsessive fears but who has a deep-felt longing to experience a redemptive vision and win back his peace of mind. Unlike Aeschylus' hero, Williams' hero is yet pursued by the Furies; thus far no divine intervention has occurred to save him and cleanse his tortured soul.

These ambiguities clearly emerge in Williams' delineation of Tom Wingfield and the dramatic pattern of *The Glass Menagerie.* But if Tom is the narrator and central character of the play, the pivotal figure is the mother Amanda; for she is instrumental in bringing her two children to such a desperate situation. She has consistently indulged in illusions and failed completely to meet life directly; and her bitter disappointments have left her impotent, as both adult and mother. Amanda's response to life generates devastating consequences for her children, crippling them psychologically and seriously inhibiting their own quests for maturity and self-realization.

From the opening scene of the play she constantly reminds everyone that she belongs to an earlier time on her family's plantation in Mississippi. . . . A woman was secure in this past time, Amanda thinks, for it was an age of chivalry and elegance. It was a time characterized by what she calls "the art of conversation" and by young ladies "possessed of a pretty face and a graceful figure" and also "a nimble wit and a tongue to meet all occasions." All too sadly, however, it is a time now irrevocably lost. Later in the play she tells Jim O'Connor, the gentleman caller of the present: "Well, in the South we had so many servants. Gone, gone, gone. All vestige of gracious living! Gone completely! I wasn't prepared for what the future brought me." Her admission that she "wasn't prepared for what the future brought me" is, of course, an explanation of her present need to live in the past by means of fantasizing: she deeply believes that she belongs to this earlier age of aristocratic life, not to the grinding daily routine of her St. Louis tenement.

Amanda Wingfield's past not only animates but also sustains her in the present, becoming in effect her point of reference for everything connected with goodness, truth, and reality. She is simply unable to break out of the framework of her dreamy recollections and to achieve any degree of perspective on them as real or imagined elements. She makes invidious comparisons between her former life and her current situation, and she emphatically rejects the present in favor of the past. Her instability is frighteningly apparent in her inability to sustain a relationship between her almost lucid moments of realism and her constant fantasizing. She vacillates from urging Laura and Tom, on the one hand, to prepare for the gentleman callers she believes are about to arrive to warning Laura, on the other, that she must get training for a business or a professional career. Amanda warns that she has seen "such pitiful cases in the South—barely tolerated spinsters living upon the grudging patronage of sister's husband or brother's wife!—stuck away in some little mousetrap of a room—encouraged by one in-law to visit another—little birdlike women without any nest—eating the crust of humility all their life!" These instances of grim realism are unfortunately rare with Amanda; she usually persists in fantasizing about the past and projecting its remembered images upon her present circumstances.

On the all-important evening when a gentleman caller finally appears, Amanda indulges in the consummate fantasy. Entering the room wearing "a girlish frock of yellowed voile with a blue silk sash," she proudly announces: "This is the dress in which I led the cotillion. Won the cakewalk twice at Sunset Hill, wore one Spring to the Governor's Ball in Jackson!" The triumph of the past is seemingly now complete, for Amanda has regressed in her fantasizing to the years of her youthful innocence as a "southern belle."

The past replaces the present; illusion overcomes reality, yet cannot reverse events. In the following scenes Jim O'Connor, the gentleman caller, is only, as Williams himself warns, "a nice, ordinary, young man" who works with Tom at the warehouse. As Laura's former high school idol, moreover, he occasions her final withdrawal from reality. When he confesses he is soon to marry a young girl he has courted for some time, all illusions are shattered. The play ends with Tom determined to leave home and go to sea, with Laura completely crushed and "huddled on the sofa," and with Amanda trying to comfort her. Williams seems to suggest in his closing stage directions that Amanda gains a degree of "dignity and tragic beauty" by her act of comforting Laura; but audiences may find it difficult to accept this assessment. It is perfectly in character for Amanda to assume a role that is only another of the bad games she constantly plays. Regardless of the individual interpretation of the ending, the play clearly shows the destructive, tragic consequences of Amanda's fantasizing, the results of which are only too apparent in the lives of Tom and Laura.

The outcome of events in *The Glass Menagerie* dramatizes the tragedy of indulging in the kinds of behavior and thinking that negate the possibilities of living fully and honestly in the present. Laura is no doubt the individual who shows the deepest personal ravages of these cruel scenes, but Amanda is still the best illustration of how such a mental condition works its corrosive destruction. Not only does she deeply and permanently injure her children but she herself is a victim of an illusory way of life— that generated by her beloved plantation South. The very nature of this civilization and her relationship to it have created in her habits and attitudes which encourage fantasies and illusions. To understand Amanda and the South, we must explore precisely what her southern background means and how its environs have fostered in her such romantic notions and wistful ideas.

The South that we encounter in *The Glass Menagerie* through Amanda's recollections is actually a pseudo-history of the region and thus a kind of myth. It is, however, a particular myth that is highly significant for Williams and for his men and women, since it functions as a mediating image by means of which his dramatic characters understand and measure their lives and current situations.

Certain major characters in all of Williams' works are trapped within a mode of thinking oriented to the past, to a psychological impulse to withdraw into a fabricated "lost" time. The present exists for these men and women only to the degree that it can be verified by constant references to the past. And the most important of his representations of the past is that of the American South, with its special commitment to a ruined former time and to a haunting awareness of a paradise now lost. In those works which develop themes and characters out of the South, beginning with *The Glass Menagerie,* Williams employs the South of history and myth as an image that mediates between what is and what might be, and thus between life caught as human expectation, desire, anxiety, and life actually realized as human creativity and individual fulfilment. Whether in memory or in fantasy, it animates and informs the consciousness of his dramatic characters, drawing them back ceaselessly into themselves and finally into some sense they have of their relationship to the past.

Williams employs the South of history and myth as an image that mediates between what is and what might be, and thus between life caught as human expectation, desire, anxiety, and life actually realized as human creativity and individual fulfilment.

—Joseph K. Davis

Elsewhere I have argued that in the popular imagination both the ante- and the post-bellum South are aspects of the American dream of the creation of a new world and the emergence of a new man who will in time bring forth a new Golden Age. The relationship between the American dream and the South, if crucial, is not actually difficult to establish and trace. According to the widely accepted view of southern history, the Old South is believed to have become, soon after settlement in the sixteenth century, a cultural region dominated by manorial plantations graced with beautiful ladies and guided by elegant gentlemen of noble birth and heraldic virtues. Despite the fact that the educated and better informed have always understood the fundamental inaccuracy and romantic idealization of this view, the illusion that the area was a land of nobility and courtly manners persists, largely untarnished by events and time. It is yet argued, in fact, that the South which fought the Civil War was, as W. J. Cash said thirty-odd years ago in *The Mind of the South,* "home of a genuine and fully realized aristocracy, coextensive and identical with the ruling class, the planters." The second view, and a corollary of the first, is that the Civil War and the thirty years following saw the destruction of civilization in the Old South, with the result that except for scattered and isolated remnants the entire structure, with its splendid men and women and its cultivated way of life, disappeared, only to be replaced by a new order of life derived from the powerful commercial and industrial interests then working to transform all of America into a modern technological nation. The Old South remains only in memory; and there it endures today, to serve in its principal features as the idealized model for worthwhile imitation and future approximation.

This account of southern history is hardly credible; it is nevertheless a very important account of the region, embodying a view of the past commonly regarded as essentially correct and true. Actually the Old South of the popular mind is best regarded as myth—but a myth vital and important in grasping the spirit of this geographical region and in seeing its relationship to its own history and to the rest of the United States. As myth this account of the South has exactly the function which Mircea Eliade in *Myth and Reality* explains as "sacred history"; namely, the transformation of the origins and development of the region—from its settlement and colonization to its deep frustrations over Negro slavery and complete defeat in war—into a rendition of its history that is mythic in form and intention. In barest outline, the Old South emerges as an almost idyllic agricultural society of genteel people and an aristocratic way of life, exemplary in its pattern and content. A visionary moment of the American dream occurred and passed; now its history is transformed into the story of a fallen order, a ruined time of nobility and heroic achievements that was vanquished and irrevocably lost. In this way the actual facts of the Old South have been translated by myth into a schemata of the birth, the flowering, and the passing of what others in an earlier era might well have called a "Golden Age."

The significance of the Old South understood as myth is considerable and far reaching in implications. It is above all a kind of pseudo-history accepted as genuine history, and thus as a view of the past by which many people—foreigners as well as Americans—orient themselves in their attempts to comprehend and relate to the American experience. Reliable, accurate history is one thing and myth quite another. (pp. 198-200)

The relationship between actual history and the way an individual looks at history are important in the successful rise of the myth of the Old South. By the middle of the nineteenth century the southern dream of empire had come painfully to grief. And by the ending decades of the nineteenth century the Southerner began to withdraw into an insular view of his region and its heritage. The still unrealized demands of the Negroes for justice and some measure of human equality, as well as the mounting tensions caused by the rapid industrialization and urbanization of the Old Confederacy, contributed significantly to the impulse to retreat into the legacy of the southern past. Now, however, the order and achievements of that earlier time are fully translated into the myth of the Old South. This tendency is only another instance of projecting on the recent past what are actually wish-fantasies of the present—here, a yearning for recovery of a lost time now transformed by means of a pseudo-myth into a marvelous and heroic era associated with the idea of a Golden Age. As a kind of history the myth will serve as deeply revered consolation and refuge for the white Southerner as he struggles with the actual heavy burdens of his daily situation and as he lives with the sharp consciousness of his defeated, ruined dreams.

The image of the South contained in *The Glass Menagerie,* as indeed in all of Williams' southern plays, is neither accurate history nor proper myth. What we are given in both cases is a falsification of history and a distortion of myth. That is, the South portrayed in Williams' works is an instance of how the popular imagination rewrites history and counterfeits myth, doing so largely out of a mentality that is incapable of handling the actual situations of life and thus of working through difficulties to establish a creative relationship between the past and the present. According to Nancy Tischler, Williams himself apparently accepts this mythopoeic reading of southern history. Certainly the image of the South he employs brilliantly serves his dramatic purposes. Unable to confront and accept their present lives, his characters are in desperate flight from time and actual history—literally, from a defeated present and thus from their fears of what they have become. None takes responsibility for his or her acts, and none is able to achieve an authentic, creative life. Trapped in time past or time future, each falls victim to illusions, illnesses, fantasies, violence—or, worse—to definite kinds of insanity. Such then are the results of repression and attempts to avoid contemporary situations.

The best dramatization of what a false historical consciousness means to an individual is Williams' portrayal of Amanda Wingfield in *The Glass Menagerie.* The view she holds of her own origins and early life in the South—or, specifically, that wistful remnant of the Old South surviving in recollections of her home at Blue Mountain, Mississippi—is so distorted by illusions and fantasizing that her integrity and character have been thoroughly undermined. The prototype of all of Williams' southern women, Amanda is directly responsible for the terrible and permanent alienation of Laura and Tom. Because she herself has withdrawn from reality, preferring rather dreams of a lost time in the South, Amanda has handed her children over to a similar, if not a worse, psychology and grim fate. *The Glass Menagerie,* in effect, gives us Williams' poignant dramatization of the dreadful human waste of illusions. The major characters in this play are so warped and their lives so distorted and perverted by fantasies that each is left with only broken fragments of what might have been.

Seen in its larger implications, the image of the South, whether approached as history or as myth, constitutes the ultimate landscape of the dislocated mind for Williams' characters. It is not merely the vital context in which his men and women exist; it is for them a final possible "environment"—the extreme of their psychological fantasies—for it must somehow provide them with the means to establish values and to measure the possibilities of life. We are hardly surprised when bitter frustrations and violence result from their efforts. (pp. 204-06)

> Joseph K. Davis, "Landscapes of the Dislocated Mind in Williams' 'The Glass Menagerie'," in Tennessee Williams: A Tribute, *edited by Jac Tharpe, University Press of Mississippi, 1977, pp. 192-206.*

Nada Zeineddine

The Glass Menagerie introduces the social and historical context within which the problems of identity of women and artists in Williams's plays can be understood and which contributes to the women's act of misconstruing their sexuality as a form of transcendence, and, subsequently, their taking on the role of the nauseated artist who cannot reconcile the ideal and realistic levels of human experience.

The Glass Menagerie is a 'memory of play'. From this fact stems the importance of the temporal framework of the play, which acts also as a formative factor in the identity of these characters because the ways in which they relate to time determine their modes of acknowledging and evading reality and illusion respectively, which in turn shapes their identity-crises, and their degree of awareness of them. To the interpreter, time becomes a question of procedure in the sense that it regulates the position of the interpreter in relation to Tom, the narrator of the 'memory play', and to Tom, the character in it interacting with his mother and sister in a basically domestic situation.

'Time' is one of the 'tricks' Tom has in his pocket. It is one of the ways by which he acts as the 'opposite of a stage magician' who will give truth 'in the pleasant disguise of illusion':

> To begin with, I turn back time. I reverse it to that quaint period, the thirties, when the huge middle class of America was matriculating in a school for the blind. Their eyes had failed them, or they had failed their eyes, and so they were having their fingers pressed forcibly down on the fiery Braille alphabet of a dissolving economy.
>
> In Spain there was revolution. Here there was only shouting and confusion.
>
> In Spain, there was Guernica. Here there were disturbances of labour, sometimes pretty violent in otherwise peaceful cities such as Chicago, Cleveland, Saint Louis . . .

This is the social background of the play.

The encroaching effect of this social background is presented as working on the lower-middle-class population and on the Wingfields as a particular example of it, in Tennessee Williams's own stage directions to the play:

> *The Wingfield apartment is in the rear of the building, one of those vast hive-like conglomerations of cellular living-units that flower as warty growths in overcrowded urban centres of lower middle-class population and are symptomatic of the impulse of this largest and fundamentally enslaved section of American society to avoid fluidity and differentiation and to exist and function as one interfused mass of automatism.*
>
> *The apartment faces an alley and is entered by a fire-escape, a structure whose name is a touch of accidental poetic truth, for all of these huge buildings are always burning with the slow and implacable fires of human desperation. The fire-escape is included in the set—that is, the landing of it and steps descending from it.*

The fire-escape is not the only 'touch of poetic truth', for the two syllables carrying the family's name could not have been more strikingly suggestive. The Wingfields seek flight in illusion but fall back on the reality which gives rise to those very illusions.

Amanda is a frustrated and domineering mother who attempts to impose her obsolete Southern values on Tom and Laura. Her attempts to overpower her children result in a loss of their individuality. At one point Tom complains that there is not one thing in his life that he can call his own. That is true, for even his individuality is smothered by the family trap set mainly by Amanda. Amanda refuses to acknowledge Laura's disability. She refuses to see her as crippled. Her attempts to launch Laura into a business career through sending her to a college are met with failure. Finding the atmosphere of a business college insensitive to her needs, Laura escapes to museums. She is incompatible with machines and significantly breaks down while taking a typing speed test.

'The scene is memory', and the episodes relived through Tom's memory centre on the attempts of Amanda to find her daughter 'a gentleman caller' who would be the 'alternative to eating the crust of humility' in the absence of a business career that would have provided some measure of security. Laura remains the passive recipient of her mother's orders, living as she is with her glass animals, her father's music—one of the remnants of him apart from a photograph in the background.

Jim O'Connor, the so-called gentleman caller, arrives. He is described by Tom as an 'emissary from a world of reality'. Although Jim, like Tom, has a job in the warehouse, he has taken up public speaking and radio engineering as means of progress in the world. Jim appreciated the 'poet' in Tom and called him 'Shakespeare', but he had never noticed that Shakespeare had a sister. He diagnoses her problem as an 'inferiority complex', dances with her in an attempt to help her surmount her shyness. In the process of the dance one of Laura's animals—a unicorn—is shattered and his horn is lost as a consequence. Jim then kisses Laura but, while leaving her suspended 'at the climax of her interior life', he informs her that he is engaged to be married. Amanda feels that Tom has played a joke on them, but Tom has the excuse that 'the warehouse is where I work, not where I know things about people'. Tom, who has been 'boiling' inside with a desire to join The Seamen's Merchant Union, escapes the family trap and the warehouse but he is 'pursued by something': it is the memory of Laura on whom the scene dissolves as she blows out her candles, for as Tom concludes, 'nowadays the world is lit by lightning!'

To understand the identity problem of the Wingfields is to question their awareness of their own plight, which would in turn depend on the temporal framework in which the characters consciously or unconsciously place themselves. The only objective standards the interpreter has are the attempts made by Tom to describe the social and historical contexts of the play, and Williams's attempts to underline certain social aspects through his stage directions, which emphasize the state of 'interfused mass' in which the lower-middle-class and the Wingfields

as part of it existed. The identity problem is one experienced collectively and individually. One of the difficulties of approaching the play is that of separating the characters' experience of identity on an individual basis, particularly when, in the language of the play, 'self' and 'selfishness' almost become synonymous because any attempt by Tom to realize his self is considered a betrayal of the interests of the group on the wider level: that is, his family. This becomes clear through Amanda's labelling of Tom as a 'selfish dreamer' and her urging him to 'overcome selfishness. Self, Self, Self, is all you ever think of', and through even Tom's inescapable use of the mother's way of seeing him as a condition for his own self-realization:

> For sixty-five dollars a month I give up all that I dream of doing and being ever! And you say self—self is all I ever think of. Why, listen, if self is what I thought of, Mother, I'd be where he is—gone! [*pointing to father's picture*] As far as the system of transportation reaches!

Seeing the characters collectively is not only a suggestion by Williams as to the social conditions of the time but is also explicit in the way Amanda sees the family unit. Amanda conceives of the necessity of 'clinging' together as a reaction against 'these trying times we live in', and an act of 'Spartan endurance'. Amanda's concept of time is rather confused, and the interpreter must always keep in mind that Williams seems to undermine the awareness she seems to have of 'these' times with her act of 'clinging' frantically to another time and place.

The characters form a kind of unity through the fact that if taken individually their means of self-assertion is a form of escape. The escapist qualities are made explicit in Williams's stage directions: Amanda's life is paranoic; therefore, she lives in her illusions. Laura is a cripple, she lives with her animals. Tom is a poet with a job in the warehouse, which at once introduces the causes and effects of his escape.

While being an 'emissary from the world of reality', Jim is himself a projection of the need to escape, thus Jim bridges the gap between illusion and reality. Jim's significance depends on the viewpoints from which the interpreter sees him: the 'now' or the 'past', but perhaps taking account of the 'now and the past' as the temporal framework of the play might afford a more comprehensive view of him.

The phrase in which Amanda describes Jim is highly suggestive of the ways in which he offers her a means of escape into the past. He is a 'gentleman caller' divested, of course, from the system of economy that went to make him so valuable in those days. He is not a planter but rather a member of the rat race. It is ironic that while the form in which Amanda sees the gentleman caller, stemming in the way she names him and the ceremonious way through which she prepares to meet him, are all part of the past and her illusions; the content of her vision of him is futuristic.

In so far as Jim is a means of escape his capacity to save her would depend on the temporal framework in which she places him:

> AMANDA. What does he do, I mean study?

TOM. Radio engineering and public speaking!

AMANDA. Then he has visions of being advanced in the world! Any young man who studies public speaking is aiming to have an executive job some day!

And radio engineering? A thing for the future!

Both of these facts are very illuminating. Those are the sort of things that a mother should know concerning any young man who comes to call on her daughter. Seriously or—not.

While Amanda cannot reconcile her past and present, she seems at least theoretically to be able to define the degree to which active interaction with time can affect the personality:

> You are the only young man that I know of who ignores the fact that the future becomes the present, the present the past, and the past turns into everlasting regret if you don't plan for it.

'Plans and provisions', as Tom puts it, are for 'young men'. She does not apply what she says, which is why Tom undermines her words with:

> I will think that over and see what I can make of it.

Amanda herself has broken with tradition. While all her callers were 'gentlemen'—and among them 'some of the most prominent young planters of the Mississippi Delta—planters and sons of planters!' she 'picked' Mr Wingfield. Amanda must believe that the gentleman caller will come to her daughter if she is to believe that she is still a Southern lady with Southern heritage which she can pass on to her daughter. But what she cannot seem to remember is that this is not Blue Mountain and there cannot be a 'flood' of callers. For Amanda to avoid the realization that past has turned into 'everlasting regret' she must plan for the future, but while on the face of it her future is done with, she can live through her children and the evidence is that she attempts to make a spectacular appearance to receive the gentleman caller. She 'resurrects' a dress from the trunk—which is a dress that reminds her of her past glory. She has worn it for social occasions and worn it on Sundays for her gentlemen callers. When Jim arrives on the scene she is full of 'Southern behaviour' and starts off with telling him about her trials and tribulations. She describes her dress to him as historical and complains about the vestiges of gracious living having 'all gone':

> I never could make a thing but angel-food cake. Well, in the South we had so many servants. Gone, gone, gone. All vestige of gracious living! Gone completely. I wasn't prepared for what the future brought me. All of my gentlemen callers were sons of planters and so of course I assumed that I would be married to one and raise my family on a large piece of land with plenty of servants. But man proposes—and woman accepts the proposal!—To vary that old, old saying a little bit—I married no planter!—That gallantly smiling gentleman over there! A telephone man who fell in love with long distance!

Amanda is probably not aware of the fact that her act of

lamenting the loss of a Southern mode of life is also an appeal to the realist in Jim to save them. By complaining to him she articulates her experiences and in so far as Jim is 'an emissary from a world of reality' her words to him serve to objectify her experience. Salvation seems to lie beyond the South. Tom must follow in his father's footsteps; Amanda must see herself against another background—a realistic one. This function of Jim is further underlined by the breaking of the unicorn's horn. Significantly, Laura's favourite glass animal is damaged not only by Jim but also by the collaborative effort of Jim and Laura to dance. Laura announces that the unicorn is now 'less freakish'. The combined effort of Jim and Laura produces a more realistic animal who can now play with the other horses.

Amanda must live vicariously. While rebuking Laura for leaving a business career, she seems to imply that there is a danger in that not only for Laura but also for Amanda as living her past and future through her daughter.

> We won't have a business career—we've given that up because it gave us nervous indigestion! What is there left but dependency all our lives? I know so well what becomes of unmarried women who aren't prepared to occupy a position. I've seen such pitiful cases in the South—barely tolerated spinsters living upon the grudging patronage of sister's husband or brother's wife!—stuck away in some little mousetrap of a room—encouraged by one in-law to visit another—little birdlike women without any nest—eating the crust of humility all their life! Is that the future that we've mapped out for ourselves? I swear it is the only alternative I can think of!

Amanda claims to live in a world of 'superior things'. She denounces instinct and reads 'filth' into D. H. Lawrence's novels, while Tom translates instinct into loving, fighting, and hunting for adventures. In so far as Amanda has a vision of herself as a transcendent woman, sublimating her passions and being on the board of a magazine which features the sublimations of women of letters, she is an artist whose attempt to escape to a world of superior things, of mind and spirit, probably stems from the realization that instinct—which belongs to animals—is such a threat. Mr Wingfield's smile appealed to Amanda, the World was enchanted and the result was that she made a tragic mistake. It is almost as if that realization of the intensity of emotions led Amanda to see instinct as detrimental. Amanda uses this transcendent vision as a means of escaping her surroundings, and her self. Amanda needs to live vicariously. That she uses D. H. Lawrence's novels as a point of departure from which to build a moral stance is in itself indicative of the literary context which emerges from Williams's plays, and acts as a point of reference or as some kind of authority which the characters use to accept or repudiate. Her critical stance towards Lawrence's novels represents the view of the traditional Southerners who fear change. From the point of view of Amanda Lawrence is insane, maybe because he presents the authentic:

> I took that horrible novel back to the library—yes! That hideous book by that insane Mr Lawrence. I cannot control the output of diseased minds or people who cater to them . . . But I

won't allow SUCH FILTH BROUGHT INTO MY HOUSE! No, no, no, no, no!

While Tom focuses on the financial aspect of owning the house, and as such sees no reason why, if he pays the rent, he cannot have any freedom within it, Amanda feels that her moral authority gives her the right. While Tom sees himself as paying the rent and making a slave of himself, he does describe his mother as trying to make her own contribution to feather the nest and plume the bird by trying to 'rope in' subscribers to one of those magazines for matrons called *The Home-maker's Companion,* 'the type of journal that features the serialized sublimations of ladies of letters who think in terms of delicate cuplike breasts, slim tapering waists, rich, creamy thighs, eyes like wood-smoke in autumn, fingers that soothe and caress like strains of music, bodies as powerful as Etruscan sculpture'. Her view of books is the wonderful 'new serial' which is to be compared in force with *Gone With the Wind,* 'It is the *Gone With the Wind* of the post-World War generation!'

For as long as Amanda and her companions can gild the lily and see sensory functions in terms of elevated objects outside the rush of time like 'strains of music' or 'sculpture', they can afford to denounce Lawrence because he sees the 'fingers' or the 'bodies' for what they are, not for what they ought to be. This discrepancy between the ideal and the realistic levels and the women's use of the first to transcend the second thus negating it, yet, by transcending it, acknowledging its power is a theme that persists in Williams's plays. It is perhaps best articulated by Alma in *Summer and Smoke,* in the image of the Gothic cathedral in which every part reaches up, 'everything seems to be straining for something out of the reach of stone—or human—fingers . . . The immense stained windows, the great arched doors that are five or six times the height of the tallest man—the vaulted ceiling and all the delicate spires—all reaching up to something beyond attainment! To me—well, that is the secret, the principle back of existence—the everlasting struggle and aspiration for more than our human limits have placed in our reach. . . . ' Alma cannot describe the cathedral in terms other than human. Even the doors are measured according to the height of man. Even though she uses human as a point of departure, like Amanda, her moral indignation is suspect because it does not realize the interdependence of the human and the divine. Amanda and Alma and Blanche [from *A Streetcar Named Desire*] have illusions about themselves, but although Laura lives in an illusory world, she is more realistic about herself and has no illusions as such. She acknowledges the charm that Jim had earlier cast on her, remembers that this happened while both were members of a choir, acknowledges she is going to be an old maid and that she is a cripple. While she escapes to a world of glass and records, she does so because it alleviates her loneliness by showing her creatures like herself—delicate yet breakable. That this process of identification with her animals is meant to be important is signified in the associations with glass and light. She is lonely, so are they. She is lonely because, like the penguins she visits in the zoo, she is a flightless bird—unable to acclimatize herself because she cannot develop with the times, yet

must live in them. But unlike the magician's trick she cannot be a bird who can swim or who can fly. She is not a 'legless creature', to borrow Williams's useful expression in *Orpheus Descending.* History or development seem to be inert for her; she can view it from a distance in a museum because it has meaning for her, it is made material; like her, it stands outside the rush of time. Williams stresses her ethereal qualities and the fact that she 'is like a piece of translucent glass touched by light'. Her mode of escape offers a contrast to that of Amanda because it is built on a realistic assessment of herself and of the relations she is born into.

Tom's use of artistic escape is built on the same premise as Amanda's—a wish to live vicariously. In fact, he attempts to define his self in relation to a stage magician. For Tom, escape lies in the very base that Amanda is trying to run away from—instinct. Tom derives his identity from that very means of escape. There is a need for him to assert his self through being a 'lover, a fighter, a hunter', three functions of instinct to him. It is a kind of negative identity which he must experience if he is to escape from the reified relations of the warehouse. Like Amanda, his self-image is derived from his evasion of reality. Like the magician's fascinating trick, he will try to find a trick that will turn reality into illusion, and make the reality of the warehouse disappear. He will get out of the '2 by 4' situation by a trick similar to the coffin trick in which a man got out without removing one nail. He will get out without removing one nail by using his Prospero-like art to get fired from the warehouse. He thus refrains from doing anything that will eradicate his reality but will avoid responsibility for his actions by getting fired. He uses art as a projection of a wish-fulfilment in the same way that Don Quixote will use a dream to restore valuable meanings to life in *Camino Real.* Then again, to evade the responsibilities of having left Laura he uses the memory play to eradicate the effects of the poem on the lid of a shoe box. It is extremely ironic that this piece of art is written on something that represents mobility to Tom, for a shoe is only something to be worn on travellers' feet and thus the meaning of it is relative to the distance that it carries its wearer. He does not go to the moon, he goes much further, for 'time is the longest distance between two places' and it is the lid of the shoe box that turns the physical distance into an intangible world of time. Space and time are interlinked through the dimension of art but both space and time hold pain for Tom, for while the cities drop behind him he is full of remorse for leaving his sister. Williams, of course, has experienced the severance of ties with his own sister.

Tom's gesture makes him less of the rebel and more of the conformist. Even his mode of escape is contributed to by the warehouse and the lid. In the opening passage Tom chooses times and spaces to indicate political or economic crises. While he selects one time axis, he moves in space to compare Guernica to America. His idea of relativity works along indicating the effectuality of a general scene in one place to the ineffectuality of it on the other. But while Tom's initial passage highlights the ineffectuality of the middle-class in America, and the dissolving economy, in the final passage he moves to the intensely subjective experience of the futility of erasing a memory because the consequences of events are indelibly marked on the mind. Yet while the objectivity claimed in the distancing effects of his statement 'I have tricks . . . ' ends on a note, that, very far from tantalizing the audience, is a means of sentimentalizing the experience, and thus would seem to miss the effect, the subjectivity of the final passage is partly led to by Tom's being a product of that very America which he criticizes and of the social system which he dislikes.

Tom is dissatisfied with the social conditions. America falls short of Guernica, and the world is waiting for bombardments. Yet he, as an individual, is an escapist while shunning the responsibility of escapism on an individual and familial level. If Tom sees himself as an escapist then he would subvert the very criticism he makes of society because he would then have to admit his complicity in whatever lack of bombardments there are in it. But the interpreter cannot argue that Tom sees himself as symptomatic, and that the escapism he embodies on an individual level reflects on the general while going to compound the fault of Americans whose eyes had failed them. Tom sees himself as an adventurer, in a way putting into practice his criticism of the lack of adventure for the masses. The movies are a form of vicarious living and the interpreter suspects that if his leaving the warehouse and the family had satisfied his yearning for adventure, he would not, as he admits in the final passage, run to the movies or a bar.

Tom is the fugitive poet and while he is alienated on several levels, and seeks cities that are torn away from the branches, there is in him enough of the critic of his times to be dissatisfied with making this 'separate peace' while being unable, because of his psychological inadequacies, to bring this beyond the level of escape. The passages in which he criticizes the conditions in America reveal a poet who is socially aware if not committed. Tom can understand the interaction between the individual and society and knows that despite the failure of the economic system, individuals who are part of it can be responsible. Tom sees that 'either their eyes had failed them or they had failed their eyes'. He is aware of complexities and contradictions. The subject of his poetry is not revealed to the interpreter. But what comes between this accurately described vision in the first passage and the alienated displaced fugitive of the last, on the level of a play, is representative of what could have made him give up his social interest: a series of encounters with the mother, and a series of 'rise and shines' inviting him to go to his coffin-like warehouse. Between the prongs of social and familial demands, Tom is drained of all but the desire to escape.

It can, of course, be argued that in so far as *The Glass Menagerie* is a memory play the exposition of the social scene is Tom's way of presenting the stage directions, and the last passage his way of concluding the action. While that is true of Tom the narrator, it is not true of Tom the character; and while the first and last passages are spoken by the narrator, Tom is only what he is as narrator by virtue of what he was and is as character, a detached observer who attempts to escape experience through the alienating effect of time: the 'past' related in the 'now' and the content of an artistic work which can be encompassed within such a framework—namely, a memory play. There is a

need to recognize the two viewpoints but not necessarily to see the distinction as clear-cut. Tom's position as narrator in the final passage, in relation to the 'memory play' is similar to Rubek's relation as 'figure' in relation to 'The Day of Resurrection'. Rubek only features as a 'figure of remorse' by virtue of his realization of corruption as the other face of purity. He thus attempts to distance the woman for the sake of total effect and to make the artist in him present the man as being in the foreground. His experiences as artist and man intermingle and he becomes what he is by virtue of experience—a figure of remorse. While the terms in which Rubek describes his art are much more oblique than Tom's and require more of an interpretive act on the part of the reader, the way Tom puts himself across is more explicit. Tom tries to put a woman in the background not because that no longer represented 'life as I now see it' but more aptly to the particular situation because the world is lit by lightning and Laura as a figure is an anachronism. Tom is unable to face the situation. He must leave her in the dark.

Amanda's and Tom's modes of finding their selves through escape share in common the typicality of the Southern experience. Amanda evades the issue of her sexuality, Tom follows in the father's footsteps—and becomes a fugitive poet. (pp. 100-10)

Nada Zeineddine, "Problems of Identity, as Experienced by the Producer, in Four Plays by Tennessee Williams," in her Because It Is My Name, *Merlin Books Ltd., 1991, pp. 90-154.*

FURTHER READING

Bibliography

McCann, John S. *The Critical Reputation of Tennessee Williams: A Reference Guide.* Boston: G. K. Hall, 1983, 430 p.
    Comprehensive guide to secondary sources on Williams published up until 1983.

Biography

Spoto, Donald. *The Kindness of Strangers: The Life of Tennessee Williams.* Boston: Little, Brown, and Co., 1985, 409 p.
    Comprehensive biography of Williams that explores the relationship between his life and work.

Criticism

Gassner, John. "Tennessee Williams: 1940-60." In his *Theatre at the Crossroads: Plays and Playwrights of the Mid-Century American Stage,* pp. 77-91. New York: Holt, Rinehart and Winston, 1960.
    Overview of Williams's career up to 1960 that includes a brief examination of *The Glass Menagerie.*

MacMullan, Hugh. "Translating *The Glass Menagerie* to Film." *Hollywood Quarterly* V, No. 1 (Fall 1950): 14-32.
    Discusses how the continuity, dramatic intent, and char-

acterization of *The Glass Menagerie* changed in director Irving Rapper's film adaptation of the play.

Nathan, George Jean. Review of *The Glass Menagerie*. In his *The Theatre Book of the Year, 1944-1945: A Record and an Interpretation,* pp. 324-27. New York: Alfred A. Knopf, 1945.

Reviews the original production of *The Glass Menagerie*, concentrating on the play's move from Chicago to New York and the actors' performances.

Scheye, Thomas E. "*The Glass Menagerie:* 'It's No Tragedy, Freckles'." In *Tennessee Williams: A Tribute,* edited by Jac Tharpe, pp. 207-13. Jackson: University Press of Mississippi, 1977.

Argues that the departure of Tom and Jim from Laura's life is not as devastating to her as critics have previously maintained.

Stang, Joanne. "Williams: Twenty Years After *Glass Menagerie.*" *The New York Times* (28 March 1965): Sec. 2, pp. 1, 3.

Interview with Williams occasioned by the twentieth anniversary of *The Glass Menagerie*.

Watson, Charles S. "The Revision of *The Glass Menagerie:* The Passing of Good Manners." *Southern Literary Journal* VIII, No. 2 (Spring 1976): 74-8.

Maintains that the changes Williams made to the "acting" edition of the play emphasize the loss of refinement associated with the old South.

Young, Michael C. "II. The Play of Memory: Reflections from *The Glass Menagerie*—An Interview." *The Tennessee Williams Newsletter* II, No. 2 (Fall 1980): 32-5.

Recounts the efforts of producer and star Eddie Dowling to bring *The Glass Menagerie* to the stage and the difficulties encountered by the actors during rehearsals for the original production.

Young, Stark. Review of *The Glass Menagerie*. In his *Immortal Shadows: A Book of Dramatic Criticism,* pp. 249-53. New York: Charles Scribner's Sons, 1948.

Review of the original production of *The Glass Menagerie* that appeared in *The New Republic* on April 16, 1945, which emphasizes Laurette Taylor's performance as Amanda.

Additional coverage of Williams's life and career is contained in the following sources published by Gale Research: *Authors in the News,* Vols. 1, 2; *Concise Dictionary of American Literary Biography, 1941-1968; Contemporary Authors,* Vols. 5-8, rev. ed., 108 [obituary]; *Contemporary Authors New Revision Series,* Vol. 31; *Contemporary Authors Bibliographical Series,* Vol. 3; *Contemporary Literary Criticism,* Vols. 1, 2, 5, 7, 8, 11, 15, 19, 30, 39, 45; *Dictionary of Literary Biography,* Vol. 7; *Dictionary of Literary Biography Documentary Series,* Vol. 4; *Dictionary of Literary Biography Yearbook: 1983;* and *Major 20th-Century Writers.*

☐ Contemporary Literary Criticism

Indexes

Literary Criticism Series
   Cumulative Author Index
Cumulative Nationality Index
Title Index, Volume 71

This Index Includes References to Entries in These Gale Series

Children's Literature Review includes excerpts from reviews, criticism, and commentary on works of authors and illustrators who create books for children.

Classical and Medieval Literature Criticism offers excerpts of criticism on the works of world authors from classical antiquity through the fourteenth century.

Contemporary Authors series encompasses five related series. *Contemporary Authors* provides biographical and bibliographical information on more than 97,000 writers of fiction and nonfiction, nonfiction, poetry, journalism, drama, and film. *Contemporary Authors New Revision Series* provides completely updated information on active authors covered in previously published volumes of *CA*. *Contemporary Authors Permanent Series* consists of updated listings for deceased and inactive authors removed from the original volumes 9-36 when those volumes were revised. *Contemporary Authors Autobiography Series* presents specially commissioned autobiographies by leading contemporary writers. *Contemporary Authors Bibliographical Series* contains primary and secondary bibliographies as well as analytical bibliographical essays by authorities on major modern authors.

Contemporary Literary Criticism presents excerpts of criticism on the works of novelists, poets, dramatists, short story writers, scriptwriters, and other creative writers who are now living or who have died since 1960.

Dictionary of Literary Biography encompasses three related series. *Dictionary of Literary Biography* furnishes illustrated overviews of authors' lives and works and places them in the larger perspective of literary history. *Dictionary of Literary Biography Documentary Series* illuminates the careers of major figures through a selection of literary documents, including letters, interviews, and photographs. *Dictionary of Literary Biography Yearbook* summarizes the past year's literary activity and includes updated entries on individual authors. A cumulative index to authors and articles is included in each new volume. *Concise Dictionary of Literary Biography* a six volume series, collects revised and updated sketches on major American authors that were originally presented in *Dictionary of Literary Biography*.

Drama Criticism provides excerpts of criticism on the works of playwrights of all nationalities and periods of literary history.

Literature Criticism from 1400 to 1800 compiles significant passages from the most noteworthy criticism on authors of the fifteenth through the eighteenth centuries.

Nineteenth-Century Literature Criticism offers significant passages from criticism on authors who died between 1800 and 1899.

Poetry Criticism presents excerpts of criticism on the works of poets from all eras, movements, and nationalities.

Short Story Criticism combines excerpts of criticism on short fiction by writers of all eras and nationalities.

Something about the Author series encompasses three related series. *Something about the Author* contains well-illustrated biographical sketches on authors and illustrators of juvenile and young adult literature from all eras. *Something about the Author Autobiography Series* presents specially commissioned autobiographies by prominent authors and illustrators of books for children and young adults. *Authors & Artists for Young Adults* provides high school and junior high school students with profiles of their favorite creative artists.

Twentieth-Century Literary Criticism contains critical excerpts by the most significant commentators on poets, novelists, short story writers, dramatists, and philosophers who died between 1900 and 1960.

Yesterday's Authors of Books for Children contains heavily illustrated entries on children's writers who died before 1961. Complete in two volumes.

Literary Criticism Series
Cumulative Author Index

This index lists all author entries in the Gale Literary Criticism Series and includes cross-references to other Gale sources. References in the index are identified as follows:

AAYA: *Authors & Artists for Young Adults,* Volumes 1-7
BLC: *Black Literature Criticism,* Volumes 1-3
CA: *Contemporary Authors* (original series), Volumes 1-136
CAAS: *Contemporary Authors Autobiography Series,* Volumes 1-15
CABS: *Contemporary Authors Bibliographical Series,* Volumes 1-3
CANR: *Contemporary Authors New Revision Series,* Volumes 1-35
CAP: *Contemporary Authors Permanent Series,* Volumes 1-2
CA-R: *Contemporary Authors* (first revision), Volumes 1-44
CDALB: *Concise Dictionary of American Literary Biography,* Volumes 1-6
CLC: *Contemporary Literary Criticism,* Volumes 1-71
CLR: *Children's Literature Review,* Volumes 1-25
CMLC: *Classical and Medieval Literature Criticism,* Volumes 1-8
DC: *Drama Criticism,* Volumes 1-2
DLB: *Dictionary of Literary Biography,* Volumes 1-114
DLB-DS: *Dictionary of Literary Biography Documentary Series,* Volumes 1-9
DLB-Y: *Dictionary of Literary Biography Yearbook,* Volumes 1980-1990
LC: *Literature Criticism from 1400 to 1800,* Volumes 1-19
NCLC: *Nineteenth-Century Literature Criticism,* Volumes 1-35
PC: *Poetry Criticism,* Volumes 1-4
SAAS: *Something about the Author Autobiography Series,* Volumes 1-14
SATA: *Something about the Author,* Volumes 1-68
SSC: *Short Story Criticism,* Volumes 1-9
TCLC: *Twentieth-Century Literary Criticism,* Volumes 1-45
WLC: *World Literature Criticism, 1500 to the Present,* Volumes 1-6
YABC: *Yesterday's Authors of Books for Children,* Volumes 1-2

A. E. 1867-1935 . . . . TCLC **3, 10**
See also Russell, George William
See also DLB 19

Abbey, Edward 1927-1989 . . . . . . CLC **36, 59**
See also CANR 2; CA 45-48;
obituary CA 128

Abbott, Lee K., Jr. 19??- . . . . CLC **48**

Abe, Kobo 1924- . . . . CLC **8, 22, 53**
See also CANR 24; CA 65-68

Abell, Kjeld 1901-1961 . . . . CLC **15**
See also obituary CA 111

Abish, Walter 1931- . . . . CLC **22**
See also CA 101

Abrahams, Peter (Henry) 1919- . . . . . CLC **4**
See also CA 57-60

Abrams, M(eyer) H(oward) 1912-. . . CLC **24**
See also CANR 13; CA 57-60; DLB 67

Abse, Dannie 1923-. . . . . CLC **7, 29**
See also CAAS 1; CANR 4; CA 53-56;
DLB 27

Achebe, (Albert) Chinua(lumogu)
1930- . . . . CLC **1, 3, 5, 7, 11, 26, 51**
See also BLC 1; CLR 20; WLC 1; CANR 6,
26; CA 1-4R; SATA 38, 40

Acker, Kathy 1948- . . . . CLC **45**
See also CA 117, 122

Ackroyd, Peter 1949- . . . . CLC **34, 52**
See also CA 123, 127

Acorn, Milton 1923- . . . . CLC **15**
See also CA 103; DLB 53

Adamov, Arthur 1908-1970 . . . . . . CLC **4, 25**
See also CAP 2; CA 17-18;
obituary CA 25-28R

Adams, Alice (Boyd) 1926- . . . CLC **6, 13, 46**
See also CANR 26; CA 81-84; DLB-Y 86

Adams, Douglas (Noel) 1952- . . . CLC **27, 60**
See also CA 106; DLB-Y 83

Adams, Francis 1862-1893 . . . . NCLC **33**

Adams, Henry (Brooks)
1838-1918 . . . . TCLC **4**
See also CA 104; DLB 12, 47

Adams, Richard (George)
1920- . . . . CLC **4, 5, 18**
See also CLR 20; CANR 3; CA 49-52;
SATA 7

Adamson, Joy(-Friederike Victoria)
1910-1980 . . . . CLC **17**
See also CANR 22; CA 69-72;
obituary CA 93-96; SATA 11;
obituary SATA 22

Adcock, (Kareen) Fleur 1934- . . . . . . CLC **41**
See also CANR 11; CA 25-28R; DLB 40

Addams, Charles (Samuel)
1912-1988 . . . . CLC **30**
See also CANR 12; CA 61-64;
obituary CA 126

Addison, Joseph 1672-1719 . . . . LC **18**
See also DLB 101

Adler, C(arole) S(chwerdtfeger)
1932- . . . . CLC **35**
See also CANR 19; CA 89-92; SATA 26

Adler, Renata 1938- . . . . CLC **8, 31**
See also CANR 5, 22; CA 49-52

Ady, Endre 1877-1919 . . . . TCLC **11**
See also CA 107

Author Index

Author Index

Author Index

Williamson, David 1932- .... **CLC 56**

Williamson, Jack 1908- .... **CLC 29**
See also Williamson, John Stewart
See also DLB 8

Williamson, John Stewart 1908-
See Williamson, Jack
See also CANR 123; CA 17-20R

Willingham, Calder (Baynard, Jr.)
1922- .... **CLC 5, 51**
See also CANR 3; CA 5-8R; DLB 2, 44

Wilson, A(ndrew) N(orman) 1950- .. **CLC 33**
See also CA 112, 122; DLB 14

Wilson, Andrew 1948-
See Wilson, Snoo

Wilson, Angus (Frank Johnstone)
1913- .... **CLC 2, 3, 5, 25, 34**
See also CANR 21; CA 5-8R; DLB 15

Wilson, August
1945- .... **CLC 39, 50, 63; DC 2**
See also BLC 3; CA 115, 122

Wilson, Brian 1942- .... **CLC 12**

Wilson, Colin 1931- .... **CLC 3, 14**
See also CAAS 5; CANR 1, 122; CA 1-4R;
DLB 14

Wilson, Edmund
1895-1972 .... **CLC 1, 2, 3, 8, 24**
See also CANR 1; CA 1-4R;
obituary CA 37-40R; DLB 63

Wilson, Ethel Davis (Bryant)
1888-1980 .... **CLC 13**
See also CA 102; DLB 68

Wilson, Harriet 1827?-?
See also BLC 3; DLB 50

Wilson, John 1785-1854......... **NCLC 5**

Wilson, John (Anthony) Burgess 1917-
See Burgess, Anthony
See also CANR 2; CA 1-4R

Wilson, Lanford 1937- .... **CLC 7, 14, 36**
See also CA 17-20R; DLB 7

Wilson, Robert (M.) 1944-........ **CLC 7, 9**
See also CANR 2; CA 49-52

Wilson, Sloan 1920- .... **CLC 32**
See also CANR 1; CA 1-4R

Wilson, Snoo 1948-............... **CLC 33**
See also CA 69-72

Wilson, William S(mith) 1932- ..... **CLC 49**
See also CA 81-84

Winchilsea, Anne (Kingsmill) Finch, Countess
of 1661-1720................. **LC 3**

Wingrove, David 1954-........... **CLC 68**
See also CA 133

Winters, Janet Lewis 1899-
See Lewis (Winters), Janet
See also CAP 1; CA 9-10

Winters, (Arthur) Yvor
1900-1968 .... **CLC 4, 8, 32**
See also CAP 1; CA 11-12;
obituary CA 25-28R; DLB 48

Winterson, Jeannette 1959-........ **CLC 64**

Wiseman, Frederick 1930-........ **CLC 20**

Wister, Owen 1860-1938 .... **TCLC 21**
See also CA 108; DLB 9, 78

Witkiewicz, Stanislaw Ignacy
1885-1939 .... **TCLC 8**
See also CA 105; DLB 83

Wittig, Monique 1935?-.......... **CLC 22**
See also CA 116; DLB 83

Wittlin, Joseph 1896-1976........ **CLC 25**
See also Wittlin, Jozef

Wittlin, Jozef 1896-1976
See Wittlin, Joseph
See also CANR 3; CA 49-52;
obituary CA 65-68

Wodehouse, (Sir) P(elham) G(renville)
1881-1975 ... **CLC 1, 2, 5, 10, 22; SSC 2**
See also CANR 3; CA 45-48;
obituary CA 57-60; SATA 22; DLB 34

Woiwode, Larry (Alfred) 1941-... **CLC 6, 10**
See also CANR 16; CA 73-76; DLB 6

Wojciechowska, Maia (Teresa)
1927- .... **CLC 26**
See also CLR 1; CANR 4; CA 9-12R;
SAAS 1; SATA 1, 28

Wolf, Christa 1929- .... **CLC 14, 29, 58**
See also CA 85-88; DLB 75

Wolfe, Gene (Rodman) 1931-....... **CLC 25**
See also CAAS 9; CANR 6; CA 57-60;
DLB 8

Wolfe, George C. 1954-........... **CLC 49**

Wolfe, Thomas (Clayton)
1900-1938 .... **TCLC 4, 13, 29**
See also CA 104; DLB 9; DLB-Y 85;
DLB-DS 2

Wolfe, Thomas Kennerly, Jr. 1931-
See Wolfe, Tom
See also CANR 9; CA 13-16R

Wolfe, Tom 1931-... **CLC 1, 2, 9, 15, 35, 51**
See also Wolfe, Thomas Kennerly, Jr.

Wolff, Geoffrey (Ansell) 1937- ..... **CLC 41**
See also CA 29-32R

Wolff, Tobias (Jonathan Ansell)
1945- .... **CLC 39, 64**
See also CA 114, 117

Wolfram von Eschenbach
c. 1170-c. 1220 .... **CMLC 5**

Wolitzer, Hilma 1930-............ **CLC 17**
See also CANR 18; CA 65-68; SATA 31

Wollstonecraft Godwin, Mary
1759-1797 .... **LC 5**
See also DLB 39

Wonder, Stevie 1950-............. **CLC 12**
See also Morris, Steveland Judkins

Wong, Jade Snow 1922-.......... **CLC 17**
See also CA 109

Woodcott, Keith 1934-
See Brunner, John (Kilian Houston)

Woolf, (Adeline) Virginia
1882-1941 .... **TCLC 1, 5, 20, 43; SSC 7**
See also CA 130; brief entry CA 104;
DLB 36, 100

Woollcott, Alexander (Humphreys)
1887-1943 .... **TCLC 5**
See also CA 105; DLB 29

Wordsworth, Dorothy
1771-1855 .... **NCLC 25**

Wordsworth, William
1770-1850 .... **NCLC 12; PC 4**
See also DLB 93, 107

Wouk, Herman 1915-......... **CLC 1, 9, 38**
See also CANR 6; CA 5-8R; DLB-Y 82

Wright, Charles 1935- .... **CLC 6, 13, 28**
See also BLC 3; CAAS 7; CANR 26;
CA 29-32R; DLB-Y 82

Wright, Charles (Stevenson) 1932-.. **CLC 49**
See also CA 9-12R; DLB 33

Wright, James (Arlington)
1927-1980 .... **CLC 3, 5, 10, 28**
See also CANR 4; CA 49-52;
obituary CA 97-100; DLB 5

Wright, Judith 1915- .... **CLC 11, 53**
See also CA 13-16R; SATA 14

Wright, L(aurali) R. 1939-........ **CLC 44**

Wright, Richard (Nathaniel)
1908-1960 ... **CLC 1, 3, 4, 9, 14, 21, 48;
SSC 2**
See also BLC 3; CA 108; DLB 76;
DLB-DS 2; CDALB 1929-1941; AAYA 5

Wright, Richard B(ruce) 1937- ...... **CLC 6**
See also CA 85-88; DLB 53

Wright, Rick 1945-
See Pink Floyd

Wright, Stephen 1946-........... **CLC 33**

Wright, Willard Huntington 1888-1939
See Van Dine, S. S.
See also CA 115

Wright, William 1930-............ **CLC 44**
See also CANR 7, 23; CA 53-56

Wu Ch'eng-en 1500?-1582? .... **LC 7**

Wu Ching-tzu 1701-1754 .... **LC 2**

Wurlitzer, Rudolph 1938?-..... **CLC 2, 4, 15**
See also CA 85-88

Wycherley, William 1640?-1716 ...... **LC 8**
See also DLB 80

Wylie (Benet), Elinor (Morton Hoyt)
1885-1928 .... **TCLC 8**
See also CA 105; DLB 9, 45

Wylie, Philip (Gordon) 1902-1971... **CLC 43**
See also CAP 2; CA 21-22;
obituary CA 33-36R; DLB 9

Wyndham, John 1903-1969 .... **CLC 19**
See also Harris, John (Wyndham Parkes
Lucas) Beynon

Wyss, Johann David 1743-1818 .. **NCLC 10**
See also SATA 27, 29

X, Malcolm 1925-1965
See Little, Malcolm

Yanovsky, Vassily S(emenovich)
1906-1989 .... **CLC 2, 18**
See also CA 97-100; obituary CA 129

Yates, Richard 1926- .... **CLC 7, 8, 23**
See also CANR 10; CA 5-8R; DLB 2;
DLB-Y 81

Yeats, William Butler
1865-1939 .... **TCLC 1, 11, 18, 31**
See also CANR 10; CA 104; DLB 10, 19

Yehoshua, A(braham) B.
1936- .... **CLC 13, 31**
See also CA 33-36R

CLC Cumulative Nationality Index

ALBANIAN
Kadare, Ismail 52

ALGERIAN
Camus, Albert 1, 2, 4, 9, 11, 14, 32, 63, 69
Cohen-Solal, Annie 50

AMERICAN
Abbey, Edward 36, 59
Abbott, Lee K., Jr. 48
Abish, Walter 22
Abrahams, Peter 4
Abrams, M. H. 24
Acker, Kathy 45
Adams, Alice 6, 13, 46
Addams, Charles 30
Adler, C. S. 35
Adler, Renata 8, 31
Ai 4, 14, 69
Aiken, Conrad 1, 3, 5, 10, 52
Albee, Edward 1, 2, 3, 5, 9, 11, 13, 25, 53
Alexander, Lloyd 35
Algren, Nelson 4, 10, 33
Allard, Janet 59
Allen, Edward 59
Allen, Woody 16, 52
Alleyne, Carla D. 65
Alta 19
Alter, Robert B. 34
Alther, Lisa 7, 41
Altman, Robert 16
Ammons, A. R. 2, 3, 5, 8, 9, 25, 57
Anaya, Rudolfo A. 23
Anderson, Jon 9
Anderson, Poul 15
Anderson, Robert 23
Angell, Roger 26
Angelou, Maya 12, 35, 64
Anthony, Piers 35

Apple, Max 9, 33
Appleman, Philip 51
Archer, Jules 12
Arendt, Hannah 66
Arnow, Harriette 2, 7, 18
Arrick, Fran 30
Ashbery, John 2, 3, 4, 6, 9, 13, 15, 25, 41
Asimov, Isaac 1, 3, 9, 19, 26
Auchincloss, Louis 4, 6, 9, 18, 45
Auden, W. H. 1, 2, 3, 4, 6, 9, 11, 14, 43
Auel, Jean M. 31
Auster, Paul 47
Bach, Richard 14
Baker, Elliott 8
Baker, Nicholson 61
Baker, Russell 31
Bakshi, Ralph 26
Baldwin, James 1, 2, 3, 4, 5, 8, 13, 15, 17, 42, 50, 67
Bambara, Toni Cade 19
Bandanes, Jerome 59
Banks, Russell 37
Baraka, Imamu Amiri 1, 2, 3, 5, 10, 14, 33
Barbera, Jack 44
Barnard, Mary 48
Barnes, Djuna 3, 4, 8, 11, 29
Barrett, William 27
Barth, John 1, 2, 3, 5, 7, 9, 10, 14, 27, 51
Barthelme, Donald 1, 2, 3, 5, 6, 8, 13, 23, 46, 59
Barthelme, Frederick 36
Barzun, Jacques 51
Baumbach, Jonathan 6, 23
Bausch, Richard 51
Baxter, Charles 45
Beagle, Peter S. 7
Beattie, Ann 8, 13, 18, 40, 63
Becker, Walter 26
Beecher, John 6

Begiebing, Robert J. 70
Behrman, S. N. 40
Belitt, Ben 22
Bell, Madison Smartt 41
Bell, Marvin 8, 31
Bellow, Saul 1, 2, 3, 6, 8, 10, 13, 15, 25, 33, 34, 63
Benary-Isbert, Margot 12
Benchley, Peter 4, 8
Benedikt, Michael 4, 14
Benford, Gregory 52
Bennett, Hal 5
Bennett, Jay 35
Benson, Jackson J. 34
Benson, Sally 17
Bentley, Eric 24
Berger, Melvin 12
Berger, Thomas 3, 5, 8, 11, 18, 38
Bergstein, Eleanor 4
Bernard, April 59
Berriault, Gina 54
Berrigan, Daniel J. 4
Berrigan, Ted 37
Berry, Chuck 17
Berry, Wendell 4, 6, 8, 27, 46
Berryman, John 1, 2, 3, 4, 6, 8, 10, 13, 25, 62
Bessie, Alvah 23
Betts, Doris 3, 6, 28
Bidart, Frank 33
Birch, Allison 65
Bishop, Elizabeth 1, 4, 9, 13, 15, 32
Bishop, John 10
Blackburn, Paul 9, 43
Blackmur, R. P. 2, 24
Blaise, Clark 29
Blatty, William Peter 2
Blessing, Lee 54
Blish, James 14

Nationality Index

Nationality Index

Nationality Index

CLC-71 Title Index

ISBN 0-8103-4448-3